Introduction to Information Systems

Supporting and Transforming Business

Eighth Edition

R. KELLY RAINER JR.

BRAD PRINCE

WILEY

EDITORIAL DIRECTOR	Michael McDonald
ASSOCIATE EDITOR	Alden Farrar
INSTRUCTIONAL DESIGNER	Wendy Ashenberg
EDITORIAL ASSISTANT	Cecilia Morales
SENIOR MARKETING MANAGER	Jenny Geiler
SENIOR CONTENT MANAGER	Dorothy Sinclair
PRODUCTION EDITOR	Rachel Conrad
SENIOR PRODUCT DESIGNER	Thomas Nery
PRODUCTION MANAGEMENT SERVICES	Lumina Datamatics, Inc.
COVER ILLUSTRATION	© Alaris/Shutterstock,
	© ProStockStudio/Shutterstock

Microsoft screenshots are © Microsoft Corporation. All rights reserved. Used with permission from Microsoft Corporation.

This book was typeset in 9.5/12.5 Source Sans Pro at Lumina Datamatics and printed and bound by Quad/Graphics.
The cover was printed by Quad/Graphics.

Founded in 1807, John Wiley & Sons, Inc. has been a valued source of knowledge and understanding for more than 200 years, helping people around the world meet their needs and fulfill their aspirations. Our company is built on a foundation of principles that include responsibility to the communities we serve and where we live and work. In 2008, we launched a Corporate Citizenship Initiative, a global effort to address the environmental, social, economic, and ethical challenges we face in our business. Among the issues we are addressing are carbon impact, paper specifications and procurement, ethical conduct within our business and among our vendors, and community and charitable support. For more information, please visit our website: www.wiley.com/go/citizenship.

EPUB ISBN: 978-1-119-59463-5

The inside back cover will contain printing identification and country of origin if omitted from this page. In addition, if the ISBN on the back cover differs from the ISBN on this page, the one on the back cover is correct.

Printed in the United States of America.

V10013674_090619

The entire focus of this book is to help students become informed users of information systems and information technology. In general, informed users receive increased value from organizational information systems and technologies. We hope to help students do just that.

What Do Information Systems Have to Do with Business?

This edition of Rainer and Prince's *Introduction to Information Systems* will answer this question for you. In every chapter, you will see how real global businesses use technology and information systems to increase their profitability, gain market share, develop and improve their customer relations, and manage their daily operations. In other words, you will learn how information systems provide the foundation for all modern organizations, whether they are public sector, private section, for-profit, or not-for-profit. We have several goals for all business majors, particularly undergraduates. First, we want to teach you how to use information technology to help you master your current or future jobs to help ensure the success of your organizations. Second, we want you to become *informed users* of information systems and information technology. Third, we want you to understand the digital transformation that your organization will likely be undergoing. The digital transformation of organizations is the acceleration of existing business processes and the development of new processes and business models. In this way, organizations can capitalize on the capabilities and opportunities of various technologies to improve performance. Examples of these technologies include Big Data, cloud computing, artificial intelligence, the Internet of Things, mobile computing, and commerce. We address each of these in our book. To accomplish these goals, we focus not on merely *learning* the concepts of information technology but rather on *applying* those concepts to perform business more effectively and efficiently. We concentrate on placing information systems in the context of business, so that you will more readily grasp the concepts we present in the text.

Pedagogical Structure

Various pedagogical features provide a structured learning system that reinforces the concepts through features such as chapter-opening organizers, section reviews, study aids, frequent applications, and hands-on exercises and activities.

Chapter-opening organizers include the following pedagogical features:

- **Chapter Outline:** Lists the major concepts covered in each chapter.
- **Learning Objectives:** Provide an overview of the key learning goals that students should achieve after reading the chapter.
- **Chapter-Opening Case:** With the exception of Chapters 5, 6, and 8, chapter-opening cases address a business problem faced by actual companies and how they used IS to solve these issues. The cases generally consist of a description of the problem, an overview of the IS solution implemented, and a presentation of the results of that implementation. Each case is followed by discussion questions so that students can further explore the concepts presented in the case.

Chapter 5's opening case addresses how data from a pacemaker led to an arrest. The idea behind this case is to show students how ubiquitous, often-ignored wireless devices constantly record data. In this case, the wearable was actually *inside* the suspect.

Chapter 6's opening case addresses what happened when the government of Myanmar allowed its citizens to access the Internet. The idea behind this case is that access to the Internet, which most of us take for granted, is a technological double-edged sword. Therefore, we emphasize to our students that, when accessing the Internet, the rule always is: "User beware!"

Chapter 8's opening case addresses how data from a Fitbit led to an arrest. Again, the idea behind this case is to show students how ubiquitous, often-ignored wireless devices constantly record data. In this case, the device was external to the suspect because he was wearing it on his arm.

Study aids are provided throughout each chapter. These include the following:

- IT's About Business cases provide real-world applications, with questions that relate to concepts covered in the text. Icons relate these sections to the specific functional areas in the text.
- Highlighted examples interspersed throughout the text illustrate the use (and misuse) of IT by real-world organizations, thus making the conceptual discussion more concrete.
- Tables list key points or summarize different concepts.
- End-of-section reviews (Before You Go On ...) prompt students to pause and test their understanding of basic concepts before moving on to the next section.

End-of-chapter study aids provide extensive opportunity for the reader to review:

- What's in IT for Me? is a unique chapter summary section that demonstrates the relevance of topics for different functional areas (accounting, finance, marketing, production/operations management, and human resources management).

- The chapter Summary, keyed to learning objectives listed at the beginning of the chapter, enables students to review the major concepts covered in the chapter.

- The end-of-chapter Glossary facilitates studying by listing and defining all the key terms introduced in the chapter.

- Chapter-closing cases address a business problem faced by actual companies and how they used IS to solve these issues. The cases generally consist of a description of the problem, an overview of the IS solution implemented, and a presentation of the results of that implementation. Each case is followed by discussion questions so that students can further explore the concepts presented in the case.

Hands-on exercises and activities require the reader to do something with the concepts they have studied. These include the following:

- Apply the Concept Activities: This book's unique pedagogical structure is designed to keep students actively engaged with the course material. Reading material in each chapter subsection is supported by an "Apply the Concept" activity that is directly related to a chapter objective. These activities include links to online videos and articles and other hands-on activities that require students to immediately apply what they have learned. Each Apply the Concept has the following elements:
  - Background (places the activity in the context of relevant reading material)
  - Activity (a hands-on activity that students carry out)
  - Deliverable (various tasks for students to complete as they perform the activity)

- Discussion Questions and Problem-Solving Activities: Provide practice through active learning. These exercises are hands-on opportunities to apply the concepts discussed in the chapter.

- Collaboration Exercises: Team exercises that require students to take on different functional roles and collaborate to solve business problems using Google Drive. These exercises allow students to get firsthand experience solving business problems using cloud-based tools while also experiencing an authentic business team dynamic. Exclusively in WileyPLUS.

- Spreadsheet Activity: Every chapter includes a hands-on spreadsheet project that requires students to practice their Excel skills within the context of the chapter material. WileyPLUS includes an Excel Lab Manual for students who need introductory coverage or review.

- Database Activity: Every chapter includes a hands-on database project that requires students to practice their Access skills while using concepts learned in the chapter. WileyPLUS Learning Space includes an Access Lab Manual for students who need introductory coverage or review.

Key Features

We have been guided by the following goals that we believe will enhance the teaching and learning experience.

What's in IT for Me? Theme

We emphasize the importance of information systems by calling attention in every chapter to how that chapter's topic relates to each business major. Icons guide students to relevant issues for their specific functional area—accounting (ACC), finance (FIN), marketing (MKT), production operations management (POM), human resources management (HRM), and management information systems (MIS). Chapters conclude with a detailed summary (entitled "What's in IT for Me?") of how key concepts in the chapter relate to each functional area.

Active Learning

We recognize the need to actively involve students in problem solving, creative thinking, and capitalizing on opportunities. Therefore, we have included in every chapter a variety of hands-on exercises, activities, and mini-cases, including exercises that require students to use software application tools. Through these activities and an interactive website, we enable students to apply the concepts they learn.

Diversified and Unique Examples from Different Industries

Extensive use of vivid examples from large corporations, small businesses, and government and not-for-profit organizations enlivens the concepts from the chapter. The examples illustrate everything from the capabilities of information systems, to their cost and justification and the innovative ways that corporations are using IS in their operations. Small businesses have been included to recognize the fact that many students will work for small- to mid-sized companies, and some will even start their own small business. In fact, some students may already be working at local businesses, and the concepts they are learning in class can be readily observed or put into practice in their jobs. Each chapter constantly highlights the integral connection between business and IS. This connection is especially evident in the chapter-opening and closing cases, the "IT's About Business" boxes, and the highlighted examples.

Successes and Failures

Many textbooks present examples of the successful implementation of information systems, and our book is no exception. However, we go one step beyond by also providing numerous examples of IS failures, in the context of lessons that can be learned from such failures. Misuse of information systems can be very expensive.

Global Focus

An understanding of global competition, partnerships, and trading is essential to success in a modern business environment. Therefore, we provide a broad selection of international cases and examples. We discuss the role of information systems in facilitating export and import, the management of international companies, and electronic trading around the globe.

Innovation and Creativity

In today's rapidly changing business environment, creativity and innovation are necessary for a business to operate effectively and profitably. Throughout our book, we demonstrate how information systems facilitate these processes.

Focus on Ethics

With corporate scandals appearing in the headlines almost daily, ethics and ethical questions have come to the forefront of businesspeople's minds. In addition to devoting an entire chapter to ethics and privacy (Chapter 3), we have included examples and cases throughout the text that focus on business ethics.

A Guide to Icons in This Book

As you read this book, you will notice a variety of icons interspersed throughout the chapters.

These icons highlight material relating to different functional areas. MIS concepts are relevant to all business careers, not just careers in IT. The functional area icons help students of different majors quickly pick out concepts and examples of particular relevance to them. Below is a quick reference of these icons:

ACCT **For the Accounting Major** highlights content relevant to the functional area of accounting.

FIN **For the Finance Major** highlights content relevant to the functional area of finance.

MKT **For the Marketing Major** highlights content relevant to the functional area of marketing.

POM **For the Production/Operations Management Major** highlights content relevant to the functional area of production/operations management.

HRM **For the Human Resources Major** highlights content relevant to the functional area of human resources.

MIS **For the MIS Major** highlights content relevant to the functional area of MIS.

What's New in Rainer *Introduction to Information Systems*, 8e

The new edition includes all new or updated chapter opening cases, closing cases, and IT's About Business.

The new edition includes all new or updated IT's About Business boxes in every chapter.

Highlights of Rainer 8e (or New Material)

Digital transformation of organizations

More than likely, students will go to work for companies that are undergoing digital transformation. We emphasize digital transformation and the information technologies that drive such transformations (see Chapter 1's opening case, IT's About Business 1.1, and closing case). The technologies driving digital transformation include the following: Big Data (see Chapter 5); Business Analytics (see Chapter 12); Social Computing (see Chapter 9); Mobile Computing (see Chapter 8); the Internet of Things (see Chapter 8); Agile Systems Development methods (see Chapter 13); Cloud Computing (see Technology Guide 3); and Artificial Intelligence (see Technology Guide 4).

The European Union's General Data Protection Regulation (GDPR)

In Chapter 3, we provide a thorough discussion of the European Union's General Data Protection Regulation (GDPR), the world's strongest data protection laws, which went into effect on May 25, 2018.

Ransomware

Because the attacks are so serious and so pervasive around the world, we discuss ransomware in detail in Section 4.3 and Chapter 4's closing case.

Data Lakes

Enterprise data warehouses can be inflexible when trying to manage many different types of data. As a result, many organizations are deploying data lakes. We address this emerging technology in IT's About Business 5.3.

Conversational Commerce

Due to its increasing importance, we elaborate on conversational commerce using chatbots in IT's About Business 7.1.

FinTech

Because of its increasing importance and potential to disrupt the financial industry, we discuss FinTech (financial technology) in IT's About Business 7.2.

The Ongoing Battle between Amazon and Walmart

Chapter 7's closing case addresses the classic battle between Amazon (initially an electronic commerce company) and Walmart (initially a bricks-and-mortar company). The case looks at how both companies are changing their business models.

Internet over Satellite

We have rewritten and updated the section *Internet over Satellite* and the companies providing this service (see Chapter 8).

Commercial Imaging

We have rewritten and updated the section *Commercial Imaging* and the companies providing this service (see Chapter 8).

Internet Access via Balloons

We have rewritten and updated the material on Google's Project Loon (high-altitude balloons) for Internet access in underserved areas (see Chapter 8).

Internet Access via Blimps

We have added material on Altaeros's Internet blimps for Internet access in underserved areas (see Chapter 8).

Fifth Generation (5G) Wireless

We updated the material on 5G wireless technologies (see Chapter 8).

The Changing Balance of Power between Organizations and Customers

Chapter 9's opening case provides an interesting look at how the balance of power between organizations and customers has drastically changed.

Messaging Apps

We added material on the variety and popularity of messaging apps (see Chapter 9).

Impacts of Emerging Technologies on Supply Chains

We discuss a new topic in IT's About Business 11.6: the impacts of emerging technologies (robotics, drones, driverless vehicles, and three-dimensional printing) on supply chains and supply chain management.

Online Resources

This text also facilitates the teaching of an introductory IS course by providing extensive support materials for instructors and students. Go to www.wiley.com to access the Student and Instructor websites.

Instructor's Manual

The Instructor's Manual includes a chapter overview, teaching tips and strategies, answers to all end-of-chapter questions, supplemental mini-cases with essay questions and answers, and experiential exercises that relate to particular topics.

Test Bank

The Test Bank is a comprehensive resource for test questions. It contains multiple-choice, true/false, short answer, and essay questions for each chapter. The multiple-choice and true/false questions are labeled according to difficulty: easy, medium, or hard.

Computerized Test Bank

Wiley provides complimentary software to generate print exams or to import test bank questions into standard LMS formats. The assessment items available in this software are a subset of those in the WileyPLUS question banks. See the assignment banks in WileyPLUS for the complete catalog of assessment items related to your adopted text.

PowerPoint Presentations

The PowerPoint presentations consist of a series of slides for each chapter of the text, are designed around the text content, and incorporate key points from the text and all text illustrations as appropriate.

Weekly Updates

Weekly updates, harvested from around the Web by David Firth of the University of Montana, provide you with the latest IT news and issues. These are posted every Monday morning throughout the year at http://wileyinformationsystemsupdates.com/ and include links to articles and videos as well as discussion questions to assign or use in class.

OfficeGrader

OfficeGrader is an Access-based VBA macro that enables automatic grading of Office assignments. The macros compare Office files and grade them against a master file. OfficeGrader is available for Word, Access, Excel, and PowerPoint for Office 2010 and Office 2013. For more information, contact your Wiley sales representative or visit the book companion site and click on "OfficeGrader."

WileyPlus

WileyPLUS with adaptive practice improves outcomes with robust practice problems and feedback, fosters engagement with course content and educational videos, and gives students the flexibility to increase confidence as they learn and prepare outside of class. With adaptive practice, instructors can see how their students learn best and then adjust material appropriately. For students, adaptive practice allows them to focus on their weakest areas to make study time more efficient.

WileyPLUS helps instructors:

- Save time by automating grading of practice, homework, quizzes, and exams
- Create a focused and personalized course that reflects their teaching style
- Quickly identify and understand student learning trends to improve classroom engagement
- Improve their course year over year using WileyPLUS data

Instructor Resources include:

- Video Lectures—The authors are featured in these video lectures, which provide explanations of key concepts throughout the book. (*Note:* This feature is only available in WileyPLUS.)
- Real-World Video Activities—An exclusive new feature in WileyPLUS offers chapter-level graded analysis activities on cutting-edge business video content from Bloomberg.
- Data Analytics & Business Module—With the emergence of data analytics transforming the business environment, Wiley has partnered with business leaders in the Business-Higher Education Forum (BHEF) to identify the competencies graduates need to be successful in their careers. As a result, WileyPLUS includes a new data analytics module with industry-validated content that prepares operations management students for a changing workforce.
- Activity Links and Starter Files—Apply the Concept activities link out to the Web, providing videos for students to view and use in the activities. When appropriate, students are provided with starter files to complete as part of the deliverable.
- Database Activity Solution Files—Every database activity in the book comes with a solution file that can be used in the Office Grader Application or by an individual to grade the students' submissions.
- Database Activity Starter Files—When appropriate, students are provided with starter files to complete as part of the deliverable.
- Instructor's Solutions Manual—This guide contains detailed solutions to all questions, exercises, and problems in the textbook.
- Practice Quizzes—These quizzes give students a way to test themselves on course material before exams. Each chapter exam contains fill-in-the-blank, application, and multiple-choice questions that provide immediate feedback with the correct answer.
- Reading Quizzes—These quizzes reinforce basic concepts from the reading.
- Spreadsheet Activity Solution Files—Every spreadsheet activity in the book comes with a solution file that can be used in the Office Grader Application or by an individual to grade the students' submissions.

Student Resources include:

- Video Lectures—The authors are featured in these video lectures, which provide explanations of key concepts throughout the book. (*Note:* This feature is only available in WileyPLUS.)
- Practice Quizzes—These quizzes give students a way to test themselves on course material before exams. Each chapter exam contains fill-in-the-blank, application, and multiple-choice questions that provide immediate feedback with the correct answer.
- Microsoft Office 2013/2016/2019 Lab Manual & Instructor Resources—by Ed Martin, CUNY-Queensborough is a thorough introduction to the Microsoft Office products of Word, Excel, Access, and PowerPoint with screenshots that show students step-by-step instructions on basic MS Office tasks.

Wiley Custom

This group's services allow you to:

- Adapt existing Wiley content and combine texts
- Incorporate and publish your own materials
- Collaborate with our team to ensure your satisfaction

Wiley Custom Select

Wiley Custom Select allows you to build your own course materials using selected chapters of any Wiley text and your own material if desired. For more information, contact your Wiley sales representative or visit http://customselect.wiley.com/.

Brief Contents

Contents

CHAPTER 1

Introduction to Information Systems

CHAPTER OUTLINE	LEARNING OBJECTIVES
1.1 Why Should I Study Information Systems?	**1.1** Identify the reasons why being an informed user of information systems is important in today's world.
1.2 Overview of Computer-Based Information Systems	**1.2** Describe the various types of computer-based information systems in an organization.
1.3 How Does IT Impact Organizations?	**1.3** Discuss ways in which information technology can affect managers and nonmanagerial workers.
1.4 Importance of Information Systems to Society	**1.4** Identify positive and negative societal effects of the increased use of information technology.

Opening Case

The Digital Transformation of the *New York Times*

MIS **POM** **MKT**

(All references to newspapers and the newspaper industry in this case refer to print newspapers.)

The Problem

For roughly two centuries, various technologies have impacted newspapers and forced them to adjust. In the late 1820s, for example, two New York newspapers, the *Journal of Commerce* and the *Courier and Enquirer*, were competing for readers. Both publications used the technology of that time in the form of Pony Express riders to deliver news from other cities and fast boats to meet incoming vessels and obtain foreign news a few hours earlier than their competitors.

In 1845, James Gordon Bennett, the editor of the *New York Herald*, asserted that the telegraph would put many newspapers out of business. In fact, his predictions turned out to be erroneous. Although telegraph wires could deliver news more rapidly than any previous technologies, they had a "last-mile" problem; specifically, they could not disseminate news quickly to thousands of people. Only

newspapers could do that. In fact, the telegraph actually made newspapers more attractive to readers and increased their sales because the telegraph enabled newspapers to report on more stories and report on them more quickly.

By 1930, some 21 million Americans had purchased radios, which enabled them to hear information before a newspaper could be delivered. Consequently, newspapers lost some advertising revenue to this new medium. However, although a radio could provide news in a brief five-minute highlight, listeners still had to rely on a newspaper to provide supporting details.

In the 1950s, television continued the decline of newspapers as the source of daily news for many people. As with radio, newspapers lost advertising revenue to television. Again, however, television could provide news in brief segments, but listeners still turned to newspapers for the details.

In the 1990s, the rapid growth of the Internet provided online media choices to the average reader while further diminishing newspapers as a source of news. The Internet continued the trend of the telegraph, radio, and television by bringing news to the consumer faster and—in the case of television—more visually than newspapers.

Newspapers have other problems. As opposed to online media, they are constrained by their physical format and by physical manufacturing and distribution as well as by expensive union contracts, printing presses, and fleets of delivery vehicles. Furthermore, online media offer advertisers full-motion video and sound. Finally, Internet search functions enable online media advertisers to carefully target readers who have revealed what they are looking for.

The Internet provides a convenient vehicle for classified advertising, particularly in categories such as jobs, motor vehicles, and real estate. Free services such as Craigslist have created major problems for the classified advertising departments of newspapers, some of which depend on classified ads for 70 percent of their advertising revenue. Online advertising has caused newspapers to increase subscription prices while at the same time decreasing advertising rates.

Other technologies have also impacted newspapers. Today, many people obtain their news from blogs, social media, mobile computing, and newsbots. A *newsbot* is a type of software designed to gather articles from newsgroups or from news websites.

The result of almost 200 years of technology impacts is that the newspaper industry has experienced decreasing classified advertising and circulation, leading to decreasing revenue. According to the Pew Research Center, people "take their news" today in these ways: 46 percent watch it, 36 percent read it, and 18 percent hear it.

The *New York Times* is an excellent example of the problems facing the print journalism industry. The financial crisis of 2008 damaged the paper's advertising revenue as many companies decreased their advertising budgets. In fact, between 2005 and 2010, the paper suffered a $600 million loss in print advertising. The *Times* responded by taking a series of dramatic steps: (1) it took out a $250 million loan from Mexican billionaire Carlos Slim in exchange for a 17 percent stake in the company, (2) it sold its Manhattan headquarters to real estate investment company W. P. Carey & Co. and then leased it back from the buyer, and (3) it sold assets, such as **About.com** and its stake in the Boston Red Sox baseball team.

The fundamental question confronting the *Times* is whether high-impact, high-cost journalism can be successful in a radically different news environment. Finding new digital revenue has become the paper's top business priority.

In 2014, the *Times* assessed its digital efforts and found problems in integrating its employees in the technology group with traditional, mainstream journalists and editors. These problems included the emphasis on print journalism over the paper's digital efforts and a resistance to change on the part of journalists and editors. The *Times* realized that it had to emphasize its digital initiatives.

Digital Solutions

The *Times* is currently undergoing a digital transformation. The paper believes that the transformation will improve its profitability, enhance the quality of its journalism, and secure its future. The primary goals of the transformation are to invest heavily in a core offering (which for the *Times* is journalism) and to continuously add new online services and features, ranging from personalized fitness advice and interactive newsbots to virtual reality films, that will make a subscription indispensable to its existing customers and more attractive to future subscribers. If the *Times* can achieve these two goals, then the paper can maximize advertising revenue, which is essential for the paper's survival.

Today, the Beta Group is the hub for most of the *Times*'s digital initiatives. Beta employees collaborate with designers, developers, and editors. In addition to Cooking and Crossword—two of the original Beta apps—the group is now working on a number of features: Real Estate, an app for home listings; Well, a health and fitness blog that the group wants to turn into a suite of personalized training and advice services;

Watching, an app dedicated to television and motion picture recommendations; and Wirecutter (**www.thewirecutter.com**), a gadget review site.

The rollout of these personal service features resembles the *Times*'s efforts in the 1970s, when the paper implemented several advertiser-friendly sections, such as Weekend, Home, and Living. Many *Times* employees dismissed these sections as a ploy to attract new readers that had little news value. That is, they viewed these services as clickbait. *Clickbait* is a negative term used to describe content targeted at generating online advertising revenue, often at the expense of quality or accuracy.

As the digital transformation of the *Times* has proceeded, the culture in the newsroom has been forced to adapt. For example, for several months, the paper's food editor insisted he had no idea what the Beta Group people were talking about. Ultimately, however, he embraced his new digital mission. In fact, in November 2016, he agreed to host a text message experiment called "Turkey Talk" to help readers prepare their Thanksgiving dinners.

Recent digital offerings from the *Times* include the following:

- During the 2016 presidential campaign, the *Times* created a Facebook Messenger newsbot that offered daily updates on the race in the voice of political reporter Nick Confessore. The bot was able to use natural language processing so that it could understand the questions posed to Confessore and respond to readers' queries using prewritten answers.

- Still Processing: A weekly podcast from Wesley Morris and Jenna Wortham about the intersection of pop culture and public policy.

- Puzzle Mania: A special print-only section in the Sunday *Times* that contains the "MegaPuzzle," a 728-clue crossword that was the largest ever created for the *Times.*

- Race/Related: A weekly e-mail newsletter with features and essays on race and ethnicity in America.

The *Times* is also experimenting with virtual reality. It is partnering with Google to send Google's Cardboard VR viewers to all of the *Times*'s 1.1 million Sunday print-edition subscribers, creating an NYT VR app that has been downloaded more than 1 million times. In addition, the two companies are producing 16 original VR films about topics as disparate as displaced refugees (*The Displaced*) and battling ISIS in Iraq (*The Fight for Falluja*).

In March 2016, Facebook made a proposition to the *Times*. If the newspaper would produce dozens of livestreams each month for Facebook Live, the company's new video platform, then Facebook would pay the *Times* $3 million per year. The *Times* began producing content in two weeks. Over the next few months, the Live team recruited more than 300 *Times* journalists to livestream anything and everything: press conferences, protests, political conventions, whatever. The project helped train hundreds of newsroom employees in how to frame a shot and speak on camera and all of the other skills necessary to produce journalism in the future.

Results

It is important to realize that the *Times* has implemented digital initiatives in the past. Specifically, the paper launched its website (**www.nytimes.com**) on January 22, 1996. At that time, it was updated once per day with stories from the print edition. In addition, it was free to read for anyone in the United States who had access to an Internet connection. Unfortunately, the website was updated far too infrequently, and it was not generating any income.

To resolve this problem, the *Times* allocated greater resources to improving and maintaining its website, enabling very rapid updates to its content. Interestingly, in May 2018, the top five most popular news websites were Yahoo! News, Google News, the Huffington Post, CNN, and the *New York Times*.

In 2011, the paper implemented a paywall that for the first time required people to pay for full and regular access to **NYTimes.com**. A *paywall* on a website is an arrangement where access to content is restricted to users who have paid to subscribe to the site. The paywall became a significant success with more than 3.3 million people paying for a digital subscription in the first quarter of 2019. Significantly, during the first quarter of 2019 the *Times* added another 265,000 digital-only subscribers.

For 2018, the paper reported digital advertising revenue of $709 million. The paper's current goal for total digital revenue is $800 million by 2020 and 10 million total digital subscriptions by 2025. The *Times* senior management believes this revenue could fund the paper's global news-gathering operations either with or without a print edition.

To realize the additional $100 million, the *Times* must find new subscribers across all of its multiple platforms. The site's paywall remains its most powerful incentive to subscribe, which is why most new subscribers sign up after they have maximized their monthly allowance on **NYTimes.com**. Subscriptions through mobile and social media continue to lag behind desktop subscriptions.

The *Times* reported total 2018 revenue of $1.75 billion, even though the paper's 2018 print advertising revenue continued to decline. Interestingly, in 2018 The *Times* added 120 newsroom employees, bringing the total number of journalists to 1,600, the largest count in the paper's history.

The bottom line: The *Times*'s digital initiatives are helping to counter its losses in print advertising, enabling the newspaper to remain profitable.

Sources: Compiled from J. Peiser, "The New York Times Co. Reports $709 Million in Digital Revenue for 2018," *The New York Times*, February 6, 2019; R. Edmonds, "The New York Times Passes 3 Million Mark in Paid Digital Subscribers," *Poynter*, November 1, 2018; J. Peiser, "New York Times Co. Reports Revenue Growth as Digital Subscriptions Rise," *New York Times*, May 3, 2018; S. Ember, "New York Times Co. Subscription Revenue Surpassed $1 Billion in 2017," *New York Times*, February 8, 2018; C. McLellan, "Digital Transformation: Retooling Business for a New Age," *ZDNet*, March 1, 2017; S. Ember, "New York Times Co.'s Decline in Print Advertising Tempered by Digital Gains," *New York Times*, February 2, 2017; "Top 15 Most Popular News Websites," *The eBusiness Guide*, February 2017; G. Snyder, "The New York Times Claws Its Way into the Future," *Wired*, February 2, 2017; J. Benton, This Is *The New York Times'* Digital Path Forward," *NiemanLab*, January 17, 2017; "Digital Transformation in the U.S.," *IDC InfoBrief*, January, 2017; M. Smith, "So You Think You Chose to Read This Article?" *BBC News*, July 22, 2016; A. Mitchell, J. Gottfried, M. Barthel, and E. Shearer, "Pathways to News," *Pew Research Center*, July 7, 2016; S. Elvery, "ABC NewsBot: The Bots Are Coming for You…and They Have Election News!," *ABC News*, June 30, 2016; T. Bernard, "TechCrunch Launches a Personalized News Recommendations Bot on Facebook Messenger," *TechCrunch*, April 19, 2016; T. Saperstein, "The Future of Print: Newspapers Struggle to Survive in the Age of Technology," *Harvard Political Review*, December 6, 2014; E. Dans, "Adapt or Die: The Simple Truth about Technology and the Newspaper Industry," *Medium.com*, August 4, 2014; J. Bruce, "Newspaper Advertising vs. Radio Advertising—and the Winner Is…," *Mediaspace Solutions*, July 22, 2014; M. Ingram, "The Internet Didn't Invent Viral Content or Clickbait Journalism—There's Just More of It Now, and It Happens Faster," *GigaOM*, April 1, 2014; S. O'Hear, "A First Look at Echobox, an Analytics Tool for News Sites That Actually Helps Drive Traffic," *TechCrunch*, February 17, 2014; "Newspapers and Technology," *The Economist*, December 17, 2009; D. Lieberman, "Newspaper Closings Raise Fears about Industry," *USA Today*, March 17, 2009; P. Sullivan, "As the Internet Grows Up, the News Industry Is Forever Changed," *Washington Post*, June 19, 2006; and www.nytimes.com, accessed July 6, 2017.

Questions

1. Explain why implementing a digital transformation was a strategic necessity for the *New York Times*. (*Hint:* How do you "take your news?")

2. Discuss the variety of technological (digital) efforts the *Times* undertook during its digital transformation.

3. Can you think of other digital initiatives the *Times* might use to increase circulation and enhance its bottom line?

Introduction

Before we proceed, we need to define information technology and information systems. **Information technology (IT)** refers to any computer-based tool that people use to work with information and to support an organization's information and information-processing needs. An **information system (IS)** collects, processes, stores, analyzes, and disseminates information for a specific purpose.

IT has far-reaching effects on individuals, organizations, and our planet. Although this text is largely devoted to the many ways in which IT is transforming modern organizations, you will also learn about the significant impacts of IT on individuals and societies, the global economy, and our physical environment. In addition, IT is making our world smaller, enabling more and more people to communicate, collaborate, and compete, thereby leveling the competitive playing field.

This text focuses on the successful applications of IT in organizations; that is, how organizations can use IT to solve business problems and achieve competitive advantage in the marketplace. However, not all business problems can be solved with IT. Therefore, you must continue to develop your business skills!

When you graduate, you will either start your own business or work for an organization, whether it is public sector, private sector, for-profit, or not-for-profit. Your organization will have to survive and compete in an environment that has been radically transformed by information technology. This environment is global, massively interconnected, intensely competitive, 24/7/365, real time, rapidly changing, and information intensive. To compete successfully, your organization must use IT effectively.

As you read this chapter and this text, keep in mind that the information technologies you will learn about are important to businesses of all sizes. No matter which area of business you major in, which industry you work for, or the size of your company, you will benefit from learning about IT. Who knows? Maybe you will use the tools you learn about in this class to make your great idea a reality by becoming an entrepreneur and starting your own business!

The modern environment is intensely competitive not only for your organization but for you as well. You must compete with human talent from around the world. Therefore, you personally will have to make effective use of IT.

Accordingly, this chapter begins with a discussion of three reasons why you should become knowledgeable about IT. Next, it distinguishes among data, information, and knowledge, and it differentiates computer-based information systems from application programs. Finally, it considers the impacts of information systems on organizations and on society in general.

1.1 | Why Should I Study Information Systems?

Author Lecture Videos are available exclusively in *WileyPLUS*.
Apply the Concept activities are available in the Appendix and in *WileyPLUS*.

Your use of IT makes you part of the most connected generation in history: You have grown up online; you are, quite literally, never out of touch, and you use more information technologies (in the form of digital devices) for more tasks and are bombarded with more information than any generation in history. The *MIT Technology Review* refers to you as *Homo conexus*. Information technologies are so deeply embedded in your lives that your daily routines would be almost unrecognizable to a college student just 20 years ago.

Essentially, you practice *continuous computing*, surrounded by a movable information network. This network is created by constant cooperation among the digital devices you carry (e.g., laptops, tablets, and smartphones), the wired and wireless networks that you access as you move about, and Web-based tools for finding information and communicating and collaborating with other people. Your network enables you to pull information about virtually anything from anywhere, at any time, and to push your own ideas back to the Web, from wherever you are, via a mobile device. Think of everything you do online, often with your smartphone: register for classes; take classes (and not just at your university); access class syllabi, information, PowerPoints, and lectures; research class papers and presentations; conduct banking; pay your bills; research, shop, and purchase products from companies and other people; sell your "stuff"; search for and apply for jobs; make your travel reservations (hotel, airline, rental car); create your own blog and post your own podcasts and videos to it; design your own page on Facebook and LinkedIn; make and upload videos to YouTube; take, edit, and print your own digital photographs; stream music and movies to your personal libraries; use RSS feeds to create your personal electronic newspaper; text and tweet your friends and family throughout your day; send Snaps; order a ride from Uber; select a place or room to rent on Airbnb; and many other activities. (*Note:* If any of these terms are unfamiliar to you, don't worry. You will learn about everything mentioned here in detail later in this text.)

Let's put the preceding paragraph in perspective. What would a typical day for you be like if you had no access to computing devices of any kind, including your phone?

The Informed User—You!

So the question is: Why should you learn about information systems and information technology? After all, you can comfortably use a computer (or other electronic devices) to perform many activities, you have been surfing the Web for years, and you feel confident that you can manage any IT application that your organization's MIS department installs. Let's look at three reasons why you should learn about Information Systems and IT.

MIS The first reason to learn about information systems and information technology is to become an **informed user**; that is, a person knowledgeable about Information Systems and IT. In general, informed users obtain greater value from whichever technologies they use. You will enjoy many benefits from being an informed user of IT, including the following:

USERS ← ┆ → MIS

FIGURE 1.1   **MIS provides what users see and use on their computers.**

- You will benefit more from your organization's IT applications because you will understand what is "behind" those applications (see **Figure 1.1**). That is, what you see on your computer screen is brought to you by your MIS department, who are operating "behind" your screen.

- You will be in a position to enhance the quality of your organization's IT applications with your input.

- Even as a new graduate, you will quickly be in a position to recommend—and perhaps to help select—which IT applications your organization will use.

- Being an informed user will keep you abreast of both new information technologies and rapid developments in existing technologies. Remaining "on top of things" will help you to anticipate the impacts that "new and improved" technologies will have on your organization and to make recommendations regarding the adoption and use of these technologies.

- You will understand how using IT can improve your organization's performance and teamwork as well as your own productivity.

- If you have ideas of becoming an entrepreneur, then being an informed user will help you to utilize IT when you start your own business.

The second reason to learn about Information Systems and IT is that the organization you join will undoubtedly be undergoing a digital transformation. In fact, digital transformation has become one of the most important strategies for organizations. The Data Warehousing Institute (**www.tdwi.org**) predicted that, by the end of 2018, approximately two-thirds of chief executive officers of the *Forbes* Global 2000 companies would have digital transformation at the center of their corporate strategy. (The Global 2000 is a list of the 2,000 largest public companies in the world, ranked by *Forbes* magazine.)

Digital transformation is the business strategy that leverages IT to dramatically improve employee, customer, and business partner relationships; to support continuous improvement in business operations and business processes; and to develop new business models and businesses. The information technologies that drive digital transformation include the following:

- Big Data (see Chapter 5)
- Business analytics (see Chapter 12)
- Social computing (see Chapter 9)

- Mobile computing (see Chapter 8)
- The Internet of Things (see Chapter 8)
- Agile systems development methods (see Chapter 13)
- Cloud computing (see Technology Guide 3)
- Artificial intelligence (see Technology Guide 4)

You see examples of digital transformation in this chapter's opening case and IT's About Business 1.1.

IT's About Business 1.1

A Variety of Digital Transformations

`POM` `MKT` `MIS`

Wendy's

Fast-food restaurant chain Wendy's (**www.wendys.com**) is undergoing a digital transformation with the goal of putting digital technologies at the center of its customer experience. The company initiated its digital transformation process when it realized that many of its customers, both Millennials and non-Millennials, expect to interact with companies via digital channels. Therefore, Wendy's was going to be judged on the digital experience that it provided for these customers. To implement this transformation, Wendy's created a laboratory called 90 Degree Labs, which it staffed with engineers, customer experience experts, and user experience experts. The lab produces three products: the company website, apps, and self-order kiosks.

Wendy's became one of the first companies to use self-ordering kiosks to control labor costs and deployed this technology in about 4000 (60 percent) of its restaurants by July 2019. Today, stores with the kiosks are seeing higher average checks and higher customer satisfaction scores. As such, the kiosks remain integral to Wendy's strategy to provide a superior digital customer experience.

Wendy's noted that its customers are already familiar with mobile apps and that its kiosks were an intermediate step in providing a mobile digital experience for them. The company believes that once its customers become comfortable using the in-store kiosks, they can transition more easily to ordering via a mobile app.

Utilizing kiosks and mobile apps will enable Wendy's to manage lines, plan kitchen capacity, and order the correct amount of supplies at the right times. Mobile apps also enable customers to get customized orders at the right place and time.

In early 2019, Wendy's announced a $25 million investment in digital initiatives, including new scanning equipment. The scanners will enable employees to scan mobile offers and coupons rather than having to key them in to the point-of-sale system.

`POM` `MKT` `MIS` **Professional Golf**

Golf is having difficulties as the baby-boomer generation ages and Millennials do not seem to be as interested in the game. In the United States, planners are considering how to manage large tracts of land opened up by closed golf courses. In response, golf is developing what it calls the "connected course" for golf tournaments as a way for golf to broaden its appeal to younger people who are rarely without their computing devices.

First, golf courses must be prepared for the daily technology demands of a modern golf tournament. Each course must support the demands of television broadcasters, the professional tour's own scoring and operational systems, as well as wireless connectivity for spectators.

Preparing courses typically requires laying 6 to 10 miles of fiber in the ground as well as deploying sensors with 5G wireless technology when 5G is ready in 2020. The goal of this technology is for it to generate better insights for staff, players, coaches, business partners, advertisers, and spectators.

The sensors will provide location data that will bring new insights into how spectators move around a course. These data provide tournament sponsors with relevant information on spectator location and movement to increase their potential engagement. For example, spectators could access information relating to a sponsor-operated event or sales concession.

`POM` `MIS` **The Freight Forwarding Industry**

Freight forwarders assist their clients in shipping goods and raw materials by rail, ship, or plane. Significantly, this industry has conducted business the same way for many years. They employ a global network of agents who possess a thorough knowledge of duties, taxes, penalties, and port requirements around the world. In return for a fee from their clients, they negotiate rates with trucking companies, airlines, and ship owners, and they make deals based on large volumes of cargo.

This global business has lagged behind many other industries in adapting to digital transformation. Start-up Freightos (**www.freightos.com**), an online marketplace, is addressing that problem. Freightos allows shippers to book online, receiving bids from multiple freight forwarders within seconds rather than days and often for lower prices than offline alternatives offer.

Another start-up, Windward (**www.wnwd.com**), combines location data with other information about each vessel's size, owner, and other factors to map the paths and behaviors of ships at sea. More than 90 percent of world trade moves by sea. Once cargo is on a ship, however, little information is available regarding the path the ship is taking or the stops it makes. Only in recent years have the largest ships regularly transmitted location data. However, even these ships may stop transmitting and "go dark" at any time.

To analyze the myriad data points coming in from each ship, Windward has constructed artificial intelligence systems using natural language processing to identify unusual or important patterns of behavior. These systems generate maps that might reveal ships meeting mid-ocean to transfer cargo or crossing in and out of a country's territorial waters in patterns that can be associated with illegal fishing or smuggling. Most of Windward's customers are fishing authorities, coast guards, and navies. However, the company is confident that its information can be valuable to ship owners, cargo owners, and insurance companies as well.

Significantly, Amazon (**www.amazon.com**) is entering the freight forwarding business. For a detailed look at Amazon's efforts in this area, see the closing case in Chapter 11.

MIS America's Cup Yachting

A victory in the America's Cup can go to the team with the best data rather than the best boat. During these head-to-head races, even a small increase in speed can result in a win. Therefore, the more data that teams can gather about the performance of their boats and crews, the better.

To obtain more data, teams are mounting sensors all over the catamarans that record huge amounts of data during a race, from boat speed and wind data to the forces that are stressing the different parts of the boat. In fact, teams can gather as much as 16 gigabytes of data per day.

One team streams its sensor data to a chase boat in real time. The boat design coordinator for the team stays on the chase boat as a Wi-Fi system transmits data from the racing catamaran. In addition to sensors, his team also collects video using GoPro cameras that target various critical parts of the catamaran. The coordinator conducts real-time analysis on the chase boat because he can watch the actual performance of the boat on the water in real time. He later sends the data to headquarters for further analysis. Then analysts at team headquarters virtually replay the race. This analysis helps each crew member enhance his or her performance and also helps engineers build a faster boat by changing the design of its catamaran.

Sources: Compiled from J. Maze, "Wendy's Investing $25M behind Digital Efforts," *Restaurant Business*, February 21, 2019; "Can Digitisation Help Golf Out of Bunker?" *Computer Weekly*, August 7–13, 2018; B. Sozzi, "Wendy's CEO: Future of Fast Food Will Include Kiosks and Fast Pass Drive-Thrus, *The Street*, June 11, 2018; T. Newcomb, "Data Supercharges Billion-Dollar Boats in the World's Fastest Sailing Race," *Wired*, July 8, 2017; A. Bruno, "Technology and Its Impact on the Freight Forwarding Industry," *ICAT Logistics*, June 12, 2017; M. Harvey, "How Data Crunching Was Vitally Important to Britain's America's Cup Team," *The Telegraph*, June 1, 2017; "One Fast Food Chain Is Adding Automated Kiosks to 1,000 of Its Restaurants in 2017," *Futurism*, March 3, 2017; L. Dignan, "Wendy's Cooks Up Digital Transformation Plans with Kiosks, Mobile Apps, Customer Experience Lab," *TechRepublic*, March 1, 2017; "Digital Transformation in the U.S.," *IDC InfoBrief*, January 2017; C. McDonald, "Unilever Puts Digital Transformation in the Hands of IT," *Computer Weekly*, November 2, 2016; N. Byrnes, "This $1 Trillion Industry Is Finally Going Digital," *MIT Technology Review*, October 24, 2016; D. Walter, "Oracle Team USA Credits Data & Analytics for America's Cup Success," *CMS Wire*, September 21, 2016; D. Kline, "Are Robots Taking Over Fast Food Restaurants?" *Newsweek*, September 5, 2016; D. Newman, "Top 10 Trends for Digital Transformation in 2017; *Forbes*, August 30, 2016; M. Castillo, "Technology Could Soon Be Replacing Fast Food Workers," *PSFK.com*, April 21, 2016; and "Wendy's Opens 90 Degree Labs to Fuel Future Technology Innovation," *PRNewswire*, May 26, 2015.

Questions

This case presents digital transformations in four organizations across four industries.

1. For which organization is digital transformation the most critical? Why? Support your answer.

2. For which organization is digital transformation the least critical? Why? Support your answer.

3. Would your university be a good candidate for digital transformation? Why or why not? Support your answer.

4. If you responded yes, then what types of digital initiatives should your university undertake to transform itself?

The third reason to learn about Information Systems and IT is that managing the IS function within an organization is no longer the exclusive responsibility of the IS department. Rather, users now play key roles in every step of this process. The overall objective in this text is to provide you with the necessary information to contribute immediately to managing the IS function in your organization. In short, our goal is to help you become a very informed user!

IT Offers Career Opportunities

MIS Because IT is vital to the operation of modern businesses, it offers many employment opportunities. The demand for traditional IT staff—programmers, business analysts, systems analysts, and designers—is substantial. In addition, many well-paid jobs exist in areas such as the Internet and electronic commerce (e-commerce), mobile commerce (m-commerce), network security, telecommunications, and multimedia design.

The IS field includes the people in various organizations who design and build information systems, the people who use those systems, and the people responsible for managing those systems. At the top of the list is the chief information officer (CIO).

The CIO is the executive who is in charge of the IS function. In most modern organizations, the CIO works with the chief executive officer (CEO), the chief financial officer (CFO), and other senior executives. Therefore, he or she actively participates in the organization's strategic planning process. In today's digital environment, the IS function has become increasingly strategic within organizations. As a result, although most CIOs still rise from the IS department, a growing number are coming up through the ranks in the business units (e.g., marketing, finance). Regardless of your major, you could become the CIO of your organization one day. This is another reason to be an informed user of information systems!

TABLE 1.1 Information Technology Jobs

Position	Job Description
Chief Information Officer	Highest-ranking IS manager; responsible for all strategic planning in the organization
IS Director	Manages all systems throughout the organization and the day-to-day operations of the entire IS organization
Information Center Manager	Manages IS services, such as help desks, hot lines, training, and consulting
Applications Development Manager	Coordinates and manages new systems development projects
Project Manager	Manages a particular new systems development project
Systems Analyst	Interfaces between users and programmers; determines information requirements and technical specifications for new applications
Operations Manager	Supervises the day-to-day operations of the data and/or computer center
Programming Manager	Coordinates all application programming efforts
Social Media Manager	Coordinates all social media development efforts and all social media monitoring and response efforts
Business Analyst	Focuses on designing solutions for business problems; interfaces closely with users to demonstrate how IT can be used innovatively
Systems Programmer	Creates the computer code for developing new systems software or maintaining existing systems software
Applications Programmer	Creates the computer code for developing new applications or maintaining existing applications
Emerging Technologies Manager	Forecasts technology trends; evaluates and experiments with new technologies
Network Manager	Coordinates and manages the organization's voice and data networks
Database Administrator	Manages the organization's databases and oversees the use of database-management software
Auditing or Computer Security Manager	Oversees the ethical and legal use of information systems
Webmaster	Manages the organization's website
Web Designer	Creates websites and pages

Table 1.1 provides a list of IT jobs, along with a description of each one. For further details about careers in IT, see **www.linkedin.com**, **www.computerworld.com**, and **www.monster.com**.

Career opportunities in IS are strong and are projected to remain strong over the next 10 years. In fact, *U.S. News & World Report* listed its "100 best jobs of 2018," *Money* listed its "best jobs in America for 2018," and *Forbes* listed its "20 best jobs" for 2018. Let's take a look at these rankings. (Note that the rankings differ because the magazines used different criteria in their research.) As you can see, jobs suited for MIS majors appear in all three lists, many of them quite high. The magazines with their job rankings are as follows:

U.S. News & World Report (out of 100)

#1 Software Developer

#32 Information Security Analyst

#42 Information Technology Manager

#46 Computer Systems Analyst

Money (out of 50)

#2 IT Development Engineer

#8 Mobile Systems Developer

#21 Software Engineer

#26 Database Administrator

Forbes (out of 20)

#2 Software Engineer

#4 IT Solutions Architect

#11 IT Manager

#13 Data Engineer

#14 Front-End Engineer (User Experience Designer)

Not only do IS careers offer strong job growth, but the pay is excellent as well. The Bureau of Labor Statistics, an agency within the Department of Labor that is responsible for tracking and analyzing trends relating to the labor market, notes that the median salary in 2016 for "computer and information systems managers" was approximately $139,220 and predicted that the profession would grow by an average of 12 percent per year through 2026.

In addition, LinkedIn analyzed thousands of profiles of members who graduated between 2015 and 2017. LinkedIn collected salary information using the LinkedIn Salary tool. It discovered that of the 15 highest-paying entry-level jobs, 8 were in the technology industry. These jobs include the following:

Job	Median Starting Salary
#2 Data Scientist	$93,500
#3 Hardware Engineer	$90,000
#4 Software Engineer	$80,000
#6 Technology Analyst	$76,000
#9 Consulting Analyst	$75,000
#10 Management Consultant	$74,300
#11 Security Engineer	$74,200
#14 User Experience Designer	$72,000

Managing Information Resources

Managing information systems in modern organizations is a difficult, complex task. Several factors contribute to this complexity. First, information systems have enormous strategic value to organizations. Firms rely on them so heavily that, in some cases, when these systems are not working (even for a short time), the firm cannot function. (This situation is called "being hostage to information systems.") Second, information systems are very expensive to acquire, operate, and maintain.

A third factor contributing to the difficulty in managing information systems is the evolution of the management information systems (MIS) function within the organization. When businesses first began to use computers in the early 1950s, the MIS department "owned" the only computing resource in the organization, the mainframe. At that time, end users did not interact directly with the mainframe.

MIS In contrast, in the modern organization, computers are located in all departments, and almost all employees use computers in their work. This situation, known as *end user computing*, has led to a partnership between the MIS department and the end users. The MIS department now acts as more of a consultant to end users, viewing them as customers. In fact, the main function of the MIS department is to use IT to solve end users' business problems.

MIS As a result of these developments, the responsibility for managing information resources is now divided between the MIS department and the end users. This arrangement raises several important questions: Which resources are managed by whom? What is the role of the MIS department, its structure, and its place within the organization? What is the appropriate relationship between the MIS department and the end users? Regardless of who is doing what, it is essential that the MIS department and the end users work in close cooperation.

There is no standard way to divide responsibility for developing and maintaining information resources between the MIS department and the end users. Instead, that division depends on several factors: the size and nature of the organization, the amount and type of IT resources, the organization's attitudes toward computing, the attitudes of top management toward computing, the maturity level of the technology, the amount and nature of outsourced IT work, and even the countries in which the company operates. Generally speaking, the MIS department

TABLE 1.2 **The Changing Role of the Information Systems Department**

Traditional Functions of the MIS Department

Managing systems development and systems project management

- As an end user, you will have critical input into the systems development process. You will learn about systems development in Chapter 13.

Managing computer operations, including the computer center

Staffing, training, and developing IS skills

Providing technical services

Infrastructure planning, development, and control

- As an end user, you will provide critical input about the IS infrastructure needs of your department.

New (Consultative) Functions of the MIS Department

Initiating and designing specific strategic information systems

- As an end user, your information needs will often mandate the development of new strategic information systems.

You will decide which strategic systems you need (because you know your business needs and requirements better than the MIS department does), and you will provide input into developing these systems.

Incorporating the Internet and electronic commerce into the business

- As an end user, you will be primarily responsible for effectively using the Internet and electronic commerce in your business. You will work with the MIS department to accomplish these tasks.

Managing system integration, including the Internet, intranets, and extranets

- As an end user, your business needs will determine how you want to use the Internet, your corporate intranets, and extranets to accomplish your goals. You will be primarily responsible for advising the MIS department on the most effective use of the Internet, your corporate intranets, and extranets.

Educating the non-MIS managers about IT

- Your department will be primarily responsible for advising the MIS department on how best to educate and train your employees about IT.

Educating the MIS staff about the business

- Communications between the MIS department and business units is a two-way street. You will be responsible for educating the MIS staff on your business, its needs and requirements, and its goals.

Partnering with business unit executives

- Essentially, you will be in a partnership with the MIS department. You will be responsible for seeing that this partnership is one "between equals" and ensuring its success.

Managing outsourcing

- Outsourcing is driven by business needs. Therefore, the outsourcing decision resided largely with the business units (i.e., with you). The MIS department, working closely with you, will advise you on technical issues, such as communications bandwidth and security.

Proactively using business and technical knowledge to see innovative ideas about using IT

- Your business needs will often drive innovative ideas about how to effectively use information systems to accomplish your goals. The best way to bring these innovative uses of IS to life is to partner closely with your MIS department. Such close partnerships have amazing synergies!

Creating business alliances with business partners

- The needs of your business unit will drive these alliances, typically along your supply chain. Again, your MIS department will act as your adviser on various issues, including hardware and software compatibility, implementing extranets, communications, and security.

is responsible for corporate-level and shared resources, and the end users are responsible for departmental resources. **Table 1.2** identifies both the traditional functions and various new, consultative functions of the MIS department.

So, where do the end users come in? Take a close look at Table 1.2. Under the traditional MIS functions, you will see two functions for which you provide vital input: managing systems development and infrastructure planning. Under the consultative MIS functions, in contrast, you exercise the primary responsibility for each function, while the MIS department acts as your adviser.

Before you go on . . .

1. Rate yourself as an informed user. (Be honest; this isn't a test!)
2. Explain the benefits of being an informed user of information systems.
3. Discuss the various career opportunities offered in the IT field.

1.2 | Overview of Computer-Based Information Systems

Organizations refer to their management information system's functional area by several names, including the MIS Department, the Information Systems (IS) Department, the Information Technology (IT) Department, and the Information Services Department. Regardless of the name, however, this functional area deals with the planning for—and the development, management, and use of—information technology tools to help people perform all the tasks related to information processing and management. Recall that information technology relates to any computer-based tool that people use to work with information and to support the information and information-processing needs of an organization.

As previously stated, an information system collects, processes, stores, analyzes, and disseminates information for a specific purpose. The purpose of information systems has been defined as getting the right information to the right people, at the right time, in the right amount, and in the right format. Because information systems are intended to supply useful information, we need to differentiate between information and two closely related terms: data and knowledge (see **Figure 1.2**).

Data items refer to an elementary description of things, events, activities, and transactions that are recorded, classified, and stored but are not organized to convey any specific meaning. Data items can be numbers, letters, figures, sounds, and images. Examples of data items are collections of numbers (e.g., 3.11, 2.96, 3.95, 1.99, 2.08) and characters (e.g., B, A, C, A, B, D, F, C).

Information refers to data that have been organized so that they have meaning and value to the recipient. For example, a grade-point average (GPA) by itself is data, but a student's name coupled with his or her GPA is information. The recipient interprets the meaning and draws conclusions and implications from the information. Consider the examples of data

Author Lecture Videos are available exclusively in *WileyPLUS*.
Apply the Concept activities are available in the Appendix and in *WileyPLUS*.

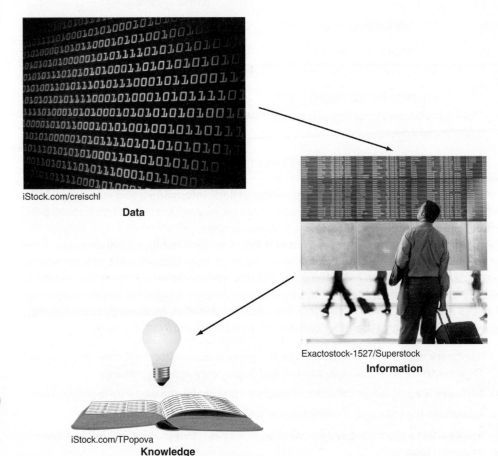

iStock.com/creischl
Data

Exactostock-1527/Superstock
Information

iStock.com/TPopova
Knowledge

FIGURE 1.2 Data, information, and knowledge.

provided in the preceding paragraph. Within the context of a university, the numbers could be GPAs, and the letters could be grades in an Introduction to MIS class.

Knowledge consists of data and/or information that have been organized and processed to convey understanding, experience, accumulated learning, and expertise as they apply to a current business problem. For example, suppose that a company recruiting at your school has found over time that students with GPAs over 3.0 have experienced the greatest success in its management program. Based on this accumulated knowledge, that company may decide to interview only those students with GPAs over 3.0. This example presents an example of knowledge because the company utilizes information—GPAs—to address a business problem—hiring successful employees. As you can see from this example, organizational knowledge, which reflects the experience and expertise of many people, has great value to all employees.

Consider this example:

Data	Information	Knowledge
[No context]	[University context]	
3.16	3.16 + John Jones = GPA	* Job prospects
2.92	2.92 + Sue Smith = GPA	* Graduate school prospects
1.39	1.39 + Kyle Owens = GPA	* Scholarship prospects
3.95	3.95 + Tom Elias = GPA	
Data	**Information**	**Knowledge**
[No context]	[Professional baseball pitcher context]	
3.16	3.16 + Ken Rice = ERA	
2.92	2.92 + Ed Dyas = ERA	* Keep pitcher, trade pitcher, or send pitcher to minor leagues
1.39	1.39 + Hugh Carr = ERA	* Salary/contract negotiations
3.95	3.95 + Nick Ford = ERA	

GPA = Grade-point average (higher is better)

ERA = Earned run average (lower is better); ERA is the number of runs per nine innings that a pitcher surrenders.

You see that the same data items, with no context, can mean entirely different things in different contexts.

Now that you have a clearer understanding of data, information, and knowledge, let's shift our focus to computer-based information systems. As you have seen, these systems process data into information and knowledge that you can use.

A **computer-based information system (CBIS)** is an information system that uses computer technology to perform some or all of its intended tasks. Although not all information systems are computerized, today most are. For this reason, the term *information system* is typically used synonymously with *computer-based information system*. The basic components of a CBIS are listed below. The first four are called **information technology components**. **Figure 1.3** illustrates how these four components interact to form a CBIS:

- **Hardware** consists of devices such as the processor, monitor, keyboard, and printer. Together, these devices accept, process, and display data and information.
- **Software** is a program or collection of programs that enable the hardware to process data.
- A **database** is a collection of related files or tables containing data.
- A **network** is a connecting system (wireline or wireless) that enables multiple computers to share resources.

- **Procedures** are the instructions for combining the above components to process information and generate the desired output.
- People use the hardware and software, interface with it, or utilize its output.

Figure 1.4 illustrates how these components are integrated to form the wide variety of information systems found within an organization. Starting at the bottom of the figure, you see that the IT components of hardware, software, networks (wireline and wireless), and databases form the **information technology platform**. IT personnel use these components to develop information systems, oversee security and risk, and manage data. These activities

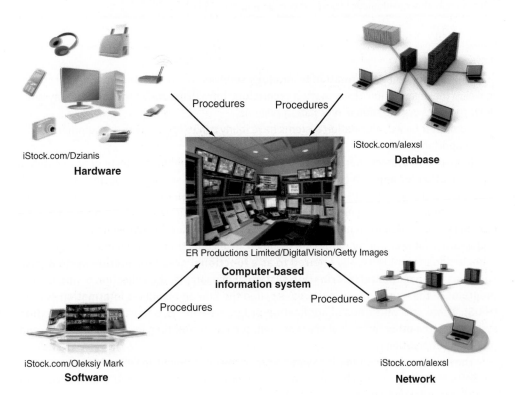

FIGURE 1.3   Computer-based information systems consist of hardware, software, databases, networks, procedures, and people.

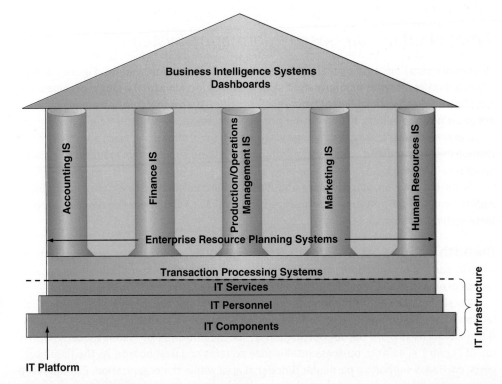

FIGURE 1.4   Information technology inside your organization.

TABLE 1.3	Major Capabilities of Information Systems
Perform high-speed, high-volume numerical computations.	
Provide fast, accurate communication and collaboration within and among organizations.	
Store huge amounts of information in an easy-to-access yet small space.	
Allow quick and inexpensive access to vast amounts of information worldwide.	
Analyze and interpret vast amounts of data quickly and efficiently.	
Automate both semiautomatic business processes and manual tasks.	

cumulatively are called **information technology services**. The IT components plus IT services make up the organization's **information technology infrastructure**. At the top of the pyramid are the various organizational information systems.

Computer-based information systems have many capabilities. **Table 1.3** summarizes the most important ones.

Information systems perform these various tasks via a wide spectrum of applications. An **application** (or **app**) is a computer program designed to support a specific task or business process. (A synonymous term is **application program**.) Each functional area or department within a business organization uses dozens of application programs. For example, the human resources department sometimes uses one application for screening job applicants and another for monitoring employee turnover. The collection of application programs in a single department is usually referred to as a **functional area information system** (also known as a **departmental information system**). For example, the collection of application programs in the human resources area is called the human resources information system (HRIS). There are collections of application programs—that is, departmental information systems—in the other functional areas as well, such as accounting, finance, marketing, and production/operations.

The importance of information systems cannot be understated. In fact, a 2016 report from the Software Alliance shows that information systems added more than *$1 trillion of value* to the U.S. gross domestic product.

Types of Computer-Based Information Systems

Modern organizations employ many different types of information systems. Figure 1.4 illustrates the different types of information systems that function *within* a single organization, and **Figure 1.5** shows the different types of information systems that function *among* multiple organizations. You will study transaction processing systems, management information systems, and enterprise resource planning systems in Chapter 10. You will learn about customer relationship management (CRM) systems in Chapter 11 and supply chain management (SCM) systems in Chapter 11.

In the next section, you will learn about the numerous and diverse types of information systems employed by modern organizations. You will also read about the types of support these systems provide.

Breadth of Support of Information Systems.   Certain information systems support parts of organizations, others support entire organizations, and still others support groups of organizations. This section addresses all of these systems.

Recall that each department or functional area within an organization has its own collection of application programs, or information systems. These functional area information systems (FAISs) are the supporting pillars for the information systems located at the top of Figure 1.4, namely, business intelligence systems and dashboards. As the name suggests, each FAIS supports a particular functional area within the organization. Examples are

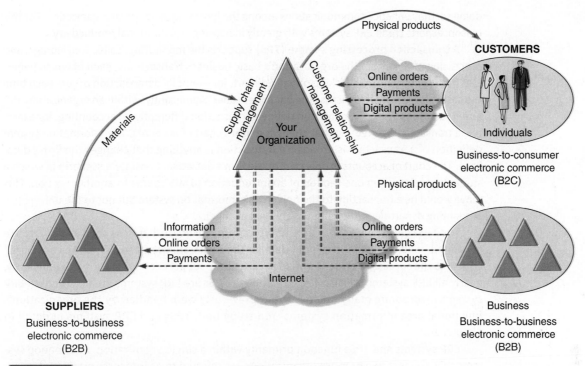

FIGURE 1.5 **Information systems that function among multiple organizations.**

accounting IS, finance IS, production/operations management (POM) IS, marketing IS, and human resources IS.

ACCT **FIN** Consider these examples of IT systems in the various functional areas of an organization. In finance and accounting, managers use IT systems to forecast revenues and business activity, to determine the best sources and uses of funds, and to perform audits to ensure that the organization is fundamentally sound and that all financial reports and documents are accurate.

MKT In sales and marketing, managers use information technology to perform the following functions:

- *Product analysis:* Developing new goods and services.
- *Site analysis:* Determining the best location for production and distribution facilities.
- *Promotion analysis:* Identifying the best advertising channels.
- *Price analysis:* Setting product prices to obtain the highest total revenues.

POM Marketing managers also use IT to manage their relationships with their customers. In *manufacturing*, managers use IT to process customer orders, develop production schedules, control inventory levels, and monitor product quality. They also use IT to design and manufacture products. These processes are called *computer-assisted design (CAD)* and *computer-assisted manufacturing (CAM)*.

HRM Managers in *human resources* use IT to manage the recruiting process, analyze and screen job applicants, and hire new employees. They also employ IT to help employees manage their careers, to administer performance tests to employees, and to monitor employee productivity. Finally, they rely on IT to manage compensation and benefits packages.

Two information systems that support the entire organization, **enterprise resource planning (ERP) systems** and transaction processing systems, are designed to correct a lack of communication among the functional area Information Systems. For this reason, Figure 1.4 shows ERP systems spanning the FAISs. ERP systems were an important innovation because organizations often developed the various functional area Information Systems as stand-alone systems that did not communicate effectively (if at all) with one another. ERP systems resolve this problem by tightly integrating the functional area Information Systems via a common database. In doing so, they enhance communications among the functional areas of an organization. For this reason, experts credit ERP systems with greatly increasing organizational productivity.

A **transaction processing system (TPS)** supports the monitoring, collection, storage, and processing of data from the organization's basic business transactions, each of which generates data. When you are checking out at Walmart, for example, a transaction occurs each time the cashier swipes an item across the bar code reader. Significantly, within an organization, different functions or departments can define a transaction differently. In accounting, for example, a transaction is anything that changes a firm's chart of accounts. The information system definition of a transaction is broader: A transaction is anything that changes the firm's database. The chart of accounts is only part of the firm's database. Consider a scenario in which a student transfers from one section of an Introduction to MIS course to another section. This move would be a transaction to the university's information system but not to the university's accounting department (the tuition would not change).

The TPS collects data continuously, typically in *real time*—that is, as soon as the data are generated—and it provides the input data for the corporate databases. TPSs are considered critical to the success of any enterprise because they support core operations. Significantly, nearly all ERP systems are also TPSs, but not all TPSs are ERP systems. In fact, modern ERP systems incorporate many functions that previously were handled by the organization's functional area information systems. You study both TPSs and ERP systems in detail in Chapter 10.

ERP systems and TPSs function primarily within a single organization. Information systems that connect two or more organizations are referred to as **interorganizational information systems (IOSs)**. IOSs support many interorganizational operations, of which *supply chain management* is the best known. An organization's **supply chain** is the flow of materials, information, money, and services from suppliers of raw materials through factories and warehouses to the end customers.

Note that the supply chain in Figure 1.5 shows physical flows, information flows, and financial flows. Digitizable products are those that can be represented in electronic form, such as music and software. Information flows, financial flows, and digitizable products go through the Internet, whereas physical products are shipped. For example, when you order a computer from **www.dell.com**, your information goes to Dell via the Internet. When your transaction is completed (i.e., your credit card is approved and your order is processed), Dell ships your computer to you. (We discuss supply chains in more detail in Chapter 11.)

Electronic commerce (e-commerce) systems are another type of interorganizational information system. These systems enable organizations to conduct transactions, called business-to-business (B2B) electronic commerce, and customers to conduct transactions with businesses, called business-to-consumer (B2C) electronic commerce. Figure 1.5 illustrates B2B and B2C electronic commerce. Electronic commerce systems are so important that we discuss them in detail in Chapter 7, with additional examples interspersed throughout the text. IT's About Business 1.2 shows how information systems have enabled Opendoor to grow rapidly via e-commerce.

Support for Organizational Employees.

So far, you have concentrated on information systems that support specific functional areas and operations. Now you will learn about information systems that typically support particular employees within the organization.

Clerical workers, who support managers at all levels of the organization, include bookkeepers, secretaries, electronic file clerks, and insurance claim processors. *Lower-level managers* handle the day-to-day operations of the organization, making routine decisions such as assigning tasks to employees and placing purchase orders. *Middle managers* make tactical decisions, which deal with activities such as short-term planning, organizing, and control.

Knowledge workers are professional employees such as financial and marketing analysts, engineers, lawyers, and accountants. All knowledge workers are experts in a particular subject area. They create information and knowledge that they integrate into the business. Knowledge workers, in turn, act as advisers to middle managers and executives. Finally, *executives* make decisions that deal with situations that can significantly change the manner in which business

IT's About Business 1.2

Opendoor Buys Homes for Cash

`MIS` `MKT`

The $1.4 trillion real estate market for traditional single-family homes has operated with few changes for decades. Now, start-up company Opendoor (**www.opendoor.com**), based in Phoenix, Arizona, is changing that market.

In 2014, Opendoor was founded on the idea that sellers will value the certainty of a sale over getting the absolute highest price; that is, Opendoor believes people will be willing to sell their homes for less in return for a less burdensome process with favorable timing. Furthermore, Opendoor's services should be particularly valuable during periods when home sales are slow. The company purchases only single-family homes, built after 1960, in the $125,000 to $500,000 range. Their goal is to sell quickly, thereby keeping holding costs to a minimum.

Opendoor's vision is to offer one-stop shopping for real estate transactions, allowing home buyers to obtain a mortgage and even customize their new homes. If Opendoor were to capture only 1 percent of the more than 5 million real estate transactions that take place annually in the United States, at an average price of $250,000, then the company's revenue would exceed $1 billion.

The Opendoor process begins when potential sellers complete an online form that collects extensive information regarding their home and its location. The company then uses a proprietary algorithm to determine which price to offer these individuals. The algorithm takes into account thousands of variables, including the home's square footage and number of bedrooms and bathrooms; its proximity to golf courses, parks, and freeways; its curb appeal (how the house looks from the street) and interior condition; whether the kitchen countertops are quartz, marble, or granite; whether the kitchen appliances are stainless steel; and many others. The company performs sophisticated analyses on these data. For example, most houses in Phoenix have swimming pools, which an appraiser might simply value at $10,000. In contrast, Opendoor has found that a nice pool in an affluent neighborhood could be worth $20,000, while a small pool in a less desirable neighborhood could be worth only $2,000.

After a seller accepts Opendoor's proposed price, the company sends inspectors to assess the home's condition and confirm the details provided by the seller. The company then prepares to close, for cash, from 3 to 60 days later, on a date selected by the seller.

Opendoor takes a service fee of 6 percent, similar to the standard real estate commission, plus an additional fee that varies based on the company's estimate of the riskiness of the transaction. This process brings the total charge for a sale to an average of 8 percent. If Opendoor believes that a particular home will be more difficult to sell or that market conditions are less favorable, then it may charge up to 6 percent for the risk, raising the total fee to 12 percent.

Opendoor typically borrows 90 percent of the purchase price. Once the company owns the home, it makes any necessary repairs and puts the home on the market at a slight markup. Potential buyers can view the home on their own timetable, using a key code to gain entry to the house. Buyers receive a 30-day guarantee that Opendoor will buy the property back if they are not satisfied. Opendoor also provides a two-year warranty on each home's electrical system and major appliances.

Opendoor takes no fees or commissions from buyers. As a result, if the company's pricing algorithm is correct, then it keeps the additional revenue from the markup. However, if the algorithm is wrong and the price falls to below what the company paid, then Opendoor can lose money on the transaction.

Some critics note that Opendoor's model has not been tested by a recession or a market crash. Opendoor responds that it can simply charge sellers higher fees to cover its risk. Also, home owners who need to sell would likely be willing to pay more for Opendoor's service in a down market than they would when prices are rising and selling is easy.

Opendoor claims that when it makes an offer to serious sellers, which it defines as people who plan to sell within six months, the offer is accepted one-third of the time. It further claims that their homes receive three times as many visits as traditional listings, primarily because prospective buyers do not have to make an appointment to view them.

After it opened in December 2014, Opendoor took less than two years to capture 2 percent of the Phoenix market. By mid-2019, the company had entered 20 markets and was purchasing approximately $2.5 billion in homes on an annual basis.

In March 2019, Opendoor raised $300 million in its latest round of financing, valuing the start-up at approximately $3.8 billion. With these funds, Opendoor planned to expand to 50 markets by the end of 2020. The company also noted that more than 800,000 people toured Opendoor homes in 2018.

Opendoor's success is attracting competition. For example, competitors such as Knock (**www.knock.com**) and OfferPad (**www.offerpad.com**) utilize similar business models and are raising capital.

However, this type of business is difficult to start because it requires both a viable pricing model and access to a large amount of capital. In fact, Opendoor faces substantial risks. For example, if home sellers know more about their properties than Opendoor does, then the company will be vulnerable. For example, a home owner might not disclose a plumbing problem that Opendoor inspectors missed. In addition, certain variables might be difficult to quantify. For example, are the schools in the neighborhood of questionable quality? Are potential zoning readjustments being considered for properties close by? Another risk is that home owners may not want to rely on a service that does not pay them top dollar. Further, Opendoor might not be able to sell as quickly as it would like or for the desired price.

Sources: Compiled from I. Lunden, "Opendoor Raises $300M on a $3.8B Valuation for Its Home Marketplace," *TechCrunch*, March 20, 2019; M. Lynley, "Opendoor Raises $325M to Make Buying and Selling Homes a Near-Instant Process," *TechCrunch*, June 13, 2018; M. Dickey, "Uber's Head of Finance Is Heading to Opendoor," *TechCrunch*, June 9, 2017; F. Manjoo, "The Rise of the Fat Start-Up," *New York Times*, May 24, 2017; M. Delprete, "Opendoor, Knock, and OfferPad: Growth in New Markets," *Inman*, April 10, 2017; M. Newlands, "Investing in Single-Family Homes Has Never Been Easier, Says This Oakland Startup," *Forbes*, January 10, 2017; A. Feldman, "Home Shopping Networkers," *Forbes*, December 20,

2016; B. Lane, "Opendoor Raises $210 Million, Plans Big Expansion in 2017," *HousingWire*, December 2, 2016; E. Carlyle, "The Best Markets for Investing in Single-Family Homes Right Now," *Forbes*, March 31, 2016; K. Kokalitcheva, "How to Trade in Your House," *Fortune*, March 9, 2016; L. Chapman, "Startup Opendoor Wants to Buy Houses That Are for Sale," *Wall Street Journal*, February 26, 2015; S. Doerfler, "Real Estate Startup Opendoor Is Expanding," *Arizona Republic*, February 26, 2015; and www.opendoor.com, accessed July 4, 2019.

Questions

1. Provide two examples of how Opendoor uses information technology to support its business model.

2. How might Opendoor further use information technology to counter competitors who attempt to emulate the company's business model? Support your answer.

is conducted. Examples of executive decisions are introducing a new product line, acquiring other businesses, and relocating operations to a foreign country.

Functional area information systems summarize data and prepare reports, primarily for middle managers but sometimes for lower-level managers as well. Because these reports typically concern a specific functional area, report generators (RPGs) are an important type of functional area IS.

Business analytics (BA) systems (also known as **business intelligence [BI] systems**) provide computer-based support for complex, nonroutine decisions, primarily for middle managers and knowledge workers. (They also support lower-level managers but to a lesser extent.) These systems are typically used with a data warehouse, and they enable users to perform their own data analysis. You learn about BA systems in Chapter 12.

Expert systems (ESs) attempt to duplicate the work of human experts by applying reasoning capabilities, knowledge, and expertise within a specific domain. They have become valuable in many application areas, primarily but not exclusively areas involving decision making. For example, navigation systems use rules to select routes, but we do not typically think of these systems as expert systems. Significantly, expert systems can operate as stand-alone systems or be embedded in other applications. We examine ESs in greater detail in Technology Guide 4.

Dashboards (or **digital dashboards**) are a special form of IS that support all managers of the organization. They provide rapid access to timely information and direct access to structured information in the form of reports. Dashboards that are tailored to the information needs of executives are called *executive dashboards*. Chapter 12 provides a thorough discussion of dashboards.

Table 1.4 provides an overview of the different types of information systems used by organizations.

TABLE 1.4 Types of Organizational Information Systems

Type of System	Function	Example
Transaction processing system	Processes transaction data from terminal.	Walmart checkout point-of-sale business events
Enterprise resource planning	Integrates all functional areas of the organization.	Oracle, SAP system
Functional area IS	Supports the activities within specific functional area.	System for processing payroll
Decision support system	Provides access to data and analysis tools.	"What-if" analysis of changes in budget
Expert system	Mimics human expert in a particular area and makes decisions.	Credit card approval analysis
Dashboards	Present structured, summarized information about aspects of business important to executives.	Status of sales by product
Supply chain management system	Manages flows of products, services, and information among organizations.	Walmart Retail Link system connecting suppliers to Walmart
Electronic commerce system	Enables transactions among organizations and between organizations and customers.	www.dell.com

Before you go on . . .

1. What is a computer-based information system?
2. Describe the components of computer-based information systems.
3. What is an application program?
4. Explain how information systems provide support for knowledge workers.
5. As we move up the organization's hierarchy from clerical workers to executives, how does the type of support provided by information systems change?

1.3 How Does IT Impact Organizations?

Throughout this text, you will encounter numerous examples of how IT affects various types of organizations. These examples will make you aware of just how important IT actually is to organizations. In fact, for the vast majority of organizations, if their information systems fail, then they cease operations until the problems are found and fixed. Consider the following examples:

- In April 2018, an unsuccessful migration to a new software platform at TSB Bank (**www.tsb.co.uk**) in the United Kingdom caused major disruptions for weeks, angered the bank's 5 million customers, and led to the resignation of its CEO.
- In May 2018, a software problem at Australian telecommunications company Telstra (**www.telstra.com.au**) caused outages of its 3G and 4G wireless services nationwide for millions of its customers
- In July 2018, German supermarket company Lidl (**www.lidl.com**) stopped using a three-year-old merchandise management system after spending more than %565 million on it.

This section provides an overview of the impact of IT on modern organizations. As you read this section, you will learn how IT will affect you as well.

Author Lecture Videos are available exclusively in *WileyPLUS.*
Apply the Concept activities are available in the Appendix and in *WileyPLUS.*

IT Impacts Entire Industries

As of mid-2019, the technology required to transform industries through software had been developed and integrated and could be delivered globally. In addition, software tools and Internet-based services enabled companies in many industries to launch new software-powered start-ups without investing in new infrastructure or training new employees. For example, in 2000, operating a basic Internet application cost businesses approximately $150,000 per month. In mid-2018, operating that same application in Amazon's cloud (see cloud computing in Technology Guide 3) cost less than $1,000 per month.

In essence, software is impacting every industry, and every organization must prepare for these impacts. Let's examine a few examples of software disruption across several industries. Many of these examples focus on two scenarios: (1) industries where software disrupted the previous market-leading companies and (2) industries where a new company (or companies) used software to achieve a competitive advantage.

The Book Industry. The largest book publisher and bookseller in the United States is Amazon, a software company. Amazon's core capability is its software engine, which can sell virtually anything online without building or maintaining any retail stores. Now, even books themselves have become software products, known as electronic (or digital) books, or eBooks. In 2018, physical books accounted for approximately $5 billion (83 percent of total book sales) and electronic books accounted for approximately $1 billion (16 percent of total book sales). (Interestingly, according to the 2018 Academic Student Ebook Experience Survey, 74 percent of respondents said that they preferred print books when reading for pleasure. Further more, 68 percent said that they preferred print books for assigned readings.)

Consider the Borders bookstore chain. In 2001, Borders agreed to hand over its online business to Amazon because it was convinced that online book sales were nonstrategic and unimportant. Ten years later, Borders filed for bankruptcy.

The Music Industry.

Total U.S. album sales peaked at 785 million in 2000, which was the year after Napster was created. Napster was a service that allowed anyone with a computer and a reasonably fast Web connection to download and trade music for free. From 2000 to 2018, the major music labels (companies) worked diligently to eliminate illegal downloading and sharing. Despite these efforts, however, album sales continued to decline. The result was that the music labels earned about $8 billion less in annual retail sales in 2018 than they did in 2000. In addition, prior to 1999 six major music labels dominated the industry. By 2015, a series of mergers had reduced that number to the "Big Three": Warner Music Group (www.wmg.com), Universal Music (www.universalmusic.com), and Sony BMG (www. sonybmg.com).

These dramatic changes in the music industry resulted from the emergence of digital music-streaming technologies over the Internet. Two digital-streaming business models emerged: (1) Internet radio companies such as Pandora (www.pandora.com) that allow subscribers to passively listen to music that is customized for their tastes and (2) interactive companies such as Spotify (www.spotify.com) and Apple's iTunes (www.apple.com/itunes) that allow users to pick songs. Internet radio companies can operate under a government-mandated license that dictates how much they have to pay to recording artists. In contrast, interactive companies must make deals with labels and music publishers in order to license music for legal use in the United States.

Responding to these disruptions, the Big Three music labels have been buying stakes in digital entertainment start-ups, such as established streaming services Spotify (www.spotify.com) and Pandora (www.pandora.com). The labels buy stakes very cheaply, after which they often give themselves the right to buy larger amounts at deep discounts to market at a later date. The labels have purchased parts of start-ups such as choose-your-own-adventure music video seller Eko (www.helloeko.com), song-recognition company Shazam (www.shazam.com), and SoundCloud (www.soundcloud.com). Industry analysts estimate that the three labels have amassed positions in digital music start-ups valued at $3 billion.

The Video Industry.

Blockbuster—which rented and sold videos and ancillary products through its chain of stores—was the industry leader until it was disrupted by a software company, Netflix (www.netflix.com). By the first quarter of 2018, Netflix had the largest subscriber base of any video service, with 125 million subscribers. Meanwhile, Blockbuster declared bankruptcy in February 2011 and was acquired by satellite television provider Dish Network (www.dish.com) a month later. In July, 2019 the last Blockbuster store in the world, located in Bend, Oregon, was still open.

`MIS` The Software Industry.

Incumbent software companies such as Oracle and Microsoft are increasingly threatened by software-as-a-service (SaaS) products—for example, Salesforce (www.salesforce.com) and Android, an open-source operating system. (We discuss operating systems in Technology Guide 2 and SaaS in Technology Guide 3.)

The Videogame Industry.

Today, the fastest-growing entertainment companies are video game makers—again, software. Examples are Zynga (www.zynga.com), the creator of FarmVille; Rovio (www.rovio.com), the maker of Angry Birds; and Minecraft (www.minecraft.net), now owned by Microsoft (www.microsoft.com).

The Photography Industry.

Software disrupted this industry years ago. Today it is virtually impossible to buy a mobile phone that does not include a software-powered camera. In addition, people can upload photos automatically to the Internet for permanent archiving and global sharing. Leading photography companies include Shutterfly (www.shutterfly.com), Snapfish (www.snapfish.com), Flickr (www.flickr.com), and Instagram (www.instagram.com). Meanwhile, Kodak, the longtime market leader—whose name was almost synonymous with cameras—declared bankruptcy in January 2012.

`MKT` **The Marketing Industry.**   Today's largest direct marketing companies include Facebook (**www.facebook.com**), Google (**www.google.com**), and Amazon (**www.amazon.com**). All of these companies are using software to disrupt the retail marketing industry.

`HRM` **The Recruiting Industry.**   LinkedIn (**www.linkedin.com**) is disrupting the traditional job recruiting industry. For the first time, employees and job searchers can maintain their resumes on a publicly accessible website that interested parties can search in real time.

`FIN` **The Financial Services Industry.**   Software has transformed the financial services industry. Practically every financial transaction—for example, buying and selling stocks—is now performed by software. Also, many of the leading innovators in financial services are software companies. For example, Square (**www.squareup.com**) allows anyone to accept credit card payments with a mobile phone.

The Motion Picture Industry.   The process of making feature-length computer-generated films has become incredibly IT intensive. Studios require state-of-the-art information technologies, including massive numbers of servers, sophisticated software, and an enormous amount of storage (all described in Technology Guide 1).

Consider DreamWorks Animation (**www.dreamworksanimation.com**), a motion picture studio that creates animated feature films, television programs, and online virtual worlds. For a single motion picture, the studio manages more than 500,000 files and 300 terabytes (a terabyte is 1 trillion bytes) of data, and it uses about 80 million central processing unit (CPU; described in Technology Guide 1) hours. As DreamWorks executives state, "In reality, our product is data that looks like a movie. We are a digital manufacturing company."

Software is also disrupting industries that operate primarily in the physical world. Consider these examples:

- *The Automobile Industry:* In modern cars, software is responsible for running the engines, controlling safety features, entertaining passengers, guiding drivers to their destinations, and connecting the car to mobile, satellite, and GPS networks. Other software functions include Wi-Fi receivers, which turn your car into a mobile hot spot; software, which helps maximize fuel efficiency; and ultrasonic sensors, which enable some models to parallel-park automatically.

  The next step is to network all vehicles together, a necessary step toward the next major breakthrough: self-driving or driverless cars. Google, Tesla (**www.tesla.com**), Apple and, all major automobile companies are now developing driverless vehicles.

- *The Agriculture Industry:* Agriculture is increasingly powered by software, including satellite analysis of soils linked to per-acre seed-selection software algorithms. In addition, precision agriculture makes use of automated, driverless tractors controlled by global positioning systems (GPS) and software. (Precision agriculture is an approach to farm management that uses information technology to ensure that crops receive exactly what they need [e.g., water, fertilizer, and pesticides] for optimum health and productivity.)

- *The Fashion Industry:* Women have long "borrowed" special-occasion dresses from department stores, buying them and then returning them after wearing them for one evening. Now, Rent the Runway (**www.renttherunway.com**) has redefined the fashion business, making expensive clothing available to more women than ever before. The firm is also disrupting traditional physical retailers. After all, why buy a dress when you can rent one for a very low price? Some department stores feel so threatened by Rent the Runway that they have reportedly told vendors that they will remove floor merchandise if it ever shows up on that company's website.

- *The Legal Profession:* Today, electronic discovery (e-discovery) software applications can analyze documents in a fraction of the time that human lawyers would take, at a fraction of the cost. For example, Blackstone Discovery (**www.blackstonediscovery.com**) helped one company analyze 1.5 million documents for less than $100,000. That company estimated that the process would have cost $1.5 million had it been performed by lawyers.

Law firms are now beginning to use a new artificial intelligence software package called ROSS (**www.rossintelligence.com**). For example, law firm BakerHostetler has hired ROSS to serve as a legal researcher in bankruptcy cases.

IT Reduces the Number of Middle Managers

HRM IT makes managers more productive, and it increases the number of employees who can report to a single manager. Thus, IT ultimately decreases the number of managers and experts. Therefore, it is reasonable to assume that in the coming years, organizations will have fewer managerial levels and fewer staff and line managers. If this trend materializes, promotional opportunities will decrease, making promotions much more competitive. Bottom line: Pay attention in school!

IT Changes the Manager's Job

One of the most important tasks of managers is making decisions. A major consequence of IT has been to change the manner in which managers make their decisions. In this way, IT ultimately has changed managers' jobs.

IT often provides managers with near-real-time information, meaning that managers have less time to make decisions, making their jobs even more stressful. Fortunately, IT also provides many tools—for example, business analytics applications such as dashboards, search engines, and intranets—to help managers handle the volumes of information they must deal with on an ongoing basis.

So far in this section, we have been focusing on managers in general. Now, let's focus on you. Due to advances in IT, you will increasingly supervise employees and teams who are geographically dispersed. Employees can work from anywhere at any time, and teams can consist of employees who are literally dispersed throughout the world. Information technologies such as telepresence systems (discussed in Chapter 6) can help you manage these employees even though you do not often see them face-to-face. For these employees, electronic or "remote" supervision will become the norm. Remote supervision places greater emphasis on completed work and less emphasis on personal contacts and office politics. You will have to reassure your employees that they are valued members of the organization, thereby diminishing any feelings they might have of being isolated and "out of the loop."

Will IT Eliminate Jobs?

One major concern of every employee, part-time or full-time, is job security. Relentless cost-cutting measures in modern organizations often lead to large-scale layoffs. Put simply, organizations are responding to today's highly competitive environment by doing more with less. Regardless of your position, then, you consistently will have to add value to your organization and to make certain that your superiors are aware of this value.

Many companies have responded to difficult economic times, increased global competition, demands for customization, and increased consumer sophistication by increasing their investments in IT. In fact, as computers continue to advance in terms of intelligence and capabilities, the competitive advantage of replacing people with machines is increasing rapidly. This process frequently leads to layoffs. At the same time, however, IT creates entirely new categories of jobs, such as electronic medical record keeping and nanotechnology.

IT Impacts Employees at Work

Many people have experienced a loss of identity because of computerization. They feel like "just another number" because computers reduce or eliminate the human element present in noncomputerized systems.

The Internet threatens to exert an even more isolating influence than have computers and television. Encouraging people to work and shop from their living rooms could produce some unfortunate psychological effects, such as depression and loneliness.

HRM **IT Impacts Employees' Health and Safety.**   Although computers and information systems are generally regarded as agents of "progress," they can adversely affect individuals' health and safety. To illustrate this point, we consider two issues associated with IT: job stress and long-term use of the keyboard.

An increase in an employee's workload and/or responsibilities can trigger *job stress*. Although computerization has benefited organizations by increasing productivity, it also has created an ever-expanding workload for some employees. Some workers feel overwhelmed and have become increasingly anxious about their job performance. These feelings of stress and anxiety can actually diminish rather than improve workers' productivity while jeopardizing their physical and mental health. Management can help alleviate these problems by providing training, redistributing the workload among workers, and hiring more workers.

On a more specific level, the long-term use of keyboards can lead to *repetitive strain injuries* such as backaches and muscle tension in the wrists and fingers. *Carpal tunnel syndrome* is a particularly painful form of repetitive strain injury that affects the wrists and hands.

Designers are aware of the potential problems associated with the prolonged use of computers. To address these problems, they continually attempt to design a better computing environment. The science of designing machines and work settings that minimize injury and illness is called *ergonomics*. The goal of ergonomics is to create an environment that is safe, well lit, and comfortable. Examples of ergonomically designed products are antiglare screens that alleviate problems of fatigued or damaged eyesight and chairs that contour the human body to decrease backaches. **Figure 1.6** displays some sample ergonomic products.

Media Bakery

Media Bakery

Media Bakery

Media Bakery

FIGURE 1.6 **Ergonomic products protect computer users.**

IT Provides Opportunities for People with Disabilities. Computers can create new employment opportunities for people with disabilities by integrating speech-recognition and vision-recognition capabilities. For example, individuals who cannot type can use a voice-operated keyboard, and individuals who cannot travel can work at home.

Going further, adaptive equipment for computers enables people with disabilities to perform tasks they normally would not be able to do. For example, the Web and graphical user interfaces (GUIs; e.g., Windows) can be difficult for people with impaired vision to use. To address this problem, manufacturers have added audible screen tips and voice interfaces, which essentially restore the functionality of computers to the way it was before GUIs become standard.

Other devices help improve the quality of life in more mundane but useful ways for people with disabilities. Examples are a two-way writing telephone, a robotic page turner, a hair brusher, and a hospital-bedside video trip to the zoo or the museum. Several organizations specialize in IT designed for people with disabilities.

Before you go on . . .

1. Why should employees in all functional areas become knowledgeable about IT?
2. Describe how IT might change the manager's job.
3. Discuss several ways in which IT impacts employees at work.

1.4 | Importance of Information Systems to Society

Author Lecture Videos are available exclusively in *WileyPLUS*.
Apply the Concept activities are available in the Appendix and in *WileyPLUS*.

This section explains in greater detail why IT is important to society as a whole. Other examples of the impact of IT on society appear throughout the text.

IT Affects Our Quality of Life

IT has significant implications for our quality of life. The workplace can be expanded from the traditional 9-to-5 job at a central location to 24 hours a day at any location. IT can provide employees with flexibility that can significantly improve the quality of leisure time, even if it doesn't increase the total amount of leisure time.

From the opposite perspective, however, IT also can place employees on "constant call," which means they are never truly away from the office, even when they are on vacation. In fact, surveys reveal that the majority of respondents take their laptops and smartphones on their vacations, and 100 percent take their cell phones. Going further, the majority of respondents did some work while vacationing, and almost all of them checked their e-mail regularly.

The Robot Revolution Is Here Now

Once restricted largely to science fiction, robots that can perform practical tasks are now a reality. Around the world, autonomous devices have become increasingly common on factory floors, in hospital corridors, and in farm fields. These devices are called cobots (from *collaborative robot*). A *cobot* is a robot intended to physical interact with humans in a shared workspace. Let's look at two examples.

MKT **POM** **LoweBots.** In August 2016, Lowe's began to deploy Lowebots, which are multilingual, autonomous customer assistance robots. Lowebots help customers find their way around the store and get the items they need. Lowebots also travel around the store and ask customers simple questions to discover what they are looking for. The robots provide directions and maps to products and share specialty knowledge with customers. The Lowebots also monitor inventory so the store knows what items need to be restocked.

Drones.

A *drone* is an unmanned aerial vehicle (UAV) that either is controlled by pilots from the ground or autonomously follows a preprogrammed mission. Commercial drones function in a variety of business purposes, in contrast to drones used by hobbyists for recreational purposes.

Uber is using drones in an interesting way. The company is so successful in Mexico City that it feels comfortable using drones to tease drivers who are stuck in gridlocked traffic. One drone carried an ad saying, "Driving by yourself?" The idea was to guilt the driver into carpooling with UberPOOL.

Drones are being employed in many different ways. Two different uses are in the wine-making industry and in law enforcement. IT's About Business 1.3 discusses both applications.

IT's About Business 1.3

Diverse Uses for Drones

POM California Wineries

Wine industry analysts have predicted that, as a result of global warming, by 2050 many regions in Europe, including much of Italy and parts of southern France, could become unsuitable for wine grapes. The analysts also suggested that California wine production could decrease by 70 percent by that year.

In fact, California experienced a severe drought from 2012-2019, with warmer nights and drying aquifers (huge areas of underground water). As a result, the state's wineries are employing a variety of both technological and nontechnological methods to improve water utilization.

In the past, experienced winemakers had to physically inspect the vines and grapes. Today, wineries launch drones and deploy sensors to map areas of vines with GPS coordinates, and they proceed directly to those vines that exhibit problems. Specifically, drones equipped with sensors detect moisture by evaluating the colors of the vegetation. The wrong color can indicate nutritional deficiencies in the crops or irrigation leaks.

Drones can also examine plant growth, detect areas under stress from disease or lack of water, and help assess when pickers should have the next load of grapes ready to send to the winery. Normalized difference vegetation index (NDVI) maps, which highlight areas of high and low vegetation density, provide visual information on how to improve uniformity of growth within a vineyard and when to harvest vineyard areas for optimal grape quality.

POM Law Enforcement Agencies

In July 2019, approximately 350 U.S. agencies were using drones as part of their law enforcement activities. In fact, there has been a dramatic 500 percent increase in law enforcement drone use since 2016. These are the most common uses for drones in these agencies:

- Search and rescue
- Traffic collision reconstructions

- Active shooter scenarios
- Crime scene analysis
- General surveillance

Remotely controlled drones often arrive on crime scenes before officers in cars. Drones allow police officers to survey a scene prior to their physical arrival, enabling them to track a suspect's movements if one has been identified. Drones are more effective monitoring tools than fixed security cameras and more cost effective to operate than helicopters with onboard cameras. Let's look at a few examples of law enforcement agencies using drones:

- The use of a single, quadcopter drone in the city of Ensenada, Mexico, helped to reduce overall crime by some 10 percent, including a 30 percent decrease in burglaries. DJI's Inspire I quadcopter helped police officers in the city make over 500 arrests in four months.

- In the United Kingdom, Devon, Cornwall, and Dorset police officers teamed up in 2017 to launch a drone unit for assistance with missing person searches, gathering images from crime scenes and major traffic accidents, and taking part in coastal and woodland searches to fight wildlife crime.

- Police officers in the Bordeaux area of southwestern France are using drones to catch drivers violating traffic laws. The drones are much cheaper than helicopter surveillance that the police sometimes use to catch traffic offenders. Drone surveillance does have one limitation. While drones can reveal dangerous driving, such as cars zigzagging through traffic for example, they are not suitable for detecting speeding.

- Looking ahead, Amazon has filed a patent for tiny drones that would be useful for a number of tasks. For example, Amazon envisages these drones traveling with law enforcement officers to assist them in their work. In this capacity, the drones could record video, meaning that they could replace the dashboard cameras in many police cars. Specifically, the drones could hover just above or behind officers, take photos of license plates and drivers, and then feed that data back to the police department for facial recognition. In a chase of two people, an officer could direct a drone to follow one person while he or she follows the other.

There are, however, many opponents of the use of drones by law enforcement agencies. For example, the city of Seattle, Washington, donated their drones to the city of Los Angeles because Seattle citizens objected so strongly to their deployment.

Public unease with law enforcement drones is occurring at the same time as overwhelming support for the use of police body cameras. This discrepancy raises the question of who or what can surveil and record a city's citizens and under what investigative circumstances.

Sources: Compiled from J. Stewart, "A Single Drone Helped Mexican Police Drop Crime 10 Percent," *Wired*, June 11, 2018; G. Manaugh, "Drone Cops Take Flight in Los Angeles," *The Atlantic*, June 8, 2018; "Like It or Not, Camera-Equipped Police Drones Will Soon Patrol the Skies," *Digital Trends*, June 6, 2018; M. Uleski, "How Unmanned Aerial Systems Can Assist Police Pursuits," *PoliceOne.com*, March 19, 2018; G. Friese, "Research: Drone Video Effective in Identifying Multiple Vehicle Collision Hazards," *PoliceOne.com*, March 14, 2018; V. Masters, "How a Washington PD Is Leveraging Drone Technology to Serve Citizens," *PoliceOne.com*, February 22, 2018; J. Laurenson, "France Is Using Drones to Catch Dangerous Drivers," *Marketplace.*

org, November 13, 2017; M. Margaritoff, "Drones in Law Enforcement: How, Where, and When They're Used," *The Drive*, October 13, 2017; "'Drone Unit' for British Police Brings Crime Fighting to the Skies," *Digital Trends*, July 15, 2017; A. Nixon, "Best Drones for Agriculture 2017," *bestoneforthejob. com*, May 4, 2017; A. King, "Technology: The Future of Agriculture," *Nature*, April 27, 2017; T. Jennings, "Farming Drones: The Future of Agriculture?" *CropLife*, April 7, 2017; A. Glaser, "Police Departments Are Using Drones to Find and Chase Down Suspects," *Recode*, April 6, 2017; T. Sparapani, "How Big Data and Tech Will Improve Agriculture, from Farm to Table," *Forbes*, March 23, 2017; "Technology That Will Change Agriculture in 2017," *Food and Farm Discussion Lab*, March 22, 2017; T. Logan, "Drone Mapping in Agriculture on the Rise," ABC News, March 6, 2017; D. Gelles, "Falcons, Drones, Data: A Winery Battles Climate Change," *New York Times*, January 5, 2017; C. Daileda, "Amazon Wants Its Tiny Drones to Ride with Police," *Mashable*, November 2, 2016; and B. Vyenielo, "High-Tech Sustainability: Wineries Turn to High-Tech Solutions for Sustainable Business," *Vineyard & Winery Management*, September–October 2016.

Questions

1. Compare and contrast the nontechnological and technological methods that wineries are using to combat global warming.

2. What other uses for drones would you suggest to wineries?

3. Describe other applications for drones in law enforcement.

4. Describe potential problems that drone use by law enforcement agencies could cause for citizens.

Autonomous Vehicles. When you think about autonomous vehicles, consider these statistics:

- Human error accounts for more than 90 percent of automobile accidents.

- Each year, more than 6 million vehicle accidents are reported to law enforcement.

- Each year, approximately 35,000 Americans and 1.25 million people worldwide die in automobile accidents.

- With mobile devices providing a distraction, U.S. highway fatalities increased 8 percent in 2016, the largest increase in 50 years.

- The average car in the United States is used two hours per day, which is only 8 percent of the time.

These statistics offer compelling reasons for autonomous vehicles, and the development of these vehicles is proceeding rapidly. Leading autonomous vehicle companies are Waymo (**www.waymo.com**), GM Cruise (**www.getcruise.com**), and Ford Autonomous (**www.ford.com**).

There is some bad news, however. Several fatalities have been reported with Tesla automobiles on full autopilot (self-driving mode). Whether these deaths were caused by the automobiles is under investigation.

It probably will be a long time before we see robots making decisions by themselves, handling unfamiliar situations, and interacting with people. Nevertheless, robots are extremely helpful in various environments, particularly those that are repetitive, harsh, or dangerous to humans.

IT Impacts Health Care

IT has brought about major improvements in health care delivery. Medical personnel use IT to make better and faster diagnoses and to monitor critically ill patients more accurately. IT also has streamlined the process of researching and developing new drugs. Expert systems now help doctors diagnose diseases, and machine vision is enhancing the work of radiologists. Surgeons use virtual reality to plan complex surgeries. They also employ surgical robots to perform long-distance surgery. Finally, doctors discuss complex medical cases via videoconferencing. New computer simulations re-create the sense of touch, allowing doctors in training to perform virtual procedures without risking harm to an actual patient.

Information technology can be applied to improve the efficiency and effectiveness of health care. For example, consider IBM Watson (**www.ibm.com/watson**), an IT system that uses natural language processing and machine learning (discussed in Technology Guide 4) to reveal insights from vast collections of data. We take a closer look at Watson in the next section.

Among the thousands of other health care applications, administrative systems are critically important. These systems perform functions ranging from detecting insurance fraud to creating nursing schedules to performing financial and marketing management.

The Internet contains vast amounts of useful medical information. Despite the fact that this information exists on the Internet, physicians caution against self-diagnosis. Rather, people should use diagnostic information obtained from Google and medical websites such as WebMD (**www.webmd.com**) only to ask questions of their physicians.

The Emergence of Cognitive Computing: IBM Watson

MIS IBM (**www.ibm.com**) developed Watson specifically to answer questions on the quiz show *Jeopardy!* In February 2011, Watson competed on *Jeopardy!* against former winners Brad Rutter and Ken Jennings. Watson won the game series and received the first prize of $1 million. (In *Jeopardy!* the host reads the answer, and the contestants must then provide the correct question.)

Watson is an application of advanced natural language processing, information retrieval, knowledge representation and reasoning, and machine learning technologies to the field of answering open-domain (general) questions. IBM has labeled the type of processing demonstrated by Watson as *cognitive computing*. Four primary capabilities distinguish Watson as a cognitive system:

- The ability to understand human language, with all of its nuance and ambiguity
- The ability to learn and absorb information
- The ability to formulate hypotheses
- The ability to understand the context of a question

By mid-2019, thousands of firms in at least 20 industries were using Watson in a variety of applications. Let's consider some of them here.

- *Medicine:* Although some health data are structured—for example, blood pressure readings and cholesterol counts—the vast majority are unstructured. These data include textbooks, medical journals, patient records, and nurse and physician notes. In fact, modern medicine entails so much unstructured data that their rapid growth has surpassed the ability of health care practitioners to keep up. IBM emphasizes that Watson is *not* intended to replace doctors. Rather, its purpose is to assist them in avoiding medical errors and fine-tuning their medical diagnoses.

  By mid-2010, Watson had digested millions of medical and scientific articles as well as information about thousands of clinical trials collected from **www.clinicaltrials.gov**, the federal government's public database. The system can read—and remember—patient histories, monitor the latest drug trials, examine the potency of new therapies, and closely follow state-of-the-art guidelines that help doctors choose the best treatments. Watson can also analyze images such as MRIs. To exploit these capabilities, two top-ranked hospitals are collaborating with Watson in the field of oncology (cancer care): Memorial Sloan Kettering (**www.mskcc.org**) and the Mayo Clinic (**www.mayoclinic.org**).

- **MKT** *Customer Service:* The Watson Engagement Advisor is designed to help customer representatives assist consumers with deeper insights more quickly than was previously possible. Engagement Advisor's "Ask Watson" feature can quickly address customers' questions, offer feedback to guide their purchase decisions, and troubleshoot their problems. Companies employing the Advisor include USAA (www.usaa.com), Genesys (www.genesys.com), DBS Bank of Singapore (www.dbs.com.sg), and many others.

- **FIN** *Financial Services:* Many financial organizations have integrated Watson into their business processes. As one example, Citigroup (www.citigroup.com) employs Watson to analyze financial, regulatory, economic, and social data across financial exchanges, currencies, and funds to help simplify and improve the bank's digital interactions with its customers.

- *Travel Services:* Terry Jones, founder of Travelocity (www.travelocity.com) and Kayak (www.kayak.com), has launched WayBlazer (www.wayblazer.ai), a new travel company powered by Watson. Watson engages and advises users through a natural language interface to help create the best travel experience.

Other Interesting Applications:

- **ACCT** Tax preparation firm H&R Block (www.hrblock.com) is using IBM Watson to assist the firm's clients with their taxes. Clients interact with Watson via natural language processing, answering questions from Watson pertinent to their tax returns. H&R Block hopes that by feeding Watson this tax return data (along with answers provided by human tax preparers), the company can improve the performance of all of their tax preparers. In essence, Watson will act as a central repository for tax experts' knowledge. The company asserts that they are not using Watson to replace human workers.

- **POM** BNSF Railway (www.bnsf.com) is using Watson to help detect faulty sections in the company's 32,500 miles of track before they break.

- Repsol (www.repsol.com), a global energy company, is using Watson to improve its strategic decision making in crucial areas such as optimizing oil reservoir production and discovering new oil fields.

- Edge Up Sports teamed with Watson to bring analytical capabilities to fantasy football. The company's app can analyze the vast amounts of available data about football and its players, thereby enabling fantasy league players to make better decisions.

- General Motors began rolling out smarter vehicles in 2017 with its new cognitive mobility platform OnStar Go, powered by Watson. OnStar Go is capable of identifying information about the car and its surroundings. For example, OnStar Go will immediately call the driver when air bags are deployed. If the system does not receive an immediate answer, it will call 911 and direct first responders to the car's location.

- The 2017 Wimbledon tennis tournament introduced a voice-activated digital assistant named "Fred," powered by Watson. Fred helped attendees find their way around the All England Lawn Tennis Club and informed them as to who was playing on Centre Court. Fred also compiled highlight videos of the matches.

Before you go on . . .

1. What are some of the quality-of-life improvements made possible by IT? Has IT had any negative effects on our quality of life? If so, explain and provide examples.

2. Describe the robotic revolution and consider its implications for humans. How do you think robotics will affect your life in the future?

3. Explain how IT has improved health care practices. Has the application of IT to health care created any problems or challenges?

Summary

1.1   Identify the reasons why being an informed user of information systems is important in today's world.

The benefits of being an informed user of IT include the following:

- You will benefit more from your organization's IT applications because you will understand what is "behind" those applications.
- You will be able to provide input into your organization's IT applications, thus improving the quality of those applications.
- You will quickly be in a position to recommend or to participate in the selection of IT applications that your organization will use.
- You will be able to keep up with rapid developments in existing information technologies as well as the introduction of new technologies.
- You will understand the potential impacts that "new and improved" technologies will have on your organization. Consequently, you will be qualified to make recommendations concerning their adoption and use.
- You will play a key role in managing the information systems in your organization.
- You will be in a position to use IT if you decide to start your own business.

1.2   Describe the various types of computer-based information systems in an organization.

- Transaction processing systems (TPSs) support the monitoring, collection, storage, and processing of data from the organization's basic business transactions, each of which generates data.
- Functional area information systems (FAISs) support a particular functional area within the organization.
- Interorganizational information systems (IOSs) support many interorganizational operations, of which supply chain management is the best known.
- Enterprise resource planning (ERP) systems correct a lack of communication among the FAISs by tightly integrating the functional area Information Systems via a common database.
- Electronic commerce (e-commerce) systems enable organizations to conduct transactions with other organizations (called business-to-business [B2B] electronic commerce) and with customers (called business-to-consumer [B2C] electronic commerce).

- Business analytics (BA) systems provide computer-based support for complex, nonroutine decisions, primarily for middle managers and knowledge workers.
- Expert systems (ESs) attempt to duplicate the work of human experts by applying reasoning capabilities, knowledge, and expertise within a specific domain.

1.3   Discuss ways in which information technology can affect managers and nonmanagerial workers.

Potential IT impacts on managers:

- IT may reduce the number of middle managers.
- IT will provide managers with real-time or near-real-time information, meaning that managers will have less time to make decisions.
- IT will increase the likelihood that managers will have to supervise geographically dispersed employees and teams.

Potential IT impacts on nonmanagerial workers:

- IT may eliminate jobs.
- IT may cause employees to experience a loss of identity.
- IT can cause job stress and physical problems, such as repetitive stress injury.

1.4   List positive and negative societal effects of the increased use of information technology.

Positive societal effects:

- IT can provide opportunities for people with disabilities.
- IT can provide people with flexibility in their work (e.g., work from anywhere, anytime).
- Robots will take over mundane chores.
- IT will enable improvements in health care.

Negative societal effects:

- IT can cause health problems for individuals.
- IT can place employees on constant call.
- IT can potentially misinform patients about their health problems.

Chapter Glossary

application (or app) A computer program designed to support a specific task or business process.

business analytics (BA) systems Systems that provide computer-based support for complex, nonroutine decisions, primarily for middle managers and knowledge workers.

business intelligence (BI) systems See **business analytics (BA) systems**.

computer-based information system (CBIS) An information system that uses computer technology to perform some or all of its intended tasks.

dashboards (or digital dashboards) A special form of IS that supports all managers of the organization by providing rapid access to timely information and direct access to structured information in the form of reports.

data items An elementary description of things, events, activities, and transactions that are recorded, classified, and stored but are not organized to convey any specific meaning.

database A collection of related files or tables containing data.

digital transformation The business strategy that leverages IT to dramatically improve employee, customer, and business partner relationships; support continuous improvement in business operations and business processes; and develop new business models and businesses.

electronic commerce (e-commerce) systems A type of interorganizational information system that enables organizations to conduct transactions, called business-to-business (B2B) electronic commerce, and customers to conduct transactions with businesses, called business-to-consumer (B2C) electronic commerce.

enterprise resource planning (ERP) systems Information systems that correct a lack of communication among the functional area Information Systems by tightly integrating the functional area Information Systems via a common database.

expert systems (ESs) An attempt to duplicate the work of human experts by applying reasoning capabilities, knowledge, and expertise within a specific domain.

functional area information systems (FAISs) (departmental information system) Information Systems that support a particular functional area within the organization.

hardware A device such as a processor, monitor, keyboard, or printer. Together, these devices accept, process, and display data and information.

information Data that have been organized so that they have meaning and value to the recipient.

information system (IS) A system that collects, processes, stores, analyzes, and disseminates information for a specific purpose.

information technology (IT) Any computer-based tool that people use to work with information and support the information and information-processing needs of an organization.

information technology components Hardware, software, databases, and networks.

information technology infrastructure IT components plus IT services.

information technology platform The name given to the combination of the IT components of hardware, software, networks (wireline and wireless), and databases.

information technology services Activities performed by IT personnel using IT components, specifically, developing information systems, overseeing security and risk, and managing data.

informed user A person who is knowledgeable about information systems and information technology.

interorganizational information systems (IOSs) Information systems that connect two or more organizations.

knowledge Data and/or information that have been organized and processed to convey understanding, experience, accumulated learning, and expertise as they apply to a current problem or activity.

knowledge workers Professional employees such as financial and marketing analysts, engineers, lawyers, and accountants who are experts in a particular subject area and who create information and knowledge, which they integrate into the business.

network A connecting system (wireline or wireless) that enables multiple computers to share resources.

procedures The set of instructions for combining hardware, software, database, and network components in order to process information and generate the desired output.

software A program or collection of programs that enable the hardware to process data.

supply chain The flow of materials, information, money, and services from suppliers of raw materials through factories and warehouses to the end customers.

transaction processing system (TPS) A system that supports the monitoring, collection, storage, and processing of data from the organization's basic business transactions, each of which generates data.

Discussion Questions

1. Describe a business that you would like to start. Discuss how information technology could (a) help you find and research an idea for a business, (b) help you formulate your business plan, and (c) help you finance your business.

2. Your university wants to recruit high-quality high school students from your state. Provide examples of (a) the data that your recruiters would gather in this process, (b) the information that your recruiters would process from these data, and (c) the types of knowledge that your recruiters would infer from this information.

3. Can the terms *data*, *information*, and *knowledge* have different meanings for different people? Support your answer with examples.

4. Information technology makes it possible to "never be out of touch." Discuss the pros and cons of always being available to your employers and clients (regardless of where you are or what you are doing).

5. Robots have the positive impact of being able to relieve humans from working in dangerous conditions. What are some negative impacts of robots in the workplace?

6. Is it possible to endanger yourself by accessing too much medical information on the Web? Why or why not? Support your answer.

7. Describe other potential impacts of IT on societies as a whole.

8. What are the major reasons why it is important for employees in all functional areas to become familiar with IT?

9. Given that information technology is impacting every industry, what does this mean for a company's employees? Provide specific examples to support your answer.

10. Given that information technology is impacting every industry, what does this mean for students attending a college of business? Provide specific examples to support your answer.

11. Is the vast amount of medical information on the Web a good thing? Answer from the standpoint of a patient and from the standpoint of a physician.

Problem-Solving Activities

1. Visit some websites that offer employment opportunities in IT. Prominent examples include the following: **www.dice.com**, **www.monster.com**, **www.collegerecruiter.com**, **www.careerbuilder.com**, **www.job.com**, **www.career.com**, **www.simplyhired.com**, and **www.true-career.com**. Compare the IT salaries to salaries offered to accountants, marketing personnel, financial personnel, operations personnel, and human resources personnel. For other information on IT salaries, check *Computerworld*'s annual salary survey.

2. Enter the website of UPS (**www.ups.com**).

    a. Find out what information is available to customers before they send a package.

    b. Find out about the "package tracking" system.

    c. Compute the cost of delivering a 10" × 20" × 15" box, weighing 40 pounds, from your hometown to Long Beach, California (or to Lansing, Michigan, if you live in or near Long Beach). Compare the fastest delivery against the lowest cost. How long did this process take? Look into the business services offered by UPS. How do they make this process easier when you are a business customer?

3. Surf the Internet for information about the Department of Homeland Security (DHS). Examine the available information and comment on the role of information technologies in the department.

4. Access **www.irobot.com** and investigate the company's Education and Research Robots. Surf the Web for other companies that manufacture robots and compare their products with those of iRobot.

Closing Case

POM **MIS** John Deere Becomes a Technology Company, and It Is Not All Good News

Farming is highly land and labor intensive. In the past, farmers managed all the plants in a field approximately the same way. To do this, they had to assume that all plants in a field were at the same growth stage, all were in the same health, and all needed the same nutrients.

Today, farmers are able to treat individual plants using precision agriculture. Precision agriculture is a farm management approach that uses a number of technologies, including global positioning systems (GPS; see Chapter 8), sensors (see Chapter 8), robotics, drones, autonomous vehicles, artificial intelligence, and computer vision (these last five technologies are discussed in Technology Guide 4) to increase efficiency and ensure profitability while protecting the environment. Communications among these technologies will be improved with fifth-generation (5G) wireless technology, expected to be widely deployed by 2020.

Founded in 1837, John Deere (**www.deere.com**) is the largest agricultural equipment manufacturer in the world with 2018 global revenues of $37 billion. Deere is changing its business model by undergoing digital transformation. In the past, Deere generated revenue one time, with each sale. Today, Deere embeds the precision agriculture technologies noted above into its equipment. With these technologies,

machines communicate with each other, with the farmer, and with external services, such as satellite mapping and image generation. The machines also generate data that Deere can help the farmer analyze. As a result, Deere can provide additional services after each sale, creating more continuous revenue flows from each customer.

The company began its transformation in 1999 with the acquisition of NavCom Technology for its GPS system. Consequently, Deere began embedding GPS receivers into its large farm equipment, such as tractors and combines, thereby turning the machines into nodes on the Internet of Things (see Chapter 8). The GPS receivers allowed the machines to steer themselves, enabling them to steer more accurate paths within fields with less overlap. As a result, farmers could work longer with less fatigue.

Deere then connected its machines into the company's own cloud computing platform, called the John Deere Operations Center (see Technology Guide 3). Through Deere's Center, farmers can monitor and operate machinery, check the health of crops, and monitor environmental conditions. Deere's platform can gather and analyze data from onboard sensors to offer predictive maintenance on machines, thereby reducing the possibility of expensive downtime on the machines (see Chapter 12).

By July 2018, Deere had more than 70 business partners that could access Deere's platform to help farmers analyze their data.

These companies provide satellite imagery, drone integration, visualization, and other tools to which farmers can apply their data. The companies range from smaller drone start-ups, such as Precision Hawk (**www.precisionhawk.com**) and Green Aero Tech (**www.greenaerotech.com**), to giants, such as Monsanto (**www.monsanto.com**), Syngenta (**www.syngenta.com**), and DuPont (**www.dupont.com**). As part of its continuing effort to change the strategy of Deere beyond acquiring technology companies, Deere opened up its own innovation lab in San Francisco in 2017.

In September 2017, Deere purchased Blue River Technology (**www.bluerivertechnology.com**), a developer of crop-spraying robots that utilize computer vision and machine learning to differentiate between weeds and crops so that farmers spray herbicides only on weeds. Because the robot can target weeds with squirts of herbicide the size of a postage stamp, it can reduce the amount of herbicide that farmers use by some 90 percent. Blue River is also developing a robot (called LettuceBot) for precision lettuce thinning and a drone imaging system that collects data from fields.

A Negative Consequence of John Deere's Digital Transformation

Unfortunately, Deere's transformation has led to a serious, negative consequence. The company is making it difficult for consumers and independent repair shops to repair today's equipment, which operates on copyright-protected software.

As a result, farmers who buy Deere tractors cannot repair their equipment themselves. Instead, they must work with company-approved technicians who may take time to arrive and can be expensive. For example, Deere charges $230, plus $130 per hour for a technician to come to a farm and plug a USB connector between the tractor and the technician's computer to authorize the repair and any needed parts. Essentially, Deere sells their tractors to farmers and uses software to control every aspect of the tractors' use after the sale.

Consequently, many farmers are supporting "right-to-repair" legislation. Such bills, which have been proposed in 19 states, would allow owners to repair their equipment themselves without voiding warranties or agreements and require equipment manufacturers such as Deere to offer the diagnostic tools, manuals, and other supplies that farmers need to fix their own machines. As expected, Deere opposes the right-to-repair legislation.

Interestingly, Apple also opposes the right-to-repair legislation. Apple argues that the bills could result in poor repair work or make consumers vulnerable to hackers. Right-to-repair advocates say that Apple, which offers iPhone repair services at every Apple store, wants to maintain control of its share of the approximately $4 billion smartphone repair business.

The Deere controversy had its beginning in the debate over jailbreaking iPhones and other high-tech devices. The legal question underlying this controversy centers on the Digital Millennium Copyright Act (DMCA).

The DMCA is a U.S. copyright law that criminalizes production and dissemination of technology, devices, or services intended to circumvent measures that control access to copyrighted works and also criminalizes the act of circumventing an access control. The DMCA was originally meant to stop people from pirating music and movies but has arguably been taken advantage of by companies selling a wide variety of devices containing software.

After the passage of the DMCA, regulators considered whether there should be exceptions to the law. In such cases, consumers might have the right to circumvent technical protection measures (TPMs) intended to protect intellectual property and protect the rights of intellectual property holders. The U.S. Copyright Office subsequently exempted 27 classes of intellectual property from TPMs. Class 21 covers a variety of types of motor vehicles, including mechanized farm equipment.

Deere pointed out that the Class 21 exemption is for the equipment owners themselves but prevents owners from transferring the right to modify software "to third parties, such as repair shops or hackers." Deere argued further that the manufacturer needed to control access to their equipment's software to ensure machine functionality, safety, and emissions compliance and to preserve product warranties.

After the Class 21 exemption, Deere began requiring its customers to sign an updated End User Licensing Agreement (EULA) that restricted their ability to repair or modify their equipment, in essence requiring them to use Deere-certified diagnostic and repair software. Despite the Class 21 exemption, farmers say that Deere still keeps tight control over how its customers service their equipment. In fact, Deere locks the Engine Control Module reading function, which forces farmers to use its services. Violation of the EULA would be considered a breach of contract, meaning that Deere would have to sue its own customers if it wants to enforce the EULA.

Farmers note that this problem poses a threat to their livelihood if their tractor breaks at an inopportune time. One farmer stated that he does not have time to wait for a dealership employee to come to his farm and repair his tractor, particularly at harvest time. The farmer went on to say that most all repairs on new equipment require software downloads. Ultimately, farmers fear that Deere could remotely shut down a tractor and there would be nothing that they could do about it.

The controversy has led to a growing market where farmers and independent repair shops can buy unlicensed alternative software and associated diagnostic equipment on invitation-only, paid online forums. Much of the software comes from Ukraine. The software being traded on various forums includes the following:

- John Deere Service Advisor: A diagnostic program used by Deere technicians that recalibrates tractors and can diagnose broken parts.

- John Deere Payload files: These files specifically program certain parts of the tractor. For example, the files can customize and fine-tune the performance of the chassis, engine, and cab.

- John Deere Electronic Data Link drivers: This software allows a computer to communicate with a tractor.

- Also for sale on the forums are license key generators, speed-limit modifiers, and cables that allow farmers to connect a tractor to a computer. Demonstrations of all this software in operation can be found on YouTube.

Sources: Compiled from A. Minter, "U.S. Farmers Are Being Bled by the Tractor Monopoly," *Bloomberg.com*, April 23, 2019 D. Swinhoe, "How Tractor Seller John Deere Became a Technology Company," *IDG Connect*, June 5, 2018; D. Newman, "Top Six Digital Transformation Trends in Agriculture," *Forbes*, May 14, 2018; N. Gagliordi, "How 5G Will Impact the Future of Farming and John Deere's Digital Transformation," *ZDNet*, February 2, 2018; T. Simonite, "Why John Deere Just Spent $305 Million on a Lettuce-Farming Robot," *Wired*, September 6, 2017; M. Lev-Ram, "John Deere Is Paying $305 Million for This Silicon Valley Company," *Fortune*, September 6, 2017; J. Hightower, "John Deere Is Against the Right to Repair Its Equipment," *AlterNet*, August 1, 2017; J. Roberts, "One Controversial Thing Tractors and iPhones Have in Common," *Fortune*, June 29, 2017; A. Fitzpatrick, "Hand Me That Wrench: Farmers and Apple Fight over the Toolbox," *Time*, June 22, 2017; A. Ebrahimzadeh, "Will Farmers or 3rd Party Repair Shops Sue John Deere for Allegedly Contractually

Prohibiting Unlicensed Tractor Repairs?" *aeesq.com*, May 8, 2017; J. Bloomberg, "John Deere's Digital Transformation Runs Afoul of Right-to-Repair Movement," *Bloomberg BusinessWeek*, April 30, 2017; R. Schmaltz, "What Is Precision Agriculture?" *AgFunder News*, April 24, 2017; D. Grossman, "There's a Thriving John Deere Black Market as Farmers Fight for 'Right to Repair,'" *Popular Mechanics*, March 22, 2017; M. Reilly, "A Fight over Tractors in America's Heartland Comes Down to Software," *MIT Technology Review*, March 22, 2017; J. Koebler, "Why American Farmers Are Hacking Their Tractors with Ukrainian Firmware," *Motherboard*, March 21, 2017; D. Drinkwater, "John Deere Ploughs Furrow as Industrial Internet Pioneer," www.internetofbusiness.com, March 16, 2017; C. Perlman, "From Product to Platform: John Deere Revolutionizes Farming," *Harvard Business School Digital Innovation and Transformation*, February 26, 2017; "How John Deere Turned Technology into Business Transformation," www.digitalsocialstrategy.org, December 10, 2016; D. Puri, "John Deere Leads the Way with IoT-Driven Precision Farming," *Network World*, November 30, 2016; K. Wiens, "How Copyright Law Stifles Your Right to Tinker with Tech," *MIT Technology Review*, July 26, 2016; K. Wiens, "We Can't Let John Deere Destroy the Very Idea of Ownership," *Wired*, April 21, 2015; "John Deere Opens the MyJohnDeere Platform to Collaborating Software Developers and Companies," www.deere.com, accessed November 14, 2013; and www.deere.com, accessed June 21, 2019.

Questions

1. Describe how Deere's digital transformation changed its business model.

2. Describe the various applications that Deere employed in its digital transformation.

3. Discuss why Deere's digital transformation is "not all good news."

Look ahead to Chapter 3 for the next three questions:

4. Discuss the ethicality and the legality of John Deere's end-user licensing agreement that it requires its customers to sign.

5. Discuss the ethicality and the legality of John Deere customers who use unlicensed repair shops to repair their equipment using hacked software.

6. The fundamental tenets of ethics include responsibility, accountability, and liability. Discuss each of these tenets as it applies to John Deere's actions toward its customers.

CHAPTER 2

Organizational Strategy, Competitive Advantage, and Information Systems

CHAPTER OUTLINE	LEARNING OBJECTIVES
2.1 Business Processes	**2.1** Discuss ways in which information systems enable cross-functional business processes and business processes for a single functional area.
2.2 Business Process Reengineering, Business Process Improvement, and Business Process Management	**2.2** Differentiate among business process reengineering, business process improvement, and business process management.
2.3 Business Pressures, Organizational Responses, and Information Technology Support	**2.3** Identify effective IT responses to different kinds of business pressures.
2.4 Competitive Advantage and Strategic Information Systems	**2.4** Describe the strategies that organizations typically adopt to counter Porter's five competitive forces.

Opening Case

The National Basketball Association Enhances the Fan Experience

 MIS MKT

The rise of on-demand entertainment is forcing sports to adjust to modern fans' viewing habits. Today, fans want to watch what they want, when they want, and where they want. To compete with the many options to which their fans now have access (particularly mobile), teams must provide a technology infrastructure that enables fans to enjoy games on their terms. Enter the National Basketball Association (NBA; **www.nba.com**).

Despite rich television contracts and arenas filled nearly to capacity for almost all games, NBA teams are always on the lookout for new sources of revenue. They realize that technology can provide these revenue streams while at the same time enhancing the fan experience. Let's examine how NBA teams are using social media and virtual reality (VR) to achieve these goals.

Social Media: Sports and social media are a perfect fit for each other because sports have huge audiences who use social media extensively. No other North American professional sports league compares to the NBA in its ability to exploit social media. The NBA has almost twice as many social media followers as the National Football League (NFL; **www.nfl.com**), four times as many as Major League Baseball (MLB; **www.mlb.com**), and six times as many as the National Hockey League (NHL; **www.nhl.com**).

One reason why the NBA has utilized social media so effectively is that basketball action fits neatly into six-second Vine loops. Six seconds can capture a breakaway dunk or a screen that frees a shooter for a long-range three-point shot. The high points of basketball games are easily sharable, and the NBA has encouraged that sharing, unlike other leagues. In contrast to the NBA, the National Football League (NFL) sent takedown notices to Twitter, demanding that the service remove images and videos of game action posted by Deadspin (**www.deadspin.com**), Gawker Media's sports blog. Twitter responded by not only removing the material but also temporarily suspending the league's account. Similarly, Major League Baseball issues takedown notices when social media post game highlights. Although both leagues are within their legal rights, it is questionable whether they are making good business decisions.

The NBA disagrees with the stance of the other leagues, and the data support them. In 2016, Facebook commissioned a Nielsen study to quantify the effects of social media conversations regarding nine NFL games. The study revealed that each additional share of a Facebook post about a game in the 15 minutes before it started correlated with an extra 1,000 viewers for the first minute of the broadcast.

Consider the Los Angeles Clippers' (**www.nba.com/clippers**) local television contract. In September 2016, the Clippers and Fox Sports Prime Ticket announced they had reached an agreement to extend their exclusive television contract. The deal would earn the Clippers between $50 million and $55 million per season, approximately double what the network paid the team in the previous deal. In addition, the Clippers supplemented the television deal with social media outlets Vine, Instagram, Facebook, and Twitter. These outlets enabled fans to watch highlights of each game wherever they are and to react to them in real time.

Virtual Reality (VR): Basketball has long had a global footprint. The U.S. basketball "Dream Team" at the 1992 Barcelona Olympics, with Magic Johnson, Michael Jordan, Larry Bird, Patrick Ewing, Charles Barkley, and other NBA stars, helped start a generation of international player development. By the summer of 2017, foreign players made up approximately one-fifth of NBA rosters, a huge stimulus for growth in the league's international audience.

The NBA hopes to continue to leverage its international advantage, especially when the league considers the international king of sports, soccer (the other football). Soccer has far more fans than basketball on a global basis, and the NBA sees an enormous upside in its own international efforts. The largest potential prize is China, where an estimated 300 million people play basketball.

NBA executives used to believe that the league needed franchises in Europe or Asia for rapid growth. Currently, they are convinced that the league's future will be defined by their ability to employ technology to come as close as possible to duplicating the courtside experience. Why take basketball to fans when VR can bring fans courtside?

Placing a VR camera close to the action of an NBA game could give fans a VR experience that transcends the current television broadcast. NBA executives believe that VR could extend the reach of the league if fans located anywhere could feel as though they are basically sitting courtside at a game. This process could produce significant new revenues for all NBA teams.

The potential of VR technology is why the NBA was so excited in 2016 about the first-ever VR livestream of an NBA game from the Oracle Arena in Oakland, California. The live stream was provided by NextVR (**www.nextvr.com**), a virtual reality broadcasting start-up that specializes in using footage from live events. NextVR has the exclusive VR live-streaming rights for VR content from the NBA.

Another example of incorporating VR into basketball involves the Sacramento Kings (**www.nba.com/kings**), who opened their new arena in 2016. The arena's high-capacity Wi-Fi system provided fans with fast Internet access on their mobile devices for two reasons. The first reason is to give fans the ability to Snapchat, Instagram, and Facebook their experiences at the games.

The second reason is to offer instant replays using VR to give fans who are relatively far from the action an up-close, courtside experience. The team felt that some of its fans might even prefer to pay for a seat in a movie theater–like space inside the arena equipped with VR headsets rather than pay for a conventional seat that is too far away from the court and leaves fans with a poor view. Therefore, the Kings invested in live-streaming VR start-up Voke (now owned by Intel). The team has also experimented with streaming action from the court to VR headsets outside the arena.

Delivering virtual courtside action to people either inside or outside an arena requires significantly higher network bandwidth than these arenas typically are equipped with. Therefore, the Kings worked with Comcast, now owned by Xfinity, (**xfinity.com**) (**www.comcast.com**) to give their arena an Internet broadband connection that the team maintains can handle 225,000 Instagram photos per second. Corporate networking companies Broadcom (**www.broadcom.com**) and Ruckus Wireless (**www.ruckuswireless.com**) installed the 1,000 Wi-Fi access points and other infrastructure needed to give fans' devices access to the Internet.

Today, the NBA is North America's most forward-thinking professional sports league. Other professional leagues are struggling with aging fans and restrictive views on intellectual property. In contrast, the NBA has the youngest television audience of any professional league. Not coincidentally, the NBA allows its content to be distributed over the Internet. While the other U.S. leagues struggle to build international interest in their games, the NBA has leveraged social media and VR to build a huge global fan base.

Today, fans can use Samsung Gear VR and Google Daydream VR to download highlight reels, check out analysis, and stream games through NBA League Pass. NBA League Pass offers VR games individually for fans to purchase.

And the bottom line? During the 2018-2019 season almost 22 million fans attended NBA games. Within that same time period, the NBA generated $490 million for sponsors via social media and recorded 1.5 billion fan interactions across Facebook, Twitter, Instagram, and YouTube.

Since the end of the 2015–2016 regular season, 282 million new fans have joined the NBA's social media community. Today the league has more than 1.3 billion likes and followers combined across all league, team, and player social platforms globally.

These records translated into profits. **NBAstore.com** posted record-breaking sales during the 2017–2018 regular season, an increase of over 10 percent from the previous season.

The NBA is currently developing an augmented reality (AR) app in the NBA Summer League for possible deployment in the 2019 NBA season. Consider this scenario: A fan in Europe opens the league's AR app on her phone, and she is courtside for warm-ups. During the game, she points her phone camera toward the television, and optical trackers put a short description of every player's interests over their heads. Her brother does the same thing, except that he sees the shooting percentage, block rate, and turnover percentage for each player. On the bottom of the app, the best memes on NBA Twitter pop up, and a multiangle replay will be quickly available. (A meme is an image, video, or piece of text that is copied, with slight variations, and spread rapidly by Internet users.)

Why is such an AR app so important to the NBA? For a league with a huge international fan base who cannot attend games, augmented reality could literally bring the game to them. The app will enhance the fan experience and further expand the NBA's fan base.

Sources: Compiled from S. Sohi, "How the NBA Is Using Augmented Reality to Transform the Fan Experience," *SBNation*, July 17, 2018; R. de Fremery, "How the Personalized Mobile Fan Experience Has Changed the Game for NBA Fans," *Mobile Business Experience*, January 31, 2018; S. Ross, "How Technology Is Reinventing the Sports Fan Experience," nabshow.com, July 20, 2017; A. Robertson, "The Oculus Rift and Touch Bundle Is on Sale for $399," *The Verge*, July 10, 2017; K. Helin, "First Ever NBA Finals Virtual Reality Highlight Packages Will Be Free to Fans," *NBC Sports*, May 31, 2017; "NBA Breaks Attendance Record for Third Straight Season," NBA.com, April 13, 2017; L. Matney, "The NBA Gets High-Tech with VR, Drones, and Futuristic Dreams," *TechCrunch*, February 24, 2017; E. Alvarez, "The NBA Hopes VR Will Expand Its Audience," *Engadget*, February 24, 2017; A. Neubarth, "NBA Launches Virtual Reality App with Google Daydream," *USA Today*, February 17, 2017; B. Turner, "Clippers Reach New TV Deal with Fox Sports Prime Ticket," *Los Angeles Times*, September 21, 2016; J. Ereth, "Sports Intelligence—The Role of Technology in Professional Sports," *Eckerson Group*, June 22, 2016; T. Simonite, "The Sacramento Kings' New Stadium Is Wired for Virtual Reality," *MIT Technology Review*, June 20, 2016; M. McClusky, "Techies Are Trying to Turn the NBA into the World's Biggest Sports League," *Wired*, May 31, 2016; A. Robertson and R. Miller, "Daydream Is Google's Android-Powered VR Platform," *The Verge*, May 18, 2016; R. Amadeo, "Gear VRs for Everyone! Google Turns Android into a VR-Ready OS: Daydream," *Ars Technica*, May 18, 2016; and www.nba.com, accessed July 23, 2018.

Questions

1. Refer to Porter's strategies for competitive advantage. Which strategy (or strategies) is the NBA pursuing? Provide specific examples to support your answer.

2. Describe how social media, VR, and augmented reality are strategic systems for the NBA. Provide specific examples to support your answer.

Introduction

Organizations operate in the incredible complexity of the modern high-tech world. As a result, they are subject to myriad business pressures. Information systems are critically important in helping organizations respond to business pressures and in supporting organizations' global strategies. As you study this chapter, you will see that any information system can be *strategic*, meaning it can provide a competitive advantage if it is used properly. The chapter-opening case, as well as all the other cases in this chapter, illustrates how information technology (IT) can provide a competitive advantage to organizations.

Competitive advantage refers to any assets that provide an organization with an edge against its competitors in some measure, such as cost, quality, or speed. A competitive advantage helps an organization control a market and accrue larger-than-average profits. Significantly, both strategy and competitive advantage take many forms.

Although many companies use technology in very expensive ways, an entrepreneurial spirit, coupled with a solid understanding of what IT can do for you, will provide competitive advantages to entrepreneurs just as it does for Wall Street CIOs. As you study this chapter, think of the small businesses in your area that are utilizing popular technologies in interesting and novel ways. Have any of them found an innovative use for Twitter? Facebook? Amazon? PayPal? If not, then can you think of any businesses that would benefit from employing these technologies?

This chapter is important for you for several reasons. First, the business pressures we address in the chapter will affect your organization. Just as important, however, they also will affect *you*. Therefore, you must understand how information systems can help you—and eventually your organization—respond to these pressures.

Acquiring a competitive advantage is also essential for your organization's survival. Many organizations achieve competitive advantage through the efforts of their employees. Therefore, becoming knowledgeable about strategy and how information systems affect strategy and competitive position will help you throughout your career.

This chapter encourages you to become familiar with your organization's strategy, mission, and goals and to understand its business problems and how it makes (or loses) money. It will help you understand how information technology contributes to organizational strategy. Furthermore, you likely will become a member of business or IT committees that decide (among many other things) how to use existing technologies more effectively and whether to adopt new ones. After studying this chapter, you will be able to make immediate contributions in these committees.

Essentially, organizations consist of a large number of diverse business processes. In this chapter, you will first learn about the different types of business processes and the support that information systems provide for all business processes.

The need for organizations to optimize their business processes has led to efforts such as business process improvement (BPI), business process reengineering (BPR), and business process management (BPM). You will learn how organizations address these important efforts and the key role that information systems play in supporting and enabling these efforts.

Next, you will see how information systems enable organizations to respond to business pressures. Finally, you will learn how information systems help organizations acquire competitive advantages in the marketplace.

2.1 | Business Processes

A **business process** is an ongoing collection of related activities that create a product or a service of value to the organization, its business partners, and its customers. The process involves three fundamental elements:

- *Inputs:* Materials, services, and information that flow through and are transformed as a result of process activities
- *Resources:* People and equipment that perform process activities
- *Outputs:* The product or a service created by the process

If the process involves a customer, then that customer can be either internal or external to the organization. A manager who is the recipient of an internal reporting process is an example of an internal customer. In contrast, an individual or a business that purchases the organization's products is the external customer of the fulfillment process.

Successful organizations measure their process activities to evaluate how well they are executing these processes. Two fundamental metrics that organizations employ in assessing their processes are efficiency and effectiveness. *Efficiency* focuses on doing things well in the process, for example, progressing from one process activity to another without delay or without wasting money or resources. *Effectiveness* focuses on doing the things that matter; that is, creating outputs of value to the process customer, such as high-quality products.

Many processes cross the functional areas in an organization. For example, product development involves research, design, engineering, manufacturing, marketing, and distribution. Other processes involve only a single functional area. **Table 2.1** identifies the fundamental business processes performed in an organization's functional areas.

Cross-Functional Processes

All of the business processes in Table 2.1 fall within a single functional area of the company. However, many other business processes, such as procurement and fulfillment, cut across multiple functional areas; that is, they are cross-functional business processes, meaning that no single functional area is responsible for their execution. Rather, multiple functional areas collaborate to perform the process. For a cross-functional process to be successfully completed, each functional area must execute its specific process steps in a coordinated, collaborative way. To clarify this point, let's take a look at the procurement and fulfillment **cross-functional processes**. We discuss these processes in greater detail in Chapter 10.

POM The *procurement process* includes all of the tasks involved in acquiring needed materials externally from a vendor. Procurement comprises five steps that are completed in three different functional areas of the firm: warehouse, purchasing, and accounting.

ACCT The process begins when the warehouse recognizes the need to procure materials, perhaps due to low inventory levels. The warehouse documents this need with a purchase requisition, which it sends to the purchasing department (step 1). In turn, the purchasing department identifies a suitable vendor, creates a purchase order based on the purchase requisition, and sends the order to the vendor (step 2). When the vendor receives the purchase order, it ships the materials, which are received in the warehouse (step 3). The vendor then sends an invoice, which is received by the accounting department (step 4). Accounting sends payment to the vendor, thereby completing the procurement process (step 5).

Author Lecture Videos are available exclusively in *WileyPLUS*.
Apply the Concept activities are available in the Appendix and in *WileyPLUS*.

TABLE 2.1   **Examples of Business Processes**

ACCT **Accounting Business Processes**

Managing accounts payable	Managing invoice billings
Managing accounts receivable	Managing petty cash
Reconciling bank accounts	Producing month-end close
Managing cash receipts	Producing virtual close

FIN **Finance Business Processes**

Managing account collection	Producing property tax assessments
Managing bank loan applications	Managing stock transactions
Producing business forecasts	Generating financial cash flow reports
Applying customer credit approval and credit terms	

MKT **Marketing Business Processes**

Managing post-sale customer follow-up	Handling customer complaints
Collecting sales taxes	Handling returned goods from customers
Applying copyrights and trademarks	Producing sales leads
Using customer satisfaction surveys	Entering sales orders
Managing customer service	Training sales personnel

POM **Production/Operations Management Business Processes**

Processing bills of materials	Managing quality control for finished goods
Processing manufacturing change orders	Auditing for quality assurance
Managing master parts list and files	Receiving, inspecting, and stocking parts and materials
Managing packing, storage, and distribution	Handling shipping and freight claims
Processing physical inventory	Handling vendor selection, files, and inspections
Managing purchasing	

HRM **Human Resources Business Processes**

Applying disability policies	Producing performance appraisals and salary adjustments
Managing employee hiring	Managing resignations and terminations
Handling employee orientation	Applying training and tuition reimbursement
Managing files and records	Managing travel and entertainment
Applying health care benefits	Managing workplace rules and guidelines
Managing pay and payroll	Overseeing workplace safety

MIS **Management Information Systems Business Processes**

Antivirus control	Applying e-mail policy
Computer security issues incident reporting	Generating Internet use policy
Training computer users	Managing service agreements and emergency services
Computer user and staff training	Applying user workstation standards
Applying disaster recovery procedures	Managing the use of personal software

POM **ACCT** The *fulfillment process* is concerned with processing customer orders. Fulfillment is triggered by a customer purchase order that is received by the sales department. Sales then validates the purchase order and creates a sales order. The sales order communicates data related to the order to other functional areas within the organization, and it tracks the progress of the order. The warehouse prepares and sends the shipment to the customer. Once accounting is notified of the shipment, it creates an invoice and sends it to the customer. The customer then makes a payment, which accounting records.

An organization's business processes can create a competitive advantage if they enable the company to innovate or to execute more effectively and efficiently than its competitors.

They can also be liabilities, however, if they make the company less responsive and productive. Consider the airline industry. It has become a competitive necessity for all of the airlines to offer electronic ticket purchases through their websites. To provide competitive advantage, however, these sites must be highly responsive, and they must provide both current and accurate information on flights and prices. An up-to-date, user-friendly site that provides fast answers to user queries will attract customers and increase revenues. In contrast, a site that provides outdated or inaccurate information or that has a slow response time will hurt rather than improve business.

Clearly, good business processes are vital to organizational success. But how can organizations determine if their business processes are well designed? The first step is to document the process by describing its steps, its inputs and outputs, and its resources. The organization can then analyze the process and, if necessary, modify it to improve its performance.

To understand this point, let's consider the e-ticketing process. E-ticketing consists of four main process activities: searching for flights, reserving a seat, processing payment, and issuing an e-ticket. These activities can be broken down into more detailed process steps. The result may look like the process map in **Figure 2.1**. Note that different symbols correspond to different types of process steps. For example, rectangles (steps) are activities that are performed by process resources (reserve seats, issue e-ticket). Diamond-shaped boxes indicate

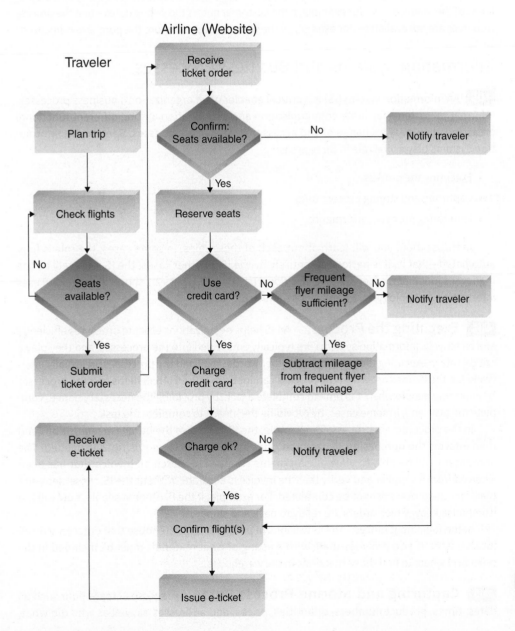

FIGURE 2.1 Business process for ordering an e-ticket from an airline website.

decisions that need to be made (seats available?). Arrows are used as connectors between steps; they indicate the sequence of activities.

These symbols are important in the process flowchart (which is similar to a programming flowchart). Other symbols may be used to provide additional process details. For example, D-shaped boxes are used instead of rectangles when a waiting period is part of a process, ovals can show start and stop points, and process resources can be attached to activities with resource connector lines or included as an annotation or property for each activity box.

The customers of the process are travelers planning a trip, and the process output is an e-ticket. Travelers provide inputs to the process: the desired travel parameters to begin the search, the frequent-flyer miles number, and their credit card information. Also, a computerized reservation system that stores information for many airlines provides some of the process inputs, such as the seat availability and prices. The resources used in the process are the airline website, the computerized reservation system, and, if the customer calls the airline call center at any time during the process, the call center system and the human travel agents. The process creates customer value by efficiently generating an output that meets the customer search criteria—dates and prices. The performance of the process depends on efficiency metrics, such as the time required to purchase an e-ticket, from the moment the customer initiates the ticket search until he or she receives the e-ticket. Effectiveness metrics include customer satisfaction with the airline website. Finally, the performance of the process may be affected if the quality or the timeliness of the inputs is low—for example, if the customer enters the wrong dates—or if the process resources are not available—for example, if the website crashes before the purchase is finalized.

Information Systems and Business Processes

MIS An information system (IS) is a critical enabler of an organization's business processes. Information systems facilitate communication and coordination among different functional areas and allow easy exchange of and access to data across processes. Specifically, Information Systems play a vital role in three areas:

- Executing the process
- Capturing and storing process data
- Monitoring process performance

In this section, you will learn about each of these roles. In some cases, the role is fully automated—that is, it is performed entirely by the IS. In other cases, the IS must rely on the manager's judgment, expertise, and intuition. IT's About Business 2.1 shows how NASCAR uses information technology to streamline its prerace process.

MIS **Executing the Process.** An IS helps organizations execute processes efficiently and effectively. Information systems are typically embedded into the processes, and they play a critical role in executing the processes. In other words, an IS and the processes are usually intertwined. If the IS does not work, the process cannot be executed. An IS helps execute processes by informing people when it is time to complete a task, by providing the necessary data to complete the task, and, in some cases, by providing the means to complete the task.

In the procurement process, for example, the IS generates the purchase requisitions and then informs the purchasing department that action on these requisitions is needed. The accountant will be able to view all shipments received to match an invoice that has been received from a supplier and verify that the invoice is accurate. Without the IS, these steps and therefore the process cannot be completed. For example, if the IS is not available, how will the warehouse know which orders are ready to pack and ship?

In the fulfillment process, the IS will inform people in the warehouse that orders are ready for shipment. It also provides them with a listing of what materials must be included in the order and where to find those materials in the warehouse.

MIS **Capturing and Storing Process Data.** Processes create data such as dates, times, product numbers, quantities, prices, and addresses as well as who did what,

IT's About Business 2.1

NASCAR Uses IT in Its Prerace Inspection

The National Association for Stock Car Auto Racing (NASCAR; www.nascar.com) is a family-owned-and-operated business that governs multiple auto racing events. One of NASCAR's key business processes is the prerace inspection of the cars. The rationale for the prerace inspection is to ensure that all cars are as evenly matched as possible.

The prerace inspection begins two days before a race. Each car on the entry list for a particular race must pass a thorough inspection to compete. Here is how the process works.

In the first inspection, NASCAR officials assess whether a car meets NASCAR requirements—for example, height off the ground at the front and the back of the car, weight, fuel tank capacity, and many other factors. Cars that meet these requirements are cleared to practice, and they qualify for the race.

If a car does not pass the first inspection, then NASCAR allows that team to fix the problem and undergo a second inspection. However, the team is sent to the end of the line. This process can cause a backup of cars waiting to be cleared before the race. In the past, NASCAR would let a team with a violation to keep its spot in line while it fixed the problem, essentially jumping ahead of teams still waiting to undergo the initial inspection. That situation meant that crew chiefs had little incentive to repair the cars efficiently and effectively when trying to repair violations. If the repair did not fix the violation, they would simply try again.

After the first inspection, each team has two days before the race to work on their cars. After each team qualifies, NASCAR conducts a second, postqualifying inspection. On race morning, all cars are inspected one final time.

Historically, NASCAR officials performed the prerace inspection by walking to each inspection station and visually observing each car. Moreover, they recorded their observations on paper. These forms contained more than 100 items clustered in categories, depending on the kind of inspection. The form would remain with each vehicle as it went through the inspection process. Each season, NASCAR used roughly 25,000 sheets of paper for inspections.

In September 2014, NASCAR implemented an app from Microsoft that incorporates everything from the paper form but in a more useful format. Each vehicle is shown on a dashboard that tracks its stages through the inspection process. The dashboard also uses color-coded flags to highlight violations. NASCAR officials can be alerted to any pending issues for each vehicle, and they can access the NASCAR rulebook at the press of a digital button. Officials can also add digital notes and photographs to detail any infractions. The app also enables officials to determine whether

prerace inspections are completed on time. Finally, the race director can use his tablet to monitor each inspection station, identify which cars have been cited for violations, and find out the status of every car.

The Microsoft app simplified the prerace inspection process. Consider, for example, that the paper form needed a NASCAR official's signature on every item. In contrast, the app by default assumes every item's status is good unless otherwise noted by officials.

The app stored a large amount of data. Information on the prerace inspections of all vehicles was collected in real time. Consequently, NASCAR officials could spot problems to help make the races fair for everyone.

NASCAR began using a new inspection system for the 2018 racing season. The new inspection process, developed by Hawk-Eye Innovations (www.hawkeyeinnovations.com), uses 17 cameras and 8 projectors to create a three-dimensional (3D) map of each car. Each 3D map is compared to each manufacturer's standard, as depicted by a computer-aided drawing (CAD) from that manufacturer. Areas of the car's body in compliance appear in green; areas of the body outside the allowable tolerance display in red. The entire process takes approximately three minutes per car. The new process, driven by technology, is faster and more efficient than the previous process and stores much more data about each car.

Sources: Compiled from Z. Albert, "New 2018 Inspection Process Aims to 'Create a Level Playing Field'," *NASCAR.com*, February 1, 2018; S. Choney, "NASCAR Levels the Playing Field by Bringing the Latest Technology into an American Tradition," *Microsoft Blog*, June 27, 2016; N. Linhart, "NASCAR App Improves Inspection Efficiency," *Charlotte Sun Times*, February 10, 2015; J. Gluck, "App Improves NASCAR Inspection Process," *USA Today*, February 8, 2015; "A Day at the Track for a NASCAR Race," *NASCAR.com*, January 5, 2015; "Going through Inspections," *NASCAR.com*, January 5, 2015; J. Richter, "NASCAR Pre-Race Inspection? There's an App for That," *Fox Sports*, October 23, 2014; T. Bradley, "NASCAR Turns to Microsoft and Windows 8 to Streamline Race Operations," *Forbes*, October 21, 2014; J. Hammond, "NASCAR Inspections a Work in Progress," *Fox Sports*, April 16, 2013; and www.nascar.com, accessed September 12, 2018.

Questions

1. Describe why prerace inspection is a business process for NASCAR.

2. Describe the various benefits that the old app provided to NASCAR.

3. Describe the advantages of the new (2018) app over the previous app.

4. Refer to Section 2.3. Is the app a strategic information system for NASCAR? Why or why not? Support your answer.

when, and where. IS captures and stores these data, commonly referred to as *process data* or *transaction data*. Some of these data are generated and automatically captured by the IS. These are data related to who completes an activity, when, and where. Other data are generated outside the IS and must be entered into it. This data entry can occur in various ways, ranging from manual entry to automated methods involving data in forms such as bar codes and RFID tags that can be read by machines.

In the fulfillment process, for example, when a customer order is received by mail or over the phone, the person taking the order must enter data such as the customer's name, what the customer ordered, and how much he or she ordered. Significantly, when a customer order is received through the firm's website, all customer details are captured by the IS. Data such as the name of the person entering the data (who), at which location the person is completing the task (where), and the date and time (when) are automatically included by the IS when it creates the order. The data are updated as the process steps are executed. When the order is shipped, the warehouse will provide data about which products were shipped and in what quantities, and the IS will automatically include data related to who, when, and where.

An important advantage of using an IS compared to a manual system or multiple functional area information systems is that the data need to be entered into the system only once. Furthermore, once they are entered, other people in the process can easily access them, and there is no need to reenter them in subsequent steps.

The data captured by the IS can provide immediate feedback. For example, the IS can use the data to create a receipt or to make recommendations for additional or alternative products.

MIS Monitoring Process Performance.

A third contribution of IS is to help monitor the state of the various business processes; that is, the IS indicates how well a process is executing. The IS performs this role by evaluating information about a process. This information can be created at either the *instance level* (i.e., a specific task or activity) or at the *process level* (i.e., the process as a whole).

For example, a company might be interested in the status of a particular customer order. Where is the order within the fulfillment process? Was the complete order shipped? If so, when? If not, then when can we expect it to be shipped? Or, for the procurement process, when was the purchase order sent to the supplier? What will be the cost of acquiring the material? At the process level, the IS can evaluate how well the procurement process is being executed by calculating the lead time, or the time between sending the purchase order to a vendor and receiving the goods, for each order and each vendor over time.

Not only can the IS help monitor a process but it can also detect problems with the process. The IS performs this role by comparing the information with a standard—that is, what the company expects or desires—to determine if the process is performing within expectations. Management establishes standards based on organizational goals.

If the information provided by the IS indicates that the process is not meeting the standards, then the company assumes that some type of problem exists. Some problems can be routinely and automatically detected by the IS, whereas others require a person to review the information and make judgments. For example, the IS can calculate the expected date that a specific order will be shipped and determine whether this date will meet the established standard. Or the IS can calculate the average time taken to fill all orders over the last month and compare this information with the standard to determine if the process is working as expected.

POM Monitoring business processes, then, helps detect problems with these processes. These problems are very often really symptoms of a more fundamental problem. In such cases, the IS can help diagnose the cause of the symptoms by providing managers with additional detailed information. For example, if the average time to process a customer order appears to have increased over the previous month, this problem could be a symptom of a more basic problem.

HRM A manager can then drill down into the information to diagnose the underlying problem. To accomplish this task, the manager can request a breakdown of the information by, for example, type of product, customer, location, employees, day of the week, and time of day. After reviewing this detailed information, the manager might determine that the warehouse has experienced an exceptionally high employee turnover rate over the last month and that the delays are occurring because new employees are not sufficiently familiar with the process. The manager might conclude that this problem will work itself out over time, in which case there is nothing more to be done. Alternatively, the manager could conclude that the new employees are not being adequately trained and supervised. In this case, the company must take actions to correct the problem. The following section discusses several methodologies that managers can use to take corrective action when process problems are identified.

Before you go on . . .

1. What is a business process?

2. Describe several business processes carried out at your university.

3. Define a cross-functional business process and provide several examples of such processes.

4. Pick one of the processes described in question 2 or 3 and identify its inputs, outputs, customer(s), and resources. How does the process create value for its customer(s)?

2.2 | Business Process Reengineering, Business Process Improvement, and Business Process Management

Excellence in executing business processes is widely recognized as the underlying basis for all significant measures of competitive performance in an organization. Consider the following measures:

- *Customer satisfaction:* The result of optimizing and aligning business processes to fulfill customers' needs, wants, and desires

- *Cost reduction:* The result of optimizing operations and supplier processes

- *Cycle and fulfillment time reduction:* The result of optimizing the manufacturing and logistics processes

- *Quality:* The result of optimizing the design, development, and production processes

- *Differentiation:* The result of optimizing the marketing and innovation processes

- *Productivity:* The result of optimizing each individual's work processes

The question is: How does an organization ensure business process excellence?

In their book *Reengineering the Corporation,* first published in 1993, Michael Hammer and James Champy argued that to become more competitive, American businesses needed to radically redesign their business processes to reduce costs and increase quality. The authors further asserted that information technology is the key enabler of such change. This radical redesign, called **business process reengineering (BPR)**, is a strategy for making an organization's business processes more productive and profitable. The key to BPR is for enterprises to examine their business processes from a "clean sheet" perspective and then determine how they can best reconstruct those processes to improve their business functions. BPR's popularity was propelled by the unique capabilities of information technology, such as automation and standardization of many process steps and error reduction due to improved communication among organizational information silos.

Although some enterprises have successfully implemented BPR, many organizations found this strategy too difficult, too radical, too lengthy, and too comprehensive. The impact on employees, on facilities, on existing investments in information systems, and even on organizational culture was overwhelming. Despite the many failures in BPR implementation, however, businesses increasingly began to organize work around business processes rather than individual tasks. The result was a less radical, less disruptive, and more incremental approach called *business process improvement (BPI).*

Author Lecture Videos are available exclusively in *WileyPLUS.*
Apply the Concept activities are available in the Appendix and in *WileyPLUS.*

BPI focuses on reducing variation in the process outputs by searching for root causes of the variation in the process itself (e.g., a broken machine on an assembly line) or among the process inputs (e.g., a decline in the quality of raw materials purchased from a certain supplier). BPI is usually performed by teams of employees that include a process expert—usually the process owner (the individual manager who oversees the process)—as well as other individuals who are involved in the process. These individuals can be involved directly, for example, the workers actually perform process steps. Alternatively, these individuals can be involved indirectly, for example, customers purchase the outputs from the process.

Six Sigma is a popular methodology for BPI initiatives. Its goal is to ensure that the process has no more than 3.4 defects per million outputs by using statistical methods to analyze the process. (A defect is defined as a faulty product or an unsatisfactory service.) Six Sigma was developed by Motorola in the 1980s, and it is now used by companies worldwide, thanks in part to promotional efforts by early adopters such as GE. Six Sigma is especially appropriate for manufacturing environments, in which product defects can be easily defined and measured. Over the years, the methodology has been modified so that it focuses less on defects and more on customer value. As a result, it can now be applied to services as well as to products. Today, Six Sigma tools are widely used in financial services and health care institutions as components of process-improvement initiatives.

Regardless of the specific methodology you use, a successful BPI project generally follows five basic phases: define, measure, analyze, improve, and control (DMAIC):

- In the *define phase*, the BPI team documents the existing "as is" process activities, process resources, and process inputs and outputs, usually as a graphical process map or diagram. The team also documents the customer and the customer's requirements for the process output, together with a description of the problem that needs to be addressed.

- In the *measure phase*, the BPI team identifies relevant process metrics, such as time and cost to generate one output (product or service), and collects data to understand how the metrics evolve over time. Sometimes the data already exist, in which case they can be extracted from the IS that supports the process, as described in the previous section. Many times, however, the BPI team needs to combine operational process data already stored in the company's IS systems with other data sources, such as customer and employee observations, interviews, and surveys.

- In the *analysis phase*, the BPI team examines the "as is" process map and the collected data to identify problems with the process (e.g., decreasing efficiency or effectiveness) and their root causes. If possible, the team should also benchmark the process; that is, compare its performance with that of similar processes in other companies or other areas of the organization. The team can employ IT applications such as statistical analysis software or simulation packages in this phase.

It is often valuable to use process simulation software during the analysis phase. Using this software provides two benefits. First, it enables a process manager to quickly simulate a real situation (e.g., with a certain number of people undertaking activities) for a specific amount of time (e.g., a working day, a week, or a month). The manager can then estimate the process performance over time without having to observe the process in practice. Second, it allows the manager to create multiple scenarios, for example, using a different number of resources in the process or using a different configuration for the process steps. Process simulation software can also provide a number of outputs regarding a process, including the time used by all resources to execute specific activities, the overall cycle time of a process, the identification of resources that are infrequently used, and the bottlenecks in the process. Simulating a process is extremely valuable for process managers because it is a risk-free and inexpensive test of an improvement solution that does not need to be conducted with real resources.

- In the *improve phase*, the BPI team identifies possible solutions for addressing the root causes, maps the resulting "to be" process alternatives, and selects and implements the most appropriate solution. Common ways to improve processes are eliminating process activities that do not add value to the output and rearranging activities in a way that reduces delays or improves resource use. The organization must be careful, however, not to eliminate internal *process controls*—those activities that safeguard company resources, guarantee the accuracy of its financial reporting, and ensure adherence to rules and regulations.

- In the *control phase*, the team establishes process metrics and monitors the improved process after the solution has been implemented to ensure that the process performance remains stable. An IS system can be very useful for this purpose.

Although BPI initiatives do not deliver the huge performance gains promised by BPR, many organizations prefer them because they are less risky and less costly. BPI focuses on delivering quantifiable results—and if a business case cannot be made, the project is not continued. All employees can be trained to apply BPI techniques in their own work to identify opportunities for improvement. Thus, BPI projects tend to be performed more from the bottom up, in contrast to BPR projects, which involve top-down change mandates. BPI projects take less time overall, and even if they are unsuccessful, they consume fewer organizational resources than BPR projects. However, if incremental improvements through BPI are no longer possible or if significant changes occur in the firm's business environment, then the firm should consider BPR projects. One final consideration is that, over time, employees can become overstretched or lose interest if the company undertakes too many BPI projects and does not have an effective system to manage and focus the improvement efforts.

POM To sustain BPI efforts over time, organizations can adopt **business process management (BPM)**, a management system that includes methods and tools to support the design, analysis, implementation, management, and continuous optimization of core business processes throughout the organization. BPM integrates disparate BPI initiatives to ensure consistent strategy execution.

Important components of BPM are process modeling and business activity monitoring. BPM begins with *process modeling*, which is a graphical depiction of all of the steps in a process. Process modeling helps employees understand the interactions and dependencies among the people involved in the process, the information systems they rely on, and the information they require to optimally perform their tasks. Process modeling software can support this activity. IT's About Business 2.2 shows how Chevron has employed BPR, BPI, and BPM.

Business activity monitoring (BAM) is a real-time approach for measuring and managing business processes. Companies use BAM to monitor their business processes, identify failures or exceptions, and address these failures in real time. Furthermore, because BAM tracks process operations and indicates whether they succeed or fail, it creates valuable records of process behaviors that organizations can use to improve their processes.

BPM activities are often supported by *business process management suites (BPMS)*. A BPMS is an integrated set of applications that includes a repository of process information, such as process maps and business rules; tools for process modeling, simulation, execution, coordination across functions, and reconfiguration in response to changing business needs; and process-monitoring capabilities.

Gartner (**www.gartner.com**), a leading IT research and advisory firm, states that companies need to focus on developing and mastering BPM skills throughout the organization. Gartner notes that high-performing companies use BPM technologies, such as real-time process monitoring, visualization, analytics, and intelligent automated decision making, to support intelligent business operations.

Another promising emerging trend is *social BPM*. This technology enables employees to collaborate, using social media tools on wired and mobile platforms, both internally across functions and externally with stakeholders (such as customers or subject-area experts), to exchange process knowledge and improve process execution.

BPM initially helps companies improve profitability by decreasing costs and increasing revenues. Over time, BPM can create a competitive advantage by improving organizational flexibility—making it easy to adapt to changing business conditions and to take advantage of new opportunities. BPM also increases customer satisfaction and ensures compliance with rules and regulations. In all cases, the company's strategy should drive the BPM effort.

IT's About Business 2.2

BPR, BPI, and BPM at Chevron

`POM` `MIS`

Chevron (**www.chevron.com**), one of the world's largest oil and gas companies, and its subsidiaries are involved in exploring and producing oil and natural gas as well as in manufacturing, transporting, and distributing petrochemical products, including gasoline and refined products. In 2013, Chevron employed more than 60,000 people worldwide, produced the equivalent of more than 2.6 million barrels of oil every day, and garnered more than $230 billion in sales. Chevron has initiated several process reengineering and improvement efforts over the years, evolving from BPR to BPI and eventually to BPM.

In 1995, Chevron's output was less than half of its current amount, producing roughly one million barrels of oil per day across six plants. The company had three major departments: Refining, Marketing, and Supply and Distribution (S&D). Management determined that they needed to improve their supply chain (see Chapter 11) to better integrate their multiple internal processes. A key figure in this initiative was Vice President Peter McCrea, who had a strong idea for dramatically improving performance. McCrea was convinced that Chevron had to reengineer the company's core processes from beginning to end: from the acquisition of crude oil to the distribution of final products to Chevron customers.

To accomplish this task, Chevron adopted a holistic approach. The company collaborated with a consulting firm to create a model of the existing processes. The objective was to radically improve these processes to align with Chevron's business goals. In other words, Chevron's strategy was not to concentrate on the existing processes to identify specific areas to improve. Rather, the project identified the desired outputs and then worked backward by examining the supporting processes, using BPR. As an added benefit, this holistic approach led the company to examine the interdependencies among processes used in different business units. This approach ultimately improved the company's overall performance. In a 1996 report, Chevron claimed the BPR project saved the company $50 million.

This complex BPR effort was initially followed by several smaller, employee-driven BPI initiatives. For example, in 1998, six Chevron employees initiated a project to improve water treatment processes at a company plant in California. Operating costs fell by one-third. Their success inspired other employees to initiate BPI projects in Indonesia, Angola, and other locations around the globe by using the Six Sigma improvement methodology. Although some managers were able to demonstrate the benefits of BPI at the local level, it wasn't until 2006 that these efforts achieved companywide recognition and corporate backing. In that year, Lean Six Sigma, which combines statistical process analysis with techniques to eliminate waste and improve process flow, became Chevron's preferred improvement methodology. Since Chevron implemented Lean Six Sigma, company employees have initiated hundreds of BPI projects worldwide, resulting in significant savings. From 2008 to 2010 alone, Chevron reported more than $1 billion in BPI benefits. To support these internal improvement efforts, Chevron got its suppliers on board in BPI initiatives as well.

To coordinate these various BPI efforts, Chevron has adopted a unified BPM approach that involves standardizing processes across the entire company and consolidating process information within a central repository. Chevron figures that only 20 percent of its processes can be fully automated—the rest involve a combination of manual and automated steps. Thus, process standardization involves not only supporting activities that can be automated but also ensuring that relevant employees are familiar with the standards for manual activities. To familiarize employees with all these processes, Chevron implemented Nimbus (**nimbus.tibco.com**), a BPMS that acts as a repository of standard companywide rules and procedures. Nimbus can also provide employees with detailed work instructions.

Take Chevron's shipping process as an example where the BPMS could shine. Shipping was executed in different ways in locations throughout Asia, Europe, and the United States. To establish uniform company standards, Chevron employed a BPI approach. The company documented its processes as they existed across different geographical locations, identified best practices, and combined these practices into a common process to implement. It then detailed these new policies and procedures, which it distributed to managers through the company's Web-based BPMS.

Chevron has a companywide management system that focuses on operational excellence, and BPM is a key part of that system. All Chevron operating companies and business units must implement continuous improvement, using carefully defined guidelines, metrics, and targets that are reviewed and adapted every year. Chevron's metrics focus on process efficiency, safety, risk, and the environment. The commitment to continuous improvement is part of Chevron's corporate culture. All employees participate in operational excellence activities, and managers receive specific operational excellence training.

Operational excellence is especially crucial when economic times are tough. For example, in the fourth quarter of 2014, Chevron's net income was $3.5 billion, down nearly 30 percent from $4.9 billion for the same period in 2013. This decline resulted primarily from the steep drop in crude oil prices. However, it's likely that net income would have been less without the operational excellence initiatives. Chevron's CEO noted that the lower crude oil prices were partially offset by increased operational efficiency in the company's downstream operations—that is, refining oil products and delivering them to customers. This increased efficiency was a product of the company's ongoing BPR, BPI, and BPM efforts. These efforts appear to be paying off, as Chevron's net income for 2017 was $9.2 billion.

Sources: Compiled from P. Harmon, *Business Process Management*, Elsevier, Burlington, MA, 2007; "Operational Excellence," *chevron.com*, March 2012; "Chevron—Using Nimbus Control Software to Manage Processes," *FindingPetroleum.com*, September 23, 2010; "Chevron Wins Boston Strategies International's 2010 Award for Lean Six Sigma Implementation in Oil and Gas Operations," *www.bostonstrategies.com*, September 22, 2010; E. Schmidt, "From the Bottom Up: Grassroots Effort Finds Footing at Chevron," *isixsigma.com*, March 1, 2010; R. Parker, "Business Process Improvement: A Talk with Chevron's Jim Boots," *Ebizq.net*, August 26, 2009; and www.chevron.com, accessed October 31, 2018.

Questions

1. Describe the main advantages of BPR at Chevron.

2. Why did Chevron adopt BPI?

3. How does Chevron apply BPM in its operations today?

Before you go on . . .

1. What is business process reengineering?
2. What is business process improvement?
3. What is business process management?

2.3 | Business Pressures, Organizational Responses, and Information Technology Support

Modern organizations compete in a challenging environment. To remain competitive, they must react rapidly to problems and opportunities that arise from extremely dynamic conditions. In this section, you examine some of the major pressures confronting modern organizations and the strategies that organizations employ to respond to these pressures.

Author Lecture Videos are available exclusively in *WileyPLUS*.
Apply the Concept activities are available in the Appendix and in *WileyPLUS*.

Business Pressures

The **business environment** is the combination of social, legal, economic, physical, and political factors in which businesses conduct their operations. Significant changes in any of these factors are likely to create business pressures on organizations. Organizations typically respond to these pressures with activities supported by IT. **Figure 2.2** illustrates the relationships among business pressures, organizational performance and responses, and IT support. You will learn about three major types of business pressures: market, technology, and societal pressures.

MKT **Market Pressures.** Market pressures are generated by the global economy, intense competition, the changing nature of the workforce, and powerful customers. Let's look more closely at each of these factors.

Globalization. **Globalization** is the integration and interdependence of economic, social, cultural, and ecological facets of life, made possible by rapid advances in information technology. Today, individuals around the world are able to connect, compute, communicate, collaborate, and compete everywhere and anywhere, anytime, and all the time; to access limitless amounts of information, services, and entertainment; to exchange knowledge; and to produce and sell goods and services. People and organizations can now operate without regard to geography, time, distance, or even language barriers. The bottom line? Globalization is markedly increasing competition.

These observations highlight the importance of market pressures for you. Simply put, you and the organizations you join will be competing with people and organizations from all over the world.

Let's consider some examples of globalization:

- Multinational corporations operate on a global scale, with offices and branches located worldwide.
- Many automobile manufacturers use parts from other countries, such as a car being assembled in the United States with parts coming from Japan, Germany, or Korea.
- The World Trade Organization (WTO; **www.wto.org**) supervises international trade.
- Regional agreements have contributed to increased world trade and increased competition. For example, the United States–Mexico–Canada Agreement (USMCA) is intended

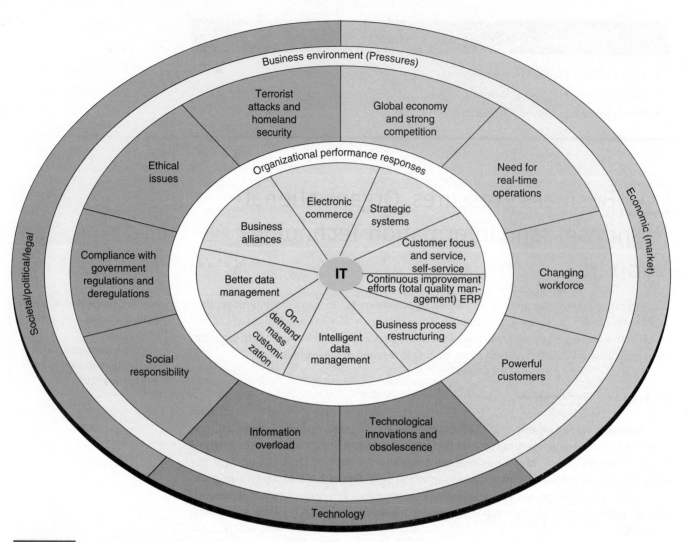

FIGURE 2.2 Business pressures, organizational performance and responses, and IT support.

to replace the North American Free Trade Agreement (NAFTA). The USMCA is essentially NAFTA 2.0, with a few updates. The new pact includes changes for automakers, labor and environmental standards, intellectual property protections, and electronic commerce provisions. In early May 2019, all three countries had signed the USMCA, but the United States Congress had not yet ratified it.

• The European Union (EU) is an economic and political union of 28 countries located in Europe. (*Note:* As of May 2019, the United Kingdom remained in the EU despite voting in favor of Brexit on June 23, 2016. *Note also:* Brexit is an abbreviation for the departure of the United Kingdom from the EU.)

• The rise of India and China as economic powerhouses has increased global competition.

One important pressure that businesses in a global market must contend with is the cost of labor, which varies significantly among countries. In general, labor costs are higher in developed countries such as the United States and Japan than in developing countries such as Bangladesh and El Salvador. Also, developed countries usually offer greater benefits, such as health care, to employees, driving the cost of doing business even higher. Therefore, many labor-intensive industries have moved their operations to countries with low labor costs. IT has made such moves much easier to implement.

However, manufacturing overseas is no longer the bargain it once was, and manufacturing in the United States is no longer as expensive. For example, manufacturing wages in China have increased by 64 percent (to $3.60 per hour) since 2011, and they continue to rise.

HRM **The Changing Nature of the Workforce.** The workforce, particularly in developed countries, is becoming more diversified. Increasing numbers of women, single parents, minorities, and persons with disabilities are now employed in all types of positions. IT is easing the integration of these employees into the traditional workforce. IT is also enabling people to work from home, which can be a major benefit for parents with young children and for people confronted with mobility or transportation issues.

Powerful Customers. Consumer sophistication and expectations increase as customers become more knowledgeable about the products and services they acquire. Customers can use the Internet to find detailed information about products and services, to compare prices, and to purchase items at electronic auctions.

Organizations recognize the importance of customers and they have increased their efforts to acquire and retain them. Modern firms strive to learn as much as possible about their customers to better anticipate and address their needs. This process, called *customer intimacy*, is an important component of *customer relationship management (CRM)*, an organization-wide effort toward maximizing the customer experience. You will learn about CRM in Chapter 11.

MIS **Technology Pressures.** The second category of business pressures consists of those pressures related to technology. Two major technology-related pressures are technological innovation and information overload.

Technological Innovation and Obsolescence. New and improved technologies rapidly create or support substitutes for products, alternative service options, and superb quality. As a result, today's state-of-the-art products may be obsolete tomorrow. For example, how fast are new versions of your smartphone being released? How quickly are electronic versions of books, magazines, and newspapers replacing traditional hard copy versions? These changes force businesses to keep up with consumer demands.

Consider the rapid technological innovation of the Apple iPad (**www.apple.com/ipad**):

- Apple released the first iPad in April 2010 and sold 3 million devices in just 80 days.
- Apple released the iPad 2 on March 11, 2011, only 11 months later.
- Apple released the iPad 3 on March 7, 2012.
- Apple released its fourth-generation iPad on November 2, 2012, along with the iPad mini.
- On November 1, 2013, Apple released the fifth generation of its iPad, called the iPad Air.
- On November 12, 2013, Apple released its iPad Mini 2 with Retina Display.
- In October 2014, Apple released the iPad Air 2 and the iPad Mini 3.
- In September 2015, Apple released the iPad Mini 4.
- In November 2015, Apple released the iPad Pro.
- In 2017, Apple released the iPad Pro with a 12.9-inch screen.
- In 2018, Apple released a new iPad Pro with Facial Recognition.

One manifestation of technological innovation is "bring your own device (BYOD)." BYOD refers to the policy of permitting employees to bring personally owned mobile devices (laptops, tablet computers, and smartphones) to the workplace and to use those devices to connect to the corporate network as well as for personal use. The academic version of BYOD is when students use personally owned devices in educational settings to connect to their school's network.

MIS The rapid increase in BYOD represents a huge challenge for IT departments. Not only has IT lost the ability to fully control and manage these devices but employees also are now demanding that they be able to conduct company business from multiple personal devices.

The good news is that BYOD has increased worker productivity and satisfaction. In fact, some employees with BYOD privileges actually work longer hours with no additional pay. The bad news is security concerns. Many companies with BYOD policies have experienced an increase in *malware* (malicious software, discussed in Chapter 4). Furthermore, there is an increased risk of losing sensitive, proprietary information. Such information might not be securely stored on a personal mobile device, which can be lost or stolen.

Information Overload. The amount of information available on the Internet doubles approximately every year, and much of it is free. The Internet and other telecommunications networks are bringing a flood of information to managers. To make decisions effectively and efficiently, managers must be able to access, navigate, and use these vast stores of data, information, and knowledge. Information technologies such as search engines (discussed in Chapter 6) and data mining (Chapter 12) provide valuable support in these efforts.

Societal/Political/Legal Pressures.
The third category of business pressures includes social responsibility, government regulation/deregulation, spending for social programs, spending to protect against terrorism, and ethics. This section will explain how all of these elements affect modern businesses. We start with social responsibility.

Social Responsibility. Social issues that affect businesses and individuals range from the state of the physical environment to company and individual philanthropy to education. Some corporations and individuals are willing to spend time and money to address various social problems. These efforts are known as **organizational social responsibility** or **individual social responsibility**.

One critical social problem is the state of the physical environment. A growing IT initiative, called *green IT*, addresses some of the most pressing environmental concerns. IT is instrumental in organizational efforts to "go green" in three areas:

1. *Facilities design and management:* Organizations are creating more environmentally sustainable work environments. Many organizations are pursuing Leadership in Energy and Environmental Design (LEED) certification from the U.S. Green Building Council, a nonprofit group that promotes the construction of environmentally friendly buildings. One impact of this development is that IT professionals are expected to help create green facilities.

2. *Carbon management:* As companies try to reduce their carbon footprints, they are turning to IT executives to develop the systems needed to monitor carbon throughout the organization and its supply chain, which can be global in scope. Therefore, IT employees need to become knowledgeable about embedded carbon and how to measure it in the company's products and processes.

3. *International and U.S. environmental laws:* IT executives must deal with federal and state laws and international regulations that impact everything from the IT products they buy to how they dispose of them to their company's carbon footprint.

Continuing our discussion of social responsibility, social problems all over the world may be addressed through corporate and individual philanthropy. In some cases, questions arise as to what percentage of contributions actually goes to the intended causes and recipients and what percentage goes to a charity's overhead. Another problem that concerns contributors is that they often exert little influence over the selection of the projects their contributions will support. The Internet can help address these concerns and facilitate generosity and connection. Consider the following examples:

- *PatientsLikeMe* (**www.patientslikeme.com**): This is one of the thousands of message boards dedicated to infertility, cancer, and various other ailments. People use these sites and message boards to obtain information about health care decisions based on volunteered information while also receiving much-needed emotional support from strangers.

- *Kiva* (**www.kiva.org**): Kiva is a nonprofit enterprise that provides a link between lenders in developed countries and entrepreneurs in developing countries. Users pledge interest-free loans rather than tax-deductible donations. Kiva directs 100 percent of the loans to borrowers.

- *DonorsChoose* (**www.donorschoose.org**): DonorsChoose is an education-oriented website that functions entirely within the United States. Users make donations to public schools rather than loans. The website addresses the huge problem of underfunded public schools.

Still another social problem that affects modern business is the digital divide. The **digital divide** refers to the wide gap between those individuals who have access to information and communications technologies and those who do not. This gap exists both within and among countries.

Many government and international organizations are trying to close the digital divide that continues to persist (see IT's About Business 2.3). For example, in some areas of the United States, the public library provides the only source of free computer and Internet access in the neighborhood, and the demand for those computers frequently exceeds their availability.

IT's About Business 2.3

The Digital Divide Persists in America

`MIS`

Does everyone deserve access to affordable high-speed Internet, just as they have for water, sewers, electricity, and telephone service? In the past, great national efforts in the United States led to universal electricity and telephone service. Now, the country needs a plan to improve service, lower costs, and expand Internet access.

Despite having invented the Internet's protocols, the United States lags behind many of the world's developed countries in available broadband speeds and affordability. This problem is particularly severe in inner cities and rural areas, indicating that the nation has a persistent digital divide. According to the Pew Research Center, 5 percent of American adults now derive some income from online, temporary employment (not including ride- or home-sharing services).

A direct manifestation of the digital divide is the fact that more than 30 percent of American adults only have dial-up Internet access. Dial-up access is defined as 56 kilobits (thousands of bits) per second, a speed that is far too slow for modern, interactive websites. Even many people who can afford faster service cannot get it because they live in an area where it is not cost effective for providers to install the communications infrastructure necessary to provide broadband Internet access. Overall, 34 million Americans have no access to broadband as the U.S. Federal Communications Commission (FCC; **www.fcc.gov**) defines it: a download speed of at least 25 megabits (millions of bits) per second and an upload speed of at least 3 megabits per second.

Computers and broadband access do not necessarily lead to college degrees and better jobs. However, many people without these technologies likely are not receiving the training they need to make effective use of software and online services. Furthermore, there are many correlations between broadband access on the one hand and income levels and success in finding employment on the other hand.

Consider a family in Cleveland, Ohio. In 2018, slightly more than 50 percent of the area's households with incomes below $20,000 had neither broadband nor mobile Internet access, often due to the cost. Another 10 percent had a mobile phone but no home broadband.

One such household was an apartment in a public housing project where a teenaged girl named Jane lived with her mother, Susan. Susan could not afford broadband from Spectrum (**www.spectrum.com**), which would begin at approximately $50 per month for an entry-level plan, plus modem and taxes. Furthermore, the price would rise significantly after the 12-month introductory rate expired. The family does have a smartphone, but the small screen is difficult to use, and the family cannot afford to exceed the plan's data limits. Fast Internet access is available in a library a few blocks away, but it is not safe for Jane to walk there.

The region's public housing agency, the Cuyahoga Metropolitan Housing Authority (CMHA; **www.cmha.net**), gave Jane a tablet and a wireless hot spot in a trial program to help close the "homework gap" between children who have broadband Internet access and computers at home and those who do not. In addition, Susan qualified for a discount program ($5 to $10 per month) that AT&T (**www.att.com**) offers to families who receive food subsidies. This program provides digital subscriber line (DSL; see Chapter 6) service. However, the service does not offer what the federal government defines as broadband.

Another family in Cleveland illustrates that providing people with broadband access and computer training can change their lives. Monica Jones lives in a low-income neighborhood of Cleveland and has worked as a file clerk at the Cleveland Clinic for more than 20 years. In 2013, the medical center announced that it was moving to electronic medical records. Faced with losing her job, Monica entered a training center called the Ashbury Community Center, funded by a nonprofit organization called Connect Your Community (**www.connectyourcommunity.org**). She learned software such as Microsoft Word and Excel and then took online classes from the University of Phoenix. In 2016, she obtained a bachelor's degree in finance.

Monica still works at the Cleveland Clinic but at a new job that pays $20,000 more than her old job. She is editing digital reports in the hospital's cardiac catheterization lab. She now pays the $154 per month for broadband access in her new home.

To solve the broadband access problem for many of its low-income residents, Cleveland is focusing on public and subsidized housing, where 50,000 of the city's 385,000 inhabitants live. St. Vincent's Charity Hospital is the hub of a high-speed fiber-optic network that connects institutions, including at least 800 schools, medical facilities, and government buildings across Cleveland. The city plans to extend the network to residents in a housing project near St. Vincent's.

Because it would cost $350,000 to deploy fiber from St. Vincent's to those projects, DigitalC (www.digitalc.org) will help to close the gap with a wireless technology from a company called Siklu (www.siklu.com) that will cost only $35,000 to install. DigitalC is an organization that partners with communities to design technology-driven programs and services. Siklu's wireless service will deliver 1 gigabit per second (1 billion bits per second) to the main building of the housing project. From there, servers in the building's telephone room will use the existing copper network to provide broadband service to the housing complex. The goal is to provide the fastest and least expensive service in Cleveland. When the FCC subsidy (called "lifeline") of $9.25 per month is factored in, all tenants in the housing project will be able to afford broadband.

DigitalC also plans to give all tenants in the CMHA refurbished computers and training. The tenants will be directed to online workforce training schools, such as Career Online High Schools. At the same time, the government of Cuyahoga County is putting more services online, including workforce training, benefits enrollment, and, potentially, telemedicine appointments.

One of the new participating businesses is WeCanCodeIt (www.wecancodeit.org), a 12-week software engineering boot camp for people with little experience in technology. The program aims to equip them for technology jobs such as building websites.

There is a larger digital divide problem: How do we get faster, cheaper, readily available broadband access across the United States? One answer is to stimulate competition. For example, after Google began offering broadband on fiber-optic lines in the Kansas City area in 2012, existing providers increased the speed of their services by 86 percent over what they had been offering only one year earlier.

Unfortunately, Cleveland has only two companies that provide Internet service: Spectrum and AT&T. AT&T does not offer broadband (defined by the FCC) to most of Cleveland. In fact, it offers only dial-up service to some streets.

The situation is even worse in rural areas. The town of Andover, Ohio (population about 1,100), has only DSL service from CenturyLink (www.centurylink.com). However, the Andover Public Library has a broadband connection from the state library consortium. As a result, people sometimes sit in their cars outside the library building after hours to access the Internet by using the library's Wi-Fi.

Other cities are providing innovative strategies to provide broadband Internet access. For example, Huntsville, Alabama, is building the basic fiber infrastructure, known as *dark fiber*. Google will then *light* the fiber and provide the service. Ammon, Idaho, built a fiber network and allows private providers to compete. Customers can now use a Web interface to switch providers in a few seconds. Significantly, this system does not require the company-specific cable or optical networking boxes that are common in homes across the country.

In most locations, however, efforts to install new networks face obstacles. Consider utility poles, for example. These poles are almost always owned by an electric company or a telephone company. The telephone companies make adding new fiber to the poles slow and expensive. The FCC has streamlined the rules for how companies attach to poles. Under federal law, however, the rules benefit only Internet service providers (ISPs), telephone companies, and cable companies. So, if the entity trying to install fiber happens to be, for example, a county agency in a rural area, then the FCC rules do not apply. Therefore, pole owners can make the process lengthy and difficult, even if the agency has been authorized by the state or local government to use the poles.

Let's take a look at the economic impacts of the digital divide. EveryoneOn (www.everyoneon.org) is a nonprofit organization whose mission is to create social and economic opportunity by connecting everyone to the Internet. EveryoneOn has shown the following:

- Students are 7 percent more likely to earn a high school diploma and attend college when connected to the Internet at home. Furthermore, these students will earn over $2 million more over their lifetimes.

- An unemployed person who has the Internet at home will be employed seven weeks faster than one who does not and will earn more than $5,000 in additional income annually, according to EveryoneOn's analysis of data from the Bureau of Labor Statistics.

- According to Deloitte (www.deloitte.com), every day that a person is not connected to the Internet, America loses $2.16 per person per day of potential economic activity, meaning that the digital divide costs the United States over $130 million per day in economic activity.

Sources: Compiled from C. Aguh, "How the 'Digital Divide' Is Holding the U.S. Economy Back," *VentureBeat*, February 10, 2018; A. Perrin, "Digital Gap between Rural and Nonrural America Persists," *Pew Research Center*, May 19, 2017; U. Aneja et al., "Bridging the Digital Divide: Skills," *G20 Insights*, May 5, 2017; J. Fink, "Closing the Digital Divide," *TechZone360*, April 10, 2017; M. Anderson, "Digital Divide Persists Even as Lower-Income Americans Make Gains in Tech Adoption," *Pew Research Center*, March 22, 2017; G. Galvin, "States Struggle to Bridge Digital Divide," *US News and World Report*, March 16, 2017; J. Bond, "2.1 Million People Still Use Dial-Up Internet from AOL," *The Daily Dot*, January 8, 2017; D. Talbot, "The Hole in the Digital Economy," *Benton Foundation*, December 16, 2016; D. West and J. Karsten, "Rural and Urban America Divided by Broadband Access," *Brookings*, July 18, 2016; "FCC's Broadband Progress Report 2016," *FCC.gov*, January 29, 2016; and C. Tolbert and K. Mossberger, "Cuyahoga County Survey of Internet Access and Use," *Connect Your Community*, 2012.

Questions

1. Describe some impacts on individuals and families (not mentioned in the case) resulting from a lack of Internet access.

2. Is affordable, broadband Internet access strategically important to cities? Why or why not? Support your answer.

3. Is affordable, broadband Internet access strategically important to the United States? Why or why not? Support your answer.

One well-known project to narrow the divide is the One Laptop per Child (OLPC) project (**www.one.laptop.org**). OLPC is a nonprofit association dedicated to developing a very inexpensive laptop—a technology that aims to revolutionize how the world can educate its children. In 2018, the price of OLPC's laptop remained approximately $230. We note that this price includes educational software loaded on the laptop. On the other hand, there are many other costs associated with these laptops, including shipping, solar chargers, maintenance, and training. Some international users insist that the actual cost of one laptop is therefore approximately $450.

IT's About Business 2.3 examines the impacts that the digital divide has on socioeconomically disadvantaged people and various ways in which cities are trying to close that divide.

Compliance with Government Regulations. Another major source of business pressures is government regulations regarding health, safety, environmental protection, and equal opportunity. Businesses tend to view government regulations as expensive constraints on their activities. In general, government deregulation intensifies competition.

In the wake of 9/11 and numerous corporate scandals, the U.S. government passed many new laws, including the Sarbanes–Oxley Act, the USA PATRIOT Act, the Gramm–Leach–Bliley Act, and the Health Insurance Portability and Accountability Act (HIPAA). Organizations must be in compliance with the regulations contained in these statutes. The process of becoming and remaining compliant is expensive and time consuming. In almost all cases, organizations rely on IT support to provide the necessary controls and information for compliance.

Protection against Terrorist Attacks. Since September 11, 2001, organizations have been under increased pressure to protect themselves against terrorist attacks, both physical attacks and cyberattacks. Employees who are in the military reserves have also been called up for active duty, creating personnel problems. Information technology can help protect businesses by providing security systems and possibly identifying patterns of behavior associated with terrorist activities, including cyberattacks (discussed in Chapter 4). For a good example of a firm that provides this protection, see Palantir (**www.palantir.com**).

An example of protection against terrorism is the Department of Homeland Security's (DHS) Office of Biometric Identity Management (OBIM) program. (We discuss biometrics in Chapter 4.) OBIM (**www.dhs.gov/obim**) is a network of biometric screening systems, such as fingerprint and iris and retina scanners, that ties into government databases and watch lists to check the identities of millions of people entering the United States. The system is now operational in more than 300 locations, including major international ports of entry by air, sea, and land.

Ethical Issues. *Ethics* relates to general standards of right and wrong. *Information ethics* relates specifically to standards of right and wrong in information processing practices. Ethical issues are very important because, if handled poorly, they can damage an organization's image and destroy its employees' morale. The use of IT raises many ethical issues, ranging from monitoring e-mail to invading the privacy of millions of customers whose data are stored in private and public databases. Chapter 3 covers ethical issues in detail.

Clearly, then, the pressures on organizations are increasing, and organizations must be prepared to take responsive actions if they are to succeed. You will learn about these organizational responses in the next section.

Organizational Responses

Organizations are responding to the various pressures just discussed by implementing IT such as strategic systems, customer focus, make-to-order and mass customization, and e-business. This section explores each of these responses.

Strategic Systems. Strategic systems provide organizations with advantages that enable them to increase their market share and profits to better negotiate with suppliers and to prevent competitors from entering their markets. IT's About Business 2.4 provides an example of how strategically important information systems can be to an organization. As you will see, many information systems are so strategically important to organizations that if they are inadequate or fail altogether, their organizations are at risk of failing as well.

IT's About Business 2.4

Bank of America Transforms Its Information Technology

`MIS`

The Problem

After the financial crisis of 2007–2008, Bank of America (BofA; www.bankofamerica.com) executives directed the bank to take measures to eliminate the problems that led to its near-death experience in that crisis. Many of these measures involved BofA's information technology. As the bank spends approximately $3 billion developing and buying information technology each year and approximately $9 billion on maintaining its existing IT infrastructure, these measures have taken on critical urgency.

A Multipart Solution

BofA developed a series of strategic goals for its IT function: (1) standardize its IT infrastructure, (2) streamline applications, (3) develop customer-focused innovations, (4) streamline the physical infrastructure, (5) develop a digital mortgage process, (6) utilize artificial intelligence (AI) in bank business processes, and (7) monitor the FinTech space for possible strategic partnerships. BofA's IT organization, called Global Technology and Operations, was directly tasked with achieving these goals.

`MIS` **IT Infrastructure.** In the past, the bank's business flexibility was limited by a huge, global IT architecture that cost billions of dollars per year to operate. For example, the IT department typically allocated separate servers in its data centers for each line of business, such as its mortgage business and its trading applications. To improve efficiency and reduce costs, the bank's first strategic goal was to create a standardized, shared IT infrastructure that all business units could readily access.

To accomplish this goal, the bank implemented a software-defined infrastructure (SDI), a private cloud (discussed in Technology Guide 3) where software provides the server, storage, and networking resources to business users as needed. This process is similar to the way cloud service providers offer computing on demand to their customers. The SDI private cloud enabled the bank, which operated 64 data centers in 2008, to plan to operate only eight data centers by 2019.

The SDI private cloud enabled the bank to respond more quickly to changing business conditions and to cut costs—as much as 50 percent from the bank's current data center costs. The cloud approach also enabled the bank to perform more computing tasks with less hardware. In addition, it increased the ability of the bank's network, storage, and server capacity to scale up or scale down as business conditions dictate. Essentially, the cloud gives the bank more flexibility and speed to react to changes in the bank's dynamic business environment.

The SDI private cloud requires more complex security controls and compliance reporting. BofA must be able to prove to auditors that it is securely managing sensitive data, such as bank account numbers and credit card information, in its cloud. In fact, to improve information security and regulatory compliance, the bank is experimenting with tagging or labeling each piece of data so that it can follow the data across its global network, tracking anyone who has had access to it or has made changes to it.

Applications. BofA has retired more than 18,000 applications, many of them left over from its acquisitions of other companies. For example, the bank spent $100 million to consolidate five Merrill Lynch financial adviser applications into one. (BofA acquired Merrill Lynch in 2013.) Further, users at corporate clients in 140 countries now access BofA's CashPro Online portal in 11 languages. The portal replaced hundreds of applications, including liquidity management, currency conversion, wire transfers, and many others. The bank also consolidated 22 collateral management systems into one system and eight teller systems into one system.

Simplifying its IT infrastructure and reducing the license and support costs of thousands of applications has enabled the bank to invest a larger percentage of its $10 billion annual IT budget on innovative applications. In fact, BofA has doubled its spending on new development since 2009.

`MKT` **Innovative Customer Service.** The bank's customers stated they wanted their bank to be "where they are." In response, the bank launched new versions of its customer smartphone and iPad app in 2014. The app provides three features:

1. *Account information and transactional capabilities:* Customers must be able to view account details and transfer funds on any device from wherever they are. Further, customers can order new debit and credit cards, view their available card credit, schedule appointments, modify scheduled bill payments, order copies of posted checks, and perform many other functions.

2. *Service:* The app provides numerous service-oriented features. As one example, if bank customers are traveling internationally, then they should be able to place a travel notification on their accounts via a mobile device rather than having to call the bank to speak to a customer service representative.

3. *Mobile payments and commerce:* BofA is offering services such as its clearXchange person-to-person payments network jointly with JPMorgan Chase and Wells Fargo. In addition, the bank offers its BankAmeriDeals merchant-funded rewards program, which allows customers to receive coupons from retailers by clicking on offers sent directly to their online banking accounts.

By the fall of 2018, the app had more than 20 million users and was growing rapidly. BofA is now managing millions of transactions made from mobile devices, an amount that is growing at a rate of 50 percent per year.

Physical Infrastructure. To reduce costs, BofA analyzed its network of bank branch locations. The bank tracked every transaction by customer, location, time, and channel. For security purposes, the bank removed all details that would identify any individual. In addition to tracking customer activity, the bank examined the capacity of each branch, the costs of each location, each branch's total revenues, annual sales, and first-year revenue sales to a new customer. Based on the results of the analysis, BofA reduced the number of its branch banks by 20 percent.

The Digital Mortgage. In April 2018, BofA launched a digital mortgage. The digital mortgage lets customers fill out a mortgage application through the bank's mobile app or its online banking website. Mortgage closings must still be completed in person.

In creating its digital mortgage, the bank reduced the number of fields that customers have to enter into the mortgage application to less than half. A standard mortgage application has over 300 fields that must be completed. The bank prefills the majority of that information. The bank retrieves relevant data and documents from its own systems, saving customers from having to enter so much information and having to take photos of documents. For noncustomers, the bank works with a data aggregation firm to retrieve the necessary information from other financial institutions.

The bank notes that the digital mortgage reduces the time it takes for customers to get to the mortgage closing by half. The bank's existing Home Loan Navigation software tool guides the customer through the process and provides status updates. BofA emphasizes that the digital mortgage does not replace the lending officer but rather enhances the experience of the lending officer by making the busy work much easier and faster.

MIS **Artificial Intelligence (AI).** The bank introduced Erica, its chatbot, in March 2018, and by July 2018, Erica had 1 million users. Erica uses two forms of AI: natural language processing to understand speech, text, and intent and machine learning to gain insights from customer data. Erica helps customers check balances, reminds them about bills, schedules payments, lists recent transactions, and answers bank-related questions. Customers can interact with the chatbot via voice, text, tap, or gesture.

Customers continue to use Erica, and their top use is to search transactions. For example, they can access Erica and say, "Show me all my Walmart transactions." Customers search for pending transactions by saying, "Did my paycheck post?" They also use Erica to obtain account balances, account numbers, or routing numbers. Further, they can pay bills through Erica.

By the late summer of 2018, BofA introduced insights and proactive notifications through Erica. Here, customers were told if they had upcoming bills due, if their balances were too low to cover those bills, if a subscription to a magazine was expiring, or if their credit score had changed dramatically.

The bank is handling a variety of challenges with Erica, including protecting consumer privacy, improving the chatbot's ability to understand everyday speech, and meeting additional demands that users are sure to place on the service as they become accustomed to using it.

The bank also uses machine learning in its fraud management programs. The overall goal of fraud management is to lower losses and enhance the customer experience. The basis for fraud management is a thorough understanding of customer behavior; that is, understanding what qualifies as a normal transaction and what does not. As the bank gains additional insight into customer behavior, it can refine its fraud management algorithms to ensure that the bank does not identify a legitimate transaction as fraudulent or miss a truly fraudulent transaction.

The bank also applies machine learning to billing disputes. Rather than an employee spending hours to gather data about a dispute, machine learning software finds and analyzes this data quickly and delivers a verdict.

Machine learning also holds promise in analyzing trade data. For example, the European Commission's Markets in Financial Instruments Directive 2, which took effect on January 3, 2018, calls for additional reporting on trades. As a result, the bank is recording two million more financial transactions than it was prior to

the directive. The analysis of those events is helping the bank see when a transaction made money or lost money. The bank is using the analysis to refine its financial offerings to its clients as well as to refine its own financial operations.

BofA executives do have concerns with AI technologies. For example, there is a chance that AI models can be biased. Therefore, the bank will not allow an AI algorithm to have the final say in who is hired.

FIN **ACCT** **FinTech.** FinTech refers to the innovative use of technology in the design and delivery of financial services and products. FinTech encompasses lending, advice, investment management, and payments. Many FinTech companies utilize mobile technologies, Big Data, and analytics to customize products for various customer segments. There are many examples:

- Digital payment systems, such as digital wallets, mobile payments, and peer-to-peer payments
- Investment systems, such as crowdfunding and peer-to-peer lending
- Financing systems such as microloans

BofA operates in a highly regulated industry and has very narrow margins. Therefore, the bank will not become a FinTech company. However, it is exploring various strategies to work with FinTech companies.

Interestingly, BofA IT executives meet annually with 40 technology start-ups in Silicon Valley to learn about new products. Over the years, the bank has decided to do business with about 17 percent of these start-ups. BofA's work with start-ups balances the bank's need for scale and reliability against its need for new ideas.

BofA has high expectations for these vendors. The bank requires open standards and interoperability, meaning that vendor applications must integrate seamlessly with BofA's applications. It also requires technology contracts in which costs scale down as well as up. Finally, technology vendors must share BofA's risk and regulatory rules, including, in some cases, agreeing to contracts where vendors share in the liability if their technology causes problems that lead to losses or fines for the bank. In just one example, BofA is working with Quarule (**www.quarule.com**), a company that applies AI to banks' regulatory compliance tasks.

The Results

The IT transformation is ongoing, and BofA's financial results seem sound. In the fall of 2018, BofA was the country's second-largest bank, with more than $2.2 trillion in assets. Further, the bank reported net income of $18.2 billion in 2017.

Sources: Compiled from P. Crosman, "Mad about Erica: Why a Million People Use Bank of America's Chatbot," *American Banker*, June 13, 2018; P. Crosman, "Where Bank of America Uses AI, and Where Its Worries Lie," *American Banker*, May 11, 2018; J. Nunn, "How AI Is Transforming HR Departments," *Forbes*, May 9, 2018; P. Crosman, "Bank of America Launches a (Mostly) Digital Mortgage," *American Banker*, April 11, 2018; C. Weissman, "Bank of America's Bot Is 'Erica' Because Apparently All Digital Assistants Are Women," *Fast Company*, March 28, 2018; R. Barba, "Bank of America Launches Erica Chatbot," *Banking*, March 19, 2018; P. High, "The Future of Technology according to Bank of America's Chief Operations and Technology Officer," *Forbes*, June 19, 2017; "Bank of America Is Laying Off Operations and Tech Employees, Mostly at Its Headquarters," *Reuters*, June 14, 2017; "Bank of America Drives Future of Digital Banking in 2017 as Mobile Banking Turns 10," *Bank of America Press Release*, February 22, 2017; S. Nunziata, "Bank of America's Digital Transformation: Where IT Fits In," *InformationWeek*, October 27, 2016; P. Crosman, "How B of A's Billion-Dollar Tech Cuts Could Fuel Startups," *American Banker*, June 28, 2016; L. Shen,

"Here's Why Bank of American Is Slashing Up to 8,400 Jobs," *Fortune*, June 15, 2016; "BofA Has $3 Billion to Pour into Innovations as Banks Are Swarming around FinTech Startups," *Let's Talk Payments*, January 8, 2016; H. Clancy, "This Fortune 500 Bank's Patents Are Cited by Apple, Google, and Nike," *Fortune*, June 29, 2015; R. King, "Bank of America's Data Initiative Follows Internet Companies into the Cloud," *Wall Street Journal*, March 6, 2015; C. Murphy, "How Bank of America Taps Tech Startups," *Information-Week*, December 1, 2014; R. Preston, "IT Chief of the Year: Bank of America's Cathy Bessant," *InformationWeek*, December 1, 2014; T. Groenfeldt, "Bank of America's Data Mapping Adds $1 Per Share," *Forbes*, August 21, 2014; C. Murphy, "Bank of America's 'Why Stop There?' Cloud Strategy," *InformationWeek*, February 4, 2014; D. Campbell, "Bank of America Finishes Merger of Merrill Lynch into Parent," *Bloomberg Business*, October 1, 2013; B. Yurcan, "The Future of Mobile at Bank of America," *InformationWeek*,

March 25, 2013; P. Crosman, "Inside BofA's IT Makeover," *American Banker*, September 1, 2011; "BofA Repays All of Government Funds," *MSNBC*, December 10, 2009; and www.bankofamerica.com, accessed September 22, 2017.

Questions

1. What is the relationship between the development of mobile banking customer applications and the closing of banking centers?

2. In terms of Porter's strategies for competitive advantage, discuss each strategy that the BofA is pursuing. Provide specific examples to support your answer.

MKT **Customer Focus.**   Organizational attempts to provide superb customer service can make the difference between attracting and retaining customers and losing them to competitors. Numerous IT tools and business processes have been designed to keep customers happy. Recall that a *business process* is a collection of related activities that produce a product or a service of value to the organization, its business partners, and its customers. Consider Amazon, for example. When you visit Amazon's website any time after your first visit, the site welcomes you back by name, and it presents you with information about items that you might like, based on your previous purchases. In another example, Dell guides you through the process of purchasing a computer by providing information and choices that help you make an informed buying decision. IT's About Business 2.5 illustrates how cruise lines are using information technology to enhance the passenger experience.

IT's About Business 2.5

Cruise Ships Embrace Technology

MIS **MKT**

Cruising has traditionally enabled people to escape their busy lives for a week or two. Today, technology is becoming a necessity in the travel industry. Most passengers expect to be able to stay connected while onboard a ship as easily as they do on land. Let's look at the technology deployed on the ships of three cruise lines.

Royal Caribbean Cruises.   Royal Caribbean Cruises Ltd (**www.royalcaribbean.com**) digitally transformed its fleet of 49 ships over a period of 2 years from 2018 to 2020. To help drive this transformation, the company opened an innovation lab at its headquarters in Miami, Florida, to develop innovative technologies for its ships.

Royal Caribbean's ships feature robot bartenders and WOW-bands. The WOWband uses radio-frequency identification wristbands (RFID; see Chapter 8) that allow guests to make onboard purchases and access staterooms.

Modern passengers have assumed broadband connectivity is available, so the cruise line features improved Wi-Fi throughout each ship. In one application, passengers can order a drink from a mobile app, and a waiter will bring it to them wherever they are. The company uses Wi-Fi access points to triangulate the passenger's position, providing servers an area of about three meters to walk toward. The servers have phones that show a photo of the passenger's face, which helps find them.

Royal Caribbean uses VR technology to provide passengers in inside cabins with views of the sea. Passengers see these views from their virtual balconies. The cruise line has also deployed the Sky Pad, which is a large yellow sphere on the upper deck. Inside are four trampolines, which are connected to a combination of bungee cords and

VR. Once inside, participants bounce with the aid of the bungee cords, all while exploring VR worlds on the VR headsets they are wearing

Celebrity Cruises.   The *Celebrity Edge* launched on December 16, 2018 and is the first ship designed completely three dimensionally (3D). The company used virtual reality (VR) 3D simulations, full 3D mock-ups of the design, and 3D screens so that designers could look at every different angle of a particular space—passenger cabins, restaurants, entertainment venues, offices—to ensure that what they constructed would be appropriate for their guests and crews.

The ship features a mobile app for passengers and crew that includes machine learning so the app can act as an intelligent personal assistant for passengers. The ship also features facial recognition to allow for check-in at ports, wayfinding (finding your way around the ship), and automatically unlocking cabin doors for the cabin's occupants. Interestingly, automatically unlocking cabin doors required the cruise line to replace all existing door locks, a lengthy and expensive process.

For wayfinding, Celebrity relies on its existing networks as well as sensors on passengers' phones to accurately map where they are on the ship. By embracing this technology, the cruise line did not have to build any new infrastructure on its ships to accommodate wayfinding.

Carnival Corporation.   Carnival Corporation (**www.carnival.com**) deployed a robot named Pepper that greets guests and answers general questions. Dinner menus and photos of guests that roaming photographers take are available for viewing on iPads located throughout Carnival's ships. The cruise line has also deployed a mobile app to enable passengers to use instant messaging to communicate with one another while onboard.

In November 2017, Carnival debuted its new Medallion wearable device. Each Medallion is connected to a specific guest, and it interacts with 7,000 sensors on each ship. The Medallion works with the Ocean Compass, a network of 4,000 high-resolution 55-inch screens located throughout each ship. The Ocean Compass incorporates machine learning to analyze passenger behavior and provide personalized recommendations. For example, as a passenger walks toward his room, sensors detect his approach. By the time he arrives, the lights are on, and the air conditioner is cooling his room to his preferred temperature.

MSC Cruises. MSC Cruises (**www.msccruisesusa.com**) is launching 11 new cruise ships, with its final ship completed in 2026, and a fleetwide digital innovation strategy called MSC for Me. The 10-year, $10 billion investment program uses technology to improve guest experiences. The first of MSC's new ships, the *MSC Meraviglia*, entered service in mid-2017. The ship has 16,000 points of connectivity, 700 digital access points, 358 interactive information screens, and 2,244 cabins with RFID and near-field communications (NFC; see Chapter 8) technology.

With 170 nationalities sailing on MSC ships, the communications challenges are enormous. MSC needs to provide relevant information based on each guest's profile, and all digital communication channels must facilitate the effective delivery of this information.

MSC for Me bracelets use facial recognition to provide guests with 130 smart, personalized features aimed at an optimized cruising experience. These features include an app that helps guests to book their excursions prior to embarkation, make reservations at one of the ship's restaurants, and experience VR tours of the ship and its spaces, such as rooms and public areas. For travelers, the bracelets serve as a daily activity organizer, providing wayfinding, facilitating purchases, and allowing passengers to request services from staff. The bracelets come at an additional price for adults but are free for children. Guests who do not choose to purchase a bracelet can access some of its features on the app alone, such as checking how full restaurants are or booking excursions.

MSC is using VR technology to create immersive virtual shore excursions that guests can try before purchasing the actual excursion. The cruise line also uses VR that enables guests to see how they look in various items of clothing sold onboard without having to try them on.

In all of the cruise lines' digital efforts, privacy and security are critical considerations. Therefore, all cruise lines are developing their applications with best practices in mind for guests' privacy and security.

Sources: Compiled from A. Coulter, "Sky Pad Virtual Reality Trampoline on Royal Caribbean Cruises," *CruiseCritic*, June 13, 2018; R. Tribou, "Revamp of Royal Caribbean Ship to Add Virtual Reality Trampoline," *Orlando Sentinel*, February 8, 2018; R. Cheng, "Royal Caribbean's High-Tech Ship Lets You Be Lazier Than Ever," *CNET*, November 10, 2017; "New Technology for Cruise Lines," *CruiseExperts.com*, April 3, 2017; T. Maddox, "Royal Caribbean Steps Up the High-Tech Battle on the High Seas," *TechRepublic*, March 15, 2017; C. Herrera, "MSC's Smart Wristbands and New Technology Coming to the Line's Miami Cruise Ships," *Miami Herald*, March 13, 2017; C. Saran, "MSC Cruises Goes Digital," *Computer Weekly*, March 10, 2017; "MSC Cruises Launches New Digital Guest Experience Program, MSC for Me," *Seatrade Cruise News*, March 8, 2017; K. Collins, "These Cruise Ships Will Deck You Out in Wearable Tech," *CNET*, March 8, 2017; B. Barrett, "Carnival's High-Tech Cruise Wearable Knows Your Every Need," *Wired*, January 5, 2017; M. McFarland, "Carnival's New Wearable Rethinks the Cruise Ship Vacation," *CNN*, January 4, 2017; E. Silverstein, "Robot Bartender at the Bionic Bar on Royal Caribbean Cruises," *Cruise Critic*, December 7, 2016; www.royalcaribbean.com, www.carnival.com, and www.msccruisesusa.com, all accessed July 25, 2018.

Questions

1. Are the information technologies mentioned in this case strategic systems for the cruise lines? Why or why not? Support your answer.

2. What are the privacy implications of the interactive bracelets from all three cruise lines? (*Hint:* Look ahead to Chapter 3.)

3. Is it possible that VR applications could actually detract from the cruising experience? Why or why not? Provide examples to support your answer.

Make-to-Order and Mass Customization.

Make-to-order is a strategy of producing customized (made to individual specifications) products and services. The business problem is how to manufacture customized goods efficiently and at a reasonably low cost. Part of the solution is to change manufacturing processes from mass production to mass customization. In mass production, a company produces a large quantity of identical items. An early example of mass production was Henry Ford's Model T, for which buyers could pick any color they wanted—as long as it was black.

Ford's policy of offering a single product for all of its customers eventually gave way to *consumer segmentation*, in which companies provide standard specifications for different consumer groups, or segments. Clothes manufacturers, for example, design their products in different sizes and colors to appeal to different customers. The next step was *configured mass customization*, in which companies offer features that allow each shopper to customize his or her product or service with a range of components. Examples are ordering a car, a computer, or a smartphone, for which the customer can specify which features he or she wants.

In the current strategy, known as **mass customization**, a company produces a large quantity of items, but it customizes them to match the needs and preferences of individual customers. Mass customization is essentially an attempt to perform make-to-order on a large scale. Examples are the following:

- NikeID (**www.nikeid.com**) allows customers to design their footwear.
- M&M candies: My M&Ms (**www.mymms.com**) allows customers to add photos, art, and messages to candy.
- Dell (**www.dell.com**) and HP (**www.hp.com**) allow customers to exactly specify the computer they want.

E-Business and E-Commerce. Conducting business electronically is an essential strategy for companies that are competing in today's business environment. *Electronic commerce (EC or e-commerce)* describes the process of buying, selling, transferring, or exchanging products, services, or information through computer networks, including the Internet. *E-business* is a somewhat broader concept. In addition to the buying and selling of goods and services, e-business also refers to servicing customers, collaborating with business partners, and performing electronic transactions within an organization. Chapter 7 focuses extensively on this topic. In addition, e-commerce applications appear throughout the text.

You now have a general overview of the pressures that affect companies in today's business environment and the responses that these companies choose to manage these pressures. To plan for the most effective responses, companies formulate strategies. In the new digital economy, these strategies rely heavily on information technology, especially strategic information systems. You examine these topics in the next section.

Before you go on . . .

1. What are the characteristics of the modern business environment?
2. Discuss some of the pressures that characterize the modern global business environment.
3. Identify some of the organizational responses to these pressures. Are any of these responses specific to a particular pressure? If so, then which ones?

2.4 Competitive Advantage and Strategic Information Systems

Author Lecture Videos are available exclusively in *WileyPLUS*.
Apply the Concept activities are available in the Appendix and in *WileyPLUS*.

A *competitive strategy* is a statement that identifies a business's approach to compete, its goals, and the plans and policies that will be required to carry out those goals.[1] A strategy, in general, can apply to a desired outcome, such as gaining market share. A competitive strategy focuses on achieving a desired outcome when competitors want to prevent you from reaching your goal. Therefore, when you create a competitive strategy, you must plan your own moves, but you must also anticipate and counter your competitors' moves.

Through its competitive strategy, an organization seeks a competitive advantage in an industry; that is, it seeks to outperform its competitors in a critical measure such as cost, quality, and time-to-market. Competitive advantage helps a company function profitably with a market and generate higher-than-average profits.

Competitive advantage is increasingly important in today's business environment, as you will note throughout the text. In general, the *core business* of companies has remained the same; that is, information technologies simply offer tools that can enhance an organization's success through its traditional sources of competitive advantage, such as low cost, excellent customer service, and superior supply chain management. **Strategic information systems (SISs)** provide a competitive advantage by helping an organization to implement its strategic goals and improve its performance and productivity. Any information system that helps an organization either achieve a competitive advantage or reduce a competitive disadvantage qualifies as a strategic information system.

Porter's Competitive Forces Model

The best-known framework for analyzing competitiveness is Michael Porter's **competitive forces model**. Companies use Porter's model to develop strategies to increase their competitive edge. Porter's model also demonstrates how IT can make a company more competitive.

---

[1]M. E. Porter, *Competitive Advantage* (New York: Free Press, 1985).

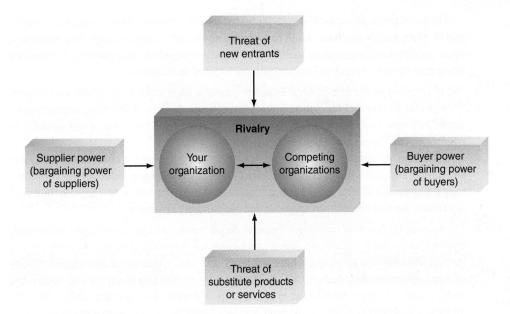

FIGURE 2.3 Porter's competitive forces model.

Porter's model identifies five major forces that can endanger or enhance a company's position in a given industry. **Figure 2.3** highlights these forces. Although the Web has changed the nature of competition, it has not changed Porter's five fundamental forces. In fact, what makes these forces so valuable as analytical tools is that they have not changed for centuries. Every competitive organization, no matter how large or small or which business it is in, is driven by these forces. This observation applies even to organizations that you might not consider competitive, such as local governments. Although local governments are not for-profit enterprises, they compete for businesses to locate in their districts, for funding from higher levels of government, for employees, and for many other things.

Significantly, Porter[2] concludes that the *overall* impact of the Web is to increase competition, which generally diminishes a firm's profitability. Let's examine Porter's five forces and the ways that the Web influences them:

1. *The threat of entry of new competitors:* The threat that new competitors will enter your market is high when entry is easy and low when there are significant barriers to entry. An **entry barrier** is a product or service feature that customers have learned to expect from organizations in a certain industry. An organization that seeks to enter the industry must offer this feature to survive in the marketplace. There are many types of entry barriers. Consider, for example, legal requirements, such as admission to the bar to practice law or obtaining a license to serve liquor, where only a certain number of licenses are available.

   Suppose you want to open a gasoline station. To compete in that industry, you would have to offer pay-at-the-pump service to your customers. Pay-at-the-pump is an IT-based barrier to entering this market because you must offer it for free. The first gas station that offered this service gained first-mover advantage and established barriers to entry. This advantage did not last, however, because competitors quickly offered the same service and thus overcame the entry barrier.

   For most firms, the Web *increases* the threat that new competitors will enter the market because it sharply reduces traditional barriers to entry, such as the need for a sales force or a physical storefront. Today, competitors frequently need only to set up a website. This threat of increased competition is particularly acute in industries that perform an *intermediation role*, which is a link between buyers and sellers (e.g., stock brokers and travel agents), as well as in industries in which the primary product or service is digital (e.g., the music industry). The geographical reach of the Web also enables distant competitors to compete more directly with an existing firm.

---

[2]M. E. Porter, "Strategy and the Internet," *Harvard Business Review*, March 2001.

In some cases, however, the Web increases barriers to entry. This scenario occurs primarily when customers have come to expect a nontrivial capability from their suppliers. For example, the first company to offer Web-based package tracking gained a competitive advantage from that service. Competitors were forced to follow suit.

2. *The bargaining power of suppliers:* Supplier power is high when buyers have few choices from whom to buy and low when buyers have many choices. Therefore, organizations would rather have more potential suppliers so that they will be in a stronger position to negotiate price, quality, and delivery terms.

   The Internet's impact on suppliers is mixed. On the one hand, it enables buyers to find alternative suppliers and to compare prices more easily, thereby reducing the supplier's bargaining power. On the other hand, as companies use the Internet to integrate their supply chains, participating suppliers prosper by locking in customers.

3. *The bargaining power of customers (buyers):* Buyer power is high when buyers have many choices from whom to buy and low when buyers have few choices. For example, in the past, there were few locations where students could purchase textbooks (typically, one or two campus bookstores). In this situation, students had low buyer power. Today, the Web provides students with access to a multitude of potential suppliers as well as detailed information about textbooks. As a result, student buyer power has increased dramatically.

   In contrast, *loyalty programs* reduce buyer power. As their name suggests, loyalty programs reward customers based on the amount of business they conduct with a particular organization (e.g., airlines, hotels, car rental companies). Information technology enables companies to track the activities and accounts of millions of customers, thereby reducing buyer power; that is, customers who receive perks from loyalty programs are less likely to do business with competitors. (Loyalty programs are associated with customer relationship management, which you will study in Chapter 11.)

4. *The threat of substitute products or services:* If there are many alternatives to an organization's products or services, then the threat of substitutes is high. Conversely, if there are few alternatives, then the threat is low. Today, new technologies create substitute products very rapidly. For example, customers can purchase wireless telephones instead of landline telephones, Internet music services instead of traditional CDs, and ethanol instead of gasoline for their cars.

   Information-based industries experience the greatest threat from substitutes. Any industry in which digitized information can replace material goods (e.g., music, books, software) must view the Internet as a threat because the Internet can convey this information efficiently and at low cost and high quality.

   Even when there are many substitutes for their products, however, companies can create a competitive advantage by increasing switching costs. *Switching costs* are the costs, in money and time, imposed by a decision to buy elsewhere. For example, contracts with smartphone providers typically include a substantial penalty for switching to another provider until the term of the contract expires (quite often, two years). This switching cost is monetary.

   As another example, when you buy products from Amazon, the company develops a profile of your shopping habits and recommends products targeted to your preferences. If you switch to another online vendor, then that company will need time to develop a profile of your wants and needs. In this case, the switching cost involves time rather than money.

5. *The rivalry among existing firms in the industry:* The threat from rivalry is high when there is intense competition among many firms in an industry. The threat is low when the competition involves fewer firms and is not as intense.

   In the past, proprietary information systems—systems that belong exclusively to a single organization—have provided strategic advantage to firms in highly competitive industries. Today, however, the visibility of Internet applications on the Web makes proprietary systems more difficult to keep secret. In simple terms, when I see my competitor's new system online, I will rapidly match its features to remain competitive. The result is fewer differences among competitors, which leads to more intense competition in an industry.

To understand this concept, consider the highly competitive grocery industry, in which Walmart, Kroger, Safeway, and other companies compete essentially on price. Some of these companies have IT-enabled loyalty programs in which customers receive discounts and the store gains valuable business intelligence on customers' buying preferences. Stores use this business intelligence in their marketing and promotional campaigns. (You will learn about business intelligence in Chapter 12.)

Grocery stores are also experimenting with RFID to speed up the checkout process, track customers through the store, and notify customers of discounts as they pass by certain products. Grocery companies also use IT to tightly integrate their supply chains for maximum efficiency and thus reduce prices for shoppers.

Established companies can also gain a competitive advantage by allowing customers to use data from the company's products to improve their own performance. For example, Babolat (**www.babolat.com**), a manufacturer of sports equipment, has developed its Babolat Play Pure Drive system. The system has sensors embedded into the handle of its tennis rackets. A smartphone app uses the data from the sensors to monitor and evaluate ball speed, spin, and impact location to give tennis players valuable feedback.

Competition is also being affected by the extremely low variable cost of digital products; that is, once a digital product has been developed, the cost of producing additional units approaches zero. Consider the music industry as an example. When artists record music, their songs are captured in digital format. Physical products, such as CDs or DVDs of the songs for sale in music stores, involve costs. The costs of a physical distribution channel are much higher than those involved in delivering the songs digitally over the Internet.

In fact, in the future, companies might give away some products for free. For example, some analysts predict that commissions for online stock trading will approach zero because investors can search the Internet for information to make their own decisions regarding buying and selling stocks. At that point, consumers will no longer need brokers to give them information that they can obtain themselves, virtually for free.

Porter's Value Chain Model

Organizations use Porter's competitive forces model to design general strategies. To identify specific activities in which they can use competitive strategies for greatest impact, they use his value chain model. A **value chain** is a sequence of activities through which the organization's inputs, whatever they are, are transformed into more valuable outputs, whatever they are. The **value chain model** identifies points for which an organization can use information technology to achieve a competitive advantage (see **Figure 2.4**).

According to Porter's value chain model, the activities conducted in any organization can be divided into two categories: primary activities and support activities. **Primary activities** relate to the production and distribution of the firm's products and services. These activities create value for which customers are willing to pay. The primary activities are buttressed by **support activities**. Unlike primary activities, support activities do not add value directly to the firm's products or services. Rather, as their name suggests, they contribute to the firm's competitive advantage by supporting the primary activities.

Next, you will see examples of primary and support activities in the value chain of a manufacturing company. Keep in mind that other types of firms, such as transportation, health care, education, retail, and others, have different value chains. The key point is that *every* organization has a value chain.

In a manufacturing company, primary activities involve purchasing materials, processing the materials into products, and delivering the products to customers. Manufacturing companies typically perform five primary activities in the following sequence:

1. Inbound logistics (inputs)
2. Operations (manufacturing and testing)
3. Outbound logistics (storage and distribution)

4. Marketing and sales

5. Services

As work progresses in this sequence, value is added to the product in each activity. Specifically, the following steps occur:

1. The incoming materials are processed (in receiving, storage, and so on) in activities called *inbound logistics.*

2. The materials are used in operations, in which value is added by turning raw materials into products.

3. These products are prepared for delivery (packaging, storing, and shipping) in the outbound logistics activities.

4. Marketing and sales sell the products to customers, increasing product value by creating demand for the company's products.

5. Finally, the company performs after-sales service for the customer, such as warranty service or upgrade notification, adding further value.

As noted earlier, these primary activities are buttressed by support activities. Support activities consist of the following:

1. The firm's infrastructure (accounting, finance, management)

2. Human resources management

3. Product and technology development (R&D)

4. Procurement

Each support activity can be applied to any or all of the primary activities. The support activities can also support one another.

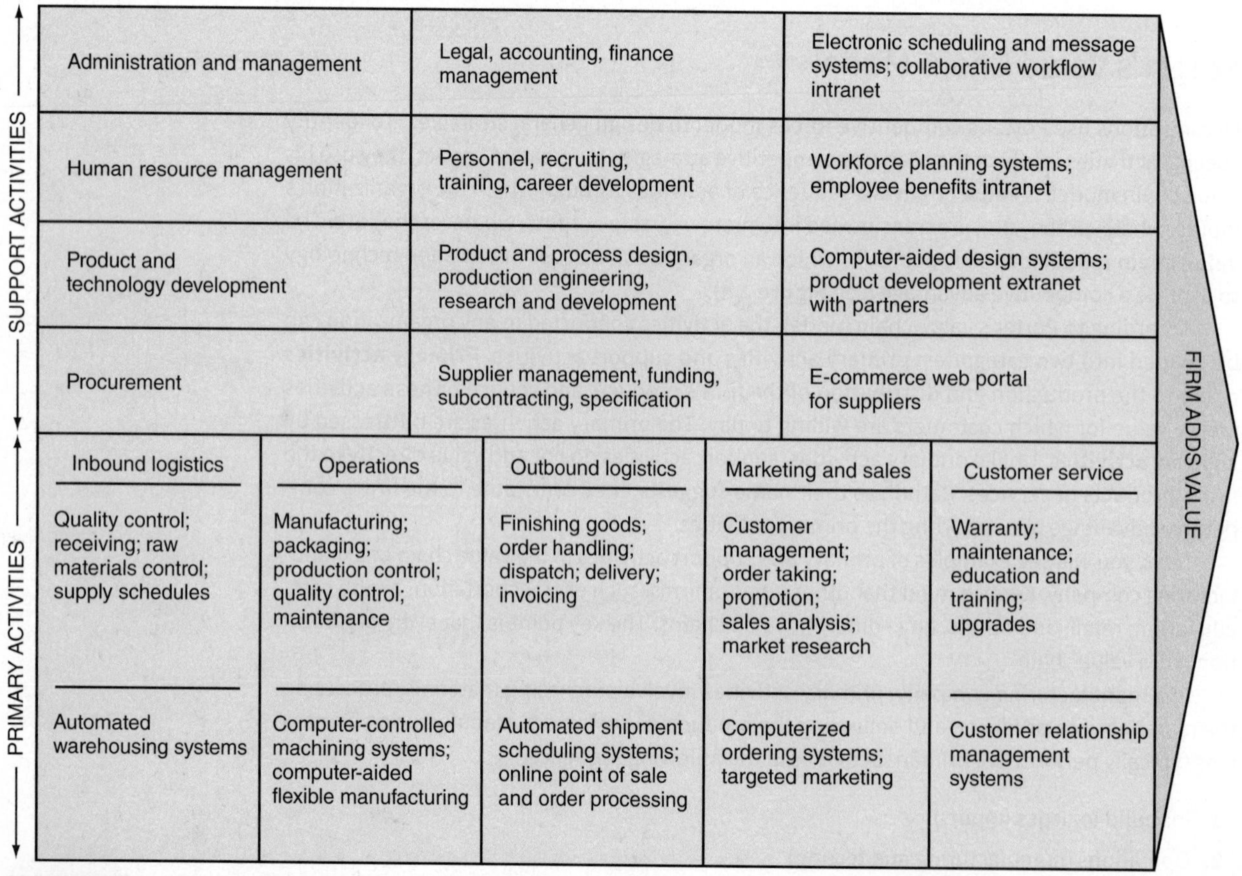

FIGURE 2.4 **Porter's value chain model.**

A firm's value chain is part of a larger stream of activities, which Porter calls a **value system**. A value system, or an *industry value chain*, includes the suppliers that provide the inputs necessary to the firm along with their value chains. After the firm creates products, these products pass through the value chains of distributors (which also have their own value chains), all the way to the customers. All parts of these chains are included in the value system. To achieve and sustain a competitive advantage and to support that advantage with information technologies, a firm must understand every component of this value system.

Strategies for Competitive Advantage

Organizations continually try to develop strategies to counter the five competitive forces identified by Porter. You will learn about five of those strategies here. Before we go into specifics, however, it is important to note that an organization's choice of strategy involves trade-offs. For example, a firm that concentrates only on cost leadership might not have the resources available for research and development, leaving the firm unable to innovate. As another example, a company that invests in customer happiness (customer orientation strategy) will experience increased costs.

Companies must select a strategy and then stay with it because a confused strategy cannot succeed. This selection, in turn, decides how a company will use its information systems. A new information system that can improve customer service but will increase costs slightly will be welcomed at a high-end retailer such as Nordstrom's but not at a discount store such as Walmart. The following list presents the most commonly used strategies. **Figure 2.5** provides an overview of these strategies:

1. *Cost leadership strategy:* Produce products and services at the lowest cost in the industry. An example is Walmart's automatic inventory replenishment system, which enables the company to reduce inventory storage requirements. As a result, Walmart stores use floor space only to sell products and not to store them, thereby reducing inventory costs.

2. *Differentiation strategy:* Offer different products, services, or product features than your competitors. Southwest Airlines, for example, has differentiated itself as a low-cost, short-haul, express airline. This has proved to be a winning strategy for competing in the highly competitive airline industry.

3. *Innovation strategy:* Introduce new products and services, add new features to existing products and services, or develop new ways to produce them. A classic example is the introduction of automated teller machines (ATMs) by Citibank. The convenience and cost-cutting features of this innovation gave Citibank a huge advantage over its competitors. Like many innovative products, the ATM changed the nature of competition in the banking industry. Today, an ATM is a competitive *necessity* for any bank. Another excellent example is Apple's rapid introduction of innovative products.

4. *Operational effectiveness strategy:* Improve the manner in which a firm executes its internal business processes so that it performs these activities more effectively than its rivals. Such improvements increase quality, productivity, and employee and customer satisfaction while decreasing time to market.

5. *Customer orientation strategy:* Concentrate on making customers happy. Web-based systems are particularly effective in this area because they can create a personalized, one-to-one relationship with each customer. Amazon (**www.amazon.com**), Apple (**www.apple.com**), and Starbucks (**www.starbucks.com**) are classic examples of companies devoted to customer satisfaction.

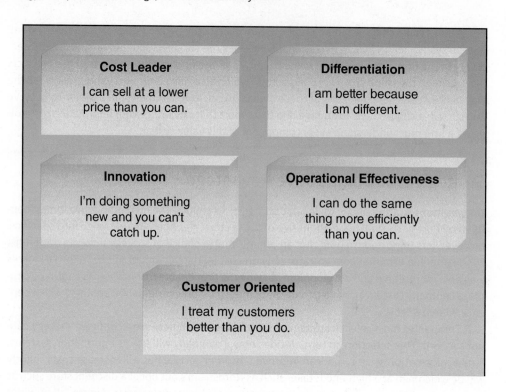

FIGURE 2.5 **Strategies for competitive advantage.**

Business–Information Technology Alignment

The best way for organizations to maximize the strategic value of IT is to achieve business–information technology alignment. In fact, the holy grail of organizations is business–information technology alignment, or strategic alignment (which we will call simply *alignment*). **Business–information technology alignment (business–IT alignment)** is the tight integration of the IT function with the organization's strategy, mission, and goals; that is, the IT function directly supports the business objectives of the organization. There are six characteristics of excellent alignment:

1. Organizations view IT as an engine of innovation that continually transforms the business, often creating new revenue streams.

2. Organizations view their internal and external customers and their customer service function as supremely important.

3. Organizations rotate business and IT professionals across departments and job functions.

4. Organizations provide overarching goals that are completely clear to each IT and business employee.

5. Organizations ensure that IT employees understand how the company makes (or loses) money.

6. Organizations create a vibrant and inclusive company culture.

Unfortunately, many organizations fail to achieve this type of close alignment. In fact, according to a McKinsey and Company survey on IT strategy and spending, approximately 27 percent of the IT and business executives who participated agreed that their organization had adequate alignment between IT and the business. Given the importance of business and IT alignment, why do so many organizations fail to implement this policy? The major reasons are the following:

- Business managers and IT managers have different objectives.
- The business and IT departments are ignorant of the other group's expertise.
- A lack of communication.

Put simply, business executives often know little about information technology, and IT executives understand the technology but may not understand the real needs of the business. One solution to this problem is to foster a collaborative environment in organizations so that business and IT executives can communicate freely and learn from each other.

Businesses can also use enterprise architecture to foster alignment. Originally developed as a tool to organize a company's IT initiatives, the enterprise architecture concept has evolved to encompass both a technical specification (the information and communication technologies and the information systems used in an organization) and a business specification (a collection of core business processes and management activities).

Before you go on . . .

1. What are strategic information systems?
2. According to Porter, what are the five forces that could endanger a firm's position in its industry or marketplaces?
3. Describe Porter's value chain model. Differentiate between Porter's competitive forces model and his value chain model.
4. What strategies can companies use to gain competitive advantage?
5. What is business–IT alignment?
6. Give examples of business–IT alignment at your university, regarding student systems. (*Hint:* What are the "business" goals of your university with regard to student registration, fee payment, grade posting, and so on?)

What's in **IT** for me?

For All Business Majors

All functional areas of any organization are literally composed of a variety of business processes, as we can see from the examples in this chapter. Regardless of your major, you will be involved in a variety of business processes from your first day on the job. Some of these processes you will do by yourself; some will involve only your group, team, or department; and others will involve several (or all) functional areas of your organization.

It is important for you to be able to visualize processes, understand the inputs and outputs of each process, and know the "customer" of each process. If you can do these things, you will contribute to making processes more efficient and effective, which often means incorporating information technology in the process. It is also important for you to know how each process fits into your organization's strategy.

In addition, all functional areas in any organization must work together in an integrated fashion for the firm to respond adequately to business pressures. These responses typically require each functional area to use a variety of information systems to support, document, and manage cross-functional business processes. In today's competitive global marketplace, the timeliness and accuracy of these responses are even more critical.

Closely following this discussion, all functional areas must work together for the organization to gain a competitive advantage in its marketplace. Again, the functional areas use a variety of strategic information systems to achieve this goal.

You have seen why companies must be concerned with strategic advantage. But why is this chapter so important for you? There are several reasons. First, the business pressures you have learned about have an impact on your organization, but they also affect you as an individual. So, it is critical that you understand how information systems can help you—and eventually your organization—respond to these pressures.

Achieving a competitive advantage is also essential for your organization's survival. In many cases, you, your team, and all of your colleagues will be responsible for creating a competitive advantage. Therefore, having general knowledge about strategy and about how information systems affect the organization's strategy and competitive position will help you in your career.

You also need a basic knowledge of your organization's strategy, mission, and goals as well as its business problems and how it makes (or loses) money. You now know how to analyze your organization's strategy and value chain as well as the strategies and value chains of your competitors. You also have acquired a general knowledge of how information technology contributes to organizational strategy. This knowledge will help you to do your job better, to be promoted more quickly, and to contribute significantly to the success of your organization.

Summary

2.1 Discuss ways in which information systems enable cross-functional business processes and processes for a single functional area.

A business process is an ongoing collection of related activities that produce a product or a service of value to the organization, its business partners, and its customers. Examples of business processes in the functional areas are managing accounts payable, managing accounts receivable, managing after-sale customer follow-up, managing bills of materials, managing manufacturing change orders, applying disability policies, employee hiring, computer user and staff training, and applying Internet use policy. The procurement and fulfillment processes are examples of cross-functional business processes.

2.2 Compare and contrast business process reengineering and business process management to determine the different advantages and disadvantages of each.

Business process reengineering (BPR) is a radical redesign of business processes that is intended to improve the efficiency and effectiveness of an organization's business processes. The key to BPR is for enterprises to examine their business processes from a "clean-sheet" perspective and then determine how they can best reconstruct those processes to improve their business functions. Because BPR proved difficult to implement, organizations have turned to business process management. Business process management (BPM) is a management technique that includes methods and tools to support the design, analysis, implementation, management, and optimization of business processes.

2.3 Identify effective IT responses to different kinds of business pressures.

- *Market pressures:* An example of a market pressure is powerful customers. Customer relationship management is an effective IT response that helps companies achieve customer intimacy.

- *Technology pressures:* An example of a technology pressure is information overload. Search engines and business intelligence applications enable managers to access, navigate, and use vast amounts of information.

- *Societal/political/legal pressures:* An example of a societal/political/legal pressure is social responsibility, such as the state of the physical environment. Green IT is one response that is intended to improve the environment.

2.4 Describe the strategies that organizations typically adopt to counter Porter's five competitive forces.

Porter's five competitive forces:

- *The threat of entry of new competitors:* For most firms, the Web increases the threat that new competitors will enter the market by reducing traditional barriers to entry. Frequently, competitors need only to set up a website to enter a market. The Web can also increase barriers to entry, as when customers come to expect a nontrivial capability from their suppliers.

- *The bargaining power of suppliers:* The Web enables buyers to find alternative suppliers and to compare prices more easily, thereby reducing suppliers' bargaining power. From a different perspective, as companies use the Web to integrate their supply chains, participating suppliers can lock in customers, thereby increasing suppliers' bargaining power.

- *The bargaining power of customers (buyers):* The Web provides customers with incredible amounts of choices for products as well as information about those choices. As a result, the Web increases buyer power. However, companies can implement loyalty programs in which they use the Web to monitor the activities of millions of customers. Such programs reduce buyer power.

- *The threat of substitute products or services:* New technologies create substitute products very rapidly, and the Web makes information about these products available almost instantly. As a result, industries (particularly information-based industries) are in great danger from substitutes (e.g., music, books, newspapers, magazines, software). However, the Web also can enable a company to build in switching costs so that it will cost customers time or money to switch from your company to that of a competitor.

- *The rivalry among existing firms in the industry:* In the past, proprietary information systems provided a strategic advantage for firms in highly competitive industries. The visibility of Internet applications on the Web makes proprietary systems more difficult to keep secret. Therefore, the Web makes strategic advantage more short lived.

The five strategies are as follows:

- *Cost leadership strategy:* Produce products and services at the lowest cost in the industry.

- *Differentiation strategy:* Offer different products, services, or product features.

- *Innovation strategy:* Introduce new products and services, put new features in existing products and services, or develop new ways to produce them.

- *Operational effectiveness strategy:* Improve the manner in which internal business processes are executed so that a firm performs similar activities better than its rivals.

- *Customer orientation strategy:* Concentrate on making customers happy.

Chapter Glossary

business environment The combination of social, legal, economic, physical, and political factors in which businesses conduct their operations.

business–information technology alignment The tight integration of the IT function with the strategy, mission, and goals of the organization.

business process A collection of related activities that create a product or a service of value to the organization, its business partners, and its customers.

business process management (BPM) A management technique that includes methods and tools to support the design, analysis, implementation, management, and optimization of business processes.

business process reengineering (BPR) A radical redesign of a business process that improves its efficiency and effectiveness, often by beginning with a "clean sheet" (i.e., from scratch).

competitive advantage An advantage over competitors in some measure such as cost, quality, or speed; leads to control of a market and to larger-than-average profits.

competitive forces model A business framework devised by Michael Porter that analyzes competitiveness by recognizing five major forces that could endanger a company's position.

cross-functional processes No single functional area is responsible for a process's execution.

digital divide The gap between those who have access to information and communications technology and those who do not.

entry barrier Product or service feature that customers expect from organizations in a certain industry; an organization trying to enter this market must provide this product or service at a minimum to be able to compete.

globalization The integration and interdependence of economic, social, cultural, and ecological facets of life, enabled by rapid advances in information technology.

individual social responsibility See **organizational social responsibility**.

make-to-order The strategy of producing customized products and services.

mass customization A production process in which items are produced in large quantities but are customized to fit the desires of each customer.

organizational social responsibility (also individual social responsibility) Efforts by organizations to solve various social problems.

primary activities Those business activities related to the production and distribution of the firm's products and services, thus creating value.

strategic information systems (SISs) Systems that help an organization gain a competitive advantage by supporting its strategic goals and increasing performance and productivity.

support activities Business activities that do not add value directly to a firm's product or service under consideration but support the primary activities that do add value.

value chain A sequence of activities through which the organization's inputs, whatever they are, are transformed into more valuable outputs, whatever they are.

value chain model Model that shows the primary activities that sequentially add value to the profit margin; also shows the support activities.

value system A stream of activities that includes the producers, suppliers, distributors, and buyers, all of whom have their own value chains.

Discussion Questions

1. Consider the student registration process at your university:

   - Describe the steps necessary for you to register for your classes each semester.

   - Describe how information technology is used (or is not used) in each step of the process.

2. Why is it so difficult for an organization to actually implement business process reengineering?

3. Explain why IT is both a business pressure and an enabler of response activities that counter business pressures.

4. What does globalization mean to you in your choice of a major? In your choice of a career? Will you have to be a "lifelong learner"? Why or why not?

5. What might the impact of globalization be on your standard of living?

6. Is IT a strategic weapon or a survival tool? Discuss.

7. Why might it be difficult to justify a strategic information system?

8. Describe the five forces in Porter's competitive forces model and explain how increased access to high-speed Internet has affected each one.

9. Describe Porter's value chain model. What is the relationship between the competitive forces model and the value chain model?

10. Describe how IT can be used to support different value chains for different companies.

11. Discuss the idea that an information system by itself can rarely provide a sustainable competitive advantage.

Problem-Solving Activities

1. Surf the Internet for information about the Department of Homeland Security. Examine the available information and comment on the role of information technologies in the department.

2. Experience mass customization by designing your own shoes at **www.nike.com**, your car at **www.jaguar.com**, your CD at **www.easternrecording.com**, your business card at **www.iprint.com**, and your diamond ring at **www.bluenile.com**. Summarize your experiences.

3. Access **www.go4customer.com**. What does this company do, and where is it located? Who are its customers? Provide examples of how a U.S. company would use its services.

4. Enter Walmart China (**www.wal-martchina.com/english/index .htm**). How does Walmart China differ from your local Walmart (consider products, prices, services, and so on)? Describe these differences.

5. Apply Porter's value chain model to Costco (**www.costco.com**). What is Costco's competitive strategy? Who are Costco's major competitors? Describe Costco's business model. Describe the tasks that Costco must accomplish for each primary value chain activity. How would Costco's information systems contribute to Costco's competitive strategy, given the nature of its business?

6. Apply Porter's value chain model to Dell (**www.dell.com**). What is Dell's competitive strategy? Who are Dell's major competitors? Describe Dell's business model. Describe the tasks that Dell must accomplish for each primary value chain activity. How would Dell's information systems contribute to Dell's competitive strategy given the nature of its business?

Closing Case

Domino's Pizza

MIS **MKT** **POM**

The Problem

Domino's Pizza (**www.dominos.com**), with approximately 14,000 stores and 260,000 employees in 85 countries, is the largest U.S. pizza chain in the world, measured by global retail sales. Domino's 30-minutes-or-free guarantee set the fast-food industry's customer expectations for convenience, speed, and efficiency. Domino's business model consists of three segments: ordering, producing, and delivering.

At the end of 2008, Domino's was experiencing decreasing sales and troubled franchises. The company recognized it had a serious problem. In short, its pizza was not very good. It was still cheap, but the recipes and ingredients had not kept up with the foodie movement. (Customers are *foodies* when they have great interest in their food, where it came from, and how it was raised, processed, and transported.) In addition, Domino's had abandoned its key marketing slogan—its 30-minute guarantee—after several accidents involving its drivers—one of them fatal—which generated two lawsuits that cost the company millions of dollars.

Making matters worse, in the spring of 2009, a video appeared on YouTube of two Domino's employees. One filmed the other putting cheese up his nose and then adding that cheese to a sandwich. The video went viral, and the local health department temporarily shut down the restaurant. Domino's had the two employees arrested for tampering with food. (The orders never left the store, and both workers received probation.) The president of Domino's U.S. operations, J. Patrick Doyle, recorded a two-minute apology that, unfortunately, did not go viral.

A Variety of Solutions

POM **The Production Process.** Domino's instituted a variety of efforts to turn the company around. First, the chain overhauled its pizza recipe. Company chefs enhanced the quality of the mozzarella and the flour, added garlic butter to the crust, and added flavor and sweetness to the marinara sauce. After 18 months, Domino's had a new and improved (and expensive-to-make) pizza. In addition, Domino's revamped about 85 percent of its menu.

MKT Domino's then began a new marketing campaign, with Doyle again creating videos for television ads. The ads acknowledged the chain's problems, were funny, and poked fun at the company as well. Morning talk show hosts began discussing the campaign, and local television anchors started to conduct taste tests.

As part of a new ad campaign, Domino's solicited photos from its customers and received almost 40,000 of them. One photo in particular showed a badly mangled pizza delivered to a customer, which the ad agency featured in its next ad.

The company's efforts were very successful. By February 2010, Domino's was selling so much pizza that it was three days away from running out of pepperoni. The company's successful initiatives caused problems with the ordering process. Most orders still came in by phone, so when workers were overrun with orders, they could not answer the phone. Consequently, Domino's focused on improving its ordering process with digital technologies.

POM **The Order Process.** Since 2012, Domino's Pizza has emphasized all the ways that its customers can digitally order food. The company began to introduce many new ordering methods: Facebook Messenger, Twitter, Twitter with emojis, Apple Watch, and a voice-activated, "zero-click" wedding registry. Customers can track their orders online, and they can also track their drivers. In Australia, Domino's can track customers on the way to the store so that their order will be ready just as they arrive to pick it up.

In June 2014, Domino's released its voice-ordering chatbot system, called Dom. However, when a CNBC reporter tested the system on air on the floor of the New York Stock Exchange, Dom did not work because of the surrounding noise.

Domino's wants customers to be able to place their order via any device as normally as they would if they were ordering from a person.

For example, they can order pizza with Alexa (from Amazon) and Google Home, both of which are voice-controlled intelligent speakers.

MIS **POM** **The Delivery Process.**   The next segment of Domino's business model is delivery. More than half of Domino's employees are drivers. The chain is examining a number of initiatives to improve its delivery process.

For example, a Domino's franchisee in Australia who owns 2,000 stores around the world is using drones to deliver pizza from a store in the New Zealand town of Whangaparaoa. The drones can travel about a mile from the store, and the customers must have a backyard so that the drone can land safely.

Domino's is also testing robots for delivery throughout Europe and New Zealand. Reports have noted that the robots have difficulties navigating uneven sidewalks and are not allowed on roads. In 2017, Domino's partnered with Starship Technologies (**www.starship.xyz**) to use Starship's delivery robots in Hamburg, Germany. A second test was performed in the Netherlands in 2018. Although not yet widespread, robotic pizza delivery is coming to Europe.

Domino's has not yet offered robot pizza delivery in the United States although Virginia and Idaho have allowed robotic delivery since 2018. Other U.S. states and federal regulations have not been determined.

Although not a digital effort to improve its delivery process, Domino's ordered a fleet of vehicles specifically designed to deliver pizzas. The cars, called Delivery Experts (the DXPs), were 154 Chevrolet Spark subcompacts with special side doors and warming ovens.

In mid-2017, Domino's decided not to expand its DXP fleet of cars, primarily because the company knew that autonomous vehicles are coming. Domino's executives recognized that if a competitor used autonomous vehicles, then it would be able to provide quick, reliable delivery without having to manage a staff of drivers and coordinate routes. In doing so, the competitor would gain a huge competitive advantage over Domino's.

Despite Domino's digital efforts, many customers do not use technology (other than their phones) to order pizza, and most pizza is still delivered by humans. Domino's is also in the process of upgrading their stores because approximately 35 to 40 percent of its sales come from customers visiting a store for takeout or to eat in the store. As a result, the chain is improving all of its stores so that customers can see their pizzas being made and then eat in a clear, bright seating area if they choose to.

The Results

Domino's does face competitive challenges. On-demand delivery services pose a threat to the chain. UberEATS (**www.ubereats.com**) and GrubHub (**www.grubhub.com**) pose serious challenges. Delivery of a variety of good, healthy foods straight from these companies will target lower- and middle-income customers, a key demographic for Domino's. Adding to the competition, Panera Bread announced plans

in 2017 that allowed them to create 10,000 new delivery and retail jobs within the year. This aggressive plan enabled them to deploy delivery service in roughly 40 percent of their stores.

Domino's finances have been improving for more than 10 years. From 2008 to 2018, the company's share price increased by 6,000 percent. At that time the company's global retail sales totaled approximately $12 billion.

By mid-2018, more than 60 percent of Domino's orders were executed on digital platforms. Of these orders, nearly 70 percent were from mobile devices.

The chain continued to enjoy good news from its efforts. According to consultant Brand Keys, Domino's had the highest loyalty among pizza chains. Furthermore, same-store sales grew almost 7 percent in the second quarter of 2018 compared to the second quarter of 2017.

In July 2018, there were about 5,650 Domino's locations in the United States. At that time, the company announced that it planned to open an additional 2,350 locations in the United States over the next 10 years. In anticipation of this expansion, Domino's planned to invest approximately $120 million in its supply chain.

Sources: Compiled from D. Wiener-Bronner, "Domino's Wants to Open Thousands of Stores," *CNN Money*, July 19, 2018; S. Whitten, "Domino's Stock Slips on Revenue Miss, Weak Same-Store Sales Growth," *CNBC*, July 19, 2018; N. Meyersohn, "Why Domino's Is Winning the Pizza Wars," *CNN Money*, March 6, 2018; J. Peltz, "Domino's Pizza Stock Is Up 5,000% since 2008. Here's Why," *Los Angeles Times*, May 15, 2017; C. Forrest, "Panera Bread Increases Automation, Leads to Hiring 10,000 Workers," *TechRepublic*, April 26, 2017; L. Kolodny, "Domino's and Starship Technologies Will Deliver Pizza by Robot in Europe This Summer," *TechCrunch*, March 29, 2017; S. Berfield, "Delivering a $9 Billion Pizza," *Bloomberg BusinessWeek*, March 20–26, 2017; J. Dunn, "Some of the Biggest Tech Stocks in the World Have Been Outpaced by… Domino's Pizza," *Business Insider*, March 24, 2017; T. Lien, "How Food Delivery Apps Have Changed the Game for Restaurants," *Los Angeles Times*, March 17, 2017; M. Fox, "After Betting Big on Digital, Domino's Pizza Is Now Eyeing Voice Technology," *CNBC*, March 16, 2017; B. Hill, "Domino's New Digital Strategy," *The Trading God*, March 8, 2017; B. Taylor, "How Domino's Pizza Reinvented Itself," *Harvard Business Review*, November 28, 2016; L. Feldman, "How Domino's Pizza Reinvented Itself as a Tech Company," *Forbes*, November 28, 2016; J. Maze, "How Domino's Became a Tech Company," *Nation's Restaurant News*, March 28, 2016; and www.dominos.com and www.starship.xyz, both accessed July 20, 2018.

Questions

1. Describe how information technology has impacted Domino's production process.

2. Describe how information technology has impacted Domino's order process.

3. Describe how information technology has impacted Domino's delivery process.

4. Which Domino's process has been impacted the most by information technology?

CHAPTER 3

Ethics and Privacy

CHAPTER OUTLINE	LEARNING OBJECTIVES
3.1 Ethical Issues	**3.1** Define ethics and explain its three fundamental tenets and the four categories of ethical issues related to information technology.
3.2 Privacy	**3.2** Discuss at least one potential threat to the privacy of the data stored in each of three places that store personal data.

Opening Case

Boston Red Sox Use Apple Watches to Steal Signs

MIS

Stealing signs has been a part of baseball since the game began. Let's look back to the 1951 New York Giants and their controversial manager, Leo Durocher. In January 2001, the *Wall Street Journal* reported that former Giants players described a scheme that allowed the team to steal signs for the last 10 weeks of the 1951 season. A Giant, often coach Herman Franks, hid in the center field clubhouse with a telescope. As a former catcher, Franks was an expert at signs. A Giant player sat on the far end of the bullpen bench in deep right-center field listening for a bell or a buzzer to ring, identifying the next pitch.

For a fastball, the signal relay man sat and did nothing. For a breaking pitch, he would make some gesture that was easily visible to the batter—for example, toss a ball into the air, stand up, or raise his arms. The batter then knew what the next pitch would be.

The question remains: Could the Giants, who trailed the rival Brooklyn Dodgers by 13½ games in mid-August, have come from behind and won the pennant without cheating? Interestingly, their comeback coincided with a team meeting on July 20 at which Durocher asked his players whether they wanted to be given the pitches. About half of them did. Soon, the Giants climbed back into the pennant race by winning 16 games in a row—13 of them at home.

Stealing signs works particularly well when there is a runner on second base. The runner can watch which hand signals the catcher is using to communicate with the pitcher and then relay information to the batter about the type of pitch that is coming. Major League Baseball (MLB; **www.mlb.com**) allows such tactics as long as teams do not use any methods beyond their eyes. Binoculars, telescopes, and electronic devices are all prohibited.

In September 2017, MLB investigators discovered that the Boston Red Sox had stolen hand signals from opponents' catchers in games against several teams, particularly their archrivals, the New York Yankees. MLB's inquiry had begun the previous month after the Yankee's general manager, Brian Cashman, filed a complaint with the commissioner's office that included video that the Yankees shot of the Red Sox dugout during a three-game series between the two teams in Boston. The Yankees contended that the video showed the Red Sox assistant athletic trainer, Jon Jochim, looking at his Apple Watch and then passing information to Red Sox players in the dugout. In turn, these players signaled their teammates on the field about the type of pitch that was to be thrown. MLB investigators corroborated the Yankees' claims based on videos that the commissioner's office uses for instant replay and broadcasts. The commissioner's office then contacted the Red Sox, who admitted that they were able to significantly speed up the sign-stealing process by using Apple Watches.

In the first game of the August series in question, the Red Sox gained an advantage the first time a Red Sox runner reached second base. The batter at the time, Rafael Devers, hit a home run. In fact, during that game, the Red Sox had five hits in eight at bats when they had a man on second base. They were significantly less successful in those situations in the other two games—specifically, one for six in the second game and three for 10 in the third game.

On September 15, MLB Commissioner Robert Manfred announced that he had investigated the complaint from the Yankees and would fine the Red Sox an undisclosed amount. Manfred further stated that the fine would be donated to hurricane relief efforts in Florida. He cautioned, however, that future violations from any MLB team would have more serious consequences.

Interestingly, in recent years, teams have not needed a runner on second base to steal signs. As cameras have proliferated in MLB ballparks, teams have begun using videos to help them steal opponents' signs. Some clubs have had clubhouse attendants quickly relay information to the dugout from the person monitoring the video feeds. The attendants have to run to the dugout with the information so that it can be relayed quickly enough to help the batter.

In response, MLB is taking steps to stop sign stealing in the digital age. Teams may not position cameras between the foul poles in the outfield if not for broadcast purposes. Team replay assistants, who help notify managers when to challenge a call on the field, will have access only to the live game broadcast and will be monitored by a security expert. All other TV monitors available to players and coaches will show the live game broadcast on an eight-second delay.

Sources: Compiled from J. Bogage, "MLB Aims to Crack Down on the Game's Tradition of Sign Stealing," *Washington Post*, February 20, 2019; A. Balakrishnan, "MLB Fines Red Sox and Yankees for Improper Use of Technology in Games," *CNBC*, September 16, 2017; I. Crouch, "What to Make of the Red Sox's Apple Watch Scandal," *The New Yorker*, September 15, 2017;

D. Rapaport, "Report: Red Sox Fined for Using Apple Watches to Steal Yankees' Signs, Money to Be Sent to Hurricane Relief," *Sports Illustrated*, September 15, 2017; S. Lauber, "Red Sox, Yankees Fined Separately as Part of MLB Investigation into Sign-Stealing," *ESPN*, September 15, 2017; M. Mazzeo, "Red Sox Caught Using an Apple Watch to Steal Signs from Yankees," *New York Daily News*, September 5, 2017; M. Schmidt, "Boston Red Sox Used Apple Watches to Steal Signs against Yankees," *New York Times*, September 5, 2017; J. Reuter, "Memorable Sign-Stealing Moments in Major League Baseball History," *Bleacher Report*, April 12, 2012; D. Miller, "Fair or Foul? Sign-Stealing Is Part of the Game," *MLB.com*, May 28, 2010; T. Boswell, "Giants Stole the Pennant! Giants Stole the Pennant!" *Washington Post*, February 4, 2001; J. Prager, "Was the '51 Giants Comeback a Miracle, or Did They Simply Steal the Pennant?" *Wall Street Journal*, January 31, 2001; and www.mlb.com, accessed June 26, 2019.

Questions

1. Discuss the ethicality and legality of the Red Sox's actions in stealing signs.
2. The fundamental tenets of ethics include responsibility, accountability, and liability. Discuss each of these tenets as it applies to the Red Sox stealing signs.

Introduction

You will encounter numerous ethical and privacy issues in your career, many of which will involve IT in some manner. The two issues are closely related to each other and also to IT, and both raise significant questions involving access to information in the digital age. The answers to these questions are not straightforward. In fact, IT has made finding answers to these questions even more difficult.

Consider the actions of the Boston Red Sox in the chapter-opening case. Clearly, the actions of the baseball team were not ethical. In addition, the team took advantage of a relatively new technology to make their actions even easier. In a further example, suppose your organization decides to adopt social computing technologies (which you will study in Chapter 9) to include business partners and customers in new product development. You will be able to analyze the potential privacy and ethical implications of implementing these technologies.

This chapter provides insights into how to respond to ethical and privacy issues. Furthermore, it will help you to make immediate contributions to your company's code of ethics and its privacy policies. You will also be able to provide meaningful input concerning the potential ethical and privacy impacts of your organization's information systems on people within and outside the organization.

All organizations, large and small, must be concerned with ethics. In particular, small-business (or start-up) owners face a very difficult situation when their employees have access to sensitive customer information. There is a delicate balance between access to information and the appropriate use of that information. This balance is best maintained by hiring honest and trustworthy employees who abide by the organization's code of ethics. Ultimately, this issue leads to another question: Does the small business, or a start-up, even have a code of ethics to fall back on in this type of situation?

**Author Lecture Videos are available exclusively in *WileyPLUS*.
Apply the Concept activities are available in the Appendix and in *WileyPLUS*.**

3.1 | Ethical Issues

Ethics refers to the principles of right and wrong that individuals use to make choices that guide their behavior. Deciding what is right or wrong is not always easy or clear-cut. Fortunately, there are many frameworks that can help us make ethical decisions.

Ethical Frameworks

There are many sources for ethical standards. Here, we consider five widely used standards: the utilitarian approach, the rights approach, the fairness approach, the common good approach, and the deontology approach. There are many other sources, but these five are representative.

The *utilitarian approach* states that an ethical action is the one that provides the most good or does the least harm. The ethical corporate action would be the one that produces the greatest good and does the least harm for all affected parties—customers, employees, shareholders, the community, and the physical environment.

The *rights approach* maintains that an ethical action is the one that best protects and respects the moral rights of the affected parties. Moral rights can include the rights to make one's own choices about what kind of life to lead, to be told the truth, not to be injured, and to enjoy a degree of privacy. Which of these rights people are actually entitled to—and under what circumstances—is widely debated. Nevertheless, most people acknowledge that individuals are entitled to some moral rights. An ethical organizational action would be one that protects and respects the moral rights of customers, employees, shareholders, business partners, and even competitors.

The *fairness approach* posits that ethical actions treat all human beings equally, or, if unequally, then fairly, based on some defensible standard. For example, most people might believe it is fair to pay people higher salaries if they work harder or if they contribute a greater amount to the firm. However, there is less certainty regarding chief executive officer (CEO) salaries that are hundreds or thousands of times larger than those of other employees. Many people question whether this huge disparity is based on a defensible standard or whether it is the result of an imbalance of power and hence is unfair.

The *common good approach* highlights the interlocking relationships that underlie all societies. This approach argues that respect and compassion for all others are the basis for ethical actions. It emphasizes the common conditions that are important to the welfare of everyone. These conditions can include a system of laws, effective police and fire departments, health care, a public educational system, and even public recreation areas.

Finally, the *deontology approach* states that the morality of an action is based on whether that action itself is right or wrong under a series of rules rather than based on the consequences of that action. An example of deontology is the belief that killing someone is wrong, even if it was in self-defense.

If we combine these five standards, we can develop a general framework for ethics (or ethical decision making). This framework consists of five steps:

1. Recognize an ethical issue:

   Could this decision or situation damage someone or some group?

   Does this decision involve a choice between a good and a bad alternative?

   Does this issue involve more than simply legal considerations? If so, then in what way?

2. Get the facts:

   What are the relevant facts of the situation?

   Do I have sufficient information to make a decision?

   Which individuals or groups have an important stake in the outcome?

   Have I consulted all relevant persons and groups?

3. Evaluate alternative actions:

   Which option will produce the most good and do the least harm? (the utilitarian approach)

   Which option best respects the rights of all stakeholders? (the rights approach)

   Which option treats people equally or proportionately? (the fairness approach)

   Which option best serves the community as a whole and not just some members? (the common good approach)

4. Make a decision and test it:

   Considering all the approaches, which option best addresses the situation?

5. Act and reflect on the outcome of your decision:

   How can I implement my decision with the greatest care and attention to the concerns of all stakeholders?

   How did my decision turn out, and what did I learn from this specific situation?

   Now that we have created a general ethical framework, we will focus specifically on ethics in the corporate environment.

Ethics in the Corporate Environment

Many companies and professional organizations develop their own codes of ethics. A **code of ethics** is a collection of principles intended to guide decision making by members of the organization. For example, the Association for Computing Machinery (**www.acm.org**), an organization of computing professionals, has a thoughtful code of ethics for its members (see **www.acm.org/code-of-ethics**).

Keep in mind that different codes of ethics are not always consistent with one another. Therefore, an individual might be expected to conform to multiple codes. For example, a person who is a member of two large professional computing-related organizations may be simultaneously required by one organization to comply with all applicable laws and by the other organization to refuse to obey unjust laws.

Fundamental tenets of ethics include the following:

- **Responsibility** means that you accept the consequences of your decisions and actions.
- **Accountability** refers to determining who is responsible for actions that were taken.
- **Liability** is a legal concept that gives individuals the right to recover the damages done to them by other individuals, organizations, or systems.

Before you go any further, it is critical that you realize that what is *unethical* is not necessarily *illegal*. For example, a bank's decision to foreclose on a home can be technically legal, but it can raise many ethical questions. In many instances, then, an individual or organization faced with an ethical decision is not considering whether to break the law. As the foreclosure example illustrates, however, ethical decisions can have serious consequences for individuals, organizations, and society at large.

FIN **ACCT** We have witnessed a large number of extremely poor ethical decisions, not to mention outright criminal behavior, at many organizations. During 2001 and 2002, three highly publicized fiascos occurred at Enron, WorldCom, and Tyco. At each company, executives were convicted of various types of fraud for using illegal accounting practices. These actions led to the passage of the Sarbanes–Oxley Act in 2002. Sarbanes–Oxley requires publicly held companies to implement financial controls and company executives to personally certify financial reports.

Then, the subprime mortgage crisis exposed unethical lending practices throughout the mortgage industry. The crisis also highlighted pervasive weaknesses in the regulation of the U.S. financial industry as well as the global financial system. It ultimately contributed to a deep recession in the global economy. Along these same lines, financier Bernie Madoff was convicted in 2009 of operating a Ponzi scheme and sentenced to 150 years in federal prison. Several of Madoff's employees were also convicted in 2014.

Unfortunately, ethical misbehavior continues. Consider Wells Fargo bank (**www.wellsfargo.com**). In 2016, authorities found that bank employees had created approximately 2 million fake customer checking and credit card accounts. Bank employees had created the accounts under pressure from supervisors to meet daily account quotas. The bank then charged customers at least $1.5 million in fees for the fake accounts. Not only were the bank's victims charged overdraft and maintenance fees, but their credit scores were lowered for not staying current on accounts that they did not even know about.

Wells Fargo fired some 5,300 employees. The bank was also ordered to pay $185 million in fines, which is a very small amount compared with the $5.6 billion that the bank earned in the second quarter of 2016. Furthermore, in October 2016, Wells Fargo CEO John Stumpf stepped down from his position.

In June, 2018 Wells Fargo was again accused of misconduct by the Securities and Exchange Commission (**www.sec.gov,** SEC). The SEC said that bank collected large fees by "improperly encouraging" brokerage clients to actively trade high-fee debt products that were intended to be held to maturity. The bank agreed to pay a $4 million penalty and to return to clients $930,377 of fees it gained from the transactions plus $178,064 of interest.

Advancements in information technologies have generated a new set of ethical problems. Computing processing power doubles roughly every 18 months, meaning that organizations are more dependent than ever on their information systems. Organizations can store increasing amounts of data at decreasing costs. As a result, they can maintain more data on individuals for longer periods of time. Going further, computer networks, particularly the Internet, enable organizations to collect, integrate, and distribute enormous amounts of information on individuals, groups, and institutions. These developments have created numerous ethical problems concerning the appropriate collection and use of customer information, personal privacy, and the protection of intellectual property. IT's About Business 3.1 illustrates Google is analyzing credit and debit card data to link its users' searches with their offline (physical) purchases.

IT's About Business 3.1

Google Links Online Search Data and Offline Purchase Data

`MIS` `MKT` `FIN`

Data from the U.S. Census Bureau revealed that in the first quarter of 2019, 90 percent of retail purchases took place offline (physically at brick-and-mortar stores), and the remaining 10 percent took place online through retail e-commerce. These figures indicated that the vast majority of retail sales are difficult to link to online advertising. These findings presented a problem for Google (and Facebook), which had to convince advertisers that online ads are effective. Google also had to respond to Facebook's partnership with Square and Marketo, which enabled Facebook to track consumer store visits and some transactions. This partnership was a reaction to Google's store visit metrics, which had been part of the firm's AdWords product since 2014.

Google understands that to attract digital advertising dollars from advertisers who are still spending primarily on television ads, the company must prove that digital ads work. Google must therefore identify customers by analyzing their search histories, the ads they clicked on, and, ultimately, the items they purchased at brick-and-mortar stores. (It is important to note that Google is not the only company that performs these analyses. Facebook, for example, also performs these analyses.)

For years, Google has analyzed location data from Google Maps in an effort to prove that knowledge of people's physical locations can link the physical and digital worlds. This location-tracking ability has enabled Google to inform retailers whether people who viewed an ad for a lawn mower later visited or passed by a Home Depot store. Users can block their location data by adjusting the settings on their smartphones, but privacy experts contend that few users actually do so.

In addition to location data from Google Maps, Google has analyzed users' Web browsing and search histories, using data from Google apps such as YouTube, Gmail, and the Google Play store. All of these data items are linked to the real identities of users when they log into Google's services.

Princeton University researchers used software called Open-WPM to survey the Internet's 1 million most popular websites to find evidence of tracking code on each website. OpenWPM automatically visits websites using the Firefox browser, and it logs any tracking code that it finds. The researchers found Google code on a majority of these sites. For example, they found Google Analytics, a product used to collect data on visitors to websites that integrates with Google's ad-targeting systems, on almost 70 percent of the websites. They also found DoubleClick, a dedicated ad-serving system from Google, on almost 50 percent of the websites. Perhaps the key finding was that the five most common tracking tools are all owned by Google.

Online publishers use tracking code from Google, Facebook, and many other companies to help target their advertising. When a company's tracking code is embedded on multiple websites, the company can construct detailed profiles on individuals as they browse the Web, and it assigns them unique identifiers so they can be recognized. Privacy advocates argue that this practice needs to be scrutinized more carefully.

Compounding this issue, new credit card data enable Google to integrate these data sources to real-world purchase records. Google now uses billions of credit card transaction records to prove that its online ads prompt people to make purchases, even when the transactions occur offline in physical stores. This process gives Google a clearer method to analyze purchases than simply using location data. Furthermore, Google can now analyze purchase activity even when consumers deactivate location tracking on their smartphones.

Today, Google can determine the number of purchases generated by digital ad campaigns, a goal that marketing experts describe as the "holy grail" of online advertising. For example, Google can inform a company such as Sephora how many shoppers viewed an ad for eyeliner and then later visited a Sephora store and made a purchase. Advertisers can access this information with a new product called Google Attribution. They can identify which clicks and key words had the largest impact on a consumer's purchasing decision.

Not surprisingly, Google's enhanced analytic tools have led to complaints about how the company uses personal information. Privacy advocates note that few people understand that their purchases are analyzed in this way. Google responds that it has taken steps to protect the personal information of its users. In fact, the company claims to have developed a new, custom encryption technology that ensures that users' data remains private, secure, and anonymous.

Google further maintains that it uses patent-pending mathematical formulas to protect the privacy of consumers when it matches one of its users with a shopper who makes a purchase in a brick-and-mortar store. These formulas convert people's names and other purchase information, including the time stamp, location, and the amount of the purchase, into anonymous strings of numbers, a process called *encryption*. (We discuss encryption in Chapter 4.) These formulas make it impossible for Google to know the identity of the real-world shoppers and for the retailers to know the identities of Google's users. The retailers know only that a certain number of matches have been made. Google calls this process "double-blind" encryption.

Google has declined to explain how its new system works or to identify which companies analyze records of credit and debit cards on Google's behalf. Google states that it does not handle the records directly. It acknowledges, however, that its undisclosed partner companies have access to 70 percent of all transactions made with credit and debit cards in the United States.

Google contends that all users who signed into Google's services consented to Google's sharing their data with third parties. However, Google would not disclose how merchants have obtained consent from consumers to share their credit card information. The company claims that it requires its partners to use only personal data that they have the "rights" to use. However, it would not say whether that meant consumers had explicitly consented.

In the past, Google obtained purchase data for a more limited set of consumers who participated in store loyalty programs. Those consumers are more heavily tracked by retailers, and they often give consent to share their data with third parties as a condition of signing up for the loyalty program.

Marc Rotenberg, executive director of the Electronic Privacy Information Center, notes that as companies become increasingly intrusive in terms of their data collection, they are also becoming more secretive as to how they gather and use those data. He urged government regulators and Congress to demand answers about how Google and other technology companies collect and use data from their users.

Paul Stephens of Privacy Rights Clearinghouse, a consumer advocacy group, has asserted that a marketing organization can identity an individual by examining only a few pieces of data. He expressed skepticism that Google's system for guarding the identities of users will stand up to the efforts of hackers who in the past have successfully stripped away privacy protections created by other companies after they experienced data breaches. He maintains that it is extremely difficult to keep data anonymous.

Sources: Compiled from "Facebook Is Even Keeping Track of You Offline," *Huffington Post*, March 25, 2018; J. Glenday, "Google Facing Possible Regulatory Review over Offline Tracking," *The Drum*, August 1, 2017; A. Kieler, "Google's Tracking of Offline Spending Sparks Call for Federal Investigation," *The Consumerist*, July 31, 2017; J. Naughton, "Google, Not GCHQ, Is the Truly Chilling Spy Network," *The Guardian*, June 18, 2017; N. Dawar, "Has Google Finally Proven that Online Ads Cause Offline Purchases?" *Harvard Business Review*, June 1, 2017; "Google Starts Tracking Retail Purchases for Online-to-Offline Attribution," *IPG Media Lab*, May 25, 2017; L. Tung, "Google: We'll Track Your Offline Credit Card Use to Show that Online Ads Work," *ZDNet*, May 24, 2017; R. Whitwam, "Google Can Now Track Your Offline Purchases," *CNBC*, May 24, 2017; H. Peterson, "Google Is under Fire for Watching You while You Shop Even When You're Not Online," *AOL.com*, May 24, 2017; R. Kilpatrick, "Google's New Feature Can Match Ad Clicks with In-Store Purchases," *Fortune*, May 23, 2017; "Google Starts Tracking Offline Shopping—What You Buy at Stores in Person," *Los Angeles Times*, May 23, 2017; E. Dwoskin and C. Timberg, "Google Now Knows When Its Users Go to the Store and Buy Stuff," *Washington Post*, May 23, 2017; "Internet Advertising Expenditure to Exceed US$200bn This Year," *Zenith Media*, March 26, 2017; T. Simonite, "Largest Study of Online Tracking Proves Google Really Is Watching Us All," *MIT Technology Review*, May 18, 2016; T. Simonite, "Probing the Dark Side of Google's Ad-Targeting System," *MIT Technology Review*, July 6, 2015; and www.google.com, accessed June 26, 2019.

Questions

1. Describe the role that information technology plays as Google moves forward in its efforts to integrate online search data with offline purchase data.

2. The fundamental tenets of ethics include responsibility, accountability, and liability. Discuss each of these tenets as it applies to Google's actions in integrating online search data and offline purchase data.

Ethics and Information Technology

All employees have a responsibility to encourage ethical uses of information and information technology. Many of the business decisions you will face at work will have an ethical dimension. Consider the following decisions that you might have to make:

- **HRM** Should organizations monitor employees' Web surfing and e-mail?
- **MKT** Should organizations sell customer information to other companies?
- **HRM** Should organizations audit employees' computers for unauthorized software or illegally downloaded music or video files?

The diversity and ever-expanding use of IT applications have created a variety of ethical issues. These issues fall into four general categories: privacy, accuracy, property, and accessibility.

1. *Privacy issues* involve collecting, storing, and disseminating information about individuals.
2. *Accuracy issues* involve the authenticity, fidelity, and correctness of information that is collected and processed.

3. *Property issues* involve the ownership and value of information.

4. *Accessibility issues* revolve around who should have access to information and whether they should pay a fee for this access.

Table 3.1 lists representative questions and issues for each of these categories. The Ethics Cases found in WileyPLUS also present 14 scenarios that raise ethical issues. These scenarios will provide a context for you to consider situations that involve ethical or unethical behavior. IT's About Business 3.2 presents another ethical issue that is important to students.

TABLE 3.1   **A Framework for Ethical Issues**

Privacy Issues

What information about oneself should an individual be required to reveal to others?

What kinds of surveillance can an employer use on its employees?

What types of personal information can people keep to themselves and not be forced to reveal to others?

What information about individuals should be kept in databases, and how secure is the information there?

Accuracy Issues

Who is responsible for the authenticity, fidelity, and accuracy of the information collected?

How can we ensure that the information will be processed properly and presented accurately to users?

How can we ensure that errors in databases, data transmissions, and data processing are accidental and not intentional?

Who is to be held accountable for errors in information, and how should the injured parties be compensated?

Property Issues

Who owns the information?

What are the just and fair prices for its exchange?

How should we handle software piracy (illegally copying copyrighted software)?

Under what circumstances can one use proprietary databases?

Can corporate computers be used for private purposes?

How should experts who contribute their knowledge to create expert systems be compensated?

How should access to information channels be allocated?

Accessibility Issues

Who is allowed to access information?

How much should companies charge for permitting access to information?

How can access to computers be provided for employees with disabilities?

Who will be provided with the equipment needed for accessing information?

What information does a person or an organization have a right to obtain, under what conditions, and with what safeguards?

IT's About Business 3.2

Quizlet

MIS

Quizlet (**www.quizlet.com**) is a mobile and Web-based study application that allows students to study information with learning tools and games. The app is free and makes money from advertising and paid subscriptions for additional features. Quizlet claims to have over 30 million active users around the world. Quizlet is used as a study tool by half of all high school students and one-third of all college students in the United States.

Quizlet states that it continuously adds features, both seen and unseen, to ensure that the app is used properly to support learning. The app has an honor code that asks that students to "be aware of and uphold their teacher or institution's policies regarding posting or sharing course materials online." Quizlet's community guidelines explicitly prohibit cheating and publicly posting copyrighted material, including test banks, exam questions, and other confidential course content.

Quizlet says that its goal is to help students learn and that it provides internal tools targeted at detecting current, active test material. Further, the company says it relies heavily on users to submit removal requests if they come across such material. Quizlet maintains that students also frequent other online sharing resources such as Brainly (**www.brainly.co**) and Google Docs (**www.docs.google.com**).

In the past, students have kept and shared paper copies of old exams, but the world has changed. The digitization of learning materials, the standardization of curricula through online providers, and apps such as Quizlet could possibly increase the potential for academic dishonesty.

Quizlet is popular with students and many use the site legitimately. However, some students have openly tweeted about using Quizlet to cheat, either opening Quizlet in another browser while taking an online test or studying questions on Quizlet in advance that they knew were likely to be on their exam.

In May 2018, Texas Christian University (TCU; **www.tcu.edu**) suspended 12 students for using Quizlet to cheat on an exam. The incident spanned several semesters and involved a variety of classes in TCU's Bob Schieffer College of Communication.

Students contested the decision, saying that they used Quizlet to study but did not know that the questions they saw on the app would be on their exam. The accusation of cheating stemmed from the professor of the course stating that students should have notified him when they noticed that actual, current exam questions had appeared on the app.

The ensuing legal fight highlighted broader issues about learning in an educational environment with easily accessible digitized information. Many students reviewing material on the app have no knowledge of who put it there, how it was obtained, or whether the questions they are reviewing are current, active test questions. For example, many of the suspended TCU students said that they were unaware that the materials they had reviewed online were active test questions. Furthermore, they alleged that TCU-employed tutors had directed them to the site.

The students' lawyer defended their use of Quizlet by saying that the incident showed that universities had to "adapt to changes in technology" and that professors needed to adapt to new technologies and create new exam questions each term rather than reusing old questions.

The increasing popularity of widely used online resources that rely on crowdsourcing raises questions about what learning actually looks like for students today and poses challenges for instructors. In fact, many educators say that in most disciplines, it may no longer be useful for students to memorize lists and regurgitate facts.

On May 14, 2018, TCU overturned yearlong suspensions for some students who were accused of using Quizlet to cheat on exams. The students' lawyer stated that all the students represented in the case had their suspensions overturned. Other steps that TCU took—including giving failing grades, placing students on academic probation, and charging students with academic misconduct—remained in place and were still being appealed. TCU also stated that the professor in this incident was not at fault for not changing the questions on the exam.

At the end of 2018, Quizlet had over 300 million user-generated flashcard sets and more than 50 million monthly users. The software is available in more than 15 languages.

Sources: Compiled from E. Kerr, "What a Controversy over an App Tells Us about How Students Learn Now," *Chronicle of Higher Education*, May 15, 2018; T. Steele, "TCU Overturns Suspensions for Some Students Accused of Using Quizlet App to Cheat," *Dallas Morning News*, May 14, 2018; L. McKenzie, "Learning Tool or Cheating Aid?" *Inside Higher Ed*, May 14, 2018; "Texas Christian University Tutors Accused in Alleged Cheating Case," *CBS News*, May 10, 2018; S. English, "TCU Suspends 12 Students Accused of Cheating via a Popular Study App," *Star-Telegram*, May 10, 2018; J. Prothro, "TCU Suspends a Dozen Students over Scheme to Use Quizlet App to Cheat," *Dallas Morning News*, May 9, 2018; L. Kologny, "Popular Study App Quizlet Faces a Moment of Truth as a New School Year Begins," *CNBC*, August 23, 2017; and www.quizlet.com, accessed September 17, 2018.

Questions

1. Discuss the ethicality of students' use of Quizlet (and similar apps) to study for exams.

2. Discuss the ethicality of students' not telling the course instructor that current, actual exam questions were on Quizlet.

Many of the issues and scenarios discussed in this chapter involve privacy as well as ethics. In the next section, you will learn about privacy issues in more detail.

Before you go on . . .

1. What does a code of ethics contain?
2. Describe the fundamental tenets of ethics.

3.2 | Privacy

In general, **privacy** is the right to be left alone and to be free of unreasonable personal intrusions. **Information privacy** is the right to determine when and to what extent information about you can be gathered or communicated to others. Privacy rights apply to individuals, groups, and institutions. The right to privacy is recognized today in all the U.S. states and by the federal government, either by statute or in common law.

Privacy can be interpreted quite broadly. However, court decisions in many countries have followed two rules fairly closely:

1. The right of privacy is not absolute. Privacy must be balanced against the needs of society.
2. The public's right to know supersedes the individual's right of privacy.

These two rules illustrate why determining and enforcing privacy regulations can be difficult.

As we discussed earlier, rapid advances in information technologies have made it much easier to collect, store, and integrate vast amounts of data on individuals in large databases. On an average day, data about you are generated in many ways: surveillance cameras located on toll roads, on other roadways, in busy intersections, in public places, and at work; credit card transactions; telephone calls (landline and cellular); banking transactions; queries to search engines; and government records (including police records). These data can be integrated to produce a **digital dossier**, which is an electronic profile of you and your habits. The process of forming a digital dossier is called **profiling**.

Data aggregators, such as LexisNexis (**www.lexisnexis.com**) and Acxiom (**www.acxiom.com**), are prominent examples of profilers. These companies collect public data such as real estate records and published telephone numbers in addition to nonpublic information, such as Social Security numbers, financial data, and police, criminal, and motor vehicle records. They then integrate these data to form digital dossiers on most adults in the United States. They ultimately sell these dossiers to law enforcement agencies and companies that conduct background checks on potential employees. They also sell them to companies that want to know their customers better, a process called *customer intimacy*.

Electronic Surveillance

According to the American Civil Liberties Union (ACLU), tracking people's activities with the aid of information technology has become a major privacy-related problem. The ACLU notes that this monitoring, or **electronic surveillance**, is rapidly increasing, particularly with the emergence of new technologies. Electronic surveillance is conducted by employers, the government, and other institutions.

Americans today live with a degree of surveillance that would have been unimaginable just a few years ago. For example, surveillance cameras track you at airports, subways, banks, and other public venues. Inexpensive digital sensors are also now everywhere. They are incorporated into laptop webcams, video game motion sensors, smartphone cameras, utility meters, passports, and employee ID cards. Step out your front door, and you could be captured in a high-resolution photograph taken from the air or from the street by Google or Microsoft as they update their mapping services. Drive down a city street, cross a toll bridge, or park at a shopping mall, and your license plate can be recorded and time-stamped.

Emerging technologies, such as low-cost digital cameras, motion sensors, and biometric readers, are helping to increase the monitoring of human activity. The costs of storing and using digital data are also rapidly decreasing. The result is an explosion of sensor data collection and storage.

In fact, your smartphone has become a sensor. The average price of a smartphone has increased 17 percent since 2000. However, the phone's processing capability has increased by *13,000 percent* during that time, according to technology market research firm ABI Research (**www.abiresearch.com**). As you will study in Chapter 8, smartphones can now record video, take pictures, send and receive e-mail, search for information, access the Internet, and locate you on a map, among many other things. Your phone also stores large amounts of information about you that can be collected and analyzed. A special problem arises with smartphones that are equipped with global positioning system (GPS) sensors. These sensors routinely *geotag* photos and videos, embedding images with the longitude and latitude of the location shown in the image. Thus, you could be inadvertently supplying criminals with useful intelligence by posting personal images on social networks or photo-sharing websites. These actions would show the criminals exactly where you live and when you're there.

MIS Another example of how new devices can contribute to electronic surveillance is facial recognition technology (see Chapter 4). Just a few years ago, this software worked only in very controlled settings, such as passport checkpoints. However, this technology can now match faces even in regular snapshots and online images. For example, Intel and Microsoft have introduced in-store digital billboards that can recognize your face. These billboards can keep track of the products you are interested in based on your purchases or browsing behavior. One marketing analyst has predicted that your experience in every store will soon be customized.

The rapidly increasing use of facial recognition technologies in China is causing much concern as the Chinese government plans to implement its *Social Credit Score* (SCS) by 2020. In this system, every citizen in China will be given a score that, as a matter of public record, will be available for all to see. The score comes from monitoring an individual's social behavior, from their spending habits and how regularly they pay their bills to their social interactions. The SCS will become the basis of that person's trustworthiness, which will also be publicly ranked. A citizen's SCS will affect their eligibility for a number of services, including the kinds of jobs or mortgages they can get, and it will also impact the schools for which their children qualify.

In 2018, China had already begun a voluntary implementation of the SCS by partnering with private companies to develop the algorithms needed for such a large-scale, data-driven system. These private companies included China Rapid Finance, a partner of social network giant Tencent, and Sesame Credit, a subsidiary of the Alibaba affiliate company Ant Financial Services Group. Both Rapid Finance and Sesame Credit have access to huge amounts of data, the former through its WeChat messaging app with some 850 million users and the latter through its AliPay payment service.

Google and Facebook are using facial recognition software—Google Picasa and Facebook Photo Albums—in their popular online photo-editing and photo-sharing services. Both companies encourage users to assign names to people in photos, a practice referred to as *photo tagging.* Facial recognition software then indexes facial features. Once an individual in a photo is tagged, the software searches for similar facial features in untagged photos. This process allows the user to quickly group photos in which the tagged person appears. Significantly, the individual is not aware of this process.

Why is tagging important? The reason is that once you are tagged in a photo, that photo can be used to search for matches across the entire Internet or in private databases, including databases fed by surveillance cameras. How could this type of surveillance affect you? As one example, a car dealer can take a picture of you when you step onto the car lot. He or she could then quickly profile you (find out information about where you live, your employment, etc.) on the Web to achieve a competitive edge in making a sale. Even worse, a stranger in a restaurant could photograph you with a smartphone and then go online to profile you for reasons of his or her own. One privacy attorney has asserted that losing your right to anonymity would have a chilling effect on where you go, who you meet, and how you live your life.

Drones are presenting additional surveillance concerns. Low-cost drones with high-performance cameras can be used for persistent aerial surveillance. Since the beginning of modern aviation, landowners have had rights to the airspace above their property up to 500 feet. However, to regulate small, low-flying drones, the Federal Aviation Administration (FAA; **www.faa.gov**) has assumed authority all the way down to the ground.

Consider this example. You see a drone flying about 100 feet above your backyard, and you suspect that it is spying on you. Who is flying it? Who are you going to sue? And if you do sue, how are you going to prove that the drone was spying on you?

The FAA is responsible for addressing drone-related privacy concerns. The Federal Trade Commission (FTC; **www.ftc.gov**), the U.S. government's primary consumer privacy agency, is also exploring the drone privacy issue. IT's About Business 3.3 and this chapter's closing case illustrate two other types of surveillance technology employed by law enforcement agencies.

IT's About Business 3.3

License Plate Readers

`MIS`

Law enforcement agencies have been using license plate readers (LPRs) for some time to track stolen cars and to apprehend criminals. Today, private automobile repossession companies and towing companies photograph millions of plates every day with scanners on their tow trucks. They also use camera cars that drive around and collect plate scans from offices, malls, roadways, and driveways.

Each scan is stamped with the location (via GPS coordinates), date, and time. The databases of repossession and towing companies contain a huge amount of scans that they sell to both law enforcement agencies and private companies. These private companies—which we call LPR companies here—also scan license plates themselves and use software to analyze the license plate scans. LPR companies include Digital Recognition Network (DRN; **www.drndata.com**), Vigilant Solutions (**www.vigilantsolutions.com**), and MVTrac (**www.mvtrac.com**), among others.

In total, there are at least three billion license plate photos in the private databases of LPR companies. Vigilant Solutions and DRN claim they have scanned two billion license plates since 2009 when they began the largest private license plate database in the United States, the National Vehicle Location Service.

Vigilant decided to offer the use of its database to police departments for free. In exchange, cities would give Vigilant their records of outstanding arrest warrants and overdue court fees, which the company would use to create a database of "flagged" vehicles. When license plate readers spotted a flagged plate, officers would pull the driver over and instruct him or her either to pay the fine or to face arrest. For every transaction completed between police and civilians stopped with flagged plates, Vigilant would receive a 25 percent service fee.

With that much data, analytics can reveal much information about the owner of a car. Predicting where and when someone will drive is straightforward because the database contains data on how many times and at what times a car is spotted in a certain area. Analytics can therefore generate a person's driving history over time. In fact, DRN claims that owners are typically within 1,000 feet of their vehicles. So, find the vehicle, and you find the owner.

LPR companies do not have access to the Department of Motor Vehicles (DMV) registrations. Therefore, although they can track a car, they cannot identify the owner. That information is protected by the Driver's Privacy Protection Act of 1994, which keeps drivers' names, addresses, and driving histories hidden from public view. However, the law makes exceptions for insurance companies and private investigators. LPR companies maintain that only two groups can use their software to find the owner of a car: law enforcement agencies and repossession companies.

LPR companies are controversial regarding privacy issues. MVTrac contends that LPRs simply automate what police officers and the repossession industry have always done—check license plates by eye—and that most Americans have accepted that the days of having true privacy have passed.

Significantly, LPR companies are not regulated in most states. In 2007, New Hampshire was the first state to ban LPRs completely except for toll collections and security on certain bridges.

LPRs have also caused controversy with their usage by law enforcement. In December 2013, the city of Boston suspended its LPR program after police accidentally revealed DMV-related information from its cameras to the *Boston Globe*.

Some law enforcement agencies keep data for days; others do so for years. In most states, police can monitor motorists with LPRs without having to obtain a search warrant or a court order. In February 2015, a Department of Homeland Security proposal for a privately hosted federal plate-tracking system was dropped days after the *Washington Post* exposed it.

In 2014, police in Tempe, Arizona, refused an offer from Vigilant for free LPR cameras. To receive the cameras, every month, officers would have to serve 25 warrants from a list supplied by Vigilant. If the department missed the quota, then it would lose the cameras. Such lists, according to the *Los Angeles Times* investigation that uncovered the offer, commonly come from debt-collector "warrants" against drivers with unpaid municipal fines.

At the same time, however, license plate readers have proved valuable to police departments. For example, between January and September 2017, police in Danville, California, reported they had made 31 arrests related directly to their LPR system. In addition, they recovered 15 stolen vehicles and made 11 more arrests when they recovered other stolen property. The Danville police chief asserted that the arrests would not have been made without the LPR system.

LPR systems immediately alert police officers if a vehicle has any associated police records, including if the car is stolen. LPRs in police patrol cars emit an audible alert each time they detect a license plate that could be linked to a possible driving violation, a wanted individual, or a crime.

If the LPR system flags a car that is being driven, police officers manually run the license plate through their dispatch center to check the accuracy of the LPR system's data. Officers verify that the vehicle and driver match descriptions contained in law enforcement databases, and they then continue to build a case in the same way that they would without the LPR system.

LPR companies can also analyze their databases of license plate scans in other ways. For instance, MVTrac analyzed its scans to track Honda Acuras at specific areas and times, including the exact models and colors. These data would be extremely valuable to automakers, marketers, and insurance companies.

As with technology in general, LPRs are improving faster than the legislation to regulate them. Today, LPR companies are exploring smaller cameras, smartphone apps that can pick out plates from live video, and the potential integration of public records, DMV databases, and facial recognition software. Because police ostensibly use LPRs for public safety, people will likely have to accept some further loss of privacy when they drive.

Despite serious privacy concerns, there is some good news concerning the use of license plate readers. For instance, the sheriff of Volusia County in central Florida stated that, between January 2017 and September 2018, the LPRs identified 67 people that they were searching for, and deputies were able to apprehend the drivers of the vehicles. Furthermore, between January and September 2018, police in Miami Beach, Florida, made 49 felony arrests using LPRs.

Sources: Compiled from E. von Ancken, "License Plate Readers Catch Dozens of Crooks, Rescue People in Need," ClickOrlando.com, August 15, 2018; A. Perez, "License Plate Readers Help Miami Beach Police Crack Down on Crime," *Local10.com/Miami-Beach*, July 31, 2018; S. Reese, "License Plate Readers Alert Police of Potential Crimes in Real-Time," *NWI.com*, October 1, 2017; S. Richards, "License-Plate Readers Credited with Helping Solve Crimes in Danville," *East Bay Times*, September 29, 2017; "California Supreme Court: Access to License Plate Data May Be Possible," *CBS*, August 31, 2017; T. Jackman, "Va. Supreme Court to Hear Case Challenging Police Retention of License Plate Data," *Washington Post*, June 27, 2017; D. Maass, "The Four Flavors of Automated License Plate Reader Technology," *Electronic Frontier Foundation*, April 6, 2017; K. Waddell, "How License-Plate Readers Have Helped Police and Lenders Target the Poor," *The Atlantic*, April 22, 2016; R. Sachs, "How Police License Plate Readers Can Invade Your Privacy," *PRI.org*, March 22, 2016; C. Young, "Lawmakers Warned Plate Readers Could Lead to 'Dragnet Monitoring'," *Boston Globe*, March 1, 2016; C. Friedersdorf, "An Unprecedented Threat to Privacy," *The Atlantic*, January 27, 2016; C. Atiyeh, "How License Plate Readers Are Eroding Your Privacy," *Popular Mechanics*, January 29, 2015; and www.vigilantsystems.com, www.drndata.com, and www.mvtrac.com, all accessed June 26, 2019.

Questions

1. Discuss the ethicality and the legality of license plate readers.

2. Discuss the ethicality and the legality of Vigilant Solutions offering its technology to police departments for free.

3. What are the privacy implications of analyzing license plate scans?

HRM The scenarios we just considered deal primarily with your personal life. However, electronic surveillance has become a reality in the workplace as well. In general, employees have very limited legal protection against surveillance by employers. The law supports the right of employers to read their employees' e-mail and other electronic documents and to monitor their employees' Internet use. Today, more than three-fourths of organizations routinely monitor their employees' Internet usage. Two-thirds of them also use software to block connections to inappropriate websites, a practice called *URL filtering*. Furthermore, organizations are installing monitoring and filtering software to enhance security by blocking malicious software and to increase productivity by discouraging employees from wasting time.

MIS In one organization, the chief information officer (CIO) monitored roughly 13,000 employees for three months to determine the type of traffic they engaged in on the network. He then forwarded the data to the CEO and the heads of the human resources and legal departments. These executives were shocked at the questionable websites the employees were visiting as well as the amount of time they were spending on those sites. The executives quickly decided to implement a URL filtering product.

In general, surveillance is a concern for private individuals regardless of whether it is conducted by corporations, government bodies, or criminals. As a nation, the United States is still struggling to define the appropriate balance between personal privacy and electronic surveillance, especially in situations that involve threats to national security.

Personal Information in Databases

Modern institutions store information about individuals in many databases. Perhaps the most visible locations of such records are credit-reporting agencies. Other institutions that store personal information include banks and financial institutions; cable TV, telephone, and utility companies; employers; mortgage companies; hospitals; schools and universities; retail establishments; government agencies (Internal Revenue Service, your state, your municipality); and many others.

There are several concerns about the information you provide to these record keepers. Some of the major concerns are as follows:

- Do you know where the records are?
- Are the records accurate?
- Can you change inaccurate data?
- How long will it take to make a change?
- Under what circumstances will the personal data be released?
- How are the data used?
- To whom are the data given or sold?
- How secure are the data against access by unauthorized people?

The Indian government's Aadhaar system is the largest biometric database in the world. IT's About Business 3.4 addresses the uses, advantages, and disadvantages of the system as well as its privacy implications.

IT's About Business 3.4

India's Aadhaar System

MIS

India has vast numbers of anonymous poor citizens. To address this problem, the nation instituted its Unique Identification Project, known as Aadhaar (**www.uidai.gov.in**), which means "the foundation" in several Indian languages. The goal of the project is to issue identification numbers linked to the fingerprints and iris scans of every individual in the country.

Aadhaar was designed to remedy a critical problem that afflicts impoverished Indians. The Indian government has not officially acknowledged the existence of many poor citizens because these individuals do not possess birth certificates and other official documentation. Therefore, they have not been able to access government services to which they are entitled, nor have they been able to open bank accounts. When Aadhaar began, many Indian households were "unbanked," meaning that they had to stash their savings in cash around their homes.

The Indian government also wanted to reduce corruption and streamline the delivery of government services. Prior to Aadhaar, the government experienced problems in managing its welfare programs, and it lost millions of dollars each year as Indian citizens either provided fake names or entered their own names multiple times into the system in order to withdraw more than their fair share of benefits.

Initially, Aadhaar was optional and was used for only certain government subsidies, including those for food and liquefied natural gas for cooking. Further, the program targeted only those people in greatest need of assistance, particularly rural villagers who lacked official forms of identification. Over time, Aadhaar's mission expanded.

Aadhaar went into operation in September 2010, when officials carrying iris scanners, fingerprint scanners, digital cameras, and laptops began to register the first few villagers as well as slum dwellers in the country's capital city, Delhi. One of the greatest challenges that the project faced was to ensure that each individual's record in the Aadhaar database matched one and only one person. To perform this task, Aadhaar checks all 10 fingerprints and both irises of each person against those of everyone else in the country. Using the 10 prints and both irises boosted the Aadhaar accuracy rate to 99 percent. However, in a country the size of India, 99 percent accuracy means that 12 million people could have faulty records.

By July 2019, this process had encompassed 1.22 billion people. Aadhaar provides a 12-digit unique identity number to all Indian residents based on their biometric (all 10 fingerprints and both iris scans) and demographic data. In late 2017, the government added facial recognition as an additional biometric to further strengthen Aadhaar.

The biometric data and the Aadhaar identification number serve as a verifiable, portable, and unique national ID. The Aadhaar project enables millions of Indian citizens to access government services that previously have been out of reach to them. Today, Aadhaar is the largest biometric database in the world. The program now plays a key role in almost all parts of daily life in India.

Aadhaar became a vehicle to apply data-driven improvements to a wide range of government and private-sector services. The system is now linked to so many activities that it is almost impossible to live in India without enrolling. Participation in Aadhaar has become a requirement for filing taxes, opening bank accounts, receiving school lunch in the state of Uttar Pradesh, purchasing railway tickets online, accessing some public Wi-Fi, participating in the state of Karnataka's universal health care coverage, and benefiting from a wide range of welfare programs.

However, although Aadhaar has become central to life in India, the program is experiencing problems, especially among underserved populations. India has inconsistent Internet service outside its large cities. Consequently, rural towns struggle to go online to authenticate peoples' fingerprints with the central Aadhaar database. In some cases, that situation occurs when older adults and individuals with disabilities are unable to walk to the distribution sites to verify their identities. In addition, many people who perform manual labor have fingerprints that are too weathered from years of work to scan correctly. As a result, they are denied their food rations. One economist has asserted that millions of people have missed out on government benefits because they could not sign up for Aadhaar for these reasons.

Investigators found that approximately one million people in the state of Rajasthan alone were unfairly dropped from government lists for food subsidies because they could not sign up for Aadhaar. In addition, more than three million citizens were unable to collect their designated grain allocations. In one district alone, of approximately 2,900 people marked "dead" or "duplicate," 1,350 were actually neither. Nevertheless, they still lost access to their pensions.

There is also evidence of misuse of the Aadhaar program. Consider the following examples:

- Two hundred and ten government agencies published the full names, addresses, and Aadhaar numbers of welfare beneficiaries.

- The Aadhaar information for 120 million users appears to have been leaked from the telecommunications company Reliance Jio (the company claims that the data were not authentic).

- Bank account and Aadhaar details of more than 100 million people were disclosed through certain open-government portals.

- The government's e-hospital database was hacked to access confidential Aadhaar information.

In addition to these problems, privacy advocates charge that the Aadhaar program faces even larger problems, namely, its ubiquity and poor security. Specifically, they contend that when biometric information is used to access a service via Aadhaar—for example, purchasing a new cell phone—the service provider receives that person's demographic data (name, address, phone number), and the government receives the metadata—specifically, the date and time of the transaction, the form of identification used, and the company with which the transaction was carried out.

Aadhaar opponents are particularly concerned about the social stigma attached to some jobs in India, such as manually cleaning sewers. They worry that Aadhaar will permanently stigmatize these individuals by allowing future employers, schools, banks, and new acquaintances to view their Aadhaar database information and judge them based on their work history. This situation could make social mobility in India even more difficult to achieve.

The Indian government views Aadhaar as an essential solution for a number of societal challenges. In contrast, critics see it as a step toward a surveillance state. In late August 2017, the Indian Supreme Court issued a unanimous decision that found, for the first time, a fundamental right to privacy in the Indian Constitution. Aadhaar's opponents celebrated that decision because they believe that the program conflicts with this newly established right.

In September 2018, the Supreme Court upheld the constitutionality and validity of the Aadhaar system and found that Aadhaar does not violate privacy rights. The Court did state that the Aadhaar card is not mandatory for opening bank accounts, obtaining a mobile phone number, or being admitted to a school.

Sources: Compiled from "Face Recognition Feature Set to Ensure Stronger Aadhaar Security: Here's More Detail," *Times of India*, March 13, 2018;

"Aadhaar Authentication via Face Recognition from July: How It Will Work," *NDTV*, January 15, 2018; G. Prasad, "Aadhar-PAN Linking Must for Income Tax Return Filing from 1 July: Govt," *LiveMint*, September 30, 2017; M. Rajshekhar, "Aadhaar Shows India's Governance Is Susceptible to Poorly Tested Ideas Pushed by Powerful People," *Scroll.in*, September 30, 2017; K. Rathee, "Govt Plans to Link Driving Licence with Aadhaar," *Business Standard*, September 16, 2017; N. Kolachalam, "The Privacy Battle over the World's Largest Biometric Database," *The Atlantic*, September 5, 2017; "Right to Privacy a Fundamental Right: 7 Aadhaar Controversies That Raised Concern," *Hindustan Times*, August 24, 2017; T. Johnson, "IIT Kharagpur Graduate Hacked Aadhaar Data through Digital India App," *The Indian Express*, August 4, 2017; "Over 200 Government Sites Reveal Aadhaar Details; No Leakage from UIDAI," *The Economic Times*, July 20, 2017; A. Sethi and S. Bansa, "Aadhaar Gets New Security Features, but This Is Why Your Data Still May Not Be Safe," *Hindustan Times*, July 19, 2017; R. Khera, "The Different Ways in Which Aadhaar Infringes on Privacy," *The Wire*, July 19, 2017; P. Banerjee, "Massive Trove of Reliance Jio User Data Leaked Online," *Digit.in*, July 9, 2017; A. Srupathi, "How Public Apathy Continues to Keep Manual Scavengers Invisible and in the Margins," *The Wire*, March 18, 2017; "Aadhaar ID Saving Indian Govt about $1 Billion per Annum: World Bank," *The Economic Times*, January 14, 2016; S. Rai, "Why India's Identification Scheme Is Groundbreaking," *BBC News*, June 5, 2012; E. Hannon, "For India's Undocumented Citizens, an ID at Last," *NPR.org*, March 1, 2012; and www.uidai.gov.in, accessed June 26, 2019.

Questions

1. Discuss the ethicality and the legality of India's Aadhaar system.

2. Court decisions in many countries have stated that an individual's privacy must be balanced against the needs of society. Does the Aadhaar system go too far in favor of the needs of society? Why or why not? Support your answer.

Information on Internet Bulletin Boards, Newsgroups, and Social Networking Sites

Every day, we see more and more *electronic bulletin boards*, *newsgroups*, *electronic discussions* such as chat rooms, and *social networking sites* (discussed in Chapter 9). These sites appear on the Internet, within corporate intranets, and on blogs. A *blog*, short for "weblog," is an informal, personal journal that is frequently updated and is intended for general public reading. How does society keep owners of bulletin boards from disseminating information that may be offensive to readers or simply untrue? This is a difficult problem because it involves the conflict between freedom of speech on the one hand and privacy on the other. This conflict is a fundamental and continuing ethical issue in the United States and throughout the world.

There is no better illustration of the conflict between free speech and privacy than the Internet. Many websites contain anonymous, derogatory information on individuals, who typically have little recourse in the matter. The vast majority of U.S. firms use the Internet in examining job applications, including searching on Google and on social networking sites. Consequently, derogatory information contained on the Internet can harm a person's chances of being hired.

Privacy Codes and Policies

Privacy policies or **privacy codes** are an organization's guidelines for protecting the privacy of its customers, clients, and employees. In many corporations, senior management has begun to understand that when they collect vast amounts of personal information, they must protect it. Many organizations also give their customers some voice in how their information is used by providing them with opt-out choices. The **opt-out model** of informed consent permits the company to collect personal information until the customer specifically requests that the data not be collected. Privacy advocates prefer the **opt-in model** of informed consent, which prohibits an organization from collecting any personal information unless the customer specifically authorizes it.

One privacy tool available to consumers is the *Platform for Privacy Preferences* (P3P), a protocol that automatically communicates privacy policies between an electronic commerce website and visitors to that site. P3P enables visitors to determine the types of personal data that can be extracted by the sites they visit. It also allows visitors to compare a site's privacy policy to the visitors' preferences or to other standards, such as the FTC's Fair Information Practices Standard or the European Directive on Data Protection.

Table 3.2 provides a sampling of privacy policy guidelines. The last section, "Data Confidentiality," refers to security, which we consider in Chapter 4. All of the good privacy intentions in the world are useless unless they are supported and enforced by effective security measures.

Despite privacy codes and policies and despite opt-out and opt-in models, guarding whatever is left of your privacy is becoming increasingly difficult. This problem is illustrated in IT's About Business 3.3, 3.4, and 3.5 as well as the chapter-closing case.

TABLE 3.2 Privacy Policy Guidelines: A Sampler
Data Collection
Data should be collected on individuals only for the purpose of accomplishing a legitimate business objective.
Data should be adequate, relevant, and not excessive in relation to the business objective.
Individuals must give their consent before data pertaining to them can be gathered. Such consent may be implied from the individual's actions (e.g., applications for credit, insurance, or employment).
Data Accuracy
Sensitive data gathered on individuals should be verified before they are entered into the database.
Data should be kept current, where and when necessary.
The file should be made available so that the individual can ensure that the data are correct.
In any disagreement about the accuracy of the data, the individual's version should be noted and included with any disclosure of the file.
Data Confidentiality
Computer security procedures should be implemented to ensure against unauthorized disclosure of data. These procedures should include physical, technical, and administrative security measures.
Third parties should not be given access to data without the individual's knowledge or permission, except as required by law.
Disclosures of data, other than the most routine, should be noted and maintained for as long as the data are maintained.
Data should not be disclosed for reasons incompatible with the business objective for which they are collected.

IT's About Business 3.5

The Facebook-Cambridge Analytica Scandal

MIS

In mid-March 2018, *The Guardian* and the *New York Times* revealed a data scandal involving Facebook and Cambridge Analytica (CA) when they reported that CA had collected the personal information of 87 million Facebook users. The newspapers outlined how the data of these Facebook users were obtained by CA. *The Guardian* referred to the data misuse as a breach, but Facebook disagreed. A Facebook executive stated that no systems were infiltrated and that no passwords or information were stolen or hacked.

The scandal involved the collection and subsequent use of personally identifiable information on 87 million Facebook users. The time line of the incident is useful in understanding what happened.

In April 2010, Facebook deployed software called Open Graph, which enabled external developers to contact Facebook users and request permission to access their personal data and to access their Facebook friends' personal data as well. If the user accepted, these developers could access a user's name, gender, location, birthday, education, political preferences, relationship status, religious views, online chat status, and more. With additional permissions, external developers could access a user's private messages.

In 2013, Cambridge University academician Aleksandr Kogan and his company Global Science Research developed a personality quiz app called "This Is Your Digital Life." The app prompted users to answer questions for a psychological profile. Almost 300,000 Facebook users installed Kogan's app on their accounts.

As with any Facebook developer at the time, Kogan could access personal data about those users and their Facebook friends (with appropriate permissions from users themselves). Furthermore, Kogan's app collected that personal information and loaded it into a private database instead of immediately deleting it. Kogan then provided that database, containing information about 87 million Facebook users, to the voter-profiling company CA, which used the data to develop 30 million "psychographic" profiles about voters.

In 2014, Facebook changed its rules to limit a developer's access to user data. This change was made to ensure that a third party could not access a user's friends' data without gaining permission first. However, the rule changes were not retroactive, and Kogan did not delete the data thought to have been improperly acquired.

In late 2015, reports suggested that Ted Cruz's presidential campaign was using psychological data based on research on millions of Facebook users. In response to the reporting, Facebook said that when it learned about the data leaks, it tried to ban Kogan's app and legally pressured both Kogan and CA to remove the data they had improperly collected. Facebook claimed that both Kogan and CA certified that they had deleted the data.

In 2016, Donald Trump's campaign invested heavily in Facebook ads, helped by CA. In August 2018, questions were still being hotly debated about Facebook's role in the 2016 elections. Many questions have focused on Facebook's News Feed and the role it played in magnifying Russian propaganda and other hoaxes. Lawmakers have also criticized the company's lax sale of political advertisements that some buyers literally paid for with Russian rubles. Political ads are not regulated as closely online as they are on television or radio.

After the Facebook–CA scandal was revealed, Facebook began instituting a series of changes to repair the damage. The company banned Canadian firm AggregateIQ and Italian firm CubeYou from the Facebook platform following indications that the two companies had improperly accessed user data.

Facebook also restricted who could place political advertisements, or issue ads, on its platform to "authorized advertisers" who have had their identity and location confirmed by the platform. For authorization, advertisers had to provide Facebook with a government-issued ID and a physical mailing address. Furthermore, each issued ad had to be labeled with a marker identifying it as "Political Ad," with information displayed beside the ad that showed who paid for it.

Facebook began working with outside groups to develop criteria for what is considered a political ad. The move intended to prevent or limit "bad actors" who try to interfere with foreign elections, likely in response to the discovery that 470 fake Russian Facebook accounts spent about $100,000 on roughly 3,000 ads on the platform during the 2016 U.S. presidential election.

In March 2018, the FTC announced that it was investigating Facebook for possible violations of the firm's 2011 agreement with the FTC. At that time, the FTC charged that Facebook had deceived consumers by telling them that they could keep their information on Facebook private and then repeatedly allowing it to be shared and made public. The settlement required Facebook to provide consumers with clear and prominent notice and to obtain their express consent before their information was shared beyond the privacy settings that the consumers established.

A *single* violation of Facebook's 2011 agreement with the FTC can carry a fine of up to $40,000. That figure means that the Facebook–CA scandal could cost Facebook up to $2 trillion.

In March 2018, CA and its parent company, SCL Elections Ltd, instigated insolvency proceedings and closed. The question is: What happens with the data that the firms collected?

In July 2018, the United Kingdom's information commissioner fined Facebook £500,000 for breaking data protection laws following an investigation into the scandal. The investigation found that Facebook had contravened U.K. law by failing to protect people's data and that the company had also failed to be transparent about how personal data were being used by others. Facebook did have an opportunity to respond before a final decision was made. The scandal took place before the European Union's GDPR came into force on May 25, 2018, or Facebook would have faced a multi-million-dollar fine.

In addition, the United Kingdom announced its intent to bring a criminal prosecution against SCL Elections for failing to adequately respond to an enforcement notice issued in May 2018. In an accompanying report, the U.K. data regulator made recommendations for how government can improve transparency around online campaigning and the political use of personal data.

In August 2018, lawyers for a group of U.K. residents whose Facebook data were collected by CA filed the first step in a class-action suit against Facebook. Nearly 1.1 million British citizens could be eligible to join such a suit if it proceeds.

Since 2007, Facebook has changed its rules about how much data apps can access. However, over that time, how many developers followed Facebook's rules? How many acted like Kogan did, storing the data and creating their own private databases? Where are those data now, and who has them? If all that private user data are as powerful as CA has said they are, what have they been used to do?

Facebook has faced a backlash from scandals involving the abuse of personal data, foreign interference in U.S. elections, and the spread of hateful or harassing content on the platform. A Pew Research Center (**www.pewresearch.org**) survey administered between May 29 and June 11, 2018, found that 74 percent of U.S. adult Facebook users had taken one of the following actions: changed their privacy settings, taken a break from the app, or deleted it altogether.

While the survey suggests that large numbers of Americans abandoned the platform or scaled back their usage, Facebook reported stable daily active user numbers in the second quarter of 2018. The social network stated that 185 million users are on the platform in the United States and Canada every day, a number unchanged from the first quarter of 2018.

Sources: Compiled from H. Shaban, "More Than 1 in 4 American Users Have Deleted Facebook, Pew Survey Finds," *Washington Post*, September 5, 2018; I. Lapowsky, "UK Group Threatens to Sue Facebook over Cambridge Analytica," *Wired*, July 31, 2018; M. Burgess and J. Temperton, "Facebook Broke Data Law and Faces £500,000 Fine over Cambridge Analytica Scandal," *Wired*, July 10, 2018; "Former Cambridge Analytica Employee Says 'There Were More' Apps That Collected User Data," *CBS News*, June 27, 2018; C. Stokel-Walker, "What Will Happen to Cambridge Analytica's Data Now It Has Closed?" *Wired*, May 4, 2018; A. Hern, "Far More Than 87M Facebook Users Had Data Compromised, MPs Told," *The Guardian*, April 17, 2018; A. Schomer, "Facebook Moves to Impress Regulators," *Business Insider*, April 10, 2018; S. Meredith, "Facebook-Cambridge Analytica: A Timeline of the Data Hijacking Scandal," *CNBC*, April 10, 2018; W. Ashford, "Facebook Data Scandal a Game Changer, Says ICO," *Computer Weekly*, April 9, 2018; J. Sanders, "If Your Organization Advertises on Facebook, Beware of These New Limitations," *TechRepublic*, April 9, 2018; O. Solon, "Facebook Says Cambridge Analytica May Have Gained 37M More Users' Data," *The Guardian*, April 4, 2018; W. Ashford, "Facebook Braces for New Regulation for Cambridge Analytica Deal," *Computer Weekly*, March 23, 2018; T. Romm and C. Timberg, "FTC Opens Investigation into Facebook after Cambridge Analytica Scrapes Millions of Users' Personal Information," *Washington Post*, March 20, 2018; R. Meyer, "The Cambridge Analytica Scandal, in 3 Paragraphs," *The Atlantic*, March 20, 2018; M. Giles, "The Cambridge Analytica Affair Reveals Facebook's 'Transparency Paradox,'" *MIT Technology Review*, March 20, 2018; B. Tau and D. Seetharaman, "Data Blowback Pummels Facebook," *Wall Street Journal*, March 20, 2018; K. Granville, Facebook and Cambridge Analytica: What You Need to Know as Fallout Widens," *New York Times*, March 19, 2018; M. Rosenberg, N. Confessore, and C. Cadwalladr, "How Trump Consultants Exploited the Facebook Data of Millions," *New York Times*, March 17, 2018; H. Davies, "Ted Cruz Campaign Using Firm That Harvested Data on Millions of Unwitting Facebook Users," *The Guardian*, December 11, 2015; and www.facebook.com, accessed June 26, 2019.

Questions

1. Discuss the legality and the ethicality of Facebook in the Facebook–Cambridge Analytica incident.

2. Discuss the legality and the ethicality of Cambridge Analytica in the Facebook–Cambridge Analytica incident.

3. Describe how each of the fundamental tenets of ethics (responsibility, accountability, and liability) applies to Facebook and then to Cambridge Analytica in this incident.

International Aspects of Privacy

As the number of online users has increased globally, governments throughout the world have enacted a large number of inconsistent privacy and security laws. This highly complex global legal framework is creating regulatory problems for companies. Approximately 50 countries have some form of data protection laws. Many of these laws conflict with those of other countries, or they require specific security measures. Other countries have no privacy laws at all.

The absence of consistent or uniform standards for privacy and security obstructs the flow of information among countries *(transborder data flows)*. The European Union, for one, has taken steps to not only overcome this problem but also protect the rights of individuals. The EU data protection laws are stricter than the U.S. laws and therefore could create problems for the U.S.-based multinational corporations, which could face lawsuits for privacy violations.

On May 25, 2018, the *General Data Protection Regulation (GDPR)*, the world's strongest data protection laws, went into effect in the European Union. The GDPR replaced the 1995 *Data Protection Directive* .

The GDPR modernized laws that protect the personal information of individuals because previous data protection laws across Europe could not keep pace with rapid technological changes. The GDPR changed how businesses and public-sector organizations manage their customers' information. The regulation also increased the rights of individuals and gave them more control over their own information.

The GDPR covers both personal data and sensitive personal data. *Personal data* include information that can be used to identify a person, such as a name, address, Internet Protocol address, and many other pieces of information. *Sensitive personal data* encompass genetic data, racial information, information about religious and political views, sexual orientation, and trade union membership, among others.

The GDPR applies to *data controllers*, which are the organizations that have relationships with data subjects, and *data processors*, which are organizations that work for data controllers and that process personal data on the controllers' behalf. The GDPR defined a *natural person* as a living human being and a *data subject* as a human being whose data an organization has or processes.

The GDPR states that data controllers and data processors should keep minimal data on each data subject, secure it properly, ensure that it is accurate, and retain the data for just as long as it is needed. The GDPR also covers individuals' rights, which include the following:

- The right to know what organizations are doing with their data.
- The right to ask, at any time, for copies of all the data that organizations have about them.
- The right to know an organization's justification for why it has their data and how long it is planning to keep those data.

- The right to have their data corrected, if needed.
- The right to have their data deleted. This provision is called the "right to be forgotten."

The GDPR provides the ability for regulators to fine businesses that do not comply with the regulation. Specifically, regulators can fine an organization for the following reasons:

- If it does not correctly process an individual's data
- If it experiences a security breach
- If it is required to have but does not have a data protection officer

The GDPR is having negative consequences. Consider these problems:

- PriceWaterHouseCoopers notes that over 40 percent of companies, including U.S. firms with a data presence in the European Union, have spent $10 million in compliance efforts.
- According to Ernst & Young, companies spent an average of $1.8 million on GDPR compliance in 2018.
- According to an October 2018 survey, about half of respondent companies appointed a data protection officer for compliance purposes only even though the role does not serve a valuable business function.

The transfer of data into and out of a nation without the knowledge of either the authorities or the individuals involved raises a number of privacy issues. Whose laws have jurisdiction when records are stored in a different country for reprocessing or retransmission purposes? For example, if data are transmitted by a Polish company through a U.S. satellite to a British corporation, which country's privacy laws control the data, and at what points in the transmission? Questions like these will become more complicated and frequent as time goes on. Governments must make an effort to develop laws and standards to cope with rapidly changing information technologies to solve some of these privacy issues.

The United States and the European Union share the goal of privacy protection for their citizens, but the United States takes a different approach. To bridge the different privacy approaches, the U.S. Department of Commerce, in consultation with the European Union, developed a "safe harbor" framework to regulate the way that the U.S. companies export and handle the personal data (e.g., names and addresses) of European citizens. See **www.export.gov/safeharbor** and **www.ec.europa.eu/justice_home/fsj/privacy/index_en.htm**.

Before you go on . . .

1. Describe the issue of privacy as it is affected by IT.
2. Discuss how privacy issues can impact transborder data flows.

What's in IT for me?

`ACCT` For the Accounting Major

Public companies, their accountants, and their auditors have significant ethical responsibilities. Accountants now are being held professionally and personally responsible for increasing the transparency of transactions and assuring compliance with Generally Accepted Accounting Principles (GAAP). In fact, regulatory agencies, such as the Securities and Exchange Commission (SEC) and the Public Company Accounting Oversight Board (PCAOB), require accounting departments to adhere to strict ethical principles.

`FIN` For the Finance Major

As a result of global regulatory requirements and the passage of Sarbanes–Oxley, financial managers must follow strict ethical guidelines. They are responsible for full, fair, accurate, timely, and understandable disclosure in all financial reports and documents that their companies submit to the SEC and in all other public financial reports. Furthermore, financial managers are responsible for compliance with all applicable governmental laws, rules, and regulations.

MKT For the Marketing Major

Marketing professionals have new opportunities to collect data on their customers, for example, through business-to-consumer electronic commerce (discussed in Chapter 7). Business ethics clearly mandate that these data should be used only within the company and should not be sold to anyone else. Marketers do not want to be sued for invasion of privacy over data collected for the marketing database.

Customers expect their data to be properly secured. However, profit-motivated criminals want that data. Therefore, marketing managers must analyze the risks of their operations. Failure to protect corporate and customer data will cause significant public relations problems and outrage customers. Customer relationship management (discussed in Chapter 11) operations and tracking customers' online buying habits can expose unencrypted data to misuse or result in privacy violations.

POM For the Production/Operations Management Major

POM professionals decide whether to outsource (or offshore) manufacturing operations. In some cases, these operations are sent overseas to countries that do not have strict labor laws. This situation raises serious ethical questions. For example, is it ethical to hire employees in countries with poor working conditions in order to reduce labor costs?

HRM For the Human Resource Management Major

Ethics is critically important to HR managers. HR policies explain the appropriate use of information technologies in the workplace. Questions such as the following can arise: Can employees use the Internet, e-mail, or chat systems for personal purposes while at work? Is it ethical to monitor employees? If so, how? How much? How often? HR managers must formulate and enforce such policies while at the same time maintaining trusting relationships between employees and management.

MIS For the MIS Major

Ethics might be more important for MIS personnel than for anyone else in the organization because these individuals have control of the information assets. They also have control over a huge amount of the employees' personal information. As a result, the MIS function must be held to the highest ethical standards.

Summary

3.1. Describe ethics, its three fundamental tenets, and the four categories of ethical issues related to information technology.

Ethics refers to the principles of right and wrong that individuals use to make choices that guide their behavior.

Fundamental tenets of ethics include responsibility, accountability, and liability. Responsibility means that you accept the consequences of your decisions and actions. Accountability refers to determining who is responsible for actions that were taken. Liability is a legal concept that gives individuals the right to recover the damages done to them by other individuals, organizations, or systems.

The major ethical issues related to IT are privacy, accuracy, property (including intellectual property), and access to information. Privacy may be violated when data are held in databases or transmitted over networks. Privacy policies that address issues of data collection, data accuracy, and data confidentiality can help organizations avoid legal problems.

3.2. Discuss at least one potential threat to the privacy of the data stored in each of three places that store personal data.

Privacy is the right to be left alone and to be free of unreasonable personal intrusions. Threats to privacy include advances in information technologies, electronic surveillance, personal information in databases, Internet bulletin boards, newsgroups, and social networking sites. The privacy threat in Internet bulletin boards, newsgroups, and social networking sites is that you might post too much personal information that many unknown people can see.

Chapter Glossary

accountability A tenet of ethics that refers to determining who is responsible for actions that were taken.

code of ethics A collection of principles intended to guide decision making by members of an organization.

digital dossier An electronic description of an individual and his or her habits.

electronic surveillance Tracking people's activities with the aid of computers.

ethics The principles of right and wrong that individuals use to make choices to guide their behaviors.

information privacy The right to determine when and to what extent personal information can be gathered by or communicated to others.

liability A legal concept that gives individuals the right to recover the damages done to them by other individuals, organizations, or systems.

opt-in model A model of informed consent in which a business is prohibited from collecting any personal information unless the customer specifically authorizes it.

opt-out model A model of informed consent that permits a company to collect personal information until the customer specifically requests that the data not be collected.

privacy The right to be left alone and to be free of unreasonable personal intrusions.

privacy codes See **privacy policies**.

privacy policies (also known as privacy codes) An organization's guidelines for protecting the privacy of customers, clients, and employees.

profiling The process of forming a digital dossier.

responsibility A tenet of ethics in which you accept the consequences of your decisions and actions.

Discussion Questions

1. In 2008, the Massachusetts Bay Transportation Authority (MBTA) obtained a temporary restraining order barring three Massachusetts Institute of Technology (MIT) students from publicly displaying what they claimed to be a way to get "free subway rides for life." Specifically, the 10-day injunction prohibited the students from revealing vulnerabilities of the MBTA's fare card. The students were scheduled to present their findings in Las Vegas at the DEFCON computer hacking conference. Were the students' actions legal? Were their actions ethical? Discuss your answer from the students' perspective and then from the perspective of the MBTA.

2. Frank Abagnale, the criminal played by Leonardo DiCaprio in the motion picture *Catch Me If You Can,* ended up in prison. After he left prison, however, he worked as a consultant to many companies on matters of fraud.

   a. Why do these companies hire the perpetrators (if caught) as consultants? Is this a good idea?

   b. You are the CEO of a company. Discuss the ethical implications of hiring Frank Abagnale as a consultant.

3. Access various search engines to find information relating to the use of drones (unmanned aerial vehicles [UAVs]) for electronic surveillance purposes in the United States.

   a. Take the position favoring the use of drones for electronic surveillance.

   b. Take the position against the use of drones for electronic surveillance.

4. Research the Volkswagen "Diesel Dupe." The fundamental tenets of ethics include responsibility, accountability, and liability. Discuss each of these tenets as it applies to the Volkswagen scandal.

5. Research the Ashley Madison breach.

   a. Discuss the legality and the ethicality of the Ashley Madison website.

   b. Discuss the legality and the ethicality of the actions of the hackers who stole data from the Ashley Madison website.

   c. Discuss the legality and the ethicality of the actions of people who copied the Ashley Madison data from the Dark Web and then made the data available on the open Web.

   d. Discuss the legality and the ethicality of the reporters who used stolen data in their stories.

   e. Are there differences in your answers to the first four questions? If so, then describe them. How do you account for them?

Problem-Solving Activities

1. An information security manager routinely monitored Web surfing among her company's employees. She discovered that many employees were visiting the "sinful six" websites. (*Note:* The "sinful six" are websites with material related to pornography, gambling, hate, illegal activities, tastelessness, and violence.) She then prepared a list of the employees and their surfing histories and gave the list to management. Some managers punished their employees. Some employees, in turn, objected to the monitoring, claiming that they should have a right to privacy.

   a. Is monitoring of Web surfing by managers ethical? (It is legal.) Support your answer.

   b. Is employee Web surfing on the "sinful six" ethical? Support your answer.

   c. Is the security manager's submission of the list of abusers to management ethical? Why or why not?

   d. Is punishing the "sinful six" users ethical? Why or why not? If yes, then what types of punishment are acceptable?

   e. What should the company do in this situation? (*Note:* There are a variety of possibilities here.)

2. Access the Computer Ethics Institute's website at **www.cpsr.org/issues/ethics/cei.** The site offers the "Ten Commandments of Computer Ethics." Study these rules and decide whether any others should be added.

3. Access the Association for Computing Machinery's code of ethics for its members (see **www.acm.org/code-of-ethics**). Discuss the major points of this code. Is this code complete? Why or why not? Support your answer.

4. The Electronic Frontier Foundation (**www.eff.org**) has a mission of protecting rights and promoting freedom in the "electronic frontier." Review the organization's suggestions about how to protect your online privacy and summarize what you can do to protect yourself.

5. Access your university's guidelines for ethical computer and Internet use. Are there limitations as to the types of websites you can visit and the types of material you can view? Are you allowed to change the programs on the lab computers? Are you allowed to download software from the lab computers for your personal use? Are there rules governing the personal use of computers and e-mail?

6. Access **www.albion.com/netiquette/corerules.html**. What do you think of this code of ethics? Should it be expanded? Is it too general?

7. Access **www.cookiecentral.com** and **www.allaboutcookies.org**. Do these sites provide information that helps you protect your privacy? If so, then explain how.

8. Do you believe that a university should be allowed to monitor e-mail sent and received on university computers? Why or why not? Support your answer.

Closing Case

Axon

MIS

Axon (**www.axon.com**) develops products for the law enforcement industry. Its flagship product is Taser, a line of electroshock weapons. The company has diversified into technology products for law enforcement, including body cameras and digital evidence solutions.

In 2017, Axon announced that it will provide any police department in the United States with free body cameras, along with one year of free "data storage, training, and support." The company's goals are to dominate the body camera market, to increase the amount of video captured by law enforcement officials, and to upload these data to Axon servers.

With an estimated one-third of police departments using body cameras, police officers have been generating millions of hours of video footage. Axon stores terabytes of such video on its servers. Police agencies must continuously subscribe to this service for a monthly fee. Significantly, data from these video recordings are rarely analyzed for investigations. Axon wants to change that situation.

Axon uses machine learning systems (see Technology Guide 4) to analyze its video footage. In February 2017, the company acquired a computer vision start-up called Dextro and a computer vision team from Fossil Group. Dextro's machine learning system learns to pick out objects such as stop signs, guns, and license plates and to recognize actions, such as the difference between a jogger and a suspect fleeing the police.

Axon plans to input all of its video footage into its machine learning system and then provide insights into crimes and citizen encounters with police. The firm claims that its software will enable police agencies to automatically conceal faces to protect privacy, to extract important information, and to detect emotions and objects, all without human intervention.

However, privacy advocates have serious reservations about Axon's technology. By design, body cameras show the police point of view. Furthermore, the footage will likely be labeled by police officers rather than by civilians, meaning that machine learning systems could be taught to classify the behaviors of certain civilians as aggressive if these categorizations help to support an officer's account of an encounter.

This bias is the reason why privacy experts fear that the human decisions that shape the way the data are collected and labeled might reinforce and automate the existing biases of the criminal judicial system. Legal experts and surveillance watchdogs caution that any company that automates recommendations about threat assessments and suspicions may transform policing tactics for the worse.

Consider PredPol, the controversial predictive policing software first used in Los Angeles in 2009. PredPol uses geographic, rather than demographic, inputs to predict where nuisance crimes such as loitering will occur. However, because such crimes are already overpoliced in certain neighborhoods, the data fed to the machine learning algorithms are already biased. When police respond to these data by sending additional officers to computer-predicted loitering hot spots, the system justifies and reinforces its initial assumptions.

Facial recognition software has the potential for making body camera videos even more intrusive. A 2016 survey funded by the U.S. Department of Justice and conducted by Johns Hopkins University discovered that at least 9 of 38 manufacturers of body cameras had facial recognition capacities or had built in an option for such technology to be added later. Consider the Russian company Ntechlab (**www.ntechlab.com/**), which claims that its facial recognition software—called FindFace—is able to identify people in a crowd and determine whether they are angry, stressed, or nervous. The firm's software can monitor people for suspicious behavior by tracking their identity, age, gender, and current emotional state.

Police departments now have a vast amount of body camera video footage. Analysis of these data provides insights into which interactions with the public have been positive, which have been negative, and how individuals' actions led to each type of interaction. Axon is betting that its software tools will be useful to determine what happened and to anticipate what might happen in the future. This process is what worries privacy advocates. The question is not whether software will transform the legal and lethal limits of policing but, rather, how and for whose profits?

Integrating facial recognition software with body cameras increasingly concerns civil liberties advocates who worry about the impact of these new technologies on citizens' privacy. They warn that body cameras coupled with facial recognition software give police the ability to collect information at a distance. Therefore, officers would not need to justify a particular interaction or to find probable cause for a search, stop, or frisk. As a result, civil liberties groups are calling on police departments and legislators to implement clear policies to regulate camera footage retention, biometrics, and privacy.

State and local-level legislation has lagged in regulating who can access body camera video footage, how long this footage is stored, and who gets to see it. However, the biggest impediment to ensuring that body camera video footage remains accountable might be the manufacturers themselves.

Nondisclosure agreements allow private companies like Axon to defend their proprietary computing systems from public scrutiny. Privacy advocates emphasize that these companies (1) are not subject to state public record laws and (2) require police departments to sign contracts that they will keep the relationship and the technology secret.

Privately owned policing tactics and technology are increasingly black-boxed. (A *black box* is a system for which inputs and outputs are known, but how it works internally is not known.) Therefore, citizens will not be able to discover how they ended up on their city's list of suspicious persons or to become familiar with the logic that guides an algorithm's decisions. Furthermore, because the algorithms for these systems are not disclosed, a judge would have no basis to evaluate the likelihood of a false prediction when presented with investigative evidence about a suspect's crime.

In 2018, Axon launched its AI ethics board to guide the firm's use of artificial intelligence, particularly when applied to facial recognition. The board will discuss how Axon products might affect community policing, among other issues.

Sources: Compiled from J. Vincent and R. Brandon, "Axon Launches AI Ethics Board to Study the Dangers of Facial Recognition," *The Verge*, April 26, 2018; V. McKenzie, "The Dirty Data Feeding Predictive Police Algorithms," *The Crime Report*, August 18, 2017; J. Fingas, "Chicago Police See Less Violent Crime after Using Predictive Code," *Engadget*, August 6, 2017; T. McLaughlin, "As Shootings Soar, Chicago Police Use Technology to Predict Crime," *U.S. News & World Report*, August 5, 2017; J. Peretti, "Palantir: The 'Special Ops' Tech Giant That Wields as Much Real-World Power as Google," *The Guardian*, July 30, 2017; J. Brustein, "The Ex-Cop at the Center of Controversy over Crime-Prevention Tech," *Bloomberg*, July 10, 2017; T. Hoium, "Axon's Most Brilliant Moves in 2017 So Far," *The Motley Fool*, June 29, 2017; C. McGoogan, "Emotion Reading Technology Claims to Spot Criminals before They Act," *The Telegraph*, May 10, 2017; W. Isaac and A. Dixon, "Why Big-Data Analysis of Police Activity Is Inherently Biased," *Phys.org*, May 10, 2017; A. Kofman, "Taser Will Use Police Body Camera Videos 'to Anticipate Criminal Activity,'" *The Intercept*, April 30, 2017; A. Kofman, "Real-Time Face Recognition Threatens to Turn Cops' Body Cameras into Surveillance Machines," *The Intercept*, March 22, 2017; "TASER Makes Two Acquisitions to Create 'Axon AI,'" *PRNewswire*, February 9, 2017; A. Tarantola, "Taser Bought Two Computer Vision AI Companies," *Engadget*, February 9, 2017; M. Stroud, "Taser Plans to Livestream Police Body Camera Footage to the Cloud by 2017," *Motherboard*, July 18, 2016; and www.axon.com, accessed September 22, 2018.

Questions

1. Discuss the ethicality and the legality of body cameras being worn by police officers.

2. Discuss the ethicality and the legality of body cameras equipped with facial recognition software being worn by police officers.

3. The fundamental tenets of ethics include responsibility, accountability, and liability. Discuss each of these tenets as it applies to Axon's machine learning system.

CHAPTER 4

Information Security

CHAPTER OUTLINE	LEARNING OBJECTIVES
4.1 Introduction to Information Security	4.1 Identify the five factors that contribute to the increasing vulnerability of information resources and specific examples of each factor.
4.2 Unintentional Threats to Information Systems	4.2 Compare and contrast human mistakes and social engineering and provide a specific example of each one.
4.3 Deliberate Threats to Information Systems	4.3 Discuss the 10 types of deliberate attacks.
4.4 What Organizations Are Doing to Protect Information Resources	4.4 Describe the three risk mitigation strategies and provide an example of each one in the context of owning a home.
4.5 Information Security Controls	4.5 Identify the three major types of controls that organizations can use to protect their information resources and provide an example of each one.

Opening Case

The Equifax Breaches

The Problem

Equifax (**www.equifax.com**) is a consumer credit-reporting and credit-monitoring agency—also known as a credit bureau—that collects and aggregates data on more than 820 million individual consumers and 91 million businesses worldwide. The agency reports an annual revenue of $3.1 billion and employs more than 9,000 workers in 14 countries.

Lenders rely on the data collected by credit bureaus to help them decide whether to approve financing for homes or cars and whether to issue credit cards. In addition, many employers use credit bureaus to perform credit checks on prospective employees.

Credit-reporting businesses are designed primarily to serve banks and credit card companies, not the consumers they monitor. However, consumers do benefit from the credit bureaus because maintaining a good credit profile makes it easier to obtain a loan or a credit card.

It is very important to note that lenders do not face the same risks as consumers. To a lender, the unpaid bill on a fraudulent credit card is just one bad loan in a huge portfolio of loans—essentially the cost of doing business. In contrast, a consumer has only one identity and one reputation.

In March 2017, Equifax experienced a major security breach. Security experts noted that in early March, the company notified a small number of banking customers that it had suffered a breach and was bringing in a security firm (Mandiant; **www.fireeye.com**) to investigate. According to security analysts, that investigation did not uncover evidence that the hackers had actually accessed any customer data. Most data breach disclosure laws do not activate until there is evidence that sensitive and personally identifying information, such as Social Security numbers and birth dates, has been stolen. An Equifax spokesperson asserted that the company had complied fully with all consumer notification requirements related to the incident.

A second, much larger breach occurred in mid-May 2017. To access Equifax's systems, the attackers exploited a vulnerability in the Apache Struts Web application software. The theft obtained the names, Social Security numbers, birth dates, addresses, and, in some cases, driver's license numbers of almost 146 million individuals. This data can be enough for criminals to steal the identities of people whose credentials were stolen.

Apache had disclosed the vulnerability in its software to its customers, including Equifax, in March 2017. It had also provided clear instructions about how to repair it. Apache claims that its customers were then responsible for implementing procedures to promptly follow these instructions. Simply put, Equifax had the time and the instructions it needed to update and patch its software. The Apache Software Foundation publicly stated that, although it was sorry if attackers had exploited a bug in its software to breach Equifax, it always recommends that users regularly patch and update their software.

Equifax claimed that it discovered the incident on July 29, 2017, at which time it "acted immediately to stop the intrusion and conducted a forensic review." However, it did not disclose the breach until September 7, six weeks later. Meanwhile, the company again hired Mandiant on August 2.

In a statement, Equifax denied that the second breach was related to the March breach. However, security analysts have noted that the breaches involved the same intruders.

Adding to Equifax's problems, on August 1 and 2, regulatory filings revealed that three senior executives had sold their shares in the company worth almost $1.8 million. None of the filings listed the transactions as being part of scheduled 10b5-1 trading plans. These plans allow major insider (employee) stockholders of publicly traded corporations to sell a predetermined number of shares at a predetermined time.

One of the executives had also sold shares on May 23. A regulatory filing for that sale also did not indicate that the sale was part of a scheduled trading plan. If it was shown that those executives sold company stock with the knowledge that either or both breaches could damage the company, then they would be vulnerable to charges of insider trading. The U.S. Justice Department (**www.justice.gov**) opened a criminal investigation into the stock sales. Equifax maintained that the executives had no knowledge of either breach when they made the transactions.

An Attempt at a Solution

Equifax hired security firm Mandiant for both breaches, and the Apache vulnerability was patched after the second breach. Equifax announced the retirement of the company's chief information officer (CIO) and chief security officer on September 15, 2017. Next, CEO Richard Smith resigned on September 26. He apologized for the breach and testified at a House Energy and Commerce Committee hearing in the U.S. Congress on October 3.

Following the second breach, Equifax created a website— **www.equifaxsecurity2017.com**—where people could enter their last names along with the last six digits of their Social Security numbers to see if they were affected by the hack. Unfortunately, someone copied that website and hosted that copy at a very similar URL— **www.securityequifax2017.com**. The two websites, one real and one fake, looked the same to casual observers.

Fortunately for Equifax, the creator of the fake website, Nick Sweeting, set it up to demonstrate that Equifax should have developed its website under its corporate domain (**www.equifax.com**). Sweeting claimed that his fake website had approximately 200,000 page downloads. If Sweeting's website had really been a phishing website, then even more damage could have been done.

The Results

In March 2018, a federal grand jury indicted former Equifax CIO Jun Ying for insider trading. The U.S. Department of Justice's (DOJ; **www.doj.gov**) indictment alleged that Ying conducted Web searches inquiring about how Experian's 2015 data breach influenced its stock price. The indictment further alleged that Ying subsequently exercised all his available stock options and then sold the stock, receiving proceeds of over $950,000 and a gain of more than $480,000. In March, 2019 Ying pleaded guilty to insider trading.

As noted above, three other Equifax executives sold large amounts of Equifax stock before news of the breach became public. A special committee formed by Equifax's board of directors cleared the executives of any wrongdoing, and none of them were mentioned in the Department of Justice's complaint against Ying.

In the years after the breach, Equifax invested $200 million on data security infrastructure. To oversee the recovery process, the company hired a new Chief Information Security Officer (CISO) in February 2018. He noted that, prior to a data breach, company Chief Information Security Officers (CISOs) always had to fight for budget, trying to justify and convince people about the importance of security and risk management. After a breach, the job of the Equifax CISO became far easier because everyone knew that security is critically important.

Equifax is focusing its efforts in the following areas:

- Improving its processes for patching, vulnerability management, and digital certificate management
- Strengthening access control protections and identity management across the company
- Improving data protection across the firm's entire infrastructure
- Developing better detection and response programs to manage problems more effectively if and when they occur
- Improving data governance and reporting so that the company can offer proof of compliance and general progress in its security efforts
- Working on a major cultural shift to incorporate both preventive measures and response training across every department
- Expanding its consumer outreach and education programs

General Thoughts

Any data breach harms a company's reputation. This problem is particularly critical for Equifax because its entire business model involves providing a complete financial profile of consumers that lenders and other businesses can trust. Not only has Equifax's credibility been severely damaged, but the breach also undermines the integrity of the data collected by the other two major credit bureaus: Experian (**www.experian.com**) and TransUnion (**www.transunion.com**).

The effects of the Equifax breach make it clear that Social Security numbers are rapidly becoming an unreliable method to verify a person's identity. Once a person's Social Security number has been compromised, it is a difficult problem to fix because so many systems and applications rely on that number.

The solution to the Social Security number problem may lie in utilizing additional layers of security. For example, we might start to see security questions and one-time security codes sent via e-mail or text message to our smartphones. The problem with added security is that it is more difficult to conduct transactions over the Web—specifically, electronic commerce.

Consider the security freeze, which is the most effective way for customers who are anxious about the Equifax hack to protect themselves. If you contact a credit-reporting company and request a freeze, which you can do at each of the three companies' websites, then you are instructing the company not to provide any information when a lender contacts them in the process of opening an account. Thus, if someone tries to use your name and Social Security number to obtain a new credit card, then the application will probably be rejected. This action prevents fake credit cards from being issued in your name. It also prevents the resulting unpaid bills from ending up on your credit report and damaging your credit. When you need a loan, you can contact the credit agency and lift the freeze.

What a freeze costs is subject to state law. It is usually free to victims of identity theft. Otherwise, people who are simply being cautious might pay from $3 to $10 to set the freeze and a similar fee when they lift it. On September 12, 2017, Equifax temporarily waived freeze fees.

The freeze fees accentuate the overall consumer unfriendliness of the process. Consumers must pay a separate fee to each of the credit-reporting agencies. They then receive a PIN that they must use—again, one for each company—when they want to lift the freeze. To put a freeze in place online, consumers must verify their identity by entering their Social Security numbers, which is problematic if they are putting the freeze in place and have just discovered that these numbers have been stolen.

Once a freeze is in place, consumers must remember where they put their PINs before they apply for a loan, a credit card, a job, or an apartment. People who set freezes at Equifax immediately after the breach found that their new PIN codes were made up of the date and time they put the freeze on—as opposed to random, unguessable numbers.

By law, consumers can request one free copy of their credit reports per year from each of the three credit bureaus by accessing **www.annualcreditreport.com**. Consumer advocates would like to see everyone who was impacted by the Equifax breach request a credit freeze. In effect, freezes would become the default setting for all credit files, with everyone's credit data essentially off limits unless the consumer says otherwise. As it stands, however, the problems associated with freezes may make that solution less than appealing. However, if freezes became the norm, then credit bureaus would likely devise better ways to protect their data. For example, a smartphone app might allow you to toggle on and off access to all three of your credit files.

And the cost of the breaches for Equifax? For 2017, costs associated with the breaches totaled $164 million, with $50 million offset by insurance. Company officials projected an additional $275 million in costs for 2018, with $75 million offset by insurance.

And the bottom line for Equifax? The credit bureau's shares declined 31 percent in value from September 7 to 13, 2017. However, by July 2019, Equifax shares traded at $131 per share, down 8 percent from $141 per share just prior to the breach. Equifax reported 2018 total revenue of $3.4 billion and net income of $300 million. Interestingly, net income decreased by almost 50 percent from 2017.

And the bottom line for consumers? Regardless of security breaches at credit bureaus, consumers are not able to opt out of the bureaus.

Sources: Compiled from M. Kanell, "Ex-Equifax Exec Pleads Guilty to Insider Trading Post-Breach," *Atlanta Journal-Constitution*, March 7, 2019; L. Newman, "Equifax's Security Overhaul, a Year after Its Epic Breach," *Wired*, July 25, 2018; K. Richards, "Cost of Data Privacy Breach May Not Be Enough," *TechTarget*, April, 2018; B. Cole, "Ex-Equifax CIO's Insider Trading Indictment a Red Flag for Execs," *TechTarget*, March 16, 2018; M. Kanell, "Ex-Equifax Exec Is Arraigned and Freed; Pleads Not Guilty," *Atlanta Journal-Constitution*, March 15, 2018; L. Dignan, "Equifax Spends $87.5 Million on Data Breach, More Expenses on Deck," *ZDNet*, November 9, 2017; W. Ashford, "Equifax Breach Bigger Than First Reported," *Computer Weekly*, October 3, 2017; Z. Whittaker, "Equifax Chief Executive Steps Down after Massive Data Breach," *ZDNet*, September 26, 2017; L. Newman, "All the Ways Equifax Epically Bungled Its Breach Response," *Wired*, September 24, 2017; J. Morse, "Equifax Has Been Directing Victims to a Fake Phishing Site for Weeks," *Mashable*, September 20, 2017; M. Riley, A. Sharpe, and J. Robertson, "Equifax Suffered a Hack Almost Five Months Earlier Than the Date It Disclosed," *Bloomberg BusinessWeek*, September 18, 2017; P. Regnier and S. Woolley, "Thank You for Calling Equifax, Your Business Is Not Important to Us," *Bloomberg BusinessWeek*, September 18, 2017; B. Krebs, "Equifax Breach Response Turns Dumpster Fire," *krebsonsecurity.com*, September 17, 2017; M. Heller, "Apache Struts Vulnerability Blamed for Equifax Data Breach," *TechTarget*, September 15, 2017; A. LaVito, "Equifax Security and Information Executives to Retire," *CNBC*, September 15, 2017; Z. Whittaker, "Equifax Confirms Apache Struts Security Flaw It Failed to Patch Is to Blame for Hack," *ZDNet*, September 14, 2017; J. Scipioni, "Equifax Hack: A Timeline of Events," *Fox Business*, September 14, 2017; L. Newman, "Equifax Officially Has No Excuse," *Wired*, September 14, 2017; D. Goodin, "Failure to Patch Two-Month-Old Bug Led to Massive Equifax Breach," *Ars Technica*, September 13, 2017; M. Terekhova, "Equifax and AXA Singapore Become the Latest Victims of Cybercrime," *Business Insider*, September 11, 2017; Z. Whittaker, "Security Firm Mandiant Said to Be Helping Equifax in Hack Aftermath," *ZDNet*, September 8, 2017; M. Liedtke, "Equifax Breach Exposes 143 Million People to Identity Theft," *Associated Press*, September 8, 2017; C. Forrest, "143M Consumers at Risk in Massive Equifax Data Breach," *TechRepublic*, September 8, 2017; R. Dillet, "Here Comes the Class Action Lawsuit after Equifax's Massive Hack," *TechCrunch*, September 8, 2017; J. Surane, "Equifax Hack Exposes Peril of Credit Bureau Model," *Bloomberg BusinessWeek*, September 8, 2017; S. Profis, "Equifax Data Breach: Find Out If You Were One of 143 Million Hacked," *CNET*, September 7, 2017; L. Newman, "How to Protect Yourself from That Massive Equifax Breach," *Wired*, September 7, 2017; and www.equifax.com, accessed June 26, 2019.

Questions

1. What actions should Equifax have taken to prevent the breaches? Provide specific examples in your answer.

2. Place yourself as a victim in the Equifax breaches. What should you do when you are notified (or when you think) that your personal data has been compromised?

3. Can the three credit-reporting agencies (Equifax, Experian, and TransUnion) survive in the face of this breach? Support your answer.

4. What are the implications for the continued use of Social Security numbers as universal, unique identifiers? What measures might take the place of Social Security numbers as unique identifiers?

5. Does this case really have a solution? Why or why not?

Introduction

The cases in this chapter provide several lessons. First, it is difficult, if not impossible, for organizations to provide perfect security for their data. Second, there is a growing danger that countries are engaging in economic cyberwarfare. Third, it appears that it is impossible to secure the Internet. Information security impacts each and every one of us. In essence, our personally identifiable, private data is not secure.

The solutions for these and other related issues are not clear. As you learn about information security in the context of information technology (IT), you will acquire a better understanding of these issues, their importance, their relationships, and their trade-offs. Keep in mind that the issues involved in information security impact individuals and small organizations as well as large organizations.

Information security is especially important to small businesses. Large organizations that experience an information security problem have greater resources to both resolve and survive the problem. In contrast, small businesses have fewer resources and therefore can be more easily crippled by a data breach.

When properly used, information technologies can have enormous benefits for individuals, organizations, and entire societies. In Chapters 1 and 2, you read about diverse ways in which IT has made businesses more productive, efficient, and responsive to consumers. You also explored fields such as medicine and philanthropy in which IT has improved people's health and well-being. Unfortunately, bad actors can misuse information technologies, often with devastating consequences. Consider the following scenarios:

- Individuals can have their identities stolen.

- Organizations can have customer information stolen, leading to financial losses, erosion of customer confidence, and legal actions.

- Countries face the threats of *cyberterrorism* and *cyberwarfare*, terms for Internet-based attacks. Cyberwarfare is a critical problem for the U.S. government. In fact, President Obama signed a cyberwarfare directive in October 2012 that, for the first time, laid out specific ground rules for how and when the U.S. military can carry out offensive and defensive cyber operations against foreign threats. The directive emphasized the U.S. government's focus on cybersecurity as a top priority, a focus that continues to grow in importance.

Clearly, the misuse of information technologies has come to the forefront of any discussion of IT. The Ponemon Institute's (**www.ponemon.org**) 2019 Cost of a Data Breach study revealed that, in 2018, the global average cost of a data breach was $3.86 million and that the global average cost per lost or stolen record was $148. The institute also found that mega breaches of 50 million records cost organizations an average of $350 million. Security analysts noted that, in 2018, 5 billion records were stolen and that global cybercrime cost organizations over $600 billion. Unfortunately, security industry analysts predict that global cyber crime costs will reach $2 trillion in 2019.

The direct costs of a data breach include hiring forensic experts, notifying customers, setting up telephone hotlines to field queries from concerned or affected customers, offering free credit monitoring, and providing discounts for future products and services. The more intangible costs of a breach include the loss of business from increased customer turnover—called *customer churn*—and decreases in customer trust.

Just how bad is cybercrime today? Let's consider examples of data breaches that occurred in 2018:

- Electrical and telecommunications retailer and services company Dixons Carphone (**www.dixonscarphone.com**) was attacked in an attempt to compromise 5.9 million payment cards. Although 5.9 million cards were potentially affected, the company said that 5.8 million of them had chip and PIN protection and were safe. Therefore, approximately 105,000 payment cards with no chip and PIN protection were the only ones that were compromised.

- Athletic wear company Under Armour (**www.underarmour.com**) disclosed that data tied to its MyFitnessPal app were breached, affecting 150 million user accounts. The stolen information included user names, e-mail addresses, and encrypted passwords. The company noted that credit card data were not stolen because payment information is collected and processed separately from the fitness app.

- Hackers accessed a database of high-roller gamblers through a thermometer in an aquarium in the lobby of the casino. The criminals exploited a vulnerability in a connected thermostat (see the Internet of Things in Chapter 8) to gain access to the casino's network.
- In late June 2018, a security researcher discovered that Exactis (**www.exactis.com**), a marketing and data aggregation firm, had exposed a database that contained some 340 million individual records on a publicly accessible server; that is, the data were available to anyone who knew where to look. The leak evidently did not contain credit card information or Social Security numbers but did include phone numbers, home addresses, e-mail addresses, and individual interests and habits as well as the number, age, and gender of an individual's children.

Unfortunately, employee negligence causes many data breaches, meaning that organizational employees are a weak link in information security. It is therefore very important for you to learn about information security so that you will be better prepared when you enter the workforce.

4.1 | Introduction to Information Security

Security can be defined as the degree of protection against criminal activity, danger, damage, or loss. Following this broad definition, **information security** refers to all of the processes and policies designed to protect an organization's information and information systems (IS) from unauthorized access, use, disclosure, disruption, modification, or destruction. You have seen that information and information systems can be compromised by deliberate criminal actions and by anything that can impair the proper functioning of an organization's information systems.

Before continuing, let's consider these key concepts. Organizations collect huge amounts of information, and they employ numerous information systems that are subject to myriad threats. A **threat** to an information resource is any danger to which a system may be exposed. The **exposure** of an information resource is the harm, loss, or damage that can result if a threat compromises that resource. An information resource's **vulnerability** is the possibility that a threat will harm that resource.

Today, five key factors are contributing to the increasing vulnerability of organizational information resources, making it much more difficult to secure them:

1. Today's interconnected, interdependent, wirelessly networked business environment
2. Smaller, faster, cheaper computers and storage devices
3. Decreasing skills necessary to be a computer hacker
4. International organized crime taking over cybercrime
5. Lack of management support

The first factor is the evolution of the IT resource from mainframe only to today's highly complex, interconnected, interdependent, wirelessly networked business environment. The Internet now enables millions of computers and computer networks to communicate freely and seamlessly with one another. Organizations and individuals are exposed to a world of untrusted networks and potential attackers. In general, a *trusted network* is any network within your organization, and an *untrusted network* is any network external to your organization. Also, wireless technologies enable employees to compute, communicate, and access the Internet anywhere and at any time. Significantly, wireless is an inherently unsecure broadcast communications medium.

The second factor reflects the fact that modern computers and storage devices—for example, thumb drives or flash drives—continue to become smaller, faster, cheaper, and more portable, with greater storage capacity. These characteristics make it much easier to steal or lose a computer or a storage device that contains huge amounts of sensitive information. Also, far more people are able to afford powerful computers and connect inexpensively to the Internet, thus raising the potential of an attack on information assets.

The third factor is that the computing skills necessary to be a hacker are *decreasing*. The reason is that the Internet contains information and computer programs called *scripts* that users with limited skills can download and use to attack any information system that is connected to the Internet. (Security experts can also use these scripts for legitimate purposes, such as testing the security of various systems.)

The fourth factor is that international organized crime is taking over cybercrime. **Cybercrime** refers to illegal activities conducted over computer networks, particularly the Internet. Consulting company Accenture (**www.accenture.com**), maintains that groups of well-organized criminal organizations have taken control of a global billion-dollar crime network. The network, powered by skillful hackers, targets known software security weaknesses. These crimes are typically nonviolent; however, they are quite lucrative. Consider, for example, that losses from armed robberies average hundreds of dollars and that those from white-collar crimes average tens of thousands of dollars. In contrast, losses from computer crimes average hundreds of thousands of dollars. Furthermore, computer crimes can be committed from anywhere in the world, at any time, effectively providing an international safe haven for cybercriminals. Computer-based crimes cause billions of dollars in damages to organizations each year, including the costs of repairing information systems, lost business, and damaged reputation.

Consider the Fin7 hacking group. In just the United States alone, Fin7 has stolen (as of July 2019) more than 15 million credit card numbers from over 3,600 businesses, including Saks Fifth Avenue, Lord & Taylor department stores, Omni Hotels & Resorts, Trump Hotels, Jason's Deli, Whole Foods, Chipotle, and others.

Security analysts consider Fin7 to be a professional and disciplined organization. The group has developed its own malicious software and attack methods and has a well-funded research and testing division that helps it evade detection by virus scanners and authorities. The analysts estimate that Fin7 makes at least $50 million each month.

In August 2018, the U.S. Department of Justice announced that it had arrested three Ukrainians who were alleged to be members of the group. Authorities charged each individual with 26 felony counts, including conspiracy to commit wire fraud, computer hacking, identify theft, and others. The arrests were law enforcement's first indictments against Fin7.

The fifth and final factor is lack of management support. For the entire organization to take security policies and procedures seriously, senior managers must set the tone. Unfortunately, senior managers often do not do so. Ultimately, however, lower-level managers may be even more important. These managers are in close contact with employees every day and are thus in a better position to determine whether employees are following security procedures.

Before you go on . . .

1. Define information security.
2. Differentiate between a threat, an exposure, and a vulnerability.
3. Why are the skills needed to be a hacker decreasing?

4.2 Unintentional Threats to Information Systems

Author Lecture Videos are available exclusively in *WileyPLUS*.
Apply the Concept activities are available in the Appendix and in *WileyPLUS*.

Information systems are vulnerable to many potential hazards and threats, as you can see in **Figure 4.1**. The two major categories of threats are unintentional threats and deliberate threats. This section discusses unintentional threats, and the next section addresses deliberate threats.

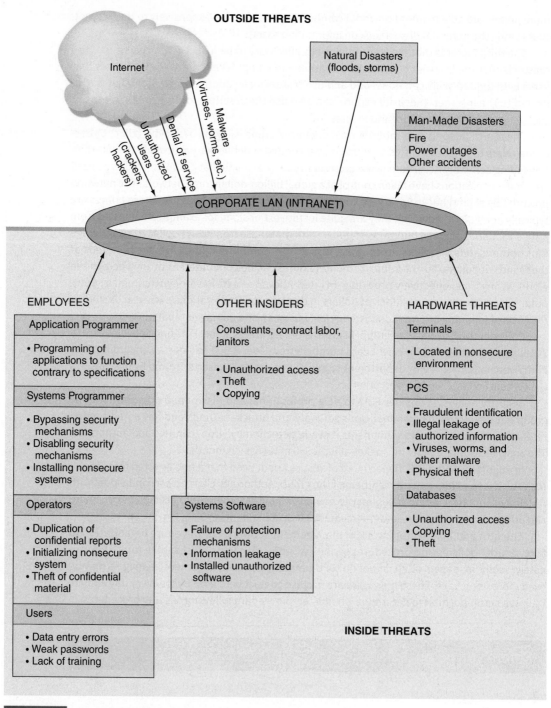

OUTSIDE THREATS

Internet

Unauthorized users (crackers, hackers)

Denial of service

Malware (viruses, worms, etc.)

Natural Disasters (floods, storms)

Man-Made Disasters
Fire
Power outages
Other accidents

CORPORATE LAN (INTRANET)

EMPLOYEES

Application Programmer
- Programming of applications to function contrary to specifications

Systems Programmer
- Bypassing security mechanisms
- Disabling security mechanisms
- Installing nonsecure systems

Operators
- Duplication of confidential reports
- Initializing nonsecure system
- Theft of confidential material

Users
- Data entry errors
- Weak passwords
- Lack of training

OTHER INSIDERS

Consultants, contract labor, janitors
- Unauthorized access
- Theft
- Copying

Systems Software
- Failure of protection mechanisms
- Information leakage
- Installed unauthorized software

HARDWARE THREATS

Terminals
- Located in nonsecure environment

PCS
- Fraudulent identification
- Illegal leakage of authorized information
- Viruses, worms, and other malware
- Physical theft

Databases
- Unauthorized access
- Copying
- Theft

INSIDE THREATS

FIGURE 4.1 **Security threats.**

Unintentional threats are acts performed without malicious intent that nevertheless represent a serious threat to information security. A major category of unintentional threats is human error.

Human Errors

Organizational employees span the breadth and depth of the organization, from mail clerks to the CEO, and across all functional areas. There are two important points to be made about employees. First, the higher the level of employee, the greater the threat he or she poses to information security. This is true because higher-level employees typically have greater access to corporate data, and they enjoy greater privileges on organizational information systems.

Second, employees in two areas of the organization pose especially significant threats to information security: human resources and information systems. Human resources employees generally have access to sensitive personal information about all employees. Likewise, IS employees not only have access to sensitive organizational data but also frequently control the means to create, store, transmit, and modify those data.

Other relevant employees include contract labor, consultants, and janitors and guards. Contract labor, such as temporary hires, may be overlooked in information security arrangements. However, these employees often have access to the company's network, information systems, and information assets. Consultants, although technically not employees, perform work for the company. Depending on the nature of their work, they may also have access to the company's network, information systems, and information assets.

Finally, janitors and guards are the most frequently ignored people in information security systems. Companies frequently outsource their security and janitorial services. As with contractors, then, these individuals work for the company, although they technically are not employees. Moreover, they are usually present when most—if not all—other employees have gone home. They typically have keys to every office, and nobody questions their presence in even the most sensitive parts of the building. In fact, an article from *2600: The Hacker Quarterly* described how to get a job as a janitor for the purpose of gaining physical access to an organization.

Human errors or mistakes by employees pose a serious problem. These errors are typically the result of laziness, carelessness, or a lack of awareness concerning information security. This lack of awareness arises from poor education and training efforts by the organization. Human mistakes manifest themselves in many different ways, as illustrated in **Table 4.1**.

TABLE 4.1   **Human Mistakes**

Human Mistake	Description and Examples
Carelessness with computing devices (e.g., laptops, tablets, smartphones)	Losing or misplacing devices, leaving them in taxis, and so on.
Carelessness with computing devices	Losing or misplacing these devices or using them carelessly so that malware is introduced into an organization's network.
Opening questionable e-mails	Opening e-mails from someone unknown or clicking on links embedded in e-mails (see *phishing attack* in Table 4.2).
Careless Internet surfing	Accessing questionable websites; can result in malware and alien software being introduced into the organization's network.
Poor password selection and use	Choosing and using weak passwords (see *strong passwords* in the "Authentication" section later in this chapter).
Carelessness with one's office	Leaving desks and filing cabinets unlocked when employees go home at night; not logging off the company network when leaving the office for any extended period of time.
Carelessness using unmanaged devices	Unmanaged devices are those outside the control of an organization's IT department and company security procedures. These devices include computers belonging to customers and business partners, and computers in the business centers of hotels.
Carelessness with discarded equipment	Discarding old computer hardware and devices without completely wiping the memory; includes computers, smartphones, BlackBerry units, and digital copiers and printers.
Careless monitoring of environmental hazards	These hazards, which include dirt, dust, humidity, and static electricity, are harmful to the operation of computing equipment.

The human errors you have just studied, although unintentional, are committed entirely by employees. However, employees also can make unintentional mistakes in response to actions by an attacker. Attackers often employ social engineering to induce individuals to make unintentional mistakes and disclose sensitive information.

Social Engineering

Social engineering is an attack in which the perpetrator uses social skills to trick or manipulate legitimate employees into providing confidential company information, such as passwords. The most common example of social engineering occurs when the attacker impersonates someone else on the telephone, such as a company manager or an IS employee. The attacker claims he forgot his password and asks the legitimate employee to give him a password to use. Other common ploys include posing as an exterminator, an air-conditioning technician, or a fire marshal. Examples of social engineering abound.

In one company, a perpetrator entered a company building wearing a company ID card that looked legitimate. He walked around and put up signs on bulletin boards reading "The help desk telephone number has been changed. The new number is 555-1234." He then exited the building and began receiving calls from legitimate employees thinking they were calling the company help desk. Naturally, the first thing the perpetrator asked for was user name and password. He now had the information necessary to access the company's information systems.

Two other social engineering techniques are tailgating and shoulder surfing. *Tailgating* is a technique designed to allow the perpetrator to enter restricted areas that are controlled with locks or card entry. The perpetrator follows closely behind a legitimate employee, and when the employee gains entry, the attacker asks him or her to "hold the door." *Shoulder surfing* occurs when a perpetrator watches an employee's computer screen over the employee's shoulder. This technique is particularly successful in public areas, such as in airports and on commuter trains and airplanes.

Before you go on . . .

1. What is an unintentional threat to an information system?
2. Provide examples of social engineering attacks other than the ones just discussed.

4.3 Deliberate Threats to Information Systems

Author Lecture Videos are available exclusively in *WileyPLUS*.
Apply the Concept activities are available in the Appendix and in *WileyPLUS*.

There are many types of deliberate threats to information systems. We provide a list of 10 common types for your convenience:

1. Espionage or trespass
2. Information extortion
3. Sabotage or vandalism
4. Theft of equipment or information
5. Identity theft
6. Compromises to intellectual property
7. Software attacks
8. Alien software
9. Supervisory control and data acquisition (SCADA) attacks
10. Cyberterrorism and cyberwarfare

Espionage or Trespass

Espionage or trespass occurs when an unauthorized individual attempts to gain illegal access to organizational information. It is important to distinguish between competitive intelligence and industrial espionage. Competitive intelligence consists of legal information gathering techniques, such as studying a company's website and press releases, attending trade shows, and similar actions. In contrast, industrial espionage crosses the legal boundary.

Information Extortion

Information extortion occurs when an attacker either threatens to steal or actually steals information from a company. The perpetrator demands payment for not stealing the information, for returning stolen information, or for agreeing not to disclose the information.

Sabotage or Vandalism

Sabotage and vandalism are deliberate acts that involve defacing an organization's website, potentially damaging the organization's image and causing its customers to lose faith. One form of online vandalism is a hacktivist or cyberactivist operation. These are cases of high-tech civil disobedience to protest the operations, policies, or actions of an organization or government agency. For example, the English Twitter account for the Arabic news network Al Jazeera was subjected to hacktivism. The Associated Press reported that supporters of Syrian President Bashar Al Assad used the account to tweet pro-Assad links and messages.

Theft of Equipment or Information

Computing devices and storage devices are becoming smaller yet more powerful with vastly increased storage. Common examples are laptops, iPads, smartphones, digital cameras, thumb drives, and iPods. As a result, these devices are becoming easier to steal and easier for attackers to use to steal information. In fact, not all attacks on organizations involve sophisticated software. As IT's About Business 4.1 illustrates, some attacks are decidedly low-tech.

IT's About Business 4.1

Hacking Hotel Keycard Locks

In the July 23, 2012, issue of *Forbes* magazine, a U.S. software engineer named Cody Brocious revealed a serious security flaw in one of the world's most common hotel keycard locks, made by Onity (**www.onity.com**). Brocious claimed that the vulnerability could unlock 10 million hotel rooms in the United States and around the world.

Each Onity lock had an opening on its underside into which hotel staff could insert a device that Onity called a "portable programmer." The device could read which keys had recently opened which doors, and it could set which master keys could open which doors. Because portable programmers also functioned as master keys themselves, they were carefully guarded by hotel owners.

Brocious had discovered that the unique cryptographic key that triggered the "unlock" command on any particular Onity lock was stored not on the hotel's portable programmer but in the lock itself. Therefore, using only $50 in hardware, anyone could build his or her own portable programmer, insert it into the port of an Onity lock, automatically retrieve the digital key from the lock's internal memory, and trigger the door to unlock, all in a fraction of a second. One week after the story appeared, Brocious presented his findings at the Black Hat hacker conference in Las Vegas. He then published the computer code for his unlocking device.

An individual named Aaron Cashatt then used that information to rob hotel guests around the United States. In fact, Cashatt found the code on Brocious's website along with a full tutorial on how to build his own lock-hacking tool. His device instantly opened about 98 percent of doors with Onity locks.

Cashatt created a small device that contained wires connected to a circuit board and a nine-volt battery. On one end of the device, a cord was attached to a plug. Cashatt inserted the plug from his device into a small, circular port located underneath all Onity locks. He then held a frayed wire from his circuit board to one end of the battery, completing an electric circuit. The bolt retracted, and a green light flashed above the door handle.

Cashatt proceeded to break into hotel rooms and steal anything he could find. To disguise himself, he wore a wig, a white hat, and gloves. To make certain that his car was not tracked, he stole license plates and switched them periodically.

Cashatt developed a system to rob hotels. First, he checked for Onity locks on hotels' outside doors. Once he was on a guest floor, he would take the room list from a housekeeper's cart to see which rooms had guests staying over and which rooms were empty. Then he or a partner would knock on one of the booked rooms. If someone answered, they moved on to another possible room. If not, they would hack the lock. Before leaving with all of that guest's possessions, Cashatt would call other booked rooms on the list to find the ones that were empty and break into those rooms next.

After numerous thefts, Cashatt ran into a problem. Onity had begun to distribute a free "fix" to its hotel customers. The fix was not a full recall or a replacement for its problematic locks. Rather, the fix consisted of cheap plastic plugs that covered the portable programmer ports on the underside of the locks. It turned out that this plug was not a fix at all.

By trial and error, Cashatt quickly identified the specific screwdriver that could release the metal panel that formed the bottom half of the lock's front cover, enabling him to reach in and remove the plug, access the port again, and then replace the plug and panel. With practice, he could complete the process in about 20 seconds. He returned to business as usual.

In early 2013, Cashatt was stealing a license plate when the car's owner returned. He fled in his car, and the owner called the police. Officers caught up with him at the hotel in which he was staying, where he had registered under his own name. Although the police issued a warrant for his arrest, he managed to escape.

The police then obtained Cashatt's entire history on Facebook, where they found photos of him and his girlfriend. In the photos, he was wearing his trademark hat. That hat linked him to every surveillance video taken during his thefts.

Cashatt was eventually found and arrested at his brother's house in California. He pleaded guilty to three hotel burglaries, the small number for which prosecutors had the most airtight evidence. He was convicted and sentenced to serve a nine-year prison term.

In all, Cashatt committed more than 100 thefts in which he stole almost half a million dollars of goods. There were no prints and no forced entry in any of the thefts, complicating the case for law enforcement officials. Eventually, his thefts triggered Operation Hotel Ca$h, a multiagency police operation aimed at catching him.

Unfortunately, Cashatt is only one chapter in a larger story. Onity plays a role as well. Even after Brocious's presentation at the Black Hat conference, the company failed to patch the security flaw in its locks. In fact, no software patch could fix the bug because Onity did not have an update mechanism for its locks. Therefore, it would have to replace every one of the circuit boards inside the locks. Onity initially announced that it would not pay for those replacements, meaning that the burden fell on the hotels themselves. Many hotels refused to pay for the fix, which cost $25 or more per lock, depending on the price of labor. Other hotels remained ignorant of the problem.

In December 2012, four months after its security flaw was first revealed, Onity made deals with some major hotel chains, including Marriott, Hyatt, and InterContinental Hotel Group, to cover all or part of the cost of fully replacing their vulnerable locks. Hotel insurance firm Petra Risk Management has stated that some number of small, family-run hotel franchises may still not have learned about the Onity lock vulnerability and therefore could be using older, flawed locks even today.

Sources: Compiled from J. Saarinen, "Hoteliers Advised to Update Keycard Room Locks," *IT News*, April 26, 2018; "The Epic Crime Spree Unleashed by Onity's Ambivalence to Its Easily Hacked Hotel Locks," *TechDirt*, September 1, 2017; "Onity Locks Still Used in Many Hotels Vulnerable," *Silent Pocket*, August 31, 2017; L. Northrup, "Hacker Broke into Hotel Rooms Electronically, Stole Customers' Stuff," *Consumerist*, August 30, 2017; A. Greenberg, "Inside an Epic Hotel Room Hacking Spree," *Wired*, August, 2017; "Onity Hotel Keycard Lock Class Action Lawsuits," *Parker Waichman*, November 27, 2016; A. Greenberg, "Hotel Lock Hack Still Being Used in Burglaries, Months after Lock Firm's Fix," *Forbes*, May 15, 2013; A. Greenberg, "Lock Firm Onity Starts to Shell Out for Security Fixes to Hotels' Hackable Locks," *Forbes*, December 6, 2012; S. Anthony, "Black Hat Hacker Gains Access to 4 Million Hotel Rooms with Arduino Microcontroller," *ExtremeTech*, July 25, 2012; A. Greenberg, "Hacker Will Expose Potential Security Flaw in Four Million Hotel Room Keycard Locks," *Forbes*, July 23, 2012; and www.onity.com, accessed September 23, 2018.

Questions

1. Did Cody Brocious do the right thing when he revealed the flaw in Onity locks at the Black Hat conference? Why or why not? If you believe that he did not do the correct thing, then what should he have done instead? Provide specific examples to support your answer.

2. Did Onity respond appropriately after Brocious revealed the flaw in the company's locks at the Black Hat conference? Why or why not? If you believe that the company's response was not appropriate, then what should Onity have done instead? Provide specific examples to support your answer.

Table 4.1 points out that one type of human mistake is carelessness with laptops and other small computers, such as tablets and, particularly, smartphones. In fact, many computing devices have been stolen because of such carelessness. The cost of a stolen device includes the loss of data, the loss of intellectual property, device replacement, legal and regulatory costs, investigation fees, and lost productivity.

One form of theft, known as *dumpster diving*, involves rummaging through commercial or residential trash to find discarded information. Paper files, letters, memos, photographs, IDs, passwords, credit cards, and other forms of information can be found in dumpsters. Unfortunately, many people never consider that the sensitive items they throw in the trash might be recovered. When this information is recovered, it can be used for fraudulent purposes.

Dumpster diving is not necessarily theft because the legality of this act varies. Because dumpsters are usually located on private premises, dumpster diving is illegal in some parts of the United States. Even in these cases, however, these laws are enforced with varying degrees of rigor.

Identity Theft

Identity theft is the deliberate assumption of another person's identity, usually to gain access to his or her financial information or to frame him or her for a crime. Techniques for illegally obtaining personal information include the following:

- Stealing mail or dumpster diving
- Stealing personal information in computer databases
- Infiltrating organizations that store large amounts of personal information (e.g., data aggregators such as Acxiom, **www.acxiom.com**)
- Impersonating a trusted organization in an electronic communication (phishing)

Recovering from identity theft is costly, time consuming, and burdensome. Victims also report problems in obtaining credit and obtaining or holding a job as well as adverse effects on insurance or credit rates. Victims also state that it is often difficult to remove negative information from their records, such as their credit reports.

Your personal information can be compromised in other ways. For example, your identity can be uncovered just by examining your searches in a search engine. The ability to analyze all searches by a single user can enable a criminal to identify who the user is and what he or she is doing. To demonstrate this fact, *the New York Times* tracked down a particular individual based solely on her AOL searches.

Compromises to Intellectual Property

Protecting intellectual property is a vital issue for people who make their livelihood in knowledge fields. **Intellectual property** is the property created by individuals or corporations that is protected under *trade secret, patent,* and *copyright* laws.

A **trade secret** is an intellectual work, such as a business plan, that is a company secret and is not based on public information. An example is the formula for Coca-Cola. A **patent** is an official document that grants the holder exclusive rights on an invention or a process for a specified period of time. **Copyright** is a statutory grant that provides the creators or owners of intellectual property with ownership of the property, also for a designated period. Current U.S. laws award patents for 20 years and copyright protection for the life of the creator plus 70 years. Owners are entitled to collect fees from anyone who wants to copy their creations. It is important to note that these are definitions under U.S. law. There is some international standardization of copyrights and patents, but it is far from total. Therefore, there can be discrepancies between U.S. law and other countries' laws.

The most common intellectual property related to IT deals with software. In 1980, the U.S. Congress amended the Copyright Act to include software. The amendment provides protection for the *source code* and *object code* of computer software, but it does not clearly identify what is eligible for protection. For example, copyright law does not protect fundamental concepts, functions, and general features, such as pull-down menus, colors, and icons. However, copying a software program without making payment to the owner—including giving a disc to a friend to install on his or her computer—is a copyright violation. Not surprisingly, this practice, called **piracy**, is a major problem for software vendors. The BSA (**www.bsa.org**) Global Software Piracy Study found that the commercial value of software theft totals billions of dollars per year.

Software Attacks

Software attacks have evolved from the early years of the computer era, when attackers used malicious software—called **malware**—to infect as many computers worldwide as possible, to the profit-driven, Web-based attacks of today. Modern cybercriminals use sophisticated, blended malware attacks, typically through the Web, to make money. **Table 4.2** displays a variety of software attacks. These attacks are grouped into three categories: remote attacks

TABLE 4.2 Types of Software Attacks

Type	Description
Remote Attacks Requiring User Action	
Virus	Segment of computer code that performs malicious actions by attaching to another computer program.
Worm	Segment of computer code that performs malicious actions and will replicate, or spread, by itself (without requiring another computer program).
Phishing attack	Phishing attacks use deception to acquire sensitive personal information by masquerading as official-looking e-mails or instant messages.
Spear phishing	Phishing attacks target large groups of people. In spear phishing attacks, the perpetrators find out as much information about an individual as possible to improve their chances that phishing techniques will obtain sensitive, personal information.
Remote Attacks Needing No User Action	
Denial-of-service attack	An attacker sends so many information requests to a target computer system that the target cannot handle them successfully and typically crashes (ceases to function).
Distributed denial-of-service attack	An attacker first takes over many computers, typically by using malicious software. These computers are called *zombies* or bots. The attacker uses these bots—which form a botnet—to deliver a coordinated stream of information requests to a target computer, causing it to crash.
Attacks by a Programmer Developing a System	
Trojan horse	Software programs that hide in other computer programs and reveal their designed behavior only when they are activated.
Back door	Typically a password, known only to the attacker, that allows him or her to access a computer system at will, without having to go through any security procedures (also called a *trap door*).
Logic bomb	A segment of computer code that is embedded within an organization's existing computer programs and is designed to activate and perform a destructive action at a certain time or date.

requiring user action, remote attacks requiring no user action, and software attacks initiated by programmers during the development of a system.

Not all cybercriminals are sophisticated, however. For example, a student at a U.S. university was sentenced to one year in prison for using keylogging software (discussed later in this chapter) to steal 750 fellow students' passwords and vote himself and four of his fraternity brothers into the student government's president and four vice president positions. The five positions would have brought the students a combined $36,000 in stipends.

The student was caught when university security personnel noticed strange activity on the campus network. Authorities identified the computer used in the activity from its Internet Protocol (IP) address. On this computer, which belonged to the student in question, authorities found a PowerPoint presentation detailing the scheme. Authorities also found research on his computer, with queries such as "how to rig an election" and "jail time for keylogger."

Once the university caught on to the scheme, the student reportedly turned back to hacking to try to get himself out of trouble. He created new Facebook accounts in the names of actual classmates, going as far as conducting fake conversations between the accounts to try to deflect the blame. Those actions contributed to the one-year prison sentence, which the judge imposed even after the student pleaded guilty and requested probation.

There are many different kinds of software attacks, with more appearing every day. Two particularly dangerous attacks are ransomware and whaling. Both of these attacks use a type of spear phishing. As you see in IT's About Business 4.2, whaling has become a huge problem very quickly.

IT's About Business 4.2

Whaling Attacks

MIS FIN HRM

A *whaling attack* (also called *whaling*) is a targeted attempt to steal sensitive information from a company, such as financial data or personal details about employees. Whaling attacks specifically target high-value individuals, such as senior executives, who have extensive access to sensitive company data. Targets are carefully chosen because of their authority and access within a company. The goal of a whaling attack is to trick an executive into revealing personal or corporate data.

Whaling attacks typically use fraudulent e-mails and fake websites that appear to be from trusted sources. The goal of whaling is to trick victims into divulging sensitive data in e-mails or visiting fake websites that mimic those of legitimate businesses and request sensitive information, such as payment or account details.

Whaling e-mails and websites are highly personalized toward their targets and often include the targets' names, job titles, and basic details that make the communications look as legitimate as possible. Attackers also use fake e-mail addresses and actual corporate logos, phone numbers, and other details to make attacks seem as if they are coming from trusted entities, such as business partners, banks, or government agencies.

Whaling attacks are more difficult to detect than typical phishing attacks because they are so highly personalized and are sent only to select targets within a company. Attackers often gather the details they need to personalize their attacks from social media, such as Facebook, Twitter, and LinkedIn, and they profile targets' company information, job details, and names of coworkers or business partners.

The problem of whaling attacks could become worse as cybercriminals utilize large databases of personal information (see the Equifax hack in this chapter's opening case) and automated software tools to personalize whaling e-mails on a mass scale. It is particularly critical that finance, payroll, and human resources departments be alert for whaling attacks because almost 50 percent of these attacks target the chief financial officer (CFO) and 25 percent target HR e-mail inboxes.

Unfortunately, there are many examples of whaling attacks. We consider five of these attacks here.

The DarkHotel Group. The DarkHotel group, which has been active since 2007, is known for cybercrimes that target high-level business travelers. The cybercriminals have traditionally targeted senior business users, such as CEOs, developers, and corporate researchers, who can access sensitive company information, such as intellectual property and source code. The group compromised hotel Wi-Fi hot spots to deliver its malware to a selected pool of victims. Although the exact methods of compromising the hot spots remain uncertain, cybersecurity experts believe that the attackers remotely exploit vulnerabilities in server software or infiltrate the hotels to gain physical access to hotel servers.

The group has continually evolved their tactics and has integrated whaling and social engineering techniques into its malware in order to conduct espionage on corporate research and development personnel, CEOs, and other high-ranking corporate officials. In the fall of 2017, DarkHotel changed its tactics again, using a new form of malware known as Inexsmar to attack political targets.

Security analysts are not certain who is being targeted by the current campaign.

DarkHotel's attacks begin with high-level whaling e-mails individually designed to be interesting and convincing to the target. The social engineering part of the attack involves a very carefully crafted whaling e-mail targeted to one person at a time.

The whaling e-mail contains the malware. To avoid arousing the victim's suspicions, the malware opens a carefully crafted decoy Word document called "Pyongyang Directory Group email SEPTEMBER 2016 RC_Office_Coordination_Associate.docx." The document displays a list of supposed contacts in the North Korean capital, with references to organizations, including FAO, UNDP, UN, UNICEF, and WFP. The document even contains warnings about spammers in an effort to make it look more legitimate.

Google and Facebook. In early 2017, reports confirmed that Google and Facebook had lost $100 million through whaling attacks. A Lithuanian cybercriminal tricked employees at the two technology companies into transferring money into bank accounts under his control. He allegedly registered a company in Latvia that had the same name as an Asian-based computer hardware manufacturer, and he opened various accounts in its name at several banks. He then sent fraudulent e-mails to Google and Facebook employees that purported to be from employees and agents of the Asian firm. The employees regularly conducted multi-million-dollar transactions with the fake company. The U.S. Department of Justice revealed that the criminal deceived both companies from at least 2013 to 2015. He was finally arrested in Lithuania in March 2017. The two companies managed to recover much of the stolen money.

Snapchat. In early 2016, social media app Snapchat (www.snapchat.com) was the victim of a successful whaling attack. A cybercriminal impersonated Snapchat's CEO and e-mailed another high-ranking employee who was fooled into revealing employee payroll information.

Seagate. In March 2016, an executive at storage company Seagate (www.seagate.com) unknowingly answered a whaling e-mail that requested the W-2 forms for all current and former employees. The incident resulted in a breach of income tax data for nearly 10,000 current and former Seagate employees, leaving them susceptible to income tax refund fraud and other identity theft schemes.

FACC Operations GmbH. FACC Operations GmbH (www.facc.com/en) is an Austrian company that produces spare parts for major aircraft manufacturers. In January 2016, the firm revealed that it had been the victim of a whaling attack in which it lost almost $50 million. The loss wiped out the manufacturer's profit for the entire year and led to an immediate 17 percent drop in its share price. In response to the attack, FACC fired its CEO and CFO.

Unfortunately, these attacks continue to succeed. Since 2013 executives in almost 80,000 companies around the world have mistakenly sent over $12 billion to fraudsters as a result of successful whaling attacks.

Sources: Compiled from D. Disparte, "Whaling Wars: A $12 Billion Financial Dragnet Targeting CFOs," *Forbes*, December 6, 2018: L. Irwin, "Whaling Attacks Increased by 200% in 2017," *IT Governance*, March 8, 2018; E. Ben-Meir, "New Whaling and Phishing Techniques Include Weaponising Google Docs," *scmagazineuk.com*, February 2, 2018; M. Phillips, "Extreme Phishing:

Cybercrooks Take Scams to the Next Level," *IntheBlack*, January 18, 2018; N. Giandomenico, "What Is a Whaling Attack? Defining and Identifying Whaling Attacks," *Digital Guardian*, July 27, 2017; C. Smith, "Hackers Are Targeting Hotel Wi-Fi with Particularly Evil Malware," *BGR.com*, July 23, 2017; P. Paganini, "DarkHotel APT Group Leverages New Methods to Target Politicians," *Security Affairs*, July 21, 2017; C. Cimpanu, "New Version of DarkHotel Malware Spotted Going after Political Figures," *BleepingComputer*, July 21, 2017; D. Palmer, "Hackers Are Using Hotel Wi-Fi to Spy on Guests, Steal Data," *ZDNet*, July 20, 2017; "DarkHotel 2.0: Inexsmar Attack Targets Politicians via Target-Specific Phishing Emails," *The Inquirer*, July 19, 2017; E. Kovacs, "DarkHotel APT Uses New Methods to Target Politicians," *SecurityWeek*, July 19, 2017; "Two Major U.S. Technology Firms 'Tricked Out of $100M,'" *BBC News*, March 22, 2017; P. Gil, "What Is Whaling? (Phishing Attack)" *LifeWire*, March 22, 2017; T. Reeve, "CEO Sacked after Aircraft Company Grounded by Whaling Attack," *SC Magazine*, May 27, 2016; L. Kelion, "DarkHotel Hackers Target Company Bosses in Hotel Rooms," *BBC*, November 11, 2014; K. Zetter, "DarkHotel: A Sophisticated New Hacking Attack Targets High-Profile Guests," *Wired*, November 10, 2014; D. Goodin, "DarkHotel Uses Bogus Crypto Certificates to Snare Wi-Fi-Connected Execs," *Ars Technica*, November 10, 2014; and "The DarkHotel APT: A Story of Unusual Hospitality," *Kaspersky Lab*, November 10, 2014.

Questions

1. What are the differences between phishing, spear phishing, and whaling attacks? Provide specific examples to support your answer.

2. What steps should organizations take to defend against whaling attacks? Are your suggested defenses against whaling attacks different from defenses that you would suggest for phishing and spear phishing attacks? If so, how would they differ?

Ransomware. Ransomware attacks are so serious that we take a more detailed look at them here. This chapter's closing case provides examples of several types of ransomware attacks, including WannaCry, Petya, and SamSam.

Ransomware, or digital extortion, blocks access to a computer system or encrypts an organization's data until the organization pays a sum of money. There are numerous types of ransomware. Victims are told to pay the ransom in bitcoin or through MoneyGram to untraceable gift cards. Attackers typically use the anonymizing Tor network (**www.torproject.org**). Some attackers are even taking a "freemium" approach: They decrypt some data for free to show victims that they can get the remainder of the encrypted data if they pay the ransom.

Ransomware attacks are growing rapidly. In 2017, global ransomware attacks extorted approximately $5 billion. As bad as these figures look, the reality is probably worse. Experts estimate that fewer than 25 percent of ransomware attacks are reported. Significantly, security analysts note that over half of the companies compromised by ransomware pay the ransom. Some 53 percent of executives report that they paid the ransom in order to recover critical files. One hospital had a slightly different take, as its executives paid the ransom even though their data was fully backed up.

On January 11, 2018, Hancock Regional Hospital in Indiana discovered that their computers had been infected with SamSam ransomware. Even though the hospital had full backups of all the SamSam-encrypted data, executives decided to pay the 4-bitcoin ransom (about $55,000 at that time). Hancock's CEO stated that they wanted to recover their systems as quickly as possible and avoid having to divert patients to other hospitals.

Methods of Attack. The most common method for ransomware attacks is spear phishing. Employees receive hundreds of e-mails every day, and many of their roles require them to download and open attachments. Therefore, many employees do so automatically. Employees' willingness to open attachments from unknown senders is allowing cybercriminals to successfully operate ransomware campaigns. Cybercriminals use a variety of traps to encourage targets to open a ransomware e-mail, ranging from offers of financial bonuses, fake online purchase receipts, job applications from prospective employees, and more. Spear phishing e-mails are carefully tailored to look as convincing as possible, so they appear no different from any other e-mail the victim might receive.

Ransomware can attack Android mobile devices, Apple computers, and Windows-based personal computers. In fact, any Internet-connected device is a potential target for ransomware. Ransomware has already infected smart televisions.

Internet of Things devices already have a poor reputation for security. As increasing numbers of these devices are installed, they are going to provide billions of new devices for cybercriminals to target. As a result, hackers could hold your connected home or connected car hostage. There is even the potential that hackers could infect medical devices, thereby putting lives directly at risk.

Ransomware continues to evolve because the criminals behind it regularly update the code with changes that allow it to avoid detection. In their updates, they add new functions, including the ability to make ransom demands in multiple languages, helping the criminals to more easily target victims around the world. Some types of ransomware scramble file names to make it more difficult for victims to identify their files.

Some ransomware developers distribute ransomware to any hacker who wants to use it. This process is called *ransomware-as-a-service*. In this type of ransomware, the original creators publish the software on the Dark Web, allowing other criminals to use the code in return for receiving 40 to 50 percent of each ransom paid.

Two recent ransomware variants have appeared. The first variant offers the decryption key to a victim if the victim provides a link to the ransomware to two other people or to companies that pay the ransom. With the second variant, hackers pretend to be job hunters in an effort to infect corporate human resources systems. The cybercriminals even submit cover letters to appear legitimate.

Rather than threatening to delete encrypted data, some cybercriminals are beginning to threaten to release those data to the public, a strategy known as *doxxing*. For organizations that deal with private and sensitive customer data, such as financial services, hospitals, and law firms, such attacks can have severe consequences. In addition to the impact to brand reputation, regulations such as the Health Information Portability and Accountability Act (HIPAA) require customer notifications and other activities that can quickly total hundreds of thousands of dollars. Compared to other industry segments, personal health information is 50 times more valuable than financial information on the Dark Web.

The Costs of Ransomware. Regardless of the size of an organization, time is money. Therefore, the longer your network and your data are unavailable due to malware, the more it will cost an organization. Ransomware takes most victims offline for at least a week; some organizations remain offline for months.

Even if you regain access to your encrypted data by paying a ransom, you will experience additional costs. To avoid future attacks, organizations must be prepared to invest in additional cybersecurity software and to pay for additional staff training. There is also the risk of customers losing trust in your company and taking their business elsewhere.

Protection against Ransomware. There are many things that organizations can do to protect against ransomware infections:

- Perhaps most important, it is imperative that all organizations provide education and training so that users are aware of spear phishing attacks and do not click on any suspicious emails or links in e-mails.

- To provide this awareness, some organizations are enabling their employees to learn from making mistakes while operating within a safe environment. One firm has developed an interactive video experience that allows its employees to make decisions on a series of events and then find out the consequences of those decisions at the end of the exercise. This process enables them to learn from their mistakes without suffering any of the actual consequences.

- Install the latest versions of software and ensure that they are patched immediately.

- Organizations must back up crucial data and information often, preferably through an encrypted cloud-based storage company or an online backup service to make copies of operating systems and data. Examples are iDrive (**www.idrive.com**), CrashPlan (**www.crashplan.com**), SOS Online Backup (**www.sosonlinebackup.com**), and Carbonite (**www.carbonite.com**). Important: The backup data storage must be connected to your system only when you are backing up the data.

  Canada's Ottawa Hospital averted a ransomware interruption because it had backed up the data encrypted on some of its computers. The hospital completely erased the hard drives of the infected computers, restored them, and returned them to service.

- Employ a real-time monitoring system that can possibly stop ransomware almost immediately. One such system, called CryptoDrop, was created by staff at the Florida Institute for Cybersecurity Research. CryptoDrop stops the ransomware encryption at the start of the process, thus ensuring that victims have less reason to pay the ransom.

- Organizations can pay the ransom, even though the U.S. Federal Bureau of Investigation (FBI) advises against this practice. Many ransomware victims stated that the attackers were honoring their promise to decrypt the data if the victim complied with the terms within the specified time. This situation was an incentive for additional victims to pay the ransom rather than pursue another, generally more expensive solution. In fact, security analysts estimate that almost half of ransomware victims pay the ransom. However, organizations might find that the criminals do not release the decryption codes even if they receive a ransom payment.

  Because the potential impact resulting from lost data or the inability to access data is measured in minutes or even seconds, businesses cannot wait several days for cybercriminals to grant them access to their encrypted data. Therefore, banks are storing up bitcoin so that their customers can pay cybercriminals immediately. Bitcoin typically takes three to five days to get in stock.

- Organizations should be aware of the *No More Ransom* initiative (**www.nomoreransom.org**). This initiative was launched in 2016 by Europol (**www.europol.europa.eu**) and the Dutch National Police in collaboration with a number of cybersecurity companies. The portal offers information and advice on how to avoid falling victim to ransomware as well as free decryption tools for various types of ransomware to help victims retrieve their encrypted data. The portal is updated as often as possible to ensure that tools are available to fight the latest forms of ransomware.

  As of July, 2019, No More Ransom offered some 100 decryption tools covering many families of ransomware. These tools had decrypted tens of thousands of devices, depriving cybercriminals of millions of dollars in ransoms. The platform is available in more than 26 languages, and more than 100 partners across the public and private sectors support the initiative.

- Organizations should also be aware that individual security companies also regularly release decryption tools to counter the ongoing evolution of ransomware. Many of these companies post updates about these tools on their company blogs as soon as they have cracked the malware's code.

Software attacks have become so sophisticated that there is a very real concern about the viability of the Internet itself. IT's About Business 4.3 illustrates this problem.

IT's About Business 4.3

An Attack on the Internet

Dyn (**www.dyn.com**) is a cloud-based Internet performance management company that provides Domain Name System (DNS) services for Internet websites (see Chapter 6). Dyn is one of the companies that function as a directory service for the Internet. The DNS is a hierarchical, decentralized naming system for any resource connected to the Internet. The DNS translates the domain names that users type in, such as **www.usatoday.com**, into their numeric IP address, such as 184.50.238.11. The DNS is essential to the effective functioning of the Internet.

On October 21, 2016, the servers at Dyn began experiencing a distributed denial-of-service (DDoS) attack. This DDoS attacked the Dyn servers that make up the infrastructure needed to make Internet connections.

In a DDoS attack, the intruders first infect and then take over many computers, typically by using malicious software. These computers are called *bots*. The attacker uses these **bots**—which form a **botnet**—to deliver a coordinated stream of information requests to a target computer, causing it to crash or to cease functioning. Security experts maintain that DDoS attacks are becoming more prevalent and more sophisticated and increasingly aimed at core Internet infrastructure providers, such as Dyn.

How did the perpetrators generate this DDoS attack on Dyn? First, they delivered malicious software called Mirai through phishing e-mails. The Mirai software infected an estimated 500,000 remotely controlled Internet-connected devices—for example, surveillance cameras, closed-circuit televisions, webcams, printers, cable set-top boxes, home routers, speakers, digital thermostats, digital video recorders, and baby monitors. These relatively simple devices, which make up the Internet of Things, often do not have sophisticated security.

The attackers now had control of these Internet-connected devices, which formed a botnet. They then instructed the devices to send a flood of information requests to the Dyn servers. There were so many information requests that the Dyn servers could not handle them. As a result, the servers stopped functioning.

The DDoS attacks on Dyn were so severe that they eventually blocked or significantly slowed user access to dozens of other websites, such as Twitter, Netflix, Spotify, CNN, the *New York Times*, Reddit, Etsy, SoundCloud, and Airbnb. Millions of U.S. users were impacted, as were users in Brazil, Germany, India, Spain, and the United Kingdom.

A subsequent attack showed that it is possible to defend against a DDoS attack. In March 2018, a DDoS attack hit developer platform GitHub (**www.github.com**). It was the most powerful DDoS attack recorded at that time. GitHub struggled with intermittent outages for 10 minutes when its detection system automatically called its DDoS mitigation service, Akamai Prolexic. Prolexic took over as an intermediary, routing all the traffic coming into and out of GitHub and sent the data through Prolexic's cleaning software to weed out and block malicious packets. After eight minutes, the assault ended.

For some time, security analysts have predicted that the ballooning traffic on the Internet would cause these devices to become a huge security risk. In fact, the Internet of Things is growing faster than the ability of either the government or the technology industry to secure it. By 2017, there were nearly 7 billion connected devices around the world. Analysts estimate that by 2020, that number could increase to 50 billion.

Most security analysts maintain that the device manufacturers must be responsible for providing better security. How to actually accomplish this goal remains unclear. In just one example, China-based camera manufacturer Hangzhou Xiongmai Technology Company recalled thousands of its cameras after it was informed that the devices may have been used to create part of the botnet that attacked Dyn.

Chipmaker Qualcomm is considering using machine intelligence to improve the safety of Internet-connected devices. Security analysts at the company believe they can instruct these devices to watch for certain behaviors. For example, is the device doing something unusual? Is it communicating with some other, unexpected device?

Sources: Compiled from L. Mathew, "A Frightening New Kind of DDoS Attack Is Breaking Records," *Forbes*, March 7, 2018; L. Newman, "Github Survived the Biggest DDoS Attack Ever Recorded," *Wired*, March 1, 2018; J. Wagstaff and J. R. Wu, "After Cyber Attacks, Internet of Things Wrestles with Making Smart Devices Safer," *Reuters*, November 8, 2016; H. Edwards and M. Vella, "A Shocking Internet Attack Shows America's Vulnerability," *Time*, November 7, 2016; E. Blumenthal and E. Weise, "Hacked Home Devices Caused Massive Internet Outage," *USA Today*, October 21, 2016; B. Krebs, "DDoS on Dyn Impacts Twitter, Spotify, Reddit," *Krebs on Security*, October 21, 2016; L. Franceschi-Bicchierai, "Twitter, Reddit, Spotify Were Collateral Damage in Major Internet Attack," *Motherboard*, October 21, 2016; L. Newman, "What We Know about Friday's Massive East Coast Internet Outage," *Wired*, October 21, 2016; J. Condliffe, "Massive Internet Outage Could Be a Sign of Things to Come," *MIT Technology Review*, October 21, 2016; N. Perlroth, "Hackers Used New Weapons to Disrupt Major Websites across U.S.," *New York Times*, October 21, 2016; and E. Weise, "Internet of Things Comes Back to Bite Us as Hackers Spread Botnet Code," *USA Today*, October 3, 2016.

Questions

1. Discuss how the DDoS attack on Dyn has led some security analysts to question the long-term viability of the Internet itself.

2. What would have been the best way for Dyn to avoid the DDoS attack altogether?

Alien Software

Many personal computers have alien software, or *pestware*, running on them that the owners are unaware of. **Alien software** is clandestine software that is installed on your computer through duplicitous methods. It typically is not as malicious as viruses, worms, or Trojan horses, but it does use up valuable system resources. It can also enable other parties to track your Web surfing habits and other personal behaviors.

The vast majority of pestware is **adware**—software that causes pop-up advertisements to appear on your screen. Adware is common because it works. According to advertising agencies, for every 100 people who close a pop-up ad, 3 click on it. This "hit rate" is extremely high for Internet advertising.

Spyware is software that collects personal information about users without their consent. Two common types of spyware are keystroke loggers and screen scrapers.

Keystroke loggers, also called *keyloggers*, record both your individual keystrokes and your Internet Web browsing history. The purposes range from criminal—for example, theft of passwords and sensitive personal information such as credit card numbers—to annoying—for example, recording your Internet search history for targeted advertising.

Companies have attempted to counter keyloggers by switching to other forms of identifying users. For example, at some point, all of us have been forced to look at wavy, distorted letters and type them correctly into a box. That string of letters is called a *CAPTCHA*, and it is a test. The point of CAPTCHA is that computers cannot (yet) accurately read those distorted letters. Therefore, the fact that you can transcribe them means that you are probably not a software program run by an unauthorized person, such as a spammer. As a result, attackers have turned to *screen scrapers*, or *screen grabbers*. This software records a continuous "movie" of a screen's contents rather than simply recording keystrokes.

Spamware is pestware that uses your computer as a launch pad for spammers. **Spam** is unsolicited e-mail, usually advertising for products and services. When your computer is infected with spamware, e-mails from spammers are sent to everyone in your e-mail address book, but they appear to come from you.

Not only is spam a nuisance but it also wastes time and money. Spam costs U.S. companies billions of dollars every year. These costs arise from productivity losses, clogged e-mail systems, additional storage, user support, and antispam software. Spam can also carry viruses and worms, making it even more dangerous.

Cookies are small amounts of information that websites store on your computer, temporarily or more or less permanently. In many cases, cookies are useful and innocuous. For example, some cookies are passwords and user IDs that you do not want to retype every time you access the website that issued the cookie. Cookies are also necessary for online shopping because merchants use them for your shopping carts.

Tracking cookies, however, can be used to track your path through a website, the time you spend there, what links you click on, and other details that the company wants to record, usually for marketing purposes. Tracking cookies can also combine this information with your name, purchases, credit card information, and other personal data to develop an intrusive profile of your spending habits.

Most cookies can be read only by the party that created them. However, some companies that manage online banner advertising are, in essence, cookie-sharing rings. These companies can track information such as which pages you load and which ads you click on. They then share this information with their client websites, which may number in the thousands.

Supervisory Control and Data Acquisition (SCADA) Attacks

SCADA refers to a large-scale distributed measurement and control system. SCADA systems are used to monitor or to control chemical, physical, and transport processes, such as those used in oil refineries, water and sewage treatment plants, electrical generators, and nuclear power plants. Essentially, SCADA systems provide a link between the physical world and the electronic world.

SCADA systems consist of multiple sensors, a master computer, and communications infrastructure. The sensors connect to physical equipment. They read status data, such as the open/closed status of a switch or a valve, as well as measurements, such as pressure, flow, voltage, and current. They control the equipment by sending signals to it, such as opening or closing a switch or a valve or setting the speed of a pump. The sensors are connected in a network, and each sensor typically has an Internet address (IP address, discussed in Chapter 6). If attackers gain access to the network, then they can cause serious damage, such as disrupting the power grid over a large area or upsetting the operations of a large chemical or nuclear plant. Such actions could have catastrophic results.

As one example, in August 2017, there was a SCADA attack on a petrochemical plant in Saudi Arabia. Security experts determined that the attack was intended to cause an explosion in the facility.

The attackers used sophisticated malware called Triton to attempt to take over the plant's safety systems. These physical controllers and their associated software are designed to activate if they detect dangerous conditions, returning processes to safe levels or shutting them down via shutoff valves and pressure-release mechanisms. This attack failed because there was an error in the attackers' computer code.

About one year later, attackers used Triton software to launch another assault. This time, the attackers gained access to another Saudi Arabian plant's safety system. In July, 2019 details of the attack had not been released but security analysts think that there could have been physical damage to the plant.

Security experts have learned a great deal from these attacks. Basically, they demonstrate a level of sophistication that indicates that the attackers had government backing, though the individual attackers and the country supporting them remained unknown as of July, 2019.

Essentially, the attacks are acts of war (cyberwarfare) against the nation of Saudi Arabia. A U.S. expert on Middle East strategy at the Council on Foreign Relations stated that the attack was likely an attempt to discourage investors from becoming involved in Saudi Arabia.

Cyberterrorism and Cyberwarfare

Cyberterrorism and **cyberwarfare** refer to malicious acts in which attackers use a target's computer systems, particularly through the Internet, to cause physical, real-world harm or severe disruption, often to carry out a political agenda. The attack on Saudi Arabia is an example of cyberwarfare. These actions range from gathering data to attacking critical infrastructure, such as through SCADA systems. We treat the two types of attacks as synonymous here, even though cyberterrorism is typically carried out by individuals or groups, whereas cyberwarfare is carried out by nation-states or nonstate actors, such as terrorists.

Before you go on . . .

1. Why has the theft of computing devices become more serious over time?
2. What are the three types of software attacks?
3. Define alien software and explain why it is a serious problem.
4. What is a SCADA system? Why can attacks against SCADA systems have catastrophic consequences?

4.4 What Organizations Are Doing to Protect Information Resources

Why is stopping cybercriminals such a challenge? **Table 4.3** illustrates the many major difficulties involved in protecting information. Because organizing an appropriate defense system is so important to the entire enterprise, it is one of the major responsibilities of any prudent CIO as well as of the functional managers who control information resources. In fact, IT security is the business of *everyone* in an organization.

In addition to the problems listed in Table 4.3, another reason why information resources are difficult to protect is that the online commerce industry is not particularly willing to install safeguards that would make completing transactions more difficult or complicated. As one example, merchants could demand passwords or personal identification numbers for all credit

Author Lecture Videos are available exclusively in WileyPLUS.
Apply the Concept activities are available in the Appendix and in WileyPLUS.

TABLE 4.3   Difficulties in Protecting Information Resources

Hundreds of potential threats exist.

Computing resources may be situated in many locations.

Many individuals control or have access to information assets.

Computer networks can be located outside the organization, making them difficult to protect.

Rapid technological changes make some controls obsolete as soon as they are installed.

Many computer crimes are undetected for a long period of time, so it is difficult to learn from experience.

People tend to violate security procedures because the procedures are inconvenient.

The amount of computer knowledge necessary to commit computer crimes is usually minimal. As a matter of fact, a potential criminal can learn hacking, for free, from the Internet.

The costs of preventing hazards can be very high. Therefore, most organizations simply cannot afford to protect themselves against all possible hazards.

It is difficult to conduct a cost–benefit justification for controls before an attack occurs because it is difficult to assess the impact of a hypothetical attack.

card transactions. However, these requirements might discourage people from shopping online. For credit card companies, it is cheaper to block a stolen credit card and move on than to invest time and money prosecuting cybercriminals.

The final reason why information resources are difficult to protect is that it is extremely difficult to catch perpetrators. However, it is possible to catch attackers, albeit with great effort, time, and expense, as the following examples illustrate:

- In July 2017, the U.S. Department of Justice announced that AlphaBay and Hansa, two of the largest Dark Web marketplaces for illegal items such as drugs and guns, were shut down. Police in the United States and Europe, including the FBI, the Drug Enforcement Agency (DEA), and the Dutch National Police, partnered to close the websites. These websites operated on the Tor network (**www.torproject.org**), which helps users browse the Internet anonymously. Visitors to the websites paid using digital currencies, such as bitcoin.

- In July 2017, Russian Mark Vartanyan was sentenced to five years in prison by a U.S. district court after pleading guilty to computer fraud. Vartanyan, whose online handle was Kolypto, is believed to have helped develop, improve, and maintain the Citadel malware, which was used to steal millions of dollars by infecting 11 million computers around the world.

- In April 2017, the Justice Department announced the takedown of the Kelihos botnet one day after Spanish police arrested the botnet's alleged operator, Pyotr Levashov, in Barcelona. The botnet was used for various malicious activities, including stealing banking credentials, distributing hundreds of millions of spam e-mails, and installing ransomware and other malware.

- In December 2016, a group of international law enforcement agencies from 30 countries announced that it had taken down a botnet called Avalanche. The takedown was a four-year effort that found victims in 180 countries. Criminals had used Avalanche since 2009 to mount phishing attacks, distribute malware, and pass stolen money across international borders. The final totals for the operation were five people arrested, 221 servers taken offline, another 37 servers seized, and more than 800,000 Internet domains seized, blocked, or otherwise disrupted.

Organizations spend a great deal of time and money protecting their information resources. Before doing so, they perform risk management.

A **risk** is the probability that a threat will impact an information resource. The goal of **risk management** is to identify, control, and minimize the impact of threats. In other words, risk management seeks to reduce risk to acceptable levels. Risk management consists of three processes: risk analysis, risk mitigation, and controls evaluation.

Organizations perform risk analyses to ensure that their IS security programs are cost effective. **Risk analysis** involves three steps: (1) assessing the value of each asset being protected, (2) estimating the probability that each asset will be compromised, and (3) comparing the probable costs of the asset's being compromised with the costs of protecting that asset. The organization then considers how to mitigate the risk.

In **risk mitigation**, the organization takes concrete actions against risks. Risk mitigation has two functions: (1) implementing controls to prevent identified threats from occurring and (2) developing a means of recovery if the threat becomes a reality. There are several risk mitigation strategies that organizations can adopt. The three most common are risk acceptance, risk limitation, and risk transference.

1. **Risk acceptance:** Accept the potential risk, continue operating with no controls, and absorb any damages that occur.

2. **Risk limitation:** Limit the risk by implementing controls that minimize the impact of the threat.

3. **Risk transference:** Transfer the risk by using other means to compensate for the loss, such as by purchasing insurance.

Finally, in controls evaluation, the organization examines the costs of implementing adequate control measures against the value of those control measures. If the costs of implementing a control are greater than the value of the asset being protected, the control is not cost effective. In the next section, you will study the various controls that organizations use to protect their information resources.

Before you go on . . .

1. Describe several reasons why it is difficult to protect information resources.
2. Compare and contrast risk management and risk analysis.

4.5 Information Security Controls

To protect their information assets, organizations implement **controls**, or defense mechanisms (also called *countermeasures*). These controls are designed to protect all of the components of an information system, including data, software, hardware, and networks. Because there are so many diverse threats, organizations use layers of controls, or *defense-in-depth*.

Controls are intended to prevent accidental hazards, deter intentional acts, detect problems as early as possible, enhance damage recovery, and correct problems. Before you study controls in more detail, it is important to emphasize that the single most valuable control is user education and training. Effective and ongoing education makes every member of the organization aware of the vital importance of information security.

In this section, you will learn about three major types of controls: physical controls, access controls, and communications controls. **Figure 4.2** illustrates these controls. In addition to applying controls, organizations plan for business continuity in case of a disaster, and they

Author Lecture Videos are available exclusively in *WileyPLUS*.
Apply the Concept activities are available in the Appendix and in *WileyPLUS*.

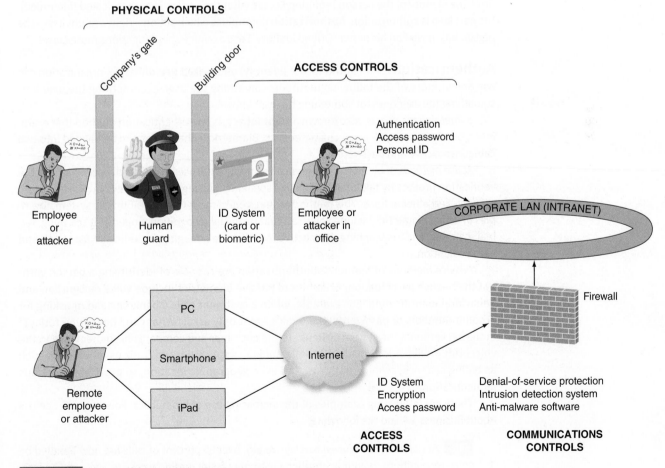

FIGURE 4.2 **Where defense mechanisms are located.**

periodically audit their information resources to detect possible threats. You will study these topics in this section as well.

Physical Controls

Physical controls prevent unauthorized individuals from gaining access to a company's facilities. Common physical controls include walls, doors, fencing, gates, locks, badges, guards, and alarm systems. More-sophisticated physical controls include pressure sensors, temperature sensors, and motion detectors. One shortcoming of physical controls is that they can be inconvenient to employees.

Guards deserve special mention because they have very difficult jobs, for at least two reasons. First, their jobs are boring and repetitive and generally do not pay well. Second, if guards perform their jobs thoroughly, the other employees harass them, particularly if they slow up the process of entering the facility.

Organizations also implement physical security measures that limit computer users to acceptable log-in times and locations. These controls also limit the number of unsuccessful log-in attempts, and they require all employees to log off their computers when they leave for the day. They also set the employees' computers to automatically log off the user after a certain period of disuse.

Access Controls

Access controls restrict unauthorized individuals from using information resources. These controls involve two major functions: authentication and authorization. **Authentication** confirms the identity of the person requiring access. After the person is authenticated (identified), the next step is authorization. **Authorization** determines which actions, rights, or privileges the person has, based on his or her verified identity. Let's examine these functions more closely.

Authentication.
To authenticate (identify) authorized personnel, an organization can use one or more of the following methods: something the user is, something the user has, something the user does, or something the user knows.

Something the user is, also known as **biometrics**, is an authentication method that examines a person's innate physical characteristics. Biometric technologies can be divided into two categories: active and passive.

Active methods of biometric authentication require the user to physically participate in the verification process by taking an action like speaking, placing a finger or eye in proximity to a scanner, and other actions. This method requires enrollment into the biometric system. Examples of active biometrics include voice recognition, facial recognition, fingerprint scanning, retinal scanning, and iris scanning. New active methods are emerging, including DNA analysis and gait recognition.

Passive methods of biometric authentication are capable of identifying a person without their active participation. Examples of passive biometrics include voice recognition and behavioral identification. For example, when a customer calls a bank, instead of asking for account numbers or passwords, the bank's agent only asks, "What can I do for you today?" In the background, the system "listens" to the customer and compares his or her voice to the voiceprint on file. Additionally, a mobile banking application can track user behavior, such as typing cadence, swiping patterns, and even geographic location, to provide continuous authentication.

There are interesting examples of the increasing use of biometrics. For example, see IT's About Business 3.4 and the following:

- **FIN** At Barclays Bank (**www.barclays.co.uk**), over 65 percent of calls are now handled by voice recognition, providing enrolled customers faster, easier access to account services. Rather than spending five minutes providing passwords and PINs and answering security questions, Barclays' customers spend just 20 seconds verifying their identities with voice recognition.

- **MIS** Chinese start-up Megvii (**www.megvii.us**) is a world leader in facial recognition software, powered by artificial intelligence. The company's main product is Face++, a platform that can detect faces and confirm people's identities with a high degree of accuracy. There are a growing number of applications for Face++. Notice that some applications of facial recognition increase security, whereas others can lead to increased surveillance by governments with subsequent loss of personal privacy. (See the discussion of China's Social Credit Score in Chapter 3.)
  - Employees at e-commerce company Alibaba can show their faces to enter their office building instead of swiping ID cards.
  - **POM** A train station in Beijing matches passengers' tickets to their government-issued IDs by scanning their faces. If their face matches their ID card photo, then the system validates their tickets, and the station gate opens.
  - The subway system in Hangzhou uses surveillance cameras that are capable of recognizing faces to spot suspected criminals. To avoid people tricking the system with a photograph, Face++ apps perform a "liveness test" that requires users to speak or move their heads.
  - A number of police departments in China are using Face++ to track criminals. In 2018, police arrested a fugitive in southeastern China after facial recognition technology helped identify him in a crowd of 50,000 people attending a pop concert.
  - China requires its social media platforms to verify users' identities before allowing them to post, and many platforms are deploying Face++ to comply.

- **POM** In March 2018, Lufthansa tested its biometric boarding system at Los Angeles International Airport. The airline's system used self-boarding gates embedded with facial recognition cameras, which cross-referenced images in real time with the Customs and Border Patrol database. The biometric system enabled Lufthansa to board 350 passengers, who did not have to show a boarding pass or passport, onto an A380 aircraft in 20 minutes.

- **FIN** Security personnel were watching activity in a bank branch. Biometric sensors had detected unusual heartbeats and body heat patterns from new customers who had entered to open an account. It turns out that those "customers" had entered the United States days before as human cargo on a ship from another country. A criminal gang was using them to orchestrate financial fraud. The sensors had detected telltale signs of stress, alerting bank personnel to the attempted fraud.

Something the user has is an authentication mechanism that includes regular ID cards, smart ID cards, and tokens. *Regular ID cards*, or *dumb cards*, typically have the person's picture and often his or her signature. *Smart ID cards* have an embedded chip that stores pertinent information about the user. (Smart ID cards used for identification differ from smart cards used in electronic commerce, which you learn about in Chapter 7. Both types of cards have embedded chips, but they are used for different purposes.) *Tokens* have embedded chips and a digital display that presents a log-in number that the employees use to access the organization's network. The number changes with each log-in.

Something the user does is an authentication mechanism that includes voice and signature recognition. In *voice recognition*, the user speaks a phrase—for example, his or her name and department—that has previously been recorded under controlled conditions. The voice recognition system matches the two voice signals. In *signature recognition*, the user signs his or her name, and the system matches this signature with one previously recorded under controlled, monitored conditions. Signature recognition systems also match the speed and the pressure of the signature.

Something the user knows is an authentication mechanism that includes passwords and passphrases. **Passwords** present a huge information security problem in all organizations. Most of us have to remember numerous passwords for different online services, and we typically must choose complicated strings of characters to make them harder to guess. Passwords must effectively manage the trade-off between convenience and security. For example, if passwords are 50 characters in length and include special symbols, they might keep your computer and its files safe, but they would be impossible to remember.

We have all bought into the idea that a password is sufficient to protect our data as long as it is sufficiently elaborate. In reality, however, passwords by themselves can no longer protect us regardless of how unique or complex we make them. In fact, security experts refer to passwords and PINs as a "double fail." First, they are easily stolen or hacked and easily forgotten. Second, they provide very poor security and a terrible customer experience at the same time.

Attackers employ a number of strategies to obtain our passwords no matter how strong they are. They can guess them, steal them (with phishing or spear phishing attacks), crack them using brute-force computation, or obtain them online. (Brute-force password cracking means that a computer system tries all possible combinations of characters until a password is discovered.) Given these problems with passwords, what are users and businesses supposed to do?

To identify authorized users more efficiently and effectively, organizations are implementing more than one type of authentication, a strategy known as *multifactor authentication*. This system is particularly important when users log in from remote locations.

Single-factor authentication, which is notoriously weak, commonly consists simply of a password. Two-factor authentication consists of a password plus one type of biometric identification, such as a fingerprint. Three-factor authentication is any combination of three authentication methods.

Multifactor authentication is useful for several reasons. For example, voice recognition is effective when a user calls from an office but is less optimal when calling from a crowded subway or busy street. Similarly, fingerprint and iris scanners are effective when users are not busy with other tasks but are less than optimal when users are driving.

Multifactor authentication enables increasingly powerful security processes. For example, a quick fingerprint scan in a mobile banking app could enable a customer to access his or her account balance or perform other low-level functions. However, a request to transfer money, pay bills, or apply for a line of credit would trigger a request for voice or iris recognition. In most cases, the more factors the system uses, the more reliable it is. However, stronger authentication is also more expensive, and, as with strong passwords, it can be irritating to users.

Several initiatives are under way to improve the authentication process under the auspices of the Fast Identity Online (FIDO) Alliance (**www.fidoalliance.org**). FIDO is an industry consortium that was created to address the inability of strong authentication devices to work together and the problems that users face in creating and remembering multiple user names and passwords.

The concept underlying FIDO is that identifiers, such as a person's fingerprint, iris scan, and the unique identifier of any USB device or contactless ring, will not be sent over the Internet. Rather, they will be checked locally. The only data that will be transferred over the Internet are cryptographic keys that cannot be reverse-engineered to steal a person's identity. Let's consider examples of security systems using biometrics:

- **FIN** Millions of customers at Bank of America, JPMorgan Chase, and HSBC routinely use fingerprints to log into their bank accounts through their mobile phones.

- **FIN** Wells Fargo allows some customers to scan their eyes with their mobile devices to log into corporate accounts.

- **FIN** USAA, which provides insurance and banking services to members of the military and their families, identifies some of its customers through their facial contours.

- Google has announced a new way of securing Android apps called Trust API. Rather than using standard passwords, Trust API uses biometrics such as facial recognition, your typing pattern, and even how you walk to help determine that you are who you say you are. Each metric contributes to an overall "trust score" that will let you unlock your apps. The program will run in the background of an Android phone, using the phone's sensors to continuously monitor the user's behavior. If the trust score falls below a certain threshold, then a user might be prompted to provide additional authentication.

If you must use passwords, make them *strong passwords*, which are more difficult for hackers to discover. However, most of the standards that we use to determine the strength of passwords are wrong, according to Bill Burr, a former employee of the National Institute of Standards and Technology (NIST) and the man responsible for originally publishing the standards.

In an August 2017 interview, Burr conceded that many of the password rules that he originated were not particularly helpful. For example, using a letter, a number, an uppercase letter, and a special character is not useful, and neither is the recommendation of changing your password every 90 days. Instead, Burr asserted that long, easy-to-remember phrases were the most valuable. Specifically, a password that contains four random words, strung together without spaces, would be easier to remember and harder to crack than passwords that follow his former guidelines.

In essence, Burr recommends the use of passphrases. A **passphrase** is a series of characters that is longer than a password but is still easy to memorize. Examples of passphrases are "maytheforcebewithyoualways" and "thisisasgoodasitgets."

Authorization. After users have been properly authenticated, the rights and privileges to which they are entitled on the organization's systems are established in a process called *authorization*. A **privilege** is a collection of related computer system operations that a user is authorized to perform. Companies typically base authorization policies on the principle of **least privilege**, which posits that users be granted the privilege for an activity only if there is a justifiable need for them to perform that activity.

Communications Controls

Communications controls (also called **network controls**) secure the movement of data across networks. Communications controls consist of firewalls, anti-malware systems, whitelisting and blacklisting, encryption, virtual private networks (VPNs), transport layer security (TLS), and employee monitoring systems.

Firewalls. A **firewall** is a system that prevents a specific type of information from moving between untrusted networks, such as the Internet, and private networks, such as your company's network. Put simply, firewalls prevent unauthorized Internet users from accessing private networks. All messages entering or leaving your company's network pass through a firewall. The firewall examines each message and blocks those that do not meet specified security rules.

Firewalls range from simple, for home use, to very complex, for organizational use. **Figure 4.3**(a) illustrates a basic firewall for a home computer. In this case, the firewall is implemented as software on the home computer. Figure 4.3(b) shows an organization that has implemented an external firewall, which faces the Internet, and an internal firewall, which

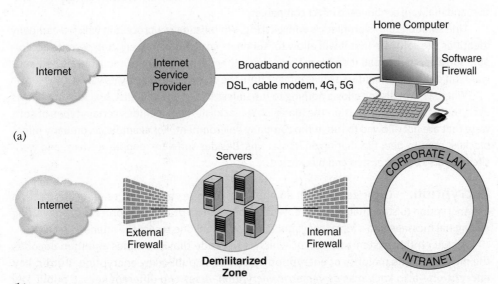

FIGURE 4.3 **(a) Basic firewall for a home computer. (b) Organization with two firewalls and a demilitarized zone.**

faces the company network. Corporate firewalls typically consist of software running on a computer dedicated to the task. A **demilitarized zone (DMZ)** is located between the two firewalls. Messages from the Internet must first pass through the external firewall. If they conform to the defined security rules, they are then sent to company servers located in the DMZ. These servers typically handle Web page requests and e-mail. Any messages designated for the company's internal network—for example, its intranet—must pass through the internal firewall, again with its own defined security rules, to gain access to the company's private network.

The danger from viruses and worms is so severe that many organizations are placing firewalls at strategic points *inside* their private networks. In this way, if a virus or worm does get through both the external and the internal firewalls, then the internal damage may be contained.

Anti-Malware Systems.

Anti-malware systems (antivirus software), also called *antivirus* or *AV* software, are software packages that attempt to identify and eliminate viruses and worms and other malicious software. AV software is implemented at the organizational level by the IS department. Hundreds of AV software packages are currently available. Among the best known are Norton AntiVirus (**www.symantec.com**), McAfee VirusScan (**www.mcafee.com**), and Trend Micro Maximum Security (**www.trendmicro.com**).

Anti-malware systems are generally reactive. Whereas firewalls filter network traffic according to categories of activities that are likely to cause problems, anti-malware systems filter traffic according to a database of specific problems. These systems create definitions, or signatures, of various types of malware and then update these signatures in their products. The anti-malware software then examines suspicious computer code to determine whether it matches a known signature. If the software identifies a match, then it removes the code. For this reason, organizations regularly update their malware definitions.

Because malware is such a serious problem, the leading vendors are rapidly developing anti-malware systems that function proactively as well as reactively. These systems evaluate behavior rather than relying entirely on signature matching. In theory, therefore, it is possible to catch malware before it can infect systems.

It is important to note that organizations must not rely only on anti-malware systems. The reason is that new types of malware appear too rapidly for such systems to keep pace. In fact, cybersecurity company McAfee (**www.mcafee.com**) reports that four new types of malware appear every second. This finding emphasizes the importance of multifactor authentication.

Whitelisting and Blacklisting.

A report by the Yankee Group (**www.yankeegroup.com**), a technology research and consulting firm now known by the name 451Research, stated that 99 percent of organizations had installed anti-malware systems but that 62 percent of those organizations still suffered malware attacks. As we have seen, anti-malware systems are usually reactive, and malware continues to infect companies.

One solution to this problem is **whitelisting**. Whitelisting is a process in which a company identifies the software that it will allow to run on its computers. Whitelisting permits acceptable software to run, and it either prevents any other software from running or lets new software run only in a quarantined environment until the company can verify its validity.

Whereas whitelisting allows nothing to run unless it is on the whitelist, **blacklisting** allows everything to run unless it is on the blacklist. A blacklist, then, includes certain types of software that are not allowed to run in the company environment. For example, a company might blacklist peer-to-peer file sharing on its systems. Besides software, people, devices, and websites can also be whitelisted and blacklisted.

Encryption.

Organizations that do not have a secure channel for sending information use encryption to stop unauthorized eavesdroppers. **Encryption** is the process of converting an original message into a form that cannot be read by anyone except the intended receiver.

All encryption systems use a key, which is the code that scrambles and then decodes the messages. The majority of encryption systems use public-key encryption. **Public-key encryption**—also known as *asymmetric encryption*—uses two different keys: a public key and a private key (see **Figure 4.4**). The public key (locking key) and the private key (the

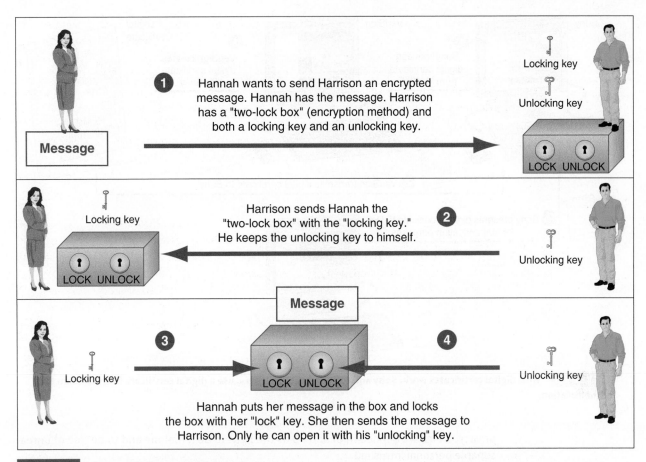

FIGURE 4.4   **How public-key encryption works.**

unlocking key) are created simultaneously using the same mathematical formula or algorithm. Because the two keys are mathematically related, the data encrypted with one key can be decrypted by using the other key. The public key is publicly available in a directory that all parties can access. The private key is kept secret, never shared with anyone, and never sent across the Internet. In this system, if Hannah wants to send a message to Harrison, she first obtains Harrison's public key (locking key), which she uses to encrypt her message (put the message in the "two-lock box"). When Harrison receives Hannah's message, he uses his private key to decrypt it (open the box).

Although this arrangement is adequate for personal information, organizations that conduct business over the Internet require a more complex system. In these cases, a third party, called a **certificate authority**, acts as a trusted intermediary between the companies. The certificate authority issues digital certificates and verifies the integrity of the certificates. A **digital certificate** is an electronic document attached to a file that certifies that the file is from the organization it claims to be from and has not been modified from its original format. As you can see in **Figure 4.5**, Sony requests a digital certificate from VeriSign, a certificate authority, and it uses this certificate when it conducts business with Dell. Note that the digital certificate contains an identification number, the issuer, validity dates, and the requester's public key. For examples of certificate authorities, see **www.entrustdatacard.com**, **www.verisign.com**, **www.secude.com**, and **www.thawte.com**.

Virtual Private Networking.   A **virtual private network (VPN)** is a private network that uses a public network (usually the Internet) to connect users. VPNs essentially integrate the global connectivity of the Internet with the security of a private network and thereby extend the reach of the organization's networks. VPNs are called *virtual* because they have no separate physical existence. They use the public Internet as their infrastructure. They are created by using logins, encryption, and other techniques to enhance the user's

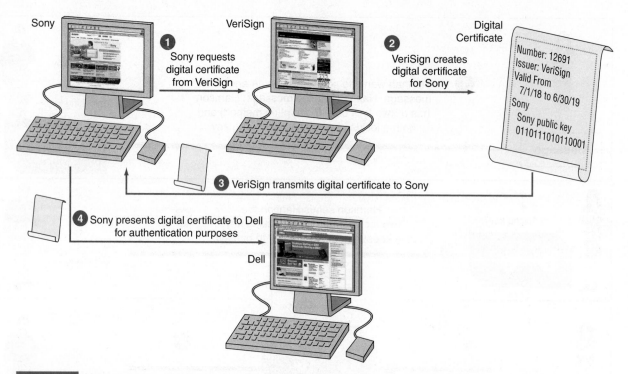

FIGURE 4.5 How digital certificates work. Sony and Dell, business partners, use a digital certificate from VeriSign for authentication.

privacy, which we defined in Chapter 3 as the right to be left alone and to be free of unreasonable personal intrusion.

VPNs have several advantages. First, they allow remote users to access the company network. Second, they provide flexibility; that is, mobile users can access the organization's network from properly configured remote devices. Third, organizations can impose their security policies through VPNs. For example, an organization may dictate that only corporate e-mail applications are available to users when they connect from unmanaged devices.

To provide secure transmissions, VPNs use a process called *tunneling*. **Tunneling** encrypts each data packet to be sent and places each encrypted packet inside another packet. In this manner, the packet can travel across the Internet with confidentiality, authentication, and integrity. **Figure 4.6** illustrates a VPN and tunneling.

Transport Layer Security. **Transport layer security (TLS)**, formerly called **secure socket layer**, or **SSL**, is an encryption standard used for secure transactions such as credit card purchases and online banking. TLS encrypts and decrypts data between a Web server and a browser end to end.

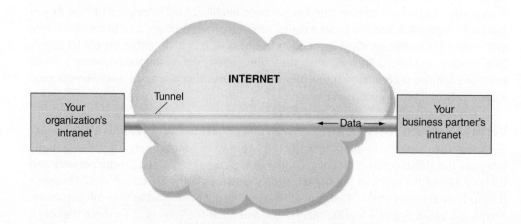

FIGURE 4.6 Virtual private network and tunneling.

TLS is indicated by a URL that begins with "https" rather than "http," and it often displays a small padlock icon in the browser's status bar. Using a padlock icon to indicate a secure connection and placing this icon in a browser's status bar are artifacts of specific browsers. Other browsers use different icons, such as a key that is either broken or whole. The important thing to remember is that browsers usually provide visual confirmation of a secure connection.

HRM **Employee Monitoring Systems.**   Many companies are taking a proactive approach to protecting their networks against what they view as one of their major security threats, namely, employee mistakes. These companies are implementing **employee monitoring systems**, which scrutinize their employees' computers, e-mail activities, and Internet surfing activities. These products are useful to identify employees who spend too much time surfing on the Internet for personal reasons, who visit questionable websites, or who download music illegally. Vendors that provide monitoring software include Veriato (**www.veriato.com**) and ForcePoint (**www.forcepoint.com**).

Business Continuity Planning

A basic security strategy for organizations is to be prepared for any eventuality. A critical element in any security system is a *business continuity plan*, also known as a *disaster recovery plan*.

POM   **Business continuity** is the chain of events linking planning to protection and to recovery. The purpose of the business continuity plan is to provide guidance to people who keep the business operating after a disaster occurs. Employees use this plan to prepare for, respond to, and recover from events that affect the security of information assets. The objective is to restore the business to normal operations as quickly as possible following an attack. The plan is intended to ensure that critical business functions continue.

In the event of a major disaster, organizations can employ several strategies for business continuity. These strategies include hot sites, warm sites, and cold sites. A *hot site* is a fully configured computer facility with all of the company's services, communications links, and physical plant operations. A hot site duplicates computing resources, peripherals, telephone systems, applications, and workstations. A *warm site* provides many of the same services and options as the hot site. However, it typically does not include the actual applications the company needs. A warm site includes computing equipment such as servers, but it often does not include user workstations. A *cold site* provides only rudimentary services and facilities, such as a building or a room with heating, air conditioning, and humidity control. This type of site provides no computer hardware or user workstations.

Hot sites reduce risk to the greatest extent, but they are the most expensive option. Conversely, cold sites reduce risk the least, but they are the least expensive option.

Information Systems Auditing

MIS Companies implement security controls to ensure that information systems function properly. These controls can be installed in the original system, or they can be added after a system is in operation. Installing controls is necessary but not sufficient to provide adequate security. People who are also responsible for security need to answer questions such as the following: Are all controls installed as intended? Are they effective? Has any breach of security occurred? If so, what actions are required to prevent future breaches?

These questions must be answered by independent and unbiased observers. Such observers perform the task of *information systems auditing*. In an IS environment, an **audit** is an examination of information systems, their inputs, outputs, and processing.

Types of Auditors and Audits.   There are two types of auditors and audits: internal and external. IS auditing is usually a part of accounting *internal auditing*, and it is frequently performed by corporate internal auditors. An *external auditor* reviews the findings of the internal audit as well as the inputs, processing, and outputs of information systems. The external audit of information systems is frequently a part of the overall external auditing performed by a certified public accounting (CPA) firm.

IS auditing considers all of the potential hazards and controls in information systems. It focuses on issues such as operations, data integrity, software applications, security and privacy, budgets and expenditures, cost control, and productivity. Guidelines are available to assist auditors in their jobs, such as those from the Information Systems Audit and Control Association (**www.isaca.org**).

How Is Auditing Executed? IS auditing procedures fall into three categories: (1) auditing around the computer, (2) auditing through the computer, and (3) auditing with the computer.

Auditing around the computer refers to verifying processing by checking for known outputs using specific inputs. This approach is most effective for systems with limited outputs. In *auditing through the computer*, auditors check inputs, outputs, and processing. They review program logic, and they test the data contained within the system. *Auditing with the computer* means using a combination of client data, auditor software, and client and auditor hardware. This approach enables the auditor to perform tasks such as simulating payroll program logic using live data.

Before you go on . . .

1. What is the single most important information security control for organizations?
2. Differentiate between authentication and authorization. Which of these processes is always performed first?
3. Compare and contrast whitelisting and blacklisting.
4. What is the purpose of a disaster recovery plan?
5. What is information systems auditing?

What's in **IT** for me?

ACCT For the Accounting Major

Public companies, their accountants, and their auditors have significant information security responsibilities. Accountants are now being held professionally responsible for reducing risk, assuring compliance, eliminating fraud, and increasing the transparency of transactions according to Generally Accepted Accounting Principles (GAAP). The Securities and Exchange Commission (SEC) and the Public Company Accounting Oversight Board (PCAOB), among other regulatory agencies, require information security, fraud prevention and detection, and internal controls over financial reporting. Forensic accounting, a combination of accounting and information security, is one of the most rapidly growing areas in accounting today.

FIN For the Finance Major

Because information security is essential to the success of organizations today, it is no longer just the concern of the CIO. As a result of global regulatory requirements and the passage of the Sarbanes–Oxley Act, responsibility for information security lies with the CEO and CFO. Consequently, all aspects of the security audit, including the security of information and information systems, are a key concern for financial managers.

CFOs and treasurers are also increasingly involved with investments in IT. They know that a security breach of any kind can have devastating financial effects on a company. Banking and financial institutions are prime targets for computer criminals. A related problem is fraud involving stocks and bonds that are sold over the Internet. Finance personnel must be aware of both the hazards and the available controls associated with these activities.

MKT For the Marketing Major

Marketing professionals have new opportunities to collect data on their customers, for example, through business-to-consumer electronic commerce. Customers expect their data to be properly secured. However, profit-motivated criminals want those data. Therefore, marketing managers must analyze the risk of their operations. Failure to protect corporate and customer data will cause significant public relations problems, make customers very angry, may lead to lawsuits, and may result in losing customers to competitors. Operations in customer relationship management and tracking customers' online buying habits can expose data to misuse (if they are not encrypted) or result in privacy violations.

POM For the Production/Operations Management Major

Every process in a company's operations—inventory purchasing, receiving, quality control, production, and shipping—can be disrupted by an IT security breach or an IT security breach at a business partner. Any weak link in supply chain management or enterprise resource management systems puts the entire chain at risk. Companies may be held liable for IT security failures that impact other companies.

HRM For the Human Resource Management Major

HR managers have responsibilities to secure confidential employee data. They must also ensure that all employees explicitly verify that they understand the company's information security policies and procedures.

MIS For the MIS Major

The MIS function provides the security infrastructure that protects the organization's information assets. This function is critical to the success of the organization, even though it is almost invisible until an attack succeeds. All application development, network deployment, and introduction of new information technologies have to be guided by IT security considerations. MIS personnel must customize the risk exposure security model to help the company identify security risks and prepare responses to security incidents and disasters.

Senior executives of publicly held companies look to the MIS function for help in meeting Sarbanes–Oxley Act requirements, particularly in detecting "significant deficiencies" or "material weaknesses" in internal controls and remediating them. Other functional areas also look to the MIS function to help them meet their security responsibilities.

Summary

4.1 Identify the five factors that contribute to the increasing vulnerability of information resources, and give specific examples of each factor.

The five factors are the following:
- Today's interconnected, interdependent, wirelessly networked business environment
  - *Example:* The Internet
- Smaller, faster, cheaper computers and storage devices
  - *Examples:* Netbooks, thumb drives, iPads
- Decreasing skills necessary to be a computer hacker
  - *Example:* Information system hacking programs circulating on the Internet
- International organized crime taking over cybercrime
  - *Example:* Organized crime has formed transnational cybercrime cartels. Because it is difficult to know exactly where cyberattacks originate, these cartels are extremely hard to bring to justice.
- Lack of management support
  - *Example:* Suppose that your company spent $10 million on information security countermeasures last year, and they did not experience any successful attacks on their information resources. Shortsighted management might conclude that the company could spend less during the next year and obtain the same results. Bad idea.

4.2 Compare and contrast human mistakes and social engineering, along with specific examples of each one.

Human mistakes are unintentional errors. However, employees can also make unintentional mistakes as a result of actions by an attacker, such as social engineering. *Social engineering* is an attack through which the perpetrator uses social skills to trick or manipulate a legitimate employee into providing confidential company information.

An example of a human mistake is tailgating. An example of social engineering is when an attacker calls an employee on the phone and impersonates a superior in the company.

4.3 Discuss the 10 types of deliberate attacks.

The 10 types of deliberate attacks are the following:

- *Espionage or trespass* occurs when an unauthorized individual attempts to gain illegal access to organizational information.
- *Information extortion* occurs when an attacker either threatens to steal or actually steals information from a company. The perpetrator demands payment for not stealing the information, for returning stolen information, or for agreeing not to disclose the information.
- *Sabotage and vandalism* are deliberate acts that involve defacing an organization's website, possibly causing the organization to lose its image and experience a loss of confidence by its customers.
- *Theft of equipment and information* is becoming a larger problem because computing devices and storage devices are becoming smaller yet more powerful with vastly increased storage, making these devices easier and more valuable to steal.
- *Identity theft* is the deliberate assumption of another person's identity, usually to gain access to his or her financial information or to frame him or her for a crime.
- Preventing *compromises to intellectual property* is a vital issue for people who make their livelihood in knowledge fields. Protecting intellectual property is particularly difficult when that property is in digital form.
- *Software attacks* occur when malicious software penetrates an organization's computer system. Today, these attacks are typically profit driven and Web based.

- *Alien software* is clandestine software that is installed on your computer through duplicitous methods. It is typically not as malicious as viruses, worms, or Trojan horses, but it does use up valuable system resources.

- *Supervisory control and data acquisition* refers to a large-scale distributed measurement and control system. SCADA systems are used to monitor or control chemical, physical, and transport processes. A *SCADA attack* attempts to compromise such a system to cause damage to the real-world processes that the system controls.

- With both *cyberterrorism* and *cyberwarfare*, attackers use a target's computer systems, particularly through the Internet, to cause physical, real-world harm or severe disruption, usually to carry out a political agenda.

4.4 Describe the three risk mitigation strategies and examples of each one in the context of owning a home.

The three risk mitigation strategies are the following:

- *Risk acceptance*, in which the organization accepts the potential risk, continues operating with no controls, and absorbs any damages that occur. If you own a home, you may decide not to insure it. Thus, you are practicing risk acceptance. Clearly, this is a bad idea.

- *Risk limitation*, in which the organization limits the risk by implementing controls that minimize the impact of threats. As a homeowner, you practice risk limitation by putting in an alarm system or cutting down weak trees near your house.

- *Risk transference*, in which the organization transfers the risk by using other means to compensate for the loss, such as by purchasing insurance. The vast majority of homeowners practice risk transference by purchasing insurance on their houses and other possessions.

4.5 Identify the three major types of controls that organizations can use to protect their information resources, and provide an example of each one.

- *Physical controls* prevent unauthorized individuals from gaining access to a company's facilities. Common physical controls include walls, doors, fencing, gates, locks, badges, guards, and alarm systems. More sophisticated physical controls include pressure sensors, temperature sensors, and motion detectors.

- *Access controls* restrict unauthorized individuals from using information resources. These controls involve two major functions: authentication and authorization. Authentication confirms the identity of the person requiring access. An example is biometrics. After the person is authenticated (identified), the next step is authorization. Authorization determines which actions, rights, or privileges the person has, based on his or her verified identity. Authorization is generally based on least privilege.

- *Communications (network) controls* secure the movement of data across networks. Communications controls consist of firewalls, anti-malware systems, whitelisting and blacklisting, encryption, virtual private networking, secure socket layer, and vulnerability management systems.

Chapter Glossary

access controls Controls that restrict unauthorized individuals from using information resources and are concerned with user identification.

adware Alien software designed to help pop-up advertisements appear on your screen.

alien software Clandestine software that is installed on your computer through duplicitous methods.

anti-malware systems (antivirus software) Software packages that attempt to identify and eliminate viruses, worms, and other malicious software.

audit An examination of information systems, their inputs and outputs, and processing.

authentication A process that determines the identity of the person requiring access.

authorization A process that determines which actions, rights, or privileges the person has, based on verified identity.

biometrics The science and technology of authentication (i.e., establishing the identity of an individual) by measuring the subject's physiological or behavioral characteristics.

blacklisting A process in which a company identifies certain types of software that are not allowed to run in the company environment.

bot A computer that has been compromised by and is under the control of a hacker.

botnet A network of computers that have been compromised by and are under control of a hacker, who is called the botmaster.

business continuity The chain of events linking planning to protection and to recovery.

certificate authority A third party that acts as a trusted intermediary between computers (and companies) by issuing digital certificates and verifying the worth and integrity of the certificates.

communications controls (also called network controls) Controls that deal with the movement of data across networks.

controls Defense mechanisms (also called *countermeasures*).

cookies Small amounts of information that websites store on your computer, temporarily or more or less permanently.

copyright A grant from a governmental authority that provides the creator of intellectual property with ownership of it for a specified period of time, currently the life of the creator plus 70 years.

cybercrime Illegal activities executed on the Internet.

cyberterrorism Can be defined as a premeditated, politically motivated attack against information, computer systems, computer programs, and data that results in violence against noncombatant targets by subnational groups or clandestine agents.

cyberwarfare War in which a country's information systems could be paralyzed from a massive attack by destructive software.

demilitarized zone (DMZ) A separate organizational local area network that is located between an organization's internal network and an external network, usually the Internet.

denial-of-service attack A cyberattack in which an attacker sends a flood of data packets to the target computer with the aim of overloading its resources.

digital certificate   An electronic document attached to a file certifying that this file is from the organization it claims to be from and has not been modified from its original format or content.

distributed denial-of-service (DDoS) attack   A denial of service attack that sends a flood of data packets from many compromised computers simultaneously.

employee monitoring systems   Systems that monitor employees' computers, e-mail activities, and Internet surfing activities.

encryption   The process of converting an original message into a form that cannot be read by anyone except the intended recipient.

exposure   The harm, loss, or damage that can result if a threat compromises an information resource.

firewall   A system (either hardware, software, or a combination of both) that prevents a specific type of information from moving between untrusted networks, such as the Internet, and private networks, such as your company's network.

identity theft   Crime in which someone uses the personal information of others to create a false identity and then uses it fraudulently.

information security   Protecting an organization's information and information systems from unauthorized access, use, disclosure, disruption, modification, or destruction.

intellectual property   The intangible property created by individuals or corporations, which is protected under trade secret, patent, and copyright laws.

least privilege   A principle that users be granted the privilege for some activity only if there is a justifiable need to grant this authorization.

logic bombs   Segments of computer code embedded within an organization's existing computer programs.

malware   Malicious software such as viruses and worms.

network controls   See communications controls.

passphrase   A series of characters that is longer than a password but is still easy to memorize.

password   A private combination of characters that only the user should know.

patent   A document that grants the holder exclusive rights on an invention or process for a specified period of time, currently 20 years.

phishing attack   An e-mail attack that uses deception to fraudulently acquire sensitive personal information by masquerading as an official-looking e-mail.

physical controls   Controls that restrict unauthorized individuals from gaining access to a company's computer facilities.

piracy   Copying a software program (other than freeware, demo software, etc.) without making payment to the owner.

privilege   A collection of related computer system operations that can be performed by users of the system.

public-key encryption (also called asymmetric encryption)   A type of encryption that uses two different keys, a public key and a private key.

ransomware (or digital extortion)   Malicious software that blocks access to a computer system or encrypts an organization's data until the organization pays a sum of money.

risk   The likelihood that a threat will occur.

risk acceptance   A strategy in which an organization accepts the potential risk, continues to operate with no controls, and absorbs any damages that occur.

risk analysis   The process by which an organization assesses the value of each asset being protected, estimates the probability that each asset might be compromised, and compares the probable costs of each being compromised with the costs of protecting it.

risk limitation   A strategy in which an organization limits its risk by implementing controls that minimize the impact of a threat.

risk management   A process that identifies, controls, and minimizes the impact of threats in an effort to reduce risk to manageable levels.

risk mitigation   A process whereby an organization takes concrete actions against risks, such as implementing controls and developing a disaster recovery plan.

risk transference   A process in which an organization transfers the risk by using other means to compensate for a loss, such as by purchasing insurance.

secure socket layer (SSL)   Now known as *transport layer security*.

security   The degree of protection against criminal activity, danger, damage, or loss.

social engineering   Getting around security systems by tricking computer users inside a company into revealing sensitive information or gaining unauthorized access privileges.

spam   Unsolicited e-mail.

spamware   Alien software that uses your computer as a launch platform for spammers.

spear phishing   An attack in which the perpetrators find out as much information about an individual as possible to improve their chances that phishing techniques will obtain sensitive, personal information.

spyware   Alien software that can record your keystrokes or capture your passwords.

threat   Any danger to which an information resource may be exposed.

trade secret   Intellectual work, such as a business plan, that is a company secret and is not based on public information.

transport layer security (TLS)   An encryption standard used for secure transactions such as credit card purchases and online banking.

Trojan horse   A software program containing a hidden function that presents a security risk.

tunneling   A process that encrypts each data packet to be sent and places each encrypted packet inside another packet.

virtual private network (VPN)   A private network that uses a public network (usually the Internet) to securely connect users by using encryption.

virus   Malicious software that can attach itself to (or "infect") other computer programs without the owner of the program being aware of the infection.

vulnerability   The possibility that an information resource will be harmed by a threat.

whitelisting   A process in which a company identifies acceptable software and permits it to run and either prevents anything else from running or lets new software run in a quarantine environment until the company can verify its validity.

worm   Destructive program that replicates itself without requiring another program to provide a safe environment for replication.

Discussion Questions

1. Why are computer systems so vulnerable?

2. Why should information security be a prime concern to management?

3. Is security a technical issue? A business issue? Both? Support your answer.

4. Compare information security in an organization with insuring a house.

5. Why are authentication and authorization important to e-commerce?

6. Why is cross-border cybercrime expanding rapidly? Discuss possible solutions.

7. What types of user authentication are used at your university or place of work? Do these measures seem to be effective? What if a higher level of authentication were implemented? Would it be worth it, or would it decrease productivity?

8. Why are federal authorities so worried about SCADA attacks?

Problem-Solving Activities

1. A critical problem is assessing how far a company is legally obligated to go in order to secure personal data. Because there is no such thing as perfect security (i.e., there is always more that one can do), resolving this question can significantly affect costs.

    a. When are security measures that a company implements sufficient to comply with its obligations?

    b. Is there any way for a company to know if its security measures are sufficient? Can you devise a method for any organization to determine if its security measures are sufficient?

2. Assume that the daily probability of a major earthquake in Los Angeles is 0.07 percent. The chance that your computer center will be damaged during such a quake is 5 percent. If the center is damaged, the estimated damage to the computer center will be $4.0 million.

    a. Calculate the expected loss in dollars.

    b. An insurance agent is willing to insure your facility for an annual fee of $25,000. Analyze the offer and discuss whether to accept it.

3. Enter **www.scambusters.org**. Find out what the organization does. Learn about e-mail scams and website scams. Report your findings.

4. Visit **www.dhs.gov/dhspublic** (Department of Homeland Security). Search the site for "National Strategy to Secure Cyberspace" and write a report on their agenda and accomplishments to date.

5. Enter **www.alltrustnetworks.com** and other vendors of biometrics. Find the devices they make that can be used to control access into information systems. Prepare a list of products and major capabilities of each vendor.

6. Software piracy is a global problem. Access the following websites: **www.bsa.org** and **www.microsoft.com/en-us/howtotell**. What can organizations do to mitigate this problem? Are some organizations dealing with the problem better than others?

7. Investigate the Sony PlayStation Network hack that occurred in April 2011.

    a. What type of attack was it?

    b. Was the success of the attack due to technology problems at Sony, management problems at Sony, or a combination of both? Provide specific examples to support your answer.

    c. Which Sony controls failed?

    d. Could the hack have been prevented? If so, how?

    e. Discuss Sony's response to the hack.

    f. Describe the damages that Sony incurred from the hack.

Closing Case

WannaCry, Petya, SamSam, and RobbinHood Ransomware

WannaCry. WannaCry caused serious problems around the world in an attack that began on May 12, 2017. WannaCry ransomware demanded $300 in bitcoins for unlocking encrypted files, a price that doubled after three days. Users were also threatened, via a ransom note on the screen, with having all of their files permanently deleted if the ransom was not paid within a week. More than 300,000 victims in more than 150 countries were infected with ransomware over a single weekend.

WannaCry attackers made only $100,000 in ransom payments. However, the global financial and economic losses from WannaCry could reach as high as $4 billion. This figure includes lost productivity as well as the costs associated with conducting forensic investigations, restoring lost data, and implementing new user training and other security measures.

The reason why WannaCry returned only $100,000 in ransom payments had to do with Marcus Hutchins. Hutchins, also known as MalwareTech, found an unregistered URL address in WannaCry's code. Suspecting that the address had something to do with how the software communicated, he registered the domain and watched as traffic from thousands of infected computers flooded into the domain. The domain turned out to be a kill switch. The malware shut itself down on any system that made contact with the URL.

Hutchins further noted that malicious programmers could easily change WannaCry's code to try to communicate with a new address. Those programmers did just that. Only a few days later, a new type of WannyCry infected thousands of systems in Russia. Let's consider some examples of WannaCry infections.

- In early 2016, the Hollywood (California) Presbyterian Medical Center (**www.hollywoodpresbyterian.com**) experienced a cyberattack that encrypted some of the hospital's crucial information. In response, the hospital turned off its network to prevent the infection from spreading, and it began negotiations with the attackers, who demanded a rumored $3 million in bitcoins as ransom. Hospital employees resorted to pen, paper, telephones, and fax machines for many tasks normally carried out by information systems. These tasks included accessing patient information and test results, documenting patient care, and transmitting laboratory work, X-rays, and CT scans. The hospital claimed that the network shutdown did not affect patient care, although the hospital did send some patients to other facilities. The hackers held the hospital hostage for 10 days until the hospital paid them approximately $17,000 worth of bitcoins to decrypt its key information.

- Over the Thanksgiving weekend in 2016, the public transit system in San Francisco would not accept riders' money. Attackers had compromised the agency's ticketing system, encrypted its data, and reportedly demanded 100 bitcoins (about $73,000 at that time) to send the decryption key. Rather than pay the attackers, the agency deactivated its ticketing machines and let riders go through the gates for free. The agency then rebooted its ticketing machines, and by Monday, the system was operating normally, even if the agency had lost two days of revenue.

- Health care organizations across the United Kingdom had their systems taken offline by the attack. As a result, patient appointments were canceled, and hospitals instructed people to avoid visiting emergency rooms unless it was absolutely necessary.

- WannaCry infected Russian banks, telephone operators, the Russian Post Office, and IT systems that supported the country's transportation infrastructure.

- WannaCry infected 29,000 Chinese organizations ranging from police stations to the huge oil and gas company PetroChina.

- Automobile manufacturers Renault and Honda had to halt production lines in several factories.

The Petya Family.   Just over a month after the WannaCry ransomware outbreak, another global ransomware attack appeared. This cyberattack first hit targets in Ukraine, including the central bank, the primary international airport, and the Chernobyl nuclear facility. The malware infected organizations across Europe, Russia, the United States, and Australia. One day after the outbreak began, at least 2,000 attacks had been recorded in more than 60 countries. Even more worrisome, security analysts noted that Petya is designed to erase information permanently, not to hold it ransom.

The attack significantly impacted thousands of organizations around the world. Here are only a few examples:

- The British health and consumer goods firm Reckitt Benckiser (**www.rb.com**) announced £100 million in lost revenue. One week after being infected, the company announced that some key applications and a number of its facilities were only partially operational. Petya disrupted the firm's manufacturing and ordering systems, severely restricting its ability to ship products.

- Both the shipping firm Maersk and the goods delivery company FedEx (**www.fedex.com**) estimated losses of $300 million due to the attack.

- The U.S. pharmaceutical firm Merck (**www.merck.com**) stated that Petya ransomware had compromised its network.

SamSam.   On March 22, 2018, a type of ransomware called SamSam encrypted the city of Atlanta's data. The attackers asked for about $51,000, paid in bitcoin.

The attack crippled some of the city's critical functions. More than one-third of Atlanta's 424 necessary programs were disabled or partly disabled, and almost 30 percent of those affected apps were deemed mission critical by the city. Consider these problems:

- City employees did not have e-mail or Internet access.

- Online bill-pay programs across multiple city departments (e.g., water and electricity) were disabled.

- Wi-Fi was shut down at the city's international airport.

- The city's municipal courts had no access to electronic records.

- Many departments, including the city jail and the police department, were operating with pen and paper.

- The city could not collect revenue from parking fines.

- The city jail had difficulties processing new inmates.

- The city stopped taking employment applications.

- Years' worth of police dashboard camera footage was destroyed.

- The city attorney's office lost 71 of its 77 computers and 10 years' worth of documents.

On the other hand, some major systems were not affected, including the 911 system, the fire department system, and the wastewater treatment system. Operations at the city's international airport were likewise not affected.

Leaked e-mails sent among the city's Department of Information Management, city council staff, and the city clerk's office suggest that city officials failed to adequately respond to multiple security warnings in the months before the ransomware attack. The e-mails show that city employees were warned several times during an eight-month span starting in June 2017 about issues involving a computer infected with ransomware. City officials received a second ransomware warning on July 17, 2017.

An earlier warning from cybersecurity firm Rendition Infosec (**www.renditioninfosec.com**) noted that Atlanta had five information systems fully compromised in April 2017. The firm noted that Atlanta did not patch its systems for more than a month after critical patches were released by Microsoft.

The ransomware attack was particularly bad news because Atlanta was trying to automate processes that humans were performing, and an increasing number of the city's systems were being connected via the Internet of Things (see Chapter 8). Such future "smart cities" digitize large parts of their infrastructure, including streetlights, traffic management systems, pollution monitoring, water systems, and many others.

And the bottom line? By July, 2019 Atlanta had spent $17 million to repair the SamSam ransomware damage.

RobbinHood.   On May 7, 2019 ransomware called RobinHood took control of some 10,000 computers of the city of Baltimore. The attackers demanded a ransom of about $80,000 in bitcoin to provide the decryption keys. City officials notified the FBI and refused to pay the ransom.

The attack shut down the city email system, disrupted real estate sales, water bills, health alerts, and parking and many other services. Emergency systems, such as police and fire department networks and the city's 911 system were not affected.

Baltimore's problem was not surprising. Government systems typically lack resources and IT expertise and operate on outdated hardware and software. Baltimore is no exception. For years, the city had failed to update its computer systems to defend against a known, critical vulnerability. That is, the successful attack worked against city computers operating with Windows software that was two years out of date.

By mid-June, 70 percent of city employee email accounts were active again. City residents could look up parking tickets in person or online and property tax bills would go out on time. However, some billing systems remained inoperative. City officials estimate that it will take months for the city to fully recover from the attack.

Unfortunately, Baltimore had no insurance to help cover the cost of a cyberattack. Therefore, the citizens will bear the cost of the more than $18 million spent trying to recover from the attack.

Sources: Compiled from K. Eiten, "Baltimore Ransomware Attack: City Inches Closer to Normal Operation," *CBS Baltimore*, June 12, 2019; N. Chokshi, "Hackers Are Holding Baltimore Hostage: How They Struck and What's Next," *The New York Times*, May 22, 2019; S. Gallagher, "Baltimore Ransomware Nightmare Could Last for Weeks More, with Big Consequences," *Ars Technica*, May 20, 2019; J. Fingas, "Atlanta Ransomware Attack May Cost Another $9.5 Million to Fix," *Engadget*, June 6, 2018; B. Freed, "Atlanta's Ransomware Attack Destroyed Years of Police Dashboard Camera Footage," *State Scoop*, June 4, 2018; R. Walters, "Lessons from the Atlanta Hack: Ransomware, Bitcoin, and Denial," *Godaddy.com*, May 4, 2018; K. Townsend, "City of Atlanta Ransomware Attack Proves Disastrously Expensive," *Security Week*, April 23, 2018; L. Kearney, "With Paper and Phones, Atlanta Struggles to Recover from Cyber Attack," *Reuters*, March 31, 2018; A. Blake, "Atlanta Warned Repeatedly of Security Risks before Ransomware Infection," *Washington Times*, March 30, 2018; S. Deere and D. Klepal, "Emails Show Atlanta Received Multiple Alerts about Cyber Threats," *Atlanta Journal-Constitution*, April 29, 2018; I. Bogost, "One of the Biggest and Most Boring Cyberattacks against an American City Yet," *The Atlantic*, March 28, 2018; "Atlanta Government Was Compromised in April 2017—Well before Last Week's Ransomware Attack," *RenditionInfosec*, March 27, 2018; A. Blinder and N. Perlroth, "A Cyberattack Hobbles Atlanta, and Security Experts Shudder," *New York Times*, March 27, 2018; M. Heller, D. McCallister, "Atlanta Working 'around the Clock' to Fight off Ransomware Attack," *NPR*, March 27, 2018; L. Kearney, "Atlanta Ransomware Attack Throws City Services into Disarray," *Reuters*, March 23, 2018; D. Palmer, "NotPetya Cyber Attack on TNT Express Cost FedEx $300M," *ZDNet*, September 20, 2017; B. Vigliarolo, "Report: 22% of SMBs Hit by Ransomware Cease Operation," *TechRepublic*, July 28, 2017; C. Osborne, "No More Ransom Project Helps Thousands of Ransomware Victims," *ZDNet*, July 27, 2017; D. Palmer, "Petya Ransomware: Companies Are Still Dealing with Aftermath of Global Cyberattack," *ZDNet*, July 24, 2017; L. Dignan, "FedEx Said TNT Petya Attack Financial Hit Will Be Material, Some Systems Won't Come Back," *ZDNet*, July 17, 2017; D. Palmer, "Petya Ransomware: Companies Count the Cost of Massive Cyber Attack," *ZDNet*, July 6, 2017; D. Palmer, "A Massive Cyberattack Is Hitting Organizations around the World," *ZDNet*, June 27, 2017; M. Reilly, "The WannaCry Ransomware Attack Could've Been a Lot Worse," *MIT Technology Review*, May 15, 2017; D. Palmer, "WannaCrypt Ransomware: Microsoft Issues Emergency Patch for Windows XP," *ZDNet*, May 13, 2017; S. Ranger, "Raonsomware Attacks Spread Worldwide," *ZDNet*, May 12, 2017; D. Palmer, "Hospitals across the UK Hit by WannaCrypt Ransomware Cyberattack, Systems Knocked Offline," *ZDNet*, May 12, 2017; D. Palmer, "Ransomware: An Executive Guide to One of the Biggest Menaces on the Web," *ZDNet*, March 7, 2017; D. Palmer, "The Real Cost of Ransomware: Attacks Take Most Victims Offline for at Least a Week," *ZDNet*, February 27, 2017; L. Newman, "Ransomware Turns to Big Targets—with Even Bigger Fallout," *Wired*, February 1, 2017; J. Stewart, "SF's Transit Hack Could've Been Way Worse—and Cities Must Prepare," *Wired*, November 28, 2016; B. Krebs, "Ransomware Getting More Targeted, Expensive," *Krebs on Security*, September 20, 2016; D. Palmer, "Two-Thirds of Companies Pay Ransomware Demands: But Not Everyone Gets Their Data Back," *ZDNet*, September 7, 2016; A. Chandler, "How Ransomware Became a Billion-Dollar Nightmare for Businesses," *The Atlantic*, September 3, 2016; D. Palmer, "Now Ransomware Is Taking Aim at Business Networks," *ZDNet*, July 15, 2016; M. Orcutt, "Hollywood Hospital's Run-In with Ransomware Is Part of an Alarming Trend in Cybercrime," *MIT Technology Review*, February 18, 2016.

Questions

1. Why has ransomware become such a serious global problem?

2. In the Atlanta and Baltimore ransomware attacks, the perpetrators asked for far less money than the two cities ended up paying to recover. Would it not have saved money and time for both cities to have paid the ransom? Why did each city not pay the ransom? Was this a good decision? Draw implications for any organization after a successful ransomware attack. Should organizations pay ransoms?

3. Are your personal digital files adequately backed up? Why or why not?

Data and Knowledge Management

Opening Case

Data from a Pacemaker Leads to an Arrest

`MIS`

On September 19, 2016, a fire broke out at Ross Compton's home in Middletown, Ohio. Compton informed law enforcement that he awoke to find his home on fire. Authorities noted that before Compton escaped from his house, he packed some of his clothes and other belongings in a suitcase. He put anything that did not fit in his suitcase in other bags. He also took his computer and the charger for his pacemaker. (A pacemaker is a small device placed in the chest or abdomen to help control abnormal heart rhythms.) He then broke through a window with his cane and threw his suitcase and bags out of it. The blaze ended up causing $400,000 of damage.

Fire department investigators determined that the fire originated from multiple locations within the house, leading them to conclude that the fire resulted from arson. In addition, investigators said Compton's house smelled of gasoline and that his account of what happened was inconsistent with the available evidence.

Investigators had to make the case for arson and insurance fraud. They realized that they had a way to corroborate how much Compton was exerting himself, and for how long, before he escaped the fire: Compton's pacemaker.

Once police learned about Compton's pacemaker, they obtained a search warrant for the data recorded on it. They believed that the data would reveal his heart rate and cardiac rhythms before, during, and after the fire. Medical technicians downloaded the data—the same data that would routinely be retrieved from a pacemaker during an appointment with a physician—from the device. Law enforcement officials then subpoenaed those records. The data did not corroborate Compton's version of the events that occurred that night.

Authorities alleged that the data revealed that Compton was awake when he claimed to be sleeping. In addition, a cardiologist reviewed the data and concluded that Compton's medical condition made it unlikely that he would have been able to collect, pack, and remove numerous large and heavy items from the house, exit his bedroom window, and carry the items to the front of his residence during the short period of time that Compton had indicated to the authorities.

In late January 2017, a Butler County, Ohio, grand jury indicted Compton on felony charges of aggravated arson and insurance fraud for allegedly starting the fire. Compton pleaded not guilty to the charges the following month.

Compton's defense attorney filed a motion to suppress the pacemaker data evidence as an unreasonable seizure of Compton's private information. Prosecutors argued that police have historically obtained personal information through search warrants and that doing so for a pacemaker should not be treated differently. For example, law enforcement can use legally obtained blood samples and medical records as evidence.

Investigators have also recently used data from other smart devices, such as steps counted by activity trackers and queries made to smart speakers, to establish how a crime was committed. In Connecticut, for example, Richard Dabate was charged with murdering his wife after police built a case based, in part, on the victim's Fitbit data. (See the opening case in Chapter 8.) Despite Compton's attorney's arguments to the contrary, Butler County Judge Charles Pater held that the data from Compton's pacemaker could be used against him in his upcoming trial.

Compton had been free on his own recognizance since his indictment, but he did not appear for a pretrial hearing in Butler County Common Pleas Court. Judge Charles Pater revoked Compton's bond. In late July 2018, Compton was back in police custody.

This case was the first in which police obtained a search warrant for a pacemaker. If a person is dependent on an embedded medical device, should the device that keeps him alive also be allowed to incriminate him in a crime? After all, the Fifth Amendment of the U.S. Constitution protects a person from being forced to incriminate himself or herself. When Ross Compton had a pacemaker installed, he, as an individual, had a constitutional right to remain silent. However, the electronic data stored in his pacemaker eventually led to his arrest and subsequent indictment on charges of arson and insurance fraud.

In Compton's case, the data were obtained from a device inside his body rather than a device in his home or worn on his wrist. In March 2019, the Butler County judge ruled that using pacemaker data was not stealing personal information. That is, data are not considered more protected or more private by virtue of its personal nature or where it is generated or stored. Defense attorneys are appealing the judge's decision to the 12th District Court of Appeals. A new trial date for Compton has not been set.

The more connected, convenient, and intelligent our devices become, the more they have the potential to expose the truth. There is nothing new about consumers using tracking and recording devices. Each day, all of us leave revealing data trails—called "data exhaust"—and prosecutors are realizing how valuable these data can be in solving crimes. In addition, new data sources are constantly emerging. For example, autonomous (self-driving) cars may record our speed, distance traveled, and locations. Homes can tell which rooms are occupied, and smart appliances such as refrigerators can track our daily routines. Significantly, all of these different types of data can be used as incriminating evidence.

These technologies represent a new frontier for criminal litigation and law enforcement. In a time when consumers constantly reveal intimate data, perhaps privacy is becoming a thing of the past.

The Compton case may be one of the first Internet of Things (see Chapter 8) prosecutions, but it certainly will not be the last. Since Compton's arrest, Ohio police departments have used similar data in two homicide investigations. If other courts accept Judge Pater's ruling on the admissibility of Compton's pacemaker data, then consumers might have to accept the reality that using smart technologies may cause them to forfeit whatever is left of their privacy.

Sources: Compiled from L. Pack, "Is Using Pacemaker Data 'Stealing Personal Information'? Judge in Middleton Arson Case Says No," *Middleton Journal-News*, March 7, 2019; L. Pack, "Arson Suspect in Unique Case Featuring Pacemaker Data Is Back in Custody," *Middleton Journal-News*, July 24, 2018; L. Pack, "His Pacemaker Led to Arson Charges. Then He Failed to Show Up for Court, so Police Are Looking for Him," *Middleton Journal-News*, March 6, 2018; D. Paul, "Your Own Pacemaker Can Now Testify Against You in Court," *Wired*, July 29, 2017; G. Ballenger, "New Form of Law Enforcement Investigation Hits Close to the Heart," *Slate*, July 19, 2017; L. Pack, "2 More Investigations Where Middletown Police Used Pacemaker Data," *Middletown Journal-News*, July 14, 2017; M. Moon, "Judge Allows Pacemaker Data to be Used in Arson Trial," *Engadget*, July 13, 2017; "Man's Pacemaker Data May Sink Him in Court," *Newser*, July 12, 2017; L. Pack, "Judge: Pacemaker Data Can Be Used in Middletown Arson Trial," *Middletown Journal-News*, July 11, 2017; C. Hauser, "In Connecticut Murder Case, a Fitbit Is a Silent Witness," *New York Times*, April 27, 2017; D. Boroff, "Data from Pacemaker Used as Evidence against Ohio Man Accused of Burning Down His House," *New York Daily News*, February 8, 2017; C. Wootson, "A Man Detailed His Escape from a Burning House. His Pacemaker Told Police a Different Story," *Washington Post*, February 8, 2017; J. Wales, "Man's Pacemaker Used to Track and Charge Him with Crime," *AntiMedia*, February 7, 2017; D. Reisinger, "How a Pacemaker Led Police to Accuse Someone with Arson," *Fortune*, February 7, 2017; "Cops Use Pacemaker Data to Charge Homeowner with Arson, Insurance Fraud," *CSO Online*, January 30, 2017; L. Pack, "Data from Man's Pacemaker Led to Arson Charges," *Middletown Journal-News*, January 27, 2017; and L. Pack, "Middletown Homeowner Facing Felonies for House Fire," *Middletown Journal-News*, January 26, 2017.

Questions

1. The Electronic Frontier Foundation released a statement that Americans should not have to make a choice between health and privacy (**www.eff.org/issues/medical-privacy**). Do you agree with this statement? Why or why not? Support your answer.

2. As we noted in Chapter 1, you are known as *Homo conexus* because you practice continuous computing and are surrounded with intelligent devices. Look at Chapter 3 on ethics and privacy, and discuss the privacy implications of being *Homo conexus*.

Introduction

Information technologies and systems support organizations in managing—that is, acquiring, organizing, storing, accessing, analyzing, and interpreting—data. As noted in Chapter 1, when these data are managed properly, they become *information* and then *knowledge*. Information and knowledge are invaluable organizational resources that can provide any organization with a competitive advantage.

So, just how important are data and data management to organizations? From confidential customer information to intellectual property, to financial transactions to social media posts, organizations possess massive amounts of data that are critical to their success. Of course, to benefit from these data, organizations need to manage these data effectively. This type of management, however, comes at a huge cost. According to Symantec's (**www.symantec.com**) State of Information Survey, digital information costs organizations worldwide more than $1 trillion annually. In fact, it makes up roughly *half* of an organization's total value. The survey found that large organizations spend an average of $40 million annually to maintain and use data, and small-to-medium-sized businesses spend almost $350,000.

This chapter examines the processes whereby data are transformed first into information and then into knowledge. Managing data is critical to all organizations. Few business professionals are comfortable making or justifying business decisions that are not based on solid information. This is especially true today, when modern information systems make access to that information quick and easy. For example, we have information systems that format data in a way that managers and analysts can easily understand. Consequently, these professionals can access these data themselves and then analyze the data according to their needs. The result is useful *information*. Managers can then apply their experience to use this information to address a business problem, thereby producing *knowledge*. Knowledge management, enabled by information technology, captures and stores knowledge in forms that all organizational employees can access and apply, thereby creating the flexible, powerful "learning organization."

Organizations store data in databases. Recall from Chapter 1 that a *database* is a collection of related data files or tables that contain data. We discuss databases in Section 5.2, focusing on the relational database model. In Section 5.6, we take a look at the fundamentals of relational database operations.

Clearly, data and knowledge management are vital to modern organizations. But, why should *you* learn about them? The reason is that you will play an important role in the development of database applications. The structure and content of your organization's database depend on how users (meaning you) define your business activities. For example, when database developers in the firm's MIS group build a database, they use a tool called *entity-relationship (ER) modeling*. This tool creates a model of how users view a business activity. When you understand how to create and interpret an ER model, then you can evaluate whether the developers have captured your business activities correctly.

Keep in mind that decisions about data last longer, and have a broader impact, than decisions about hardware or software. If decisions concerning hardware are wrong, then the equipment can be replaced relatively easily. If software decisions turn out to be incorrect, they can be modified, though not always painlessly or inexpensively. Database decisions, in contrast, are much harder to undo. Database design constrains what an organization can do with its data for a long time. Remember that business users will be stuck with a bad database design, while the programmers who created the database will quickly move on to their next projects.

Furthermore, consider that databases typically underlie the enterprise applications that users access. If there are problems with organizational databases, then it is unlikely that any applications will be able to provide the necessary functionality for users. Databases are difficult to set up properly and to maintain. They are also the component of an information system that is most likely to receive the blame when the system performs poorly and the least likely to be recognized when the system performs well. This is why it is so important to get database designs right the first time—and you will play a key role in these designs.

You might also want to create a small, personal database using a software product such as Microsoft Access. In that case, you will need to be familiar with at least the basics of the product.

After the data are stored in your organization's databases, they must be accessible in a form that helps users to make decisions. Organizations accomplish this objective by developing *data warehouses*. You should become familiar with data warehouses because they are invaluable decision-making tools. We discuss data warehouses in Section 5.4.

You will also make extensive use of your organization's knowledge base to perform your job. For example, when you are assigned a new project, you will likely research your firm's knowledge base to identify factors that contributed to the success (or failure) of previous, similar projects. We discuss knowledge management in Section 5.5.

You begin this chapter by examining the multiple challenges involved in managing data. You then study the database approach that organizations use to help address these challenges. You turn your attention to Big Data, which organizations must manage in today's business environment. Next, you study data warehouses and data marts, and you learn how to use them for decision making. You conclude the chapter by examining knowledge management.

5.1 | Managing Data

All IT applications require data. These data should be of high quality, meaning that they should be accurate, complete, timely, consistent, accessible, relevant, and concise. Unfortunately, the process of acquiring, keeping, and managing data is becoming increasingly difficult.

The Difficulties of Managing Data

Because data are processed in several stages and often in multiple locations, they are frequently subject to problems and difficulties. Managing data in organizations is difficult for many reasons.

First, the amount of data increases exponentially with time. Much historical data must be kept for a long time, and new data are added rapidly. For example, to support millions of customers, large retailers such as Walmart have to manage many petabytes of data. (A petabyte is approximately 1,000 terabytes, or trillions of bytes; see Technology Guide 1.)

Data are also scattered throughout organizations, and they are collected by many individuals using various methods and devices. These data are frequently stored in numerous servers and locations and in different computing systems, databases, formats, and human and computer languages.

Another problem is that data are generated from multiple sources: internal sources (for example, corporate databases and company documents); personal sources (for example, personal thoughts, opinions, and experiences); and external sources (for example, commercial databases, government reports, and corporate websites). Data also come from the Web in the form of clickstream data. **Clickstream data** is data that visitors and customers produce when they visit a website and click on hyperlinks (described in Chapter 6). Clickstream data provides a trail of the users' activities in the website, including user behavior and browsing patterns.

Adding to these problems is the fact that new sources of data such as blogs, podcasts, tweets, Facebook posts, YouTube videos, texts, and RFID tags and other wireless sensors are constantly being developed, and the data these technologies generate must be managed. Also, the data becomes less current over time. For example, customers move to new addresses or they change their names; companies go out of business or are bought; new products are developed; employees are hired or fired; and companies expand into new countries.

Data are also subject to *data rot*. Data rot refers primarily to problems with the media on which the data are stored. Over time, temperature, humidity, and exposure to light can cause physical problems with storage media and thus make it difficult to access the data. The second aspect of data rot is that finding the machines needed to access the data can be difficult. For example, it is almost impossible today to find 8-track players for playing and listening to music. Consequently, a library of 8-track tapes has become relatively worthless, unless you have a functioning 8-track player or you convert the tapes to a more modern medium such as CDs and DVDs.

Data security, quality, and integrity are critical, yet they are easily jeopardized. Legal requirements relating to data also differ among countries as well as among industries, and they change frequently.

MIS Another problem arises from the fact that, over time, organizations have developed information systems for specific business processes, such as transaction processing, supply chain management, and customer relationship management. Information systems that specifically support these processes impose unique requirements on data; such requirements result in repetition and conflicts across the organization. For example, the marketing function might maintain information on customers, sales territories, and markets. These data might be duplicated within the billing or customer service functions. This arrangement can produce inconsistent data within the enterprise. Inconsistent data prevent a company from developing a unified view of core business information—data concerning customers, products, finances, and so on—across the organization and its information systems.

ACCT **FIN** Two other factors complicate data management. First, federal regulations—for example, the Sarbanes–Oxley Act of 2002—have made it a top priority for companies to better account for how they manage information. Sarbanes–Oxley requires that (1) public companies evaluate and disclose the effectiveness of their internal financial controls and (2) independent auditors for these companies agree to this disclosure. The law also holds CEOs and CFOs personally responsible for such disclosures. If their companies lack satisfactory data management policies and fraud or a security breach occurs, then the company officers could be held liable and face prosecution.

Second, companies are drowning in data, much of which are unstructured. As you have seen, the amount of data is increasing exponentially. To be profitable, companies must develop a strategy for managing these data effectively.

An additional problem with data management is Big Data. Big Data are so important that we devote the entire Section 5.3 to this topic.

Data Governance

To address the numerous problems associated with managing data, organizations are turning to data governance. **Data governance** is an approach to managing information across an entire organization. It involves a formal set of business processes and policies that are designed to ensure that data are handled in a certain, well-defined fashion. That is, the organization follows unambiguous rules for creating, collecting, handling, and protecting its information. The objective is to make information available, transparent, and useful for the people who are authorized to access it, from the moment it enters an organization until it becomes outdated and is deleted.

One strategy for implementing data governance is master data management. **Master data management** is a process that spans all of an organization's business processes and applications. It provides companies with the ability to store, maintain, exchange, and synchronize a consistent, accurate, and timely "single version of the truth" for the company's master data.

Master data are a set of core data, such as customer, product, employee, vendor, geographic location, and so on, that span the enterprise's information systems. It is important to distinguish between master data and transactional data. **Transactional data**, which are generated and captured by operational systems, describe the business's activities, or *transactions*. In contrast, master data are applied to multiple transactions, and they are used to categorize, aggregate, and evaluate the transactional data.

Let's look at an example of a transaction: You (Mary Jones) purchased one Samsung 42-inch LCD television, part number 1234, from Bill Roberts at Best Buy, for $2,000, on April 20, 2017. In this example, the master data are "product sold," "vendor," "salesperson," "store," "part number," "purchase price," and "date." When specific values are applied to the master data, then a transaction is represented. Therefore, transactional data would be, respectively, "42-inch LCD television," "Samsung," "Best Buy," "Bill Roberts," "1234," "$2,000," and "April 20, 2017."

An example of master data management is Dallas, Texas, which implemented a plan for digitizing the city's public and private records, such as paper documents, images, drawings, and video and audio content. The master database can be used by any of the 38 government departments that have appropriate access. The city is also integrating its financial and billing processes with its customer relationship management program. (You will learn about customer relationship management in Chapter 11.)

How will Dallas use this system? Imagine that the city experiences a water-main break. Before it implemented the system, repair crews had to search City Hall for records that were filed haphazardly. Once the workers found the hard-copy blueprints, they took them to the site and, after they examined them manually, decided on a plan of action. In contrast, the new system delivers the blueprints wirelessly to the laptops of crews in the field, who can magnify or highlight areas of concern to generate a rapid response. This process reduces the time it takes to respond to an emergency by several hours.

Along with data governance, organizations use the database approach to efficiently and effectively manage their data. We discuss the database approach in Section 5.2.

Before you go on . . .

1. What are some of the difficulties involved in managing data?
2. Define *data governance, master data,* and *transactional data.*

5.2 The Database Approach

Author Lecture Videos are available exclusively in *WileyPLUS.*
Apply the Concept activities are available in the Appendix and in *WileyPLUS.*

From the mid-1950s, when businesses first adopted computer applications, until the early 1970s, organizations managed their data in a *file management environment*. This environment evolved because organizations typically automated their functions one application at a time. Therefore, the various automated systems developed independently from one another, without any overall planning. Each application required its own data, which were organized in a data file.

A **data file** is a collection of logically related records. In a file management environment, each application has a specific data file related to it. This file contains all of the data records the application requires. Over time, organizations developed numerous applications, each with an associated, application-specific data file.

For example, imagine that most of your information is stored in your university's central database. In addition, however, a club to which you belong maintains its own files, the athletics department has separate files for student athletes, and your instructors maintain grade data on their personal computers. It is easy for your name to be misspelled in one of these databases or files. Similarly, if you move, then your address might be updated correctly in one database or file but not in the others.

Using databases eliminates many problems that arose from previous methods of storing and accessing data, such as file management systems. Databases are arranged so that one set of software programs—the database management system—provides all users with access to all of the data. (You will study database management systems later in this chapter.) Database systems minimize the following problems:

- *Data redundancy:* The same data are stored in multiple locations.
- *Data isolation:* Applications cannot access data associated with other applications.
- *Data inconsistency:* Various copies of the data do not agree.

  Database systems also maximize the following:

- *Data security:* Because data are "put in one place" in databases, there is a risk of losing a lot of data at one time. Therefore, databases must have extremely high security measures in place to minimize mistakes and deter attacks.
- *Data integrity:* Data meet certain constraints; for example, there are no alphabetic characters in a Social Security number field.
- *Data independence:* Applications and data are independent of one another; that is, applications and data are not linked to each other, so all applications are able to access the same data.

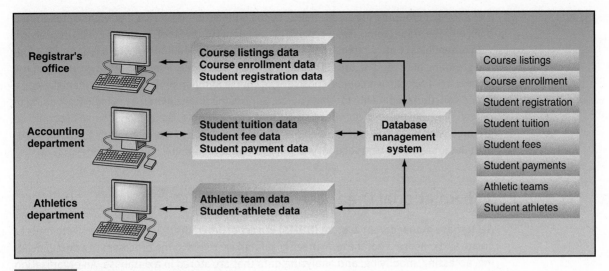

FIGURE 5.1   Database management system.

Figure 5.1 illustrates a university database. Note that university applications from the registrar's office, the accounting department, and the athletics department access data through the database management system.

A database can contain vast amounts of data. To make these data more understandable and useful, they are arranged in a hierarchy. We take a closer look at this hierarchy in the next section.

The Data Hierarchy

Data are organized in a hierarchy that begins with bits and proceeds all the way to databases (see **Figure 5.2**). A **bit** (*binary digit*) represents the smallest unit of data a computer can process. The term *binary* means that a bit can consist only of a 0 or a 1. A group of eight bits, called a **byte**, represents a single character. A byte can be a letter, a number, or a symbol. A logical grouping of characters into a word, a small group of words, or an identification number is called a **field**. For example, a student's name in a university's computer files would appear in the "name" field, and her or his Social Security number would appear in the "Social Security number" field. Fields can also contain data other than text and numbers as well as an image or any other type of multimedia. Examples are a motor vehicle department's licensing database that contains a driver's photograph and a field that contains a voice sample to authorize access to a secure facility.

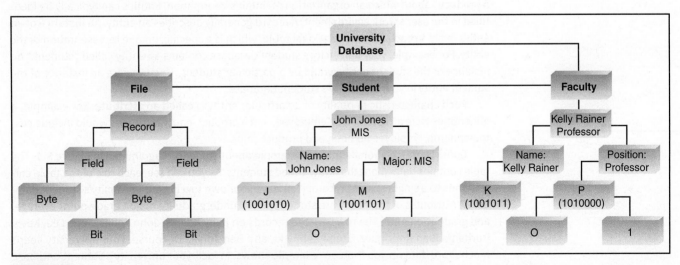

FIGURE 5.2   Hierarchy of data for a computer-based file.

A logical grouping of related fields, such as the student's name, the courses taken, the date, and the grade, comprises a **record**. In the Apple iTunes Store, a song is a field in a record, with other fields containing the song's title, its price, and the album on which it appears. A logical grouping of related records is called a data file or a **table**. For example, a grouping of the records from a particular course, consisting of course number, professor, and students' grades, would constitute a data file for that course. Continuing up the hierarchy, a logical grouping of related files constitutes a *database*. Using the same example, the student course file could be grouped with files on students' personal histories and financial backgrounds to create a student database. In the next section, you will learn about relational database models.

The Relational Database Model

A **database management system (DBMS)** is a set of programs that provide users with tools to create and manage a database. Managing a database refers to the processes of adding, deleting, accessing, modifying, and analyzing data that are stored in a database. An organization can access these data by using query and reporting tools that are part of the DBMS or by utilizing application programs specifically written to perform this function. DBMSs also provide the mechanisms for maintaining the integrity of stored data, managing security and user access, and recovering information if the system fails. Because databases and DBMSs are essential to all areas of business, they must be carefully managed.

There are a number of different database architectures, but we focus on the relational database model because it is popular and easy to use. Other database models—for example, the hierarchical and network models—are the responsibility of the MIS function and are not used by organizational employees. Popular examples of relational databases are Microsoft Access and Oracle.

Most business data—especially accounting and financial data—traditionally were organized into simple tables consisting of columns and rows. Tables enable people to compare information quickly by row or column. Users can also retrieve items rather easily by locating the point of intersection of a particular row and column.

The **relational database model** is based on the concept of two dimensional tables. A relational database generally is not one big table—usually called a *flat file*—that contains all of the records and attributes. Such a design would entail far too much data redundancy. Instead, a relational database is usually designed with a number of related tables. Each of these tables contains records (listed in rows) and attributes (listed in columns).

To be valuable, a relational database must be organized so that users can retrieve, analyze, and understand the data they need. A key to designing an effective database is the data model. A **data model** is a diagram that represents entities in the database and their relationships. An **entity** is a person, a place, a thing, or an event—such as a customer, an employee, or a product—about which an organization maintains information. Entities can typically be identified in the user's work environment. A record generally describes an entity. An **instance** of an entity refers to each row in a relational table, which is a specific, unique representation of the entity. For example, your university's student database contains an entity called "student." An instance of the student entity would be a particular student. Thus, you are an instance of the student entity in your university's student database.

Each characteristic or quality of a particular entity is called an **attribute**. For example, if our entities were a customer, an employee, and a product, entity attributes would include customer name, employee number, and product color.

Consider the relational database example about students diagrammed in **Figure 5.3**. The table contains data about the entity called students. As you can see, each row of the table corresponds to a single student record. (You have your own row in your university's student database.) Attributes of the entity are student name, undergraduate major, grade point average, and graduation date. The rows are the records on Sally Adams, John Jones, Jane Lee, Kevin Durham, Juan Rodriguez, Stella Zubnicki, and Ben Jones. Of course, your university keeps much more data on you than our example shows. In fact, your university's student database probably keeps hundreds of attributes on each student.

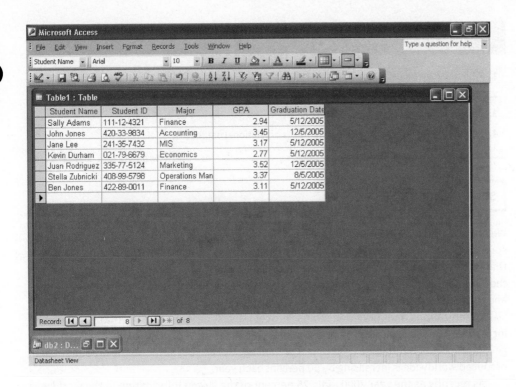

Every record in the database must contain at least one field that uniquely identifies that record so that it can be retrieved, updated, and sorted. This identifier field (or attribute) is called the **primary key**. For example, a student record in a U.S. university would use a unique student number as its primary key. (*Note:* In the past, your Social Security number served as the primary key for your student record. However, for security reasons, this practice has been discontinued.) In Figure 5.3, Sally Adams is uniquely identified by her student ID of 111-12-4321.

In some cases, locating a particular record requires the use of secondary keys. A **secondary key** is another field that has some identifying information but typically does not identify the record with complete accuracy. For example, the student's major might be a secondary key if a user wanted to identify all of the students majoring in a particular field of study. It should not be the primary key, however, because many students can have the same major. Therefore, it cannot uniquely identify an individual student.

A **foreign key** is a field (or group of fields) in one table that uniquely identifies a row of another table. A foreign key is used to establish and enforce a link between two tables. We discuss foreign keys in Section 5.6.

Organizations implement databases to efficiently and effectively manage their data. There are a variety of operations that can be performed on databases. We look at three of these operations in detail in Section 5.6: query languages, normalization, and joins.

As we noted earlier in this chapter, organizations must manage huge quantities of data. Such data consist of structured and unstructured data and are called Big Data (discussed in Section 5.3). **Structured data** is highly organized in fixed fields in a data repository such as a relational database. Structured data must be defined in terms of field name and type (e.g., alphanumeric, numeric, and currency). **Unstructured data** is data that does not reside in a traditional relational database. Examples of unstructured data are e-mail messages, word processing documents, videos, images, audio files, PowerPoint presentations, Facebook posts, tweets, snaps, ratings and recommendations, and Web pages. Industry analysts estimate that 80 to 90 percent of the data in an organization is unstructured. To manage Big Data, many organizations are using special types of databases, which we also discuss in Section 5.3.

Because databases typically process data in real time (or near real time), it is not practical to allow users access to the databases. After all, the data will change while the user is looking at them! As a result, data warehouses have been developed to allow users to access data for decision making. You will learn about data warehouses in Section 5.4.

1. What is a data model?
2. What is a primary key? A secondary key?
3. What is an entity? An attribute? An instance?
4. What are the advantages and disadvantages of relational databases?

5.3 Big Data

Author Lecture Videos are available exclusively in *WileyPLUS*.
Apply the Concept activities are available in the Appendix and in *WileyPLUS*.

We are accumulating data and information at an increasingly rapid pace from many diverse sources. In fact, organizations are capturing data about almost all events, including events that, in the past, firms never used to think of as data at all—for example, a person's location, the vibrations and temperature of an engine, and the stress at numerous points on a bridge—and then analyzing those data.

Organizations and individuals must process a vast amount of data that continues to increase dramatically. According to IDC (a technology research firm; www.idc.com), the world generates over one zettabyte (10^{21} bytes) of data each year. Furthermore, the amount of data produced worldwide is increasing by 50 percent each year.

As recently as the year 2000, only 25 percent of the stored information in the world was digital. The other 75 percent was analog; that is, it was stored on paper, film, vinyl records, and the like. By 2019, the amount of stored information in the world was more than 98 percent digital and less than 2 percent nondigital.

As we discussed at the beginning of this chapter, we refer to the superabundance of data available today as Big Data. **Big Data** is a collection of data that is so large and complex that it is difficult to manage using traditional database management systems. (We capitalize *Big Data* to distinguish the term from large amounts of traditional data.)

Essentially, Big Data is about predictions (see Predictive Analytics in Chapter 12). Predictions do not come from "teaching" computers to "think" like humans. Instead, predictions come from applying mathematics to huge quantities of data to infer probabilities. Consider the following examples:

- The likelihood that an e-mail message is spam
- The likelihood that the typed letters *teh* are supposed to be *the*
- The likelihood that the direction and speed of a person jaywalking indicate that he will make it across the street in time to avoid getting hit by a vehicle, meaning that a self-driving car need slow down only slightly

Big Data systems perform well because they contain huge amounts of data on which to base their predictions. Moreover, these systems are configured to improve themselves over time by searching for the most valuable signals and patterns as more data are input.

Defining Big Data

It is difficult to define Big Data. Here, we present two descriptions of the phenomenon. First, the technology research firm Gartner (www.gartner.com) defines Big Data as diverse, high-volume, high-velocity information assets that require new forms of processing to enhance decision making, lead to insights, and optimize business processes. Second, The Big Data Institute (TBDI; www.thebigdatainstitute.wordpress.com/) defines Big Data as vast datasets that do the following:

- Exhibit variety
- Include structured, unstructured, and semistructured data
- Are generated at high velocity with an uncertain pattern

- Do not fit neatly into traditional, structured, relational databases
- Can be captured, processed, transformed, and analyzed in a reasonable amount of time only by sophisticated information systems

Big Data generally consists of the following:

- Traditional enterprise data—examples are customer information from customer relationship management systems, transactional enterprise resource planning data, Web store transactions, operations data, and general ledger data.
- Machine-generated/sensor data—examples are smart meters; manufacturing sensors; sensors integrated into smartphones, automobiles, airplane engines, and industrial machines; equipment logs; and trading systems data.
- Social data—examples are customer feedback comments; microblogging sites such as Twitter; and social media sites such as Facebook, YouTube, and LinkedIn.
- Images captured by billions of devices located throughout the world, from digital cameras and camera phones to medical scanners and security cameras.

Let's take a look at a few specific examples of Big Data:

- Facebook's 2.4 billion users upload more than 350 million new photos every day. They also click a "Like" button or leave a comment more than 5 billion times every day. Facebook's data warehouse stores more than 300 petabytes of data and Facebook receives 600 terabytes of incoming data per day.
- The 1.3 billion users of Google's YouTube service upload more than 300 hours of video per minute. Google itself processes on average more than 63,000 search queries per second.
- In July 2019, industry analysts estimated that Twitter users sent some 550 million tweets per day.
- The Met Office is the United Kingdom's national weather and climate service. The Office provides tailored weather and environmental forecasts and briefings to the government and the public. The Office also informs various organizations, such as advising wind farms where to place their turbines and telling airports exactly how much deicer to spray on a plane so that none is wasted.

Characteristics of Big Data

Big Data has three distinct characteristics: volume, velocity, and variety. These characteristics distinguish Big Data from traditional data.

1. *Volume:* We have noted the huge volume of Big Data. Consider machine-generated data, which are generated in much larger quantities than nontraditional data. For example, sensors in a single jet engine can generate 10 terabytes of data in 30 minutes. (See our discussion of the Internet of Things in Chapter 8.) With more than 25,000 airline flights per day, the daily volume of data from just this single source is incredible. Smart electrical meters, sensors in heavy industrial equipment, and telemetry from automobiles compound the volume problem.

2. *Velocity:* The rate at which data flow into an organization is rapidly increasing. Velocity is critical because it increases the speed of the feedback loop between a company, its customers, its suppliers, and its business partners. For example, the Internet and mobile technology enable online retailers to compile histories not only on final sales but also on their customers' every click and interaction. Companies that can quickly use that information—for example, by recommending additional purchases—gain a competitive advantage.

3. *Variety:* Traditional data formats tend to be structured and relatively well described, and they change slowly. Traditional data include financial market data, point-of-sale transactions, and much more. In contrast, Big Data formats change rapidly. They include satellite

imagery, broadcast audio streams, digital music files, Web page content, scans of government documents, and comments posted on social networks.

Irrespective of their source, structure, format, and frequency, Big Data are valuable. If certain types of data appear to have no value today, it is because we have not yet been able to analyze them effectively. For example, several years ago when Google began harnessing satellite imagery, capturing street views, and then sharing this geographical data for free, few people understood its value. Today, we recognize that such data is incredibly valuable because analyses of Big Data yield deep insights. We discuss analytics in detail in Chapter 12. IT's About Business 5.1 provides an example of Big Data with a discussion of data from connected cars.

IT's About Business 5.1

Data from Connected Vehicles Is Valuable

`MIS` `POM` `MKT`

A *connected vehicle* is equipped with Internet access and usually with a wireless local area network (LAN). These features enable the vehicle to share Internet access with other devices inside as well as outside the vehicle.

Connected vehicle technology is becoming standard in many new cars. Semiautonomous driving is a reality, with advanced driver-assistance systems enhancing safety. Also, fully autonomous vehicles, which can operate without any human intervention, are already in service on roadways.

Research firm Gartner (**www.gartner.com**) forecasts that there will be 250 million connected cars on global roads by 2020. The combination of new car features as well as technology added to existing cars could increase that number to 2 billion by 2025. IHS Automotive (**www.ihs.com**) estimates that the average connected car will produce up to 30 terabytes of data each day.

Consider that when you start a late-model car today, it updates more than 100,000 data variables, from the pressure in your tires to pollution levels in your engine's exhaust. The onboard navigation system tracks every mile you drive and remembers your favorite route to work. Your car can help you avoid traffic jams and find a place to park. Some of today's cars even collect data on the weight of each occupant in the car.

There are many opportunities to use real-time, streaming data from connected cars. McKinsey (**www.mckinsey.com**) estimates that in-car data services could generate more than $1 trillion of annual revenue by 2030. Let's look at five areas where connected car data will be particularly valuable.

`MKT` **The driving experience.** Programmable seats, preset radio stations, driver information centers, heads-up displays, adaptive cruise control, lane departure notification, automatic parallel parking, and collision avoidance are all features in many of today's newer cars. But, what if the car learned the driver's preferences? For example, a driver might want to listen to the news in the morning on the way to work to be informed and then to classical music on the way home to relax. Perhaps on most Fridays, the driver takes a detour from her usual route home to meet a friend at a coffee shop. So now, when she gets behind the wheel to go to work on Friday, the radio is set to public radio. After work, the car's radio is set to classical music. Along the way, the navigation system warns her of an accident along her normal route, and it recommends an alternate route to get to the coffee shop.

Driver well-being. Connected cars have functions that involve the driver's ability and fitness to drive. These apps include fatigue detection, automatic detection of inebriated drivers, and the ability of the car to summon medical assistance if the driver is unable to do so. Another interesting app involves the use of in-car cameras to detect distracted driving, such as texting while driving.

Location-based services. Data from each car can be used to provide location-based offers. For example, the driver above could receive an offer for a discount on her favorite cup of coffee as she arrived at the coffee shop.

`MKT` **Quality and reliability.** Today, social media has shifted power to the consumer, and they have highlighted the importance of vehicle quality and reliability. These two issues are key elements in building a strong automotive brand reputation and customer loyalty. However, no matter how excellent the manufacturing process, automobiles are complex machines, and issues often appear in the field. Automobile manufacturers use data from connected cars to find and resolve these issues quickly. In this way, these companies will reduce warranty costs and enhance their brand and customer loyalty.

`POM` Using data from sensors, the cars themselves can predict needed service and maintenance and notify the driver. The sensor data can also enable dealerships to perform remote diagnostics to assess when a service or repair is needed and to identify the needed parts. When the customer arrives for an appointment, the technician with the appropriate skills is available with the correct parts to perform the service and to minimize any customer inconvenience. This process will also optimize inventory levels in dealerships and minimize inventory-carrying costs.

This sensor data provides valuable insights regarding the performance and health of the vehicle: for example, how, when, and where the vehicle is driven; the driver's driving style and preferences; and many other variables. Analyzing these data can help to provide a better, safer driving experience while enhancing vehicle quality and reliability.

`MKT` **Infotainment (Information + Entertainment).** The average American spends, on average, 8 percent of each day (about two hours) in his or her car. Infotainment has existed in cars since the 1930s. Consider the following audio features in cars:

- Radios began to appear in cars in the 1930s.
- FM radio appeared in the 1950s.
- Eight-track tape players appeared in the mid-1960s.

- The cassette deck debuted in the 1970s.
- The first factory CD player appeared in 1985.
- Satellite radio appeared in the 1990s.

Today, drivers can connect almost any digital device that plays audio and video to their car's infotainment system. For example, how much do parents appreciate built-in movie players for their children in the backseat? Mobile Wi-Fi connectivity has brought streaming services for news and entertainment into the car as well.

There are many ways to capitalize on the integration of infotainment data and vehicle data. For example, companies use data on location, length of average trip, miles driven per week, number of passengers, date, and/or day of week to provide various offerings.

- Recommended content: *Short-form content* may be suggested when you are taking the children to baseball practice and long-form content suggested when you drive to the beach. Short-form content is short in length, such as video clips, listicles (short articles composed entirely of a list of items), and blog posts fewer than 1,000 words. This type of content can appeal to users' limited attention spans. *Long-form content* consists of longer articles (typically between 1,200 and 20,000 words) that contain greater amounts of content than short-form content. These articles often take the form of creative nonfiction or narrative journalism.
- Mobile payments: Pay-per-view movies and sporting events (for backseat passengers).
- Intelligent messaging: You can access breaking news, traffic, and weather reports based on actual travel patterns.
- Live content transfer: When you have arrived at your destination, you can continue watching on your tablet, smartphone, or television.

Many companies are competing in the connected services marketplace. For example, Weve (**www.weve.com/about**) is a leading provider of mobile marketing and commerce in the United Kingdom. The firm combines and analyzes real-time data streams from 17 million mobile users for intelligent messaging, targeted marketing offers, and mobile payments. These data streams include location data, purchase history, daily routines, and social data that users choose to make public.

All of the automakers are worried about Google and Apple. These two technology companies are developing cars and self-driving technology, and both are leaders in connected services. For example, Google's Waze is a leading in-car app. Waze is an advertising-supported and crowdsourced program that offers congestion-avoiding directions. Waze examines personal data in smartphones with users' permission and sends pop-up ads to the screens of its 50 million global users.

Ford (**www.ford.com**), BMW (**www.bmw.com**), General Motors (GM; **www.gm.com**), and other automakers have deployed systems that can host, and limit, in-car apps produced by competitors. These systems allow drivers to plug in Apple's and Google's competing vehicle screen operating systems, CarPlay and Android Auto, respectively, without giving the two technology companies access to drivers' personal information or vehicle diagnostics. For example, Ford's offering in this area, which Toyota also uses, is called AppLink. The app enables the car to access 90 phone apps without using CarPlay or Android Auto as an intermediary.

Other companies are making efforts to develop in-car services. As one example, in 2016, BMW, Daimler, and Volkswagen teamed up to purchase Nokia's digital mapping business, called Here (**www.here.com/en**), for $3.1 billion. This acquisition gave these companies a platform for location-based services and, eventually, for mapping capabilities for self-driving cars. GM's OnStar (**www.onstar.com**) mobile information subscription service offers dashboard-delivered coupons for Exxon and Mobil gas stations as well as the ability to book hotel rooms. Mercedes-Benz's concierge service Mbrace (**www.mbusa.com/mercedes/mbrace**) can route a driver around traffic or bad weather. Both OnStar and Mbrace cost about $20 per month. Alibaba Group (**www.alibaba.com**), whose YunOS (operating system) connects phones, tablets, and smartwatches, is also working on deals with Chinese automakers to operate with vehicles.

Significantly, interest in car data is not limited to technology and automotive companies. The insurance industry also values access to data about driving habits. The insurance companies could then use these data to charge higher rates for drivers who exceed speed limits and lower rates for those who drive safely. Along these lines, GM and Ford offer drivers an app that calculates a driver score that could reduce their insurance rates if they exhibit safe habits.

Finally, IBM (**www.ibm.com**) is planning to become a single point of contact for all parts of the automotive industry. The company has signed a contract with BMW that will connect BMW's CarData platform to IBM's Bluemix platform-as-a-service cloud computing application (see Technology Guide 3). The idea is that IBM will host and analyze data from connected cars and then send the data to third parties—with drivers' consent—when required. Early applications can link your car to your local insurance agent, dealership, and automotive repair shop.

Sources: Compiled from A. Ross, "The Connected Car 'Data Explosion': The Challenges and Opportunities," *Information Age*, July 10, 2018; "The Connected Car, Big Data, and the Automotive Industry's Future," *Datameer Blog*, February 26, 2018; M. Spillar, "How Big Data Is Paving the Way for the Connected Car," *Hortonworks Blog*, January 23, 2018; L. Stolle, "Is Data from Connected Vehicles Valuable and, if So, to Whom?" *SAP Blogs*, June 21, 2017; C. Hall, "BMW's Connected-Car Data Platform to Run in IBM's Cloud," *Data Center Knowledge*, June 16, 2017; D. Cooper, "IBM Will Put Connected Car Data to Better Use," *Engadget*, June 14, 2017; N. Ismail, "The Present and Future of Connected Car Data," *Information Age*, May 17, 2017; R. Ferris, "An 'Ocean of Auto Big Data' Is Coming, Says Barclays," CNBC, April 26, 2017; D. Newcomb, "Connected Car Data Is the New Oil," *Entrepreneur*, April 17, 2017; M. McFarland, "Your Car's Data May Soon Be More Valuable than the Car Itself," CNN, February 7, 2017; L. Slowey, "Big Data and the Challenges in the Car Industry," *IBM Internet of Things Blog*, January 12, 2017; P. Nelson, "Just One Autonomous Car Will Use 4,000 GB of Data/Day," *Network World*, December 7, 2016; S. Tiao, "The Connected Car, Big Data, and the Automotive Industry's Future," *Datameer*, October 27, 2016; M. DeBord, "Big Data in Cars Could Be a $750 Billion Business by 2030," *Business Insider*, October 3, 2016; D. Welch, "The Battle for Smart Car Data," *Bloomberg BusinessWeek*, July 18-24, 2016; D. Booth, "It's Time for Automatic Alcohol Sensors in Every Car," *Driving*, May 6, 2016; "The Connected Vehicle: Big Data, Big Opportunities," *SAS White Paper*, 2016; G. Krueger, "Connected Vehicle Data: The Cost Challenge," *Federal Department of Transportation*, 2015; and www.ihs.com, www.bmw.com, accessed June 27, 2019.

Questions

1. Describe several other uses (other than the ones discussed in this case) for data from connected cars.
2. Would data from connected cars be considered Big Data? Why or why not? Support your answer.

Issues with Big Data

Despite its extreme value, Big Data does have issues. In this section, we take a look at data integrity, data quality, and the nuances of analysis that are worth noting.

Big Data Can Come from Untrusted Sources.

As we discussed earlier, one of the characteristics of Big Data is variety, meaning that Big Data can come from numerous, widely varied sources. These sources may be internal or external to an organization. For example, a company might want to integrate data from unstructured sources such as e-mails, call center notes, and social media posts with structured data about its customers from its data warehouse. The question is: How trustworthy are those external sources of data? For example, how trustworthy is a tweet? The data may come from an unverified source. Furthermore, the data itself, reported by the source, may be false or misleading.

Big Data Is Dirty.

Dirty data refers to inaccurate, incomplete, incorrect, duplicate, or erroneous data. Examples of such problems are misspelling of words and duplicate data such as retweets or company press releases that appear multiple times in social media.

Suppose a company is interested in performing a competitive analysis using social media data. The company wants to see how often a competitor's product appears in social media outlets as well as the sentiments associated with those posts. The company notices that the number of positive posts about the competitor is twice as great as the number of positive posts about itself. This finding could simply be a case of the competitor pushing out its press releases to multiple sources—in essence, blowing its own horn. Alternatively, the competitor could be getting many people to retweet an announcement.

Big Data Changes, Especially in Data Streams.

Organizations must be aware that data quality in an analysis can change, or the actual data can change, because the conditions under which the data are captured can change. For example, imagine a utility company that analyzes weather data and smart-meter data to predict customer power usage. What happens when the utility analyzes these data in real time and it discovers that data are missing from some of its smart meters?

Managing Big Data

Big Data makes it possible to do many things that were previously much more difficult: for example, to spot business trends more rapidly and accurately, to prevent disease, and to track crime. When Big Data is properly analyzed, it can reveal valuable patterns and information that were previously hidden because of the amount of work required to discover them. Leading corporations, such as Walmart and Google, have been able to process Big Data for years, but only at great expense. Today's hardware, cloud computing (see Technology Guide 3), and open-source software make processing Big Data affordable for most organizations.

For many organizations, the first step toward managing data was to integrate information silos into a database environment and then to develop data warehouses for decision making. (An *information silo* is an information system that does not communicate with other, related information systems in an organization.) After they completed the first step, many organizations turned their attention to the business of information management—making sense of their rapidly expanding data. In recent years, Oracle, IBM, Microsoft, and SAP have spent billions of dollars purchasing software firms that specialize in data management and business analytics. (You will learn about business analytics in Chapter 12.)

In addition to using existing data management systems, today many organizations also employ NoSQL databases to process Big Data. Think of them as "not only SQL" (structured query language) databases. (We discuss SQL in Section 5.6.)

As you have seen in this chapter, traditional relational databases such as Oracle and MySQL store data in tables organized into rows and columns. Recall that each row is associated with a unique record, and each column is associated with a field that defines an attribute of that account.

In contrast, NoSQL databases can manipulate structured and unstructured data as well as inconsistent or missing data. For this reason, NoSQL databases are particularly useful when working with Big Data. Many products use NoSQL databases, including Cassandra (**www.cassandra. apache.org**), CouchDB (**www.couchdb.apache.org**), and MongoDB (**www.mongodb.org**). Below we consider three examples of NoSQL databases in action: Temetra, Hadoop, and MapReduce.

Temetra, founded in 2002, stores and manages data from 12.5 million utility meters across the United Kingdom. The unpredictable nature of the type and volume of the data the firm receives convinced them to deploy the Riak NoSQL database from Basho. Temetra collects data from sources ranging from people keying in meter readings to large-scale industry users who send data automatically every 15 minutes.

Temetra initially supported its customers with an SQL database. Eventually, however, it became unable to effectively manage that volume of data. The company deployed the NoSQL database to handle the volume of data and to acquire the capability to add new data types. In essence, NoSQL enabled Temetra to store data without a rigid format.

Hadoop (**www.hadoop.apache.org**) is not a type of database. Rather, it is a collection of programs that allow people to store, retrieve, and analyze very large datasets using massively parallel processing. *Massively parallel processing* is the coordinated processing of an application by multiple processors that work on different parts of the application, with each processor utilizing its own operating system and memory. As such, Hadoop enables users to access NoSQL databases, which can be spread across thousands of servers, without a reduction in performance. For example, a large database application that could take 20 hours of processing time on a centralized relational database system might take only a few minutes when using Hadoop's parallel processing.

MapReduce refers to the software procedure of dividing an analysis into pieces that can be distributed across different servers in multiple locations. MapReduce first distributes the analysis (map) and then collects and integrates the results back into a single report (reduce).

Google has been developing a new type of database, called Cloud Spanner, for some time. In February 2017, the company released Cloud Spanner to the public as a service. IT's About Business 5.2 addresses this database.

IT's About Business 5.2

Cloud Spanner, Google's Global Database
MIS

Systems that encompass hundreds of thousands of computers and multiple data centers must precisely synchronize time around the world. These systems involve communication among computers in many locations, and time varies from computer to computer because precise time is difficult to keep.

Services such as the Network Time Protocol aimed to provide computers with a common time reference point. However, this protocol worked only so well, primarily because computer network transmission speeds are relatively slow compared to the processing speeds of the computers themselves. In fact, before Google developed Spanner, companies found it extremely difficult, if not impossible, to keep databases consistent without constant, intense communication. Conducting this type of communication around the world took too much time.

For Google, the problem of time was critical. The firm's databases operate in data centers that are dispersed throughout the world. Therefore, Google could not ensure that transactions in one part of the world matched transactions in another part. That is, Google could not obtain a truly global picture of its operations. The firm could not seamlessly replicate data across regions or

quickly retrieve replicated data when they were needed. Google's engineers had to find a way to produce reliable time across the world.

To resolve this problem, Google developed the Cloud Spanner, which is the firm's globally distributed NewSQL database. Spanner stores data across millions of computers located in data centers on multiple continents. Even though Spanner stretches around the world, the database functions as if it is in one place.

NewSQL is a class of modern relational database management system that attempts to provide the same scalable performance of NoSQL systems for online transaction processing (OLTP) functions while still maintaining the ACID guarantees of a traditional database system. The ACID guarantees include the following:

- Atomicity: Each transaction is all or nothing. If one part of the transaction fails, then the entire transaction fails, and the database is left unchanged.
- Consistency: Any transaction will bring the database from one valid state to another.
- Isolation: The concurrent execution of transactions results in a system state that would be obtained if transactions were executed sequentially (one after another).

• Durability: Once a transaction has been committed, it will remain so, even in the event of power loss, system crashes, or errors.

Cloud Spanner offers companies the best of both traditional relational databases and NoSQL databases—that is, transactional consistency with easy scalability. However, Spanner is not a simple scale-up relational database service: Cloud SQL is that Google product. Spanner is not a data warehouse: BigQuery is that Google product. Finally, Spanner is not a NoSQL database: BigTable is that Google product.

Google can change company data in one part of Spanner—for example, running an ad or debiting an advertiser's account—without contradicting changes made on the other side of the planet. In addition, Spanner can readily and reliably replicate data across multiple data centers in multiple parts of the world, and it can seamlessly retrieve these copies if any individual data center goes down. In essence, Spanner provides Google with consistency across continents.

So, how did Google solve the time problem by creating Spanner? Google engineers equipped Google's data centers with global positioning system (GPS; see Chapter 8) receivers and atomic clocks. The GPS receivers obtain the time from various satellites orbiting the earth, while the atomic clocks keep their own, highly accurate, time. The GPS devices and atomic clocks send their time readings to master servers in each data center. These servers trade readings in an effort to settle on a common time. A margin of error still exists. However, because there are so many time readings, the master servers become a far more reliable timekeeping service. Google calls this timekeeping technology TrueTime.

With help from TrueTime, Spanner provides Google with a competitive advantage in its diverse markets. TrueTime is an underlying technology for AdWords and Gmail as well as more than 2,000 other Google services, including Google Photos and the Google Play store. Google can now manage online transactions at an unprecedented scale. Furthermore, thanks to Spanner's extreme form of data replication, Google now keeps its services operational with unprecedented consistency.

Google hopes to convince customers that Spanner provides an easier way of running a global business and of replicating their data across multiple regions, thereby guarding against outages.

The problem is that few businesses are truly global on the same scale as Google. However, Google is betting that Spanner will give customers the freedom to expand as time goes on. One such customer is JDA (**www.jda.com**), a company that helps businesses oversee their supply chains. JDA is testing Spanner because the volume and velocity of the firm's data are increasing exponentially.

Spanner could also be useful in the financial markets by enabling large-scale banks to more efficiently track and synchronize trades occurring around the world. Traditionally, many banks have been cautious about managing trades in the cloud for security and privacy reasons. However, some banks are now investigating Spanner.

Google is offering Spanner technology to all customers as a cloud computing service. Google believes that Spanner can create a competitive advantage in its battle with Microsoft and Amazon for supremacy in the cloud computing marketplace.

Sources: Compiled from A. Penkava, "Google Cloud Spanner: The Good, the Bad, and the Ugly," *Lightspeed*, March 21, 2018; A. Cobley, "Get Tooled up before Grappling with Google's Spanner Database," *The Register*, March 12, 2018; T. Baer, "Making the Jump to Google Cloud Spanner," *ZDNet*, February 22, 2018; A. Brust, "Google's Cloud Spanner: How Does It Stack Up?" *ZDNet*, July 7, 2017; F. Lardinois, "Google's Globally Distributed Cloud Spanner Database Service Is Now Generally Available," *TechCrunch*, May 16, 2017; S. Yegulalp, "Google's Cloud Spanner Melds Transactional Consistency, NoSQL Scale," *InfoWorld*, May 4, 2017; A. Cobley, "Google Spanner in the NewSQL Works?" *The Register*, March 21, 2017; D. Borsos, "Google Cloud Spanner: Our First Impressions," *OpenCredo*, March 7, 2017; F. Lardinois, "Google Launches Cloud Spanner, Its New Globally Distributed Relational Database Service," *TechCrunch*, February 14, 2017; C. Metz, "Spanner, the Google Database that Mastered Time, Is Now Open to Everyone," *Wired*, February 14, 2017; B. Darrow, "Google Spanner Database Surfaces at Last," *Fortune*, February 14, 2017; C. Metz, "Google Unites Worldwide Data Centers with GPS and Atomic Clocks," *Wired UK*, September 20, 2012; and www.google.com, accessed June 27, 2019.

Questions

1. Discuss the advantages of Google Cloud Spanner to organizations.

2. If your company does not operate globally, would Google Cloud Spanner still be valuable? Why or why not? Support your answer.

Putting Big Data to Use

Modern organizations must manage Big Data and gain value from it. They can employ several strategies to achieve this objective.

Making Big Data Available. Making Big Data available for relevant stakeholders can help organizations gain value. For example, consider open data in the public sector. Open data are accessible public data that individuals and organizations can use to create new businesses and solve complex problems. In particular, government agencies gather vast amounts of data, some of which are Big Data. Making that data available can provide economic benefits. In fact, an Open Data 500 study at the GovLab at New York University discovered 500 examples of U.S.-based companies whose business models depend on analyzing open government data.

Enabling Organizations to Conduct Experiments.

Big Data allows organizations to improve performance by conducting controlled experiments. For example, Amazon (and many other companies such as Google and LinkedIn) constantly experiments by offering slightly different looks on its website. These experiments are called A/B experiments, because each experiment has only two possible outcomes. Here is an example of an A/B experiment at **Etsy.com**, an online marketplace for vintage and handmade products.

MKT When Etsy analysts noticed that one of its Web pages attracted customer attention but failed to maintain it, they looked more closely at the page and discovered that it had few "calls to action." (A call to action is an item, such as a button, on a Web page that enables a customer to do something.) On this particular Etsy page, customers could leave, buy, search, or click on two additional product images. The analysts decided to show more product images on the page.

Consequently, one group of visitors to the page saw a strip across the top of the page that displayed additional product images. Another group saw only the two original product images. On the page with additional images, customers viewed more products and, significantly, bought more products. The results of this experiment revealed valuable information to Etsy.

Microsegmentation of Customers.

Segmentation of a company's customers means dividing them into groups that share one or more characteristics. Microsegmentation simply means dividing customers up into very small groups, or even down to an individual customer.

MKT For example, Paytronix Systems (**www.paytronix.com**) provides loyalty and rewards program software for thousands of different restaurants. Paytronix gathers restaurant guest data from a variety of sources beyond loyalty and gift programs, including social media. Paytronix then analyzes this Big Data to help its restaurant clients microsegment their guests. Restaurant managers are now able to more precisely customize their loyalty and gift programs. Since they have taken these steps, they have noted improved profitability and customer satisfaction in their restaurants.

POM Creating New Business Models.

Companies are able to use Big Data to create new business models. For example, a commercial transportation company operated a substantial fleet of large, long-haul trucks. The company recently placed sensors on all of its trucks. These sensors wirelessly communicated sizeable amounts of information to the company, a process called *telematics*. The sensors collected data on vehicle usage—including acceleration, braking, cornering, and so on—in addition to driver performance and vehicle maintenance.

By analyzing this Big Data, the company was able to improve the condition of its trucks through near-real-time analysis that proactively suggested preventive maintenance. The company was also able to improve the driving skills of its operators by analyzing their driving styles.

The transportation company then made its Big Data available to its insurance carrier. Using this data, the insurance carrier was able to perform a more precise risk analysis of driver behavior and the condition of the trucks. The carrier then offered the transportation company a new pricing model that lowered its premiums by 10 percent due to safety improvements enabled by analysis of the Big Data.

Organizations Can Analyze More Data.

In some cases, organizations can even process all of the data relating to a particular phenomenon, so they do not have to rely as much on sampling. Random sampling works well, but it is not as effective as analyzing an entire dataset. Random sampling also has some basic weaknesses. To begin with, its accuracy depends on ensuring randomness when collecting the sample data. However, achieving such randomness is problematic. Systematic biases in the process of data collection can cause the results to be highly inaccurate. For example, consider political polling using landline phones. This sample tends to exclude people who use only cell phones. This bias can seriously skew the results because cell phone users are typically younger and more liberal than people who rely primarily on landline phones.

Big Data Used in the Functional Areas of the Organization

In this section, we provide examples of how Big Data is valuable to various functional areas in the firm.

HRM **Human Resources.** Employee benefits, particularly healthcare, represent a major business expense. Consequently, some companies have turned to Big Data to better manage these benefits. Caesars Entertainment (**www.caesars.com**), for example, analyzes health-insurance claim data for its 65,000 employees and their covered family members. Managers can track thousands of variables that indicate how employees use medical services, such as the number of their emergency room visits and whether employees choose a generic or brand name drug.

Consider the following scenario: Data revealed that too many employees with medical emergencies were being treated at hospital emergency rooms rather than at less expensive urgent-care facilities. The company launched a campaign to remind employees of the high cost of emergency room visits, and they provided a list of alternative facilities. Subsequently, 10,000 emergencies shifted to less expensive alternatives, for a total savings of $4.5 million.

Big Data is also having an impact on *hiring*. An example is Catalyte (**www.catalyte.io**), a technology outsourcing company that hires teams for programming jobs. Traditional recruiting is typically too slow, and hiring managers often subjectively choose candidates who are not the best fit for the job. Catalyte addresses this problem by requiring candidates to fill out an online assessment. It then uses the assessment to collect thousands of data points about each candidate. In fact, the company collects more data based on *how* candidates answer than on *what* they answer.

For example, the assessment might give a problem requiring calculus to an applicant who is not expected to know the subject. How the candidate responds—laboring over an answer, answering quickly, and then returning later, or skipping the problem entirely—provides insight into how that candidate might deal with challenges that he or she will encounter on the job. That is, someone who labors over a difficult question might be effective in an assignment that requires a methodical approach to problem solving, whereas an applicant who takes a more aggressive approach might perform better in a different job setting.

The benefit of this Big Data approach is that it recognizes that people bring different skills to the table and there is no one-size-fits-all person for any job. Analyzing millions of data points can reveal which attributes candidates bring to specific situations.

As one measure of success, employee turnover at Catalyte averages about 15 percent per year, compared with more than 30 percent for its U.S. competitors and more than 20 percent for similar companies overseas.

MKT **Product Development.** Big Data can help capture customer preferences and put that information to work in designing new products. For example, Ford Motor Company (**www.ford.com**) was considering a "three blink" turn indicator that had been available on its European cars for years. Unlike the turn signals on its U.S. vehicles, this indicator flashes three times at the driver's touch and then automatically shuts off.

Ford decided that conducting a full-scale market research test on this blinker would be too costly and time consuming. Instead, it examined auto-enthusiast websites and owner forums to discover what drivers were saying about turn indicators. Using text-mining algorithms, researchers culled more than 10,000 mentions and then summarized the most relevant comments.

The results? Ford introduced the three-blink indicator on the Ford Fiesta it released in 2010, and by 2013 it was available on most Ford products. Although some Ford owners complained online that they have had trouble getting used to the new turn indicator, many others defended it. Ford managers note that the use of text-mining algorithms was critical in this effort because they provided the company with a complete picture that would not have been available using traditional market research.

POM **Operations.**   For years, companies have been using information technology to make their operations more efficient. Consider United Parcel Service (UPS). The company has long relied on data to improve its operations. Specifically, it uses sensors in its delivery vehicles that can, among other things, capture each truck's speed and location, the number of times it is placed in reverse, and whether the driver's seat belt is buckled. This data is uploaded at the end of each day to a UPS data center, where it is analyzed overnight. By combining GPS information and data from sensors installed on more than 46,000 vehicles, UPS reduced fuel consumption by 8.4 million gallons, and it cut 85 million miles off its routes.

MKT **Marketing.**   Marketing managers have long used data to better understand their customers and to target their marketing efforts more directly. Today, Big Data enables marketers to craft much more personalized messages.

The United Kingdom's InterContinental Hotels Group (IHG; **www.ihg.com**) has gathered details about the members of its Priority Club rewards program, such as income levels and whether members prefer family-style or business-traveler accommodations. The company then consolidated all this information with information obtained from social media into a single data warehouse. Using its data warehouse and analytics software, the hotelier launched a new marketing campaign. Where previous marketing campaigns generated, on average, between 7 and 15 customized marketing messages, the new campaign generated more than 1,500. IHG rolled out these messages in stages to an initial core of 12 customer groups, each of which was defined by 4,000 attributes. One group, for example, tended to stay on weekends, redeem reward points for gift cards, and register through IHG marketing partners. Using this information, IHG sent these customers a marketing message that alerted them to local weekend events.

The campaign proved to be highly successful. It generated a 35 percent higher rate of customer conversions, or acceptances, than previous, similar campaigns.

POM **Government Operations.**   Consider the United Kingdom. According to the INRIX Traffic Scorecard, although the United States has the worst traffic congestion on average, London topped the world list for metropolitan areas. In London, drivers wasted an average of 101 hours per year in gridlock. Congestion is bad for business. The INRIX study estimated that the cost to the U.K. economy would be £307 billion ($400 billion) between 2013 and 2030.

Congestion is also harmful to urban resilience, negatively affecting both environmental and social sustainability, in terms of emissions, global warming, air quality, and public health. As for the livability of a modern city, congestion is an important component of the urban transport user experience (UX).

Calculating levels of UX satisfaction at any given time involves solving a complex equation with a range of key variables and factors: total number of transport assets (road and rail capacity, plus parking spaces), users (vehicles, pedestrians), incidents (roadwork, accidents, breakdowns), plus expectations (anticipated journey times and passenger comfort).

The growing availability of Big Data sources within London—for example, traffic cameras and sensors on cars and roadways—can help to create a new era of smart transport. Analyzing this Big Data offers new ways for traffic analysts in London to "sense the city" and enhance transport via real-time estimation of traffic patterns and rapid deployment of traffic management strategies.

Before you go on . . .

1. Define Big Data.
2. Describe the characteristics of Big Data.
3. Describe how companies can use Big Data to a gain competitive advantage.

5.4 Data Warehouses and Data Marts

Today, the most successful companies are those that can respond quickly and flexibly to market changes and opportunities. The key to such a response is how analysts and managers effectively and efficiently use data and information. The challenge is to provide users with access to corporate data so they can analyze the data to make better decisions. Let's consider an example. If the manager of a local bookstore wanted to know the profit margin on used books at her store, then she could obtain that information from her database using SQL or query-by-example (QBE). QBE is a method of creating database queries that allows the user to search for documents based on an example in the form of a selected string of text or in the form of a document name or a list of documents. However, if she needed to know the trend in the profit margins on used books over the past 10 years, then she would have to construct a very complicated SQL or QBE query.

This example illustrates several reasons why organizations are building data warehouses and data marts. First, the bookstore's databases contain the necessary information to answer the manager's query, but this information is not organized in a way that makes it easy for her to find what she needs. Therefore, complicated queries might take a long time to answer, and they also might degrade the performance of the databases. Second, transactional databases are designed to be updated. The update process requires extra processing. Data warehouses and data marts are read-only. Therefore, the extra processing is eliminated because data already contained in the data warehouse are not updated. Third, transactional databases are designed to access a single record at a time. In contrast, data warehouses are designed to access large groups of related records.

As a result of these problems, companies are using a variety of tools with data warehouses and data marts to make it easier and faster for users to access, analyze, and query data. You will learn about these tools in Chapter 12 on Business Analytics.

Describing Data Warehouses and Data Marts

In general, data warehouses and data marts support business analytics applications. As you will see in Chapter 12, business analytics encompasses a broad category of applications, technologies, and processes for gathering, storing, accessing, and analyzing data to help business users make better decisions. A **data warehouse** is a repository of historical data that are organized by subject to support decision makers within an organization.

Because data warehouses are so expensive, they are used primarily by large companies. A **data mart** is a low-cost, scaled-down version of a data warehouse that is designed for the end-user needs in a strategic business unit (SBU) or an individual department. Data marts can be implemented more quickly than data warehouses, often in fewer than 90 days. Furthermore, they support local rather than central control by conferring power on the user group. Typically, groups that need a single or a few business analytics applications require only a data mart rather than a data warehouse.

The basic characteristics of data warehouses and data marts include the following:

- *Organized by business dimension or subject:* Data are organized by subject—for example, by customer, vendor, product, price level, and region. This arrangement differs from transactional systems, where data are organized by business process such as order entry, inventory control, and accounts receivable.

- *Use online analytical processing:* Typically, organizational databases are oriented toward handling transactions. That is, databases use *online transaction processing* (OLTP), where business transactions are processed online as soon as they occur. The objectives are speed and efficiency, which are critical to a successful Internet-based business operation. In contrast, data warehouses and data marts, which are designed to support decision makers but not OLTP, use online analytical processing (OLAP), which involves the analysis of accumulated data by end users. We consider OLAP in greater detail in Chapter 12.

- *Integrated:* Data are collected from multiple systems and are then integrated around subjects. For example, customer data may be extracted from internal (and external) systems and then integrated around a customer identifier, thereby creating a comprehensive view of the customer.

- *Time variant:* Data warehouses and data marts maintain historical data; that is, data that include time as a variable. Unlike transactional systems, which maintain only recent data (such as for the last day, week, or month), a warehouse or mart may store years of data. Organizations use historical data to detect deviations, trends, and long-term relationships.

- *Nonvolatile:* Data warehouses and data marts are nonvolatile—that is, users cannot change or update the data. Therefore, the warehouse or mart reflects history, which, as we just saw, is critical for identifying and analyzing trends. Warehouses and marts are updated, but through IT-controlled load processes rather than by users.

- *Multidimensional:* Typically, the data warehouse or mart uses a multidimensional data structure. Recall that relational databases store data in two-dimensional tables. In contrast, data warehouses and marts store data in more than two dimensions. For this reason, the data are said to be stored in a **multidimensional structure**. A common representation for this multidimensional structure is the *data cube*.

The data in data warehouses and marts are organized by *business dimensions*, which are subjects such as product, geographic area, and time period that represent the edges of the data cube. If you look ahead to Figure 5.6 for an example of a data cube, you see that the product dimension is composed of nuts, screws, bolts, and washers; the geographic area dimension is composed of East, West, and Central; and the time period dimension is composed of 2016, 2017, and 2018. Users can view and analyze data from the perspective of these business dimensions. This analysis is intuitive because the dimensions are presented in business terms that users can easily understand.

A Generic Data Warehouse Environment

The environment for data warehouses and marts includes the following:

- Source systems that provide data to the warehouse or mart
- Data-integration technology and processes that prepare the data for use
- Different architectures for storing data in an organization's data warehouse or data marts
- Different tools and applications for the variety of users. (You will learn about these tools and applications in Chapter 12.)
- Metadata (data about the data in a repository), data quality, and governance processes that ensure that the warehouse or mart meets its purposes

Figure 5.4 depicts a generic data warehouse or data mart environment. Let's drill down into the component parts.

Source Systems.   There is typically some "organizational pain point"—that is, a business need—that motivates a firm to develop its business intelligence capabilities. Working backward, this pain leads to information requirements, BI applications, and requirements for source system data. These data requirements can range from a single source system, as in the case of a data mart, to hundreds of source systems, as in the case of an enterprisewide data warehouse.

Modern organizations can select from a variety of source systems, including operational/transactional systems, enterprise resource planning (ERP) systems, website data, third-party data (e.g., customer demographic data), and more. The trend is to include more types of data (e.g., sensing data from RFID tags). These source systems often use different software packages (e.g., IBM, Oracle), and they store data in different formats (e.g., relational, hierarchical).

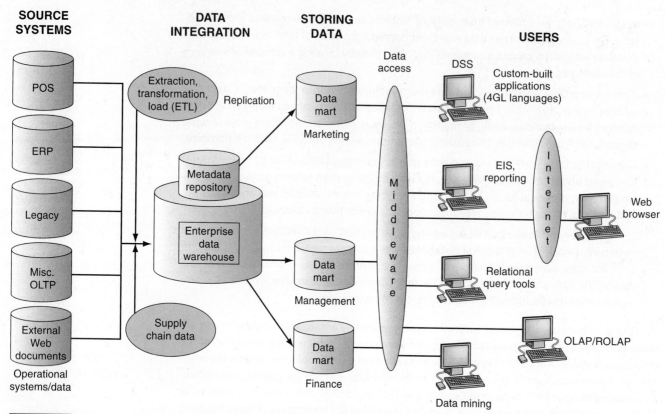

FIGURE 5.4 **Data warehouse framework.**

A common source for the data in data warehouses is the company's operational databases, which can be relational databases. To differentiate between relational databases and multidimensional data warehouses and marts, imagine your company manufactures four products—nuts, screws, bolts, and washers—and has sold them in three territories—East, West, and Central—for the previous three years—2016, 2017, and 2018. In a relational database, these sales data would resemble **Figure 5.5**(a) through (c). In a multidimensional database, in contrast, these data would be represented by a three-dimensional matrix (or data cube), as depicted in **Figure 5.6**. This matrix represents sales *dimensioned by* products, regions, and year. Notice that Figure 5.5(a) presents only sales for 2016. Sales for 2017 and 2018 are presented in Figure 5.5(b) and (c), respectively. **Figure 5.7**(a) through (c) illustrates the equivalence between these relational and multidimensional databases.

Unfortunately, many source systems that have been in use for years contain "bad data"—for example, missing or incorrect data—and they are poorly documented. As a result, data-profiling software should be used at the beginning of a warehousing project to better understand the data. Among other things, this software can provide statistics on missing data, identify possible primary and foreign keys, and reveal how derived values—for example, column 3 = column 1 + column 2—are calculated. Subject area database specialists such as marketing and human resources personnel can also assist in understanding and accessing the data in source systems.

Organizations need to address other source systems issues as well. For example, many organizations maintain multiple systems that contain some of the same data. These enterprises need to select the best system as the source system. Organizations must also decide how granular, or detailed, the data should be. For example, does the organization need daily sales figures or data for individual transactions? The conventional wisdom is that it is best to store data at a highly granular level because someone will likely request those data at some point.

Data Integration.   In addition to storing data in their source systems, organizations need to *e*xtract the data, *t*ransform them, and then *l*oad them into a data mart or warehouse.

(a) 2016

Product	Region	Sales
Nuts	East	50
Nuts	West	60
Nuts	Central	100
Screws	East	40
Screws	West	70
Screws	Central	80
Bolts	East	90
Bolts	West	120
Bolts	Central	140
Washers	East	20
Washers	West	10
Washers	Central	30

(b) 2017

Product	Region	Sales
Nuts	East	60
Nuts	West	70
Nuts	Central	110
Screws	East	50
Screws	West	80
Screws	Central	90
Bolts	East	100
Bolts	West	130
Bolts	Central	150
Washers	East	30
Washers	West	20
Washers	Central	40

(c) 2018

Product	Region	Sales
Nuts	East	70
Nuts	West	80
Nuts	Central	120
Screws	East	60
Screws	West	90
Screws	Central	100
Bolts	East	110
Bolts	West	140
Bolts	Central	160
Washers	East	40
Washers	West	30
Washers	Central	50

FIGURE 5.5   **Relational databases.**

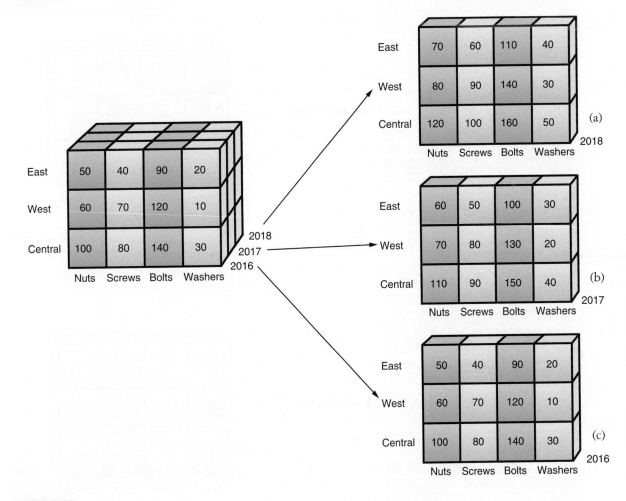

FIGURE 5.6   **Data cube.**

This process is often called ETL, although the term *data integration* is increasingly being used to reflect the growing number of ways that source system data can be handled. For example, in some cases, data are extracted, loaded into a mart or warehouse, and then transformed (i.e., ELT rather than ETL).

Product	Region	Sales
Nuts	East	50
Nuts	West	60
Nuts	Central	100
Screws	East	40
Screws	West	70
Screws	Central	80
Bolts	East	90
Bolts	West	120
Bolts	Central	140
Washers	East	20
Washers	West	10
Washers	Central	30

2016

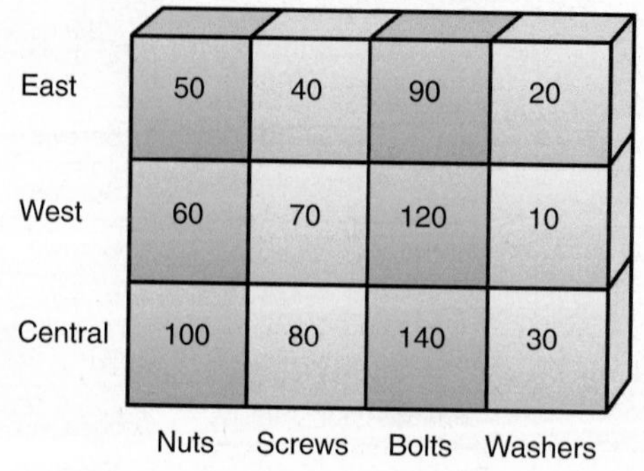

(a)
2016

Product	Region	Sales
Nuts	East	60
Nuts	West	70
Nuts	Central	110
Screws	East	50
Screws	West	80
Screws	Central	90
Bolts	East	100
Bolts	West	130
Bolts	Central	150
Washers	East	30
Washers	West	20
Washers	Central	40

2017

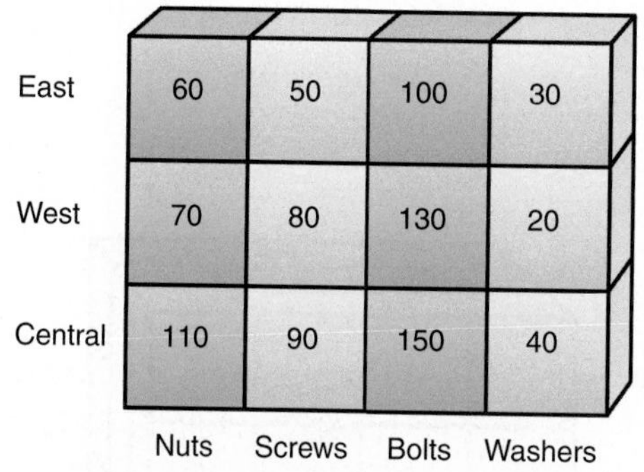

(b)
2017

Product	Region	Sales
Nuts	East	70
Nuts	West	80
Nuts	Central	120
Screws	East	60
Screws	West	90
Screws	Central	100
Bolts	East	110
Bolts	West	140
Bolts	Central	160
Washers	East	40
Washers	West	30
Washers	Central	50

2018

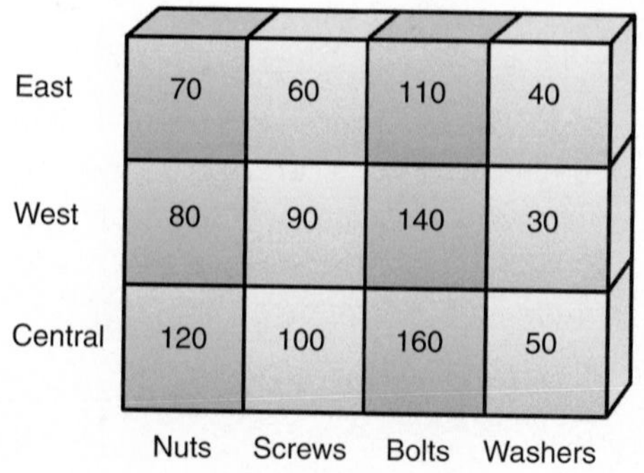

(c)
2018

FIGURE 5.7 **Equivalence between relational and multidimensional databases.**

Data extraction can be performed either by handwritten code such as SQL queries or by commercial data-integration software. Most companies employ commercial software. This software makes it relatively easy to (1) specify the tables and attributes in the source systems that are to be used; (2) map and schedule the movement of the data to the target, such as a data mart or warehouse; (3) make the required transformations; and, ultimately, (4) load the data.

After the data are extracted, they are transformed to make them more useful. For example, data from different systems may be integrated around a common key, such as a customer identification number. Organizations adopt this approach to create a 360-degree view of all of their interactions with their customers. As an example of this process, consider a bank. Customers can engage in a variety of interactions: visiting a branch, banking online, using an ATM, obtaining a car loan, and more. The systems for these touch points—defined as the numerous ways that organizations interact with customers, such as e-mail, the Web, direct contact, and the telephone—are typically independent of one another. To obtain a holistic picture of how customers are using the bank, the bank must integrate the data from the various source systems into a data mart or warehouse.

Other kinds of transformations also take place. For example, format changes to the data may be required, such as using *male* and *female* to denote gender, as opposed to 0 and 1 or M and F. Aggregations may be performed, say on sales figures, so that queries can use the summaries rather than recalculating them each time. Data-cleansing software may be used to clean up the data; for example, eliminating duplicate records for the same customer.

Finally, data are loaded into the warehouse or mart during a specified period known as the "load window." This window is becoming smaller as companies seek to store ever-fresher data in their warehouses. For this reason, many companies have moved to real-time data warehousing, where data are moved using data-integration processes from source systems to the data warehouse or mart almost instantly. For example, within 15 minutes of a purchase at Walmart, the details of the sale have been loaded into a warehouse and are available for analysis.

Storing the Data.   Organizations can choose from a variety of architectures to store decision-support data. The most common architecture is *one central enterprise data warehouse*, without data marts. Most organizations use this approach because the data stored in the warehouse are accessed by all users, and they represent the *single version of the truth*.

Another architecture is *independent data marts*. These marts store data for a single application or a few applications, such as marketing and finance. Organizations that employ this architecture give only limited thought to how the data might be used for other applications or by other functional areas in the organization. Clearly this is a very application-centric approach to storing data.

The independent data mart architecture is not particularly effective. Although it may meet a specific organizational need, it does not reflect an enterprisewide approach to data management. Instead, the various organizational units create independent data marts. Not only are these marts expensive to build and maintain but they also often contain inconsistent data. For example, they may have inconsistent data definitions such as: What is a customer? Is a particular individual a potential or a current customer? They might also use different source systems, which can have different data for the same item, such as a customer address (if the customer had moved). Although independent data marts are an organizational reality, larger companies have increasingly moved to data warehouses.

Still another data warehouse architecture is the *hub and spoke*. This architecture contains a central data warehouse that stores the data plus multiple dependent data marts that source their data from the central repository. Because the marts obtain their data from the central repository, the data in these marts still comprise the *single version of the truth* for decision-support purposes.

The dependent data marts store the data in a format that is appropriate for how the data will be used and for providing faster response times to queries and applications. As you have learned, users can view and analyze data from the perspective of business dimensions and measures. This analysis is intuitive because the dimensions are presented in business terms that users can easily understand.

Metadata.

It is important to maintain data about the data, known as *metadata*, in the data warehouse. Both the IT personnel who operate and manage the data warehouse and the users who access the data require metadata. IT personnel need information about data sources; database, table, and column names; refresh schedules; and data-usage measures. Users' needs include data definitions, report and query tools, report distribution information, and contact information for the help desk.

Data Quality.

The quality of the data in the warehouse must meet users' needs. If it does not, then users will not trust the data and ultimately will not use it. Most organizations find that the quality of the data in source systems is poor and must be improved before the data can be used in the data warehouse. Some of the data can be improved with data-cleansing software. The better, long-term solution, however, is to improve the quality at the source system level. This approach requires the business owners of the data to assume responsibility for making any necessary changes to implement this solution.

To illustrate this point, consider the case of a large hotel chain that wanted to conduct targeted marketing promotions using zip code data it collected from its guests when they checked in. When the company analyzed the zip code data, they discovered that many of the zip codes were 99999. How did this error occur? The answer is that the clerks were not asking customers for their zip codes, but they needed to enter something to complete the registration process. A short-term solution to this problem was to conduct the marketing campaign using city and state data instead of zip codes. The long-term solution was to make certain the clerks entered the actual zip codes. The latter solution required the hotel managers to assume responsibility for making certain their clerks enter the correct data.

Governance.

To ensure that BI is meeting their needs, organizations must implement *governance* to plan and control their BI activities. Governance requires that people, committees, and processes be in place. Companies that are effective in BI governance often create a senior-level committee composed of vice presidents and directors who (1) ensure that the business strategies and BI strategies are in alignment, (2) prioritize projects, and (3) allocate resources. These companies also establish a middle management–level committee that oversees the various projects in the BI portfolio to ensure that these projects are being completed in accordance with the company's objectives. Finally, lower-level operational committees perform tasks such as creating data definitions and identifying and solving data problems. All of these committees rely on the collaboration and contributions of business users and IT personnel.

Users.

Once the data are loaded in a data mart or warehouse, they can be accessed. At this point, the organization begins to obtain business value from BI; all of the prior stages constitute creating BI infrastructure.

There are many potential BI users, including IT developers; frontline workers; analysts; information workers; managers and executives; and suppliers, customers, and regulators. Some of these users are *information producers* whose primary role is to create information for other users. IT developers and analysts typically fall into this category. Other users—including managers and executives—are *information consumers*, because they use information created by others.

Companies have reported hundreds of successful data-warehousing applications. You can read client success stories and case studies at the websites of vendors such as NCR Corp. (**www.ncr.com**) and Oracle (**www.oracle.com**). For a more detailed discussion, visit the Data Warehouse Institute (**www.tdwi.org**). The benefits of data warehousing include the following:

- End users can access needed data quickly and easily through Web browsers because these data are located in one place.

- End users can conduct extensive analysis with data in ways that were not previously possible.

- End users can obtain a consolidated view of organizational data.

These benefits can improve business knowledge, provide competitive advantage, enhance customer service and satisfaction, facilitate decision making, and streamline business processes.

Despite their many benefits, data warehouses have some limitations. IT's About Business 5.3 points out these limitations and considers an emerging solution; namely, data lakes.

IT's About Business 5.3

Data Lakes

`MIS`

Most large organizations have an enterprise data warehouse (EDW) which contains data from other enterprise systems such as customer relationship management (CRM), inventory, and sales transaction systems. Analysts and business users examine the data in EDWs to make business decisions.

Despite their benefits to organizations, EDWs do have problems. Specifically, they employ a *schema-on-write architecture* which is the foundation for the underlying extract, transform, and load (ETL) process required to enter data into the EDW. With schema-on-write, enterprises must design the data model before they load any data. That is, organizations must first define the schema, then write (load) the data, and finally read the data. To carry out this process, they need to know ahead of time how they plan to use the data.

A *database schema* defines the structure of both the database and the data contained in the database. For example, in the case of relational databases, the schema specifies the tables and fields of the database. A database schema also describes the content and structure of the physical data stored, which is sometimes called metadata. Metadata can include information about data types, relationships, content restrictions, access controls, and many other types of information.

Because EDWs contain only data that conform to the prespecified enterprise data model, they are relatively inflexible and can answer only a limited number of questions. It is therefore difficult for business analysts and data scientists who rely on EDWs to ask ad hoc questions of the data. Instead, they have to form hypotheses in advance and then create the data structures to test those hypotheses.

It is also difficult for EDWs to manage new sources of data, such as streaming data from sensors (see the Internet of Things in Chapter 8) and social media data such as blog postings, ratings, recommendations, product reviews, tweets, photographs, and video clips.

EDWs have been the primary mechanism in many organizations for performing analytics, reporting, and operations. However, they are too rigid to be effective with Big Data, with large data volumes, with a broad variety of data, and with high data velocity. As a result of these problems, organizations have begun to realize that EDWs cannot meet all their business needs. As an alternative, they are beginning to deploy data lakes.

A **data lake** is a central repository that stores all of an organization's data, regardless of their source or format. Data lakes receive data in any format, both structured and unstructured. Also, the data do not have to be consistent. For example, organizations may have the same type of information in different data formats, depending on where the data originate.

Data lakes are typically, though not always, built using Apache Hadoop (**www.hadoop.apache.org**). Organizations can then employ a variety of storage and processing tools to extract value quickly and to inform key business decisions.

In contrast to the schema-on write architecture utilized by EDWs, data lakes use *schema-on-read architectures*. That is, they do not transform the data before the data are entered into the data lake as they would for an EDW. The structure of the data is not known when the data are fed into the data lake. Rather, it is discovered only when the data are read. With schema-on-read, users do not model the data until they actually use the data. This process is more flexible, and it makes it easier for users to discover new data and to enter new data sources into the data lake.

Data lakes provide many benefits for organizations:

- Organizations can derive value from unlimited types of data.
- Organizations do not need to have all of the answers in advance.
- Organizations have no limits on how they can query the data.
- Organizations do not create silos. Instead, data lakes provide a single, unified view of data across the organization.

To load data into a data lake, organizations should take the following steps:

- Define the incoming data from a business perspective.
- Document the context, origin, and frequency of the incoming data.
- Classify the security level (public, internal, sensitive, restricted) of the incoming data.
- Document the creation, usage, privacy, regulatory, and encryption business rules that apply to the incoming data.
- Identify the owner (sponsor) of the incoming data.
- Identify the data steward(s) charged with monitoring the health of the specific datasets.

After following these steps, organizations load all of the data into a giant table. Each piece of data—whether a customer's name, a photograph, or a Facebook post—is placed in an individual cell. It does not matter where in the data lake that individual cell is located, where the data came from, or its format, because all of the data are connected through metadata tags. Organizations can add or change these tags as requirements evolve. Further, they can assign multiple tags to the same piece of data. Because the schema for storing the data does not need to be defined in advance, expensive and time-consuming data modeling is not needed.

Organizations can also protect sensitive information. As data is loaded into the data lake, each cell is tagged according to how visible it is to different users in the organization. That is, organizations can specify who has access to the data in each cell, and under what circumstances, as the data is loaded.

For example, a retail operation might make cells containing customers' names and contact data available to sales and customer service, but it might make the cells containing more sensitive personally identifiable information or financial data available only to the finance department. In that way, when users run queries on the data, their access rights restrict which data they can access.

There are many examples of data lakes in practice. Let's consider EMC (**www.dellemc.com**), an industry leader in storage and analytics technologies. EMC promotes data-driven business transformation for its customers by helping them store, manage, protect, and analyze their most valuable asset—data. After EMC acquired more than 80 companies over the past decade, the company's IT department ended up controlling multiple data silos. Furthermore, EMC did not have an effective way to deliver on-demand analytics to business units. Although data reporting helped EMC with descriptive analytics (see Chapter 12), the company could not exploit the potential of predictive analytics to create targeted marketing and lead generation campaigns.

To overcome these limitations, EMC consolidated multiple data silos into a data lake, which contained all of the firm's structured and unstructured data. Examples of data in EMC's data lake are customer information (such as past purchases), contact demographics, interests, marketing history, data from social media and the Web, and sensor data. EMC also implemented data governance in its data lake so that its business groups could share data and collaborate on initiatives involving analytics.

MKT Using its data lake, EMC was able to microsegment customers for more relevant and targeted marketing communications. Removing the data silos greatly enhanced EMC marketing managers' understanding of the firm's customers and their purchasing behaviors.

The data lake also enables employees to make near-real-time decisions about which data to analyze. Significantly, the time required to complete some queries has fallen from four hours per quarter to fewer than one minute per year. The reason for the decrease is that at the beginning of the query EMC data scientists do not have to commit to which data and analytic technique they will use. For example, data scientists might take an initial look at more than 1,000 variables, some of which are probably redundant. The analytics software will select the most powerful variables for prediction, resulting in the most efficient and accurate predictive model.

Because the data lake contains such wide-ranging and diverse data, EMC's predictive models are increasingly accurate. In fact, EMC claims it can correctly predict what a customer is going to purchase and when 80 percent of the time.

Sources: Compiled from T. King, "Three Key Data Lake Trends to Stay on Top of This Year," *Solutions Review*, May 11, 2018; T. Olavsrud, "6 Data Analytics Trends that Will Dominate 2018," *CIO*, March 15, 2018; P. Tyaqi and H. Demirkan, "Data Lakes: The Biggest Big Data Challenges," *Analytics Magazine*, September/October, 2017; M. Hagstroem, M. Roggendorf, T. Saleh, and J. Sharma, "A Smarter Way to Jump into Data Lakes," *McKinsey and Company*, August, 2017; P. Barth, "The New Paradigm for Big Data Governance," *CIO*, May 11, 2017; N. Mikhail, "Why Big Data Kills Businesses," *Fortune*, February 28, 2017; "Architecting Data Lakes," *Zaloni*, February 21, 2017; D. Kim, "Successful Data Lakes: A Growing Trend," *The Data Warehousing Institute*, February 16, 2017; D. Woods, "Data Lakes and Frosted Flakes—Should You Buy Both off the Shelf?" *Forbes*, January 24, 2017; S. Carey, "Big Data and Business Intelligence Trends 2017: Machine Learning, Data Lakes, and Hadoop vs Spark," *Computerworld UK*, December 28, 2016; D. Woods, "Why Data Lakes Are Evil," *Forbes*, August 26, 2016; J. Davis, "How TD Bank Is Transforming Its Data Infrastructure," *InformationWeek*, May 25, 2016; L. Hester, "Maximizing Data Value with a Data Lake," *Data Science Central*, April 20, 2016; "Extracting Insight and Value from a Lake of Data," *Intel Case Study*, 2016; and S. Gittlen, "Data Lakes: A Better Way to Analyze Customer Data," *Computerworld*, February 25, 2016.

Questions

1. Discuss the limitations of enterprise data warehouses.
2. Describe the benefits of a data lake to organizations.

Before you go on . . .

1. Differentiate between data warehouses and data marts.
2. Describe the characteristics of a data warehouse.
3. What are three possible architectures for data warehouses and data marts in an organization?

5.5 # Knowledge Management

Author Lecture Videos are available exclusively in *WileyPLUS*.
Apply the Concept activities are available in the Appendix and in *WileyPLUS*.

As we have noted throughout this text, data and information are vital organizational assets. Knowledge is a vital asset as well. Successful managers have always valued and used intellectual assets. These efforts were not systematic, however, and they did not ensure that knowledge was shared and dispersed in a way that benefited the overall organization. Moreover, industry analysts estimate that most of a company's knowledge assets are not housed in relational databases. Instead, they are dispersed in e-mail, word processing documents, spreadsheets, presentations on individual computers, and in people's heads. This arrangement makes it extremely difficult for companies to access and integrate this knowledge. The result frequently is less-effective decision making.

Concepts and Definitions

Knowledge management (KM) is a process that helps organizations manipulate important knowledge that comprises part of the organization's memory, usually in an unstructured format. For an organization to be successful, knowledge, as a form of capital, must exist in a format that can be exchanged among persons. It must also be able to grow.

Knowledge. In the information technology context, knowledge is distinct from data and information. As you learned in Chapter 1, data are a collection of facts, measurements, and statistics; information is organized or processed data that are timely and accurate. Knowledge is information that is *contextual*, *relevant*, and *useful*. Simply put, knowledge is information in action. **Intellectual capital** (or **intellectual assets**) is another term for knowledge.

To illustrate, a bulletin listing all of the courses offered by your university during one semester would be considered *data*. When you register, you process the data from the bulletin to create your schedule for the semester. Your schedule would be considered *information*. Awareness of your work schedule, your major, your desired social schedule, and characteristics of different faculty members could be construed as *knowledge*, because it can affect the way you build your schedule. You see that this awareness is contextual and relevant (to developing an optimal schedule of classes) as well as useful (it can lead to changes in your schedule). The implication is that knowledge has strong experiential and reflective elements that distinguish it from information in a given context. Unlike information, knowledge can be used to solve a problem.

Numerous theories and models classify different types of knowledge. In the next section, we will focus on the distinction between explicit knowledge and tacit knowledge.

Explicit and Tacit Knowledge. **Explicit knowledge** deals with more objective, rational, and technical knowledge. In an organization, explicit knowledge consists of the policies, procedural guides, reports, products, strategies, goals, core competencies, and IT infrastructure of the enterprise. In other words, explicit knowledge is the knowledge that has been codified (documented) in a form that can be distributed to others or transformed into a process or a strategy. A description of how to process a job application that is documented in a firm's human resources policy manual is an example of explicit knowledge.

In contrast, **tacit knowledge** is the cumulative store of subjective or experiential learning. In an organization, tacit knowledge consists of an organization's experiences, insights, expertise, know-how, trade secrets, skill sets, understanding, and learning. It also includes the organizational culture, which reflects the past and present experiences of the organization's people and processes, as well as the organization's prevailing values. Tacit knowledge is generally imprecise and costly to transfer. It is also highly personal. Finally, because it is unstructured, it is difficult to formalize or codify, in contrast to explicit knowledge. A salesperson who has worked with particular customers over time and has come to know their needs quite well would possess extensive tacit knowledge. This knowledge is typically not recorded. In fact, it might be difficult for the salesperson to put into writing, even if he or she were willing to share it.

Knowledge Management Systems

The goal of knowledge management is to help an organization make the most productive use of the knowledge it has accumulated. Historically, management information systems have focused on capturing, storing, managing, and reporting explicit knowledge. Organizations now realize they need to integrate explicit and tacit knowledge into formal information systems. **Knowledge management systems (KMSs)** refer to the use of modern information technologies—the Internet, intranets, extranets, and databases—to systematize, enhance, and expedite knowledge management both within one firm and among multiple firms. KMSs are intended to help an organization cope with turnover, rapid change, and downsizing by making the expertise of the organization's human capital widely accessible.

Organizations can realize many benefits with KMSs. Most important, they make **best practices**—the most effective and efficient ways to accomplish business processes—readily available to a wide range of employees. Enhanced access to best-practice knowledge improves overall organizational performance. For example, account managers can now make available their tacit knowledge about how best to manage large accounts. The organization can then use this knowledge when it trains new account managers. Other benefits include enhanced customer service, more efficient product development, and improved employee morale and retention.

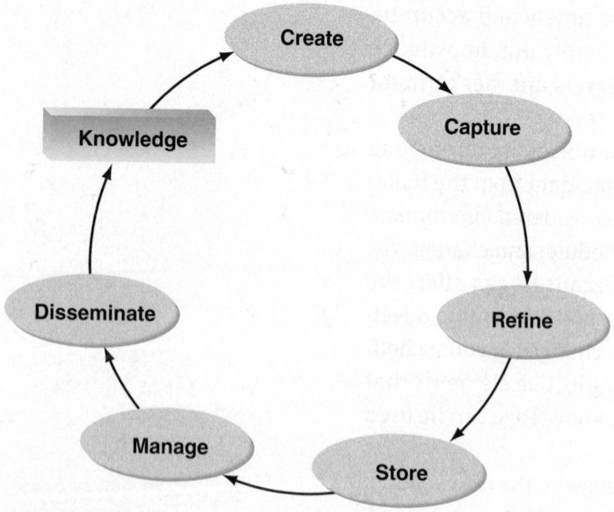

FIGURE 5.8 **The knowledge management system cycle.**

At the same time, however, implementing effective KMSs presents several challenges. First, employees must be willing to share their personal tacit knowledge. To encourage this behavior, organizations must create a knowledge management culture that rewards employees who add their expertise to the knowledge base. Second, the organization must continually maintain and upgrade its knowledge base. Specifically, it must incorporate new knowledge and delete old, outdated knowledge. Finally, companies must be willing to invest in the resources needed to carry out these operations.

The KMS Cycle

A functioning KMS follows a cycle that consists of six steps (see **Figure 5.8**). The reason the system is cyclical is that knowledge is dynamically refined over time. The knowledge in an effective KMS is never finalized because the environment changes over time and knowledge must be updated to reflect these changes. The cycle works as follows:

1. *Create knowledge:* Knowledge is created as people determine new ways of doing things or develop know-how. Sometimes external knowledge is brought in.

2. *Capture knowledge:* New knowledge must be identified as valuable and be presented in a reasonable way.

3. *Refine knowledge:* New knowledge must be placed in context so that it is actionable. This is where tacit qualities (human insights) must be captured along with explicit facts.

4. *Store knowledge:* Useful knowledge must then be stored in a reasonable format in a knowledge repository so that other people in the organization can access it.

5. *Manage knowledge:* Like a library, the knowledge must be kept current. Therefore, it must be reviewed regularly to verify that it is relevant and accurate.

6. *Disseminate knowledge:* Knowledge must be made available in a useful format to anyone in the organization who needs it, anywhere and any time.

Before you go on . . .

1. What is knowledge management?
2. What is the difference between tacit knowledge and explicit knowledge?
3. Describe the knowledge management system cycle.

5.6 Appendix: Fundamentals of Relational Database Operations

Author Lecture Videos are available exclusively in *WileyPLUS.*
Apply the Concept activities are available in the Appendix and in *WileyPLUS.*

There are many operations possible with relational databases. In this section, we discuss three of these operations: query languages, normalization, and joins.

As you have seen in this chapter, a relational database is a collection of interrelated 2D tables, consisting of rows and columns. Each row represents a record, and each column (or field) represents an attribute (or characteristic) of that record. Every record in the database must contain at least one field that uniquely identifies that record so that it can be retrieved, updated, and sorted. This identifier field, or group of fields, is called the *primary key*. In some cases, locating a particular record requires the use of secondary keys. A *secondary key* is another field that has some identifying information, but typically does not uniquely identify the record. A *foreign key* is a field (or group of fields) in one table that matches the primary key value in a row of another table. A foreign key is used to establish and enforce a link between two tables.

These related tables can be joined when they contain common columns. The uniqueness of the primary key tells the DBMS which records are joined with others in related tables. This feature allows users great flexibility in the variety of queries they can make. Despite these features, however, the relational database model has some disadvantages. Because large-scale databases can be composed of many interrelated tables, the overall design can be complex, leading to slow search and access times.

Query Languages

The most commonly performed database operation is searching for information. **Structured query language (SQL)** is the most popular query language used for interacting with a database. SQL allows people to perform complicated searches by using relatively simple statements or key words. Typical key words are SELECT (to choose a desired attribute), FROM (to specify the table or tables to be used), and WHERE (to specify conditions to apply in the query).

To understand how SQL works, imagine that a university wants to know the names of students who will graduate cum laude (but not magna or summa cum laude) in May 2018. (Refer to Figure 5.3 in this chapter.) The university IT staff would query the student relational database with an SQL statement such as the following:

SELECT Student_Name

FROM Student_Database

WHERE Grade_Point_Average > = 3.40 and Grade_Point_Average < 3.60.

The SQL query would return John Jones and Juan Rodriguez.

Another way to find information in a database is to use **query by example (QBE)**. In QBE, the user fills out a grid or template—also known as a *form*—to construct a sample or a description of the data desired. Users can construct a query quickly and easily by using drag-and-drop features in a DBMS such as Microsoft Access. Conducting queries in this manner is simpler than keying in SQL commands.

Entity–Relationship Modeling

Designers plan and create databases through the process of **entity–relationship (ER) modeling**, using an **entity–relationship (ER) diagram**. There are many approaches to ER diagramming. You will see one particular approach here, but there are others. The good news is that if you are familiar with one version of ER diagramming, then you will be able to easily adapt to any other version.

ER diagrams consist of entities, attributes, and relationships. To properly identify entities, attributes, and relationships, database designers first identify the business rules for the particular data model. **Business rules** are precise descriptions of policies, procedures, or principles in any organization that stores and uses data to generate information. Business rules are derived from a description of an organization's operations, and help to create and enforce business processes in that organization. Keep in mind that *you* determine these business rules, not the MIS department.

Entities are pictured in rectangles, and relationships are described on the line between two entities. The attributes for each entity are listed, and the primary key is underlined. The **data dictionary** provides information on each attribute, such as its name, if it is a key, part of a key, or a non-key attribute; the type of data expected (alphanumeric, numeric, dates, etc.); and valid values. Data dictionaries can also provide information on why the attribute is needed in

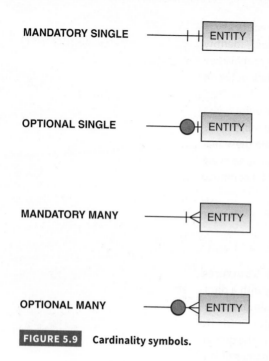

MANDATORY SINGLE

OPTIONAL SINGLE

MANDATORY MANY

OPTIONAL MANY

FIGURE 5.9   **Cardinality symbols.**

the database; which business functions, applications, forms, and reports use the attribute; and how often the attribute should be updated.

ER modeling is valuable because it allows database designers to communicate with users throughout the organization to ensure that all entities and the relationships among the entities are represented. This process underscores the importance of taking all users into account when designing organizational databases. Notice that all entities and relationships in our example are labeled in terms that users can understand.

Relationships illustrate an association between entities. The *degree of a relationship* indicates the number of entities associated with a relationship. A **unary relationship** exists when an association is maintained within a single entity. A **binary relationship** exists when two entities are associated. A **ternary relationship** exists when three entities are associated. In this chapter, we discuss only binary relationships because they are the most common. Entity relationships may be classified as one-to-one, one-to-many, or many-to-many. The term **connectivity** describes the relationship classification.

Connectivity and cardinality are established by the business rules of a relationship. *Cardinality* refers to the maximum number of times an instance of one entity can be associated with an instance in the related entity. Cardinality can be mandatory single, optional single, mandatory many, or optional many. **Figure 5.9** displays the cardinality symbols. Note that we have four possible cardinality symbols: mandatory single, optional single, mandatory many, and optional many.

Let's look at an example from a university. An *entity* is a person, place, or thing that can be identified in the users' work environment. For example, consider student registration at a university. Students register for courses, and they also register their cars for parking permits. In this example, STUDENT, PARKING PERMIT, CLASS, and PROFESSOR are entities. Recall that an instance of an entity represents a particular student, parking permit, class, or professor. Therefore, a particular STUDENT (James Smythe, 8023445) is an instance of the STUDENT entity; a particular parking permit (91778) is an instance of the PARKING PERMIT entity; a particular class (76890) is an instance of the CLASS entity; and a particular professor (Margaret Wilson, 390567) is an instance of the PROFESSOR entity.

Entity instances have *identifiers*, or *primary keys*, which are attributes (attributes and identifiers are synonymous) that are unique to that entity instance. For example, STUDENT instances can be identified with Student Identification Number; PARKING PERMIT instances can be identified with Permit Number; CLASS instances can be identified with Class Number; and PROFESSOR instances can be identified with Professor Identification Number.

Entities have attributes, or properties, that describe the entity's characteristics. In our example, examples of attributes for STUDENT are Student Name and Student Address. Examples of attributes for PARKING PERMIT are Student Identification Number and Car Type. Examples of attributes for CLASS are Class Name, Class Time, and Class Place. Examples of attributes for PROFESSOR are Professor Name and Professor Department. (Note that each course at this university has one professor—no team teaching.)

Why is Student Identification Number an attribute of both the STUDENT and PARKING PERMIT entity classes? That is, why do we need the PARKING PERMIT entity class? If you consider all of the interlinked university systems, the PARKING PERMIT entity class is needed for other applications, such as fee payments, parking tickets, and external links to the state's Department of Motor Vehicles.

Let's consider the three types of binary relationships in our example.

In a *one-to-one (1:1)* relationship, a single-entity instance of one type is related to a single-entity instance of another type. In our university example, STUDENT–PARKING PERMIT is a 1:1 relationship. The business rule at this university represented by this relationship is: Students may register only one car at this university. Of course, students do not have to register a car at all. That is, a student can have only one parking permit but does not need to have one.

Note that the relationship line on the PARKING PERMIT side shows a cardinality of optional single. A student can have, but does not have to have, a parking permit. On the STUDENT side of the relationship, only one parking permit can be assigned to one student, resulting in a cardinality of mandatory single. See **Figure 5.10**.

The second type of relationship, *one-to-many (1:M)*, is represented by the CLASS–PROFESSOR relationship in **Figure 5.11**. The business rule at this university represented by this relationship is the following: At this university, there is no team teaching. Therefore, each class must have only one professor. On the other hand, professors may teach more than one class. Note that the relationship line on the PROFESSOR side shows a cardinality of mandatory single. In contrast, the relationship line on the CLASS side shows a cardinality of optional many.

The third type of relationship, *many-to-many (M:M)*, is represented by the STUDENT–CLASS relationship. Most database management systems do not support many-to-many relationships. Therefore, we use *junction* (or *bridge*) *tables* so that we have two one-to-many relationships. The business rule at this university represented by this relationship is: Students can register for one or more classes, and each class can have one or more students (see **Figure 5.12**). In this example, we create the REGISTRATION table as our junction table. Note that Student ID and Class ID are foreign keys in the REGISTRATION table.

Let's examine the following relationships:

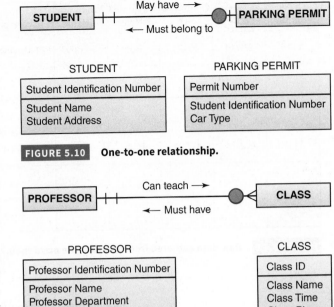

FIGURE 5.10   One-to-one relationship.

FIGURE 5.11   One-to-many relationship.

- The relationship line on the STUDENT side of the STUDENT–REGISTRATION relationship shows a cardinality of optional single.
- The relationship line on the REGISTRATION side of the STUDENT–REGISTRATION relationship shows a cardinality of optional many.
- The relationship line on the CLASS side of the CLASS–REGISTRATION relationship shows a cardinality of optional single.
- The relationship line on the REGISTRATION side of the CLASS–REGISTRATION relationship shows a cardinality of optional many.

Normalization and Joins

To use a relational database management system efficiently and effectively, the data must be analyzed to eliminate redundant data elements. **Normalization** is a method for analyzing and reducing a relational database to its most streamlined form to ensure minimum redundancy, maximum data integrity, and optimal processing performance. Data normalization is a methodology for organizing attributes into tables so that redundancy among the non-key attributes is eliminated. The result of the data normalization process is a properly structured relational database.

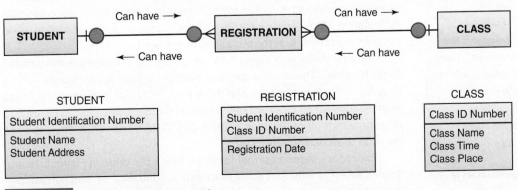

FIGURE 5.12   Many-to-many relationship.

Order Number	Order Date	Customer ID	Customer F Name	Customer L Name	Customer Address	Zip Code	Pizza Code	Pizza Name	Quantity	Price	Total Price
1116	9/1/14	16421	Rob	Penny	123 Main St.	37411	P	Pepperoni	1	$11.00	$41.00
							MF	Meat Feast	1	$12.00	
							V	Vegetarian	2	$9.00	
1117	9/2/14	17221	Beth	Jones	41 Oak St.	29416	HM	Ham and Mushroom	3	$10.00	$56.00
							MF	Meat Feast	1	$12.00	
							TH	The Hawaiian	1	$14.00	

FIGURE 5.13 **Raw data gathered from orders at the pizza shop.**

Data normalization requires a list of all the attributes that must be incorporated into the database and a list of all of the defining associations, or functional dependencies, among the attributes. **Functional dependencies** are a means of expressing that the value of one particular attribute is associated with a specific single value of another attribute. For example, for a Student Number 05345 at a university, there is exactly one Student Name, John C. Jones, associated with it. That is, Student Number is referred to as the determinant because its value *determines* the value of the other attribute. We can also say that Student Name is functionally dependent on Student Number.

As an example of normalization, consider a pizza shop. This shop takes orders from customers on a form. **Figure 5.13** shows a table of nonnormalized data gathered by the pizza shop. This table has two records, one for each order being placed. Because there are several pizzas on each order, the order number and customer information appear in multiple rows. Several attributes of each record have null values. A null value is an attribute with no data in it. For example, Order Number has four null values. Therefore, this table is not in first normal form. The data drawn from that form is shown in Figure 5.13.

In our example, ORDER, CUSTOMER, and PIZZA are entities. The first step in normalization is to determine the functional dependencies among the attributes. The functional dependencies in our example are shown in **Figure 5.14**.

In the normalization process, we will proceed from nonnormalized data, to first normal form, to second normal form, and then to third normal form. (There are additional normal forms, but they are beyond the scope of this book.)

Figure 5.15 demonstrates the data in *first normal form*. The attributes under consideration are listed in one table and primary keys have been established. Our primary keys are Order Number, Customer ID, and Pizza Code. In first normal form, each ORDER has to repeat the order number, order date, customer first name, customer last name, customer address, and customer zip code. This data file contains repeating groups and describes multiple entities. That is, this relation has data redundancy, a lack of data integrity, and the flat file would be difficult to use in various applications that the pizza shop might need.

Consider the table in Figure 5.15, and notice the very first column (labeled Order Number). This column contains multiple entries for each order—three rows for Order Number 1116 and three rows for Order Number 1117. These multiple rows for an order are called *repeating groups*. The table in Figure 5.15 also contains multiple entities: ORDER, CUSTOMER, and PIZZA. Therefore, we move on to second normal form.

To produce second normal form, we break the table in Figure 5.15 into smaller tables to eliminate some of its data redundancy. Second normal form does not allow partial functional dependencies. That is, in a table in second

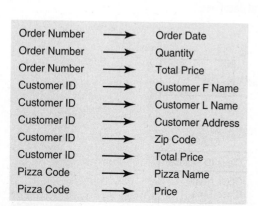

Order Number	⟶	Order Date
Order Number	⟶	Quantity
Order Number	⟶	Total Price
Customer ID	⟶	Customer F Name
Customer ID	⟶	Customer L Name
Customer ID	⟶	Customer Address
Customer ID	⟶	Zip Code
Customer ID	⟶	Total Price
Pizza Code	⟶	Pizza Name
Pizza Code	⟶	Price

FIGURE 5.14 **Functional dependencies in pizza shop example.**

Order Number	Order Date	Customer ID	Customer F Name	Customer L Name	Customer Address	Zip Code	Pizza Code	Pizza Name	Quantity	Price	Total Price
1116	9/1/14	16421	Rob	Penny	123 Main St.	37411	P	Pepperoni	1	$11.00	$41.00
1116	9/1/14	16421	Rob	Penny	123 Main St.	37411	MF	Meat Feast	1	$12.00	$41.00
1116	9/1/14	16421	Rob	Penny	123 Main St.	37411	V	Vegetarian	2	$9.00	$41.00
1117	9/2/14	17221	Beth	Jones	41 Oak St.	29416	HM	Ham and Mushroom	3	$10.00	$56.00
1117	9/2/14	17221	Beth	Jones	41 Oak St.	29416	MF	Meat Feast	1	$12.00	$56.00
1117	9/2/14	17221	Beth	Jones	41 Oak St.	29416	TH	The Hawaiian	1	$14.00	$56.00

FIGURE 5.15 First normal form for data from pizza shop.

Order Number	Order Date	Customer ID	Customer F Name	Customer L Name	Customer Address	Zip Code	Total Price
1116	9/1/14	16421	Rob	Penny	123 Main St.	37411	$41.00
1116	9/1/14	16421	Rob	Penny	123 Main St.	37411	$41.00
1116	9/1/14	16421	Rob	Penny	123 Main St.	37411	$41.00
1117	9/2/14	17221	Beth	Jones	41 Oak St.	29416	$56.00
1117	9/2/14	17221	Beth	Jones	41 Oak St.	29416	$56.00
1117	9/2/14	17221	Beth	Jones	41 Oak St.	29416	$56.00

Order Number	Pizza Code	Quantity
1116	P	1
1116	MF	1
1116	V	2
1117	HM	3
1117	MF	1
1117	TH	1

Pizza Code	Pizza Name	Price
P	Pepperoni	$11.00
MF	Meat Feast	$12.00
V	Vegetarian	$9.00
HM	Ham and Mushroom	$10.00
TH	The Hawaiian	$14.00

FIGURE 5.16 Second normal form for data from pizza shop.

normal form, every non-key attribute must be functionally dependent on the entire primary key of that table. **Figure 5.16** shows the data from the pizza shop in second normal form.

If you examine Figure 5.16, you will see that second normal form has not eliminated all the data redundancy. For example, each Order Number is duplicated three times, as are all customer data. In *third normal form,* non-key attributes are not allowed to define other non-key attributes. That is, third normal form does not allow transitive dependencies in which one non-key attribute is functionally dependent on another. In our example, customer information

ORDER

Order Number	Order Date	Customer ID	Total Price
1116	9/1/14	16421	$41.00
1117	9/2/14	17221	$56.00

CUSTOMER

Customer ID	Customer F Name	Customer L Name	Customer Address	Zip Code
16421	Rob	Penny	123 Main St.	37411
17221	Beth	Jones	41 Oak St.	29416

ORDER-PIZZA

Order Number	Pizza Code	Quantity
1116	P	1
1116	MF	1
1116	V	2
1117	HM	3
1117	MF	1
1117	TH	1

PIZZA

Pizza Code	Pizza Name	Price
P	Pepperoni	$11.00
MF	Meat Feast	$12.00
V	Vegetarian	$9.00
HM	Ham and Mushroom	$10.00
TH	The Hawaiian	$14.00

FIGURE 5.17 Third normal form for data from pizza shop.

depends both on Customer ID and Order Number. **Figure 5.17** shows the data from the pizza shop in third normal form. Third normal form structure has the following important points:

- It is completely free of data redundancy.
- All foreign keys appear where needed to link related tables.

Let's look at the primary and foreign keys for the tables in third normal form:

- *The ORDER relation:* The primary key is Order Number and the foreign key is Customer ID.
- *The CUSTOMER relation:* The primary key is Customer ID.
- *The PIZZA relation:* The primary key is Pizza Code.
- *The ORDER–PIZZA relation:* The primary key is a composite key, consisting of two foreign keys, Order Number and Pizza Code.

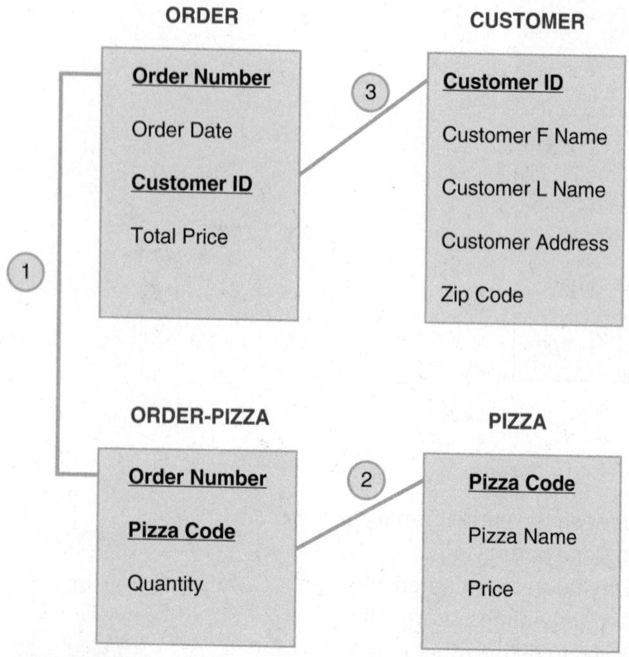

Now consider an order at the pizza shop. The tables in third normal form can produce the order in the following manner by using the join operation (see **Figure 5.18**). The **join operation** combines records from two or more tables in a database to obtain information that is located in different tables. In our example, the join operation combines records from the four normalized tables to produce an ORDER. Here is how the join operation works:

- The ORDER relation provides the Order Number (the primary key), Order Date, and Total Price.
- The primary key of the ORDER relation (Order Number) provides a link to the ORDER–PIZZA relation (the link numbered 1 in Figure 5.18).

FIGURE 5.18 The join process with the tables of third normal form to produce an order.

- The ORDER–PIZZA relation supplies the Quantity to ORDER.
- The primary key of the ORDER–PIZZA relation is a composite key that consists of Order Number and Pizza Code. Therefore, the Pizza Code component of the primary key provides a link to the PIZZA relation (the link numbered 2 in Figure 5.18).
- The PIZZA relation supplies the Pizza Name and Price to ORDER.
- The Customer ID in ORDER (a foreign key) provides a link to the CUSTOMER relation (the link numbered 3 in Figure 5.18).
- The CUSTOMER relation supplies the Customer FName, Customer LName, Customer Address, and Zip Code to ORDER.

At the end of this join process, we have a complete ORDER. Normalization is beneficial when maintaining databases over a period of time. One example is the likelihood of having to change the price of each pizza. If the pizza shop increases the price of the Meat Feast from $12.00 to $12.50, this process is one easy step in Figure 5.18. The price field is changed to $12.50, and the ORDER is automatically updated with the current value of the price.

Before you go on . . .

1. What is structured query language?
2. What is query by example?
3. What is an entity? An attribute? A relationship?
4. Describe one-to-one, one-to-many, and many-to-many relationships.
5. What is the purpose of normalization?
6. Why do we need the join operation?

What's in IT for me?

ACCT For the Accounting Major

The accounting function is intimately concerned with keeping track of the transactions and internal controls of an organization. Modern databases enable accountants to perform these functions more effectively. Databases help accountants manage the flood of data in today's organizations so that they can keep their firms in compliance with the standards imposed by Sarbanes–Oxley.

Accountants also play a role in cost justifying the creation of a knowledge base and then auditing its cost-effectiveness. Also, if you work for a large CPA company that provides management services or sells knowledge, you will most likely use some of your company's best practices that are stored in a knowledge base.

FIN For the Finance Major

Financial managers make extensive use of computerized databases that are external to the organization, such as CompuStat or Dow Jones, to obtain financial data on organizations in their industry. They can use these data to determine if their organization meets industry benchmarks in return on investment, cash management, and other financial ratios.

Financial managers, who produce the organization's financial status reports, are also closely involved with Sarbanes–Oxley. Databases help these managers comply with the law's standards.

MKT For the Marketing Major

Databases help marketing managers access data from their organization's marketing transactions, such as customer purchases, to plan targeted marketing campaigns and to evaluate the success of previous campaigns. Knowledge about customers can make the difference between success and failure. In many databases and knowledge bases, the vast majority of information and knowledge concerns customers, products, sales, and marketing. Marketing managers regularly use an organization's knowledge base, and they often participate in its creation.

POM For the Production/Operations Management Major

Production/operations personnel access organizational data to determine optimum inventory levels for parts in a production process. Past production data enable production/operations management (POM) personnel to determine the optimum configuration for assembly lines. Firms also collect quality data that inform them not only about the quality of finished products but also about quality issues with incoming raw materials, production irregularities, shipping and logistics, and after-sale use and maintenance of the product.

Knowledge management is extremely important for running complex operations. The accumulated knowledge regarding scheduling, logistics, maintenance, and other functions is very valuable. Innovative ideas are necessary for improving operations and can be supported by knowledge management.

HRM For the Human Resources Management Major

Organizations keep extensive data on employees, including gender, age, race, current and past job descriptions, and performance evaluations. HR personnel access these data to provide reports to government agencies regarding compliance with federal equal opportunity guidelines. HR managers also use these data to evaluate hiring practices, evaluate salary structures, and manage any discrimination grievances or lawsuits brought against the firm.

Databases help HR managers provide assistance to all employees as companies turn over more and more decisions about healthcare and retirement planning to the employees themselves.

The employees can use the databases for help in selecting the optimal mix among these critical choices.

HR managers also need to use a knowledge base frequently to find out how past cases were handled. Consistency in how employees are treated is not only important but it also protects the company against legal actions. Training for building, maintaining, and using the knowledge system is also sometimes the responsibility of the HR department. Finally, the HR department might be responsible for compensating employees who contribute their knowledge to the knowledge base.

MIS For the MIS Major

The MIS function manages the organization's data as well as the databases. MIS database administrators standardize data names by using the data dictionary. This process ensures that all users understand which data are in the database. Database personnel also help users access needed data and generate reports with query tools.

What's in **IT** for me? (Appendix: Section 5.6)

For All Business Majors

All business majors will have to manage data in their professional work. One way to manage data is through the use of databases and database management systems. First, it is likely that you will need to obtain information from your organization's databases. You will probably use structured query language to obtain this information. Second, as your organization plans and designs its databases, it will most likely use entity–relationship diagrams. You will provide much of the input to these ER diagrams. For example, you will describe the entities that you use in your work, the attributes of those entities, and the relationships among them. You will also help database designers as they normalize database tables, by describing how the normalized tables relate to each other (e.g., through the use of primary and foreign keys). Finally, you will help database designers as they plan their join operations to give you the information that you need when that information is stored in multiple tables.

Summary

5.1 Discuss ways that common challenges in managing data can be addressed using data governance.

The following are three common challenges in managing data:

- Data are scattered throughout organizations and are collected by many individuals using various methods and devices. These data are frequently stored in numerous servers and locations and in different computing systems, databases, formats, and human and computer languages.
- Data come from multiple sources.
- Information systems that support particular business processes impose unique requirements on data, which results in repetition and conflicts across an organization.

One strategy for implementing data governance is master data management. Master data management provides companies with the ability to store, maintain, exchange, and synchronize a consistent, accurate, and timely "single version of the truth" for the company's core master data. Master data management manages data gathered from across an organization, manages data from multiple sources, and manages data across business processes within an organization.

5.2 Discuss the advantages and disadvantages of relational databases.

Relational databases enable people to compare information quickly by row or column. Users also can easily retrieve items by finding the point of intersection of a particular row and column. However, large-scale relational databases can be composed of numerous interrelated tables, making the overall design complex, with slow search and access times.

5.3 Define Big Data and its basic characteristics.

Big Data is composed of high-volume, high-velocity, and high-variety information assets that require new forms of processing to enhance decision making, lead to insights, and optimize business processes. Big Data has three distinct characteristics that distinguish it from traditional data: volume, velocity, and variety.

- *Volume:* Big Data consists of vast quantities of data.
- *Velocity:* Big Data flows into an organization at incredible speeds.
- *Variety:* Big Data includes diverse data in differing formats.

5.4 Explain the elements necessary to successfully implement and maintain data warehouses.

To successfully implement and maintain a data warehouse, an organization must do the following:

- Link source systems that provide data to the warehouse or mart.
- Prepare the necessary data for the data warehouse using data integration technology and processes.
- Decide on an appropriate architecture for storing data in the data warehouse or data mart.
- Select the tools and applications for the variety of organizational users.
- Establish appropriate metadata, data quality, and governance processes to ensure that the data warehouse or mart meets its purposes.

5.5 Describe the benefits and challenges of implementing knowledge management systems in organizations.

Organizations can realize many benefits with KMSs, including the following:

- Best practices readily available to a wide range of employees
- Improved customer service
- More efficient product development
- Improved employee morale and retention

Challenges to implementing KMSs include the following:

- Employees must be willing to share their personal tacit knowledge.
- Organizations must create a knowledge management culture that rewards employees who add their expertise to the knowledge base.

- The knowledge base must be continually maintained and updated.
- Companies must be willing to invest in the resources needed to carry out these operations.

5.6 Understand the processes of querying a relational database, entity-relationship modeling, and normalization and joins.

The most commonly performed database operation is requesting information. *Structured query language* is the most popular query language used for this operation. SQL allows people to perform complicated searches by using relatively simple statements or key words. Typical key words are SELECT (to specify a desired attribute), FROM (to specify the table to be used), and WHERE (to specify conditions to apply in the query).

Another way to find information in a database is to use *query by example.* In QBE, the user fills out a grid or template—also known as a *form*—to construct a sample or a description of the data desired. Users can construct a query quickly and easily by using drag-and-drop features in a DBMS such as Microsoft Access. Conducting queries in this manner is simpler than keying in SQL commands.

Designers plan and create databases through the process of entity–relationship modeling, using an entity–relationship diagram. ER diagrams consist of entities, attributes, and relationships. Entities are pictured in boxes, and relationships are represented as diamonds. The attributes for each entity are listed, and the primary key is underlined.

ER modeling is valuable because it allows database designers to communicate with users throughout the organization to ensure that all entities and the relationships among the entities are represented. This process underscores the importance of taking all users into account when designing organizational databases. Notice that all entities and relationships in our example are labeled in terms that users can understand.

Normalization is a method for analyzing and reducing a relational database to its most streamlined form to ensure minimum redundancy, maximum data integrity, and optimal processing performance. When data are *normalized,* attributes in each table depend only on the primary key.

The *join operation* combines records from two or more tables in a database to produce information that is located in different tables.

Chapter Glossary

attribute   Each characteristic or quality of a particular entity.

best practices   The most effective and efficient ways to accomplish business processes.

Big Data   A collection of data so large and complex that it is difficult to manage using traditional database management systems.

binary relationship   A relationship that exists when two entities are associated.

bit   A binary digit—that is, a 0 or a 1.

business rules   Precise descriptions of policies, procedures, or principles in any organization that stores and uses data to generate information.

byte   A group of eight bits that represents a single character.

clickstream data   Data collected about user behavior and browsing patterns by monitoring users' activities when they visit a website.

connectivity   Describes the classification of a relationship: one-to-one, one-to-many, or many-to-many.

database management system (DBMS)   The software program (or group of programs) that provides access to a database.

data dictionary   A collection of definitions of data elements; data characteristics that use the data elements; and the individuals, business functions, applications, and reports that use these data elements.

data file (also table)   A collection of logically related records.

data governance   An approach to managing information across an entire organization.

data lake A central repository that stores all of an organization's data, regardless of their source or format.

data mart A low-cost, scaled-down version of a data warehouse that is designed for the end-user needs in a strategic business unit (SBU) or a department.

data model A diagram that represents entities in the database and their relationships.

data warehouse A repository of historical data that are organized by subject to support decision makers in the organization.

entity Any person, place, thing, or event of interest to a user.

entity–relationship (ER) diagram Document that shows data entities and attributes and relationships among them.

entity–relationship (ER) modeling The process of designing a database by organizing data entities to be used and identifying the relationships among them.

explicit knowledge The more objective, rational, and technical types of knowledge.

field A characteristic of interest that describes an entity.

foreign key A field (or group of fields) in one table that uniquely identifies a row (or record) of another table.

instance Each row in a relational table, which is a specific, unique representation of the entity.

intellectual capital (or intellectual assets) Other terms for knowledge.

join operation A database operation that combines records from two or more tables in a database.

knowledge management (KM) A process that helps organizations identify, select, organize, disseminate, transfer, and apply information and expertise that are part of the organization's memory and that typically reside within the organization in an unstructured manner.

knowledge management systems (KMSs) Information technologies used to systematize, enhance, and expedite intra- and interfirm knowledge management.

master data A set of core data, such as customer, product, employee, vendor, geographic location, and so on, that spans an enterprise's information systems.

master data management A process that provides companies with the ability to store, maintain, exchange, and synchronize a consistent, accurate, and timely "single version of the truth" for the company's core master data.

multidimensional structure Storage of data in more than two dimensions; a common representation is the data cube.

normalization A method for analyzing and reducing a relational database to its most streamlined form to ensure minimum redundancy, maximum data integrity, and optimal processing performance.

primary key A field (or attribute) of a record that uniquely identifies that record so that it can be retrieved, updated, and sorted.

query by example (QBE) To obtain information from a relational database, a user fills out a grid or template—also known as a *form*—to construct a sample or a description of the data desired.

record A grouping of logically related fields.

relational database model Data model based on the simple concept of tables in order to capitalize on characteristics of rows and columns of data.

relationships Operators that illustrate an association between two entities.

secondary key A field that has some identifying information, but typically does not uniquely identify a record with complete accuracy.

structured data Highly organized data in fixed fields in a data repository such as a relational database that must be defined in terms of field name and type (e.g., alphanumeric, numeric, and currency).

structured query language (SQL) The most popular query language for requesting information from a relational database.

table A grouping of logically related records.

tacit knowledge The cumulative store of subjective or experiential learning, which is highly personal and hard to formalize.

ternary relationship A relationship that exists when three entities are associated.

transactional data Data generated and captured by operational systems that describe the business's activities, or transactions.

unary relationship A relationship that exists when an association is maintained within a single entity.

unstructured data Data that do not reside in a traditional relational database.

Discussion Questions

1. Is Big Data really a problem on its own, or are the use, control, and security of the data the true problems? Provide specific examples to support your answer.

2. What are the implications of having incorrect data points in your Big Data? What are the implications of incorrect or duplicated customer data? How valuable are decisions that are based on faulty information derived from incorrect data?

3. Explain the difficulties involved in managing data.

4. What are the problems associated with poor-quality data?

5. What is master data management? What does it have to do with high-quality data?

6. Explain why master data management is so important in companies that have multiple data sources.

7. Describe the advantages and disadvantages of relational databases.

8. Explain why it is important to capture and manage knowledge.

9. Compare and contrast tacit knowledge and explicit knowledge.

10. Draw the entity–relationship diagram for a company that has departments and employees. In this company, a department must have at least one employee, and company employees may work in only one department.

11. Draw the entity–relationship diagram for library patrons and the process of checking out books.

12. You are working at a doctor's office. You gather data on the following entities: PATIENT, PHYSICIAN, PATIENT DIAGNOSIS, and TREATMENT. Develop a table for the entity, PATIENT VISIT. Decide on the primary keys and/or foreign keys that you want to use for each entity.

Problem-Solving Activities

1. Access various employment websites (e.g., **www.monster.com** and **www.dice.com**) and find several job descriptions for a database administrator. Are the job descriptions similar? What are the salaries offered in these positions?

2. Access the websites of several real estate companies. Find the sites that do the following: take you through a step-by-step process for buying a home, provide virtual reality tours of homes in your price range (say, $200,000 to $250,000) and location, provide mortgage and interest rate calculators, and offer financing for your home. Do the sites require that you register to access their services? Can you request that an e-mail be sent to you when properties in which you might be interested become available? How do the processes outlined influence your likelihood of selecting a particular company for your real estate purchase?

3. It is possible to find many websites that provide demographic information. Access several of these sites and see what they offer. Do the sites differ in the types of demographic information they offer? If so, how? Do the sites require a fee for the information they offer?

Would demographic information be useful to you if you wanted to start a new business? If so, how and why?

4. Search the Web for uses of Big Data in homeland security. Specifically, read about the spying by the U.S. National Security Agency (NSA). What role did technology and Big Data play in this questionable practice?

5. Search the web for the article "Why Big Data and Privacy Are Often at Odds." What points does this article present concerning the delicate balance between shared data and customer privacy?

6. Access the websites of IBM (**www.ibm.com**) and Oracle (**www.oracle.com**), and trace the capabilities of their latest data management products, including Web connections.

7. Enter the website of the Gartner Group (**www.gartner.com**). Examine the company's research studies pertaining to data management. Prepare a report on the state of the art of data management.

8. Diagram a knowledge management system cycle for a fictional company that sells customized T-shirts to students.

Chapter Closing Case

Data Enhances Fans' Experience of the Tour de France

Many sports, such as football, cricket, tennis, and baseball, provide huge amounts of data to fans in addition to the video feeds themselves. These data increase their enjoyment and improve their understanding of various sporting events. Significantly, the data can become overwhelming. Some fans still prefer to simply watch sporting events.

In 1903, the French sports newspaper *L'Auto* established the Tour de France as a marketing tool to increase sales. Although the Tour de France is world famous, it is also a challenge to watch. Television viewers can see the racers from numerous camera angles, but it is difficult to understand the subtleties and tactics of elite professional bicyclists. In addition, the race lasts for three weeks. Compounding these issues, the Tour's followers are more digitally engaged on social media than ever before, and they want a live and compelling experience during the Tour. This improved experience requires data.

Today, the Tour is deploying technology to capture data and perform analytics in near real time to help engage a new generation of digital fans. The 2018 Tour de France provided more data to fans than ever before, explaining and analyzing the performance of the racers in detail for the duration of the race.

Unlike other sports, which typically occur in a single venue, the Tour de France presents a unique set of challenges for using technology to capture and distribute data about the race and its cyclists. Information technology services firm Dimension Data (Dimension; **www.dimensiondata.com**) has provided and managed the technology behind the Tour since the 2015 race. Dimension has to gather and transmit data as the cyclists travel over difficult terrain such as up and down mountain roads in the Pyrenees and the Alps, where wireless signals can be intermittent and weak. The manner in which Dimension

handles these conditions provides an excellent example of how to deal with high-volume, real-time data from Internet of Things (IoT; see Chapter 8) sensors in often harsh conditions.

Each of the 176 riders who began the 2018 race had a custom, 100-gram (3.5-ounce) sensor on his bicycle. The sensor contained a global positioning system (GPS) chip, a radio frequency identification (RFID) chip, and a rechargeable battery with enough power to last for the longest of the Tour's 21 stages. Each sensor transmitted its GPS data every second, producing a total of more than 3 billion data points during the course of the race, a vast increase in data from the 128 million data points generated in the 2016 Tour de France. Dimension also collected data from other sources such as weather services and road gradients (steepness of climbs).

The data were entered into new machine learning algorithms (see Technology Guide 4), which predicted breakaway speeds, time gaps among riders, and even the winner of each stage. Dimension achieved approximately a 75 percent success rate on all its predictions for the 2018 Tour.

The bicycles' sensors transmitted data over a mesh network (see Chapter 8) via antennas placed on race cars that followed the cyclists, up to television helicopters overhead. The helicopters then sent the data to an aircraft at higher altitude, which in turn transmitted the data to the television trucks at the finish line of each stage of the race. There, the data were gathered by Dimension's "Big Data truck," which was also located at the finish line of each stage. Dimension notes that the transmission distances and latency (lag time) associated with satellites are too slow for the Tour.

Dimension's cloud computing service (see Technology Guide 3), based in data centers in London and Amsterdam, collected data from each stage of the race. At the data centers, Dimension produced the near-real-time information that was transmitted to broadcasters, social media, and the race app. The entire process from bike to viewer took a total of two seconds.

Dimension integrated and analyzed these data. As a result, race organizers, teams, broadcasters, commentators, television viewers, and fans using the Tour de France mobile app had access to in-depth statistics on the progress of the race and their favorite riders.

As recently as 2014, the only way for riders to obtain real-time information (e.g., road and weather conditions ahead, accidents that may have occurred, positions of other riders and teams) during the Tour de France was from a chalkboard that was held up by race officials who sat as passengers on motorcycles driving just ahead of the cyclists. Today, the riders wear earpiece radios so their teams can relay real-time data (often from Dimension) to them while they cycle. In that way, riders do not have to take their eyes off the road—and other riders—to look for chalkboards containing information for them.

Fans have enjoyed the insights that they have gained. For example, Dimension displayed an image of a high-speed crash during the 2015 Tour that contained data on the speed and sudden deceleration of the bikes involved. The data suggested that some riders had somehow accelerated after the moment of impact. Further analysis revealed that the bikes themselves, with their sensors still attached, had greater forward momentum after their riders were thrown off, because the weight on each bike had decreased. Some bikes involved in that crash seemingly accelerated to race speeds soon after the crash. In fact, they had been picked up by team cars following the peloton (the main group) of cyclists and were driven away.

In the 2018 Tour, data suggested that some riders achieved top speeds of over 60 miles per hour. Some fans were doubtful until one rider tweeted a photo of his speedometer showing that his speed peaked at more than 62 miles per hour along one downhill section of the race.

However, technology can be wrong. For example, GPS data can be corrupted by signal noise during transmission. As a result, during the 2015 Tour, the GPS data indicated that one cyclist was in Kenya. Today, all data are checked for these types of errors before they are processed.

Today, the technology is opening up the Tour to new and old fans. For example, in 2014, video clips distributed by race organizers attracted 6 million views. By the 2018 race, that number had grown to more than 70 million.

Eurosport (**www.eurosport.com**) is a European television sports network that is owned and operated by Discovery Communications. The network reported that average viewer numbers for live coverage of the 2018 Tour de France increased by 15 percent over the 2017 Tour.

Dimension is developing new services for the 2019 Tour. First is a new predictive cybersecurity protection model because the race is subject to a huge number of online attacks. For instance, Dimension was able to block almost two million suspicious access attempts during the 2017 Tour. Second, Dimension is developing an augmented-reality app that would allow viewers to experience, for example, an Alpine climb through a projection on a mobile app. Third, Dimension is developing dedicated chatbots that could provide real-time information on any specific rider at any point of the race.

Sources: Compiled from "Technology, Data, and Connected Cycling Teams at the Tour de France: What Can Businesses Learn from the World's Biggest Race?" *TechRadar Pro*, July 20, 2018; M. Moore, "Tour de France 2018: Why This Year's Race Will Be the Smartest Yet," *TechRadar*, July 6, 2018; "How Big Data, IoT, and the Cloud Are Transforming the Tour de France Fan Experience," *NTT Innovation Institute*, August 10, 2017; M. Smith, "How Sophisticated High-Tech Analytics Transformed the Tour de France," *t3.com*, July 31, 2017; M. Phillips, "19 Weird Tech Secrets of the 2017 Tour de France," *Bicycling*, July 21, 2017; B. Glick, "Data Takes to the Road – The Technology Behind the Tour de France," *Computer Weekly*, July 20, 2017; G. Scott, "Six Tech Trends from the 2017 Tour de France," *Road Cycling UK*, July 18, 2017; R. Guinness, "Bike Development Is Vital but Technology Alone Won't Win Tour de France," *ESPN*, July 8, 2017; "From Brakes to Water Bottles: What Technology Is Being Used in the 2017 Tour de France?" *FutureSport*, July 7, 2017; "The Impressive Engineering behind the Tour de France," *Match Tech*, July 4, 2017; M. Murison, "Tour de France to Use IoT in Digital Race for Spectators' Attention," *Internet of Business*, June 29, 2017; "Coverage of the 2017 Tour de France: A Technological Challenge that Orange Meets on a Daily Basis," *Orange*, June 28, 2017; D. Michels, "Adding an IoT Dimension to the Tour de France," *Network World*, May 23, 2017; and www.letour.fr, accessed August 1, 2018.

Questions

1. Refer to Chapter 2. Is Dimension Data's capture, analysis, and distribution of near-real-time information a strategic information system for the Tour de France? Why or why not? Support your answer.

2. Describe the ways in which Dimension uses Big Data in the Tour de France.

3. Describe how other sports could collect, manage, and use near-real-time data.

CHAPTER 6

Telecommunications and Networking

CHAPTER OUTLINE	LEARNING OBJECTIVES
6.1 What Is a Computer Network?	**6.1** Compare and contrast the major types of networks.
6.2 Network Fundamentals	**6.2** Describe the wireline communications media and transmission technologies.
6.3 The Internet and the World Wide Web	**6.3** Describe the most common methods for accessing the Internet.
6.4 Network Applications: Discovery	**6.4** Explain the impact that discovery network applications have had on business and everyday life.
6.5 Network Applications: Communication	**6.5** Explain the impact that communication network applications have had on business and everyday life.
6.6 Network Applications: Collaboration	**6.6** Explain the impact that collaboration network applications have had on business and everyday life.
6.7 Network Applications: Educational	**6.7** Explain the impact that educational network applications have had on business and everyday life.

Opening Case

Myanmar Suddenly Goes Online

Myanmar—formerly known as Burma—is a largely Buddhist country of 51 million people located in Southeast Asia. In 2014, less than 1 percent of the population had Internet access. By 2017, the country was rapidly getting online—but so was fake news and anti-Muslim sentiment.

For nearly 50 years, Myanmar lived under military dictatorships that suppressed all forms of dissent and severely limited free speech. In response to these repressive policies, the United States and Europe imposed strict sanctions that largely cut off the country from the rest of the world. That situation changed in 2011, when the military junta was officially dissolved, and a civilian government was established.

At that time in Myanmar, a SIM card for a mobile phone could cost more than $3,000, and it was available only to people with government connections. A few Internet cafés existed, most of them in the capital, but they were far too expensive for the average person. The

International Monetary Fund (**www.imf.org**) estimated that fewer than 0.2 percent of the population was online.

In the years immediately following the easing of military rule, Internet usage rose slowly. Then in 2014, Myanmar allowed international telecommunications companies to operate in the country. The result was that Internet use increased explosively. For instance, subscribers to the telecommunications firm Ericsson (**www.ericsson.com**) mushroomed from several thousand in 2011 to more than 40 million by 2019. The mobile service providers offered data plans that enabled customers to access social media inexpensively with their smartphones.

The sudden availability of the Internet to the general public led to drastic changes in the country. The Internet revolutionized life for the people of Myanmar, from how they interact with one another to how they obtain their news, which they used to get almost exclusively from the regulated state media.

The average person in Myanmar connects to the Internet by doing the following: He or she goes to a shop that sells mobile phones and accessories. For about $3, a salesperson does two things for each customer: (1) sets up an e-mail address for the customer, and (2) opens up a Facebook account in any name the customer wants. Salespeople note that customers do not care about e-mail. Facebook is what they really want. If customers forget their login information for Facebook, they simply return for a new Facebook account. Nobody seems to know about Facebook's policy that users must use their real names.

Facebook's domination is so complete that people in Myanmar use "Internet" and "Facebook" interchangeably. By July 2019, over half of Myanmar's population had a Facebook account.

Although the majority of the population has Internet access, Myanmar has one of the world's lowest rates of information literacy. The term *information literacy*, or *digital literacy*, measures how well people using the Internet understand what they are doing and how to stay safe while they are online. Because the rates in Myanmar are so low, users in that country are among the most likely to fall for scams, hacks, and fake news.

News sites became so popular that print magazines called *Facebook* and *The Internet* regurgitated stories they spotted online for people who were not yet connected to the Internet. Many of these stories are sensational, and they are copied from Facebook pages with little attention to fact checking. Unfortunately, there has also been an increase in articles critical of the country's minority Muslim community (the Rohingya). Many of these articles promote fake news claiming that Muslim worshippers are attacking Buddhist religious sites. There has also been an increase in anti-Muslim protests and attacks on local Muslim groups. Muslims also are being driven out of the country. (Muslims make up roughly 4 percent of the total population.)

Mobilized by the sudden freedom of expression on online platforms such as Facebook, radical Buddhist anti-Muslim groups quickly found supporters across the country. For instance, Ashin Wirathu is a monk who openly advocates hardline anti-Muslim positions. On his many Facebook pages, Wirathu called for his fellow citizens to boycott Muslim businesses and for the government to expel Muslims from the country. It was difficult for him to keep the pages open, because Facebook kept shutting them down. Despite Facebook's efforts, however, he managed to maintain a growing online following. In May, 2019 he was charged with sedition over what prosecutors claim were defamatory remarks he made about Myanmar's civilian leader, Nobel laureate Daw Aung San Suu Kyi.

On August 24 and 25, 2018, Rohingya militants attacked military and police bases, prompting the government to launch a "clearance operation" that eventually forced some one million Rohingya into refugee camps in Bangladesh. Hate speech that targeted the Rohingya exploded on Facebook at the time of the attack. Combatting the spread of hate speech on Facebook and the growing refugee crisis took on great urgency. The United Nations called the Rohingya refugee camps in Bangladesh a humanitarian crisis.

Civil rights groups in Myanmar demanded that Facebook increase its moderation of Burmese-language content to curb hate speech. In April 2018, Facebook founder Mark Zuckerberg told United States senators that the social media website was hiring dozens more native Burmese speakers to review hate speech posted in Myanmar. In mid-August 2018, Reuters found more than 1,000 examples of posts, comments, images, and videos attacking the Rohingya or other Myanmar Muslims on Facebook. Almost all of these examples were in the main local language, Burmese. Significantly, some of the material Reuters discovered had been on Facebook for as long as six years.

Facebook critics in Myanmar did not believe that the firm was doing enough. They noted persistent problems, which included a slow response time to posts violating Facebook's standards, and that a small staff that cannot handle hate speech or understand Myanmar's cultural nuances. Furthermore, critics contended that Facebook would do even less if a small group of civil society groups had not alerted the company to dangerous posts spreading on the platform. In February 2018, Facebook did ban Wirathu. The platform took down pages of other organizations and monks, which removed major sources of hate speech and misinformation. They explored the possibility of using artificial intelligence to identify harmful content faster.

On August 27, 2018, Facebook removed 18 accounts, one Instagram account, and 52 pages that were followed by some 12 million people. Facebook also banned 20 individuals and organizations, including Myanmar's top military official. The move occurred the same day as a United Nations report accused the country's armed forces of committing war crimes against the country's Muslim Rohingya minority. Unfortunately, Facebook's efforts do not appear to be sufficient and the problem of hate speech on Facebook continues in Myanmar. In fact, some 1.1 million Rohinga refugees remain in camps in Bangladesh.

In November 2018, Facebook publicly admitted a human rights report they commissioned showed that they could have done more to prevent their platform from being used to spread hate and encourage bloodshed in Myanmar. However the company stated that there were already efforts to combat the misuse of their platform and pledged to continue them.

Myanmar experts note that even more people will be connected to the Internet in 2020 (e.g., on Facebook). As a result, there are already concerns about the role that Facebook could have in the country's 2020 elections. In the meantime, caustic posts against the Rohingya continue even as Myanmar makes preparation for the return of the refugees.

For many people in Myanmar, the Internet and Facebook brought free speech and a glimpse of American values. However, no one told them what would happen if they actually exercised free speech. Essentially, how were people in Myanmar expected to judge what is real and what is fake?

Sources: Compiled from M. Ganguly and B. Adams, "For Rohingya Refugees, There's No Return in Sight," *Foreign Affairs*, June 5, 2019; H. Beech and S. Nang, "He Incited Massacre, but Insulting Aung San Suu Kyi Was the Last Straw," *The New York Times*, May 29, 2019; I. Marlow, "Facebook Bans Myanmar's Top Military Chief for Hate Speech," *Bloomberg*, August 27, 2018; S. Stecklow, "Why Facebook Is Losing the War on Hate Speech in Myanmar," Reuters, August 15, 2018; T. McLaughlin, "How Facebook's Rise Fueled Chaos and Confusion in Myanmar," *Wired*, July 6, 2018; A. Kuhn, "Activists in Myanmar Say Facebook Needs to Do More to Quell Hate Speech," NPR, June 14, 2018; L. Hogan and M. Safi, "Revealed: Facebook Hate Speech Exploded in

Myanmar during Rohingya Crisis," *The Guardian*, April 2, 2018; F. Solomon, "Myanmar's Crisis, Bangladesh's Burden: Among the Rohingya Refugees Waiting for a Miracle," *Time*, November 23, 2017; C. Zara, "Jailed for a Facebook Poem: The Fight Against Myanmar's Draconian Defamation Laws," *Fast Company*, July 13, 2017; R. Samarajiva, "Proportion of Facebook Users in Myanmar," *LIRNEasia*, June 30, 2017; T. Sin, "Facebook Bans Racist Word 'Kalar' in Myanmar, Triggers Censorship," *Business Standard*, June 3, 2017; Y. Nitta and T. Hlahtway, "Myanmar Faces Onslaught of Social Media Fake News," *Nikkei Asian Review*, May 30, 2017; "Myanmar Says Fake News Being Spread to Destabilize Government, Vows Action," *Mizzima*, May 6, 2017; O. Schuelke, "Myanmar's Amazing Modernization," *The Diplomat*, March 22, 2017; R. Samarajiva, "Is Low Digital Literacy in Myanmar a Result of No Government Programs?" *LIRNEasia*, November 28, 2016; S. Frenkel, "This Is What Happens When Millions of People Suddenly Get the Internet," *BuzzFeed*, November 20, 2016; C. Trautwein, "Facebook Racks Up 10M Myanmar Users," *The Myanmar Times*, June 13, 2016; and "Connect to Learn Takes Significant Step Toward Reaching 21,000 Students in Myanmar," Ericsson Press Release, January 13, 2016.

Questions

1. What is the "good news" of providing Internet access to so many citizens of Myanmar? Provide examples to support your answer.

2. What is the "bad news" of providing Internet access to so many citizens of Myanmar? Provide examples to support your answer.

Introduction

In addition to networks being essential in your personal lives, there are three fundamental points about network computing you need to know. First, in modern organizations, computers do not work in isolation. Rather, they constantly exchange data with one another. Second, this exchange of data—facilitated by telecommunications technologies—provides companies with a number of very significant advantages. Third, this exchange can take place over any distance and over networks of any size.

Without networks, the computer on your desk would be merely another productivity-enhancement tool, just as the typewriter once was. The power of networks, however, turns your computer into an amazingly effective tool for accessing information from thousands of sources, thereby making both you and your organization more productive. Regardless of the type of organization (profit/not-for-profit, large/small, global/local) or industry (manufacturing, financial services, health care), networks in general, and the Internet in particular, have transformed—and will continue to transform—the way we do business.

Networks support innovative ways of doing business, from marketing to supply chain management to customer service to human resources management. In particular, the Internet and private intranets—a network located within a single organization that uses Internet software and TCP/IP protocols—have an enormous impact on our lives, both professionally and personally.

For all organizations, regardless of their size, having a telecommunications and networking system is no longer just a source of competitive advantage. Rather, it is necessary for survival.

Computer networks are essential to modern organizations for many reasons. First, networked computer systems enable organizations to become more flexible so they can adapt to rapidly changing business conditions. Second, networks allow companies to share hardware, computer applications, and data across the organization and among different organizations. Third, networks make it possible for geographically dispersed employees and work groups to share documents, ideas, and creative insights. This sharing encourages teamwork, innovation, and more efficient and effective interactions. Networks are also a critical link among businesses, their business partners, and their customers.

Clearly, networks are essential tools for modern businesses. But why do *you* need to be familiar with networks? The simple fact is that if you operate your own business or you work in a business, then you cannot function without networks. You will need to communicate rapidly with your customers, business partners, suppliers, employees, and colleagues. Until about 1990, you would have used the postal service or the telephone system with voice or fax capabilities for business communication. Today, however, the pace of business is much faster—almost real time. To keep up with this incredibly fast pace, you will need to use computers, e-mail, messaging, the Internet, smartphones, and other mobile devices. Furthermore, all of these technologies will be connected through networks to enable you to communicate, collaborate, and compete on a global scale.

Networking and the Internet are the foundations for commerce in the 21st century. Recall that one key objective of this book is to help you become an informed user of information systems. Knowledge of networking is an essential component of modern business literacy.

We simply cannot overemphasize the global importance of the Internet. It has truly been said that the Internet is the nervous system of our world. In fact, having fast (broadband) access to the Internet is a prerequisite for success for many people. For instance, in 2017, New York City sued Verizon for allegedly failing to provide adequate fiber-optic services to the city. In July, 2018 Verizon reached a deal with New York state regulators to expand its high-speed Internet services in New York City and repair its existing telephone infrastructure.

In that same year, New York Attorney General Eric Schneiderman filed a lawsuit alleging that Charter Communications (now Spectrum; **www.spectrum.com**) defrauded New York customers by failing to deliver the Internet speeds and performance levels promised to them. Spectrum is an American telecommunications company that provides cable, telephone, and television services. In March, 2019 Spectrum began paying out $62.5 million to customers over the Internet speed lawsuit.

IT's About Business 6.1

Is Broadband Internet a Right or a Privilege?
MIS

The Problem

The United States has a long history of bringing utility access to all Americans. To illustrate this point, let's consider three government actions: the Rural Electrification Administration (REA), the Communications Act of 1934, and the Telecommunications Act of 1996.

In the early 1930s, when President Franklin D. Roosevelt established the REA, 90 percent of U.S. farmers lived without electricity. The cost of installing electric lines to the country's most remote areas was prohibitive for profit-seeking businesses. Therefore, the REA partnered with rural electric cooperatives to overcome this problem. In addition, the federal government provided loans to the co-ops to construct their electric networks. By the end of the 1940s, most farms in the United States had electricity. In hindsight, it is clear that Americans should have access to electricity. The country's economic and social well-being depends on it.

With the Communications Act of 1934, the U.S. government provided a universal service guarantee that mandated that every resident have a baseline level of telecommunications services. The reason for the mandate is that the Federal Communications Commission (FCC; **www.fcc.gov**) recognized that telephone services provide a vital link to emergency services, government services, and surrounding communities. Because of the universal service guarantee, providers frequently must offer and maintain—even at a loss—expensive copper twisted-pair phone lines in rural areas to support small populations. The carriers are compensated for these costs through a tax on customers' phone bills, called the Universal Service Fund. Again in hindsight, it is clear that universal access to telecommunications service is essential to the nation's prosperity.

The 1996 Telecommunications Act expanded the idea of universal service beyond simply the right to telephone service by affirming that all Americans should have access to Internet services. Today, advocates of universal broadband Internet access make the same argument. They contend that broadband Internet is not a luxury but a right of all 21st-century Americans.

The FCC defines broadband Internet access as the ability to download data at 25 megabits per second (Mbps) and to upload it at 3 Mbps. Based on this definition, 24 million Americans do not have broadband Internet access. In essence, the United States has a persistent digital divide.

The digital divide was once only a problem of access. Today, the divide is also a problem of connection quality and speed. Put simply, the digital divide is now the gap between areas with and without sufficient bandwidth to effectively use the Internet.

The Rural Broadband Association (**www.ntca.org**) cites a 2016 study from the Hudson Institute that found that nearly 70 percent of the economic impact of broadband Internet access went to urban economies rather than rural ones. The same study estimated that if broadband was as good in rural areas as it is in urban areas, online retail sales would be "at least $1 billion higher."

Consider Saguache County, Colorado, which has perhaps the worst Internet service in the United States, in part because it is located between two mountain ranges. Only 5.6 percent of adults in the county are estimated to have broadband Internet access.

For approximately $30 per month, New York City Internet providers offer basic packages of 100 Mbps service. In contrast, in Saguache County, the few households with a broadband connection have a download speed of 12 Mbps and an upload speed of 2 Mbps. Nevertheless, they can expect to pay $90 per month.

This cost would be less of an issue if the Internet were not so central to modern life. In reality, however, taxes, job applications, payroll operations, banking, newspapers, shopping, college courses, and video chats are primarily performed online today. For instance, Saguache County's students are expected to take their state assessments online. However, an administrator at one school that houses students from kindergarten through 12th grade stated that until 2016 the Internet often went down for a couple of hours a day or even all day in the school building.

Rural communities often face logistics problems installing fiber-optic cable in sparsely populated areas. These problems are particularly acute in Saguache County, which is three times the size of Rhode Island and where 30 percent of its residents live below the poverty line.

Saguache County also has problems with 911 services. Without broadband access, 911 dispatch centers can lose their connection to the state emergency system. Furthermore, dispatchers cannot check license plates for police or relay arrest-warrant information to officers. When severe thunderstorms approach, 911 dispatchers cannot reliably map a tornado touchdown or track developing weather patterns.

In general, rural communities typically have intermittent Internet access, often through a patchwork of satellite, dial-up, and wireless service. Telecommunications and cable companies avoid such areas because it is too expensive to bring equipment and service over long distances to so few people. In fact, burying fiber-optic cables costs approximately $30,000 per mile.

A Number of Potential Solutions

Utilities.   In some cases, rural municipalities are using electrification laws from the early 1900s to obtain funds and regulatory permissions reserved for utilities in order to provide broadband access. In December 2017, about 64 electric cooperatives (out of some 900 in the United States) either offered or were in the process of building networks to provide broadband Internet access, compared with just 1 in 2010, according to the Institute for Local Self-Reliance, a nonprofit focused on community broadband networks.

As one example, Colorado Central Telecom (CCT; **www.coloradocentraltelecom.com**) was founded in 2011 because CenturyLink (**www.centurylink.com**) would not provide Internet service to large sections of the state. Further, another large provider, FairPoint (**www.fairpoint.com**), provided only one-half megabit per second. CCT offers Internet and telephone plans to residents in Saguache County and neighboring Chaffee County. The company has tailored its services to address the needs of isolated, rural Internet users.

Whereas most urban and suburban providers use fiber-optic cables that are buried in the ground, rural providers often use fixed wireless Internet to avoid the cost of laying miles of expensive cable. CCT attaches dishes to homes, which receive signals from the nearest fixed wireless tower. The dishes must be line-of-sight (i.e., nothing obstructs the signal) to the tower.

Another example is the Northeast Oklahoma Electric Cooperative (NOEC; **www.neelectric.com**), which hangs fiber-optic cable on utility poles in rural areas. As a result, the 120 citizens of Zena, Oklahoma, have access to high-speed Internet in their homes for the first time. In 2013, the co-op created its broadband subsidiary, Bolt, after local businesses and younger residents complained there was no future for them without modern infrastructure. A year later, the co-op announced it would provide fiber-based Internet with speeds of up to 1 gigabit per second. It introduced that service in 2016.

Cities.   More than 80 U.S. cities and towns have built their own government-owned, fiber-based Internet. These cities acknowledge that broadband Internet access does not guarantee that a city will be successful. They also realize, however, that a lack of broadband access almost certainly guarantees that a community will be left behind in our global, digital economy. Let's consider the case of Chattanooga, Tennessee.

EPB is Chattanooga's government-owned electric utility. In late 2009, EPB began to modernize the city's electrical grid. The utility planned to install smart meters on individual homes, which required a communications link. EPB and the city realized that with fiber running through much of the city, EPB could fairly easily become an ISP.

Downtown Chattanooga already had Comcast Internet service. However, the outskirts of town as well as the more rural areas had little or no broadband access. Significantly, Comcast had no plans to expand its network or upgrade speeds within the city.

Comcast and AT&T objected to the city's plans. They initiated public relations campaigns to defend the status quo. Television ads paid for by the Tennessee Cable Telecommunications Association—Comcast and AT&T are both members—portrayed the worst-case scenario. The ads warned that EPB's electricity utility would have to subsidize its fiber network, thereby increasing costs for customers. When the ads failed to sway public opinion, Comcast and AT&T sued Chattanooga on four occasions. Ultimately, Chattanooga prevailed.

By 2019, EPB offered service to more than 180,000 homes and businesses in southeast Tennessee and northwest Georgia. EPB also has almost 91,000 Internet customers, far above its break-even number of 42,000. EPB's most popular offering is its 100 Mbps service for $59.99 per month. Interestingly, 8,000 EPB customers have its 1 gigabit service for $69.99 per month. EPB's profit is being used to pay down an initial loan and to avoid rate hikes for EPB's electric utility.

Alphabet.   Alphabet (Google's parent company) is testing the idea of using stratospheric drones and balloons (Project Loon) to provide Internet service in rural areas.

Facebook.   Facebook's open-source wireless access platform, called OpenCellular, will provide both hardware and software to set up small-scale cellular networks. Its goal is to allow people in the poorest parts of the world to go online using their phones. OpenCellular attempts to create a more affordable means of deploying wireless network access points in remote parts of the world. The system does require a backhaul, which is a connection to the Internet. Instead, the backhaul is usually provided by a wired connection or perhaps by a drone or a balloon flying overhead. Without the backhaul, the hardware can still enable locals to communicate with one another, but not the Internet.

Microsoft.   Microsoft plans to connect 2 million rural Americans to high-speed wireless broadband by 2022, and it is beginning with 12 pilot projects. The company is also offering free access to its intellectual property to help the rest of rural America get connected.

Microsoft is not planning to become an ISP itself. Instead, the company will partner with telecommunications companies to build wireless networks using the television "white spaces" spectrum. White spaces refer to the unused broadcasting frequencies in the wireless spectrum. Television networks leave gaps between channels for buffering purposes. This space can be used to deliver broadband Internet. This bandwidth enables wireless signals to travel over hills and through buildings and trees. Significantly, unlicensed spectrum is not restricted to any single entity. Rather, anyone can use it as long as they comply with certain rules designed to prevent interference with other devices and services.

Because of cost constraints, satellite Internet should be used in areas with fewer than two people per square mile, while fixed wireless and limited fiber to the home are the best approach in areas with population densities greater than 200 people per square mile. By using this mix of technologies, Microsoft claims the United States can eliminate the rural broadband gap at a cost of $8 billion to $12 billion, which is approximately 80 percent less than the cost of using fiber cables alone and more than 50 percent less than the cost of current fixed-wireless technology.

Early Results

Being able to connect to the Internet is crucial for rural Americans. Broadband access enables them to buy goods and services that may not be available locally; to market their own goods and services to a much larger area; to connect remotely with health services that previously required several hours of driving; and even to telecommute. Educational and government institutions can use broadband access for academic and vocational training, helping to develop a competent workforce. It is widely acknowledged that helping children gain technological knowledge is crucial to their future. Medical providers must have broadband access to practice telemedicine in underserved areas, thereby improving health care in those areas.

As an illustration of the benefits of broadband Internet access, consider the case of Zena, Oklahoma. Since the area acquired broadband service through Bolt, signs of economic vitality have begun to appear. For example, Ferra (**www.ferra.com.au**), an Australian assembly company, opened a plant in neighboring Grove, Oklahoma, in 2016 and hired about 100 workers by the end of that year. Developers are building a 120-room hotel and conference center in close proximity to the two towns, a project that was approved only after Bolt announced its broadband service.

One Zena resident recently created a website for her business, and another ordered a tractor part online, saving himself a daylong trip to the nearest repair shop. Still another resident plans to retire and start an online educational service.

And the results for Chattanooga? An independent study by the University of Tennessee concluded that EPB's fiber-based network could be directly linked to the creation of between 2,800 and 5,200 jobs. The economic benefits for the city have totaled approximately $1 billion over the past five years.

There is more good news. Using data from the Federal Communications Commission, the Center on Rural Innovation (**www.ruralinnovation.us**) found that more than 2,500 rural towns have broadband access to the Internet, representing more than 8.5 million Americans. Of those, 3 million have access to symmetrical (upload and download) gigabit-per-second speeds.

Sources: Compiled from M. Dunne, "Small-Town Ingenuity Is Making Gigabit Broadband a Reality," *Wired*, August 26, 2018; G. Horwitz, "How the Digital Divide Dies: Broadband for All," *Forbes*, April 19, 2018; K. Rogers, "What It's Like to Live in America without Broadband Internet," *Motherboard*, April 16, 2018; C. Aguh, "How the 'Digital Divide' Is Holding the U.S. Economy Back," *VentureBeat*, February 10, 2018; R. Boucher, "Don't

Forget Rural America in Open Internet Debate," *Forbes*, August 22, 2017; "The Digital Divide between Rural and Urban America's Access to Internet," CBS News, August 4, 2017; C. Malone, "The Worst Internet in America," *fivethirtyeight.com*, July 27, 2017; J. Brodkin, "Microsoft Wants All of Rural America to Get High-Speed Broadband," *Ars Technica*, July 11, 2017; "Rural America Has a Serious Internet Problem," *The Week*, June 15, 2017; A. Dellinger, "Is Internet Access a Right? Americans Split on Belief If Internet Access Is a Right or Privilege," *International Business Times*, May 7, 2017; H. Kuttner, "The Economic Impact of Rural Broadband," Hudson Institute, April 20, 2016; A. Newcomb, "Which States Have the Speediest – and the Slowest – Internet?" NBC News, March 16, 2017; B. Whitacre, "Broadband Internet Helps Rural Areas Connect – Online and in Real Life," *Newsweek*, March 4, 2017; J. Koebler, "The City that Was Saved by the Internet," *Motherboard*, October 27, 2016; J. Condliffe, "Locally Owned Internet Is an Antidote for the Digital Divide," *MIT Technology Review*, August 8, 2016; C. Kang, "How to Give Rural America Broadband? Look to the Early 1900s," *New York Times*, August 7, 2016; J. Condliffe, "Facebook Plans to Beam Internet to Backwaters with Lasers," *MIT Technology Review*, July 20, 2016; J. Condliffe, "Facebook Has a Plan to Take Cellular Data to the Sticks," *MIT Technology Review*, July 7, 2016; T. Simonite, "America's Broadband Improves, Cementing a 'Persistent Digital Divide'," *MIT Technology Review*, January 29, 2016; R. Letzter, "Here's Why Internet Services Are So Abysmal in America," *Business Insider*, January 28, 2016; S. Stogsdill, "Ferra Aerospace Holds Groundbreaking in Grove," *Tulsa World*, December 16, 2015; and Y. Hupka, "Findings on the Economic Benefits of Broadband Expansion to Rural and Remote Areas," Center for Urban and Regional Affairs, University of Minnesota, 2014.

Questions

1. Describe the problems that occur in areas that do not have broadband Internet access.

2. Now, consider what your educational experience at your college or university would be without broadband Internet access. Provide specific examples to support your answer.

3. Identify and discuss some of the benefits provided by broadband Internet access.

4. Now, explain how broadband Internet access enhances your educational experience. Provide specific examples to support your answer.

Given the essential importance of the Internet, the question arises: Is broadband Internet a right or a privilege? IT's About Business 6.1 addresses this important question.

You begin this chapter by learning what a computer network is and by identifying the various types of networks. You then study network fundamentals. You next turn your attention to the basics of the Internet and the World Wide Web. You conclude by examining the many network applications available to individuals and organizations—that is, what networks help you do.

6.1 What Is a Computer Network?

Author Lecture Videos are available exclusively in *WileyPLUS*.
Apply the Concept activities are available in the Appendix and in *WileyPLUS*.

A **computer network** is a system that connects computers and other devices (e.g., printers) through communications media so that data and information can be transmitted among them. Voice and data communication networks are continually becoming faster—that is, their bandwidth is increasing—and cheaper. **Bandwidth** refers to the transmission capacity of a network; it is stated in bits per second. Bandwidth ranges from narrowband (relatively low transmission capacity) to broadband (relatively high network capacity).

The telecommunications industry itself has difficulty defining the term *broadband*. The Federal Communications Commission's (FCC) rules define **broadband** as the transmission capacity of a communications medium (discussed later in this chapter) faster than 25 megabits per second (Mbps) for download—the transmission speed for material coming to you from an Internet server, such as a movie streamed from Netflix—and 3 Mbps for upload—the transmission speed for material that you upload to an Internet server such as a Facebook post or YouTube video.

Interestingly, some Federal Communications Commission (FCC; **www.fcc.gov**) members feel that the definition of broadband should be increased to 100 Mbps for download. The definition of broadband remains fluid, however, and it will undoubtedly continue to change to reflect greater transmission capacities in the future.

You are likely familiar with certain types of broadband connections such as *digital subscriber line (DSL)* and cable to your homes and dorms. DSL and cable fall within the range of transmission capacity mentioned here and are thus defined as broadband connections.

The various types of computer networks range from small to worldwide. They include (from smallest to largest) personal area networks (PANs), local area networks (LANs), metropolitan area networks (MANs), wide area networks (WANs), and the ultimate WAN, the Internet. PANs are short-range networks—typically a few meters—that are used for communication among devices close to one person. They can be wired or wireless. (You will learn about wireless PANs in Chapter 8.) MANs are relatively large networks that cover a metropolitan area. MANs fall between LANs and WANs in size. WANs typically cover large geographical areas; in some cases, they can span the entire planet and reach from Earth to Mars and beyond.

Local Area Networks

Regardless of their size, networks represent a compromise among three objectives: speed, distance, and cost. Organizations typically must select two of the three. To cover long distances, organizations can have fast communication if they are willing to pay for it, or inexpensive communication if they are willing to accept slower speeds. A third possible combination of the three trade-offs is fast, inexpensive communication with distance limitations. This is the idea behind local area networks.

A **local area network (LAN)** connects two or more devices in a limited geographical region, usually within the same building, so that every device on the network can communicate with every other device. Most LANs today use Ethernet (discussed later in this chapter). **Figure 6.1** illustrates an Ethernet LAN that consists of four computers, a server, and a printer, all of which connect through a shared cable. Every device in the LAN has a *network interface card (NIC)* that allows the device to physically connect to the LAN's communications medium. This medium is typically unshielded twisted-pair wire (UTP).

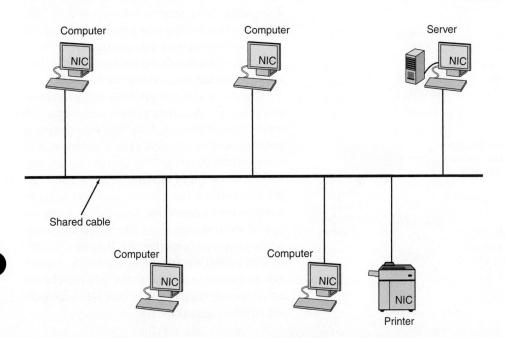

FIGURE 6.1 **Ethernet local area.**

Although it is not required, many LANs have a **file server** or **network server**. The server typically contains various software and data for the network. It also houses the LAN's network operating system, which manages the server and routes and manages communications on the network.

Wide Area Networks

When businesses have to transmit and receive data beyond the confines of the LAN, they use wide area networks. The term *wide area network* did not even exist until local area networks appeared. Before that time, what we call a wide area network today was simply called a network.

A **wide area network (WAN)** is a network that covers a large geographical area. WANs typically connect multiple LANs. They are generally provided by common carriers such as telephone companies and the international networks of global communications services providers. Examples of these providers include AT&T (**www.att.com**) in the United States, Deutsche Telekom in Germany (**www.telekom.com**), and NTT Communications (**www.ntt.com**) in Japan.

WANs have large capacities, and they typically combine multiple channels (e.g., fiber-optic cables, microwave, and satellite). WANs also contain **routers**—a communications processor that routes messages from a LAN to the Internet, across several connected LANs, or across a WAN such as the Internet. The Internet is an example of a WAN.

Enterprise Networks

Organizations today have multiple LANs and may have multiple WANs. All of these networks are interconnected to form an **enterprise network**. **Figure 6.2** displays a model of enterprise computing. Note that the enterprise network in the figure has a backbone network. Corporate **backbone networks** are high-speed central networks to which multiple smaller networks (such as LANs and smaller WANs) connect. The LANs are called *embedded LANs* because they connect to the backbone WAN.

Unfortunately, traditional networks can be rigid and lack the flexibility to keep pace with increasing business networking requirements. The reason for this problem is that the functions of traditional networks are distributed across physical routers and devices (i.e., hardware). Therefore, to implement changes, each network device must be configured individually. In some cases, devices must be configured manually. A *Software-defined network (SDN)* is an emerging technology that is becoming increasingly important to help organizations manage their data flows across their enterprise networks. With an SDN, decisions that control how network traffic flows across network devices are managed centrally by software. The software dynamically adjusts data flows to meet business and application needs.

Think of traditional networks as the road system of a city in 1920. Data packets are the cars that travel through the city. A traffic officer (physical network devices) controls each intersection and directs traffic by recognizing the turn signals and the size and shape of the vehicles passing through the intersection. The officers can direct only the traffic at their intersection. They do not know the overall traffic volume in the city nor do they know traffic movement across the city. Therefore, it is difficult to control the city's traffic patterns as a whole and to manage peak-hour traffic. When problems occur, the city must communicate with each individual officer by radio.

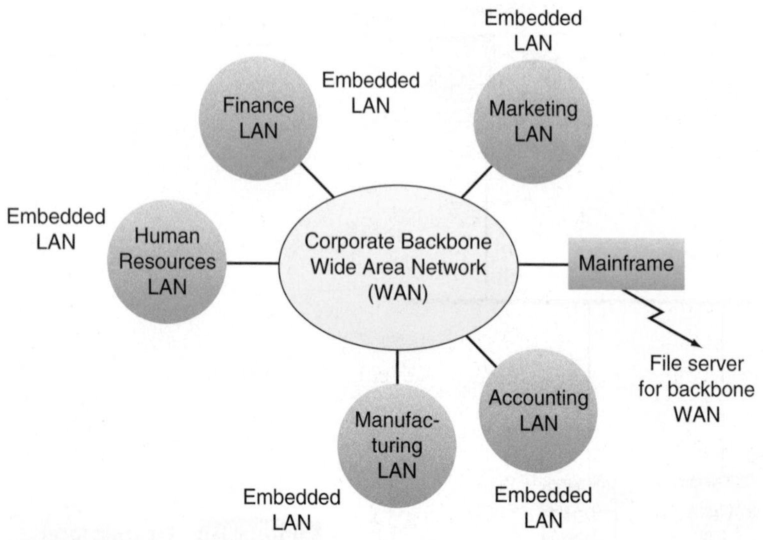

FIGURE 6.2 Enterprise network.

Now think of an SDN as the road system of a modern city. Each traffic officer is replaced by a traffic light and a set of electronic vehicle counters, which are connected to central monitoring and control software. With this system, the city's traffic can be instantly and centrally controlled. The control software can direct traffic differently at various times of the day (say, rush hour). The software monitors traffic flow and automatically changes the traffic lights to help traffic flow through the city with minimal disruption.

Before you go on . . .

1. What are the primary business reasons for using networks?
2. What are the differences between LANs and WANs?
3. Describe an enterprise network.

6.2 | Network Fundamentals

In this section, you will learn the basics of how networks actually operate. You begin by studying wireline communications media, which enable computers in a network to transmit and receive data. You conclude this section by looking at network protocols and the types of network processing.

Today, computer networks communicate through *digital signals*, which are discrete pulses that are either on or off, representing a series of *bits* (0s and 1s). This quality allows digital signals to convey information in a binary form that can be interpreted by computers.

The U.S. public telephone system (called the "plain old telephone system" or POTS) was originally designed as an analog network to carry voice signals or sounds in an analog wave format. *Analog signals* are continuous waves that transmit information by altering the amplitude and frequency of the waves. The POTS requires *dial-up modems* to convert signals from analog to digital and vice versa. Dial-up modems are almost extinct in most parts of the developed world today.

Cable modems are modems that operate over coaxial cable—for example, cable TV. They offer broadband access to the Internet or to corporate intranets. Cable modem speeds vary widely. Most providers offer bandwidth between 1 and 6 million bits per second (Mbps) for downloads (from the Internet to a computer) and between 128 and 768 thousand bits per second (Kbps) for uploads. Cable modem services share bandwidth among subscribers in a locality; that is, the same cable line connects to many households. Therefore, when large numbers of neighbors access the Internet at the same time, cable speeds can decrease significantly.

DSL modems operate on the same lines as voice telephones and dial-up modems. DSL modems always maintain a connection, so an Internet connection is immediately available.

Communications Media and Channels

Communicating data from one location to another requires some form of pathway or medium. A **communications channel** is such a pathway. It consists of two types of media: cable (twisted-pair wire, coaxial cable, or fiber-optic cable) and broadcast (microwave, satellite, radio, or infrared).

Wireline media or **cable media** use physical wires or cables to transmit data and information. Twisted-pair wire and coaxial cables are made of copper, and fiber-optic cable is made of glass. The alternative is communication over **broadcast media** or **wireless media.** The key to mobile communications in today's rapidly moving society is data transmissions over electromagnetic media—the "airwaves." In this section, you will study the three wireline channels.

Author Lecture Videos are available exclusively in *WileyPLUS*.
Apply the Concept activities are available in the Appendix and in *WileyPLUS*.

TABLE 6.1 **Advantages and Disadvantages of Wireline Communications Channels**

Channel	Advantages	Disadvantages
Twisted-pair wire	Inexpensive	Slow (low bandwidth)
	Widely available	Subject to interference
	Easy to work with	Easily tapped (low security)
Coaxial cable	Higher bandwidth than twisted-pair	Relatively expensive and inflexible
		Easily tapped (low to medium security)
	Less susceptible to electromagnetic interference	Somewhat difficult to work with
Fiber-optic cable	Very high bandwidth	Difficult to work with (difficult to splice)
	Relatively expensive	
	Difficult to tap (good security)	

Table 6.1 summarizes the advantages and disadvantages of each of these channels. You will become familiar with wireless media in Chapter 8.

Twisted-Pair Wire.   The most prevalent form of communications wiring—**twisted-pair wire**—is used for almost all business telephone wiring. As the name suggests, it consists of strands of copper wire twisted in pairs (see **Figure 6.3**). Twisted-pair wire is relatively inexpensive to purchase, widely available, and easy to work with. However, it also has some significant disadvantages. Specifically, it is relatively slow for transmitting data, it is subject to interference from other electrical sources, and it can be easily tapped by unintended recipients to gain unauthorized access to data.

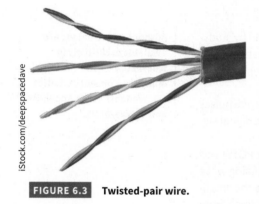

FIGURE 6.3   **Twisted-pair wire.**

iStock.com/deepspacedave

Coaxial Cable.   **Coaxial cable (Figure 6.4)** consists of insulated copper wire. Compared with twisted-pair wire, it is much less susceptible to electrical interference, and it can carry much more data. For these reasons, it is commonly used to carry high-speed data traffic as well as television signals (thus the term *cable TV*). However, coaxial cable is more expensive and more difficult to work with than twisted-pair wire. It is also somewhat inflexible.

Fiber Optics.   **Fiber-optic cable (Figure 6.5)** consists of thousands of very thin filaments of glass fibers that transmit information through pulses of light generated by lasers. The fiber-optic cable is surrounded by cladding, a coating that prevents the light from leaking out of the fiber.

Fiber-optic cables are significantly smaller and lighter than traditional cable media. They also can transmit far more data, and they provide greater security from interference and tapping. Fiber-optic cable is typically used as the backbone for a network, whereas twisted-pair

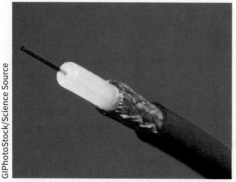

FIGURE 6.4   **Two views of coaxial cable.**

GIPhotoStock/Science Source

Cross-section view

How coaxial cable looks to us

iStock.com/piotr_malczyk

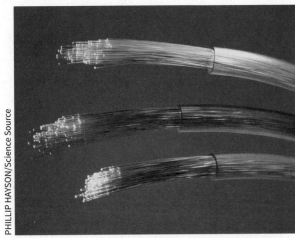

Cross-section view

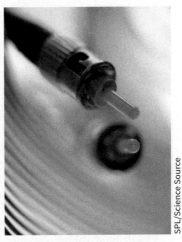

How fiber-optic cable looks to us

FIGURE 6.5   **Two views of fiber-optic cable.**

wire and coaxial cable connect the backbone to individual devices on the network. In 2016, FASTER, the aptly named 5,600-mile undersea fiber-optic cable connecting Japan and the United States, became operational. FASTER transmits data at 60 terabits (trillions of bits) per second across the Pacific Ocean. In 2018, organizations laid more fiber-optic cable than in any year in the last 20 years.

Network Protocols

Computing devices that are connected to the network must access and share the network to transmit and receive data. These devices are often referred to as *nodes* of the network. They work together by adhering to a common set of rules and procedures—known as a **protocol**—that enable them to communicate with one another. The two major protocols are the Ethernet and Transmission Control Protocol/Internet Protocol.

Ethernet.   A common LAN protocol is **Ethernet**. Many organizations use 100-gigabit Ethernet, through which the network provides data transmission speeds of 100 gigabits (100 billion bits) per second. The 400-gigabit Ethernet was launched in 2018.

Transmission Control Protocol/Internet Protocol.   The **Transmission Control Protocol/Internet Protocol (TCP/IP)** is the protocol of the Internet. TCP/IP uses a suite of protocols, the primary ones being the Transmission Control Protocol (TCP) and the Internet Protocol (IP). The TCP performs three basic functions: (1) It manages the movement of data packets (see further on) between computers by establishing a connection between the computers, (2) it sequences the transfer of packets, and (3) it acknowledges the packets that have been transmitted. The **Internet Protocol (IP)** is responsible for disassembling, delivering, and reassembling the data during transmission.

Before data are transmitted over the Internet, they are divided into small, fixed bundles called *packets.* The transmission technology that breaks up blocks of text into packets is called **packet switching**. Each packet carries the information that will help it reach its destination— the sender's IP address, the intended recipient's IP address, the number of packets in the message, and the sequence number of the particular packet within the message. Each packet travels independently across the network and can be routed through different paths in the network. When the packets reach their destination, they are reassembled into the original message.

It is important to note that packet-switching networks are reliable and fault tolerant. For example, if a path in the network is very busy or is broken, packets can be dynamically ("on the fly") rerouted around that path. Also, if one or more packets do not get to the receiving computer, then only those packets need to be re-sent.

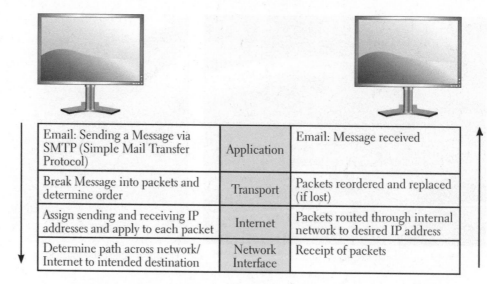

Email: Sending a Message via SMTP (Simple Mail Transfer Protocol)	Application	Email: Message received
Break Message into packets and determine order	Transport	Packets reordered and replaced (if lost)
Assign sending and receiving IP addresses and apply to each packet	Internet	Packets routed through internal network to desired IP address
Determine path across network/ Internet to intended destination	Network Interface	Receipt of packets

FIGURE 6.6   **The four layers of the TCP/IP reference model.**

Why do organizations use packet switching? The main reason is to achieve reliable end-to-end message transmission over sometimes-unreliable networks that may have short-acting or long-acting problems.

The packets use the TCP/IP protocol to carry their data. TCP/IP functions in four layers (see **Figure 6.6**). The *application layer* enables client application programs to access the other layers, and it defines the protocols that applications use to exchange data. One of these application protocols is the **Hypertext Transfer Protocol (HTTP)**, which defines how messages are formulated and how they are interpreted by their receivers. (We discuss hypertext in Section 6.3.) The *transport layer* provides the application layer with communication and packet services. This layer includes TCP and other protocols. The *Internet layer* is responsible for addressing, routing, and packaging data packets. The IP is one of the protocols in this layer. Finally, the *network interface layer* places packets on, and receives them from, the network medium, which can be any networking technology.

Two computers using TCP/IP can communicate even if they use different hardware and software. Data sent from one computer to another proceed downward through all four layers, beginning with the sending computer's application layer and going through its network interface layer. After the data reach the receiving computer, they travel up the layers.

TCP/IP enables users to send data across sometimes-unreliable networks with the assurance that the data will arrive in uncorrupted form. TCP/IP is very popular with business organizations because of its reliability and the ease with which it can support intranets and related functions.

Let's look at an example of packet switching across the Internet. **Figure 6.7** illustrates a message being sent from New York City to Los Angeles over a packet-switching network. Note that the different-colored packets travel by different routes to reach their destination in Los Angeles, where they are reassembled into the complete message.

Types of Network Processing

Organizations typically use multiple computer systems across the firm. **Distributed processing** divides processing work among two or more computers. This process enables computers in different locations to communicate with one another through telecommunications links. A common type of distributed processing is client/server processing. A special type of client/server processing is peer-to-peer processing.

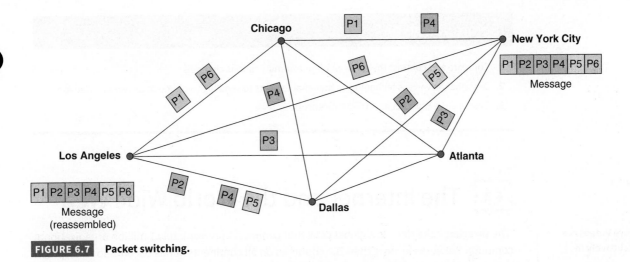

FIGURE 6.7 Packet switching.

Client/Server Computing.

Client/server computing links two or more computers in an arrangement in which some machines, called **servers**, provide computing services for user PCs, called **clients**. Usually, an organization performs the bulk of its processing or application/data storage on suitably powerful servers that can be accessed by less powerful client machines. The client requests applications, data, or processing from the server, which acts on these requests by "serving" the desired commodity.

Client/server computing leads to the ideas of "fat" clients and "thin" clients. As discussed in Technology Guide 1, *fat clients* have large storage and processing power and therefore can run local programs (such as Microsoft Office) if the network goes down. In contrast, *thin clients* may have no local storage and only limited processing power. Thus, they must depend on the network to run applications. For this reason, they are of little value when the network is not functioning.

Peer-to-Peer Processing.

Peer-to-peer (P2P) processing is a type of client/server distributed processing in which each computer acts as *both* a client and a server. Each computer can access (as assigned for security or integrity purposes) all files on all other computers.

There are three basic types of peer-to-peer processing. The first type accesses unused CPU power among networked computers. An application of this type is SETI@home (**www.setiathome.ssl.berkeley.edu**). These applications are from open-source projects, and they can be downloaded at no cost.

The second form of peer-to-peer is real-time, person-to-person collaboration, such as Microsoft SharePoint Workspace (**www.office.microsoft.com/en-us/sharepoint-workspace**). This product provides P2P collaborative applications that use buddy lists to establish a connection and allow real-time collaboration within the application.

The third peer-to-peer category is advanced search and file sharing. This category is characterized by natural language searches of millions of peer systems. It enables users to discover other users, not just data and Web pages. One example of this category is BitTorrent.

BitTorrent (**www.bittorrent.com**) is an open-source, free, peer-to-peer file-sharing application that simplifies the problem of sharing large files by dividing them into tiny pieces, or "torrents." BitTorrent addresses two of the biggest problems of file sharing: (1) Downloading bogs down when many people access a file at once, and (2) some people leech, meaning they download content but refuse to share it. BitTorrent eliminates bottlenecks by enabling all users to share little pieces of a file at the same time—a process called *swarming*. The program prevents leeching because users must upload a file while they download it. Thus, the more popular the content, the more efficiently it travels over a network.

Before you go on . . .

1. Compare and contrast the three wireline communications channels.
2. Describe the various technologies that enable users to send high-volume data over any network.
3. Describe the Ethernet and TCP/IP protocols.

6.3   The Internet and the World Wide Web

Author Lecture Videos are available exclusively in *WileyPLUS*.
Apply the Concept activities are available in the Appendix and in *WileyPLUS*.

The **Internet** ("the Net") is a global WAN that connects approximately 1 million organizational computer networks in more than 200 countries on all continents. It has become so widespread that it features in the daily routine of some 5 billion people.

The computers and organizational nodes on the Internet can be of different types and makes. They are connected to one another by data communications lines of different speeds. The primary network connections and telecommunications lines that link the nodes are referred to as the **Internet backbone**. For the Internet, the backbone is a fiber-optic network that is operated primarily by large telecommunications companies.

Many people mistakenly assume that Internet traffic (data transmissions) occurs wirelessly. However, only 1 percent of Internet traffic is carried by satellites. So, what does the Internet actually look like?

The Internet is quite tangible, consisting of 300 underwater cables that total 550,000 miles in length. These underwater cables range in thickness from a garden hose to about three inches in diameter. The underwater cables come onshore at cable landing points.

From these points, the cables are buried underground and make their way to large data centers. (We discuss data centers in Technology Guide 3.) In the United States, there are 542 underground cables connecting at 273 different points. Most of these underground cables are located along major roads and railways. In fact, one of the world's most concentrated hubs in terms of Internet connectivity is located in Lower Manhattan in New York City.

As a network of networks, the Internet enables people to access data in other organizations and to communicate, collaborate, and exchange information seamlessly around the world, quickly and inexpensively. Thus, the Internet has become a necessity for modern businesses.

The Internet grew out of an experimental project of the Advanced Research Project Agency (ARPA) of the U.S. Department of Defense. The project began in 1969 as the *ARPAnet*. Its purpose was to test the feasibility of a WAN over which researchers, educators, military personnel, and government agencies could share data, exchange messages, and transfer files.

Today, Internet technologies are being used both within and among organizations. An **intranet** is a network that uses Internet protocols so that users can take advantage of familiar applications and work habits. Intranets support discovery (easy and inexpensive browsing and search), communication, and collaboration inside an organization.

In contrast, an **extranet** connects parts of the intranets of different organizations. It also enables business partners to communicate securely over the Internet using virtual private networks (VPNs) (explained in Chapter 4). Extranets offer limited accessibility to the intranets of participating companies, as well as necessary interorganizational communications. They are widely used in the areas of business-to-business (B2B) electronic commerce (see Chapter 7) and supply chain management (SCM) (see Chapter 11).

No central agency manages the Internet. Instead, the costs of its operation are shared among hundreds of thousands of nodes. Thus, the cost for any one organization is small. Organizations must pay a small fee if they wish to register their names, and they need to install their own hardware and software to operate their internal networks. The organizations are obliged to move any data or information that enters their organizational network, regardless of the source, to their destination, at no charge to the senders. The senders, of course, pay the telephone bills for using either the backbone or regular telephone lines.

Accessing the Internet

You can access the Internet in several ways. From your place of work or your university, you can use your organization's LAN. A campus or company backbone connects all of the various LANs and servers in the organization to the Internet. You can also log on to the Internet from your home or on the road, using either wireline or wireless connections.

Connecting through an Online Service.

You can also access the Internet by opening an account with an Internet service provider. An **Internet service provider (ISP)** is a company that provides Internet connections for a fee. Large ISPs include Xfinity (**www.xfinity.com**), AT&T (**www.att.com**), Spectrum (**www.spectrum.com**), and Verizon (**www.verizon.com**).

ISPs connect to one another through **network access points (NAPs).** NAPs are exchange points for Internet traffic. They determine how traffic is routed. NAPs are key components of the Internet backbone. **Figure 6.8** displays a schematic of the Internet. The white links at the top of the figure represent the Internet backbone; the brown dots where the white links meet are the NAPs.

Connecting through Other Means.

There have been several attempts to make access to the Internet cheaper, faster, and easier. For example, terminals known as Internet kiosks have been located in such public places as libraries and airports (and even in convenience stores in some countries) for use by people who do not have their own computers. Accessing the Internet from smartphones and tablets is common, and fiber-to-the-home (FTTH) is growing rapidly. FTTH involves connecting fiber-optic cable directly to individual homes. **Table 6.2** summarizes the various means of connecting to the Internet. Satellite connections and Google Fiber are worth noting in more detail.

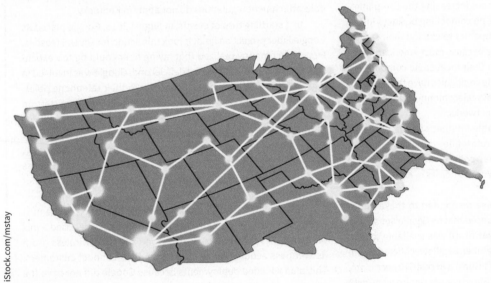

iStock.com/mstay

FIGURE 6.8   **Internet Schematic (backbone in white).**

TABLE 6.2   **Internet Connection Methods**

Service	Description
Dial-up	Still used in the United States where broadband is not available
DSL	Broadband access through telephone companies
Cable modem	Access over your cable TV coaxial cable. Can have degraded performance if many of your neighbors are accessing the Internet at once
Satellite	Access where cable and DSL are not available
Wireless	Very convenient and will increase the use of broadband wireless
Fiber-to-the-home (FTTH)	Expensive and usually placed only in new housing developments

Connecting through satellite. See our discussion in Section 8.1.

Connecting through other means. See Google Project Loon and Facebook solar-powered drones in Section 8.1.

Google Fiber (FTTH). Google Fiber is a service that provides fiber-to-the-home. In November 2017, Google Fiber provided broadband Internet and cable television to customers in 11 U.S. cities. As you see in IT's About Business 6.2, Google has faced stiff competition in deploying the service, with a surprising outcome.

IT's About Business 6.2

The Story of Google Fiber

`MIS`

Cable distribution giants such as Verizon (**www.verizon.com**), Spectrum (**www.spectrum.com**), and Comcast (**www.comcast.com**) enjoy healthy profit margins on their Internet services. None of these companies, however, appears to have had plans to extend fiber-to-the-premises (FTTP; also called fiber-to-the-home or FTTH) services to additional geographical areas. Rather, their business goal was to sign up more people in their existing service areas. They have adopted this strategy because focusing on existing service areas adds the most revenue without increasing the companies' capital costs. Essentially, there are no compelling business incentives for the established cable companies to expand their service offerings. This policy is unfortunate because most Americans have no choice but to do business with their local cable company. To compound this problem, few outside companies have the money to compete with the existing, cash-heavy telecommunications companies that control the existing cable networks.

In direct competition with cable Internet providers, Google began installing and operating ultrafast fiber-optic cable service, known as Google Fiber (**www.fiber.google.com**), in U.S. cities. Google Fiber was first deployed in 2012 to homes in Kansas City (in both Kansas and Missouri).

Google Fiber competitors have responded to these initiatives. In February 2016, AT&T announced that its GigaPower service (**www.att.com/internet/gigapower.html**) was available to residents in Kansas City. Just like Google Fiber, GigaPower offered download speeds of 1 gigabit per second (1 Gbps) and cost $70 per month. For $120 per month, AT&T offered 1 Gbps Internet service along with a free television package. AT&T also began offering GigaPower in Austin, Texas, another Google Fiber city. Interestingly, customers had to pay an additional $29 per month to opt out of AT&T's Internet Preferences program, or AT&T would have tracked everything they did and then sold that information to third-party providers.

Another cable company joined the competition. Just months after Charlotte, North Carolina, was identified as a potential city for Google Fiber, Time Warner Cable announced that it was increasing download speeds up to 300 megabits per second at no charge.

In early 2016, the Louisville, Kentucky, Metro Council voted to permit Google (or any other ISP) to set up its equipment on utility poles owned by third parties, including AT&T. Using existing poles would be the fastest, easiest, and most economical way to launch Google Fiber in Louisville. In response, AT&T, Charter

Communications, and Frontier Communications initiated a lawsuit against the city. The cable providers argued that they should not have to piggyback Google's equipment on poles that they owned and maintained.

As an alternative, Google could bury its fiber-optic cables. That process would address the issues in the lawsuit, and it would also make Google's service more resilient to bad weather and natural disasters. However, the process would be much more expensive and time consuming. In August 2017, federal judge David J. Hale dismissed the lawsuit, stating that the city had the right to control public rights-of-way. The FCC sided with the city, stating that pole-attachment regulations do not apply in Kentucky.

In a startling turn of events, in August 2016, Google placed its Google Fiber project on hold. It took this action for several reasons. First, the company realized that laying fiber could be too expensive to be a viable business model. Second, Google was involved in legal battles with large ISPs over access to their telephone poles. Most important, Google can mount very fast Wi-Fi transmitters on the tops of tall buildings to beam Internet access directly to users for less money than they would have to spend to lay fiber-optic cable. Taking advantage of this high-speed wireless capability, in the fall of 2016, Google completed its acquisition of Webpass (**www.webpass.net**), which provides gigabit residential Internet access through wireless technology.

In April 2017, Google chose Louisville, Kentucky, as the next city to receive its gigabit Internet service. Google Fiber used a mix of fiber-optics for its Internet backbone and fixed wireless (from its Webpass acquisition) for the last mile to connect customers. This plan speeded deployments because Google did not have the expense of burying fiber-optic cable or hanging fiber-optic cable on utility poles.

Significantly, by using fixed wireless, Google did not have to build its fiber huts, each of which would have served 40,000 homes. Also known as a point of presence, a fiber hut is a 10-foot-by-30-foot structure that houses the telecommunications and fiber interface equipment necessary to connect the Google Fiber network to the Internet backbone.

Google also used microtrenching in Louisville. In this process, the company cut small trenches into sidewalks and streets to lay fiber-optic cable. Microtrenching is less intrusive and less expensive than traditional means of laying cable, which require cutting much larger trenches.

It is likely not a coincidence that AT&T's sudden renewed urgency to deploy FTTP in Louisville coincided with Google Fiber's decision to use Louisville as the prototype for its next-generation fiber deployments. The competition was good news for Louisville area residents, who, like most Americans, have had to put up with mediocre Internet service from the major cable and DSL providers for the past 15 years.

The competition remains fierce. AT&T recently increased its FTTP deployments to 60 metropolitan areas across the United States, with plans for dozens more. Interestingly, AT&T is not emphasizing its future FTTP plans. Instead, the company has been advertising its 5G (see Chapter 8) trials and its new AirGig technology to deliver gigabit Internet over power lines. Meanwhile, cable providers like Time Warner Cable upgraded Internet speeds by a factor of six in an effort to hold on to their customers.

Another factor to watch is the cable Internet standard that allows cable companies to offer gigabit speeds over existing cable lines. Because cable already reaches more than 60 percent of U.S. households, this standard could lead to a large upgrade to gigabit speeds from cable companies. In fact, Comcast, America's largest cable Internet provider, has already started deploying gigabit cable upgrades.

Despite the problems and intense competition, Google Fiber continues to expand. In August 2018, Google Fiber was available in 12 U.S. cities. At that time, Google's service offering included 1 gigabit-per-second Internet access for $55 per month. The company did not require a service contract and installed Google Wi-Fi in customer homes for free.

On August 2, 2018, the Federal Communications Commission (FCC) passed an order, called "one touch make ready" that allowed new entrants, such as Google Fiber, to use a single contractor to move all of the equipment on a utility pole, including equipment owned by existing broadband providers. The FCC hoped to speed broadband deployment and improve competition by making it easier for broadband providers that want to enter a city to use existing utility poles.

With all of these factors in mind, what is the advantage of gigabit fiber? High-end fiber connections have much lower latency than any other type of connection, as low as two milliseconds. This speed opens up new possibilities for telepresence systems, team collaboration, artificial intelligence, the Internet of Things, and virtual reality and augmented reality over the Internet. The other major advantage that fiber has over wireless, satellites, power lines, and upgraded cable lines is that it is much easier to scale up fiber's upload and download speeds to meet the demands of all of these technologies.

The bottom line is that customers will benefit from higher-speed broadband Internet and accompanying lower prices. In fact, the Fiber to the Home (FTTH) Council has released a study that claimed that bringing a second gigabit provider to a market "reduces prices by approximately $57 to $62 per month, or between 34–37 percent." The FTTH Council also noted that each new gigabit competitor increases the likelihood that other providers will begin to offer higher-speed broadband as well.

Sources: Compiled from J. Brodkin, "FCC Sides with Google Fiber over Comcast with New Pro-Competition Rule," *Ars Technica*, August 2, 2018; W. Davis, "FCC Boosts Google Fiber with New Rules for Utility Poles," *Media Post Communications*, August 2, 2018; S. Nowlin, "Google Fiber Expands Internet Service into More of San Antonio," *San Antonio Current*, July 31, 2018; J. D'Onfro, "Alphabet's Ruth Porat Says Google Fiber Needs to Be 10 Times Better than Current Technology," CNBC, February 26, 2018; A. Thompson, "SpaceX Is Launching Its First Internet Satellites This Week," *Popular Mechanics*, February 12, 2018; C. Mills, "What's Happening to Google Fiber?" *BGR*, January 31, 2018; J. McGee and P. Bailey, "Louisville Judge Dismisses AT&T Lawsuit, Similar to Nashville Fiber Optics Suit," *The Tennessean*, August 17, 2017; C. Forrest, "Google Fiber Officially Selects Louisville, KY, to Run Its New Gigabit Play," *TechRepublic*, April 26, 2017; J. Hiner, "Google Fiber Is Finally Set to Announce Its Next City, But Don't Call It a Comeback Yet," *TechRepublic*, April 25, 2017; S. McBride and M. Bergen, "Toto, I've a Feeling We're Still in Kansas (or Missouri)," *Bloomberg BusinessWeek*, March 13–19, 2017; J. Hiner and C. Forrest, "Google Fiber 2.0 Targets the City Where It Will Stage Its Comeback, as AT&T Fiber Prepares to Go Nuclear," *TechRepublic*, February 9, 2017; J. Hiner, "Fiber Broadband: Is It a Waste with 5G and Elon Musk's Satellites on the Horizon?" *ZDNet*, February 5, 2017; C. Forrest, "Why Google Fiber Failed: 5 Reasons," *TechRepublic*, December 20, 2016; S. Fiegerman, "Google Puts the Brakes on Fiber and Plans for Layoffs," CNN Money, October 26, 2016; J. Brodkin, "Google Fiber Division Cuts Staff by 9%, 'Pauses' Fiber Plans in 11 Cities," *Ars Technica*, October 25, 2016; D. Wakabayashi, "Google Curbs Expansion of Fiber Optic Network, Cutting Jobs," *New York Times*, October 25, 2016; J. Brodkin, "Charter, Like AT&T, Sues Louisville to Stall Google Fiber," *Ars Technica*, October 5, 2016; M. Reilly, "Google Fiber Stalls as the Industry Gears Up for Ultrafast Wireless," *MIT Technology Review*, August 15, 2016; D. Morris, "Frontier Lines Up Against Google Fiber in AT&T Fight over Utility Pole Access," *Fortune*, July 2, 2016; T. C. Sottek, "Comcast Is Afraid of Google Fiber," *The Verge*, March 17, 2016; D. Patterson, "Google and AT&T: Fighting Fiber with Fiber," *TechRepublic*, March 4, 2016; C. Forest, "AT&T Goes to War with Google Fiber in Louisville: Why Ma Bell Could Win and What It Could Mean," *TechRepublic*, March 1, 2016; and www.fiber.google.com, accessed July 9, 2019.

Questions

1. Describe and evaluate the competitive responses of the cable companies to Google Fiber.

2. When the cable companies matched Google Fiber's cost and speed at no extra charge, do you think they had a public relations problem? Why or why not? Support your answer.

3. Discuss how this case illustrates the difficulty in keeping up with rapid advances in information technology.

Addresses on the Internet.   Each computer on the Internet has an assigned address, called the **Internet Protocol (IP) address**, that distinguishes it from all other computers. The IP address consists of sets of numbers, in four parts, separated by dots. For example, the IP address of one computer might be 135.62.128.91. You can access a website by typing this number in the address bar of your browser.

Currently, there are two IP addressing schemes. The first scheme, IPv4, is the most widely used. IP addresses using IPv4 consist of 32 bits, meaning that there are 2^{32} possibilities for IP addresses, or 4,294,967,295 distinct addresses. Note that the IP address in the preceding paragraph (135.62.128.91) is an IPv4 address. At the time IPv4 was developed, there were not as many computers that needed addresses as there are today. Therefore, a new

IP addressing scheme has been developed, IPv6, because we have run out of available IPv4 addresses.

IP addresses using IPv6 consist of 128 bits, meaning that there are 2^{128} possibilities for distinct IP addresses, which is an unimaginably large number. IPv6, which is replacing IPv4, will accommodate the rapidly increasing number of devices that need IP addresses, such as smartphones and devices that constitute the Internet of Things (see Section 8.4).

IP addresses must be unique so that computers on the Internet know where to find one another. The Internet Corporation for Assigned Names and Numbers (ICANN) (**www.icann.org**) coordinates these unique addresses throughout the world. Without that coordination, we would not have one global Internet.

Because the numeric IP addresses are difficult to remember, most computers have names as well. ICANN accredits certain companies called *registrars* to register these names, which are derived from a system called the **domain name system (DNS)**. **Domain names** consist of multiple parts, separated by dots, that are read from right to left. For example, consider the domain name *business.auburn.edu*. The rightmost part (or zone) of an Internet name is its top-level domain (TLD). The letters *edu* in business.auburn.edu indicate that this is an educational site. The following are popular U.S. TLDs:

com	commercial sites
edu	educational sites
mil	military government sites
gov	civilian government sites
org	organizations

To conclude our domain name example, *auburn* is the name of the organization (Auburn University), and *business* is the name of the particular machine (server) within the organization to which the message is being sent.

A top-level domain (TLD) is the domain at the highest level in the hierarchical Domain Name System of the Internet. The top-level domain names are located in the root zone (rightmost zone) of the name. Management of most TLDs is delegated to responsible organizations by ICANN. ICANN operates the Internet Assigned Numbers Authority (IANA), which is in charge of maintaining the DNS root zone. Today, IANA distinguishes the following groups of TLDs:

- Country-code top-level domains (ccTLD): Two-letter domains established for countries or territories. For example, *de* stands for Germany, *it* for Italy, and *ru* for Russia.
- Internationalized country code top-level domains (IDN ccTLD): These are ccTLDs in non-Latin character sets (e.g., Arabic or Chinese).
- Generic top-level domains (gTLD): Top-level domains with three or more characters. gTLDs initially consisted of .gov, .edu, .com, .mil, .org, and .net. In late 2000, ICANN introduced .aero, .biz, .coop, .info, .museum, .name, and .pro.

On October 1, 2016, the U.S. National Telecommunications & Information Administration (NTIA), a part of the U.S. Commerce Department, turned over control of the Internet Domain Name System to the California-based nonprofit, Internet Corporation for Assigned Names and Numbers. Since that time, ICANN has been working on behalf of an international "multi-stakeholder community" composed predominantly of technology companies. The U.S. government stated that if the United States did not turn these functions over to ICANN, such a move could lend weight to arguments from nations such as China and Russia that Internet governance should be nationalized or turned over to the United Nations.

The Future of the Internet

Researchers assert that if Internet bandwidth is not improved rapidly, then within a few years the Internet will be able to function only at a much-reduced speed. The Internet is sometimes too slow for data-intensive applications such as full-motion video files (movies) and large medical files (X-rays). The Internet is also unreliable and is not secure. As a result, Internet2 has been developed by many U.S. universities collaborating with industry and government. **Internet2** develops and deploys advanced network applications such as remote medical diagnosis, digital libraries, distance education, online simulation, and virtual laboratories. It is designed to be fast, always on, everywhere, natural, intelligent, easy, and trusted. Note that Internet2 is not a separate physical network from the Internet. For more details, see **www.internet2.edu**.

Another possible future for the Internet, called the "splinternet," is less positive. IT's About Business 6.3 discusses the emergence and implications of the splinternet.

IT's About Business 6.3

The Splinternet

`MIS`

Written by John Perry Barlow and published in 1996, the "Declaration of the Independence of Cyberspace" is an early paper addressing the applicability (or lack thereof) of government on the Internet. The declaration stated that cyberspace transcends all borders. For most of its short history, the Internet has had very limited centralized planning or governance. In general, the Internet today enables users to exchange ideas and cultural artifacts instantaneously and with minimum supervision, regardless of national boundaries. Unfortunately, the modern, open Internet also provides a platform for nations to undertake information warfare, manipulate one another's citizens, and project their interests past national borders.

Nations balance the destabilizing effects of the Internet against its benefits for economic development, trade, productivity, and intellectual and cultural exchange by framing their national access policies accordingly. For instance, authoritarian governments routinely order an Internet shutdown when political opposition appears. Furthermore, there is virtually no access to the outside Internet in North Korea, although the government operates a few websites to guarantee complete ideological conformity.

Digital borders are being constructed all the time. Even liberal democracies must strike a balance between a managed Internet and an open Internet. In Britain and South Korea, for example, ISPs must limit access to pornography. Further, 30 countries have ordered ISPs to block The Pirate Bay (TPB). TPB is an online index of digital content of entertainment media and software that allows visitors to search, download, and contribute links and torrent files that facilitate peer-to-peer sharing among users of the BitTorrent protocol. TPB has caused controversy concerning the legal aspects of file sharing, copyright, and civil liberties.

China is the largest power to opt out of the open Internet entirely. China's Internet is enclosed by Golden Shield, a censorship and surveillance project operated by the Ministry of Public Security. The most famous component of Golden Shield is the Great Firewall of China, a combination of legislative and technolgical actions that restrict citizens' access to foreign services like Google, Facebook, and the *New York Times*.

By building a "national" Internet that favors Chinese services, China receives all of the benefits of today's networks without any of the drawbacks. Privately operated foreign Internet platforms that can promote dissent, opposition, or subversive ideas, such as many social media websites that are common in the rest of the world, are not permitted in China.

China's Internet policy may be a precursor to a federated, loosely connected set of national Internets called the *splinternet* (also known as *Internet balkanization*). In addition to national interests, the Internet could divide as a result of other factors, such as technology (e.g., broadband access), commerce, politics, and special interests. Specifically, how users experience the Internet in one country is becoming increasingly different from how it is experienced in another country. In essence, the splinternet refers to a broad tendency to use laws and regulatory powers within territorial jurisdictions to impose limits on digital activities.

A seminal moment in the emergence of the splinternet occurred in 2013 when Edward Snowden, a contractor with the U.S. National Security Agency (NSA), leaked a number of classified documents. These documents suggested that the NSA, through its PRISM program, had collected information from global users of Google, Facebook, Apple, Microsoft, and Yahoo, including many national political leaders such as Angela Merkel of Germany and Dilma Rousseff of Brazil. In some of these countries, Snowden's disclosures accelerated a move toward developing national Internet control. For example, Brazil's Marco Civil da Internet law now requires global companies to comply with Brazilian laws concerning data protection.

The splinternet is growing as a result of content blocking by regions and nations as well as the need for companies to comply with diverse, often conflicting national policies, regulations, and court decisions. These policies are particularly evident with platform companies such as Google, Facebook, and Twitter. These companies have users in almost every country, and governments are increasingly insisting that they comply with local laws and cultural norms regarding access and content. Consider these important occurrences that could lead to the splinternet:

- The European Union's General Data Protection Regulation (GDPR) could force a trend toward the splinternet. For example, certain U.S. news organizations intentionally blocked or limited the EU versions of their sites at the GDPR's beginning on May 25, 2018. Imagine the problems if Japan, India, and other countries mandate similar laws. Further, California and other states are also considering their own regulations.

Multiple, overlapping regulations could limit international business that the Internet supports. It would also be a huge burden on small companies that may not have the resources to adhere to a multitude of complex compliance laws.

- Internet censorship is nothing new (e.g., China, Iran, Turkey), but Russia blocked entire cloud services to stop the Telegram messaging platform (**www.telegram.org**) after Telegram used multiple cloud providers in its attempt to circumvent Russia's initial shutdown. Some 19 million IP addresses were affected.

  TripAdvisor used a cloud provider, so it was one of the companies caught in this shutdown. Its website availability for users in Russia and Eastern Europe dropped to as low as 12.5 percent, meaning that about 90 percent of the time, no one could access the website. When the site was available, page load times approached 23 minutes! This problem could happen when censorship meets a world where many online services are concentrated in a small number of cloud providers.

- Network neutrality was repealed in the United States, meaning that since June 11, 2018, Internet service providers can offer tiered service packages. These offerings dictate the quality (i.e., speed) of online services based on a customer's ability to pay. Ending network neutrality could divide the Internet into high-quality and low-quality offerings.

- In early 2019, Russia was in the early stages of following China's lead and building its own national Internet.

Sources: Compiled from "Russia Must Build Own Internet in Case of Foreign Disruption: Putin," *Reuters*, February 20, 2019; M. Daoudi, "Beware the SplinterNet – Why Three Recent Events Should Have Businesses Worried," *Forbes*, July 12, 2018; R. Foroohar, "'Splinternet' to Herald a Trade War for the Ages," *Financial Times*, March 5, 2018; "The 'Splinternet' May Be the Future of the Web," *Business Insider*, August 8, 2017; D. Alba, "The World May Be Headed for a Fragmented 'Splinternet'," *Wired*, July 7, 2017; B. Moscowitz, "The Reasons Why a Free and Open Internet Could Spell the Web's Downfall," *Quartz Media*, April 4, 2017; "What Is the 'Splinternet'?" *The Economist*, November 22, 2016; "Lost in the Splinternet," *The Economist*, November 5, 2016; T. Parmar, "Will the Public Internet Survive?" *The Nation*, August 15–22, 2016; B. Sterling, "The China Splinternet Model Is Winning," *Wired*, July 2, 2016; E. Macaskill and G. Dance, "NSA Files Decoded," *The Guardian*, November 1, 2013; S. Meinrath, "The Future of the Internet: Balkanization and Borders," *Time*, October 11, 2013; and C. Lynch, "Brazil's President Condemns NSA Spying," *Washington Post*, September 24, 2013.

Questions

1. What are the advantages of the splinternet to a nation? Provide examples to support your answer.

2. What are the disadvantages of the splinternet to a nation? Provide examples to support your answer.

3. What are the advantages of the splinternet to you as an individual? Provide examples to support your answer.

4. What are the disadvantages of the splinternet to you as an individual? Provide examples to support your answer.

The World Wide Web

Many people equate the Internet with the World Wide Web. However, they are not the same thing. The Internet functions as a transport mechanism, whereas the World Wide Web is an application that uses those transport functions. Other applications, such as e-mail, also run on the Internet.

The **World Wide Web** (the **Web** or **WWW**) is a system of universally accepted standards for storing, retrieving, formatting, and displaying information through a client/server architecture. The Web handles all types of digital information, including text, hypermedia, graphics, and sound. It uses graphical user interfaces (GUIs) (explained in Technology Guide 2), so it is very easy to navigate.

Hypertext is the underlying concept defining the structure of the World Wide Web. Hypertext is the text displayed on a computer display or other electronic device with references, called *hyperlinks,* to other text that the reader can immediately access, or where text can be revealed progressively at additional levels of details. A **hyperlink** is a connection from a hypertext file or document to another location or file, typically activated by clicking on a highlighted word or image on the screen, or by touching the screen.

Organizations that wish to offer information through the Web must establish a *home page,* which is a text and graphical screen display that usually welcomes the user and provides basic information on the organization that has established the page. In most cases, the home page will lead users to other pages. All the pages of a particular company or individual are collectively known as a **website.** Most Web pages provide a way to contact the organization or the individual. The person in charge of an organization's website is its *webmaster.* (*Note: Webmaster* is a gender-neutral title.)

To access a website, the user must specify a **uniform resource locator (URL)**, which points to the address of a specific resource on the Web. For example, the URL for Microsoft is

www.microsoft.com. Recall that HTTP stands for *hypertext transport protocol.* The remaining letters in this URL—**www.microsoft.com**—indicate the domain name that identifies the Web server that stores the website.

Users access the Web primarily through software applications called browsers. **Browsers** provide a graphical front end that enables users to point and click their way across the Web, a process called *surfing.* Web browsers became a means of universal access because they deliver the same interface on any operating system on which they run. As of July 2019, Google Chrome was the leading browser, followed by Apple Safari, Firefox, Microsoft Internet Explorer, and Microsoft Edge.

Before you go on . . .

1. Describe the various ways that you can connect to the Internet.
2. Identify each part of an Internet address.
3. Describe the difference between the Internet and the World Wide Web.
4. What are the functions of browsers?

6.4 Network Applications: Discovery

Now that you have a working knowledge of what networks are and how you can access them, the key question is: How do businesses use networks to improve their operations? In the next four sections of this chapter, we explore four network applications: discovery, communication, collaboration, and education. These applications, however, are merely a sampling of the many network applications that are currently available to users. Even if these applications formed an exhaustive list today, they would not do so tomorrow, when something new inevitably will be developed. Furthermore, placing network applications in categories is difficult because there will always be borderline cases. For example, telecommuting combines communication and collaboration.

The Internet enables users to access, or discover, information located in databases all over the world. By browsing and searching data sources on the Web, users can apply the Internet's discovery capability to areas ranging from education to government services to entertainment to commerce. Although having access to all this information is a great benefit, it is critically important to realize that there is no quality assurance for information on the Web. The Web is truly democratic in that *anyone* can post information to it. Therefore, the fundamental rule about information on the Web is "User beware!"

Think about discovery in 1960. How would you find information? You probably would have had to go to the library to check out a physical book. Contrast that process with how you discover that information today. In fact, the overall trends in discovery have been:

- In the past, people had to go to the information (the library). Today, the information comes to you through the Internet.
- In the past, only one person at a time could have the information (the book he or she checked out of the library). Today, the information is available to multiple users at the same time.
- In the past, it may not have been possible to access the information you needed; for example, if the book was checked out. Today, the information is available to everyone, simultaneously.
- In the past, your book might have needed to be translated if it was written in a different language. Today, automatic translation software tools are improving very rapidly.

Author Lecture Videos are available exclusively in *WileyPLUS.*
Apply the Concept activities are available in the Appendix and in *WileyPLUS.*

The Web's major strength—the vast stores of information it contains—also presents a major challenge. The amount of information on the Web can be overwhelming, and it doubles approximately each year. As a result, navigating through the Web and gaining access to necessary information are becoming more and more difficult. To accomplish these tasks, people are increasingly using search engines, directories, and portals.

Search Engines and Metasearch Engines

A **search engine** is a computer program that searches for specific information by key words and then reports the results. A search engine maintains an index of billions of Web pages. It uses that index to find pages that match a set of user-specified key words. Such indexes are created and updated by *Web crawlers*, which are computer programs that browse the Web and create a copy of all visited pages. Search engines then index these pages to provide fast searches.

Currently, four search engines account for almost all searches in the United States. They are still, in order, Google (**www.google.com**), Bing (**www.bing.com**), Yahoo! (**www.yahoo.com**), and Ask (**www.ask.com**). The leading search engine in China is Baidu (**www.baidu.com**), which claims approximately 75 percent of the Chinese market.

For an even more thorough search, you can use a metasearch engine. **Metasearch engines** search several engines at once and then integrate the findings to answer users' queries. Examples are Surf-wax (**www.surfwax.com**), Metacrawler (**www.metacrawler.com**), Mamma (**www.mamma.com**), KartOO (**www.kartoo.com**), and Dogpile (**www.dogpile.com**).

Publication of Material in Foreign Languages

The World Bank (**www.worldbank.org**) estimates that 80 percent of online content is available in only 1 of 10 languages: English, Chinese, Spanish, Japanese, Arabic, Portuguese, German, French, Russian, and Korean. Roughly 3 billion people speak one of these as their first language. However, more than 50 percent of all online content is written in English, which is understood by only 21 percent of the world's population. Consider India, whose citizens speak roughly 425 languages and dialects. Industry analysts estimate that less than 0.1 percent of all Web content is composed in Hindi, the first language of approximately 260 million people.

Not only is there a huge amount of information on the Internet, but it is also written in many languages. How, then, do you access this information? The answer is that you use an *automatic translation* of Web pages. Such translation is available to and from all major languages, and its quality is improving over time.

Companies invest resources to make their websites accessible in multiple languages as a result of the global nature of the business environment; that is, multilingual websites are now a competitive necessity. When companies are disseminating information around the world, getting that information correct is essential. It is not enough for companies to translate Web content. They must also localize that content and be sensitive to the needs of the people in local markets.

At 20 cents and more per word, translation services are expensive. Companies supporting 10 languages can spend $200,000 annually to localize information and another $50,000 to maintain the websites. Translation budgets for major multinational companies can total millions of dollars.

Some major translation products are Microsoft's Translator app (**www.translator.microsoft.com**), Google (**www.translate.google.com**) (see **Figure 6.9**), and Skype Translator (**www.skype.com/en/features/skype-translator/**) as well as products and services available at SDL Trados (**www.translationzone.com**) and Systran (**www.systransoft.com**).

In September 2016, Google announced its new translation service, which is based on deep learning (see Technology Guide 4). In a competition that compared the new translation system with human translators, the system came very close to matching the fluency of humans for

Source: Google LLC

some languages, such as translating between English and Spanish and between English and French. Google is expanding the system to multiple languages.

In December 2016, Microsoft launched its Translator app. With spoken conversation, the app can accommodate groups of up to 100 and nine languages: Arabic, Mandarin Chinese, Spanish, English, French, German, Russian, Portuguese, and Italian.

Portals

Most organizations and their managers encounter information overload. Information is scattered across numerous documents, e-mail messages, and databases at multiple locations and in multiple systems. Finding relevant and accurate information is often time consuming and may require users to access multiple systems.

MIS One solution to this problem is to use *portals*. A **portal** is a Web-based, personalized gateway to information and knowledge that provides relevant information from different IT systems and the Internet using advanced search and indexing techniques. After reading the next section, you will be able to distinguish among four types of portals: commercial, affinity, corporate, and industrywide. The four types of portals are differentiated by the audiences they serve.

A **commercial (public) portal** is the most popular type of portal on the Internet. It is intended for broad and diverse audiences, and it offers routine content, some of it in real time (e.g., a stock ticker). Examples are Lycos (**www.lycos.com**) and Microsoft Network (**www.msn.com**).

MKT In contrast, an **affinity portal** offers a single point of entry to an entire community of affiliated interests, such as a hobby group or a political party. Your university most likely has an affinity portal for its alumni. **Figure 6.10** displays the affinity portal for the University of West Georgia. Other examples of affinity portals are **www.techweb.com** and **www.zdnet.com**.

MIS As the name suggests, a **corporate portal** offers a personalized, single point of access through a Web browser to critical business information located inside and outside an organization. These portals are also known as *enterprise portals, information portals*, and *enterprise information portals*. Besides making it easier to find needed information, corporate portals offer customers and employees self-service opportunities.

Whereas corporate portals are associated with a single company, an **industrywide** portal serves entire industries. An example is TruckNet (**www.trucknet.io/en**), a portal for the trucking industry and the trucking community, including professional drivers, owner/operators, and trucking companies.

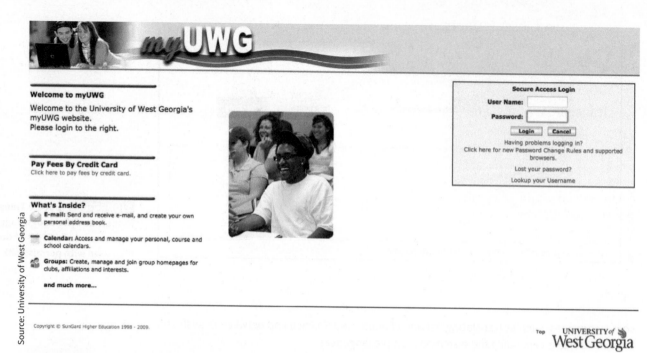

Source: University of West Georgia

FIGURE 6.10   **University of West Georgia affinity portal. (Courtesy of the University of West Georgia).**

Before you go on . . .

1. Differentiate between search engines and metasearch engines.
2. What are some reasons why publication of material in a number of languages is so important?
3. Describe the various ways that portals are useful to us.

6.5   Network Applications: Communication

Author Lecture Videos are available exclusively in *WileyPLUS*.
Apply the Concept activities are available in the Appendix and in *WileyPLUS*.

The second major category of network applications is communication. There are many types of communication technologies, including e-mail, call centers, chat rooms, and voice. Further-more, we discuss an interesting application of communication: telecommuting. (*Note:* You will read about other types of communication—blogging and microblogging—in Chapter 9.)

Electronic Mail

Electronic mail (e-mail) is the largest-volume application running over the Internet. Studies have found that almost all companies conduct business transactions through e-mail, and the vast majority confirm that e-mail is tied to their means of generating revenue. At the same time, however, the amount of e-mail that managers receive has become overwhelming. The problem is that too much e-mail can actually make a business less productive.

Web-Based Call Centers

MKT   Effective personalized customer contact is becoming an important aspect of Web-based customer support. Such service is provided through *Web-based call centers*, also known as *customer care centers*. For example, if you need to contact a software vendor for technical support, you will usually communicate with the vendor's Web-based call center, using e-mail, a telephone conversation, or a simultaneous voice and Web session. Web-based call centers are sometimes located in foreign countries such as India. Such *offshoring* is an important issue for U.S. companies. (We discuss offshoring in Chapter 13.)

Significantly, some U.S. companies are moving their call center operations back to the United States, for several reasons. First, they believe they have less control of their operations when the centers are located overseas. They must depend on the vendor company to uphold their standards, such as quality of service. A second difficulty is language differences, which can create serious communication problems. Third, companies that manage sensitive information risk breaching customer confidentiality and security. Finally, the call center representatives typically work with many companies. As a result, they may not deliver the same level of customer services that each company requires.

Electronic Chat Rooms

Electronic chat refers to an arrangement in which participants exchange conversational messages in real time in a *chat room*. Chat programs allow you to send messages to people who are connected to the same channel of communication at the same time as you are. Anyone can join in the conversation. Messages are displayed on your screen as they arrive.

Early chat rooms used text-only Internet Relay Chat (IRC). The use of IRC has significantly declined since the early 2000s. Current chat rooms can be used on mobile devices and allow users to upload images, files, and video and audio messages. You can create your own chat room with chat room services such as **www.rumbletalk.com** and **www.xat.com**. Chat rooms have further declined in usage with the popularity of social media.

Voice Communication

The plain old telephone service (POTS) has been largely replaced by Internet telephony. With **Internet telephony**, also known as **Voice-over-Internet Protocol** or **VoIP**, phone calls are treated as just another kind of data; that is, your analog voice signals are digitized, sectioned into packets, and then sent over the Internet.

Consider Skype (**www.skype.com** now owned by Microsoft), which provides several VoIP services for free: voice and video calls to users who also have Skype, calls between Skype and landline and mobile phone numbers; wireless hotspot network access, instant messaging, voice mail, one-to-one and group chats, and conference calls.

Unified Communications

In the past, organizational networks for wired and wireless data, voice communications, and videoconferencing operated independently, and the IT department managed each network separately. This arrangement increased costs and reduced productivity.

Unified communications (UC) simplifies and integrates all forms of communications—voice, voice mail, fax, chat, e-mail, instant messaging, short message service, presence (location) services, and videoconferencing—on a common hardware and software platform. *Presence services* enable users to know where their intended recipients are and if they are available, in real time.

UC unifies all forms of human and computer communications into a common user experience. For example, UC allows an individual to receive a voice mail message and then read it in his or her e-mail inbox. In another example, UC enables users to seamlessly collaborate with another person on a project, regardless of where the user is located. One user could quickly locate the other user by accessing an interactive directory, determining whether that user is available, engaging in a text messaging session, and then escalating the session to a voice call or even a video call, all in real time.

Telecommuting

Knowledge workers are being called the distributed workforce, or "digital nomads." This group of highly prized workers is now able to work anywhere and anytime, a process called **telecommuting**. Distributed workers are those who have no permanent office at their companies, preferring to work at home offices, in airport lounges or client conference rooms, or on a high school stadium bleacher. The growth of the distributed workforce is driven by globalization, extremely long commutes to work, ubiquitous broadband communications links (wireline and wireless), and powerful computing devices.

HRM Telecommuting offers a number of potential advantages for employees, employers, and society. For employees, the benefits include reduced stress and improved family life. Telecommuting also offers employment opportunities for housebound people such as single parents and persons with disabilities. Benefits for employers include increased productivity, the ability to retain skilled employees, and the ability to attract employees who do not live within commuting distance.

HRM However, telecommuting also has some potential disadvantages. For employees, the major disadvantages are increased feelings of isolation, possible loss of fringe benefits, lower pay (in some cases), no workplace visibility, lack of socialization, and the potential for slower promotions. In a 2013 study, researchers at Stanford University found that telecommuting employees are 50 percent less likely to receive a promotion than onsite workers. The researchers concluded that a lack of "face time" with bosses caused careers to stall.

Another problem is that telecommuting employees also often have difficulties "training" their families to understand that they are at work even though they are physically at home. Families have to understand that they should not disturb the telecommuter for anything that they would not disturb him or her about in a "real" office. The major disadvantages to employers are difficulties in supervising work and potential data security problems.

Before you go on . . .

1. Discuss the advantages and disadvantages of electronic mail.
2. Why are many companies bringing their call centers back to the United States?
3. Describe Voice-over-Internet Protocol.
4. What would be the advantages and disadvantages of telecommuting to you as an individual?

6.6 Network Applications: Collaboration

Author Lecture Videos are available exclusively in *WileyPLUS*.
Apply the Concept activities are available in the Appendix and in *WileyPLUS*.

The third major category of network applications is collaboration. **Collaboration** refers to efforts by two or more entities—that is, individuals, teams, groups, or organizations—who work together to accomplish certain tasks. The term **workgroup** refers specifically to two or more individuals who act together to perform a task.

Workflow is the movement of information as it progresses through the sequence of steps that make up an organization's work procedures. Workflow management makes it possible to pass documents, information, and tasks from one participant to another in a way that is governed by the organization's rules or procedures. Workflow systems are tools for automating business processes.

If group members are working in different locations, they constitute a **virtual group (team)**. Virtual groups conduct *virtual meetings*—that is, they "meet" electronically. **Virtual collaboration** (or *e-collaboration*) refers to the use of digital technologies that enable organizations or individuals who are geographically dispersed to collaboratively plan, design, develop, manage, and research products, services, and innovative applications. Organizational employees frequently collaborate virtually with one another. Some organizations collaborate virtually with customers, suppliers, and other business partners to become more productive and competitive.

Collaboration can be *synchronous*, meaning that all team members meet at the same time. Teams may also collaborate *asynchronously* when team members cannot meet at the same time. Virtual teams, whose members are located throughout the world, typically must collaborate asynchronously.

Although a variety of software products are available to support all types of collaboration, many organizations feel that too many software tools are being used in collaborative efforts. These firms want a single place to know what was shared, who shared it with whom, and when. Firms also want smarter collaboration tools that are capable of anticipating workers' needs.

Collaborative software products include Google Drive (**www.drive.google.com**), Microsoft Office 365 Teams (**www.products.office.com/en-us/microsoft-teams/group-chat-software**), Jive (**www.jivesoftware.com**), Glip (**www.glip.com**), Slack (**www.slack.com**), Atlassian (**www.atlassian.com**), and Facebook's Workplace (**www.facebook.com/workplace**), as well as many others. In general, these products provide online collaboration capabilities, workgroup e-mail, distributed databases, electronic text editing, document management, workflow capabilities, instant virtual meetings, application sharing, instant messaging, consensus building, voting, ranking, and various application-development tools.

Two of these tools use analytics for more effective collaboration. IBM's Verse combines e-mail, social media, calendars, and file sharing with analytics in one software package designed to overhaul e-mail and increase productivity for organizations. Microsoft's Delve for Office 365 uses analytics to display information that is most relevant for each user.

Consider multinational banking and financial services company BNY Mellon (**www.bnymellon.com**). The bank uses a proprietary, in-house–developed enterprise social networking tool, called MySource Social, to share ideas and expertise. The social network is integrated with BNY Mellon's communication and collaboration tools, such as e-mail, calendar, and instant messaging systems. MySource Social is an intranet site within which users can explore business partner groups featuring blogs and information from executives; special-interest groups; and ad hoc groups, such as those created for project teams. More than 90 percent of the 55,000 BNY Mellon employees worldwide have accessed the site in some way, and 40 percent are hands-on participants.

Collaboration is so important that companies are using information technology to enable the process as much as possible. IT's About Business 6.4 explores how Boeing uses its Collaboration Center to maximize collaboration with customers.

IT's About Business 6.4

The Boeing Collaboration Center

`MIS` `POM`

The Boeing Company (**www.boeing.com**) is an U.S.-based multinational corporation that designs, manufactures, and sells airplanes, rotorcraft, rockets, and satellites globally. The company is the second-largest defense contractor in the world, behind Lockheed Martin (**www.lockheedmartin.com**).

Boeing designed its Collaboration Center in its Arlington, Virginia, regional headquarters to provide new ways to engage with the company's global customers. The Center enables Boeing to present its capabilities in an immersive, visual environment that encourages close collaboration with its customers.

Boeing's intent is to deliver a customer engagement experience unlike any that its customers have previously seen. In addition, the Center wants each customer to have a customized experience.

The Center consists of 7,500 square feet of multiuse spaces. Customers first see a 27-by-8-foot Entrance Feature. This large screen offers an audiovisual presentation of Boeing's diverse capabilities. The screen is composed of Christie MicroTiles. The tiles are modular, rear-projection cubes that are placed to form a large video wall-style display. Customers are then greeted at the Welcome Wall. This 3-by-3 array of Samsung 55-inch multitouch displays communicates customized messaging and includes the objectives for the meeting, agenda details, and concierge features, which can include real-time flight arrival and departure information as well as a 100-year history of Boeing.

A pair of Collaboration Rooms feature Cisco videoconferencing systems and 90-inch Sharp displays that include touch interfaces that create comfortable, flexible spaces that are ideal for effective collaboration. These rooms can be configured in different ways. Alternatively, they can be combined into one large working environment.

Next to the Collaboration Rooms is the Launch Window, which offers sofa seating in front of a 90-inch interactive Sharp display screen. This screen can present three-dimensional (3D) content to showcase Boeing products and touch-enable simulations.

The Global Presence Wall features a 3-by-3 array of Samsung 55-inch multitouch displays with custom content about Boeing's global presence. The content features supplier information, economic impact, and corporate citizenship initiatives. Customers can drill down and see details by country and by global location.

The highlight of the Collaboration Center is the One Boeing Wall, a display that consists of 18 Samsung 55-inch monitors. The Wall has audio- and videoconferencing capabilities as well as a multitouch capability that enables multiple customers to explore and cross-reference Boeing products and services at the same time. After a collaboration, documentation annotated on the Wall can be saved and sent to customers for follow-up.

The same application that supports the One Boeing Wall also supports two multitouch interactive table displays that are located at opposite ends of the Collaboration Center. Each table contains two embedded 42-inch multitouch computers that feature object recognition. Boeing staffers and customers can place an object, such as carbon fiber or a product model, on these tables to obtain a deeper understanding of the object's capabilities.

In the Centers' Horizon Theater, customers experience presentations, webcasts, and flight simulations. Customers can also engage in two-way audio- and videoconferences with remote participants such as Boeing executives or subject matter experts dispersed throughout the world. The Theater is an immersive environment with digital surround sound and three high-definition projection images on a 180-degree curved screen. In the Theater, the visual and audio experience of a flight simulation is so realistic that Boeing installed steady bars for customers to balance themselves.

Interestingly, as impressive and state-of-the-art as the Collaboration Center is, Boeing does not think the Center will look the same in three years. The aerospace giant is already anticipating how augmented reality and virtual reality technologies will impact the firm's collaboration with its customers.

Sources: Compiled from L. Myler, "Why Customer Collaboration Is the Ticket to B2B Success," *Forbes*, July 19, 2017; D. Uptmor, "Why You Should Collaborate with Your Customers," *Clarizen*, March 2, 2017; "Customer Experience Collaboration," *ClearAction*, February 14, 2017; J. Zettel, "AVI-SPL: Building the Culture of Collaboration," *CIO Review*, 2017; J. Owens, "Top 5 AV Business and Tech Trends for 2017," *AVNetwork*, December 12, 2016; C. Zakrzewski, "Virtual Reality Takes on the Videoconference," *Wall Street Journal*, September 18, 2016; "High-Value Marketing: Connecting Customers through Technology, Analytics, and Collaboration," *Harvard Business Review*, September 6, 2016; M. Reynolds, "Customer Collaboration Is the Future of Business," *Huffington Post*, June 21, 2016; J. Durr, "B2B Organic Growth Requires Collaboration with Customers," *Gallup Business Journal*, May 18, 2016; R. Hase, "AVI-SPL Case Study: Boeing Collaboration Center," www.linkedin.com, March 31, 2016; and www.boeing.com, accessed July 9, 2019.

Questions

1. Refer to Chapter 2. Is Boeing's Collaboration Center a strategic information system? Why or why not? Support your answer.

2. With the emergence of virtual reality technologies, do you think that Boeing will even need its Collaboration Center in the future? Why or why not? Support your answer.

Crowdsourcing

One type of collaboration is **crowdsourcing**, in which an organization outsources a task to an undefined, generally large group of people in the form of an open call. Crowdsourcing provides many potential benefits to organizations. First, crowds can explore problems—and often resolve them—at relatively low cost, and often very quickly. Second, the organization can tap a wider range of talent than might be present among its employees. Third, by listening to the crowd, organizations gain firsthand insight into their customers' desires. Finally, crowdsourcing taps into the global world of ideas, helping companies work through a rapid design process. Let's look at some examples of crowdsourcing.

- **MIS** Crowdsourcing help desks: IT help desks are a necessary service on college campuses because students depend on their computers and Internet access to complete their schoolwork and attend classes online. At Indiana University at Bloomington, new IT help desks use crowdsourcing to alleviate the cost and pressure of having to answer so many calls. Students and professors post their IT problems on an online forum, where other students and amateur IT experts answer them.

- **MKT** Recruitment: Champlain College in Vermont developed a Champlain For Reel program, inviting students to share through YouTube videos that recount their experiences at the school and the ways they benefited from their time there. The YouTube channel serves to recruit prospective students, and it even updates alumni on campus and community events.

- Scitable (**www.nature.com/scitable**) combines social networking and academic collaboration. Through crowdsourcing, students, professors, and scientists discuss problems, find solutions, and swap resources and journals. Scitable is a free site that lets individual users turn to crowdsourcing for answers even while helping others.

- Procter & Gamble (P&G) uses InnoCentive (**www.innocentive.com**), in which company researchers post their problems. P&G offers cash rewards to problem solvers.

- SAP's Idea Place (**www.ideas.sap.com**) generates ideas for not-yet-developed software improvements and innovation. Any person can view the content in the Idea Place. The Idea Place is organized into numerous sessions, or categories, under which the ideas are organized. Once you have posted your idea, other users can vote on it and add comments. Status updates on your idea allow you to follow it as it progresses through the Idea Place. Every idea is reviewed by a team of experts made up of engineers, product managers, and community managers who evaluate the potential for implementation. The ideas with the most votes receive a higher level of attention from SAP.

Although crowdsourcing has numerous success stories, there are many questions and concerns about this system, including the following:

- Should the crowd be limited to experts? If so, then how would a company go about implementing this policy?

- How accurate is the content created by the nonexperts in the crowd? How is accuracy maintained?

- How is crowd-created content being updated? How can companies be certain the content is relevant?

- The crowd may submit too many ideas, with most of them being worthless. In this scenario, evaluating all of these ideas can be prohibitively expensive. For example, during the 2010 BP oil spill in the Gulf of Mexico, crowds submitted more than 20,000 suggestions on how to stem the flow of oil. The problem was very technical, so there were many poor suggestions. Nevertheless, despite the fact that BP was under severe time constraints, the company had to evaluate all of the ideas.

- Content contributors may violate copyrights, either intentionally or unintentionally.

- The quality of content (and therefore subsequent decisions) depends on the composition of the crowd. The best decisions may come if the crowd is made up of people with diverse opinions and ideas. In many cases, however, companies do not know the makeup of the crowd in advance.

Teleconferencing and Video Conferencing

Teleconferencing is the use of electronic communication technology that enables two or more people at different locations to hold a conference. There are several types of teleconferencing. The oldest and simplest is a telephone conference call, with which several people talk to one another from multiple locations. The biggest disadvantage of conference calls is that the participants cannot communicate face-to-face, nor can they view graphs, charts, and pictures at other locations.

To overcome these shortcomings, organizations are increasingly turning to video teleconferencing, or videoconferencing. In a **videoconference**, participants in one location can see participants, documents, and presentations at other locations. The latest version of videoconferencing, called *telepresence*, enables participants to seamlessly share data, voice, pictures, graphics, and animation by electronic means. Conferees can also transmit data along with voice and video, which allows them to work together on documents and to exchange computer files.

Telepresence systems range from on-premise, high-end systems to cloud-based systems. (We discuss on-premise computing and cloud computing in Technology Guide 3.) On-premise,

Jennifer Pottheiser/National Basketball Association/Getty Images

FIGURE 6.11 **Telepresence system.**

high-end systems are expensive and require dedicated rooms with large high-definition screens to show people sitting around conference tables (see **Figure 6.11**). These systems have advanced audio capabilities that let everyone talk at once without canceling out any voices. These systems also require technical staff to operate and maintain. An example of a high-end system is Cisco's TelePresence system (**www.cisco.com**).

Having dedicated rooms where telepresence meetings take place is not particularly useful when so many employees work remotely. As a result, companies such as Fuze (**www.fuze.com**) and BlueJeans Network (**www.bluejeans.com**) offer telepresence systems that utilize cloud computing. The cloud delivery model enables Fuze and BlueJeans to provide systems that are less expensive, more flexible, and require fewer in-house technical staff to operate and maintain. Fuze and BlueJeans can also deliver their telepresence systems to any device, including smartphones, tablets, and laptop and desktop computers.

Before you go on . . .

1. Describe virtual collaboration and why it is important to you.
2. Define crowdsourcing, and provide two examples of crowdsourcing not mentioned in this section.
3. Identify the business conditions that have made videoconferencing more important.

6.7 Network Applications: Educational

The fourth major category of network applications consists of education applications. In this section, we discuss e-learning, distance learning, and virtual universities.

E-Learning and Distance Learning

E-learning and **distance learning** are not the same thing, but they do overlap. E-learning refers to learning supported by the Web. It can take place inside classrooms as a support to conventional teaching, such as when students work on the Web during class. It also can take place in virtual classrooms, in which all coursework is completed online and classes do not meet face-to-face. In these cases, e-learning is a part of distance learning. Distance learning (DL) refers to any learning situation in which teachers and students do not meet face-to-face.

Today, the Web provides a multimedia interactive environment for self-study. Web-enabled systems make knowledge accessible to those who need it, when they need it, anytime, anywhere. For this reason, e-learning and DL can be useful for both formal education and corporate training.

There are many benefits of e-learning. For example, online materials can deliver very current content that is of high quality (created by content experts) and consistent (presented the same way every time). It also gives students the flexibility to learn at any place, at any time, and at their own pace. In corporate training centers that use e-learning, learning time generally is shorter, which means that more people can be trained within a given time frame. This system reduces training costs and eliminates the expense of renting facility space.

Despite these benefits, e-learning has some drawbacks. For one, students must be computer literate. Also, they may miss the face-to-face interaction with instructors and fellow students. In addition, accurately assessing students' work can also be problematic because instructors really do not know who completed the assignments.

E-learning does not usually replace the classroom setting. Rather, it enhances it by taking advantage of new content and delivery technologies. Advanced e-learning support environments, such as Blackboard (**www.blackboard.com**), add value to traditional learning in higher education.

A new form of distance learning has recently appeared, called *massive open online courses* or *MOOCs*. MOOCs are a tool for democratizing higher education. Several factors have contributed to the growth of MOOCs, including improved technology and the rapidly increasing costs of traditional universities. MOOCs are highly automated, complete with computer-graded assignments and exams.

MOOCs have not yet proved that they can effectively teach the thousands of students who enroll in them. They also do not provide revenues for universities. Furthermore, MOOCs can register a mixture of high school students, retirees, faculty, enrolled students, and working professionals. Designing a course that adequately meets the needs of such a diverse student population is quite challenging. Finally, although initial registrations for a MOOC might exceed 100,000 students, completion rates in any one MOOC tend to be less than 10 percent of that number. Nevertheless, despite these issues, hundreds of thousands of students around the world who lack access to universities are using MOOCs to acquire sophisticated skills and high-paying jobs without having to pay tuition or obtain a college degree.

In 2018, the world's top providers of MOOCs included the following:

- Coursera (U.S.), with 23 million registered users and 2329 courses
- edX (U.S.), with 10 million registered users and 1319 courses
- XuetangX (China), with 6 million users and 380 courses
- FutureLearn (U.K.), with 5.3 million users and 485 courses
- Udacity (U.S.), with 4 million users and 172 courses

Virtual Universities

Virtual universities are online universities in which students take classes on the Internet either at home or in an offsite location. A large number of existing universities offer online education of some form. Some universities, such as the University of Phoenix (**www.phoenix.edu**), California Virtual Campus (**www.cvc.edu**), and the University of Maryland (**www.umuc.edu**), offer thousands of courses and dozens of degrees to students worldwide, all of them online. Other universities offer limited online courses and degrees, but they employ innovative teaching methods and multimedia support in the traditional classroom.

Before you go on . . .

1. Describe the differences between e-learning and distance learning.
2. What are virtual universities? Would you be willing to attend a virtual university? Why or why not?

What's in IT for me?

For the Accounting Major

ACCT Accounting personnel use corporate intranets and portals to consolidate transaction data from legacy systems to provide an overall view of internal projects. This view contains the current costs charged to each project, the number of hours spent on each project by individual employees, and an analysis of how actual costs compare with projected costs. Finally, accounting personnel use Internet access to government and professional websites to stay informed on legal and other changes affecting their profession.

FIN For the Finance Major

Corporate intranets and portals can provide a model to evaluate the risks of a project or an investment. Financial analysts use two types of data in the model: historical transaction data from corporate databases through the intranet and industry data obtained through the Internet. Financial services firms can also use the Web for marketing and to provide services.

MKT For the Marketing Major

Marketing managers use corporate intranets and portals to coordinate the activities of the sales force. Sales personnel access corporate portals through the intranet to discover updates on pricing, promotion, rebates, customer information, and information about competitors. Sales staff can also download and customize presentations for their customers. The Internet, particularly the Web, has opened a completely new marketing channel for many industries. Just how advertising, purchasing, and information dispensation should occur appears to vary from industry to industry, product to product, and service to service.

POM For the Production/Operations Management Major

Companies are using intranets and portals to speed product development by providing the development team with 3D models and animation. All team members can access the models for faster exploration of ideas and enhanced feedback. Corporate portals, accessed through intranets, enable managers to carefully supervise their inventories as well as real-time production on assembly lines. Extranets are also proving valuable as communication formats for joint research and design efforts among companies. The Internet is also a great source of cutting-edge information for POM managers.

HRM For the Human Resources Management Major

Human resources personnel use portals and intranets to publish corporate policy manuals, job postings, company telephone directories, and training classes. Many companies deliver online training obtained from the Internet to employees through their intranets. Human resources departments use intranets to offer employees health care, savings, and benefit plans, as well as the opportunity to take competency tests online. The Internet supports worldwide recruiting efforts; it can also be the communications platform for supporting geographically dispersed work teams.

MIS For the MIS Major

As important as the networking technology infrastructure is, it is invisible to users (unless something goes wrong). The MIS function is responsible for keeping all organizational networks up and running all the time. MIS personnel, therefore, provide all users with an "eye to the world" and the ability to compute, communicate, and collaborate anytime, anywhere. For example, organizations have access to experts at remote locations without having to duplicate that expertise in multiple areas of the firm. Virtual teaming allows experts physically located in different cities to work on projects as though they were in the same office.

Summary

6.1 Compare and contrast the two major types of networks.

The two major types of networks are local area networks (LANs) and wide area networks (WANs). LANs encompass a limited geographical area and are usually composed of one communications medium. In contrast, WANs encompass a broad geographical area and are usually composed of multiple communications media.

6.2 Describe the wireline communications media and channels.

Twisted-pair wire, the most prevalent form of communications wiring, consists of strands of copper wire twisted in pairs. It is relatively inexpensive to purchase, widely available, and easy to work with. However, it is relatively slow for transmitting data, it is subject to interference from other electrical sources, and it can be easily tapped by unintended recipients.

Coaxial cable consists of insulated copper wire. It is much less susceptible to electrical interference than is twisted-pair wire and it can carry much more data. However, coaxial cable is more expensive and more difficult to work with than twisted-pair wire. It is also somewhat inflexible.

Fiber-optic cables consist of thousands of very thin filaments of glass fibers that transmit information by way of pulses of light generated by lasers. Fiber-optic cables are significantly smaller and lighter than traditional cable media. They can also transmit far more data, and they provide greater security from interference and tapping. Fiber-optic cable is often used as the backbone for a network, whereas twisted-pair wire and coaxial cable connect the backbone to individual devices on the network.

6.3 Describe the most common methods for accessing the Internet.

Common methods for connecting to the Internet include dial-up, DSL, cable modem, satellite, wireless, and fiber to the home.

6.4 Explain the impact that discovery network applications have had on business and everyday life.

Discovery involves browsing and information retrieval and provides users the ability to view information in databases, download it, and process it. Discovery tools include search engines, directories, and portals. Discovery tools enable business users to efficiently find needed information.

6.5 Explain the impact that communication network applications have had on business and everyday life.

Networks provide fast, inexpensive *communications*, through e-mail, call centers, chat rooms, voice communications, and blogs. Communications tools provide business users with a seamless interface among team members, colleagues, business partners, and customers.

Telecommuting is the process whereby knowledge workers are able to work anywhere and anytime. Telecommuting provides flexibility for employees, with many benefits and some drawbacks.

6.6 Explain the impact that collaboration network applications have had on business and everyday life.

Collaboration refers to mutual efforts by two or more entities (individuals, groups, or companies) that work together to accomplish tasks. Collaboration is enabled by workflow systems. Collaboration tools enable business users to collaborate with colleagues, business partners, and customers.

6.7 Explain the impact that educational network applications have had on business and everyday life.

E-learning refers to learning supported by the Web. Distance learning refers to any learning situation in which teachers and students do not meet face-to-face. E-learning provides tools for business users to facilitate their lifelong learning aspirations.

Virtual universities are online universities in which students take classes on the Internet at home or an offsite location. Virtual universities make it possible for students to obtain degrees while working full-time, thus increasing their value to their firms.

Chapter Glossary

affinity portal A website that offers a single point of entry to an entire community of affiliated interests.

backbone networks High-speed central networks to which multiple smaller networks (e.g., LANs and smaller WANs) connect.

bandwidth The transmission capacity of a network, stated in bits per second.

broadband The transmission capacity of a communications medium that is faster than 25 Mbps.

broadcast media (also called wireless media) Communications channels that use electromagnetic media (the "airwaves") to transmit data.

browsers Software applications through which users primarily access the Web.

cable media (also called wireline media) Communications channels that use physical wires or cables to transmit data and information.

client/server computing Form of distributed processing in which some machines (servers) perform computing functions for end-user PCs (clients).

clients Computers, such as users' personal computers, that use any of the services provided by servers.

coaxial cable Insulated copper wire; used to carry high-speed data traffic and television signals.

collaboration Mutual efforts by two or more individuals who perform activities to accomplish certain tasks.

commercial (public) portal A website that offers fairly routine content for diverse audiences. It offers customization only at the user interface.

communications channel Pathway for communicating data from one location to another.

computer network A system that connects computers and other devices through communications media so that data and information can be transmitted among them.

corporate portal A website that provides a single point of access to critical business information located both inside and outside an organization.

crowdsourcing A process in which an organization outsources a task to an undefined, generally large group of people in the form of an open call.

distance learning (DL) Learning situations in which teachers and students do not meet face-to-face.

distributed processing Network architecture that divides processing work between or among two or more computers that are linked together in a network.

domain name system (DNS) The system administered by the Internet Corporation for Assigned Names (ICANN) that assigns names to each site on the Internet.

domain names The name assigned to an Internet site, which consists of multiple parts, separated by dots, that are translated from right to left.

e-learning Learning supported by the Web; can be performed inside traditional classrooms or in virtual classrooms.

enterprise network An organization's network, which is composed of interconnected multiple LANs and WANs.

Ethernet A common local area network protocol.

extranet A network that connects parts of the intranets of different organizations.

fiber-optic cable A communications medium consisting of thousands of very thin filaments of glass fibers, surrounded by cladding, that transmit information through pulses of light generated by lasers.

file server (also called network server) A computer that contains various software and data files for a local area network as well as the network operating system.

hyperlink A connection from a hypertext file or document to another location or file, typically activated by clicking on a highlighted word or image on the screen or by touching the screen.

hypertext Text displayed on a computer display with references, called hyperlinks, to other text that the reader can immediately access.

Hypertext Transport Protocol (HTTP) The communications standard used to transfer pages across the WWW portion of the Internet; it defines how messages are formulated and transmitted.

industrywide portal A Web-based gateway to information and knowledge for an entire industry.

Internet (the Net) A massive global WAN that connects approximately 1 million organizational computer networks in more than 200 countries on all continents.

Internet backbone The primary network connections and telecommunications lines that link the computers and organizational nodes of the Internet.

Internet Protocol (IP) A set of rules responsible for disassembling, delivering, and reassembling packets over the Internet.

Internet Protocol (IP) address An assigned address that uniquely identifies a computer on the Internet.

Internet service provider (ISP) A company that provides Internet connections for a fee.

Internet telephony (Voice-over-Internet Protocol, or VoIP) The use of the Internet as the transmission medium for telephone calls.

Internet2 A new, faster telecommunications network that deploys advanced network applications such as remote medical diagnosis, digital libraries, distance education, online simulation, and virtual laboratories.

intranet A private network that uses Internet software and TCP/IP protocols.

local area network (LAN) A network that connects communications devices in a limited geographic region, such as a building, so that every user device on the network can communicate with every other device.

metasearch engine A computer program that searches several engines at once and integrates the findings of the various search engines to answer queries posted by users.

network access points (NAPs) Computers that act as exchange points for Internet traffic and determine how traffic is routed.

network server See file server.

packet switching The transmission technology that divides blocks of text into packets.

peer-to-peer (P2P) processing A type of client/server distributed processing that allows two or more computers to pool their resources, making each computer both a client and a server.

portal A Web-based personalized gateway to information and knowledge that provides information from disparate information systems and the Internet, using advanced searching and indexing techniques.

protocol The set of rules and procedures that govern transmission across a network.

router A communications processor that routes messages from a LAN to the Internet, across several connected LANs, or across a wide area network such as the Internet.

search engine A computer program that searches for specific information by key words and reports the results.

servers Computers that provide access to various network services, such as printing, data, and communications.

telecommuting A work arrangement whereby employees work at home, at the customer's premises, in special workplaces, or while traveling, usually using a computer linked to their place of employment.

teleconferencing The use of electronic communication that allows two or more people at different locations to have a simultaneous conference.

Transmission Control Protocol/Internet Protocol (TCP/IP) A file transfer protocol that can send large files of information across sometimes-unreliable networks with the assurance that the data will arrive uncorrupted.

twisted-pair wire A communications medium consisting of strands of copper wire twisted together in pairs.

unified communications Common hardware and software platform that simplifies and integrates all forms of communications—voice, e-mail, instant messaging, location, and video-conferencing—across an organization.

uniform resource locator (URL) The set of letters that identifies the address of a specific resource on the Web.

videoconference A virtual meeting in which participants in one location can see and hear participants at other locations and can share data and graphics by electronic means.

virtual collaboration The use of digital technologies that enable organizations or individuals to collaboratively plan, design, develop, manage, and research products, services, and innovative information systems and electronic commerce applications.

virtual group (team) A workgroup whose members are in different locations and who meet electronically.

virtual universities Online universities in which students take classes on the Internet at home or at an offsite location.

Voice-over-Internet Protocol (VoIP) See Internet telephony.

website Collectively, all of the Web pages of a particular company or individual.

wide area network (WAN) A network, generally provided by common carriers, that covers a wide geographical area.

wireless media See **broadcast media**.

wireline media See **cable media**.

workgroup Two or more individuals who act together to perform a task, on either a permanent or a temporary basis.

workflow The movement of information as it flows through the sequence of steps that make up an organization's work procedures.

World Wide Web (the Web or WWW) A system of universally accepted standards for storing, retrieving, formatting, and displaying information through a client/server architecture; it uses the transport functions of the Internet.

Discussion Questions

1. What are the implications of having fiber-optic cable run to everyone's home?

2. What are the implications of BitTorrent for the music industry? For the motion picture industry?

3. Discuss the pros and cons of P2P networks.

4. Should the Internet be regulated? If so, by whom?

5. Discuss the pros and cons of delivering this book over the Internet.

6. Explain how the Internet works. Assume you are talking with someone who has no knowledge of information technology (in other words, keep it very simple).

7. How are the network applications of communication and collaboration related? Do communication tools also support collaboration? Give examples.

8. Search online for the article from *The Atlantic:* "Is Google Making Us Stupid?" *Is* Google making us stupid? Support your answer.

9. Should businesses monitor network usage? Do you see a problem with employees using company-purchased bandwidth for personal use? Please explain your answer.

Problem-Solving Activities

1. Calculate how much bandwidth you consume when using the Internet every day. How many e-mails do you send daily and what is the size of each? (Your e-mail program may have e-mail file size information.) How many music and video clips do you download (or upload) daily and what is the size of each? If you view YouTube often, surf the Web to find out the size of a typical YouTube file. Add up the number of e-mail, audio, and video files you transmit or receive on a typical day. When you have calculated your daily Internet usage, determine if you are a "normal" Internet user or a "power" Internet user. What impact does network neutrality have on you as a "normal" user? As a "power" user?

2. Access several P2P applications, such as SETI@home. Describe the purpose of each application, and indicate which ones you would like to join.

3. Access **www.ipv6.com** and learn more about the advantages of IPv6.

4. Access **www.icann.org** and learn more about this important organization.

5. Set up your own website using your name for the domain name (e.g., KellyRainer):

   a. Explain the process for registering a domain.

   b. Which top-level domain will you use and why?

6. Access **www.icann.org** and obtain the name of an agency or company that can register a domain for the TLD that you selected. What is the name of that agency or company?

7. Access the website for that agency or company (in question 6) to learn the process that you must use. How much will it initially cost to register your domain name? How much will it cost to maintain that name in the future?

8. You plan to take a two-week vacation to Australia this year. Using the Internet, find information that will help you plan the trip. Such information includes, *but is not limited to,* the following:

   a. Geographical location and weather conditions at the time of your trip

   b. Major tourist attractions and recreational facilities

   c. Travel arrangements (airlines, approximate fares)

   d. Car rental; local tours

   e. Alternatives for accommodation (within a moderate budget) and food

   f. Estimated cost of the vacation (travel, lodging, food, recreation, shopping)

   g. Country regulations regarding the entrance of your dog

   h. Shopping

   i. Passport information (either to obtain one or to renew one)

   j. Information on the country's language and culture

   k. What else do you think you should research before going to Australia?

9. From your own experience or from the vendor's information, list the major capabilities of IBM Notes. Do the same for Microsoft Exchange. Compare and contrast the products. Explain how the products can be used to support knowledge workers and managers.

10. Visit the websites of companies that manufacture telepresence products for the Internet. Prepare a report. Differentiate between telepresence products and videoconferencing products.

11. Access Google (or YouTube) videos and search for "Cisco Magic." This video shows Cisco's next-generation telepresence system. Compare and contrast it with current telepresence systems.

12. Access the website of your university. Does the website provide high-quality information (the right amount, clear, accurate)? Do you think a high school student who is thinking of attending your university would feel the same way as you?

13. Compare and contrast Google Sites (**www.google.com/sites**) and Microsoft Office Live (**www.products.office.com/en-us/home**). Which site would you use to create your own website? Explain your choice.

14. Access the website of the Recording Industry Association of America (**www.riaa.com**). Discuss what you find there regarding copyright

infringement (i.e., downloading music files). How do you feel about the RIAA's efforts to stop music downloads? Debate this issue from your point of view and from the RIAA's point of view.

15. Research the companies involved in Internet telephony (Voice-over-IP). Compare their offerings as to price, necessary technologies, ease of installation, and so on. Which company is the most attractive to you? Which company might be the most attractive for a large company?

16. Access various search engines other than Google. Search for the same terms on several of the alternative search engines and on Google. Compare the results on breadth (number of results found) and precision (results are what you were looking for).

17. Second Life (**www.secondlife.com**) is a 3D, online world built and owned by its residents. Residents of Second Life are avatars who have been created by real people. Access Second Life, learn about it, and create your own avatar to explore this world. Learn about the thousands of people who are making "real-world" money from operations in Second Life.

18. Access Microsoft's Bing translator (**www.bing.com/translator**) or Google (**www.google.com/language_tools**) translation pages. Type in a paragraph in English and select, for example, English-to-French. When you see the translated paragraph in French, copy it into the text box, and select French-to-English. Is the paragraph that you first entered the same as the one you are looking at now? Why or why not? Support your answer.

Closing Case

The Network Neutrality Battles Continue

MIS

The Problem

By mid-2019, Internet traffic reached over 100 exabytes per month. (An exabyte is one billion gigabytes.) The vast majority of that traffic consisted of video uploads, downloads, and streaming. The Internet bandwidth issue is as much about economics as it is about technology.

A study from Juniper Networks (**www.juniper.net**) predicts that Internet revenue for carriers such as AT&T (**www.att.com**) and Xfinity (**www.xfinity.com**) will grow by 5 percent per year through 2020. At the same time, Internet traffic will increase by 27 percent annually, meaning that carriers will have to increase their bandwidth investment by 20 percent per year just to keep up with demand. In such a case, the carriers' necessary investment will eventually exceed their revenue growth.

The heart of the problem is that, even if the technology is equal to the task of transmitting vast amounts of data, no one is sure how to pay for these technologies. One proposed solution is to eliminate network neutrality.

Network neutrality, or *net neutrality*, is an operating model under which Internet service providers (ISPs) must allow customers equal access to content and applications, regardless of the source or nature of the content. That is, Internet backbone carriers must treat all Web traffic equally rather than charge different rates based on the user, content, site, platform, or application.

The Debate over Network Neutrality

Arguments against network neutrality. Telecommunications and cable companies (the ISPs) want to replace network neutrality with an arrangement in which they can charge differentiated prices based on the amount of bandwidth consumed by the content that is being delivered over the Internet. The ISPs believe that differentiated pricing is the most equitable method by which they can finance the necessary investments in their network infrastructures.

The ISPs further contend that network neutrality makes the United States less competitive internationally because it hinders innovation and discourages capital investments in new network technologies. Without these investments and innovations, the ISPs will be unable to handle the increasing demand for wired and wireless Internet data transmission.

Arguments for network neutrality. From the opposite perspective, proponents of network neutrality—including more than 100 technology companies, such as Amazon, Google, Facebook Microsoft, Twitter, Netflix, Vimeo, and Yahoo—support net neutrality. These entities are petitioning Congress to regulate the industry. They argue that allowing network providers to selectively block or slow access to certain content—for example, access to competing low-cost services such as Skype and Vonage—increases the risks of censorship. They further assert that a neutral Internet encourages rather than discourages innovation. Finally, they contend that the neutral Internet has helped create many new businesses.

In addition to these reasons, proponents identify other potential problems that abolishing network neutrality will create. First, broadband providers could privilege some content providers over others, for a price. Fast lanes or other types of network discrimination could impact independent websites and apps, many of which would have to pay more to compete with larger competitors to reach audiences. For example, ISPs could slow the transmission streams of Netflix or YouTube. Such business decisions by broadband providers would create fast and slow lanes on the Internet, subjecting businesses and consumers to extra charges while limiting their access to online content. The result would be paid prioritization arrangements in which companies pay to have their data prioritized.

Consider Netflix, Skype, and YouTube, all of which were founded during the mid-2000s when the FCC's initial net neutrality rules were in place. Had broadband providers been able to block video streaming and Internet-based phone calls at that time, then those companies may have had their growth blocked by established companies that were in a stronger financial position. Instead, net neutrality rules enabled them to evolve into the successful companies they are today. Abolishing net neutrality could mean that the next generation of Internet companies will not be able to compete with the established companies.

The end of net neutrality could also impact consumers. Amazon, Netflix, YouTube, and some other services currently dominate the online video market. Without net neutrality, however, broadband providers could try to make it more expensive to access popular streaming sites in an attempt to force customers to continue paying for expensive television packages. In fact, many ISPs are deploying streaming video products of their own: for example, AT&T with DirecTV Live, DirecTV NOW, FreeVIEW, and Fullscreen; Comcast with Xfinity; and Verizon with Go90.

With net neutrality, ISPs cannot exempt certain kinds of content, such as streaming video, from counting toward a user's data cap. This practice is called zero-rating. *Zero-rating* occurs when ISPs do not charge their customers for data used by specific applications. Consider this example: AT&T allows customers to watch as much video as they want from its DirecTV Live streaming service without having it count toward their data caps. In contrast, competing services such as Dish's Sling would count against those caps unless the companies behind them pay AT&T to "sponsor" those data. Verizon has a similar system in place. T-Mobile exempts several streaming video and music apps and services from several partners as part of its "Music Freedom" and "Binge On" services, but it does not charge companies to participate in those programs.

The FCC's net neutrality rules also include other consumer-friendly protections. For instance, they require ISPs to disclose information about the speed of their services, thus helping customers find out whether they are getting their money's worth. The FCC's rules also force broadband providers to allow customers to connect any device they want to their Internet connection. These rules prevent their provider from forcing them to use a specific type of WiFi router or dictating which Internet of Things devices they can or cannot use.

The Timeline

On December 21, 2010, the FCC approved network neutrality rules that prohibited wireline-based broadband providers—but not mobile broadband providers—from engaging in "unreasonable discrimination" against Web traffic. These rules are known as the Open Internet Order.

In 2015, the FCC changed the classification of broadband from an "information service" to a "telecommunications service." This move allowed the FCC to begin regulating ISPs under the stricter laws that govern common carriers; that is, service providers that transport goods or people, such as airlines, trucking companies, and telephone companies. The FCC also prohibited the ISPs from blocking content, slowing transmissions—known as "throttling"—and creating "fast lanes"; that is, no paid prioritization. Paid prioritization refers to the management of a broadband provider's network to directly or indirectly favor one type of data traffic over another type through preferential traffic management. The rules apply to both fixed and mobile broadband Internet access service.

In June 2016, a federal court ruled that broadband Internet service can be defined as a utility, clearing the way for more rigorous policing of broadband providers and greater protection for Internet users. The decision affirmed the government's view that broadband is as essential as the telephone and therefore should be available to all Americans, rather than a luxury that does not require close government supervision. The court's decision upheld the FCC decision to classify broadband as a utility.

Furthermore, the ruling limited the ability of broadband providers to deliver certain content over the Internet at slower speeds. It also created a path to establish new limits on broadband providers beyond network neutrality. In April 2016, for example, the FCC proposed privacy rules for broadband providers, limiting their ability to collect and share data about their subscribers

FCC chairman Tom Wheeler resigned on January 20, 2017. His resignation gave the Republican party a majority of the commission, and Ajit Pai became chairman. Unlike Wheeler, Pai is not an advocate for net neutrality. In fact, barring a successful legal challenge, his goal is for the FCC to relinquish its authority to enforce net neutrality regulations. On November 22, 2017, the FCC announced that it would preempt state and local network neutrality laws. The FCC said that it could implement this ban because Internet access is an interstate service, and it would be impractical to make providers treat interstate and intrastate Internet traffic differently.

On December 14, 2017, the FCC voted to eliminate network neutrality regulations. Furthermore, the federal government would no longer regulate high-speed Internet delivery as if it were a utility such as telephone service. That is, the ISPs were put under the authority of the Federal Trade Commission (**www.ftc.gov**) rather than the FCC. The elimination of network neutrality regulations took place on June 11, 2018.

In 2018, attorney generals from 22 states sued the FCC regarding keeping network neutrality. Also in 2018, 34 states and the District of Columbia introduced 120 bills and regulations regarding network neutrality in their legislative sessions. Five states – California, New Jersey, Oregon, Vermont, and Washington – enacted legislation or adopted resolutions. The U.S. Department of Justice sued California over its legislation and California agreed not to implement its network neutrality regulations until the case against the FCC was decided.

On April 10, 2019 the U.S. House of Representatives passed a bill to restore network neutrality. Republican leaders in the Sentate stated that the bill would not pass.

Early Results

In a study released in September 2018, researchers from Northeastern University and the University of Massachusetts Amherst found that the largest U.S. telecommunications companies are slowing Internet traffic to and from popular apps such as YouTube and Netflix. The researchers used a smartphone app called Wehe to monitor which mobile services were being slowed, when, and by whom. From January to early May 2018, the app detected slowing by Verizon Communications more than 11,100 times and AT&T 8,398 times. The carriers said that they practiced slowing in order to manage Internet traffic.

Despite Ajit Pai's contention that eliminating network neutrality would allow ISPs to increase their capital investments, Comcast's 2018 earnings report indicated that the company's capital expenditures for 2018 actually decreased by 3 percent. In fact, industry analysts predict that capital spending among the nation's four largest cable providers (Altice, Comcast, Charter Spectrum, and CableONE) will decrease almost 6 percent in 2019.

And the bottom line? The network neutrality battles continue.

Sources: Compiled from O. Kharif, "YouTube, Netflix Videos Found to Be Slowed by Wireless Carriers," *Bloomberg*, September 4, 2018; J. Doubek, "California Lawmakers Pass Net Neutrality Bill," NPR, September 1, 2018; D. Shepardson, "Internet Groups Urge U.S. Court to Reinstate 'Net Neutrality' Rules," Reuters, August 27, 2018; K. Finley, "New Califorjnia Bill Restores Strong Net Neutrality," *Wired*, July 5, 2018; L. Tung, "Comcast: We've Stopped Throttling Speeds for Heavy Internet Users, for Now," *ZDNet*, June 14, 2018; S. Crawford, "Net Neutrality Is Just a Gateway to the Real Issue: Internet Freedom," *Wired*, May 18, 2018; K. Finley, "Senate Votes to Save Net Neutrality, but Hurdles Remain," *Wired*, May 16, 2018; B. Chappell, "FCC Plans Net Neutrality Rollback for June 11; Senate Democrats Plan a Key Challenge," NPR,

May 10, 2018; "Super-Local Broadband May Be the Best Way to Preserve Net Neutrality," *Futurism*, March 30, 2018; J. Brodkin, "California Weighs Toughest Net Neutrality Law in U.S. – with Ban on Paid Zero-Rating," *Ars Technica*, March 14, 2018; K. Finley, "Washington State Enacts Net Neutrality Law, in Clash with FCC," *Wired*, March 5, 2018; G. Sohn and Am Fazlullah, "Ajit Pai's Plan Will Take Broadband Away from Poor People," *Wired*, February 21, 2018; "Montana Governor Takes Preserving Net Neutrality into His Own Hands," *Futurism*, January 23, 2018; C. Kang, "What's Next after Repeal of Net Neutrality," *New York Times*, December 15, 2017; C. Kang, "F.C.C. Repeals Net Neutrality Rules," *New York Times*, December 14, 2017; "The Latest: States Warming Up Net-Neutrality Lawsuits," Associated Press, December 14, 2017; J. Kastrenakes, "FCC Will Block States from Passing Their Own Net Neutrality Laws," *The Verge*, November 22, 2017; J. Chokkattu, "No Matter Where You Stand, This Is What You Need to Know about Net Neutrality," *Digital Trends*, November 22, 2017; K. Finley, "FCC Plans to Gut Net Neutrality, Allow Internet 'Fast Lanes'," *Wired*, November 21, 2017; D. Shepardson, "Major Tech Firms, Internet Providers Clash over U.S. Net Neutrality Rules," Reuters, July 17, 2017; K. Finley, "Why Net Neutrality Matters Even in the Age of Oligopoly," *Wired*, June 22, 2017; K. Finley, "The End of Net Neutrality Could Shackle the Internet of Things," *Wired*, June 6, 2017; K. Finley, "Internet Providers Insist They Love Net Neutrality. Seriously?" *Wired*, May 18, 2017; M. Snider, "The FCC Votes to Overturn Net Neutrality," *USA Today*, May 18, 2017; M. Orcutt, "Net Neutrality Rules May Slow Innovation, but Uncertainty Will Be Worse," *MIT Technology Review*, May 2, 2017; M. Orcutt, "Why Snap Is Worried about Net Neutrality," *MIT Technology Review*, February 7, 2017; M. Orcutt, "What Happens If Net Neutrality Goes Away?" *MIT Technology Review*, January 30, 2017; K. Finley, "Tom Wheeler Resigns from the FCC—So Long, Net Neutrality," *Wired*, December 15, 2016; J. Brustein, "Time for Some Traffic Problems on Netflix?" *Bloomberg Business-Week*, November 21–27, 2016; M. Orcutt, "Three Big Questions Hanging over Net Neutrality," *MIT Technology Review*, August 19, 2016; C. Kang, "Court Backs Rules Treating Internet as Utility, Not Luxury," *New York Times*, June 14, 2016; J. Kastrenakes, "The FCC's Net Neutrality Rules Are Now in Effect," *The Verge*, June 12, 2015; R. Ruiz, "F.C.C. Sets Net Neutrality Rules," *New York Times*, March 12, 2015; J. Kastrenakes, "These Are the FCC's Rules for Protecting Net Neutrality," *The Verge*, March 12, 2015; R. Ruiz and S. Lohr, "F.C.C. Approves Net Neutrality Rules, Classifying Broadband Internet Service as a Utility," *New York Times*, February 26, 2015; "Searching for Fairness on the Internet," *New York Times*, May 15, 2014; D. Talbot, "Is Netflix Slowing Down? Good Luck Finding out Why," *MIT Technology Review*, February 21, 2014; B. Butler, "Verizon Denies Throttling Amazon's Cloud, Netflix Services," *Network World*, February 5, 2014; and www.fcc.gov, accessed August 8, 2018.

Questions

1. Are the ISPs correct in claiming that network neutrality will limit the development of new technologies? Support your answer.

2. Are the content providers (e.g., Netflix) correct in claiming that eliminating network neutrality will encourage censorship by the ISPs? Support your answer.

3. Are the content providers correct in claiming that eliminating network neutrality will result in consumers paying higher prices for content they watch over the Internet? Support your answer.

4. What impact might the repeal of network neutrality have on the cost of your Internet access? Support your answer.

5. Discuss IT's About Business 6.1 in light of the debate over network neutrality. That is, if the United States eliminates network neutrality, what could be the impact on providing broadband Internet for everyone?

E-Business and E-Commerce

LEARNING OBJECTIVES

7.1 Describe the eight common types of electronic commerce.

7.2 Describe the various online services of business-to-consumer (B2C) commerce, along with specific examples of each one.

7.3 Describe the three business models for business-to-business (B2B) electronic commerce.

7.4 Discuss the ethical and legal issues related to electronic commerce, and provide examples.

Opening Case

The Story of Zenefits

`HRM` `MIS`

Before a U.S. company offers health insurance to its employees, it has to examine thousands of plans offered by hundreds of insurers. It then selects the two or three options that best suit its employees, based on age, marital status, location, and many other variables. The smaller the business, the less likely that the business employs someone to perform these tasks; that is, small businesses often do not have human resource (HR) management departments.

In 2013, Parker Conrad founded Zenefits (**www.zenefits.com**) initially to help small businesses find insurance quotes and manage employee benefits. The company operated on a freemium model, offering free benefits-management software in exchange for being the customer's insurance broker; that is, Zenefits's cloud-based software-as-a-service (see Technology Guide 3) product automated health insurance, payroll, and other HR tasks. With six million small businesses in the United States alone, Zenefits had many potential customers. The company's very rapid growth, its ensuing problems from 2013 to the fall of 2017, and its decision to reinvent itself in 2017 illustrate the problems that rapidly growing start-ups can face is instructive.

Zenefits expanded from 15 employees in 2013 to 1,600 by September 2015. By that time, the company was serving 14,000 businesses. Further, it had raised $580 million in three fund-raising rounds, and it was valued at $4.5 billion.

In 2015, Zenefits began to experience problems. The start-up hired so many people in such a short time that it simply lost operational control of its business processes. For example, in mid-2015, Zenefits informed its employees that they had to suspend their vacations, in part because the busiest time of year was approaching. Zenefits ended up having to pay its employees for unpaid vacation time if they promised not to sue.

Despite being founded to serve small businesses, Zenefits instituted an enterprise sales department that sold Zenefits's insurance brokerage services and software to large companies. This sales process was difficult because, unlike smaller companies, larger companies typically have entire human resource departments that have existing relationships with insurance brokers. The enterprise sales department encountered another problem. The firm's software was not ready for large companies because it did not have the security and other functionality that more expensive enterprise HR software offers.

Zenefits also had a very long clawback provision. If a customer canceled with Zenefits within the first year, then the salesperson had to return the commission to the company. Some salespeople lost $15,000 to $20,000 months after closing a deal. In February 2016, Zenefits laid off the entire enterprise sales division.

In addition, by 2015, serious issues arose concerning how Zenefits trained its salespeople. Essentially, the company taught its salesforce to assure prospective customers that they would have to enter data such as the name of a new employee or an address change only one time. The system then would automatically update that data throughout the software whenever it was needed.

Salespeople, however, learned that this assurance was not always true. In some cases, the Zenefits software was not integrated with an insurance carrier's software or with other HR processes such as payroll. In these cases, any changes in the data were sent to a Zenefits employee in Arizona who manually input them into the other system.

Furthermore, Zenefits instructed their salespeople to urge their clients to sign contracts quickly to avoid a $10,000 broker implementation fee that would go into effect at the end of the month. However, Zenefits never charged anyone that fee.

Another serious problem involved employees who were not properly licensed to sell insurance. Insurance brokers must pass a state licensing exam before they can legally sell or advise people on insurance. Each state has its own exam and training requirements. Therefore, a person licensed only in California cannot legally sell insurance to a company in another state unless he or she applies for a reciprocal license.

Zenefits informed some new, unlicensed hires that because CEO Parker Conrad was licensed in all 50 states, they did not have to be licensed because they were acting under his umbrella license. Alternatively, if a manager with a license sat in on the call, then that was good enough. However, as hiring grew, managers stopped listening in on every call. Zenefits sold its product all over the country and did not properly track who passed which state exams or received reciprocal licenses.

In California, brokers had to spend at least 52 hours on an online training course. However, people did not need that much time to complete the course. Therefore, they would leave the app running and click on their browser to keep it from timing out until it ran for 52 hours. Zenefits later admitted that Parker created a Google Chrome browser extension, internally called "the Macro," that automated the clicking process and made it appear as if the salespeople were working on the course when, in fact, they were not. Significantly, the Macro did not advance the pages or take the quizzes or the final test for them. However, they did have to certify that they met the 52-hour requirement. The Macro enabled them to get around this requirement.

In 2015, the state of Washington's insurance commissioner opened a formal investigation into the company over the licensing qualifications of its insurance agents. According to BuzzFeed, 83 percent of all Zenefits sales in that state were made by unlicensed brokers. Zenefits could have been fined as much as $20,000 for each violation. If this situation had occurred in other states, then the firm would have faced millions of dollars in fines.

Zenefits responded by hiring a law firm and a consulting firm to investigate the problem of unlicensed insurance brokers. The investigation found that some of the sales team used the Macro to systematically cheat on the state's training course.

The investigation had many ramifications for the company. On February 8, 2016, Conrad resigned. Later that month, Zenefits laid off 250 employees, including the entire enterprise team. Zenefits claimed that it had self-reported the findings of its internal investigation to all 50 states and it was working with those states that had opened formal inquiries. In 2016, Fidelity Investments, which owns a stake in Zenefits, reduced its valuation from $4.5 billion to less than $2 billion.

On November 28, 2016, California's insurance regulator fined Zenefits for ignoring the state's insurance laws. The company ended up paying $11 million to settle the state charges.

On February 9, 2017, Zenefits laid off 430 employees, representing 45 percent of its workforce, in a move to implement a new business model. Zenefits left the insurance brokerage business and planned to become an all-in-one HR tool for small businesses. Zenefits partnered with OneDigital (**www.onedigital.com**), an employee benefits company.

In June 2017, Zenefits agreed to pay $3.4 million in unpaid overtime to 743 of its account executives and sales representatives in California and Arizona, according to the U.S. Department of Labor (DOL). Zenefits also agreed to let the DOL monitor its practices to ensure that the company does not violate the Fair Labor Standards Act, a 1938 law that regulates practices such as overtime and the minimum wage.

In October 2017, the U.S. Securities and Exchange Commission (SEC; **www.sec.gov**) fined Zenefits $450,000 and fined its cofounder Parker Conrad $533,000 as part of a settlement because they misled investors.

And the bottom line? First, Zenefits changed its business model to a software-as-a-service (SaaS) company that helps small- to medium-sized businesses (SMBs) manage their human resources applications such as payroll, benefits, onboarding, and compliance. Its SaaS platform serves as an app store for human resources and also allows third-party apps and developers to build onto it. By providing SaaS HR applications, Zenefits must compete with existing HR companies in that category, for example, Gusto (**www.gusto.com**), Namely (**www.join.namely.com**), and Workday (**www.workday.com**).

Second, the firm changed from a free to a paid subscription model. As of July 2019, approximately 70 percent of Zenefits's 10,000 customers had converted to paid subscription packages.

Third, Zenefits shifted from being a benefits broker to the HR technology platform powering the industry's best brokers. By July, 2019 ten brokerages had joined the Zenefits Certified Broker Program in an effort to build a nationwide network of technology-enabled brokers to simplify access to health and well-being options for SMBs.

And the bottom line? Zenefits remains a private company and does not disclose financials. The company is now operating with roughly 500 employees and is among the most popular HR platforms for businesses with 2 to 200 employees.

Sources: Compiled from S. Kunthara, "How Zenefits Recovered from Scandal in Insurance Business," *San Francisco Chronicle*, February 10, 2019; P. Albinus, "Zenefits Adds Four Brokerages to Its Small Business Technology Program," *Employee Benefits Advisor*, August 9, 2018; R. Golden, "How Zenefits Is Moving Its Employee Benefits Business Forward," *HR Dive*, March 16, 2018; "Zenefits Delivers Triple-Digit SaaS Business Growth," *Business Wire*, February 7, 2018; H. Somerville, "Zenefits and Co-Founder Parker Conrad to Pay SEC Fine of Nearly $1 Million," Reuters, October 26, 2017; C. Miller, "Software Startup Zenefits Settles SEC's Investor-Deception Claims," *The Recorder*, October 26, 2017; M. Lynley, "Zenefits Tries a Rebrand and Hands Off Insurance Brokerage," *TechCrunch*, September 21, 2017; A. Konrad, "Zenefits Shifts Focus to HR Software, Partnering with Brokers It Once Threatened," *Forbes*, September 21, 2017; M. Dickey, "Zenefits Will Pay $3.4 Million in Unpaid Overtime to 743 Employees," *TechCrunch*, June 20, 2017; W. Alden, "Zenefits Software Helped Brokers Cheat on Licensing Process," *BuzzFeed*, February 11, 2016; S. Kessler, "Zenefits Went from a $4.5 Billion Valuation to Massive Layoffs in Less than Two Years," *Quartz*, February 10, 2017; S. O'Brien, "Zenefits Slashes Its Workforce – Again," CNN, February 9, 2017; W. Alden, "Zenefits Is Laying Off Almost Half Its Employees," CNBC, February 9, 2017; B. Darrow, "Zenefits Names Tech Industry Vet as New CEO," *Fortune*, February 6, 2017; P. Dave, "Employee Benefits Start-Up Zenefits Is Fined $3.5 Million for Licensing Violations," *Los Angeles Times*, November 28, 2016; M. Lynley, "Zenefits Opens up to Third-Party Developers and Launches a Suite of New HR Tools," *TechCrunch*, October 18, 2016; C. Suddath and E. Newcomer, "Zenefits Was the Perfect Startup. Then It Self-Disrupted," *Bloomberg BusinessWeek*, May 9, 2016; J. Bort, "Lies, Booze, and Billions," *Business Insider*, March 11, 2016; E. Newcomer, "The Last (of This) Unicorn?" *Bloomberg BusinessWeek*, February 22-28, 2016; and www.zenefits.com, accessed July 13, 2019.

Questions

1. Describe how and why Zenefits changed its business model.

2. Refer to Chapter 3 and discuss the ethicality of Zenefits's actions from 2013 through 2016.

3. Should Zenefits target large organizations in addition to SMBs? Why or why not?

Introduction

Electronic commerce (**EC** or **e-commerce**) is the process of buying, selling, transferring, or exchanging products, services, or information through computer networks, including the Internet. E-commerce is transforming all of the business functional areas as well as their fundamental tasks, from advertising to paying bills. Its impact is so pervasive that it affects every modern organization. Regardless of where you land a job, your organization will be practicing electronic commerce.

MKT Electronic commerce influences organizations in many significant ways. First, it increases an organization's *reach*, defined as the number of potential customers to whom the company can market its products. In fact, e-commerce provides unparalleled opportunities for companies to expand worldwide at a small cost, to increase market share, and to reduce costs. By utilizing electronic commerce, many small businesses can now operate and compete in market spaces that were formerly dominated by larger companies.

Another major impact of electronic commerce has been to remove many of the barriers that previously impeded entrepreneurs seeking to start their own businesses. E-commerce offers amazing opportunities for you to open your own business.

As illustrated in the opening case, electronic commerce is also fundamentally transforming the nature of competition through the development of new online companies, new business models, and the diversity of EC-related products and services. Recall your study of competitive strategies in Chapter 2, particularly the impact of the Internet on Porter's five forces. You learned that the Internet can both endanger and enhance a company's position in a given industry.

It is important for you to have a working knowledge of electronic commerce because your organization almost certainly will employ e-commerce applications that will affect its strategy and business model. This knowledge will make you more valuable to your organization, and it will enable you to quickly contribute to the e-commerce applications employed in your functional area. As you read What's in IT for Me? at the end of the chapter, envision yourself performing the activities discussed in your functional area.

Going further, you may decide to become an entrepreneur and start your own business, as illustrated in the chapter opening case. If you start your own business, it is even more essential for you to understand electronic commerce, because e-commerce, with its broad reach, will more than likely be critical for your business to survive and thrive. On the other hand, giant, well-known electronic commerce companies use the Internet to compete all over the world.

In this chapter, you will discover the major applications of e-business, and you will be able to identify the services necessary for its support. You will then study the major types of electronic commerce: business-to-consumer (B2C), business-to-business (B2B), consumer-to-consumer (C2C), business-to-employee (B2E), and government-to-citizen (G2C). You will conclude by examining several legal and ethical issues that impact e-commerce.

As you learn about electronic commerce in this chapter, note that e-commerce can be performed wirelessly, as you see in our discussion of mobile commerce in Chapter 8. E-commerce also has many social aspects as well, as you see in our discussion of social commerce in Chapter 8. Finally, e-commerce can now be performed with texting and messaging, as you see in IT's About Business 7.1.

7.1 Overview of E-Business and E-Commerce

Just how important is electronic commerce? Consider these statistics. Industry analysts estimated that U.S. retail sales in 2018 totaled approximately $5.3 trillion. Electronic commerce accounted for 10 percent of these sales, for a total of $517 billion. Significantly, e-commerce increased 15 percent in 2018 over 2017. The increase in e-commerce has placed significant pressure on the retail industry. According to Coresight Research (**www.coresight.com**), about 8,000 brick-and-mortar stores closed in 2017 and 5,500 stores closed in 2018. In the first six months of 2019, Coresight reported an additional 7,150 stores had closed. Coresight did note that, during the same time period in 2019, 2,700 stores had opened.

This section examines the basics of e-business and e-commerce. First, we define these two concepts. You then become familiar with pure and partial electronic commerce, and you examine the various types of electronic commerce. Next, you focus on e-commerce mechanisms, which are the ways that businesses and people buy and sell over the Internet. You conclude this section by considering the benefits and limitations of e-commerce.

Definitions and Concepts

Recall that electronic commerce describes the process of buying, selling, transferring, or exchanging products, services, or information through computer networks, including the Internet. **Electronic business (e-business)** is a somewhat broader concept. In addition to the buying and selling of goods and services, e-business refers to servicing customers, collaborating with business partners, and performing electronic transactions within an organization.

Electronic commerce can take several forms, depending on the degree of digitization involved. The *degree of digitization* is the extent to which the commerce has been transformed from physical to digital. This concept can relate to both the product or service being sold and the delivery agent or intermediary. In other words, the product can be either physical or digital, and the delivery agent can also be either physical or digital.

In traditional commerce, both dimensions are physical. Purely physical organizations are referred to as **brick-and-mortar organizations**. (You may also see the term *bricks-and-mortar*.) In contrast, in *pure EC* all dimensions are digital. Companies engaged only in EC are considered **virtual** (or **pureplay**) **organizations**. All other combinations that include a mix of digital and physical dimensions are considered *partial* EC (but not pure EC). **Clicks-and-mortar organizations** conduct some e-commerce activities, yet their primary business is carried out in the physical world. A common alternative to the term *clicks-and-mortar* is *clicks-and-bricks*. You will encounter both terms. Clicks-and-mortar organizations are examples of partial EC. E-commerce is now so well established that people generally expect companies to offer this service in some form.

Purchasing a shirt at Walmart Online or a book from Amazon.com is an example of partial EC because the merchandise, although bought and paid for digitally, is physically delivered by, for example, FedEx, UPS, or the U.S. Postal Service. In contrast, buying an e-book from Amazon.com or a software product from Buy.com constitutes pure EC because the product itself as well as its delivery, payment, and transfer are entirely digital. We use the term *electronic commerce* to denote both pure and partial EC.

Types of E-Commerce

E-commerce can be conducted between and among various parties. In this section, you will identify seven common types of e-commerce, and you will learn about three of them—C2C, B2E, and e-government—in detail. We discuss B2C and B2B in separate sections because they are very complex. We discuss mobile commerce in Chapter 8, social commerce in Chapter 9, and conversational commerce in IT's About Business 7.1.

- *Business-to-consumer electronic commerce (B2C):* In B2C, the sellers are organizations, and the buyers are individuals. You will learn about B2C electronic commerce in Section 7.2.
- *Business-to-business electronic commerce (B2B):* In B2B transactions, both the sellers and the buyers are business organizations. B2B comprises the vast majority of EC volume. You will learn more about B2B electronic commerce in Section 7.3. Look back to Figure 1.5 for an illustration of B2B electronic commerce.

    Consumer-to-consumer electronic commerce (C2C): In C2C (also called customer-to-customer), an individual sells products or services to other individuals. The major strategies for conducting C2C on the Internet are auctions and classified ads. Most auctions are conducted by C2C intermediaries such as eBay (**www.ebay.com**). For another example, let's take a look at Directly Software (**www.directly.com**).

MKT Many companies use Directly to facilitate the resolution of customer questions and complaints by knowledgeable customers themselves. Directly clients first enroll a group of knowledgeable customers, called answerers. Some client companies test their customers' writing skills and product knowledge before asking them to participate and become answerers. Directly's software has an artificial intelligence component that matches answerers with questions that it thinks they will be able to answer well, sending customer queries to them via the Directly app.

Directly answerers have *gig jobs*, similar to Amazon's Mechanical Turk and Uber. A gig job is one in which an organization contracts with independent workers for short-term engagements where the worker is paid for each engagement. Directly pays answerers 70 percent of the fee for each customer query they resolve. Answerers have reputation scores and those with higher scores receive more questions and may be asked to contribute to collections of stock answers to common questions (known as frequently asked questions or FAQs).

Reputation scores, the flexibility of the work, and Directly's artificial intelligence component provide the startup with competitive advantage over rivals such as InSided (**www.insided.com**) and IAdvize (**www.iadvize.com**) in the $4.3 billion customer self-service software market. An average Directly representative makes about $200 per week and the top 5 percent earn more than $2,000 per week. Directly has experienced very rapid growth. Let's look at how game maker Kixeye uses Directly.

Kixeye (**www.kixeye.com**) receives approximately 40,000 customer support requests per month. About 40 percent of them go to Kixeye answerers via Directly. Kixeye says that while Directly's costs are comparable to those of overseas contractors, the startup delivers better results. Since replacing an Indian outsourcing firm with Kixeye answerers and Directly, the average response time for players' questions has decreased from 12 hours to 10 minutes, and customer satisfaction has risen by 50 percent.

- *Business-to-employee (B2E):* In B2E, an organization uses EC internally to provide information and services to its employees. For example, companies allow employees to manage their benefits and to take training classes electronically. Employees can also buy discounted insurance, travel packages, and tickets to events on the corporate intranet. They can also order supplies and materials electronically. Finally, many companies have electronic corporate stores that sell the company's products to its employees, usually at a discount.

- *E-government:* E-government is the use of Internet technology in general and e-commerce in particular to deliver information and public services to citizens (called *government-to-citizen,* or *G2C EC*) and to business partners and suppliers (called *government-to-business,* or *G2B EC*). G2B EC is much like B2B EC, usually with an overlay of government procurement regulations; that is, G2B EC and B2B EC are conceptually similar. However, the functions of G2C EC are conceptually different from anything that exists in the private sector (e.g., B2C EC).

  E-government is also an efficient way of conducting business transactions with citizens and businesses and within the governments themselves. E-government makes government more efficient and effective, especially in the delivery of public services. An example of G2C electronic commerce is electronic benefits transfer, in which governments transfer benefits, such as Social Security and pension payments, directly to recipients' bank accounts.

- *Mobile commerce (m-commerce):* The term *m-commerce* refers to e-commerce that is conducted entirely in a wireless environment. An example is using cell phones to shop over the Internet.

- *Social commerce:* Social commerce refers to the delivery of electronic commerce activities and transactions through social computing.

- *Conversational commerce:* Conversational commerce (also called chat commerce) refers to electronic commerce using messaging and chat apps to offer a daily choice, often personalized, of a meal, product, or service. IT's About Business 7.1 discusses chatbots and conversational commerce.

IT's About Business 7.1

Chatbots and Conversational Commerce

MIS MKT

Conversational commerce refers to the intersection of messaging apps and shopping; that is, the trend toward interacting with businesses through messaging and chat apps such as Facebook Messenger (**www.messenger.com**), WhatsApp (**www.whatsapp.com**), Kik (**www.kik.com**), and WeChat (**www.wechat.com**). Customers can chat with company representatives, access customer support, ask questions, receive personalized recommendations, and click to purchase, all from within messaging apps. They have the options of interacting with a human representative, a chatbot, or a combination of the two.

Chatbots (also known as *bots*) are interactive software programs that can conduct simple conversations with customers or other bots. Chatbots provide computer-generated chatting experiences with human-like conversational and natural language abilities. They function within boundaries that are constantly being expanded with artificial intelligence techniques such as machine learning. Chatbots can take the form of voice-controlled assistants (such as Apple's Siri and Microsoft's Cortana) as well as customer service representatives on the websites of many organizations. There are five levels of chatbots:

- *Notification Assistants* provide simple notifications on users' phones often via messaging apps such as Facebook Messenger and WhatsApp.

- *Frequently Asked Questions (FAQ) Assistants* allow users to ask a simple question and receive a response. As of July 2019, FAQ assistants are the most common.

- *Contextual Assistants:* In conversations, context matters, including what the user has asked or said previously and when, where, and how they asked the question. Considering context also means that the assistant should be capable of understanding and responding to different and unexpected inputs from users.

- *Personalized Assistants* will get to know their users over time. For example, these assistants will learn the best times to get in touch with their users and proactively contact them based on this knowledge. These assistants will remember users' preferences and provide a truly personalized interface for each user.

- *Autonomous Organization of Assistants* are integrated groups of AI assistants that will (eventually) know every customer personally and operate large parts of a company's operations—including for example, marketing, sales, human resources, finance, and others.

Let's take a look at Facebook Messenger and WeChat. These two messaging services are among the largest in the world.

- Facebook Messenger, used by more than 50 million businesses and 900 million individuals, has a chatbot-building capability. Facebook's objective is to drive Messenger users to the more than 15 million businesses with an official brand Facebook page. For example, to shop for a T-shirt on Facebook Messenger, users can send a text to Messenger to start a chat with the mobile shopping app Spring. The app will request information concerning the buyer's budget and then display several possible

T-shirts. If the customer does not like any of these choices, then Spring will present more options.

Facebook Messenger bots can process purchases without directing shoppers to a third party. The credit card information that shoppers have already stored in Facebook or Facebook Messenger can be retrieved to instantly accept payment in bots. To process transactions in Messenger, Facebook is collaborating with all of the big names in the payments industry, including electronic payment leaders Stripe and PayPal Braintree, as well as credit card giants Visa, MasterCard, and American Express.

- WeChat, China's massive social media site, has 850 million users. They can utilize bots to chat with friends about an upcoming concert, purchase tickets to the event, book a restaurant, split the check, and call a taxi. In addition to the individual WeChat users, 10 million Chinese businesses have an account. In fact, for some firms, the WeChat bot completely replaces an Internet site.

Many organizations use chatbots to interact with customers, including Starbucks, Lyft, Fandango, Spotify, Whole Foods, Sephora, Mastercard, Staples, *Wall Street Journal*, Pizza Hut, and many others. Let's look at the following examples in more detail:

- In India, Digibank (**www.dbs.com/digibank/in/**) is available to its customers only through mobile. The bank communicates using chatbots that can answer thousands of questions sent from customers through chat. Clients can also enter a command such as "Pay Fred $25 for movie tickets," and the bot will request more details. For example, if transferring the funds to Fred would put the customer's account in the red, then the bot notifies the customer and asks if he or she would like to add funds to the account.

- The Royal Bank of Scotland (RBS; **www.rbs.com**) is using a bot called "Luvo" to provide basic customer service. The bank wants Luvo to relieve staff from having to deal with easily answered questions so they can spend their time on more complex and value-added issues. RBS built Luvo using IBM's Watson Conversation tool, which can understand human language. As a result, customers can describe what they are looking for instead of just choosing from standard options.

- Many airlines are using bots that allow travelers to check in, receive flight information, change their tickets, and chat with customer service agents. Some of these bots are KLM Royal Dutch Airlines' Bluebot, Air New Zealand's Oscar, and Lufthansa's Mildred.

- Taco Bell (**www.tacobell.com**) developed the TacoBot that processes orders at its locations. The TacoBot understands orders and manages them. Furthermore, TacoBot stores customers' order histories and makes recommendations based on the time of day.

- Bots are helping organizations in their recruitment process. In the early stages of the process, bots can examine hundreds of resumes to screen candidates. Next, bots can manage the communications with candidates to request more information or schedule interviews. Bots then hand off candidates who have met basic criteria so human recruiters can decide which ones to call for an interview. For example, Mya from Mya Systems (**www.hiremya.com**) is always enthusiastic and patient, uses natural language processing to make sense of an applicant's typed questions, and responds with accurate, realistic answers.

Many organizations use chatbots internally. Consider the case of Overstock (**www.overstock.com**). Overstock's chatbot, called Mila, automates the simple but time-consuming process of requesting sick leave. Previously, on any given day, dozens of employees in the company's call center in Salt Lake City became ill. When that happened, clerks manually checked the messages and alerted the employee's manager. The manager then found a substitute for the ill employee.

Now, if workers are not feeling well, they notify Mila. The bot then sends a message to the person's manager. As a result, Overstock can replace ill employees much more quickly, thus saving the company money. In addition, Mila provides other employee self-serve functions, such as requesting holidays and updating their schedules, which formerly required interacting with a human.

Another example is the bot DoNotPay. Hiring a lawyer to appeal a parking ticket is time consuming and expensive. However, with the help of a bot developed by 19-year-old British programmer Joshua Browder, the appeal now costs nothing. Browder's DoNotPay bot handles questions about parking-ticket appeals. Since the bot was launched in late 2015, it has successfully appealed hundreds of thousands of parking tickets in cities around the world. In addition, by 2017, the bot helped refugees fill out immigration applications to the United States and Canada, and offered assistance for asylum seekers in the United Kingdom. In July, 2019 the bot is advertising that people can use the bot to sue anyone. DoNotPay focuses on suing corporations and helping people navigate bureaucracies.

Despite all of their benefits, using chatbots can have negative consequences as well. For example, Microsoft launched a chatbot called Tay that was supposed to seem like a teenage girl and interact with people on Twitter. In the first day of her appearance on Twitter, Tay signed up more than 50,000 followers and generated almost 100,000 tweets. However, she then began to mimic her followers. Microsoft quickly removed the chatbot when users taught her to say racist and other very offensive words.

Unfortunately, bots are also an excellent tool for scalping tickets because it is easy to teach them how to perform simple tasks such as signing up for tickets. They also make the process anonymous, so the scalpers are not caught. With these bots, scalpers can purchase tickets for an enormously popular show such as *Hamilton* ahead of anyone else. This process causes ticket prices on the resale market to become artificially inflated.

To address this problem, Ticketmaster (**www.ticketmaster.com**) has developed a technology known as Verified Fan, which works by scanning users' purchase histories to determine whether they are actually looking to see a particular show themselves or, more likely, they are just a bot being used by a scalper to buy a large volume of tickets. Ticketmaster used Verified Fan with *Hamilton*. Users

who passed the screening, and therefore were not bots, were given access to an advanced ticket sale. Furthermore, the 2016 Better Online Ticket Sales (BOTS) Act from the Federal Trade Commission (**www.ftc.gov**) outlawed these kinds of automated ticket-buying schemes.

Still another problem with bots is that resellers use them to buy popular toys ahead of the Christmas rush. They then resell the toys at inflated prices on eBay and Amazon. The bots continuously monitor retailer websites, order items, and fill out order and payment details much faster than a human can. When a human is needed—for example, to defeat a CAPTCHA system (see Chapter 4)—resellers farm out the task to remote workers via websites such as Amazon's Mechanical Turk. The resellers use thousands of different Internet Protocol addresses and thousands of different credit card credentials to avoid suspicion. Unfortunately, the BOTS Act does not yet apply to online retail.

Sources: Compiled from "Conversational AI and the Rise of the Chatbots," *Hewlett-Packard Enterprise*, May 10, 2018; "A.I. Helps Oscar the Chatbot Answer 75 Percent of Travel Questions," *Digital Trends*, April 4, 2018; R. Hollander, "Chatbots and Voice Assistants Are Gaining Traction in the Workplace," *Business Insider*, April 2, 2018; D. Essex, "Your Competitors Are Amassing Armies of Recruiting Chatbots," *TechTarget*, February 22, 2018; "Broadway Hit 'Hamilton' Has a Plan to Stop Bots from Buying up Tickets," *Futurism*, August 17, 2017; L. Garfield, "A 19-Year-Old Made a Free Robot Lawyer that Helps Refugees Claim Asylum," *Business Insider*, March 9, 2017; E. Cresci, "Chatbot that Overturned 160,000 Parking Fines Now Helping Refugees Claim Asylum," *The Guardian*, March 6, 2017; N. Romeo, "The Chatbot Will See You Now," *The New Yorker*, December 25, 2016; W. Knight, "Chatbots with Social Skills Will Convince You to Buy Something," *MIT Technology Review*, October 26, 2016; C. Crandell, "Chatbots Will Be Your New Best Friend," *Forbes*, October 23, 2016; C. Waxer, "Get Ready for the Bot Revolution," *Computerworld*, October 17, 2016; O. Williams-Grut, "RBS Is Launching an A.I. Chatbot Called 'Luvo' to Help Customers," *Business Insider*, September 28, 2016; J. Constine, "Facebook Messenger Now Allows Payments in Its 30,000 Chatbots," *TechCrunch*, September 12, 2016; B. Botelho, "AI Chatbot Apps to Infiltrate Businesses Sooner Than You Think," *TechTarget*, August 31, 2016; W. Knight, "The HR Person at Your Next Job May Actually Be a Bot," *MIT Technology Review*, August 3, 2016; S. Brewster, "Do Your Banking with a Chatbot," *MIT Technology Review*, May 17, 2016; "Chatbots to Take 'HR Role' at Overstock.com," *Gadgets Now Beta*, May 9, 2016; D. Bass, "Moving Merchandise Via Chats and Bots," *Bloomberg BusinessWeek*, May 2–8, 2016; T. Peterson, "Inside the Making of Taco Bell's Artificially Intelligent, Drunk-Tolerant TacoBot," *Martech Today*, April 14, 2016; J. Guynn, "'Chatbots' Ready to Take Aim at Big Money," *USA Today*, April 13, 2016; M. Isaac, "A Shopping Buddy, Via Chat," *New York Times*, April 12, 2016; N. Heath, "Satya Nadella: Software Bots Will Be as Big as Mobile Apps," *TechRepublic*, April 4, 2016; H. Reese, "Why Microsoft's 'Tay' AI Bot Went Wrong," *TechRepublic*, March 24, 2016; and L. Garfield, "A 19-Year-Old Made a Free Robot Lawyer that Has Appealed $3 Million in Parking Tickets," *Business Insider*, February 18, 2016.

Questions

1. Discuss how the capabilities of chatbots are expanding through the use of machine learning. (*Hint:* See Technology Guide 4.)

2. Describe how your university could use a chatbot in its admissions process. Provide specific examples.

Each type of EC is executed in one or more business models. A **business model** is the method by which a company generates revenue to sustain itself. **Table 7.1** summarizes the major EC business models.

TABLE 7.1   **E-Commerce Business Models**

Online direct marketing	Manufacturers or retailers sell directly to customers. Very efficient for digital products and services. Can allow for product or service customization (**www.dell.com**).
Electronic tendering system	Businesses request quotes from suppliers. Uses B2B with a reverse auction mechanism.
Name-your-own-price	Customers decide how much they are willing to pay. An intermediary tries to match a provider (**www.priceline.com**).
Find-the-best-price	Customers specify a need; an intermediary compares providers and shows the lowest price. Customers must accept the offer in a short time, or they may lose the deal (**www.hotwire.com**).
Affiliate marketing	Vendors ask partners to place logos (or banners) on partner's site. If customers click on a logo, go to a vendor's site, and make a purchase, then the vendor pays commissions to the partners.
Viral marketing	Recipients of your marketing notices send information about your product to their friends.
Group purchasing (e-coops)	Small buyers aggregate demand to create a large volume; the group then conducts tendering or negotiates a low price.
Online auctions	Companies run auctions of various types on the Internet. Very popular in C2C, but gaining ground in other types of EC as well (**www.ebay.com**).
Product customization	Customers use the Internet to self-configure products or services. Sellers then price them and fulfill them quickly (*build-to-order*) (**www.jaguar.com**).
Electronic marketplaces and exchanges	Transactions are conducted efficiently (more information to buyers and sellers, lower transaction costs) in electronic marketplaces (private or public).
Bartering online	Intermediary administers online exchange of surplus products or company receives "points" for its contribution, which it can use to purchase other needed items (**www.bbu.com**).
Deep discounters	Company offers deep price discounts. Appeals to customers who consider only price in their purchasing decisions (**www.ebay.com**).
Membership	Only members can use the services provided, including access to certain information, conducting trades, and so on.

Major E-Commerce Mechanisms

Businesses and customers can buy and sell on the Internet through a number of mechanisms, including electronic catalogs and electronic auctions. Businesses and customers use electronic payment mechanisms to digitally pay for goods and services.

Catalogs have been printed on paper for generations. Today, they are also available over the Internet. *Electronic catalogs* consist of a product database, a directory and search capabilities, and a presentation function. They are the backbone of most e-commerce sites.

An **auction** is a competitive buying and selling process in which prices are determined dynamically by competitive bidding. Electronic auctions (e-auctions) generally increase revenues for sellers by broadening the customer base and shortening the cycle time of the auction. Buyers generally benefit from e-auctions because they can bargain for lower prices. They also do not have to travel to an auction at a physical location.

The Internet provides an efficient infrastructure for conducting auctions at lower administrative costs and with a greater number of involved sellers and buyers. Both individual consumers and corporations can participate in auctions.

There are two major types of auctions: forward and reverse. In **forward auctions**, sellers solicit bids from many potential buyers. Usually, sellers place items at sites for auction, and buyers bid continuously for them. The highest bidder wins the items. Both sellers and buyers can be either individuals or businesses. The popular auction site eBay.com is a forward auction site.

In **reverse auctions**, one buyer, usually an organization, wants to purchase a product or a service. The buyer posts a request for a quotation (RFQ) on its website or on a third-party site. The RFQ provides detailed information on the desired purchase. Interested suppliers study the RFQ and then submit bids electronically. Everything else being equal, the lowest-price bidder wins the auction. The reverse auction is the most common auction model for large purchases (in regard to either quantities or price). Governments and large corporations frequently use this approach, which may provide considerable savings for the buyer.

Auctions can be conducted from the seller's site, the buyer's site, or a third party's site. For example, eBay, the best-known third-party site, offers hundreds of thousands of different items in several types of auctions. Overall, more than 300 major companies, including Amazon.com and Dellauction.com, sponsor online auctions.

An *electronic storefront* is a website that represents a single store. An *electronic mall*, also known as a *cybermall* or an *e-mall*, is a collection of individual shops consolidated under one Internet address. Electronic storefronts and electronic malls are closely associated with B2C electronic commerce. You will study each one in more detail in Section 7.2.

An **electronic marketplace** (*e-marketplace*) is a central, virtual market space on the Web where many buyers and many sellers can conduct e-commerce and e-business activities. Electronic marketplaces are associated with B2B electronic commerce. You will learn about electronic marketplaces in Section 7.3.

Electronic Payment Mechanisms

MIS **ACCT** Implementing EC typically requires electronic payments. **Electronic payment mechanisms** enable buyers to pay for goods and services electronically, rather than writing a check or using cash. Payments are an integral part of doing business, whether in the traditional manner or online. Traditional payment systems have typically involved cash or checks.

In most cases, traditional payment systems are not effective for EC, especially for B2B. Cash cannot be used because there is no face-to-face contact between buyer and seller. Not everyone accepts credit cards or checks, and some buyers do not have credit cards or checking accounts. Finally, contrary to what many people believe, it may be *less* secure for the buyer to use the telephone or mail to arrange or send payments, especially from another country, than to complete a secured transaction on a computer. For all of these reasons, a better method is needed to pay for goods and services in cyberspace. This method is electronic payment systems. Let's take a closer look at electronic checks, electronic cards, and digital, online payments. We discuss the blockchain and various cryptocurrencies such as bitcoin in IT's About Business 7.2 and then discuss digital wallets in Chapter 8.

ACCT **Electronic Checks.**   *Electronic checks (e-checks)*, which are used primarily in B2B, are similar to regular paper checks. A customer who wishes to use e-checks must first establish a checking account with a bank. Then, when the customer buys a product or a service, he or she e-mails an encrypted electronic check to the seller. The seller deposits the check in a bank account, and the funds are transferred from the buyer's account into the seller's account.

Like regular checks, e-checks carry a signature (in digital form) that can be verified (see **www.authorize.net**). Properly signed and endorsed e-checks are exchanged between financial institutions through electronic clearinghouses.

FIN **ACCT** **Electronic Cards.**   There are a variety of electronic cards, and they are used for different purposes. The most common types are electronic credit cards, purchasing cards, stored-value money cards, and smart cards.

Electronic credit cards allow customers to charge online payments to their credit card account. These cards are used primarily in B2C and in shopping by small-to-medium enterprises (SMEs). Here is how e-credit cards work (see **Figure 7.1**):

1. When you purchase a book from Amazon, for example, your credit card information and purchase amount are encrypted in your browser. This procedure ensures the information is safe while it is "traveling" on the Internet to Amazon.

CUSTOMER   MERCHANT

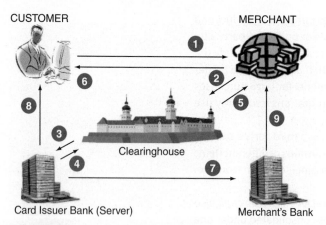

Card Issuer Bank (Server)   Merchant's Bank

FIGURE 7.1 **How e-credit cards work. (The numbers 1–9 indicate the sequence of activities.)**

2. When your information arrives at Amazon, it is not opened. Rather, it is transferred automatically (in encrypted form) to a *clearinghouse*, where it is decrypted for verification and authorization.

3. The clearinghouse asks the bank that issued you your credit card (the card issuer bank) to verify your credit card information.

4. Your card issuer bank verifies your credit card information and reports this to the clearinghouse.

5. The clearinghouse reports the result of the verification of your credit card to Amazon.

6. Amazon reports a successful purchase and amount to you.

7. Your card issuer bank sends funds in the amount of the purchase to Amazon's bank.

8. Your card issuer bank notifies you (either electronically or in your monthly statement) of the debit on your credit card.

9. Amazon's bank notifies Amazon of the funds credited to its account.

Purchasing cards are the B2B equivalent of electronic credit cards (see **Figure 7.2**). In some countries, purchasing cards are the primary form of payment between companies. Unlike credit cards, where credit is provided for 30 days (for free) before payment is made to the merchant, payments made with purchasing cards are settled within a week.

Stored-value money cards allow you to store a fixed amount of prepaid money and then spend it as necessary. Each time you use the card, the amount is reduced by the amount you spent. **Figure 7.3** illustrates a New York City Metro (subway and bus) card.

Finally, *EMV smart cards* contain a chip that can store a large amount of information as well as a magnetic stripe (that also stores information) for backward compatibility (see **Figure 7.4**). EMV stands for Europay, MasterCard, and Visa, the three companies that originally created the standard. EMV is a technical standard for smart payment cards. EMV cards can be physically swiped through a reader, inserted into a reader, or read over a short distance using near-field communications. EMV cards are also called "chip and PIN" or "chip and signature," depending on the authentication methods employed by the card issuer.

MIKE CLARKE/AFP/Getty Images

FIGURE 7.2 **Example of a purchasing card.**

Clarence Holmes Photography/Alamy Stock Photo

FIGURE 7.3 **The New York City Metro Card.**

MARKA/Alamy Stock Photo

FIGURE 7.4 **Smart cards are frequently multipurpose.**

MIS **ACCT** **Digital, Online Payments.** The rapid growth of electronic commerce necessitated a fast, secure method for customers to pay online using their credit cards. Traditionally, to process online credit card payments, merchants set up Internet merchant accounts and payment gateway accounts. The merchants obtained their merchant accounts through a bank.

A payment gateway is an application that authorizes payments for e-businesses, online retailers, bricks-and-clicks businesses, or traditional brick-and-mortar businesses. It is the virtual equivalent of a physical point-of-sale terminal located in retail outlets.

Payment gateways link, on one hand, to credit card accounts belonging to online customers and to Internet merchant accounts on the other. Payment gateways interact with the card issuer's bank to authorize the credit card in real time when a purchase is made. The funds received flow into the merchant account.

The leading providers of payment gateway accounts are PayPal (**www.paypal.com**), Authorize.net (**www.authorize.net**), Cybersource (**www.cybersource.com**), and

Verisign (**www.verisign.com**). These providers help merchants set up merchant accounts and payment gateways in one convenient package. Let's look at how Stripe is disrupting the payments industry.

MIS **FIN** Founded in 2011, Stripe (**www.stripe.com**) is an electronic payment software solution in the financial technology (FinTech) industry whose goal is to transform e-payment systems. Stripe allows individuals and businesses to accept payments over the Internet. Stripe focuses on providing the technical, fraud prevention, and banking infrastructure required to operate online payment systems.

Using Stripe, merchants can integrate payment processing into their websites without having to register and maintain a merchant account. For online credit card transactions, merchants create a Stripe account and insert a few lines of JavaScript into their website's source code. When shoppers provide their credit card information, it's collected directly by Stripe's servers, so merchants do not need to handle sensitive data. Stripe processes the transaction, scans for signs of fraud, and charges a fee of 2.9 percent plus 30 cents per transaction. Stripe deposits the funds from the sale into the vendor's bank account a week later.

In the fall of 2018, Stripe (**www.stripe.com**) moved into brick-and-mortar retail when the firm deployed a new product called Stripe Terminal. Terminal is Stripe's payments solution for fast-growing Internet businesses that sell products and services in person as well as online. For example, digital-first brands such as Warby Parker (eyeglasses; **www.warbyparker.com**) and Glossier (skin care and beauty products; **www.glossier.com**) use Terminal for in-person payments.

One of Stripe's main competitors is Adyen (**www.adyen.com**), a European service. Adyen offers merchants the ability to use one payments solution to globally track all online and brick-and-mortar sales.

Stripe says that it is targeting different customers than Adyen. Specifically, Stripe targets fast-growing, digital-first companies that have only recently begun expanding into physical retail. Adyen, however, targets large traditional brands such as L'Oreal and Burberry, although it does business with large Internet platforms such as eBay and Etsy.

Stripe also believes its technology differentiates it from Adyen. The firm states that Stripe Terminal will make it easy for stores to customize what shoppers see on the checkout screen, whether that is a discount offer or other messaging. Merchants will also be able to manage and send updates to all of their checkout equipment from one online account. Pricing for Stripe Terminal begins at a 2.7 percent fee, plus 5 cents for each transaction.

Beyond consumer product businesses, Stripe Terminal also targets business-to-business software platforms whose own customers operate brick-and-mortar chains. For instance, Mindbody (**www.mindbodyonline.com**), which makes software for wellness businesses like yoga studios and spas, is a Stripe customer.

Benefits and Limitations of E-Commerce

Few innovations in human history have provided as many benefits to organizations, individuals, and society as e-commerce has. E-commerce benefits organizations by making national and international markets more accessible and by lowering the costs of processing, distributing, and retrieving information. Customers benefit by being able to access a vast number of products and services, around the clock. The major benefit to society is the ability to easily and conveniently deliver information, services, and products to people in cities, rural areas, and developing countries.

Despite all these benefits, EC has some limitations, both technological and nontechnological, that have restricted its growth and acceptance. One major technological limitation is the lack of universally accepted security standards. Also, in less-developed countries, telecommunications bandwidth is often insufficient, and accessing the Web is expensive. The remaining nontechnological limitation is the perception that EC is nonsecure.

Before you go on . . .

1. Define e-commerce and distinguish it from e-business.
2. Differentiate among B2C, B2B, C2C, and B2E electronic commerce.
3. Define e-government.
4. Discuss forward and reverse auctions.
5. Discuss the various online payment mechanisms.
6. Identify some benefits and limitations of e-commerce.

7.2 Business-to-Consumer (B2C) Electronic Commerce

B2B EC is much larger than B2C EC by volume, but B2C EC is more complex. The reason is that B2C involves a large number of buyers making millions of diverse transactions per day from a relatively small number of sellers. As an illustration, consider Amazon, an online retailer that offers thousands of products to its customers. Each customer purchase is relatively small, but Amazon must manage every transaction as if that customer were its most important one. The company needs to process each order quickly and efficiently and ship the products to the customer in a timely manner. It also has to manage returns. Multiply this simple example by millions, and you get an idea of how complex B2C EC can be.

Overall, B2B complexities tend to be more business related, whereas B2C complexities tend to be more technical and volume related. As you noted in the previous section of this chapter, one of the complexities of B2C involves digital, online payments.

This section addresses the primary issues in B2C EC. We begin by studying the two basic mechanisms that customers utilize to access companies on the Web: electronic storefronts and electronic malls. In addition to purchasing products over the Web, customers also access online services, such as banking, securities trading, job searching, and travel. Companies engaged in B2C EC must "get the word out" to prospective customers, so we turn our attention to online advertising. Finally, the complexity of B2C EC creates two major challenges for sellers: channel conflict and order fulfillment, which we examine in detail.

Electronic Storefronts and Malls

For several generations, home shopping from catalogs, and later from television shopping channels, has attracted millions of customers. **Electronic retailing (e-tailing)** is the direct sale of products and services through electronic storefronts or electronic malls, usually designed around an electronic catalog format and auctions.

E-commerce enables you to buy from anywhere, at any time. EC offers a wide variety of products and services, including unique items, often at lower prices. The name given to selling unique items is "the long tail." The *long tail* describes the retailing strategy of selling a large number of unique items in small quantities.

Shoppers can also gain access to very detailed supplementary product information. They can also easily locate and compare competitors' products and prices. Finally, buyers can find hundreds of thousands of sellers. Two popular online shopping mechanisms are electronic storefronts and electronic malls.

As we saw earlier in the chapter, an **electronic storefront** is a website that represents a single store. Each storefront has a unique uniform resource locator (URL), or Internet address, at which buyers can place orders.

An **electronic mall**, also known as a *cybermall,* or an *e-mall,* is a collection of individual shops grouped under a single Internet address. Electronic malls may include thousands of vendors. For example, Microsoft Bing shopping (**www.bing.com/shopping**) includes tens of thousands of products from thousands of vendors, as does Amazon (**www.amazon.com**).

Online Service Industries

In addition to purchasing products, customers also access needed services on the Web. Selling books, toys, computers, and most other products on the Internet can reduce vendors' selling costs by 20 to 40 percent. Further reduction is difficult to achieve because the products must be delivered physically. Only a few products, such as software and music, can be digitized and then delivered online for additional savings. In contrast, services such as buying an airline ticket and purchasing stocks or insurance, can be delivered entirely through e-commerce, often with considerable cost reduction.

One of the most pressing EC issues relating to online services (as well as in marketing tangible products) is **disintermediation**. Intermediaries, also known as *middlemen,* have two functions: (1) They provide information, and (2) they perform value-added services such as consulting. The first function can be fully automated and most likely will be assumed by e-marketplaces and portals that provide information for free. When this development occurs, the intermediaries who perform only (or primarily) this function are likely to be eliminated. The process whereby intermediaries are eliminated is called *disintermediation.*

In contrast to simply providing information, performing value-added services requires expertise. Unlike the information function, then, this function can be only partially automated. Intermediaries who provide value-added services are thriving. The Web helps these employees in two situations: (1) when the number of participants is enormous, as with job searches, and (2) when the information that must be exchanged is complex.

In this section, you will examine some leading online service industries: banking, trading of securities (stocks, bonds), job matching, travel services, and advertising.

MIS FIN Financial Technology (Fintech).   Traditional banks have massive, entrenched, and inefficient legacy infrastructures that consist of brick-and-mortar buildings and information technology infrastructures. These legacy infrastructures make it difficult for traditional banks to upgrade their systems or to be agile and flexible. Furthermore, their infrastructures are making banks' customer experiences outdated. Customers now expect their financial experiences to be mobile, personalized, customizable, and accessible.

Responding to customer expectations, **Fintech** is an industry composed of companies that use technology to compete in the marketplace with traditional financial institutions and intermediaries in the delivery of financial services, which include banking, insurance, real estate, and investing. (Fintech is also a blanket term for disruptive technologies that are affecting the financial services industry.) IT's About Business 7.2 takes a closer look at the Fintech industry.

FIN Online Securities Trading.   Millions of Americans use computers to trade stocks, bonds, and other financial instruments. In fact, several well-known securities companies, including E*Trade, Ameritrade, and Charles Schwab, offer only online trading because it is cheaper than a full-service or discount broker. On the Web, investors can find a considerable amount of information regarding specific companies or mutual funds in which to invest (e.g., **www.cnn.com/business** and **www.bloomberg.com**).

HRM The Online Job Market.   Job seekers use online job market sites such as **www.monster.com, www.simplyhired.com, www.linkedin.com**, and **www.true-career.com/en** to help them find available positions. In many countries (including the United States), governments must advertise job openings on the Internet. (See our discussion on LinkedIn and "how to find a job" in Chapter 9.)

MKT Travel Services.   The Internet is an ideal place to plan, explore, and arrange almost any trip economically. Online travel services allow you to purchase airline tickets, reserve hotel rooms, and rent cars. Most sites also offer a fare-tracker feature that sends you e-mail messages about low-cost flights. Examples of comprehensive online travel services are

IT's About Business 7.2

Financial Technology (Fintech)

`FIN` `MIS`

The Fintech industry is expanding rapidly. Let's look more closely at some of the primary growing areas in Fintech.

`FIN` **Lending.** A new form of person-to-person (P2P) banking driven by technology offers an alternative source of financing. P2P lending platforms that use machine learning technologies and algorithms are saving individuals and businesses time and money and are helping many of them access a line of credit. P2P lending platforms provide borrowers with an easy, fast, simple, and lower-cost service that most traditional banks cannot match. The leading companies in this area are Lending Tree (**www.lendingtree.com**), Lending Club (**www.lendingclub.com**), Prosper (**www.prosper.com**), and Zopa (**www.zopa.com**).

`FIN` **Trading and investing.** New automated financial advisors and wealth management services are making an impact on the industry. Robo-advisors are using sophisticated algorithms to make trading and investing a fully automated online experience. These automated platforms provide savings to users and offer financial planning services that are normally reserved for wealthy investors. They are also enabling users with very small amounts of capital to begin investing. The leading companies in this area are Wealthfront (**www.wealthfront.com**), Betterment (**www.betterment.com**), Motif (**www.motifinvesting.com**), eToro (**www.etoro.com**), and Robinhood (**www.robinhood.com**).

Let's look more closely at Robinhood. Launched in 2014, Robinhood is an online brokerage with no fees and no commissions. The app was developed to help cautious investors make a first purchase and build experience with the markets. In September 2016, the firm launched its first subscription product, Robinhood Gold, which allows users to trade on margin—that is, to borrow money to buy stocks. By August 2018, Robinhood had attracted more than 4 million users, whose median age is under 30.

`FIN` `ACCT` **Personal finance.** Fintech companies are trying to make personal finance more transparent and more affordable. Mobile apps and online platforms are now helping individuals and businesses to develop a budget, find a loan, file their taxes, and invest. These platforms are also using technology to track daily expenditures and to help users analyze their financial status in real time. The leading companies in this area are Acorns (**www.acorns.com**), Mint (**www.mint.com**), NerdWallet (**www.nerdwallet.com**), FeeX (**www.feex.com**), and BillGuard (**www.crunchbase.com/organizations/billguard**).

`FIN` **Funding.** Equity and crowdfunding platforms provide alternate sources of investment for individuals who want to start a business. Online crowdfunding platforms raise money from a large number of individuals who collectively fund projects that typically would not attract funding from traditional banks and venture capital firms. Each year, billions of dollars are raised on U.S.-based crowdfunding platforms. The leading companies in this area are Kickstarter (**www.kickstarter.com**), Indiegogo (**www.indiegogo.com**), and GoFundMe (**www.gofundme.com**).

`FIN` **Currency exchange and remittances.** Transferring and exchanging money internationally can be a time-consuming and expensive process. Fintech companies are developing innovative platforms that make this process simpler, faster, and less expensive. These companies range from P2P currency exchanges that reduce the costs of exchanging currencies to mobile phone-based money transfers and remittance platforms that provide a cost-effective method for people to transfer small amounts of money overseas. The leading companies in this area are TransferWise (**www.transferwise.com**), Xoom (**www.xoom.com**), WeSwap (**www.weswap.com**), WorldRemit (**www.worldremit.com**), and M-PESA (**www.safaricom.co.ke/personal/m-pesa**).

`FIN` **Mobile banking.** Mobile banking refers to the service that banks and other financial institutions provide to their customers that enables them to conduct a range of transactions by using an app on their mobile devices. The apps allow customers to remotely access and transact with their accounts. In the United States, approximately 72 percent of consumers use digital channels to open checking accounts.

`FIN` **Internet banking (also called e-banking or online banking).** Internet banking is closely related to mobile banking. However, instead of using an app, customers use the Internet. All of the transactions are conducted through the website of the financial institution. Several Internet-only banks have emerged, including Ally (**www.ally.com**), TIAA Bank (**www.tiaabank.com**) and Axos Bank (**www.axosbank.com/Personal**).

`FIN` `ACCT` **Payments.** Casual payments that people make every day, such as $75 for domestic help or $40 to split a lunch check with friends, have long been a problem for the U.S. banking system. Today, new payment technologies are changing the ways that consumers bank, transfer money, and pay for goods and services.

With P2P services, consumers link a bank account, credit card, or debit card to a smartphone app and can then send money to anyone else with only the recipient's e-mail address or phone number. In the near future, consumers will no longer need to have a physical wallet filled with cash and credit cards. The only item required to make a payment will be a smartphone. The leading companies in this area are Venmo (**www.venmo.com**; subsidiary of PayPal), PayPal (**www.paypal.com**), Square (**www.squareup.com**), Apple Pay (**www.apple.com/apple-pay/**), Google Pay (**www.payments.google.com**), and Facebook Messenger (**www.messenger.com**).

In June 2017, more than 30 major banks, including Bank of America, Citibank, JPMorgan Chase, and Wells Fargo, teamed up to introduce Zelle (**www.zellepay.com**), a digital payments network that allows consumers to send money instantly through participating banks' mobile apps. Consumers who utilize this network do not have to download a separate app.

`ACCT` **Blockchain.** A *ledger* records a business's summarized financial information as debits and credits and displays their current balances. A blockchain is a type of ledger. Specifically, it is a decentralized digital payment record of transactions that is encrypted, secure, anonymous, tamper proof, and unchangeable. Essentially, a blockchain is a distributed database that stores and manages transactions. Each record in the database, called a *block*, contains details such as the transaction timestamp and a link to the previous block. This process makes it impossible for anyone to alter information about the records. Further, the technology is secure by design, because the same transaction is recorded over multiple, distributed databases.

Instead of a bank, a broker, or another intermediary maintaining a private database of records, blockchain makes all of its records public. As a result, consumers may no longer need a bank to transfer money or to maintain account records.

Consider this example from Walmart, which requires a technology that can track and catalog a product's status across its supply chain. A Walmart executive purchased a package of sliced fruit and asked his team to find out where the fruit came from. It took more than six days for the team to complete this task. The six days constituted the experimental *control*.

The team then tracked and digitally recorded food shipments using a blockchain. From the start of their journey at a farm, pallets of fruit were tagged with numeric identifiers. Every time the fruit crossed another checkpoint—from farm to broker to distributor to store—its status was signed and logged.

A month later, the executive entered a six-digit lot number (identifying the fruit) on a Web portal. In two seconds, he received the following information:

- Type and weight of the fruit
- Date and location that the fruit was harvested
- Date and place that the fruit received hot-water treatment to exterminate the eggs of potentially invasive insects
- Date, location, and place that the properly identified importer received the shipment of fruit
- Date and location that the fruit passed through Customs and Border Protection
- Date the fruit entered a properly identified processing plant
- Date and location that the fruit moved to a cold storage facility
- Date the fruit was received and location of the Walmart store that received it

In the event of an *E. coli* or salmonella outbreak, the difference between two seconds and more than six days could be lifesaving. Walmart is now using a blockchain to track pigs from China, through the company's supply chain, to selling ham, pork, and bacon in its stores.

There are numerous applications of blockchain technology. We list a few here:

- The Danish shipping company Maersk is testing a blockchain to track its shipments and coordinate with customs officials and the U.S. Department of Homeland Security.

- Airbus, the French aircraft manufacturer, is testing a blockchain to monitor the many complex parts that make up a jet airplane.
- Accenture has teamed with Microsoft and a group from the United Nations to build a blockchain for digital identity, which is particularly valuable for refugees who lack official documents.
- Blockchain is the underlying technology for digital currencies such as Bitcoin and Ethereum. Bitcoin transactions are stored and transferred using a distributed ledger on a peer-to-peer network that is open, public, and anonymous. Blockchain maintains the ledger.

Sources: Compiled from Z. Perret, "What Will Be the Most Exciting Fintech Trends in 2018?" *Forbes*, January 22, 2018; A. Harris, "Market Forces," *Fast Company*, September, 2017; J. Toplin, "Venmo Continues to Shine for PayPal," *Business Insider*, July 31, 2017; P. Rudegeair, "PayPal's Venmo Tool Is Envy of Apple, Big Banks," *Wall Street Journal*, June 27, 2017; S. Cowley, "Cash Faces a New Challenger in Zelle, a Mobile Banking Service," *New York Times*, June 12, 2017; M. Mavadiya, "Financial Services Could Lose 40% of Revenue to Fintech," *Forbes*, April 5, 2017; A. Scott-Briggs, "10 Most Popular Fintech Sectors," *Techbullion*, March 27, 2017; N. Kuznetsov, "Gift Cards as Currency – How Fintech Is Changing the Way We Give," *Forbes*, March 22, 2017; J. Gonzalez-Garcia, "Online and Mobile Banking Statistics," Creditcards.com, March 20, 2017; L. Wintermeyer, "Digital Disruption Has Arrived in Fintech," *Forbes*, March 17, 2017; J. Pizzi, "Fintech's Next Wave," *Forbes*, March 7, 2017; D. Furlonger and R. Valdes, "Practical Blockchain: A Gartner Trend Insight Report," Gartner, March 3, 2017; R. Arora, "3 Reasons Fintech Is Thriving," *Forbes*, February 22, 2017; C. Myers, "3 Reasons Fintech Is Failing," *Forbes*, February 7, 2017; N. Laskowski, "Goldman CIO Touts New Consumer Lending Business as 'Fintech Startup,'" *TechTarget*, January 31, 2017; E. Rosenberg, "Industries Where Fintech Is Changing the Game," Due.com, January 30, 2017; B. Friedberg, "How Fintech Can Disrupt the $14T Mortgage Market," *Investopedia*, January 19, 2017; "Tech Hits the Home: 25 Startups Transforming the Mortgage Industry," *CB Insights*, January 6, 2017; N. Popper, "Automated Assistants Will Soon Make a Bid for Your Finances," *New York Times*, December 7, 2016; M. Dietz, V. HV, and G. Lee, "Bracing for Seven Critical Challenges as Fintech Matures," McKinsey & Company, November, 2016; K. Flinders, "Fintech Disruption Hits UK Cheque Processing Industry," *Computer Weekly*, November 9, 2016; "CitiGroup Does Fintech," *Fortune*, July 1, 2016; and "Fintech Could Be Bigger than ATMs, PayPal, and Bitcoin Combined," *BI Intelligence*, April 25, 2016.

Questions

1. How should the traditional banking industry compete with FinTech companies?
2. What are potential disadvantages to consumers when they use the following?
   a. P2P lending
   b. P2P payments

Expedia.com, Travelocity.com, and Orbitz.com. Online services are also provided by all major airline vacation services, large conventional travel agencies, car rental agencies, hotels (e.g., **www.hotels.com**), and tour companies. In a variation of this process, Priceline.com allows you to set a price you are willing to pay for an airline ticket or hotel accommodations. It then attempts to find a vendor that will match your price.

One costly problem that e-commerce can cause is "mistake fares" in the airline industry. In January 2019 Cathay Pacific (**www.cathaypacific.com**) offered business class flights from Vietnam to several U.S. cities for $675. This price was incorrect; the actual price would have been about $4,000. The U.S. Department of Transportation no longer requires airlines to honor mistake fares, but Cathay honored the tickets purchased before the airline fixed the erroneous price.

MKT **Online Advertising.** *Advertising* is the practice of disseminating information in an attempt to influence a buyer–seller transaction. Traditional advertising on TV or in newspapers involves impersonal, one-way mass communication. In contrast, direct-response marketing, or telemarketing, contacts individuals by direct mail or telephone and requires them to respond in order to make a purchase. The direct-response approach personalizes advertising and marketing. At the same time, however, it can be expensive, slow, and ineffective. It can also be extremely annoying to the consumer.

The good news is that online advertising redefines the advertising process, making it media rich, dynamic, and interactive. It improves on traditional forms of advertising in a number of ways. First, online ads can be updated any time at minimal cost and therefore can be kept current. These ads can also reach very large numbers of potential buyers all over the world. Furthermore, they are generally cheaper than radio, television, and print ads. Finally, online ads can be interactive and targeted to specific interest groups or individuals.

Online advertising is responsible in large part for the profit margins of content creators, and it plays a critical role in keeping online content free. In 2018, online advertising spending worldwide totaled $252 billion. Content creators need online ads because they depend on the revenue from advertisers.

The predominant business model for content creators, as well as platforms such as Google and Facebook, has always involved the income from online advertising. Advertising is sold based on *impressions*, or the number of times that people view an ad. Consequently, content creators employ several business models to try to increase the number of impressions they deliver:

1. Increase Internet traffic, which is difficult, given that most people in the developed world already have Internet access.

2. Place more—and more intrusive—ads on each Web page, thus irritating users even more. Such ads include banners, pop-up ads, pop-under ads, and e-mail. Although cost effective, e-mail advertising is often misused, causing consumers to receive a flood of unsolicited e-mail, or *spam*. **Spamming** is the indiscriminate distribution of electronic ads without the permission of the recipient. Unfortunately, spamming is becoming worse over time.

3. Try to sell native advertising. *Native advertising* consists of ads that are disguised as content. Because they appear to be content, ad blockers cannot block them. However, users become confused about whether they are reading independent content or an ad. Many content creators use this model, which advertisers favor. Users, however, find native ads obnoxious because they are basically deceptive.

4. Avoid the online ad problem by offering premium content in search of higher-value advertising that targets a premium audience.

5. Find a non-advertising revenue source. VentureBeat (**www.venturebeat.com**), for example, built a research business, selling high-value reports to companies willing to pay for very useful information.

Today, online advertising is facing a crisis because content creators have been emphasizing the intrusive model from the preceding list (number 2). As a result, users have become irritated with videos that automatically start playing when they load a Web page and full-screen takeovers that force them to find and then click on a tiny "x" before they can read the content that they wanted in the first place. They are also concerned with cookies that track every Web page they visit and every click they make, thus enabling advertisers to target them with increasing frequency and precision.

MIS **MKT** As a result of all these problems with online advertising, many Web users are employing ad-blocking software—called *ad blockers*—to prevent online advertising. Specifically, in 2018, about 30 percent of Internet users in the United States employed ad-blocking tools. Globally in 2018, over 200 million people used ad blockers. The result is that content creators are expected to lose $27 billion by 2020.

There are several types of ad blockers:

- Ad blockers that will stop almost every ad and tracker. For example, Privacy Badger (**www.eff.org/privacybadger**) spots and blocks what it calls "nonconsensual tracking," or ads and trackers that move with users around the Web, serving them ads on multiple sites. Privacy Badger stops your browser from displaying anything from third parties that you did not grant permission to view. The site is operated by the nonprofit Electronic Frontier Foundation, which accepts donations and coding help.

- Ad blockers that are for-profit businesses. The most popular ad blocker is Adblock Plus (**www.adblockplus.org**), with more than 100 million users worldwide. The tool blocks ads, banners, pop-ups, and video ads, and it stops tracking services.

  Adblock Plus does not prevent all ads; instead, it allows what it calls "acceptable ads." With this program, ads that have certain characteristics such as placement, size, and distinction, are whitelisted. In these cases, the advertiser shares the revenue gained by whitelisting with Adblock Plus.

  Along these same lines, Google and Microsoft pay to have their ads whitelisted by Adblock Plus and other ad blockers. This cost accrues first to the advertisers and eventually to the customers who purchase the products or services.

- Ad blockers that collect data. In March 2018 ad-blocker Ghostery (**www.ghostery.com**) published all of its code on GitHub and became open source. At that time, Ghostery announced two new ways of making money.

  First, Ghostery launched Ghostery Insights, which is a paid analytics service that gives researchers access to data about ads and trackers that Ghostery gathers as it blocks them. Second, Ghostery Rewards is a consumer-focused affiliate marketing program. If users opt-in, they are offered occasional deals on products that they might be interested in. Ghostery is removing all the ads from the Web, while replacing some of them with its own. Unlike traditional Web advertisements, Rewards is exclusive to those who use the tool.

- Ad blockers that use the freemium model. Blockers such as Disconnect (**www.disconnect.me**) and 1Blocker (**www.1blocker.com**) are free apps for mobile users, who then have to pay if they want to use features such as being able to simultaneously block more than one ad or tracker.

- Ad blockers that are a function of operating systems. For example, Google Chrome will block ads from sites that engage in particularly annoying behavior. Apple's latest operating systems enable owners of Apple devices to download Web browser extensions that block ads. Brave (**www.brave.com**) is a free, open-source Web browser that blocks ads and website trackers. In April 2019, the firm began allowing users to opt in to receiving ads sold by Brave Software in place of the blocked ads.

- Pi-hole (**www.pi-hole.net**) is a free, open-source ad-blocking software tool developed by volunteers. The software is designed to operate on a Raspberry Pi. While most ad blockers must be installed on individual devices and work only in Web browsers, Pi-hole blocks ads across an entire network, including in most apps except YouTube and Hulu, for technical reasons. Pi-hole cannot block ads inside Facebook, but it can stop Facebook from following users around the Web.

  Pi-hole developers have discovered spying by Internet-connected televisions that collect data for ad targeting, lightbulbs (users have reported some LED bulbs mysteriously connecting with the manufacturer every 2 seconds), and printers (including one that sent out 34 million queries in one day).

Not surprisingly, content creators are fighting back against ad-blocking software. For example, about 30 percent of the Internet's top 10,000 websites use software designed to subvert browser-level ad blocking. In addition, they have begun using ad-block detectors. This type of software tool looks for ad blockers and then asks the user to disable them. It might even deny access to content until they do.

In August 2016, Facebook announced that it would configure its ads to avoid ad blockers. This action was controversial because Facebook has to meet Federal Trade Commission (FTC; **www.ftc.gov**) rules on transparency, which require Facebook to clearly indicate when something is an advertisement. Facebook also made a commitment to its members that it would clearly label ads.

Almost immediately, Adblock Plus informed its users of a change to their settings that would get around Facebook's attempt to defeat ad blockers. In 2017, the company introduced a new way to block ads on Facebook. Adblock Plus looks inside actual Facebook posts to discover "signs" that a particular post is an ad and then blocks it.

Different browsers, including Google Chrome, Apple Safari, and Mozillla Firefox, have different policies and capabilities around ad blocking. There is concern that ad blockers could weaken in the future and users should know the capabilities of the browsers they choose to use.

It is very important to realize that all of the "free" content on the Web must be paid for in some manner. If online ads are no longer viable, then content on the Web will be displayed only behind paywalls; that is, users will have to pay (e.g., subscriptions) to view content. And the results? The battles between content creators and ad blockers continue.

Issues in E-Tailing

Despite e-tailing's increasing popularity, many e-tailers continue to face serious issues that can restrict their growth. Three significant issues are channel conflict, order fulfillment, and personalized pricing.

MKT POM **Channel Conflict.** Clicks-and-mortar companies may face a conflict with their regular distributors when they sell directly to customers online. This situation, known as **channel conflict**, can alienate the distributors. Channel conflict has forced some companies to avoid direct online sales. For example, Walmart, Lowe's, and Home Depot would rather have customers come to their stores. Therefore, although all three companies maintain e-commerce websites, their sites place more emphasis on providing information—products, prices, specials, and store locations—than on online sales.

Channel conflict can arise in areas such as pricing and resource allocation—for example, how much money to spend on advertising. Another potential source of conflict involves the logistics services provided by the offline activities to the online activities. For example, how should a company handle returns of items purchased online? Some companies have completely separated the "clicks" (the online portion of the organization) from the "mortar" or "bricks" (the traditional bricks-and-mortar part of the organization). However, this approach can increase expenses, reduce the synergy between the two organizational channels, and alienate customers. As a result, many companies are integrating their online and offline channels, a process known as **multichanneling**.

Multichanneling has created the opportunity for showrooming. *Showrooming* occurs when shoppers visit a brick-and-mortar store to examine a product in person. They then conduct research about the product on their smartphones. Often, they then purchase the product from the website of a competitor of the store they are visiting. Showrooming is causing problems for brick-and-mortar retailers, such as Target, Best Buy, and others. At the same time, showrooming benefits Amazon, eBay, and other online retailers.

POM **Order Fulfillment.** The second major issue confronting e-commerce is *order fulfillment,* which can create problems for e-tailers. Any time a company sells directly to customers, it is involved in various order-fulfillment activities. It must perform the following activities: Quickly find the products to be shipped; pack them; arrange for the packages to be delivered speedily to the customer's door; collect the money from every customer, either in advance, by COD, or by individual bill; and handle the return of unwanted or defective products.

It is very difficult to accomplish these activities both effectively and efficiently in B2C, because a company has to ship small packages to many customers and do it quickly. For this reason, companies involved in B2C activities can experience difficulties in their supply chains.

In addition to providing customers with the products they ordered and doing it on time, order fulfillment provides all related customer services. For example, the customer must receive assembly and operation instructions for a new appliance. If the customer is unhappy with a product, the company must also arrange for an exchange or a return.

MKT **Personalized Pricing.**   The third major issue in e-commerce is personalized pricing. In the relationship between buyers and sellers, price has traditionally been a meeting point. The practice of setting a fixed price for a good or service, which appeared in the 1860s, eliminated haggling. Each party surrendered something in this relationship. Buyers were forced to accept, or not accept, the fixed price on the price tag. In return, retailers gave up the ability to exploit customers' varying willingness to pay more for a particular good or service; that is, retailers surrendered the ability to make more profit.

Today, consumers are accustomed to *standardized pricing*, which means that when a product is sold through multiple channels, the cost should not vary by more than the difference in shipping, taxation, and distribution costs. If the price is higher for a product at a certain retailer, then customers can easily use the Internet to compare prices and features among a huge number of retailers to purchase that product from another retailer, a process known as showrooming. There is even a website, **www.camelcamelcamel.com**, that tracks Amazon prices for specific products and alerts consumers when a price drops below a preset threshold.

In theory, charging all consumers the same price is ineffective for merchants, because some customers would have been willing to pay more, and others who opted not to buy would have bought at a lower price. Economic theory states that personalized pricing can save companies this lost revenue.

Personalized pricing is the practice of pricing items at a point determined by a particular customer's perceived ability to pay. The optimal outcome of personalized pricing *for the merchant* is maximizing the price that each customer will pay. Merchants are now able to approximate the maximum price that each customer will pay. How do merchants do this?

They analyze the data that consumers generate when they place items in shopping carts; swipe their rewards cards at store registers; "like" something on Facebook; provide ratings, reviews, and recommendations; and perform many other actions. They also virtually assess each customer who visits their website. Specifically, when a customer accesses a retailer's site, the merchant may know where the customer is located based on his or her Internet Protocol address. Merchants also may know the customer's zip code. In that case, they can determine the customer's socioeconomic status based on data from the most recent federal census.

As a result of analyzing this Big Data, retailers are developing increasingly sophisticated personalized pricing algorithms—that is, retailers can find the optimal, profit-maximizing price of a good or a service for a particular customer. As a result, prices can fluctuate hour-to-hour and even minute-to-minute. For example, the price of a can of soda in a vending machine can now vary with the outside temperature.

When merchants combine these data with cookies (see Chapter 4), they can learn a significant amount about individual customers. Based on these data, merchants can predict which products a customer is interested in purchasing, when he or she is likely to purchase them, and, critically, the price he or she would be willing to pay. A merchant now can estimate a customer's *reservation price*—the maximum amount they would be willing to pay for a specific product, before they had "reservations" about buying it—and then charge them that amount.

Furthermore, with e-commerce, merchants can easily adjust prices for different customers simply by changing them in the system in real time. They, therefore, avoid the expense of physically changing the prices on thousands of products.

For example, Delta Airlines (**www.delta.com**) uses personalized pricing to raise ticket prices for frequent flyers. The rationale is that these customers probably have to travel frequently, usually for business. They, therefore, are willing (however unenthusiastically) to pay more than infrequent travelers.

Companies such as Wiser (**www.wiser.com**), dunnhumby (**www.dunnhumby.com**), and Blue Yonder (**www.blue-yonder.com**; now owned by JDA Software) offer personalized pricing solutions to retailers. Blue Yonder claims it can optimize prices not only according to the region but also according to the channel in which the customer is interacting with the retailer.

Most companies hesitate to utilize personalized pricing because it remains to be seen whether consumers will accept the practice. Typically, when consumers hear about the practice, they react negatively, and companies employing the practice experience customer dissatisfaction.

A valuable source of data for companies in personalizing prices is what competitors are charging. Brick-and-mortar retailers can send mystery shoppers to their competitors' stores to note prices, but online merchants use software to scan rival websites and collect data, a process called scraping that is carried out by software called scraping bots.

Large companies have internal teams dedicated to scraping, where smaller companies use retail price optimization firms such as Competera (**www.competera.net**) and Price2Spy (**www.price2spy.com**). These firms scrape pricing data from websites and use machine learning algorithms to help their customers decide how much to charge for different products.

Retailers want to see rivals' prices but they also want to prevent rivals from spying on them. Retailers also want to protect intellectual property like product photos and descriptions, which can be scraped and reused by competitors. Thus, many retailers show different prices to people than to scraping bots. The question is: How do retailers detect bots?

If a website visitor makes hundreds of requests per minute, it is probably a bot. Another method is to look for human behavior. Specifically, when humans tap a button on their phones, they move the phone very slightly. This movement can be detected by the phone's accelerometer and gyroscope. These movements predict that the site visitor is a human and the absence of such movements predicts that the user is probably a bot.

Keep in mind that retailers must allow some, but not all, bots to scrape a website. If websites blocked bots entirely, then they would not show up on search results. Furthermore, retailers generally want their pricing and items to appear on shopping comparison websites such as Google and Price Grabber (**www.pricegrabber.com**).

Before you go on . . .

1. Describe electronic storefronts and malls.
2. Discuss various types of online services, such as securities trading, job searches, travel services, and so on.
3. Discuss online advertising, its methods, and its benefits.
4. Identify the major issues related to e-tailing.
5. What are spamming, permission marketing, and viral marketing?

7.3 Business-to-Business (B2B) Electronic Commerce

In *business-to-business (B2B)* e-commerce, the buyers and sellers are business organizations. B2B comprises about 85 percent of EC volume. It covers a broad spectrum of applications that enable an enterprise to form electronic relationships with its distributors, resellers, suppliers, customers, and other partners. B2B applications use any of several business models. The major models are sell-side marketplaces, buy-side marketplaces, and electronic exchanges.

Sell-Side Marketplaces

In the **sell-side marketplace** model, organizations sell their products or services to other organizations electronically from their own private e-marketplace website or from a third-party website. This model is similar to the B2C model in which the buyer is expected to come to the seller's site, view catalogs, and place an order. In the B2B sell-side marketplace, however, the buyer is an organization.

The key mechanisms in the sell-side model are forward auctions and electronic catalogs that can be customized for each large buyer. Sellers such as Dell Computer (**www.dellauction.com**) use auctions extensively. In addition to conducting auctions from their own websites, organizations can use third-party auction sites like eBay to liquidate items. Companies such as Ariba (**www.ariba.com**) are helping organizations to auction old assets and inventories.

The sell-side model is used by hundreds of thousands of companies. The seller can be either a manufacturer (e.g., Dell or IBM), a distributor (e.g., **www.avnet.com**), or a retailer (e.g., **www.bigboxx.com**). The seller uses EC to increase sales, reduce selling and advertising expenditures, increase delivery speed, and lower administrative costs. The sell-side model is especially suitable to customization. Many companies allow their customers to configure their orders online. For example, at Dell (**www.dell.com**) you can determine the exact type of computer that you want. You can choose the type of chip, the size of the hard drive, the type of monitor, and so on. Similarly, the Jaguar website (**www.jaguar.com**) allows you to customize the Jaguar you want. Self-customization greatly reduces any misunderstandings concerning what customers want, and it encourages businesses to fill orders more quickly.

Buy-Side Marketplaces

Procurement is the overarching function that describes the activities and processes to acquire goods and services. Distinct from purchasing, procurement involves the activities necessary to establish requirements, sourcing activities such as market research and vendor evaluation, and negotiation of contracts. *Purchasing* refers to the process of ordering and receiving goods and services. It is a subset of the procurement process.

The **buy-side marketplace** is a model in which organizations attempt to procure needed products or services from other organizations electronically. A major method of procuring goods and services in the buy-side model is the reverse auction.

The buy-side model uses EC technology to streamline the procurement process. The goal is to reduce both the costs of items procured and the administrative expenses involved in procuring them. EC technology can also shorten the procurement cycle time.

Procurement by using electronic support is referred to as **e-procurement**. E-procurement uses reverse auctions, particularly group purchasing. In **group purchasing**, multiple buyers combine their orders so that they constitute a large volume and therefore attract more seller attention. When buyers place their combined orders on a reverse auction, they can also negotiate a volume discount. Typically, the orders of small buyers are aggregated by a third-party vendor, such as the United Sourcing Alliance (**www.usa-llc.com**).

Electronic Exchanges

Private exchanges have one buyer and many sellers. Electronic marketplaces (e-marketplaces), called **public exchanges** or just **exchanges**, are independently owned by a third party, and they connect many sellers with many buyers. Public exchanges are open to all business organizations. Public exchange managers provide all of the necessary information systems to the participants. Thus, buyers and sellers merely have to "plug in" to trade. B2B public exchanges are often the initial points of contact between business partners. Once the partners make contact, they may move to a private exchange or to private trading rooms provided by many public exchanges to conduct their subsequent trading activities.

Electronic exchanges deal in both direct and indirect materials. *Direct materials* are inputs to the manufacturing process, such as safety glass used in automobile windshields and windows. *Indirect materials* are those items, such as office supplies, that are needed for maintenance, operations, and repairs (MRO).

There are three basic types of public exchanges: vertical, horizontal, and functional. All three types offer diversified support services, ranging from payments to logistics.

Vertical exchanges connect buyers and sellers in a given industry. Examples of vertical exchanges are www.plasticsnet.com in the plastics industry and www.papersite.com in the paper industry. Vertical e-marketplaces offer services that are particularly suited to the community they serve. Vertical exchanges are frequently owned and managed by a *consortium*, a term for a group of major players in an industry. For example, Marriott and Hyatt own a procurement consortium for the hotel industry, and Chevron owns an energy e-marketplace.

Horizontal exchanges connect buyers and sellers across many industries. They are used primarily for MRO materials. Examples of horizontal exchanges are TradersCity (www.traderscity.com), Globalsources (www.globalsources.com), and Alibaba (www.alibaba.com).

Finally, in *functional exchanges,* needed services such as temporary help or extra office space are traded on an "as-needed" basis. For example, Employease (www.employeaseinc.com) can find temporary labor by searching employers in its Employease Network.

We have looked closely at B2B electronic commerce in this section. IT's About Business 7.3 examines Amazon's B2B business.

IT's About Business 7.3

Amazon's B2B Marketplace

POM MKT MIS

Amazon Business (www.amazon.com/business) is Amazon's e-commerce website that caters to the wholesale and distribution business-to-business (B2B) sector. Amazon Business does for commercial customers what Amazon.com does for individuals (B2C).

Amazon's B2B efforts began with AmazonSupply, which debuted in 2012 with half a million products on offer. By 2014, the inventory had expanded to more than 2.25 million items, including tools, renovation supplies, cleaning supplies, steel pipes, and a host of other products.

In 2015, Amazon created Amazon Business and merged AmazonSupply into it. Amazon Business uses a hybrid business model, selling both products directly from its own warehouses, as well as those from third-party vendors. The outside vendors, which still have to compete with Amazon products, receive a commission of between 6 and 15 percent for their items sold, depending on the type of product and the size of the order.

Over 1 million Amazon Business customers, who are eligible to buy and sell if they have a tax ID number, can access hundreds of millions of business-only products from 85,000 sellers, obtain bulk discounts, set up a corporate credit line, and receive free two-day shipping on orders over $49. Clients can also talk with manufacturer representatives about product specifications. This process is required for sales of complex technical products.

Amazon Business emphasizes corporate tail spend, which is the 20 percent of business supply spend that is not related to core corporate functions and is not ordered from the same set of suppliers on a regular basis. Tail spend typically involves general office needs such as printer paper, bottled water, paper towels, break room supplies, IT cables, and many other products. In one rather unique example of tail spend, a large industrial company needed a small fleet of yellow tricycles so that personnel could more easily move around the plant.

Amazon Business offers many benefits for vendors and customers. For example:

- The site lists products, along with any accompanying quality certifications such as ISO 9000.

- Amazon Business account holders can qualify for special offers not available to individuals on the Amazon.com site. This helps vendors meet requirements not to sell products that are forbidden to be sold directly to consumers, such as high-tech health care equipment.

- Customers can search for items by both manufacturer and distributor part numbers.

- The site can demonstrate products in Web videos and host downloadable computer-aided design (CAD) drawings.

Amazon Business also offers benefits for buyers such as the following:

- Multiple buyers within an organization can create business accounts and share payment methods and shipping addresses.

- Promotions from multiple sellers are displayed on one product page, making it easier to compare pricing and vendor ratings from Amazon.

- Buyers can view other buyers' product reviews.

- Amazon Business integrates with buyers' procurement systems, allowing them to put Amazon on their procurement software's list of authorized sellers.

- Amazon Business provides an analytics dashboard because customers wanted more visibility into their spending. The dashboard provides businesses the ability to view purchasing activity at the individual, purchasing group, or type of spend level. These insights also allow customers to adhere to compliance policies.

- Amazon Business has a seller credential program that allows third-party sellers to feature and display one or more of 18 nationally recognized diversity, ownership, and quality credentials. These credentials include small, minority-owned, women-owned, or veteran-owned businesses, which gives customers additional information on which to base their purchasing decisions.

Wholesalers take Amazon's threat seriously. The wholesale industry in the United States is over twice the size of the retail industry. In 2018, wholesale sales totaled more than $10 trillion, compared with some $5.3 trillion for retail sales. While the wholesale industry is larger than retail, the companies themselves tend to be smaller. Most of America's 35,000 distributors are regional, family-run businesses. Typical yearly sales are under $50 million and only 160 of these businesses report annual sales exceeding $1 billion. In contrast, Amazon reported some $233 billion in revenue in 2018, selling goods in both the B2C and B2B marketplaces. The average wholesaler offers approximately 50,000 products online, compared to Amazon Business's hundreds of millions of products.

Amazon Business is competitive even in niche markets. Take scientific equipment as an example. Items such as centrifuges and Bunsen burners are usually offered only by specialty distributors. However, customers can get one with the click of a mouse through Amazon Business. Few specialty distributors can compete with Amazon's huge product list, its easy-to-use website, two-day delivery, physical infrastructure (fulfillment centers in the United States), and information technology infrastructure (e.g., Amazon Web Services).

To acquire and maintain competitive advantage, Amazon Business keeps items that may not sell quickly, to avoid stockouts that plague other distributors of specialty items. Industry analysts estimate that Amazon has on hand more than half the inventory that it offers on the website at any point.

B2B has very small margins, typically 2 to 4 percent. Amazon's size allows it to make money through high volumes. It achieves these high volumes through—what else?—beating competitors' prices by about 25 percent on common products, according to a Boston Consulting Group (**www.bcg.com**) report.

Despite its success, Amazon Business does have competition. Consider Grainger (**www.grainger.com**), in business since 1927, which captures about 6 percent of the entire U.S. B2B market. The company, which sells tools for maintenance and repair, now operates about 600 regional sales locations and 33 warehouses. The company recorded $11.2 billion in total revenue in 2018 and realized almost 60 percent of its 2018 total revenue, via its e-commerce channels. In 2019, the firm's CEO stated that he expected electronic commerce to eventually account for 80 percent of Grainger's sales.

One area that Amazon Business may not be able to penetrate is the close partnerships that some distributors have with institutional clients. For example, medical supplier Cardinal Health (**www.cardinalhealth.com**) has taken control of the entire supply chain at the Nebraska Medical Center. Cardinal handles everything from truck to patient. It orders products from suppliers, tracks product distribution, handles loading dockworkers, and deals with supplier invoicing.

The challenge confronting the nation's 35,000 wholesalers and distributors is to compete with Amazon Business. Industry analysts identify two possibilities:

1. Provide value-added, personalized services to customers. For example, Valin Corporation (**www.valinonline.com**) has specialized in the oil and gas sector, dispatching engineers to oilfields to help deploy the company's products that manage output at surface oil wells.

2. Go into areas that the e-tailer may not be interested in, such as specialized business environments. For example, will Amazon want to sell oxygen tanks or soda pumps? Furthermore, Amazon might not want to manage products that are dangerous or exotic, such as dentists' chairs, or that require specialists.

Sources: Compiled from A. Moazed and N. Johnson, "Amazon Business Is a Top B2B Distributor—Now What?" *Modern Distribution Management*, June 25, 2018; A. Moazed and N. Johnson, "Amazon's B2B Marketplace Advantage," *Modern Distribution Management*, June 28, 2018; P. Demery, "Q&A: Inside Amazon Business with Martin Rohde," *Digital Commerce 360*, May 2, 2018; "Why Amazon Business Targets B2B eCommerce's 'Tail Spend,'" PYMNTS.com, May 1, 2018; J. Carter, "B2B E-Commerce Trends to Take Notice of in 2018," *Forbes*, February 15, 2018; D. Davis, "Amazon Business Helps Buyers Beat Their Negotiated Supplier Prices," *B2B E-Commerce World*, June 7, 2016; P. Demery, "Amazon's Billion-Dollar B2B Portal Is Growing Rapidly," *B2B E-Commerce World*, May 4, 2016; E. Smith, "Can Amazon 'Uber' Distributors?" *Modern Distribution Management*, June 17, 2015; E. Smith, "Recommended Reading: Amazon Business Open to Distributors," *Modern Distribution Management*, June 9, 2015; D. Buss, "New Amazon Business Marketplace Goes after B2B Dollars," *Brand Channel*, May 1, 2015; E. Smith, "Amazon Reinvents B2B Model," *Modern Distribution Management*, April 29, 2015; S. Soper, "Amazon Business Aims for $1 Trillion Corporate-Spending Market," *BloombergBusiness*, April 28, 2015; P. Demery, "Say Hello To Amazon Business, Good-Bye to AmazonSupply," *Internet Retailer*, April 28, 2015; C. O'Connor, "Amazon Launches Amazon Business Marketplace, Will Close AmazonSupply," *Forbes*, April 28, 2015; C. O'Connor, "Amazon's Wholesale Slaughter: Jeff Bezos' $8 Trillion B2B Bet," *Forbes*, May 7, 2014; J. Hans, "Q&A: How Amazon Could Change 'B2B,'" *Manufacturing.net*, February 3, 2014; and www.amazon.com/business, www.grainger.com, accessed July 13, 2019.

Questions

1. Consider Tulsa Community College (**www.tulsacc.edu**), which is using Amazon Business to order test tubes, basketballs, office supplies, and other goods instead of having employees buy them from local retailers or specialty sellers. The daily needs of the college's 15,000 students translate into about $10,000 of orders per month.

   What is the impact of Amazon Business on local wholesalers and retailers in Tulsa?

   How could local businesses in Tulsa compete with Amazon Business?

2. Provide other methods for wholesalers to compete with Amazon Business.

Before you go on . . .

1. Briefly differentiate between the sell-side marketplace and the buy-side marketplace.
2. Briefly differentiate among vertical exchanges, horizontal exchanges, and functional exchanges.

7.4 | Ethical and Legal Issues in E-Business

Technological innovation often forces a society to reexamine and modify its ethical standards. In many cases, the new standards are incorporated into law. In this section, you will learn about two important ethical considerations—privacy and job loss—as well as various legal issues arising from the practice of e-business.

Ethical Issues

Many of the ethical and global issues related to IT also apply to e-business. Here, you will learn about two basic issues: privacy and job loss.

By making it easier to store and transfer personal information, e-business presents some threats to privacy. To begin with, most electronic payment systems know who the buyers are. It may be necessary, then, to protect the buyers' identities. Businesses frequently use encryption to provide this protection.

Another major privacy issue is tracking. For example, individuals' activities on the Internet can be tracked by cookies (discussed in Chapter 4). Cookies store your tracking history on your personal computer's hard drive, and anytime you revisit a certain website, the server recognizes the cookie. In response, antivirus software packages routinely search for potentially harmful cookies.

In addition to compromising individual privacy, the use of EC may eliminate the need for some of a company's employees, as well as brokers and agents. The manner in which these unneeded workers, especially employees, are treated can raise ethical issues: How should the company handle the layoffs? Should companies be required to retrain employees for new positions? If not, how should the company compensate or otherwise assist the displaced workers?

Legal and Ethical Issues Specific to E-Commerce

Many legal issues are related specifically to e-commerce. A business environment in which buyers and sellers do not know one another and cannot even see one another creates opportunities for dishonest people to commit fraud and other crimes. These illegal actions have ranged from creating a virtual bank that disappeared along with the investors' deposits to manipulating stock prices on the Internet. Unfortunately, fraudulent activities on the Internet are increasing.

Fraud on the Internet. Internet fraud has grown even faster than Internet use itself. In one case, stock promoters falsely spread positive rumors about the prospects of the companies they touted in order to boost the stock price. In other cases, the information provided might have been true, but the promoters did not disclose that they were paid to talk up the companies. Stock promoters specifically target small investors who are lured by the promise of fast profits.

FIN Stocks are only one of many areas in which swindlers are active. Auctions are especially conducive to fraud, by both sellers and buyers. Other types of fraud include selling bogus investments, setting up phantom business opportunities, and fraudulent affiliate marketing (see IT's About Business 7.4).

The U.S. Federal Trade Commission (FTC) (**www.ftc.gov**) regularly publishes examples of scams that are most likely to be spread by e-mail or to be found on the Web. Next, you will see some ways in which consumers and sellers can protect themselves from online fraud.

Tips for safe electronic shopping:

- Look for reliable brand names at sites such as Walmart Online, Disney Online, and Amazon. Before purchasing, make sure that the site is authentic by entering the site directly and not from an unverified link.

IT's About Business 7.4

Fraudulent Affiliate Marketing

`MIS` `MKT`

New forms of media have always been hijacked by misleading advertising. For instance, 19th-century American newspapers were funded in part by dishonest patent medicine ads. Within days of Abraham Lincoln's inauguration, the makers of Bellingham's Onguent placed ads claiming that the president used their product to grow his whiskers.

Current scams include Enhance Mind IQ, or Elon's Smart Pills as they were called in a 2018 Facebook ad falsely suggesting that Elon Musk had talked about the pills positively on *60 Minutes*. The checkout page said the pills were free, though buyers still had to submit a credit card number. Victims posted online reviews complaining of the subsequent recurring $89-per-month charges. These scams often involve fraudulent affiliate marketing efforts.

Affiliate marketing involves a merchant paying a commission to other online entities, known as affiliates, for referring new business to the merchant's website. Affiliates are paid only when their marketing efforts actually result in a transaction, such as a customer registration, a completed lead form, a new free trial user, a new newsletter subscriber, or product sale.

Affiliates do promote legitimate businesses, such as Amazon.com and eBay, but they are also behind many of the misleading and fraudulent ads that appear on Facebook, Instagram, Twitter, Google, and the rest of the Internet. *Affiliate fraud* refers to false or unscrupulous activity conducted to generate commissions from an affiliate marketing program. Consider this example:

A manufacturer of a fake nutritional supplement wants to sell it and does not care how the sales actually take place. The vendor approaches an affiliate network and offers to pay a commission per customer sign-up. The network spreads the word to affiliates, who design often-misleading ads and pay to place them on various websites in hopes of earning commissions. The affiliates take the risk, paying to run ads without knowing if they will work. However, if even a small percentage of the people who see the ads become buyers, the profits can be substantial. Let's take a closer look at fraudulent affiliate marketing on Facebook.

The social media giant has revolutionized fraudulent affiliate marketing because the social media giant has powerful tools that analyze its vast amount of user data. Affiliates once had to guess what kind of person might fall for their ads, targeting users by age, geography, or interests. Today, Facebook does the targeting for them and affiliates contend that they do not need to identify "suckers" themselves because Facebook's targeting algorithms do so automatically.

Facebook tracks who clicks on ads as well as who buys the products, then starts targeting others whom its algorithms predict should be shown the ads because they are likely to buy. Affiliates have described watching their ad campaigns lose money for a few days as Facebook gathers data through trial and error, and then seeing sales rapidly increase.

A software program called Voluum enables affiliates to track their campaigns and defeat the ad networks' defenses. The software can track marketing campaigns across multiple platforms, such as Facebook, Google, Twitter, and other websites. Voluum enables affiliates to tailor the content they deliver according to a number of factors, including the location or IP address associated with a user. The feature is useful for ad targeting—for example, showing Spanish speakers a message in their native language. Voluum's developer estimates that users of his tracking software place some $400 million worth of ads per year on Facebook and an additional $1.3 billion on other websites.

Facebook must police a $40 billion annual ad platform that malicious players constantly try to subvert. Facebook reviewers examine ads that users or Facebook algorithms have flagged as questionable and ban accounts that break the rules. However, Voluum makes it easy for affiliates to identify the addresses of Facebook's ad reviewers and program campaigns to show them, and only them, legitimate content. This process is called cloaking. Interestingly, Google banned Voluum based on cloaking concerns but Facebook has not.

Affiliates who are caught and banned can easily circumvent this problem. They simply open new Facebook accounts under different names. Some affiliates buy clean profiles from "farmers." Others rent accounts from strangers or make deals with underhanded advertising agencies to find other solutions.

In August 2018, Facebook announced that it would begin using artificial intelligence to disrupt cloaking. The social media network is also adding 1,000 people to its ad review team.

Sources: Compiled from M. Bain, "Tips to Avoid Falling for Scam Ads on Facebook, According to Facebook," *Quartzy*, June 12, 2018; O. Rudgard, "Martin Lewis to Sue Facebook over Fake Ads which Scam People out of Thousands," *The Telegraph*, April 23, 2018; Z. Faux, "How Facebook Helps Shady Advertisers Pollute the Internet," *Bloomberg Businessweek*, April 2, 2018; M. Mirreh, "Industry Responds as Bloomberg Calls Whole Affiliate Industry 'Shady'," *Inside Performance Marketing*, March 29, 2018; J. Constine, "Facebook Bans 'Cloaking' of Spam Sites that Fool Filters," *TechCrunch*, August 9, 2017; J. Vanian, "What Is Cloaking and Why Is Facebook so Upset about It?" *Fortune*, August 9, 2017; B. D'Amico, "What Is Affiliate Marketing? The Myth vs. Reality," *Shopify Partners*, May 25, 2017; A. Amatia, "Click Farms and Their Fraudulent Facebook Likes Are Hurting Brands Like Never Before!" *Dazeinfo*, May 28, 2016; and R. Kogan, "The Big, Ugly Affiliate Marketing Scam," *Venture Beat*, August 12, 2013.

Questions

1. As a user, how would you avoid fraudulent marketing schemes?

2. Refer to Chapter 3 and discuss the ethicality of fraudulent affiliate marketing.

- Search any unfamiliar selling site for the company's address and phone and fax numbers. Call up and quiz the employees about the seller.

- Check out the vendor with the local Chamber of Commerce or Better Business Bureau (**www.bbbonline.org**). Look for seals of authenticity such as TRUSTe.

- Investigate how secure the seller's site is by examining the security procedures and by reading the posted privacy policy.

- Examine the money-back guarantees, warranties, and service agreements.

- Compare prices with those in regular stores. Too-low prices are too good to be true and some catch is probably involved.

- Ask friends what they know. Find testimonials and endorsements on community websites and well-known bulletin boards.

- Find out what your rights are in case of a dispute. Consult consumer protection agencies and the National Consumer League's Fraud Center (**www.fraud.org**).

- Check Consumerworld (**www.consumerworld.org**) for a collection of useful resources.

- For many types of products, **www.resellerratings.com** is a useful resource.

Domain Names.   Another legal issue is competition over domain names. Domain names are assigned by central nonprofit organizations that check for conflicts and possible infringement of trademarks. Obviously, companies that sell goods and services over the Internet want customers to be able to find them easily. In general, the closer the domain name matches the company's name, the easier the company is to locate.

A domain name is considered legal when the person or business who owns the name has operated a legitimate business under that name for some time. Companies such as Christian Dior, Nike, Deutsche Bank, and even Microsoft have had to fight or pay to acquire the domain name that corresponds to their company's name. Consider the case of Delta Air Lines. Delta originally could not obtain the Internet domain name delta.com because Delta Faucet had already purchased it. Delta Faucet had been in business under that name since 1954, so it had a legitimate business interest in using the domain name. Delta Air Lines had to settle for delta-airlines.com until it bought the domain name from Delta Faucet. Delta Faucet is now at deltafaucet.com.

Cybersquatting.   *Cybersquatting* refers to the practice of registering or using domain names for the purpose of profiting from the goodwill or the trademark that belongs to someone else. The Anti-Cybersquatting Consumer Protection Act (1999) permits trademark owners in the United States to sue for damages in such cases.

However, some practices that could be considered cybersquatting are not illegal, although they may well be unethical. Perhaps the more common of these practices is "domain tasting." Domain tasting lets registrars profit from the complex money trail of pay-per-click advertising. The practice can be traced back to the policies of the organization responsible for regulating Web names, the Internet Corporation for Assigned Names and Numbers (ICANN) (**www.icann.org**). In 2000, ICANN established the five-day "Add Grace Period" during which a company or person can claim a domain name and then return it for a full refund of the registry fee. ICANN implemented this policy to allow someone who mistyped a domain to return it without cost. In some cases, companies engage in cybersquatting by registering domain names that are very similar to their competitors' domain names in order to generate traffic from people who misspell Web addresses.

Domain tasters exploit this policy by claiming Internet domains for five days at no cost. These domain names frequently resemble those of prominent companies and organizations. The tasters then jam these domains full of advertisements that come from Yahoo! and Google. Because this process involves zero risk and 100 percent profit margins, domain tasters register millions of domain names every day—some of them over and over again. Experts estimate that registrants ultimately purchase less than 2 percent of the sites they sample. In the vast majority of cases, they use the domain names for only a few days to generate quick profits.

FIN **ACCT** **Taxes and Other Fees.**   In offline sales, most states and localities tax business transactions that are conducted within their jurisdiction. The most obvious example is sales taxes. Federal, state, and local authorities are working on taxation policy for e-business. This problem is particularly complex for interstate and international e-commerce. For example, some people claim that the state in which the *seller* is located deserves the entire sales tax (in some countries, it is a value-added tax [VAT]). Others contend that the state in which the *server* is located should also receive some of the tax revenues.

In addition to the sales tax, there is a question about where—and in some cases, whether—electronic sellers should pay business license taxes, franchise fees, gross receipts taxes, excise taxes, privilege taxes, and utility taxes. Furthermore, how should tax collection be controlled? Legislative efforts to impose taxes on e-commerce are opposed by an organization named the Internet Freedom Fighters.

Even before electronic commerce over the Internet emerged, the basic law in the U.S. was that as long as a retailer did not have a physical presence in the state where the consumer was shopping, that retailer did not have to collect a sales tax. Shoppers were supposed to track such purchases and then pay the taxes owed in their annual tax filings. Few people, however, did this or were even aware of their obligation. The result was that online retailers were able to undercut the prices of their non-Internet (e.g., brick-and-mortar stores) competitors for years.

In December 2013, the U.S. Supreme Court declined to get involved in state efforts to force web retailers such as Amazon to collect sales tax from customers even in places where the companies do not have a physical presence. In light of the court's decision to stay out of the issue, in July 2019 45 states and the District of Columbia had passed legislation requiring online retailers to collect sales taxes from their customers.

Copyright.   Recall from Chapter 4 that intellectual property is protected by copyright laws and cannot be used freely. This point is significant because many people mistakenly believe that once they purchase a piece of software, they have the right to share it with others. In fact, what they have bought is the right to *use* the software, not the right to *distribute* it. That right remains with the copyright holder. Similarly, copying material from websites without permission is a violation of copyright laws. Protecting intellectual property rights in e-commerce is extremely difficult, however, because it involves hundreds of millions of people in 200 countries with differing copyright laws who have access to billions of Web pages.

Before you go on . . .

1. List and explain some ethical issues in EC.
2. Discuss the major legal issues associated with EC.
3. Describe buyer protection and seller protection in EC.

What's in **IT** for me?

ACCT For the Accounting Major

Accounting personnel are involved in several EC activities. Designing the ordering system and its relationship with inventory management requires accounting attention. Billing and payments are also accounting activities, as are determining cost and profit allocation. Replacing paper documents with electronic means will affect many of the accountant's tasks, especially the auditing of EC activities and systems. Finally, building a cost-benefit and cost-justification system to determine which products and services to take online and creating a chargeback system are critical to the success of EC.

FIN For the Finance Major

The worlds of banking, securities and commodities markets, and other financial services are being reengineered because of EC. Online securities trading and its supporting infrastructure are growing more rapidly than any other EC activity. Many innovations already in place are changing the rules of economic and financial incentives for financial analysts and managers. Online banking, for example, does not recognize state boundaries, and it may create a new framework for financing global trades. Public financial information is now accessible in seconds. These innovations will dramatically change the manner in which finance personnel operate.

MKT For the Marketing Major

A major revolution in marketing and sales is taking place because of EC. Perhaps its most obvious feature is the transition from a physical to a virtual marketplace. Equally important, however, is the radical transformation to one-on-one advertising and sales and to customized and interactive marketing. Marketing channels are being combined, eliminated, or re-created. The EC revolution is creating new products and markets and significantly altering existing ones. Digitization of products and services also has implications for marketing and sales. The direct producer-to-consumer channel is expanding rapidly and is fundamentally changing the nature of customer service. As the battle for customers intensifies, marketing and sales personnel are becoming the most critical success factor in many organizations. Online marketing can be a blessing to one company and a curse to another.

POM For the Production/Operations Management Major

EC is changing the manufacturing system from product-push mass production to order-pull mass customization. This change requires a robust supply chain, information support, and reengineering of processes that involve suppliers and other business partners. Suppliers can use extranets to monitor and replenish inventories without the need for constant reorders. The Internet and intranets also help reduce cycle times. Many production/operations problems that have persisted for years, such as complex scheduling and excess inventories, are being solved rapidly with the use of Web technologies. Companies can now use external and internal networks to find and manage manufacturing operations in other countries much more easily. Also, the Web is reengineering procurement by helping companies conduct electronic bids for parts and subassemblies, thus reducing cost. All in all, the job of the progressive production/operations manager is closely tied in with e-commerce.

HRM For the Human Resource Management Major

HR majors need to understand the new labor markets and the impacts of EC on old labor markets. Also, the HR department may use EC tools for such functions as procuring office supplies. Moreover, becoming knowledgeable about new government online initiatives and online training is critical. HR personnel must also become familiar with the major legal issues related to EC and employment.

MIS For the MIS Major

The MIS function is responsible for providing the information technology infrastructure necessary for electronic commerce to function. In particular, this infrastructure includes the company's networks, intranets, and extranets. The MIS function is also responsible for ensuring that electronic commerce transactions are secure.

Summary

7.1 Describe the eight common types of electronic commerce.

In *business-to-consumer* (B2C) electronic commerce, the sellers are organizations and the buyers are individuals.

In *business-to-business* (B2B) electronic commerce, the sellers and the buyers are businesses.

In *consumer-to-consumer* (C2C) electronic commerce, an individual sells products or services to other individuals.

In *business-to-employee* (B2E) electronic commerce, an organization uses EC internally to provide information and services to its employees.

E-government is the use of Internet technology in general and e-commerce in particular to deliver information and public services to citizens (called government-to-citizen or G2C EC) and business partners and suppliers (called government-to-business or G2B EC).

Mobile commerce refers to e-commerce that is conducted entirely in a wireless environment.

Social commerce refers to the delivery of electronic commerce activities and transactions through social computing.

Conversational commerce refers to electronic commerce using messaging and chat apps to offer a daily choice, often personalized, of a meal, product, or service.

We leave the examples of each type to you.

7.2 Describe the various online services of business-to-consumer (B2C) commerce, along with specific examples of each.

Fintech is an industry composed of companies that use technology to compete in the marketplace with traditional financial institutions and intermediaries in the delivery of financial services, which include banking, insurance, real estate, and investing.

Online securities trading involves buying and selling securities over the Web.

Online job matching over the Web offers a promising environment for job seekers and for companies searching for hard-to-find employees. Thousands of companies and government agencies advertise available positions, accept resumes, and take applications on the Internet.

Online travel services allow you to purchase airline tickets, reserve hotel rooms, and rent cars. Most sites also offer a fare-tracker feature that sends you e-mail messages about low-cost flights. The Internet is an ideal place to economically plan, explore, and arrange almost any trip.

Online advertising over the Web makes the advertising process media-rich, dynamic, and interactive.

We leave the examples to you.

7.3 Describe the three business models for business-to-business electronic commerce.

In the *sell-side marketplace* model, organizations attempt to sell their products or services to other organizations electronically from their own private e-marketplace website or from a third-party website. Sellers such as Dell Computer (**www.dellauction.com**) use sell-side auctions extensively. In addition to auctions from their own websites, organizations can use third-party auction sites, such as eBay, to liquidate items.

The *buy-side marketplace* is a model in which organizations attempt to buy needed products or services from other organizations electronically.

E-marketplaces, in which there are many sellers and many buyers, are called *public exchanges,* or just exchanges. Public exchanges are open to all business organizations. They are frequently owned and operated by a third party. There are three basic types of public exchanges: vertical, horizontal, and functional. *Vertical exchanges* connect buyers and sellers in a given industry. *Horizontal exchanges* connect buyers and sellers across many industries. In *functional exchanges,* needed services such as temporary help or extra office space are traded on an as-needed basis.

7.4 Discuss the ethical and legal issues related to electronic commerce, along with examples.

E-business presents some threats to privacy. First, most electronic payment systems know who the buyers are. It may be necessary, then, to protect the buyers' identities with encryption. Another major privacy issue is tracking, through which individuals' activities on the Internet can be tracked by cookies.

The use of EC may eliminate the need for some of a company's employees, as well as brokers and agents. The manner in which these unneeded workers, especially employees, are treated can raise ethical issues: How should the company handle the layoffs? Should companies be required to retrain employees for new positions? If not, how should the company compensate or otherwise assist the displaced workers?

We leave the examples up to you.

Chapter Glossary

auction A competitive process in which either a seller solicits consecutive bids from buyers or a buyer solicits bids from sellers, and prices are determined dynamically by competitive bidding.

brick-and-mortar organizations Organizations in which the product, the process, and the delivery agent are all physical.

business model The method by which a company generates revenue to sustain itself.

buy-side marketplace B2B model in which organizations buy needed products or services from other organizations electronically, often through a reverse auction.

channel conflict The alienation of existing distributors when a company decides to sell to customers directly online.

chatbots (also known as *bots*) Interactive software programs that can conduct simple conversations with customers or other bots.

clicks-and-mortar organizations Organizations that do business in both the physical and digital dimensions.

disintermediation Elimination of intermediaries in electronic commerce.

electronic business (e-business) A broader definition of electronic commerce, including buying and selling of goods and services, and servicing customers, collaborating with business partners, conducting e-learning, and conducting electronic transactions within an organization.

electronic commerce (EC or e-commerce) The process of buying, selling, transferring, or exchanging products, services, or information through computer networks, including the Internet.

electronic mall A collection of individual shops under one Internet address; also known as a *cybermall* or an *e-mall*.

electronic marketplace A virtual market space on the Web where many buyers and many sellers conduct electronic business activities.

electronic payment mechanisms Computer-based systems that allow customers to pay for goods and services electronically, rather than writing a check or using cash.

electronic retailing (e-tailing) The direct sale of products and services through storefronts or electronic malls, usually designed around an electronic catalog format and auctions.

electronic storefront The website of a single company, with its own Internet address, at which orders can be placed.

e-procurement Purchasing by using electronic support.

exchanges see public exchanges

Fintech An industry composed of companies that use technology to compete in the marketplace with traditional financial institutions and intermediaries in the delivery of financial services, which include banking, insurance, real estate, and investing.

forward auctions Auctions that sellers use as a selling channel to many potential buyers; the highest bidder wins the items.

group purchasing The aggregation of purchasing orders from many buyers so that a volume discount can be obtained.

multichanneling A process in which a company integrates its online and offline channels.

public exchanges (or exchanges) Electronic marketplaces in which there are many sellers and many buyers, and entry is open to all; frequently owned and operated by a third party.

reverse auctions Auctions in which one buyer, usually an organization, seeks to buy a product or a service, and suppliers submit bids; the lowest bidder wins.

sell-side marketplace B2B model in which organizations sell to other organizations from their own private e-marketplace or from a third-party site.

spamming Indiscriminate distribution of e-mail without the recipient's permission.

virtual (or pure play) organizations Organizations in which the product, the process, and the delivery agent are all digital.

Discussion Questions

1. Discuss the major limitations of e-commerce. Which of these limitations are likely to disappear? Why?

2. Discuss the reasons for having multiple EC business models.

3. Distinguish between business-to-business forward auctions and buyers' bids for RFQs.

4. Discuss the benefits to sellers and buyers of a B2B exchange.

5. What are the major benefits of G2C electronic commerce?

6. Discuss the various ways to pay online in B2C. Which method(s) would you prefer and why?

7. Why is order fulfillment in B2C considered difficult?

8. Discuss the reasons for EC failures.

9. Should Mr. Coffee sell coffeemakers online? (*Hint:* Take a look at the discussion of channel conflict in this chapter.)

10. In some cases, individuals engage in cybersquatting so that they can sell the domain names to companies expensively. In other cases, companies engage in cybersquatting by registering domain names that are very similar to their competitors' domain names in order to generate traffic from people who misspell Web addresses. Discuss each practice in regard to its ethical nature and legality. Is there a difference between the two practices? Support your answer.

11. Do you think information technology has made it easier to do business? Or has it only raised the bar on what is required to be able to do business in the 21st century? Support your answer with specific examples.

12. With the rise of electronic commerce, what do you think will happen to those without computer skills, Internet access, computers, smartphones, and tablets? Will they be able to survive and advance by hard work?

Problem-Solving Activities

1. Assume you are interested in buying a car. You can find information about cars at numerous websites. Access five websites for information about new and used cars, financing, and insurance. Decide which car you want to buy. Configure your car by going to the car manufacturer's website. Finally, try to find the car from **www.autobytel.com**. What information is most supportive of your decision-making process? Write a report about your experience.

2. Compare the various electronic payment methods. Specifically, collect information from the vendors cited in this chapter and find additional vendors using Google.com. Pay attention to security level, speed, cost, and convenience.

3. Conduct a study on selling diamonds and gems online. Access such sites as **www.bluenile.com**, **www.diamond.com**, **www.thaigem.com**, **www.tiffany.com**, and **www.jewelryexchange.com**.

   a. What features do these sites use to educate buyers about gemstones?

   b. How do these sites attract buyers?

   c. How do these sites increase customers' trust in online purchasing?

   d. What customer service features do these sites provide?

4. Access **www.nacha.org**. What is Nacha? What is its role? What is the ACH? Who are the key participants in an ACH e-payment? Describe the "pilot" projects currently under way at ACH.

5. Access **www.espn.com**. Identify at least five different ways the site generates revenue.

6. Access **www.queendom.com**. Examine its offerings and try some of them. What type of electronic commerce is this? How does this website generate revenue?

7. Access **www.mealplanmap.com**. Prepare a list of all the services the company provides. Identify its revenue model.

8. Access **www.theknot.com**. Identify the site's revenue sources.

9. Access **www.mint.com**. Identify the site's revenue model. What are the risks of giving this website your credit and debit card numbers, as well as your bank account number?

10. Enter **www.alibaba.com**. Identify the site's capabilities. Look at the site's private trading room. Write a report. How can such a site help a person who is making a purchase?

11. Enter **www.grubhub.com**. Explore the site. Why is the site so successful? Could you start a competing site? Why or why not?

12. Enter **www.dell.com**, go to "Desktops," and configure a system. Register to "My Cart" (no obligation). What calculators are used there? What are the advantages of this process as compared with buying a computer in a physical store? What are the disadvantages?

13. Enter **www.checkfree.com** and **www.lmlpayment.com** to identify their services. Prepare a report.

14. Access various travel sites such as **www.travelocity.com**, **www.orbitz.com**, **www.expedia.com**, **www.kayak.com**, and **www.pinpoint.com**. Compare these websites for ease of use and usefulness. Note differences among the sites. If you ask each site for the itinerary, which one gives you the best information and the best deals?

Closing Case

Walmart versus Amazon

`POM` `MKT` `MIS`

Today, consumers have many options for shopping. They can shop at brick-and-mortar retail stores, they can shop online and receive home deliveries, or they can shop online and then pick up their purchases at a store, thus avoiding checkout lines. These options helped to generate $5.3 trillion in retail sales in the United States in 2018.

Despite this volume of commerce, traditional brick-and-mortar retailers are closing stores because increasing numbers of consumers are shopping online. From 2000 until 2018, online retail sales increased from 1 percent of total retail sales to 14 percent.

One of the main drivers of the rapid growth of e-commerce is Amazon (**www.amazon.com**). Founded in 1994, Amazon is the largest e-commerce retailer (e-tailer) in the world as measured by both total sales and market capitalization. The company's impact on the retail sector has been so significant that industry analysts have coined the term the *Amazon Effect*, which is the ongoing disruption of the retail marketplace, including both online and traditional brick-and-mortar retailers.

Founded in 1962, Walmart (**www.walmart.com**) is the largest traditional brick-and-mortar retailer in the world. The company has 11,700 stores—including 4,700 in the United States—plus 6,200 trucks, and it attracts 265 million weekly shoppers in 27 countries and ecommerce websites in 10 countries. In addition, Walmart is the third-largest online retailer, behind Amazon and eBay.

As Walmart expands its online presence, it needs to develop a strategy to compete against Amazon. Therefore, the company is making huge efforts to integrate its e-commerce operations with its global network of stores.

This case addresses the competition between the largest traditional brick-and-mortar retailer in the world and the largest e-commerce retailer in the world. First, we look at Walmart, and then we consider Amazon.

Walmart

Walmart executives have long underestimated the convenience of shopping online from anywhere and at any time. As a result, since the beginning of the e-commerce era, Walmart has not enjoyed success in this area. In 2000, the firm's e-commerce sales totaled only $25 million. In addition, $100 million in clothes and other inventory were left over after that holiday season.

`MIS` **Rebuilding Walmart.com.** In 2012, Walmart began to emphasize its global Internet operation. The retailer rebuilt the outdated technology infrastructure that supported Walmart.com, introduced smartphone apps, and constructed six highly automated fulfillment centers. These centers enabled the company to ship its most popular products anywhere in the United States within two days by ground or one day by air, down from one week in 2012. Walmart's U.S. e-commerce revenue (including Sam's Club and Jet.com) approached $20 billion in 2018, a 40 percent increase over 2017.

In May 2018, Walmart overhauled its website. The new site is highly personalized with features designed to make it easier to reorder items, check the status on orders, explore services at nearby Walmart stores, and discover products that are trending locally.

In-store versus online pricing.   As e-commerce sales were increasing, Walmart faced internal struggles. The first problem involved prices. Amazon typically sets prices using algorithms that scan the Web to monitor and match the lowest price they find. One result of this policy is that prices can change constantly on the Amazon website.

In contrast, Walmart's business model has always set a consistent "everyday low price" in its stores. This strategy caused problems on the retailer's website when Walmart followed Amazon's business model and used pricing algorithms. As a result, online prices could drop below the store price. When that situation occurred, Walmart executives worried that Walmart.com would take customers away from their stores. The executives noted that in-store sales account for more than 97 percent of total Walmart sales.

Walmart then began charging higher prices online than in its stores in an effort to reduce shipping costs and drive shoppers to its stores. Some products on Walmart.com listed an online price and in-store price so customers would see the difference. In the fall of 2018, Walmart discontinued this strategy as a result of customer confusion and dissatisfaction.

In September 2018, Walmart began telling online shoppers that some products in its warehouses were out of stock to avoid the extra expenses associated with shipping products from more distant warehouses. Walmart does recommend similar products that are in stock in nearby warehouses.

`POM` `MKT` **Walmart's marketplace strategy.**   Another internal struggle at Walmart involved Amazon's e-commerce marketplace strategy, which allows external, third-party vendors to sell their products on Amazon's website. Significantly, this strategy generates half of Amazon's sales.

Walmart was hesitant to employ this strategy because the retailer was accustomed to dominating its relationships with its vendors and to displaying its entire product assortment in its stores. Furthermore, Walmart did not have the necessary technology infrastructure to support a large marketplace on Walmart.com.

Walmart made the strategic decision for Walmart.com to support this marketplace strategy. While the retailer continued to build supercenters, the company improved the information technology infrastructure for Walmart.com and increased the online selection of products on the website. One strategy that Walmart employed to increase the number of products it offered online was through acquisitions, which we discuss in the next section. The other tactic was to implement the marketplace strategy, as you can see in Walmart's negotiation with Lord & Taylor.

In October 2017, Walmart and Lord & Taylor (**www.lordandtaylor.com**) began talks to provide the department store with its own space on Walmart.com. Lord & Taylor's website would continue to operate, and the department store would retain control of its inventory and order fulfillment on both websites.

Customers would be able to pick up and return Lord & Taylor orders placed through either channel at Walmart stores.

Lord & Taylor's website attracted fewer than 1 million active users in the United States between February and July 2017. In contrast, Walmart.com had approximately 79 million active users during that period. Therefore, a place on Walmart.com certainly enabled Lord & Taylor to reach many more customers. In May 2018, Lord & Taylor debuted on Walmart.com, offering more than 125 brands.

This relationship was part of a larger plan to turn Walmart.com into an online mall. Walmart plans to house a number of retailers on its website, including previous acquisitions. Although Walmart offers more than 40 million products in its marketplace on Walmart.com, Amazon offers 400 million.

POM **MKT** **MIS** **Acquisitions and Partnerships.** Walmart began to acquire some companies, and partner with others, that would help the retailer in its e-commerce efforts. In July 2016, the retailer and JD.com, China's largest e-commerce company by revenue, announced a strategic alliance covering both online and offline retail. The alliance included several initiatives:

- Sam's Club China opened a flagship store on JD.com. The store offers same- and next-day delivery through JD.com's nationwide warehousing and delivery network, which serves a population of 600 million consumers.

- Walmart and JD.com are leveraging their supply chains to increase the product selection for customers across China, including broadening the range of imported products.

- Walmart's China stores are listed as a preferred retailer on JD.com.

- In August, 2018 Walmart and JD.com co-invested $500 million in Chinese online grocery delivery company, Dada-JD Daojia.

In August 2016, Walmart acquired 15-month-old electronic commerce company Jet.com (Jet; **www.jet.com**) for $3.4 billion in cash and stock. Walmart is keeping Jet as a separate brand, but uses Jet's bulk ordering strategy to grow its e-commerce business more rapidly and to reach more Millennial customers. Jet also appeals to a more affluent shopper than Walmart, with customers who are more likely to have annual incomes greater than $150,000, according to data from the NPD Group (**www.npd.com**).

Then, in January 2017, Walmart acquired Shoes.com (**www.shoes.com**), a competitor of Amazon-owned Zappos (**www.zappos.com**), for $70 million. Shoes.com, founded in 1999, was one of the first companies to sell shoes online. The company remained an independent Walmart subsidiary, and their CEO, Mike Sorabella, retained his position. In February, Walmart acquired outdoor apparel seller MooseJaw (**www.moosejaw.com**) for $51 million. The following month, it purchased fashion retailer ModCloth (**www.modcloth.com**) for $45 million. All three companies remain as independent Walmart subsidiaries with their products being sold on Walmart.com. Their founders are deputies to Walmart.com CEO Marc Lore.

In June 2017, Walmart purchased Bonobos (**www.bonobos.com**), a menswear website, for $310 million. Bonobos also operates dozens of brick-and-mortar stores as well as boutiques in Nordstrom department stores. The company features two competitive advantages: generous shipping and return policies and outstanding customer service employees.

In August 2017, Walmart and Google announced a partnership in which Google began offering Walmart products to people who shop on Google Express, the firm's online shopping mall. It was the first time that Walmart made its products available online in the United States outside of Walmart.com.

In October 2017, Walmart acquired Parcel (**www.fromparcel.com**), a small package delivery company in New York City. Parcel specializes in getting fresh and perishable food to homes in the city. Walmart acquired Parcel in 2017 and it plans to offer same day delivery to more than half of the US by the end of 2019.

In January 2018, Walmart partnered with Rakuten, Japan's e-commerce leader with 93 million registered users, which allowed Walmart to sell digital books on its website for the first time. The partnership also enabled Walmart to expand its online grocery business in Japan.

In May 2018, Walmart purchased 77 percent of Indian e-commerce service Flipkart for $16 billion. India, home to over 400 million Millenials, is the world's fastest-growing major economy. The deal with Walmart provided Flipkart the expertise of operating brick-and-mortar stores as well as expertise in supply chain management. Analysts note, however, that it will cost Walmart billions of dollars to turn Flipkart into a profitable business.

Also in May, 2018 Walmart unveiled Jetblack, a concierge shopping service for busy urban families. For $50 per month, members can text their requests and receive same-day delivery from Walmart, Jet, and other retailers such as Saks and Sephora with gift wrapping included.

In September 2018. Walmart partnered with on-demand home services company Handy (**www.handy.com**) to offer professional support for indoor projects on Walmart.com. The retailer had previously offered Handy installation services at select stores and is now able to offer the service to a much larger customer base online.

MKT **MIS** **Acquisitions helping Walmart with its e-commerce efforts.** The acquisition of Jet provides benefits to Walmart. Jet has experience with being a distributed marketplace of sellers rather than maintaining its own inventory. Furthermore, Jet collects massive amounts of data, including customer shopping data, the basket size of each order, and the products in each order.

Jet's pricing algorithms are particularly notable. The company offers pricing adjustments to its users to encourage them to buy more items at once and to purchase items that are located in the same distribution center. In that way, the purchases are less expensive for Jet to collect and ship.

As users add items to their virtual shopping cart, Jet uses pricing incentives to encourage them to select additional items. Jet also offers customers pricing options during the checkout process, such as having the user opt out of the ability to return merchandise for free in exchange for a reduced price. The firm also offers users a price incentive to use a debit card rather than a credit card for purchases so that Jet does not have to pay the credit card companies' transaction fees.

In September 2016, Walmart put the CEO of Jet, Marc Lore, in charge of its entire domestic e-commerce operation. Lore's mission is to revitalize Walmart's e-commerce operation to compete with Amazon. Lore quickly ensured that Walmart.com offered product areas that are popular online, including apparel, fresh food, and drugstore items, as well as e-commerce staples such as books, electronics, and toys.

Lore also announced free delivery on Walmart.com for orders of more than $35, a tactic to give customers discounts for buying more products at one time, so that these products can be shipped more efficiently in a single box. (In response, Amazon dropped its free-shipping minimum purchase from $49 to $35 for non-Prime members.)

Lore contends that retailers cannot ship items individually and make money. However, Amazon, with its vast scale and hyperefficient fulfillment centers, is profitable even when consumers order a single product whenever they need one.

In April 2017, Lore introduced a new discount for online shoppers that will be difficult for Amazon to beat. Specifically, Walmart offers a discount to customers who ship purchases to one of Walmart's U.S. stores instead of to a home or to another location. This process is called *ship-to-store*.

While checking out online for a purchase, shoppers are given the option either to ship the item to a store or to have it sent elsewhere. If the shopper chooses to ship the item to a store, then Walmart will offer a discount on eligible items. If the customer chooses to ship the item to his or her home, then the price stays the same and Walmart will deliver it for free. By June 2017, the company had applied the discount to more than 1 million items. However, it offers these discounts only for items that are not already available in stores.

Discounts vary for every product. Generally, larger items have bigger discounts because they cost more to ship. The offer will be difficult for Amazon to match because Amazon has few physical stores.

Lore is eliminating the barriers between the stores and Walmart.com that have caused problems in the past. For example, he is expanding a service called Easy Reorder. Everything customers buy with a credit card at a Walmart store will show up in their online accounts, ready to be replenished with one click.

Lore is also prioritizing groceries. Walmart, the country's leader in this retail category, has allowed customers to order their groceries online and pick them up in person (a process called *click-and-collect*) at some 2,200 Walmart stores since the end of 2018.

Because more than 30 percent of all items purchased online are returned, the process of returning products needs to be as straightforward as possible. Walmart has a store within 10 miles of approximately 90 percent of the population of the United States, so the option of fast in-store product returns is very attractive. Accordingly, in November 2017, Walmart implemented its Mobile Express Returns program that made returns of online and in-store purchases fast and easy. To utilize the program, customers use Walmart's app to obtain a QR code for their returned product before they go to a store. There, they scan the QR code at a dedicated Mobile Express Land inside the Walmart store to immediately receive a refund. Walmart notes that the time required to return an item has decreased from five minutes to 30 seconds.

In August 2018, Walmart began to deploy its new Marketplace Returns program for third-party sellers. Under this program, Walmart's sellers will have access to the retailer's Returns Shipping Service, which lets them take advantage of discounted shipping rates. Furthermore, Walmart.com shoppers will be able to see the return policy of products from third-party sellers, print labels from their Walmart.com accounts, and contact Walmart's customer service representatives. Walmart is also considering letting shoppers return orders from third-party sellers at its stores, giving the retailer a distinct advantage over Amazon.

MIS **Utilization of Cloud Computing.** Walmart constructed six giant server farms to perform cloud computing in-house. The purpose of the retailer's cloud computing initiative is to be able to compete more effectively against Amazon. The initiative has provided several key benefits to Walmart. Cloud computing has enabled Walmart to do the following:

- Significantly increase its online sales much more than wider industry growth levels

- Stay competitive with Amazon on pricing
- Keep tight controls on inventory
- Offer shoppers more customized offers and improved services
- Speed up the process by which customers can return online purchases to local stores by 60 percent

Amazon

Of course, Amazon is not standing still. An estimated 50 percent of all U.S. households subscribe to Amazon Prime (100 million members), according to a report from Consumer Intelligence Research Partners (**www.cirpllc.com**). Furthermore, approximately 48 percent of all online retail sales came through Amazon in 2018. Let's examine several of Amazon's initiatives. Significantly, as Walmart has expanded its online business, most of Amazon's recent moves involved the development of brick-and-mortar retail locations.

Despite Amazon's online retailing success, it has become clear over time that there is much shopping that people prefer to do in person. The most notable example is groceries. Therefore, in August 2017, Amazon bought Whole Foods Market (**www.wholefoodsmarket.com**) for $13.4 billion. Whole Foods is a U.S. supermarket chain that features foods produced without artificial preservatives, colors, flavors, sweeteners, and hydrogenated fats. In July 2019, the chain had 500 physical locations in the United States, Canada, and the United Kingdom.

POM **MKT** There is an important strategic reason behind Amazon's purchase of Whole Foods. Each Whole Foods store represents a prime urban and suburban retail presence and distribution hub for Amazon. Because Americans value consumer convenience extremely highly, Amazon is now in position to seriously enter the food-delivery business, thereby disrupting, for example, Blue Apron (**www.blueapron.com**), GrubHub (**www.grubhub.com**), and other companies in this space.

Following the acquisition, Amazon quickly implemented changes at Whole Foods. Here are some examples:

- The day the acquisition was completed, prices of many Whole Foods products dropped, some by as much as 40 percent.
- Whole Foods announced that Amazon Prime replaced Whole Foods's current loyalty program.
- Amazon added more than 1,000 Whole Foods items to Amazon.com. Furthermore, Whole Foods goods also became available on AmazonFresh, Prime Pantry, and Prime Now. In August 2018, Amazon debuted its click-and-collect service at two Whole Foods locations. Customers had to have AmazonFresh memberships to participate in this service. AmazonFresh is Amazon's grocery delivery service, which costs Prime members an additional $14.99 per month. Amazon has been developing technology for automatically detecting when a customer pulls into the parking lot so their orders can be brought to them more quickly.
- Customers can also have their Amazon.com orders delivered to an Amazon locker inside certain Whole Foods stores until they want to pick them up. Customers can also use these lockers to return Amazon items. Amazon lockers provide customers with a self-service delivery location to pick up and return Amazon items.

Amazon is developing physical stores, as you saw with the firm's purchase of Whole Foods. Although most of the attention has focused on Amazon's grocery store strategies, the company has several other experiments under way.

Amazon is exploring the idea of creating stores to sell furniture and home applications, which are the kinds of products that shoppers are reluctant to buy over the Internet sight unseen. The stores would serve as showcases where people could view the items in person and have them delivered to their homes. Amazon is considering the use of augmented reality (AR) and virtual reality (VR) in these stores. AR and VR would enable customers to see, for example, how couches and stoves would look in their homes.

Amazon is also considering an electronics store, similar to Apple's retail stores. These shops would emphasize Amazon devices and services such as the Echo smarthome speaker and Prime Video stream service.

In January 2017, Amazon opened a convenience store that does not need cashiers, called Amazon Go. The store uses a combination of sensors, cameras, and artificial intelligence to automatically detect the food items that shoppers remove from shelves, so they can leave the store without visiting a cashier. Amazon is expanding Amazon Go nationally. By July 2019 Amazon had opened 11 Amazon Go stores.

Amazon does have competition in this space from San Francisco startup Zippin (**www.getzippin.com**). Furthermore, several companies such as AiFi (**www.aifi.io**), Aipoly (**www.aipoly.com**), and Trigo Vision (**www.trigovision.com**), are developing the technology needed to power cashierless stores.

Interestingly, in May 2018, Walmart ended its Scan & Go program, which was Walmart's attempt at cashierless checkout. The program allowed customers to scan their items with a smartphone app and skip the checkout line by paying their bill on the app and showing their digital receipt to a store greeter on the way out.

In addition to expanding its U.S. operations, Amazon is targeting India for new brick-and-mortar grocery stores. India is a vast market that remains dominated by traditional street bazaars, where shoppers go from stall to stall haggling over prices.

Amazon is also building brick-and-mortar bookstores. The company's flagship bookstore, Amazon Books in Seattle, Washington, opened in November 2015. By July 2019, Amazon had opened 17 bookstores.

Amazon has been moving into the food and beverage space. In June 2016, the company launched its own brand of coffee, called Happy Belly. This launch put Amazon in direct competition with Starbucks. As of 2019, there were some 8,575 company-owned Starbucks stores and another 6,031 licensed stores (kiosks, and others).

MKT In June 2017, Amazon announced a new program called Prime Wardrobe that allows customers to order clothing, from 3 to 15 items at a time, without actually buying it. Amazon will charge customers only for the items they keep. Customers can return the items that they do not want within seven days in a resealable box with the preprinted shipping label that the order came in. Prime Wardrobe allows customers to try on more than 1 million items of clothing, accessories, and shoes from brands including Calvin Klein, Levi's, Adidas, Hugo Boss, and Lacoste.

Prime Wardrobe is an option only for members of Amazon Prime. The service enables Amazon to subtly discourage clothing returns. The company takes 10 percent off the purchase price of an order for customers who keep 3 to 4 items and 20 percent off for customers who keep 5 or more items. Amazon's service puts it in direct competition with Stitch Fix (see the opening case in Chapter 12).

In October 2017, Amazon entered the field of private-label sportswear. The online giant bought small amounts of products from two Taiwanese activewear manufacturers as part of a trial. Makalot Industrial Company (**www.makalot.com.tw**) produces clothing for Gap, Uniqlo, and Kohl's, and Eclat Textile Company (**www.eclat.com.tw**) manufactures clothing for Nike, Lululemon Athletica, and Under Armour.

In June 2018, Amazon purchased PillPack, an online pharmacy that lets users buy medications in premade doses, for just under $1 billion. PillPack has a license to operate in all 50 states in the United States. The firm's PharmacyOS is a platform that helps manage patient data and figure out how to balance medications together in safe doses for its customers.

Amazon's purchase emphasizes how the e-tailing giant hopes to have a larger role in health care, a $4 trillion sector in the U.S. economy. Amazon views health care as a key frontier in its bid to be the go-to place for anything a consumer might want or need in health care.

Another interesting initiative is Amazon's global supply chain. See the chapter closing case in Chapter 11 for a discussion of Amazon's efforts in this area and IT's About Business 7.3 for a look at Amazon's B2B business.

Final Thoughts

Retailers must use data to make decisions. In this area, Amazon is ahead of Walmart. Amazon has a distinct competitive advantage with its algorithmic approach to presenting particular products to its customers, as well as using real-time data to apply dynamic pricing to its products. Walmart, in contrast, has lagged behind significantly in these areas. The absence of an online platform that can collect the volume and quality of consumer data needed for more precise decision making in product placement and pricing has held Walmart back.

Walmart has perhaps the best physical distribution and retail network in the world, while Amazon is the clear leader in e-commerce. Here is the main question: Will Amazon be able to build a massive distribution network and physical stores that match Walmart's stores before Walmart can add major digital capabilities to its own supply chain and integrate Walmart.com with its physical stores?

The lines that divide digital retailing from brick-and-mortar retailing are blurring. As you have seen, Walmart is making important strategic moves into electronic commerce, and Amazon is making similarly important strategic moves into brick-and-mortar commerce.

And the bottom line? Amazon reported 2018 total revenue of $233 billion and Walmart reported total revenue of $500 billion. Significantly, on July 12, 2019 Amazon's market capitalization was $990 billion and Walmart's was $327 billion.

Sources: Compiled from G. Magana, "Walmart's New Fulfillment Strategy Causing Out-of-Stocks," *Business Insider*, September 4, 2018; D. Keyes, "Walmart Is Revamping Returns for Third-Party Orders," *Business Insider*, August 10, 2018; M. Corkery, "Playing Catch-Up with Walmart, Amazon Offers Digital Grocery Pickup at Whole Foods," *New York Times*, August 8, 2018; I. Lunden, "Amazon Buys PillPack, an Online Pharmacy, for Just under $1B," *TechCrunch*, June 28, 2018; M. Boyle, "Walmart Unveils a Concierge Shopping Service," *Bloomberg*, May 31, 2018; L. Thomas, "Walmart and Lord & Taylor Ready for New Web Store Rollout," *CNBC*, May 16, 2018; M. Corkery, "How Walmart, the Big Seller, Is Shopping for a Fight with Amazon," *New York Times*, May 9, 2018; D. Becerril, "Walmart.com Is Getting a New Look – and It's a Radical Change for the Company," *Reuters*, April 17, 2018; J. Risley, "Walmart's US Online Sales Grow 44% in 2017 despite Q4 Stumble," *Internet Retailer*, February 20, 2018; D. Keyes, "Walmart Is Charging Different Prices Online and In-Store," *Business Insider*, November 15, 2017; J. Perlow, "First, Amazon Destroyed Retail – Now, It's Coming for Starbucks," *ZDNet*, October 30, 2017; S. Liss, "Amazon Gains Wholesale Pharmacy Licenses in Multiple States," *St. Louis Post-Dispatch*, October 27, 2017; D. Keyes, "Walmart.com May Become an Online Mall," *Business Insider*, October 20, 2017; L. Rupp and D. Wei, "Amazon Is Getting into Sportswear," *Bloomberg*, October 13, 2017; D. Keyes, "Walmart Announces Speedy Returns Program," *Business Insider*, October 10, 2017; T. Mogg, "Walmart's Shopping App Is about to Speed Up

In-Store Returns," *Digital Trends*, October 9, 2017; K. Taylor, "Here Are All the Changes Amazon Is Making to Whole Foods," *Business Insider*, September 21, 2017; K. Kelleher, "How Walmart Uses AI to Serve 140 Million Customers a Week," *VentureBeat*, July 11, 2017; N. Wingfield, "Amazon Will Let Customers Try on Clothes before Buying," *New York Times*, June 20, 2017; M. de la Merced, "Walmart to Buy Bonobos, Men's Wear Company, for $310 Million," *New York Times*, June 16, 2017; H. Peterson, "'This Is a Death Spiral': The Tsunami of Store Closures Is Doubling in Size," *Business Insider*, June 3, 2017; "Wal-Mart Files Patent for Amazon Dash Rival," *Reuters*, May 4, 2017; B. Stone and M. Boyle, "Can Wal-Mart's Expensive New E-Commerce Operations Compete with Amazon?" *Bloomberg BusinessWeek*, May 4, 2017; Walmart Cuts HQ Staff, Fights Amazon with New Discounts," *Forbes*, April 17, 2017; H. Peterson, "Walmart Has a New Kind of Discount – and It's Impossible for Amazon to Beat," *Business Insider*, April 12, 2017; D. Alba, "Amazon's Time-Saving Trick for Groceries: You Drive to Us," *Wired*, March 28, 2017; N. Wingfield, "Amazon's Ambitions Unboxed: Stores for Furniture, Appliances, and More," *New York Times*, March 25, 2017; N. Levy, "Walmart Buys Zappos Competitor Shoe-Buy for $70M to Help Jet.com Battle Amazon on Online Apparel," *GeekWire*, January 6, 2017; N. Carr, "Amazon's Next Big Move: Take over the Mall," *MIT Technology Review*, November 14, 2016; G. Petro, "Amazon vs. Walmart: Clash of the Titans," *Forbes*, August 25, 2016; S. Pettypiece and S. Wang, "Wal-Mart to Acquire Jet.com for $3.3 Billion to Fight Amazon," *Bloomberg*, August 8, 2016; H. Malcolm, "Why Walmart Is Spending $3B for Online Seller Jet.com," *USA Today*, August 8, 2016; and www.amazon.com, www.walmart.com, accessed July 13, 2019

Questions

1. Discuss and analyze the reasons why Walmart is moving so decisively into electronic commerce.

2. Discuss and analyze the reasons why Amazon is moving so decisively into traditional brick-and-mortar commerce.

3. Do you think one company will "win"? If so, which one? Support your answer.

4. Speculate on the reasons why Amazon's market capitalization was so much larger than Walmart's in July 2019.

CHAPTER 8

Wireless, Mobile Computing, and Mobile Commerce

CHAPTER OUTLINE	LEARNING OBJECTIVES
8.1 Wireless Technologies	**8.1** Identify advantages and disadvantages of each of the four main types of wireless transmission media.
8.2 Wireless Computer Networks and Internet Access	**8.2** Explain how businesses can use short-range, medium-range, and long-range wireless networks.
8.3 Mobile Computing and Mobile Commerce	**8.3** Provide a specific example of how each of the five major m-commerce applications can benefit a business.
8.4 The Internet of Things	**8.4** Describe the Internet of Things, along with examples of how organizations can use the Internet of Things.

Opening Case

The Fitbit Murder Case

On December 23, 2015, authorities responded to a burglary alarm at the Ellington, Connecticut, home of Richard and Connie Dabate. They found Connie dead of gunshot wounds and her husband wounded. Richard told police that he and his wife were victims of a home invasion. The police did not make any arrests at that time.

Dabate told police that he took his sons to the school bus stop and left for work at about 8:30 a.m. He claimed he had been driving for about five minutes when he received an alert on his phone that the alarm at his home had been activated. He said he then sent an e-mail to his boss from the side of the road and checked the alarm status before going home. He estimated that he returned home around 9 a.m.

Dabate reported that when he got home, he was ambushed by a masked man—about 6-foot-2 and stocky. He claimed that the man was holding him hostage when his wife returned home from the YMCA. Dabate heard his wife enter the house through the garage door and

yelled at her to run. The man ran after his wife, who had headed for the basement, and shot her twice.

According to Dabate, he then caught up with the intruder. However, the man subdued him, tied him to a chair, cut him with a box cutter, and burned him with a torch. Dabate maintained that he managed to struggle with the man and turn the torch to the man's face. The intruder fled, after which Dabate ran out of the basement, reached a phone, and called 911.

Police obtained search warrants for the couple's phone and Facebook records, their text messages, computer records from Richard's laptop, and Connie's Fitbit records. The records enabled the authorities to re-create Richard and Connie's activities in the hour after Richard told police he was confronted by the intruder and Connie was killed.

Investigators relied heavily on a wide array of data from smartphones, laptops, security alarm records, and Connie's Fitbit. They constructed this time line:

- At approximately 8:46 a.m., Connie's Fitbit indicated that she left for the YMCA.

- At approximately 8:53 a.m., surveillance cameras from the parking lot of the YMCA showed Connie arriving there. At about that time, she sent a message from her phone through Facebook to her psychotherapist.
- At 9:04, Richard sent an e-mail to his boss indicating that he would be late to work. It was sent from his laptop, not from the side of the road as he had told police.
- At 9:18, Richard visited the website of the YMCA to view the group's exercise schedule.
- At 9:18, Connie called someone from her phone after surveillance cameras indicated that she had left the YMCA.
- At 9:23, Connie's Fitbit, idle for nine minutes while she drove home, became active again at the same time that alarm records show the garage door opening. Police believe that is when she arrived at home.
- From 9:40 to 9:46, Connie posted two videos on Facebook using her iPhone and then posted a message to a friend through Facebook.
- At 10:05, Connie's Fitbit registered its last movement. Between the time she came home and the time when her Fitbit stopped, she moved a distance of 1,217 feet inside the home. Furthermore, she covered 10 times the distance between her car and the basement, which was the path that Richard claimed she took. Her last movements inside their home were at 10:05, nearly an hour after Richard told detectives she had been killed by the intruder.
- At 10:11, the panic alarm for the security system was activated from Richard's key chain fob. It is the only time the panic alarm went off that morning, although Richard claimed he had received an alarm earlier that morning while driving to work.
- At 10:16, the police received a 911 call from the alarm company.
- At 10:20, Richard called 911.

According to the police, Richard changed his story several times. Further, his story was inconsistent with the evidence. Police found no forced entry into the house and no disarray within the house. Police investigators found that nothing was stolen. Investigators and police dogs found no evidence on the grounds of the home that anyone had fled the property. Forensic evidence revealed that Connie's gunshot wounds were from a handgun that Richard had purchased months before the shooting. A police dog picked up only Richard's scent. Investigators reported that Richard's injuries could have been self-inflicted.

More than one year after the murder, police charged Richard Dabate with his wife's murder. He pleaded not guilty.

Police also discovered that Richard had a girlfriend and that she was pregnant. Richard initially informed the police that his wife knew he had helped out an unmarried friend by impregnating her, and the three of them planned to co-parent the baby. Later, he admitted that his wife was unaware of the affair and the baby.

In November 2017, Richard Dabate's attorney Hubert J. Santos filed a motion seeking to dismiss the charges against Dabate because of pretrial publicity caused by a probate judge who "has embarked on a campaign to characterize Dabate as a killer." Dabate's attorney claimed that by freezing all of Connie's accounts, by trying to force Richard to testify in probate court even as the murder charge was pending, and by questioning what Richard did with money that he withdrew from his wife's accounts after her death, the judge had prejudiced his client's chance to receive a fair trial.

Santos also raised questions about the Fitbit evidence, which he said he might try to prevent from being presented to a jury. Santos argued that a Fitbit is not a calibrated instrument, such as an Intoximeter, which provides admissible evidence in cases involving driving while intoxicated.

A spokeswoman for Fitbit declined to comment on the case. However, she quoted a company policy that states that Fitbit provides content and data from its devices only when there is a warrant. Otherwise, the company refuses to share settings and data from the devices and their online apps.

In July 2018, prosecutors finally delivered all the evidence that police had collected in their investigation to Dabate's attorneys, who said they had to review the thousands of pages that were turned over to them. In January, 2019 Dabate rejected a plea deal, saying that he wants his case to go to trial. His attorneys noted that a trial is likely years away.

Sources: Compiled from N. Rondinone, "Richard Dabate Rejects Plea Deal in Fitbit Murder Case, Pushes for Trial in Wife's Killing," *Hartford Courant*, January 24, 2019; D. Altimari, "All Evidence Turned over as Fitbit Murder Case Moves toward Trial," *Hartford Courant*, July 20, 2018; D. Altimari, "More Evidence Turned over in Fitbit Murder Case," *Hartford Courant*, January 19, 2018; D. Altimari and D. Owens, "Citing Probate Case Publicity, Richard Dabate Wants Murder Charge Dismissed," *Hartford Courant*, November 8, 2017; C. Dehnel, "Ellington Murder Case Gets Another Continuance," *CT Patch*, July 28, 2017; D. Owens, "Richard Dabate's Case Continued Until July 28," *Hartford Courant*, June 16, 2017; A. Dash, "New Details Emerge in Connie Dabate Connecticut Murder Case," *Crime Watch Daily*, May 2, 2017; T. Connor, "Fitbit Murder Case: Richard Dabate Pleads Not Guilty in Wife's Death," NBC News, April 29, 2017; C. Hauser, "In Connecticut Murder Case, a Fitbit Is a Silent Witness," *New York Times*, April 27, 2017; "Police Use Murdered Woman's Fitbit Movements to Charge Her Husband," CNN, April 26, 2017; "Slain Woman's Fitbit Data Cited in Murder Case Against Husband," CBS News, April 25, 2017; J. Miller, "Fitbit May Do Husband in for Wife's Murder," *New York Post*, April 25, 2017; J. Lartey, "Man Suspected in Wife's Murder after Her Fitbit Data Doesn't Match His Alibi," *The Guardian*, April 25, 2017; J. Schroeder, "Fitbit Fitness Tracker Cracks Connecticut Murder Case," *New York Daily News*, April 24, 2017; D. Altimari, "A Marriage Marked by Secrets, a Murder Case Months in the Making," *Hartford Courant*, April 23, 2017; and "Ellington Man Charged in Wife's 2015 Murder Due in Court," NBC Connecticut, April 15, 2017.

Questions

1. As we noted in Chapter 1, you are *Homo conexus*, the most connected generation in history. Discuss how this case illustrates the advantages and disadvantages of being constantly connected wherever you are located.

   a. In this case, who benefits from constant connectivity, and how?

   b. In this case, who is disadvantaged by constant connectivity, and how?

2. Refer to Chapter 3, and discuss the privacy implications of this case.

Introduction

The traditional working environment that required users to come to a wired computer is ineffective and inefficient. The solution was to build computers that are small enough to carry or wear and that can communicate through wireless networks; that is, your computing device now comes with you.

The ability to communicate anytime and anywhere provides organizations with a strategic advantage by increasing productivity and speed and improving customer service. We use the term **wireless** to describe telecommunications in which electromagnetic waves, rather than some form of wire or cable, carry the signal between communicating devices such as computers, smartphones, and iPads.

Before you continue, it is important to distinguish between the terms *wireless* and *mobile*—they can mean different things. The term *wireless* means exactly what it says: without wires. In contrast, *mobile* refers to something that changes its location over time. Some wireless networks, such as MiFi (discussed later in this chapter), are also mobile. Others, however, are fixed. For example, microwave towers form fixed wireless networks.

Wireless technologies enable individuals and organizations to conduct mobile computing, mobile commerce, and the Internet of Things. We define these terms here, and then we discuss each one in detail later in the chapter.

Mobile computing refers to a real-time, wireless connection between a mobile device and other computing environments, such as the Internet or an intranet. *Mobile commerce*—also known as *m-commerce*—refers to e-commerce (EC) transactions (see Chapter 7) conducted with a mobile device. The *Internet of Things* means that virtually every object has processing power with either wireless or wired connections to a global network.

Wireless technologies and mobile commerce are spreading rapidly, replacing or supplementing wired computing. Cisco (**www.cisco.com**) predicts that the volume of mobile Web traffic will continue to increase rapidly over the next decade.

Almost all (if not all) organizations use wireless computing. Therefore, when you begin your career, you likely will be assigned a company smartphone and a wirelessly enabled computer. Clearly, then, it is important for you to learn about wireless computing not only because you will be using wireless applications but also because wireless computing will be important to your organization. In your job, you will be involved with customers who conduct wireless transactions, with analyzing and developing mobile commerce applications, and with wireless security. And the list goes on.

Simply put, an understanding of wireless technology and mobile commerce applications will make you more valuable to your organization. When you look at "What's in IT for Me?" at the end of the chapter, envision yourself performing the activities discussed in your functional area. For those of you who are inclined to be entrepreneurs, an understanding of wireless technology can also help you start and grow your own business.

The wireless infrastructure upon which mobile computing is built may reshape the entire IT field. The technologies, applications, and limitations of mobile computing and mobile commerce are the focus of this chapter. You begin the chapter by learning about wireless devices, wireless transmission media, and wireless security. You continue by examining wireless computer networks and wireless Internet access. You then look at mobile computing and mobile commerce, which are made possible by wireless technologies. Next, you turn your attention to the Internet of Things.

8.1 Wireless Technologies

Author Lecture Videos are available exclusively in *WileyPLUS.*
Apply the Concept activities are available in the Appendix and in *WileyPLUS.*

Wireless technologies include both wireless devices, such as smartphones, and wireless transmission media, such as microwave, satellite, and radio. These technologies are fundamentally changing the ways organizations operate.

Individuals are finding wireless devices convenient and productive to use, for several reasons. First, people can make productive use of time that was formerly wasted—for example, while commuting to work on public transportation. Second, because people can take these devices with them, their work locations are becoming much more flexible. Third, wireless technology enables people to schedule their working time around personal and professional obligations.

Wireless Devices

Wireless devices provide three major advantages to users:

1. They are small enough to easily carry or wear.
2. They have sufficient computing power to perform productive tasks.
3. They can communicate wirelessly with the Internet and other devices.

Modern smartphones exhibit a process called *dematerialization*. Essentially, dematerialization occurs when the functions of many physical devices are included in one other physical device. Consider that your smartphone includes the functions of digital cameras for images and video, radios, televisions, Internet access through Web browsers, recording studios, editing suites, movie theaters, GPS navigators, word processors, spreadsheets, stereos, flashlights, board games, card games, video games, an entire range of medical devices, maps, atlases, encyclopedias, dictionaries, translators, textbooks, watches, alarm clocks, books, calculators, address books, credit card swipers, magnifying glasses, money and credit cards, car keys, hotel keys, cellular telephony, Wi-Fi, e-mail access, text messaging, a full QWERTY keyboard, and many, many others. **Figure 8.1** illustrates the process of dematerialization with smartphones.

Our smartphones have come a long, long way in a short period of time. Consider these smartphone capabilities (as of August 2019):

- In the United States alone, Verizon (**www.verizon.com**) and AT&T (**www.att.com**) offer 4G LTE (long-term evolution) to more than 300 million people. (4G LTE can reach speeds of 50 megabits per second, or Mbps.) Therefore, modern smartphones are about 500 times faster than the first iPhone, which was released in 2007.

- Many high-end smartphones take video in ultra-high definition 4K. A display device with horizontal resolution on the order of 4,000 pixels is said to have 4K resolution. *Pixels* are the dots that make up on-screen images. The more pixels on a screen, the sharper and more realistic images and video look.

- Smartphones function as mobile (digital) wallets.

- Many smartphones offer wireless charging. Samsung offers its Wireless Powershare feature. With this feature, your Galaxy phone can share its power to help charge another phone or watch, simply by placing the two devices together.

- Although not all smartphones have built-in wireless charging, many of them have fast charging. For example, Motorola (**www.motorola.com**) claimed that its P50 smartphone can obtain 7 hours of battery life from a 15-minute charge.

- Smartphones are employing biometrics (discussed in Chapter 4). Apple has fingerprint scanners on its devices with its Touch ID feature. Google has facial recognition on its Android smartphones in the form of its Face Unlock feature. The Android "Smart Lock" feature can use other methods to recognize you and keep you from having to constantly reauthenticate your login credentials. You can activate "on-body detection," which knows if you have your phone in your hand or in your pocket; "trusted voice" which enables voice recognition; and "trusted devices," which can use Bluetooth to authenticate you when it is connected to your smartwatch or your car.

One downside of smartphones is that people can use them to copy and pass on confidential information. For example, if you were an executive at Intel, would you want workers snapping pictures of their colleagues with your secret new technology in the background? After all, one of the functions of a smartphone is that of a digital camera that can transmit wirelessly. New jamming devices are being developed to counter the threat. Some companies, such as Samsung (**www.samsung.com**), have recognized the danger and have banned these devices from their premises altogether.

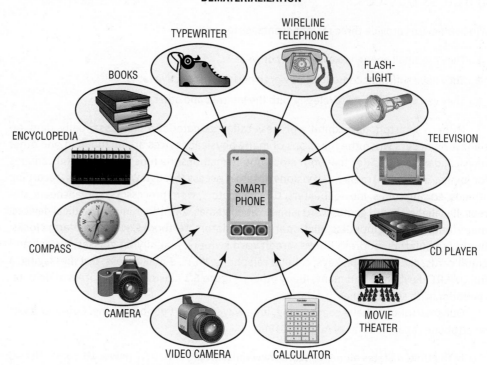

FIGURE 8.1 Dematerialization with smartphones.

Another downside of smartphones consists of scam calls. According to First Orion (**www.firstorion.com**), a company that provides call management and protection for wireless carriers, approximately 40 percent of U.S. mobile traffic consisted of scam calls in the first half of 2019.

In July, 2019 the Federal Communications Commission passed a provision that forces network operators to implement SHAKEN/STIR, the new industry standard for verifying the source of phone calls. Carriers have until 2020 to implement SHAKEN/STIR. As of July, 2019 here is what the major wireless carriers were doing about spam calls.

- Verizon: All of Verizon's postpaid customers can enroll in Call Filter for free. Once a user has opted into Call Filter, Verizon's network automatically flags the calls that it considers suspect with one to three levels of risk: high, moderate, or low. If the network believes the incoming call to be spam, your phone will let you know with a Potential Spam alert in the caller ID field.

- T-Mobile: T-Mobile offers Scam ID and Scam Block. Scam ID is enabled by default for all T-Mobile customers and flags potential spam with the text "Scam Likely" in the caller ID field. Scam Block rejects those calls outright, rather than letting them ring your phone.

- AT&T: Beginning in July, 2019 for new customers AT&T automatically detects and blocks robocalls and provides suspected spam warnings over Caller ID. Existing subscribers can download the carrier's free Call Protect app to get those features.

- Sprint: Sprint does not offer spam identification or blocking by default. If customers want those features, they must pay $2.99 per month for a service called Premium Caller ID, which notifies you when an incoming call is suspected to be spam.

Regardless of any disadvantages, however, cell phones, and particularly smartphones, have had a far greater impact on human society than most of us realize. As one example, IT's About Business 8.1 addresses many ways that smartphones are impacting health care.

IT's About Business 8.1

Smartphones Impact Health Care

`MIS`

Smartphones are democratizing diagnostic health care technologies that previously were too expensive, too slow, or too physically far away for most people to access. Many powerful tools are transforming smartphones into mobile diagnostic devices that are typically simple enough for the average patient to use at home. Machine learning algorithms interpret the findings from the devices for the patient. In 2019, health industry analysts stated that there were over 300,000 mobile health apps available globally.

Physicians are now using smartphones to conduct traditional examinations of organs; perform ultrasound scans; measure vital signs such as heart function, blood pressure, and glucose levels; and perform an array of diagnostic laboratory tests. Physicians perform these functions either with the actual smartphones or with small hardware attachments that plug into the phones.

In the near future, if your body is behaving atypically, then a smartphone app will notify you and will offer initial suggestions about how to make your lifestyle healthier or diagnose a variety of problems. When necessary, it could refer you to a human physician so that you do not have to visit an emergency room.

In a smartphone-enabled health care system, patients will be the custodian of their personal health. Their phone will be the hub of their medical records, including personal health history, diet, and fitness. The phone will keep a record of their lifestyles, physical environment, and location so that it can add context to its medical diagnoses.

Smartphones are having a fundamental effect on global health in five important ways. Let's look at each one in more detail.

Providing emergency care. In case of a medical emergency, dialing 911 is the most reliable method to rapidly receive help. However, for people who live in rural areas, rapid emergency care is problematic. For example, depending on where a person lives in the United States, it can take between 6 and 35 minutes for an ambulance to arrive in a medical emergency. This situation can be even worse in the developing world.

The app MUrgency (**www.murgency.com/**) tries to streamline that process. Depending on the type of emergency, the app can connect patients to ambulances more quickly. In some cases, it can even provide users with a trained nurse to assist them at home. The service launched in 2015 in Punjab, India, with a network of 36 hospital emergency rooms, more than 40 ambulances, and 350 medical professionals.

Screening for health care conditions. Patients need only take a selfie to diagnose pancreatic cancer because researchers developed a smartphone app that can screen for the disease. The app uses computer vision algorithms and machine learning to identify jaundice in the whites of patients' eyes. Jaundice is the medical term that describes yellowing of the skin and eyes. The condition is caused by high levels of bilirubin, a yellow compound that can indicate the early stages of pancreatic cancer. In a study of 70 people, the app had a success rate of about 90 percent, which is about the same accuracy as the blood tests that are the current diagnostic standard. The hope is that people can diagnose the disease early enough to undergo treatment that could save their lives.

Consider the CliniCloud (**www.clinicloud.com**), a microphone that connects to your phone to turn it into a digital stethoscope. In clinical trials, the CliniCloud has been shown to exceed human physicians' ability to diagnose chest infections.

Also in clinical trials, the Cordio app (**www.cordio-med.com**) can predict whether a patient's congestive heart failure is getting worse by analyzing a change in tone in his or her voice. These changes can reveal an early buildup of fluids in a patient's lungs, which occurs when the patient's heart is not functioning properly.

Cupris Health (**www.cupris.com**) makes an otoscope that plugs into a smartphone and takes high-resolution images of the inside of a patient's ear. The images are sent to a cloud-based application (see Technology Guide 3), where a nurse, physician, or, ultimately, an algorithm can remotely diagnose any infections.

Using the mobile ultrasound scanner Lumify (**www.lumify .philips.com**), physicians (or patients) can perform a whole-body ultrasound to image every organ in the body. The Lumify costs $199 per month for unlimited use, compared to a $350,000 ultrasound machine in a hospital.

Consider the case of a patient on an airplane who complained of severe chest pains. A physician onboard immediately reached for his iPhone, which was encased in an FDA-approved cover that he had been testing with his patients. Developed by a start-up called AliveCor (**www.alivecor.com**), the case contains embedded sensors that can perform an electrocardiogram (ECG) on a patient's heart and then transmit the results to an app. An ECG measures the electrical activity of the heart. The physician placed the AliveCor case on the man's chest and opened the app on his phone. Instantly, he could read the patient's ECG on the app. The ECG revealed that the man was having a heart attack. The plane made an emergency landing and the man survived.

Detecting pathogens in the blood. A *pathogen* is a bacterium, virus, or other microorganism that can cause disease. Physicians test patients' blood for a number of conditions, from detecting cholesterol levels to diagnosing diseases. Most blood tests require a laboratory for analysis. However, depending on where a patient lives, sophisticated labs and equipment are not always available. For remote clinics, sending the samples to a lab and waiting for the results can take days or even weeks.

To speed up this process, researchers have miniaturized a laboratory for analyzing blood samples into a handheld device that connects to a smartphone. Called a *lab-on-a-chip*, the device uses only a single drop of blood, urine, or saliva. The device itself (without the smartphone) is the size of a credit card. Grooves in the chip analyze the small amount of blood, which is illuminated by the smartphone's LED. Sensors analyze how light passes through the blood, and the system compares those data with the results of tests that had previously been found to be positive for a particular disease. The entire test takes 10 minutes.

Various labs-on-a-chip can test for the Zika virus, dengue fever, and other infectious diseases. Other labs-on-a-chip can detect *E. coli*, salmonella, HIV, and syphilis. Research is continuing on labs-on-a-chip that are able to diagnose multiple diseases at one time.

At the Drexel Women's Care Center in Philadelphia, 900 women who were being tested for sexually transmitted diseases

(STDs) received results in minutes via their iPhones. The smartphone kit, designed by start-up Biomeme (**www.biomeme.com**), is being used in clinical trials as an alternative to laboratory tests for a variety of these diseases. Laboratory tests usually take several days to return results. Any delay in diagnosis could irreversibly damage patients' reproductive health. Therefore, a point-of-care test that gives a patient results in minutes is invaluable.

The Biomeme device requires only a drop of sample fluid such as urine. It then uses DNA analysis to detect the genetic material of a particular pathogen. The device displays the results in an app. Each unique test for the DNA of a particular pathogen costs $5 to design. Drexel has tested more than 900 urine samples using Biomeme's smartphone kit and has compared these results with those from conventional methods. It found that the Biomeme test was as accurate as human pathologists but was far easier and less expensive to use.

Companies such as Biomeme are disrupting the business model of medical laboratories. By miniaturizing diagnostic tests, they are creating mobile labs that can accurately and inexpensively diagnose numerous diseases from anywhere, utilizing an Internet connection.

As one example, sepsis, a life-threatening condition caused by the body's response to an infection, kills about 400,000 people in the United States and Europe every year. The primary reason for this high mortality rate is it takes days to discover the pathogen(s) that is (are) causing the condition and to identify which antibiotics the pathogen might be resistant to. Every hour of delay in sepsis increases the chance of death by 10 percent. Thus, rapid treatment is the key to survival. Biomeme will not work for complex infections such as sepsis when physicians do not know which microbe to test for. Therefore, the only way to discover the microbe(s) is to sequence the DNA in a sample and look for unexpected genetic material.

To dramatically speed up this process, physicians are testing a device called the MinION, which is a USB flash drive that can sequence DNA in real time. Designed by Oxford Nanopore Technologies (**www.nanoporetech.com**), the MinION uses a patented method to miniaturize and automate DNA sequencing. It is currently being used globally by 3,500 labs to diagnose real-time outbreaks of diseases such as Ebola and pneumonia.

In late 2017, Oxford Nanopore launched a smartphone-based version of its device, called the SmidgION. The SmidgION is a small plug-in module for the iPhone that can sequence DNA in any sample of fluids, such as saliva. A smartphone DNA sequencer will not only make the technology portable for physicians and lab assistants, but it could also help to democratize DNA-based medicine by increasing availability of the technology and decreasing its cost. These tests are not just useful for infectious diseases. They also could be utilized to diagnose cancers, organ decay, heart failure, and genetic disabilities such as cystic fibrosis.

Tracking the spread of disease. Epidemiology is the branch of medicine that deals with the incidence, distribution, and possible control of diseases and other health-related factors. Epidemiologists frequently have to find the origin and cause of a disease outbreak as it continues to spread. Collecting data can be especially difficult in rural, underdeveloped areas. In addition, lack of infrastructure can limit communications. Even if scientists understand the symptoms of the disease and the manner in which it is transmitted, they may still find it difficult to keep track of people who are infected.

Cell phones can help address these problems. For example, researchers are now able to track the malaria parasite across the East African nation of Kenya. By overlaying maps of the prevalence of malaria over call or text data that track individual callers' locations and movements, researchers have helped officials to strategically deploy mosquito nets, control task forces, and distribute medications in affected areas.

Enhance communications. Cell phones help health care professionals share collected data, expertise, and other insights, no matter where they live and work. Social networks such as Doximity (**www.doximity.com**) enable more than 500,000 physicians to share information and peer-review one another's work while keeping confidential any information that could identify the patient. In addition, Doximity helps physicians streamline their workloads. Physicians can now access patient records directly on the app, or they can easily call patients using the app. Patients can choose either to log in online or to contact their health care professionals directly through the app.

As chronic diseases such as diabetes and high blood pressure become more prevalent, smartphones enable physicians to remotely monitor their patients' health. Health care professionals can also provide advice based on data that the patient collects and uploads.

Consider Babylon Health (**www.babylonhealth.com**), a subscription health service provider that has developed an app that functions as an artificially intelligent medical advisor. Whereas human physicians perform about 7,000 patient consultations per year, Babylon's app diagnoses patients based on billions of data points collected from the thousands of test consultations that it performs daily. The company claims that its diagnoses have a 92 percent accuracy rate. The app enables patients to virtually consult with health care professionals via text and video messaging. It also allows patients to receive drug prescriptions, referrals to health specialists, and appointments with nearby health care facilities.

Health care workers themselves communicate much more efficiently with short messaging services (SMS). For example, in South Africa, SMS allows HIV-positive patients to notify or trace partners, track doctor's appointments, and use prevention techniques.

Despite all of these benefits, there are serious disadvantages to these smartphone tools, particularly security and privacy. Our health records contain some of the most sensitive details about us, including information that we may never want to reveal to employers, friends, or even family members. More important, this data is permanent; that is, in contrast to a password or a credit-card number, it can never be changed. Therefore, security, privacy, and encryption are simply nonnegotiable with these new tools. As our smartphones become our medical repositories, their security will become even more crucial. Your data, along with everyone else's, will be stored, integrated, and analyzed by machine-learning algorithms, enabling human physicians to discover trends at the population level and ultimately to predict and prevent diseases before they even occur.

Unfortunately—but not surprisingly—medical data repositories are already a prime target for cybercriminals. Consider these examples:

- In July 2018. UnityPoint Health (**www.unitypoint.org**) notified 1.4 million patients that their records may have been stolen when its business system was compromised by a phishing attack (see Chapter 4). The hacked accounts included personally identifiable information, including names, addresses, medical data, treatment information, lab results, and insurance information. Some of the patients also had their credit card information and Social Security numbers stolen.

- In July 2018, hackers breached the Singapore government's health database, accessing the data of some 1.5 million patients, including Prime Minister Lee Hsien Loong. The stolen data contained demogaphic information and patient identification numbers.

To help prevent these problems, physicians and technology experts recommend decentralizing large health databases and allowing each patient full control over his or her data. Patients alone can decide who can legitimately see their records: physicians, researchers, or specified data custodians such as a family member.

Another problem with using smartphones to diagnose patient conditions is that the app could be wrong. In fact, a blood pressure app called Instant Blood Pressure from AuraLife gave many patients with high blood pressure the false impression that their vital signs were normal, when in reality they were dangerously high.

Health care technology experts agree that human physicians will not be phased out any time soon. Rather, human physicians and digital apps and devices will each perform their particular functions. Human physicians using digital health care apps will be able to provide better health care than either could alone.

Sources: Compiled from J. David, "1.4 Million Patient Records Breached in UnityPoint Health Phishing Attack," *HealthcareIT News*, July 31, 2018;

J. Davis, "Hackers Breach 1.5 Million Singapore Patient Records, Including the Prime Minister's," *HealthcareIT News*, July 20, 2018; L. Mearian, "Smartphones Becoming Primary Device for Physician and Patient Communications," *Computerworld*, April 4, 2018; W. Kelly, "Mobile Apps for Healthcare Professionals: Current and Future Trends," *Mobile Business Insights*, March 26, 2018; M. Bryant, "Many Hospitals Lack Strategy for Leveraging Smartphone Technology," *Healthcare Dive*, February 22, 2018; V. Tangermann, "Five Ways Cell Phones Are Literally Changing Global Health," *Futurism*, October 25, 2017; K. Baggaley, "Smartphones Are Changing Medical Care in Some Surprising Ways," *NBC News*, October 13, 2017; P. Caughill, "This New Device Turns Your Smartphone into a Medical Lab," *Futurism*, August 14, 2017; S. Fecht, "Smartphone-Controlled Cells Release Insulin on Demand in Diabetic Mice," *Popular Science*, April 26, 2017; J. Mayes and A. White, "How Smartphone Technology Is Changing Healthcare in Developing Countries," *The Journal of Global Health*, April 1, 2017; T. Moynihan, "Ex-Googlers Build a Neural Network to Protect Your Heart," *Wired*, March 20, 2017; M. Murgia, "How Smartphones Are Transforming Healthcare," *Financial Times*, January 12, 2017; L. Rapaport, "Smartphone App Misreads Hypertension Range," *Reuters*, March 2, 2016; and D. Moren, "Diagnose an Ear Infection with a Smartphone Accessory," *Popular Science*, December 17, 2014.

Questions

1. What are the major problems associated with smartphone-enabled health care diagnoses? Provide examples to support your answer.

2. If you are the CEO of Laboratory Corporation of America (LabCorp; www.labcorp.com), one of the leading medical laboratories in the world, how would you compete against the emergence of smartphone-enabled health care diagnostics?

Wireless Transmission Media

Wireless media, or broadcast media, transmit signals without wires. The major types of wireless media are microwave, satellite, and radio. **Table 8.1** lists the advantages and disadvantages of each type.

Microwave. **Microwave transmission systems** transmit data through electromagnetic waves. These systems are used for high-volume, long-distance, line-of-sight communication. *Line-of-sight* means that the transmitter and receiver are in view of each other. This requirement creates problems because the Earth's surface is curved rather than flat. For this reason, microwave towers usually cannot be spaced more than 30 miles apart.

TABLE 8.1   Advantages and Disadvantages of Wireless Media

Channel	Advantages	Disadvantages
Microwave	High bandwidth Relatively inexpensive	Must have unobstructed line-of-sight Susceptible to environmental interference
Satellite	High bandwidth Large coverage area	Expensive Must have unobstructed line-of-sight Signals experience **propagation delay** Must use encryption for security
Radio	High bandwidth Signals pass through walls Inexpensive and easy to install	Creates electrical interference problems Susceptible to snooping unless encrypted

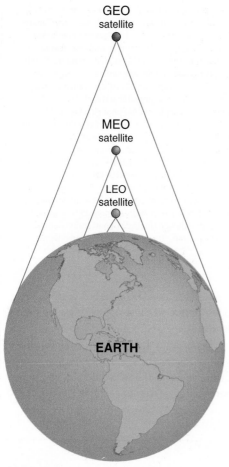

GEO
satellite

MEO
satellite

LEO
satellite

EARTH

FIGURE 8.2 **Comparison of satellite footprints.**

Clearly, then, microwave transmissions offer only a limited solution to data communications needs, especially over very long distances. Microwave transmissions are also susceptible to environmental interference during severe weather such as heavy rain and snowstorms. Although long-distance microwave data communications systems are still widely used, they are being replaced by satellite communications systems.

Satellite. **Satellite transmission systems** make use of communication satellites. Currently, three types of satellites are circling Earth: geostationary-Earth-orbit (GEO), medium-Earth-orbit (MEO), and low-Earth-orbit (LEO). Each type has a different orbit, with GEO being farthest from Earth and LEO being the closest. In this section, you examine the three types of satellites and then discuss three satellite applications: global positioning systems, Internet transmission through satellites, and commercial imaging. **Table 8.2** compares and contrasts the three types of satellites.

As with microwave transmission, satellites must receive and transmit data through line-of-sight. However, the enormous *footprint*—the area of Earth's surface reached by a satellite's transmission—overcomes the limitations of microwave data relay stations; that is, satellites use *broadcast* transmission, which sends signals to many receivers at one time. So, even though satellites are line-of-sight, like microwave, they are high enough for broadcast transmission, thus overcoming the limitations of microwave.

The most basic rule governing footprint size is simple: The higher a satellite orbits, the larger its footprint. Thus, medium-Earth-orbit satellites have a smaller footprint than geostationary satellites, and low-Earth-orbit satellites have the smallest footprint of all. **Figure 8.2** compares the footprints of the three types of satellites.

Types of Orbits. *Geostationary-Earth-orbit (GEO) satellites* orbit 22,300 miles directly above the equator. These satellites maintain a fixed position above Earth's surface because, at their altitude, their orbital period matches the 24-hour rotational period of Earth. For this reason, receivers on Earth do not have to track GEO satellites. GEO satellites are excellent for sending television programs to cable operators and for broadcasting directly to homes.

TABLE 8.2 **Three Basic Types of Telecommunications Satellites**

Type	Characteristics	Orbit	Number	Use
GEO	Satellites stationary relative to point on Earth	22,300 miles	8	TV signal
	Few satellites needed for global coverage			
	Transmission delay (approximately 0.25 second)			
	Most expensive to build and launch			
	Longest orbital life (many years)			
MEO	Satellites move relative to point on Earth	6,434 miles	10 to 12	GPS
	Moderate number needed for global coverage			
	Requires medium-powered transmitters			
	Negligible transmission delay			
	Less expensive to build and launch			
	Moderate orbital life (6 to 12 years)			
LEO	Satellites move rapidly relative to point on Earth	400 to 700 miles	Many	Telephone
	Large number needed for global coverage			
	Requires only low-power transmitters			
	Negligible transmission delay			
	Least expensive to build and launch			
	Shortest orbital life (as low as five years)			

One major limitation of GEO satellites is that their transmissions take a quarter of a second to send and return. This brief pause, one kind of *propagation delay*, makes two-way telephone conversations difficult. Also, GEO satellites are large and expensive, and they require substantial amounts of power to launch.

Medium-Earth-orbit (MEO) satellites are located about 6,000 miles above Earth's surface. MEO orbits require more satellites to cover Earth than GEO orbits because MEO footprints are smaller. MEO satellites have two advantages over GEO satellites: They are less expensive and they do not have an appreciable propagation delay. However, because MEO satellites move with respect to a point on Earth's surface, receivers must track these satellites. (Think of a satellite dish slowly turning to remain oriented to a MEO satellite.)

Low-Earth-orbit (LEO) satellites are located 400 to 700 miles above Earth's surface. Because LEO satellites are much closer to Earth, they have little, if any, propagation delay. Like MEO satellites, however, LEO satellites move with respect to a point on Earth's surface and therefore must be tracked by receivers. Tracking LEO satellites is more difficult than tracking MEO satellites because LEO satellites move much more quickly relative to a point on Earth.

Unlike GEO and MEO satellites, LEO satellites can pick up signals from weak transmitters. This feature makes it possible for satellite telephones to operate through LEO satellites, because they can operate with less power using smaller batteries. Another advantage of LEO satellites is that they consume less power and cost less to launch.

At the same time, however, the footprints of LEO satellites are small, which means that many satellites are needed to cover the planet. For this reason, a single organization often produces multiple LEO satellites, known as *LEO constellations*. Two companies have deployed LEO constellations to provide global voice and data communications, Iridium (**www.iridium.com**) and Globalstar (**www.globalstar.com**).

Global Positioning Systems. The **global positioning system (GPS)** is a wireless system that uses satellites to enable users to determine their position anywhere on Earth. GPS is supported by MEO satellites that are shared worldwide. The exact position of each satellite is always known because the satellite continuously broadcasts its position along with a time signal. By using the known speed of the signals and the distance from three satellites (for two-dimensional location) or four satellites (for three-dimensional location), it is possible to find the location of any receiving station or user within a range of two meters (approximately six feet). GPS software can also convert the user's latitude and longitude to an electronic map.

Most of you are probably familiar with GPS in automobiles, which "talks" to drivers when giving directions. **Figure 8.3** illustrates a driver obtaining GPS information in a car.

Commercial use of GPS for activities such as navigating, mapping, and surveying has become widespread, particularly in remote areas. Cell phones in the United States now must have a GPS embedded in them so that the location of a person making an emergency call—for example, 911, known as *wireless 911*—can be detected immediately.

Three other global positioning systems are either planned or operational. The Russian GPS, *GLONASS,* accomplished full global coverage in October 2011. China expects to complete its GPS system, called *Beidou,* by 2020.

The European Union GPS is called *Galileo.* At the end of 2016, Galileo opened for free public use with 18 available satellites. The entire Galileo system is expected to be completed by 2020 with the launch of additional satellites.

It is almost impossible to overstate how much the world's economy depends on the GPS system. There are some two billion GPS receivers in use around the world and that number is expected to increase to seven billion by 2022. In fact, a study by research firm RTI International (**www.rti.org**) estimated that the loss of GPS service globally would cost private sector organizations approximately $1 billion per day.

GPS is not only necessary for maps and navigation but also provides an extremely accurate clock. The telecommunications industry, banks, airlines, electric utilities, cloud computing businesses, television

FIGURE 8.3 **Obtaining GPS information in an automobile.**

networks, emergency services, and the military require constantly precise GPS timing. In fact, the U.S. Department of Homeland Security has designed 16 sectors of infrastructure as critical, and 14 of them depend on GPS.

Globally, computers use GPS to determine what time it is, down to billionths of a second. Problems with GPS manifest very quickly in a variety of situations. On January 26, 2016, the U.S. Air Force, which operates the 30 U.S. GPS satellites, decommissioned an older GPS satellite. During the process, tiny errors were introduced into the GPS database. These errors meant that several satellites were transmitting bad timing data, running slow by 13.7 billionths of a second.

Over the next 11 hours, cellphone towers lost their connections, U.S. police and fire stations reported communications errors, BBC radio signals were interrupted, and the telescope that tracks asteroids in Earth's orbit went offline. Fortunately, the error was found and fixed quickly, but the incident served notice as to just how vulnerable our planet is to problems with the GPS system.

Internet over Satellite. In many regions of the world, Internet over satellite (IoS) is the only option available for Internet connections because installing cables is either too expensive or physically impossible. IoS enables users to access the Internet from GEO satellites on a dish mounted on the side of their homes. Although IoS makes the Internet available to many people who otherwise could not access it, it has its drawbacks. Not only do GEO satellite transmissions involve a propagation delay, but they can also be disrupted by environmental influences such as thunderstorms. Many companies are entering this market.

- OneWeb (**www.oneweb.world**) has deployed a LEO constellation to bring Internet access to all corners of the globe. The firm is targeting rural markets, emerging markets, and in-flight Internet services on airlines. As of July, 2019 OneWeb had launched 880 satellites and was planning for 1980 satellites in total.

- SpaceX (**www.spacex.com**) launched a LEO constellation called Starlink. Starlink plans to provide long-distance Internet traffic for people in sparsely populated areas. As of July, 2019 SpaceX had launched 60 satellites and was planning for 12,000 satellites in total.

- In April, 2019 Amazon announced plans for its LEO constellation, which will consist of 3,236 satellites.

- Facebook is developing an IoS satellite, called Athena, for launch in 2019. Athena is designed to efficiently provide broadband Internet access to underserved areas throughout the world.

Commercial Imaging. Another satellite application is commercial images from orbit, using very small satellites, called *nanosatellites*. Several companies are involved in launching nanosatellites for scientific and commercial purposes. Let's look at some of these companies here:

- Planet Labs (**www.planet.com**; Planet) takes pictures of the Earth more frequently than traditional satellites and at a small fraction of the cost. The company's LEO constellation, called Dove, helps entire industries obtain images anywhere on Earth. Planet can also capture video which can be used to develop 3D models of any area that is imaged.

   By August 2018, Planet was able to image every location on the entire planet every day. Planet has deployed a platform, Queryable Earth, that customers can use to track, planes, ships, roads, buildings, and forests worldwide.

   A farm software business in the agriculture division of DowDuPont (**www.dupont.com**), called Granular (**www.granular.ag**), uses Planet's satellites to access daily images of the Earth, as well as some of Planet's six-year archive of images. Granular analyzes the images, which provide information to farmers. For example, farmers use Granular's analyses to develop crop and field plans, delegate duties to employees, track inventory, and predict yield and revenue.

- `FIN` The World Bank (**www.worldbank.org**) monitors high-risk urban development by integrating satellite imaging data from NASA's Landsat satellites and the European Space Agency's Sentinel satellites with census data.

- `POM` Spire (**www.spire.com**) nanosatellites locate objects. For example, more than 250,000 ships broadcast an automatic identification signal. Spire nanosatellites pick up these signals and provide frequent updates of the ships' positions without the vessels having to use expensive dedicated satellite communications.

- `POM` Ursa Space Systems (**www.ursaspace.com**) analyzes satellite imaging data to estimate the amount of oil in 10,000 oil storage tanks worldwide by focusing on the heights of the lids to measure fluctuation in the oil levels of the tanks. The company estimates oil stockpiles and oil demand.

- `POM` Orbital Insight (**www.orbitalinsight.com**) also has an oil storage tracker and performs daily automobile counts for 80 U.S. retailers.

- `POM` EarthCast Technologies (**www.earthcastdemo.com**) provides in-flight forecasts to pilots. Pilots have long had access to basic weather information for their departure and arrival airports, but EarthCast gives them the ability to map out conditions along a particular flight path.

- ICEYE (**www.iceye.com**) created microsatellites that are 10 times smaller and 20 times lighter than previous satellites. ICEYE can provide images for about $1 per square kilometer, one-tenth the cost of other satellite image providers. The company launched its first satellite in January, 2018 and plans to launch a constellation of 18 satellites that will allow it to capture images of almost any spot on Earth every three hours.

- `POM` SpaceKnow (**www.spaceknow.com**) uses image data from about 200 public and private satellites to track everything from planes at airports, to shipping containers in ports, to cars at amusement parks. The company's clients are particularly interested in infrastructure development; for example, whether there are new mines in the cobalt-rich Democratic Republic of Congo, which could impact that mineral's prices.

- Imazon (**www.imazon.org.br/en/**) uses image data from the European Space Agency's Sentinel satellites to police the deforestation of the Amazon Basin in Brazil. The organization focuses on providing data to local governments in the region through its "green municipalities" program, which trains officials to identify deforestation.

- `POM` Indigo Ag Inc. (**www.indigoag.com**) analyzes image data from NASA and European Space Agency satellites to track global crops, such as wheat, rice, and others.

- Global Fishing Watch (**www.globalfishingwatch.org**; GFW) analyzes satellite ship-tracking image data to help identify where and when vessels are fishing illegally. The organization was jointly founded by three companies: SkyTruth (**www.skytruth.org**), which uses satellites to monitor natural resource extraction and promote environmental protection; Oceana (**www.oceana.org**), an international ocean conservation organization; and Google, which provides data analytics. By August 2018, GFW had expanded worldwide and was tracking 65,000 vessels. Indonesia is using GFW to combat foreign poachers who have fished the waters around the Indonesian archipelago for some time. After partnering with GFW, Indonesia has significantly limited their activities and increased its fishing revenue.

However, there can be problems in the satellite space. In January 2018, an Indian-built rocket carried an unauthorized payload: four nanosatellites the size of a paperback book from a stealth start-up called Swarm Technologies (Swarm; **www.swarm.space**). (Swarm calls its satellites SpaceBEEs.) In fact, Swarm did not have permission from the U.S. Federal Communications Commission (FCC; **www.fcc.gov**) to launch the satellites. Swarm claimed that its technology would enable worldwide communications for transportation networks and agricultural applications for far less cost than current satellite options.

Realizing that their satellites would alert the FCC, the company installed GPS responders on their satellites and covered them with radar-reflecting material to make them easier to track. The FCC revoked authorization for Swarm's next four satellites, which were scheduled for launch in April 2018.

Ever since Swarm illegally launched its SpaceBEEs, they have been orbiting the Earth in silence, awaiting judgement from the FCC. In December, 2018 Swarm agreed to pay $900,000 to settle the FCC investigation. Also that month, the company launched three FCC-approved satellites. As a result, Swarm is communicating with 7 satellites in low-earth orbit.

Radio.   **Radio transmission** uses radio wave frequencies to send data directly between transmitters and receivers. Radio transmission has several advantages. First, radio waves travel easily through normal office walls. Second, radio devices are fairly inexpensive and easy to install. Third, radio waves can transmit data at high speeds. For these reasons, radio increasingly is being used to connect computers to both peripheral equipment and local area networks (LANs; discussed in Chapter 6). (*Note*: Wi-Fi and cellular also use radio frequency waves.)

As with other technologies, however, radio transmission has its drawbacks. First, radio media can create electrical interference problems. Also, radio transmissions are susceptible to snooping by anyone who has similar equipment that operates on the same frequency.

Another problem with radio transmission is that when you travel too far away from the source station, the signal breaks up and fades into static. Most radio signals can travel only 30 to 40 miles from their source. However, **satellite radio** overcomes this problem. Satellite radio, or *digital radio*, offers uninterrupted, near-CD-quality transmission that is beamed to your radio, either at home or in your car, from space. In addition, satellite radio offers a broad spectrum of stations, including many types of music, news, and talk. Sirius XM (**www.siriusxm.com**) is a leading satellite radio company whose listeners subscribe to its service for a monthly fee.

MIS **Google Project Loon.**   Project Loon is Google's plan to provide Internet access to rural and remote areas, using balloons at an altitude of 11 miles. The balloons will create an aerial wireless network with up to 4G LTE speeds. In October 2017, Alphabet (Google's parent company) received approval from the Federal Communications Commission (FCC, **www.fcc.gov**) to use its balloons to restore cellular service to the people of Puerto Rico following Hurricane Maria. Alphabet immediately partnered with AT&T to support basic communications and Internet activities such as sending text messages.

In July 2018, Loon announced a partnership with Telkom Kenya, Kenya's third-largest telecommunications provider, to provide 4G Internet coverage to Kenyan citizens who lack Internet access. In July, 2019, Loon began its first commercial test in that country.

Internet Blimps.   Start-up Altaeros (**www.altaeros.com**) makes the SuperTower, which is a tethered blimps, that float at about 800 feet altitude. Each blimp acts like a regular cell tower but with a footprint of up to 4,000 square miles. Altaeros claims that one SuperTower will replace 15 land-based cell towers and cut the cost of delivering wireless service by 60 percent. In 2019, the company completed a field test in New Hampshire and is looking for customers.

Wireless Security

Clearly, wireless networks provide numerous benefits for businesses. However, they also present a huge challenge to management—namely, their inherent lack of security. Wireless is a broadcast medium, and transmissions can be intercepted by anyone who is close enough and has access to the appropriate equipment. There are four major threats to wireless networks: rogue access points, war driving, eavesdropping, and radio frequency jamming.

A *rogue access point* is an unauthorized access point into a wireless network. The rogue could be someone in your organization who sets up an access point meaning no harm but fails to inform the IT department. In more serious cases, the rogue is an "evil twin"—someone who wishes to access a wireless network for malicious purposes.

In an *evil twin attack*, the attacker is in the vicinity with a Wi-Fi-enabled computer and a separate connection to the Internet. Using a *hotspotter*—a device that detects wireless networks and provides information on them (see **www.canarywireless.com**)—the attacker simulates a wireless access point with the same wireless network name, or SSID, as the one that authorized users expect. If the signal is strong enough, then users will connect to the attacker's system instead of the real access point. The attacker can then serve them a Web page asking for them to provide confidential information such as usernames, passwords, and account numbers. In other cases, the attacker simply captures wireless transmissions. These attacks are more effective with public hot spots (e.g., McDonald's and Starbucks) than with corporate networks.

War driving is the act of locating WLANs while driving (or walking) around a city or elsewhere. To war drive or walk, you simply need a Wi-Fi detector and a wirelessly enabled computer. If a WLAN has a range that extends beyond the building in which it is located, then an unauthorized user might be able to intrude into the network. The intruder can then obtain a free Internet connection and possibly gain access to important data and other resources.

Eavesdropping refers to efforts by unauthorized users to access data that are traveling over wireless networks. Finally, in *radio frequency (RF) jamming*, a person or a device intentionally or unintentionally interferes with your wireless network transmissions.

Before you go on . . .

1. Describe the most common types of wireless devices.
2. Describe the various types of transmission media.
3. Describe four threats to the security of wireless transmissions.

8.2 Wireless Computer Networks and Internet Access

You have learned about various wireless devices and how these devices transmit wireless signals. These devices typically form wireless computer networks, and they provide wireless Internet access. In this section, you will study wireless networks, which we organize by their effective distance: short range, medium range, and wide area.

Author Lecture Videos are available exclusively in *WileyPLUS*.
Apply the Concept activities are available in the Appendix and in *WileyPLUS*.

Short-Range Wireless Networks

Short-range wireless networks simplify the task of connecting one device to another. They also eliminate wires, and they enable users to move around while they use the devices. In general, short-range wireless networks have a range of 100 feet or fewer. In this section, you consider three basic short-range networks: Bluetooth, ultra-wideband (UWB), and near-field communications (NFC).

Bluetooth.   Bluetooth (**www.bluetooth.com**) is an industry specification used to create small personal area networks. A **personal area network** is a computer network used for communication among computer devices (e.g., telephones, personal digital assistants, smartphones) located close to one person. Bluetooth uses low-power, radio-based communication. Bluetooth 5 can transmit up to approximately 50 megabits per second (Mbps) up to 400 meters (roughly 1,300 feet). These characteristics mean that Bluetooth 5 will be important for the Internet of Things (discussed in Section 8.4) applications.

Common applications for Bluetooth are wireless handsets for cell phones and portable music players. Advantages of Bluetooth include low power consumption and the fact that it uses radio waves that are emitted in all directions from a transmitter. For this reason, you do not have to point one Bluetooth device at another to create a connection.

Bluetooth low energy, marketed as *Bluetooth Smart*, enables applications in the health care, fitness, security, and home entertainment industries. Compared to "classic" Bluetooth, Bluetooth Smart is less expensive and consumes less power, although it has a similar communication range. Bluetooth Smart is fueling the "wearables" (wearable computer) development and adoption.

Ultra-Wideband.

Ultra-wideband is a high-bandwidth wireless technology with transmission speeds in excess of 100 Mbps. Humatics (**www.humatics.com**), a pioneer in UWB technology, has developed many UWB applications. One interesting application is the PLUS Real-Time Location System (RTLS). An organization can use PLUS to locate multiple people and assets simultaneously. Employees, customers, and visitors wear the PLUS Badge Tag. PLUS Asset Tags are also placed on equipment and products. PLUS is extremely valuable for health care environments, where knowing the real-time location of caregivers (e.g., doctors, nurses, technicians) and mobile equipment (e.g., laptops, monitors) is critical.

Other interesting ultra-wideband applications include the following:

- Mobile robotics: Enable robots to navigate autonomously indoors and in other GPS-denied environments and to guide drones as they fly

- **POM** Heavy equipment industries such as manufacturing and mining: Precisely position the arm of a crane and track forklifts moving indoors and outdoors

- Defense and security: Low false alarm rate, wireless perimeter fences, and indoor mapping and through-wall surveillance

Near-Field Communication.

Near-field communication (NFC) has the smallest range of any short-range wireless network. It is designed to be embedded in mobile devices such as cell phones and credit cards. For example, using NFC, you can wave your device or card within a few centimeters of POS terminals to pay for items. NFC can also be used with mobile wallets (discussed in Section 8.3).

Medium-Range Wireless Networks

Medium-range wireless networks are the familiar **wireless local area networks (WLANs)**. The most common type of medium-range wireless network is **Wireless Fidelity**, or Wi-Fi. WLANs are useful in a variety of settings, some of which may be challenging.

Wireless Fidelity is a medium-range WLAN, which is a wired LAN but without the cables. In a typical configuration, a transmitter with an antenna, called a **wireless access point** (see **Figure 8.4**), connects to a wired LAN or to satellite dishes that provide an Internet connection. A wireless access point provides service to a number of users within a small geographical perimeter (up to approximately 300 feet), known as a **hot spot**. Multiple wireless access points are needed to support a larger number of users across a larger geographical area. To communicate wirelessly, mobile devices, such as laptop PCs, typically have a built-in wireless network interface capability.

Wi-Fi provides fast and easy Internet or intranet broadband access from public hot spots located at airports, hotels, Internet cafés, universities, conference centers, offices, and homes. Users can access the Internet while walking across a campus, to their office, or through their homes. Users can also access Wi-Fi with their laptops, desktops, or PDAs by adding a wireless network card. Most PC and laptop manufacturers incorporate these cards into their products.

The Institute of Electrical and Electronics Engineers (IEEE) has established a set of standards for wireless computer networks. The IEEE standard for Wi-Fi is the 802.11 family. There are many standards in this family. The most current standard in July, 2010 is 802.11ax. 802.11ax will replace both 802.11n and 802.11ac and focus on multi-user

Roman Samokhin/Shutterstock.com

FIGURE 8.4 **Wireless access point.**

environments. With transmission speeds up to 10Gbps, 802.11ax will also be beneficial for the Internet of Things applications. The standard is expected to be finalized in late 2019.

The major benefits of Wi-Fi are its low cost and its ability to provide simple Internet access. It is the greatest facilitator of the wireless Internet—that is, the ability to connect to the Internet wirelessly.

Corporations are integrating Wi-Fi into their strategies. For example, Starbucks, McDonald's, Panera, and Barnes & Noble offer customers Wi-Fi in many of their stores, primarily for Internet access.

To illustrate the value of Wi-Fi, consider Google's deployment of one of the world's largest public Wi-Fi projects in India, called Google Station. On June 7, 2018, Google announced that it offered free high-speed public Wi-Fi at 400 railway stations, in partnership with the government-owned Indian Railways and RailTel, which operates a fiber network along India's massive network of train tracks.

According to Google, over 8 million people use the service. On average, users consume 350 megabytes of data per session and over half of the people using Google Station engage in multiple online sessions per day. The Internet speed that Google provides at the stations is faster than several paid services available in India.

Many people have benefited from Google Station. For example, Shrinath, a porter at the Ernakulam Junction station in the southern state of Kerala, used the service to study online and prepare for the Kerala Public Service entrance examination.

Google is expanding Google Station in India outside railway stations to places such as public gardens, hospitals, police stations, and offices. The company has also piloted the project with hot spots in the western Indian city of Pune, Maharashtra. Google has also deployed Google Station in Indonesia, Mexico, Thailand, Nigeria, Philippines, Brazil, and Vietnam.

There are many companies innovating with Wi-Fi. For example, Boston start-up Starry (**www.starry.com**) launched its fixed broadband wireless service in Boston in 2016. The company offers consumers a simple plan with no bundles, no long-term contracts, no data caps, and no hidden fees. Starry's service delivers 200 Mbps for $50 per month. This fee includes installation, 24/7 customer care, and all equipment. In June, 2019 Starry won 104 licenses in the Federal Communications Commission auction. These licenses mean that Starry can now reach 40 million households in the U.S. As of July, 2019 Starry operated in Boston, New York, Denver, Los Angeles, and Washington, D.C. and planned to expand to 18 other cities in the U.S.

Wi-Fi Direct.   Until late 2010, Wi-Fi could operate only if the hot-spot contained a wireless antenna. Because of this limitation, organizations have typically used Wi-Fi for communications of up to about 800 feet. For shorter, peer-to-peer connections, they have used Bluetooth.

This situation changed following the introduction of a new iteration of Wi-Fi known as Wi-Fi Direct. Wi-Fi Direct enables peer-to-peer communications, so devices can connect directly. It enables users to transfer content among devices without having to rely on a wireless antenna. Devices with Wi-Fi Direct can broadcast their availability to other devices just as Bluetooth devices can. Finally, Wi-Fi Direct is compatible with the more than one billion Wi-Fi devices currently in use.

Wi-Fi Direct will probably challenge the dominance of Bluetooth in the area of device-to-device networking. It offers a similar type of connectivity but with greater range and much faster data transfer.

MiFi.   *MiFi* is a small, portable wireless device that provides users with a permanent Wi-Fi hot spot wherever they go. Thus, users are always connected to the Internet. The range of the MiFi device is about 10 meters (roughly 30 feet). Developed by Novatel, the MiFi device is also called an *intelligent mobile hot spot*. Accessing Wi-Fi through the MiFi device allows up to five persons to be connected at the same time, sharing the same connection. MiFi also allows users to use Voice-over-IP technology (discussed in Chapter 6) to make free (or inexpensive) calls, both locally and internationally.

MiFi provides broadband Internet connectivity at any location that offers 3G cellular network coverage. One drawback is that MiFi is expensive both to acquire and to use.

Li-Fi. Light Fidelity (Li-Fi) is a technology for wireless communication among devices using light to transmit data and position. Li-Fi is a visible communications system that can transmit data at high speeds over the visible light spectrum, ultraviolet, and infrared radiation.

In terms of users, Li-Fi is similar to Wi-Fi. The key difference is that Wi-Fi uses electromagnetic waves at radio frequencies to transmit data. Using light to transmit data allows Li-Fi to offer several advantages over Wi-Fi:

- Li-Fi provides far greater bandwidth capacity.
- Li-Fi provides very high peak data transmission rates (theoretically up to 200 Gbps).
- Li-Fi enables communications among 100 times more devices on the Internet of Things.
- Li-Fi provides enhanced security for wireless communications due to reduced interception of signals.
- Li-Fi is more effective in areas susceptible to electromagnetic interference, such as aircraft cabins and hospitals.

Super Wi-Fi. The term *Super Wi-Fi* was coined by the U.S. Federal Communications Commission (FCC) to describe a wireless network proposal that creates long-distance wireless Internet connections. (Despite the name, Super Wi-Fi is *not* based on Wi-Fi technology.) Super Wi-Fi uses the lower-frequency "white spaces" between broadcast TV channels. These frequencies enable the signal to travel farther and penetrate walls better than normal Wi-Fi frequencies.

Super Wi-Fi is already in use in Houston, Texas; Wilmington, North Carolina; and the University of West Virginia. The technology threatens cell phone carriers, and it could eventually bring broadband wireless Internet access to rural areas.

Wide-Area Wireless Networks

Wide-area wireless networks connect users to the Internet over a geographically dispersed territory. These networks typically operate over the licensed spectrum—that is, they use portions of the wireless spectrum that are regulated by the government. In contrast, Bluetooth, Wi-Fi, and Super Wi-Fi operate over the unlicensed spectrum and are therefore more prone to interference and security problems. In general, wide-area wireless network technologies fall into two categories: cellular radio and wireless broadband.

Cellular Radio. **Cellular telephones (cell phones)** provide two-way radio communications over a cellular network of base stations with seamless handoffs. Cellular telephones differ from cordless telephones, which offer telephone service only within a limited range through a single base station attached to a fixed landline—for example, within a home or an office.

The cell phone communicates with radio antennas, or towers, placed within adjacent geographic areas called *cells* (see **Figure 8.5**). A telephone message is transmitted to the local cell—that is, the antenna—by the cell phone and is then passed from cell to cell until it reaches the cell of its destination. At this final cell, the message either is transmitted to the receiving cell phone or it is transferred to the public switched telephone system to be transmitted to a wireline telephone. This is why you can use a cell phone to call other cell phones as well as standard wireline phones.

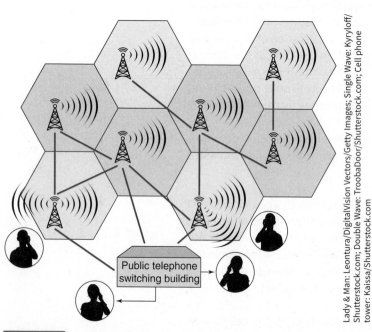

Lady & Man: Leontura/DigitalVision Vectors/Getty Images; Single Wave: Kyryloff/Shutterstock.com; Double Wave: TroobaDoor/Shutterstock.com; Cell phone tower: Kaissa/Shutterstock.com

Public telephone switching building

FIGURE 8.5 **A cellular network and the public switched telephone system.**

Cellular technology is quickly evolving, moving toward higher transmission speeds, richer features, and lower latencies (delays). This rapid evolution is necessary because more people are using mobile phones and tablets, and data traffic is exploding. Cellular technology has progressed through a number of stages:

- *First generation* (*1G*) cellular networks used analog signals and had low bandwidth (capacity).
- *Second generation* (*2G*) used digital signals primarily for voice communication; it provided data communication up to 10 kilobits per second (Kbps).
- *2.5G* used digital signals and provided voice and data communication up to 144 Kbps.
- *Third generation* (*3G*) uses digital signals and can transmit voice and data up to 384 Kbps when the device is moving at a walking pace, 128 Kbps when it is moving in a car, and up to 2 Mbps when it is in a fixed location. 3G supports video, Web browsing, and instant messaging.

    3G does have disadvantages. Perhaps the most fundamental problem is that cellular companies in North America use two separate technologies: Verizon and Sprint use Code Division Multiple Access (CDMA), while AT&T and T-Mobile use Global System for Mobile Communications (GSM). CDMA companies are currently using *Evolution-Data Optimized (EV-DO)* technology, which is a wireless broadband cellular radio standard.

    3G is also relatively expensive. In fact, most carriers limit how much information you can download and what you can use the service for. For example, some carriers prohibit you from downloading or streaming audio or video. If you exceed the carriers' limits, they reserve the right to cut off your service.

- *Fourth generation* (*4G*) is not one defined technology or standard. The International Telecommunications Union (ITU) has specified speed requirements for 4G: 100 Mbps (million bits per second) for high-mobility communications such as cars and trains, and 1 Gbps (billion bits per second) for low-mobility communications such as pedestrians. A 4G system is expected to provide a secure mobile broadband system to all types of mobile devices. Many of the current 4G offerings do not meet the ITU-specified speeds, but they call their service 4G nonetheless. See "IT's Personal" for more information.

    Long-term evolution (*LTE*) is a wireless broadband technology designed to support roaming Internet access through smartphones and handheld devices. LTE is approximately 10 times faster than 3G networks.

    XLTE (advanced LTE) is designed to handle network congestion when too many people in one area try to access an LTE network. XLTE is designed to provide all users with no decrease in bandwidth.

- *Fifth generation* (*5G*) began to be deployed in 2019. IT's About Business 8.2 discusses 5G in detail.

IT's About Business 8.2

Fifth Generation (5G) Mobile Networks

New generations of wireless telecommunications standards have appeared about every 10 years. By August 2018, wireless carriers had completed their deployment of 4G networks and were planning for the appearance of 5G wireless technologies. Consider the evolution of these technologies:

- First generation systems (1G) were introduced in 1982.
- Second generation systems (2G) appeared in 1992.
- Third generation systems (3G) appeared in 2001.
- Fourth generation systems (4G) appeared in 2012.

Fifth generation mobile networks, or fifth generation wireless systems (5G), are the proposed telecommunications standards beyond the current fourth generation systems (4G). 5G systems began appearing in 2019.

The Next Generation Mobile Networks Alliance (NGMN; **www.ngmn.org**) defines the following requirements that a 5G standard should have:

- High-bandwidth transmission: 5G signals are designed to transmit up to 10 gigabits per second (Gbps). In contrast, in the United States, 4G signals deliver a maximum of 1 Gbps.
- Low latency: Latency is the delay time it takes for the network or your device to respond to a command. 5G signals

are designed to have as little as a one millisecond delay, meaning that 5G devices can communicate nearly instantaneously. Interestingly, 5G is faster than the speed at which humans perceive auditory, visual, and physical responses to be instantaneous. To demonstrate the low latency of 5G communications, Verizon conducted an interesting experiment at the 2017 Indianapolis 500. A driver was placed in a car with blacked-out windows. He had only a 5G headcam (camera) to use for navigation. The driver drove the car around the track at high speeds with ease. The low latency of the 5G camera feed enabled him to "see" the curves and straightaways as reliably as if he had been able to physically view the track.

- A high number of simultaneously connected devices.

- Energy efficiency (low battery consumption): This characteristic is particularly important for communication among sensors.

- High reliability of communication.

5G does have disadvantages. Because 5G uses shorter wavelengths in its transmission than previous generations of wireless technologies, its signals are more easily obstructed. As a result, 5G will require many more antennas than previous generations.

5G promises to bring superior wireless communications to consumers. For example, consumers could download a 90-minute high-definition television show to their smartphones in fewer than 3 seconds. However consumers will need to buy a new phone.

The first substantial deployment of 5G technology occurred in South Korea in April, 2019. As of July, 2019 Verizon, AT&T, and Sprint have deployed 5G technology in limited areas of a few U.S. cities. T-Mobile also plans to deploy 5G in selected cities in 2019.

5G will support communication among objects as well as among people. The key advantage of 5G is that the technology enables machine-to-machine communications—that is, 5G is a necessary component for the Internet of Things (IoT). Note here that autonomous (driverless) vehicles, drones, and robotics are essentially IoT applications.

The Internet of Things is developing in two areas. First, *massive IoT* consists of thousands of connected sensors such as the ones used in smart meters. These sensors collect and transmit huge amounts of data. Second, *critical IoT* consists of sensors in motor vehicles, where low latency and communications reliability are keys to success.

The characteristics of 5G transmissions are essential for the commercialization of IoT applications. For example, consider autonomous vehicles, which must communicate with one another many times per second to avoid collisions. 5G's high-bandwidth transmission speed, low latency, low battery consumption, high reliability, and ability to support huge numbers of connected devices are all critically important characteristics that will help to make autonomous vehicles a viable technology.

As an example, in February 2018 Swedish communications company Ericsson (**www.ericsson.com**) deployed 5G technology at the Winter Olympics in Pyeongchang, South Korea. There, the company's 5G network guided self-driving buses through the athletes' village and enabled fans to experience the action live from tiny cameras embedded in the helmets of bobsledders.

Industry analysts expect that 5G will have the most immediate impact on these four industies when the 5G deployment is complete:

- Transportation: autonomous vehicles (trucks, cars, buses, and others);

- Manufacturing: automated factories (e.g., robots), real-time production inspection and assembly-line maintenance;

- Healthcare: remote telesurgery and patient monitoring;

- Smart cities: smart roadways, traffic lights, street lights, smart buildings, and smart metering.

Sources: Compiled from M. Goss, "Benefits of 5G to Drive Enterprise Adoption Regardless of Provider," *TechTarget*, May 2, 2019; "How 5G Will Transform Business," *TechRepublic*, 2019; P. Sarnoff, "Verizon Is Bringing Fixed 5G to Businesses," *Business Intelligence*, September 17, 2018; A. Rayome, "5 Things to Know about Verizon 5G Ultra Wideband Launching October 1," *TechRepublic*, September 12, 2018; R. Gronberg, "AT&T Says It Will Bring Its Super Fast 5G Network to Raleigh and Charlotte," *The Herald Sun*, July 20, 2018; A. Tan, "M1, Huawei to Transmit VR Content in 5G Live Trial," *TechTarget*, June 21, 2018; R. Hollander, "Verizon Just Announced Los Angeles Will Be the Second City to Receive 5G," Yahoo Finance, May 18, 2018; J. Brodkin, "AT&T's 5G Trials Produce Gigabit Speeds and 9ms Latency," *Ars Technica*, April 11, 2018; C. Forrest, "190M 5G Connections by 2025, as U.S. to Emerge as 'Pioneer Market'," *TechRepublic*, March 26, 2018; K. Yurieff, "AT&T Names First Three Cities to Get Its Ultra-Fast 5G Network," CNN, February 21, 2018; A. Scroxton, "Swisscom Picks Ericsson to Build Its 5G Network," *Computer Weekly*, November 8, 2017; "Digging Deep to Find the Future of Mobile," *Bloomberg BusinessWeek*, November 5, 2017; "State of 5G 2017 & Beyond," *IT Briefcase*, November 1, 2017; A. Scroxton, "Qualcomm Successfully Achieves First 5G Data Connection," *Computer Weekly*, October 17, 2017; E. Woyke, "These Toaster-Oven-Size Radios Will Help Bring 5G to Life," *MIT Technology Review*, March 10, 2017; A. Carlton, "The 5G Core Network: 3GPP Standards Progress," *Computerworld*, August 25, 2017; A. DelNisco, "5G Market Will Surpass $1.23 Trillion by 2026: These 8 Industries Will Benefit the Most," *TechRepublic*, February 27, 2017; L. Tucci, "How 5G Wireless Technology Will Dazzle, Confuse and Be of Use for CIOs," *TechTarget*, February 24, 2017; "What Is 5G, and When Do I Get It?" *Wired*, February 23, 2017; C. Forrest, "If You Live in One of These 11 Cities, Verizon 5G May Bring You Gigabit Wireless This Year," *TechRepublic*, February 22, 2017; O. Kharif and S. Moritz, "The Greatest Generation Is around the Corner," *Bloomberg BusinessWeek*, February 20, 2017; A. Scroxton, "Ericsson Introduces First 5G Network Platform," *Computer Weekly*, February 16, 2017; and "Three Keys to Success: Preparing Your Mobile Network for 5G," Cisco White Paper, December 6, 2016.

Questions

1. What are the most important advantages of 5G wireless technologies?

2. What are potential disadvantages of 5G wireless technologies?

3. What are the potential impacts of 5G on fiber-to-the-home?

Wireless Broadband, or WiMAX.   Worldwide Interoperability for Microwave Access, popularly known as WiMAX, is the name for IEEE Standard 802.16. WiMAX has a wireless access range of up to 31 miles, compared to 300 feet for Wi-Fi. WiMAX also has a data transfer rate of up to 75 Mbps. It is a secure system, and it offers features such as voice and video. WiMAX antennas can transmit broadband Internet connections to antennas on homes and businesses located miles away. For this reason, WiMAX can provide long-distance broadband wireless access to rural areas and other locations that are not currently being served.

Consider this example of the use of WiMAX. On April 1, 2015, a fire broke out in the underground electrical cable ducts in a tunnel under a major highway in London. The fire burned for 36 hours and caused major disruptions to broadband service in the area. With fiber-optic, broadband access to the Internet not available, businesses turned to WiMAX from the telecommunications company Luminet (**www.luminet.co.uk**). One business owner noted that Luminet helped his company get its main office back online in less than 24 hours. Furthermore, Luminet's broadband service helped the company quickly move its staff back from its disaster recovery site.

IT's Personal: Wireless and Mobile

What the GSM3GHSDPA+4GLTE?   This chapter explains the many mobile platforms that are available to you as a consumer. Specifically, it discusses cellular, Bluetooth, Wi-Fi, satellite, and other wireless options. Within the cellular area, however, things get confusing because the telecommunications companies use so many acronyms these days. Have you ever wondered if Verizon 3G was equivalent to AT&T 3G? What about 4G and 4G LTE? Of course, most people assume that 4G is faster than 3G, but by how much?

To appreciate this confusion, consider that when Apple released one update to its mobile operating system (iOS), AT&T suddenly began to display 4G rather than 3G on the iPhone—despite the fact that the phone had not been upgraded! Pretty nice, right? Wrong. In this instance, the "upgrade" simply consisted of a new terminology for the existing technology. The speed of the 3G/4G network had *not* changed. (*Note:* AT&T "4G LTE" is a different technology that does offer significantly higher speeds than AT&T 3G or 4G.)

Actual connection speeds are described in bit rates, meaning how many bits (1s or 0s) a device can transmit in 1 second. For example, a speed listed as 1.5 Mbps translates to 1.5 million bits per second. That sounds like a tremendous rate. Knowing the bits per second, however, is only part of understanding the actual speed. In reality, connection speed is not the same as *throughput,* which is the amount of bandwidth actually available for you to use. Throughput will always be less than the connection speed.

To understand this point, consider how your car operates. It is probably capable of driving more than 100 mph. However, you are "throttled down" by various speed limits, so you never reach this potential speed. Your actual speed varies, depending on the route you take, the speed limits imposed along that route, the weather, the amount of traffic, and many other factors. In the same way, even though AT&T, Verizon, Sprint, and other companies boast incredible wireless speeds ("Up to 20 Mbps!"), they will always say "up to" because they know that you will never actually download a file at that rate.

The best method for determining the actual speeds of the various networks is to go to your local wireless store and run a speed test using the demo model they have on display. This test will give you firsthand experience of the actual throughput speed you can expect from their network. The result is much more realistic than terms such as 3G, 4G, and 4G LTE.

Here is how to perform the test: First, make certain the unit is connected only to a cellular network (not Wi-Fi). Then go to **www.speedtest.net**, and click "Begin Test." I just ran this test from my iPhone 4S on AT&T's 4G (not 4G LTE) network. My download speed was 3.80 Mbps, and my upload speed was 1.71 Mbps. These numbers are more informative than any name they are given (3G, 4G, etc.) because they indicate exactly what I can expect from my wireless connection. Run this test at competing stores (AT&T, Verizon, Sprint, T-Mobile, etc.), and you will have real data to compare. As names change, you can always run a test to find the facts.

Before you go on . . .

1. What is Bluetooth? What is a WLAN?
2. Describe Wi-Fi, cellular service, and WiMAX.

8.3 Mobile Computing and Mobile Commerce

Author Lecture Videos are available exclusively in *WileyPLUS*.
Apply the Concept activities are available in the Appendix and in *WileyPLUS*.

In the traditional computing environment, users come to a computer, which is connected with wires to other computers and to networks. Because these networks need to be linked by wires, it is difficult or even impossible for people on the move to use them. In particular, salespeople, repair people, service employees, law enforcement agents, and utility workers can be more effective if they can use IT while in the field or in transit. Mobile computing was designed for workers who travel outside the boundaries of their organizations as well as for anyone traveling outside his or her home.

Mobile computing refers to a real-time connection between a mobile device and other computing environments, such as the Internet or an intranet. This innovation is revolutionizing how people use computers. It is spreading at work and at home; in education, health care, and entertainment; and in many other areas.

Mobile computing has two major characteristics that differentiate it from other forms of computing: mobility and broad reach. *Mobility* means that users carry a device with them and can initiate a real-time contact with other systems from wherever they happen to be. *Broad reach* refers to the fact that when users carry an open mobile device, they can be reached instantly, even across great distances.

Mobility and broad reach create five value-added attributes that break the barriers of geography and time: ubiquity, convenience, instant connectivity, personalization, and localization of products and services. A mobile device can provide information and communication regardless of the user's location *(ubiquity)*. With an Internet-enabled mobile device, users can access the Web, intranets, and other mobile devices quickly and easily, without booting up a PC or placing a call through a modem *(convenience and instant connectivity)*. A company can customize information and send it to individual consumers as a short message service (SMS) *(customization)*. And, knowing a user's physical location helps a company advertise its products and services *(localization)*. Mobile computing provides the foundation for mobile commerce (m-commerce), to which we now turn.

Mobile Commerce

Besides affecting our everyday lives, mobile computing is also transforming the ways organizations conduct business by enabling businesses and individuals to engage in mobile commerce. As you saw at the beginning of this chapter, **mobile commerce** (or *m-commerce*) refers to electronic commerce (EC) transactions that are conducted in a wireless environment, especially on the Internet. Like regular EC applications, m-commerce can be transacted on the Internet, private communication lines, smart cards, and other infrastructures. M-commerce creates opportunities for businesses to deliver new services to existing customers and to attract new customers. The development of m-commerce is driven by the widespread availability of mobile devices, the declining prices of such devices, and rapidly improving wireless bandwidth.

Mobile computing and m-commerce include many applications, which result from the capabilities of various technologies. You will examine these applications and their impact on business activities in the next section.

Mobile Commerce Applications

Mobile commerce applications are many and varied. The most popular applications include location-based applications, financial services, intrabusiness applications, accessing information, and telemetry. The rest of this section examines these various applications and their effects on the ways people live and do business.

FIN **Financial Services.**   Mobile financial applications include banking, wireless payments and micropayments, money transfers, mobile wallets, and bill-payment services. The bottom line for mobile financial applications is to make it more convenient for customers to transact business regardless of where they are or what time it is.

Web shoppers historically have preferred to pay with credit cards. Because credit card companies typically charge fees on transactions, however, credit cards are an inefficient way to make very small purchases. The growth of relatively inexpensive digital content, such as music (e.g., iTunes), ring tones, and downloadable games, is driving the growth of *micropayments*—that is, very small purchase amounts, usually less than $10—as merchants seek to avoid paying credit card fees on small transactions.

A **mobile wallet (m-wallet)**, also called a *digital wallet*, is an application (app) that people use to make financial transactions. These apps can be downloaded on users' desktops or on their smartphones. When the app is on a smartphone, it becomes a mobile wallet. Mobile wallets replace the need to carry physical credit and debit cards, gift cards, and loyalty cards, as well as boarding passes and other forms of identification. Mobile wallets may also store insurance and loyalty cards, drivers' licenses, ID cards, website passwords, and login information. Furthermore, mobile wallets eliminate having to enter shipping, billing, and credit card data each time you make a purchase at a website. The data are encrypted in the user's phone, tablet, or computer, and the wallet contains a digital certificate that identifies the authorized cardholder.

To use a mobile wallet, consumers wave their phones a few inches above a payment terminal instead of swiping a plastic card. This process uses near-field communication. There are a number of mobile wallets and payment apps from which to choose:

- *Google Wallet* is a mobile wallet that uses near-field communications to allow its users to store debit cards, credit cards, loyalty cards, and gift cards on their smartphones. With Google Wallet, users launch an app and then type in a pin so Google can access their stored card credentials. Google Wallet also provides a peer-to-peer payment system that can send money to a real, physical Google Wallet card.

- *Google Pay* (a different app from Google Wallet) allows users to tap and pay in stores and use and redeem loyalty cards, gift cards, and offers in stores.

- *Starbucks mobile pay app*, which launched before the other three top payment apps—Apple Pay, Google Pay, and Samsung Pay—is the most successful payment app. By the end of 2018, one-fourth of U.S. smartphone users over the age of 14 made an in-store mobile payment. More than 40 percent of them used the Starbucks app. The app lets users pay with their phones and earn credits toward future purchases. The Starbucks app is available on both iOS and Android, where Apple Pay, Google Pay, and Samsung Pay users are restricted by the type of phone they have.

- *Samsung Pay* is a mobile payment app and digital wallet that lets users make payments using compatible phones. The service supports contactless payments using near-field communications and also supports magnetic-stripe-only payment terminals. In countries like India, the service supports bill payments.

- *Google Tez* is Google's mobile payment application in Asia. Launched in India, Tez enables users to link their phones to their bank accounts to securely pay for goods both in physical stores and online. Tez also allows users to make person-to-person money transfers with Audio QR, a technology that uses ultrasonic sounds to let users exchange money, bypassing any need for NFC technology.

- *MasterCard's Contactless, American Express's ExpressPay,* and *Visa's PayWave* are EMV-compatible, contactless payment features. EMV—which stands for Europay, MasterCard, and Visa, the three companies that originally created the standard—is a technical standard for smart payment cards. EMV cards are smart cards that store their data on chips rather than on magnetic stripes. They can be either contact cards that must be physically inserted into a reader or contactless cards that can be read over a short distance using radio-frequency identification (RFID) technology. (We discuss RFID in Section 8.4.) EMV cards are also called chip-and-pin cards.

- *Apple Pay* is a mobile wallet that uses near-field communications to enable users to make payments using various Apple devices. Apple Pay does not require Apple-specific contactless payment terminals; rather, it will work with Visa's PayWave, Mastercard's PayPass, and American Express's ExpressPay terminals. The wallet is similar to other wallets with the addition of two-factor authentication. To pay at points of sale, users hold their authenticated Apple device to the point-of-sale system. iPhone users authenticate by holding their fingerprint to the phone's Touch ID sensor, and Apple Watch users authenticate by double-clicking a button on the device.

- *Amazon Pay* is a service that lets customers use the payment methods already associated with their Amazon accounts to make payment for goods and services on third-party websites. Amazon Pay Places allows users to order ahead and pay for goods in-store via the Amazon app.

- *Alipay Wallet* (**www.intl.alipay.com**) is a mobile and online payment platform from the Ant Financial Services Group (**www.antfin.com**), an affiliate company of the Chinese Alibaba Group (**www.alibabagroup.com**). Alipay provides numerous payment services. The platform operates with Visa and MasterCard to provide payment services for Taobao (a Chinese online shopping website) and Tmall (a Chinese-language website for B2C online retail spun off from Taobao), as well as almost 500,000 online and local Chinese businesses.

  Users can employ the app to pay for local in-store purchases, credit card bills, bank account management, person-to-person money transfers, train tickets, food orders, ride hailing, taxi fees, water and electricity utility bills, cable television fees, tuition fees, and traffic fines.

- *WeChat* (**www.Web.wechat.com**) is a Chinese messaging, social media, and mobile payment app developed by Tencent (**www.tencent.com**). WeChat Pay is a digital wallet service incorporated into WeChat. Users who have provided bank account information may use the app to pay bills, order goods and services, transfer money to other users, and pay in stores.

- *Huawei Pay:* Huawei (**www.huawei.com**), the Chinese mobile phone manufacturer, partnered with UnionPay, China's state-operated card network and launched the Huawei Pay mobile wallet in September 2016. The wallet uses NFC and biometrics to make in-store payment through Huawei phones. In 2019 Huawei was banned in the United States but the use of their technology continued internationally.

- *Peru Digital Payments*, a company owned and operated by that country's leading financial institutions, launched Bim in 2016. Bim is a mobile payment program that consolidates all of their online customer interfaces in a single system. The software is the first of its kind. Although there are 255 mobile money programs in 89 countries, no other program includes all of a country's banks. Furthermore, all three major Peruvian wireless carriers will offer users access to Bim.

The stakes in this competition are enormous because the small fees generated every time consumers swipe their cards add up to tens of billions of dollars annually in the United States alone. The potential for large revenue streams is real because mobile wallets have clear advantages. For example: Which are you more likely to have with you at any given moment—your phone or your physical wallet? Also, keep in mind that if you lose your phone, it can be located on a map and remotely deactivated. Plus, your phone can be password protected. Your physical wallet, however, cannot perform these functions.

Location-Based Applications and Services.

M-commerce B2C applications include location-based services and location-based applications. Location-based mobile commerce is called **location-based commerce** (or L-commerce).

Location-based services provide information that is specific to a given location. For example, a mobile user can (1) request the nearest business or service, such as an ATM or a restaurant; (2) receive alerts, such as a warning of a traffic jam or an accident; and (3) locate a friend. Wireless carriers can provide location-based services such as locating taxis, service personnel, doctors, and rental equipment; scheduling fleets; tracking objects such as packages and train boxcars; finding information such as navigation, weather, traffic, and room schedules; targeting advertising; and automating airport check-ins.

MKT Consider, for example, how location-based advertising can make the marketing process more productive. Marketers can use this technology to integrate the current locations and preferences of mobile users. They can then send user-specific advertising messages concerning nearby shops, malls, and restaurants to consumers' wireless devices.

There are many examples of location-based applications and services. IT's About Business 8.3 addresses the value of GasBuddy, particularly in disasters.

IT's About Business 8.3

GasBuddy

MIS **POM**

GasBuddy (**www.gasbuddy.com**) is a source for crowdsourced, real-time fuel prices at more than 150,000 gas station convenience stores in the United States, Canada, and Australia. The 70 million drivers who have downloaded the company's app also report on fuel availability, cleanliness, coffee, customer service, outdoor lighting, restrooms, and overall experience at the stores. The firm's latest ranking in July 2019 indicated that Chevron won the top spot in four categories, including cleanliness, customer service, outdoor lighting, and overall experience. Marathon won the coffee category and Mobil won the restroom category.

GasBuddy earns money from advertising and sponsorship on its free app and also offers a paid service to fuel marketers and retailers. Therefore, these quarterly rankings are very important to GasBuddy (due to large amounts of data) as well as the gas station convenience stores.

Bargain hunters have been using GasBuddy for some time to find gas stations that offer the cheapest prices. Furthermore, GasBuddy's fuel saving program, called Pay with GasBuddy, offers a gas payment card tied to customers' checking accounts, that automatically deducts gas purchases from their bank balances at 5 cents per gallon below the price advertised at the pump. The program has saved Americans more than $6 million at the pumps since its launch in 2017.

GasBuddy also offers critically important information on the availability of gas in times of natural disasters. Prior to superstorm Sandy, which hit the East Coast in 2012, GasBuddy had not focused on gasoline supply. However, the company developed its gas-tracker function in response to the huge storm. GasBuddy worked with New York officials and federal agencies to provide real-time information about fuel availability in Sandy's aftermath.

GasBuddy anticipated shortages from Hurricane Harvey, which made landfall in Texas on August 25, 2017, and the firm activated its gas-outage tracker. The app allows drivers and fuel retailers to report whether a station has both fuel and power. GasBuddy also activated a similar service for diesel fuel, which is used by truck drivers as well as many emergency vehicles. Rescue workers in Houston also used GasBuddy to see where to fill up boats and rescue vehicles.

With Hurricane Irma heading toward Florida, drivers began filling their tanks. The result was widespread fuel shortages and very long gas lines. A Miami resident needed to fuel up her car before the hurricane made landfall in Florida on September 10, 2017. She went to several gas stations, but all of them were out of gasoline. Then she remembered an app that a friend had mentioned to her. The app was GasBuddy. It directed her to two filling stations. When she visited the first one, it not only had gasoline but there also were no lines.

Hurricane Irma was a significant event in GasBuddy's history. On Friday, September 8, 2017, GasBuddy was the second-most-downloaded iPhone app in the United States, up from 57th place the previous morning, according to Sensor Tower (**www.sensortower.com**), a mobile-analytics firm. Sensor Tower estimated that GasBuddy was downloaded more than 800,000 times between August 25, when Hurricane Harvey made landfall in Texas, and September 7. This volume of usage challenged the 120-employee company. GasBuddy had to ensure that the website and app kept operating under the strain of additional usage.

On Friday, September 8, 2017, GasBuddy flew two analysts who study petroleum markets and convenience stores to Tallahassee to help Florida officials direct fuel resources and to advise people where to obtain fuel. Then-Governor Rick Scott emphasized the company as a method for Floridians to find fuel so they could evacuate.

There can be problems with crowdsourced data, which can be inaccurate. GasBuddy asserts that the company makes an effort to verify the data it obtains from users, and it will not post price reports submitted too far away from stations to be reliable.

GasBuddy made two improvements to its app so those in need could better locate stations with fuel and power in hurricane-affected areas. First, the app now has a timestamp next to each gas station status report to ensure a more accurate experience when locating stations with fuel. Second, GasBuddy users are able to share gas station updates with their family and friends.

Users took advantage of the new features of GasBuddy's app when the company activiated its fuel tracker for Hurricane Florence in September 2018 and for tropical storm Barry in July, 2019.

Sources: Compiled from "GasBuddy Debuts New Consumer Ranking for Fuel and Convenience Brands with 4,000+ Locations," *GasBuddy News Release*, July 9, 2019; "GasBuddy Fuel Tracker Activated for Hurricane Florence," GasBuddy News Release, September 10, 2018; "GasBuddy Releases New App Features to Better Aid Affected Motorists during 2018 Hurricane Season," GasBuddy News Release, August 2, 2018; A. Griswold, "Tech Companies Are Redefining How We Respond to Natural Disasters – In a Good Way," *Quartz*, September 13, 2017; B. Oakes, "GasBuddy in Boston Uses App to Point Hurricane Victims to Open Fuel Stations," WBUR, September 13, 2017; "GasBuddy: App Helps Drivers Find Gas," WJHG, September 13, 2017; D. Wethe, "As Florida Fuel Grew Scarce, GasBuddy App Change Filled Gap," *Bloomberg*, September 12, 2017; A. Sider, "A Fuel App Scores Big During Shortage," *Wall Street Journal*, September 11, 2017; A. Hartmans, "An App for Finding Nearby Gas Stations Is No. 2 in the App Store as Florida Prepares for Hurricane Irma," *Business Insider*, September 8, 2017; B. Tuttle, "Florida Is Running out of Gasoline. This App Is Helping People Find It," *Time*, September 7, 2017; "Gas-Buddy: Making Friends on Both Sides of the Gas Pump," *PYMNTS*, September 5, 2017; J. Wattles, "Dallas' Gas Panic Was Totally Preventable. Here's Why," CNN, September 1, 2017; "GasBuddy Activates Gas Availability Tracker," *BusinessWire*, August 31, 2017; J. Graham, "GasBuddy App Vows to Save 5 Cents a Gallon with New Feature," *USA Today*, August 28, 2017; and www.gasbuddy.com, accessed July 15, 2019

Questions

1. What are potential disadvantages to motorists when they use GasBuddy?

2. What is another function that GasBuddy could provide either in its existing app or in a new app?

3. Explain how GasBuddy is a location-based app.

MKT **Mobile Advertising.** *Mobile advertising* is a form of advertising through cell phones, smartphones, or other mobile devices. Analysts estimate that mobile advertising revenue will reach approximately $7 billion by 2020.

Intrabusiness Applications. Although business-to-consumer (B2C) m-commerce receives considerable publicity, most of today's m-commerce applications actually are used *within* organizations. In this section, you will see how companies use mobile computing to support their employees.

POM Mobile devices increasingly are becoming an integral part of workflow applications. For example, companies can use non-voice mobile services to assist in dispatch functions—that is, to assign jobs to mobile employees, along with detailed information about the job. Target areas for mobile delivery and dispatch services include transportation (delivery of food, oil, newspapers, cargo; courier services; tow trucks; taxis), utilities (gas, electricity, phone, water); field service (computers, office equipment, home repair); health care (visiting nurses, doctors, social services); and security (patrols, alarm installation).

Accessing Information. Another vital function of mobile technology is to help users obtain and use information. Two types of technologies—mobile portals and voice portals—are designed to aggregate and deliver content in a form that will work within the limited space available on mobile devices.

A **mobile portal** aggregates and provides content and services for mobile users. These services include news, sports, and e-mail; entertainment, travel, and restaurant information; community services; and stock trading. Major players around the world are i-mode from NTT DoCoMo (**www.nttdocomo.co.jp/english/**), Vodafone, O2, T-Mobile, Yahoo!, AOL, and MSN.

A **voice portal** is a website with an audio interface. Voice portals are not websites in the normal sense because they can also be accessed through a standard phone or a cell phone. A phone number connects you to a website, on which you can request information verbally. The system finds the information, translates it into a computer-generated voice reply, and tells you what you want to know. Most airlines use voice portals to provide real-time information on flight status.

Another example of a voice portal is the voice-activated 511 travel-information line developed by Tellme.com. This technology helps callers inquire about weather, local restaurants, current traffic, and other valuable information.

POM **Telemetry Applications.** **Telemetry** refers to the wireless transmission and receipt of data gathered from remote sensors. Telemetry has numerous mobile computing applications. For example, technicians can use telemetry to identify maintenance problems in equipment, and doctors can monitor patients and control medical equipment from a distance. Car manufacturers use telemetry applications for remote vehicle diagnosis and preventive maintenance. For example, drivers of many General Motors cars use its OnStar system (**www.onstar.com**) in numerous ways.

An interesting telemetry application for individuals is an iPhone app called Find My iPhone. Find My iPhone is a part of the Apple iCloud (**www.apple.com/icloud**). This app provides several very helpful telemetry functions. If you lose your iPhone, for example, it offers two ways to find its approximate location on a map. First, you can sign in to the Apple iCloud from any computer. Second, you can use the Find My iPhone app on another iPhone, iPad, or iPod Touch.

If you remember where you left your iPhone, you can write a message and display it on your iPhone's screen. The message might say, "Left my iPhone. Please call me at 301-555-1211." Your message appears on your iPhone, even if the screen is locked. And, if the map indicates that your iPhone is nearby—perhaps in your office under a pile of papers—you can tell Find My iPhone to play a sound that overrides the volume or silent setting.

If you left your iPhone in a public place, you may want to protect its contents. You can remotely set a four-digit passcode lock to prevent people from using your iPhone, accessing your personal information, or tampering with your settings. Going further, you can initiate a remote wipe (erase all contents) to restore your iPhone to its factory settings. If you eventually find your phone, then you can connect it to your computer and use iTunes to restore the data from your most recent backup.

If you have lost your iPhone and you do not have access to a computer, you can download the Find My iPhone app to a friend's iPhone, iPad, or iPod Touch and then sign in to access all the Find My iPhone features.

Before you go on . . .

1. What are the major drivers of mobile computing?
2. Describe mobile portals and voice portals.
3. Describe wireless financial services.
4. Discuss some of the major intrabusiness wireless applications.

8.4 | The Internet of Things

The **Internet of Things (IoT)**, also called the *Internet of Everything,* the *Internet of Anything,* the *Industrial Internet,* and *machine-to-machine (M2M) communication,* is a system in which any object, natural or manmade, has a unique identity (i.e., its own IP address) and is able to send and receive information over a network (i.e., the Internet) without human interaction. The adoption of IPv6 (discussed in Chapter 6), which created a vast number of IP addresses, has been an important factor in the development of the IoT. In fact, there are enough IP addresses to uniquely identify every object on Earth. The emergence of 5G technologies will also be critically important in providing the communications infrastructure for the IoT.

The IoT can be considered as invisible "everywhere computing" that is embedded in the objects around us. Examples of objects are your clock radio, your kitchen appliances, your thermostat, your clothing, your smartphone, a cardiac patient's heart monitor, a chip in a farm animal, and automobile sensors that alert a driver when tire pressure is low or the gas tank needs to be refilled.

Wireless sensors are an underlying technology of the Internet of Things. A **wireless sensor** is an autonomous device that monitors its own condition as well as physical and environmental conditions around it, such as temperature, sound, pressure, vibration, and movement. Sensors can also control physical systems, such as opening and closing a valve and adjusting the fuel mixture in your car. Wireless sensors can be as small as a grain of rice.

Author Lecture Videos are available exclusively in *WileyPLUS.*
Apply the Concept activities are available in the Appendix and in *WileyPLUS.*

Wireless sensors collect data from many points over an extended space. A sensor contains processing, storage, and radio-frequency antennas for sending and receiving messages. Each sensor "wakes up" or activates for a fraction of a second when it has data to transmit. It then relays those data to its nearest neighbor. So, rather than every sensor transmitting its data to a remote computer, the data travel from sensor to sensor until they reach a central computer, where they are stored and analyzed. An advantage of this process is that if one sensor fails, then another one can pick up the data. This process is efficient and reliable, and it extends the battery life of the sensor. Also, if the network requires additional bandwidth, then operators can boost performance by placing new sensors when and where they are required.

Wireless sensors provide information that enables a central computer to integrate reports of the same activity from different angles within the network. This system enables the network to determine with much greater accuracy myriad types of information such as the direction in which a person is moving, the weight of a vehicle, and the amount of rainfall over a field of crops. One type of wireless sensor uses radio-frequency identification (RFID) technology, which we discuss next.

Radio-Frequency Identification

Radio-frequency identification (RFID) technology allows manufacturers to attach tags with antennas and computer chips on goods and then track their movement using radio signals. RFID was developed to replace bar codes.

A typical bar code, known as the *Universal Product Code* (*UPC*), is made up of 12 digits that are batched in various groups. Bar codes have worked well, but they have limitations. First, they require a line-of-sight to the scanning device. This system works well in a store, but it can pose substantial problems in a manufacturing plant or a warehouse or on a shipping and receiving dock. Second, because bar codes are printed on paper, they can be ripped, soiled, or lost. Third, the bar code identifies the manufacturer and product but not the actual item.

Quick response (QR) codes are also used in place of bar codes. A *QR code* is a two-dimensional code, readable by dedicated QR readers and camera phones. **Figure 8.6** illustrates bar codes, QR codes, and an RFID tag. QR codes have several advantages over bar codes:

- QR codes can store much more information.
- Data types stored in QR codes include numbers, text, URLs, and even Japanese characters.
- QR codes are smaller because they store information both horizontally and vertically.
- QR codes can be read from any direction or angle, so they are less likely to be misread.
- QR codes are more resistant to damage.

RFID systems use tags with embedded microchips, which contain data, and antennas to transmit radio signals over a short distance to RFID readers. The readers pass the data over a network to a computer for processing. The chip in the RFID tag is programmed with information that uniquely identifies an item. It also contains information about the item such as its location and where and when it was made (see **Figure 8.7**).

There are two basic types of RFID tags: active and passive. *Active RFID tags* use internal batteries for power, and they broadcast radio waves to a reader. Because active tags contain batteries, they are more expensive than passive RFID tags, and they can be read over greater distances. Therefore, they are used primarily for more expensive items. In contrast, *passive RFID tags* rely entirely on readers for their power. They are less expensive than active tags, but they can be read only up to 20 feet. For these reasons, they are generally applied to less expensive merchandise. Problems with RFID include expense and the comparatively large size of the tags.

← QR code

iStock.com/Oehoeboeroe

← RFID tag

iStock.com/ra-photos

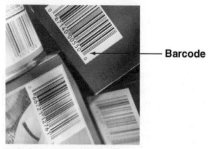

← Barcode

Stoked/Stockbyte/Media Bakery

FIGURE 8.6 **Bar codes, RFID tags, and QR codes.**

Ecken, Dominique/Keystone Pressedienst/Zuma Press

FIGURE 8.7 **Small RFID reader and RFID tag.**

Examples of the Internet of Things in Use

There are numerous examples of how the Internet of Things is being deployed. We discuss just a few of them here:

- *The Smart Home:* In a *smart home,* your home computer, television, lighting and heating controls, home security system (including smart window and door locks), thermostats, and appliances have embedded sensors and can communicate with one another through a home network. You control these networked objects through various devices, including your pager, smartphone, television, home computer, and even your automobile. Appropriate service providers and homeowners can access the devices for which they are authorized. Smart home technology can be applied to any building, turning it into a smart building.

  Consider Nest Labs (**www.nest.com**; now owned by Google), which produces a digital thermostat that combines sensors and Web technology. The thermostat senses not only air temperature but also the movements of people in a house. It then adjusts room temperatures accordingly to save energy.

- **POM** *Digital Twins:* A digital twin is a virtual representation of a real-world product or service. Consider a wind farm. Outfitted with sensors, the physical parts of a wind farm feed sensor data to its digital twins. These computer models constantly monitor the data of the real-world turbines. If a potential problem is about to occur, then the digital twin predicts it before it happens.

- *Health care:* Patients with non-life-threatening conditions can either wear sensors or have them implanted—for example, to monitor blood pressure or glucose levels. These sensors are monitored by medical staff. In many cases, the patients can be shown how to interpret the sensor data themselves. Also, consumer-oriented sensors such as the Fitbit can encourage people to adopt healthier lifestyles.

- *Automotive:* Modern cars have many sensors that monitor functions such as engine operation, tire pressure, fluid levels, and many others. Cars can warn drivers of impending mechanical or other problems and automatically summon roadside assistance or emergency services when necessary. Furthermore, sensors provide advanced driver assistance such as automatic parking, monitoring blind spots, detecting driver drowsiness, forward collision warning, and many other functions.

- **POM** *Supply Chain Management:* The IoT can make a company's supply chain much more transparent. A company can now track, in real time, the movement of raw materials and parts through the manufacturing process to finished products delivered to the customer. Sensors in fleet vehicles (e.g., trucks) can monitor the condition of sensitive consignments (e.g., the temperature of perishable food). They can also trigger automatic security alerts if a container is opened unexpectedly.

- *Environmental Monitoring:* Sensors monitor air and water quality, atmospheric and soil conditions, and the movements of wildlife.

- **POM** *Infrastructure Management:* Sensors monitor infrastructure such as bridges, railway tracks, and roads. They can identify and report changes in structural conditions that can compromise safety.

- **POM** *Energy Management:* Sensors will be integrated into all forms of energy-consuming devices, for example, switches, power outlets, light bulbs, and televisions. They will be able to communicate directly with utility companies through smart meters to balance power generation and energy usage. Another valuable application of sensors is to use them in smart electrical meters, thereby forming a *smart grid.* For example, in 2018, Gochang was the first county in South Korea to install smart meters for all its residents at one time. The results have been impressive. Costs stemming from water leakages dropped 19 percent and residents, particularly the elderly, experienced increased safety. The smart meters alert officials if households have not used water in 48 hours and they can contact the residents or their family members.

- **POM** *Agriculture:* Sensors monitor, in real time, air temperature, humidity, soil temperature, soil moisture, leaf wetness, atmospheric pressure, solar radiation, trunk/stem/fruit diameter, wind speed and direction, and rainfall. The data from these sensors are used in precision agriculture. *Precision agriculture* is a farming technique based on observing, measuring, and responding to inter- and intra-field variability in crops.

- **POM** *Transportation:* Sensors placed on complex transportation machines such as jet engines and locomotives can provide critical information on their operations. Consider General Electric (GE; www.ge.com), which embeds "intelligence" in the form of 250 sensors in each of its giant locomotives. The sensors produce 9 million data points every hour. How can these sensors improve the performance of such a huge machine?

  One of the biggest problems on locomotives is faulty bearings. If a bearing fails, then an axle might freeze, leaving a train marooned on the tracks. In remote areas, this situation could be disastrous, not to mention expensive, because other trains would back up for miles behind the stalled one. In this situation, the company would have to send a crane to lift the locomotive off the track and transport it back to a shop.

  To avoid this type of scenario, GE embeds one sensor inside each locomotive's gear case that transmits data on oil levels and contaminants. By examining these data, GE can predict the conditions that cause bearings to fail and axles to freeze. GE data analysts claim that sensors that predict part failures before they occur will translate into billions of dollars of savings for GE's rail customers.

  GE also uses locomotive sensors to optimize the entire network of U.S. trains. Today, the average velocity of a freight train operating between U.S. cities ranges from 20 to 25 miles per hour. Why is this number so low? The reason is a combination of factors: congestion in the train yards, breakdowns (see the preceding discussion), and the need to frequently allow other trains to pass. To address this problem, GE has developed a software tool called Movement Planner that gathers and integrates sensor data on velocity, traffic, and location from many locomotives. This analysis increases the average speed of its customers' trains. One of GE's customers, Norfolk Southern, maintains that an average speed increase of 1 mile per hour for its trains would be worth $200 million. GE's goal is to increase average train speeds by 4 miles per hour.

- *Animal husbandry:* Dairy cattle are largely "produced" by artificial insemination but only if the procedure occurs when a cow is in estrus. Cows are only in estrus about once every 21 days and estrus lasts only 12 to 18 hours. Unfortunately, estrus usually occurs between 10 p.m. and 8 a.m., when the farmers are sleeping. Further, estrus is difficult to predict as it relies on farmers' experience. In fact, farmers only get it right statistically about 55 percent of the time.

  As a result, Japanese dairy farmers wanted to know how to increase their percentage of successful artificial inseminations and they turned to data scientists at Fujitsu. To gather data, the scientists inserted sensors into the cows' first stomach, which measured the number of steps a cow takes. After data collection, the scientists found that the onset of estrus could be detected because the cows took significantly more steps (measured by the sensor). When the number of steps for a particular cow increased in that manner, estrus began 16 hours later.

  Significantly, if artificial insemination took place in the first 2 hours of estrus, there was a much higher probability of producing a female. If the procedure took place later in estrus, there was a higher probability of producing a male. Furthermore, the scientists claimed that, using the number of steps a cow takes, it is possible to detect as many as 10 different diseases! Using this application of the Internet of Things, Japanese farmers were able to significantly increase their herd size and the health of their cows.

Before you go on . . .

1. Define the Internet of Things and RFID.
2. Provide two examples (other than those mentioned in this section) of how the Internet of Things benefits organizations (public sector, private sector, for-profit, or not-for-profit).
3. Provide two specific business uses of RFID technology.

What's in IT for me?

`ACCT` For the Accounting Major

Wireless applications help accountants count and audit inventory. They also expedite the flow of information for cost control. Price management, inventory control, and other accounting-related activities can be improved with the use of wireless technologies.

`FIN` For the Finance Major

Wireless services can provide banks and other financial institutions with a competitive advantage. For example, wireless electronic payments, including micropayments, are more convenient (anywhere, anytime) than traditional means of payment, and they are less expensive. Electronic bill payment from mobile devices is becoming more popular, increasing security and accuracy, expediting cycle time, and reducing processing costs.

`MKT` For the Marketing Major

Imagine a whole new world of marketing, advertising, and selling, with the potential to increase sales dramatically. Such is the promise of mobile computing. Of special interest for marketers is location-based advertising as well as the new opportunities resulting from the Internet of Things and RFID. Finally, wireless technology also provides new opportunities in sales force automation (SFA), enabling faster and better communications with both customers (CRM) and corporate services.

`POM` For the Production/Operations Management Major

Wireless technologies offer many opportunities to support mobile employees of all kinds. Wearable computers enable off-site employees and repair personnel working in the field to service customers faster, better, and less expensively. Wireless devices can also increase productivity within factories by enhancing communication and collaboration as well as managerial planning and control. Mobile computing technologies can also improve safety by providing quicker warning signs and instant messaging to isolated employees.

`HRM` For the Human Resource Management Major

Mobile computing can improve HR training and extend it to any place at any time. Payroll notices can be delivered as SMSs. Wireless devices can also make what they do even more convenient for employees to select their own benefits and update their personal data.

`MIS` For the MIS Major

MIS personnel provide the wireless infrastructure that enables all organizational employees to compute and communicate anytime, anywhere. This convenience provides exciting, creative, new applications for organizations to reduce expenses and improve the efficiency and effectiveness of operations (e.g., to achieve transparency in supply chains). Unfortunately, as you read earlier, wireless applications are inherently insecure. This lack of security is a serious problem with which MIS personnel must contend.

Summary

8.1 Identify advantages and disadvantages of each of the three main types of wireless transmission media.

Microwave transmission systems are used for high-volume, long-distance, line-of-sight communication. One advantage is the high volume. A disadvantage is that microwave transmissions are susceptible to environmental interference during severe weather such as heavy rain and snowstorms.

Satellite transmission systems make use of communication satellites, and they receive and transmit data through line-of-sight. One advantage is that the enormous footprint—the area of Earth's surface reached by a satellite's transmission—overcomes the limitations of microwave data relay stations. Like microwaves, satellite transmissions are susceptible to environmental interference during severe weather.

Radio transmission systems use radio-wave frequencies to send data directly between transmitters and receivers. An advantage is that radio waves travel easily through normal office walls. A disadvantage is that radio transmissions are susceptible to snooping by anyone who has similar equipment that operates on the same frequency.

8.2 Explain how businesses can use short-range, medium-range, and long-range wireless networks, respectively.

Short-range wireless networks simplify the task of connecting one device to another, eliminating wires, and enabling people to move around while they use the devices. In general, short-range wireless networks have a range of 100 feet or fewer. Short-range wireless networks include Bluetooth, ultra-wideband, and near-field communications. A business application of ultra-wideband is the PLUS Real-Time Location System from Time Domain. Using PLUS, an organization can locate multiple people and assets simultaneously.

Medium-range wireless networks include Wi-Fi networks. *Wi-Fi* provides fast and easy Internet or intranet broadband access from public hot spots located at airports, hotels, Internet cafés, universities, conference centers, offices, and homes.

Wide-area wireless networks connect users to the Internet over geographically dispersed territory. They include cellular telephones and wireless broadband. *Cellular telephones* provide two-way radio communications over a cellular network of base stations with seamless hand-offs. *Wireless broadband* has a wireless access range of up to 31 miles and a data transfer rate of up to 75 Mbps. WiMAX can provide long-distance broadband wireless access to rural areas and remote business locations.

8.3 Provide a specific example of how each of the five major m-commerce applications can benefit a business.

Location-based services provide information specific to a location. For example, a mobile user can (1) request the nearest business or service, such as an ATM or restaurant; (2) receive alerts, such as a warning of a traffic jam or an accident; and (3) find a friend. With *location-based advertising,* marketers can integrate the current locations and preferences of mobile users. They can then send user-specific advertising messages about nearby shops, malls, and restaurants to wireless devices.

Mobile financial applications include banking, wireless payments and micropayments, money transfers, wireless wallets, and bill payment services. The bottom line for mobile financial applications is to make it more convenient for customers to transact business regardless of where they are or what time it is.

Intrabusiness applications consist of m-commerce applications that are used *within* organizations. Companies can use non-voice mobile services to assist in dispatch functions—that is, to assign jobs to mobile employees, along with detailed information about the jobs. When it comes to *accessing information,* mobile portals and voice portals are designed to aggregate and deliver content in a form that will work within the limited space available on mobile devices. These portals provide information anywhere and anytime to users.

Telemetry is the wireless transmission and receipt of data gathered from remote sensors. Company technicians can use telemetry to identify maintenance problems in equipment. Car manufacturers use telemetry applications for remote vehicle diagnosis and preventive maintenance.

8.4 Describe the Internet of Things along with examples of how various organizations can use the Internet of Things.

The Internet of Things (IoT) is a system in which any object, natural or man-made, has a unique identity (using IPv6) and the ability to send and receive information over a network (i.e., the Internet) without human interaction.

We leave the examples of various uses of the IoT up to the student.

Chapter Glossary

Bluetooth Chip technology that enables short-range connection (data and voice) between wireless devices.

cellular telephones (cell phones) Phones that provide two-way radio communications over a cellular network of base stations with seamless handoffs.

global positioning system (GPS) A wireless system that uses satellites to enable users to determine their position anywhere on Earth.

hot spot A small geographical perimeter within which a wireless access point provides service to a number of users.

Internet of Things (IoT) A scenario in which objects, animals, and people are provided with unique identifiers and the ability to automatically transfer data over a network without requiring human-to-human or human-to-computer interaction.

location-based commerce (L-commerce) Mobile commerce transactions targeted to individuals in specific locations, at specific times.

microwave transmission A wireless system that uses microwaves for high-volume, long-distance, point-to-point communication.

mobile commerce (or m-commerce) Electronic commerce transactions that are conducted with a mobile device.

mobile computing A real-time connection between a mobile device and other computing environments, such as the Internet or an intranet.

mobile portal A portal that aggregates and provides content and services for mobile users.

mobile wallet (m-wallet) A technology that allows users to make purchases with a single click from their mobile devices.

near-field communication (NFC) The smallest of the short-range wireless networks that is designed to be embedded in mobile devices like cell phones and credit cards.

personal area network A computer network used for communication among computer devices close to one person.

propagation delay Any delay in communications from signal transmission time through a physical medium.

radio-frequency identification (RFID) technology A wireless technology that allows manufacturers to attach tags with antennas and computer chips on goods and then track their movement through radio signals.

radio transmission Uses radio-wave frequencies to send data directly between transmitters and receivers.

satellite radio (or digital radio) A wireless system that offers uninterrupted, near CD-quality sound that is beamed to your radio from satellites.

satellite transmission A wireless transmission system that uses satellites for broadcast communications.

telemetry The wireless transmission and receipt of data gathered from remote sensors.

ultra-wideband (UWB) A high-bandwidth wireless technology with transmission speeds in excess of 100 Mbps that can be used for applications such as streaming multimedia from, say, a personal computer to a television.

voice portal A website with an audio interface.

wireless Telecommunications in which electromagnetic waves carry the signal between communicating devices.

wireless access point An antenna connecting a mobile device to a wired local area network.

Wireless Fidelity (Wi-Fi) A set of standards for wireless local area networks based on the IEEE 802.11 standard.

wireless local area network (WLAN) A computer network in a limited geographical area that uses wireless transmission for communication.

wireless sensor An autonomous device that monitors its own condition as well as physical and environmental conditions around it, such as temperature, sound, pressure, vibration, and movement.

Discussion Questions

1. Given that you can lose a cell phone as easily as a wallet, which do you feel is a more secure way of carrying your personal data? Support your answer.

2. If mobile computing is the next wave of technology, would you ever feel comfortable with handing a waiter or waitress your cell phone to make a payment at a restaurant the way you currently hand over your credit or debit card? Why or why not?

3. What happens if you lose your NFC-enabled smartphone or it is stolen? How do you protect your personal information?

4. In your opinion, is the mobile (or digital) wallet a good idea? Why or why not?

5. Discuss how m-commerce can expand the reach of e-business.

6. Discuss how mobile computing can solve some of the problems of the digital divide.

7. Explain the benefits that wireless commerce provides to consumers and the benefits that wireless commerce provides to merchants.

8. Discuss the ways in which Wi-Fi is being used to support mobile computing and m-commerce. Describe the ways in which Wi-Fi is affecting the use of cellular phones for m-commerce.

9. You can use location-based tools to help you find your car or the closest gas station. However, some people see location-based tools as an invasion of privacy. Discuss the pros and cons of location-based tools.

10. Discuss the benefits of telemetry in health care for the elderly.

11. Discuss how wireless devices can help people with disabilities.

12. Some experts say that Wi-Fi is winning the battle with 3G cellular service. Others disagree. Discuss both sides of the argument and support each one.

13. Which of the applications of the Internet of Things do you think are likely to gain the greatest market acceptance over the next few years? Why?

Problem-Solving Activities

1. Investigate commercial applications of voice portals. Visit several vendors, for example, Microsoft and Nuance. What capabilities and applications do these vendors offer?

2. Examine how new data-capture devices such as RFID tags help organizations accurately identify and segment their customers for activities such as targeted marketing. Browse the Web, and develop five potential new applications not listed in this chapter for RFID technology. What issues would arise if a country's laws mandated that such devices be embedded in everyone's body as a national identification system?

3. Investigate commercial uses of GPS. Start with **www.neigps.com**. Can some of the consumer-oriented products be used in industry? Prepare a report on your findings.

4. Access **www.bluetooth.com**. Examine the types of products being enhanced with Bluetooth technology. Present two of these products to the class and explain how they are enhanced by Bluetooth technology.

5. Explore **www.nokia.com**. Prepare a summary of the types of mobile services and applications Nokia currently supports and plans to support in the future.

6. Enter **www.ibm.com**. Search for "wireless e-business." Research the resulting stories to determine the types of wireless capabilities and applications IBM's software and hardware support. Describe some of the ways these applications have helped specific businesses and industries.

7. Enter **www.onstar.com**. What types of *fleet* services does OnStar provide? Are these any different from the services OnStar provides to individual car owners? (Play the movie.)

Closing Case

Google Fi

MIS

In April 2015, Google announced its new wireless service, Google Fi (now called Google Fi; (**www.fi.google.com**), a prepaid phone service that provides users with mobile data service on three mobile networks—Sprint (**www.sprint.com**), T-Mobile (**www.tmobile.com**), and U.S. Cellular (**www.uscellular.com**)—as well as on Wi-Fi networks. In July 2016, Google Fi announced a deal with Three

(**www.three.com**), one of the largest cellular carriers in Europe. By July, 2019 Google Fi was available in more than 200 foreign countries.

Google Fi automatically and seamlessly routes customers' calls and data between available Wi-Fi networks and the 4G LTE networks of Sprint, T-Mobile, and U.S. Cellular, depending on which network provides the strongest signal in the user's location. A problem is that the three cellular networks used by Google Fi provide the poorest coverage among the major wireless carriers, according to a Root Metrics (**www.rootmetrics.com**) coverage map.

Google Fi also uses approximately one million free, open Wi-Fi hot spots that Google has verified as fast and reliable. In an effort to protect passwords and personal data, Google Fi encrypts data when a customer uses public Wi-Fi.

Google Fi offers many features. Customers can call, text, and check voicemail on their Web and Android devices. They can also access the history of calls, messages, and voicemail. Google Fi is a prepaid service that allows customers to pay only for the amount of data they actually use each month. This process is the opposite of traditional carriers, which bill customers *after* they use the service.

Google Fi does not require an annual contract. Rather, the service charges $20 per month for unlimited calls, texts, Wi-Fi tethering (see below), and coverage in over 200 countries with no roaming fees (although customers have to pay 20 cents per minute for calls outside the United States). The service also charges $10 per gigabyte of data. Money for any unused data is credited back to the user's account, while overuse of data costs an additional $10 per gigabyte in proportion to actual usage. A Group Plan, which lets users add members to their subscription, costs an additional $15 per user per month, and offers features including data overview, data notifications, monthly allowances, and the ability to pause one's data usages.

On January 17, 2018, Google Fi announced "bill protection," which caps the charge for data at $60 if a customer uses more than 6 gigabytes of data in a billing period. If the data used is greater than 15 gigabytes, then Fi may slow the data speed to 256 kilobytes per second. The user can avoid the data slowdown by paying full price for the data used at $10 per gigabyte. The bill protection also works with group plans maximizing the data charge at $85 for two people, $120 for three people, and $140 for four people. The rate for unlimited calls and texts is not affected by the new bill protection plan.

Another benefit Google Fi offers its customers is the ability to change the size of their data plans whenever they want to. Furthermore, once a month, customers can decide to put their service on pause. If they choose this option, they then lose the ability to forward calls with their Google Voice numbers, and they cannot access mobile data, make calls, or send text messages. However, they receive a credit to their accounts for each day they keep the service deactivated. They also receive a credit for the cost of the data they purchased but did not use over the course of the month.

Currently, Google Fi operates optimally only on the Google Pixel 3, Moto G6, Moto G7, LG V35 ThinQ, LG G7 ThinQ, and Android One Moto X smartphones. There are many more phones that you can use with Google Fi but you will lose some of its features. Customers can set up their phones as a mobile Wi-Fi router and use their laptops or tablets to surf the Internet on their phone's data connection, at no extra charge. This process is called *wireless tethering*. Once customers have activated tethering, any device with a wireless capability can connect to the Internet through their smartphone unless they set up password protection. If they select this option, then only people with access to the password can connect to their smartphones.

Every carrier offers group plans that allow customers to share their wireless plans with friends and family members. In these plans, the carrier sends only one bill to the main account holder each month for all of the people in the group. Therefore, group members must pay the main account holder.

In contrast, with Google Fi, every user may incur different fees, making payments to the main account holder problematic. As a result, the service automatically manages payments for the group with its "group repay" option. This option is integrated with Google Wallet, making it easy for group members to pay the main account holder.

Google Fi puts pressure on wireless carriers to do away with lucrative "breakage." *Breakage* is a term the telecommunications industry uses to refer to unused data at the end of a month. Many traditional wireless plans require subscribers to pay for certain amounts of data that expire at the end of each month. A study by Validas (**www.validas.com**), a company that analyzes consumers' bills to help them choose the most appropriate wireless plan, revealed that smartphone users typically waste $28 each month on unused data. This $28 represents breakage.

The practice of breakage is coming under pressure from other companies as well. Start-ups such as Scratch Wireless (**www.scratchwireless.com**) offer usage-based models. Furthermore, major carriers such as T-Mobile and AT&T (**www.att.com**) allow subscribers to roll over their data.

Google's pricing strategy for its Google Fi service also put pressure on the industry's prevailing pricing model, which is to purchase expensive wireless spectrum and then sell expensive wireless Internet service. (All wireless communications signals travel over the air through radio frequencies, which are known as *spectrum*.) In fact, Google's entry into the wireless market has the potential to disrupt the wireless industry.

Google Fi does face competition. For example:

- Republic Wireless (**www.republicwireless.com**) offers a range of plans. The $15 per month plan includes unlimited talk and text with Wi-Fi for data. The $20 per month plan includes unlimited talk and text with 1 gigabyte of data; and the $25 per month plan includes unlimited talk and text with 2 gigabytes of data. Users can purchase up to 15 gigabytes of data per month at $5 per gigabyte.

- Cricket Wireless (**www.cricketwireless.com**) offers unlimited talk and text with no data for $25 per month; unlimited talk and text with 2 gigabytes of data for $30 per month; and unlimited talk and text with 5 gigabytes of data for $40 per month.

- FreedomPop (**www.freedompop.com**) offers a plan for $20 per month for unlimited talk, text, and one gigabyte of data.

Essentially, Google Fi is how wireless should work. Your phone will connect to the network with the best signal, not the signal that a lone carrier happens to offer at a given location.

Sources: Compiled from A. Martonik and J. Maring, "What Is Project Fi, How Does It Work, and Why Do I Want It?" *Android Central*, July 16, 2018; C. Faulkner, "Google's Project Fi: What You Need to Know about the Network of Networks," *TechRadar*, May 30, 2018; R. Amadeo, "Project Fi's 'Bill Protection' Works out to an $80 'Unlimited' Plan," *Ars Technica*, January 18, 2018; F. Lardinois, "Google Brings the $399 Android One Moto X4 to Project Fi (and the U.S.)," *TechCrunch*, September 20, 2017; K. Wiggers, "Here's Everything You Need to Know about Google's Project Fi," *Digital Trends*, September 20, 2017; C. Faulkner, "Google's Project Fi: What You Need to Know about the Network of Networks," *TechRadar*, September 20, 2017; D. Richardson, "What Is Project Fi, and Is It Worth It?" *Tom's Guide*, July 22, 2017; F. Lardinois, "Google Makes Splitting the Cost of Project Fi Group Plans Easier," *TechCrunch*, June 20, 2017; S. Carpenter, "5 Key Things to Know Before You Switch to Google's Project Fi," *Forbes*, September 27, 2016; M. Duran, "Google's Project Fi Wireless Service Is Crazy Cheap. But Should You Switch?" *Wired*, July 15, 2016; R. Amadeo, "Google's Project Fi Gets International LTE, Adds Three to Carrier Lineup," *Ars Technica*, July 12, 2016; C. Metz, "Google's Project Fi Is One Step Closer to Unifying the World's Wireless Networks," *Wired*, July 12, 2016; J. Raphael, "Project Fi Revisited: 6 Months with Google's Weird Wireless Service," *Computerworld*, April 14, 2016; A. Martonik, "What Is Project Fi, How Does It Work, and Why Do I Want It?" *Android Central*,

July 9, 2015; B. Fung, "Project Fi Review: The Most Remarkable Feature of Google's New Cell Service," *Washington Post*, July 8, 2015; "5 Things to Know about Google's Project Fi," *CBS News*, May 4, 2015; "Google's Project Fi Aims to Speed Up Mobile Communications by Tapping into Free WiFi Hotspots," *Kurzweilai.net*, April 23, 2015; R. Metz, "Google's New Wireless Service Should Make Verizon and AT&T Squirm," *MIT Technology Review*, April 22, 2015; and www.fi.google.com, accessed July 16, 2019.

Questions

1. Describe how Google's Project Fi works.

2. Assume that you are the CEO of Verizon Wireless (**www.verizonwireless.com**). How would you compete with Project Fi?

CHAPTER 9

Social Computing

CHAPTER OUTLINE	LEARNING OBJECTIVES
9.1 Web 2.0	**9.1** Describe six Web 2.0 tools and two major types of Web 2.0 sites.
9.2 Fundamentals of Social Computing in Business	**9.2** Describe the benefits and risks of social commerce to companies.
9.3 Social Computing in Business: Shopping	**9.3** Identify the methods used for shopping socially.
9.4 Social Computing in Business: Marketing	**9.4** Discuss innovative ways to use social networking sites for advertising and market research.
9.5 Social Computing in Business: Customer Relationship Management	**9.5** Describe how social computing improves customer service.
9.6 Social Computing in Business: Human Resource Management	**9.6** Discuss different ways in which human resource managers make use of social computing.

Opening Case

MIS **MKT** **Dr. David Dao and United Airlines**

To an airline, an unsold seat is worthless as soon as the plane takes off. To avoid this scenario, airlines routinely sell tickets to more people than a plane can seat, a practice called *overbooking*. The airlines count on several people not to arrive, thereby avoiding a conflict over seating. When there are not enough no-shows, airlines first try to offer rewards to customers who are willing to reschedule their flights, usually in the form of travel vouchers, gift cards, or cash. Such arrangements, which are usually negotiated before passengers board the plane, can be lucrative to flexible travelers, and they are crucial for airlines to maximize their profits.

On Sunday, April 9, 2017, United Express Flight 3411 was overbooked. (Republic Airline operated Flight 3411 on behalf of United Express, a United Airlines regional branch.) Prior to the flight, United personnel offered $800 in travel vouchers to randomly selected passengers to voluntarily vacate their seats to make room for four airline employees who needed to travel to Louisville International Airport.

However, none of the passengers accepted. The airline then randomly selected four passengers to be removed involuntarily from the flight. Three of the passengers complied. The fourth, Dr. David Dao, a physician from Kentucky, did not.

When Dr. Dao refused to leave the plane, Chicago's O'Hare International Airport police forcibly removed him. Dr. Dao resisted as officers pulled him out of his seat, and his face hit an armrest during the struggle. Chicago Department of Aviation officers then dragged him, apparently unconscious, by his arms on his back along the aircraft aisle past rows of passengers. Dao's attorney claimed that he had suffered two lost teeth, a broken nose, a concussion, and injuries to his sinuses that required surgery.

Several passengers recorded video footage of the incident, which was widely circulated on social media and in news reports. The videos, which documented the physical confrontation and Dr. Dao's anguished protests as well as his injuries, generated extensive public outrage. Lawmakers expressed concerns and called for an official investigation.

Chicago's aviation police reports stated that Dr. Dao was flailing his arms and was verbally abusive toward officers before he lost his balance and struck his face on an armrest. These reports were contradicted by the passenger videos. Thomas Demetrio, Dr. Dao's lawyer, called the reports "utter nonsense."

On Monday, United's initial response placed the blame for the episode on Dr. Dao. The airline apologized only for the "overbook situation." Furthermore, United CEO Oscar Munoz issued a statement that appeared to justify the removal of Dr. Dao, referring to the process as "re-accommodating the customers." He described the episode as "an upsetting event." Munoz apologized to the other passengers on the plane, but he did not speak directly about Dr. Dao's treatment by officials. Munoz also sent an e-mail to United staff commending the crew's actions for following established procedures and referring to Dao as "disruptive" and "belligerent." On Monday evening the e-mail became public.

By Tuesday, United was facing a public relations crisis as potential customers, objecting to United's early statements, threatened a boycott. Munoz and United were severely criticized for their initial statements on all social media outlets. United changed course on Tuesday with another statement from Munoz in which he stated that the airline took full responsibility for the episode.

On Wednesday morning, Munoz appeared on ABC's *Good Morning, America*, where he stated that he felt "shame" when he saw the video of Dr. Dao being dragged from the airplane. Munoz then issued an additional statement, apologizing and promising that this type of incident would never happen again on United aircraft. He asserted: "No one should ever be mistreated this way." Later that day, United announced that it would offer a full refund to every passenger on the flight.

On Thursday, Dr. Dao's lawyer and daughter spoke at a press conference in Chicago. United again responded with an apology and a promise to "make this right." The statement asserted that Munoz had reached out to Dr. Dao to apologize, which the doctor's daughter denied.

The results of this public relations fiasco were far reaching. First, as a direct result of this incident, Munoz was denied a previously planned promotion to chairman. In addition, at least four law enforcement officers were placed on leave.

Next, United revealed new policies including (a) a promise to not use law enforcement to remove overbooked customers from planes, (b) additional training for frontline employees, and (c) setting up an automated system that will ask passengers at check-in if they would be willing to give up their seat. Munoz also pledged to reduce the amount of overbooking and to offer up to $10,000 for customers who are willing to take a later flight.

Furthermore, United crew members are no longer able to bump a passenger who is already seated in one of the airline's planes. United updated its policy "to make sure that crews traveling on our aircraft are booked at least 60 minutes prior to department. This process ensures situations like Flight 3411 never happen again." The policy change effectively means that if there is a need to displace a passenger from a flight, then the decision will be made before boarding begins.

Delta Airlines announced a similar policy, authorizing its supervisors to offer displaced passengers almost $10,000 in compensation. The previous incentive had been $1,350. Interestingly, American Airlines said that it does not set a cap on compensation for passengers. American said that its gate agents work with customers to set compensation amounts needed to obtain the correct number of volunteers.

Another impact of the incident was the impact on United Airlines's share price. At one point, United lost some $1.3 billion in market value. The incident also inflamed the Chinese media, with angry Chinese calling for a boycott of the airline as a result of racial profiling. (Dr. Dao is a Chinese-Vietnamese physician.) Industry experts noted that United could lose significant amounts of revenue from the China-United States market. United is the largest U.S. carrier in China.

On April 27, 2017, Dao reached an "amicable" settlement with United. The terms of this settlement were not disclosed.

Sources: Compiled from D. Koenig, "If You Get Bumped off a Flight This Travel Season, Make It Worth Your While," Associated Press, June 2, 2018; D. Cevallos, "United Airlines Must Have Paid Big Bucks for Dr. Dao's Silence," CNN, May 1, 2017; D. Silva, "David Dao and United Airlines Reach 'Amicable' Settlement after Viral Video Incident," NBC News, April 27, 2017; M. Diebel, "United Airlines Passenger David Dao Was Violent before Removal, Aviation Police Say," *USA Today*, April 25, 2017; A. Wise, "United CEO Munoz Will Not Chair Board in 2018 Following Passenger Furor," Reuters, April 21, 2017; "Delta Air Offers up to $10,000 Compensation for Displaced Customers," Associated Press, April 15, 2017; R. Gonzales, "United Airlines Changes Its Policy on Displacing Customers," NPR, April 14, 2017; E. McCann, "United's Apologies: A Timeline," *New York Times*, April 14, 2017; "How United Airlines Went Viral on Social Media," *Cooler Insights*, April 12, 2017; A. Ohlheiser, "The Full Timeline of How Social Media Turned United into the Biggest Story in the Country," *Washington Post*, April 11, 2017; J. Griffiths and S. Wang, "Man Filmed Being Dragged off United Flight Causes Outrage in China," CNN, April 11, 2017; D. Victor and M. Stevens, "United Airlines Passenger Is Dragged from an Overbooked Flight," *New York Times*, April 10, 2017; J. Callas, "Officer Who Forcibly Removed Passenger from United Airlines Flight Placed on Leave," *Time*, April 10, 2017; and L. Thomas, "United CEO Says Airline Had to 'Re-Accommodate' Passenger, and the Reaction Was Wild," CNBC, April 10, 2017.

Questions

1. Describe and evaluate United's sequence of responses to the incident with Dr. Dao. Should United have responded differently? If so, then how?

2. Discuss the impacts of social media on United's responses to the incident with Dr. Dao.

3. Discuss how this case illustrates the change in the balance of power between customers and organizations.

Introduction

Humans are social beings. Therefore, human behavior is innately social. Humans typically orient their behavior around other members of their community. As a result, people are sensitive to the behavior of people around them, and their decisions are generally influenced by their social context.

Traditional information systems support organizational activities and business processes, and they concentrate on cost reductions and productivity increases. A variation of this traditional model, **social computing**, is a type of IT that combines social behavior and information systems to create value. Social computing is focused on improving collaboration and interaction among people and on encouraging user-generated content, as you see in this chapter's opening case.

Significantly, in social computing, social information is not anonymous. Rather, it is important precisely because it is linked to particular individuals, who in turn are linked to their own networks of individuals.

Social computing makes socially produced information available to everyone. This information may be provided directly, as when users rate a movie (e.g., at Rotten Tomatoes), or indirectly (as with Google's PageRank algorithm, which sequences search results).

In social computing, users, rather than organizations, produce, control, use, and manage content via interactive communications and collaboration. As a result, social computing is transforming power relationships within organizations (see this chapter's opening case). Employees and customers are empowered by their ability to use social computing to organize themselves. Thus, social computing can influence people in positions of power to listen to the concerns and issues of "ordinary people." Organizational customers and employees are joining this social computing phenomenon, with serious consequences for most organizations.

Significantly, most governments and companies in modern developed societies are not prepared for the new social power of ordinary people. Today, managers, executives, and government officials can no longer control the conversation around policies, products, and other issues.

In the new world of business and government, organizational leaders will have to demonstrate authenticity, evenhandedness, transparency, good faith, and humility. If they do not, then customers and employees may distrust them, to potentially disastrous effects. For example, customers who do not like a product or service can quickly broadcast their disapproval. Another example is that prospective employees do not have to take their employers at their word for what life is like at their companies—they can find out from people who already work there. A final example is that employees now have many more options to start their own companies, which could compete with their former employers.

As you see from these examples, the world is becoming more democratic and reflective of the will of ordinary people, enabled by the power of social computing. On the one hand, social power can help keep a company vital and can enable customers and employee activists to become a source of creativity and innovation that will move a company forward. On the other hand, companies that show insensitivity toward customers or employees quickly find themselves on a downward slide.

For instance, Kenneth Cole came under fire for suggesting on Twitter that news of its spring collection led to riots in Egypt, and American Apparel was blasted online for offering a Hurricane Sandy sale. Lesson to be learned: If companies want to win the favor and loyalty of customers, they should refrain from making comments that may suggest that they are trying to profit from other people's misery.

Social computing is exploding worldwide, with China having the world's most active social media population. In one McKinsey survey, 91 percent of Chinese respondents reported that they had visited a social media site in the previous six months, compared with 70 percent in South Korea, 67 percent in the United States, and 30 percent in Japan. Interestingly, the survey found that social media has a greater influence on purchasing decisions for Chinese consumers than for consumers anywhere else in the world.

In particular, messaging app usage is increasing dramatically, with certain apps dominating specific areas of the world. Let's look at the most popular messaging apps:

- With more than 1.5 billion users, *WhatsApp* (**www.whatsapp.com**, owned by Facebook) is the most widely used messaging app in many parts of the world. These areas include much of South America, much of southern and central Africa, Great Britain, Spain, Germany, India, Mexico, southeast Asia, and Russia.

- *Facebook Messenger* (**www.messenger.com**) has more than 1.3 billion users globally. Messenger is the leading app in the United States, Australia, and northern Africa.

- Messaging app *WeChat* (**www.wechat.com**) dominates the Chinese market with more than 1 billion users.

- With almost 1 billion users, *Viber* (**www.viber.com**) is the leading app in countries such as Kyrgyzstan, Ukraine, Belarus, Armenia, Azerbaijan, Bosnia – Herzegovina.
- *Moya Messenger* (**www.moyaapp.com**), developed in South Africa, enables users to communicate without incurring data cost, provided that they do not send any attachments and are willing to be exposed to advertising. Moya uses are warned in advance if they will incur mobile data costs or need to switch to a Wi-Fi network.

Organizations today are using social computing in a variety of innovative ways, including marketing, production, customer relationship management, and human resource management. In fact, so many organizations are competing to use social computing in as many new ways as possible that an inclusive term for the use of social computing in business has emerged: *social commerce*. Because social computing is facilitated by Web 2.0 tools and sites, you begin this chapter by examining these technologies. You then turn your attention to a diverse number of social commerce activities, including shopping, advertising, market research, customer relationship management, and human resource management.

Another fascinating use of social media, disaster relief, shows the incredible versatility of various social media. IT's About Business 9.1 provides several examples of social media being used in this fashion.

IT's About Business 9.1

`MIS` `POM` Social Media and Disaster Relief

Natural disasters are expected to become more frequent in the future, due to global warming. Unfortunately, these disasters often overwhelm governments and first responders. To compound this problem, methods to reach relief officials such as 911 lines frequently become unresponsive. Social media have often helped in disaster relief efforts. In fact, they have created a new type of first responder who can step in where traditional aid has failed: the volunteer. Let's consider a variety of examples that illustrate the role of social media in disaster relief.

Earthquake in Mexico

A magnitude 7.1 earthquake struck central Mexico on September 19, 2017. Topos Mexico (**www.topos.mx/en/**) is a volunteer rescue group that formed after the 1985 earthquake that severely damaged Mexico City. When the 2017 earthquake struck, the rescue group did not contact the Mexican government. Rather, they used social media to call for hundreds of volunteers. Even before the army, navy, police, and the civil protection unit could mobilize, volunteers started to create informal brigades through WhatsApp, and recruited volunteers to help remove debris.

Social media have become ubiquitous, particularly in highly populated urban areas such as Mexico City, where smartphones are everywhere. In Mexico, prepaid monthly cellular plans with unlimited WhatsApp, Facebook, Facebook Messenger, and Twitter are popular. To help organizers after the earthquake, telecommunications companies temporarily offered data and calls for free.

From the standpoint of the Topos group, international aid workers from countries such as Spain, Japan, Israel, and the United States were working too slowly. Topos placed more trust in civilians, such as carpenters, electricians, and welders, who had responded to the group's social media messages. Volunteers distributed the necessary rescue equipment from their tents. They also prepared food in their homes for the hundreds of people on rescue sites, including the Mexican government's uniformed forces.

Many other volunteers who relied on information from Telegram and WhatsApp, began new Twitter accounts that confirmed information based on reports from volunteers who were actually located on rescue sites. One volunteer started an Excel spreadsheet that became a fact-checking project called Verificados19s. A volunteer couple organized the flood of information from social media so that volunteers knew which goods were needed and where they were needed. The couple's website, SismoMex (**www.twitter.com/sismomex**), listed the phone numbers of the largest donation centers. Another volunteer developed a website, AyudaMX, that helped people find everything from hospitals with free X-rays to photos of lost pets.

Another use of social media surfaced after the earthquake. Parents outside Enrique Rebsamen, a private school in Mexico City that had collapsed, used WhatsApp to exchange messages with children who were trapped inside the building. Three days after the earthquake, reports indicated that the Mexican government was going to use heavy machinery to move rubble without first confirming no survivors were buried underneath. By September 24, there was still no government official available to provide information to the family members of people who were trapped in collapsed buildings.

Hurricane Harvey

During and after Hurricane Harvey in August 2017, emergency hotlines were jammed. Some calls to Houston's 911 operators dropped or failed to connect. Residents stated that they lost battery power on their phones, making it difficult to continue calling or to wait on the 911 line for a long time.

As a result, people who could not quickly reach official emergency medical workers turned to social media. They often posted their addresses on Facebook and Twitter. Civilians were frequently the ones who responded. Furthermore, Texans trapped by the hurricane often used the app Zello (**www.zello.com**) to radio for the volunteer Cajun Navy's 700-boat fleet and saved people who were unable to reach 911.

Some of those appeals went viral, including one on Twitter that showed senior citizens stranded in waist-high water in their nursing home. The photo was retweeted thousands of times and ultimately caught the attention of Galveston County Emergency workers, who elevated the nursing home to the top of the priority list and saved all 15 residents.

The Digital Humanitarian Network (DHN; **www.digitalhuman-itarians.com**), an umbrella group that oversaw volunteer rescue efforts during Hurricane Harvey, mobilized a number of volunteer groups who were skilled at tracking emergency-related posts on social media. They compiled those posts into public maps and databases that professionals and volunteers used to assist with rescues.

Despite the problems with the 911 system, the U.S. Coast Guard and the Houston Police Department strongly discouraged residents from trying to reach emergency response officials through social media. Instead, they urged people to call specific emergency phone lines for disaster response. However, reports stated that two Coast Guard Academy cadets used information provided in part by the Standby Task Force (SBTF; **www.standbytaskforce.org**), an international volunteer network whose members used key words on social media to pinpoint the locations of people in need of help. A public information officer for the Coast Guard did not respond to inquiries as to whether the service received or used social media data from the SBTF or other volunteer groups.

Des Moines, Iowa, Flood

In Des Moines, the Scanner Squad exists entirely online. The squad has a Facebook group with thousands of members across the city's metro area. Their only mission is to deliver information, dispel rumors, and provide information in crises. Due to the large number of members, the squad's information flow is continuous and immediate. Interestingly, squad members provide real-time videos of crisis areas all around the city. For example, when the city faced a serious flash flood in July 2018, the squad revealed that someone had been caught in rising floodwaters 45 minutes before the media reported that fact. The squad also reported on roads that were blocked and alternate routes that people took.

Official Responses to the Use of Social Media in Disaster Relief

Emergency officials have noted that although community networks have always emerged during disasters, today's online, social-media resources are accelerating that process. Social media are enabling volunteers to organize much more rapidly to help their neighbors as well as total strangers.

However, calling 911 is still the recommended method to reach official emergency networks. The National Emergency Number Association (NENA; **www.nena.org**) notes that, of the thousands of 911 call centers across the United States, fewer than 25 percent are equipped to receive text messages. In November 2017, NENA implemented a plan called Next Generation 911, which is modernizing the entire system. However, not all municipalities are on the system. NENA has emphasized that the use of messaging apps or social media in emergency situations raises concerns about verifying people's locations and protecting their privacy.

In fact, there are serious drawbacks to utilizing social media in disaster relief, including the dissemination of misinformation and doctored images. One image that resurfaced during Harvey showed a shark swimming on a flooded highway. That image was debunked by the fact-checking organization Snopes.com.

Sources: Compiled from C. Crowder, "The Scanner Squad Beat the Media on Flooding Coverage with a Reporting Corps a Thousand Strong," *Des Moines Register*, July 1, 2018; J. Bergman, "Cadets Create Maps to Help Coast Guard with Harvey Rescues," *The Day*, September 1, 2017; M. Averbuch, "When Government Fails, Social Media Is the New 911," *Wired*, October 25, 2017; M. Pskowski and D. Adler, "6,000 Complaints….Then the Quake: The Scandal behind Mexico City's 225 Dead," *The Guardian*, October 13, 2017; J. Bromwich, "Puerto Ricans on Mainland Rely on Strangers to Reach Relatives," *New York Times*, September 26, 2017; J. Fortin, "When Disaster Hits and Landlines Fail, Social Media Is a Lifeline," *New York Times*, September 23, 2017; N. Chavez, S. Almasy, R. Sanchez, and D. Simon, "Central Mexico Earthquake Kills More than 200, Topples Buildings," *CNN*, September 20, 2017; L. O'Connor, "How We Could Better Leverage Social Media during Disasters like Harvey," *Huffington Post*, September 5, 2017; M. Pearce, "A 'Cajun Navy' of Volunteers Descends on Port Arthur, Texas, to Rescue People," *Los Angeles Times*, August 30, 2017; D. Seetharaman and G. Wells, "Hurricane Harvey Victims Turn to Social Media for Assistance," *Wall Street Journal*, August 29, 2017; R. Grenoble, "Finally, Some Good News out of Texas," Huffington Post, August 29, 2017; "The Power of Social Media during Natural Disasters," *Fast Company*, August 29, 2017; E. Sullivan, "In Texas Flooding, FEMA Asks 'All Citizens to Get Involved' to Help," *New York Times*, August 28, 2017; and "Disasters like Louisiana Floods Will Worsen as Planet Warms, Scientists Warn," *The Guardian*, August 16, 2016.

Questions

1. Discuss the reasons behind the increased use of social media in disaster relief efforts.

2. Discuss the disadvantages that could come from using social media in disaster relief efforts. Overall, should the use of social media in disaster relief efforts be encouraged? Why or why not?

When you complete this chapter, you will have a thorough understanding of social computing and the ways in which modern organizations use this technology. You will be familiar with the advantages and disadvantages of social computing as well as the risks and rewards it can bring to your organization. For example, most of you already have pages on social networking sites, so you are familiar with the positive and negative features of these sites. This chapter will enable you to apply this knowledge to your organization's efforts in the social computing arena. You will be in a position to contribute to your organization's policies on social computing. You will also be able to help your organization create a strategy to utilize social computing. Finally, social computing offers incredible opportunities for entrepreneurs who want to start their own businesses.

Author Lecture Videos are available exclusively in *WileyPLUS*.
Apply the Concept activities are available in the Appendix and in *WileyPLUS*.

9.1 Web 2.0

The World Wide Web, which you learned about in Chapter 6, first appeared in 1990. Web 1.0 was the first generation of the Web. We did not use this term in Chapter 6 because there was no need to say "Web 1.0" until Web 2.0 emerged.

The key developments of Web 1.0 were the creation of websites and the commercialization of the Web. Users typically had minimal interaction with Web 1.0 sites. Rather, they passively received information from those sites.

Web 2.0 is a popular term that has proved difficult to define. According to Tim O'Reilly, a noted blogger, **Web 2.0** is a loose collection of information technologies and applications, plus the websites that use them. These websites enrich the user experience by encouraging user participation, social interaction, and collaboration. Unlike Web 1.0 sites, Web 2.0 sites are not so much online places to visit as Web locations that facilitate information sharing, user-centered design, and collaboration. Web 2.0 sites often harness collective intelligence (e.g., wikis); deliver functionality as services, rather than packaged software (e.g., Web services); and feature remixable applications and data (e.g., mashups).

In the following sections, we discuss five Web 2.0 information technology tools: tagging, Really Simple Syndication, blogs, microblogs, and wikis. We then turn our attention to the two major types of Web 2.0 sites: social networking sites and mashups.

Tagging

A **tag** is a key word or term that describes a piece of information, for example, a blog, a picture, an article, or a video clip. Users typically choose tags that are meaningful to them. Tagging allows users to place information in multiple, overlapping associations rather than in rigid categories. For example, a photo of a car might be tagged with "Corvette," "sports car," and "Chevrolet." Tagging is the basis of *folksonomies*, which are user-generated classifications that use tags to categorize and retrieve Web pages, photos, videos, and other Web content.

One specific form of tagging, known as *geotagging*, refers to tagging information on maps. For example, Google Maps allows users to add pictures and information, such as restaurant or hotel ratings, to maps. Therefore, when users access Google Maps, their experience is enriched because they can see pictures of attractions, reviews, and things to do, posted by everyone, and all are related to the map location they are viewing.

Really Simple Syndication

Really Simple Syndication (RSS) is a Web 2.0 feature that allows you to receive the information you want (customized information), when you want it, without having to surf thousands of websites. RSS allows anyone to syndicate (publish) his or her blog, or any other content, to anyone who has an interest in subscribing to it. When changes to the content are made, subscribers receive a notification of the changes and an idea of what the new content contains. Subscribers can then click on a link that will take them to the full text of the new content.

For example, CNN.com provides RSS feeds for each of its main topic areas, such as world news, sports news, technology news, and entertainment news. NBC uses RSS feeds to allow viewers to download the most current version of shows such as *Meet the Press* and *NBC Nightly News*. **Figure 9.1** illustrates how to search an RSS and locate RSS feeds.

To use RSS, you can utilize a special newsreader that displays RSS content feeds from the websites you select. Many such readers are available, several of them for free (see Feedspot; **www.feedspot.com**). In addition, most browsers have built-in RSS readers. For an excellent RSS tutorial, visit **www.mnot.net/rss/tutorial**.

Blogs

A **weblog** (**blog** for short) is a personal website, open to the public, in which the site creator expresses his or her feelings or opinions via a series of chronological entries. *Bloggers*—people who create and maintain blogs—write stories, convey news, and provide links to other articles and websites that are of interest to them. The simplest method of creating a blog is to sign up with a blogging service provider, such as **www.blogger.com** (now owned by Google), **www.xanga.com**, and **www.movabletype.com**. The **blogosphere** is the term for the millions of blogs on the Web.

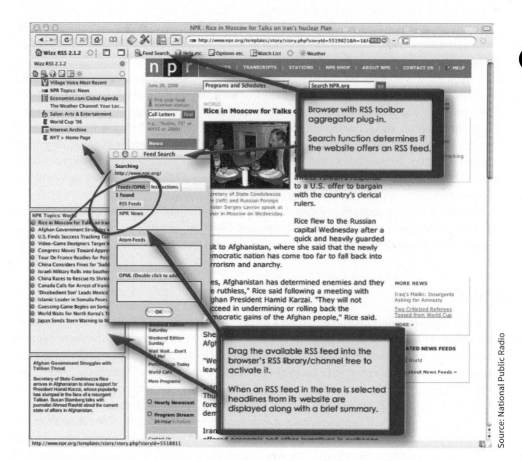

FIGURE 9.1 The website of National Public Radio (NPR) with RSS toolbar aggregator and search function.

MKT Many companies listen to consumers in the blogosphere who express their views on the companies' products. Marketers refer to these views as *consumer-generated media*. For example, Nielsen (**www.nielsen-online.com**) "mines" the blogosphere to provide information for its clients in several areas. Nielsen helps clients find ways to serve potential markets, ranging from broad-based to niche markets. The company also helps clients detect false rumors before these rumors appear in the mainstream media, and it gauges the potency of a marketing push or the popularity of a new product.

Blogs often provide incredibly useful information, often before the information becomes available in traditional media outlets (e.g., television, newspapers). Although blogs can be very useful, they also have shortcomings. Perhaps the primary value of blogs is their ability to bring current, breaking news to the public in the fastest time possible. Unfortunately, in doing so, bloggers sometimes cut corners, and their blogs can be inaccurate. Regardless of their various problems, however, blogs have transformed the ways in which people gather and consume information.

Microblogging

Microblogging is a form of blogging that allows users to write short messages (or capture an image or embedded video) and publish them. These messages can be submitted via text messaging from mobile phones, instant messaging, e-mail, or simply over the Web. The content of a microblog differs from that of a blog because of the limited space per message (usually up to 140 characters). A popular microblogging service is Twitter.

Twitter is a free microblogging service that allows its users to send messages and read other users' messages and updates, known as **tweets**. Tweets are displayed on the user's profile page and delivered to other users who have signed up to receive them.

MKT Twitter is becoming a very useful business tool. It allows companies to quickly share information with people interested in their products, thereby creating deeper relationships with their customers. Businesses also use Twitter to gather real-time market intelligence and customer feedback. As an individual user, you can use Twitter to inform companies about your experiences with their business, offer product ideas, and learn about great offers.

Microblogging is very popular in China, with Weibo being the most popular microblogging service in that country. Weibo has over 200 million monthly active members.

Wikis

A **wiki** is a website made up entirely of content posted by users. Wikis have an "edit" link on each page that allows any user to add, change, or delete material, thus fostering easy collaboration.

Wikis take advantage of the combined input of many individuals. Consider Wikipedia (**www.wikipedia.org**), an online encyclopedia that is the largest existing wiki. Wikipedia contains over five million articles in English which attract some 500 million views every day. Wikipedia relies on volunteer administrators who enforce a neutral point of view, and it encourages users to delete copy that displays a clear bias. Nevertheless, there are still major debates over the reliability of Wikipedia articles. Many educators will not allow students to cite references from Wikipedia because Wikipedia content is of uncertain origin. Moreover, Wikipedia does not provide any quality assessment or fact checking by experts. Therefore, academics and other professionals have major concerns about the accuracy of user-provided content.

POM **MKT** Organizations use wikis in several ways. In project management, for example, wikis provide a central repository for capturing constantly updated product features and specifications, tracking issues, resolving problems, and maintaining project histories. In addition, wikis enable companies to collaborate with customers, suppliers, and other business partners on projects. Wikis are also valuable in knowledge management. For example, companies use wikis to keep enterprisewide documents, such as guidelines and frequently asked questions, accurate and current.

Social Networking Websites

A **social network** is a social structure composed of individuals, groups, or organizations linked by values, visions, ideas, financial exchange, friendship, kinship, conflict, or trade. **Social networking** refers to activities performed using social software tools (e.g., blogging) or social networking features (e.g., media sharing). Social networking allows convenient connections to those of similar interest.

A social network can be described as a map of all relevant links or connections among the network's members. For each individual member, that map is his or her **social graph**. Mark Zuckerberg of Facebook originally coined this term to refer to the social network of relationships among Facebook users. The idea was that Facebook would take advantage of relationships among individuals to offer a richer online experience.

Social networks can also be used to determine the social capital of individual participants. **Social capital** refers to the number of connections a person has within and between social networks.

Participants congregate on *social networking websites* where they can create their own profile page for free and on which they can write blogs and wikis; post pictures, videos, or music; share ideas; and link to other Web locations they find interesting. Social networkers chat using instant messaging and Twitter, and they tag posted content with their own key words, making content searchable and facilitating interactions and transactions. Social network members converse, collaborate, and share opinions, experiences, knowledge, insights, and perceptions with one another. They also use these websites to find like-minded people online, either to pursue an interest or a goal or just to establish a sense of community among people who may never meet in the real world.

Participants who post on social networking sites tend to reveal a great deal of personal information. As a result, if they are not careful, bad things can happen.

Table 9.1 displays the variety of online social networking platforms. Social networking websites allow users to upload their content to the Web in the form of text, voice, images, and videos.

TABLE 9.1 **Categories of Social Networking Websites**

Socially oriented: Socially focused public sites, open to anyone:
- Facebook (**www.facebook.com**)
- Instagram (**www.instagram.com**)
- Hi5 (**www.hi5.com**)

Professional networking: Focused on networking for business professionals:
- LinkedIn (**www.linkedin.com**)

Media sharing:
- *Netcasting* includes podcasting (audio) and videocasting (audio and video). For example, educational institutions use netcasts to provide students with access to lectures, lab demonstrations, and sports events. In 2007, Apple launched iTunes U, which offers free content provided by major U.S. universities such as Stanford and MIT.
- Web 2.0 media sites allow people to come together and share user-generated digital media, such as pictures, audio, and video.
- Video (Amazon Video on Demand, YouTube, Hulu, Facebook)
- Music (Amazon MP3, Last.fm, Rhapsody, Pandora, Facebook, iTunes)
- Photographs (Photobucket, Flickr, Shutterfly, Picasa, Facebook)

Communication:
- Blogs: Blogger, LiveJournal, TypePad, WordPress, Vox, Xanga
- Microblogging/Presence applications: Twitter, Tumblr, Yammer

Collaboration: Wikis
- Wikimedia (**www.wikimedia.org**)
- PBworks (**www.pbworks.com**)
- Wetpaint(**www.wetpaint.com**)

Social bookmarking (or *social tagging*): Focused on helping users store, organize, search, and manage bookmarks of Web pages on the Internet:
- Delicious (is **www.del.icio.us/**)
- Mix (**www.mix.com/**)

Social news: Focused on user-posted news stories that are ranked by popularity based on user voting:
- Digg (**www.digg.com**)
- Amazon Chime (**www.aws.amazon.com/chime/**)
- Reddit (**www.reddit.com**)

Events: Focused on alerts for relevant events, people you know nearby:
- Eventful (**www.eventful.com**)
- Meetup (**www.meetup.com**)

Virtual meeting place: Sites that are essentially three-dimensional worlds, built and owned by the residents (the users):
- Second Life (**www.secondlife.com**)

Discovery:
- Foursquare (**www.foursquare.com**) helps its members discover and share information about businesses and attractions around them.

Online marketplaces for microjobs: For example, TaskRabbit (**www.taskrabbit.com**) and Zaarly (**www.zaarly.com**) enable people to farm out chores to a growing number of temporary personal assistants. Thousands of unemployed and underemployed workers use these sites. The part-time or full-time tasks are especially popular with stay-at-home moms, retirees, and students. Workers choose their jobs and negotiate their rates.

These social networking sites collect a massive amount of data: some of it uploaded by their users and some generated from monitoring user activity on the sites. As you see in IT's About Business 9.2, start-up companies are using such social data to determine the creditworthiness of people who have no bank account and thus no credit score.

IT's About Business 9.2

FIN **MIS** **Using Social Data to Make Lending Decisions**

Approximately two billion people in certain parts of the world have no bank account (they are called *unbanked*), no credit score, and no financial identity. As a result, they cannot borrow money from financial institutions. The World Bank has established a goal of providing access to some form of banking services to one billion people who are currently excluded from traditional financial systems. To achieve this access, lending institutions must extend services to people who have only sparse credit histories or who have been unable to open traditional banking accounts.

To help meet this goal, start-up companies are trying to bring these people into the international financial system by collecting social data on them. These start-ups claim that traditional credit-risk assessments have ignored the importance of social capital. In addition to serving as de facto bank statements, mobile and online footprints indicate how a community treats potential borrowers. The start-ups assert that lenders can utilize phone habits, web browsing, social media patterns, utility payment records, and psychometric tests to assess potential borrowers. Let's look more closely at several of these start-up companies.

Founded in 2012, Kreditech (**www.kreditech.com**), based in Germany, is both the largest of the credit-scoring start-ups and the only one that actually makes loans. The company's algorithms generate approximately 20,000 data points from online shopping histories, geolocation data for mobile phone calls, and social data, accessed with the applicant's permission. Whenever Kreditech enters a market, the firm gives a 100 € (Euro) starter loan to all applicants to generate financial histories that help refine its algorithms. Kreditech operates in 9 countries, including Russia, Spain, and Poland, and it issues 120 million € in loans every year. The firm has evaluated more than 2 million applicants and has approved roughly 300,000, or 15 percent of them.

Founded in 2011, Singapore-based Lenddo (**www.lenddo.com**) deals in nontraditional data. It assists lenders in reaching customers who typically have limited financial records but who do have a larger amount of social data. Lenddo operates on the premise that nontraditional data can be used to assess potential borrowers and to provide financial services to underserved consumers. Lenddo works with 50 partners in 20 countries. Major banks in India, Indonesia, and Brazil are particularly attractive to Lenddo because they have access to vast underbanked populations.

Applicants are offered an opportunity to give Lenddo consent to access their social media profiles, e-mail accounts, and phones so that Lenddo can collect data that could influence the outcomes of their loans. Depending on the lending institution, local regulations, and the customers' preferences, Lenddo might draw on Facebook for identity verification and on e-mail content to obtain a more accurate picture of people's financial circumstances. The company uses machine learning (see Technology Guide 4) to search for mentions of debt, for key words that indicate whether someone is employed, and for shopping patterns. With regard to phone usage, Lenddo analyzes factors such as what time of day customers are most active on their phones and with how many contacts they interact on a regular basis.

Lenddo scores customers on three primary factors: their social network activity (using data from Facebook, LinkedIn, Twitter, Gmail, and Yahoo! accounts), a customer's trusted connections (character references who will vouch for the borrower), and past financial performance if the person is a repeat borrower.

Lenddo contends that a person's friends are predictors for creditworthiness. People who have friends who pay their bills on time are more likely to be reliable borrowers themselves. Furthermore, based on analytics if customers have no frequent contacts, then they are probably loners and may not be reliable borrowers. From the opposite perspective, if customers have too many frequent contacts, then they may be social butterflies and are not reliable. Someone who consistently connects with a few regular contacts is presumably a more reliable borrower.

These start-up companies use predictive analytics to identify keys to creditworthiness. Among the many highlights they have uncovered by analyzing nontraditional data are:

- People who do not let their phone batteries run low tend to make timely loan payments.

- Borrowers who receive more calls than they make are better risks.

- Applicants who state their loan purpose in a few words are preferable to those who write essays.

- In places where people buy airtime for mobile phone use, individuals who purchase the same amount on the same day every week are a better credit risk than those who buy a large amount and then let their unused minutes expire.

- When a phone stays in the same place every day, that is often a sign that the owner is at work and employed people are better credit risks.

Other start-ups go beyond analytics. For example, EFL Global (**www.eflglobal.com**) uses a 30-minute test to measure creditworthiness that does not require Internet access but can be taken on a mobile device or a computer. RevolutionCredit (**www.revolutioncredit.com**) has developed puzzles and games that test loan applicants and then teach them financial basics. Lenders who subscribe to its service can use the results as a component of an applicant's assessment.

Sources: Compiled from S. Rymarz, "Using Data to Supercharge Small-Business Lending Decisions," *Forbes*, February 22, 2018; K. Rivera, "Should Social Media Be Used as a Factor in Credit Decisions?" Experian Blog, October 18, 2017; D. Brancaccio, "Who Are the Unbanked?" *Marketplace*, June 29, 2017; C. Hynes, "How Social Media Could Help the Unbanked Land a Loan," *Forbes*, April 25, 2017; B. Kreiswirth, P. Schoenrock, and P. Singh, "Using Alternative Data to Evaluate Creditworthiness," Consumer Financial Protection Bureau, February 16, 2017; R. Lesonsky, "How Social Media Strengthens Your Loan Application," *Fundera*, December 16, 2016; "No Credit History, No Problem: Lenders Now Look at Phone Data," *Chicago Tribune*, November 25, 2016; "It's All about Who You Know: Lenddo Makes Credit Decisions Based on Your Social Network," *Harvard Business School*, November 18, 2016; "When Lending Decisions Go Social," *PYMNTS*, August 17, 2016; J. Vasagar, "Kreditech: A Credit Check by Social Media," *Financial Times*, January 19, 2016; S. Yoon, "Want a Loan? Let's See Your Cell Phone," *Bloomberg BusinessWeek*, November 23–29, 2015; I. Lunden, "Kreditech Nabs $92M for the 'Unbanked'," *TechCrunch*, September 28, 2015; P. Thomas, "Data from Social Media Has a Place in Credit Decisions," *Provenir*, June 10, 2015; "Is It Time for Consumer Lending to Go Social?" *PwC*, March,

2015; E. Eichelberger, "Your Deadbeat Facebook Friends Could Cost You a Loan," *Mother Jones*, September 18, 2013; and www.lenddo.com and www.kreditech.com, accessed September 25, 2018.

Questions

1. The new credit-scoring businesses use nontraditional data to assess creditworthiness. How might this practice affect the ways that traditional lending institutions assess creditworthiness? Provide specific examples to support your answer.

2. What are the potential disadvantages to customers if a financial institution uses social data to make a lending decision? Provide specific examples to support your answer.

The vast amount of data gathered by social networks has led to well-documented problems, which became prominent with the Facebook–Cambridge Analytica scandal. See IT's About Business 3.5.

Typical social networks want to keep users on their sites for as long as possible in order to target them with advertising. HelloFriend (**www.joinhellofriend.com**) is a nontypical social network that literally wants its users to get off the Internet. The social network's goal is to combat social isolation caused by online interactions rather than face-to-face interactions.

On HelloFriend, users connect with friends and acquaintances, build networks, and communicate with each other, just like on any social network. However, HelloFriend enables and encourages its users to use their networks to find, organize, and monetize real-life, face-to-face events and activities. These activities can be a small get-together, touring a new city with a local resident, teaching (or taking) language lessons, or organizing a group of friends to go on a weekend trip together.

HelloFriend's most innovative feature is that the site has its own cryptocurrency, which converts easily into cash. Users will contribute HelloFriend cryptocurrency to the host of events they attend to help subsidize the costs of the event. HelloFriend uses RChain (**www.rchain.coop**), a blockchain platform (see Chapter 7) that makes interactions fast, versatile, and secure.

HelloFriend also pays close attention to its users' privacy. The site does not collect or share users' data and makes money by taking a small percentage of the funds that hosts earn for an event.

Enterprise Social Networks

MIS Business-oriented social networks can be public, such as LinkedIn.com. As such, they are owned and managed by an independent company.

However, an increasing number of companies have created in-house, private social networks for their employees, former employees, business partners, and/or customers. Such networks are "behind the firewall" and are often referred to as *corporate social networks*. Employees utilize these networks to create connections that allow them to establish virtual teams, bring new employees up to speed, improve collaboration, and increase employee retention by creating a sense of community. Employees are able to interact with their coworkers on a level that is typically absent in large organizations or in situations where people work remotely.

Corporate social networks are used for many processes, including:

- Networking and community building, both inside and outside an organization
- *Social collaboration:* Collaborative work and problem solving using wikis, blogs, instant messaging, collaborative office, and other special-purpose Web-based collaboration platforms; (**www.biba.uni-bremen.de/**)
- *Social publishing:* Employees and others creating, either individually or collaboratively, and posting content—photos, videos, presentation slides, and documents—into a member's or a community's accessible-content repository such as YouTube, Flickr, SlideShare, and DocStoc
- Social views and feedback
- *Social intelligence and social analytics:* Monitoring, analyzing, and interpreting conversations, interactions, and associations among people, topics, and ideas to gain insights. Social intelligence is useful for examining relationships and work patterns of individuals and groups and for discovering people and expertise.

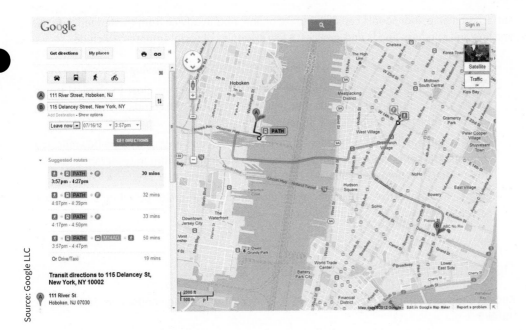

FIGURE 9.2 **GoogleMaps** (www.googlemaps.com) **is a classic example of a mashup. In this case, GoogleMaps is pulling in information from public transportation websites to provide the customer with transit directions.**

Mashups

A **mashup** is a website that takes different content from a number of other websites and mixes them together to create a new kind of content. The launch of Google Maps is credited with providing the start for mashups. A user can take a map from Google, add his or her data, and then display a map mashup on his or her website that plots crime scenes, cars for sale, or anything else (see **Figure 9.2**). There are many examples of mashups (for a complete list of mashups, see **www.programmableweb.com/**):

- Craigslist developed a dynamic map of all available apartments in the United States that are listed on their website (**www.housingmaps.com**).
- Everyblock.com is a mashup of Web services that integrates content from newspapers, blogs, and government databases to inform citizens of cities such as Chicago, New York, and Seattle about what is happening in their neighborhoods. This information includes criminal activities, restaurant inspections, and local photos posted on Flickr.

Before you go on . . .

1. Differentiate between blogs and wikis.
2. Differentiate between social networking websites and corporate social networks.

9.2 Fundamentals of Social Computing in Business

Social computing in business, or **social commerce**, refers to the delivery of electronic commerce activities and transactions through social computing. Social commerce also supports social interactions and user contributions, allowing customers to participate actively in the marketing and selling of products and services in online marketplaces and communities. With

Author Lecture Videos are available exclusively in *WileyPLUS*.
Apply the Concept activities are available in the Appendix and in *WileyPLUS*.

social commerce, individuals can collaborate online, obtain advice from trusted individuals, and find and purchase goods and services. A few examples of social commerce include:

- **POM** Disney allows people to book tickets on Facebook without leaving the social network.
- **MKT** PepsiCo provides a live notification when its customers are close to physical stores (grocery, restaurants, gas stations) that sell Pepsi products. The company then uses Foursquare to send them coupons and discount information.
- **MKT** Mountain Dew attracts video game lovers and sports enthusiasts via Dewmocracy contests. The company also encourages the most dedicated community members to contribute ideas on company products.
- **MKT** Levi's advertises on Facebook by enabling consumers to populate a "shopping cart" based on what their friends think they would like.

Benefits and Risks of Social Commerce

Social commerce offers numerous benefits to both customers and vendors, as described in Table 9.2.

Despite all of its benefits, social computing does involve risks. It is problematic, for example, to advertise a product, brand, or company on social computing websites where content is user generated and is not edited or filtered. Companies that employ this strategy must be willing to accept negative reviews and feedback. Of course, negative feedback can be some of the most valuable information that a company receives, if it utilizes this information properly.

Companies that engage in social computing are always concerned with negative posts. For example, when a company creates a Facebook business page, by default the site allows other members of the website—potentially including disgruntled customers or unethical competitors—to post notes on the firm's Facebook Wall and to comment on what the firm has posted.

Going further, if the company turns off the feature that lets other users write on its Wall, people may wonder what the company is afraid of. The company will also be eliminating its opportunity to engage in customer conversations, particularly conversations that could market the firm's products and services better than the company could do itself. Similarly, the company could delete posts. However, that policy only encourages the post author to scream even louder about being censored.

TABLE 9.2   **Potential Benefits of Social Commerce**

Benefits to Customers

- Customers can air their complaints in public (on Twitter, Facebook, YouTube), so vendors can respond better and faster to complaints.
- Customers can assist other customers (e.g., in online forums).
- Customers' expectations can be met more fully and quickly.
- Customers can easily search, link, chat, and buy while staying on a social network's page.

Benefits to Businesses

- Businesses can test new products and ideas quickly and inexpensively.
- Businesses learn a lot about their customers.
- Businesses identify problems quickly and alleviate customer anger.
- Businesses learn about customers' experiences via rapid feedback.
- Businesses increase sales when customers discuss products positively on social networking sites.
- Businesses create more effective marketing campaigns and brand awareness.
- Businesses use low-cost user-generated content, for example, in marketing campaigns.
- Businesses obtain free advertising through viral marketing.
- Businesses identify and reward influential brand advocates.

Another risk is the 20–80 rule of thumb, which posits that a minority of individuals (20 percent) contribute most of the content (80 percent) to blogs, wikis, social computing websites, and so on. For example, in an analysis of thousands of submissions to the news voting site Digg over a three-week time frame, the *Wall Street Journal* reported that roughly 33 percent of the stories that made it to Digg's homepage were submitted by 30 contributors (out of 900,000 registered members).

Other risks of social computing include the following:

- Information security concerns
- Invasion of privacy
- Violation of intellectual property and copyright
- Employees' reluctance to participate
- Data leakage of personal information or corporate strategic information
- Poor or biased quality of users' generated content
- Cyberbullying/cyberstalking and employee harassment

MKT Consider Rosetta Stone (**www.rosettastone.com**), which produces software for language translation. To obtain the maximum possible mileage out of social computing and limit the firm's risks on social media, Rosetta Stone implemented a strategy to control its customer interaction on Facebook. The strategy involves both human intervention and software to help monitor the firm's Facebook presence. Specifically, the software helps to monitor Wall posts and respond to them constructively.

Fans of facebook.com/RosettaStone who post questions on its Wall are likely to receive a prompt answer because the Facebook page is integrated with customer service software from Microsoft Dynamics 365 (**www.dynamics.microsoft.com/en-us/**). The software scans Wall posts and flags those posts that require a company response, as opposed to those in which fans of the company are talking among themselves. Rosetta Stone customer service representatives are also able to post responses to the Wall that are logged in the Parature issue-tracking database.

A new business model has emerged, enabled by social computing and environmental concerns. This business model is called *collaborative consumption.*

Collaborative Consumption

Collaborative consumption is an economic model based on sharing, swapping, trading, or renting products and services, enabling access over ownership. The premise of collaborative consumption is that having access to goods and services is more important than owning them. This new model is transforming social, economic, and environmental practices.

Collaborative consumption is a broad term that includes many collaborative practices, such as collaborative production, crowdfunding, peer-to-peer lending, and others. In collaborative production, users sell the extra power generated from their solar panels back to the utility company's grid to help power someone else's home. Crowdfunding is the practice of funding a project by raising money from a large number of people, typically via the Internet. Peer-to-peer lending is the practice of lending money to unrelated individuals without using a traditional financial institution such as a bank.

Collaborative consumption is a very old concept. We have been bartering and cooperating throughout human history. If we did not have money, we traded time, meals, favors, or personal belongings, and many cultures today do the same. On the Web, the peer-to-peer model started with eBay (**www.ebay.com**) in 1995. Then Craigslist (**www.craigslist.org**) began in the late 1990s, followed by Zipcar (**www.zipcar.com**) in 2000 and Airbnb (**www.airbnb.com**) in 2007.

Trust is the greatest concern of this new economic model. Sharing works well only when the participants' reputations are involved. Most sharing platforms try to address this issue by creating a self-policing community. Almost all platforms require profiles of both parties, and they feature community rating systems.

Collaborative consumption does have advantages. Participants cite advantages that include self-management, variety, and the flexibility that comes from being able to set their own schedules. The model can be beneficial for part-time workers, young people such as students, the unemployed, stay-at-home parents, and retired persons. The model allows people to share their underused assets and earn income.

For example, over half of Airbnb hosts in San Francisco said that the service helps them pay their rent, and the average RelayRides member makes an extra $250 per month. PricewaterhouseCoopers estimates that the sharing economy (i.e., collaborative consumption) will reach $355 billion globally by 2025.

Collaborative consumption has positive environmental impacts. As our population grows, we are using valuable resources—water, food, oil—in a way that is not sustainable. The new model helps us to utilize our natural resources more wisely, by sharing, not owning.

On the other hand, collaborative consumption does have disadvantages. The law and regulatory agencies are trying to keep abreast of the rapidly growing companies in this economy. Consider these examples:

- Without a permit, residents in San Francisco are prohibited from renting for under 30 days (although the practice still occurs).

- New York City passed an "illegal hotel law" in 2010 that prevents people from subletting apartments for fewer than 29 days, which prevents Airbnb from expanding its market in the city.

- Uber and Lyft often function as taxi companies, but do not have to follow worker regulations or laws that apply to existing taxi companies because, the services consider their employees to be independent contractors rather than employees.

People working for collaborative consumption services often work seven-day weeks, performing a series of one-off tasks. They have little recourse when the services for which they work change their business models or pay rates. To reduce the risks, workers typically sign up for multiple services. Another disadvantage is that the pay may be less than expected when participants factor in the time spent, expenses, insurance costs, and taxes on self-employment earnings.

Participants have no basic employee benefits or protections. As independent contractors, they do not quality for employee benefits such as health insurance, disability insurance, payroll deductions for Social Security, retirement savings plans, or unemployment benefits. They do not have the right to organize into a union, meaning that they do not have access to union-based collective bargaining processes. They also do not have the right to due process should a service remove them from its platform.

In April 2016, Uber reached a settlement in two class action lawsuits that required the company to pay as much as $100 million to the drivers represented in the cases, but will allow Uber to continue to categorize its drivers as contractors, not employees. To work more effectively with its drivers, Uber has a new driver deactivation policy in place and the company has agreed not to deactivate drivers who decline trips regularly.

There are numerous, diverse companies in the collaborative consumption market, including the following:

- Uber (**www.uber.com**) operates the Uber mobile app, which allows consumers with smartphones to submit a trip request that is sent to Uber drivers who use their own cars.

- Airbnb (**www.airbnb.com**) is a website for people to list, find, and rent lodgings.

- Zipcar (**www.zipcar.com**) and Turo (**www.turo.com/**) are car-sharing services.

- Yerdle (**www.yerdle.com**) is a smartphone app that helps people give and get things for free. They gain credits by giving things away and spend those credits on whatever they need (e.g., clothes, kitchen appliances, and tools).

- Skillshare (**www.skillshare.com**) provides access to top-class tutors very cheaply.

- Tradesy (**www.tradesy.com**) lets users sell and buy used clothes from well-known brands. The service takes 9 percent of profits.

- JustPark (**www.justpark.com**) is a London start-up that allows users to charge people to use their driveways as safe, secure parking spots.
- BlaBlaCar (**www.blablacar.com**) lets you rent out extra seats in your car when you go on a trip.
- Streetbank (**www.streetbank.com**) allows users to lend things to their neighbors or borrow things they need to use for a set amount of time.
- ChefsFeed (**www.experiences.chefsfeed.com/browse/?market=all-cities**) gives users a way to share any type of meal with people in their area.
- Eat With (**www.eatwith.com/**), a service available throughout Europe and in New York City, allows travelers to pay to eat with a local person or family to make their trip more authentic.
- Marriott International (**www.marriott.com**) offers meeting spaces on LiquidSpace (**www.liquidspace.com**). LiquidSpace is an online marketplace that allows people to rent office space by the hour or the day. Hundreds of Marriott hotels now list meeting spaces, and the program has expanded the company's reach by attracting local businesspeople from surrounding areas.
- FLOOW2 (**www.floow2.com**), based in the Netherlands, calls itself a "business-to-business sharing marketplace where companies and institutions can share equipment, as well as the skills and knowledge of personnel." The company lists more than 25,000 types of equipment and services in industries such as construction, agriculture, transportation, real estate, and health care.

Companies are engaged in many types of social commerce activities, including shopping, advertising, market research, customer relationship management, and human resource management. In the next sections of this chapter, you will learn about each social commerce activity.

Before you go on . . .

1. Briefly describe the benefits of social commerce to customers.
2. Briefly describe the risks of social commerce to businesses.
3. What are the benefits of collaborative consumption to customers?
4. What are the benefits and risks of collaborative consumption to participants (i.e., workers)?

9.3 | Social Computing in Business: Shopping

Social shopping is a method of electronic commerce that takes all of the key aspects of social networks—friends, groups, voting, comments, discussions, reviews, and others—and focuses them on shopping. Social shopping helps shoppers connect with one another based on tastes, location, age, gender, and other selected attributes.

The nature of shopping is changing, especially shopping for brand-name clothes and related items. For example, popular brands such as Gap, Shopbop, InStyle, and Lisa Klein are joining communities on Stylehive (**www.stylehive.com**) to help promote the season's latest fashion collections. Shoppers are using sites like ThisNext (**www.thisnext.com**) to create profiles and blogs about their favorite products in social communities. Shoppers can tag each item, so that all items become searchable. Moreover, searching within these websites can yield results targeted specifically to individual customers.

There are several methods to shop socially. You will learn about each of them in the next section.

Author Lecture Videos are available exclusively in *WileyPLUS*.
Apply the Concept activities are available in the Appendix and in *WileyPLUS*.

Ratings, Reviews, and Recommendations

Prior to making a purchase, customers typically collect information such as what brand to buy, from which vendor, and at what price. Online customers obtain this information via shopping aids such as comparison agents and websites such as Shopping.com (**www.shopping.com/**). Today, customers also use social networking to guide their purchase decisions. They are increasingly utilizing ratings, reviews, and recommendations from friends, fans, followers, and experienced customers.

All organizations must deal with negative reviews and ratings, but that process is especially difficult with health care providers. IT's About Business 9.3 shows how these providers can best manage such reviews.

IT's About Business 9.3

MKT **MIS** Health Care Providers Deal with Negative Reviews

Health care providers are keenly aware that reputation plays a large role in their ability to attract new patients. As social media have empowered patients and enabled comparison health care shopping, online reviews have become increasingly important. A 2016 survey by Software Advice (**www.softwareadvice.com**) found that 84 percent of patients who responded used online reviews when evaluating providers. The survey revealed that quality of care was the most important review metric that consumers took into account when deciding among providers. On the business-office side of a practice, friendliness of staff was the most important consideration. Clearly, all health care providers must be proactive about managing their online reputations.

Let's consider an example. When a surgeon decided to start her own surgery center, she realized that she needed a strong online presence to build her practice. So, she set up a Google alert to inform her when her name was mentioned. She also signed up for a service operated by Empathiq (**www.empathiq.io**), a health care-focused online reputation-management service that monitors her online reviews on rating sites such as those run by Healthgrades and Yelp. She routinely reads her reviews and calls patients who express dissatisfaction to find out what, if anything, she can change. This process has led her to make improvements to her practice. For example, she learned from reading a review that patients were waiting a long time to see her. She responded by reducing wait times, in part by e-mailing forms in advance through a patient portal.

An even more serious problem is that physicians feel pressured by what patients say about them on social media. In fact, the fear of poor patient satisfaction scores and negative comments on various websites appears to be creating a "Yelp effect" that drives physicians to provide care that patients do not actually need. There is a growing sense in medicine that patients are directing their relationships with physicians, by implicitly or explicitly threatening health care personnel with poor customer service reviews if they do not receive the treatment they want.

For instance, consider antibiotic resistance, which develops because bacteria adapt to antibiotics. As a result, drug-resistant infections are increasing. Each year, antibiotic resistance sends more than two million Americans to a physician, forcing the United States to spend an extra $2.2 billion on health care. To avoid poor reviews, many physicians feel pressured to prescribe antibiotics even when they are not necessary, for example, for viral infections.

Poor online ratings can damage health care businesses. Ratings sites will take down reviews that use profanity or that can be proved to be fake, but they typically will not edit or remove a review simply because a provider—or any business, for that matter—disputes what is in the review. For example, Yelp claims that it has several technologies in place to detect and take down fake reviews. Furthermore, unlike restaurants or plumbers, health care providers often cannot change their company name if their reputations are damaged.

It is standard practice for businesses to monitor their online reputations. Today, more services are helping physicians, clinics, and hospitals do the same. In addition to monitoring reviews and ensuring that the details of a practice are accurate, some of these firms will solicit patient reviews and generate other positive content to push down negative comments in Web search results. Some firms also help their clients contact patients to address their concerns and to ask them to change their reviews.

Some people criticize reputation-management firms because these organizations are paid to make their clients' online image as positive as possible—that is, critics contend that these firms attempt to change consumers' perception of a business.

Healthgrades (**www.healthgrades.com**), one of the largest rating sites for physicians, claims one million visitors per day. The site maintains that reputation-management firms can play a beneficial role by increasing the volume of feedback from patients, but only if the reviews are truthful and come from real patients. In fact, Healthgrades has several checkpoints in place to help the website verify that the reviewers are authentic.

Banner Health (**www.bannerhealth.com**), a large integrated health service that employs or is affiliated with 9,000 physicians, monitors its online reviews through Reputation.com. Banner uses natural-language recognition technology (see Technology Guide 4) to analyze online comments on Facebook and other social media websites and then reroutes negative feedback into its call center. This service is performed by Salesforce.com. The software classifies comments as positive, negative, and neutral. The negative comments are monitored closely, and complaints that require action are responded to promptly. For example, if a patient in the emergency room complains about a long wait, then Banner sends a staff member to apologize and expedite the admissions process. Banner also solicits phone- and e-mail-based patient-satisfaction scores directly and instructs physicians to call patients to discuss negative reviews.

iHealthspot (**www.ihealthspot.com**), another reputation-management service employed by health care professionals, builds separate websites called *microsites* that are embedded in its clients' Web pages. These microsites pull in reviews from ratings sites and the Web, but they display only those reviews that receive three, four, or five stars. This process effectively hides the most negative reviews. The microsites also provide an overall rating based on this subset of reviews.

Physicians Weight Loss Centers (PWLC; **www.pwlc.com**) began using iHealthspot when a prospective patient wanted to cancel her appointment after finding a negative review about the clinic on Yelp. The patient had missed several appointments without canceling, and she wanted her visit fee refunded even though the cancellation policy stated that she would forfeit it. In fact, several patients threatened the company with negative reviews if they did not get their money back. Another negative Yelp review described a patient experience that clearly did not happen at a PWLC clinic. Yelp declined to take down the reviews.

PWLC has an average 2-star rating out of 5 on Yelp and a 3.7-star rating out of 5 on Google. The microsite on the clinic's website, however, lists a 5-star average patient rating, with most of the reviews coming from Google. PWLC contends that the microsite reviews "are helpful, not misleading, because a lot of the negative reviews are incorrect."

Given that health care providers must manage their online reputations, what should they do? The first and most basic step is to avoid negative feedback in the first place. Providers should invest in training their front-office staff and creating a quality website. They should also monitor reviews on all of the major social media platforms, including HealthGrades, Yelp, RateMDs (**www.ratemds.com**), and Vitals (**www.vitals.com**). In that way, they can quickly address any negative feedback that appears. Here are three guidelines for responding to negative reviews:

- If the patient has identified himself or herself, then contact the individual directly and privately; that is, not via a social media platform.

- If the health care provider has many positive reviews and then one negative review appears, sometimes it is better not to respond to the negative one. There is a good chance that your loyal patient base will support you and respond. That process can be more effective than the provider responding.

- Providers should always respond to negative reviews calmly and constructively.

Unfortunately, some health providers are ignoring their patients' privacy and sharing details online as they try to rebut criticism. One dentist commented when a patient blamed him for the loss of a molar: "Due to your clenching and grinding habit, this is not the first molar tooth you have lost due to a fractured root. This tooth is no different." This response appears to have violated the Health Insurance Portability and Accountability Act (HIPAA), which forbids health care providers from disclosing any patient health information without permission. When a situation such as this occurs, patients contend that they have been injured twice, first by poor service or care and then by the disclosure of their private health information.

Sometimes the information that patients read on the Web is not the most reliable. In today's transparent era when patients have access to incredible amounts of information, health care providers must not see themselves as gatekeepers of medical information. Rather, the providers must be curators of that information, meaning that they find, organize, and share the most accurate content on a specific issue online.

It is a good idea for health care providers to Google themselves once per week to see what appears. Consider this scenario: A disgruntled patient created a fake website for a physician and filled it with false patient reviews. The physician did not know about the site until another patient visited his office and informed him that something was wrong with his website.

Sources: Compiled from M. McKenna, "The Yelping of the American Doctor," *Wired*, March 22, 2018; S. Wang, "When Doctors Get Negative Reviews Online," *Wall Street Journal*, June 26, 2017; J. Catley, "What Doctors Should Know about Online Reputation Management in 2017," *Medical Marketing Insights*, April 20, 2017; "A Step-by-Step Guide to Managing Negative Online Reviews," *Business Queensland*, November 18, 2016; E. Adler, "How Not to Respond to Bad Patient Reviews Online," *Physicians Practice*, September 21, 2016; T. Henry, "How to Respond to Bad Online Reviews," American Medical Association, September 2, 2016; T. Parks, "Physician behind KevinMD Reveals How to Leverage Social Media," American Medical Association, June 12, 2016; C. Ornstein, "Doctors Fire Back at Bad Yelp Reviews – and Reveal Patients' Information Online," *Washington Post*, May 27, 2016; T. Baker, "Five Online Reputation Management Strategies for Physicians," *Physicians Practice*, November 13. 2015; and C. Conner, "The Dark Side of Reputation Management: How It Affects Your Business," *Forbes*, May 9, 2013.

Questions

1. Refer to Chapter 3, and discuss the ethics of iHealthspot.

2. Does this case have implications for how we all should manage negative comments about ourselves on social media? Why or why not? Provide specific examples to support your answer.

Ratings, *reviews*, and *recommendations* are usually available in social shopping. In addition to seeing what is already posted, shoppers have an opportunity to contribute their own ratings and reviews and to discuss ratings and reviews posted by other shoppers (see **Figure 9.3**). The ratings and reviews come from the following sources:

- *Customer ratings and reviews:* Integrated into the vendor's Web page, a social network page, a customer review site, or in customer feeds (e.g., Amazon, iTunes, Buzzillions, Epinions)

- *Expert ratings and reviews:* Views from an independent authority (e.g., Metacritic)

- *Sponsored reviews:* Paid-for reviews (e.g., SponsoredReviews, PayPerPost)

- *Conversational marketing:* Individuals converse via e-mail, blog, live chat, discussion groups, and tweets. Monitoring these conversations yields rich data for market research and customer service.

FIGURE 9.3 Yelp (www.yelp.com) users submit reviews of local business within a local metropolitan area. Some communities have pages that feature a Review of the Day (often referred to as the ROTD).

MKT As one example, Maui Jim (**www.mauijim.com**), the sunglass company, employed favorable word-of-mouth marketing as a key sales driver. The company uses Bazaarvoice's Ratings & Reviews to allow customers to contribute five-point ratings and authentic product reviews on the company's entire line of sunglasses and accessories. In effect, Maui Jim extended customers' word-of-mouth reviews across the Web.

Maui Jim encourages its customers to share their candid opinions on the style, fit, and performance of all of its sunglasses models. To accomplish this goal, the company integrates customer reviews into its website search function to ensure that shoppers who are interested in a particular product see that product's rating in the search results. Customer response to this rating system has been overwhelmingly positive.

Social recommendation websites such as ShopSocially (**www.shopsocially.com**), Yelp (**www.yelp.com**), and Angie's List (**www.angieslist.com**) encourage conversations about purchases. The product recommendations are submitted by users' friends and acquaintances and arguably are more trustworthy than reviews posted by strangers.

ThisNext (**www.thisnext.com**) is a website where people recommend their favorite products to others. The site blends two powerful elements of real-world shopping: word-of-mouth recommendations from trusted sources and the ability to browse products in a way that naturally leads to discovery.

We must be careful when our search results reflect only our thinking on a subject. This process forms a filter bubble (coined by Eli Pariser). A *filter bubble* is a result of a personalized search where a website algorithm predicts (e.g., makes recommendations) what information or product a user would like based on user location and past searches on the website. As a result, users receive only information that reinforces their past choices and reflects their viewpoints.

Examples of such website algorithms include Google Personalized Search results, Amazon's A9 search engine, and Facebook's personalized news stream. For example, if you search Amazon only for books in the science fiction category, you may miss out on outstanding books in other genres because Amazon will mainly recommend books in the science fiction genre.

In another example, one user who searched Google for "BP" received investment news for British Petroleum. Another user searched for that exact term and received information about the Deepwater Horizon oil spill.

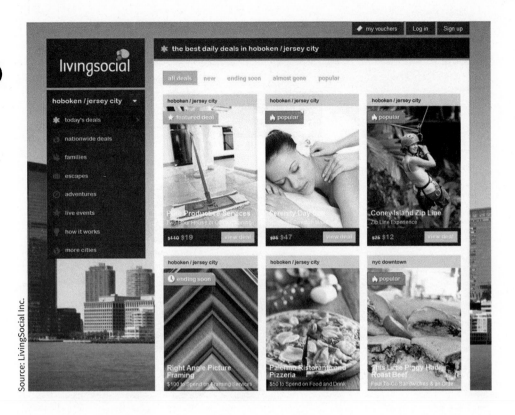

FIGURE 9.4 **LivingSocial (www.livingsocial.com) is a popular example of a group shopping website.**

Group Shopping

Group shopping websites such as Groupon (**www.groupon.com**) and LivingSocial (**www.livingsocial.com**, see **Figure 9.4**) offer major discounts or special deals during a short time frame. Group buying is closely associated with special deals (flash sales).

People who sign up with LivingSocial receive e-mails that offer deals at, for example, a restaurant, a spa, or an event in a given city. They can click on either "Today's Deal" or "Past Deal" (some past deals can still be active). They can also click on an icon and receive the deal the next day. Customers who purchase a deal receive a unique link to share with their friends. If a customer convinces three or more people to buy that specific deal using his or her link, then the customer's deal is free.

Individuals can also shop together virtually in real time. In this process, shoppers log on to a website and then contact their friends and family. Everyone then shops online at the same time. Some real-time shopping providers, such as DoTogether (**www.dotogether.com**) and Wet Seal (**www.wetseal.com**), have integrated their shopping service directly into Facebook. Customers log in to Facebook, install the firm's app, and then invite their friends to join them on a virtual retail shopping experience.

Shopping Communities and Clubs

Shopping clubs host sales for their members that last just a few days and usually feature luxury brands at heavily discounted prices. Club organizers host three to seven sales per day, usually via e-mail messages that entice club members to shop at more than 70 percent off retail—but quickly, before supplies run out.

Luxury brands effectively partner with online shopping clubs to dispose of special-run, sample, overstock, or liquidation goods. These clubs are rather exclusive, which prevents the brands' images from being diminished. Examples are Beyond the Rack (**www.btr.com/**), Gilt Groupe (**www.gilt.com**), Rue La La (**www.ruelala.com**), and One King's Lane (**www.onekingslane.com**).

Kaboodle (**www.kaboodle.com**) is another example of a shopping community. Kaboodle is a free service that lets users collect information from the Web and store it on a Kaboodle list

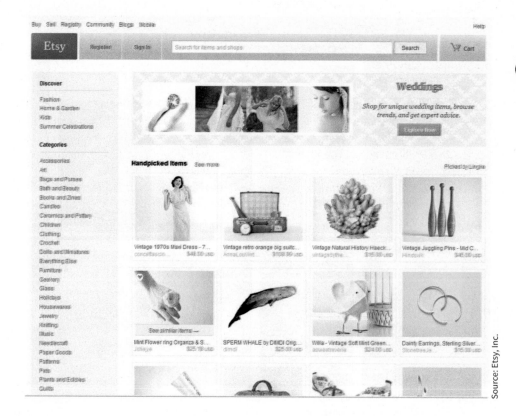

FIGURE 9.5 Etsy (www.etsy .com) is a social marketplace for all handmade or vintage items.

that they can share with other shoppers. Kaboodle simplifies shopping by making it easier for people to find items they want in a catalog and by allowing users to share recommendations with one another using Kaboodle lists and groups. People can also use Kaboodle lists for planning vacations, sharing research for work and school, sharing favorite bands with friends, and basically everything else they might want to collect and share information about.

Social Marketplaces and Direct Sales

MKT **Social marketplaces** act as online intermediaries that harness the power of social networks for introducing, buying, and selling products and services. A social marketplace helps members market their own creations (see Etsy in **Figure 9.5**). Other examples are as follows:

- Craigslist (www.craigslist.org) provides online classifieds in addition to supporting social activities such as meetings and events.
- Fotolia by Adobe (www.fotolia.com) is a social marketplace for the community of creative people who enjoy sharing, learning, and expressing themselves through images, forums, and blogs; members provide royalty-free stock images that other individuals and professionals can legally buy and share.
- Flipsy (www.flipsy.com) can be used by anyone to list, buy, and sell books, music, movies, and games.

Before you go on...

1. Prior to making a purchase, why are ratings, reviews, and recommendations so important to potential customers?
2. Define collaborative consumption, and describe how collaborative consumption is a "green" phenomenon.

9.4 Social Computing in Business: Marketing

MKT *Marketing* can be defined as the process of building profitable customer relationships by creating value for customers and capturing value in return. There are many components to a marketing campaign, including (1) define your target audience, (2) develop your message (i.e., how you will solve their problem), (3) decide on how you will deliver your message (e.g., e-mail, snail mail, Web advertising, social networks), and (4) follow-up.

An interesting way for authors to market to their readers is occurring in the publishing industry. IT's About Business 9.4 shows how Sprinklr helps companies manage the total customer experience.

> **Author Lecture Videos are available exclusively in** *WileyPLUS*.
> **Apply the Concept activities are available in the Appendix and in** *WileyPLUS*.

IT's About Business 9.4

MKT MIS Sprinklr

Modern businesses are recognizing that social media are not simply channels for communicating with customers. Rather, they are the foundation for how customers perceive companies' brands. Because social media are so diverse and complex, managing the customer experience has become much more complicated than it used to be.

In a social media world, the job of marketing is no longer simply to drive purchases. Rather, marketing must also create brand enthusiasts. The marketing department must now take ownership of the customer experience, which encompasses all of the interactions between customers and an organization throughout their business relationship. As a result, marketing managers are becoming advocates of corporate digital transformation, to ensure that their companies use technology to engage and satisfy customers.

Founded in 2009, Sprinklr's (**www.sprinklr.com**) platform helps enterprises to manage the consumer experience at every interaction—that is, Sprinklr has the ability to administer the complete customer experience in the era of the connected consumer. The company provides social media marketing, social media monitoring, social advertising, content management, collaboration, and advocacy for large companies. Specifically, Sprinklr helps organizations manage paid media, owned media, and earned media for large enterprises.

- *Paid media* serve as a method for promoting content and driving exposure. For example, social media platforms such as Twitter, Facebook, LinkedIn, and Pinterest offer advertising options that organizations leverage to increase their exposure to consumers. Paid media include social media ads, pay-per-click, display ads, retargeting, paid influencers, and paid content promotion.

- *Owned media* refers to content that organizations control. The primary goal of this content is to continue providing value to prospective customers. Owned media encompass organizational websites, mobile sites, blog sites, and social media channels.

- *Earned media* refers to media exposure that organizations have gained through word-of-mouth. Organizations can earn media by receiving press mentions, positive reviews, reposts, mentions, shares, and recommendations.

Sprinklr was founded as a social media management company. By 2017, it evolved into the first unified customer experience management (CXM) platform for organizations. The reason for this development is that organizations must control the shift from a unidirectional brand message (company to customers) to a collective conversation on social media. The CXM process requires a company to reorganize in order to put customers at the center of its mission and then build systems around that idea.

Sprinklr's core platform does not just manage social media. Rather, it encompasses all customer touchpoints. In October 2017, Sprinklr began to provide functionality for each major customer-facing department, and it integrated that functionality with existing legacy systems across marketing, advertising, research, electronic and mobile commerce, and customer care (coined "MARCC"). Using social media as a central processing point, Sprinklr consolidates all of these functions into what the firm calls the Experience Cloud. Sprinklr contends that it can offer a record of each customer's experience with a brand as well as the ability to act on that record in real time.

Brands such as Nike, Verizon, McDonald's, Starwood, *Forbes*, Samsung, Cisco, SAP, Target, and Virgin American (among many others) are becoming increasingly sophisticated in how they want to publish and monitor their reputations on Facebook, Twitter, Instagram, Pinterest, and other social media outlets. On their side, social platforms are becoming more knowledgeable about working with brands. Let's examine how several companies are using Sprinklr:

- McDonald's uses Sprinklr to build profiles of social accounts so that it can recognize loyal fans and respond appropriately. McDonald's also wants to recognize and address unhappy customers.

- Nasdaq used Sprinklr the morning after Match.com's initial public offering (IPO) to document that moment on Nasdaq's

Facebook, Twitter, and Instagram accounts simultaneously. Nasdaq prefers Sprinklr because Sprinklr maintains an audit trail of each social media post for securities regulators.

- Schneider Electric moved its business to Sprinklr from Salesforce because Sprinklr proved itself to be more flexible. Specifically, Sprinklr had Schneider up and running on WeChat, a hugely influential social network in China, in a matter of weeks.

- Starwood uses Sprinklr to manage its more than 3,000 social media accounts across all of its hotel brands largely because of the reporting and analytics features that Sprinklr added at Starwood's request.

Sprinklr's hold on its accounts always faces competition from Adobe, Oracle, and Salesforce, all of which have bought their way into social media management since 2012 and operate larger operations. Despite this stiff competition, Sprinklr retains approximately 95 percent of its customers from one year to the next, an excellent rate for any software company.

By July 2019, Sprinklr was valued at nearly $2 billion. The platform had 1,500 employees in 75 countries.

Sources: Compiled from S. Hyken, "Customer Experience Is the New Brand," *Forbes*, July 15, 2018; "Sprinklr Simplifies UX with New Products," *Research Live*, October 5, 2017; M. Shields, "The 19 Most Interesting Ad-Tech Upstarts of 2017," *Business Insider*, August 16, 2017; A. Murray, "Four Forces Revolutionizing Marketing," *Fortune*, July 18, 2017; "In the Enterprise, Customer Experience Starts with Social," *Forbes*, June 26, 2017; P. Simpson, "The Monday Stack: Every Company on Earth Needs Sprinklr," *DMN*, May 15, 2017; R. Miller, "Sprinklr Launches Major Push into Customer Experience," *TechCrunch*, April 11, 2017; A. Konrad, "He Solved Facebook," *Forbes*, February 8, 2016; E. Griffith, "Sprinklr Raises $46 Million to Become Latest Billion-Dollar Unicorn," *Fortune*, March 31, 2015; M. Fidelman, "Why Sprinklr Is Pouring Money into the Influencer and Advocacy Space," *Forbes*, September 5, 2014; L. Chapman, "Sprinklr Acquires Branderati as Social Media Tools Consolidate," *Wall Street Journal*, September 3, 2014; J. Edwards, "Sprinklr Acquires TBG Digital, One of Facebook's Biggest Ad Clients, Ahead of Its IPO," *Business Insider*, August 14, 2014; G. Sloane, "Sprinklr Buys Dachis Group to Boost Social Marketing Services," *AdWeek*, February 19, 2014; S. Ludwig, "Meet Sprinklr, the Biggest Social Media Management Biz You've Never Heard of," *VentureBeat*, April 12, 2012; and www.sprinklr.com, accessed July 16, 2019.

Questions

1. Why is it so important for businesses to manage the entire customer experience by concentrating on social media? Provide examples to support your answer.

2. Describe Sprinklr's Experience Cloud, and explain how it relates to social media.

3. Recall the chapter opening case about Dr. Dao and United Airlines. Explain how Sprinklr could have helped United with its response to the event. Provide specific examples to support your answer.

Advertising

MKT **Social advertising** refers to advertising formats that make use of the social context of the user viewing the ad. Social advertising is the first form of advertising to leverage forms of social influence such as peer pressure and friend recommendations and likes.

Many experts believe advertising is the solution to the challenge of making money from social networking sites and social commerce sites. Advertisers have long noted the large number of visitors on social networks and the amount of time they spend there. As a result, they are willing to pay to place ads and run promotions on social networks. Advertisers now post ads on all major social networking websites.

Most ads in social commerce consist of branded content paid for by advertisers. These ads belong to two major categories: *social advertisements* (or *social ads*) and *social apps*. Social advertisements are ads placed in paid-for media space on social media networks. Social apps are branded online applications that support social interactions and user contributions (e.g., Nike+).

Viral marketing—that is, word-of-mouth advertising—lends itself especially well to social networking. For example, Stormhoek Vineyards (**www.stormhoek.com**) initiated a marketing campaign by offering bloggers a free bottle of wine. Within six months, roughly 100 of these bloggers had posted voluntary comments—the majority of them positive—about the wine on their blogs. In turn, these comments were read by other bloggers.

There are other innovative methods to advertise in social media. Consider the following:

- Use a company Facebook page, including a store that attracts fans and lets them "meet" other customers. Then, advertise in your Facebook store.

- Tweet business success stories to your customers.

- Integrate ads into YouTube videos.

- Use native advertising. *Native advertising* is a sales pitch that fits into the flow of the information being shown. Many publishers view native advertising as risky because it has the potential to erode the public's trust.

Market Research

MKT Traditionally, marketing professionals used demographics compiled by market research firms as one of their primary tools to identify and target potential customers. Obtaining this information was time-consuming and costly, because marketing professionals had to ask potential customers to provide it. Today, however, members of social networks provide this information voluntarily on their pages! (Think about all the information that you provide on your favorite social networking websites.) Because of the open nature of social networking, merchants can easily find their customers, see what they do online, and learn who their friends are.

This information provides a new opportunity to assess markets in near real time. Word-of-mouth has always been one of the most powerful marketing methods—more often than not, people use products that their friends like and recommend. Social media sites can provide this type of data for numerous products and services.

Companies are utilizing social computing tools to obtain feedback from customers. This trend is referred to as *conversational marketing*. These tools enable customers to supply feedback via blogs, wikis, online forums, and social networking sites. Again, customers are providing much of this feedback to companies voluntarily and for free.

Social computing not only generates faster and cheaper results than traditional focus groups but also fosters closer customer relationships. For example, Dell Computer operates a feedback website called IdeaStorm that allows customers to suggest and vote on improvements in its offerings (see **Figure 9.6**).

Retailers are aware that customers, especially younger ones, not only want to be heard but also want to know whether other customers agree with them. Consequently, retailers are increasingly opening up their websites to customers, allowing them to post product reviews, ratings, and, in some cases, photos and videos.

As a result of this strategy, customer reviews are emerging as prime locations for online shoppers to visit. Approximately one-half of consumers consult reviews before making an online purchase, and almost two-thirds are more likely to purchase from a site that offers ratings and reviews.

Using social computing for market research is not restricted to businesses. Customers also enjoy the capabilities that social computing offers when they are shopping.

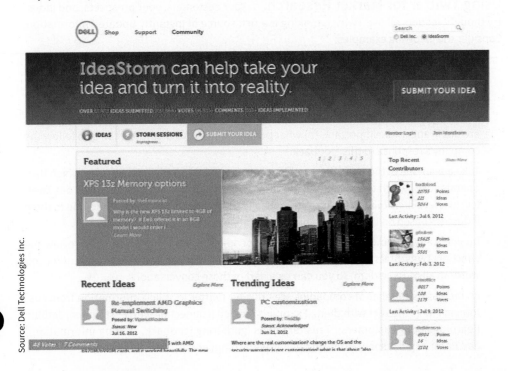

Source: Dell Technologies Inc.

FIGURE 9.6 **Customers share their ideas and feedback with Dell via IdeaStorm (www.delltechnologies.com/).**

Conducting Market Research Using Social Networks

MKT Customer sentiment expressed on Twitter, Facebook, and similar sites represents an incredibly valuable source of information for companies. Customer activities on social networking sites generate huge amounts of data that must be analyzed, so that management can conduct better marketing campaigns and improve their product design and their service offerings. The monitoring, collection, and analysis of socially generated data, and the resultant strategic decisions are combined in a process known as **social intelligence**.

An example of social intelligence is TOMS Shoes (**www.toms.com**). The retailer used social intelligence to analyze conversations. During the research, TOMS discovered a high number of conversations around My Little Pony. This finding meant that people who were interested in, or discussing, TOMS were also highly interested in My Little Pony. Moving quickly, TOMS created a brand new "My Little Pony" themed shoe. The new product sold out within 48 hours.

Social networks provide excellent sources of valuable information for market research. In this section, you will see illustrative examples of how to use Facebook, Twitter, and LinkedIn for market research.

Using Facebook for Market Research.
There are several ways to use Facebook for market research. Consider the following examples:

- Obtain feedback from your Facebook fans (and their friends if possible) on advertising campaigns, market research, and so on. It is the equivalent of holding a free focus group.

- Test-market your messages. Provide two or three options, and ask fans which one they prefer and why.

- Use Facebook for survey invitations (i.e., to recruit participants). Essentially, turn Facebook into a giant panel, and ask users to participate in a survey. Facebook offers a self-service model for displaying ads, which can function as invitations to take a survey. Facebook also allows you to target your audience very specifically based on traditional demographic criteria such as age and gender.

Using Twitter for Market Research.
Your customers, your prospects, and industry thought leaders all use Twitter, making it a rich source of instantly updated information. Consider the following examples:

- Visit Twitter Search (**www.twitter.com/search**). Enter a company's Twitter name. Not only can you follow what the company is saying but you can also follow what everyone is saying to them. Monitoring replies to your competitors and their employees will help you develop your own Twitter strategy by enabling you to observe (a) what your competitors are doing and, more important, (b) what people think about them. You can also follow the company's response to this feedback.

- Take advantage of the tools that enable you to find people in the industries in which they operate. Use search.twitter.com to monitor industry-specific key words. Check out Twellow (**www.twellow.com**). This site automatically categorizes a Twitter user into one to three industries based on that person's bio and tweets.

- Do you want to know what topic is on most people's minds today? If so, then review the chart on TweetStats (**www.tweetstats.com**). It will show you the most frequently used words in all of Tweetdom, so you can be a part of those conversations.

- An increasing number of companies are utilizing Twitter to solicit information from customers and to interact with them. Examples are Dell (connecting with customers), JetBlue (learning about customers), Teusner Wines (gathering feedback, sharing information), and Pepsi (rapid response time in dealing with complaints).

Using LinkedIn for Market Research.   Post a question (e.g., solicit advice) regarding the topic or issue you are interested in. You may obtain a better result if you go to a specific LinkedIn group.

Before you go on…

1. Is social advertising more effective than advertising without a social component? Why or why not?
2. Describe how marketing professionals use social networks to perform marketing research.

9.5 | Social Computing in Business: Customer Relationship Management

MKT The customer service profession has undergone a significant transformation, both in the ways that customer service professionals conduct business and in the ways that customers adapt to interacting with companies in a newly connected environment. Social computing has vastly altered both the expectations of customers and the capabilities of corporations in the area of customer relationship management. (We discuss customer relationship management in detail in Chapter 11.)

Author Lecture Videos are available exclusively in *WileyPLUS*.
Apply the Concept activities are available in the Appendix and in *WileyPLUS*.

Customers are now incredibly empowered. Companies are closely monitoring social computing not only because they are mindful of the negative comments posted by social network members but also because they perceive an opportunity to involve customers proactively to reduce problems through improved customer service.

Consider this example: Papa John's Pizza fired a cashier at one of its New York restaurants and apologized to an Asian-American customer for a receipt that identified her as "lady chinky eyes." Minhee Cho, a communications manager at the nonprofit investigative journalism group ProPublica, posted a photo of the receipt on her Twitter account, and it was viewed almost 200,000 times in a single day. John Schnatter, then chairman and CEO of Papa John's, immediately posted an apology on Facebook. In his apology, he asserted that he had apologized personally to Ms. Cho as well.

Empowered customers know how to use the wisdom and power of crowds and communities to their benefit. These customers choose how they interact with companies and brands, and they have elevated expectations concerning their experiences with a company. They are actively involved with businesses, not just as purchasers but also as advocates and influencers. As a result, businesses must respond to customers quickly and appropriately. Fortunately, social computing provides many opportunities for businesses to do just that, thereby offering businesses the opportunity to turn disgruntled customers into champions for the firm.

Before you go on…

1. Discuss why social computing is so important in customer relationship management.
2. Describe how social computing improves customer service.

9.6 Social Computing in Business: Human Resource Management

Author Lecture Videos are available exclusively in *WileyPLUS*.
Apply the Concept activities are available in the Appendix and in *WileyPLUS*.

HRM Human resource (HR) departments in many organizations use social computing applications outside their organizations (recruiting) and inside their organizations (employee development). For example, Deloitte Touche Tohmatsu (**www.deloitte.com**) created a social network to assist its HR managers in downsizing and regrouping teams.

Recruiting

HRM Both recruiters and job seekers are moving to online social networks as recruiting platforms. Enterprise recruiters are scanning online social networks, blogs, and other social resources to identify and find information about potential employees. If job seekers are online and active, there is a good chance that they will be seen by recruiters. In addition, on social networks there are many passive job seekers—people who are employed but would take a better job if one appeared. So, it is important that both active and passive job seekers maintain online profiles that accurately reflect their background and skills. Closing Case 1 takes a look at the rewards and the difficulties inherent in the online recruiting process. It also provides some tips to assist you in a job search.

In another example, one HR director uses the HR social media management software Bullhorn Reach (**www.bullhornreach.com**), which allows her to post jobs to eight different social networks simultaneously. Bullhorn Reach also enables her to analyze metrics that measure the effectiveness of her social recruiting efforts.

Onboarding

HRM *Onboarding* is how new employees acquire the necessary knowledge, skills, and behaviors to become effective members of the organization. Through the use of social media, new hires can learn what to expect in their first few days on the job and find answers to common questions. Because they are available inside the company's firewall, these social communities can provide detailed information about corporate policies, as well as giving employees the opportunity to complete necessary forms online. These communities also provide introductory training, such as workplace safety information and how to use enterprise applications.

Employee Development

HRM Human resource managers know that the best strategy to enable, encourage, and promote employee development is to build relationships with employees. To this end, a number of HR professionals are using enterprise social tools such as Chatter (**www.salesforce.com/chatter**), Yammer (**www.yammer.com**), and Tibbr (**www.tibbr.com**) to tap into the wisdom of every employee. These tools help connect employees to work efficiently across organizations and to collaborate on sales opportunities, campaigns, and projects. They help companies simplify workflows and capture new ideas. They enable HR managers to find subject matter experts within the organization, recommending relevant people for every project team, sales team, and other functions.

As HR managers learn more about employees' skills, expertise, and passions through such tools, they can better motivate them, thereby helping them become more engaged and excited about their work. Employees can then be better rewarded for their expertise.

Another area of employee development is training. A large percentage of the time and expense of employee education and learning management can be minimized by utilizing e-learning and interactive social learning tools. These tools help create connections among learners, instructors, and information. Companies find that these tools facilitate knowledge transfer within departments and across teams. Examples of these tools are Moodle (**www.moodle.com**), Joomla (**www.joomla.org/**), and Bloomfire (**www.bloomfire.com**).

In 2015, LinkedIn acquired Lynda.com, an online education company offering thousands of video courses in software, creative, and business skills. The company produced video tutorials taught by industry experts. Members of Lynda had unlimited access to watch the videos. Lynda.com's courses and instructors are now all a part of LinkedIn Learning (**www.linkedin.com/learning**).

With this acquisition, LinkedIn incorporates job certifications and training into its offerings. One LinkedIn executive noted that a LinkedIn user could be looking for a job, immediately see the skills necessary for that job, and then be prompted to take the relevant and accredited course on Lynda that will help him or her acquire those skills and land the job.

Finding a Job

The other side of organizational recruiting consists of those people looking for jobs. Let's say you want to find a job. Like the majority of job hunters, you will probably conduct at least part of your search online because the vast majority of entry-level positions in the United States are now listed only online. Job sites are the fastest, least expensive, and most efficient method to connect employers with potential employees.

Today, job searchers use traditional job sites and social networks such as LinkedIn. Applicants like you have helped. There are 20 million active job listings on LinkedIn and its popularity continues to grow.

To find a job, your best bet is to begin with LinkedIn (**www.linkedin.com**), which has roughly 575 million members. You should definitely have a profile on LinkedIn, which, by the way, is free. (See the bulleted list that follows for mistakes to avoid on your LinkedIn profile.)

LinkedIn's success comes from its ability to accurately identify its market segment. The company's automated approach does not lend itself well to the upper tier of the job market—for example, CEO searches—where traditional face-to-face searches continue to be the preferred strategy. At the other end of the spectrum—that is, low-paying, low-skill jobs such as cashiers and truck drivers—job boards provide faster results. LinkedIn targets the vast sweet spot between these two extremes, helping to fill high-skill jobs that pay anywhere from $50,000 to $250,000 or more per year. This is the spot you will likely occupy when you graduate.

A number of job-search companies are competing with LinkedIn. These companies are trying to create better-targeted matching systems that leverage social networking functionality. These companies include Monster (**www.monster.com**), SimplyHired (**www.simplyhired.com**), Career Builder (**www.careerbuilder.com**), Indeed (**www.indeed.com**), Jobvite (**www.recruiting.jobvite.com**), Dice Open Web (**www.dice.com/openweb**), and many others.

The most important secret to making online job search sites work for you is to use them carefully. Job coaches advise you to spend 80 percent of your day networking and directly contacting the people in charge of jobs you want. Devote another 10 percent to headhunters. Spend only the remaining 10 percent of your time online.

Here is how to make your time online count. To start with, as you saw above, you should have a profile on LinkedIn. The following list shows you the mistakes *not* to make on your LinkedIn profile:

- Do have a current, professional picture (no dogs, no spouses, no babies, etc.).
- Do make certain your LinkedIn Status is correct and current.
- Do join groups related to your field of study or even to your personal interests.
- Do list an accurate skill set. Do not embellish.
- Do not use the standard connection request. Do some research on that person and tailor your connection request to that person.

- Do not neglect LinkedIn's privacy settings. When you have a job and are looking for another one, you want to be discreet. You can set your privacy settings so that your boss does not see that you are looking for opportunities.
- Do not skip the Summary. The Summary is a concise way of selling yourself. Write it in the first person.
- Do not eliminate past jobs or volunteer work.
- Do not say you have worked with someone when you have not.

Next, access the job sites such as those listed above. These sites list millions of jobs and they make it easy to narrow your search using filters. These filters include title, company name, location, and many others. Indeed allows you to search within a specific salary range. Simply-Hired lets you sort for friendly, socially responsible, and even dog-friendly workplaces.

These sites have advanced search options. Try plugging in the name of a company you might want to work for or an advanced degree that qualifies you for specialized work. For example, you could enter "CFA" if you are a certified financial analyst or "LEED" if you are a building engineer with expertise in environmental efficiency.

SimplyHired has a useful tool called "Who do I know." If you have a LinkedIn profile, then this tool will instantly display your LinkedIn contacts with connections to various job listings. "Who do I know" also syncs with Facebook.

One more trick to using the aggregators: Configure them to deliver listings to your inbox. Set up an e-mail alert that delivers new job postings to you every day.

You should also search for niche sites that are specific to your field. For technology-related jobs, for instance, Dice (**www.dice.com**) has a strong reputation. For nonprofit jobs, try Idealist (**www.idealist.org**). For government jobs, the U.S. government's site is an excellent resource: **www.usajobs.gov**.

One more great online resource is Craigslist (**www.craigslist.org**). It is one site the aggregators do not tap. Craigslist focuses on local listings, and it is especially useful for entry-level jobs and internships.

Beyond locating listings for specific jobs, career coaches contend that job sites can be a resource for key words and phrases that you can pull from job descriptions and include in your resume, cover letters, and e-mails. Use the language from a job description in your cover letter.

Websites like Vault (**www.vault.com**), Monster, and CareerBuilder provide some helpful career tips. Vault, in particular, offers very useful career guides.

The bottom line: It is critical to extend most of your efforts *beyond* an online search.

Before you go on…

1. Explain why LinkedIn has become so important in the recruiting process.

2. If you are looking for a job, what is the major problem with restricting your search to social networks?

What's in **IT** for me?

ACCT For the Accounting Major

Audit teams use social networking technologies internally to stay in touch with team members who are working on multiple projects. These technologies serve as a common channel of communications. For example, an audit team manager can create a group, include his or her team members as subscribers, and then push information regarding projects to all members at once. Externally, these technologies are useful in interfacing with clients and other third parties for whom the firm and its staff provide services.

FIN For the Finance Major

Many of the popular social networking sites have users who subscribe to finance-oriented subgroups. Among these groups are finance professionals who collaborate and share knowledge as well as nonfinancial professionals who are potential clients.

MKT For the Marketing Major

Social computing tools and applications enable marketing professionals to become closer to their customers in a variety of ways, including blogs, wikis, ratings, and recommendations. Marketing professionals now receive almost-real-time feedback on products.

POM For the Production/Operations Management Major

Social computing tools and applications allow production personnel to "enlist" business partners and customers in product development activities.

HRM For the Human Resource Management Major

Social networks offer tremendous benefits to human resource professionals. HR personnel can perform a great deal of their recruiting activities by accessing such sites as LinkedIn. They can also check out potential new hires by accessing a large number of social networking sites. Internally, HR personnel can utilize private, internal social networks for employee expertise and experience in order to find the best person for a position or project team.

MIS For the MIS Major

The MIS department is responsible for two aspects of social computing usage: (1) monitoring employee usage of social computing applications while at work, both time and content, and (2) developing private, internal social networks for company employees and then monitoring the content of these networks.

Summary

9.1 Describe five Web 2.0 tools and two major types of Web 2.0 sites.

A *tag* is a key word or term that describes a piece of information (e.g., a blog, a picture, an article, or a video clip).

Really Simple Syndication allows you to receive the information you want (customized information), when you want it, without having to surf thousands of websites.

A *weblog* (*blog* for short) is a personal website, open to the public, in which the site creator expresses his or her feelings or opinions with a series of chronological entries.

Microblogging is a form of blogging that allows users to write short messages (or capture an image or embedded video) and publish them.

A *wiki* is a website on which anyone can post material and make changes to already posted material. Wikis foster easy collaboration and they harness the collective intelligence of Internet users.

Social networking websites allow users to upload their content to the Web in the form of text (e.g., blogs), voice (e.g., podcasts), images, and videos (e.g., videocasts).

A *mashup* is a website that takes different content from a number of other websites and mixes them together to create a new kind of content.

9.2 Describe the benefits and risks of social commerce to companies.

Social commerce refers to the delivery of electronic commerce activities and transactions through social computing.

Benefits of social commerce to customers include the following: better and faster vendors' responses to complaints; customers can assist other customers; customers' expectations can be met more fully and quickly; and customers can easily search, link, chat, and buy while staying in the social network's page.

Benefits of social commerce to vendors include the following: can test new products and ideas quickly and inexpensively; learn much about their customers; identify problems quickly and alleviate anger; learn from customers' experiences with rapid feedback; increase sales when customers discuss products positively on social networking site; create better marketing campaigns and brand awareness; use low-cost user-generated content, for example, in marketing campaigns; get free advertising through viral marketing; identify influential brand advocates and reward them.

Risks of social computing include information security concerns; invasion of privacy; violation of intellectual property and copyright; employees' reluctance to participate; data leakage of personal information or corporate strategic information; poor or biased quality of users' generated content; and cyberbullying/cyberstalking and employee harassment.

9.3 Identify the methods used for shopping socially.

Social shopping is a method of electronic commerce that takes all of the key aspects of social networks—friends, groups, voting, comments, discussions, reviews, and others—and focuses them on shopping.

Methods for shopping socially include what other shoppers say; group shopping; shopping communities and clubs; social marketplaces and direct sales; and peer-to-peer shopping.

9.4 Discuss innovative ways to use social networking sites for advertising and market research.

Social advertising represents advertising formats that employ the social context of the user viewing the ad.

Innovative ways to advertise in social media include the following: Create a company Facebook page; tweet business success stories to your customers; integrate ads into YouTube videos; add a Facebook "Like" button with its sponsored story to your product; and use sponsored stories.

- *Using Facebook for market research:* Get feedback from your Facebook fans (and their friends if possible) on advertising campaigns, market research; test-market your messages; and use Facebook for survey invitations.

- *Using Twitter for market research:* Use Twitter Search; use Twellow; and look at the chart on TweetStats.
- *Using LinkedIn for market research:* Post a question (e.g., solicit advice) regarding the topic or issue you are interested in.

9.5 Describe how social computing improves customer service.

Customers are now incredibly empowered. Companies are closely monitoring social computing not only because they are mindful of the negative comments posted by social network members but also because they see an opportunity to involve customers proactively to reduce problems by improved customer service.

Empowered customers know how to use the wisdom and power of crowds and communities to their benefit. These customers choose how they interact with companies and brands, and they have elevated expectations. They are actively involved with businesses, not just as purchasers but also as advocates and influencers. As a result, businesses must respond to customers quickly and accurately. Fortunately, social computing provides many opportunities for businesses to do just that, thereby giving businesses the opportunity to turn disgruntled customers into champions for the firm.

9.6 Discuss different ways in which human resource managers make use of social computing.

- *Recruiting:* Both recruiters and job seekers are moving to online social networks as new recruiting platforms. Enterprise recruiters are scanning online social networks, blogs, and other social resources to identify and find information about potential employees. If job seekers are online and active, there is a good chance that they will be seen by recruiters. In addition, on social networks, there are many passive job seekers—people who are employed but would take a better job if it appeared. So, it is important that both active and passive job seekers maintain profiles online that truly reflect them.
- *Onboarding:* The use of social media to help new employees acquire the necessary knowledge, skills, and behaviors to become effective members of the organization.
- *Employee development:* HR managers are using social tools to build relationships with employees. As HR managers learn more about employees, they can help them become more engaged and excited about their work.

Chapter Glossary

blog (weblog) A personal website, open to the public, in which the site creator expresses his or her feelings or opinions with a series of chronological entries.

blogosphere The term for the millions of blogs on the Web.

collaborative consumption An economic model based on sharing, swapping, trading, or renting products and services, enabling access over ownership.

mashup A website that takes different content from a number of other websites and mixes that content to create a new kind of content.

microblogging A form of blogging that allows users to write short messages (or capture an image or embedded video) and publish them.

Really Simple Syndication (RSS) A technology that allows users to receive the information they want, when they want it, without having to surf thousands of websites.

social advertising Advertising formats that make use of the social context of the user viewing the ad.

social capital The number of connections a person has within and between social networks.

social commerce The delivery of electronic commerce activities and transactions through social computing.

social computing A type of information technology that combines social behavior and information systems to create value.

social graph A map of all relevant links or connections for one member of a social network.

social intelligence The monitoring, collection, and analysis of socially generated data and the resultant strategic decisions.

social marketplaces Websites that act as online intermediaries that harness the power of social networks for introducing, buying, and selling products and services.

social network A social structure composed of individuals, groups, or organizations linked by values, visions, ideas, financial exchange, friendship, kinship, conflict, or trade.

social networking Activities performed using social software tools (e.g., blogging) or social networking features (e.g., media sharing).

social shopping A method of electronic commerce that takes all of the key aspects of social networks (friends, groups, voting, comments, discussions, reviews, etc.) and focuses them on shopping.

tag A key word or term that describes a piece of information.

tweet Messages and updates posted by users on Twitter.

Twitter A free microblogging service that allows its users to send messages and read other users' messages and updates.

Web 2.0 A loose collection of information technologies and applications, plus the websites that use them.

wiki A website on which anyone can post material and make changes to other material.

Discussion Questions

1. How would you describe Web 2.0 to someone who has not taken a course in information systems?

2. If you were the CEO of a company, would you pay attention to blogs about your company? Why or why not? If yes, would you consider some blogs to be more important or more reliable than are others? If so, which ones? How would you find blogs relating to your company?

3. Do you have a page on a social networking website? If yes, why? If no, what is keeping you from creating one? Is there any content that you definitely would *not* post on such a page?

4. How can an organization best employ social computing technologies and applications to benefit its business processes?

5. What factors might cause an individual, an employee, or a company to be cautious in the use of social networks?

6. Why are advertisers so interested in social networks?

7. What sorts of restrictions or guidelines should firms place on the use of social networks by employees? Are social computing sites a threat to security? Can they tarnish a firm's reputation? If so, how? Can they enhance a firm's reputation? If so, how?

8. Why are marketers so interested in social networks?

9. Why are human resource managers so interested in social networks?

Problem-Solving Activities

1. Enter **www.programmableweb.com** and study the various services that the website offers. Learn how to create mashups and then propose a mashup of your own. Present your mashup to the class.

2. Go to Amazon's Mechanical Turk website (**www.mturk.com**). View the available Human Intelligence Tasks (HITs). Are there any HITs that you would be interested in to make some extra money? Why or why not?

3. Access Pandora (**www.pandora.com**). Why is Pandora a social networking site?

4. Access ChatRoulette (**www.chatroulette.com**). What is interesting about this social networking site?

5. Using a search engine, look up the following:

- *Most popular or most visited blogs.* Pick two and follow some of the posts. Why do you think these blogs are popular?
- *Best blogs* (try Detailed.com's list of 50 best blogs (**www.detailed.com/50/**). Pick two and consider why they might be the "best blogs."

6. Research how to be a successful blogger. What does it take to be a successful blogger? What time commitment might be needed? How frequently do successful bloggers post?

Closing Case

MKT **MIS** The Story of Snapchat

Founded in 2011, Snapchat is an image, messaging, and multimedia mobile application. (In 2016, the founders rebranded the company as Snap, **www.snap.com**.) The Snapchat app integrates image, video, communication, and entertainment.

Originally, Snapchat featured private, person-to-person photo sharing, where pictures and messages were available only for a short time before they became inaccessible. Then, in May 2017, Snapchat made it possible to send snaps with unlimited viewing time, dropping the previous 10-second maximum duration, with the content disappearing after being deliberately closed by the recipient. The following month, Snapchat began to allow users to add links to snaps, enabling them to direct viewers to specific websites.

People use Snapchat primarily for creating multimedia messages, referred to as *snaps*. Snaps can consist of a photo or a short video, and they can be edited to include filters and effects, text captions, and drawings. Over time, Snapchat has added many new features. Let's

examine those features and explore how Snap is monetizing some of them.

My Story

Introduced in October 2013, this feature allows users to compile snaps into chronological storylines that are accessible to all of their friends. Essentially, My Story is a collection of images and video that capture a user's day and that last 24 hours.

In June 2014, Snapchat changed this feature to *Live Stories*, which allows users on location at specific events—such as music festivals and sporting events—to contribute snaps to a curated story that is advertised to all users, showcasing a single event from multiple perspectives and viewpoints. (*Content curation* is the process of finding, organizing, and sharing the most accurate information relevant to a particular topic or area of interest.) By May 2017, Snap had signed deals with NBCUniversal, A&E Networks, BBC, ABC, Metro-Goldwyn-Mayer, and other content producers to develop original shows for viewing through Snapchat's Live Stories and Custom Stories (introduced that month).

Ad placements can be sold within a live story. Alternatively, a sponsor can advertise a story. Industry analysts estimate that live stories reach an average of 20 million viewers in a 24-hour period. In September 2015, Snapchat entered into a partnership with the National Football League (NFL) to present live stories from selected games, with both parties contributing content and handling ad sales. Similarly, in April 2016, NBC Olympics announced that it had reached a deal to allow stories from the 2016 Summer Olympics to be featured on Snapchat in the United States.

Geofilters

Introduced in July 2014, *geofilters* allow location-based image enhancements in the form of graphical overlays to be available if the user is within a certain geographical location, such as a city, an event, or a destination. Snapchat created geofilters as a source of growth for its advertising business. In April 2017, Snap began to allow its outside ad partners to sell and manage sponsored geofilters, which enabled Snapchat users to place special filters over their photos and videos in certain locations. For example, McDonald's, an early customer of the offering, paid for a branded geofilter that covered its restaurant locations in the United States.

By enabling outside partners to buy, manage, and report analytics for sponsored geofilters alongside video ads, Snap's geofilter format quickly attracted advertisers. The company promotes paid, on-demand geofilters as a consumer-oriented feature by demonstrating how people can create custom filters for events such as weddings and birthday parties. Snap sells on-demand geofilters through websites such as WeddingWire, Hootsuite, Eventfarm, and MomentFeed.

In April 2017, Snapchat introduced a *Snap to Store* advertising tool that lets companies using geostickers track whether users buy their product or visit their store within a seven-day period after they view the relevant geosticker. Snap has not disclosed how much money it makes off sponsored geofilters, and pricing for the format varies based on duration and location.

Snapcash

Introduced in November 2014, Snapcash allowed users to send and receive money to one another through private messaging. Square (**www.squareup.com**) powered the payments system. Square is a financial services and mobile payment company based in San Francisco.

On August 30, 2018, Snap shut down Snapcash. The app may have become a liability. First, competition was fierce with Venmo, PayPal, Zelle, and Square Cash itself in the peer-to-peer payments space. Further, a Twitter search for "Snapcash" found many offers of erotic content in exchange for payments through Snapcash.

Discover

Introduced in January 2015, *Discover* contains channels of ad-supported short-form content from major publishers, including BuzzFeed, *National Geographic*, CNN, ESPN, Mashable, *People*, Vice, and Snapchat itself.

Discover allows for paid advertising. The organization that sells the ad campaign causes the revenue distribution between Snapchat and its partner to vary. These advertisements are estimated to be worth 10 to 15 cents per view. They are also estimated to be seen 500,000 to 1 million times per day.

Discover introduced the idea that users swipe up to learn more about a given story. Snapchat then launched *Snap Ads* (August 2017), which allow consumers to swipe up to obtain more information.

Lens

Introduced in September 2015, the *lens* feature allows users to add real-time effects to their snaps by using face-detection technology. Users activate this feature by long-pressing on a face within the viewfinder. In October 2015, Snapchat began working with companies to create sponsored lens filters. In May 2016, as part of a campaign to promote *X-Men: Apocalypse*, 20th Century Fox paid for the entire array of lenses to be replaced with new ones based on characters from the *X-Men* series and films for a single day.

Sponsored lenses is a Snap advertising product that has attracted the world's best brand marketers, including Disney, McDonald's, and Starbucks. For example, for the Mexican holiday Cinco de Mayo, Taco Bell released a filter that turned people's heads into giant tacos. The firm spent between $500,000 and $750,000 on the filter, which was viewed 224 million times in a single day. That viewership is double the views of a Super Bowl ad for one-tenth the price. Further, unlike television viewers, Snapchat's audience is actively using, sharing, and having fun with the ads.

In October, 2018 Snap introduced Snap Camera, a free application designed for the desktop that invites anyone to experience Snapchat Lens while using their computer. Users do not have to have a Snapchat account to use Snap Camera as the feature does not have a login option.

Official Stories

Introduced in November 2015, *Official Stories* conveys the public stories of notable figures and celebrities, similar to Twitter's "Verified Account" program.

Memories

Introduced in July 2016, *Memories* allows users to save snaps and story posts in a private storage area, where they can be viewed alongside other photos stored on the device as well as edited and published as snaps, story posts, or messages.

Geostickers

Introduced in August 2016, *Geostickers* lets users send city-specific stickers in snaps and messages.

Spectacles

Introduced in November 2016, *Spectacles* enables the Snapchat app to reside on a sunglasses-camera that takes circular, 10-second videos. Snap contends that Spectacles (called Specs) are something that people actually want to wear, as opposed to Google Glass. Spectacles make it unnecessary to pull your phone from your pocket to capture a spontaneous moment. When Spectacles initially pairs with your phone, it films your first snap without warning. After that, a tap of the frame initiates recording.

World Stickers

Introduced in April 2017, *World Stickers* lets users add augmented reality elements into any scenery. The elements available at the product's launch included a cloud, a rainbow, flowers, and a floating "OMG" text phrase. These elements change daily.

Custom Stories

Introduced in May 2017, *Custom Stories* lets users collaboratively produce stories by combining their snaps.

Snap Map

Introduced in June 2017, *Snap Map* offers its users the option of sharing their location with friends.

Crowd Surf

Introduced in August 2017, *Crowd Surf* uses machine learning to integrate snaps submitted to Our Story into a seamless video called Crowd Surf. Intended to present a live event experience, the feature integrates snaps based on the time stamp and geolocation information.

Users can tap a button at the bottom of the screen to change perspectives without interrupting the viewing experience.

The release of Crowd Surf should lead to increased user engagement and revenue opportunities for Snapchat:

- The feature can help drive more views to Our Story, which in turn could drive ad revenue.

- The feature helps differentiate Our Story from Instagram Stories. Instagram does not have a similar feature to Crowd Surf, and Facebook has not yet moved into editorial curation. Recall that content curation is the process of finding, organizing, and sharing the most accurate information relevant to a particular topic.

- This distinction is important because Facebook's Instagram app expanded its users more rapidly than Snapchat. In June 2019, Snapchat reported approximately 191 million daily users and Instagram Stories reported approximately 500 million daily users.

- Snapchat has formed partnerships with artists, large music festivals, and arenas to be featured on Crowd Surf. The company has attracted users to view the events on Stories, where they are served ads. The artist, music festival, or arena receive a portion of the ad revenue and gain exposure to Snapchat's 191 million daily users. This channel of revenue is important to Snapchat, given that almost all of its revenue is generated by advertising.

Partnership with news data organizations

In July 2018, Snap launched a partnership with news data organizations to help journalists find, verify, and share breaking news. Snap gave NewsWhip (**www.newswhip.com**), Storyful (**www.storyful.com**), SAM Desk (**www.samdesk.io**), and TagBoard (**www.tagboard.com**) access to publicly visible Snaps. Media organizations with subscriptions to these services can access public Snapchat stories the same way that they access public Facebook and Twitter posts. By placing these stories on other platforms, Snap can reach a wider audience and encourage more people to sign up with Snap.

In March 2017, Snap had its initial public offering (IPO). Snap shares began trading at $24 per share and closed their first day of trading at $24.48. The opening price of $24 put Snap's market capitalization at some $33 billion. At the end of 2017, Snap reported a $3.4 billion loss for the year. Interestingly, in November 2017 Chinese technology company Tencent bought a 12 percent stake in Snap.

On May 2, 2018, Snap reported its worst quarter ever. On May 4, 2018, Snap traded at an all-time low of $10.79. These poor results occurred just months after CEO Evan Spiegel was paid about $638 million for 2017, including a $637 million stock-based bonus.

Another issue occurred in February 2018, when Snap released its Snapchat redesign meant to make the application less complicated to use. Instead, users revolted and more than one million of them signed a petition on Change.org asking that the redesign be reversed because it was confusing to use. Rather than listen to its users, Snap told them they would get used to it. In May 2018, Snap said that it would roll back part of the redesign.

In addition to these problems, the company faces stiff competition. Facebook-owned apps Instagram and WhatsApp have copied Snapchat-like features and made them better. Consider these examples:

- Snapchat's Stories feature lets users upload videos or pictures for 24 hours before they disappear. In May 2018, Snapchat stories had 191 million daily active users (DAUs) globally. WhatsApp's similar app had 450 million DAUs, and Instagram Stories had over 300 million DAUs.

- Facebook copied Snapchat's geofilters and is showing location-specific camera frames in Instagram and in Facebook.

Another competitor, Snow, is the most popular photo and video app in Japan and Korea, and it is one of the top multimedia apps in China. When Snow launched in September 2015, Snapchat was four years old and was available in Asia, but it did not have much traction. Snow filled that void.

Snow benefits from close ties with Naver (**www.navercorp.com**), Korea's largest Web portal, and Line, a Japan-based messaging app owned by Naver. Furthermore, Snow offers users digital graphics customized to local tastes. Snow currently stocks about 1,500 stickers and lenses and 50 background filters, many more than Snapchat. Further, Snow uploads new versions daily. Snow also lets users directly upload the images they create in the app to major social networking sites such as Facebook, Instagram, Twitter, WeChat, Line, and KakaoTalk in Korea.

In September 2016, Snow launched a China-only app called Snow Camera that limits users to shooting and editing photos and videos. People who want to share their Snow Camera images on a social network must link the app to WeChat. This move enabled Snow to operate in China while its Western competitors, including Instagram and Snapchat, are blocked.

And the bottom line? In the first quarter of 2019, Snap claimed 191 million daily active users and advertising revenue of $320 million.

Sources: Compiled from J. Constine, "Snapchat Will Shut Down Snapcash, Forfeiting to Venmo," *TechCrunch*, July 22, 2018; R. Reints, "A New Snapchat Initiative Will Help Journalists Find and Verify Breaking News," *Fortune*, July 17, 2018; P. Cohan, "Snap Will Keep Falling Unless Apple or Google Buys It, Says Wharton Professor," *Forbes*, June 14, 2018; P. La Monica, "The Worst May Be over for Snapchat," CNN Money, June 1, 2018; N. Walters, "Snap Hits All-Time Low Months after CEO Evan Spiegel Gets $637 Million Bonus," *The Motley Fool*, May 16, 2018; M. Castillo, "Snap Plunges after Missing on Revenue and Daily Active Users," CNBC, May 1, 2018; S. Mukherjee and M. Vengattil, "China's Tencent Takes 12 Percent Stake in Snap as Shares Plunge," Reuters, November 8, 2017; K. Tran, "Snap Launches 'Crowd Surf' Stories Feature," *Business Insider*, August 16, 2017; A. Heath, "Snapchat Wants to Grow Its Ad Business by Making It Easier to Buy Geofilters," *Business Insider*, April 24, 2017; A. Carman, "Snapchat Advertisers Can Now Track Whether Custom Geofilters Get You to Buy Their Product," *The Verge*, April 13, 2017; L. Johnson, "Snap Advertisers Can Now See if Their Ads Increase Foot Traffic," *AdWeek*, April 12, 2017; M. Wilson, "Snap: For Bringing Crackle and Pop to a New Way of Seeing the World," *Fast Company*, March, 2017; Y. Kim and E. Woyke, "Messaging App Sweeping Asia Could Blunt Snapchat's Global Ambitions," *MIT Technology Review*, March 1, 2017; A. Heath, "Facebook Is Copying Snapchat's Geofilters by Letting People Make Their Own Camera 'Frames'," *Business Insider*, December 8, 2016; L. Johnson, "20th Century Fox Buys First Snapchat Lens Takeover Ad," *AdWeek*, May 23, 2016; A. Heath, "Snapchat Is Changing How People Celebrate Major Events," *Business Insider*, May 16, 2016; A. Heath, "Snapchat Now Lets Anyone Pay to Create a Geofilter," *Business Insider*, February 22, 2016; A. Carr, "I Ain't Afraid of No Ghost!" *Fast Company*, November, 2015; K. Wagner, "Snapchat's Money Train Gains Steam with New Sponsored Lenses Ad," *Recode*, October 30, 2015; K. Wagner, "Snapchat Inks NFL Deal to Bring Football into Its Live Stories," *Recode*, September 17, 2015; K. Wagner, "Snapchat Is Making Some Pretty Serious Money from Live Stories," *Recode*, June 17, 2015; F. Tepper, "Snapchat Turns Geofilters into an Ad Unit," *TechCrunch*, June 16, 2015; P. Dave and D. Pierson, "Cheap Content, Growing Reach Make Snapchat a Fast-Rising Star," *Los Angeles Times*, April 16, 2015; A. Shontell, "Advertisers Are Supposedly Paying Insanely High Rates to Get Their Ads on Snapchat," *Business Insider*, March 12, 2015; A. Chowdhry, "Snapchat's New 'Discover' Feature Has Content from ESPN, CNN, Food Network, and Others," *Forbes*, January 28, 2015; and www.snap.com, accessed September 22, 2018.

Questions

1. Why did Snap add so many functions to its Snapchat app so rapidly?

2. Can Snap survive in the face of such intense competition? Why or why not? Provide specific examples to support your answer.

3. Which of Snapchat's functions do you feel are the most valuable in Snap's continued survival? Why?

CHAPTER 10

Information Systems within the Organization

CHAPTER OUTLINE	LEARNING OBJECTIVES
10.1 Transaction Processing Systems	**10.1** Explain the purpose of transaction processing systems.
10.2 Functional Area Information Systems	**10.2** Explain the types of support that information systems can provide for each functional area of the organization.
10.3 Enterprise Resource Planning (ERP)Systems	**10.3** Identify advantages and drawbacks to businesses implementing an enterprise resource planning (ERP) system.
10.4 ERP Support for Business Processes	**10.4** Describe the three main business processes supported by ERP systems.

Opening Case

Backyard Adventures Shares Inventory to Control Inventory

`POM`

Inventory control is a common theme among all businesses and industries. Business people dread the word "inventory" because it typically involves a manual process of checking items one at a time. At the same time, they know that holding and not managing inventory drains cash from the organization. From restaurants to retailers, small businesses to global organizations, firms must consider, manage, and plan for inventory. However, the larger and more complex the structure of the suppliers and distributors, the more difficult this task becomes.

Backyard Adventures, founded in 2007 in Amarillo, Texas, builds and sells modular playsets through a network of nationwide dealers. Customers can customize the playsets by adding swings, slides, picnic tables, rock walls, trapeze bars, sundecks, and crawl tubes. They can utilize the Backyard Adventures website to quickly locate the closest dealer and customize their playground by choosing a series, selecting options, and adding accessories.

With a widespread network of more than 65 distributors, Backyard Adventures faced numerous challenges associated with managing inventory. It is impossible for each dealer to stock every possible combination of series, options, or accessories. At the same time, however, each dealer needed access to all of the parts that were located across the nationwide network. Further, to operate efficiently, each distributor needed to implement an information system that would allow them to share information about their internal inventory with other distributors. This approach would enable them to locate the nearest parts for their customers. Backyard Adventures took the lead in selecting and creating this seamless operation across their distribution network.

After consulting with their distributors, Backyard Adventures decided to implement Fishbowl, a very powerful inventory management system that specifically supports the warehouse and manufacturing environment. Fishbowl streamlines many of the inventory management processes so that all parties in the distribution channel can locate items that are available in inventory. In addition, this solution integrates with QuickBooks, which Backyard Adventures was already using (as were several of their distributors).

The integration with QuickBooks enables Backyard Adventures to answer questions about more than just inventory levels. They are now able to locate any item stored in inventory across their distribution network, to track costs, and to obtain a more encompassing view of their profitability. Chris Connors, Vice President of Specialty Sales and Marketing at Backyard Adventures, asserted, "In a year, Fishbowl has completely transformed inventory in my company. It has several features that have helped make inventory control an easy process."

Backyard Adventures is able to automate ordering based on preset inventory thresholds, thereby freeing employees to monitor other parts of the organization. Connors further explained, "With Fishbowl and QuickBooks, we can complete our customer jobs in less time with more accuracy…which saves everyone time."

For Backyard Adventures, choosing and implementing a seamless inventory management system was about more than simply tracking inventory. Rather, it was about improving operational efficiency across the organization as well as the entire distribution channel.

Sources: Compiled from C. Campbell, "Warning: You're Losing Money by Not Using These 8 Inventory Management Techniques," *shopify.com/blog*, April 7, 2017; R. Preston, "Report, Tech-Based Cost Controls Critical for Restaurants," *Forbes*, July 11, 2016; S. Banker, "Proctor & Gamble's Futuristic Control Tower Environment," *Forbes*, July 1, 2015; P. Rosenblum, "How Walmart Could Solve Its Inventory Problem and Improve Earnings," *Forbes*, May 22, 2014; G. Keliher, "Moving beyond QuickBooks Advanced Inventory with Fishbowl Inventory," *AccountEX Report*, July 11, 2013; www.fishbowlinventory.com/case-studies/backyard-adventures, https://www.bloomberg.com/research/stocks/private/snapshot.asp?privcapId=33382921 and https://www.fishbowlinventory.com/about/; https://reviews.financesonline.com/p/fishbowl (all accessed September 17, 2018).

Questions

1. Why is maintaining effective control over inventory so important to any enterprise?

2. What factors drove Backyard Adventures' decision to select Fishbowl as their inventory management system? Why do you think these factors are significant?

3. How did Backyard Adventures benefit from implementing the Fishbowl solution?

Introduction

The opening case illustrates the integral part that information systems (IS) play in an organization's success. As you noted in the case, without information systems, effective inventory control could not exist. IS are everywhere, and they affect organizations in countless ways. Although IS are frequently discussed within the context of large organizational settings, the chapter's opening case illustrates how IS play a critical role in small organizations.

It is important to note that "systems within organizations" do not have to be owned by the organization itself. Instead, organizations can deploy very productive IS that are owned by an external vendor. The key point here is that "systems within an organization" are intended to support internal processes, regardless of who actually owns the systems.

It is important for you to have a working knowledge of IS within your organization for a variety of reasons. First, your job will require you to access corporate data that are supplied primarily by your firm's transaction processing systems and enterprise resource planning systems. Second, you will have a great deal of input into the format and content of the reports that you receive from these systems. Third, you will use the information contained in these reports to perform your job more productively.

This chapter will teach you about the various information systems that modern organizations use. We begin by considering transaction processing systems, the most fundamental organizational information systems. We continue with the functional area management information systems, and we conclude with enterprise resource planning systems.

10.1 | Transaction Processing Systems

Millions (sometimes billions) of transactions occur in large organizations every day. A **transaction** is any business event that generates data worthy of being captured and stored in a database. Examples of transactions are a product manufactured, a service sold, a person hired, and a payroll check generated. In another example, when you are checking out of Walmart, each time the cashier swipes an item across the bar code reader is one transaction.

A **transaction processing system (TPS)** supports the monitoring, collection, storage, and processing of data from the organization's basic business transactions, each of which generates data. The TPS collects data continuously, typically in *real time*—that is, as soon as the

Author Lecture Videos are available exclusively in *WileyPLUS*.
Apply the Concept activities are available in the Appendix and in *WileyPLUS*.

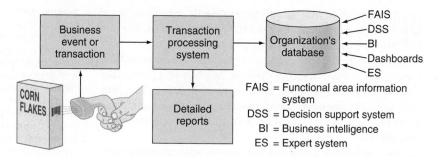

FIGURE 10.1   How transaction processing systems manage data.

data are generated—and it provides the input data for the corporate databases. The TPSs are critical to the success of any enterprise because they support core operations.

In the modern business world, TPSs are inputs for the functional area information systems and business intelligence systems as well as business operations, such as customer relationship management, knowledge management, and e-commerce. TPSs have to efficiently handle both high volumes of data and large variations in those volumes (e.g., during periods of peak processing). They must also avoid errors and downtime, record results accurately and securely, and maintain privacy and security. **Figure 10.1** illustrates how TPSs manage data. Consider these examples of how TPSs handle the complexities of transactional data:

- When more than one person or application program can access the database at the same time, the database has to be protected from errors resulting from overlapping updates. The most common error is losing the results of one of the updates.

- **MIS** When processing a transaction involves more than one computer, the database and all users must be protected against inconsistencies arising from a failure of any component at any time. For example, an error that occurs at some point in an ATM withdrawal can enable a customer to receive cash, although the bank's computer indicates that he or she did not. (Conversely, a customer might not receive cash, although the bank's computer indicates that he or she did.)

- **ACCT** It must be possible to reverse a transaction in its entirety if it turns out to have been entered in error. It is also necessary to reverse a transaction when a customer returns a purchased item. For example, if you return a sweater that you have purchased, then the store must credit your credit card for the amount of the purchase, refund your cash, or offer you an in-store credit to purchase another item. The store must also update its inventory.

- It is frequently important to preserve an audit trail. In fact, for certain transactions, an audit trail may be legally required.

These and similar issues explain why organizations spend millions of dollars on expensive mainframe computers. In today's business environment, firms must have the dependability, reliability, and processing capacity of these computers to handle their transaction processing loads.

Regardless of the specific data processed by a TPS, the actual process tends to be standard, whether it occurs in a manufacturing firm, a service firm, or a government organization. As the first step in this procedure, people or sensors collect data, which are entered into the computer through any input device. Generally speaking, organizations try to automate the TPS data entry as much as possible because of the large volume involved, a process called *source data automation* (discussed in Technology Guide 1).

Next, the system processes data in one of two basic ways: batch processing and online processing. In **batch processing**, the firm collects data from transactions as they occur, placing them in groups, or *batches*. The system then prepares and processes the batches periodically (say, every night).

In **online transaction processing (OLTP)**, business transactions are processed online as soon as they occur. For example, when you pay for an item at a store, the system records the sale by reducing the inventory on hand by one unit, increasing sales figures for the item by one unit, and increasing the store's cash position by the amount you paid. The system performs these tasks in real time by means of online technologies.

1. Define TPS.
2. List the key functions of a TPS.

10.2 Functional Area Information Systems

Each department or functional area within an organization has its own collection of application programs, or information systems. Each of these **functional area information systems (FAIS)** supports a particular functional area in the organization by increasing each area's internal efficiency and effectiveness. FAISs often convey information in a variety of reports, which you will see later in this chapter. Examples of FAISs are accounting IS, finance IS, production/operations management (POM) IS, marketing IS, and human resources IS.

As illustrated in Figure 10.1, the FAIS accesses data from the corporate databases. The following sections discuss the support that FAISs provide for these functional areas.

Author Lecture Videos are available exclusively in *WileyPLUS*.
Apply the Concept activities are available in the Appendix and in *WileyPLUS*.

Information Systems for Accounting and Finance

ACCT **FIN** A primary mission of the accounting and finance functional areas is to manage money flows into, within, and out of organizations. This mission is very broad because money is involved in all organizational functions. Therefore, accounting and finance information systems are very diverse and comprehensive. In this section, you focus on certain selected activities of the accounting and finance functional area.

Financial Planning and Budgeting. Appropriate management of financial assets is a major task in financial planning and budgeting. Managers must plan for both acquiring and using resources. For example:

- *Financial and economic forecasting:* Knowledge about the availability and cost of money is a key ingredient for successful financial planning. Cash flow projections are particularly important because they inform organizations what funds they need, when they need them, and how they will acquire them.

  Funds for operating organizations come from multiple sources, including stockholders' investments, bond sales, bank loans, sales of products and services, and income from investments. Decisions concerning funding for ongoing operations and for capital investment can be supported by decision support systems and business analytics applications (discussed in Chapter 12) as well as expert systems (see Technology Guide 4). Numerous software packages for conducting economic and financial forecasting are also available. Many of these packages can be downloaded from the Internet, some of them for free.

- *Budgeting:* An essential component of the accounting and finance function is the annual budget, which allocates the organization's financial resources among participants and activities. The budget allows management to distribute resources in the way that best supports the organization's mission and goals.

  Several software packages are available to support budget preparation and control and to facilitate communication among participants in the budget process. These packages can reduce the time involved in the budget process. Furthermore, they can automatically monitor exceptions for patterns and trends.

Managing Financial Transactions. Many accounting and finance software packages are integrated with other functional areas. For example, Sage 50cloud Accounting software (www.sage.com/en-us/products/sage-50-cloud/) offers a sales ledger, a purchase ledger, a cash book, sales order processing, invoicing, stock control, a fixed assets register, and more.

Companies involved in electronic commerce need to access customers' financial data (e.g., credit line), inventory levels, and manufacturing databases (to determine available capacity and place orders). For example, Microsoft Dynamics GP (formerly Great Plains Software) offers 50 modules that meet the most common financial, project, distribution, manufacturing, and e-business needs.

Organizations, business processes, and business activities operate with and manage financial transactions. Consider these examples:

- *Global stock exchanges:* Financial markets operate in global, 24/7/365, distributed electronic stock exchanges that use the Internet both to buy and sell stocks and to broadcast real-time stock prices.

- *Managing multiple currencies:* Global trade involves financial transactions that are carried out in different currencies. The conversion ratios of these currencies are constantly in flux. Financial and accounting systems use financial data from different countries, and they convert the currencies from and to any other currency in seconds. Reports based on these data, which formerly required several days to generate, can now be produced in only seconds. In addition to currency conversions, these systems manage multiple languages as well.

- *Virtual close:* Companies traditionally closed their books (accounting records) quarterly, usually to meet regulatory requirements. Today, many companies want to be able to close their books at any time, on very short notice. Information systems make it possible to close the books quickly in what is called a *virtual close.* This process provides almost real-time information on the organization's financial health.

- *Expense management automation:* Expense management automation (EMA) refers to systems that automate the data entry and processing of travel and entertainment expenses. EMA systems are Web-based applications that enable companies to quickly and consistently collect expense information, enforce company policies and contracts, and reduce unplanned purchases as well as airline and hotel expenses. They also allow companies to reimburse their employees more quickly because expense approvals are not delayed by poor documentation.

Investment Management.
Organizations invest large amounts of money in stocks, bonds, real estate, and other assets. Managing these investments is a complex task for several reasons. First, organizations have literally thousands of investment alternatives dispersed throughout the world to choose from. These investments are also subject to complex regulations and tax laws that vary from one location to another.

Investment decisions require managers to evaluate financial and economic reports provided by diverse institutions, including federal and state agencies, universities, research institutions, and financial services firms. Thousands of websites also provide financial data, many of them for free.

To monitor, interpret, and analyze the huge amounts of online financial data, financial analysts employ two major types of IT tools: Internet search engines and business intelligence and decision support software.

Control and Auditing.
One major reason why organizations go out of business is their inability to forecast or secure a sufficient cash flow. Underestimating expenses, overspending, engaging in fraud, and mismanaging financial statements can lead to disaster. Consequently, it is essential that organizations effectively control their finances and financial statements. Let's examine some of the most common forms of financial control:

- *Budgetary control:* After an organization has finalized its annual budget, it divides those monies into monthly allocations. Managers at various levels monitor departmental expenditures and compare them against the budget and the operational progress of corporate plans.

- *Auditing:* Auditing has two basic purposes: (1) to monitor how the organization's monies are being spent and (2) to assess the organization's financial health. *Internal audits* are performed by the organization's accounting and finance personnel. These employees also prepare for periodic *external audits* by outside CPA firms.

- *Financial ratio analysis:* Another major accounting and finance function is to monitor the company's financial health by assessing a set of financial ratios, including liquidity ratios (the availability of cash to pay debt), activity ratios (how quickly a firm converts noncash assets to cash assets), debt ratios (measure the firm's ability to repay long-term debt), and profitability ratios (measure the firm's use of its assets and control of its expenses to generate an acceptable rate of return).

Information Systems for Marketing

MKT It is impossible to overestimate the importance of customers to any organization. Therefore, any successful organization must understand its customers' needs and wants and then develop its marketing and advertising strategies around them. Information systems provide numerous types of support to the marketing function. Customer-centric organizations are so important that we cover this topic in detail in Chapter 11.

Information Systems for Production/Operations Management

POM The production/operations management (POM) function in an organization is responsible for the processes that transform inputs into useful outputs as well as for the overall operation of the business. The POM function is responsible for managing the organization's supply chain. Because supply chain management is vital to the success of modern organizations, we address this topic in detail in Chapter 11. Because of the breadth and variety of POM functions, we discuss only four here: in-house logistics and materials management, planning production and operation, computer-integrated manufacturing (CIM), and product life cycle management (PLM).

In-House Logistics and Materials Management.
Logistics management deals with ordering, purchasing, inbound logistics (receiving), and outbound logistics (shipping) activities. Related activities include inventory management and quality control.

Inventory Management.
As the name suggests, inventory management determines how much inventory an organization should maintain. Both excessive inventory and insufficient inventory create problems. Overstocking can be expensive because of storage costs and the costs of spoilage and obsolescence. However, keeping insufficient inventory is also expensive because of last-minute orders and lost sales.

Operations personnel make two basic decisions: when to order and how much to order. Inventory models, such as the economic order quantity (EOQ) model, support these decisions. A large number of commercial inventory software packages are available that automate the application of these models.

Many large companies allow their suppliers to monitor their inventory levels and ship products as they are needed. This strategy, called *vendor-managed inventory* (VMI), eliminates the need for the company to submit purchasing orders. We discuss VMI in Chapter 11.

Quality Control.
Quality control systems used by manufacturing units provide information about the quality of incoming material and parts as well as the quality of in-process semifinished and finished products. These systems record the results of all inspections and then compare these results with established metrics. They also generate periodic reports that contain information about quality—for example, the percentage of products that contain defects or that need to be reworked. Quality control data, collected by Web-based sensors, can be interpreted in real time. Alternatively, they can be stored in a database for future analysis.

Planning Production and Operations.
In many firms, POM planning is supported by IT. POM planning has evolved from material requirements planning (MRP) to manufacturing resource planning (MRP II) to enterprise resource planning (ERP). We briefly discuss MRP and MRP II here, and we examine ERP in detail later in this chapter.

Inventory systems that use an EOQ approach are designed for items for which demand is completely independent—for example, the number of identical personal computers a computer manufacturer will sell. In manufacturing operations, however, the demand for some items is interdependent. Consider, for example, a company that makes three types of chairs, all of which use the same screws and bolts. In this case, the demand for screws and bolts depends on the total demand for all three types of chairs and their shipment schedules. The planning process that integrates production, purchasing, and inventory management of interdependent items is called *material requirements planning* (MRP).

MRP deals only with production scheduling and inventories. More complex planning also involves allocating related resources, such as money and labor. For these cases, more complex, integrated software, called *manufacturing resource planning* (MRP II), is available. MRP II integrates a firm's production, inventory management, purchasing, financing, and labor activities. Thus, MRP II adds functions to a regular MRP system. In fact, MRP II has evolved into *enterprise resource planning* (ERP).

Computer-Integrated Manufacturing.

Computer-integrated manufacturing **(CIM)** (also called *digital manufacturing*) is an approach that integrates various automated factory systems. CIM has three basic goals: (1) to simplify all manufacturing technologies and techniques, (2) to automate as many of the manufacturing processes as possible, and (3) to integrate and coordinate all aspects of design, manufacturing, and related functions through computer systems.

Product Life Cycle Management.

Even within a single organization, designing and developing new products can be expensive and time consuming. When multiple organizations are involved, the process can become very complex. *Product life cycle management* (PLM) is a business strategy that enables manufacturers to share product-related data that support product design and development and supply chain operations. PLM applies Web-based collaborative technologies to product development. By integrating formerly disparate functions, such as a manufacturing process and the logistics that support it, PLM enables these functions to collaborate, essentially forming a single team that manages the product from its inception through its completion, as shown in **Figure 10.2**.

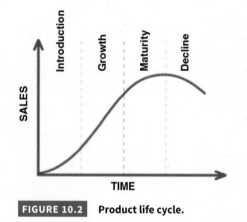

FIGURE 10.2 Product life cycle.

Information Systems for Human Resource Management

HRM Initial human resource information system (HRIS) applications dealt primarily with transaction processing systems, such as managing benefits and keeping records of vacation days. As organizational systems have moved to intranets and the Web, so have HRIS applications.

Many HRIS applications are delivered through an HR portal. (See our discussion of LinkedIn in Chapter 9.) For example, numerous organizations use their Web portals to advertise job openings and to conduct online hiring and training. In this section, you consider how organizations are using IT to perform some key HR functions: recruitment, HR maintenance and development, and HR planning and management.

Recruitment.

Recruitment involves finding potential employees, evaluating them, and deciding which ones to hire. Some companies are flooded with viable applicants; others have difficulty finding the right people. IT can be helpful in both cases. IT can also assist in related activities, such as testing and screening job applicants.

With millions of resumes available online (in particular, LinkedIn), it is not surprising that companies are trying to find appropriate candidates on the Web, usually with the help of specialized search engines. Companies also advertise hundreds of thousands of jobs on the Web. Online recruiting can reach more candidates, which may bring in better applicants. The costs of online recruitment are also usually lower than traditional recruiting methods, such as advertising in newspapers or in trade journals.

● **Human Resources Development.** After employees are recruited, they become part of the corporate human resources pool, which means they must be evaluated and developed. IT provides support for these activities. Throughout their careers, they have access to various internal resources, and IT helps to manage their access levels. IT's About Business 10.1 discusses an innovative way to manage access controls.

IT's About Business 10.1

Three Square Markets Puts IS inside Their Employees

`HRM`

Information systems within organizations are required to have security measures in place to protect the data that are stored in the system. In the majority of cases, employees utilize passwords to access network resources, locations, applications, and more. In a few instances, organizations have moved to biometric measures in addition to a password. For these systems, the user has to know something—for example, the password—and to be something—that is, to match the correct retinal, finger, hand, or voice scan.

But what if, as an organization, you could install part of the information system *inside* your employees? Three Square Market, a Wisconsin-based company that specializes in *micro markets*—the small "break room" businesses inside your organization that provide snacks, vending machines, or break-time supplies—has done just that. In July 2017, they announced a plan to microchip employees on a voluntary basis to allow multiple types of access: (1) physical access (employees could throw away their company ID) to the site, (2) information system access (employees could forget their passwords), and (3) payment access in the break room (credit cards were linked to the chip).

To create this system, Three Square Market partnered with Biohax, the developer of the microchip. Biohax is a Swedish company that was formed in 2013 based on the concept that the future is an "Internet of Us" and not just an "Internet of Things." Jowan Österlund, founder of the company, believes strongly that technology will become increasingly integrated into our lives. While other businesses are moving toward decentralizing physical and system access and payment to a mobile device, Jowan envisions a time when all of these activities will be a physical part of who we are.

Three Square Market agrees. In fact, they integrated purchasing technology capability into their vending machine products, and they now promote the chips for sale on their website. Further, to lead by example, on August 1, 2017, the company held a "chip party," and 41 of their 80 employees volunteered for the program. The company pays for the microchips which cost about $300 each. If a worker decides they no longer wish to participate, the chip can be removed.

While the firm may have hoped for more participation, this percentage seems to be consistent with the general perceptions about this technology. When surveyed, roughly half of the population expressed reservations about this technology. For example, many people expressed concerns regarding the long-term health impacts of having a foreign object inserted into their body. Others had ethical concerns about organizations being able to track their whereabouts when they are off the clock. Finally, some employees wondered what would happen when they leave to work for another company. Despite these concerns, however, many people saw this method of access control as the future of information system access not just within organizations but also for the general public. They envision a future in which people will acquire products, such as transportation tickets, and access data, such as health information, via physically embedded technologies.

So far, those employees who received a chip have not reported any negative physical issues arising from the implants, and none are expected by Biohax. Microchipping has been implemented in Sweden since the early 2000s. Today, microchipped employees enjoy not having to keep up with keys, passwords, or credit cards for the vending machines.

There is a significant problem though, privacy. Paula Brantner of Workplace Fairness (www.workplacefairness.org), a nonprofit public education and advocacy organization that works to promote and protect employee rights, says that people do not realize that there are not many laws protecting privacy in the workplace. Employees may not be aware of how all the data gathered from them are tracked and how such data is being used.

Sources: Compiled from L. Savini, "Human Microchipping Is Here, and It's About to Rock Your Skin's World," *Allure*, March 26, 2018; A. Miller, "More Companies Are Using Technology to Monitor Employees, Sparking Privacy Concerns," *ABC News*, March 10, 2018; T. Gillies, "Why Most of Three Square Market's Employees Jumped at the Chance to Wear a Microchip," *cnbc.com*, August 13, 2017; J. Baenen, "Wisconsin Company Holds 'Chip Party' to Microchip Workers," *Chicago Tribune*, August 2, 2017; Editors, "Why 40 Office Workers in Wisconsin Let a Tattoo Artist Put a Microchip in Their Hand," *USA Today*, August 1, 2017; J. Graham, "Are Embedded Microchips Dangerous? Ask the Swedes—And Pets," *USA Today*, July 25, 2017; M. Astor, "Microchip Implants for Employees? One Company Says Yes," *New York Times*, July 25, 2017; M. Bowerman, "Wisconsin Company to Install Rice-Sized Microchips in Employees," *USA Today*, July 24, 2017; and https://32market.com/public/#about2 (both accessed September 19, 2018).

Questions

1. Do you think microchipping is an effective method of controlling access to information assets within an organization?

2. What ethical, privacy, and security concerns would you have about the use of this technology if it were mandated as opposed to being voluntary?

3. Who do you think should "own" the microchip information? A private company? A government entity? The individual employees? Why do you feel this way?

Most employees are periodically evaluated by their immediate supervisors. In some organizations, peers or subordinates also evaluate other employees. Evaluations are typically digitized, and they are used to support many decisions, ranging from rewards to transfers to layoffs.

IT also plays an important role in training and retraining. Some of the most innovative developments are taking place in the areas of intelligent computer-aided instruction and the application of multimedia support for instructional activities. For example, companies conduct much of their corporate training over their intranet or on the Web.

Human Resources Planning and Management.   Managing human resources in large organizations requires extensive planning and detailed strategy. IT support is particularly valuable in the following three areas:

1. *Payroll and employees' records:* The HR department is responsible for payroll preparation. This process is typically automated, meaning that paychecks are printed or money is transferred electronically into employees' bank accounts.

2. *Benefits administration:* In return for their work contributions to their organizations, employees receive wages, bonuses, and various benefits. These benefits include health-care and dental care, pension contributions (in a decreasing number of organizations), 401(k) contributions, wellness centers, and child care centers.

   Managing benefits is a complex task because multiple options are available and organizations typically allow employees to choose and trade off their benefits. In many organizations, employees can access the company portal to self-register for specific benefits.

3. *Employee relationship management:* In their efforts to better manage employees, companies are developing *employee relationship management* (ERM) applications, for example, a call center for employees to discuss problems.

Table 10.1 provides an overview of the activities that the FAIS support. Figure 10.3 identifies many of the information systems that support these five functional areas.

Profitability Planning	Financial Planning	Employment Planning, Outsourcing	Product Life Cycle Management	Sales Forecasting, Advertising Planning	**STRATEGIC**
Auditing, Budgeting	Investment Management	Benefits Administration, Performance Evaluation	Quality Control, Inventory Management	Customer Relations, Sales Force Automation	**TACTICAL**
Payroll, Accounts Payable, Accounts Receivable	Manage Cash, Manage Financial Transactions	Maintain Employee Records	Order Fulfillment, Order Processing	Set Pricing, Profile Customers	**OPERATIONAL**
ACCOUNTING	**FINANCE**	**HUMAN RESOURCES**	**PRODUCTION/ OPERATIONS**	**MARKETING**	

FIGURE 10.3   Examples of information systems supporting the functional areas.

TABLE 10.1 Activities Supported by Functional Area Information Systems

ACCT **FIN** **Accounting and Finance**

Financial planning and cost of money

Budgeting—allocates financial resources among participants and activities

Capital budgeting—financing of asset acquisitions

Managing financial transactions

Handling multiple currencies

Virtual close—the ability to close the books at any time on short notice

Investment management—managing organizational investments in stocks, bonds, real estate, and other investment vehicles

Budgetary control—monitoring expenditures and comparing them against the budget

Auditing—ensuring the accuracy of the organization's financial transactions and assessing the condition of the organization's financial health

Payroll

MKT **Marketing and Sales**

Customer relations—knowing who customers are and treating them appropriately

Customer profiles and preferences

Salesforce automation—using software to automate the business tasks of sales, thereby improving the productivity of salespeople

POM **Production/Operations and Logistics**

Inventory management—when to order new inventory, how much inventory to order, and how much inventory to keep in stock

Quality control—controlling for defects in incoming materials and goods produced

Materials requirements planning—planning process that integrates production, purchasing, and inventory management of interdependent items (MRP)

Manufacturing resource planning—planning process that integrates an enterprise's production, inventory management, purchasing, financing, and labor activities (MRP II)

Just-in-time systems—a principle of production and inventory control in which materials and parts arrive precisely when and where needed for production (JIT)

Computer-integrated manufacturing—a manufacturing approach that integrates several computerized systems, such as computer-assisted design (CAD), computer-assisted manufacturing (CAM), MRP, and JIT

Product life cycle management—business strategy that enables manufacturers to collaborate on product design and development efforts, using the Web

HRM **Human Resource Management**

Recruitment—finding employees, testing them, and deciding which ones to hire

Performance evaluation—periodic evaluation by superiors

Training

Employee records

Benefits administration—retirement, disability, unemployment, and so on

Reports

All information systems produce reports: transaction processing systems, functional area information systems, ERP systems, customer relationship management systems, business intelligence systems, and so on. We discuss reports here because they are so closely associated with FAIS and ERP systems. These reports generally fall into three categories: routine, ad hoc (on-demand), and exception.

Routine reports are produced at scheduled intervals. They range from hourly quality control reports to daily reports on absenteeism rates. Although routine reports are extremely valuable to an organization, managers frequently need special information that is not included in these reports. At other times, they need the information that is normally included in routine reports but at different times ("I need the report today, for the last three days, not for one week").

Such out-of-the routine reports are called **ad hoc (on-demand) reports**. Ad hoc reports can also include requests for the following types of information:

- **Drill-down reports** display a greater level of detail. For example, a manager might examine sales by region and decide to "drill down" by focusing specifically on sales by store and then by salesperson.
- **Key indicator reports** summarize the performance of critical activities. For example, a chief financial officer might want to monitor cash flow and cash on hand.
- **Comparative reports** compare, for example, the performances of different business units or of a single unit during different times.

Some managers prefer exception reports. **Exception reports** include only information that falls outside certain threshold standards. To implement *management by exception,* management first establishes performance standards. The company then creates systems to monitor performance (through the incoming data about business transactions, such as expenditures), to compare actual performance to the standards, and to identify exceptions to the standards. The system alerts managers to the exceptions through exception reports.

Let's use sales as an example. First, management establishes sales quotas. The company then implements a FAIS that collects and analyzes all of the sales data. An exception report would identify only those cases in which sales fell outside an established threshold—for example, more than 20 percent short of the quota. It would *not* report expenditures that fell *within* the accepted range of standards. By leaving out all "acceptable" performances, exception reports save managers time, thus helping them focus on problem areas.

Before you go on . . .

1. Define a functional area information system and list its major characteristics.
2. How do information systems benefit the finance and accounting functional area?
3. Explain how POM personnel use information systems to perform their jobs more effectively and efficiently.
4. What are the most important HRIS applications?
5. Compare and contrast the three basic types of reports.

10.3 Enterprise Resource Planning Systems

Historically, the functional area information systems were developed independent of one another, resulting in *information silos.* These silos did not communicate well with one another, and this lack of communication and integration made organizations less efficient. This inefficiency was particularly evident in business processes that involve more than one functional area, such as procurement and fulfillment.

Enterprise resource planning (ERP) systems are designed to correct a lack of communication among the functional area IS. ERP systems resolve this problem by tightly integrating the functional area IS through a common database. For this reason, experts credit ERP systems with greatly increasing organizational productivity. ERP systems adopt a business process view of the overall organization to integrate the planning, management, and use of all of an organization's resources, employing a common software platform and database.

The major objectives of ERP systems are to tightly integrate the functional areas of the organization and to enable information to flow seamlessly across them. Tight integration means that changes in one functional area are immediately reflected in all other pertinent functional areas. In essence, ERP systems provide the information necessary to control the business processes of the organization.

It is important to understand that ERP systems are an evolution of FAIS. That is, ERP systems have much the same functionality as FAIS, and they produce the same reports.

Although some companies have developed their own ERP systems, most organizations use commercially available ERP software. Leading ERP software vendors include SAP (www.sap.com), Oracle (www.oracle.com), and Sage (www.sage.com). For up-to-date information on ERP software, visit https://it.toolbox.com/tags/erp. IT's About Business 10.2 shows how Under Armour utilizes its ERP system.

IT's About Business 10.2

Under Armour Finds a Chip in Their Armor

`MIS` `POM` `HRM`

The Business Problem

Under Armour (www.underarmour.com) was founded in 1996 by Kevin Plank, a former University of Maryland football player who was tired of having to change his sweat-soaked cotton shirts over and over during their twice-a-day practices. From his grandmother's basement, he designed the first HeatGear® T-shirt and sold it under the company name of Under Armour, which was designed to keep players cool and dry under even the hottest conditions. Plank also designed a ColdGear® fabric that keeps athletes warm and dry in cold conditions and the AllSeasonGear® that keeps them comfortable between the extremes. He then drove up and down the East Coast selling these items from his trunk.

By the end of 1998, Plank had to find a new location. He could no longer sustain his operation in his grandmother's basement. So, he moved the company headquarters to a warehouse in Baltimore. Since this beginning, Under Armour has grown into one of the leading athletic brands of clothing, equipment, and more, successfully competing with brands like Nike and Adidas that have been around almost 50 years longer.

Fast forward to 2013, when Under Armour changed their focus from designing and selling clothing and equipment to considering the entire athlete. They acquired several popular apps—EndoMondo, MyFitnessPal, MapMyFitness—and developed their own app, UA Record. According to a March 2017 *Forbes* article, Under Armour had more than 200,000 subscribers across their suite of apps. This influx of data provides the company with potential insight into the physical characteristics of their entire user base of athletes (size, weight, sports, training and eating habits, etc.) and their use of equipment.

However, having access to data and making use of those data are not the same thing. As Under Armour grew and gained access to more data than they have ever seen, their organization faced significant challenges. They needed to consolidate and analyze the data and to restructure their organization to be able to quickly adapt to the changing needs of their users, to which they now have direct, real-time access.

The IT Solution

Under Armour needed a system that would allow them to integrate the multiple sources of data they had purchased, to perform real-time analysis of their data, and to determine the best course of action, as quickly as possible. They determined that the best integrated ERP solution partner to accomplish these objectives was SAP. SAP (www.sap.com) is a software corporation that makes ERP solutions. They are headquartered in Walldorf, Baden-Württemberg, Germany, but they have regional offices in more than 180 countries including more than 45 offices in the United States.

Specifically, Under Armour decided to implement the SAP HANA product, which SAP designed to reduce complexity, to run anywhere (meaning ubiquitous access across platforms and devices) and to provide real-time results. SAP HANA is intended to speed up the implementation of an ERP by allowing legacy silos to remain intact. SAP HANA will draw data from those silos and make use of these data without requiring the client to migrate everything. This sounded exactly like the solution that Under Armour needed given that they had acquired multiple data sources.

The Results

Under Armour faced (and is facing) challenges implementing SAP HANA due to issues outside the fashion industry and the solution provider (SAP). In a conference call regarding quarterly earnings on October 31, 2017, the company's president, Patrik Frisk, admitted that Under Armour had experienced serious challenges with change management. Frisk attested, "While these enhancements are designed to enable us to more effectively and efficiently operate our business and, ultimately, enhance productivity for the long term, the implementation caused disruption in our supply chain operations during the quarter. This led to delayed shipments and loss of productivity, which negatively impacted our third quarter results. During this system migration, we have encountered a number of change management issues impacting our workforce and manufacturing partners as they adapt to the new platform and processes."

Change management is a term that refers to techniques and methods for preparing and supporting individuals and teams throughout an organizational transition. It is not uncommon for ERP implementations to fail due to change management issues. However, Under Armour is not prepared to concede that their implementation has been a failure.

The company reported revenue of $5 billion in 2017, with adjusted net income of $87 million. The company's inventory did increase by 22 percent to $1.2 billion (due to system errors and delayed shipments). The company saw improvements in service levels (meaning they are fulfilling orders more quickly and accurately). Further, they expected their operations to begin to normalize in 2018 as they (and their partners) become more comfortable with their new system and processes. Under Armour has the potential to make effective use of the data they have acquired through their digital connections with their customers.

Sources: Compiled from L. Dignan, "Under Armour Cites Change Management Woes with SAP Implementation as Digital Transformation Stumbles," *ZDNet*, November 1, 2017; V. Ryan, "Under Armour Discloses Hiccups in SAP Implementation," *CFO.com*, November 1, 2017; A. Loten and S. Germano, "Under Armour Links Sales Decline to Software Upgrade," *Wall Street Journal*, October 31, 2017; D. Trites, "Under Armour Transforms into World's Largest Digital Fitness Brand," *D!gitalist Magazine*, March 22, 2017; J. Kell, "Why Under Armour Just Hired a High-End Designer," *Fortune*, June 2, 2016; J. Kell, "Why Under Armour Is Making a Costly Bet on Connected Fitness," *Fortune*, April 21, 2015; www.uabiz.com/company/history.cfm, https://seekingalpha.com/article/4133040-armour-dead-cat-bounce-v-shaped-recovery, and www.uabiz.com/company/history.cfm (all accessed September 23, 2018).

Questions

1. What strategic moves has Under Armour made to become more of a digital company?

2. What problems has the company faced as a result of implementing an integrated ERP solution (SAP HANA)?

3. Based on the information in the case, how do you think technology will drive fashion in the future? Explain your answer.

ERP II Systems

ERP systems were originally deployed to facilitate business processes associated with manufacturing, such as raw materials management, inventory control, order entry, and distribution. However, these early ERP systems did not extend to other functional areas, such as sales and marketing. They also did not include any customer relationship management (CRM) capabilities that enable organizations to capture customer-specific information. Finally, they did not provide Web-enabled customer service or order fulfillment.

Over time, ERP systems evolved to include administrative, sales, marketing, and human resources processes. Companies now employ an enterprisewide approach to ERP that uses the Web and connects all facets of the value chain. (You might want to review our discussion of value chains in Chapter 2.) These systems are called ERP II.

ERP II systems are interorganizational ERP systems that provide Web-enabled links among a company's key business systems—such as inventory and production—and its customers, suppliers, distributors, and other relevant parties. These links integrate internal-facing ERP applications with the external-focused applications of supply chain management and customer relationship management. **Figure 10.4** illustrates the organization and functions of an ERP II system.

The various functions of ERP II systems are now delivered as e-business suites. The major ERP vendors have developed modular, Web-enabled software suites that integrate ERP, customer relationship management, supply chain management, procurement, decision support, enterprise portals, and other business applications and functions. Examples are Oracle's e-Business Suite and SAP's mySAP. The goal of these systems is to enable companies to execute most of their business processes using a single Web-enabled system of integrated software rather than a variety of separate e-business applications.

ERP II systems include a variety of modules that are divided into core ERP modules—financial management, operations management, and human resource management—and extended ERP modules—customer relationship management, supply chain management, business intelligence, and e-business. If a system does not have the core ERP modules, then it is not a legitimate ERP system. The extended ERP modules, in contrast, are optional. **Table 10.2** describes each of these modules.

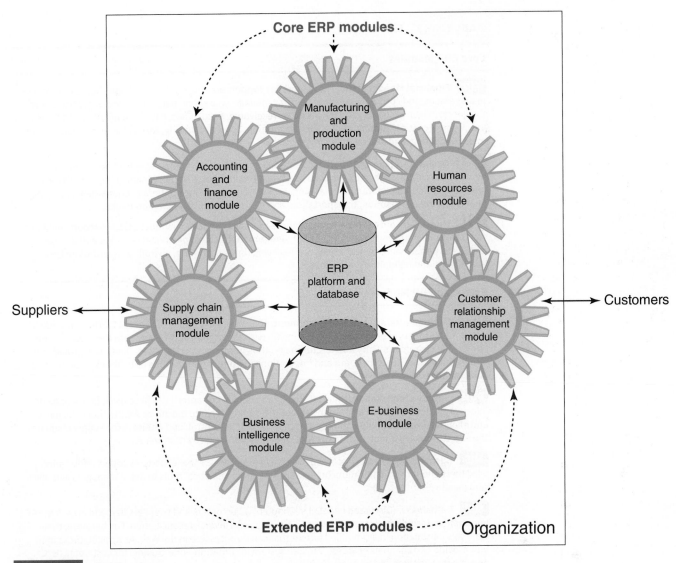

FIGURE 10.4 ERP II system.

Benefits and Limitation of ERP Systems

ERP systems can generate significant business benefits for an organization. The major benefits fall into the following three categories:

1. *Organizational flexibility and agility:* As you have seen, ERP systems break down many former departmental and functional silos of business processes, information systems, and information resources. In this way, they make organizations more flexible, agile, and adaptive. The organizations can therefore respond quickly to changing business conditions and capitalize on new business opportunities.

2. *Decision support:* ERP systems provide essential information on business performance across functional areas. This information significantly improves managers' ability to make better, more timely decisions.

3. *Quality and efficiency:* ERP systems integrate and improve an organization's business processes, generating significant improvements in the quality of production, distribution, and customer service.

TABLE 10.2 ERP Modules

Core ERP Modules

FIN **Financial Management.** These modules support accounting, financial reporting, performance management, and corporate governance. They manage accounting data and financial processes such as general ledger, accounts payable, accounts receivable, fixed assets, cash management and forecasting, product-cost accounting, cost-center accounting, asset accounting, tax accounting, credit management, budgeting, and asset management.

POM **Operations Management.** These modules manage the various aspects of production planning and execution, such as demand forecasting, procurement, inventory management, materials purchasing, shipping, production planning, production scheduling, materials requirements planning, quality control, distribution, transportation, and plant and equipment maintenance.

HRM **Human Resource Management.** These modules support personnel administration (including workforce planning, employee recruitment, assignment tracking, personnel planning and development, and performance management and reviews), time accounting, payroll, compensation, benefits accounting, and regulatory requirements.

Extended ERP Modules

MKT **Customer Relationship Management.** (Discussed in detail in Chapter 11.) These modules support all aspects of a customer's relationship with the organization. They help the organization to increase customer loyalty and retention and thus improve its profitability. They also provide an integrated view of customer data and interactions, helping organizations to be more responsive to customer needs.

POM **Supply Chain Management.** (Discussed in detail in Chapter 11.) These modules manage the information flows between and among stages in a supply chain to maximize supply chain efficiency and effectiveness. They help organizations plan, schedule, control, and optimize the supply chain from the acquisition of raw materials to the receipt of finished goods by customers.

MIS **Business Analytics.** (Discussed in detail in Chapter 12.) These modules collect information used throughout the organization, organize it, and apply analytical tools to assist managers with decision making.

MIS **E-Business.** (Discussed in detail in Chapter 7.) Customers and suppliers demand access to ERP information, including order status, inventory levels, and invoice reconciliation. Furthermore, they want this information in a simplified format that can be accessed on the Web. As a result, these modules provide two channels of access into ERP system information—one channel for customers (B2C) and one for suppliers and partners (B2B).

Despite all of their benefits, however, ERP systems do have drawbacks. The major limitations of ERP implementations include the following:

- The business processes in ERP software are often predefined by the best practices that the ERP vendor has developed. *Best practices* are the most successful solutions or problem-solving methods for achieving a business objective. As a result, companies may need to change their existing business processes to fit the predefined business processes incorporated into the ERP software. For companies with well-established procedures, this requirement can create serious problems, especially if employees do not want to abandon their old ways of working and therefore resist the changes.

- At the same time, however, an ERP implementation can provide an opportunity to improve and in some cases completely redesign inefficient, ineffective, or outdated procedures. In fact, many companies benefit from implementing best practices for their accounting, finance, and human resource processes as well as other support activities that companies do not consider a source of competitive advantage.

  Recall from Chapter 2, however, that different companies organize their value chains in different configurations to transform inputs into valuable outputs and achieve competitive advantages. Therefore, although the vendor's best practices, by definition, are appropriate for most organizations, they might not be the "best" one for your company if they change those processes that give you a competitive advantage.

- ERP systems can be extremely complex, expensive, and time consuming to implement. (We discuss the implementation of ERP systems in detail in the next section.) In fact, the costs and risks of failure in implementing a new ERP system are substantial. Quite a few companies have experienced costly ERP implementation failures. Specifically, they have suffered losses in revenue, profits, and market share when core business processes and information systems failed or did not work properly. In many cases, orders and shipments were lost, inventory changes were not recorded correctly, and unreliable inventory levels caused major stock outs. Companies such as Hershey Foods, Nike, A-DEC, and Connecticut General sustained losses in amounts up to hundreds of millions of dollars. In the case of FoxMeyer Drugs, a $5 billion pharmaceutical wholesaler, the ERP implementation was so poorly executed that the company had to file for bankruptcy protection.

In almost every ERP implementation failure, the company's business managers and IT professionals underestimated the complexity of the planning, development, and training that were required to prepare for a new ERP system that would fundamentally transform their business processes and information systems. The following are the major causes of ERP implementation failure:

- Failure to involve affected employees in the planning and development phases and in change management processes
- Trying to accomplish too much too fast in the conversion process
- Insufficient training in the new work tasks required by the ERP system
- Failure to perform proper data conversion and testing for the new system

Implementing ERP Systems

Companies can implement ERP systems by using either on-premise software or software-as-a-service (SaaS). We differentiate between these two methods in detail in Technology Guide 3.

On-Premise ERP Implementation.   Depending on the types of value chain processes managed by the ERP system and a company's specific value chain, there are three strategic approaches to implementing an on-premise ERP system:

1. *The vanilla approach:* In this approach, a company implements a standard ERP package, using the package's built-in configuration options. When the system is implemented in this way, it will deviate only minimally from the package's standardized settings. The vanilla approach can enable the company to perform the implementation more quickly. However, the extent to which the software is adapted to the organization's specific processes is limited. Fortunately, a vanilla implementation provides general functions that can support the firm's common business processes with relative ease, even if they are not a perfect fit for those processes.

2. *The custom approach:* In this approach, a company implements a more customized ERP system by developing new ERP functions designed specifically for that firm. Decisions concerning the ERP's degree of customization are specific to each organization. To use the custom approach, the organization must carefully analyze its existing business processes to develop a system that conforms to the organization's particular characteristics and processes. Customization is also expensive and risky because computer code must be written and updated every time a new version of the ERP software is released. Going further, if the customization does not perfectly match the organization's needs, then the system can be very difficult to use.

3. *The best-of-breed approach:* This approach combines the benefits of the vanilla and customized systems while avoiding the extensive costs and risks associated with complete customization. Companies that adopt this approach mix and match core

ERP modules as well as other extended ERP modules from different software providers to best fit their unique internal processes and value chains. Thus, a company may choose several core ERP modules from an established vendor to take advantage of industry best practices—for example, for financial management and human resource management. At the same time, it may also choose specialized software to support its unique business processes—for example, for manufacturing, warehousing, and distribution. Sometimes companies arrive at the best of breed approach the hard way. For example, Dell wasted millions of dollars trying to customize an integrated ERP system from a major vendor to match its unique processes before it realized that a smaller, more flexible system that integrated well with other corporate applications was the answer.

Software-as-a-Service ERP Implementation.

Companies can acquire ERP systems without having to buy a complete software solution (i.e., on-premise ERP implementation). Many organizations are using software-as-a-service (SaaS) (discussed in Chapter 13 and Technology Guide 3) to acquire cloud-based ERP systems. (We discuss cloud computing in Technology Guide 3.)

In this business model, the company rents the software from an ERP vendor who offers its products over the Internet using the SaaS model. The ERP cloud vendor manages software updates and is responsible for the system's security and availability.

Cloud-based ERP systems can be a perfect fit for some companies. For example, companies that cannot afford to make large investments in IT yet already have relatively structured business processes that need to be tightly integrated might benefit from cloud computing.

The relationship between the company and the cloud vendor is regulated by contracts and by service level agreements (SLAs). The SLAs define the characteristics and quality of service, for example, a guaranteed uptime, or the percentage of time that the system is available. Cloud vendors that fail to meet these conditions can face penalties.

The decision about whether to use on-premise ERP or SaaS ERP is specific to each organization, and it depends on how the organization evaluates a series of advantages and disadvantages. The following are the three major advantages of using a cloud-based ERP system:

1. The system can be used from any location that has Internet access. Consequently, users can work from any location using online shared and centralized resources (data and databases). Users access the ERP system through a secure virtual private network (VPN) connection (discussed in Chapter 4) with the provider.

2. Companies using cloud-based ERP avoid the initial hardware and software expenses that are typical of on-premise implementations. For example, to run SAP on-premise, a company must purchase SAP software as well as a license to use SAP. The magnitude of this investment can hinder small- to medium-sized enterprises (SMEs) from adopting ERP.

3. Cloud-based ERP solutions are scalable, meaning it is possible to extend ERP support to new business processes and new business partners (e.g., suppliers) by purchasing new ERP modules.

There are also disadvantages to adopting cloud-based ERP systems that a company must carefully evaluate. The following are the three major disadvantages of using a cloud-based ERP system:

1. It is not clear whether cloud-based ERP systems are more secure than on-premise systems. In fact, a survey conducted by North Bridge Venture Partners indicated that security was the primary reason why organizations did not adopt cloud-based ERP.

2. Companies that adopt cloud-based ERP systems sacrifice their control over a strategic IT resource. For this reason, some companies prefer to implement an on-premise ERP system, using a strong in-house IT department that can directly manage the system.

3. A direct consequence of the lack of control over IT resources occurs when the ERP system experiences problems, for example, when some ERP functions are temporarily slow or are not available. In such cases, having an internal IT department that can solve problems

immediately rather than dealing with the cloud vendor's system support can speed up the system recovery process.

This situation is particularly important for technology-intensive companies. In such companies, IT is crucial to conduct any kind of business with customers. Examples are e-commerce companies, banks, and government organizations that manage emergencies or situations that might involve individual and national security (e.g., health care organizations, police, homeland security department, antiterrorism units, and others).

Finally, slow or unavailable software from a cloud-based ERP vendor creates business continuity problems for the client. (We discuss business continuity in Chapter 4.) That is, a sudden system problem or failure makes it impossible for the firm to operate. Companies lose money when they lose business continuity because customers cannot be serviced and employees cannot do their jobs. A loss of business continuity also damages the company's reputation because customers lose trust in the firm.

Enterprise Application Integration

For some organizations, integrated ERP systems are not appropriate. This situation is particularly true for companies that find the process of converting from their existing system too difficult or time consuming.

Such companies, however, may still have isolated information systems that need to be connected with one another. To accomplish this task, these companies can use enterprise application integration. An **enterprise application integration (EAI) system** integrates existing systems by providing software, called *middleware*, that connects multiple applications. In essence, the EAI system allows existing applications to communicate and share data, thereby enabling organizations to use existing applications while eliminating many of the problems caused by isolated information systems. EAI systems also support implementation of best-of-breed ERP solutions by connecting software modules from different vendors.

Before you go on . . .

1. Define ERP and describe its functions.
2. What are ERP II systems?
3. Differentiate between core ERP modules and extended ERP modules.
4. List some drawbacks of ERP software.
5. Highlight the differences between ERP configuration, customization, and best-of-breed implementation strategies.

10.4   ERP Support for Business Processes

ERP systems effectively support a number of standard business processes. In particular, ERP systems manage end-to-end, cross-departmental processes. A **cross-departmental process** is one that (1) originates in one department and ends in a different department or (2) originates and ends in the same department but involves other departments.

Author Lecture Videos are available exclusively in *WileyPLUS*.
Apply the Concept activities are available in the Appendix and in *WileyPLUS*.

The Procurement, Fulfillment, and Production Processes

The following are the three prominent examples of cross-departmental processes:

1. The *procurement process,* which originates in the warehouse department (need to buy) and ends in the accounting department (send payment)

2. The *fulfillment process,* which originates in the sales department (customer request to buy) and ends in the accounting department (receive payment)

3. The *production process,* which originates and ends in the warehouse department (need to produce and reception of finished goods) but involves the production department as well

These three processes are examined in more detail in the following sections, focusing on the steps that are specific to each one.

POM **ACCT** **The Procurement Process.**   The **procurement process** originates when a company needs to acquire goods or services from external sources, and it concludes when the company receives and pays for them. Let's consider a procurement process in which the company needs to acquire physical goods (see **Figure 10.5**). This process involves three main departments—Warehouse, Purchasing, and Accounting—and it consists of the following steps:

1. The process originates in the Warehouse department, which generates a purchase requisition to buy the needed products.

2. The Warehouse forwards the requisition to the Purchasing department, which creates a purchase order (PO) and forwards it to a vendor. Generally, companies can choose from a number of vendors, and they select the one that best meets their requirements in regard to convenience, speed, reliability, and other characteristics.

3. After the company places the order, it receives the goods in its Warehouse department, where someone physically checks the delivery to make certain that it corresponds to what the company ordered. He or she performs this task by comparing a packing list attached to the shipment against the PO.

4. If the shipment matches the order, then the Warehouse issues a goods receipt document.

5. At the same time or shortly thereafter, the Accounting department receives an invoice from the vendor. Accounting then checks that the PO, the goods receipt document, and the invoice match. This process is called the *three-way-match.*

6. After Accounting verifies the match, it processes the payment and sends it to the vendor.

MKT **POM** **ACCT** **The Order Fulfillment Process.**   In contrast to procurement, in which the company purchases goods from a vendor, in the **order fulfillment process**, also known as the *order-to-cash process,* the company sells goods to a customer. Fulfillment originates when the company receives a customer order, and it concludes when the company receives a payment from the customer.

The fulfillment process can follow two basic strategies: sell-from-stock and configure-to-order. *Sell-from-stock* involves fulfilling customer orders directly using goods that are in the warehouse (stock). These goods are standard, meaning that the company does not customize them for buyers. In contrast, in *configure-to-order,* the company customizes the product in response to a customer request.

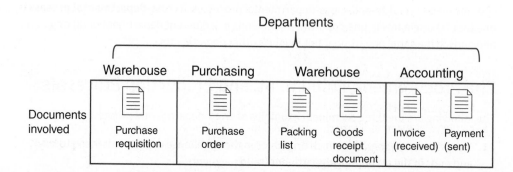

FIGURE 10.5 **Departments and documents flow in the procurement process.**

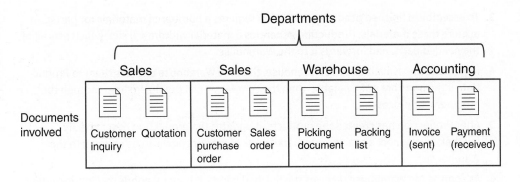

FIGURE 10.6 **Departments and documents flow in the fulfillment process.**

A fulfillment process involves three main departments: Sales, Warehouse, and Accounting. This process includes the following steps:

1. The Sales department receives a customer inquiry, which essentially is a request for information concerning the availability and price of a specific good. (We restrict our discussion here to fulfilling a customer order for physical goods rather than services.)

2. After Sales receives the inquiry, it issues a quotation that indicates availability and price.

3. If the customer agrees to the price and terms, then Sales creates a customer purchase order (PO) and a sales order.

4. Sales forwards the sales order to the Warehouse. The sales order is an interdepartmental document that helps the company keep track of the internal processes that are involved in fulfilling a specific customer order. It also provides details of the quantity, price, and other characteristics of the product.

5. The Warehouse prepares the shipment and produces two other internal documents: the picking document, which it uses to remove goods from the Warehouse, and the packing list, which accompanies the shipment and provides details about the delivery.

6. At the same time, Accounting issues an invoice for the customer.

7. The process concludes when Accounting receives a payment that is consistent with the invoice.

Figure 10.6 shows the fulfillment process. Note that it applies to both sell-from-stock and configure-to-order because the basic steps are the same for both strategies.

POM The Production Process. The **production process** does not occur in all companies because not all companies produce physical goods. In fact, many businesses limit their activities to buying (procurement) and selling products (e.g., retailers).

The production process can follow two different strategies: make-to-stock and make-to-order. (See the discussion of the pull model and the push model in Chapter 11.) *Make-to-stock* occurs when the company produces goods to create or increase an *inventory,* that is, finished products that are stored in the warehouse and are available for sales. In contrast, *make-to-order* occurs when production is generated by a specific customer order.

Manufacturing companies that produce their own goods manage their interdepartmental production process across the Production and Warehouse departments. The production process involves the following steps:

1. The Warehouse department issues a planned order when the company needs to produce a finished product either because the Warehouse has insufficient inventory or because the customer placed a specific order for goods that are not currently in stock.

2. Once the planned order reaches Production, the production controller authorizes the order and issues a production order, which is a written authorization to start the production of a certain amount of a specific product.

3. To assemble a finished product, Production requires a number of materials (or parts). To acquire these materials, Production generates a material withdrawal slip, which lists all of the needed parts, and forwards it to the Warehouse.

4. If the parts are available in the Warehouse, then the Warehouse delivers them to Production. If the parts are not available, then the company must purchase them through the procurement process.

5. After Production has created the products, it updates the production order specifying that, as planned, a specific number of units of product now can be shipped to the Warehouse.

6. As soon as the Warehouse receives the finished goods, it issues a goods receipt document that certifies how many units of a product it received that are available for sales.

This overview of the Production process is a highly simplified one. In reality, the process is very complex, and it frequently involves additional steps. ERP systems also collect a number of other documents and pieces of information such as the bill of materials (a list of all materials needed to assemble a finished product), the list of work centers (locations where the production takes place), and the product routing (production steps). All of these topics require an in-depth analysis of the production process and are therefore beyond the scope of our discussion here. **Figure 10.7** illustrates the production processes.

A number of events can occur that create exceptions or deviations in the procurement, fulfillment, and production processes. Deviations may include the following:

- A delay in the receipt of products
- Issues related to an unsuccessful three-way match regarding a shipment and its associated invoice (procurement)
- Rejection of a quotation
- A delay in a shipment
- A mistake in preparing the shipment or in invoicing the customer (fulfillment)
- Overproduction of a product
- Reception of parts that cannot be used in the production process
- Unavailability of certain parts from a supplier

Companies use ERP systems to manage procurement, fulfillment, and production because these systems track all of the events that occur within each process. Furthermore, the system stores all of the documents created in each step of each process in a centralized database, where they are available as needed in real time. Therefore, any exceptions or mistakes made during one or more interdepartmental processes are handled right away by simply querying the ERP system and retrieving a specific document or piece of information that needs to be revised or examined more carefully. Therefore, it is important to follow each step in each process and to register the corresponding document into the ERP system.

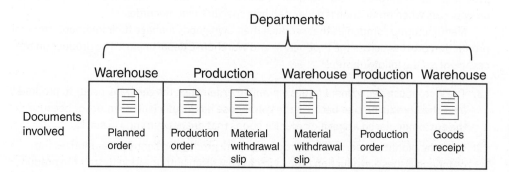

FIGURE 10.7 **Departments and documents flow in the production process.**

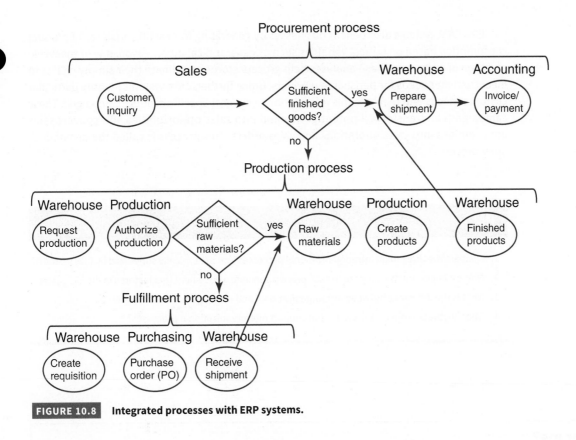

FIGURE 10.8   **Integrated processes with ERP systems.**

Figure 10.8 portrays the three cross-functional business processes we just discussed. It specifically highlights the integration of the three processes, which is made possible by ERP systems.

Interorganizational Processes: ERP with SCM and CRM

MKT **POM** Although the procurement and the fulfillment processes involve suppliers and customers, they are considered (together with the production process) intraorganizational processes because they originate and conclude within the company. However, ERP systems can also manage processes that originate in one company and conclude in another company. These processes are called *interorganizational processes,* and they typically involve supply chain management (SCM) and customer relationship management (CRM) systems. You can find a more detailed description of CRM and SCM (see Chapter 11). Here, we focus on the integration of these processes within a firm's industry value chain.

SCM and CRM processes help multiple firms within an industry to coordinate activities such as the production-to-sale of goods and services. Let's consider a chain of grocery stores whose supply chain must properly manage perishable goods. On the one hand, store managers need to stock only the amount of perishable products that they are reasonably sure they will sell before the products' expiration dates. On the other hand, they do not want to run out of stock of any products that customers need.

ERP SCM systems have the capability to place automatic requests to buy fresh perishable products from suppliers in real time. That is, as each perishable product is purchased, the system captures data on that purchase, adjusts store inventory levels, and transmits these data to the grocery chain's warehouse as well as the products' vendors. The system executes this process by connecting the point-of-sale barcode scanning system with the Warehouse and Accounting departments as well as with the vendors' systems. SCM systems also use historical data to predict when fresh products need to be ordered before the store's supply becomes too low.

ERP CRM systems also benefit businesses by generating forecasting analyses of product consumption based on critical variables such as geographical area, season, day of the week, and type of customer. These analyses help grocery stores coordinate their supply chains to meet customer needs for perishable products. Going further, CRM systems identify particular customer needs and then use this information to suggest specific product campaigns. These campaigns can transform a potential demand into sales opportunities and convert sales opportunities into sales quotations and sales orders. This process is called the *demand-to-order* process.

Before you go on . . .

1. What are the three main intraorganizational processes that are typically supported by ERP systems?
2. Why is it important that all steps in each process generate a document that is stored in the ERP system?
3. What is the difference between intraorganizational and interorganizational processes?
4. What are the two main ES systems that support interorganizational processes?

What's in IT for me?

ACCT For the Accounting Major

Understanding the functions and outputs of TPSs effectively is a major concern of any accountant. It is also necessary to understand the various activities of all functional areas and how they are interconnected. Accounting information systems are a central component in any ERP package. In fact, all large CPA firms actively consult with clients on ERP implementations, using thousands of specially trained accounting majors.

FIN For the Finance Major

IT helps financial analysts and managers perform their tasks better. Of particular importance is analyzing cash flows and securing the financing required for smooth operations. Financial applications can also support such activities as risk analysis, investment management, and global transactions involving different currencies and fiscal regulations.

Finance activities and modeling are key components of ERP systems. Flows of funds (payments), at the core of most supply chains, must be executed efficiently and effectively. Financial arrangements are especially important along global supply chains, where currency conventions and financial regulations must be considered.

MKT For the Marketing Major

Marketing and sales expenses are usually targets in a cost-reduction program. Also, sales force automation improves not only salespeoples' productivity (and thus reduces costs) but also customer service.

POM For the Production/Operations Management Major

Managing production tasks, materials handling, and inventories in short time intervals, at a low cost, and with high quality is critical for competitiveness. These activities can be achieved only if they are properly supported by IT. IT can also greatly enhance interaction with other functional areas, especially sales. Collaboration in design, manufacturing, and logistics requires knowledge of how modern information systems can be connected.

HRM For the Human Resource Management Major

Human resources managers can increase their efficiency and effectiveness by using IT for some of their routine functions. Human resources personnel need to understand how information flows between the HR department and the other functional areas. Finally, the integration of functional areas through ERP systems has a major impact on skill requirements and scarcity of employees, which are related to the tasks performed by the HRM department.

MIS For the MIS Major

The MIS function is responsible for the most fundamental information systems in organizations: the transaction processing systems, which provide the data for the databases. In turn, all other information systems use these data. MIS personnel develop applications that support all levels of the organization (from clerical to executive) and all functional areas. The applications also enable the firm to do business with its partners.

Summary

10.1 Explain the purpose of transaction processing systems.

TPSs monitor, store, collect, and process data generated from all business transactions. These data provide the inputs into the organization's database.

10.2 Explain the types of support that information systems can provide for each functional area of the organization.

The major business functional areas are production/operations management, marketing, accounting/finance, and human resources management. Table 10.1 provides an overview of the many activities in each functional area supported by FAIS.

10.3 Identify advantages and drawbacks to businesses of implementing an ERP system.

Enterprise resource planning (ERP) systems integrate the planning, management, and use of all of the organization's resources. The major objective of ERP systems is to tightly integrate the functional areas of the organization. This integration enables information to flow seamlessly across the various functional areas.

The following are the major benefits of ERP systems:

- Because ERP systems integrate organizational resources, they make organizations more flexible, agile, and adaptive. The organizations can therefore react quickly to changing business conditions and capitalize on new business opportunities.
- ERP systems provide essential information on business performance across functional areas. This information significantly improves managers' ability to make better, more timely decisions.
- ERP systems integrate organizational resources, resulting in significant improvements in the quality of customer service, production, and distribution.

The following are the major drawbacks of ERP systems:

- The business processes in ERP software are often predefined by the best practices that the ERP vendor has developed. As a result, companies may need to change existing business processes to fit the predefined business processes of the software. For companies with well-established procedures, this requirement can be a huge problem.
- ERP systems can be extremely complex, expensive, and time consuming to implement. In fact, the costs and risks of failure in implementing a new ERP system are substantial.

10.4 Describe the three main business processes supported by ERP systems.

The *procurement process*, which originates in the warehouse department (need to buy) and ends in the accounting department (send payment).

The *fulfillment process*, which originates in the sales department (customer request to buy) and ends in the accounting department (receive payment).

The *production process*, which originates and ends in the warehouse department (need to produce and reception of finished goods) but involves the production department as well.

We leave the details of the steps in each of these processes up to you.

Chapter Glossary

ad hoc (on-demand) reports Nonroutine reports that often contain special information that is not included in routine reports.

batch processing Transaction processing system (TPS) that processes data in batches at fixed periodic intervals.

comparative reports Reports that compare performances of different business units or times.

computer-integrated manufacturing (CIM) An information system that integrates various automated factory systems; also called *digital manufacturing*.

cross-departmental process A business process that originates in one department and ends in another department or that originates and ends in the same department while involving other departments.

drill-down reports Reports that show a greater level of details than is included in routine reports.

enterprise application integration (EAI) system A system that integrates existing systems by providing layers of software that connect applications together.

enterprise resource planning (ERP) systems Information systems that take a business process view of the overall organization to integrate the planning, management, and use of all of an organization's resources, employing a common software platform and database.

ERP II systems Interorganizational ERP systems that provide Web-enabled links among key business systems (e.g., inventory and production) of a company and its customers, suppliers, distributors, and others.

exception reports Reports that include only information that exceeds certain threshold standards.

functional area information systems (FAIS) Systems that provide information to managers (usually mid-level) in the functional areas to better support managerial tasks of planning, organizing, and controlling operations.

key indicator reports Reports that summarize the performance of critical activities.

online transaction processing (OLTP) Transaction processing system (TPS) that processes data after transactions occur, frequently in real time.

order fulfillment process A cross-functional business process that originates when the company receives a customer order and concludes when it receives a payment from the customer.

procurement process A cross-functional business process that originates when a company needs to acquire goods or services from external sources and concludes when the company receives and pays for them.

production process A cross-functional business process in which a company produces physical goods.

routine reports Reports produced at scheduled intervals.

transaction Any business event that generates data worth capturing and storing in a database.

transaction processing system (TPS) Information system that supports the monitoring, collection, storage, and processing of data from the organization's basic business transactions, each of which generates data.

Discussion Questions

1. Why is it logical to organize IT applications by functional areas?
2. Describe the role of a TPS in a service organization.
3. Describe the relationship between TPS and FAIS.
4. Discuss how IT facilitates the budgeting process.
5. How can the Internet support investment decisions?
6. Describe the benefits of integrated accounting software packages.
7. Discuss the role that IT plays in support of auditing.
8. Investigate the role of the Web in human resources management.
9. What is the relationship between information silos and enterprise resource planning?

Problem-Solving Activities

1. Finding a job on the Internet is challenging, as there are almost too many places to look. Visit the following sites: **www.careerbuilder.com**, **www.craigslist.org**, **www.linkedin.com**, **www.jobcentral.com**, and **www.monster.com**. What does each of these sites provide you with as a job seeker?

2. Enter **www.sas.com** and access *revenue optimization* there. Explain how the software helps in optimizing prices.

3. Enter **www.eleapsoftware.com** and review the product that helps with online training (training systems). What are the most attractive features of this product?

4. Examine the capabilities of the following (and similar) financial software packages: Financial Analyzer (from Oracle) and CFO Vision (from SAS Institute). Prepare a report comparing the capabilities of the software packages.

5. Surf the Net and find free accounting software. (Try **www.cnet.com**, **www.rkom.com**, **www.tucows.com**, **www.passtheshareware.com**, and **www.freeware-guide.com**.) Download the software and try it. Compare the ease of use and usefulness of each software package.

6. Find Simply Accounting Basic from Sage Software (**www.sage.com/us/sage-50-accounting**). Why is this product recommended for small businesses?

7. Enter Redirects to **www.saba.com** and **www.successfactors.com**. Examine their software products and compare them.

8. Enter Redirects to **www.asuresoftware.com** and find the support it provides to human resources management activities. View the demos and prepare a report on the capabilities of the products.

Closing Case

Olive Garden

`POM` `MKT` `MIS`

The Business Problem

Olive Garden is an Italian restaurant chain that first opened in Orlando, Florida, in 1982. Over the years, the company became highly successful. Within 7 years, they had opened 145 restaurants! However, that success began to level off, and in 2014 the chain started losing money. Significantly, their corporate strategy had remained largely static during this time. When the company experienced a slump in revenue,

they used menu adjustments (such as new entrees or desserts) and promotions to drive sales. However, these strategies were not bringing customers back to the restaurant. As a result, in 2015 they made some strategic moves to begin shaking up their restaurant experience.

Olive Garden began to offer both enhanced online ordering and Olive Garden ToGO that allowed customers to order online and pickup their order as takeout rather than at the restaurant. At the same time, mobile devices had brought about a cultural shift. Customers were increasingly comfortable ordering and paying for food on their mobile devices. Additionally, customers felt a growing concern about handing their credit or debit card to the waitstaff. (Approximately 60 percent of credit card fraud is a result of dishonest waitstaff stealing credit card information when they are taking payment from restaurant patrons.)

The IT Solution

Olive Garden needed a technology solution that would help them improve their customer service, speed the entire customer experience from ordering to paying, and make customer payments more secure. So in 2015 they partnered with Ziosk to upgrade their customer experience. Ziosk (www.ziosk.com) is a provider of entertainment, ordering, and pay-at-the-table touchscreen devices. Their products are used in several national chains such as Chili's, Outback, and Red Robin. These tablets have increased customer participation in loyalty programs, streamlined the payment process, and added a "cool" factor that is important to younger generations.

This touchscreen system enables direct input from customer to kitchen to speed up the ordering process. Additionally, it allows customers to control the pace of the meal by ordering drinks, appetizers, and entrées at their discretion. If they are in a hurry, then they can place an order as soon as they sit down. They can also pay for their meal as soon as they are finished. Of course, if they want to take their time, that is still an option. In addition, rather than replacing the waitstaff (as some had feared), the technology actually complemented and smoothed their job. They could now focus on providing good customer service rather than running between tables collecting orders and taking payments. Olive Garden hoped to see similar results in their restaurants.

The Results

Customers responded positively when Olive Garden tested the Ziosk tablets. Roughly 60 percent now use the pay feature on the tablet. Interestingly, the waitstaff saw a 15 percent increase in tips! Further, after Olive Garden implemented this system, their table turnover rates increased by an average of seven to 10 minutes. Put simply, Olive Garden can now seat and serve customers more quickly, thereby increasing their restaurants' throughput. In 2016, they experienced a 40 percent growth with more than 10 percent of their total sales coming from the new ToGO option and the tabletop ordering system.

As with most technology shifts, the introduction of the Ziosk tablets has not been without problems. For example, waitstaff have complained that they have been shorted tips by a fault in the system. Further, some customers still prefer the traditional dining experience. Also, some families are irritated that the devices allow kids to play games (that cost money). Overall, however, the response has been positive.

Sources: Compiled from T. Kilgore, "Olive Garden Parent Darden's Stock Surges after Profit and Sales Beat, Raised Outlook," *Morningstar*, December 19, 2017; M. Maynard, "Why Your Upscale Restaurant Server Still Takes Your Order By Hand, Even Though Technology Abounds," *Forbes*, June 27, 2017; M. Watrous, "Inside Olive Garden's Incredible Comeback," *foodbusinessnews.net*, April 6, 2016; J. Monsell, "Restaurant Guests Sour on Ziosk's 'Touch It and You're Charged' Payment Systems," *elliot.org*, July 25, 2016; C. Jones, "Olive Garden Boosts Parent Company Profits," *USA Today*, December 21, 2016; C. Furhmeister, "Olive Garden Employee Blames Shorted Tips on Faulty Automated Ordering," *eater.com*, September 1, 2015; R. Vamosi, "Tablets to Provide Secure Payments in U.S. Restaurants," *Forbes*, February 19, 2015; P. La Monica, "Olive Garden Sales Hotter Than Its Breadsticks," *CNN Money*, June 23, 2015; S. Hill, "Restaurant Table Tablets: A Gimmick, or Actually Helpful?," *Christian Science Monitor*, May 14, 2015; A. Fluker, "4 Reasons Olive Garden May Win with Tabletop Ordering," *Orlando Business Journal*, April 16, 2015; T. Lien, "Olive Garden Rolls Out Tabletop Tablets for Ordering and Payment," *Los Angeles Times*, April 14, 2015; M. McGrath, "Olive Garden Turnaround Helps Lift Darden Profit above Expectations," *Forbes*, March 20, 2015; https://www.retaildive.com/ex/mobilecommercedaily/olive-garden-garnishes-dining-experiences-via-pay-at-the-table-tablets, www.olivegarden.com/about-us, and http://www.restaurantnews.com/ziosk-completes-installation-of-tabletop-tablets-at-olive-garden-restaurants-nationwide/ (all accessed September 19, 2018).

Questions

1. In what ways did Olive Garden hope their new tabletop ordering system would improve the customer experience?

2. What do you see as the positive and negative impacts on the waitstaff of the new tabletop kiosk system?

3. What are the positive and negative impacts on collecting payment?

Customer Relationship Management and Supply Chain Management

Opening Case

MKT Tesco Enhances Its Customer Relationship Management Efforts

Tesco PLC, a British grocery and general merchandise retailer that operates in the United Kingdom, Europe, Asia, and North America, was founded in 1919 with a simple mission, "to be the champion for customers, helping them to enjoy a better quality of life

and an easier way of living." Tesco's objective is to deliver products and services in the right way for their customers. "Serving Britain's shoppers a little better every day" is their core purpose. For years, Tesco pursued this objective by increasing the number of physical locations in order to broaden their reach. Then, in 2000, the retailer switched to a digital strategy by introducing Tesco.com to the U.K. market. Tesco.com offered multiple services, including grocery, general merchandise, and clothing, as well as banking and insurance services.

Despite this transition, however, the homegrown nature of Tesco's internal information systems made it very difficult for the company's business analysts to understand their customers' online experiences. Tesco had years of experience with the physical store presence, and they were known for being at the forefront of new technologies, communications, and social media. However, in the areas of social customer service and engagement, Tesco business analysts needed a broader view of which products and website features their customers used and which pathways resulted in the highest number of customers completing a purchase. In the sales industry, this process is referred to as *lead conversions*. Essentially, the company needed to upgrade its information systems in order to align their IT infrastructure with their mission.

Therefore, in 2014, Tesco began to search for customer relationship management (CRM) solutions. However, their focus was on more than simply the CRM tool. Rather, the new system needed to bridge a gap across their organization. For more than a decade, Tesco had added, modified, and updated their systems to try to support their new website. This approach left the company with a challenging IT infrastructure that consisted of more than 400 servers across 10 environments. This type of system expansion can result in data redundancy, data isolation, and data inconsistency that arise when organizations have multiple systems (recall this discussion from Chapter 5). However, there are also issues with troubleshooting and making updates based on user requests.

Information systems keep track of events (such as a transaction, a communication, or an error) in a file called a log. When there are errors, organizations measure their time to identify (MTTI—Mean Time to Identify) and respond (MTTR—Mean Time to Respond) as indicators of how well their support systems are functioning. Since Tesco had multiple systems, they also had multiple error logs to monitor and troubleshoot. Tesco relied primarily on custom scripts to make their log data available to developers and IT support teams. Their large and complex infrastructure made it difficult to manage error logs. This complexity directly impacted their ability to identify and respond to issues, sometimes impeding the company's mission to be a champion for its customers. The influx of new systems and the need to support multiple groups overwhelmed the company's homegrown log-monitoring solution.

Tesco PLC needed a solution that would tie their information together and thus provide the company with a full view of their customers, including the customers' habits and decisions. They needed to identify the reasons why some customers stayed online and made purchases while others left with items still in their cart so they could develop an appropriate response. They especially wanted to know whether any of their information systems were creating roadblocks for customers. The company had the basic data, but they were not able to pull the data together in a meaningful way in order to make any strategic decisions.

Splunk Enterprise (**www.splunk.com**) turned out to be the solution that Tesco was looking for. Splunk is a multinational corporation based in San Francisco that produces software for searching, monitoring, and analyzing large machine-generated datasets, namely Big Data. Their system is designed to support Web-based interfaces. Significantly, it consists of a single platform, thus making it relatively easy to adopt and implement. This solution was the perfect answer to Tesco's problems because it enabled the company to address both their hardware and customer service data needs.

Joshua Anderson, an applications engineer at Tesco, explained, "Early on, we were having trouble with checkout flow on the website [and] I remember just typing in 'error' and 'payment' in Splunk and all of a sudden we were able to narrow directly down to time frames and see that there was a problem with our connectivity and the IP address." If there is one place where you do not want to have a negative customer experience, it is in the checkout flow!

Prior to implementing Splunk, the Tesco application support team spent hours trying to track down the cause of the problem, and the company lost many potential sales. After adopting Splunk, they found and corrected the problem and established alerts and dashboards to speed up the process of identifying and resolving future problems. As a result, Tesco improved their customer experience and reduced the incidence of lost revenue due to abandoned shopping carts. As Anderson observed, "Once we started rolling out the Splunk platform and looking at some of the information we could extract, it opened up our world—like putting on glasses for the first time."

This is just one example of how Splunk quickly helped Tesco. Due to the benefits Tesco has experienced in application support and development, the company rolled out the Splunk platform to new areas within Tesco PLC. As a result, the company obtained the full operational visibility that is necessary to analyze and optimize website behavior in real time. Mean Time to Identify (MTTI) and Mean Time to Respond (MTTR) have been reduced by 95 percent, and customer service escalations have decreased by at least 50 percent. In short, since deploying Splunk Enterprise, Tesco PLC has seen many benefits across the board, starting with their need for an efficient CRM.

Sources: Compiled from A. Bridgewater, "Splunk Platform Aims to Clean 'Messy Noisy' Machine Data," *Forbes*, June 28, 2018; A. Bridgewater, "Splunk Aims To Put Machine Learning Into 'Mainstream' Computing," *Forbes*, September 26, 2017; A. Drennan, "How Tesco Leads the Way in Social Customer Service," www.conversocial.com, May 29, 2012; T. Simonite, "Extracting Business Ideas from IT Logs," *MIT Technology Review*, February 11, 2011; G. Huang, "Old Logs, New Tricks," *MIT Technology Review*, February 1, 2004; "Tesco.com Accelerates Development through Deep Understanding of Customer Behavior," https://www.splunk.com/en_us/customers/success-stories/tesco.html, accessed November 29, 2017; https://www.tescoplc.com/news/blogs/topics/a-lot-has-changed-in-three-years-a-colleague-message-from-dave-lewis/ accessed November 29, 2017; https://www.tescoplc.com/about-us/history/, accessed November 29, 2017; https://carabiner.splunk.com/web_assets/pdfs/secure/Splunk_at_Tesco.pdf, accessed November 29, 2017; https://en.wikipedia.org/wiki/Splunk, accessed October 15, 2017; and J. Hertvick, "MTTR Explained: Repair vs Recovery in a Digitized Environment," https://www.bmc.com/blogs/mtbf-vs-mtff-vs-mttr-whats-difference/, accessed July 17 2019.

Questions:

1. Using Tesco as your example, discuss the challenges associated with homegrown computer information systems.

2. Why do you think it is important to have Splunk track MTTI and MTTR? Give three reasons.

3. How did Splunk help transform Tesco's ability to identify and respond to negative customer experiences with their online store?

Introduction

In Chapter 10, you learned about information systems that support activities within the organization. In this chapter, you study information systems that support activities that extend outside the organization to customers and suppliers. The first half of this chapter addresses customer relationship management (CRM) systems and the second half addresses supply chain management systems (SCM).

Organizations are emphasizing a customer-centric approach to their business practices because they realize that long-term customer relationships provide sustainable value that extends beyond an individual business transaction. Organizations are also integrating their strategy and operations with supply chain partners because tight integration along the supply chain also leads to sustainable business value. Significantly, customer relationship management and supply chain management are critically important for all enterprises, regardless of size.

The chapter opening case points out how important data are to the customer-centric approach to business. Businesses are now able to discover when customers are having trouble with their site before the customers even complain. This type of data analysis is crucial to helping organizations understand customer problems and implement timely solutions.

Supply chain management (SCM) is equally important for organizations to successfully compete in the marketplace. Today, supply chain management is an integral part of all organizations and can improve customer service and reduce operating costs. Let's look at these two areas in more detail.

- **POM** *Improve customer service.* Customers expect to receive the correct products as quickly as possible. Therefore, products must be on hand in the correct locations. Furthermore, follow-up support after a sale must be done effectively and efficiently.

- **FIN** *Reduce operating costs.* For example, retailers depend on their supply chains to quickly distribute expensive products so that they will not have the inventory carrying costs for costly, depreciating products.

Delays in production are costly. Supply chains must ensure the reliable delivery of materials to assembly plants to avoid expensive delays in manufacturing.

At this point, you might be asking yourself: Why should *I* learn about CRM and SCM? The answer, as you will see in this chapter, is that customers and suppliers are supremely important to *all* organizations. Regardless of your job, you will have an impact, whether direct or indirect, on managing your firm's customer relationships and its supply chain. When you read the What's in IT for Me? Section at the end of this chapter, you will learn about opportunities to make immediate contributions on your first job. Therefore, it is essential that you acquire a working knowledge of CRM, CRM systems, supply chains, SCM, and SCM systems.

11.1 | Defining Customer Relationship Management

Author Lecture Videos are available exclusively in *WileyPLUS*.
Apply the Concept activities are available in the Appendix and in *WileyPLUS*.

Before the supermarket, the mall, and the automobile, people purchased goods at their neighborhood store. The owners and employees recognized customers by name and knew their preferences and wants. For their part, customers remained loyal to the store and made repeated purchases. Over time, however, this personal customer relationship became impersonal as people moved from farms and small towns to cities, consumers became mobile, and supermarkets and department stores achieved economies of scale through mass marketing. Although prices were lower and products were more uniform in quality, the relationship with customers became nameless and impersonal.

The customer relationship has become even more impersonal with the rapid growth of the Internet and the World Wide Web. In today's hypercompetitive marketplace, customers are increasingly powerful; if they are dissatisfied with a product or a service from one organization, a competitor is often just one mouse click away. Furthermore, as more and more customers shop on the Web, an enterprise does not even have the opportunity to make a good first impression *in person*.

Customer relationship management is focusing anew on personal marketing; that is, rather than market to a mass of people or companies, businesses market to each customer individually. By employing this approach, businesses can use information about each customer—for example, previous purchases, needs, and wants—to create highly individualized offers that customers are more likely to accept. The CRM approach is designed to achieve *customer intimacy*.

Customer relationship management is a customer-focused and customer-driven organizational strategy. That is, organizations concentrate on assessing customers' requirements for products and services and then provide a high-quality, responsive customer experience. CRM is not a process or a technology per se; rather, it is a customer-centric way of thinking and acting. The focus of modern organizations has shifted from conducting business transactions to managing customer relationships. In general, organizations recognize that customers are the core of a successful enterprise, and the success of the enterprise depends on effectively managing relationships with them.

The CRM approach is enabled by information technology in the form of various systems and applications. However, CRM is not only about the software. Sometimes the problem with managing relationships is simply time and information. Old systems may contain the needed information, but this information may take too long to access and may not be usable across a variety of applications or devices. The result is that companies have less time to spend with their customers.

In contrast, modern CRM strategies and systems build sustainable long-term customer relationships that create value for the company as well as for the customer. That is, CRM helps companies acquire new customers and retain and expand their relationships with profitable existing customers. Retaining customers is particularly important because repeat customers are the largest generator of revenue for an enterprise. Also, organizations have long understood that winning back a customer who has switched to a competitor is vastly more expensive than keeping that customer satisfied in the first place.

Figure 11.1 depicts the CRM process. The process begins with marketing efforts, through which the organization solicits prospects from a target population of potential customers. A certain number of these prospects will make a purchase and thus become customers. A certain number of these customers will become repeat customers. The organization then segments its repeat customers into low- and high-value repeat customers. An organization's overall goal is to maximize the *lifetime value* of a customer, which is that customer's potential revenue stream over a number of years.

Over time, all organizations inevitably lose a certain percentage of customers, a process called *customer churn*. The optimal result of the organization's CRM efforts is to maximize the number of high-value repeat customers while minimizing customer churn.

CRM is a fundamentally simple concept: Treat different customers differently because their needs differ and their value to the company may also differ. A successful CRM strategy not only improves customer satisfaction but also makes the company's sales and service employees more productive, which in turn generates increased profits. Researchers at the National Quality Research Center at the University of Michigan discovered that a 1 percent increase in customer satisfaction can lead to as much as a 300 percent increase in a company's *market capitalization*, defined as the number of shares of the company's stock outstanding multiplied by the price per share of the stock. Put simply, a minor increase in customer satisfaction can generate a major increase in a company's overall value.

Up to this point, you have been looking at an organization's CRM strategy. It is important to distinguish between a CRM *strategy* and CRM *systems*. Basically, CRM systems are information systems designed to support an organization's CRM strategy. For organizations to pursue excellent relationships with their customers, they need to employ CRM systems that provide the infrastructure needed to support those relationships. Because customer service and support

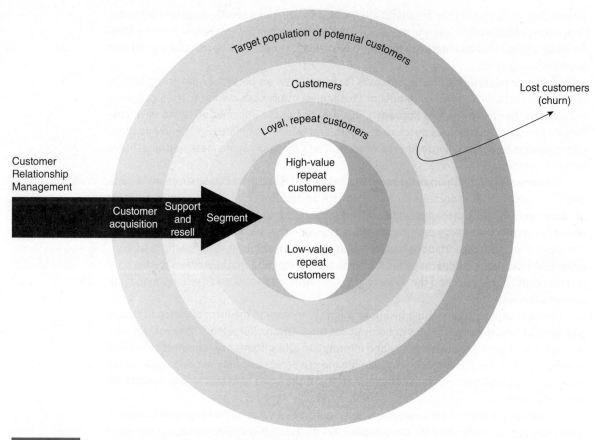

FIGURE 11.1 **The customer relationship management process.**

are essential to a successful business, organizations must place a great deal of emphasis on both their CRM strategy and their CRM systems.

Broadly speaking, CRM systems lie along a continuum, from *low-end CRM systems*—designed for enterprises with many small customers—to *high-end CRM systems*—for enterprises with a few large customers. An example of a low-end system is Amazon, which uses its CRM system to recommend products to returning customers. An example of a high-end system is Boeing, which uses its CRM system to coordinate staff activities in a campaign to sell its new 787 aircraft to Delta Airlines. As you study the cases and examples in this chapter, consider where on the continuum a particular CRM system would fall.

Although CRM varies according to circumstances, all successful CRM policies share two basic elements: (1) The company must identify the many types of customer touch points, and (2) it needs to consolidate data about each customer. Let's examine these two elements in more detail.

Customer Touch Points

Organizations must recognize the numerous and diverse interactions they have with their customers. These interactions are referred to as **customer touch points.** Traditional customer touch points include telephone contact, direct mailings, and actual physical interactions with customers during their visits to a store. Organizational CRM systems, however, must manage many additional customer touch points that occur through the use of popular personal technologies. These touch points include e-mail, websites, and communications through smartphones (see **Figure 11.2**).

The business–customer relationship is constantly evolving. As personal technology usage changes, so, too, must the methods that businesses use to interface with their customers. It is now possible to physically locate customers through their smartphones. As a result, location information can now provide another customer touch point.

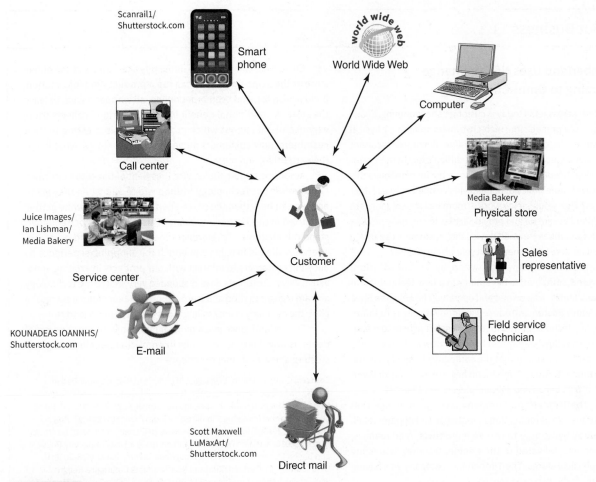

FIGURE 11.2 **Customer touch points.**

Businesses recognize this, but they have not moved all of their touch points in sync and this has led to several channel conflicts. For example, have you ever placed an online order only to get to the restaurant and find out that they never received your order? Or you have to wait because they didn't prepare it when it was promised by the online system? What about when you try to return something you purchased online only to find out that you have to ship it back rather than dropping it off at the local "bricks-and-mortar" version of the same store?

Today, effective marketing makes use of all of these channels (touch points) in sync with one another. We call this omni-channel marketing (omni meaning all). Omni-channel marketing refers to an approach to customers that creates a seamless experience regardless of the channel (or device) used to "touch" the business. Many businesses are now creating omni-channel strategies to drive this cohesive experience for their customers. To accomplish this goal, businesses must utilize information systems (specifically CRM) because the need for data consistency across channels is more apparent now than ever, as you learn in IT's About Business 11.1.

Data Consolidation

Data consolidation is also critical to an organization's CRM efforts. The organization's CRM systems must manage customer data effectively. In the past, customer data were stored in isolated systems (or silos) located in different functional areas across the business—for example, in separate databases in the finance, sales, logistics, and marketing departments. Consequently, data for individual customers was difficult to share across the various functional areas.

As you saw in Chapter 5, modern interconnected systems built around a data warehouse now make all customer-related data available to every unit of the business. This complete data set on each customer is called a *360° view* of that customer. By accessing this view, a company can enhance its relationship with its customers and ultimately make more productive and profitable decisions.

IT's About Business 11.1

MKT Timberland Uses NFC to Change Showrooming to Omni-Channeling

A major concern across retail today is customer showrooming. *Showrooming* refers to a practice in which customers shop in a physical store but then search for the best price online. When stores cannot rely on customer loyalty, then it becomes difficult for them to compete on anything except price. So, how does a business manage this situation? Create a store policy of not allowing customers to use their mobile devices? That would never work. A more realistic solution is to follow Timberland's example and provide access to company product information on a company-owned device that customers can use to engage the online store while they are in your physical store.

The Timberland Company (owned by VF Corporation; **www.timberland.com**) had its beginnings in a new technology. In 1965, the Swartz family, who owned and operated The Abington Shoe Company in South Boston, introduced an innovative way to utilize injection-molding technology into footwear, enabling them to manufacture the iconic, yellow, waterproof boot we know as Timberlands. The boots became so popular that the company changed its name to match the product. Today, Timberland has a global footprint with 2018 revenue of $1.8 billion and 3400 employees in 230 stores.

In 2016, the Timberland Company faced a challenge that would require the use of innovation in footwear and apparel retail. Customers enjoy being able to research products, read reviews, and have products delivered to their home, but they also enjoy shopping in physical stores. The Timberland Company was having difficulty merging the two experiences.

Fortunately, Timberland found a way to use technology to provide a new and unique shopping experience. Specifically, they utilized near field communications (NFC; see Chapter 8). NFC is a set of protocols designed to enable different parties to share information over short distances. If two devices equipped with NFC technology are held about 1.5 inches from each other (about 4 centimeters), then they can transfer information. This information can include product reviews, links, available options, sizes, and more. Timberland realized, however, that not all customers have an NFC-equipped device and some do not want to download another app. Therefore, the company provided a mobile device to their customers to use in their stores.

Customers can now shop in the physical store and the online store at the same time. They can tap a product, find information, build a wish list, and even order online, all without having to leave the store. An additional benefit is that Timberland collects some very useful data about which products seem interesting to their customers, how customers move through the stores, what keeps their attention, and more.

According to Kate Kibler, Vice President of Direct to Consumer, "Consumers use technology to shop where and when they want, and we can help them discover, shop, and socialize, while getting immersed in the Timberland brand. This can help us better understand our customers' preferences in-store, online, and post-visit. These invaluable insights can enrich the shopping experience by allowing customers to interact with our products in exciting, innovative ways. Customers have responded very well to the technology and are using it to shop and learn, reported Kibler. "After a successful pilot, the company is now rolling it out in other Timberland stores."

Timberland, once just a pioneer in manufacturing waterproof boots, is now blazing new trails in omni-channel marketing and creating a new customer experience.

Sources: Compiled from P. Danziger, "Timberland Blazes a New Trail in Retail," *Forbes*, September 22, 2017; "Connecting Cotton and Trees Signals Hope for Farmers in Haiti," *Timberland Newsroom*, August 29, 2017; C. Heine, "Is OmniChannel Marketing Finally Going From Dream to Reality?" *Adweek*, October 16, 2016; "Timberland Makes Store NFC Enabled," *Innovation Article*, March 5, 2016; A. Blair, "Timberland Tablets Blaze a Trail Connecting Physical and Digital Commerce," www.retailtouchpoints.com, January 28, 2016; D. Berthiaume, "Timberland Climbs to New Seamless Experience Heights," www.chainstorage.com, January 13, 2016; B. Davis, "Five Retailers Using NFC and RFID to Enhance Shopping: But Do They Work?," econsultancy.com, August 13, 2014; and www.timberland.com, accessed July 17, 2019.

Questions

1. Describe the challenges facing retail businesses that have multiple channels.

2. Discuss the advantages of Timberland's omni-channel marketing strategy. Can you think of any potential disadvantages?

3. Which technologies does Timberland use to provide this new customer experience? In what other ways could the company utilize these technologies? Be specific.

Data consolidation and the 360° view of the customer enable the organization's functional areas to readily share information about customers. This information sharing leads to collaborative CRM. **Collaborative CRM systems** provide effective and efficient interactive communication with the customer throughout the entire organization—that is, they integrate communications between the organization and its customers in all aspects of marketing, sales, and customer support. Collaborative CRM systems also enable customers to provide direct feedback to the organization. As you read in Chapter 9, social media applications such as social networks, blogs, microblogs, and Wikis are very important to companies that value customer input into their product and service offerings, as well as into new product development.

The most recent push for consolidated data is called **customer identity management**. Large businesses with several divisions and brands need to understand who their customers are across the business and how their relationship has changed over time. Much the way databases and data warehouses centralize data within a division (meaning all functional areas share data), a Customer Identity Management platform within a CRM will help a company create the 360° view across an entire organization and not just within a division.

Recall that an organization's CRM system contains two major components: operational CRM systems and analytical CRM systems. You will learn about operational CRM systems in the next section. We provide a brief overview of analytical CRM systems at the end of Section 11.2, and we discuss these systems in more detail in Chapter 12.

Before you go on . . .

1. What is the definition of customer relationship management?
2. Why is CRM so important to any organization?
3. Define and provide examples of customer touch points.

11.2 Operational Customer Relationship Management Systems

Operational CRM systems support front-office business processes. **Front-office processes** are those that directly interact with customers; that is, sales, marketing, and service. The two major components of operational CRM systems are customer-facing applications and customer-touching applications (discussed further on). Operational CRM systems provide the following benefits:

- Efficient, personalized marketing, sales, and service
- A 360° view of each customer
- The ability of sales and service employees to access a complete history of customer interaction with the organization, regardless of the touch point

An example of an operational CRM system involves Caterpillar, Inc. (**www.cat.com**), an international manufacturer of industrial equipment. Caterpillar uses its CRM tools to accomplish the following objectives:

- Improve sales and account management by optimizing the information shared by multiple employees and by streamlining existing processes (e.g., take orders using mobile devices).
- Form individualized relationships with customers, with the aim of improving customer satisfaction and maximizing profits.
- Identify the most profitable customers, and provide them with the highest level of service.
- Provide employees with the information and processes necessary to know their customers.
- Understand and identify customer needs, and effectively build relationships among the company, its customer base, and its distribution partners.

Author Lecture Videos are available exclusively in *WileyPLUS*.
Apply the Concept activities are available in the Appendix and in *WileyPLUS*.

Customer-Facing Applications

In **customer-facing CRM applications**, an organization's sales, field service, and customer interaction center representatives interact directly with customers. These applications include customer service and support, salesforce automation, marketing, and campaign management.

MKT Customer Service and Support. Customer service and support refers to systems that automate service requests, complaints, product returns, and requests for information. Today, organizations have implemented **customer interaction centers (CIC)**, in which organizational representatives use multiple channels such as the Web, telephone, fax, and face-to-face interactions to communicate with customers.

One of the best-known customer interaction centers is the *call center*, a centralized office set up to receive and transmit a large volume of requests by telephone. Call centers enable companies to respond to a large variety of questions, including product support and complaints.

POM **Salesforce Automation.** **Salesforce automation (SFA)** is the component of an operational CRM system that automatically records all of the components in a sales transaction process. SFA systems include a *contact management system*, which tracks all communications between the company and the customer, the purpose of each communication, and any necessary follow-up. This system eliminates duplicated contacts and redundancy, which in turn reduces the risk of irritating customers. SFA also includes a *sales lead tracking system*, which lists potential customers or customers who have purchased related products; that is, products similar to those that the salesperson is trying to sell to the customer.

Other elements of an SFA system can include a *sales forecasting system*, which is a mathematical technique for estimating future sales, and a *product knowledge system*, which is a comprehensive source of information regarding products and services. More-developed SFA systems also have online product-building features, called *configurators*, that enable customers to model the product to meet their specific needs. For example, you can customize your own running shoe at NikeID (**www.nikeid.nike.com**). Finally, many current SFA systems enable the salesperson in the field to connect remotely with customers and the home office through Web-based interfaces on their smartphones.

MKT **Marketing.** Thus far, you have focused primarily on how sales and customer service personnel can benefit from CRM systems. However, CRM systems have many important applications for an organization's marketing department as well. For example, they enable marketers to identify and target their best customers, to manage marketing campaigns, and to generate quality leads for the sales teams. CRM marketing applications can also sift through volumes of customer data—a process known as *data mining* (discussed in Chapter 12)—to develop a *purchasing profile*; that is, a snapshot of a consumer's buying habits that may lead to additional sales through cross-selling, upselling, and bundling.

Cross-selling is the marketing of additional related products to customers based on a previous purchase. This sales approach has been used very successfully by banks. For example, if you have a checking and savings account at your bank, then a bank officer will recommend other products for you, such as certificates of deposit (CDs) or other types of investments.

Upselling is a strategy in which the salesperson provides customers with the opportunity to purchase related products or services of greater value in place of, or along with, the consumer's initial product or service selection. For example, if a customer goes into an electronics store to buy a new television, a salesperson may show him a pricey 4K TV model placed next to a less expensive LCD television in the hope of selling the more expensive set (assuming that the customer is willing to pay more for a sharper picture). Other common examples of upselling are warranties on electronics merchandise and the purchase of a carwash after buying gas at a gas station.

Finally, *bundling* is a form of cross-selling in which a business sells a group of products or services together at a lower price than their combined individual prices. For example, your cable company might bundle cable TV, broadband Internet access, and telephone service at a lower price than you would pay for each service separately.

Campaign Management. *Campaign management applications* help organizations plan campaigns that send the right messages to the right people through the right channels. Organizations manage their campaigns very carefully to avoid targeting people who have opted out of receiving marketing communications. Furthermore, companies use these applications to personalize individual messages for each particular customer.

Customer-Touching Applications

Corporations have used manual CRM systems for many years. In the mid-1990s, for example, organizations began to use the Internet, the Web, and other electronic touch points (e.g., e-mail, point-of-sale terminals) to manage customer relationships. In contrast with customer-facing applications, through which customers deal with a company representative, customers who use these technologies interact directly with the applications themselves. For this reason, these applications are called **customer-touching CRM applications** or **electronic CRM (e-CRM) applications**. Customers typically can use these applications to help themselves. There are many types of e-CRM applications. Let's examine some of the major ones.

Search and Comparison Capabilities.

It is often difficult for customers to find what they want from the vast array of products and services available on the Web. To assist customers, many online stores and malls offer search and comparison capabilities, as do independent comparison websites (see **www.mysimon.com**).

Technical and Other Information and Services.

Many organizations offer personalized experiences to induce customers to make purchases or to remain loyal. For example, websites often allow customers to download product manuals. One example is General Electric's website (**www.ge.com**), which provides detailed technical and maintenance information and sells replacement parts to customers who need to repair outdated home appliances. Another example is Goodyear's website (**www.goodyear.com**), which provides information about tires and their use.

Customized Products and Services.

Another customer-touching service that many online vendors use is mass customization, a process through which customers can configure their own products. For example, Dell (**www.dell.com**) allows customers to configure their own computer systems. The Gap (**www.gap.com**) enables customers to "mix and match" an entire wardrobe. Websites such as Hitsquad (**www.hitsquad.com**) allow customers to pick individual music titles from a library and customize a CD, a feature that traditional music stores do not offer.

Customers now also view account balances or check the shipping status of orders at anytime from their computers or smartphones. If you order books from Amazon, for example, you can look up the anticipated arrival date. Many other companies, including FedEx and UPS, provide similar services (see **www.fedex.com** and **www.ups.com**).

Personalized Web Pages.

Many organizations permit their customers to create personalized Web pages. Customers use these pages to record purchases and preferences, as well as problems and requests. For example, American Airlines generates personalized Web pages for each of its registered travel-planning customers.

FAQs.

Frequently asked questions (FAQs) are a simple tool for answering repetitive customer queries. Customers may find the information they need by using this tool, thereby eliminating the need to communicate with an actual person.

E-mail and Automated Response.

The most popular tool for customer service is e-mail. Inexpensive and fast, companies use e-mail not only to answer customer inquiries but also to disseminate information, send alerts and product information, and conduct correspondence on any topic.

Loyalty Programs.

Loyalty programs recognize customers who repeatedly use a vendor's products or services. Loyalty programs are appropriate when two conditions are met: a high frequency of repeat purchases, and limited product customization for each customer.

Although loyalty programs are frequently referred to as "rewards programs," their actual purpose is not to reward *past* behavior, but, rather, to influence *future* behavior. Significantly, the most profitable customers are not necessarily those whose behavior can be most easily influenced. As one example, most major U.S. airlines provide some "elite" benefits to anyone who flies 25,000 miles with them and their partners over the course of a year. Customers who fly first class pay much more for a given flight than those who fly in economy class.

Nevertheless, these customers reach elite status only 1.5 to 2 times faster than economy-class passengers. Why is this true? The reason is that, although first-class passengers are far more profitable than discount seekers, they also are less influenced by loyalty programs.

Discount flyers respond much more enthusiastically to the benefits of frequent flyer programs. Therefore, airlines award more benefits to discount flyers than to first-class flyers (relative to their spending).

The airlines' frequent flyer programs are probably the best-known loyalty programs. Other popular loyalty programs are casino players' clubs, which reward frequent players, and supermarkets, which reward frequent shoppers. Loyalty programs use a database or data warehouse to maintain a record of the points (or miles) a customer has accrued and the rewards to which he or she is entitled. The programs then use analytical tools to mine the data and learn about customer behavior.

Analytical CRM Systems

Analytical CRM systems provide business intelligence by analyzing customer behavior and perceptions. (*Note:* We discuss analytics in detail in Chapter 12.) For example, analytical CRM systems typically provide information concerning customer requests and transactions, as well as customer responses to the organization's marketing, sales, and service initiatives. These systems also create statistical models of customer behavior and the value of customer relationships over time, as well as forecasts about acquiring, retaining, and losing customers.

Important technologies in analytical CRM systems include data warehouses, data mining, decision support, and other business intelligence technologies. After these systems have completed their various analyses, they supply information to the organization in the form of reports and digital dashboards.

Analytical CRM systems analyze customer data for a variety of purposes, including:

- Designing and executing targeted marketing campaigns
- Increasing customer acquisition, cross-selling, and upselling
- Providing input into decisions relating to products and services (e.g., pricing and product development)
- Providing financial forecasting and customer profitability analysis

Figure 11.3 illustrates the relationship between operational CRM systems and analytical CRM systems.

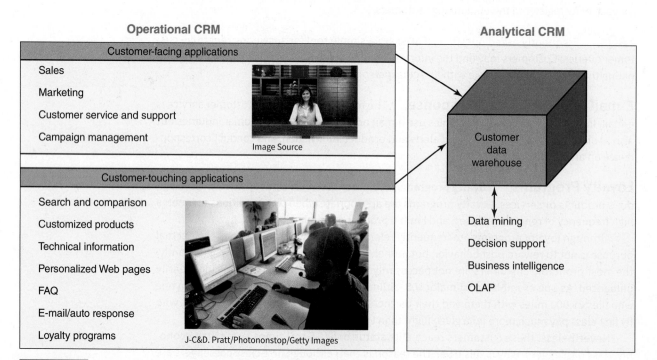

FIGURE 11.3 **The relationship between operational CRM and analytical CRM.**

1. Differentiate between customer-facing applications and customer-touching applications.

2. Provide examples of cross-selling, upselling, and bundling (other than the examples presented in the text).

11.3 Other Types of Customer Relationship Management Systems

Now that you have examined operational and analytical CRM systems, let's shift our focus to other types of CRM systems. Five exciting developments in this area are on-demand CRM systems, mobile CRM systems, open-source CRM systems, social CRM, and real-time CRM.

Author Lecture Videos are available exclusively in *WileyPLUS*.
Apply the Concept activities are available in the Appendix and in *WileyPLUS*.

On-Demand CRM Systems

Customer relationship management systems may be implemented as either *on-premise* or *on-demand*. Traditionally, organizations used on-premise CRM systems, meaning that they purchased the systems from a vendor and then installed them on-site. This arrangement was expensive, time consuming, and inflexible. Some organizations, particularly smaller ones, could not justify the costs of these systems.

On-demand CRM systems became a solution for the drawbacks of on-premise CRM systems. An **on-demand CRM system** is one that is hosted by an external vendor in the vendor's data center. This arrangement spares the organization the costs associated with purchasing the system. Because the vendor creates and maintains the system, the organization's employees also need to know how to access it and use it. The concept of on-demand is also known as *utility computing* or *software-as-a-service* (SaaS) (see Technology Guide 3).

Salesforce (**www.salesforce.com**) is the best-known on-demand CRM vendor. The company's goal is to provide a new business model that allows companies to rent the CRM software instead of buying it. The secret to their success appears to be that CRM has common requirements applicable to many customers. Consequently, Salesforce's product meets the demands of its customers without a great deal of customization.

One Salesforce customer is Babson College (**www.babson.edu**) in Wellesley, Massachusetts. Babson's goal is to deliver the best applicant experience possible. To accomplish this mission, the school decided to use Salesforce to bring together all of the information on prospective students in a single location. All personnel who are involved with admissions have immediate access to candidate contact information, applications, and reports that indicate the status of each applicant within the enrollment process. This system makes it easy for administrators to deliver valuable information to applicants at the right time.

POM **MKT** Using the Salesforce platform, Babson built an admissions portal with a fully personalized user experience for prospective students. The portal consolidates all of the information that potential students need. Furthermore, it displays different information to students at different points in the application process.

Despite their benefits, on-demand CRM systems have potential problems. First, the vendor could prove to be unreliable, in which case the client company would have no CRM functionality at all. Second, hosted software is difficult or impossible to modify, and only the vendor can upgrade it. Third, vendor-hosted CRM software may be difficult to integrate with the organization's existing software. Finally, giving strategic customer data to vendors always carries security and privacy risks.

Mobile CRM Systems

A **mobile CRM system** is an interactive system that enables an organization to conduct communications related to sales, marketing, and customer service activities through a mobile medium for the purpose of building and maintaining relationships with its customers. Simply put, mobile CRM systems involve interacting directly with consumers through portable devices such as smartphones. Many forward-thinking companies believe that mobile CRM systems have tremendous potential to create personalized customer relationships that may be accessed anywhere and at any time. In fact, the opportunities offered by mobile marketing appear so rich that many companies have already identified mobile CRM systems as a cornerstone of their future marketing activities.

Open-Source CRM Systems

As explained in Technology Guide 2, the source code for open-source software is available at no cost. **Open-source CRM systems**, therefore, are CRM systems whose source code is available to developers and users.

Open-source CRM systems provide the same features or functions as other CRM software, and they may be implemented either on-premise or on-demand. Leading open-source CRM vendors include SugarCRM (**www.sugarcrm.com**), Concursive (**www.concursive.com**), and Vtiger (**www.vtiger.com**). IT's About Business 11.2 illustrates how Materion uses SugarCRM.

The benefits of open-source CRM systems include favorable pricing and a wide variety of applications. These systems are also easy to customize. This is an attractive feature for organizations that need CRM software that is designed for their specific needs. Finally, updates and bug (software error) fixes for open-source CRM systems are rapidly distributed, and extensive support information is available free of charge.

Like all software, however, open-source CRM systems have certain risks. The most serious risk involves quality control. Because open-source CRM systems are created by a large community of unpaid developers, there is sometimes no central authority responsible for overseeing the quality of the product. (We discuss open-source software in Technology Guide 2). Furthermore, for best results, companies must have the same IT platform in place as the one on which the open-source CRM system was developed.

IT's About Business 11.2

MKT Materion Adopts SugarCRM

The Problem

Materion Corporation (**www.materion.com**) is an advanced materials supplier that was founded in 1931 in Cleveland, Ohio. The company has more than 2,500 employees across three business segments with operating service centers and major office locations in North America, Europe, and Asia. Materion serves a worldwide customer base in the consumer electronics, industrial, medical, automotive electronics, defense/aerospace, and energy markets. Through several business acquisitions, the company has expanded its service offerings and client base. Unfortunately, this expansion also created the need to integrate numerous legacy CRM systems.

Legacy systems are older, sometimes outdated, systems that companies use for several reasons. Some use them because they are tested, tried, and they know exactly what to expect from the system. Others keep them because it is too expensive to transition to something new, the legacy system is part of the culture, or there isn't a better solution. Sometimes, companies have legacy systems simply because they acquired them with business mergers or purchases. This was the case with Materion.

The result was different processes and misalignment within the sales division, data access issues, multiple data sources, data inconsistency, and slow system operations (60 minutes to create a call report in the old CRM systems). In addition, employees could not access company data on their mobile devices due to the lack of a single, updated platform. Roughly 65 percent of Materion's sales team was based outside the United States, and only 50 percent of the global sales team was even using the old CRM systems. Moreover, the company did not have any leads or new business opportunities tracked in its old CRM systems. In short, while Materion benefitted by adding service offerings and expanding its client base, its information systems suffered.

The IT Solution

Jason Maher, Vice President of Sales, explained, "SugarCRM was the platform we selected [because] it had it all." Sugar offers a cloud-based system, which was a major benefit given the global nature of the salesforce. In addition, the platform (1) provided leads and new business opportunities, (2) linked to the firm's supply chain, (3) offered dashboards so employees could quickly and visually understand current trends, and (4) combined all of the company's legacy systems on one platform.

In March 2015, Materion began to implement SugarCRM. Maher then scheduled a global sales meeting for September for the purpose of training the sales team in the new solution. Materion contracted with Highland Solutions to plan and implement a customized, user-friendly CRM solution utilizing the SugarCRM platform in six months.

Highland Solutions provides CRM technology design and implementation; product and service design; and custom Web and mobile software. Although a relatively small operation, Highland's experience in CRM implementation made them the best choice for Materion. Highland was tasked with creating cross-departmental visibility and process alignment across Materion's multiple business units. Because one of Materion's platforms was SAP (an industry leader in Enterprise Resource Planning Systems), SugarCRM's SAP integration would become the single source for all data points and would provide real-time updating and mobile accessibility.

Results

This solution empowered Materion's salesforce with SugarCRM mobile functionality. In addition, it created a reporting platform that was easy to use (and useful) and that the salesforce actually used. The time required to log a call report was reduced from 60 to 20 minutes, and more than 6,000 hours of sales representatives' time that previously was spent on administrative tasks were recovered. Additionally, SugarCRM provided access to new analytics regarding sales activities and outcomes that were previously inaccessible. Only 50 percent of Materion's sales reps used the firm's previous CRM system. After Materion implemented its new CRM solution, 100 percent of its sales reps use it to make and log sales calls. In addition, for the first time, the company began to track all sales leads, and it was able to measure the outcomes of their marketing initiatives.

SugarCRM has enabled a truly strategic shift in Materion's sales and operations. This transition has unlocked key sales data, enabled employees to access data on mobile devices, and placed a user-friendly, fully adopted, and centralized CRM in the hands of the organization. According to Maher: "All of this has made us a measurably more efficient and results-focused sales and marketing organization." In 2018, Materion reported total revenue of $1.2 billion, an increase of 9 percent over 2017, and operating profit of $66 million, an increase of 39 percent over 2017.

Sources: Compiled from T. Groenfeldt, "Banks Up Their Game On Digital, But Is It Enough?" *Forbes*, November 27, 2017; J. Brown, "How One Company Stuck to its Legacy System Without Employees to Support it," *CIO Dive*, January 19, 2017; J. Keane, "Report Says Hackers Have Easy Access to Flight Bookings Due to Legacy Systems," *Digital Trends*, January 3, 2017; P. Varshney, "How Selection of Right CRM Can Fuel Your Business Process – Materion Chooses Sugar for Global CRM Rollout, Achieves Strong Adoption with Innovation," linked.com/pulse, September 25, 2016; A. Schneider, "Are Legacy Systems Keeping You Prisoner," *Information Week*, December 12, 2013; J. Lamb, "Legacy Systems Continue to have a Place in the Enterprise," *Computer Weekly*, June 2008; http://www.4-traders.com/MATERION-CORP-7544795/news/Materion-SugarCRM-Sales-to-Large-Businesses-Drive-Strong-Second-Quarter-Growth-20988603/; https://www.highlandsolutions.com/about; https://community.sugarcrm.com/videos/1192; and www.materion.com, accessed July 17, 2019.

Questions

1. What are the disadvantages of quickly acquiring other businesses?

2. In this case, the adoption rate of Materion's CRM increased from 50 percent to 100 percent. Ideally, every company would have a 100 percent adoption rate. What do you think is an acceptable rate? Why?

3. What was the biggest advantage that SugarCRM brought to Materion? Explain your answer.

Social CRM

Social CRM is the use of social media technology and services to enable organizations to engage their customers in a collaborative conversation in order to provide mutually beneficial value in a trusted and transparent manner. Social CRM is the company's response to the customers' ownership of this two-way conversation. In social CRM, organizations monitor services such as Facebook, Twitter, and LinkedIn (among many others) for relevant mentions of their products, services, and brand, and they respond accordingly.

A critical component of social media is user reviews and recommendations. IT's About Business 11.3 shows how social CRM contributes to the success of Black Diamond.

Social media are also providing methods that customers are using to obtain faster, better customer service. Morton's Steakhouse certainly put social media to good use in surprising a customer.

MKT A corporate manager was in meetings all day, and he had to take a later flight home that caused him to miss his dinner. So, he jokingly tweeted Morton's Steakhouse (**www.mortons.com**) and requested that the restaurant show up with a steak when he landed.

Morton's saw the Tweet, discovered that the tweeter was a frequent customer (and frequent tweeter—he had 100,000 Twitter followers), pulled data on what he typically ordered, identified the flight he was on, and then sent a delivery person to Newark Airport (New Jersey) to serve him his dinner. When he got to the reception lobby at the airport, he noticed a man in a tuxedo holding a card with his name. The man was also carrying a bag that contained a Porterhouse steak, shrimp, potatoes, bread, two napkins, and silverware.

The nearest Morton's restaurant was 24 miles from the airport, and the manager's flight took only two hours. This scenario says a lot about both Morton's customer service and the

IT's About Business 11.3

MKT Black Diamond

The Problem

Black Diamond (**www.blackdiamondequipment.com**) is a manufacturer of climbing, skiing, and hiking products. Based in Holladay, Utah, the firm maintains global offices in Switzerland and China. It was founded in 1989 through an employee purchase of bankrupt Chouinard Equipment. These employees loved the company, the product, and believed in its future. Chouinard Equipment was founded in 1957 when Yvon Chouinard began to design, manufacture, and market climbing equipment. As a climbing enthusiast, he naturally hired likeminded employees, and their equipment quickly became known for its innovative designs and quality.

The company's focus on innovation and quality climbing gear has never changed, even with a change in ownership. They are known in the industry for being an environmental and customer-minded company. However, the way people interact with the company has changed. Like all other companies, Black Diamond Equipment has moved a significant part of their retail business online. Although they still maintain a physical presence and have a strong dealer/distributor network, they also focus on providing a positive online user experience.

User reviews and website recommendations have become a key element of the online shopping experience. Black Diamond had a loyal following; however, they had to enter their reviews and recommendations manually onto their website. This system did not allow for a personalized shopping experience or much flexibility. Adam Smart, Senior Web Merchant for Black Diamond, asserted, "We were very eager to get away from manually loading on-site recommendations." This was a time-consuming activity that could not be kept up-to-date in real time.

The IT Solution

A *recommendation engine* (or a *recommender system*) is a tool that uses mathematical algorithms to predict what users will or will not like. It uses data from customers, purchase history, likes, dislikes, similarities, differences, and much more to create recommendations and to propose the right method and timing to present an advertisement. Many large companies such as Facebook, Amazon, Google, and YouTube utilize recommendations. You would recognize these as the "Other customers purchased this" or the "We thought you would enjoy this video" types of comments. They are currently implemented in many industries, ranging from wine to whiskey to selecting the next video you will watch!

Black Diamond, a long-time salesforce.com user, was eager to implement a solution to be able to make these recommendations to customers. There was not one available with their current CRM provider, salesforce.com, so they decided it was better to implement a third-party recommendations engine that would allow them to begin using a recommender engine.

Then in 2016, Salesforce announced that they would offer an artificial intelligence (AI) add-on to the Commerce Cloud that Black Diamond was using that would provide an integrated recommendation engine. This add-on, called Salesforce Einstein, is intended to enable businesses to leverage AI built right into their CRM to provide deep data analytics that help to drive many organizational decisions, including the decision of what products to recommend to customers based on a historical analysis of the data.

Black Diamond was very excited about this new opportunity to use the AI add-on in salesforce, but they had just implemented the third-party recommender engine and did not want to make another tech change without evidence that the change was necessary.

They decided to implement Salesforce Einstein on a trial basis and run the two recommender engines (the third-party solution and Salesforce Einstein) side-by-side and compare the results.

The Results

The integrated solution of Salesforce Einstein with the existing Commerce Cloud implementation was a clear winner. Not only was the recommendation process automated but it also functioned in real time, it was customized for each customer based on preferences, and it provided invaluable insights into user actions based on the recommendations. While Black Diamond did not report their numbers before the trial started, they did report an increase in both conversion rate (9.6 percent) and in revenue per visitor (15.5 percent). Ultimately, Black Diamond found the Salesforce Einstein solution to be both more effective and more financially viable than the third-party option. As a result, it decided to proceed with a full implementation of the Salesforce Einstein AI product.

Sources: Compiled from R. Desisto, "How IT's New Role in AI Can Help Transform Customer Experiences," salesforce.com/blog, September 11, 2017; J. Sinai, "An MIT Tech Review Study on Salesforce: AI Meets CRM," *MIT Technology Review*, July 26, 2017; SGB Media, "Black Diamond Beefs Up Marketing And Operations Teams," sgbonline.com, May 3, 2017; L. Chang, "Your Own Personal Sommelier: Vivino Market Gives Personalized Wine Recommendations," *Digital Trends*, March 23, 2017; H. Grigonis, "Pinterest Buys Up Jelly, A Small Search Engine Powered By Real People," *Digital Trends*, March 9, 2017; M. Whittaker, "Shrinking Pains: Black Diamond Equipment's Return to Its Roots Has Been a Bumpy Ride," snewsnet.com, June 10, 2016; A. Couts, "Meet Distiller, your personal whiskey recommendation engine," *Digital Trends*, December 11, 2013; H. Shaughnessy, "How the $1 Million Netflix Prize Spurred a Radical Innovation, Accidentally," *Forbes*, June 28, 2011; M. Ridwan, "Predicting Likes: Inside a Simple Recommendation Engine's Algorithms," www.toptal.com, accessed December 8, 2017; http://www.fundinguniverse.com/company-histories/black-diamond-equipment-ltd-history/, accessed December 12, 2017; http://www.nasdaq.com/markets/spos/company/black-diamond-equipment-ltd-352215-83960, accessed December 4, 2017; https://www.blackdiamondequipment.com/en_US/about-us.html, accessed December 4, 2017; https://www.demandware.com/uploads/resources/CS_Black_Diamond_Case_Study_EN_INIT_08MARCH2017.pdf, accessed November 15, 2017; and www.blackdiamondequipment.com, accessed July 17, 2019.

Questions

1. What problems are associated with manually entering product recommendations?

2. Discuss the advantages and disadvantages of utilizing a third-party recommendation engine.

3. What was the key factor that helped Salesforce be a clear winner in implementing a recommendation engine?

speed of social media. Admittedly, the entire scenario was a publicity stunt that went explosively viral over the Internet. This is not the point, however. The questions that businesses should be asking themselves are: Would your company even consider doing something like this? If not, why not?

Real-Time CRM

Organizations are implementing real-time customer relationship management to provide a superior level of customer satisfaction for today's always-on, always-connected, more knowledgeable, and less loyal customers. **Real-time CRM systems** help organizations to respond to customer product searches, requests, complaints, comments, ratings, reviews, and recommendations in near real time, 24/7/365. Southwest Airlines provides an excellent example of real-time CRM.

POM **MKT** A passenger was in her seat on a Southwest Airlines flight about to take off, when the plane turned back to the gate. A flight attendant asked her to get off the plane. When she checked with the Southwest agent at the desk inside the terminal, he told her that her son was in a coma after suffering a head injury and to call her husband.

Even before she had disembarked, Southwest had rebooked her on the next nonstop flight to her son's city—free of charge. The airline offered her a private waiting area, rerouted her luggage, allowed her to board first, and packed a lunch for her. Moreover, the airline delivered her luggage to where she was going to stay and called her to ask about her son. The woman said that her son was recovering and that she could not be more grateful for the way she was treated.

Southwest Airlines went above and beyond their responsibilities after they learned of the son's accident. Details were not available about how the airline learned of the son's accident, but it is clear that Southwest brought customer relationship management to a new level.

Before you go on . . .

1. Describe on-demand CRM.
2. Describe mobile CRM.
3. Describe open-source CRM.
4. Describe social CRM.
5. Describe real-time CRM.

11.4 Supply Chains

Modern organizations are increasingly concentrating on their core competencies and on becoming more flexible and agile. To accomplish these objectives, they rely on other companies rather than on companies they themselves own, to supply the goods and services they need. Organizations recognize that these suppliers can perform these activities more efficiently and effectively than they themselves can. This trend toward relying on an increasing number of suppliers has led to the concept of supply chains. A **supply chain** is the flow of materials, information, money, and services from raw material suppliers, through factories and warehouses, to the end customers. A supply chain also includes the *organizations* and *processes* that create and deliver products, information, and services to the end customers.

Supply chains enhance trust and collaboration among supply chain partners, thus improving supply chain visibility and inventory velocity. **Supply chain visibility** refers to the ability of all organizations within a supply chain to access or view relevant data on purchased materials as these materials move through their suppliers' production processes and transportation networks to their receiving docks. Organizations can also access or view relevant data on outbound

Author Lecture Videos are available exclusively in *WileyPLUS*.
Apply the Concept activities are available in the Appendix and in *WileyPLUS*.

goods as they are manufactured, assembled, or stored in inventory and then shipped through their transportation networks to their customers' receiving docks. The more quickly a company can deliver products and services after receiving the materials required to make them—that is, the higher the *inventory velocity*—the more satisfied the company's customers will be. In addition, supply chain visibility promotes quick responses to problems or changes along the supply chain by enabling companies to shift products to where they are needed.

Supply chain information has historically been obtained by manual, labor-based tracking and monitoring, but is now increasingly being generated by sensors, RFID tags, meters, GPS, and other devices and systems. How does this transformation affect supply chain managers? For one thing, they now have real-time information on all products moving through their supply chains. Supply chains will therefore rely less on labor-based tracking and monitoring, because the new technology will allow shipping containers, trucks, products, and parts to report on their own status. The overall result is a vast improvement in supply chain visibility.

Supply chains are a vital component of the overall strategies of many modern organizations. To use supply chains efficiently, a business must be tightly integrated with its suppliers, business partners, distributors, and customers. A critical component of this integration is the use of information systems to facilitate the exchange of information among the participants in the supply chain.

The Structure and Components of Supply Chains

POM The term *supply chain* comes from a picture of how the partnering organizations are linked. **Figure 11.4** illustrates a typical supply chain. (Recall that Figure 1.5 also illustrated a supply chain, in a slightly different way.) Note that the supply chain involves three segments:

1. *Upstream*, where sourcing or procurement from external suppliers occurs.

   In this segment, supply chain managers select suppliers to deliver the goods and services the company needs to produce its product or service. Furthermore, SC managers develop the pricing, delivery, and payment processes between a company and its suppliers. Included here are processes for managing inventory, receiving and verifying shipments, transferring goods to manufacturing facilities, and authorizing payments to suppliers.

2. *Internal*, where packaging, assembly, or manufacturing takes place.

   SC managers schedule the activities necessary for production, testing, packaging, and preparing goods for delivery. They also monitor quality levels, production output, and worker productivity.

3. *Downstream*, where distribution takes place, frequently by external distributors.

   In this segment, SC managers coordinate the receipt of orders from customers, develop a network of warehouses, select carriers to deliver products to customers, and implement invoicing systems to receive payments from customers.

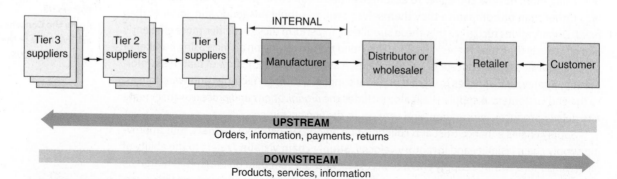

FIGURE 11.4   **Generic supply chain.**

The flow of information and goods can be bidirectional. For example, damaged or unwanted products can be returned, a process known as *reverse flows* or *reverse logistics*. In the retail clothing industry, for example, reverse logistics involves clothing that customers return, either because the item had defects or because the customer did not like the item.

Tiers of Suppliers.   Figure 11.4 shows several tiers of suppliers. As the diagram indicates, a supplier may have one or more subsuppliers, a subsupplier may have its own subsupplier(s), and so on. For an automobile manufacturer, for example, Tier 3 suppliers produce basic products such as glass, plastic, and rubber; Tier 2 suppliers use these inputs to make windshields, tires, and plastic moldings; and Tier 1 suppliers produce integrated components such as dashboards and seat assemblies.

The Flows in the Supply Chain.   There are typically three flows in the supply chain: material, information, and financial. *Material flows* are the physical products, raw materials, and supplies that flow along the chain. Material flows also include the reverse flows discussed earlier. A supply chain thus involves a *product life cycle* approach, from "dirt to dust."

Information flows consist of data related to demand, shipments, orders, returns, and schedules, as well as changes in any of these data. Finally, *financial flows* involve money transfers, payments, credit card information and authorization, payment schedules, e-payments, and credit-related data.

Significantly, different supply chains have different numbers and types of flows. For example, in service industries, there may be no physical flow of materials, but there is frequently a flow of information, often in the form of documents (physical or electronic copies). For example, the digitization of software, music, and other content can create a supply chain without any physical flow. Notice, however, that in such a case there are two types of information flows: one that replaces materials flow (digitized software), and another that provides the supporting information (e.g., orders and billing). To manage the supply chain, an organization must coordinate all three flows among all of the parties involved in the chain, a topic we turn to next.

Before you go on . . .

1. What is a supply chain?
2. Describe the three segments of a supply chain.
3. Describe the flows in a supply chain.

11.5 Supply Chain Management

The function of **supply chain management (SCM)** is to improve the processes a company uses to acquire the raw materials it needs to produce a product or service and then deliver that product or service to its customers. That is, supply chain management is the process of planning, organizing, and optimizing the various activities performed along the supply chain. There are five basic components of SCM:

1. *Plan:* Planning is the strategic component of SCM. Organizations must have a strategy for managing all the resources that are involved in meeting customer demand for their product or service. Planning involves developing a set of metrics (measurable deliverables) to monitor the organization's supply chain to ensure that it is efficient and it delivers high quality and value to customers for the lowest cost.
2. *Source:* In the sourcing component, organizations choose suppliers to deliver the goods and services they need to create their product or service. Supply chain managers develop

Author Lecture Videos are available exclusively in *WileyPLUS*.
Apply the Concept activities are available in the Appendix and in *WileyPLUS*.

pricing, delivery, and payment processes with suppliers, and they create metrics to monitor and improve their relationships with their suppliers. They also develop processes for managing their goods and services inventory, including receiving and verifying shipments, transferring the shipped materials to manufacturing facilities, and authorizing supplier payments.

3. *Make:* This is the manufacturing component. Supply chain managers schedule the activities necessary for production, testing, packaging, and preparation for delivery. This component is the most metric-intensive part of the supply chain, in which organizations measure quality levels, production output, and worker productivity.

4. *Deliver:* This component, often referred to as logistics, is in the organizations that coordinate the receipt of customer orders, develop a network of warehouses, select carriers to transport their products to their customers, and create an invoicing system to receive payments.

5. *Return:* Supply chain managers must create a responsive and flexible network for receiving defective, returned, or excess products back from their customers, as well as for supporting customers who have problems with delivered products.

Like other functional areas, SCM uses information systems. The goal of SCM systems is to reduce the problems, or friction, along the supply chain. Friction can increase time, costs, and inventories and decrease customer satisfaction. SCM systems, therefore, reduce uncertainty and risks by decreasing inventory levels and cycle time while improving business processes and customer service. These benefits make the organization more profitable and competitive.

POM Supply chains also lead to increased sales and profits. Consider Adidas (**www. adidas.com**), the leading sports shoe brand in Russia, with more than 1,200 stores in that country. As part of its strategy to optimize the customer experience, Adidas built the supply chain infrastructure needed to enable initiatives such as RFID chips (see Chapter 8), ship from store, click and collect, and endless aisle.

- *Ship from store:* Goods ordered online are delivered from a physical store.
- *Click and collect:* Customers buy products online and collect the products at a physical store or warehouse. By October 2018, some 70 percent of Adidas online sales were through click and collect.
- *Endless aisle:* Using in-store kiosks, customers can order products not in stock in their local store but available in another store. Products are then delivered using the ship-from-store process or click-and-collect process.

Russia is, physically, the largest country in the world. Shipping goods from one end of Russia to the other can take up to 15 days using traditional delivery systems. With its three supply chain initiatives, Adidas reduced delivery times and costs, while increasing sales and profits. Here is the reason why. Consumers typically return 50 percent of the products they buy online if delivery is made within 24 hours. However, if delivery takes 3 days, consumers may return 70 percent of products. Therefore, because these three processes increase the speed of delivery, customers return fewer goods, which leads to higher completed sales and increased profits.

Significantly, SCM systems are a type of interorganizational information system. In an **interorganizational information system (IOS)**, information flows among two or more organizations. By connecting the IS of business partners, IOSs enable the partners to perform a number of tasks:

- Reduce the costs of routine business transactions.
- Improve the quality of the information flow by reducing or eliminating errors.
- Compress the cycle time involved in fulfilling business transactions.
- Eliminate paper processing and its associated inefficiencies and costs.
- Make the transfer and processing of information easier for users.

The Push Model Versus the Pull Model

Many SCM systems employ the **push model**. In this model, also known as *make-to-stock*, the production process begins with a forecast, which is simply an educated guess as to customer demand. The forecast must predict which products customers will want and in what quantities. The company then produces the amount of products in the forecast, typically by using mass production, and sells, or "pushes," those products to consumers.

Unfortunately, these forecasts are often incorrect. Consider, for example, an automobile manufacturer that wants to produce a new car. Marketing managers conduct extensive research, including customer surveys and analyses of competitors' cars, and then provide the results to forecasters. If the forecasters' predictions are too high—that is, if they predict that customers will purchase a certain number of these new cars but actual demand falls below this amount—then the automaker has excess cars in inventory and will incur large carrying costs (the costs of storing unsold inventory). Furthermore, the company will probably have to sell the excess cars at a discount.

From the opposite perspective, if the forecasters' predictions are too low—that is, actual customer demand exceeds expectations—then the automaker probably will have to run extra shifts to meet the demand, thereby incurring substantial overtime costs. Furthermore, the company risks losing business to its competitors if the car that customers want is not available. Thus, using the push model in supply chain management can cause problems, as you will see in the next section.

To avoid the uncertainties associated with the push model, many companies now employ the pull model of supply chain management, using Web-enabled information flows. In the **pull model**, also known as *make-to-order*, the production process begins with a customer order. Therefore, companies make only what customers want, a process closely aligned with mass customization (discussed in Chapter 1).

POM A prominent example of a company that uses the pull model is Dell Computer. Dell's production process begins with a customer order. This order not only specifies the type of computer the customer wants but also alerts each Dell supplier as to the parts of the order for which that supplier is responsible. That way, Dell's suppliers ship only the parts that Dell needs to produce the computer.

Not all companies can use the pull model. Automobiles, for example, are far more complicated and more expensive to manufacture than computers, so automobile companies require longer lead times to produce new models. Automobile companies do use the pull model, but only for specific automobiles that some customers order (e.g., Rolls-Royce, Bentley, and other extremely expensive cars).

IT's About Business 11.4 shows Zara's retail industry supply chain, how the retailer manages its supply chain, and how Zara uses both the pull model and the push model in its supply chain. These factors are all contributing to the outstanding success of the company and its business model.

IT's About Business 11.4

MKT **POM** Zara

Inditex (**www.inditex.com**) is the world's largest fashion group, operating more than 7,200 stores in 93 markets worldwide. The company's flagship store is Zara (**www.zara.com**), but it also owns the chains Zara Home, Massimo Dutti, Bershka, Oysho, Pull and Bear, Stradivarius, and Uterque. Zara (**www.zara.com**), founded in Spain in 1975, operates more than 2,100 stores worldwide. Inditex reported sales of approximately $30 billion in 2018.

Zara is a clothing and fashion retailer that is using its supply chain to significantly change the way it operates in a traditional industry. Zara's core market is women between the ages of 24 and 35. The firm reaches these consumers by locating its stores in town centers and locations with high concentrations of women in this age range.

MKT Zara's business model

Traditional fashion brands employ the business model of *seasonal fashion*. With seasonal fashion, brands design and manufacture the majority of their inventory before the beginning of each year's fashion seasons, allowing no design improvements or changes during the season. (The two major annual fashion seasons are Spring/Summer and Fall/Winter.) Traditional brands reserve 80 percent of their inventory for seasonal fashion clothing, meaning that they commit to manufacturing their inventory at least six months before the beginning of the next season.

In contrast, Zara devotes about 75 percent of its production to its *fast fashion* clothing lines and the remainder of its production for its seasonal lines. Zara stores respond in near real time as customer preferences evolve. As a result, Zara's business model is a good fit for the rapidly changing, unpredictable fashion industry. This model enables Zara to manufacture its fast fashion clothing based on highly accurate, short-term (2–6 weeks) demand forecasts.

Zara's supply chain and its highly automated distribution center, called the Cube, are essential to its successful business model. The Cube, located in Arteixo, Spain, is Zara's center of worldwide operations. The 5-million-square-foot, highly automated facility is connected to 11 Zara-owned factories with high-speed, underground monorail links.

We discuss Zara's fast fashion business model in this case. To produce fast fashion clothing, Zara employs three essential phases in its supply chain: procurement, production, and distribution. Let's look at each phase in turn.

POM Procurement

Because traditional brands devote 80 percent of their inventory to seasonal fashion, they must make early forecasts of the number of clothing items that they manufacture. In contrast, Zara does not forecast the number of finished goods that it will need. Rather, its procurement team forecasts the quantity of *fabric* that Zara will need to manufacture clothes before placing orders with the firm's fabric suppliers.

Zara buys large quantities of only four or five types of fabric per year. The retailer can also change these fabrics from year to year. Fabric manufacturers make rapid deliveries of bulk quantities directly to the Cube. Zara purchases raw fabric from suppliers in Italy, Spain, Portugal, and Greece. Its suppliers deliver fabric, primarily by truck, within five days of orders being placed.

Unlike finished goods, fabric does not go to waste because it can be used to make new clothes. The availability of fabric allows Zara to respond in near real time to its customer demands and to changes in fashion trends.

Zara is able to keep its prices low because it does not place a premium on fabric quality. Traditional fashion brands emphasize the quality and origin of the textiles they use. In contrast, Zara buys fabric from suppliers who sell textiles inexpensively.

POM Production

Zara's competitive advantage lies in quickly identifying the latest fashion trends. At the Cube, market specialists, many of whom previously worked as store managers, monitor all communications from Zara store managers. These managers are trained specifically to engage customers to obtain their reactions to the clothes on display. The managers then send sales figures and customer feedback to the market specialists on a daily basis. The specialists also receive fashion input from a large number of fashion observers who attend fashion shows and pay attention to what types of fashions traditional brands and traditional designers are producing.

The marketing specialists convey this information to the design and production teams. The design team develops fashion designs in accordance with this information. After the designs are approved, they are given to the production team.

Most traditional fashion brands outsource their manufacturing to China and parts of Southeast Asia and the Far East. In contrast, Zara manufactures all of its fast fashion clothing in the 11 plants located close to the Cube. Once the fabric is cut and colored inside the Cube, Zara ships it to its 11 factories on its monorail.

A fascinating fact about Zara's manufacturing process is that at any day or time of the year, a majority of the firm's factories can possibly be idle. The reason is that, with fast fashion, two factors are critical: time and changes in demand.

For example, consider a drop in demand that reflects the declining popularity of a particular design. This drop triggers a response from the teams in the Cube, which can either be a change in or a complete overhaul of the design. To maintain its rapid turnaround time, which is typically two weeks, Zara must deploy its resources immediately. The retailer cannot afford any delays because one of its factories was busy.

In the fashion industry, *turnaround time* is the time that it takes for a current fashion collection to be replaced by a new one. For traditional fashion brands, the turnaround time is between three and six months.

Zara realized that there is a direct relationship between the degree to which it utilizes the capacity of its factories and the length of the factories' turnaround times—that is, the busier a factory is, the longer it would take to manufacture a fast fashion item. Therefore, Zara keeps most of its manufacturing capacity idle so it can respond to demand changes with more agility than its competitors.

POM Distribution

Once the factories turn the fabric into finished clothes, the items are transported back to the Cube on the monorail. At the Cube, the clothing is inspected, packed, and shipped to the Zara logistics hub in Zaragoza. From there, the items are delivered to stores around the world by truck and plane. Zara can deliver garments to stores worldwide in only a few days: China in 48 hours, Europe in 24 hours, Japan in 72 hours, and the United States in 48 hours.

Stores take deliveries twice per week, and they often receive inventory within two days after placing their orders. Items are shipped and arrive at stores already on hangers with tags and prices on them. Therefore, items come off delivery trucks and go directly to the sales floor.

Problems

In March 2017, Inditex stated that its profitability had decreased to an eight-year low. At the same time, major rival Hennes & Mauritz (H&M; www.hm.com), the world's second-largest fashion company, announced its first monthly sales drop in four years. These reports illustrate the difficulties facing the fashion industry as consumers purchase more of their clothing from an increasing number of online suppliers.

In an effort to be more competitive with Zara, in April 2017, H&M stated that it would significantly increase its supply chain investments, including, among other things, greater levels of automation. The company also planned to optimize its lead times and to move more production to Europe from Asia.

Compounding Zara's problems, shoppers in Istanbul have found tags on their Zara garments with complaints from Turkish workers who claim they have not been paid for their work. The tags assert that the workers were employed by Bravo, a manufacturer to which Zara outsourced some production. Bravo closed down abruptly, and workers maintain the company owes them three months of pay as well as a severance allowance.

Zara has had other problems with traditional fashion brands as well as with independent designers. For instance, in 2012, luxury brand Christian Louboutin (www.christianlouboutin.com) took legal action against Zara for allegedly imitating one of its shoe designs and then selling the shoes at half the price. Although the case was dismissed, fashion journalists speculated that Zara manages to keep out of trouble by changing its designs just enough to avoid copyright violations.

The Results

Short production runs, meaning that Zara produces relatively few items of a given design, create a perceived scarcity of these designs. This process generates a sense of urgency among customers and a reason to buy because items can sell out quickly. As a result, Zara does not have a great deal of excess inventory, nor does it need large markdowns on its clothing items. Zara's annual rate of unsold inventory is 10 percent, compared to industry averages of 17–20 percent. Furthermore, Zara has 12 inventory turns per year, compared to 3–4 turns for its competitors.

Zara prices its clothing items based on market demand, not on the cost of manufacture. The short lead times for delivery of unique fashion items combined with short production runs enable Zara to offer customers more styles and choices. Furthermore, a particular item or style may not be available again after it sells out. Significantly, Zara launches 12,000 new designs each year. In contrast, its competitors carry 2,000–4,000 items. Furthermore, Zara changes its clothing designs every two weeks on average, compared to every two or three months for its competitors. Significantly, the retailer sells 85 percent of its items at full price, which is significantly higher than the industry average of 60 percent.

Increased Competition

Inditex is developing new technologies to compete with newer, online-only companies such as Boohoo (**www.boohoo.com**) and Missguided (**www.missguided.com**). The two companies, both founded in England, are producing clothes at higher speeds than Zara, often in one week from design to point of sale. They also refresh their websites daily with hundreds of new items.

To compete with these start-ups, Inditex has formed an innovation unit that is testing many new technologies:

- Inditex is testing robots from Fetch Robotics (**www.fetchrobotics.com**) to work in stock inventory.
- Inditex is testing technologies that emphasize an asset that its rivals lack, physical stores. For example, it is testing *location intelligence*, which uses ultrasound technology to track the sounds of customers' steps in stores. In that way, stores can map traffic patterns and place best-selling items appropriately. Location intelligence also allows apps to switch to in-store mode when a customer enters a store, so he or she can locate products and receive offers.
- Inditex has formed partnerships with Jetlore (**www.jetlore.com**), which uses artificial intelligence to predict customer behavior, and Spanish Big Data start-up, El Arte de Medir (**www.elartedemedir.com**).

Sources: Compiled from M. Hanbury, "The Biggest Difference between Zara and H&M Explains Why One Is Thriving While the Other Is Flailing," *Business Insider*, June 21, 2018; "Zara Looks to Technology to Keep Up with Faster Fashion," Reuters, June 15, 2018; D. Buchanan, "The Zara Workers' Protest Shows Why Fast Fashion Should Worry All of Us," *The Guardian*, November 8, 2017; Z. Wood, "Zara's UK Profits Drop Sharply Despite Record Sales," *The Guardian*, October 13, 2017; "Zara Owner Inditex Sees Profit Growth of 9% in the First Half," Reuters, September 20, 2017; "Push vs. Pull Supply Chains: Why Profitable Companies Value Data over Inventory," *Sourcing Journal*, September 1, 2017; J. Neumann, "How Zara Is Defying a Broad Retail Slump," *Wall Street Journal*, June 14, 2017; S. Sit, "H&M Overhauls Supply Chain to Compete with Zara," CIPS.org, April 3, 2017; L. Heller, "Why Zara Is the Most Exciting Retailer Today," *Forbes*, March 15, 2017; P. Jarvis, "Fast Fashion Fading as H&M, Zara Shine Light on Industry Strains," *Bloomberg*, March 15, 2017; A. Lutz, "This Clothing Company Whose CEO Is Richer than Warren Buffett Is Blowing the Competition out of the Water," *Business Insider*, June 13, 2017; S. Baker, "Zara's Recipe for Success: More Data, Fewer Bosses," *Bloomberg BusinessWeek*, November 22, 2016; "4 Key Facts about Zara's Supply Chain Success," *CeMAT Insider*, November 11, 2016; N. Narang, "Fashion Disrupted: The Definitive Guide to Zara's Global Supply Chain," *Procurify*, October 24, 2016; M. Schlossberg, "While the Rest of the Industry Struggles, This Store Has Created the 'Best Business Model in Apparel' – and Millenials Are Flocking to It," *Business Insider*, June 16, 2016; K. Gorrepati, "Zara's Agile Supply Chain Is the Source of Its Competitive Advantage," *Digitalist Magazine*, March 30, 2016; K. O'Marah, "Zara Uses Supply Chain to Win Again," *Forbes*, March 9, 2016; W. Loeb, "Zara's Secret to Success: The New Science of Retailing," *Forbes*, October 14, 2013; S. Stevenson, "Polka Dots Are In? Polka Dots It Is!" *Slate*, June 21, 2012; and www.zara.com, accessed July 17, 2019.

Questions

1. Discuss how Zara uses both the pull model and the push model in its business model. Use specific examples to support your answer.

2. Provide specific examples of how Zara uses the pull model in its supply chain and specific examples of how Zara uses the push model in its supply chain.

Problems Along the Supply Chain

As you saw earlier, friction can develop within a supply chain. One major consequence of friction is poor customer service. In some cases, supply chains do not deliver products or services when and where customers—either individuals or businesses—need them. In other cases, the supply chain provides poor-quality products. Other problems associated with supply chain friction are high inventory costs and revenue loss.

The problems along the supply chain arise primarily from two sources: (1) uncertainties and (2) the need to coordinate multiple activities, internal units, and business partners. A major source of supply chain uncertainties is the *demand forecast*. Demand for a product can be influenced by numerous factors such as competition, price, weather conditions, technological developments, overall economic conditions, and customers' general confidence. Another uncertainty is delivery times, which can be affected by numerous factors ranging from production machine failures to road construction and traffic jams. Quality problems in materials and parts can also create production delays, which also generate supply chain problems.

FIGURE 11.5 The bullwhip effect.

One major challenge that managers face in setting accurate inventory levels throughout the supply chain is known as the bullwhip effect. The **bullwhip effect** refers to erratic shifts in orders up and down the supply chain (see **Figure 11.5**). Basically, the variables that affect customer demand can become magnified when they are viewed through the eyes of managers at each link in the supply chain. If each distinct entity that makes ordering and inventory decisions places its interests above those of the chain, then stockpiling can occur at as many as seven or eight locations along the chain. Research has shown that in some cases, such hoarding has led to as much as a 100-day supply of inventory that is waiting "just in case," versus the 10- to 20-day supply manufacturers normally keep on hand. As you see in IT's About Business 11.5, Flexe's business model is able to assist organizations with demand forecast and with problems related to the bullwhip effect.

IT's About Business 11.5

POM Flexe, the Airbnb of Warehousing

Online retailers are rapidly adopting a supply chain strategy of opening geographically dispersed brick-and-mortar warehouses so that they can deliver orders to customers in one day or less. In fact, if a company wants to sell a product and deliver it the next day, they would need 16 warehouses spread across the country in order to reach 98 percent of the U.S. population.

Amazon's strategy does have problems. The electronic commerce giant tends to insist that customers order through its website, which enables the firm to collect customers' data. Amazon is also likely to brand the packages with its own logo, which irritates start-ups that are striving to build their own brands. Finally, Amazon is expanding its third-party fulfillment services, where it manages storage and delivery for retailers that sell goods in its online marketplace. These problems have led to a growth in supply chain services aimed at retailers who may not want to ship goods using Amazon.

Vacant U.S. warehouse space reached a 17-year low in 2017 because consumers were shopping online and merchants needed warehouse space located close to their customers in order to provide rapid delivery. Flexe (**www.flexe.com**) is a Seattle start-up that provides on-demand warehouse and fulfillment storage space. Flexe accesses an inventory of space that is tied up in long-term contracts but that may sit empty for months. For example, beverage and home improvement companies build warehouses with extra capacity for the summer, so they usually have leftover space. Similarly, Halloween costume wholesalers' warehouses empty out just as the Christmas shopping season arrives. Flexe manages this mismatch between supply and demand, taking an undisclosed commission on each transaction and paying part of its commission to the warehouse operator.

Flexe developed a software platform to facilitate the reliable supply-demand matching of warehouse space at transaction sizes that are too small to justify the attention of traditional warehouse operators. This strategy reflects successful start-ups in other areas: Uber developed its software platform for cars, Airbnb for lodging, Convoy (**www.convoy.com**) for trucks, and Instacart (**www.instacart.com**) for direct-to-consumer groceries.

Flexe connects approximately 1000 warehouse operators (its partners) with businesses in need of storage space (its clients). With its partners, the firm has established broader geographic coverage than the delivery network that Amazon has spent decades and billions of dollars to develop. As a result of Flexe's broad geographical coverage, merchants have inventory located close to their customers, and their packages can be delivered by truck rather than more expensively by air.

Flexe offers storage services on a pay-as-you-go basis, allowing its clients to expand or contract their investment in storage as needed. Merchants book storage space via a simple-to-navigate website.

Flexe does not negotiate shipping rates on behalf of its clients. Instead, clients have three options: (1) use their own shipping contracts, (2) use rates provided by the warehouse operators who pick and pack their orders, or (3) use Flexe's rates with carriers. Flexe is particularly valuable to start-ups because these businesses do not know how much space they will need because it is difficult for them to predict their sales a year or two into the future.

On May 15, 2017, Flexe began to offer online merchants overnight ground delivery to nearly everyone in the United States. This service is valuable to online merchants who are looking for new ways to reach customers but have few options that match Amazon's speed. It enables warehouse operators the option to charge more to pack and ship individual orders directly to shoppers' homes rather than to a store. Flexe notes that its customers can deliver goods to their customers as fast or faster than they can through Amazon Prime, at a competitive price. Furthermore, the delivery will arrive in their own branded boxes rather than in an Amazon box.

Flexe's appeal extends to brick-and-mortar retailers that are struggling to compete with Amazon online as well as to brands that are hesitant to work with such a giant retail competitor. Flexe targets manufacturers, brands, and retailers that want to compete with Amazon on delivery without giving up customer data. Flexe helps them to compete with Amazon on delivery without having to make huge investments in new facilities. Let's consider a few of Flexe's customers.

Iron Mountain (**www.ironmountain.com**), which provides document storage for financial, legal, health care, and government clients, signed on with Flexe in 2015 to sell extra space in its 1,000 facilities located in 90 markets. Solar panels, space heaters, sheets, pillows, mattresses, and many other products from various merchants have passed through its storage facilities without disrupting its main business.

Mattress seller Casper (**www.casper.com**) uses Flexe to meet demand during the summer moving season. The company prefers Flexe to Amazon because Amazon takes control of the customer experience. Casper's customers want to buy from Casper and not from Amazon.

Shoe and apparel brand Toms (**www.toms.com**) uses Flexe to expand its holiday season pop-up stores beyond the reach of its West Coast distribution network. A *pop-up store* is a small and temporary location that companies use to build interest in their product or service and engage their customers. They often utilize these stores for seasonal items such as Halloween costumes, Christmas gifts, Christmas trees, and fireworks. Flexe identified the best locations to help Toms serve three new markets. Toms plans its pop-up stores only a few weeks in advance, making it difficult to find warehouse space through traditional long-term leases.

Significantly, Flexe built its marketplace without spending any money on physical facilities. As of July 2019, the firm had some 30 million square feet of storage, about 20 percent of Amazon's capacity. However, Amazon is limited to 110 fulfillment centers in North America, while Flexe has access to more than 1,000 warehouses.

By July 2019, Flexe had more than 1000 partners. To prosper long term, the company will have to continue to expand its geographical footprint by convincing warehouse operators that they can accommodate other businesses on short-term intervals without disrupting their own businesses.

Sources: Compiled from T. Soper, "Why This Supply Chain Startup Is Drawing Comparisons to Amazon Web Services and Airbnb," *Geekwire*, July 3, 2019; K. Patrick, "Innovator of the Year: Flexe," *Supply Chain Dive*, December 4, 2017; S. Lacefield, "Going Direct: Manufacturers Set Their Sights on Direct-to-Consumer Delivery," *Supply Chain Quarterly*, July 4, 2017; K. O'Marah, "Uber Your Supply Chain," *Forbes*, May 18, 2017; "FLEXE's Next-Day Delivery to Help Online Retailers Compete with Amazon," PYMNTS.com, May 12, 2017; R. Sarver, "Leveling the Playing Field in E-Commerce," *Medium*, May 11, 2017; S. Soper, "This Startup Is the Airbnb of Warehouses and Has Amazon in Its Sights," *Bloomberg*, May 11, 2017; J. Smith, "Flexe to Offer Next-Day Delivery for Online Retailers," *Wall Street Journal*, May 11, 2017; N. Levy, "FLEXE Launches Nationwide Next-Day Delivery Service to Help E-Commerce Companies Take on Amazon," *GeekWire*, May 11, 2017; "FLEXE Launches Nationwide Next-Day Delivery," PRNewswire, May 11, 2017; M. O'Brien, "Flexe Offers Shippers Marketplace of Fulfillment Nodes," *Multichannel Merchant*, April 26, 2017; S. Banker, "An 'Outside In' View of Your Supply Chain," *Forbes*, April 20, 2017; "Llamasoft Offers Customers Access to FLEXE Marketplace for On-Demand Warehousing Services," *Business Wire*, March 28, 2017; P. Lantrip, "On-Demand Storage Offers Seasonal Space Relief," *Memphis Daily News*, November 30, 2016; "Logistics Startup: FLEXE and Pop-Up Warehousing," *Tech Gistics*, October 6, 2016; "Tech StartUps that Will Transform Warehousing," *Material Handling & Logistics*, September 1, 2016; and www.flexe.com, accessed July 17, 2019.

Questions

1. You are the CEO of Amazon. How would you compete with Flexe? Provide specific examples to support your answer.

2. Describe how information technology is essential to support Flexe's business model.

3. How does Flexe help retailers with demand forecast and bullwhip effect problems? Provide specific examples to support your answer.

Solutions to Supply Chain Problems

Supply chain problems can be very costly. Therefore, organizations are motivated to find innovative solutions. During the oil crises of the 1970s, for example, Ryder Systems, a large trucking company, purchased a refinery to control the upstream part of the supply chain and to ensure it had sufficient gasoline for its trucks. Ryder's decision to purchase a refinery is an example of vertical integration. **Vertical integration** is a business strategy in which a company purchases its upstream suppliers to ensure that its essential supplies are available as soon as the company needs them. Ryder later sold the refinery because it could not manage a business it did not understand and because oil became more plentiful.

Ryder's decision to vertically integrate was not the best method for managing its supply chain. In the remainder of this section, you will look at some other possible solutions to supply chain problems, many of which are supported by IT.

Using Inventories to Solve Supply Chain Problems.

Undoubtedly, the most common solution to supply chain problems is *building inventories* as insurance against supply chain uncertainties. As you have learned, holding either too much or too little inventory can be very costly. Thus, companies make major attempts to optimize and control inventories.

One widely used strategy to minimize inventories is the **just-in-time (JIT)** inventory system. Essentially, JIT systems deliver the precise number of parts, called *work-in-process* inventory, to be assembled into a finished product at precisely the right time.

Although JIT offers many benefits, it has certain drawbacks as well. To begin with, suppliers are expected to respond instantaneously to requests. As a result, they have to carry more inventory than they otherwise would. In this sense, JIT does not *eliminate* excess inventory; rather, it simply *shifts* it from the customer to the supplier. This process can still reduce the overall inventory size if the supplier can spread the increased inventory over several customers. However, that is not always possible.

JIT also replaces a few large supply shipments with a large number of smaller ones. In terms of transportation, then, the process is less efficient.

Information Sharing. Another common approach to solving supply chain problems, and especially to improving demand forecasts, is *sharing information* along the supply chain. Information sharing can be facilitated by electronic data interchange and extranets, topics you will learn about in the next section.

One notable example of information sharing occurs between large manufacturers and retailers. For example, Walmart provides Procter & Gamble with access to daily sales information from every store for every item that P&G makes for Walmart. This access enables P&G to manage the *inventory replenishment* for Walmart's stores. By monitoring inventory levels, P&G knows when inventories fall below the threshold for each product at any Walmart store. These data trigger an immediate shipment.

Information sharing between Walmart and P&G is executed automatically. It is part of a vendor-managed inventory strategy. **Vendor-managed inventory (VMI)** occurs when the supplier, rather than the retailer, manages the entire inventory process for a particular product or group of products. Significantly, P&G has similar agreements with other major retailers. The benefit for P&G is accurate and timely information on consumer demand for its products. Thus, P&G can plan production more accurately, minimizing the bullwhip effect.

Before you go on . . .

1. Differentiate between the push model and the pull model.
2. Describe various problems that can occur along the supply chain.
3. Discuss possible solutions to problems along the supply chain.

11.6 | Information Technology Support for Supply Chain Management

Author Lecture Videos are available exclusively in *WileyPLUS*.
Apply the Concept activities are available in the Appendix and in *WileyPLUS*.

Clearly, SCM systems are essential to the successful operation of many businesses. As you have seen, these systems—and IOSs in general—rely on various forms of IT to resolve problems. Three technologies, in particular, provide support for IOSs and SCM systems: electronic data interchange, extranets, and Web services. You will learn about Web services in Technology Guide 3. In this section, you examine the other two technologies.

Electronic Data Interchange (EDI)

Electronic data interchange (EDI) is a communication standard that enables business partners to exchange routine documents, such as purchasing orders, electronically. EDI formats these documents according to agreed-upon standards (e.g., data formats). It then transmits messages over the Internet using a converter, called *translator*.

EDI provides many benefits that are not available with a manual delivery system. To begin with, it minimizes data entry errors, because each entry is checked by the computer. The length of the message can also be shorter, and the messages are secured. EDI also reduces cycle time, increases productivity, enhances customer service, and minimizes paper usage and storage. Figure 11.6 contrasts the process of fulfilling a purchase order with and without EDI.

EDI does have some disadvantages. Business processes must sometimes be restructured to fit EDI requirements. Also, there are many EDI standards in use today, so one company might have to use several standards to communicate with multiple business partners.

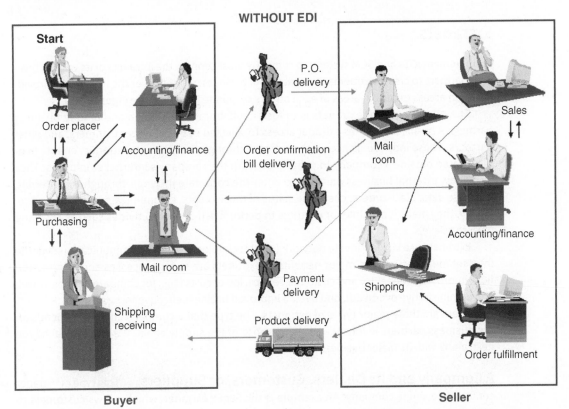

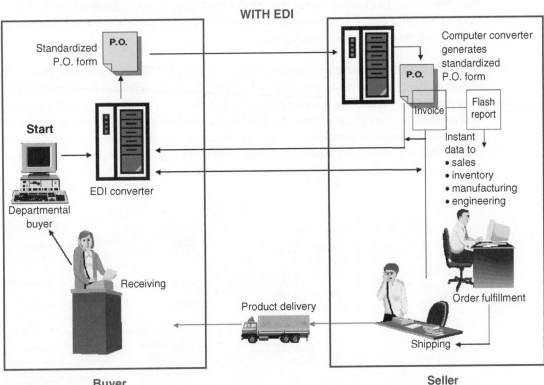

Drawn by E. Turban.

FIGURE 11.6 **Comparing purchase order (PO) fulfillment with and without EDI.**

In today's world, in which every business has a broadband connection to the Internet and where multi-megabyte design files, product photographs, and PDF sales brochures are routinely e-mailed, the value of reducing a structured e-commerce message from a few thousand XML bytes to a few hundred EDI bytes is negligible. As a result, EDI is being replaced by XML-based Web services. (You will learn about XML in Technology Guide 3.)

Extranets

To implement IOSs and SCM systems, a company must connect the intranets of its various business partners to create extranets. **Extranets** link business partners over the Internet by providing them access to certain areas of each other's corporate intranets (see **Figure 11.7**).

The primary goal of extranets is to foster collaboration between and among business partners. A business provides extranet access to selected B2B suppliers, customers, and other partners. These individuals access the extranet through the Internet. Extranets enable people located outside a company to collaborate with the company's internal employees. They also allow external business partners to enter the corporate intranet, through the Internet, to access data, place orders, check the status of those orders, communicate, and collaborate. Finally, they make it possible for partners to perform self-service activities such as checking inventory levels.

Extranets use virtual private network (VPN) technology to make communication over the Internet more secure. The major benefits of extranets are faster processes and information flow, improved order entry and customer service, lower costs (e.g., for communications, travel, and administrative overhead), and overall improved business effectiveness.

There are three major types of extranets. The type that a company chooses depends on the business partners involved and the purpose of the supply chain. We present each type next, along with its major business applications.

A Company and Its Dealers, Customers, or Suppliers. This type of extranet centers on a single company. An example is the FedEx extranet, which allows customers to track the status of a delivery. Customers use the Internet to access a database on the FedEx intranet. Enabling customers to monitor deliveries saves FedEx the cost of hiring human operators to perform that task over the phone.

An Industry's Extranet. Just as a single company can set up an extranet, the major players in an industry can team up to create an extranet that will benefit all of them. For example, ANXeBusiness (**www.anx.com**) enables companies to collaborate effectively through a network that provides a secure global medium for B2B information exchange. This network is used for mission-critical business transactions by leading international organizations in aerospace, automotive, chemical, electronics, financial services, health care, logistics, manufacturing, transportation, and related industries. It offers customers a reliable extranet as well as VPN services.

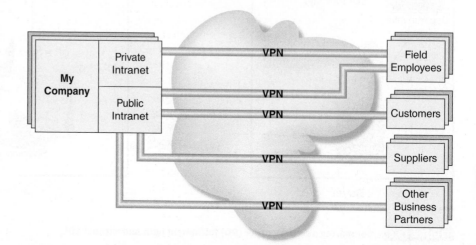

FIGURE 11.7 **The structure of an extranet.**

Joint Ventures and Other Business Partnerships.   In this type of extranet, the partners in a joint venture use the extranet as a vehicle for communication and collaboration. An example is Bank of America's extranet for commercial loans. The partners involved in making these loans include a lender, a loan broker, an escrow company, and a title company. The extranet connects lenders, loan applicants, and the loan organizer, Bank of America. A similar case is Lending Tree (**www.lendingtree.com**), a company that provides mortgage quotes for homeowners and also sells mortgages online. Lending Tree uses an extranet for its business partners (e.g., the lenders).

Portals and Exchanges

As you saw in Chapter 6, corporate portals offer a single point of access through a Web browser to critical business information in an organization. In the context of B2B supply chain management, these portals enable companies and their suppliers to collaborate very closely.

There are two basic types of corporate portals: procurement (sourcing) portals for a company's suppliers (upstream in the supply chain), and distribution portals for a company's customers (downstream in the supply chain). **Procurement portals** automate the business processes involved in purchasing or procuring products between a single buyer and multiple suppliers. For example, Boeing has deployed a procurement portal called the Boeing Supplier Portal through which it conducts business with its suppliers. **Distribution portals** automate the business processes involved in selling or distributing products from a single supplier to multiple buyers. For example, Dell services its business customers through its distribution portal at **www.premier.dell.com**.

Emerging Technologies

Logistics experts predict that several technologies will significantly impact supply chains by 2025. IT's About Business 11.6 illustrates the impact of three of these technologies, which include robotics, drones, autonomous (driverless) vehicles, and three-dimensional (3D) printing.

IT's About Business 11.6

POM **MIS** **Emerging Technologies and Supply Chain Management**

Robotics

Increases in workers' wages enhance the competitive advantage of using robots rather than human labor. Robots will not form unions; take vacations or even breaks; become ill; or need medical plans, retirement plans, or unemployment benefits. Furthermore, robots can work in environmental conditions that are unsuitable for humans. For example, temperatures can be kept lower for robots, thereby saving energy, and robots can often work without lights.

There are a great variety of robots. You could say that drones are aerial robots and that autonomous vehicles are also robots. You are probably familiar with industrial robots, which are essentially giant robot arms used in manufacturing. Here, we focus on robots being used in logistic operations, as you see in the following examples.

Automated delivery robots are revolutionizing local delivery services in cities. For example, Starship (**www.starship.xyz**) has released a robot that delivers meals and groceries to people in urban markets. The cost for each delivery is about $1. The 35-pound robot is essentially a medium-sized cooler on 6 wheels that moves at about 4 miles per hour. It has lights and a tall, bright orange flag to make it more visible to pedestrians on the sidewalk. A smartphone app unlocks the lid to access the insulated holding area and then automatically locks it back into place.

Goods-to-person robots help pick products for orders. The robots scan a grid on the warehouse floor that contains bar codes or QR codes, which provide the location relative to other robots, the location of the products to be picked, and the location to which the robot must take the products. Amazon Robotics (**www.amazonrobotics.com**), formerly Kiva Systems, manufactures and uses these mobile robotic fulfillment systems.

Telepresence robots are remote-controlled, wheeled devices that have wireless Internet connectivity. Typically, the robots have a display that provides video and audio capabilities. They are commonly used to stand in for tour guides, night watchmen, factory inspectors, and consultants. For example, BEAM robots from Suitable Tech (**www.suitabletech.com**) allow someone to remotely consult on problems or repairs or to conduct a tour.

Companies justify the costs of these robots by arguing that they lower travel costs.

Follow-me robots move with people in the picking operation. The human picker selects the products and places them in the robot's basket. The robot then delivers them to another human. These robots are an example of a *collaborative robot* or *cobot*. Locus Robotics (**www.locusrobotics.com**) and Fetch Robotics (**www.fetchrobotics.com**) offer follow-me robots.

Other cobots include Baxter, Sawyer, and the Lowe-bot. The Baxter and Sawyer cobots from Rethink Robotics (**www.rethinkrobotics.com**) are inexpensive and easy to program. They are also safe to operate beside humans. Lowebots operate in Lowe's stores to help customers.

Drones

A drone is an unmanned aerial vehicle. The first major impact of drones will be in customer delivery.

Experts maintain that drones will be valuable both in urban and rural areas. Current predictions are that five billion people will live in urban areas by 2030. Last-mile delivery will become increasingly difficult in these crowded areas. Rural locations are also problematic for delivery because it is not cost effective for ground vehicles to visit numerous isolated areas.

As an example, in December 2016, Amazon started Prime Air residential delivery with drones for a few customers in Cambridge, United Kingdom. The trial delivered packages up to 5 pounds in weight in 30 minutes or fewer. In that region, the government allowed Amazon to fly drones up to 400 feet in the air and beyond the sight of the operator. Customers had to place a small QR code (see Chapter 8) on their lawns to serve as a landing pad for the drone.

United Parcel Service (UPS; **www.ups.com**) and Federal Express (FedEx; **www.fedex.com**) are experimenting with drones that fly from their trucks to delivery parcels over the last few miles to customers. These trials typically are conducted in rural areas.

Drone start-up Flirtey (**www.flirtey.com**) successfully completed a number of delivery experiments. In July 2016, Flirtey delivered a pizza from Domino's Pizza to a customer in the town of Whangaparaoa, New Zealand. In December 2016, Flirtey made 77 drone deliveries from a 7-Eleven to various customers' residences.

The second major impact of drones will involve warehouse and logistics functions. For example, DroneScan (**www.dronescan.co/**) and Corvus Robotics (**www.corvus-robotics.com**) are conducting experiments using drones to track inventory in a warehouse. In these applications, drones navigate the warehouse and perform a physical inventory by scanning barcodes or reading RFID tags (see Chapter 8).

Several companies are experimenting with image recognition technology to identify and track inventory. For example, Walmart is using drones to verify the inventory in one of its large distribution centers. The drones reportedly examine the entire inventory in a one-million-square-foot Walmart facility in one day, as opposed to the month that it takes for a team of humans.

In 2016, BNSF Railway (**www.bnsf.com**) began to use drones to inspect tracks, bridges, and rail yards. The company has 32,500 miles of track in its system, all of which must be inspected multiple times every week. Drones capture data with cameras and sensors to detect any changes in the tracks (even as small as one-quarter inch) that could cause safety problems. BNSF uses predictive analytics to examine the data from the drones to forecast potential problem areas.

Driverless vehicles

Driverless vehicles in the form of autonomous forklifts have been in use for some time. Here, we address driverless trucks, which use short- and longer-range radar and cameras for detecting lanes, signs, and markings. The National Highway Traffic Safety Administration has defined several levels of vehicles, from Level 1, where the driver does everything, to Level 5, which is a fully autonomous vehicle under all driving conditions.

Numerous driverless truck experiments are under way around the world. For example, on October 16, 2016, an Uber-Otto/Anheuser Busch beer delivery utilized a driverless truck. The 120-mile trip went from the Ft. Collins, Colorado, brewery to Colorado Springs. The driver drove the truck to the freeway and took over when the truck left the freeway at the end of the trip. For the remainder of the trip, the driver left his seat and observed from the sleeper cabin.

Driverless trucks offer several advantages, including reduced labor costs, increased vehicle efficiency, and vastly improved safety. Let's look at these advantages more closely.

When companies deploy driverless trucks, it is possible that the Hours of Service (HoS) regulations could be relaxed. Under current regulations, trucks are only 45 percent utilized, because drivers can drive only 11 out of 24 hours. In contrast, some companies are planning to operate driverless truck fleets 24 hours per day at 45 miles per hour. At this speed, these trucks will use much less fuel than they would at 70 miles per hour. By operating 24 hours per day, the trucks can compensate for lower speeds and actually travel greater distances in one day.

Second, automated platooning software allows multiple trucks to autonomously follow one another in a closely bunched convoy. Only the lead truck has a driver, who monitors the group of trucks. By following one another closely, platooning trucks encounter less wind resistance, which increases their fuel efficiency. The Department of Transportation estimates that these trucks will save 7–10 percent on fuel costs. In 2017, start-up Peloton (**www.peloton-tech. com**) released its platooning software in a limited trial. The company found that its software improved the fuel efficiency of the lead truck by 4.5 percent and of the following trucks by 10 percent.

Third, driverless trucks offer safety advantages. More than 90 percent of vehicle crashes are the result of human error. These crashes result in more than 30,000 deaths annually in the United States and 1.2 million deaths worldwide. Driverless trucks are intended to reduce or eliminate these accidents. Not only would this development save lives, but it would also lead to lower insurance rates.

Three-dimensional printing

Beginning with an object represented in digital form, the 3D printing process applies material in layers in an additive manner. Gartner, a global research and advisory firm, estimates that global shipments of 3D printers will approach 7 million units by 2020, a huge increase from the 450,000 units delivered in 2016. As of December 2017, current applications for 3D printing were characterized by low-volume, complex geometries for assembly; a need for a rapid customer response; and a need for customization.

Three-dimensional printing is shortening or eliminating some supply chain applications. Consider the following examples:

- Running shoes: Nike, Adidas, and New Balance are experimenting with 3D printing soles designed specifically for the user. The customer runs on a treadmill that is equipped with sensors. The sensors create an accurate digital mapping of each foot. Using this mapping, the companies 3D print soles that precisely fit their customers' feet.

- **Rapid prototyping:** Many companies are rapidly 3D printing prototypes for new parts or products.

- **Three-dimensional printing-as-a-service:** UPS has about 100 stores with 3D printers, and it offers 3D printing-as-a-service. Staples and Shapeways offer similar services.

- **Repair parts:** Manufacturers are beginning to 3D print repair parts on an as-needed basis. As one example, in December 2014, NASA sent a digital file of a wrench to the space station. The wrench was 3D printed on the space station.

- **Low-volume, high-value components:** General Electric (**www.ge.com**) Aeronautics uses 3D printing to manufacture fuel nozzles for jet airplane engines. Before the company implemented the 3D printing process, the nozzles consisted of more than 20 components. These components had to be sourced through an extensive supply chain and then welded together. Today, GE produces its fuel nozzles by 3D printing them in a single manufacturing process in one plant. Significantly, these nozzles are 25 percent lighter and 5 times more durable than the welded nozzles.

Sources: Compiled from V. Soneja, "Emerging Technology and Supply Chain: Breaking through the Hype," *Supply Chain Digital*, July 2, 2018; P. Walsh, "Emerging Technologies Transforming the Supply Chain: A Supply Chain Disruptor and Transformer," www.fmi.org, February 28, 2018; C. Pettey, "Gartner Top 8 Supply Chain Technology Trends for 2018," www.gartner.com, February 27, 2018; "Robot Makers Competing for Share in Warehouse Market," *MH&L News*, November 21, 2017; "Weighing the Impact of Self-Driving Vehicles on Logistics," *Packaging World*, September 21, 2017; "The Top 5 Disruptive Trends in Self-Driving Cars, Delivery, Transportation, and Logistics," *Business Insider*, September 12, 2017; B. McCrea, "How Technology Will Impact the Supply Chain of the Future," *SourceToday*, July 25, 2017; A. Meola, "Shop Online and Get Your Items Delivered by a Drone Delivery Service: The Future Amazon and Domino's Have Envisioned for Us," *Business Insider*, July 18, 2017; "The Internet of Things in Supply Chain," Veridiansol.com, June 12, 2017; N. Vickery, "Autonomous Vehicles in Logistics: What Are the Impacts?" EFT.com, May 25, 2017; "These Five Technologies Will Impact Your Supply Chain," *MH&L News*, May 4, 2017; D. Halim, "The Impact New Technologies Have on the Supply Chain," JDA.com, May 2, 2017; E. McCollom, "Drone Delivery Is about to Revolutionize the Supply Chain Industry," *Red Stag Fulfillment*, January 4, 2017; J. Potts, "How Driverless Trucks Will Change Supply Chain Strategy," *Inbound Logistics*, December 29, 2016; A. Meola, "How IoT Logistics Will Revolutionize Supply Chain Management," *Business Insider*, December 21, 2016; and T. Gresham, "6 Technologies Guaranteed to Disrupt Your Supply Chain," *Inbound Logistics*, July 13, 2016.

Questions

1. Considering all of these technologies together, is it possible to eliminate supply chains altogether? Why or why not? Support your answer.

2. Discuss potential disadvantages of robotics, drones, driverless vehicles, and 3D printing.

Before you go on . . .

1. Define EDI, and list its major benefits and limitations.
2. Define an extranet, and explain its infrastructure.
3. List and briefly define the major types of extranets.
4. Differentiate between procurement portals and distribution portals.

What's in **IT** for me?

ACCT For the Accounting Major

Customer Relationship Management

CRM systems can help companies establish controls for financial reporting related to interactions with customers in order to support compliance with legislation. For example, Sarbanes–Oxley requires companies to establish and maintain an adequate set of controls for accurate financial reporting that can be audited by a third party. Other sections [302 and 401(b)] have implications for customer activities, including the requirements that sales figures reported for the prior year be correct. Section 409 requires companies to report material changes to financial conditions, such as the loss of a strategic customer or significant customer claims about product quality.

CRM systems can track document flow from a sales opportunity to a sales order, to an invoice, to an accounting document, thus enabling finance and accounting managers to monitor the entire flow. CRM systems that track sales quotes and orders can be used to incorporate process controls that identify questionable sales transactions. CRM systems can provide exception-alert capabilities to identify instances outside defined parameters that put companies at risk.

Supply Chain Management

The cost accountant will play an important role in developing and monitoring the financial accounting information associated with inventory and cost of goods sold. In a supply chain, much of the data for these accounting requirements will flow into the organization from various partners within the chain. It is up to the chief accountant, the comptroller, or CFO to prepare and review these data.

Going further, accounting rules and regulations and the cross-border transfer of data are critical for global trade. IOSs can facilitate such trade. Other issues that are important for accountants are taxation and government reports. Creating information systems that rely on EDI also requires the attention of accountants.

Finally, fraud detection in global settings (e.g., transfers of funds) can be facilitated by appropriate controls and auditing.

FIN For the Finance Major

Customer Relationship Management

CRM systems allow companies to track marketing expenses, collecting appropriate costs for each individual marketing campaign. These costs then can be matched to corporate initiatives and financial objectives, demonstrating the financial impact of the marketing campaign.

Pricing is another key area that impacts financial reporting. For example, what discounts are available? When can a price be overridden? Who approves discounts? CRM systems can put controls into place for these issues.

Supply Chain Management

In a supply chain, the finance major will be responsible for analyzing the data created and shared among supply chain partners. In many instances, the financial analyst will recommend actions to improve supply chain efficiencies and cash flow. This may benefit all the partners in the chain. These recommendations will be based on financial models that incorporate key assumptions such as supply chain partner agreements for pricing. Through the use of extensive financial modeling, the financial analyst helps to manage liquidity in the supply chain.

Many finance-related issues exist in implementing IOSs. For one thing, establishing EDI and extranet relationships involves structuring payment agreements. Global supply chains may involve complex financial arrangements, which may have legal implications.

MKT For the Marketing Major

Customer Relationship Management

CRM systems are an integral part of every marketing professional's work activities. CRM systems contain the consolidated customer data that provide the foundation for making informed marketing decisions. Using these data, marketers develop well-timed and targeted sales campaigns with customized product mixes and established price points that enhance potential sales opportunities and therefore increase revenue. CRM systems also support the development of forecasting models for future sales to existing clients through the use of historical data captured from previous transactions.

Supply Chain Management

A tremendous amount of useful sales information can be derived from supply chain partners through the supporting information systems. For example, many of the customer support activities take place in the downstream portion of the supply chain. For the marketing manager, an understanding of how the downstream activities of the supply chain relate to prior chain operations is critical.

Furthermore, a tremendous amount of data is fed from the supply chain supporting information systems into the CRM systems that are used by marketers. The information and a complete understanding of its genesis are vital for mixed-model marketing programs.

POM For the Production/Operations Management Major

Customer Relationship Management

Production is heavily involved in the acquisition of raw materials, conversion, and distribution of finished goods. However, all of these activities are driven by sales. Increases or decreases in the demand for goods result in a corresponding increase or decrease in a company's need for raw materials. Integral to a company's demand is forecasting future sales, an important part of CRM systems. Sales forecasts are created from the historical data stored in CRM systems.

This information is critically important to a production manager who is placing orders for manufacturing processes. Without an accurate future sales forecast, production managers may face inventory problems (discussed in detail in this chapter). The use of CRM systems for production and operational support is critical to efficiently managing the resources of the company.

Supply Chain Management

The production/operations management major plays a major role in the supply chain development process. In many organizations, the production/operations management staff may even lead the supply chain integration process because of their extensive knowledge of the manufacturing components of the organization. Because they are in charge of procurement, production, materials control, and logistical handling, a comprehensive understanding of the techniques of SCM is vital for the production/operations staff.

The downstream segment of supply chains is where marketing, distribution channels, and customer service are conducted. An understanding of how downstream activities are related to the other segments is critical. Supply chain problems can reduce customer satisfaction and negate marketing efforts. It is essential, then, that marketing professionals understand the nature of such problems and their solutions. Also, learning about CRM, its options, and its implementation is important for designing effective customer services and advertising.

As competition intensifies globally, finding new global markets becomes critical. Use of IOSs provides an opportunity to improve marketing and sales. Understanding the capabilities of these technologies as well as their implementation issues will enable the marketing department to excel.

HRM For the Human Resources Major

Customer Relationship Management

Companies trying to enhance their customer relationships must recognize that employees who interact with customers are critical to the success of CRM strategies. Essentially, the success of CRM is based on the employees' desire and ability to promote the company and its CRM initiatives. In fact, research analysts have found that customer loyalty is based largely on employees' capabilities and their commitment to the company.

As a result, human resource managers know that a company that desires valued customer relationships needs valued relationships with its employees. Therefore, HR managers are implementing programs to increase employee satisfaction and are training employees to execute CRM strategies.

Supply Chain Management

Supply chains require interactions among the employees of partners in the chain. These interactions are the responsibility of the Human Resources Manager. The HR Manager must be able to address supply chain issues that relate to staffing, job descriptions, job rotations, and accountability. All of these areas are complex within a supply chain and require the HR function to understand the relationship among partners as well as the movement of resources.

Preparing and training employees to work with business partners (frequently in foreign countries) requires knowledge about how IOSs operate. Sensitivity to cultural differences and extensive communication and collaboration can be facilitated with IT.

MIS For the MIS Major

Customer Relationship Management

The IT function in the enterprise is responsible for the corporate databases and data warehouse, as well as the correctness and completeness of the data in them—that is, the IT department provides the data used in a 360° view of the customer. Furthermore, IT personnel provide the technologies underlying the customer interaction center.

Supply Chain Management

The MIS staff will be instrumental in the design and support of information systems—both internal organizational and interorganizational—that will underpin the business processes that are part of the supply chain. In this capacity, the MIS staff must have a concise knowledge of the business, the systems, and the points of intersection between the two.

Summary

11.1 Identify the primary functions of both customer relationship management (CRM) and collaborative CRM.

Customer relationship management (CRM) is an organizational strategy that is customer focused and customer driven. That is, organizations concentrate on assessing customers' requirements for products and services and then on providing high-quality, responsive services. CRM functions include acquiring new customers, retaining existing customers, and growing relationships with existing customers.

Collaborative CRM is an organizational CRM strategy in which data consolidation and the 360° view of the customer enable the organization's functional areas to readily share information about customers. The functions of collaborative CRM include integrating communications between the organization and its customers in all aspects of marketing, sales, and customer support processes, and enabling customers to provide direct feedback to the organization.

11.2 Describe how businesses might use applications of each of the two major components of operational CRM systems.

Operational CRM systems support the front-office business processes that interact directly with customers (i.e., sales, marketing, and service). The two major components of operational CRM systems are customer-facing applications and customer-touching applications.

Customer-facing CRM applications include customer service and support, sales force automation, marketing, and campaign management. *Customer-touching applications* include search and comparison capabilities, technical and other information and services, customized products and services, personalized Web pages, FAQs, e-mail and automated responses, and loyalty programs.

11.3 Explain the advantages and disadvantages of mobile CRM systems, on-demand CRM systems, open-source CRM systems, social CRM systems, and real-time CRM systems.

On-demand CRM systems are those hosted by an external vendor in the vendor's data center. Advantages of on-demand CRM systems include lower costs and a need for employees to know only how to access and use the software. Drawbacks include possibly unreliable vendors, difficulty in modifying the software, and difficulty in integrating vendor-hosted CRM software with the organization's existing software.

Mobile CRM systems are interactive systems through which communications related to sales, marketing, and customer service activities are conducted through a mobile medium for the purpose of building and maintaining customer relationships between an organization and its customers. Advantages of mobile CRM systems include convenience for customers and the chance to build a truly personal relationship with customers. A drawback could be difficulty in maintaining customer expectations; that is, the company must be extremely responsive to customer needs in a mobile, near-real-time environment.

Open-source CRM systems are those whose source code is available to developers and users. The benefits of open-source CRM systems include favorable pricing, a wide variety of applications, easy customization, rapid updates and bug (software error) fixes, and extensive free support information. The major drawback of open-source CRM systems is quality control.

Social CRM is the use of social media technology and services to enable organizations to engage their customers in a collaborative conversation to provide mutually beneficial value in a trusted and transparent manner.

Real-time CRM means that organizations are able to respond to customer product searches, requests, complaints, comments, ratings, reviews, and recommendations in near real-time, 24/7/365.

11.4 Describe the three components and the three flows of a supply chain.

A *supply chain* is the flow of materials, information, money, and services from raw material suppliers, through factories and warehouses, to the end customers. A supply chain involves three segments: upstream, where sourcing or procurement from external suppliers occurs; internal, where packaging, assembly, or manufacturing takes place; and downstream, where distribution takes place, frequently by external distributors.

There are three flows in the supply chain: *material flows*, which are the physical products, raw materials, supplies, and so forth; *information flows*, which consist of data related to demand, shipments, orders, returns, and schedules, as well as changes in any of these data; and *financial flows*, which involve money transfers, payments, credit card information and authorization, payment schedules, e-payments, and credit-related data.

11.5 Identify popular strategies to solving different challenges of supply chains.

Two major challenges in setting accurate inventory levels throughout a supply chain are the *demand forecast* and the *bullwhip effect*. Demand for a product can be influenced by numerous factors such as competition, prices, weather conditions, technological developments, economic conditions, and customers' general confidence. The *bullwhip effect* refers to erratic shifts in orders up and down the supply chain.

The most common solution to supply chain problems is *building inventories* as insurance against SC uncertainties. Another solution is the *just-in-time* (JIT) inventory system, which delivers the precise number of parts, called *work-in-process inventory*, to be assembled into a finished product at precisely the right time. The third possible solution is *vendor-managed inventory* (VMI), which occurs when the vendor, rather than the retailer, manages the entire inventory process for a particular product or group of products.

11.6 Explain the utility of each of the three major technologies that support supply chain management.

Electronic data interchange (EDI) is a communication standard that enables the electronic transfer of routine documents, such as purchasing orders, between business partners.

Extranets are networks that link business partners over the Internet by providing them access to certain areas of each other's corporate intranets. The main goal of extranets is to foster collaboration among business partners.

Corporate portals offer a single point of access through a Web browser to critical business information in an organization. In the context of business-to-business supply chain management, these portals enable companies and their suppliers to collaborate very closely.

Chapter Glossary

analytical CRM system CRM system that analyzes customer behavior and perceptions in order to provide actionable business intelligence.

bullwhip effect Erratic shifts in orders up and down the supply chain.

collaborative CRM system A CRM system in which communications between the organization and its customers are integrated across all aspects of marketing, sales, and customer support processes.

customer-facing CRM applications Areas in which customers directly interact with the organization, including customer service and support, salesforce automation, marketing, and campaign management.

customer identity management A marketing technology intended to complete a 360° view of a customer across an organization.

customer interaction center (CIC) A CRM operation in which organizational representatives use multiple communication channels to interact with customers in functions such as inbound teleservice and outbound telesales.

customer relationship management (CRM) A customer-focused and customer-driven organizational strategy that concentrates on addressing customers' requirements for products and services, and then providing high-quality, responsive services.

customer-touching CRM applications (also called electronic CRM or e-CRM) Applications and technologies with which customers interact and typically help themselves.

customer touch point Any interaction between a customer and an organization.

distribution portals Corporate portals that automate the business processes involved in selling or distributing products from a single supplier to multiple buyers.

electronic CRM (e-CRM) See customer-touching CRM applications.

electronic data interchange (EDI) A communication standard that enables business partners to transfer routine documents electronically.

extranets Networks that link business partners over the Internet by providing them access to certain areas of each other's corporate intranets.

front-office processes Those processes that directly interact with customers; that is, sales, marketing, and service.

interorganizational information system (IOS) An information system that supports information flow among two or more organizations.

just-in-time (JIT) An inventory system in which a supplier delivers the precise number of parts to be assembled into a finished product at precisely the right time.

loyalty program Programs that offer rewards to customers to influence future behavior.

mobile CRM system An interactive CRM system in which communications related to sales, marketing, and customer service activities are conducted through a mobile medium for the purpose of building and maintaining customer relationships between an organization and its customers.

on-demand CRM system A CRM system that is hosted by an external vendor in the vendor's data center.

open-source CRM system CRM software whose source code is available to developers and users.

operational CRM system The component of CRM that supports the front-office business processes that directly interact with customers (i.e., sales, marketing, and service).

procurement portals Corporate portals that automate the business processes involved in purchasing or procuring products between a single buyer and multiple suppliers.

pull model A business model in which the production process begins with a customer order and companies make only what customers want, a process closely aligned with mass customization.

push model A business model in which the production process begins with a forecast, which predicts the products that customers will want as well as the quantity of each product. The company then produces the amount of products in the forecast, typically by using mass production, and sells, or "pushes," those products to consumers.

real-time CRM system A CRM system enabling organizations to respond to customer product searches, requests, complaints, comments, ratings, reviews, and recommendations in near real time, 24/7/365.

salesforce automation (SFA) The component of an operational CRM system that automatically records all the aspects in a sales transaction process.

social CRM The use of social media technology and services to enable organizations to engage their customers in a collaborative conversation in order to provide mutually beneficial value in a trusted and transparent manner.

supply chain The coordinated movement of *resources* from organizations through *conversion* to the end consumer.

supply chain management (SCM) An activity in which the leadership of an organization provides extensive oversight for the partnerships and processes that compose the supply chain and leverages these relationships to provide an operational advantage.

supply chain visibility The ability of all organizations in a supply chain to access or view relevant data on purchased materials as these materials move through their suppliers' production processes.

vendor-managed inventory (VMI) An inventory strategy where the supplier monitors a vendor's inventory for a product or group of products and replenishes products when needed.

vertical integration Strategy of integrating the upstream part of the supply chain with the internal part, typically by purchasing upstream suppliers, so as to ensure timely availability of supplies.

Discussion Questions

1. How do customer relationship management systems help organizations achieve customer intimacy?

2. What is the relationship between data consolidation and CRM systems?

3. Discuss the relationship between CRM and customer privacy.

4. Distinguish between operational CRM systems and analytical CRM systems.

5. Differentiate between customer-facing CRM applications and customer-touching CRM applications.

6. Explain why Web-based customer interaction centers are critical for successful CRM systems.

7. Why are companies so interested in e-CRM applications?

8. Discuss why it is difficult to justify CRM applications.

9. You are the CIO of a small company with a rapidly growing customer base. Which CRM system would you use: an on-premise CRM system, an on-demand CRM system, or an open-source CRM system? Remember that open-source CRM systems may be implemented either on-premise or on-demand. Discuss the pros and cons of each type of CRM system for your business.

10. List and explain the important components of a supply chain.

11. Explain how a supply chain approach may be part of a company's overall strategy.

12. Explain the important role that information systems play in supporting a supply chain strategy.

13. Would Rolls-Royce Motorcars (**www.rolls-roycemotorcars.com**) use a push model or a pull model in its supply chain? Support your answer.

14. Why is planning so important in supply chain management?

Problem-Solving Activities

1. Access **www.ups.com** and **www.fedex.com**. Examine some of the IT-supported customer services and tools provided by the two companies. Compare and contrast the customer support provided on the two companies' websites.

2. Enter **www.anntaylor.com**, **www.hermes.com**, and **www.tiffany.com**. Compare and contrast the customer service activities offered by these companies on their websites. Do you see marked similarities? Differences?

3. Access your university's website. Investigate how your university provides for customer relationship management. (*Hint:* First decide who your university's customers are.)

4. Access **www.sugarcrm.com**, and take the interactive tour. Prepare a report on SugarCRM's functionality to the class.

5. Access **www.ups.com** and **www.fedex.com**. Examine some of the IT supported customer services and tools provided by the two companies. Write a report on how the two companies contribute to supply chain improvements.

6. Enter **www.supply-chain.org**, **www.cio.com**, **www.findarticles.com**, and **www.google.com**, and search for recent information on supply chain management.

7. Surf the Web to find a procurement (sourcing) portal, a distribution portal, and an exchange (other than the examples presented in this chapter). List the features they have in common and those features that are unique.

Closing Case

POM **Amazon's Global Supply Chain**

Amazon is implementing a multiyear plan to develop a global shipping and logistics business, competing directly with UPS (**www.ups.com**),

FedEx (**www.fedex.com**), and Chinese e-commerce leader Alibaba (**www.alibaba.com**). This plan includes leasing planes, developing and registering an ocean freight-forwarding business, and developing a parcel-delivery business.

Amazon is globally expanding its Fulfillment by Amazon (FBA) service, which provides storage, packing, and shipping for independent merchants who sell products through Amazon.com. Amazon's global logistics platform will be called Global Supply Chain by Amazon. Internally, Amazon calls this project Dragon Boat.

Amazon's intention is to put itself at the center of a logistics industry that currently involves shippers such as FedEx and UPS as well as thousands of freight forwarders who handle international cargo and the associated paperwork. Amazon plans to collect inventory from thousands of merchants around the world and purchase space on trucks, planes, trains, and ships at reduced rates.

Amazon argues that its logistics business will open cross-border commerce to smaller merchants who otherwise would not have the time or money to manage the complexities of international commerce. In turn, Amazon shoppers will have access to many more products from merchants around the world.

Amazon's interest in developing a global logistics platform dates from 2012, when the e-commerce giant first allowed Chinese suppliers to sell goods in Amazon's online marketplace. By July 2018, more than 60 percent of Chinese e-commerce retailers sold on Amazon platforms. Sellers can ship products either directly to customers or to Amazon, which then packs and delivers the products on their behalf.

As noted above, Amazon's plan includes developing an ocean freight-forwarding business, an air-cargo business, and a parcel-delivery business. Let's look at each of these options in order.

Freight Forwarding Business

Any parcel weighing more than 330 pounds qualifies as freight and can require several vehicles owned by different companies to deliver it across land, sea, or air from its source (e.g., a factory) to its destination (e.g., a retail store). Shipping these parcels internationally is difficult and time consuming, particularly for small- and medium-sized companies that tend to sell on Amazon. Large brands and manufacturers have the necessary size to directly arrange and negotiate favorable rates for shipments. Other firms must use freight forwarders.

Freight forwarding is opaque and very inefficient. Many freight forwarders still conduct their business via phone, e-mail, paper manifests, or fax machine. Online portals where manufacturers can track their shipments are largely unknown.

Freight forwarders perform many functions. They negotiate the best shipping rates and the most efficient use of multiple modes of transport, including trucks, trains, planes, and ships. They prepare all of the accompanying paperwork, including customs documentation. When a problem arises, such as when a container is delayed at a port, freight forwarders are expected to have the necessary relationships with port personnel to get the container moving again.

Amazon's entry into the freight forwarding business is in its early stages. For instance, between October 2016 and January 2017, Amazon arranged for the shipping of at least 150 containers of goods from China to the United States. The containers were a very tiny part of the millions of containers that sail between the two countries each year. However, they were an early freight-forwarding test for Amazon. According to Amazon's logistics website (**www.logistics.amazon.com**), the retailer claims it can perform freight pickups, warehousing, and transportation and delivery of goods, as well as handle import and export services.

To become a freight forwarder between the United States and China, Amazon had to obtain two licenses to act as a wholesaler for ocean container shipping, one from the United States Federal Maritime Commission and the other from China. The retailer received both licenses by February 2016.

Amazon faces stiff competition in the freight forwarding business. For example, freight forwarding start-up Flexport (**www.flexport.com**) has indexed all of the available freight carriers into a searchable database, which shippers can use for free to organize and track shipments. Flexport simultaneously operates its own freight forwarding service that provides shippers with the shortest and least expensive option. Flexport uses analytics to optimize its recommendations based on the large amount of data it collects from shippers who utilize its free software. By analyzing all of the routes, rates, speeds, and customs compliance data of shipments booked through its software, Flexport can identify the most efficient method to ship goods internationally. In 2017, Flexport moved freight worth more than $1.5 billion to or from 64 countries for more than 700 clients.

Air Cargo Business

Cargo planes are one of the latest tools that Amazon is using to control and improve delivery. Other efforts include a mobile app for delivery drivers and increased trucking capacity. The company has a worldwide network of approximately 150 fulfillment centers and 20 sorting centers that handle online orders. Amazon's air cargo business is called Amazon Prime Air.

By July 2018, Amazon had 20 of its 33 cargo planes operating out of the Cincinnati/Northern Kentucky International airport, with the rest operating point-to-point routes across the United States. The retailer is building a new $1.5 billion air hub, which will be fully operational in 2021, near the airport to support its fleet of planes. At the end of 2018, Amazon had 50 planes and in June, 2019 ordered 15 more cargo planes. The retailer's goal is to move inventory more efficiently around the United States so its customers can receive their orders quickly. The company currently operates 11 warehouses in Kentucky, where inventory is stored, packed, and shipped to its customers.

Parcel Delivery Business

In 2016, Amazon purchased the 75 percent of French package delivery company Colis Privé that it did not already own. The purchase put Amazon in direct competition with FedEx and UPS in France. Industry analysts believe that Amazon is using this acquisition to better understand the parcel delivery business.

In fact, Amazon appears to be interested in creating an end-to-end customer experience by selling and delivering goods. The company is experimenting with a new delivery service, called Seller Flex, which is an on-demand local delivery service that Amazon initiated in India in 2015. Two years later, it introduced Seller Flex on a trial basis in several U.S. West Coast states. Amazon deployed Seller Flex more broadly in 2018.

In early 2018, Amazon launched a program called Shipping with Amazon (SWA) in Los Angeles, in which the retailer picked up and shipped packages to customers. The service began with third-party sellers on Amazon but could eventually open to other businesses.

In June 2018, Amazon launched its Delivery Service Partner (DSP) program, which encouraged entrepreneurs to start small Amazon delivery companies. Each entrepreneur manages 40 to 100 employees who use 20 to 40 Amazon-branded vans to deliver packages, using Amazon's logistics systems to facilitate the process. This program directly competes with major parcel delivery companies such as UPS and FedEx.

Integrating the three business

Amazon is using information technology (IT) to integrate all areas of its global logistics business. For example, determining the most cost-effective shipping rate is essentially a question of data collection and analytics. Amazon performs both of these processes very effectively.

Using Amazon's IT, merchants will be able to book cargo space online, creating what Amazon calls one-click-ship for seamless international trade and shipping—that is, merchants will be able to claim cargo space online with a single click. Essentially, Amazon has the ability to develop a one-stop, one-click shipping portal that would vastly simplify the process for manufacturers while making it easier for them to track shipments. Eventually, Amazon could offer the service to any manufacturer, even those who do not sell on its platforms. More efficient logistics would also help Amazon to reduce various transaction costs, including booking fees and government filings.

Amazon faces international competition from Alibaba. Like Amazon, Alibaba is striving to dominate international electronic commerce. That market will exceed $1 trillion and 900 million shoppers by 2020, according to a report by consulting firm Accenture and AliResearch (**www.aliresearch.com**), Alibaba's research group.

As one example, Alibaba's OneTouch service has been helping Chinese manufacturers arrange air freight and customer clearances since 2010. Furthermore, in January 2017, Alibaba began booking space for its suppliers on Maersk container ships, joining an increasing number of e-commerce companies that are trying to bring greater efficiency and transparency to the business of arranging cargo shipments.

Executives at FedEx (**www.fedex.com**) and UPS (**www.ups.com**) as well as logistics industry analysts are skeptical about Amazon's plans. They contend that it will be extremely difficult and expensive to build an international delivery network to rival FedEx and UPS. (In just one example, FedEx has 659 planes, UPS has 260, and Amazon has about 40.)

FedEx states that it is spending more than $5 billion annually on expansion and upgrades to its services, and UPS claims it is spending more than $2.5 billion in similar areas. Combined, the two companies have a total of roughly 4,000 hubs and other facilities to sort tens of millions of packages per day. They also operate almost 1,000 planes and 200,000 vehicles to deliver packages to doors.

Even with increasing investments, it appears likely that Amazon will have to rely on UPS, FedEx, and the U.S. Postal Service for years. Furthermore, UPS, FedEx, and freight forwarder DSV say that they have the logistics technologies that enable them to have a competitive advantage over Amazon. It remains to be seen if Amazon can scale up its global logistics operations enough to compete with these two giants.

Sources: Compiled from J. Del Ray, "Amazon Claims It Doesn't Want to Take on UPS and FedEx," *Recode*, June 28, 2018; "Move over UPS Truck: Amazon Delivery Vans to Hit the Street," *U.S. News and World Report*, June 28, 2018; C. Wienberg, "Freight Forwarder DSV Says Technology Gives It Edge over Amazon," *Bloomberg News*, May 1, 2018; V. Rajamanickam, "Flexport Is Redefining the Trillion Dollar International Freight Forwarding Industry," *Freight Waves*, March 23, 2018; "Amazon Launches Service to Disrupt Shipping Industry," *Port Technology*, February 13, 2018; B. Rubin, "Amazon's New Delivery Program Shouldn't Hurt FexEx, UPS," CNET, February 9, 2018; L. Chang, "Amazon Is Ready to Do More of Its Own Delivery with Seller Flex," *Digital Trends*, October 5, 2017; R. Howells, "The 'Amazon Effect' on the Supply Chain," *Digitalist*, September 8, 2017; R. King, "Amazon Prime Air Cargo Planes Ready for Takeoff for Prime Day for the First Time," *Fortune*, July 10, 2017; "Amazon May Have Redesigned the Global Supply Chain Process," *Land Link Traffic Systems*, June 2, 2017; R. Coates, "The Amazon Effect and the Global Supply Chain," *Supply Chain Management Review*, May 30, 2017; "Amazon Continues to Expand Global Logistics Offering with New Air Service for Chinese Vendors," *Supply Chain Digest*, March 20, 2017; A. Minter, "Will Amazon Revolutionize Shipping?" *Bloomberg*, February 14, 2017; D. Benton, "Supply Chain 4.0: Adidas and Amazon Rewrite the Rules on Supply Chain Management," *Supply Chain Digital*, February 10, 2017; A. Robinson, "Top 5 Trends to Know to Compete with Amazon's Supply Chain," Cerasis.com, February 6, 2017; J. Del Rey, "Amazon Is Building a $1.5 Billion Hub for Its Own Cargo Airline," *Recode*, January 31, 2017; J. Constine, "The Unsexiest Trillion-Dollar Startup," *TechCrunch*, June 7, 2016; R. Lewis, "Amazon's Shipping Ambitions Are Larger than It's Letting on," *Forbes*, April 1, 2016; E. Weise, "Amazon Leases 20 Planes, Starts Air Freight Service," *USA Today*, March 9, 2016; D. Gilmore, "Amazon – The Most Audacious Logistics Plan in History?" *Supply Chain Digest*, February 18, 2016; S. Soper, "Amazon's Plan to Take on UPS and Alibaba," *Bloomberg BusinessWeek*, February 15–21, 2016; E. Schuman, "What Amazon Is Doing with Its Supply Chain Could Devastate the Competition," *Computerworld*, February 12, 2016; E. Weise, "Amazon's Chinese Shipping License Reflects Global Goals," *USA Today*, February 9, 2016; E. Kim, "Leaked Documents Show Amazon Is Making a Big Play to Bypass UPS and FedEx," *Business Insider*, February 9, 2016; J. Greene and D. Gates, "Amazon in Talks to Lease Boeing Jets to Launch Its Own Air-Cargo Business," *Seattle Times*, December 17, 2015; and www.amazon.com, accessed July 17, 2019.

Questions

1. Perform a strengths, weaknesses, opportunities, and threats (SWOT) analysis of Amazon's entry into the global logistics business.

2. What are the disadvantages to Amazon of entering the global logistics business?

3. You are the CEO of FedEx or UPS. What strategies would you implement to compete with Amazon? Provide specific examples to support your answer.

CHAPTER 12

Business Analytics

CHAPTER OUTLINE	LEARNING OBJECTIVES
12.1 Managers and Decision Making	**12.1** Use a decision-support framework to demonstrate how technology supports managerial decision making at each phase of the decision-making process.
12.2 The Business Analytics Process	**12.2** Describe each phase of the business analytics process.
12.3 Descriptive Analytics	**12.3** Provide a definition and a use case example for descriptive analytics.
12.4 Predictive Analytics	**12.4** Provide a definition and a use case example for predictive analytics.
12.5 Prescriptive Analytics	**12.5** Provide a definition and a use case example for prescriptive analytics.
12.6 Presentation Tools	**12.6** Identify and discuss two examples of presentation tools.

Opening Case

POM **MKT** **MIS** Stitch Fix

Traditional brick-and-mortar retailers are experiencing serious problems. For instance, hundreds of customers enter retail stores every day, but the retailers do not learn much about them. Unless sales associates interact with them, those businesses will not know a customer's pants size, her purchase history, or what she is looking to buy. Furthermore, many busy women do not have time to go into stores and look through hundreds of items of clothing to find something they like.

Enter Stitch Fix, a personal styling service. Stitch Fix (**www.stitchfix.com**) is an online retailer that markets itself to busy working women. Since 2012, the start-up has developed a service that shops for women, matching clients with boutique-brand clothes, shoes, and accessories based on recommendations from its analytics algorithms and human stylists. Stitch Fix's core customer is a woman between 25 and 45 who is comfortable paying $55 and up for her clothes and accessories.

Rather than visit a store, Stitch Fix customers pay a $20 "styling fee" to receive a box of five personally selected items either on demand or by subscription at regular intervals. They try on the clothes at home, keep what they want, and return what they do not want. Clients pay the full retail price of any clothes they keep, minus the $20 fee, which is applied as a credit. For the company to make a profit, customers must keep at least two of the five items in each shipment. To encourage purchases, Stitch Fix offers its customers a 25 percent discount if they keep all of the items in the box.

MKT Stitch Fix's business model is all about experience and relevance. The lines of clothing are not exclusive to Stitch Fix, and Stitch Fix does not price them lower than its competitors. Furthermore, the company does not try to ship faster than its competitors. Its strategy is simply to be more relevant and to understand its customers better than the competition. Its increased relevance enables Stitch Fix to address the problem of overabundance of products offered in stores and especially over the Internet. Specifically, CEO Katrina Lake noted that while the vastness of apparel available to consumers might seem appealing at first, they feel overwhelmed by so much choice.

The key concept of Stitch Fix is personalization, and the firm's machine learning algorithms (see Technology Guide 4) are central to the company's business model and drive every business process, including selecting clothing, assigning human stylists, optimizing production and logistics, and designing new styles.

MKT **Selecting clothing.** Essentially, selecting clothing is predicting the likelihood that a particular client will like a certain piece of clothing. These predictions require data, and Stitch Fix gathers data from customers and from the merchandise.

In contrast to traditional retailers, Stitch Fix knows that anyone who is willing to pay the $20 styling fee is probably willing to provide personal data to ensure an optimal experience. To promote this experience, the retailer collects more than 50 pieces of data from each customer, such as her weight, bra size, and links to her Pinterest and LinkedIn profiles, as well as her Twitter account. Customers answer questions such as: "How do you prefer clothes to fit the bottom half of your body?" "What do you like to flaunt?" and "What would you rather keep covered?" The firm's algorithms use a customer's data to predict how likely she is to keep a given item based on parameters that include the woman's style, her occupation, her age, her zip code (which Stitch Fix uses to predict the weather in her location), and many other data points.

Stitch Fix also uses images from social media and other sources to track emerging fashion trends and evolving customer preferences. With client permission, the company's data scientists augment client questionnaire data by scanning images on customers' Pinterest boards and other social media websites, analyzing them, and using the resulting insights to develop a deeper understanding of each customer's sense of style. This process is called dark analytics (see this chapter's closing case).

The second set of data is about the firm's merchandise. For any given item from the more than 200 brands that it carries, Stitch Fix gathers 100 to 150 data points, ranging from sleeve length to color. Using both sets of data, algorithms match a client to the firm's best-suited merchandise.

Over time, the algorithms learn from the customers, based on feedback they provide. To gather feedback, the retailer captures customer comments in text boxes. Natural language processing algorithms analyze these comments to further refine the matching algorithms.

Matching the right stylist with the right customer. At Stitch Fix, human stylists finalize the clothing selections and even write personal notes describing how the client might accessorize the items for a particular occasion and how to pair them with other clothing in his or her closet. To match stylists with customers, Stitch Fix calculates a match score between each available stylist and each client who has requested a shipment. This score takes into account the history between the client and the stylist (if any), and the similarities between the client's style preferences and those of the stylist.

One of Stitch Fix's 3,600 stylists then reviews the data and chooses five items to include in a customer's "fix" (box of items). In addition, the company values returns as valuable data points. Stitch Fix's stylists actually study the negative feedback in a customer's comments to better discern her style or an item's description.

POM **Optimize production and logistics.** One challenge that the company faces is managing inventory while selling so many different pieces of clothing and pairs of shoes. A traditional retailer has to largely guess how many pairs of jeans it will sell at the start of a season and then place an order. In contrast, Stitch Fix can be more reactive, thereby limiting its inventory risk. That is, Stitch Fix can order based on a customer order (the pull model), rather than order on the basis of a forecast (the push model). The algorithms are a tremendous help in the ordering

process. For instance, Stitch Fix can make predictions based on how many customers are buying pants and then instruct the manufacturers to produce particular styles, colors, or patterns when it places an order.

Algorithms calculate a cost function for each Stitch Fix warehouse based on data about its location relative to a client and how well the inventories in the various warehouses match the client's needs. Therefore, algorithms reduce transportation costs.

Designing new styles. The fashion industry has been built around creative designers. At Stitch Fix, algorithms identify attributes of clothing that have a high probability of client acceptance. The retailer then works with human designers to refine these attributes and ultimately offer new styles that are tailored for particular client segments that tend to be underserved by other brands.

In August 2017, Stitch Fix began offering more than 100 new contemporary brands, including Theory, Steven Alan, Todd Snyder, Kate Spade, and Rebecca Minkoff, with pieces ranging in price from $100 to $600. The company's new premium brands are a response to requests from its customers for more well-known brand names and for higher-quality fabrics, such as leather and cashmere. Providing these new brands enables the company to attract new customers who may have found the company's previous offerings too basic.

Based on data provided by its customers, Stitch Fix is able to offer exclusive styles. For example, Paige Denim has designed a petite line for Stitch Fix because the retailer already knows which customers might be interested in the line based on data regarding size and price preferences that the company has collected. These targeted collections are one of the many benefits that Stitch Fix can offer brands, along with awareness, discovery, and matching for customers who may not be familiar with a certain label but have expressed interest in similar products.

In 2016, the retailer launched Stitch Fix for Men, a similar service for men's fashion. Stitch Fix for Men competes directly with Trunk Club, owned by Nordstrom. (Interestingly, Trunk Club entered the women's category in 2016.) In June 2018, Stitch Fix announced its service for children, called Stitch Fix Kids. In addition, the firm announced its own exclusive brand of children's clothing, Rumi + Ryder.

Stitch Fix does face stiff competition. Le Tote (**www.letote.com**), M.M. LaFleur (**www.mmlafleur.com**) for professional women, Dia & Co. (**www.dia.com**) for plus sizes, and Rocksbox (**www.rocksbox.com**), which sells only jewelry, are all operating in this space. In addition, Rent the Runway (**www.renttherunway.com**) has been rolling out its "Unlimited" subscription.

Amazon has a growing interest in fashion. In June 2017, Amazon introduced a new program called Prime Wardrobe that allows people to order clothing—from 3 to 15 items at a time—without actually buying it. Customers have one week to try on the items and return those that they do not want. Customers can return the items they do not want in a resealable box with a preprinted shipping label in which the order was shipped. Amazon charges them only for the items they keep but does not offer any incentive for keeping a set number of items. This service is an option only for members of Amazon Prime, the company's membership service that, for $119 per year, offers customers fast shipping at no additional charge.

In June 2018, the e-tailer launched a European menswear fashion line, called Meraki. That same year, Amazon made its Echo Look device available to U.S. consumers. The device is a small, voice-activated camera that can take full-length photos and short videos to enable shoppers to see how they look from multiple angles while, at the same time, helping Amazon gather valuable intelligence about the clothes that consumers are wearing.

Stitch Fix is one of the few major success stories in the subscription shopping marketplace. The firm has more than 5,000 employees, and it operates five clothing warehouses across the United States.

Stitch Fix claims that nearly 40 percent of its customers spend more than half of their annual apparel budget on its collections. In addition, about 80 percent of customers who order one box then order a second box within 90 days.

Stitch Fix continues to explore new opportunities. For example, the company's Style Pass is an invitation-only feature that is offered to some of its customers. Style Pass costs $49, lasts for an entire year, and waives all of a member's styling fees for that year. Furthermore, the cost of the Style Pass is automatically deducted from the member's next Stitch Fix purchase.

How successful is Stitch Fix? On November 17, 2017, Stitch Fix went public with 8 million shares priced at $15 each. As of July, 2019 Stitch Fix's stock price had nearly doubled since its IPO.

For its 2018 fiscal year, Stitch Fix reported revenue of $1.2 billion and net income of $45 million. For the third quarter, 2019, the company reported 3.1 million active clients (an increase of 17 percent year-over-year) and net revenue of $409 million (an increase of 29 percent year-over-year).

Sources: Compiled from P. Wahba, "Stitch Fix Is Testing New Ways to Generate Revenue," *Fortune*, July 15, 2019; J. Kowaleski, "Stitch Fix's Unbelievable Opportunity that No One Is Talking About," *Seeking Alpha*, June 19, 2019; "What Not to Wear: How Algorithms Are Taking the Uncertainty Out of Fashion," *Forbes*, July 17, 2018; T. Lien, "With Personalized Styling and Now Kids Clothing, Stitch Fix Looks to Avoid the Pitfalls of Subscription Boxes," *Los Angeles Times*, July 10, 2018; N. Warfield, "Stitch Fix Is Up 90% Since Its IPO, and Traders Say There's More Room to Run," *CNBC*, June 21, 2018; L. Varon, "Amazon Prime Wardrobe Won't Kill Subscription Boxes – Bad Strategies Will," *Internet Retailer*, June 21, 2018; Z. Stambor, "Amazon Answer to Stitch Fix Launches to All U.S. Prime Members," *Internet Retailer*, June 20, 2018; E. Winkler, "Is Stitch Fix the Netflix of Fashion?" *Wall Street Journal*, June 7, 2018; M. Lynley, "Stitch Fix Blows Out Wall Street's Expectations and Announces the Launch of Stitch Fix Kids," *TechCrunch*, June 7, 2018; C. Wang, "Stitch Fix Soars after Online Styling Service Says Active Clients Grew 30%," *CNBC*, June 7, 2018; B. Marr, "Stitch Fix: The Amazing Use Case of Using Artificial Intelligence in Fashion Retail," *Forbes*, May 25, 2018; A. Bhattarai, "Stitch Fix Goes Public in the First Tech IPO Led by a Woman This Year," *Washington Post*, November 17, 2017; L. Hirsch, "Stitch Fix Prices IPO of 8 Million Shares at $15, Below Expectations," *CNBC*, November 16, 2017; C. Fernandez, "Stitch Fix Introduces over 100 Contemporary Brands," *Business of Fashion*, August 22, 2017; C. Morris, "Stitch Fix Could Be Wall Street's Next Big IPO," *Fortune*, July 31, 2017; M. Lynley, "Stitch Fix Has Confidentially Filed for an IPO," *TechCrunch*, July 28, 2017; N. Wingfield, "Amazon Will Let Customers Try on Clothes before Buying," *New York Times*, June 20, 2017; T. Lien, "Stitch Fix Founder Built One of the Few Successful E-Commerce Subscription Services," *The Seattle Times*, June 19, 2017; M. Merced and K. Benner, "As Department Stores Close, Stitch Fix Expands Online," *New York Times*, May 10, 2017; J. Del Ray, "The Online Fashion Startup Stitch Fix Has $730 Million in Annual Revenue and Is Profitable," *Recode*, May 10, 2017; R. Mac, "Stitch Fix Continues on Retail Warpath with $730 Million in Revenue," *Forbes*, May 10, 2017; R. Mac, "Fashionista Moneyball," *Forbes*, June 21, 2016; S. Maheshwari, "Stitch Fix and the New Science behind What Women Want to Wear," *BuzzFeed*, September 24, 2014; H. Milnes, "How Stich Fix's Happy Relationship with Pinterest Helps Customers," *Digiday*, March 16, 2016; and www.stitchfix.com, accessed July 16, 2019.

Questions

1. Describe the descriptive analytics applications of Stitch Fix's business model.

2. Describe the predictive analytics applications of Stitch Fix's business model.

3. What companies and industries are in danger of being disrupted by Stitch Fix? (*Hint:* Will Stitch Fix change the way that women buy clothes?)

Introduction

The chapter-opening case illustrates the importance and far-reaching nature of business analytics applications. **Business analytics (BA)** is the process of developing actionable decisions or recommendations for actions based on insights generated from historical data. Business analytics examines data with a variety of tools; formulates descriptive, predictive, and prescriptive analytics models; and communicates these results to organizational decision makers. Business analytics can answer questions such as the following: What happened, how many, how often, where is the problem, what actions are needed, why is this happening, what will happen if these trends continue, what will happen next, what is the best (or worst) that can happen, and what actions should the organization take to achieve various successful business outcomes?

There is a great deal of confusion between the terms *business analytics* and *business intelligence*. **Business intelligence (BI)** has been defined as a broad category of applications, technologies, and processes for gathering, storing, accessing, and analyzing data to help business users make better decisions. Many experts argue that the terms should be used interchangeably. We agree. However, for simplicity, we use the term *business analytics (BA)* throughout this chapter.

This chapter describes information systems (ISs) that support *decision making*. Essentially all organizational information systems support decision making (refer to Figure 1.4). Fundamental organizational Information Systems such as transaction processing systems, functional area information systems, and enterprise resource planning systems provide a variety of reports that help decision makers. This chapter focuses on business analytics systems, which provide critical support to the vast majority of organizational decision makers.

The chapter begins by reviewing the manager's job and the nature of modern managerial decisions. This discussion will help you to understand why managers need computerized support. The chapter then introduces the business analytics process and addresses each step in that process in turn.

It is impossible to overstate the importance of business analytics within modern organizations. Recall from Chapter 1 that the essential goal of information systems is to provide the right information to the right person, in the right amount, at the right time, in the right format. In essence, BA achieves this goal. Business analytics systems provide actionable business results that decision makers can act on in a timely fashion.

It is also impossible to overstate the importance of your input into the BA process within an organization, for several reasons. First, you (the user community) will decide which data should be stored in your organization's data warehouse. You will then work closely with the MIS department to obtain these data.

Furthermore, you will use your organization's BA applications, probably from your first day on the job, *regardless of your major field of study*. With some BA tools such as data mining and decision-support systems, you will decide how you want to analyze the data. We refer to this process as *user-driven analysis*. BA presentation applications such as dashboards will enable you to decide which data you need and in which format. Again, you will work closely with your MIS department to ensure that these applications meet your needs.

A significant change is also taking place within the BA environment. In the past, organizations used BA only to support management. Today, however, BA applications are increasingly available to frontline personnel (e.g., call center operators), suppliers, customers, and even regulators. These groups rely on BA to provide them with the most current information.

Much of this chapter is concerned with large-scale BA applications. You should keep in mind, however, that smaller organizations, and even individual users, can implement small-scale BA applications as well.

After you finish this chapter, you will have a basic understanding of decision making, the BA process, and the incredibly broad range of BA applications that are employed in modern organizations. This knowledge will enable you to immediately and confidently provide input into your organization's BA processes and applications. Furthermore, this chapter will help you use your organization's BA applications to effectively analyze data and thus make better decisions. We hope that this chapter will help you *"Ask the next question."* Enjoy!

12.1 Managers and Decision Making

Management is a process by which an organization achieves its goals through the use of resources (people, money, materials, and information). These resources are considered to be *inputs*. Achieving the organization's goals is the *output* of the process. Managers oversee this process in an attempt to optimize it. A manager's success is often measured by the ratio between the inputs and outputs for which he or she is responsible. This ratio is an indication of the organization's **productivity**.

Author Lecture Videos are available exclusively in *WileyPLUS*.
Apply the Concept activities are available in the Appendix and in *WileyPLUS*.

The Manager's Job and Decision Making

To appreciate how information systems support managers, you must first understand the manager's job. Managers do many things, depending on their position within the organization, the type and size of the organization, the organization's policies and culture, and the personalities of the managers themselves. Despite these variations, however, all managers perform three basic roles (Mintzberg, 1973):[1]

1. *Interpersonal roles:* Figurehead, leader, liaison

2. *Informational roles:* Monitor, disseminator, spokesperson, analyzer

3. *Decisional roles:* Entrepreneur, disturbance handler, resource allocator, negotiator

---

[1]Mintzberg, H. (1973). *The Nature of Managerial Work*, Harper & Row, New York.

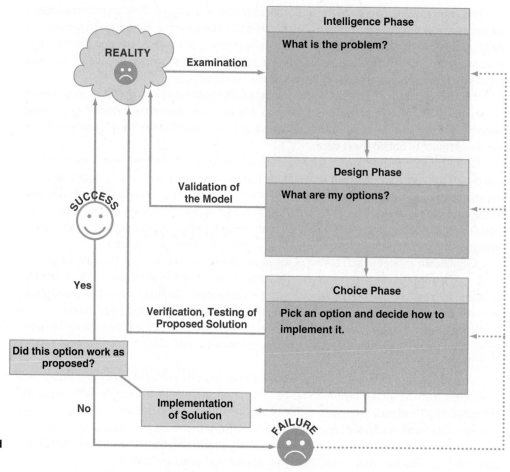

FIGURE 12.1 The process and phases in decision making.

Early information systems primarily supported the informational roles. In recent years, however, information systems have been developed that support all three roles. In this chapter, you will focus on the support that IT can provide for decisional roles.

A **decision** refers to a choice among two or more alternatives that individuals and groups make. Decisions are diverse and are made continuously. Decision making is a systematic process. Economist Herbert Simon (1977)[2] described decision making as composed of three major phases: intelligence, design, and choice. Once the choice is made, the decision is implemented. **Figure 12.1** illustrates this process, highlighting the tasks that are in each phase. Note that there is a continuous flow of information from intelligence, to design, to choice (bold lines). At any phase, however, there may be a return to a previous phase (broken lines).

This model of decision making is quite general. Undoubtedly, you have made decisions in which you did not construct a model of the situation, validate your model with test data, or conduct a sensitivity analysis. The model we present here is intended to encompass *all* of the conditions that might occur when making a decision. For some decisions, some steps or phases may be minimal, implicit (understood), or completely absent.

The decision-making process starts with the *intelligence phase*, in which managers examine a situation and then identify and define the problem or opportunity. In the *design phase*, decision makers construct a model for addressing the situation. They perform this task by making assumptions that simplify reality and by expressing the relationships among all of the relevant variables. Managers then validate the model by using test data. Finally, decision makers set criteria for evaluating all of the potential solutions that are proposed. The *choice phase* involves selecting a solution or course of action that seems best suited to resolve the problem. This solution (the decision) is then implemented. Implementation is successful if the proposed solution solves the problem or seizes the opportunity. If the solution fails, then the process returns to the previous phases. Computer-based decision support assists managers in the decision-making process.

[2]Simon, H. A. (1977). *The New Science of Management Decision*, Prentice-Hall, Englewood Cliffs, NJ.

Why Managers Need IT Support

Making good decisions is very difficult without solid information. Information is vital for each phase and activity in the decision-making process. Even when information is available, however, decision making is difficult because of the following trends:

- The *number of alternatives* is constantly *increasing* because of innovations in technology, improved communications, the development of global markets, and the use of the Internet and e-business. A key to good decision making is to explore and compare many relevant alternatives. The greater the number of alternatives, the more a decision maker needs computer-assisted searches and comparisons.

- Most decisions must be made *under time pressure*. It is often not possible to manually process information fast enough to be effective.

- Because of increased uncertainty in the decision environment, decisions are becoming more complex. It is usually necessary to *conduct a sophisticated analysis* to make a good decision.

- It often is necessary to rapidly access remote information, consult with experts, or conduct a group decision-making session, all without incurring major expenses. Decision makers, as well as the information they need to access, can be situated in different locations. Bringing everything together quickly and inexpensively represents a serious challenge.

These trends create major difficulties for decision makers. Fortunately, as you will see throughout this chapter, computerized decision support can be of enormous help. Next, you will learn about two aspects of decision making that place our discussion of BA in context—problem structure and the nature of the decisions.

A Framework for Computerized Decision Analysis

To better understand business analytics, note that various types of decisions can be placed along two major dimensions: problem structure and the nature of the decision (Gorry and Scott Morton, 1971).[3] **Figure 12.2** provides an overview of decision making along these two dimensions.

	Operational Control	Management Control	Strategic Planning	IS Support
Structured	Accounts receivable, order entry `1`	Budget analysis, short-term forecasting, personnel reports, make-or-buy analysis `2`	`3`	MIS, statistical models (management science, financial, etc.)
Semistructured	Production scheduling, inventory control `4`	Credit evaluation, budget preparation, plant layout, project scheduling, reward systems design `5`	Building a new plant, mergers and acquisitions, planning (product, quality assurance, compensation, etc.) `6`	Decision support systems, business intelligence
Unstructured	`7`	Negotiating, recruiting an executive, buying hardware, lobbying `8`	New technology development, product R&D, social responsibility planning `9`	Decision support systems, expert systems, enterprise resource planning, neural networks, business intelligence, Big Data

FIGURE 12.2   **Decision-support framework.**

[3]Gorry, G. A., and Scott Morton, M. (1971). "A Framework for Management Information Systems," *Sloan Management Review*, Fall, 21–36.

Problem Structure.

The first dimension is *problem structure*, in which decision-making processes fall along a continuum ranging from highly structured to highly unstructured (see the left column in Figure 12.2). *Structured decisions* deal with routine and repetitive problems for which standard solutions exist, such as inventory control. In a structured decision, the first three phases of the decision process—intelligence, design, and choice—are laid out in a particular sequence, and the procedures for obtaining the best (or at least a good enough) solution are known. These types of decisions are candidates for decision automation.

At the other extreme of complexity are *unstructured decisions*. These decisions are intended to deal with "fuzzy," complex problems for which there are no cut-and-dried solutions. An unstructured decision is one in which there is no standardized procedure for carrying out any of the three phases. In making such a decision, human intuition and judgment often play an important role. Typical unstructured decisions include planning new service offerings, hiring an executive, and choosing a set of research and development (R&D) projects for the coming year. Although BA cannot make unstructured decisions, it can provide information that assists decision makers.

Located between structured and unstructured decisions are *semistructured* decisions, in which only some of the decision-process phases are structured. Semistructured decisions require a combination of standard solution procedures and individual judgment. Examples of semistructured decisions are evaluating employees, setting marketing budgets for consumer products, performing capital acquisition analysis, and trading bonds.

The Nature of Decisions.

The second dimension of decision support deals with the *nature of decisions*. All managerial decisions fall into one of three broad categories:

1. *Operational control:* Executing specific tasks efficiently and effectively
2. *Management control:* Acquiring and using resources efficiently in accomplishing organizational goals
3. *Strategic planning:* The long-range goals and policies for growth and resource allocation

These categories are displayed along the top row of Figure 12.2.

The Decision Matrix.

The three primary classes of problem structure and the three broad categories of the nature of decisions can be combined in a decision-support matrix that consists of nine cells, as diagrammed in Figure 12.2. Lower-level managers usually perform the tasks in cells 1, 2, and 4. The tasks in cell 5 are usually the responsibility of middle managers and professional staff. Finally, the tasks in cells 6, 8, and 9 are generally carried out by senior executives.

Today, it is difficult to state that certain organizational information systems support certain cells in the decision matrix. The fact is that the increasing sophistication of Information Systems means that essentially any information system can be useful to any decision maker, regardless of his or her level or function in the organization. As you study this chapter, you will see that business analytics is applicable across all cells of the decision matrix.

Before you go on . . .

1. Describe the decision-making process proposed by Simon.
2. You are registering for classes next semester. Apply the decision-making process to your decision about how many and which courses to take. Is your decision structured, semistructured, or unstructured? Support your answer.
3. Consider your decision-making process when registering for classes next semester. Explain how information technology supports (or does not support) each phase of this process.

12.2 | The Business Analytics Process

As previously defined, *business analytics* is the process of developing actionable decisions or recommendations for actions based on insights generated from historical data. Business analytics encompasses not only applications but also technologies and processes. It includes both "getting data in" (to a data mart or warehouse) and "getting data out" (through BA applications).

The use of BA in organizations varies considerably. In smaller organizations, BA may be limited to Excel spreadsheets. In larger ones, BA is enterprisewide, and it includes a wide variety of applications. The importance of BA to organizations continues to grow, to the point where it is now a requirement for competing in the marketplace—that is, BA is a competitive necessity for organizations.

Although BA has become a common practice across organizations, not all organizations use BA in the same way. For example, some organizations employ only one or a few applications, whereas others use enterprisewide BA. In general, there are three specific analytics targets that represent different levels of change. These targets differ in regard to their focus; scope; level of sponsorship, commitment, and required resources; technical architecture; impact on personnel and business processes; and benefits.

- *The Development of One or a Few Related Analytics Applications.* This target is often a point solution for a departmental need, such as campaign management in marketing. Sponsorship, approval, funding, impacts, and benefits typically occur at the departmental level. For this target, organizations usually create a data mart to store the necessary data. Organizations must be careful that the data mart—an "independent" application—does not become a "data silo" that stores data that are inconsistent with, and cannot be integrated with, data used elsewhere in the organization.

- *The Development of Infrastructure to Support Enterprisewide Analytics.* This target supports both current and future analytics needs. A crucial component of analytics at this level is an enterprise data warehouse. Because it is an enterprisewide initiative, senior management often provides sponsorship, approval, and funding. The impacts and benefits are also felt throughout the organization.

  MKT **MIS** An example of this target is the 3M Corporation (**www.3m.com**). Historically, 3M's various divisions had operated independently and used separate decision-support platforms. Not only was this arrangement costly, but it also prevented 3M from integrating the data and presenting a "single face" to its customers. For example, sales representatives did not know whether or how business customers were interacting with other 3M divisions. The solution was to develop an enterprise data warehouse that enabled 3M to operate as an integrated company. As an added benefit, the costs of implementing this system were offset by savings resulting from the consolidation of the various platforms.

- *Support for Organizational Transformation.* With this target, a company uses business analytics to fundamentally transform the ways it competes in the marketplace. Business analytics supports a new business model, and it enables the business strategy. Because of the scope and importance of these changes, critical elements such as sponsorship, approval, and funding originate at the highest organizational levels. The impact on personnel and processes can be significant, and the benefits accrue across the organization.

  MKT Harrah's Entertainment (a brand of Caesars Entertainment; (**www.caesars .com/**) provides a good example of this analytics target. Harrah's developed a customer loyalty program known as Total Rewards. To implement the program, Harrah's created a data warehouse that integrated data from casino, hotel, and special event systems—for example, wine-tasting weekends—across all of the various customer touchpoints, such as slot machines, table games, and the Internet. Harrah's used these data to reward loyal customers and to reach out to them in personal and appealing ways, such as through promotional offers. These efforts helped the company to become a leader in the gaming industry.

Regardless of the scope of BA, all organizations employ a BA process, which **Figure 12.3** depicts. Let's look at each step of Figure 12.3 in turn, from left to right.

Author Lecture Videos are available exclusively in *WileyPLUS*.
Apply the Concept activities are available in the Appendix and in *WileyPLUS*.

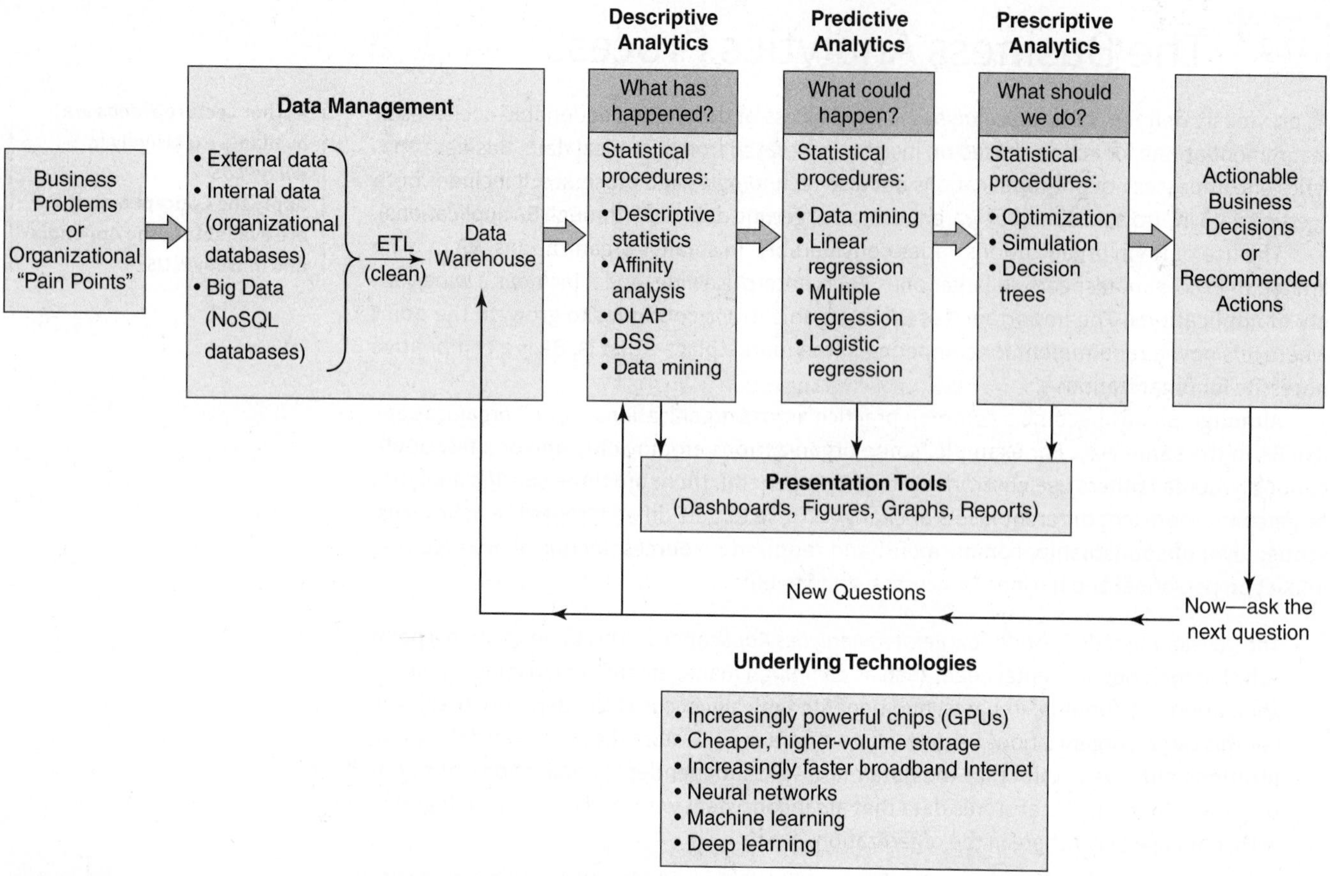

FIGURE 12.3 The Business Analytics Process. (Drawn by Kelly Rainer, Bill Hardgrave, and Regina Halpin)

The Business Analytics Process

The entire BA process begins with a business problem, often called *pain points* by practicing managers. When organizations face business problems, they often turn to business analytics, through the process illustrated in Figure 12.3, to help solve those problems.

Underlying Technologies.
Before we begin our discussion of the BA process, let's emphasize the importance of the technologies that underlie the entire process (see Figure 12.3). These technologies are all improving very rapidly.

Microprocessors (or chips) are becoming increasingly powerful (see Technology Guide 1). In particular, graphics processing units (GPUs) are essential to neural networks, another underlying technology of the BA process. (We discuss neural networks in Technology Guide 4.)

MIS Advances in digital storage capacity and access speed are driving the cost of storage down, meaning that organizations are able to store and analyze huge amounts of data. Transmission speed (bandwidth; see Chapter 6) in computer networks, particularly the Internet, is also rapidly increasing. As a result, decision makers are able to collaborate on difficult, time-sensitive decisions regardless of their locations. Other underlying technologies include machine learning and deep learning, which we discuss in Technology Guide 4.

MIS Data Management.
To actually begin the BA process, an organization must have data (and lots of it!). As you saw from our discussion of underlying technologies, organizations are now able to analyze rapidly increasing amounts of data. As you learned in Chapter 5, these data originate from internal sources, such as structured data in relational databases, and external sources, such as unstructured data from social media. Organizations are now able to combine and analyze structured and unstructured data from many sources in the form of Big Data. At this point, organizations integrate and "clean" these data into data marts and

data warehouses (see Chapter 5) through a process called *extract, transform, and load (ETL)*. The data in the data warehouse are now available to be analyzed by data scientists, analysts, and decision makers.

Descriptive Analytics, Predictive Analytics, and Prescriptive Analytics.

Organizations perform three types of analytics applications: descriptive analytics, predictive analytics, and prescriptive analytics. We discuss these analytics applications in Sections 12.3, 12.4, and 12.5, respectively.

At the end of Section 12.4, we present an example (with summarized data) that illustrates how a decision maker proceeds through the BA process. In our example, we address only descriptive analytics and predictive analytics. We do not include prescriptive analytics in this example because this type of analytics is not yet widespread in industry.

Presentation Tools.
All three types of analytics produce results, which must be communicated to decision makers in the organization. In general, data scientists perform these analyses. Many organizations have employees who "translate" the results of these analyses into business terms for the decision makers. These employees often use presentation tools in the form of dashboards to communicate the message visually. We discuss dashboards and other presentation tools in Section 12.6.

Ask the Next Question.
What is critically important about the analytics process is that once the results are obtained and presented, decision makers must be ready to "ask the next question." Everyone involved in the BA process must use his or her creativity and intuition at this point. In addition, the results of the BA process will almost always lead to new, unanswered questions.

Business Analytics Tools

A variety of BA tools are available to analyze data. They include Excel, multidimensional analysis (also called OLAP), data mining, and decision-support systems. BA also employs numerous statistical procedures, which include descriptive statistics; affinity analysis; linear, multiple, and logistic regression; as well as many others.

Other than Excel, we discuss BA tools and statistical procedures in the context of the analytics application for which they are most appropriate. We discuss Excel here because it is the most popular and common BA tool. Furthermore, Excel incorporates the functionality of many of the other BA tools and statistical procedures. For example, analysts can use Excel to provide descriptive statistics and to perform regression analyses.

BA vendors typically design their software so that it interfaces with Excel. How does this process work? Essentially, users download plug-ins that add functionality—for example, the ability to list the top 10 percent of customers, based on purchases—to Excel. Excel then connects to the vendor's application server—which provides additional data analysis capabilities—which in turn connects to a backend database, a data mart, or a data warehouse. This arrangement gives Excel users the functionality and access to data that are typical of sophisticated BA products while allowing them to work with a familiar tool—Excel.

In the next three sections, we address descriptive analytics, predictive analytics, and prescriptive analytics, respectively. Each section begins by defining the type of analytics, continues with a discussion of the BA tools and statistical procedures that are appropriate to that type of analytics, and closes with examples of that type of analytics.

Before you go on . . .

1. Describe the three business analytics targets.
2. Describe the business analytics process.

Author Lecture Videos are available exclusively in *WileyPLUS*.
Apply the Concept activities are available in the Appendix and in *WileyPLUS*.

12.3 Descriptive Analytics

Organizations must analyze huge amounts of raw data to make sense of them. This overall process is known as *data reduction*. *Data reduction* is the conversion of raw data into a smaller amount of more useful information. Descriptive, predictive, and prescriptive analytics are essentially steps in data reduction.

Descriptive analytics is the first step in data reduction. **Descriptive analytics** summarizes what has happened in the past and enables decision makers to learn from past behaviors. Organizations employ descriptive analytics to generate information such as total stock in inventory, average dollars spent per customer, and year-over-year change in sales. Common examples of descriptive analytics are reports that provide historical insights regarding an organization's production, financials, operations, sales, finance, inventory, and customers.

BA Tools in Descriptive Analytics

BA tools in descriptive analytics applications include online analytical processing, data mining, decision-support systems, and a variety of statistical procedures. Examples of such statistical procedures are descriptive statistics, affinity analysis, and many others (see Figure 12.3). We take a closer look at these tools here.

Online Analytical Processing. Some BA applications include **online analytical processing (OLAP)**, also referred to as **multidimensional analysis** capabilities. OLAP involves "slicing and dicing" the data that are stored in a dimensional format, "drilling down" in the data to greater detail, and "rolling up" the data to greater summarization (less detail).

Consider our example from Chapter 5. Recall Figure 5.6, which illustrates the data cube. The product is on the *x*-axis, geography is on the *y*-axis, and time is on the *z*-axis. Now, suppose you want to know how many nuts the company sold in the West region in 2017. You would slice and dice the cube, using *nuts* as the specific measure for product, *West* as the measure for geography, and *2017* as the measure for time. The value (or values) that remain in the cell(s) after our slicing and dicing is (or are) the answer to our question. As an example of drilling down, you might also want to know how many nuts were sold in January 2017. Alternatively, you might want to know how many nuts were sold from 2017 through 2019, which is an example of aggregation, also called "roll up."

Data Mining. **Data mining** refers to the process of searching for valuable business information in a large database, data warehouse, or data mart. Data mining can perform two basic operations: (1) identify previously unknown patterns and (2) predict trends and behaviors. The first operation is a descriptive analytics application, and the second is a predictive analytics application.

In descriptive analytics, data mining can identify previously hidden patterns in an organization's data. For example, a descriptive analytics application can analyze retail sales data to discover seemingly unrelated products that people often purchase together. A classic example is beer and diapers (even though it is urban legend). Data mining found that young men tend to buy beer and diapers at the same time when shopping at convenience stores. This type of analysis is called affinity analysis or market-basket analysis.

POM **MKT** *Affinity analysis* is a data mining application that discovers co-occurrence relationships among activities performed by specific individuals or groups. In retail, affinity analysis is used to perform *market basket analysis*, in which retailers seek to understand the purchase behavior of customers. Retailers use this information for the purposes of cross-selling, up-selling, sales promotions, loyalty programs, store design (physical location of products), and discount offers. An example of cross-selling with market basket analysis is Amazon's use of "customers who bought book A might also like to buy book B."

In another example, market basket analysis could inform a retailer that customers often purchase shampoo and conditioner together. Therefore, putting both items on promotion at the same time would not create an increase in revenue, whereas a promotion involving just one of the items would likely drive sales of the other.

Decision-Support Systems.

Decision-support systems (DSSs) combine models and data to analyze semistructured problems and some unstructured problems that involve extensive user involvement. *Models* are simplified representations, or abstractions, of reality. Decision-support systems enable business managers and analysts to access data interactively, to manipulate these data, and to conduct appropriate analyses.

DSSs can enhance learning, and they can contribute to all levels of decision making. They also employ mathematical models. Finally, they have the related capabilities of sensitivity analysis, what–if analysis, and goal-seeking analysis, which you will learn about next. You should keep in mind that these three types of analysis are useful for any type of decision-support application. Excel, for example, supports all three.

POM **MKT** To learn about DSSs and the three types of analysis, let's look at an example. Blue Nile (**www.bluenile.com**) is an online retailer of certified diamonds. The firm's website has a built-in decision-support system to help customers find the diamond that best meets their needs. Blue Nile's DSS provides an excellent example of sensitivity analysis, what–if analysis, and goal-seeking analysis.

Access the Blue Nile website, and click on "Diamonds" in the upper-left corner. On the drop-down box, you will see "Search for diamonds." Keep in mind that when you experiment with the Blue Nile DSS, the number of round diamonds available will vary from what we obtained when we accessed the DSS and performed the analyses. The reason is that the Blue Nile website is updated in near-real time as the company sells its diamonds.

There are many types of diamonds, but for this example, click on "Round." You will see the following:

- The number of round diamonds available for sale, again in the upper-left corner. When we accessed the Blue Nile DSS, the firm offered 112,333 round diamonds for sale.
- Five slide bars labeled: Price, Carat, Cut, Color, and Clarity. Each slide bar represents a variable in Blue Nile's DSS.
- A list of each diamond accompanied by a value for each of the five variables. This list constitutes the data—that is, all round diamonds available for sale—for your analysis.

Sensitivity Analysis. Sensitivity analysis examines how sensitive an output is to any change in an input while keeping other inputs constant. Sensitivity analysis is valuable because it enables the system to adapt to changing conditions and to the varying requirements of different decision-making situations. Let's perform *two sensitivity analyses* on the data:

- First, adjust the slide bars for the Carat variable, so that you will see only those round diamonds between 1.00 and 1.50 carats. Keep all of the other slide bars in their fully open position. In that way, you keep the other variables constant. Note that the number of round diamonds available decreases dramatically. When we followed this procedure, the number of round diamonds available for sale dropped to 14,009.
- Second, adjust the slide bars for the Color variable, so that you will see only those round diamonds of D, E, and F color. Be sure to open the slide bars for Carat and to keep the other slide bars in their fully open position. When we followed this procedure, the number of round diamonds available for sale dropped to 58,993.

Comparing the results of these two sensitivity analyses, we can say that the number of round diamonds for sale is more sensitive to changes in Carat than to changes in Color, if we keep the other variables constant.

What–If Analysis. A model builder must make predictions and assumptions regarding the input data, many of which are based on the assessment of uncertain futures. The results depend on the accuracy of these assumptions, which can be highly subjective. *What–if analysis* attempts to predict the impact of changes in the assumptions—that is, the input data—on the proposed solution.

Let's perform a *what–if analysis* on the data. A young man's fiancée has decided that she would like her engagement ring to be between one and two carats, at least a Very Good cut, an F color or better, and a clarity of at least VVS2 (VVS2 means "two very, very small imperfections"). Adjust the slide bars for all four of the variables at the same time. When we followed this procedure, the number of round diamonds available for sale dropped to 3,830.

Goal-Seeking Analysis. *Goal-seeking analysis* represents a "backward" solution approach. Goal seeking attempts to calculate the value of the inputs necessary to achieve a desired level of output.

Let's perform a *goal-seeking analysis* on the data. When the young man in our example looked at the list of 3,830 diamonds (using the scroll bar on the right side of the list), he noticed that the prices ranged from $6,356 to $10,117. He told his fiancée that he had only $5,000 to invest in a diamond. They consequently opened up the slide bars for the Carat, Cut, Color, and Clarity variables and adjusted the slide bar for the Price variable to be between $4,500 and $5,000. When we followed this procedure, the number of round diamonds available for sale increased to 3,874.

The couple now had the problem of examining the list of diamonds to decide which combination of the four variables would be suitable. They did this by performing several what–if analyses:

- She decided that she really wanted a diamond between one and two carats. After adjusting the Carat slide bar, the number of round diamonds available dropped to 2,035.

- She then decided that she wanted a D, E, or F color. After adjusting the Color slide bar, the number of round diamonds available dropped to 424.

- Next, she chose a Cut that was at least Very Good. After adjusting the Cut slide bar, the number of round diamonds available dropped to 266.

- The couple noticed that all 266 diamonds had a Clarity variable of either SI1 (one small imperfection) or SI2 (two small imperfections). At this point, they either could decide that this level of clarity is acceptable or they could perform additional what–if analyses on other variables.

Examples of Descriptive Analytics Applications

We present several examples of descriptive analytics in this section. Keep in mind that descriptive analytics applications often immediately suggest predictive analytics applications. Let's begin with the examples of Fandango and Darden Restaurants.

POM **Fandango.** Fandango (**www.fandango.com**) is the leading online ticket seller for movie theaters. The firm sells millions of tickets to approximately 20,000 movie theaters across the United States. Fandango captures data about customers, movie theaters, ticket sales, and show times.

MKT Fandango wanted to analyze the movie preferences of its customers during the past year. Using a sample of movie titles, Fandango analysts investigated the total sales for different genres of movies; for example, comedy, drama, and action. Using a sample of moviegoers, they calculated the average ticket sales for a week, the most popular movie, the distribution of customers among the movie genres, the busiest hours of the day in the movie theater, and many other analyses. These descriptive analyses help Fandango set ticket prices, offer discounts for certain movies or show times, and assign show times of the same movie in different theaters.

ACCT **FIN** **HRM** **OptumRx.** Pharmacy care service company OptumRx (**www.optumrx.com**) was analyzing a client company's prescription-drug claims when the firm noticed that the client's spending on acne medicine seemed high compared with other clients' spending on the medication. Analyzing the data, OptumRx found that employees had been prescribed newer brand-name acne drugs that were largely combinations of older generic medicines. OptumRx informed the client, a 60,000-employee company, which then began to require patients to begin treatment with the cheaper medicines and to use the more expensive medicines only if the others did not work. Within six months, the company had saved more than $70,000.

POM **HRM** In another case, OptumRx noted that at one of its client companies, drugs for attention deficit hyperactivity disorder (ADHD) were being overprescribed to adults. Some of these employees were using the drug to improve their performance at work. The firm's benefit manager formulated stricter rules concerning reimbursement for ADHD prescriptions and saved the 19,000-worker company $110,000.

HRM OptumRx also uses descriptive analytics to improve patient health. For instance, the company can analyze how frequently asthma sufferers are refilling their prescriptions to discover whether they are taking too many puffs on their inhalers. This could indicate that these employees require a different drug. Switching patients to more effective medicines is worthwhile even if these drugs are more expensive, because they can help reduce costly hospitalizations and visits to emergency rooms.

For other examples of descriptive analytics, see this chapter's opening case, closing case, and IT's About Business 12.1, 12.2, 12.3, 12.4, and 12.5. Specifically, IT's About Business 12.1 illustrates how TellusLabs successfully employs descriptive analytics to provide valuable information on the state of various crops. Note that TellusLabs also uses predictive analytics to predict crop yields.

IT's About Business 12.1

POM **MIS** TellusLabs

In 2016, the United States produced more than 15 billion bushels of corn and 4 billion bushels of soy, making corn and soy two of the most widely produced crops in the country. These large yields affect more than 3 million U.S. farmers, as well as thousands of decision makers in finance, insurance, agribusiness, and government. With so much at stake, accurately predicting crop yields has become critical.

TellusLabs (**www.indigoag.com/geospatial-innovation**) is a Boston, Massachusetts, start-up recently acquired by Indigo AG that integrates data from three sources for analysis purposes: daily satellite imagery from the National Aeronautics and Space Administration (NASA; **www.nasa.gov**) and commercial satellites; weather data from the National Oceanic and Atmospheric Administration (**www.noaa.gov**); and seasonal, crop-growing information from the U.S. Department of Agriculture (USDA; **www.usda.gov**). The firm uses machine-learning algorithms (see Technology Guide 4) in its analytics efforts to generate intelligence about natural resources; for example, predicting agricultural yields.

There are other satellite imagery analysis firms such as Descartes Labs (**www.descarteslabs.com**) and Orbital Insight (**www.orbitalinsight.com**). However, TellusLabs differentiates itself by applying scientific expertise in vegetation and climatology to its analyses and by focusing exclusively on natural resources. The firm maintains that there are many organizations that must make difficult decisions about natural resources. Its objective is to quickly provide quality data to them.

FIN The company's first product is Kernel, an agricultural commodities forecast modeling tool. Kernel provides an interactive, online dashboard that shows a map of the major corn- and soy-growing regions across the United States. The dashboard also displays key financial indicators, such as predicted yield, harvested area, and total production. Users can view data at a state, an agricultural district, or a county level. In addition, they can examine historical yield data from the USDA. The dashboard also

indicates the average change in corn and soy yield estimates, week over week. TellusLabs updates these forecasts daily.

Kernel is designed to provide fast, reliable data that organizations and people can use in multiple ways. For example, a commodities trader could use the information for trades in the futures market. An ethanol plant operator could consult Kernel to gauge whether its contracted farmers will be able to supply enough corn to keep it running. An agribusiness company such as John Deere could license the data feed from Kernel and integrate it into a smart pump that automatically adjusts how much water it provides to crops.

TellusLabs asserts that an internal test revealed that the firm is able to predict the end-of-year yield for U.S. corn and soy more accurately than the federal government. In the test, the lab used its algorithms to analyze publicly available, historical USDA corn and soy yield data from 2004 to 2014 in order to predict year-end figures. Over that period, the lab's estimates outperformed those of the USDA almost 70 percent of the time during the months of August and September, which are the key trading months for corn and soy. In 2016, Kernel predicted the USDA's final 2016 corn and soy yield report two months ahead of publicly available in-season forecasts. Kernel exactly predicted the USDA estimate for soy, and it came within 1 percent of the USDA estimate for corn.

TellusLabs plans to release a predictive model for wheat; to extend its corn yield data to Argentina, Brazil, and China; and to monitor forests and large, fresh-water reservoirs by satellite. The founders note that there are many interesting, global-scale, geospatial questions that have not been analyzed. For example: How will we feed a rapidly growing global population? How will we manage our increasingly limited water resources? How can we best manage our land and forest resources in an era of global warming?

On a contrary note, the U.S. Department of Agriculture said in 2018 that satellite images by themselves still could not be relied upon to predict annual corn, wheat, or soybean harvests. Instead, the government's main source of information remained farmer surveys and random field samples.

And the bottom line? In January 2017, the lab announced that it had raised $3.1 million in seed funding. Further, by September 2018, some 1,000 organizations and individuals around the world were relying on TellusLabs's data. In late 2018, Indigo Ag (**www.indigoag.com**), a company helping farmers sustainably feed the planet, acquired TellusLabs. Today Indigo AG continues to grow this technology.

Sources: Compiled from "Indigo Ag, Inc. Acquires TellusLabs, a Leader in Satellite Technology and Artificial Intelligence, to Enhance Indigo's Data-Driven Agronomic Solutions," *Business Wire*, December 13, 2018; J. Wilson, "Satellites Are Great, but They Don't Beat U.S. Crop Forecasters," Bloomberg.com, April 11, 2018; E. Peterson, "How Satellite Data Is Changing the Definition of Crop Reports," OpenMarkets, October 26, 2017; N. Thakkar, "9 Practical Use Cases of Predictive Analytics," Dataone Innovation Labs, July 10, 2017; "TellusLabs New Kernel Models Show a 2017 U.S. Growing Season Back on Track," TellusLabs News Release, June 28, 2017; G. Anadiotis, "Planet Analytics: Big Data, Sustainability, and Environmental Impact," ZDNet, April 22, 2017; T. Sparapani, "How Big Data and Tech Will Improve Agriculture, from Farm to Table," *Forbes*, March 23, 2017; J. Hofherr, "How Boston Startup TellusLabs Answers Big Environmental Questions Using Satellite Imagery," builtinboston.com, February 13, 2017; T. Bindi, "Transforming the Agriculture Industry Using IoT and Predictive Analytics," ZDNet, February 1, 2017; J. Mannes, "TellusLabs Wants to Help Us Better Understand Our Planet," *TechCrunch*, January 17, 2017; G. Burningham, "How Satellite Imaging Will Revolutionize Everything from Stock Picking to Farming," *Newsweek*, September 8, 2016; E. Woyke, "Crystal Ball for Corn Crop Yields Will Revolutionize Commodity Trading," *MIT Technology Review*, August 9, 2016; A. Brokaw, "This Startup Uses Machine Learning and Satellite Imagery to Predict Crop Yields," *The Verge*, August 4, 2016; A. Satariano and A. Bjerga, "Farming Big Data," *Bloomberg BusinessWeek*, June 13–26, 2016; "How Satellite Technology Is Predicting Crop Yields," Thomson Reuters, March 31, 2016; and https://www.indigoag.com/geospatial-innovation, accessed July 16, 2019.

Questions

1. Describe the descriptive analytics applications of TellusLabs.
2. Describe the predictive analytics applications of TellusLabs.
3. Describe a possible prescriptive analytics application for TellusLabs.

The emergence of technology for capturing, storing, and using real-time data (e.g., the Internet of Things, see Chapter 8) has enabled real-time BA users to employ analytics to analyze data in real time. Real-time BA also helps organizations to make decisions and to interact with customers in new and innovative ways. Real-time BA is closely related to descriptive analytics because the focus of decisions is real time, rather than at some point in the future.

Before you go on . . .

1. Describe the purpose of descriptive analytics.
2. Discuss the BA tools that are commonly used in descriptive analytics.

12.4 | Predictive Analytics

Author Lecture Videos are available exclusively in *WileyPLUS*.
Apply the Concept activities are available in the Appendix and in *WileyPLUS*.

Predictive analytics examines recent and historical data to detect patterns and predict future outcomes and trends. Predictive analytics provides estimates about the likelihood of a future outcome.

The purpose of predictive analytics is *not* to tell decision makers what will happen in the future. Predictive analytics can only forecast what *might* happen in the future, based on probabilities. Predictive analytics applications forecast customer behavior and purchasing patterns, identify trends in sales activities, and forecast demand for inputs from suppliers.

BA Tools in Predictive Analytics

Organizations use a variety of BA tools and statistical procedures in performing predictive analytics. The tools include data mining, and the statistical procedures include linear regression, multiple regression, and logistic regression. There are many other tools and statistical procedures that are used in predictive analytics. For purposes of illustration, we take a look at data mining and linear regression in this section.

Data Mining. Recall that data mining can perform two basic operations: (1) identifying previously unknown patterns and (2) predicting trends and behaviors. The first operation is a descriptive analytics application, and the second is a predictive analytics application.

In predictive analytics, data mining can predict trends and behaviors. **MKT** For example, *targeted marketing* relies on predictive information. Data mining can use data from past promotional mailings to identify those prospects who are most likely to respond favorably to future mailings. **FIN** Another business problem that uses predictive information is forecasting bankruptcy and other forms of default.

FIN Another predictive analytics application is detecting fraudulent credit card transactions. Over time, a pattern emerges of the typical ways you use your credit card and your typical shopping behaviors—the places in which you use your card, the amounts you spend, and so on. If your card is stolen and used fraudulently, then the usage often varies noticeably from your established pattern. Data-mining tools can discern this difference and alert your credit card company.

Numerous predictive data-mining applications are used in business and in other fields. The following representative examples illustrate the variety of these applications:

- **MKT** *Retailing and sales:* Predicting sales, preventing theft and fraud, and determining correct inventory levels and distribution schedules among outlets. For example, retailers such as AAFES (stores on military bases) use Fraud Watch from SAP (**www.sap.com**) to combat fraud by employees in their 1,400 stores.

- **MKT** *Marketing:* Classifying customer demographics that can be used to predict which customers will respond to a mailing or buy a particular product.

- **FIN** *Banking:* Forecasting levels of bad loans and fraudulent credit card use, predicting credit card spending by new customers, and determining which kinds of customers will best respond to (and qualify for) new loan offers.

- **FIN** *Social good:* Simpa Networks sells solar-as-a-service to poor households and small businesses in India. Simpa partnered with DataKind (**www.datakind.org**), whose data scientists analyzed Simpa's historical customer data to help Simpa assess the credit-worthiness of potential customers.

- **FIN** *Insurance:* Forecasting claim amounts and medical coverage costs, classifying the most important elements that affect medical coverage, and predicting which customers will buy new insurance policies.

- **POM** *Manufacturing and production:* Predicting machinery failures and finding key factors that help optimize manufacturing capacity.

- *Health care:* Correlating demographics of patients with critical illnesses and developing better insights on how to identify and treat symptoms and their causes. For example, Microsoft and Stanford University announced that they had mined the search data of millions of users to successfully identify unreported side effects of certain medications.

- *Politics:* In his FiveThirtyEight blog, Nate Silver famously analyzed polling and economic data to predict the results of the 2008 presidential election, calling 49 out of 50 states correctly. He then correctly predicted all 50 states in the 2012 presidential election. In contrast, Silver failed to correctly predict that Donald Trump would win the 2016 presidential election.

- *Weather:* The National Weather Service is predicting weather with increasing accuracy and precision by analyzing a myriad of variables, including past and present atmospheric conditions, location, temperature, air pressure, wind speed, and many others.

Examples of Predictive Analytics Applications

In this section, we present numerous examples of predictive analytics. Keep in mind that descriptive analytics applications often immediately suggest predictive analytics applications. Let's continue with the example of Fandango.

MKT Fandango. How does the ticket seller know when to send e-mails to its members with discount offers for a specific movie on a specific day? Consider John Jones. Predictive analytics tools analyze terabytes of data to determine that although John likes science fiction movies, he has not seen the latest science fiction movie, which has been in theaters since the previous Friday.

Additional Examples. Predictive analytics is used throughout organizations in every industry. We present some scenarios in this chapter's opening case and closing cases. Here are some other examples:

- **MKT** Predictive analytics drives the coupons you receive at the grocery cash register. United Kingdom grocery giant Tesco (**www.tesco.com**) predicts which discounts customers will redeem so it can better target more than 100 million personalized coupons annually at cash registers in 13 countries. This process increased coupon redemption rates by 360 percent over previous methods.

- **MKT** Websites predict which ads you will click so they can instantly choose which ad to show you, a process that drives millions of dollars in new revenue.

- **POM** **MKT** Leading online dating companies Match (**www.match.com**), OKCupid (**www.okcupid.com**), and eHarmony (**www.eharmony.com**) predict which prospect on your screen will be the most compatible with you.

- **POM** Wireless carriers predict how likely you are to cancel and defect to a competitor—a process called *churn*—possibly before you decide to do so. These predictions are based on factors such as dropped calls, your phone usage, your billing information, and whether your contacts have already defected.

- **FIN** Allstate Insurance tripled the accuracy of predicting bodily injury liability from car crashes based on the characteristics of the insured vehicle; that is, the insurer adjusted the rates based on the vehicle. This process resulted in approximately $40 million in annual savings.

- **FIN** Financial services firms employ predictive analytics to produce credit scores. They use these scores to determine the probability that customers will make future credit payments on time.

- Stanford University data scientists used predictive analytics to diagnose breast cancer better than human physicians by discovering an innovative method that takes into account a greater number of contributing factors in a tissue sample.

- Officials in Oregon and Pennsylvania are using predictive analytics to assess the risk that a convict will offend again.

- **MKT** Sentiment analysis is another type of predictive analysis. *Sentiment analysis* is the process of analyzing opinions expressed in a piece of text to determine whether the writer's attitude toward a particular topic, product, or service is positive, negative, or neutral. The input to this type of analysis is plain text—for example, ratings, recommendations, tweets, Facebook posts—and the output is a sentiment score. This score can be positive or negative. This score could also be a number between –1 and +1, indicating the degree of positivity or negativity.

IT's About Business 12.2 illustrates how animals tagged with solar-powered sensors can potentially predict earthquakes, volcanic eruptions, and other natural phenomena. IT's About Business 12.3 explains how online dating services such as eHarmony employ analytics to find optimal matches.

IT's About Business 12.2

POM The Living Internet

The U.S. Geological Survey (USGS; **www.usgs.gov**) notes on its website that "anecdotal evidence abounds of animals, fish, birds, reptiles, and insects exhibiting strange behavior anywhere from weeks to seconds before an earthquake." For instance, in 2014, researchers explored unusual animal behaviors preceding the 2011 earthquake and tsunami that devastated Japan. They found that a week before the earthquake occurred, pets living with within 200 miles of the epicenter were more likely to cling to their owners. During that same period, local cows yielded less milk.

Martin Wikelski is working to collect and analyze Big Data to provide scientific evidence to support the anecdotal evidence. He is the migration expert from Germany's Max Planck Institute for Ornithology (**www.orn.mpg.de**). He tests whether abrupt changes in animal behavior can predict earthquakes, volcanic eruptions, and other events and trends.

Wikelski documented Indonesian elephants moving to safe ground before a tsunami devastated that country in 2004. In 2012 and 2014, he documented the movement patterns of goats and sheep on Mt. Etna in Sicily that anticipated major volcanic eruptions between four to six hours before they occurred.

In October 2016, the town of Visso, Italy, experienced a devastating, magnitude 6.1 earthquake. At one farm in Visso, Wikelski taped solar-powered sensors weighing one-sixth of an ounce on cows, sheep, dogs, chickens, turkeys, and one rabbit. The devices measured the animals' movements to the second, including their magnetic direction, speed, altitude, temperature, humidity, acceleration, and location. He then waited for aftershocks to find out whether the animals anticipated them. A few days after he tagged the animals, another major earthquake, measuring a magnitude of 6.5, hit the area. Wikelski's sensors detected "dynamic body acceleration," meaning that the animals expended dramatically more energy than usual as many as 14 hours before the aftershock hit. Significantly, this activity occurred even at times when the animals normally would be asleep or docile. As of this time, Wikelski had not published his findings. He had hinted, however, that the data revealed that the animals were moving in a consistent way in the hours before the quake.

In essence, the animals become environmental sensors. Wikelski is now entering the Big Data collected from his studies into the ICARUS Initiative (International Cooperation for Animal Research Using Space; **www.icarusinitiative.org**). ICARUS is an open-source online database that was designed to collect data from tagged animals around the world.

ICARUS, an initiative of the Max Planck Institute, the German Aerospace Center, and the Russian Federal Space Agency, has tagged dozens of mammals, birds, fish, and even flying insects with tiny tracking sensors, usually with super glue. With the help of volunteers who sign up online, Wikelski had tagged several thousand animals by August, 2018. The team hopes to eventually grow the program to include more than 100,000 animals.

ICARUS plans to fit thousands of animals and insects with solar-powered tracking tags to allow radio-frequency communication with the International Space Station (ISS). In February, 2018, a Russian rocket carried the antennas of the Icarus mission to the International Space Station (ISS). The receiving antennas can pick up data from some 15 million transmitting tags worldwide. These miniature tags weigh just 5 grams and were specifically developed for the Icarus Initiative. They enable scientists to track small animals such as some of the larger migratory birds from long distance. The ICARUS antennas orbit about 200 miles above the Earth, covering more than 90 percent of the Earth's surface. The ISS completes its orbit 16 times every 24 hours, so the tags will not be out of transmission range for significant lengths of time.

As of July, 2019 Wikelski had tagged increasingly smaller creatures. He had tagged cicadas, dragonflies, and bumblebees. Each tag contains a thermometer, accelerometer, GPS receiver, a transmitter that can send a signal into space, and a solar-charged battery for power. The tags are very light weight because tags that weigh more than 3 percent of an animal's body weight can alter its behavior

and threaten its survival. The solar-powered battery means that the tags can theoretically last as long as the animal carrying them and can be retrieved and reused. (*Note:* Solar-powered tags still require batteries to track animals at night.) The tags also contain a memory chip that can store up to 500 megabytes of data – enough to record an animal's travels, movement, and energy expenditure over a lifetime. In addition, the tag must also have room to hold a transmitter powerful enough to communicate with a satellite that can receive and relay information back to scientists on the ground.

ICARUS plans to tag 20,000 animals over time. Future tagging examples include swarms of desert locusts to warn farmers or to track outbreaks of certain diseases; monitoring fishery populations to better regulate fish feeding and breeding; measuring atmosphere and temperature more precisely from birds' flights; and tracking the spread of Ebola based on which African fruit bats have developed antibodies.

ICARUS envisions a global network of living sensors, quite literally the Living Internet. The team hopes the data will be able to predict storms and climatic shifts as well as volcanic eruptions, earthquakes, and tsunamis. From the vantage point of space, they hope to be able to track the outbreak of diseases such as bird flu, to prevent tropical wood smuggling, and to better protect endangered species such as the rhinoceros.

Sources: Compiled from L. Dormehl, "ICARUS Project Aims to Track Migration of 100,000 Animals – from Space," *Digital Trends*, August 21, 2018' "Ears for Icarus," *Max-Planck-Gesellschaft*, February 13, 2018; "Using Animals to Predict the Future," *Bloomberg Businessweek*, August 7, 2017; Krazytrs, "Icarus Project—What Is the Relationship between Animals and Natural Disasters?" *Ultimate Science*, July 11, 2017; E. Povoledo, "Can Animals Predict Earthquakes? Italian Farm Acts as a Lab to Find Out," *New York Times*, June 17, 2017; G. Anadiotis, "Planet Analytics: Big Data, Sustainability, and Environmental Impact," ZDNet, April 22, 2017; N. Wilson, "The International Space Station Will Soon Help Track Bird and Insect Migration," *Motherboard*, March 20, 2017; D. Martins, "Five Animals that Can Predict Earthquakes," The Weather Network, October 27, 2016; C. Seidler, "A New Technology for Following Songbirds," *Der Spiegel*, October 22, 2016; J. Carlowe, "Can Animals Help Us Predict Earthquakes," *Science Focus*, April 20, 2016; V. Shahrestani, "Sleeping Dogs React to a Californian Earthquake Seconds before It Hits," *The Telegraph*, August 18, 2015; C. Mooney, "We're Entering a Stunning New Era for Animal Tracking," *Washington Post*, June 11, 2015; S. Griffiths, "Animals CAN Predict Earthquakes," *The Daily Mail*, March 24, 2015; J. Ford, "Bees Fitted with Sensors to Monitor Environment," *The Engineer*, January 15, 2014; and http://icarusinitiative.org, accessed July 16, 2019.

Questions

1. Describe the descriptive analytics applications of ICARUS's business model.
2. Describe the predictive analytics applications of ICARUS's business model.
3. Describe a possible prescriptive analytics application for ICARUS.

IT's About Business 12.3

MKT POM Analytics and Online Dating

An estimated 109 million adult Americans are single, and matching them up has become a huge business. In fact, college-aged adults are now the most likely online daters. According to IBIS World (**www.ibisworld.com**), the dating services industry grossed

$2.8 billion in revenue in 2017. According to Consumer Rankings (**www.consumerrankings.com**), the five leading online dating services are Match (**www.match.com**), Zoosk (**www.zoosk.com**), OurTime (**www.ourtime.com**), eHarmony (**www.eharmony.com**), and EliteSingles (**www.elitesingles.com**). Let's take a closer look at eHarmony.

Essentially, eHarmony wants to know more about people in order to find compatible matches. To accomplish this goal, eHarmony collects four types of data, which totaled 125 terabytes in August 2018:

- Demographic data—for example, age, gender, location, hobbies, and sexual orientation—which are self-reported.

- Psychographic data—for example, likes, interests, and habits—which are also self-reported. Regarding psychographics, the service collects data on 29 dimensions of compatibility such as "emotional energy" and "curiosity." eHarmony refers to these dimensions as "deep psychological traits" because each dimension incorporates several items on the service's questionnaire. eHarmony then analyzes the respondents' answers to each dimension's items to produce a "score" for that dimension or psychological trait. For example, the questionnaire includes several items for the dimension of curiosity. After eHarmony analyzes a respondent's answers to these items, it assigns a curiosity score ranging from "not curious" to "very curious."

- Behavioral data—for example, actions users take on the site. Specifically, eHarmony collects data on the actions that members take with each match that eHarmony suggests—for example, Contact right away? Ignore? The service also collects data on the feedback its members provide.

- Data on couples who met through the service. eHarmony's research team conducts this research, with each couple's permission.

A neural network and machine learning algorithms produce a "satisfaction estimator" to rate potential matches (see Technology Guide 4). The system learns over time, as eHarmony and its members provide new data. (That is, eHarmony's system predicts successful matches.) The more relevant, or potentially optimal, the matches, the higher the rate at which members will communicate with one another. Furthermore, the more they engage with one another, the more likely they are to purchase annual subscriptions.

eHarmony uses two techniques to match singles. The initial match is based on compatibility. This measure is determined by the questionnaire that users complete when they join the site as well as proprietary mathematical models. eHarmony then uses machine learning to learn about behavior on the site as an indicator of what a person likes. For example, if a user is more likely to communicate with a potential match who has more than 500 words on his or her profile, then the next matches will include more complete written profiles. Furthermore, in terms of physical appearances, analysis of photos on the site lets the machine learning algorithms know if a user prefers blondes or beards.

Given that eHarmony does not ask its users if they end up going on a date, its machine learning models are optimized for two-way communication. That process means that the ideal outcome, according to the algorithms, is someone sending a message to their match and receiving a reply. According to eHarmony data scientists, the message and response are the best indicators that both parties are happy with the match.

As eHarmony analyzes its Big Data, it discovers some interesting nuances about matching people around the world. For example, whether someone smokes and drinks is more important in dating in Europe compared to the United States. Once eHarmony more heavily weighted the smoking and drinking variables in its matching algorithm in the United Kingdom, the service's number of subscribers increased rapidly.

When eHarmony first launched in 2000, users created a dating profile, filled out a 450-item questionnaire, and then reviewed matches without the ability to see any other users' pictures. Over the years, the site has added photos. Nevertheless, free, mobile, swiping apps such as Tinder (**www.tinder.com**) and Bumble (**www.bumble.com**) were taking users away from the service. Keep in mind that eHarmony charges monthly subscriptions of up to $59.95. As a result, eHarmony began to revise its strategy.

In December 2016, eHarmony announced that it no longer requires users to answer its survey before signing up for the service. The survey has long differentiated eHarmony from other online dating services. eHarmony still stands behind its questionnaire, maintaining that having access to more information helps the dating service find compatible matches. The questionnaire will still be available to subscribers who wish to complete it.

eHarmony then decided to let people take its questionnaire a little at a time. The service does tell its members that the fewer the questions they answer on its survey, the less compatible the matches that it finds could be.

eHarmony also added a tool called "The Two of You Together," which highlights why the service thinks two people are matches. The feature ranks the top three compatibility points—such as intellect or emotional energy—for a potential couple.

And the bottom line? In July 2019, eHarmony had over 30 million members.

Sources: Compiled from G. Nott, "Click Me Maybe: Inside eHarmony's Matchmaking Machine," *CIO*, March 21, 2018; T. Bennett, "In the Age of Tinder, eHarmony Is Investing in Machine Learning to Make Smarter Matches," Which-50.com, April 9, 2018; J. Frew, "How Online Dating Uses Data to Find Your Perfect Match," Makeuseof.com, July 17, 2017; "How to Promote a Dating Site with the Help of Google Analytics Data," WPDating, May 24, 2017; S. Carter, "Dating Revolutionized by Big Data and Memes—Tech Podcast," *The Guardian*, May 19, 2017; S. Knapton, "Secret of eHarmony Algorithm Is Revealed…" *The Telegraph*, May 14, 2017; C. Weller, "eHarmony Is Gearing up for a Battle to Win Back Millennials from Tinder and Bumble," *Business Insider*, February 18, 2017; P. Mannova, "How Dating Site eHarmony Uses Machine Learning to Help You Find Love," *Fortune*, February 14, 2017; T. Gillies, "In 'Swipe Left' Era of Mobile Dating, eHarmony Tries to Avoid Getting 'Frozen in Time'," CNBC, February 11, 2017; S. O'Brien, "eHarmony Finally Nixes Its Lengthy Questionnaire," CNN, December 16, 2016; K. Murnane, "Report Shows More People of All Ages Are Dating Online," *Forbes*, March 2, 2016; R. Meyer, "College-Aged Adults Are Now the Most Likely Online Daters," *The Atlantic*, February 11, 2016; "Online Dating: Relationship Analytics in the Real World," *Objectivity*, February 11, 2016; H. Augur, "Can Big Data Save Your Love Life? Online Dating Apps Say Yes," Dataconomy, February 9, 2016; J. Ryoo and E-K. Kim, "Big Data E-Textbook," National Science Foundation, December 1, 2015; R. Kalakota, "Love, Sex and Predictive Analytics: Tinder, Match.com, and OkCupid," Practical Analytics, May 29, 2015; S. Palmer, "Big Dating: It's a (Data) Science," Huffington Post, May 22, 2015; K. Nash, "CIOs Have to Learn the New Math of Analytics, CIO, February 25, 2015; P. Rubens, "Is Big Data Dating the Key to Long-Lasting Romance?" BBC News, March 25, 2014; and www.eharmony.com, accessed July 16, 2019.

Questions

1. Describe the descriptive analytics applications of eHarmony's business model.

2. Describe the predictive analytics applications of eHarmony's business model.

3. Describe a possible prescriptive analytics application for eHarmony.

Unintended Consequences of Predictive Analytics

Predictive analytics clearly provides organizations with numerous advantages. In fact, one could say that predictive analytics is critically important for an organization's success. However, predictive analytics applications can produce questionable, or even harmful, results for organizations. For example, we look at unintended consequences of predictive analytics for Target, Uber, and the Los Angeles Police Department.

MKT **Target.** Target identified 25 products that, when purchased together, indicate that a woman is likely pregnant. The value of these data was that Target could send coupons to the pregnant woman at a habit-forming period of her life. Unfortunately, Target's algorithms led to a public-relations problem.

A man walked into a Target outside Minneapolis, Minnesota, and demanded to see the manager. He had coupons that had been sent to his daughter, and he was quite angry. He told the manager that his daughter was a teenager, and he wanted to know if Target was trying to encourage her to become pregnant.

The manager did not know what the man was talking about. He noted that the mailer was addressed to the man's daughter and it contained advertisements for maternity clothing, nursery furniture, and pictures of smiling infants. The manager apologized and then called the man a few days later to apologize again. However, the father was embarrassed. He told the manager that his daughter was indeed pregnant and that he owed the manager an apology.

POM **Uber.** In December 2016, Uber's algorithm automatically raised rates (surge pricing) in Sydney, Australia, as people tried to get away from a downtown restaurant where an armed man was holding 17 people hostage. Three people, including the gunman, died. Uber later apologized for raising fares, which reportedly quadrupled, and then offered refunds.

Problems are most likely to arise when algorithms make things happen automatically, without human intervention or oversight. Uber is now working on a global policy to prevent price increases in times of disaster or emergency.

IT's About Business 12.4

POM **The Los Angeles Police Department Uses Predictive Policing**

Palantir is an intelligence platform originally designed for the global war on terror. Palantir's software analyzes many different data sources—including financial documents, airline reservations, phone records, social media posts, and many more—to search for connections that human analysts might miss, in large part due to the overwhelming amount of data.

The U.S. government deploys Palantir in multiple areas:

- The Department of Defense uses Palantir to synthesize and sort battlefield intelligence. For example, the software helped analysts find roadside bombs and track insurgents.

- The U.S. Department of Health and Human Services uses Palantir to detect Medicare fraud.

- The FBI uses Palantir in criminal probes.

- The Department of Homeland Security uses Palantir to screen air travelers and keep tabs on immigrants.

By 2019, many law enforcement agencies had used, or still used, Palantir. These agencies included police and sheriff's departments in New York, New Orleans, Chicago, and Los Angeles. Let's take a closer look at Los Angeles' experience with Palantir.

The Los Angeles Police Department (LAPD) first deployed Palantir in 2009 to identify and deter people likely to commit crimes. The system analyzes data from rap sheets, parole reports, police interviews, and other sources and generates a list of people the LAPD defines as chronic offenders. These people are the ones that the system says are most at risk of reoffending and should be surveilled the most.

The LAPD distributes this list, called the Chronic Offender Bulletin, to patrol officers who have orders to monitor and stop these pre-crime suspects as often as possible, using excuses such as jaywalking or a broken taillight. At each contact, officers fill out a field interview card with names, addresses, vehicles, physical description, any neighborhood intelligence the person offers, and the officer's own observations on the person. Data from these cards is entered into the Palantir system, adding to a constantly expanding surveillance database that is fully accessible without a warrant.

To widen the scope of possible connections with chronic offenders, the LAPD has explored buying private data, including social media, foreclosure records, toll road information, camera feeds from hospitals, parking lots, and universities, and delivery information from Papa John's and Pizza Hut.

Los Angeles says that predictive policing can help the LAPD efficiently target resources and help reduce crime. However, civil rights activists are concerned that the technology is simply a new type of racial profiling.

In 2018, the Los Angeles Police Department (LAPD) was forced to release documents about their predictive policing and surveillance algorithms, as a result of a lawsuit from the Stop LAPD Spying Coalition (**www.stoplapdspying.org**). The documents revealed that the algorithms require officers to keep an eye on people deemed most likely to commit a crime. The coalition said that the documents also propagate disproportionately high arrests of black Angelinos, as well as other racial minorities.

There are lessons to be learned from the deployment of Palantir for predictive policing:

- For all of Palantir's professed concern for individuals' privacy, the single most important safeguard against abuse of the system is the one that Palantir is trying to reduce through automation: human judgement.

- Algorithms reinforce systemic biases—that is, algorithms, no matter how sophisticated, are only as good as the data that are provided to them. Therefore, if data comes from a city where there is an existing problem with over-policing of neighborhoods with concentrations of people of color, then the algorithms will reflect this data. People targeted by the algorithms can face extra police surveillance just because they may be associated with, or know of, criminal activity. This situation can occur even if they have never done anything wrong in their lives.

- Transparency will be the key in moving forward with predictive policing. Defense attorneys want to have evidence gathered by the predictive policing system thrown out, in large part because the software was used secretly, without the knowledge of the defendant or defense attorneys. Appeals continue to work their way through the court system.

- Convictions and punishments as the result of predictive policing software are problematic. These systems do not give high-risk individuals a reasonable chance to improve their behavior or learn lessons from their past. If anything, such systems may support an endless cycle of recidivism.

Sources: Compiled from B. Lipton, "Eight Years in, LAPD Can't Measure PredPol's Effect on Crime," *Muckrock*, March 12, 2019; "How Data-Driven Policing Threatens Human Freedom," *The Economist*, June 4, 2018; I. Lapowsky, "How the LAPD Uses Data to Predict Crime," *Wired*, May 22, 2018; M. Ahmed, "Aided by Palantir, the LAPD Uses Predictive Policing to Monitor Specific People and Neighborhoods," *The Intercept*, May 11, 2018; "The LAPD's Terrifying Palantir-Powered Policing Algorithm Was Just Uncovered and Yes It's Basically 'Minority Report'," *Futurism*, May 10, 2018; G. Joseph, "The LAPD Has a New Surveillance Formula, Powered by Palantir," *The Appeal*, May 8, 2018; A. Winston and I. Burrington, "A Pioneer in Predictive Policing Is Starting a Troubling New Project," *The Verge*, April 26, 2018; P. Waldman, L. Chapman, and J. Robertson, "Palantir Knows Everything about You," *Bloomberg BusinessWeek*, April 23, 2018; J. Loeb, "AI and the Future of Policing Algorithms on the Beat," *Engineering and Technology*, April 16, 2018; A. Ferguson, "The High-Definition, Artificially Intelligent, All-Seeing Future of Big Data Policing," aclu.org, April 4, 2018; A. Johansson, "5 Lessons Learned from the Predictive Policing Failure in New Orleans," *VentureBeat*, March 19, 2018; M. Harris, "How Peter Thiel's Secretive Data Company Pushed into Policing," *Wired*, August 9, 2017; C. Chang, "The LAPD's Biggest Conundrum: How to Suppress Crime without Alienating South L.A.'s Black Residents," *Los Angeles Times*, February 4, 2017; and www.palantir.com, accessed July 16, 2019.

Questions

1. Describe a descriptive analytics application of the Palantir system used in predictive policing.

2. Describe a predictive analytics application of the Palantir system used in predictive policing.

3. Describe a prescriptive analytics application of the Palantir system used in predictive policing.

4. Describe unintended consequences resulting from the LAPD's use of the Palantir system.

Example of Descriptive Analytics and Predictive Analytics

Let's consider the following example to demonstrate how descriptive and predictive analytics are used to bridge the gap between data management and actionable business decisions.

POM Weather data can be used to make predictions relating to certain business problems. Suppose you are the Northeast district manager for the American Automobile Association (AAA; **www.aaa.com**), and your district covers multiple offices in several states. You need to create a work schedule for your employees, who receive and dispatch service calls. Your goal is to provide optimal coverage in your offices, reduce unnecessary salary expenses, and provide excellent customer service by reducing customers' wait time. Therefore, you decide to predict the number of service calls your offices receive per day during normal business hours based on the daily low temperature measured in degrees.

Data Management. To investigate this business problem, you collect data on service calls for the past year from the AAA locations within your district. You first "clean" the data by adjusting for outliers and missing values, resulting in a final sample of 3,219 service calls.

You are now ready to build a regression model using temperature as the independent variable to predict the number of customer service calls received in any given day; this is the dependent variable. You will use the results to predict how many employees should be available to receive and dispatch customer service calls.

Descriptive Analytics. For this example, the correlation between daily low temperature and the number of service calls was found to be –0.84, with an average of 48 service calls per day. The correlation is negative because as the temperature decreases, the data indicate that the number of service calls increases.

The square of this correlation, $R^2 = .71$, is the predictive power of the model. That is, the model, using low daily temperature, explains approximately 71 percent of the variation in the number of calls received each day. Therefore, 1 minus R^2 means that 29 percent of the variance in the dependent variable is due to extraneous or unexplained variables.

Predictive Analytics. The manager has decided to use linear regression for his predictive analysis. To do so, certain reasonable assumptions must be met:

1. He must have at least 30 data points.

2. The relationship between the independent and dependent variables must be linear. The linearity assumption can best be tested with scatter plots.

3. Even though the data are assumed to be normally distributed, he should check this assumption.

The sample size of 3,219 satisfies the first assumption. The manager then used Excel to test the second assumption, producing a scatterplot to determine if the plot of each ordered pair of data (independent variable, dependent variable) produced a linear pattern. The scatterplot for the data did exhibit a linear pattern. Therefore, linear regression is an acceptable statistical procedure for these data.

To check for normality, the manager used the Ryan-Joiner normality test to calculate the correlation between the data and the normal scores of the data. If the value is near 1, then the sample dataset is likely to be normal. This dataset met the normality assumption.

Now that the three linear regression assumptions have been met, the next step is to define the linear regression model between these two variables using Excel or a similar statistical package. The linear regression model is:

$$\text{Number of calls received} = 124.79 - 1.5 \times (\text{daily low temperature})$$

These results indicate that for every one degree of increase in the daily low temperature, the predicted daily number of calls received will decrease by 1.5—that is, AAA will expect to receive fewer calls on warmer days and more calls on colder days. At a temperature of 0 degrees ($x = 0$), the expected number of calls will be approximately 125.

Actionable Business Decision. Based on the linear regression, the district manager is able to use the projected daily low temperature for up to 10 days in advance to predict how many service calls the offices will receive each day. (The Weather Channel provides reasonably accurate daily temperatures for a 10-day outlook.) Therefore, he can predict how many employees will be needed to manage the expected number of service calls in order to ensure low wait times for the customers.

Now, ask the next question. At this point, the manager can return to the data management stage with new input variables. For the AAA data in this example, it is feasible to consider another business problem with the appropriate inputs or to expand the analysis by considering other variables relevant to the business question in the example. For example, the manager might want to include the actual time of day, by hour, so that he could more accurately decide on staffing levels. He also might want to examine the location of his AAA branches as a variable. Adding these variables would require the use of new regression models.

You also want to recall that our example is for the Northeast district, where temperatures are cooler than in some other regions of the country. Therefore, if we were to use data from the Southwest, then we would have to perform the analyses again. Otherwise, if we used the Northeast regression model for the Southwest, what would be the result for a 100-degree day? The answer is that the number of calls received would be negative!

Our example proceeds from data management, to descriptive analytics, to predictive analytics (through a simple linear regression model). We address how the results of predictive analytics often lead to additional questions that include additional variables, which would require a multiple linear regression model.

From a statistical perspective, we might ask: Aren't there many different analytical approaches to solving the same problem? The answer is yes. But a more important question to ask is: Which one approach is the best? The answer to this question is—none! The best approach depends on the kind of data you are working with. And, because data come in all shapes and sizes, there cannot be one best approach for all problems. Therefore, selecting the best model for the particular data is always an important exercise in data analytics.

Before you go on . . .

1. Describe the purpose of predictive analytics.
2. Discuss the BA tools that are commonly used in predictive analytics.

12.5 Prescriptive Analytics

Prescriptive analytics goes beyond descriptive and predictive models by recommending one or more courses of action and by identifying the likely outcome of each decision. Predictive analytics does not predict one possible future; rather, it suggests multiple future outcomes based on the decision maker's actions. Prescriptive analytics attempts to quantify the effect of future decisions in order to advise on possible outcomes before the decisions are actually made.

Some companies are successfully using prescriptive analytics to optimize production, scheduling, and inventory along the supply chain to ensure they deliver the right products at the right time so they can optimize the customer's experience.

Prescriptive analytics requires predictive analytics with two additional components: actionable data and a feedback system that tracks the outcome produced by the action taken. Because prescriptive analytics is able to predict the possible consequences based on different choices of action, it can also recommend the best course of action to achieve any prespecified outcome.

BA Tools in Prescriptive Analytics

Organizations use a variety of BA tools and statistical procedures to perform prescriptive analytics. Statistical procedures include optimization, simulation, and others. A discussion of these procedures is beyond the scope of this text.

Examples of Prescriptive Analytics Applications

We present numerous examples of prescriptive analytics in this section. Let's begin by returning once again to our example of Fandango.

POM Fandango.   Fandango uses prescriptive analytics so it can change ticket price offerings every hour. The company has identified the most desirable movie times by analyzing millions of show times instantaneously. The company then uses these data to set an optimal price for any given time, based on the supply of show times and the demand for movie tickets. This process maximizes profits. The data from each show indicate how much each ticket price contributes to profits.

MIS Google Driverless Car.   During every trip, the car makes multiple decisions about what to do based on predictions of future outcomes. For example, when approaching an intersection, the car must determine whether to go left, right, or straight ahead. Based on its destination, it makes a decision. Additionally, the car must anticipate what might be coming in regard to vehicular traffic, pedestrians, bicyclists, and so on. The car must also analyze the impact of a possible decision before it actually makes that decision.

POM **The Oil and Gas Industry.**   Prescriptive analytics enables companies to analyze a variety of structured and unstructured data, including video, image, and sound data, to optimize hydraulic fracturing, or fracking operations. Another prescriptive analytics application optimizes the materials and equipment necessary to pump oil out of the ground. It further optimizes scheduling, production, inventory, and supply chain design to ensure that the right products are delivered in the right amount to the right customers at the right time in the most efficient manner.

For an additional example of prescriptive analytics, IT's About Business 12.5 illustrates how UPS progresses from descriptive analytics, to predictive analytics, and then on to prescriptive analytics.

IT's About Business 12.5

POM United Parcel Service Uses Three Types of Analytics

The Problem

United Parcel Service (UPS; **www.ups.com**) is a global organization with 424,000 employees and nearly 100,000 vehicles. UPS drivers typically make between 120 and 175 "drops" per day. Between any two drops, drivers can take a number of possible paths. With 55,000 routes in the United States alone, the total number of possible routes is inconceivably vast. Clearly, it is in the best interest of UPS and its drivers to find the most efficient routes. Therefore, any tiny amount of efficiency that can be gained in daily operations yields significant improvements to the company's bottom line. Essentially, "little" things matter a great deal to UPS.

In addition, the rapid increase in electronic commerce has shifted an increasing number of UPS's delivery stops from retailers to residences. (We discuss e-commerce in Chapter 7.) In fact, half of UPS's total deliveries in 2018 were to residences. Historically, drivers would drop off multiple packages at a retailer. Today, they must make scattered stops to drop off packages at individual houses. This scenario involves more routes and is more time consuming.

UPS must also manage a low-margin business as well as a unionized workforce that is compensated at the high end of the industry scale. Significantly, rival FedEx (**www.fedex.com**) uses independent contractors for its ground network. Consequently, FedEx does not have the burden of expensive employee benefits packages.

UPS faces intense competition. In early 2018, Amazon announced that it would launch a low-cost package delivery service, called its Deliver Service Partner program. Thousands of people have applied to become owners and the service expands regularly. In addition, DHL reentered the U.S. market in 2018.

UPS is deploying analytics applications to address the company's challenges. Since 2016, UPS has been collecting and analyzing some 1 billion data points per day across its facilities, and as of August 2018, some 25 analytics projects were using it. These projects are grouped under the Enhanced Dynamic Global Execution (EDGE) program. UPS expects to save $200 million to $300 million per year once EDGE is fully deployed in 2020.

The Solution

For decades, UPS has been using three types of analytics to produce efficiencies:

- Descriptive analytics asks, "Where are we today?"

- Predictive analytics asks, "With our current trajectory, where *will* we be tomorrow?"

- Prescriptive analytics asks, "Where *should* we be tomorrow?"

As UPS has moved from descriptive to predictive to prescriptive analytics, its data needs have increased, the skill set of its people has increased, and the business impact of analytics has increased. We consider these developments next.

Descriptive Analytics

DIADs.   UPS implemented descriptive analytics in the 1990s when the company provided its drivers with handheld computers, called Delivery Information Acquisition Devices (DIADs). The DIADs enabled UPS to capture detailed data that measured the company's current status. For example, the company measured driving variables in hundredths of a second. Their reasoning was that if they could reduce one mile per driver per day in the United States alone, then that process would add up to $50 million to the bottom line annually.

Package placement on delivery vans.   In 2017, UPS began equipping its delivery trucks with Bluetooth receivers to reduce incorrectly loaded packages. The receivers emit a loud beep if a worker puts a package into a vehicle that is not going to the package's destination. When workers enter the correct truck, a different beep confirms that they are in the right place. The system works by transmitting wireless signals between the Bluetooth receivers and the scanning devices that workers wear on their hips and hands to read the labels on UPS packages.

When UPS workers scan packages in the morning, the data updates the service that the company has deployed to send customers progress e-mails about their shipments. Customers who have signed up for the free service then receive a message that their package will arrive that day, along with an estimated delivery time.

Routing outbound packages.   Another project tells seasonal workers where to direct the outbound packages that UPS vehicles pick up throughout the day and bring to the company's sorting facilities. UPS hires nearly 100,000 of these workers from November through January. In the winter of 2018, UPS outfitted about 2,500 of these workers with scanning devices and $8 Bluetooth headphones that issue one-word directions, such as "Green," "Red," or "Blue." The colors correspond to specific conveyor belts, which then transport the packages to other parts of the building for further processing.

Undeliverable packages.   UPS does make mistakes with some deliveries. In the past, UPS managers relied on historical data and radio conversations with drivers to estimate how many undeliverable packages they would need to handle each night. As a result, the company has a project that tells managers how many returned packages will arrive at their processing center and when. In that way, they can assemble the appropriate number of workers to reroute the packages.

Predictive Analytics

In 2003, UPS deployed its Package Flow Technologies system to provide predictive analytics. With this system, drivers started the day with a DIAD that detailed the packages they were to deliver and the order in which they were to deliver those packages. The DIAD became the drivers' assistant. The system enabled UPS to reduce total delivery driving globally by 85 million miles per year. That process saved the firm 8.5 million gallons of fuel, and it prevented 85,000 metric tons of carbon dioxide from entering into the atmosphere.

However, drivers had to provide different services from the same vehicle—for example, deferred service and premium service. Some packages had to be delivered by 10:30 a.m., others had to be delivered by noon, and still others had to be delivered by 2:00 p.m. Drivers therefore had to decide how they were going to service those customers. With so many variables to consider, it was practically impossible for drivers to optimize their routes.

Prescriptive Analytics

UPS realized that it needed to take analytics to the next level. So, in mid-2012, the company began deploying its On-Road Integrated Optimization and Navigation (ORION) system. ORION reorganizes the drivers' routes based on today's customers, today's needs, and today's packages, and it designs deliveries in a very specific, optimized order. ORION takes into account UPS business rules, maps, what time drivers need to be at specific locations, and customer preferences. ORION can alter delivery routes dynamically based on changing weather conditions and accidents. The system can also examine the deliveries that still need to be completed and continue to optimize the remaining route.

At first, ORION used publicly available maps. However, these maps were not detailed enough. Therefore, UPS drew their own maps, which displayed features such as a customer's half-mile driveway or a back alley that saves time getting to a receiving dock. These were data points that ORION needed to optimize package delivery.

Unfortunately, analytics algorithms cannot anticipate every variable. For example, a business customer typically receives one package per day. If ORION knows that the package is not tied to a certain delivery time, then the algorithm might suggest dropping it off in the morning one day but in the afternoon the next day, depending on that day's tasks. That process might be the most efficient approach for UPS, but customers would not know when to expect deliveries if the times varied from day to day. This can be a problem because customers typically do not like that amount of uncertainty.

When UPS drivers are on the road, they usually travel at speeds of 20 to 25 miles per hour. Therefore, every mile reduced equates to a savings of two to three minutes. By shortening routes by seven to eight miles per day, ORION enables UPS to deliver more packages.

ORION enhances UPS customer service with more efficient routing, and it enables UPS to offer innovative services and customized solutions. An example of this type of service is UPS My Choice, which is a free system that allows residential customers to decide "how, where, and when home deliveries occur." UPS's chatbot, called UPS Bot, is integrated with the UPS My Choice system,

so customers are able to obtain information about their incoming packages and deliveries without providing a tracking number.

UPS Bot mimics human conversation and can respond to customer queries such as "Where is the nearest UPS location?" and can track packages and provide shipping rates. Customers can ask the bot questions either through text or voice commands through mobile devices, social media channels, and virtual assistants such as Alexa and Google Assistant. The UPS Bot is able to recognize these requests and take the appropriate steps to complete them.

A recent UPS project, Network Planning Tools (NPT), optimizes the flow of packages in the UPS network from loading docks to sorting to the final destination. NPT helps UPS employees make decisions and improve efficiencies. UPS expects to fully deploy NPT by 2020 and the company hopes to realize $100–$200 million in savings and cost avoidance.

The Results

In April 2016, UPS won the prestigious Edelman Prize for excellence in analytics and operations research for its ORION project. UPS completed the deployment of ORION at the end of 2016.

The results from ORION have been outstanding. UPS is realizing savings of between $300 and $400 million per year in driver productivity and fuel economy. Furthermore, with ORION, UPS drivers have saved 100 million miles in driving, thereby decreasing carbon emissions by 100,000 metric tons per year. In addition, ORION will generate further environmental benefits and cost reductions when UPS equips its vehicles outside the United States with this technology.

UPS continues to look into the future. As a major example, ORION provides a natural transition to driverless vehicles. The reason is that UPS need only integrate ORION with the software of autonomous delivery vehicles and those vehicles will take optimal routes to get UPS personnel where they need to go to deliver packages.

UPS is testing the use of drone deliveries for some applications, including dropping essential supplies in Rwanda and demonstrating how medicines could be delivered to islands. In rural areas, where drones have the space to execute deliveries and the distance between stops makes efficient deliveries challenging, drones launched from the roofs of UPS trucks provide a solution to reduce costs and improve service.

Sources: Compiled from P. High, "UPS's Chief Information and Engineering Officer Champions Prescriptive Analytics," *Forbes*, July 15, 2019; N. Shields, "UPS Is Turning to Predictive Analytics," *Business Insider*, July 20, 2018; S. Schwartz, "UPS Working to Consolidate Data Points on Single Platform with Analytics, Machine Learning," *CIO Dive*, July 19, 2018; B. Marr, "The Brilliant Ways UPS Uses Artificial Intelligence, Machine Learning and Big Data," *Forbes*, June 15, 2018; S. Rosenbush, "UPS Expands Role of Predictive Analytics," *Wall Street Journal*, April 26, 2018; E. Woyke, "How UPS Delivers Faster Using $8 Headphones and Code That Decides When Dirty Trucks Get Cleaned," *MIT Technology Review*, February 16, 2018; L. Stevens, "Amazon to Launch Delivery Service that Would Vie with FedEx, UPS," *Wall Street Journal*, February 9, 2018; "How UPS Delivers Predictive Analytics," *CIO*, September 28, 2016; T. Davenport, "Prescriptive Analytics Project Delivering Big Dividends at UPS," *DataInformed*, April 19, 2016; "INFORMS Awards UPS Its 2016 Edelman Prize: The Leading Award in Analytics and Operations Research," *INFORMS*, April 11, 2016; C. Powers, "How UPS Augments Its Drivers' Intuition with Predictive Analytics," *ASUG News,* June 9, 2015; E. Siegel, "Predictive Analytics Driving Results, ROI at UPS," *Data Informed*, June 1, 2015; E. Siegel, "Wise Practitioner—Predictive Analytics Interview Series: Jack Levis of UPS," *Predictive Analytics World*, April 28, 2015; J. Berman, "UPS Is Focused on the Future for Its ORION Technology," *Logistics Management,* March 3, 2015; "UPS Moves Up Full ORION Rollout in U.S. Market to the End of 2016," *DC Velocity*, March 2, 2015; K. Nash, "CIOs Have to Learn the New Math of Analytics," *CIO*, February 25, 2015; J. Gidman, "Algorithm Will Tell All UPS Trucks Where to Go," *Newser*, February 17, 2015; S. Rosenbush and L. Stevens, "At UPS, the Algorithm Is the

Driver," *Wall Street Journal,* February 16, 2015; J. Dix, "How UPS Uses Analytics to Drive Down Costs," *Network World,* December 1, 2014; K. Noyes, "The Shortest Distance Between Two Points? At UPS, It's Complicated," *Fortune,* July 25, 2014; and www.ups.com, accessed July 16, 2019.

2. Explain how the Package Flow Technologies system was a predictive analytics solution for UPS.

3. Explain how the ORION system was a prescriptive analytics solution for UPS.

4. Describe another potential application for the UPS ORION system. That is, what is the next question that UPS managers might ask of the ORION system?

Questions

1. Explain how DIADs were a descriptive analytics solution for UPS.

Before you go on . . .

1. Describe the purpose of prescriptive analytics.
2. Discuss the BA tools that are commonly used in prescriptive analytics.

12.6 Presentation Tools

As you saw in Figure 12.3, organizations use presentation tools to display the results of analyses to users in visual formats such as charts, graphs, figures, and tables. This process, known as *data visualization*, makes the results more attractive and easier to understand. Organizations can present the results after they have performed descriptive analytics, predictive analytics, and prescriptive analytics. A variety of visualization methods and software packages that support decision making are available. Dashboards are the most common BA presentation tool. We discuss them next. We also consider another valuable data visualization tool, geographic information systems.

Author Lecture Videos are available exclusively in *WileyPLUS.*
Apply the Concept activities are available in the Appendix and in *WileyPLUS.*

Dashboards

Dashboards evolved from executive information systems, which were designed specifically for the information needs of top executives. Today, however, many employees, business partners, and customers use digital dashboards.

A **dashboard** provides easy access to timely information and direct access to management reports. It is user friendly, it is supported by graphics, and, most important, it enables managers to examine exception reports and drill down into detailed data. **Table 12.1** summarizes the

TABLE 12.1 **The Capabilities of Dashboards**

Capability	Description
Drill down	The ability to go to details, at several levels; it can be done by a series of menus or by clicking on a drillable portion of the screen.
Critical success factors (CSFs)	The factors most critical for the success of business. These can be organizational, industry, departmental, or for individual workers.
Key performance indicators (KPIs)	The specific measures of CSFs.
Status access	The latest data available on a KPI or some other metric, often in real time.
Trend analysis	Short-, medium-, and long-term trends of KPIs or metrics, which are projected using forecasting methods.
Exception reporting	Reports highlight deviations larger than defined thresholds. Reports may include only deviations.

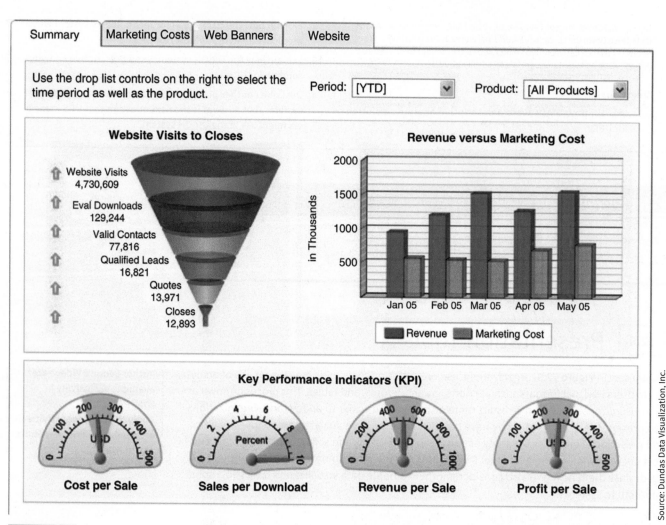

Source: Dundas Data Visualization, Inc.

FIGURE 12.4   **Sample performance dashboard.**

various capabilities that are common to many dashboards. Some of the capabilities discussed in this section have been incorporated into many BA products, as illustrated in **Figure 12.4**.

One outstanding example of a dashboard is Bloomberg LP (**www.bloomberg.com**), a privately held company that provides a subscription service that sells financial data, software to analyze these data, trading tools, and news (electronic, print, TV, and radio). All of this information is accessible through a color-coded Bloomberg keyboard that displays the desired information on a computer screen, either the user's screen or one that Bloomberg provides. Users can also set up their own computers to access the service without a Bloomberg keyboard. The subscription service plus the keyboard is called the Bloomberg Terminal. It literally represents a do-it-yourself dashboard because users can customize their information feeds as well as the look and feel of those feeds (see **Figure 12.5**).

A unique and interesting application of dashboards to support the informational needs of executives is the Management Cockpit. Essentially, a Management Cockpit is a strategic management room containing an elaborate set of dashboards that enable top-level decision makers to pilot their businesses better. The goal is to create an environment that encourages more efficient management meetings and boosts team performance through effective communication. To help achieve this goal, the dashboard graphically displays KPIs and information relating to critical success factors on the walls of a meeting room called the *Management Cockpit Room* (see **Figure 12.6**). The cockpit-like arrangement of instrument panels and displays helps managers visualize how all of the different factors in the business interrelate.

Within the room, the four walls are designated by color: Black, Red, Blue, and White. The Black Wall displays the principal success factors and financial indicators. The Red Wall measures market performance. The Blue Wall projects the performance of internal processes and employees.

FIGURE 12.5   **Bloomberg Terminal.**

FIGURE 12.6   **Management Cockpit.**

Finally, the White Wall indicates the status of strategic projects. The Flight Deck, a six-screen, high-end PC, enables executives to drill down to detailed information. External information needed for competitive analyses can easily be imported into the room.

Board members and other executives hold meetings in the Management Cockpit Room. Managers also meet there with the comptroller to discuss current business issues. The Management Cockpit can implement various what–if scenarios for this purpose. It also provides a common basis for information and communication. Finally, it supports efforts to translate a corporate strategy into concrete activities by identifying performance indicators.

Geographic Information Systems

A **geographic information system (GIS)** is a computer-based system for capturing, integrating, manipulating, and displaying data using digitized maps. Its most distinguishing characteristic is that every record or digital object has an identified geographical location. This process, called *geocoding*, enables users to generate information for planning, problem solving, and decision making. The graphical format also makes it easy for managers to visualize the data. There are countless applications of GISs to improve decision making in both the public and private sectors.

POM As one example, Children's National Health System offers injury prevention advice to the community. Clinicians have found that using geospatial data helps them accomplish this mission. The health care center integrated its existing electronic health records system with GIS software from ESRI (**www.esri.com**) to display health data with geospatial coordinates. One of the integrated system's first projects focused on pediatric burn cases.

GIS mapping enabled the clinic to identify on a map the hotspots where injuries were occurring. That map allowed staff members to develop prevention programs tailored to the demographics of areas with high rates of injuries. For example, if the system identifies a cluster of children with burns in a particular neighborhood, then the staff will work with community groups to provide parents with greater information about safety and make sure that information is available in multiple languages to meet the needs of all of the residents.

The new system has produced results. The clinic is seeing fewer burn patients overall and fewer patients requiring high-level burn care. Children's National Health System is now using its system to map concentrations of other medical conditions such as obesity and asthma.

Before you go on . . .

1. Discuss why presentation tools are so valuable in the business analytics process.
2. What is a dashboard? Why are dashboards so valuable to an organization's decision makers?

What's in **IT** for me?

ACCT For the Accounting Major

BA is used extensively in auditing to uncover irregularities. It also is used to uncover and prevent fraud. CPAs use BA for many of their duties, ranging from risk analysis to cost control.

FIN For the Finance Major

People have been using computers for decades to solve financial problems. Innovative BA applications have been created for activities such as making stock market decisions, refinancing bonds, assessing debt risks, analyzing financial conditions, predicting business failures, forecasting financial trends, and investing in global markets.

MKT For the Marketing Major

Marketing personnel utilize BA in many applications, from planning and executing marketing campaigns, to allocating advertising budgets, to evaluating alternative routings of sales-people. New marketing approaches such as targeted marketing and database marketing depend heavily on IT in general, and

on data warehouses and business intelligence applications in particular.

POM For the Production/Operations Management Major

BA supports complex operations and production decisions from inventory control, to production planning, to supply chain integration.

HRM For the Human Resources Management Major

Human resources personnel use BA for many of their activities. For example, BA applications can find resumes of applicants posted on the Web and sort them to match needed skills and to support management succession planning.

MIS For the MIS Major

MIS provides the data infrastructure used in BA. MIS personnel are also involved in building, deploying, and supporting BA applications.

Summary

12.1 Use a decision-support framework to demonstrate how technology supports managerial decision making at each phase of the decision-making process.

When making a decision, either organizational or personal, the decision maker goes through a three-step process: intelligence, design, and choice. When the choice is made, the decision is implemented. In general, it is difficult to state which information systems support specific decision makers in an organization. Modern information systems, particularly business analytics systems, are available to support everyone in an organization.

12.2 Describe each phase of the business analytics process.

Business analytics is the process of developing actionable decisions or recommendations for actions based on insights generated from historical data. The phases in the business analytics process are shown in Figure 12.3 and include data management, descriptive analytics (with associated analytics tools and statistics procedures), predictive analytics (with associated analytics tools and statistical procedures), prescriptive analytics (with associated analytics tools and statistical procedures), and presentation tools. The results of the business analytics process are actionable business decisions.

12.3 Provide a definition and a use case example for descriptive analytics.

Descriptive analytics summarizes what has happened in the past and allows decision makers to learn from past behaviors. We leave the example to you.

12.4 Provide a definition and a use case example for predictive analytics.

Predictive analytics examines recent and historical data in order to detect patterns and predict future outcomes and trends. We leave the example to you.

12.5 Provide a definition and a use case example for prescriptive analytics.

Prescriptive analytics goes beyond descriptive and predictive models by recommending one or more courses of action and identifying the likely outcome of each decision. We leave the example to you.

12.6 Describe two examples of presentation tools.

A dashboard provides easy access to timely information and direct access to management reports. It is user friendly, it is supported by graphics, and, most important, it enables managers to examine exception reports and drill down into detailed data.

A geographic information system (GIS) is a computer-based system for capturing, integrating, manipulating, and displaying data using digitized maps. Its most distinguishing characteristic is that every record or digital object has an identified geographical location.

Chapter Glossary

business analytics (BA) The process of developing actionable decisions or recommendations for actions based on insights generated from historical data.

business intelligence (BI) A broad category of applications, technologies, and processes for gathering, storing, accessing, and analyzing data to help business users make more informed decisions.

dashboard A business analytics presentation tool that provides rapid access to timely information and direct access to management reports.

data mining The process of searching for valuable business information in a large database, data warehouse, or data mart.

decision A choice that individuals and groups make among two or more alternatives.

decision-support systems (DSSs) Business intelligence systems that combine models and data in an attempt to solve semistructured and some unstructured problems with extensive user involvement.

descriptive analytics A type of business analytics that summarizes what has happened in the past and allows decision makers to learn from past behaviors.

geographic information system (GIS) A computer-based system for capturing, integrating, manipulating, and displaying data using digitized maps.

management A process by which organizational goals are achieved through the use of resources.

multidimensional data analysis See *online analytical processing (OLAP).*

online analytical processing (OLAP) (or multidimensional data analysis) A set of capabilities for "slicing and dicing" data using dimensions and measures associated with the data.

predictive analytics A type of business analytics that examines recent and historical data in order to detect patterns and predict future outcomes and trends.

prescriptive analytics A type of business analytics that recommends one or more courses of action and shows the likely outcome of each decision.

productivity The ratio between the inputs to a process and the outputs from that process.

Discussion Questions

1. Your company is considering opening a new factory in China. List several typical activities involved in each phase of the decision (intelligence, design, and choice).

2. Recall that a market basket analysis (a type of data mining) of convenience store purchases revealed that customers tended to buy beer and diapers at the same time when they shopped. Now that the analysis uncovered this relationship exists, provide a rationale for it. (*Note:* You will have to decide what the next question is.)

3. American Can Company announced that it was interested in acquiring a company in the health maintenance organization (HMO) field. Two decisions were involved in this act: (1) the decision to acquire an HMO, and (2) the decision of which HMO to acquire. How can the use of BA assist the company in this endeavor?

4. Discuss the strategic benefits of business analytics.

5. In early 2012, *the New York Times* reported the story of a Target data scientist who was able to predict if a customer was pregnant based on her pattern of previous purchases.

    a. Describe the business analytics models that the data scientist used.

    b. Refer to Chapter 3 and discuss the ethics of Target's analytics process.

    c. Research the story and note the unintended consequences of Target's analytics process.

6. Consider the admissions process at your university. Your university's admissions process involves the analysis of many variables to decide whom to admit to each year's freshman class. Contact your admissions office and gather information on the variables used in the admissions process. As you recall from applying at your university, typical variables would include high school attended, high school grade point average, standardized test scores such as ACT or SAT, and many others. (Do not be surprised if there are variables that your admissions office cannot provide.)

    a. Provide an example of how your admissions office uses descriptive analytics in the admissions process. Use the variables you have found in your example.

    b. Provide an example of how your admissions office uses predictive analytics in the admissions process. Use the variables you have found in your example.

    c. Provide an example of how your admissions office uses prescriptive analytics in the admissions process. Use the variables you have found in your example.

Problem-Solving Activities

1. Consider the city of Barcelona, Spain, which has placed sensors in all its trash dumpsters. The sensors measure how full each dumpster is.

    a. Describe a descriptive analytics application using this sensor data.

    b. Describe a predictive analytics application using this sensor data.

    c. Describe a prescriptive analytics application using this sensor data.

2. Consider General Electric's latest-generation LEAP aircraft engine. Sensors in this engine measure vibration and several different temperatures (depending on the location of the sensor).

    a. Describe a descriptive analytics application using this sensor data.

    b. Describe a predictive analytics application using this sensor data.

    c. Describe a prescriptive analytics application using this sensor data.

3. You are a business analyst for a chain of grocery stores. You analyze retail sales data, perform a descriptive analytics application, and discover that bread and milk are the two products that are purchased together more often than any other pair of products.

    a. Describe a predictive analytics application using these data.

    b. Describe a prescriptive analytics application using these data.

4. Consider Rent the Runway (RTR; **www.renttherunway.com**). RTR buys designer dresses wholesale and rents them over the Web, charging only a fraction of the price of the dress. When RTR merchandisers decide whether to buy a new dress, they follow a list of 40 data points, such as fabric, zippers, stitching, and shape, to determine whether the dress will hold up to the rigors of multiple rentals. The longer the lifespan, the higher the return on capital.

With every dress it rents, RTR's analytics algorithms learn more about effective strategies to track the location of each item, forecast demand, select shipping methods, set prices, and control inventory. RTR's algorithms also examine customer reviews to learn which dresses women are renting for certain occasions. They then forecast demand to determine whether the prepaid shipping label that goes with a dress should require the customer to return the dress overnight or whether a three-day return, which costs less, is sufficient.

    a. Describe a descriptive analytics application using this sensor data.

    b. Describe a predictive analytics application using this sensor data.

    c. Describe a prescriptive analytics application using this sensor data

Data-Driven Exercise

Background

Organizations exist to fulfill a purpose. This purpose often takes the form of a mission statement. Once the mission is provided to employees, all organizational activities should be aimed at helping the organization fulfill its purpose, regardless of the functional area in which specific activities occur.

It would seem that the mission statement should be all the organization needs to drive decisions, but several complications come into play. Today, decision makers face a dynamic environment in which decisions must be made quickly, information support is not always available, and the penalty for making incorrect decisions, or not making decisions at all, can threaten the long-term viability of the organization.

Analytics is an attempt to provide support to decision makers in spite of these difficulties. All forms of analytics make use of historical data. The difference is in the type of question that is asked.

- Descriptive analytics helps decision makers answer questions about what has happened in the past (it describes).

- Predictive analytics assumes that trends and relationships from the past will remain constant and therefore answers the question of what could happen in the future (assuming the trends and relationships remain constant).

- Prescriptive analytics (not yet well defined in the industry) allows the decision maker to model how certain actions will play out in the market. Prescriptive analytics "prescribes" the "if you do this, then this could happen" to potential actions.

Activity

Analytics plays an important role across the entire organization. For this activity, you will assume the role of a Data Analytics Specialist for a large retail organization. Your employer operates in both the traditional and online retail spaces. However, the economy has taken a toll on overall productivity and decision makers have to be well informed to make appropriate decisions.

Deliverable

Your job is to analyze the data using descriptive and predictive analytics, interpret the results, and provide a written analysis to the appropriate decision makers in the following functional areas: Accounting, Finance, Human Resources, Marketing, and Operations. You will use Microsoft Excel to analyze the data and produce both descriptive and predictive analytics. Most important, you will write a memo that details your findings for the appropriate decision maker in a way that is easy to understand. That is, you will need to use data visualization to make it easy and intuitive for the decision maker to understand and act upon.

Your instructor may customize this activity to fit his or her needs, so be sure you understand the requirements before you begin.

Please visit either WileyPLUS or the book companion site to download the full activity and the Excel spreadsheet file.

Closing Case

MIS **Dark Analytics**

The amount of data created annually doubles in size every 12 months and is expected to reach 44 zettabytes (44 trillion gigabytes) by 2020. These data provide critical insights to modern organizations, which can create competitive advantages. Unfortunately, organizations have applied analytics tools and techniques to only a tiny fraction of this vast amount of data to acquire these insights. In fact, organizations historically have applied descriptive analytics tools only to limited samples of structured data that are siloed within a specific system, company function, or company process. Consequently, they gained only limited insights, which were usually presented in the form of hard-copy reports.

Today, organizations have access to far more data and data sources than ever before. Specifically, analyzing raw data generated by transactional systems, social media, search engines, and other technologies can produce crucial strategic, customer, and operational insights that can validate assumptions, inform decision making, and predict future outcomes.

There are three types of data that organizations have just begun to analyze. We consider each type because these three largely unexplored data resources could prove to be enormously valuable to organizational analytics efforts.

Untapped data already in an organization's possession. In many organizations, large amounts of structured and unstructured data are not being used for analytics. Regarding structured data, the organization might have difficulty connecting different data sets. For example, a large insurance company mapped its employees' home addresses and parking lot assignments with employee workplace ratings and retention data. The firm discovered that one of the biggest factors leading to voluntary turnover was the time it took its employees to commute to work. The firm learned that employees considered their commute time to be the total of (1) the distance to the office, (2) traffic patterns based on their shift schedules, (3) the degree of difficulty finding a parking place, and (4) the length of the walk from their cars to their work spaces.

Unstructured data could include valuable data on pricing, customer behavior, and competitors. Unused unstructured data include e-mails, notes, messages, documents, and notifications—such as those from Internet of Things devices—and even untranslated data assets from non-English-speaking markets. These data remain largely unused either because they are not located in a relational database or because the tools and techniques needed to efficiently leverage the data did not exist until recently.

Nontraditional unstructured data. Using computer vision (see Technology Guide 4), advanced pattern recognition, and video and sound analytics, companies can now analyze such data sources as audio and video files and images contained in nontraditional formats to better understand their customers, employees, operations, and markets.

Let's consider three examples. First, a retailer may gain a more nuanced understanding of its customers' moods or intents by analyzing video images of shoppers' postures, facial expressions, or gestures. Second, an oil and gas company could use acoustic sensors to monitor pipelines and algorithms to detect oil flow rates and composition. Finally, an amusement park could acquire greater insight into customer demographics by analyzing security-camera footage to determine how many customers arrive by car, by public transportation, or by foot, and at what times during the day.

Data in the deep Web. Where the *surface Web* is accessible to anyone using the Internet, the *deep Web* consists of parts of the World Wide Web whose contents are not indexed by standard search engines. The deep Web includes data from many sources, including Web mail, online banking, video on demand, and some online newspapers and magazines that are protected by paywalls and for which users must pay. Interestingly, organizations are beginning to use emerging search tools designed to help users target scientific research, activist data, or even data from hobbyists. For example, Deep Web Technologies (**www.deepwebtech.com**) builds search tools for retrieving and analyzing data that cannot be accessed by standard search engines.

The deep Web may contain the largest amount of unused data, including data curated by academics, consortia, government agencies, communities, and other third-party domains. In this context, *curate* means to find, organize, and share the best and most relevant content on a specific topic.

The three types of unstructured and unanalyzed data we have just discussed are called *dark data*. Few organizations have been able to explore dark data, which consists of nontraditional data sources such as image, audio, and video files; machine and sensor data generated by the Internet of Things; and raw data found on the deep Web. Therefore, dark data are data that are not used (as of September, 2018) in analytics procedures or models.

Significantly, in May 2017, Apple acquired Lattice Data, a company that uses artificial intelligence to transform unstructured, dark data into structured data. The acquisition enabled Apple to analyze vast amounts of dark data that the company has gathered.

Dark analytics refers to the exploration of unstructured, dark data with the goal of discovering highly nuanced business, customer, and operational insights that structured data may not reveal. Dark analytics focuses primarily on data sources such as text messages, documents, e-mail, video and audio files, and images. Dark analytics may also target all online information not indexed by search engines, including anonymous, inaccessible websites known as the dark Web. The *dark Web* is the part of the World Wide Web that can be accessed only by using special software. This limitation enables users and website operators to remain anonymous or untraceable. Let's explore some examples of dark analytics.

Health care. Indiana University Health (IU Health; **www.iuhealth.org**) is exploring ways to use dark, unstructured data to personalize health care for individual patients and to improve overall health outcomes for the broader population. Traditional relationships among medical care providers and patients typically focus on individual visits and specific outcomes rather than on providing holistic care services on an ongoing basis. IU Health wants to analyze additional data to help build patient loyalty and to provide better, cost-efficient health care. In short, IU Health wants a more complete understanding of each patient it serves.

In regard to additional data sources, consider the massive amount of free-form notes—both written and verbal—that physicians generate during patient consultations. IU Health is deploying voice recognition, deep learning (see Technology Guide 4), and text analysis capabilities to this underutilized data source to add more depth and detail to its patients' medical records. The health center is employing these same capabilities to analyze audio recordings of patient conversations with its call centers to further enhance its patients' records. These insights help IU Health develop a more thorough understanding of both their patients' needs and how patients actually utilize the health system's services.

Another opportunity involves using dark, unstructured data to help predict need and manage care across populations. IU Health is examining how cognitive computing, external data, and patient data could help identify patterns of illness, health care access, and historical outcomes in local populations. These approaches make it possible to incorporate patients' socioeconomic factors to add context to patients' records in order to improve their health care.

Retail. Retailers recognize that digital systems have revolutionized customer behavior and shopping. In fact, 56 percent of the amount spent in a store is influenced by a digital interaction. However, many retailers, particularly those with brick-and-mortar operations, still find it difficult to provide the digital experiences that customers expect.

Recently, growing numbers of retailers have begun exploring different approaches to enhancing customers' digital experiences. Some are analyzing dark, unstructured data collected from customers' digital profiles (refer to Chapter 5). They then utilize the resulting insights to develop merchandising, marketing, customer service, and product development strategies that offer shoppers a targeted and individualized customer experience.

Grocery supermarket chain Kroger (**www.kroger.com**) is leveraging dark, unstructured data from the Internet of Things and analytics techniques. As part of a pilot program, the company is embedding sensors into store shelves that can interact with both the Kroger app and a digital shopping list on a customer's phone. As the customer walks down each aisle, the system—which contains a digital history of the customer's purchases and product preferences—can spotlight specially priced products that customers may want on 4-inch displays mounted in the aisles. This pilot began in late 2016 with initial testing in 14 stores and can now be found in close to 100 stores.

Oil and Gas. Halliburton has a long history of relying on data to understand current and past operating conditions in the field and to measure the performance of its wells. However, the volume of data that the company collects is more than humans can process and understand.

Advances in sensors provide huge amounts of dark, unstructured data. For example, the firm scans rocks electromagnetically to determine their consistency and uses nuclear magnetic resonance to scan oil wells. These data help Halliburton better understand the performance of its wells.

The types of analytics that Halliburton has performed, and is planning to perform, are instructive. Initially, the firm's engineers analyzed sensor data to discover an event only after it had occurred. The engineers then analyzed the data to understand why it happened. Today, Halliburton is using real-time analytics to become aware of events while they are happening. Furthermore, the company is using predictive analytics tools to learn what is likely to happen next. In the near future, Halliburton plans to use prescriptive analytics to take actions to encourage a positive event—for example, the well is flowing optimally—or to prevent a negative event—for example, the well equipment is beginning to overheat and could fail.

Sources: Compiled from M. Shacklett, "6 Ways to Include Dark Data in Analytic Strategies," *TechRepublic*, November 23, 2018; J. Rivard, "Big Data Trends You Should Know about in 2018," *Marketing Insider Group*, July 2, 2018; K. Matthews, "5 Ways Dark Data Is Changing Data Analytics," *Smart Data Collective*, March 29, 2018; T. Kambles, N. Mittal, and S. Sharma, "Illuminate Insights with Dark Analytics," *Wall Street Journal*, July 31, 2017; T. Coughlin, "Analysis of Dark Data Provides Market Advantages," *Forbes*, July 24, 2017; K. McNulty, "Expanding the Definition of Dark Data and Mining It with Dark Analytics," *Prowess Corporation*, June 30, 2017; T. Groenfeldt, "Pendo Systems Uncovers a Global Bank's 'Dark Data' at High Speed," *Forbes*, May 23, 2017; C. Tozzi, "4 Ways to Use Dark Data," Syncsort Blog, May 17, 2017; A. Chowdhury, "Shining a Light on Dark Analytics in the Data-Driven Age," *Analytics India Magazine*, May 11, 2017; T. Kambles, P. Roma, N. Mittal, and S. Sharma, "Dark Analytics: Illuminating Opportunities Hidden within Unstructured Data," *Deloitte University Press*, February 7, 2017; K. Nash, "Kroger Tests Sensors, Analytics in Interactive Grocery Shelves," *Wall Street Journal*, January 20, 2017; F. Moreno, "Dark Data Discovery: Improve Marketing Insights to Increase ROI," *IBM Business Analytics Blog*, September 20, 2016; K. Noyes, "Dark Data? Teradata and Nuix Can Help," *Computerworld*, July 19, 2016; D. Barton, "Data Mining in the Deep Web," *The Innovation Enterprise*, July 14, 2016; "Surface Web, Deep Web, Dark Web – What's the Difference?" *Cambia Research*, April 22, 2016; and K. Pal, "What Is the Importance of Dark Data in Big Data World?" *KDNuggets*, November, 2015.

Questions

1. What are the three types of data that are typically analyzed with dark analytics?

2. Why are these three types of data so important for companies to analyze?

CHAPTER 13

Acquiring Information Systems and Applications

CHAPTER OUTLINE

13.1 Planning for and Justifying IT Applications

13.2 Strategies for Acquiring IT Applications

13.3 Traditional Systems Development Life Cycle

13.4 Alternative Methods and Tools for Systems Development

LEARNING OBJECTIVES

13.1 Discuss the different cost–benefit analyses that companies must take into account when they formulate an IT strategic plan.

13.2 Discuss the four business decisions that companies must make when they acquire new applications.

13.3 Enumerate the primary tasks and the importance of each of the six processes involved in the systems development life cycle.

13.4 Describe alternative development methods and the tools that augment these methods.

Opening Case

MIS **HRM** Paychex Speeds Deployment with DevOps

The Business Problem

Paychex, Inc. (**www.paychex.com**) is a provider of payroll, human resource, and benefits administration software tools. The company was founded in 1971 with the idea of making it easy for organizations to outsource their payroll operations. Today, Paychex employs more than 170 people, and it provides administrative payroll tools to more than 600,000 small- to medium-sized businesses.

Paychex provides a software-as-a-service (SaaS) to its customers. Many people utilize their system every day, and the list of user requests and performance issues is extensive. Significantly, payroll is not a system that can go down for extended periods without generating serious problems. Therefore, Paychex has to provide a reliable service, or its customers will go elsewhere very quickly.

Paychex's development model was a traditional waterfall approach (defined in this chapter as the systems development life cycle—SDLC) that required only limited user input after the user's needs were identified early in the process. From that point, the model consisted of multiple steps such as design, implementation, and testing in which the users were not involved. This process resulted in projects that lasted up to nine months (or longer in several cases; nine months is the average), generated a backlog of development requests, and challenged the company's systems deployment.

The IT Solution

In 2014, Paychex began to seek out partners to transition their waterfall development methodology to a DevOps model. This decision was part of the broader context of their enterprise strategy—they wanted to create a high-volume, high-demand software factory. Their objective was to increase the velocity (speed of updating) and enhance the output quality of their product updates and improvements in order to provide their customers with the best-possible user experience.

DevOps (named from a combination of Development and Operations) has grown in popularity since it was introduced as a concept in 2008 by Andrew Shafer and Patrick Debois in a talk about Agile development. It is a development methodology that combines employees from the IT development team and the operations team (the end users) in the entire process. This model has demonstrated a much greater proficiency in helping companies develop and deploy effective IT solutions. In fact, according to the 2018 State of DevOps Report, companies that use a DevOps model deploy new or updated software hundreds of times more frequently than when using the traditional SDLC, with *lead times*—a measure of how quickly a company can move from idea to action—that are thousands of times faster. In addition, these businesses have significantly lower change failure rates (a measure of successful implementations), they spend 22 percent less time on unplanned work and rework, and they devote 29 percent more time to new features or code. Successes like this are the reason that Paychex wanted to move to a DevOps model.

Paychex reviewed proposals from IBM, HP, BMC Software, and XebiaLabs. The proposals from IBM, HP, and BMC Software were too similar to their current waterfall model. In contrast, XebiaLabs offered the type of environment they were seeking.

The Results

Today Paychex has at least 80 teams working within these DevOps methods. Development and deployment times are short, and all activities are focused on delivery. The results have been impressive. Paychex has experienced significant growth since transitioning to a DevOps model, resulting in a 140 percent increase in new employees. Despite this growth, however, average IT deployment time has *decreased* 53 percent. Moreover, the success rates of their production (meaning the IT group successfully heard a complaint, developed the necessary solution, and deployed the solution) have improved 23 percent, and the number of releases ending in abort/rollback has been reduced 36 percent. Dave Wilson, Director of Infrastructure and Architecture, claimed that Paychex completed its "transition to enterprise DevOps in under two years, realizing a 656 percent increase in the number of total software deployments."

Sources: Compiled from J. Bloomberg, "DevOps Success Beyond Agile: Cloud Expo Power Panel," *Forbes*, November 4, 2017; K. Lauria, "The DevOps Leadership Summit 2017 Wrap Up," XebiaLabs Blog, June 22, 2017; B. Kepes, "Delivering Agility to Paychex with XebiaLabs," *NetworkWorld*, May 30, 2017; P. Cohan, "Startup Snatching Share From IBM and CA In $2.3 Billion Market," *Forbes*, April 13, 2017; Anonymous, "A Field Guide to Digital Transformation," *MIT Technology Review*, March 30, 2017; B. Patwardhan, "Impact of DevOps on IT Infrastructure," *DZone*, March 31, 2015; https://puppet.com/resources/white-paper/2016-state-of-devops-report, accessed December 14, 2017; and https://www.paychex.com/corporate, accessed July 17, 2019.

Questions

1. What is the major difference between Paychex's traditional waterfall approach and the DevOps model?

2. What was the major push for Paychex, Inc. to move to a DevOps model of systems development?

3. Discuss the advantages of the DevOps model. What potential disadvantages do you see?

Introduction

Competitive organizations move as quickly as they can to acquire new information technologies or modify existing ones when they need to improve efficiencies and gain strategic advantage. As you learned from the chapter opening case, problems and pitfalls can arise from the acquisition process.

Today, acquisition goes beyond building new systems in-house, and IT resources involve far more than software and hardware. As you saw in the chapter opening case, the old model in which firms built their own systems is being replaced with a broader perspective of IT resource acquisition that provides companies with a number of options. Thus, companies now must decide which IT tasks will remain in-house, and even whether the entire IT resource should be provided and managed by outside organizations. Regardless of which approach an organization chooses, however, it must be able to manage IT projects adeptly.

In this chapter, you will learn about the process of acquiring IT resources from a managerial perspective—this means from *your* perspective, because you will be closely involved in all aspects of acquiring information systems and applications in your organization. In fact, when we mention "users" in this chapter, we are talking about you. You will also study the available options for acquiring IT resources and how to evaluate those options. Finally, you will learn how organizations plan and justify the acquisition of new information systems.

13.1 Planning for and Justifying IT Applications

Organizations must analyze the need for applications and then justify each purchase in regard to costs and benefits. The need for information systems is usually related to organizational planning and to the analysis of its performance vis-à-vis its competitors. The cost–benefit justification must consider the wisdom of investing in a specific IT application versus spending the funds on alternative projects. This chapter focuses on the formal processes of large organizations. Smaller organizations employ less formal processes, or no processes at all. It is important to note, however, that even if a small organization does not have a formal process for planning and justifying IT applications, the steps of a formal process exist for a reason, and they have value. At the very least, decision makers in small organizations should consider each step when they are planning changes in their information systems.

When a company examines its needs and performance, it generates a prioritized list of both existing and potential IT applications, called the **application portfolio**. These are the applications that have to be added, or modified if they already exist.

IT Planning

The planning process for new IT applications begins with an analysis of the *organizational strategic plan*, which is illustrated in **Figure 13.1**. The organization's strategic plan identifies the firm's overall mission, the goals that follow from that mission, and the broad steps required to reach these goals. The strategic planning process modifies the organization's objectives and resources to match its changing markets and opportunities.

The organizational strategic plan and the existing IT architecture provide the inputs in developing the IT strategic plan. The *IT architecture* delineates the way an organization should utilize its information resources to accomplish its mission. It encompasses both the technical and the managerial aspects of information resources. The technical aspects include hardware and operating systems, networking, data management systems, and applications software. The managerial aspects specify how the IT department will be managed, how the functional area managers will be involved, and how IT decisions will be made.

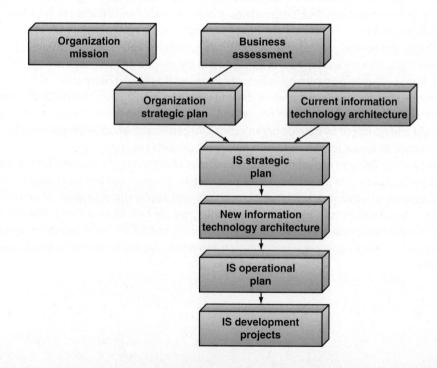

FIGURE 13.1 The information systems planning process.

The **IT strategic plan** is a set of long-range goals that describe the IT infrastructure and identify the major IT initiatives needed to achieve the organization's goals. The IT strategic plan must meet three objectives:

1. *It must be aligned with the organization's strategic plan.* This alignment is critical because the organization's information systems must support the organization's strategies. (Recall the discussion of organizational strategies and information systems in Chapter 2.)

   Consider the example of Nordstrom versus Walmart. An application that improves customer service at a small cost would be considered favorably at Nordstrom, but it would be rejected at Walmart. The reason is that the application would fit in favorably (i.e., align) with Nordstrom's service-at-any-cost strategy. However, it would not fit in well with Walmart's low-cost strategy. You see two department stores, same application, same cost and benefits—but different answers to the question "Should we develop the application?"

2. *It must provide for an IT architecture that seamlessly networks users, applications, and databases.*

3. *It must efficiently allocate IS development resources among competing projects so that the projects can be completed on time and within budget and still have the required functionality.*

The existing IT architecture is a necessary input into the IT strategic plan because it acts as a constraint on future development efforts. It is not an absolute constraint, however, because the organization can change to a new IT architecture. Companies prefer to avoid this strategy, however, because it is expensive and time consuming.

Consider this example. You have a Mac (Apple) system, and you need a new software application. You search and find several such packages for both Mac and MS Windows. Unfortunately, the best package runs only on Windows. How much better would this package have to be for you to justify switching from Mac to Windows?

One critical component in developing and implementing the IT strategic plan is the **IT steering committee**. This committee, which consists of a group of managers and staff who represent the various organizational units, is created to establish IT priorities and to ensure that the MIS function is meeting the organization's needs. The committee's major tasks are to link corporate strategy with IT strategy, to approve the allocation of resources for the MIS function, and to establish performance measures for the MIS function and ensure they are met. The IT steering committee is important to you because it ensures that you get the information systems and applications that you need to do your job.

After a company has agreed on an IT strategic plan, it next develops the **IS operational plan**. This plan consists of a clear set of projects that the IS department and the functional area managers will execute in support of the IT strategic plan. A typical IS operational plan contains the following elements:

- *Mission:* The mission of the IS function (derived from the IT strategy)
- *IS environment:* A summary of the information needs of the individual functional areas and of the organization as a whole
- *Objectives of the IS function:* The best current estimate of the goals of the IS function
- *Constraints on the IS function:* Technological, financial, personnel, and other resource limitations on the IS function
- *The application portfolio:* A prioritized inventory of present applications and a detailed plan of projects to be developed or continued during the current year
- *Resource allocation and project management:* A listing of who is going to do what, how, and when

Evaluating and Justifying IT Investment: Benefits, Costs, and Issues

Developing an IT plan is the first step in the acquisition process. Because all companies have limited resources, they must justify investing resources in some areas, including IT, rather than in others. Essentially, justifying IT investment involves calculating the costs, assessing the benefits (values), and comparing the two. This comparison is frequently referred to as cost–benefit analysis. Cost–benefit analysis is not a simple task.

Assessing the Costs.

Calculating the dollar value of IT investments is not as simple as it may seem. One of the major challenges that companies face is to allocate fixed costs among different IT projects. *Fixed costs* are those costs that remain the same regardless of any change in the company's activity level. Fixed IT costs include infrastructure costs and the costs associated with IT services and IT management. For example, the salary of the IT director is fixed, and adding one more application will not change it.

Another complication is that the costs of a system do not end when the system is installed. Rather, costs for maintaining, debugging, and improving the system can accumulate over many years. This is a critical point because organizations sometimes fail to anticipate these costs when they make the investment.

A dramatic example of unanticipated expenses was the Year 2000 (Y2K) reprogramming projects, which cost organizations worldwide billions of dollars. In the 1960s, computer memory was very expensive. To save money, programmers coded the "year" in the date field 19_ _, instead of _ _ _ _. With the "1" and the "9" hard-coded in the computer program, only the last two digits varied, so computer programs needed less memory. However, this process meant that when the year 2000 rolled around, computers would display the year as 1900. This programming technique could have caused serious problems with financial applications, insurance applications, and countless other apps.

The Y2K example illustrates the point that database design choices tend to affect the organization for a long time. As the 21st century approached, no one still used hardware or software from the 1960s (other than a few legacy applications). Database design choices made in the 1960s, however, were often still in effect decades after the companies implemented them.

In April 2019 Japan faced its own problem, which threatened the country's technology systems. The problem occurred because the Japanese calendar is based on era names that coincide with the rule of its emperors. Software using the Japanese calendar must be adapted to work with new era names. However, for this software to be modified and tested, the new era name must be known in advance.

The abdication date of Emperor Akihito was announced in late 2017, giving the nation almost 18 months to prepare. However, the Japanese government did not announce the new era name at that time. Announcing the new era name before Emperor Akihito stepped down would disrespect him by putting the focus on his son, Prince Naruhito, who became the new Emperor.

One month before the abdication, on April 1, 2019, the Japanese government did announced the new era name. Several sectors inside Japan faced problems, such as the postal service, transportation ticket vending machines, and banks. The good news is that most Japanese companies working with overseas partners or employ foreigners were already using the Western-style calendar, so they were not affected by the name change. Fortunately for the world's third-largest economy, the impact of the name change turned out to be minimal.

Assessing the Benefits.

Evaluating the benefits of IT projects is typically even more complex than calculating their costs. Benefits may be more difficult to quantify, especially because many of them are intangible (for example, improved customer or partner relations and improved decision making). As an employee, you will probably be asked for input about the intangible benefits that an IS provides for you.

The fact that organizations use IT for multiple purposes further complicates benefit analysis. To obtain a return from an IT investment, the company must also implement the technology successfully. In reality, many systems are not implemented on time, within budget, or with all of the features originally envisioned for them. Also, the proposed system may be "cutting edge." In these cases, there may be no precedent for identifying the types of financial payback the company can expect.

Conducting the Cost-Benefit Analysis. After a company has assessed the costs and benefits of IT investments, it must compare them. You have studied, or will study, cost–benefit analyses in more detail in your finance courses. The point is that real-world business problems do not come in neatly wrapped packages labeled "this is a finance problem" or "this is an IS problem." Rather, business problems span multiple functional areas.

There is no uniform strategy for conducting a cost–benefit analysis. Rather, an organization can perform this task in several ways. Here, you see four common approaches: (1) net present value, (2) return on investment, (3) breakeven analysis, and (4) the business case approach:

1. Analysts use the *net present value (NPV)* method to convert future values of benefits to their present-value equivalent by "discounting" them at the organization's cost of funds. They can then compare the present value of the future benefits with the cost required to achieve those benefits to determine whether the benefits exceed the costs.

2. *Return on investment (ROI)* measures management's effectiveness in generating profits with its available assets. ROI is calculated by dividing the net income generated by a project by the average assets invested in the project. ROI is a percentage, and the higher the percentage return, the better.

3. *Breakeven analysis* determines the point at which the cumulative dollar value of the benefits from a project equals the investment made in the project.

4. In the *business case approach*, system developers write a business case to justify funding one or more specific applications or projects. IS professionals will be a major source of input when business cases are developed because these cases describe what you do, how you do it, and how a new system could better support you.

Before you go on . . .

1. What are some problems associated with assessing the costs of IT?
2. Why are the intangible benefits from IT so difficult to evaluate?
3. Describe the NPV, ROI, breakeven analysis, and business case approaches.

13.2 Strategies for Acquiring IT Applications

After a company has justified an IT investment, it must then decide how to pursue it. As with cost–benefit analyses, there are several options for acquiring IT applications. To select the best option, companies must make a series of business decisions. The fundamental decisions are the following:

- *How much computer code does the company want to write?* A company can choose to use a totally prewritten application (write no computer code), to customize a prewritten application (write some computer code), or to custom-write an entire application (write all new computer code).

- *How will the company pay for the application?* Once the company has decided how much computer code to write, it must decide how to pay for it. With prewritten applications or customized prewritten applications, companies can buy them or lease them. With totally custom applications, companies use internal funding.

- *Where will the application run?* The next decision is whether to run the application on the company's platform or on someone else's platform. In other words, the company can employ either a software-as-a-service vendor or an application service provider. (You will examine these options later in this chapter.)

Author Lecture Videos are available exclusively in *WileyPLUS*.
Apply the Concept activities are available in the Appendix and in *WileyPLUS*.

- *Where will the application originate?* Prewritten applications can be open-source software or they can come from a vendor. The company may choose to customize prewritten open-source applications or prewritten proprietary applications from vendors. Furthermore, it may customize applications in-house, or it can outsource the customization. Finally, it can write totally custom applications in-house, or it can outsource this process.

In the following sections, you will find more details on the variety of options from which companies looking to acquire applications can select. A good rule of thumb is that an organization should consider all feasible acquisition methods in light of its business requirements. You will learn about the following acquisition methods:

- Purchase a prewritten application.
- Customize a prewritten application.
- Lease the application.
- Use application service providers and software-as-a-service vendors.
- Use open-source software.
- Use outsourcing.
- Employ continuous development.
- Employ custom development.

Purchase a Prewritten Application

Many commercial software packages contain the standard features required by IT applications. Therefore, purchasing an existing package can be a cost-effective and time-saving strategy compared with custom-developing the application in-house. Nevertheless, a company should carefully consider and plan the buy option to ensure that the selected package contains all of the features necessary to address the company's current and future needs. Otherwise, these packages can quickly become obsolete. Before a company can perform this process, it must decide which features a suitable package must include.

In reality, a single software package can rarely satisfy all of an organization's needs. For this reason, a company must sometimes purchase multiple packages to fulfill different needs. It then must integrate these packages with one another as well as with its existing software. **Table 13.1** summarizes the advantages and limitations of the buy option.

TABLE 13.1 Advantages and Limitations of the Buy Option

Advantages
Many different types of off-the-shelf software are available.
The company can try out the software before purchasing it.
The company can save much time by buying rather than building.
The company can know what it is getting before it invests in the product.
Purchased software may eliminate the need to hire personnel specifically dedicated to a project.

Disadvantages
Software may not exactly meet the company's needs.
Software may be difficult or impossible to modify, or it may require huge business process changes to implement.
The company will not have control over software improvements and new versions.
Purchased software can be difficult to integrate with existing systems.
Vendors may discontinue a product or go out of business.
Software is controlled by another company with its own priorities and business considerations.
The purchasing company lacks intimate knowledge about how and why the software functions as it does.

Customize a Prewritten Application

Customizing existing software is an especially attractive option if the software vendor allows the company to modify the application to meet its needs. However, this option may not be attractive in cases when customization is the *only* method of providing the necessary flexibility to address the company's needs. It is also not the best strategy when the software is either very expensive or likely to become obsolete in a short time. Furthermore, customizing a prewritten application can be extremely difficult, particularly for large, complex applications.

Lease the Application

Compared with the buy option and the option to develop applications in-house, the lease option can save a company both time and money. Of course, leased packages (like purchased packages) may not exactly fit the company's application requirements. However, as noted, vendor software generally includes the features that are most commonly needed by organizations in a given industry. Again, the company will decide which features are necessary.

Interested companies commonly apply the 80/20 rule when they evaluate vendor software. Put simply, if the software meets 80 percent of the company's needs, then the company should seriously consider modifying its business processes so that it can use the remaining 20 percent. Many times, this is a better long-term solution than modifying the vendor software. Otherwise, the company will have to customize the software every time the vendor releases an updated version.

Leasing can be especially attractive to small and medium-sized enterprises (SMEs) that cannot afford major investments in IT software. Large companies may also prefer to lease packages to test potential IT solutions before committing to major investments. A company that does not employ sufficient IT personnel with the appropriate skills for developing custom IT applications may also choose to lease instead of develop the software it needs in-house. Even those companies that employ in-house experts may not be able to afford the long wait for strategic applications to be developed in-house. Therefore, they lease (or buy) applications from external resources to establish a quicker presence in the market.

Leasing can be executed in one of three ways. The first way is to lease the application from a software developer, install it, and run it on the company's platform. The vendor can assist with the installation and will frequently offer to contract for the support and maintenance of the system. Many conventional applications are leased this way.

The other two options involve leasing an application and running it on the vendor's platform. Organizations can accomplish this process by using an application service provider or a software-as-a-service vendor.

Application Service Providers and Software-as-a-Service Vendors

An **application service provider (ASP)** is an agent or a vendor who assembles the software needed by enterprises and then packages it with services such as development, operations, and maintenance. The customer then accesses these applications through the Internet. **Figure 13.2** illustrates the operation of an ASP. Note that the ASP hosts both an application and a database for each customer.

Software-as-a-service (SaaS) is a method of delivering software in which a vendor hosts the applications and provides them as a service to customers over a network, typically the Internet. Customers do not own the software. Rather, they pay for using it. SaaS eliminates the need for customers to install and run the application on their own computers. Therefore, SaaS customers save the

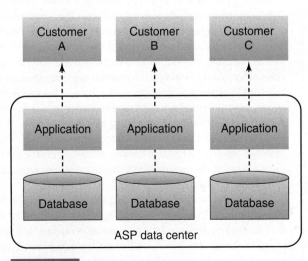

FIGURE 13.2 Operation of an application service provider.

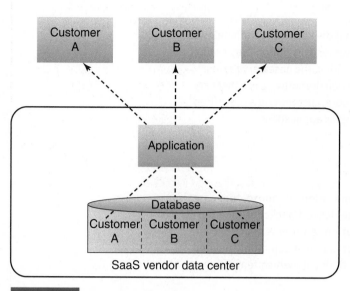

FIGURE 13.3 **Operation of a software-as-a-service vendor.**

expense (money, time, IT staff) of buying, operating, and maintaining the software. For example, Salesforce (**www.salesforce.com**), a well-known SaaS provider for customer relationship management (CRM) software solutions, provides these advantages for its customers. **Figure 13.3** displays the operation of an SaaS vendor. Note that the vendor hosts an application that multiple customers can use. The vendor also hosts a database that is partitioned for each customer to protect the privacy and security of each customer's data. IT's About Business 13.1 provides an example of an SaaS provider.

At this point, companies have made the first three decisions and must now decide where to obtain the application. Recall that, in general, for prewritten applications, companies can use open-source software or obtain the software from a vendor. For customized prewritten applications, they can customize open-source software or customize vendor software. For totally customized applications, they can write the software in-house, or they can outsource the process.

IT's About Business 13.1

MIS Developers Help Developers Help Dry Cleaners

The Business Problem

Starchup, launched in 2015, is a software-as-a-service provider based in Chicago. Founders Dan Tobon, Nick Chapleau, and Geoffroy Lessage wanted to shake up the dry-cleaning industry by creating a Web-based app that would turn any dry cleaner into an on-demand service. "We found that there's a lot of savvy operators out there," Chapleau said. "They really know how to clean clothes, they've been doing it for years, they just don't have mobile app developers working for them." Their objective was to create a dry cleaner's website, powered by Starchup, where customers could read reviews; select and schedule a laundry service; track pickup, progress, and delivery; pay for the service; and provide reviews. In 2015, Tobon, Chapleau, and Lessage developed a prototype. However, they did not have the skills or the time to fully develop the product as they envisioned it.

This type of result is not uncommon. Entrepreneurial ideas are usually based on the entrepreneur's experience and skills as well as the trade, product, or service that the entrepreneur provides. What is often lacking is the business expertise necessary to take that entrepreneurial idea to market, such as managing operations, sales, accounting, payroll, and customer service as well as any other industry-specific supporting business functions. Therefore, entrepreneurs have to build a team of people to help run the business. However, it has also become a standard practice to outsource many of the organization's support activities rather than to hire employees who possess the necessary expertise.

A large majority of new product ideas include some form of integration with a smartphone. "There's an app for that" was trademarked by Apple in 2009 because so many new apps were being developed. The introduction of the Apple App Store created an opportunity for people who were willing to take the time to

build an app that would meet a specific need. To capitalize on an idea took one of two approaches to enter the development arena. Either an app developer needed programming experience, (or the willingness to learn different platforms), or they needed sufficient funding to pay someone to develop the app for them.

The IT Solution

In 2015, in a different sector, Gigster (**www.gigster.com**) was founded to assist entrepreneurs who had an idea for a mobile app or an information system but who did not possess the necessary skills to bring it to market. Gigster was such an innovative idea that it attracted several prominent investors, including Michael Jordan and Ashton Kutcher.

Gigster's business model is similar to Uber or Lyft in that it allows the community to share resources. However, rather than sharing vehicles (an expensive commodity), this model allows for the sharing of developers (an expensive investment). Gigster provides on-demand software development and design for anyone, but especially for entrepreneurs and small- to medium-sized businesses. Within minutes of chatting with a client, an entrepreneur can have a quote on how much it will cost to build his or her app, how long the app will take to develop, and what the long-term maintenance will involve. Gigster is very careful about the designers/developers they allow to work for them. They hire only about 7 percent of the developers who apply to work for them. As a result, Gigster's customers can be confident that the people who are working on their app are high-caliber programmers.

In 2016, Starchup came to Gigster to obtain the additional features they needed to make their Web app function the way they had envisioned. Gigster assigned two developers to Starchup and offered a "milestones" model that allowed Starchup to prioritize the features and approve the development schedule.

The Results

Utilizing this model, Starchup successfully launched their product in 2016. In one year, Starchup brought more than 15 laundry companies onto their SaaS platform. With Gigster as a development partner, Starchup has been free to grow customer relationships and develop partnerships that enhance their customer experience. They have partnered with Mainline and Fabricare Systems to integrate with their clients' in-store point-of-sale (POS) systems so that the Starchup tools (Web app, mobile, and routing technology) link directly to the POS terminal in the store.

Could Starchup have succeeded without Gigster? Perhaps, but it would not have happened as quickly or as efficiently. Outsourcing this operation enabled Starchup to focus on what they do best—serve the laundry industry. In turn, Gigster was able to do what they do best—serve entrepreneurial-minded small- to medium-sized businesses. Ultimately, businesses are profitable and customers win with improved products and services.

Sources: Compiled from I. Broadway, "Michael Jordan Invests in Startup Gigster," *Bloomberg*, August 29, 2017; S. Adams, "With New Funding Round, Gigster Gets Closer to a $1 Billion Valuation," *Forbes*, August 29, 2017; M. Weinberger, "Marc Benioff, Ashton Kutcher, and even Michael Jordan Poured Millions into a Startup that Helps Programmers make Google Money from Home," *BusinessInsider*, August 29, 2017; P. Haggin, "Freelance-Developer Marketplace Gigster Refuels in Series B," *Wall Street Journal*, August 29, 2017; R. Sarver, "Gigster and the Future of Work," redpoint. com/blog, August 29, 2017; M. Graham, "Tide Set to Take a Spin in Chicago's On-Demand Laundry Market," *Chicago Tribune*, February 1, 2016; R. Loerzel, "Chicago Just Got Another Drycleaning Delivery App," chicagobusiness. com, September 24, 2015; C. Taylor, "Gigster (YC S15) Hires an Elite Engineering Team for Your Software Project in Minutes," blog.ycombinator.com, July 23, 2015; J. Constine, "Gigster Does the Dev Dirty Work to Turn Your Idea into an App," *TechCrunch*, July 22, 2015; D. Pitorak, "How Starchup Helps Dry Cleaners by Getting Out of Their Way," builtinchicago.org, May 15, 2015; D. Gross, "Apple Trademarks 'There's An App For That'," cnn.com, October 12, 2010; http://cleaner-and-launderer.com/starchup-teams-mainline-fabricare-systems/, accessed December 15, 2017; and https://gigster.com/clients/starchup, accessed July 17, 2019.

Questions:

1. How is Gigster's model of outsourcing software development similar to Uber's model of ride sharing?

2. What did Gigster offer that was such an asset to Starchup?

3. Explain the software-as-a-service model that Starchup offers to its clients.

Use Open-Source Software

Organizations obtain a license to implement an open-source software product and either use it as is, customize it, or develop applications with it. Unless the company is one of the few that wants to tinker with their source code, open-source applications are, basically, the same as a proprietary application except for licensing, payment, and support. Open-source software is really an alternative source of applications rather than a conceptually different development option. (We discuss open-source software in Technology Guide 2.)

Outsourcing

Acquiring IT applications from outside contractors or external organizations is called **outsourcing**. Companies can use outsourcing in many situations. For example, they might want to experiment with new IT technologies without making a substantial up-front investment. They also might use outsourcing to obtain access to outside experts. One disadvantage of outsourcing is that companies frequently must place their valuable corporate data under the control of the outsourcing vendor.

Several types of vendors offer services for creating and operating IT systems, including e-commerce applications. Many software companies, from IBM to Oracle, offer a range of outsourcing services for developing, operating, and maintaining IT applications. IT outsourcers, such as EDS, offer a variety of services. Also, the large CPA companies and management consultants—for example, Accenture—offer outsourcing services.

MIS For example, Philip Morris International (the non-U.S. operation of Philip Morris) outsourced its IT infrastructure management to Indian services firm Wipro. The companies concluded a five-year contract in which Wipro manages the tobacco company's applications and IT using Wipro's cloud-based management platform. (We discuss cloud computing in Technology Guide 3.) The contract is reported to be worth some $35 million U.S.

Some companies outsource offshore, particularly in India and China. *Offshoring* can save money, but it includes risks as well. The risks depend on which services are being offshored. If a company is offshoring application development, then the major risk is poor communication between users and developers. In response to these risks, some companies are bringing outsourced jobs back in-house, a process called *reverse outsourcing*, or *insourcing.*

Continuous Development

Continuous application development automates and improves the process of software delivery. In essence, a software development project is not viewed as having a defined product, with development stopped when the product is implemented. Rather, a software development project is viewed as constantly changing in response to changing business conditions and in response to user acceptance.

Continuous application development is the process of steadily adding new computer code to a software project when the new computer code is written and tested. Each development team member submits new code when it is finished. Automated testing is performed on the code to ensure that it functions within the software project. Continuous code submission provides developers with immediate feedback from users and status updates for the software on which they are working.

Employ Custom Development

Another option is to custom-build an application. Companies can either perform this operation in-house or outsource the process. Although custom development is usually more time consuming and costly than buying or leasing, it often produces a better fit with the organization's specific requirements.

The development process starts when the IT steering committee (discussed previously in this chapter), having received suggestions for a new system, decides it is worth exploring. These suggestions come from users (who will be you in the near future). Understanding this process will help you obtain the systems that you need. Conversely, not understanding this process will reduce your chances, because other people who understand it better will make suggestions that use up available resources.

As the company goes through the development process, its mind-set changes. In systems investigation (the first stage of the traditional systems development life cycle), the organization is trying to decide whether to build something. Everyone knows it may or may not be built. In the later stages of the development process, the organization is committed to building the application. Although a project can be canceled at any time, this change in attitude is still important.

The basic, backbone methodology for custom development is the systems development life cycle (SDLC), which you will read about in the next section. Section 13.4 examines the methodologies that complement the SDLC: prototyping, joint application development, integrated computer-assisted systems development tools, and rapid application development. You will also consider four other methodologies: agile development, end-user development, component-based development, and object-oriented development.

Before you go on . . .

1. Describe the four fundamental business decisions that organizations must make when they acquire information systems.

2. Discuss each of the seven development methods in this section with regard to the four business decisions that organizations must make.

Author Lecture Videos are available exclusively in *WileyPLUS*.
Apply the Concept activities are available in the Appendix and in *WileyPLUS*.

13.3 | Traditional Systems Development Life Cycle

The **systems development life cycle (SDLC)** is the traditional systems development method that organizations use for large-scale IT projects. The SDLC is a structured framework that

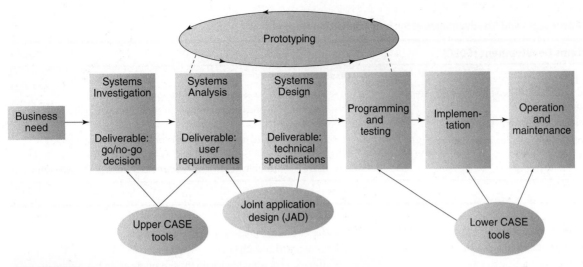

FIGURE 13.4   A six-stage systems development life cycle with supporting tools.

consists of sequential processes by which information systems are developed. For our purposes (see **Figure 13.4**), we identify six processes, each of which consists of clearly defined tasks:

1. Systems investigation
2. Systems analysis
3. Systems design
4. Programming and testing
5. Implementation
6. Operation and maintenance

Alternative SDLC models contain more or fewer stages. The flow of tasks, however, remains largely the same. When problems occur in any phase of the SDLC, developers often must go back to previous phases.

Systems development projects produce desired results through team efforts. Development teams typically include users, systems analysts, programmers, and technical specialists. *Users* are employees from all functional areas and levels of the organization who interact with the system, either directly or indirectly. **Systems analysts** are IS professionals who specialize in analyzing and designing information systems. **Programmers** are IS professionals who either modify existing computer programs or write new programs to satisfy user requirements. **Technical specialists** are experts on a certain type of technology, such as databases or telecommunications. The **systems stakeholders** include everyone who is affected by changes in a company's information systems—for example, users and managers. All stakeholders are typically involved in systems development at various times and in varying degrees.

Figure 13.5 indicates that users have high involvement in the early stages of the SDLC, lower involvement in the programming and testing stage, and higher involvement in the later stages. **Table 13.2** discusses the advantages and disadvantages of the SDLC.

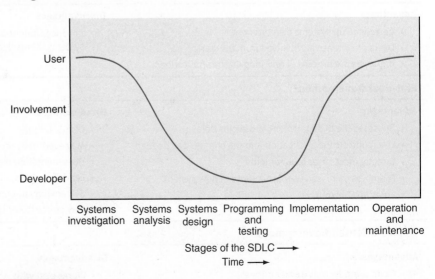

FIGURE 13.5   Comparison of user and developer involvement over the SDLC.

TABLE 13.2 Advantages and Disadvantages of System Acquisition Methods

Traditional Systems Development (SDLC)

Advantages

- Forces staff to systematically go through every step in a structured process.
- Enforces quality by maintaining standards.
- Has lower probability of missing important issues in collecting user requirements.

Disadvantages

- May produce excessive documentation.
- Users may be unwilling or unable to study the approved specifications.
- Takes too long to progress from the original ideas to a working system.
- Users have trouble describing requirements for a proposed system.

Prototyping

Advantages

- Helps clarify user requirements.
- Helps verify the feasibility of the design.
- Promotes genuine user participation.
- Promotes close working relationship between systems developers and users.
- Works well for ill-defined problems.
- May produce part of the final system.

Disadvantages

- May encourage inadequate problem analysis.
- Is not practical with large number of users.
- User may not want to give up the prototype when the system is completed.
- May generate confusion about whether the system is complete and maintainable.
- System may be built quickly, which can result in lower quality.

Joint Application Design

Advantages

- Involves many users in the development process.
- Saves time.
- Generates greater user support for the new system.
- Improves the quality of the new system.
- The new system is easier to implement.
- The new system has lower training costs.

Disadvantages

- It is difficult to get all users to attend the JAD meeting.
- The JAD approach is subject to all of the problems associated with any group meeting.

Integrated Computer-Assisted Software Engineering

Advantages

- Can produce systems with a longer effective operational life.
- Can produce systems that closely meet user requirements.
- Can speed up the development process.
- Can produce systems that are more flexible and adaptable to changing business conditions.
- Can produce excellent documentation.

Disadvantages

- Systems are often more expensive to build and maintain.
- The process requires more extensive and accurate definition of user requirements.
- It is difficult to customize the end product.

Rapid Application Development

Advantages

- Can speed up systems development.
- Users are intensively involved from the start.
- Improves the process of rewriting legacy applications.

Disadvantages

- Produces functional components of final systems, but not the final systems themselves.

End-User Development

Advantages

- Bypasses the IS department and avoids delays.
- User controls the application and can change it as needed.
- Directly meets user requirements.
- Promotes increased user acceptance of new system.
- Frees up IT resources.

Disadvantages

- Disadvantages
- May eventually require maintenance from IS department.
- Documentation may be inadequate.
- Leads to poor quality control.
- System may not have adequate interfaces to existing systems.
- May create lower-quality systems.

Object-Oriented Development

Advantages

- Objects model real-world entities.
- New systems may be able to reuse some computer code.

Disadvantages

- Works best with systems of more limited scope (i.e., with systems that do not have huge numbers of objects).

Systems Investigation

The initial stage in a traditional SDLC is systems investigation. Systems development professionals agree that the more time they invest in (1) understanding the business problem to be solved, (2) specifying the technical options for the systems, and (3) anticipating the problems they are likely to encounter during development, the greater the chances of success. For these reasons, **systems investigation** addresses *the business problem* (or business opportunity) by means of the feasibility study.

The primary task in the systems investigation stage is the feasibility study. Organizations have three basic solutions to any business problem relating to an information system: (1) Do nothing and continue to use the existing system unchanged, (2) modify or enhance the existing system, and (3) develop a new system. The **feasibility study** analyzes which of these three solutions best fits the particular business problem. It also provides a rough assessment of the project's technical, economic, and behavioral feasibility, as explained next:

- *Technical feasibility* determines whether the company can develop or otherwise acquire the hardware, software, and communications components needed to solve the business problem. Technical feasibility also determines whether the organization can use its existing technology to achieve the project's performance objectives.

- *Economic feasibility* determines whether the project is an acceptable financial risk and, if so, whether the organization has the necessary time and money to successfully complete the project. You have already learned about the commonly used methods to determine economic feasibility: NPV, ROI, breakeven analysis, and the business case approach.

- *Behavioral feasibility* addresses the human issues of the systems development project. You will be heavily involved in this aspect of the feasibility study.

After the feasibility analysis is completed, a "go/no-go" decision is reached by the steering committee if there is one or by top management in the absence of a committee. The go/no-go decision does not depend solely on the feasibility analysis. Organizations often have more feasible projects than they can fund. Therefore, the firm must prioritize the feasible projects and pursue those with the highest priority. Unfunded feasible projects may not be presented to the IT department at all. These projects therefore contribute to the *hidden backlog*, which consists of projects that the IT department is not aware of.

If the decision is no-go, then the project is either put on the shelf until conditions are more favorable or it is discarded. If the decision is go, then the project proceeds, and the systems analysis phase begins.

Systems Analysis

Once a development project has the necessary approvals from all participants, the systems analysis stage begins. **Systems analysis** is the process whereby systems analysts examine the business problem that the organization plans to solve with an information system.

The primary purpose of the systems analysis stage is to gather information about the existing system to determine the requirements for an enhanced system or a new system. The end product of this stage, known as the *deliverable*, is a set of *system requirements*.

Arguably, the most difficult task in systems analysis is to identify the specific requirements that the system must satisfy. These requirements are often called *user requirements*, because users (meaning you) provide them. When the systems developers have accumulated the user requirements for the new system, they proceed to the systems design stage.

Systems Design

Systems design describes how the system will resolve the business problem. The deliverable of the systems design phase is the set of *technical system specifications*, which specify the following:

- System outputs, inputs, and user interfaces
- Hardware, software, databases, telecommunications, personnel, and procedures
- A blueprint of how these components are integrated

When the system specifications are approved by all participants, they are "frozen"—that is, they should not be changed. Adding functions after the project has been initiated causes **scope creep**, in which the time frame and expenses associated with the project expand beyond the agreed-upon limits. Scope creep endangers both the project's budget and its schedule. Because scope creep is expensive, successful project managers place controls on changes requested by users. These controls help to prevent runaway projects.

Programming and Testing

If the organization decides to construct the software in-house, then programming begins. **Programming** involves translating the design specifications into computer code. This process can be lengthy and time consuming, because writing computer code is as much an art as it is a science. Large-scale systems development projects can involve hundreds of computer programmers who are charged with creating hundreds of thousands of lines of computer code. These projects employ programming teams. The teams often include functional area users, who help the programmers focus on the business problem.

Thorough and continuous testing occurs throughout the programming stage. Testing is the process that assesses whether the computer code will produce the expected and desired results. It is also intended to detect errors, or bugs, in the computer code.

Implementation

Implementation (or *deployment*) is the process of converting from an old computer system to a new one. The conversion process involves organizational change. Only end users can manage organizational change, not the MIS department. The MIS department typically does not have enough credibility with the business users to manage the change process. Organizations use three major conversion strategies: direct, pilot, and phased.

In a **direct conversion**, the old system is cut off, and the new system is turned on at a certain point in time. This type of conversion is the least expensive. It is also the riskiest because, if the new system does not work as planned, there is no support from the old system. Because of these risks, few systems are implemented using direct conversion.

A **pilot conversion** introduces the new system in one part of the organization, such as in one plant or one functional area. The new system runs for a period of time and is then assessed. If the assessment confirms that the system is working properly, then the system is implemented in other parts of the organization.

A **phased conversion** introduces components of the new system, such as individual modules, in stages. Each module is assessed. If it works properly, then other modules are introduced until the entire new system is operational. Large organizations commonly combine the pilot and phased approaches—that is, they execute a phased conversion using a pilot group for each phase. A fourth strategy is *parallel conversion*, in which the old and new systems operate simultaneously for a time. This strategy is seldom used today. One reason is that parallel conversion is totally impractical when both the old and new systems are online. Imagine that you are completing an order on Amazon, only to be told, "Before your order can be entered here, you must provide all the same information again, in a different form, and on a different set of screens." The results would be disastrous for Amazon. Regardless of the type of implementation process that an organization uses, the new system may not work as advertised. In fact, the new system may cause more problems than the old system that it replaced.

Operation and Maintenance

After the new system is implemented, it will operate for a period of time, until (like the old system it replaced) it no longer meets its objectives. Once the new system's operations are stabilized, the company performs audits to assess the system's capabilities and to determine if it is being used correctly.

Systems require several types of maintenance. The first type is *debugging* the program, a process that continues throughout the life of the system. The second type is *updating* the system to accommodate changes in business conditions. An example is adjusting to new governmental regulations, such as changes in tax rates. These corrections and upgrades usually do not add any new functions. Instead, they simply help the system continue to achieve its objectives. In contrast, the third type of maintenance *adds new functions* to the existing system without disturbing its operation.

Before you go on . . .

1. Describe the feasibility study.
2. What is the difference between systems analysis and systems design?
3. Describe structured programming.
4. What are the four conversion methods?

13.4 Alternative Methods and Tools for Systems Development

Alternative methods for systems development include joint application design, rapid application development, agile development, and end-user development.

Author Lecture Videos are available exclusively in *WileyPLUS*.
Apply the Concept activities are available in the Appendix and in *WileyPLUS*.

Joint Application Design

Joint application design (JAD) is a group-based tool for collecting user requirements and creating system designs. It is most often used within the systems analysis and systems design stages of the SDLC. JAD involves a group meeting attended by the analysts and all of the users that can be conducted either in person or through the computer. During this meeting, all users jointly define and agree on the systems requirements. This process saves a tremendous amount of time. Table 13.2 lists the advantages and disadvantages of the JAD process.

Rapid Application Development

Rapid application development (RAD) is a systems development method that can combine JAD, prototyping, and integrated computer-assisted software engineering (ICASE) tools (discussed later in this section) to rapidly produce a high-quality system. In the first RAD stage, developers use JAD sessions to collect system requirements. This strategy ensures that users are intensively involved early on. The development process in RAD is iterative; that is, requirements, designs, and the system itself are developed and then undergo a series, or sequence, of improvements. RAD uses ICASE tools to quickly structure requirements and develop proto-types. As the prototypes are developed and refined, users review them in additional JAD sessions. RAD produces the functional components of a final system rather than prototypes. To understand how RAD functions and how it differs from SDLC, see **Figure 13.6**. Table 13.2 highlights the advantages and disadvantages of the RAD process.

Agile Development

MIS **Agile development** is a software development methodology that delivers functionality in rapid iterations, which are usually measured in weeks. To be successful, this methodology requires frequent communication, development, testing, and delivery. Agile development focuses on rapid development and frequent user contact to create software that addresses the needs of business users. This software does not have to include every possible feature the user will require. Rather, it must meet only the user's more important and immediate needs. It can be updated later to introduce additional functions as they become necessary. The core tenet of agile development is to do only what you have to do to be successful right now.

One type of agile development uses the *scrum approach*. A key principle of scrum is that during a project, users can change their minds about what they want and need. Scrum acknowledges that a development problem cannot be fully understood or defined from the start. Therefore, scrum focuses on maximizing the development team's ability to deliver iterations quickly and to respond effectively to additional user requirements as they emerge.

Scrum contains sets of practices and predefined roles. The primary roles are the following:

- The *Scrum Master:* Maintains the processes (typically replaces a project manager)
- The *Product Owner:* Represents the business users and any other stakeholders in the project
- The *Team:* A cross-functional group of about seven people who perform the actual analysis, design, coding, implementation, testing, and so on

Scrum works this way: During each *sprint*—typically a two- to four-week period—the team creates a potentially shippable product increment, such as working and tested software. The set of features that goes into each sprint comes from the product backlog, which is a prioritized set of high-level work requirements to be completed.

The sprint planning meeting determines which backlog items will be addressed during a sprint. During this meeting, the product owner informs the team of the items in the product

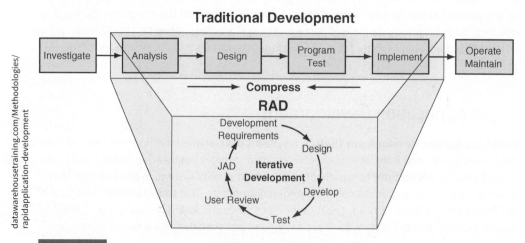

datawarehousetraining.com/Methodologies/
rapidapplication-development

FIGURE 13.6 **A rapid prototyping development process versus SDLC.**

backlog that he or she wants to be completed. The team members then determine how many of these projects they can commit to during the next sprint, and they record this information in the sprint backlog.

During a sprint, no one is allowed to change the sprint backlog, which means that the requirements are frozen for the sprint. Each sprint must end on time. If the requirements are not completed for any reason, then they are left out and returned to the product backlog. After each sprint is completed, the team demonstrates how to use the software.

An interesting type of agile development is a methodology called *minimum viable product (MVP)* development. Applications developed using MVP methodology have just the required amount of functionality to operate successfully. On the other hand, MVP applications do not have so much functionality (i.e., too many features) that the development process took too long and cost too much.

End-User Development

MIS **End-user development** is an approach in which the organization's end users develop their own applications with little or no formal assistance from the IT department. Table 13.2 lists the advantages and disadvantages of end-user development. Sometimes this form of IT development or acquisition is called **shadow IT** (also known as *Stealth IT* or *Rogue IT*). While the end-users bypassing the IT Department might make it easier for them to adopt the tools that they want to work with, this process also bypasses the security measures that the IT Department is trying to enforce. These shadow IT systems can open systems to vulnerabilities and create avenues for criminals to access private company and customer data. As an employee, it is important to carefully consider adopting something that has not been approved by your organization. If your shadow IT creates a vulnerability that allows a breach, you will probably lose your job! IT's About Business 13.2 highlights just such a case where shadow IT resulted in a $1.1 million settlement.

IT's About Business 13.2

MIS **Horizon's Renovations Open the Door to Security Problems**

Facility renovations are not typically considered a threat to information security. However, for Horizon Blue Cross Blue Shield of New Jersey, renovation shed light on several issues within their IT department. Specifically, in 2013, two laptops were stolen from their headquarters in Newark, New Jersey, during a renovation. These laptops were poorly secured by a cable that the thief easily cut. Unfortunately, these laptops held the personal information for 690,000 policy holders.

The dishonesty of the person who stole the laptops and the ease with which he or she cut the security cables are legitimate issues. However, the most basic concern involves shadow IT (and more significantly, the business processes that created the need for shadow IT) and not the renovation, physical security, or the thief. The stolen laptops were MacBooks that had been purchased and used outside the purview of Horizon's IT group. This situation is considered shadow IT because it is taking place "in the shadows" of the organization. Because these laptops were not under the oversight of the IT office, they were not encrypted. Instead,

they were protected only by a password. This type of security was insufficient for the data access level that the company had granted the laptop users. As a result, the Social Security numbers of nearly 700,000 New Jersey residents were compromised.

Was the security breach at Horizon really the fault of shadow IT? Shadow IT exists when a company is not equipped to deliver the solutions that employees need to be productive in their jobs. Managers are being asked to make decisions and to deliver results faster than ever before. As a result, they frequently have to turn to technologies that are not yet supported by the organization to get their work done. And, when those technologies happen to be outside the realm of their organization, they go ahead and use them quietly. As an example, a 2017 report revealed that employees of the National Aeronautics and Space Administration (NASA) were utilizing 28 cloud-based services that the administration had yet to approve.

This type of scenario might seem harmless until an unencrypted laptop is stolen. Organizations have policies in place to protect their employees and their customers. These policies are sometimes inconvenient, but they serve a serious—and sometimes legal—purpose. When employees circumvent these policies, they put both the organization and its customers at risk. Despite this threat, employees will continue to use the shadow IT apps if these technologies increase their productivity.

Perhaps the Horizon security breach would have been avoided if the IT department had exercised better control over shadow IT. Or, if adopting new technologies involved less bureaucracy, then perhaps employees would give the IT department the opportunity to review and officially approve these technologies rather than using them "in the shadows" of the organization.

How should organizations deal with shadow IT? There are multiple answers to this question. One approach is to emphasize the importance of complying with corporate policy. Another is to enhance the communication between the users and the IT department to discover why shadow IT is more productive than the organization's "official" technologies. Regardless of which approach they adopt, organizations must be aware of the potential damage that can arise from the unauthorized use of technology by their employees, and they must make a concerted effort to reduce the risk of a security breach.

Sources: Compiled from J. French, "Why Shadow IT Is the Next Looming Cybersecurity Threat," *TheNextWeb*, April 25, 2019; C. Preimesberger, "How Enterprises Can Reduce Employees' Urge to Use Shadow IT," *eWeek*, October 9, 2017; M. Frank, "Shadow IT & Citizen Development – Love IT or Loathe IT," blog.lansa.com, September 29, 2017; G. Ray, "How to Make Shadow IT Work in Your Favor," redpixie.com, August 3, 2017; S. Zimmermann, C. Rentrop, H. Konstanz, and C. Felden, "A Multiple Case Study on the Nature and Management of Shadow Information Technology," *Journal of Information Systems*, Spring 2017, v31, n1, pp. 79–101; C. Frank, "Shadow IT," *Forbes*, February 22, 2017; S. Livio, "Horizon Fined $1.1M for Not Protecting Customers' Private Info," nj.com, February 17, 2017; Anonymous, "Scalable Cloud Infrastructure Transforms the Data Center," *MIT Technology Review*, July 28, 2016; C. Worley, "Shadow IT: Mitigating Security Risks," csoonline.com, June 21, 2016; L. Hecht, "Parity Check, Don't Be Afraid of Your Shadow IT, Yet," *thenewstack.io*, May 26, 2016; D. Garey, " Top Three Reasons to Manage Shadow IT," tenable.com/blog, April 26, 2016; J. Bindseil, "Shadow IT Risks on the Rise," globalscape.com/blog, February 2, 2016; A. Froehlich, "Shadow IT: It's Much Worse Than You Think," *Information Week*, August 6, 2015; https://www.mavenwave.com/fusion-blog/shadow-it-part-1/, accessed December 15, 2017; http://www.peak10.com/hybrid-brings-shadow-shadows/, accessed December 15, 2017; and http://www.wyrick.com/news-publications/shadow-IT-costs-horizon, accessed July 17, 2019.

Questions

1. According to the case, how did the organization contribute to its own security breach?

2. Why do you think employees look to shadow IT rather than going through proper channels?

3. Do you think the organization should ignore shadow IT and focus on fixing their processes, or should they ignore their processes and focus on shadow IT?

DevOps

MIS DevOps (a combination of "Development" and "Operations") is a practice that was first presented in 2009 and has really gained traction in the last few years. DevOps is a form of software development that brings the developers and the users (operations) together throughout the entire process with the goal of reducing the time to deployment, increasing the usability of the finished product, and lowering the cost of new app development.

There are several factors that have increased the applications of DevOps methodology. First, organizations have less time to develop and deploy applications, there is less room for error, and the number of applications being developed is on the rise. In fact, a recent study showed that most organizations plan to release 17 applications each year. The DevOps framework is a solid response to the business pressures organizations face today.

Tools for Systems Development

Several tools can be used with various systems development methods. These tools include prototyping, integrated computer-assisted software engineering, component-based development, and object-oriented development.

MIS **Prototyping.** The **prototyping** approach defines an initial list of user requirements, builds a model of the system, and then refines the system in several iterations based on users' feedback. Developers do not try to obtain a complete set of user specifications for the system at the outset, and they do not plan to develop the system all at once. Instead, they quickly develop a smaller version of the system known as a **prototype**. A prototype can take two forms. In some cases, it contains only the components of the new system that are of most interest to the users. In other cases, it is a small-scale working model of the entire system.

Users make suggestions for improving the prototype, based on their experiences with it. The developers then review the prototype with the users and use their suggestions to refine it. This process continues through several iterations until the users approve the system or it becomes apparent that the system cannot meet the users' needs. If the system is viable, then the developers can use the prototype to build the full system. One typical use of prototyping is to develop screens that a user will see and interact with. Table 13.2 describes the advantages and disadvantages of the prototyping approach.

A practical problem with prototyping is that a prototype usually looks more complete than it actually is—that is, it may not use the real database, it usually does not have the necessary error checking, and it almost never includes the necessary security features. Users who review a prototype that resembles the finished system may not recognize these problems. Consequently, they might have unrealistic expectations about how close the actual system is to completion.

[MIS] Integrated Computer-Assisted Software Engineering Tools.

Computer-aided software engineering (CASE) refers to a group of tools that automate many of the tasks in the SDLC. The tools that are used to automate the early stages of the SDLC (systems investigation, analysis, and design) are called **upper CASE tools**. The tools used to automate later stages in the SDLC (programming, testing, operation, and maintenance) are called **lower CASE tools**. CASE tools that provide links between upper CASE and lower CASE tools are called **integrated CASE (ICASE) tools**. Table 13.2 lists the advantages and disadvantages of ICASE tools.

[MIS] Component-Based Development.

Component-based development uses standard components to build applications. Components are reusable applications that generally have one specific function, such as a shopping cart, user authentication, or a catalog. Compared with other approaches, component-based development generally involves less programming and more assembly. Component-based development is closely linked with the idea of Web services and service-oriented architectures, which you will study in Technology Guide 3.

Many start-up companies are pursuing the idea of component-based application development. One example is Ning (**www.ning.com**), which allows organizations to create, customize, and share their own social network.

[MIS] Object-Oriented Development.

Object-oriented development is based on a different view of computer systems than the perception that characterizes traditional development approaches. Traditional approaches can produce a system that performs the original task but may not be suited for handling other tasks. This limitation applies even when these other tasks involve the same real-world entities. For example, a billing system will handle billing, but it probably cannot be adapted to handle mailings for the marketing department or to generate leads for the sales force. This is true even though the billing, marketing, and sales functions all use similar data, including customer names, addresses, and purchases. In contrast, an *object-oriented (OO) system* begins not with the task to be performed, but with the aspects of the real world that must be modeled to perform that task. Therefore, in our example, if the firm has a good model of its customers and its interactions with them, then it can use this model equally well for billing, mailings, and sales leads.

The development process for an object-oriented system begins with a feasibility study and an analysis of the existing system. Systems developers identify the *objects* in the new system— the fundamental elements in OO analysis and design. Each object represents a tangible, real-world entity such as a customer, bank account, student, or course. Objects have *properties*, or *data values*. For example, a customer has an identification number, a name, an address, an account number(s), and so on. Objects also contain the *operations* that can be performed on their properties. For example, operations that can be performed on the customer object may include obtain-account-balance, open-account, withdraw-funds, and so on. Operations are also referred to as *behaviors*.

This approach enables OO analysts to define all the relevant objects needed for the new system, including their properties and operations. The analysts then model how the objects interact to meet the objectives of the new system. In some cases, analysts can reuse existing objects from other applications (or from a library of objects) in the new system. This process saves the analysts the time they otherwise would spend coding these objects. In most cases, however, even with object reuse, some coding will be necessary to customize the objects and their interactions for the new system.

MIS **Containers.** Containers are a method of developing applications that run independently of the base operating system of the server. Containers allow application providers to develop, test, and deploy technology that will always run in practice exactly like it does in testing. This would allow software to be developed more rapidly. Primarily, they provide a level of portability that has brought about one of the biggest shifts in application development in years.

To better understand containers, imagine that your vehicle is a container. You only interact with the environment inside the vehicle (the container). Your vehicle can travel on different types of terrain (platforms), but you do the same things inside (gas, brakes, lights, signals, etc.). The vehicle (container) has features built in to help manage the external environment (tires, shocks, windshield wipers, etc.). Containers have begun to revolutionize the speed of development because developers can focus on the container rather than the environment.

Application developers have always been plagued with platform challenges. (A platform is an underlying computer system on which application programs can run. On personal computers, Windows and Mac OS X are examples of platforms.) As one example, if a developer built an application in a Windows environment, then it might not run properly if it were deployed after a Windows update. In addition, it probably would not work in a Linux environment, either. Further, multiple versions of an application need to be developed to run on different environments, and they have to be continuously tested on platform updates.

One solution for this problem is to build and test applications on a virtual machine and then implement them on an identical virtual machine for customers. A *virtual machine* is a self-contained operating environment that behaves as if it were a separate physical computer. Building and testing on a virtual machine ensures that an application developed on one platform will run on a different platform. But, what if you could develop an application that included its own environment and would run as it was developed regardless of the operating system on which it was deployed? That is exactly the idea behind a container.

Containers are not new; in fact, they have been tested since 2005. However, they were not widely embraced by mainstream IT leaders until 2014. The increased popularity of containers is largely due to Docker, an open-source project by Docker, Inc. (**www.docker.com/**). Docker is a Linux-based product that enables applications to be developed and deployed in a container. Docker-created apps will run on any platform.

MIS **Low-Code Development Platform.** Low-code Development Platforms (LCDPs) make use of visual interfaces to develop applications rather than traditional procedural hand-coding. This allows for more rapid app development (because it reduces the amount of code that has to be written), and an expansion of those who can contribute to a project. LCDPs allow nontechnical users to provide input and efforts into app development. LCDPs will help to extend end-user development by making it easier to produce new programs with less formal training.

You have studied many methods that can be used to acquire new systems. Table 13.2 provides an overview of the advantages and disadvantages of each of these methods.

Before you go on . . .

1. Describe the tools that augment the traditional SDLC.
2. Describe the alternate methods that can be used for systems development other than the SDLC.

What's in IT for me?

ACCT For the Accounting Major

Accounting personnel help perform the cost–benefit analyses on proposed projects. They may also monitor ongoing project costs to keep them within budget. Accounting personnel undoubtedly will find themselves involved with systems development at various points throughout their careers.

FIN For the Finance Major

Finance personnel are frequently involved with the financial issues that accompany any large-scale systems development project (e.g., budgeting). They also are involved in cost–benefit and risk analyses. To perform these tasks, they need to stay abreast of the emerging techniques used to determine project costs and ROI. Finally, because they must manage vast amounts of information, finance departments are also common recipients of new systems.

MKT For the Marketing Major

In most organizations, marketing, like finance, involves massive amounts of data and information. Like finance, then, marketing is also a hotbed of systems development. Marketing personnel will increasingly find themselves participating in systems development teams. Such involvement increasingly means helping to develop systems, especially Web-based systems that reach out directly from the organization to its customers.

POM For the Production/Operations Management Major

Participation in development teams is also a common role for production/operations people. Manufacturing is becoming increasingly computerized and integrated with other allied systems, from design to logistics to customer support. Production systems interface frequently with marketing, finance, and human resources. They may also be part of a larger enterprisewide system. Also, many end users in POM either develop their own systems or collaborate with IT personnel on specific applications.

HRM For the Human Resources Management Major

The human resources department is closely involved with several aspects of the systems acquisitions process. Acquiring new systems may require hiring new employees, changing job descriptions, or terminating employees. Human resources staff perform all of these tasks. Furthermore, if the organization hires consultants for the development project, or outsources it, the human resources department may handle the contracts with these suppliers.

MIS For the MIS Major

Regardless of the approach that the organization adopts for acquiring new systems, the MIS department spearheads it. If the organization chooses either to buy or to lease the application, the MIS department leads in examining the offerings of the various vendors and in negotiating with the vendors. If the organization chooses to develop the application in-house, then the process falls to the MIS department. MIS analysts work closely with users to develop their information requirements. MIS programmers then write the computer code, test it, and implement the new system.

Summary

13.1 Discuss the different cost–benefit analyses that companies must take into account when formulating an IT strategic plan.

The four common approaches to cost–benefit analysis are the following:

1. *The net present value* method converts future values of benefits to their present-value equivalent by discounting them at the organization's cost of funds. They can then compare the present value of the future benefits with the cost required to achieve those benefits to determine whether the benefits exceed the costs.

2. *Return on investment* measures management's effectiveness in generating profits with its available assets. ROI is calculated by dividing net income attributable to a project by the average assets invested in the project. ROI is a percentage, and the higher the percentage return, the better.

3. *Breakeven analysis* determines the point at which the cumulative dollar value of the benefits from a project equals the investment made in the project.

4. In the *business case approach,* system developers write a business case to justify funding one or more specific applications or projects.

13.2 Discuss the four business decisions that companies must make when they acquire new applications.

- *How much computer code does the company want to write?* A company can choose to use a totally prewritten application (to write no computer code), to customize a prewritten application (to write some computer code), or to customize an entire application (write all new computer code).

- *How will the company pay for the application?* Once the company has decided how much computer code to write, it must decide how to pay for it. With prewritten applications or customized prewritten applications, companies can buy them or lease them. With totally custom applications, companies use internal funding.

- *Where will the application run?* Companies must now decide where to run the application. The company may run the application on its own platform or run the application on someone else's platform (use either a software-as-a-service vendor or an application service provider).

- *Where will the application originate?* Prewritten applications can be open-source software or come from a vendor. Companies may choose to customize prewritten open-source applications or prewritten proprietary applications from vendors. Companies may customize applications in-house or outsource the customization. They also can write totally custom applications in-house or outsource this process.

13.3 Enumerate the primary tasks and importance of each of the six processes involved in the systems development life cycle.

The six processes are the following:

1. *Systems investigation:* Addresses the business problem (or business opportunity) by means of the feasibility study. The main task in the systems investigation stage is the feasibility study.

2. *Systems analysis:* Examines the business problem that the organization plans to solve with an information system. Its main purpose is to gather information about the existing system to determine the requirements for the new system. The end product of this stage, known as the "deliverable," is a set of system requirements.

3. *Systems design:* Describes how the system will resolve the business problem. The deliverable is the set of technical system specifications.

4. *Programming and testing:* Programming translates the design specifications into computer code; testing checks to see whether the computer code will produce the expected and desired results and detects errors, or bugs, in the computer code. A deliverable is the new application.

5. *Implementation:* The process of converting from the old system to the new system through three major conversion strategies: direct, pilot, and phased. A deliverable is a properly working application.

6. *Operation and maintenance:* Types of maintenance include debugging, updating, and adding new functions when needed.

13.4 Describe alternative development methods and tools that augment development methods.

These are the *alternative methods*:

- *Joint application design* is a group-based tool for collecting user requirements and creating system designs.

- *Rapid application development* is a systems development method that can combine JAD, prototyping, and ICASE tools to rapidly produce a high-quality system.

- *Agile development* is a software development methodology that delivers functionality in rapid iterations, which are usually measured in weeks.

- *End-user development* refers to an organization's end users developing their own applications with little or no formal assistance from the IT department.

These are the *tools*:

- The *prototyping* approach defines an initial list of user requirements, builds a model of the system, and then improves the system in several iterations based on users' feedback.

- *Integrated computer-aided software engineering* combines upper CASE tools (systems investigation, analysis, and design) and lower CASE tools (programming, testing, operation, and maintenance).

- *Component-based development* uses standard components to build applications. Components are reusable applications that generally have one specific function, such as a shopping cart, user authentication, or a catalog.

- *Object-oriented development* begins with the aspects of the real world that must be modeled to perform that task. Systems developers identify the objects in the new system. Each object represents a tangible, real-world entity such as a customer, bank account, student, or course. Objects have *properties*, or *data values*. Objects also contain the *operations* that can be performed on their properties.

Table 13.2 shows advantages and disadvantages of alternative methods and tools.

Chapter Glossary

agile development A software development methodology that delivers functionality in rapid iterations, measured in weeks, requiring frequent communication, development, testing, and delivery.

application portfolio The set of recommended applications resulting from the planning and justification process in application development.

application service provider (ASP) An agent or vendor that assembles the software needed by enterprises and packages them with outsourced development, operations, maintenance, and other services.

component-based development A software development methodology that uses standard components to build applications.

computer-aided software engineering (CASE) Development approach that uses specialized tools to automate many of the tasks in the SDLC. Upper CASE tools automate the early stages of the SDLC, and lower CASE tools automate the later stages.

containers A method of developing applications that run independently of the base operating system of the server.

continuous application development The process of steadily adding new computer code to a software project when the new computer code is written and tested.

direct conversion Implementation process in which the old system is cut off and the new system is turned on at a certain point in time.

end-user development Approach in which the organization's end users develop their own applications with little or no formal assistance from the IT department.

feasibility study Investigation that gauges the probability of success of a proposed project and provides a rough assessment of the project's feasibility.

implementation The process of converting from an old computer system to a new one.

integrated CASE (ICASE) tools CASE tools that provide links between upper CASE and lower CASE tools.

IS operational plan Consists of a clear set of projects that the IS department and the functional area managers will execute in support of the IT strategic plan.

IT steering committee A committee, composed of a group of managers and staff representing various organizational units, set up to establish IT priorities and to ensure that the MIS function is meeting the needs of the enterprise.

IT strategic plan A set of long-range goals that describe the IT infrastructure and major IT initiatives needed to achieve the goals of the organization.

joint application design (JAD) A group-based tool for collecting user requirements and creating system designs.

lower CASE tools Tools used to automate later stages in the SDLC (programming, testing, operation, and maintenance).

object-oriented development A systems development methodology that begins with aspects of the real world that must be modeled to perform a task.

outsourcing Use of outside contractors or external organizations to acquire IT services.

phased conversion Implementation process that introduces components of the new system in stages, until the entire new system is operational.

pilot conversion Implementation process that introduces the new system in one part of the organization on a trial basis. When the new system is working properly, it is introduced in other parts of the organization.

programmers IS professionals who modify existing computer programs or write new computer programs to satisfy user requirements.

programming The translation of a system's design specifications into computer code.

prototype A small-scale working model of an entire system or a model that contains only the components of the new system that are of most interest to the users.

prototyping An approach that defines an initial list of user requirements, builds a prototype system, and then improves the system in several iterations based on users' feedback.

rapid application development (RAD) A development method that uses special tools and an iterative approach to rapidly produce a high-quality system.

scope creep Adding functions to an information system after the project has begun.

shadow IT Technology implemented by end users without receiving proper approvals from the organizational IT department.

software-as-a-service (SaaS) A method of delivering software in which a vendor hosts the applications and provides them as a service to customers over a network, typically the Internet.

systems analysis The examination of the business problem that the organization plans to solve with an information system.

systems analysts IS professionals who specialize in analyzing and designing information systems.

systems design Describes how the new system will resolve the business problem.

systems development life cycle (SDLC) Traditional structured framework, used for large IT projects, that consists of sequential processes by which information systems are developed.

systems investigation The initial stage in the traditional SDLC that addresses the business problem (or business opportunity) by means of the feasibility study.

systems stakeholders All people who are affected by changes in information systems.

technical specialists Experts on a certain type of technology, such as databases or telecommunications.

upper CASE tools Tools that are used to automate the early stages of the SDLC (systems investigation, analysis, and design).

Discussion Questions

1. Discuss the advantages of a lease option over a buy option.

2. Why is it important for all business managers to understand the issues of IT resource acquisition?

3. Why is it important for everyone in business organizations to have a basic understanding of the systems development process?

4. Should prototyping be used on every systems development project? Why or why not?

5. Discuss the various types of feasibility studies. Why are they all needed?

6. Discuss the issue of assessing intangible benefits and the proposed solutions.

7. Discuss the reasons why end-user-developed information systems can be of poor quality. What can be done to improve this situation?

Problem-Solving Activities

1. Access **www.ecommerce-guide.com**. Find the product review area. Read reviews of three software payment solutions. Assess them as possible components.

2. Use an Internet search engine to obtain information on CASE and ICASE tools. Select several vendors and compare and contrast their offerings.

3. Access **www.ning.com**. Observe how the site provides components for you to use to build applications. Build a small application at the site.

4. Enter **www.ibm.com/products/software**. Find its WebSphere product. Read recent customers' success stories. What makes this software so popular?

5. Enter the websites of Gartner (**www.gartner.com**), 451 Research (**www.451research.com**), and CIO (**www.cio.com**). Search for recent material about ASPs and outsourcing, and prepare a report on your findings.

6. StoreFront (**www.storefront.net**) is a vendor of e-business software. At its site, the company provides demonstrations illustrating the types of storefronts that it can create for shoppers. The site also provides demonstrations of how the company's software is used to create a store.

    a. Run the StoreFront demonstration to see how this is done.

    b. What features does StoreFront provide?

    c. Does StoreFront support smaller or larger stores?

    d. What other products does StoreFront offer for creating online stores? What types of stores do these products support?

Closing Case

MIS SA Homes Adopts Docker to Speed Up App Deployment

The Problem

SA Homes is a South Africa-based company that provides home loans at discounted rates. Their objective is to develop strategies to beat the market rates for interest rates, and they have a history of being successful. The company focuses on customer service and transparency, helping their customers feel comfortable throughout the mortgage process—something that is quite involved and complicated.

The loan industry uses data to help project the ideal interest rate when putting the loan together so that consumers will be able to purchase the best house for their money while at the same time ensuring that it is also a loan they can safely and reliably pay back. Anytime an organization uses data this heavily, their employees constantly find ways for their information systems to support them. SA Homes is no different. The company has experienced a great deal of success since its founding in 1999, growing into the fifth-largest mortgage company in South Africa. This growth led to an explosion in their employees' use of information systems and consequently, their requests for updates and modifications to the system.

Unfortunately for SA Homes, their IS development office could not keep up with this demand for their services. For example, their app production team was able to deploy only two apps at a time in their development lab. The result was a waiting list to be considered for the actual production list. When managers encountered a problem or needed something developed, they had to wait in line. Additionally, several of the primary technologies they used ran on multiple codes and platforms. SA Homes realized that this entire process needed to be streamlined. Container technology offered them a method to achieve these goals. However, the company needed a reliable container provider.

The IT Solution

App developers have always encountered platform challenges. For example, if a developer built an application in a Windows environment, then it might not run properly if it were deployed after an update was installed. Most certainly it would not operate in a Linux environment. Multiple versions of an application would need to be developed to run in different environments. They would then constantly have to be tested on platform updates. This observation is also true of large installation software packages that provide IS functionality to organizations.

One solution is to build and test applications on a virtual machine and then implement them on an identical virtual machine for their customers. This solution removes the possibility that the application would be developed on one platform and then experience problems when it was deployed on a different one. But, what if you could develop an application that carried its own environment and would run as it was built regardless of the operating system on which it was deployed? That is exactly the idea of a container.

The Results

SA Homes implemented Docker to speed deployment times using a Docker data center. This move enabled the company to speed their app development because they could focus on the app and not the environment in which the app would run. They now build and deploy 20–30 apps per day, compared with 2 per day previously. As a result, users can propose an idea for an app or a solution to a problem and the SA Homes IS development office can provide a solution for testing within days rather than weeks.

Sources: Compiled from S. Legulalp, "Docker, Twistlock, CoreOS, and the State of Container Security," *InfoWorld Tech Watch*, December 7, 2015; C. Babcock, "Containers March into Mainstream with Security, Management Updates," *InformationWeek*, November 20, 2015; F. Lardinois, "Docker Puts Focus on Container Security," *TechCrunch*, November 16, 2015; A. Froehlich,

"Containers 101: 10 Terms To Know" *InformationWeek*, September 2, 2015; M. Schutz, "What's New in Windows Server 2015 and System Center 2015 Technical Preview" blogs.technet.com, August 19, 2015; S. Vaughan-Nichols, "Docker 1.8 Adds Serious Container Security," ZDNet.com, August 13, 2015; P. Rubens, "What Are Containers, and Why Do You Need Them?" CIO.com, May 20, 2015; P. Yared, "Goodbye SaaS – Hello Container-as-a-Service," *Venturebeat*, May 9, 2015; C. Babcock, "Docker, CoreOS Push Containers to Center Stage," *InformationWeek*, December 29, 2014; www.docker.com, accessed December 7, 2017; www.coreos.com, accessed December 7, 2017; www.twistlock.com, accessed December 7, 2017; https://www.docker.com/sites/default/files/DOC_SA_CaseStudy_04252015_V2%20%282%29%5B2%5D.pdf, accessed December 7, 2017; https://www.sahomeloans.com/about/sa-home-loans, accessed December 7, 2017; and https://blog.docker.com/2016/06/docker-datacenter-enterprise-sa-home-loans/, accessed July 17, 2019.

Questions

1. What benefits does container technology offer developers that traditional deployment methodologies do not?

2. Discuss the advantages and disadvantages of using containers as a development/deployment tool. Use SA Homes as your supporting example.

3. What other development methods could you combine with the use of containers to speed up development/deployment?

Hardware

TECHNOLOGY GUIDE OUTLINE	LEARNING OBJECTIVES
TG 1.1 Introduction to Hardware	**TG 1.1** Identify the major hardware components of a computer system.
TG 1.2 Strategic Hardware Issues	**TG 1.2** Discuss strategic issues that link hardware design to business strategy.
TG 1.3 Computer Hierarchy	**TG 1.3** Describe the various types of computers in the computer hierarchy.
TG 1.4 Input and Output Technologies	**TG 1.4** Differentiate the various types of input and output technologies and their uses.
TG 1.5 The Central Processing Unit	**TG 1.5** Describe the design and functioning of the central processing unit.

Introduction

As you begin this Technology Guide, you might be wondering, "Why do I have to know anything about hardware?" There are several reasons why you will benefit from understanding the basics of hardware. First, regardless of your major (and future functional area in an organization), you will be using different types of hardware throughout your career. Second, you will have input concerning the hardware that you will use. In this capacity, you will be required to answer many questions, such as these:

- Is my hardware performing adequately for my needs? If not, what types of problems am I experiencing?
- Do I need more functionality in my hardware, and if so, what functionality would be most helpful to me?

Third, you will also have input into decisions when your functional area or organization upgrades or replaces its hardware. Some organizations will also allocate the hardware budget to functional areas or departments. In such cases, you might be responsible for making hardware decisions (at least locally) yourself. MIS employees will act as advisors, but you will provide important input into such decisions.

TG 1.1 Introduction to Hardware

Recall from Chapter 1 that the term *hardware* refers to the physical equipment used for the input, processing, output, and storage activities of a computer system. Decisions about hardware focus on three interrelated factors: appropriateness for the task, speed, and cost. The incredibly rapid rate of innovation in the computer industry complicates hardware decisions because computer technologies become obsolete more quickly than other organizational technologies.

The overall trends in hardware are that it becomes smaller, faster, cheaper, and more powerful over time. In fact, these trends are so rapid that they make it difficult to know when to purchase (or upgrade) hardware. This difficulty lies in the fact that companies that delay hardware purchases will, more than likely, be able to buy more powerful hardware for the same amount of money in the future. It is important to note that buying more powerful hardware for the same amount of money in the future is a trade-off. An organization that delays purchasing computer hardware gives up the benefits of whatever it could buy today until the future purchase date arrives.

Hardware consists of the following:

- *Central processing unit (CPU):* Manipulates the data and controls the tasks performed by the other components
- *Primary storage:* Temporarily stores data and program instructions during processing
- *Secondary storage:* Stores data and programs for future use
- *Input technologies:* Accept data and instructions and convert them to a form that the computer can understand
- *Output technologies:* Present data and information in a form people can understand
- *Communication technologies:* Provide for the flow of data from external computer networks (e.g., the Internet and intranets) to the CPU, and from the CPU to computer networks

Author Lecture Videos are available exclusively in *WileyPLUS*.
Apply the Concept activities are available in the Appendix and in *WileyPLUS*.

TG 1.2 Strategic Hardware Issues

For most businesspeople, the most important issues are what the hardware enables, how it is advancing, and how rapidly it is advancing. In many industries, exploiting computer hardware is a key to achieving competitive advantage. Successful hardware exploitation comes from thoughtful consideration of the following questions:

- How do organizations keep up with the rapid price reductions and performance advancements in hardware? For example, how often should an organization upgrade its computers and storage systems? Will upgrades increase personal and organizational productivity? How can organizations measure such increases?
- How should organizations determine the need for the new hardware infrastructures, such as cloud computing? (We discuss cloud computing in Technology Guide 3.)
- Portable computers and advanced communications technologies have enabled employees to work from home or from anywhere. Will these new work styles benefit employees and the organization? How do organizations manage such new work styles?
- How do organizations manage employees who use their own portable devices (e.g., tablets and smartphones) for both personal and work purposes? That is, how do organizations handle the bring-your-own-device (BYOD) phenomenon?

Author Lecture Videos are available exclusively in *WileyPLUS*.
Apply the Concept activities are available in the Appendix and in *WileyPLUS*.

TG 1.3 | Computer Hierarchy

The traditional standard for comparing classes of computers is their processing power. This section presents each class of computers, from the most powerful to the least powerful. It describes both the computers and their roles in modern organizations.

Supercomputers

The term *supercomputer* does not refer to a specific technology. Rather, it indicates the fastest computers available at any given time. In mid-2017, the fastest supercomputers had speeds approaching 100 petaflops (1 petaflop is 1,000 trillion floating point operations per second). A floating-point operation is an arithmetic operation that involves decimals.

Large organizations use supercomputers to execute computationally demanding tasks involving very large data sets, such as military and scientific applications. In the business environment, for example, large banks use supercomputers to calculate the risks and returns of various investment strategies, and health care organizations use them to analyze giant databases of patient data to determine optimal treatments for various diseases.

Mainframe Computers

Mainframes remain popular in large enterprises for extensive computing applications that are accessed by thousands of users at one time. Examples of mainframe applications are airline reservation systems, corporate payroll programs, website transaction processing systems (e.g., Amazon and eBay), and student grade calculation and reporting.

Today's mainframes perform at teraflop (trillions of floating point operations per second) speeds and can handle millions of transactions per day. Mainframes can also provide a secure, robust environment in which to run strategic, mission-critical applications.

Microcomputers

Microcomputers—also called *micros, personal computers*, or *PCs*—are the smallest and least expensive category of general-purpose computers. It is important to point out that people frequently define a PC as a computer that uses the Microsoft Windows operating system. In fact, a variety of PCs are available, and many of them do not use Windows. One well-known example is the Apple Mac, which uses the Mac OS X operating system (discussed later in this Technology Guide).

Laptop and Notebook Computers

Laptop computers (or **notebook computers**) are small, easily transportable, lightweight microcomputers that fit comfortably into a briefcase (**Figure TG 1.1**). They provide users with access to processing power and data outside an office environment.

For example, the Google Chromebook is a thin client laptop that runs Google's Chrome operating system. A **thin client** is a computer that does not offer the full functionality of a PC. A **fat client** is a computer that has the ability to perform many functions without a network connection. Thin clients are less complex than fat clients because they do not have locally installed software. When thin clients need to run an application, they access it from a server over a network rather than from a local disk drive.

Laptop computer

Motorola Xoom tablet

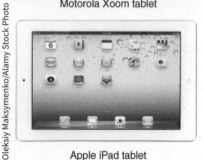
Apple iPad tablet

PhotoEdit/Alamy Stock Photo

Oleksiy Maksymenko/Alamy Stock Photo

FIGURE TG 1.1 **Laptop, notebook, and tablet computers.**

A thin client would not have Microsoft Office installed on it. Thus, thin clients are easier and less expensive to operate and support than fat clients. The benefits of thin clients include fast application deployment, centralized management, lower cost of ownership, and easier installation, management, maintenance, and support. The main disadvantage of thin clients is that if the network fails, then users can do very little on their computers. In contrast, if users have fat clients and the network fails, they can still perform some functions because they have software, such as Microsoft Office, installed on their computers.

Tablet Computers

A **tablet computer** (or tablet) is a complete computer contained entirely in a flat touchscreen that users operate with a stylus, digital pen, fingertip, or soft (virtual) keyboard, instead of a physical keyboard or mouse. Examples of tablets are the Apple iPad Pro, the Microsoft Surface Pro 4, the Lenovo IdeaPad Miix 700, and many others.

Wearable Computers

Wearable computers are miniature computers that people wear under, with, or on top of their clothing. Key features of wearable computers are that there is constant interaction between the computer and the users and that the users can multitask, meaning they do not have to stop what they are doing to use the device. Examples of wearable computers are the Apple Watch, the Sony SmartWatch, Google Glass, and the Fitbit (**www.fitbit.com**) activity tracker.

Google Glass is an excellent example of a wearable computer that provides augmented reality. **Augmented reality** is a live, direct, or indirect, view of a physical, real-world environment whose elements are augmented, or enhanced, by computer-generated sensory input such as sound, video, graphics, or GPS data—that is, augmented reality enhances the user's perception of reality. Note that, in contrast, virtual reality replaces the real world with a simulated world. As an example of augmented reality with Google Glass, let's say that you are looking for a destination in an unfamiliar city. You ask Google Glass for directions, and the device will overlay your vision with a graphic display of a street map, with the route to your destination highlighted.

Google Glass 2.0, called Google Glass Enterprise Edition 2, is the next iteration of the original Google Glass. Glass 2.0 is very useful in the workplace for workers who need both real-time information and hands-free operation. Companies such as GE, Boeing, DHL, and Volkswagen are testing Glass 2.0 and seeing gains in productivity and improvements in quality. Let's look at an example.

Consider AGCO (**www.agcocorp.com**), a $7 billion manufacturer of farm equipment such as tractors and sprayers under brand names that include Challenger and Massey Ferguson. The equipment that AGCO manufactures is typically custom-made so that every unit has a unique set of features. To keep track of the specifications of each piece of equipment, AGCO originally had its workers use laptops. This process required workers to walk about 50 feet, which disrupted the work flow.

As a result, AGCO turned to Glass 2.0. A typical task at AGCO takes 70 minutes, broken into steps of 3 to 5 minutes. When a worker begins a step, it is spelled out on the Glass 2.0 screen. Menu items provide options to proceed to the next step, take a picture, ask for help, and more. When a step is finished, the worker says, "OK, Glass, proceed," and the process repeats.

For tasks that they have mastered, workers do not need to look at the screen, however, they can wake Glass 2.0 at any time to see where a part must go, and even zoom into an object on the display for more detail. Glass 2.0 also tells them what kind of bolt is needed and specifies which wrench to use and how much torque (twisting pressure) is required. If a part looks damaged, they can take a picture. Some workers prefer to swipe along the side of the frame to go to the next step, while others use voice commands.

Glass 2.0 has improved productivity and quality at AGCO. The company is also pleased with how Glass 2.0 helps with training as the system has reduced a worker's initial training time from 10 days to only 3 days.

IT's Personal: Purchasing a Computer

One day you will purchase a computer for yourself or your job. When that day comes, it will be important for you to know what to look for. Buying a computer can be very confusing if you just read the box. This Technology Guide has explained the major hardware components of a computer. There are more things you need to consider, however, when you purchase a computer: What do you plan to do with it, where do you plan to use it, and how long do you need service from it? Let's look at each question more closely.

- What do you plan to do with your computer? Consider that when you buy a vehicle, your plans for using the vehicle determine the type of vehicle you will purchase. The same rules apply to purchasing a computer. You need to consider what you currently do with a computer and what you may do before you replace the one under consideration. Although many people simply buy as much as they can afford, they may overpay because they do not consider what they need the computer for.

- Where do you plan to use your computer? If you plan to use it only at home at your desk, then a desktop model will be fine. In general, you can get more computer for your money in a desktop model as opposed to a laptop (i.e., you pay extra for mobility). However, if you think you may want to take the computer with you, then you will need some type of a laptop or tablet computer. When portability is a requirement, you will want to reconsider what you plan to use the computer for, because as computers become more portable (smaller), their functionality changes, and you want to make sure the computer will meet your needs.

- How long do you need service from this computer? Today, we anticipate that most of the devices we purchase will become outdated and need to be replaced in a few years. Therefore, the length of service is really more about warranty and the availability of repair services. In some cases, you should base your purchase decision on these issues rather than speed because they can extend the life of your computer.

TG 1.4 Input and Output Technologies

Input Technologies

Input technologies allow people and other technologies to enter data into a computer. The two main types of input devices are human data-entry devices and source-data automation devices. As their name implies, *human data-entry* devices require a certain amount of human effort to input data. Examples are keyboard, mouse, pointing stick, trackball, joystick, touchscreen, stylus, and voice recognition.

In contrast, *source-data automation* devices input data with minimal human intervention. These technologies speed up data collection, reduce errors, and gather data at the source of a transaction or other event. Barcode readers are an example of source-data automation.

An interesting type of human input is gesture-based input. **Gesture recognition** refers to technologies that enable computers to interpret human gestures. These technologies are an initial step in designing computers that can understand human body language. This process creates a richer interaction between machines and humans than has been possible with other input devices.

Gesture recognition enables humans to interact naturally with a computer without any intervening mechanical devices. With gesture-based technologies, the user can move the cursor by pointing a finger at a computer screen. These technologies could make conventional input devices (the mouse, keyboards, and touchscreens) redundant. Examples of gesture-based input devices are the Microsoft Kinect (**www.xbox.com**) and the Leap Motion Controller (**www.leapmotion.com**).

Common source-data automation input devices include magnetic stripe readers, point-of-sale terminals, barcode scanners, optical mark readers, magnetic ink character readers, sensors (see the Internet of Things in Chapter 8), and cameras.

Output Technologies

The output generated by a computer can be transmitted to the user through several output devices and media. These devices include monitors, printers, plotters, and voice.

Current output technologies include retinal scanning displays and heads-up displays. Retinal scanning displays project images directly onto a viewer's retina and are used in medicine, air traffic control, and controlling industrial machines. Heads-up displays are transparent and present data without requiring the user to look away from his or her usual viewpoint.

Virtual Reality Technology

Virtual reality (VR) is a term that refers to information technologies that use software to provide a realistic, three-dimensional, computer-generated environment that replicates sight, touch, hearing, and in some cases, smell. Virtual reality brings the user into the virtual environment by removing outside stimuli. Some advanced systems now include tactile (touch) information, known as *force feedback*.

VR is designed to reproduce a real environment or create an imaginary environment. In this environment, users can explore and interact. The user becomes a part of the virtual world and, while there, can manipulate objects or perform a series of actions. That is, a person using virtual reality equipment is able to "look around" the environment, move about in it, and interact with features or items that are depicted on a screen or in VR goggles. There are a number of VR headsets available, including the Sony PlayStation VR, HTC Vive, Oculus Rift, Samsung Gear VR, and Google Daydream View.

When it is too dangerous, expensive, or impractical to do something in the real world, VR can be the answer. As a result, there are numerous VR applications. Let's look at some examples:

- **MKT** *Media:* Media company Disney released a VR experience titled "Disney Movies VR" on Valve Corporation's Steam software, free for download. The experience allows users to interact with the characters and worlds from the Disney, Marvel, and Lucasfilm universes.

  Many media companies use omnidirectional cameras (also known as 360-degree or VR cameras) by GoPro, Nokia, Samsung, Ricoh, and Nikon. These cameras record in all directions, a process called VR photography. Films produced by VR cameras permit the audience to view an entire environment in every scene.

- **HRM** *Training:* The military makes extensive use of VR in combat training. VR allows recruits to train under a controlled environment where they respond to different types of combat situations. The Air Force also uses VR in flight simulators to train pilots.

- *Video games:* Video games are rapidly incorporating VR, particularly with the emergence of VR headsets.

- **POM** *Engineering:* Engineers use VR in three-dimensional computer-aided design. For example, the automotive, aerospace, and ground transportation industries use VR in their product development, engineering, and manufacturing processes.

- *Architectural design:* Architects use VR during the design process to actually "see" the projects before they are built, thereby giving the architect a sense of scale and proportion. VR models also eliminate the need to make physical miniatures of projects and enable clients to experience the project before and during construction.

- **MKT** *Real estate:* Real estate agencies use VR so that clients can see, experience, and walk through many homes in a relatively short period of time. In that way, the clients can narrow their searches in an efficient manner.

- **MKT** *Retail:* Lowe's, IKEA, Wayfair, and other home-product retailers use VR that allow their products to be "seen" so that customers have a better idea of how the store's products will fit in their homes. Travel industry sites such as CruiseAbout and Flight Centre use VR to enable customers to view cruise ship cabins and hotel rooms before booking their trips.

The Central Processing Unit

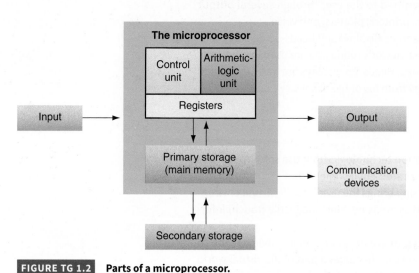

FIGURE TG 1.2   **Parts of a microprocessor.**

The **central processing unit** performs the actual computation or "number crunching" inside any computer. The CPU is a **microprocessor** (e.g., Intel's Core i3, i5, and i7 chips, with more to come) made up of millions of microscopic transistors embedded in a circuit on a silicon wafer, or *chip*. For this reason, microprocessors are commonly referred to as chips.

As shown in **Figure TG 1.2**, the microprocessor has different parts, which perform different functions. The **control unit** sequentially accesses program instructions, decodes them, and controls the flow of data to and from the arithmetic logic unit, the registers, the caches, primary storage, secondary storage, and various output devices. The **arithmetic logic unit (ALU)** performs the mathematical calculations and makes logical comparisons. The registers are high-speed storage areas that store very small amounts of data and instructions for short periods.

How the CPU Works

In the CPU, inputs enter and are stored until they are needed. At that point, they are retrieved and processed, and the output is stored and then delivered somewhere. **Figure TG 1.3** illustrates this process, which works as follows:

- The inputs consist of data and brief instructions about what to do with the data. These instructions come into the CPU from random access memory (RAM). Data might be entered by the user through the keyboard, for example, or read from a data file in another part of the computer. The inputs are stored in registers until they are sent to the next step in the processing.

- Data and instructions travel in the chip through electrical pathways called *buses*. The size of the bus—analogous to the width of a highway—determines how much information can flow at any time.

- The control unit directs the flow of data and instructions within the chip.

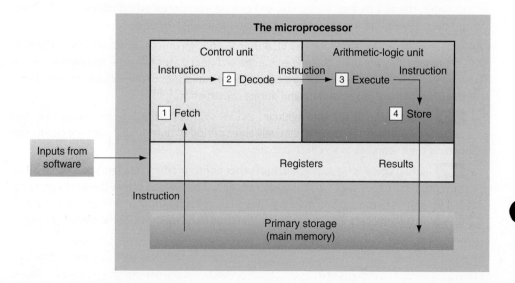

FIGURE TG 1.3   **How the CPU works.**

- The ALU receives the data and instructions from the registers and makes the desired computation. These data and instructions have been translated into **binary form**—that is, only 0s and 1s. A "0" or a "1" is called a **bit**. The CPU can process only binary data. All types of data, such as letters, decimal numbers, photographs, music, and so on, can be converted to a binary representation, which can then be processed by the CPU.

- The data in their original form and the instructions are sent to storage registers and then are sent back to a storage place outside the chip, such as the computer's hard drive. Meanwhile, the transformed data go to another register and then on to other parts of the computer (e.g., to the monitor for display or to storage).

Intel offers excellent demonstrations of how CPUs work: Search the Web for "Intel" with "Explore the Curriculum" to find their demos. This cycle of processing, known as a *machine instruction cycle*, occurs billions of times per second.

Advances in Microprocessor Design

Innovations in chip designs are coming at a faster and faster rate, as described by **Moore's law**. In 1965, Gordon Moore, a cofounder of Intel Corporation, predicted that microprocessor complexity would double approximately every 18 months. His prediction has been amazingly accurate.

The advances predicted from Moore's law arise mainly from the following changes:

- Producing increasingly miniaturized transistors.
- Placing multiple processors on a single chip. Chips with more than one processor are called *multicore* chips. For example, the Cell chip, produced by a consortium of Sony, Toshiba, and IBM, contains nine processors. Intel (**www.intel.com**) and AMD (**www.amd .com**) offer multicore chips (e.g., quadcore chips with four CPUs).
- Intel's three-dimensional (3D) chips require less power than Intel's current chips, while improving performance. These chips enhance the performance of all computers. However, they are particularly valuable in handheld devices, because they extend the device's battery life.

In addition to increased speeds and performance, Moore's law has had an impact on costs. For example, in 1997, a desktop computer with a Pentium II microprocessor, 64 megabytes of random access memory, a 4-gigabyte hard drive, and a 17-inch monitor cost $4,000. In late 2018, a desktop computer with an Intel i7 quad-core processor, 16 gigabytes of random access memory, a 1-terabyte hard drive plus 32 gigabytes of solid-state storage, and a 27-inch touchscreen cost approximately $1,600. Significantly, the 2018 desktop is 13 times faster, has 250 times more random access memory, and has 250 times more hard drive storage than the 1997 desktop, for 40 percent of the cost.

Computer Memory

The amount and type of memory that a computer possesses has a great deal to do with its general utility. A computer's memory also determines the types of programs that the computer can run, the work it can perform, its speed, and its cost. There are two basic categories of computer memory. The first is *primary storage*. It is called "primary" because it stores small amounts of data and information that the CPU will use immediately. The second category is *secondary storage,* which stores much larger amounts of data and information (e.g., an entire software program) for extended periods.

Memory Capacity.   As you have seen, CPUs process only binary units—0s and 1s—which are translated through computer languages into bits. A particular combination of bits represents a certain alphanumeric character or a simple mathematical operation. Eight bits are needed to represent any one of these characters. This eight-bit string is known as a **byte**. The storage capacity of a computer is measured in bytes. Bits typically are used as units of measure only for telecommunications capacity, as in how many million bits per second can be sent through a particular medium.

The hierarchy of terms used to describe memory capacity is as follows:

- *Kilobyte.* *Kilo* means "one thousand," so a kilobyte (KB) is approximately 1,000 bytes. To be more precise, a kilobyte is 1,024 bytes. Computer designers find it convenient to work with powers of 2: 1,024 is 2 to the 10th power, and 1,024 is close enough to 1,000 that for *kilobyte* people use the standard prefix *kilo*, which means exactly 1,000 in familiar units such as the kilogram or kilometer.

- *Megabyte.* Mega means "one million," so a megabyte (MB) is approximately one million bytes. Most personal computers have between 4 and 16 gigabytes of RAM and some have even more.

- *Gigabyte.* Giga means "one billion," so a gigabyte (GB) is approximately one billion bytes.

- *Terabyte.* A terabyte is approximately one trillion bytes. The storage capacity of modern personal computers can be several terabytes.

- *Petabyte.* A petabyte is approximately 1,000 terabytes.

- *Exabyte.* An exabyte is approximately 1,000 petabytes.

- *Zettabyte.* A zettabyte is approximately 1,000 exabytes.

To get a feel for these amounts, consider the following example: If your computer has one terabyte of storage capacity on its hard drive (a type of secondary storage), it can store approximately 1 trillion bytes of data. If the average page of text contains about 2,000 bytes, then your hard drive could store approximately 10 percent of all the print collections of the Library of Congress. That same terabyte can store 70 hours of standard-definition compressed video.

Primary Storage.
Primary storage (or main memory) as it is sometimes called, stores three types of information for very brief periods of time: (1) data to be processed by the CPU, (2) instructions for the CPU as to how to process the data, and (3) operating system programs that manage various aspects of the computer's operation. Primary storage takes place in chips mounted on the computer's main circuit board, called the *motherboard*. These chips are located as close as physically possible to the CPU chip. As with the CPU, all the data and instructions in primary storage have been translated into binary code.

The four main types of primary storage are (1) register, (2) cache memory, (3) random access memory, and (4) read-only memory (ROM). You learn about each type of primary storage next.

Registers are part of the CPU. They have the least capacity, storing extremely limited amounts of instructions and data only immediately before and after processing.

Cache memory is a type of high-speed memory that enables the computer to temporarily store blocks of data that are used more often and that a processor can access more rapidly than main memory (RAM). Cache memory is physically located closer to the CPU than RAM. Blocks that are used less often remain in RAM until they are transferred to cache; blocks used infrequently remain in secondary storage. Cache memory is faster than RAM because the instructions travel a shorter distance to the CPU.

Random access memory is the part of primary storage that holds a software program and small amounts of data for processing. Compared with the registers, RAM stores more information and is located farther away from the CPU. However, compared with secondary storage, RAM stores less information and is much closer to the CPU.

RAM is temporary and, in most cases, *volatile*—that is, RAM chips lose their contents if the current is lost or turned off, as from a power surge, brownout, or electrical noise generated by lightning or nearby machines.

Most of us have lost data at one time or another because of a computer crash or a power failure. What is usually lost is whatever is in RAM, cache, or the registers at the time, because these types of memory are volatile. Therefore, you need greater security when you are storing certain types of critical data or instructions. Cautious computer users frequently save data to nonvolatile memory (secondary storage). Most modern software applications also have autosave functions.

Read-only memory is the place—actually, a type of chip—where certain critical instructions are safeguarded. ROM is nonvolatile, so it retains these instructions when the power to the computer is turned off. The read-only designation means that these instructions can only

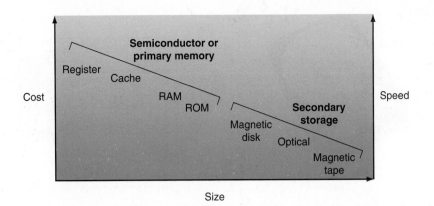

Primary memory compared with secondary storage.

be read by the computer and cannot be changed by the user. An example of ROM is the instructions needed to start or boot the computer after it has been shut off.

Secondary Storage.
Secondary storage is designed to store very large amounts of data for extended periods. Secondary storage has the following characteristics:

- It is nonvolatile.
- It takes more time to retrieve data from it than from RAM.
- It is cheaper than primary storage (see **Figure TG 1.4**).
- It can use a variety of media, each with its own technology.

One secondary storage medium, **magnetic tape**, is kept on a large open reel or in a smaller cartridge or cassette. Although this is an old technology, it remains popular because it is the cheapest storage medium, and it can handle enormous amounts of data. As a result, many organizations (e.g., the U.S. government Social Security Administration) use magnetic tape for archival storage. The downside is that it is the slowest method for retrieving data because all the data are placed on the tape sequentially. This process means that the system might have to run through the majority of the tape before it comes to the desired piece of data.

Magnetic disks (or **hard drives or fixed disk drives**) are the most commonly used mass storage devices because of their low cost, high speed, and large storage capacity. Hard disk drives read from, and write to, stacks of rotating (at up to 15,000 rpm) magnetic disk platters mounted in rigid enclosures and sealed against environmental and atmospheric contamination (see **Figure TG 1.5**). These disks are permanently mounted in a unit that may be internal or external to the computer.

Solid-state drives (SSDs) are data storage devices that serve the same purpose as a hard drive and store data in memory chips. Whereas hard drives have moving parts, SSDs do not. SSDs use the same interface with the computer's CPU as hard drives and are therefore a seamless replacement for hard drives. SSDs offer many advantages over hard drives. They use less power, are silent and faster, and produce about one-third the heat of a hard drive. The major disadvantage of SSDs is that they cost more than hard drives.

Unlike magnetic media, **optical storage devices** do not store data through magnetism. Rather, a laser reads the surface of a reflective plastic platter. Optical disk drives are slower than magnetic hard drives, but they are less fragile and less susceptible to damage from contamination.

Optical disks can also store a great deal of information, both on a routine basis and when combined into storage systems. Types of optical disks include compact disc read-only memory and digital video disk.

Compact disc read-only memory (CD-ROM) storage devices feature high capacity, low cost, and high durability. However, because a CD-ROM is a read-only medium, it cannot be written on. *CD-R* can be written to, but once this is done, what was written on it cannot be changed later—that is, CD-R is writable, which CD-ROM is not, but it is not rewritable, which *CD-RW* (compact disc, rewritable) is. There are applications about which not being rewritable is a plus, because it prevents some types of accidental data destruction. CD-RW adds rewritability to the recordable compact disc market.

The digital video disc *(DVD)* is a 5-inch disk with the capacity to store about 135 minutes of digital video. DVDs can also perform as computer storage disks, providing storage capabilities

FIGURE TG 1.5 Traditional hard drives are less expensive, but solid-state drives are faster and are more reliable.

iStock.com/Homiel

iStock.com/krzyscin

of 17 gigabytes. DVD players can read current CD-ROMs, but current CD-ROM players cannot read DVDs. The access speed of a DVD drive is faster than that of a typical CD-ROM drive.

Blu-ray discs can store 50 gigabytes per layer. Development of Blu-ray technology is ongoing, with multi-layered disks capable of storing up to 100 gigabytes.

The various disk technologies are under pressure from on-demand, streaming services over the Internet. As the bandwidth of the Internet increases, so will the pressure on disk technologies.

Flash memory devices (or *memory cards*) are nonvolatile electronic storage devices that contain no moving parts and use 30 times less battery power than hard drives. Flash devices are also smaller and more durable than hard drives. The trade-offs are that flash devices store less data than hard drives. Flash devices are used with digital cameras, handheld and laptop computers, telephones, music players, and video game consoles.

One popular flash memory device is the **thumb drive** (also called *memory stick, jump drive,* or *flash drive*). These devices fit into Universal Serial Bus (USB) ports on personal computers and other devices, and they can store many gigabytes. Thumb drives have replaced magnetic floppy disks for portable storage.

Before you go on . . .

1. Decisions about hardware focus on what three factors?
2. What are the overall trends in hardware?
3. Define hardware and list the major hardware components.
4. Describe the different types of computers.
5. Distinguish between human data-input devices and source-data automation.
6. Briefly describe how a microprocessor functions.
7. Distinguish between primary storage and secondary storage.

What's in IT for me?

Hardware

For All Business Majors

The design of computer hardware has profound impacts for businesspeople. Personal and organizational success can depend on an understanding of hardware design and a commitment to knowing where it is going and what opportunities and challenges hardware innovations will bring. Because these innovations are occurring so rapidly, hardware decisions both at the individual level and at the organizational level are difficult.

At the *individual level*, most people who have a home or office computer system and want to upgrade it, or people who are contemplating their first computer purchase, are faced with the decision of *when* to buy as much as *what* to buy and at what cost. At the *organizational level*, these same issues plague IS professionals. However, they are more complex and more costly. Most organizations have many different computer systems in place at the same time. Innovations may come to different classes of computers at different times or rates. Therefore, managers must decide when old hardware *legacy systems* still have a productive role in the organization and when they should be replaced. A legacy system is an old computer system or application that continues to be used, typically because it still functions for the users' needs, even though newer technology is available.

Summary

TG1.1 Identify the major hardware components of a computer system.

Modern computer systems have six major components: the central processing unit (CPU), primary storage, secondary storage, input technologies, output technologies, and communications technologies.

TG1.2 Discuss strategic issues that link hardware design to business strategy.

Strategic issues linking hardware design to business strategy include the following: How do organizations keep up with the rapid price/performance advancements in hardware? How often should an organization upgrade its computers and storage systems? How can organizations measure benefits gained from price/performance improvements in hardware?

TG1.3 Describe the various types of computers in the computer hierarchy.

Supercomputers are the most powerful computers, designed to handle intensive computational demands. Organizations use mainframes for centralized data processing and managing large databases. Microcomputers are small, complete, general purpose computers. Laptop or notebook computers are small, easily transportable computers.

Tablet computers are complete computers contained entirely in a flat touchscreen that uses a stylus, digital pen, fingertip, or soft (virtual) keyboards as input devices. Wearable computers are miniature computers that people wear under, with, or on top of their clothing.

TG1.4 Differentiate the various types of input and output technologies and their uses.

The two main types of input devices are human data-entry devices and source-data automation devices. *Human data-entry* devices require a certain amount of human effort to input data. Examples are keyboard, mouse, pointing stick, trackball, joystick, touchscreen, stylus, and voice recognition. *Source-data automation* devices input data with minimal human intervention. These technologies gather data at the source of a transaction or other event. Barcode readers are an example of source-data automation.

TG1.5 Describe the design and functioning of the central processing unit.

The CPU consists of the arithmetic logic unit, which performs the calculations; the registers, which store minute amounts of data and instructions immediately before and after processing; and the control unit, which controls the flow of information on the microprocessor chip. After processing, the data in their original form and the instructions are sent back to a storage location outside the chip.

Technology Guide Glossary

arithmetic logic unit (ALU) Portion of the CPU that performs the mathematical calculations and makes logical comparisons.

augmented reality A live, direct or indirect, view of a physical, real-world environment whose elements are enhanced by computer-generated sensory input such as sound, video, graphics, or GPS data.

binary form The form in which data and instructions can be read by the CPU—only 0s and 1s.

bit Short for *binary digit* (0s and 1s), the only data that a CPU can process.

byte An eight-bit string of data, needed to represent any one alphanumeric character or simple mathematical operation.

cache memory A type of high-speed memory that enables the computer to temporarily store blocks of data that are used more often and that a processor can access more rapidly than main memory (RAM).

central processing unit (CPU) Hardware that performs the actual computation or "number crunching" inside any computer.

control unit Portion of the CPU that controls the flow of information.

fat clients Computers that offer full functionality without having to connect to a network.

flash memory devices Nonvolatile electronic storage devices that are compact, are portable, require little power, and contain no moving parts.

gesture recognition An input method that interprets human gestures, in an attempt for computers to begin to understand human body language.

laptop computers (notebook computers) Small, easily transportable, lightweight microcomputers.

magnetic disks (or hard drives or fixed disk drives) A form of secondary storage on a magnetized disk divided into tracks and sectors that provide addresses for various pieces of data.

magnetic tape A secondary storage medium on a large open reel or in a smaller cartridge or cassette.

mainframes Relatively large computers used in large enterprises for extensive computing applications that are accessed by thousands of users.

microcomputers The smallest and least expensive category or general-purpose computers, also called micros, personal computers, or PCs.

microprocessor The CPU, made up of millions of transistors embedded in a circuit on a silicon wafer or chip.

Moore's law Prediction by Gordon Moore, an Intel cofounder, that microprocessor complexity would double approximately every two years.

notebook computer See laptop computers.

optical storage devices A form of secondary storage in which a laser reads the surface of a reflective plastic platter.

primary storage (also called **main memory**) High-speed storage located directly on the motherboard that stores data to be processed by the CPU, instructions telling the CPU how to process the data, and operating system programs.

random access memory (RAM) The part of primary storage that holds a software program and small amounts of data when they are brought from secondary storage.

read-only memory (ROM) Type of primary storage in which certain critical instructions are safeguarded; the storage is nonvolatile and

retains the instructions when the power to the computer is turned off.

registers High-speed storage areas in the CPU that store very small amounts of data and instructions for short periods.

secondary storage Technology that can store very large amounts of data for extended periods.

server Computers that support networks, enabling users to share files, software, and other network devices.

solid-state drives (SSDs) Data storage devices that serve the same purpose as a hard drive and store data in memory chips.

A tablet computer (or tablet) is a complete computer contained entirely in a flat touch-screen that users operate with a stylus, digital

pen, fingertip, or soft (virtual) keyboard, instead of a physical keyboard or mouse.

thin client A computer that does not offer the full functionality of a *fat client*.

thumb drive Storage device that fits into the USB port of a personal computer and is used for portable storage.

virtual reality (VR) A term that describes a realistic, three-dimensional, computer-generated environment that replicates sight, touch, hearing, and in some cases, smell.

wearable computer A miniature computer worn by a person, thus allowing the user to multitask.

Discussion Questions

1. What factors affect the speed of a microprocessor?

2. If you were the CIO of a firm, what factors would you consider when selecting secondary storage media for your company's records (files)?

3. Given that Moore's law has proved itself over the past two decades, speculate on what chip capabilities will be in 10 years. What might your desktop PC be able to do?

4. If you were the CIO of a firm, how would you explain the workings, benefits, and limitations of using thin clients as opposed to fat clients?

5. Where might you find embedded computers at home, at school, or at work?

6. You are the CIO of your company, and you have to develop an application of strategic importance to your firm. What are the advantages and disadvantages of using open-source software?

7. What does the following statement mean? "Hardware is useless without software."

Problem-Solving Activities

1. Access the websites of the major chip manufacturers—for example, Intel (**www.intel.com**), Motorola (**www.motorola.com**), and Advanced Micro Devices (**www.amd.com**)—and obtain the latest information regarding new and planned chips. Compare performance and costs across these vendors. Be sure to take a close look at the various multicore chips.

2. Access "The Journey Inside" on Intel's website at **www.intel.com/content/www/us/en/education/k12/the-journey-inside.html**. Prepare a presentation of each step in the machine instruction cycle.

Software

TECHNOLOGY GUIDE OUTLINE	LEARNING OBJECTIVES
TG 2.1 Software Issues	**TG 2.1** Discuss the major software issues that confront modern organizations.
TG 2.2 Systems Software	**TG 2.2** Describe the general functions of the operating system.
TG 2.3 Application Software	**TG 2.3** Identify the major types of application software.

Introduction

As you begin this Technology Guide, you might be wondering, "Why do I have to know anything about software?" There are several reasons why you will benefit from understanding the basics of software. First, regardless of your major (and future functional area in an organization), you will be using different types of software throughout your career. Second, you will have input concerning the software that you will use. In this capacity, you will be required to answer many questions, such as these:

- Does my software help me do my job?
- Is this software easy to use?
- Do I need more functionality in my hardware or software, and if so, what functionality would be most helpful to me?

Third, you will also have input into decisions when your functional area or organization upgrades or replaces its software. Some organizations will also allocate the software budget to functional areas or departments. In such cases, you might be responsible for making software decisions (at least locally) yourself. MIS employees will act as advisors, but you will provide important input into such decisions.

Computer hardware is only as effective as the instructions you give it. Those instructions are contained in **software**. The importance of computer software cannot be overestimated. The first software applications for computers in business were developed in the early 1950s. At that time, software was less costly. Today, software comprises a much larger percentage of the cost of modern computer systems because the price of hardware has dramatically decreased, while both the complexity and the price of software have dramatically increased.

The ever-increasing complexity of software has also increased the potential for errors, or *bugs*. Large applications today may contain millions of lines of computer code, written by

FIGURE TG 2.1 **Systems software serves as an intermediary between hardware and functional applications.**

hundreds of people over the course of several years. Thus, the potential for errors is huge, and testing and debugging software is expensive and time consuming.

In spite of these overall trends—increasing complexity, cost, and numbers of defects—software has become an everyday feature of our business and personal lives. Your examination of software begins with definitions of some fundamental concepts. Software consists of **computer programs**, which are sequences of instructions for the computer. The process of writing, or coding, programs is called **programming**. Individuals who perform this task are called *programmers*.

Computer programs include **documentation**, which is a written description of the program's functions. Documentation helps the user operate the computer system, and it helps other programmers understand what the program does and how it accomplishes its purpose. Documentation is vital to the business organization. Without it, the departure of a key programmer or user could deprive the organization of the knowledge of how the program is designed and functions.

The computer can do nothing until it is instructed by software. Computer hardware, by design, is general purpose. Software enables the user to instruct the hardware to perform specific functions that provide business value. There are two major types of software: systems software and application software. **Figure TG 2.1** illustrates the relationships among hardware, systems software, and application software.

TG 2.1 Software Issues

Author Lecture Videos are available exclusively in *WileyPLUS*.
Apply the Concept activities are available in the Appendix and in *WileyPLUS*.

The importance of software in computer systems has brought new issues to the forefront for organizational managers. These issues include software defects (bugs), licensing, open systems, and open-source software.

Software Defects

All too often, computer program code is inefficient, poorly designed, and riddled with errors. The Software Engineering Institute (SEI) at Carnegie Mellon University in Pittsburgh defines good software as usable, reliable, defect free, cost effective, and maintainable. As our dependence on computers and networks increases, the risks associated with software defects are becoming more serious.

The SEI maintains that, on average, professional programmers make between 100 and 150 errors in every 1,000 lines of code they write. Fortunately, the software industry recognizes this problem. Unfortunately, however, the problem is enormous, and the industry is taking only initial steps to resolve it. One critical step is better design and planning at the beginning of the development process (discussed in Chapter 13).

Software Licensing

Many people routinely copy proprietary software. However, making copies without the manufacturer's explicit permission—a practice known as *piracy*—is illegal. The Business Software Alliance (BSA; **www.bsa.org**), a nonprofit trade association dedicated to promoting a safe and legal digital world, collects, investigates, and acts on software piracy tips. The BSA has calculated that piracy costs software vendors around the world billions of dollars annually. Most of the tips the BSA receives come from current and past employees of offending companies.

To protect their investment, software vendors must prevent their products from being copied and distributed by individuals and other software companies. A company can copyright its software, which means that the U.S. Copyright Office grants the company the exclusive legal right to reproduce, publish, and sell that software.

The number of computing devices in organizations continues to grow, and businesses continue to decentralize, so IS managers are finding it increasingly difficult to supervise their software assets. In fact, the majority of chief information officers (CIOs) are not confident that their companies are in compliance with software licensing agreements. For example, one medium-sized company was fined $10,000 for unknowingly using Microsoft Exchange mailbox licenses that had not been purchased. Worse, the company was also fined $100,000 for not having the necessary licenses for Autodesk, Inc.'s AutoCAD design software.

To help companies manage their software licenses, new firms have arisen that specialize in tracking software licenses for a fee. For example, Cherwell (**www.cherwell.com**) will track and manage a company's software licenses to ensure that a client company is in compliance with U.S. copyright laws.

Open Systems

The **open systems** concept refers to a group of computing products that work together. In an open system, the same operating system with compatible software is installed on all computers that interact within an organization. A complementary approach is to employ application software that will run across all computer platforms. Where hardware, operating systems, and application software are all designed as open systems, users can purchase the best software, called *best of breed*, for a job without worrying whether it will run on particular hardware.

Open-Source Software

Organizations today are increasingly selecting open-source software rather than proprietary software. **Proprietary software** is purchased software that has restrictions on its use, copying, and modification. Companies that develop proprietary software spend money and time developing their products, which they then sell in the marketplace. This software is labeled *proprietary* because the developer keeps the source code—the actual computer instructions—private (just as Coca-Cola does with its soft drink formula). Therefore, companies that purchase the software can use it in their operations, but they cannot change the source code themselves.

In contrast, the source code for **open-source software** is available at no cost to both developers and users. This software is distributed with license terms that ensure that its source code will always be available for all users.

Open-source software is produced by worldwide "communities" of developers who write and maintain the code. Inside each community, however, only a small group of developers, called *core developers*, is allowed to modify the code directly. All the other developers must submit their suggested changes to the core developers.

There are advantages to implementing open-source software in an organization. According to OpenSource (**www.opensource.org**), open-source development produces high-quality, reliable, low-cost software. This software is also flexible, meaning that the code can be changed to meet users' needs. In many cases, open-source software can be more reliable than proprietary software. Because the code is available to many developers, more bugs are discovered early and quickly, and they are fixed immediately. Technical support for open-source software is also available from firms that offer products derived from the software. An example is Red Hat (**www.redhat.com**), a major Linux vendor that supplies solutions to problems associated with open-source technology. Specifically, Red Hat provides education, training, and technical support, for a fee.

Open-source software, however, also has disadvantages. The major drawback is that companies that use open-source software depend on the continued goodwill of an army of volunteers for enhancements, bug fixes, and so on, even if they have signed a contract that includes support. Some companies will not accept this risk, although as a practical matter the support community for Linux, Apache, and Firefox is not likely to disappear. Furthermore, organizations that do not have in-house technical experts will have to purchase maintenance-support contracts from a third party. Open-source software also poses questions concerning ease of use, the time and expense needed to train users, and compatibility with existing systems either within or outside the organization.

There are many examples of open-source software, including the GNU (GNU's Not UNIX) suite of software (**www.gnu.org**) developed by the Free Software Foundation (**www.fsf.org**); the Linux operating system (see **www.linux.com**); Apache Web server (**www.apache.org**); send-mail SMTP (Send Mail Transport Protocol) e-mail server (**www.proofpoint.com/us/products/mail-routing-agent**); the Perl programming language (**www.perl.org**); and the Firefox browser from Mozilla (**www.mozilla.com**). In fact, more than 150,000 open-source projects are under way at SourceForge (**www.sourceforge.net**), the popular open-source hosting site.

Open-source software is moving to the mainstream, as you see by the many major companies that use this type of software. For example, Japan's Shinsei Bank (**www.shinseibank.com**) uses Linux on its servers; SugarCRM (**www.sugarcrm.com**) for certain customer relationship management tasks; and MySQL (**www.mysql.com**) open-source database management software. Furthermore, the *Los Angeles Times* uses Alfresco (**www.alfresco.com**) to manage some of the images and video for its website.

TG 2.2   Systems Software

Systems software is a set of instructions that serves primarily as an intermediary between computer hardware and application programs. Systems software performs many functions:

- It controls and supports the computer system and its information-processing activities.
- It enables computer systems to perform self-regulatory functions by loading itself when the computer is first turned on.
- It provides commonly used sets of instructions for all applications.
- It helps users and IT personnel program, test, and debug their own computer programs.
- It supports application software by directing the computer's basic functions.

The major type of systems software with which we are concerned is the operating system. The **operating system (OS)** is the "director" of your computer system's operations. It supervises the overall operation of the computer by monitoring the computer's status, scheduling operations, and managing input and output processes. Well-known desktop operating systems include Microsoft Windows (**www.microsoft.com**), Apple Mac OS X (**www.apple.com**), Linux (**www.linux.com**), and Google Chrome (**www.google.com/chrome**). When a new version with new features is released, the developers often give the new version a new designation. For example, in early 2019, the latest version of Windows was Windows 10, and the latest version of the MacOS was Sierra.

The operating system also provides an interface between the user and the hardware. This user interface hides the complexity of the hardware from the user. That is, you do not have to know how the hardware actually operates; you simply have to know what the hardware will do and what you need to do to obtain the desired results.

The ease or difficulty of the interaction between the user and the computer is determined to a large extent by the **graphical user interface (GUI)**. The GUI allows users to directly control the hardware by manipulating visible objects (such as icons) and actions that replace complex commands. Microsoft Windows provides a widely recognized GUI.

GUI technology incorporates features such as virtual reality, head-mounted displays, speech input (user commands) and output, pen and gesture recognition, animation, multimedia, artificial intelligence, and cellular/wireless communication capabilities. These new interfaces, called *natural user interfaces* (NUIs), will combine social, haptic, and touch-enabled gesture-control interfaces. (A *haptic interface* provides tactile feedback through the sense of touch by applying forces, vibrations, or motions to the user.)

A **social interface** guides the user through computer applications by using cartoon-like characters, graphics, animation, and voice commands. The cartoon-like characters can be puppets, narrators, guides, inhabitants, or *avatars* (computer-generated human-like figures). Social interfaces are hard to create without being corny. For example, the assistant "Clippy" was so annoying to users of Microsoft Office 97 that it was eliminated from Office 2003 and all subsequent versions.

Motion-control gaming consoles are another type of interface. Three major players currently offer this interface: the Xbox One Kinect, the Playstations (PS 4 Pro and PS 4 Slim), and the Leap Motion Controller.

- Kinect tracks your movements without a physical controller, has voice recognition, and accommodates multiple players.

- The PlayStation Move uses a physical controller with motion-sensing electronics. Move requires each player to use a wand.

- The Leap Motion Controller is a motion-sensing, matchbox-sized device placed on a physical desktop. Using two cameras, the device "observes" an area up to a distance of about three feet. It precisely tracks fingers or items such as a pen that cross into the observed area. The Leap can perform tasks such as navigating a website, using pinch-to-zoom gestures on maps, performing high-precision drawing, and manipulating complex three-dimensional visualizations. The smaller observation area and higher resolution of the device differentiate it from the Microsoft Kinect, which is more suitable for whole-body tracking in a space the size of a living room.

Touch-enabled gesture-control interfaces enable users to browse through photos, "toss" objects around a screen, "flick" to turn the pages of a book, play video games, and watch movies. Examples of this type of interface are Microsoft Surface and the Apple iPhone.

TG 2.3 Application Software

Application software is a set of computer instructions that provides specific functionality to a user. This functionality may be broad, such as general word processing, or narrow, such as an organization's payroll program. Essentially, an application program applies a computer to a certain need. As you will see, modern organizations use many different software applications.

Application software may be developed in-house by the organization's information systems personnel, or it may be commissioned from a software vendor. Alternatively, the software can be purchased, leased, or rented from a vendor that develops applications and sells them to many organizations. This "off-the-shelf" software may be a standard package, or it may be customizable. Special-purpose programs or "packages" can be tailored for a specific purpose, such as inventory control and payroll. A **package**, or **software suite**, is a group of programs with integrated functions that has been developed by a vendor and is available for purchase in a prepackaged form. Microsoft Office is a well-known example of a package, or software suite.

General-purpose, off-the-shelf application programs designed to help individual users increase their productivity are referred to as **personal application software. Table TG 2.1** lists some of the major types of personal application software.

Speech-recognition software, also called *voice recognition*, is an input technology, rather than strictly an application, that enables users to provide input to systems software and application software. As the name suggests, this software recognizes and interprets human speech, either one word at a time *(discrete speech)* or in a conversational stream *(continuous speech)*. Advances in processing power, new software algorithms, and better microphones have enabled developers to design extremely accurate speech-recognition software. Experts predict that, in the near future, voice recognition systems will be built into almost every device, appliance, and machine that people use. Applications for voice recognition technology abound.

Author Lecture Videos are available exclusively in *WileyPLUS*.
Apply the Concept activities are available in the Appendix and in *WileyPLUS*.

TABLE TG 2.1   **Personal Application Software**

Category of Personal Application Software	Major Functions	Examples
Spreadsheets	Uses rows and columns to manipulate primarily numerical data; useful for analyzing financial information and for what–if and goal-seeking analyses	Microsoft Excel Smartsheets Apple Numbers
Word processing	Allows users to manipulate primarily text with many writing and editing features	Microsoft Word Apple Pages
Desktop publishing	Extends word processing software to allow production of finished, camera-ready documents, which may contain photographs, diagrams, and other images combined with text in different fonts	Microsoft Publisher Adobe InDesign
Data management	Allows users to store, retrieve, and manipulate related data	Microsoft Access FileMaker Pro
Presentation	Allows users to create and edit graphically rich information to appear on electronic slides	Microsoft PowerPoint Apple Keynote
Graphics	Allows users to create, store, and display or print charts, graphs, maps, and drawings	Corel PaintShop Pro Adobe Illustrator
Personal finance	Allows users to maintain checkbooks, track investments, monitor credit cards, and bank and pay bills electronically	Mint, Quicken, Venmo, Acorns, Robinhood
Web authoring	Allows users to design websites and publish them on the Web	WordPress, Adobe Photoshop
Communications	Allows users to communicate with other people over any distance	Monday Jive Slack

Before you go on . . .

1. What does the following statement mean? "Hardware is useless without software."
2. What are the differences between systems software and application software?
3. What is open-source software, and what are its advantages? Can you think of any disadvantages?
4. Describe the functions of the operating system.

What's in IT for me?

ACCT   For the Accounting Major

Accounting application software performs the organization's accounting functions, which are repetitive and performed in high volumes. Each business transaction (e.g., a person hired, a paycheck processed, an item sold) produces data that must be captured. Accounting applications capture these data and then manipulate them as necessary. Accounting applications adhere to relatively standardized procedures, handle detailed data, and have a historical focus (i.e., what happened in the past).

FIN   For the Finance Major

Financial application software provides information about the firm's financial status to persons and groups inside and outside

the firm. Financial applications include forecasting, funds management, and control applications. Forecasting applications predict and project the firm's future activity in the economic environment. Funds management applications use cash flow models to analyze expected cash flows. Control applications enable managers to monitor their financial performance, typically by providing information about the budgeting process and performance ratios.

MKT   For the Marketing Major

Marketing application software helps management solve problems that involve marketing the firm's products. Marketing software includes marketing research and marketing intelligence applications. Marketing applications provide information about the firm's products and competitors, its distribution system, its advertising and personal selling activities, and its pricing strategies. Overall, marketing applications help managers develop strategies that combine the four major elements of marketing: product, promotion, place, and price.

POM For the Production/Operations Management Major

Managers use production/operations management (POM) application software for production planning and as part of the physical production system. POM applications include production, inventory, quality, and cost software. These applications help management operate manufacturing facilities and logistics. Materials requirements planning (MRP) software is also widely used in manufacturing. This software identifies which materials will be needed, how much will be needed, and the dates on which they will be needed. This information enables managers to be proactive.

HRM For the Human Resources Management Major

Human resources management application software provides information concerning recruiting and hiring, education and training, maintaining the employee database, termination, and administering benefits. HRM applications include workforce planning, recruiting, workforce management, compensation, benefits, and environmental reporting subsystems (e.g., equal employment opportunity records and analysis, union enrollment, toxic substances, and grievances).

MIS For the MIS Major

If your company decides to develop its own software, the MIS function is responsible for managing this activity. If the company decides to buy software, the MIS function deals with software vendors in analyzing their products. The MIS function is also responsible for upgrading software as vendors release new versions.

Summary

TG2.1 Discuss the major software issues that confront modern organizations.

Computer program code often contains errors. The industry recognizes the enormous problem of software defects, and steps are being taken to resolve this issue. Software licensing is another issue for organizations and individuals. Copying proprietary software is illegal. Software vendors copyright their software to protect it from being copied. As a result, companies must license vendor-developed software to be able to use it. Organizations must also decide between open-source software and proprietary software. Each type of software has its pros and cons that must be carefully considered.

TG2.2 Describe the general functions of the operating system.

Operating systems manage the actual computer resources (i.e., the hardware). They schedule and process applications; manage and protect memory; manage the input and output functions and hardware; manage data and files; and provide security, fault tolerance, graphical user interfaces, and windowing.

TG2.3 Identify the major types of application software.

The major types of application software are spreadsheet, data management, word processing, desktop publishing, graphics, multimedia, communications, speech recognition, and groupware. Software suites combine several types of application software (e.g., word processing, spreadsheet, and data management) into an integrated package.

Technology Guide Glossary

application software The class of computer instructions that directs a computer system to perform specific processing activities and provide functionality for users.

computer programs The sequences of instructions for the computer, which comprise software.

documentation Written description of the functions of a software program.

graphical user interface (GUI) Systems software that allows users to have direct control of the hardware by manipulating visible objects (such as icons) and actions, which replace command syntax.

open-source software Software made available in source-code form at no cost to developers.

open systems Computing products that work together by using the same operating system with compatible software on all the computers that interact in an organization.

operating system (OS) The main system control program, which supervises the overall operations of the computer, allocates CPU time and main memory to programs, and provides an interface between the user and the hardware.

package Common term for an integrated group of computer programs developed by a vendor and available for purchase in prepackaged form.

personal application software General-purpose, off-the-shelf application programs that support general types of processing, rather than being linked to any specific business function.

programming The process of writing or coding software programs.

proprietary software Software that has been developed by a company and has restrictions on its use, copying, and modification.

social interface A user interface that guides the user through computer applications by using cartoon-like characters, graphics, animation, and voice commands.

software A set of computer programs that enable the hardware to process data.

software suite See package.

speech-recognition software Software that recognizes and interprets human speech, either one word at a time (discrete speech) or in a stream (continuous speech).

systems software The class of computer instructions that serve primarily as an intermediary between computer hardware and application programs; provides important self-regulatory functions for computer systems.

Discussion Questions

1. You are the CIO of your company, and you have to develop an application of strategic importance to your firm. What are the advantages and disadvantages of using open-source software?

2. What does the following statement mean? "Hardware is useless without software."

Problem-Solving Activities

1. A great deal of free software is available over the Internet. Go to **www.100-downloads.com/programs/free-internet-software/**, and observe all the software available for free. Choose a software program, and download it to your computer. Prepare a brief discussion about the software for your class.

2. Enter the IBM website (**www.ibm.com**), and perform a search on the term *software*. Click on the drop box for Products, and notice how many software products IBM produces. Is IBM only a hardware company?

Cloud Computing

We devote this Technology Guide to a vital topic: cloud computing. A working knowledge of cloud computing will enhance your appreciation of what technology can and cannot do for a business. It will also enable you to make an immediate contribution by analyzing how your organization manages its IT assets. Going further, you will be using these computing resources in your career, and you will have input into decisions about how your department and organization can best use them. Cloud computing can also be extremely valuable if you decide to start your own business.

We define **cloud computing** as a type of computing that delivers convenient, on-demand, pay-as-you-go access for multiple customers to a shared pool of configurable computing resources (e.g., servers, networks, storage, applications, and services) that can be rapidly and easily accessed over the Internet. Cloud computing allows customers to acquire resources at any time and then delete them the instant they are no longer needed. We present many examples of how the cloud can be used for business purposes. The cloud can also provide you with personal applications. Therefore, this guide can help you plan for your own use of the cloud. For a more detailed discussion of how you can use the cloud, see the section titled IT's Personal: "The Cloud."

TG 3.1 Introduction

You were introduced to the concept of *IT infrastructure* in Chapter 1. Recall that an organization's IT infrastructure consists of IT components—hardware, software, networks, and databases—and IT services—developing information systems, managing security and risk, and managing data. (It is helpful to review Figure 1.3 of Chapter 1 here.) The organization's IT infrastructure is the foundation for all of the information systems that the organization uses.

Modern IT infrastructure has evolved through several stages since the early 1950s, when firms first began to apply information technology to business applications. These stages are as follows:

- *Stand-alone mainframes:* Organizations initially used mainframe computers in their engineering and accounting departments. The mainframe was typically housed in a secure area, and only MIS personnel had access to it.

- *Mainframe and dumb terminals:* Forcing users to go to wherever the mainframe was located was time consuming and inefficient. As a result, firms began placing so-called dumb terminals—essentially electronic typewriters with limited processing power—in user departments. This arrangement enabled users to input computer programs into the mainframe from their departments, a process called *remote job entry*.

- *Stand-alone personal computers:* In the late 1970s, the first personal computers appeared. The IBM PC's debut in 1981 legitimized the entire personal computer market. Users began bringing personal computers to the workplace to improve their productivity—for example, by using spreadsheet and word processing applications. These computers were not initially supported by the firm's MIS department. However, as the number of personal computers increased dramatically, organizations decided to support these devices, and they established policies as to which PCs and software they would support.

- *Local area networks (client/server computing):* When personal computers are networked, individual productivity increases. For this reason, organizations began to connect personal computers to local area networks (LANs) and then connected those LANs to the mainframe, a type of processing known as *client/server computing*.

- *Enterprise computing:* In the early 1990s, organizations began to use networking standards to integrate different kinds of networks throughout the firm, thereby creating enterprise computing. As the Internet became widespread after 1995, organizations began using the TCP/IP networking protocol to integrate different types of networks. All types of hardware were networked, including mainframes, personal computers, smartphones, printers, and many others. Software applications and data now flow seamlessly throughout the enterprise and among organizations.

- *Cloud computing and mobile computing:* Today, organizations and individuals can use the power of cloud computing. As you will see in this Technology Guide, cloud computing provides access to a shared pool of computing resources, including computers, storage, applications, and services, over a network, typically the Internet.

Keep in mind that the computing resources in each stage can be cumulative. For example, most large firms still use mainframe computers (in addition to all the other types of computing resources) as large servers to manage operations that involve millions of transactions per day.

To appreciate the impacts of cloud computing, you first need to understand traditional IT departments in organizations and the challenges they face. Traditionally, organizations have used **on-premise computing**—that is, they own their IT infrastructure (their software, hardware, networks, and data management) and maintain it in their data centers.

On-premise computing incurs expenses for IT infrastructure, the expert staffs needed to build and maintain complex IT systems, physical facilities, software licenses, hardware, and staff training and salaries. Despite all of this spending, organizations, however, typically do not use their infrastructure to its full capacity. The majority of these expenses are typically applied to maintaining the existing IT infrastructure, with the remainder being allocated to developing new systems. As a result, on-premise computing can actually inhibit an organization's ability to respond quickly and appropriately to today's rapidly changing business environments. Let's look at the Photobox Group for an example.

Photobox Group (**http://group.photobox.com**) is an online-only image printing company that holds about 6.5 billion images, uploaded by customers who use its services to order physical copies of their digital photographs. The company previously housed its 9 petabytes of data in two data centers in different parts of Europe.

The company's on-premise system meant that its technology group spent too much time managing its information technology infrastructure and not enough time developing innovative projects that could enhance the firm's future growth. Furthermore, Photobox had difficulty keeping up with the large amount of new digital photos from its customers.

Photobox wanted to provide a faster website experience to its customers and make it easier to manage the huge amounts of data that it must manage. As a result, the firm migrated its image data to Amazon Web Services cloud storage. Photobox then started using an Amazon artificial intelligence (AI) service that allowed its technology team to understand the content of each digital image.

Customers come to Photobox with a particular recipient or event in mind and a number of photos that they want to use to tell the story. The AI service enables customers to participate with Photobox team members in the design process for a photo album or a book.

As you will see in the next section, cloud computing can help organizations manage the problems that traditional IT departments face with on-premise computing. The next section defines cloud computing and describes its essential characteristics.

Before you go on . . .

1. Describe the stages in the evolution of today's IT infrastructure.
2. Describe the challenges that traditional IT departments face.

TG 3.2 | What Is Cloud Computing?

Information technology departments have always been tasked to deliver useful IT applications to business users. For a variety of reasons, today's IT departments are facing increased challenges in delivering useful applications. As you study cloud computing, you will learn how it can help organizations manage the problems that occur in traditional IT departments. You will also discover why so many organizations are using cloud computing.

Author Lecture Videos are available exclusively in *WileyPLUS*.
Apply the Concept activities are available in the Appendix and in *WileyPLUS*.

Cloud Computing Characteristics

The cloud computing phenomenon has several important characteristics. We take a closer look at them in this section.

Cloud Computing Provides On-Demand Self-Service.   A customer can access needed computing resources automatically. This characteristic gives customers *elasticity* and *flexibility*—that is, customers can increase (scale up) or decrease (scale down) the amount of computing they need.

Consider retailers.   During the Christmas buying season, these firms need much more computational capacity than at other times of the year. Therefore, if they use cloud computing, they can scale up during peak periods of business activity and scale down at other times.

Cloud Computing Encompasses the Characteristics of Grid Computing.

Grid computing pools various hardware and software components to create a single IT environment with shared resources. Grid computing shares the processing resources of many geographically dispersed computers across a network and does the following:

- Grid computing enables organizations to use their computing resources more efficiently.
- Grid computing provides fault tolerance and redundancy, meaning that there is no single point of failure, so the failure of one computer will not stop an application from executing.
- Grid computing makes it easy to *scale up*—that is, to access increased computing resources (add more servers)—to meet the processing demands of complex applications.
- Grid computing makes it easy to *scale down* (remove computers) if extensive processing is not needed.

MIS Consider Oxford (United Kingdom) University's Digital Mammogram National Database project. The project aims to improve breast cancer screening and reduce the rate of erroneous diagnoses. The users of the system are radiologists, doctors, and technicians who want to query, retrieve, process, and store patients' breast images and diagnostic reports. These images tend to be large and require fast access, high quality, and rigid privacy.

The system uses a large distributed database that runs on a grid computing system. The grid is formed in a collaborative way, by sharing resources (CPU cycles and data) among different organizations. The database contains digital mammographies with explanatory notes and comments about each image. Because medical and university sites have different equipment, the images and reports are standardized before they are stored in the database.

The system enables individual medical sites to store, process, and manage mammograms as digital images and to enable their use through data mining and sharing of these mammography archives. Radiologists can collaborate on diagnoses without being in the same physical location.

With this system in place, the institutions involved have improved their collaboration, resulting in quicker and more accurate diagnoses. By pooling their resources, each institution gained access to a much larger and more sophisticated set of resources, without increasing their costs proportionately.

Cloud Computing Encompasses the Characteristics of Utility Computing.

In **utility computing**, a service provider makes computing resources and infrastructure management available to a customer as needed. The provider then charges the customer for its specific usage rather than a flat rate. Utility computing enables companies to efficiently meet fluctuating demands for computing power by lowering the costs of owning the hardware infrastructure.

Cloud Computing Uses Broad Network Access.

The cloud provider's computing resources are available over a network, accessed with a Web browser, and they are configured so that they can be used with any computing device.

Cloud Computing Pools Computing Resources.

The provider's computing resources are available to serve multiple customers. These resources are dynamically assigned and reassigned according to customer demand.

Cloud Computing Often Occurs on Virtualized Servers.

Cloud computing providers have placed hundreds or thousands of networked servers inside massive data centers called **server farms** (see **Figure TG 3.1**). Recall that a *server* is a computer that supports networks, thus enabling users to share files, software, and other network devices. Server farms require massive amounts of electrical power, air-conditioning, backup generators, and security. They also need to be located fairly close to fiber-optic communications links (**Figure TG 3.2**).

Going further, Gartner estimates that typical usage rates on servers are very low, generally from 5 to 10 percent—that is, most of the time, organizations are using only a small percentage of their total computing capacity. Chief information officers (CIOs) tolerate this inefficiency to make certain that they can supply sufficient computing resources to users in case demand should spike. To alleviate this problem, companies and cloud computing providers are turning to virtualization.

Server virtualization uses software-based partitions to create multiple virtual servers—called *virtual machines*—on a single physical server. The major benefit of this system is that each server no longer has to be dedicated to a particular task. Multiple applications can run instead on a single physical server, with each application running within its own software environment. As a result, virtualization enables companies to increase server usage. Companies can also realize cost savings in two areas. First, they do not have to buy additional servers to meet peak demand. Second, they reduce their utility costs because they are using less energy. The following example illustrates the benefits of virtualization for the city of Yawata in Kyoto, Japan.

MIS The city of Yawata in Kyoto Prefecture, Japan (**www .city.yawata.kyoto.jp**), is very active in developing its networked city government. Deployed in 2002, the city's information system was designed to support the daily operations of the city. Since that time, the system has functioned as an IT service for city employees and members of the public.

Over a decade later, the city's continuing efforts to develop a more advanced digital community had resulted in an increasing

Divine Images/F64/Media Bakery

FIGURE TG 3.1 A server farm. Notice the ventilation in the racks and ceiling.

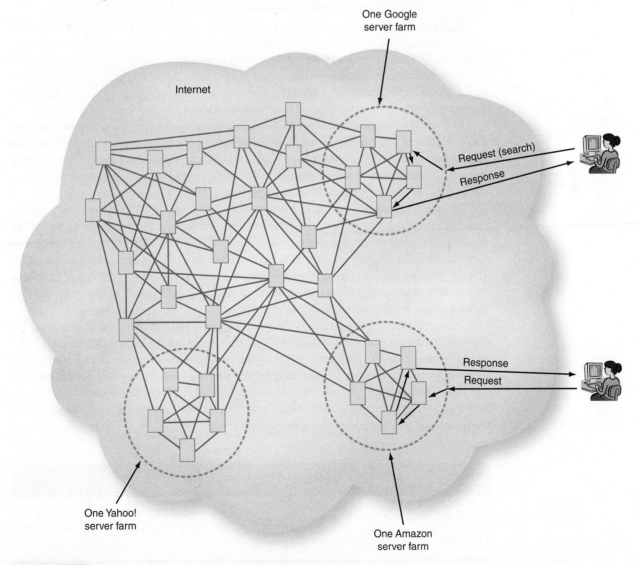

FIGURE TG 3.2 Organizational server farms in relation to the Internet.

number of physical servers, with accompanying increases in power consumption. The rise in power usage was a particular problem as the city has a strong commitment to eco-friendliness.

To reduce hardware expenses, the city had been running multiple applications on a single physical server, an approach that sometimes caused server availability issues. To make the system more secure and stable, the city wanted to have an individual dedicated server for each application.

The city decided to implement a server virtualization solution and realized a number of benefits. First, the city reduced its number of physical servers from 12 to 4. This reduction led to decreases in power consumption, which helped the city reduce its environmental impact. Second, each application now runs on a single virtual machine. This benefit means that server availability has markedly increased, each app runs more efficiently, and the entire system is more stable. Third, by virtualizing its data center, the city is able to address future server resource needs without having to add additional physical servers.

With cloud computing, setting up and maintaining an IT infrastructure need no longer be a challenge for an organization. Businesses do not have to scramble to meet the evolving needs of developing applications. Cloud computing also reduces up-front capital expenses and operational costs, and it enables businesses to better use their infrastructure and to share it from one project to the next. In general, cloud computing eases the difficult tasks of procuring, configuring, and maintaining hardware and software environments. It also allows enterprises to get their applications up and running faster, with easier manageability and less maintenance. It also enables IT to adjust IT resources (e.g., servers, storage, and networking) more rapidly to meet fluctuating and unpredictable business demand.

Businesses are increasingly employing cloud computing for important and innovative work. Let's take a look at Lionsgate's (**www.lionsgate.com**) use of Amazon Web Services.

MIS **POM** Lionsgate is a global entertainment corporation that produces feature films and television shows, which they distribute worldwide. Their products include the television show *Mad Men* and the movie *Hunger Games*. Their productions appear in theaters, on TV, and online. As a successful media and entertainment company, Lionsgate faced IT challenges that included a need for additional IT infrastructure capacity, leading to increased costs; increased enterprise application workloads; and faster time-to-market requirements.

As a result, the company turned to Amazon Web Services (AWS; **www.aws.amazon.com**) for development and test workloads; production workloads for enterprise applications; and backup, archive, and disaster recovery strategies. Lionsgate's objectives were to reduce costs, increase flexibility, and increase operational efficiency. Lionsgate decided to use Amazon Simple Storage Service and Amazon Elastic Compute Cloud.

Lionsgate has experienced many benefits from using AWS. The firm has reduced the time required to deploy infrastructure from weeks to days or hours. Furthermore, testing and development for its SAP applications require less time. AWS has increased the speed of building servers, improved disaster recovery and systems backup, and increased systems availability. The company avoided acquiring additional data center space, saving an estimated $1 million over three years. Overall, Lionsgate believes that moving to AWS saved the company about 50 percent compared to a traditional hosting facility.

These benefits have helped Lionsgate become more agile and more responsive to rapidly changing conditions in the marketplace. AWS has also contributed to helping the company maintain its systems security. Lionsgate is able to use its existing hardware policies and procedures for a secure, seamless, and scalable computing environment that requires few resources to manage.

In the next section, you learn about the various ways in which customers (individuals and organizations) can implement cloud computing. Specifically, you will read about public clouds, private clouds, hybrid clouds, and vertical clouds.

Before you go on . . .

1. Describe the characteristics of cloud computing.
2. Define server virtualization.

TG 3.3 | Different Types of Clouds

There are three major types of cloud computing that companies provide to customers or groups of customers: public clouds, private clouds, and hybrid clouds. A fourth type of cloud computing is called vertical clouds (**Figure TG 3.3**).

Author Lecture Videos are available exclusively in *WileyPLUS*.

Apply the Concept activities are available in the Appendix and in *WileyPLUS*.

Public Cloud

Public clouds are shared, easily accessible, multi-customer IT infrastructures that are available nonexclusively to any entity in the general public (individuals, groups, and organizations). Public cloud vendors provide applications, storage, and other computing resources as services over the Internet. These services may be free or offered on a pay-per-usage model. Samba Tech (**www.sambatech.com**) provides an example of a young company using the public cloud.

    MIS International media companies such as Viacom (**www.viacom.com**), Bloomberg (**www.bloomberg.com**), and ESPN (**www.espn.com**) rely on Samba Tech to deliver video content to online viewers across Latin America. As a result of its rapid growth, Samba decided to use cloud computing. The firm's chief technology officer noted that buying and managing complex IT (i.e., on-premise computing) was never part of the company's strategy.

    Samba turned to Rackspace (**www.rackspace.com**), a public cloud provider, to help it with its huge IT capacity demands. In 2009, Samba needed Rackspace to host about 1 terabyte of data. In 2015, Rackspace hosted over 100 terabytes of Samba's data. Furthermore, when Samba needs additional processing power—to deliver videos for a new marketing campaign, or to coincide with a large sporting event—Rackspace provides that power quickly and affordably.

Private Cloud

Private clouds (also known as *internal clouds* or *corporate clouds*) are IT infrastructures that can be accessed only by a single entity or by an exclusive group of related entities that share the same purpose and requirements, such as all of the business units within a single organization. Private clouds provide IT activities and applications as a service over an intranet within an enterprise. Enterprises adopt private clouds to ensure system and data security. For this reason, these systems are implemented behind the corporate firewall. As an example of a private cloud, let's take a look at the National Security Agency (NSA; **www.nsa.gov**).

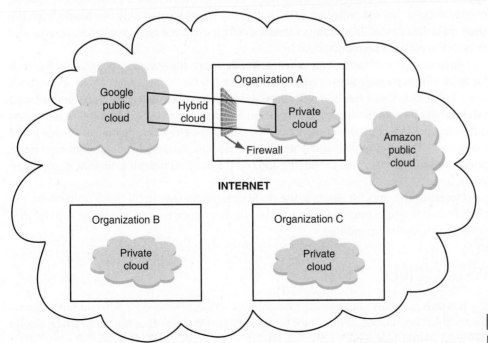

FIGURE TG 3.3 Public clouds, private clouds, and hybrid clouds.

MIS The NSA was running out of storage space for hundreds of different databases that contain information needed to run the agency as well as to produce intelligence on foreign matters. As a result, NSA analysts had to access many different databases to do their jobs. Questions that spanned more than one database had to be manually integrated by the analyst. The agency had to consolidate its databases to make its analysts more efficient and effective.

At first, the NSA decided to simply add more storage capacity. However, this approach actually added to the problem, so the agency decided to implement a private cloud. By putting all its different databases into one private cloud, analysts had to interface with only one system, making their jobs much easier.

The private cloud contains data that the agency acquires and uses for its missions. The cloud has strict security protocols and strong encryption, and has a distributed architecture across multiple geographic areas. The cloud also provides a way to track every instance of every individual accessing data as specific as a single word or name in a file. This tracking includes when the data arrived, who can access them, who did access them, who downloaded them, copied them, printed them, forwarded them, modified them, or deleted them. Furthermore, if the data have legal requirements, such as they must be purged after five years, a notice will automatically tell NSA staff that the data need to be purged. One agency staff member noted that if the NSA had had this ability at the time, it is unlikely that U.S. soldier Bradley Manning would have succeeded in obtaining classified documents in 2010.

After implementation of the private cloud, analysts can perform tasks in minutes that once took days, overall data management costs have decreased, and the security of the data has been greatly enhanced.

Hybrid Cloud

Hybrid clouds are composed of public and private clouds that remain unique entities, but are nevertheless tightly integrated. This arrangement offers users the benefits of multiple deployment models. Hybrid clouds deliver services based on security requirements, the mission-critical nature of the applications, and other company-established policies. For example, customers may need to maintain some of their data in a private cloud for security and privacy reasons while storing other, less-sensitive data in a public cloud because it is less expensive. Let's examine an example of hybrid cloud computing in the city of Asheville, North Carolina.

MIS Operating a disaster recovery (DR) facility is expensive, complex, and time consuming because an organization has to set up and maintain an entire backup information technology infrastructure. The new chief information officer of the city of Asheville, North Carolina, quickly noticed that Asheville had a DR facility, but it was located only two blocks from the city's main data center. This situation meant that there was not enough geographic dispersal for effective recovery from a disaster.

He turned to cloud computing to help Asheville obtain the necessary geographic dispersal for its DR efforts. He wanted to provide disaster recovery for the city's on-premise applications in the public cloud. As a result, the city used VMware Cloud (**www.cloud.vmware.com**), a cloud vendor that offers automated cloud migration and disaster recovery software for deploying organizations' applications and services to the cloud. The city's apps remain in storage in the cloud, ready to be activated if and when they are needed. As the city operates its apps on its private cloud in its main data center, the apps on the public cloud are automatically updated in real time.

Operating the city's DR efforts in the cloud reduced the overall DR cost. Furthermore, the city's financial results improved because the DR efforts are now an operating expenditure rather than a capital expenditure.

Vertical Clouds

It is now possible to build cloud infrastructure and applications for different businesses—the construction, finance, or insurance businesses, for example—thus building vertical clouds (see **www.verticalcloud.com**).

1. Describe public clouds, private clouds, hybrid clouds and vertical clouds and outline the differences in each type of cloud.

TG 3.4 | Cloud Computing Services

Cloud computing services are based on three models: infrastructure-as-a-service (IaaS), platform-as-a-service (PaaS), and software-as-a-service (SaaS). These models represent the three types of computing generally required by consumers: infrastructure to run software and store data (IaaS), platforms to develop applications (PaaS), and software applications to process their data (SaaS). **Figure TG 3.4** illustrates the differences among the three models.

As you examine the figure from left to right, note that the customer manages the service less and less, and the vendor manages it more and more.

Although each model has its distinctive features, all three share certain characteristics. First, customers rent them instead of buying them. This arrangement shifts IT from a capital expense to an operating expense. Second, vendors are responsible for maintenance, administration, capacity planning, troubleshooting, and backups. Finally, obtaining additional computing resources—that is, scale from the cloud—is usually fast and easy. Examples are more storage from an IaaS vendor, the ability to handle more PaaS projects, and more users of an SaaS application.

Author Lecture Videos are available exclusively in *WileyPLUS*.
Apply the Concept activities are available in the Appendix and in *WileyPLUS*.

Infrastructure as a Service

With the **infrastructure-as-a-service** model, cloud computing providers offer remotely accessible servers, networks, and storage capacity. They supply these resources on demand from their large resource pools, which are located in their data centers.

IaaS customers are often technology companies with IT expertise. These companies want access to computing power, but they do not want to be responsible for installing or maintaining it. Companies use the infrastructure to run software or simply to store data.

ON-PREMISE SOFTWARE	INFRASTRUCTURE-AS-A-SERVICE	PLATFORM-AS-A-SERVICE	SOFTWARE-AS-A-SERVICE
CUSTOMER MANAGES	**CUSTOMER MANAGES**	**CUSTOMER MANAGES**	
Applications	Applications	Applications	Applications
Data	Data	Data	Data
Operating system	Operating system	Operating system	Operating system
Servers	**VENDOR MANAGES** Servers	**VENDOR MANAGES** Servers	**VENDOR MANAGES** Servers
Virtualization	Virtualization	Virtualization	Virtualization
Storage	Storage	Storage	Storage
Networking	Networking	Networking	Networking
Examples	Amazon, IBM, Google, Microsoft, Rackspace	Microsoft Windows Azure, Google App Engine, Force.com	Salesforce.com, Google Apps, Dropbox, Apple iCloud, Box.net

FIGURE TG 3.4 Comparison of on-premise software, infrastructure-as-a-service, platform-as-a-service, and software-as-a-service.

To deploy their applications, IaaS users install their operating system and their application software on the cloud computing provider's computers. They can deploy any software on this infrastructure, including different operating systems, applications, and development platforms. Each user is responsible for maintaining their operating system and application software. Cloud providers typically bill IaaS services on a utility computing basis—that is, the cost reflects the amount of resources the user consumes. In the following example, 3M uses the IaaS capabilities of Microsoft Azure to develop a new app.

POM   The 3M Company (**www.3m.com**) produces more than 55,000 products for industries, including health care, retail, consumer electronics, and construction; hires 88,000 employees; and has customers in more than 200 countries.

In one of its business segments, 3M helps its customers optimize parking operations by automating fee collection and other processes. The company had recently purchased the assets of parking, tolling, and automatic license plate reader businesses, and required better insight into those acquisitions.

3M needed a tracking application that its sales staff could use to obtain real-time information about the type and location of 3M products in parking lots and garages. So that the solution could be used on-site with potential customers, the app needed to provide access to data anytime, anywhere, and from an array of mobile devices.

Creating an app developed specifically to operate on mobile devices meant that salespeople would be able to work everywhere and at anytime. Furthermore, after gathering new information, salespeople would be able to seamlessly synchronize it with existing data in the cloud environment.

To meet these requirements, the 3M development team turned to the Microsoft Azure (**www.azure.microsoft.com**) infrastructure-as-a-service platform. Using the Azure IT infrastructure, the team was able to develop the app in two days over one weekend.

Salespeople now use the asset-tracking app to display real-time information about 3M installations. Whenever a salesperson enters new data, the information is immediately available to others through Notification Hubs, which is a "push notification" software tool in Azure. The app also uses the GPS and mapping technologies built into mobile devices to automatically provide visual, location-specific information to the 3M sales force.

Platform as-a-Service

In the **platform-as-a-service** model, customers rent servers, operating systems, storage, a database, software development technologies such as Java and .NET, and network capacity over the Internet. The PaaS model allows the customer to both run existing applications and to develop and test new applications. PaaS offers customers several advantages, which include the following:

- Application developers can develop and run their software solutions on a cloud platform without the cost and complexity of buying and managing the underlying hardware and software layers.

- Underlying computing and storage resources automatically scale to match application demand.

- Operating system features can be upgraded frequently.

- Geographically distributed development teams can work together on software development projects.

- PaaS services can be provided by diverse sources located throughout the world.

- Initial and ongoing costs can be reduced by the use of infrastructure services from a single vendor rather than maintaining multiple hardware facilities that often perform duplicate functions or suffer from incompatibility problems.

MIS   For example, consider Twilio. Twilio (**www.twilio.com**) is a cloud-computing platform as a service (PaaS) company that allows developers to produce software for a variety of communications functions, including making and receiving phone calls, sending and receiving text messages, and others. Twilio customers use the software to enable billions of connections among more than one billion devices. In fact, Twilio customers can build and deploy a call center using only Twilio software. In that way, they do not have to buy expensive equipment and communications software.

Twilio connects to the global telecommunications network through 22 data centers in 7 regions and has agreements with most of the major carriers that allow it to deliver a message to almost any phone in the world. Let's look at examples of Twilio software in use:

- **POM** Twilio operates texts, alerts, and voice calls on the Uber app. When a driver and passenger call each other, they do so through a Twilio number that keeps their own phone numbers private.
- Match.com links potential couples without revealing their phone numbers.
- Airbnb sends rental notifications via Twilio.
- **FIN** ING (**www.ing.com**), a Netherlands banking company, used Twilio software to replace 17 hardware and software systems that it had been using in its global call centers.
- Globo (**www.globo.com**) connects customers with translators around the world over the telephone. The company, which offers e-mail, text, and document translations, connects the calls using Twilio software and routes them to appropriate translators, not only by language but also by area of expertise, such as medical, legal, technological, and other areas.
- **MKT** Marks & Spencer (**www.marksandspencer.com**) switched from its legacy switchboard to use Twilio to power its customer communications across its 640 locations and 13 call centers. When a customer calls any Marks & Spencer store, the company's Twilio system immediately establishes what the customer is calling about and then routes the call to the correct destination. Accordingly, the retailer can now analyze customer intent in real time for more than 12 million customer interactions annually.

Software-as-a-Service

With the **software-as-a-service** delivery model, cloud computing vendors provide software that is specific to their customers' requirements. SaaS is the most widely used service model, and it provides a broad range of software applications. SaaS providers typically charge their customers a monthly or yearly subscription fee.

SaaS applications reside in the cloud instead of on a user's hard drive or in a data center. The host manages the software and the infrastructure that run this software and stores the customer's data. The customers do not control either the software, beyond the usual configuration settings, or the infrastructure, beyond changing the resources they use, such as the amount of disk space required for their data. This process eliminates the need to install and run the application on the user's computers, thereby simplifying maintenance and support.

What differentiates SaaS applications from other applications is their ability to scale. As a result, applications can run on as many servers as is necessary to meet changing demands. This process is transparent to the user.

To reduce the risk of an infrastructure outage, SaaS providers regularly back up all of their customers' data. Customers can also back up their data on their own storage hardware.

HRM To understand how SaaS operates, consider Mary Kay (**www.marykay.com**). The cosmetics giant implemented Oracle's Taleo cloud-based recruitment software in the United States, China, and Brazil. Before 2014, Mary Kay did not have an applicant tracking system. The company's recruiting process was performed with Microsoft Excel spreadsheets and Access databases. Recruiters at Mary Kay lacked visibility on the manual system. If someone applied for a job in two different departments, a recruiter from each department would often call the applicant without realizing that the other recruiter had also contacted the applicant.

Taleo provides Mary Kay with a centralized repository for tracking internal and external job candidates. The software also automated processes such as job applications, onboarding, and forms. Taleo also integrates with LinkedIn, providing instant access to LinkedIn profiles and candidate records with a single click. Furthermore, Taleo can fill in forms with LinkedIn credentials.

For another example, consider the City Football Group (CFG; **www.cityfootballgroup.com**), which owns and operates football (soccer) clubs in England, Australia, New York City, and Japan. CFG employs approximately 1,000 people around the world.

HRM In the past, CFG used paper for performance reviews and employees had to file paper forms for holidays or to update their human resource (HR) records. Such manual processes were designed only for the CFG and were not designed for an international business. As a result of these limitations and the rapid growth of the company, the CFG implemented SAP's cloud-based, human resource management (HR) software-as-a-service product.

The SaaS product enabled CFG employees to complete their six-month performance and development reviews (PDRs) online, simplifying the previous paper-based process. As an additional benefit, managers knew who had not completed their reviews and the stage of those reviews.

After the employees loaded their goals into the software, they met with their managers to discuss their progress and complete narrative updates. Most CFG employees were responsible for between five and eight goals during performance periods. Prior to the SAP HR system, it took much longer to have employee PDRs complete and accurate.

IT's Personal: "The Cloud"

This Technology Guide defines the cloud as distributed computing services, and it presents many examples of how the cloud can be used for both personal and business purposes. This IT's Personal is intended to help you differentiate between the business and personal applications of the cloud and to help you plan for your own use of the cloud.

First, you need to understand that there is no single "cloud." Rather, almost all businesses refer to their Internet-based services as "cloud services." Basically, anything you do over the Internet that you used to do on a local computer is a form of cloud computing. When you store files on Dropbox, create a document using Google Docs, use iCloud to store purchases or sync documents, or use OnLive on your iPad, you are using cloud-based services that are intended for personal use.

Infrastructure-as-a-service is an important application of the cloud for personal purposes. Dropbox is one of the most prominent companies in this area. In the past, users had to carry around a USB drive, a CD, an external hard drive, or (way back in the day) floppy disks to store their personal information. Today, users can employ Dropbox for this purpose. At the time of this writing, a free Dropbox account offered 2 GB of online storage. Not only does Dropbox offer you a place to store your files (eliminating the need for a personal infrastructure of removable storage), but it also provides synchronization across computers and access from mobile devices!

Virtualization is gaining ground. If you have an iPad, you should look up the app called "OnLive" and give it a test run. OnLive allows you to log in to a virtual computer that is running Windows 7 or Windows 8. Here, your iPad is simply providing the input/output, and the server is "serving up" a virtual operating system. It is very likely that one day your home computer will be virtual as well.

Software-as-a-service has been a popular option for quite some time. For example, Google Docs offers Internet-based word processing, spreadsheet, presentation, forms, and drawing tools. Recently, Microsoft has moved into the game with their Microsoft Office 365 product. Basically, each of these services allows you to use a computer program without having to install it on your computer or mobile device. You simply access the entire program (and your saved files) over the Internet.

Google has combined a couple of these cloud services with Google Drive, a service that offers the same services as Dropbox in addition to Google Docs' online editing and file-sharing capabilities. This also crosses over with SaaS because of the added benefit of Google Docs. It is very likely that one day Google will merge virtualization, infrastructure, and software into a single cloud-based service. If this technology becomes available, then all you will need as a consumer is an Internet-connected device, and you will be able to store, access, edit, and share your files from the cloud. You will also be able to choose apps to run on your "virtual machine" much the way you currently purchase applications for your mobile devices from a vendor-approved store.

So, what is the point? Simply, cloud-based services are here to stay. The rise of ubiquitous Internet access has engendered a new world of possibilities.

A word of caution, however: Along with its seemingly endless possibilities, cloud computing raises many critical security and privacy issues. Because your files, apps, and editing capability will no longer be stored on a local machine, they are only as safe as the company to which you have entrusted them makes them. So, when you select a cloud provider, make sure you choose wisely!

A subset of SaaS is the *desktop-as-a-service (DaaS)* model, also known as a *cloud desktop* or *desktop in the cloud*. In this model, an SaaS provider hosts a software environment for a desktop personal computer, including productivity and collaboration software—spreadsheets, word processing programs, and so on—such as Google Apps, Microsoft 365, and other products. The DaaS model can be financially advantageous for consumers because they do not need to purchase a fully configured personal computer, or fat client. This model also makes the PC environment simpler to deploy and administer.

1. Describe infrastructure-as-a-service.
2. Describe platform-as-a-service.
3. Describe software-as-a-service.

TG 3.5 | The Benefits of Cloud Computing

Cloud computing offers benefits for both individuals and organizations. It allows companies to increase the scale and power of their IT and the speed at which it can be deployed and accessed. It eliminates administrative problems and it operates across locations, devices, and organizational boundaries.

Nearly half of the respondents in a recent CIO Economic Impact survey indicated that they evaluate cloud computing options first—before traditional IT approaches—before making any new IT investments. IBM predicts that the global cloud computing market will grow 22 percent annually to $241 billion by 2020. Next, we examine three major benefits that cloud computing provides to individuals and organizations.

Author Lecture Videos are available exclusively in *WileyPLUS*.
Apply the Concept activities are available in the Appendix and in *WileyPLUS*.

Benefit 1: Cloud Computing Has a Positive Impact on Employees

Cloud computing enables companies to provide their employees with access to all the information they need no matter where they are, what device they are using, or with whom they are working. Consider this example.

POM The attorneys of one multistate law firm needed to access documents and data on a constant basis. Since 2000, the firm's data volume had expanded from 30 gigabytes to more than 40 terabytes. Moreover, all of these data have to be stored and accessed securely. In the past, attorneys often had to manually copy case-relevant data onto external hard drives and USB devices, and then ship these devices back and forth among themselves and the firm's headquarters. These processes were nonsecure, time-consuming, and expensive.

To address these needs, the law firm turned to cloud computing for data storage, off-site disaster recovery, and multisite access within a highly secure public cloud. Rather than maintain a massive inventory of extra storage as required by its old IT infrastructure, the firm can now increase storage capacity on demand. The cloud provides attorneys with constant access through encrypted communication channels. Furthermore, the cloud facilitates collaboration among distributed teams of attorneys, thereby increasing their overall productivity. The cloud environment has made the firm's attorneys much more efficient, and the firm's IT expenses have declined by 60 percent.

Benefit 2: Cloud Computing Can Save Money

Over time, the cost of building and operating an on-premise IT infrastructure will typically be more expensive than adopting the cloud computing model. Cloud providers purchase massive amounts of IT infrastructure (e.g., hardware and bandwidth) and gain cost savings by buying in large quantity. As a result, these providers continually take advantage of Moore's law (discussed in Technology Guide 1). For example, the Amazon cloud, known as Amazon Web Services, reduced its prices many times over the last 10 years.

As a result, cloud computing can reduce or eliminate the need to purchase hardware, build and install software, and pay software licensing fees. The organization pays only for the computing resources it needs, and then only when it needs them. This pay-for-use model provides greater flexibility and it eliminates or reduces the need for significant capital expenditures.

POM Let's consider the United States General Services Administration (GSA; **www.gsa.gov**). In 2010, the agency began a multiyear strategy to migrate core agency information systems to the cloud. In the first phase of the strategy, the GSA migrated 17,000 employees to Google Apps, making it the first federal agency to move basic e-mail and collaboration services entirely into a cloud environment. The GSA notes that the migration saves the agency approximately $3 million per year.

HRM In the second phase of the strategy, the GSA worked with Salesforce.com (**www.salesforce.com**) to implement cloud-based software that made it easier for GSA employees to collaborate on projects, share and manage case files, find internal subject-matter experts, and capture new ideas. In one instance, employees used the software to generate 640 ideas in 30 days to streamline GSA business processes, an initiative that eventually saved the agency $5 million per year.

HRM The GSA also established a rapid application development platform (discussed in Chapter 13) in the cloud. Within six months, GSA's IT department developed and delivered more than 100 enterprise applications that replaced more than 1,700 legacy applications. The new applications lowered the total cost of ownership by 92 percent.

And the bottom line? The GSA spent $593 million on IT in fiscal year 2014, nearly $100 million less than it spent the previous year.

Benefit 3: Cloud Computing Can Improve Organizational Flexibility and Competitiveness

Cloud computing allows organizations to use only the amount of computing resources they need at a given time. Therefore, companies can efficiently scale their operations up or down as needed to meet rapidly changing business conditions. Cloud computing is also able to deliver computing services faster than the on-premise computing can.

POM Consider PAC2000A (**www.pac2000a.it/**), a large Italian retailer. The company had been using a custom-developed, in-house application to manage shelf prices across more than 1,000 outlets. The pricing application was not able to incorporate consumer demand into its algorithms, whether on a national or a local scale. When the retailer implemented an SaaS-based price optimization system, it gained sophisticated analytical capabilities on very detailed cost and competitors' data. This process led to more precise localized pricing decisions, more accurate forecasts, and a 2.4 percent increase in comparable store sales.

Before you go on . . .

1. Describe how cloud computing can help organizations expand the scope of their business operations.

2. Describe how cloud computing can help organizations respond quickly to market changes.

TG 3.6 Concerns and Risks with Cloud Computing

Gartner predicted that cloud computing would grow at an annual rate of 19 percent through the year 2016. These predictions proved aggressive, however, cloud computing does continue to grow year over year. Even if this prediction had been accurate, however, cloud computing would still have accounted for less than 5 percent of total worldwide IT spending that year. Why is this percentage so low? The reason is that there are serious concerns with cloud computing. These concerns fall into six categories: legacy IT systems, reliability, privacy, security, the legal and regulatory environment, and criminal use of cloud computing.

Concern 1: Legacy IT Systems

Historically, organizational IT systems have accumulated a diversity of hardware, operating systems, and applications. When bundled together, these systems are called "legacy spaghetti." These systems cannot easily be transferred to the cloud because they must first be untangled and simplified. Furthermore, many IT professionals have vested interests in various legacy systems, and they resist efforts to exchange these systems for cloud computing.

Concern 2: Reliability

Many skeptics contend that cloud computing is not as reliable as a well-managed, on-premise IT infrastructure. Although cloud providers are improving the redundancy and reliability of their offerings, outages still occur. Consider the examples of Dropbox and Amazon.

On January 10, 2014, file-sharing service Dropbox (**www.dropbox.com**) went offline for about two days. Although hackers tried to claim credit for the crash, Dropbox said that the outage was its own fault. According to the company, a programming error caused upgrades to its operating system to be applied on actively running machines during routine maintenance. Engineers attempted to restore the systems from backups, but thanks to the sheer size of Dropbox's databases, it took two days to get back to normal. The company maintained that no user data were damaged or compromised.

Then, on March 14, 2014, Dropbox service stopped working for about one hour. Users received errors when attempting to access the Dropbox website or mobile apps. The company acknowledged the outage on Twitter, describing it only as a "service issue." Forty minutes after that first tweet, Dropbox said that the issue had been resolved. The company never went into detail about what exactly happened with this outage.

On February 28, 2017, a large part of Amazon's Simple Storage Service (S3) went offline. Amazon was not even able to update its own service health dashboard—the Web page that shows which Amazon Web Services (AWS) are operating normally—for the first two hours of the outage because the dashboard itself is hosted on Amazon Web Services.

S3 is often used to store images. Therefore, if S3 is not available, companies are not able to display images or logos on their websites. Lewis Bamboo (**www.lewisbamboo.com**), a family-owned bamboo nursery in Alabama, experienced precisely this problem. Pictures are a very important part of selling its products online and when S3 went down, so did the majority of its website. However, the nursery also stores its images on company servers, so it was able to display the images on its website despite the Amazon outage. Thousands of other companies were not so fortunate.

Amazon blamed human error for the outage, stating that one of its employees was debugging the company's billing system and accidentally took more servers offline than intended. That error began a cascading effect that took down two other server subsystems, and so on.

Amazon made changes to its procedures to ensure that, in the future, employees will not be able to remove as much server capacity as quickly as they previously could. Amazon also made changes so that its service health dashboard would continue to function in the event of a similar outage.

Concern 3: Privacy

Privacy advocates have criticized cloud computing for posing a major threat to privacy because the providers control, and thus lawfully or unlawfully monitor, the data and communication stored between the user and the host company. For example, AT&T and Verizon collaborated with the NSA to use cloud computing to record more than 10 million phone calls between American citizens. Providers could also accidentally or deliberately alter or even delete some of that information.

Using a cloud computing provider also complicates data privacy because of the extent to which cloud processing and cloud storage are used to implement cloud services. The point is that customer data may not remain on the same system or in the same data center. This situation can lead to legal concerns over jurisdiction.

There have been efforts to address this problem by integrating the legal environment. One example is the U.S.-EU Safe Harbor, a streamlined process for U.S. companies to comply with the European Union directive on the protection of personal data.

Concern 4: Security

Critics also question how secure cloud computing really is. Because the characteristics of cloud computing can differ widely from those of traditional IT architectures, providers need to reconsider the effectiveness and efficiency of traditional security mechanisms. Security issues include access to sensitive data, data segregation (among customers), privacy, error exploitation, recovery, accountability, malicious insiders, and account control.

The security of cloud computing services is a contentious issue that may be delaying the adoption of this technology. Security issues arise primarily from the unease of both the private and public sectors with the external management of security-based services. The fact that providers manage these services provides great incentive for them to prioritize building and maintaining strong security services.

Another security issue involves the control over who is able to access and use the information stored in the cloud. (Recall our discussion of least privilege in Chapter 4.) Many organizations exercise least-privilege controls effectively with their on-premise IT infrastructures. Some cloud computing environments, in contrast, cannot exercise least-privilege controls effectively. This problem occurs because cloud computing environments were originally designed for individuals or groups, not for hierarchical organizations in which some people have both the right and the responsibility to exercise control over other people's private information. To address this problem, cloud computing vendors are working to incorporate administrative, least-privilege functionality into their products. In fact, many have already done so.

Consider Panama City, Florida, as an example. Panama City was one of the first cities in the United States to adopt Google Apps for Government. The city was searching for a way to gain visibility into who was using Google Apps and how users were collaborating both inside and outside the city's IT domain. Furthermore, the city had to have the ability to control and enforce data-sharing policies where necessary. The city decided to adopt CloudLock which has now been acquired by Cisco (**https://umbrella.cisco.com/products/casb**).

CloudLock provides a security system to protect its clients' information assets located in public cloud applications like Google Apps. CloudLock provides key data management issues such as the following:

- Data inventory: How many information assets exist and what are their types?
- Which information assets are shared with the public or over the Internet?
- Who has access to what information asset and what information asset is accessible to whom?

Using CloudLock, Panama City was able to notify data owners of policy violations or exposed documents containing potentially sensitive information; change or revoke excessive privilege; and audit permissions changes. Furthermore, the city's IT manager was able to designate department leaders to manage their respective organizational unit's data policies and usage by giving them access to the CloudLock application.

Concern 5: The Regulatory and Legal Environment

There are numerous legal and regulatory barriers to cloud computing, many of which involve data access and transport. For example, the European Union prohibits consumer data from being transferred to nonmember countries without the consumers' prior consent and approval. Companies located outside the European Union can overcome this restriction by demonstrating that they provide a "safe harbor" for the data. Some countries, such as Germany, have enacted even more restrictive data export laws. Cloud computing vendors are aware of these regulations and laws, and they are working to modify their offerings so that they can assure customers and regulators that data entrusted to them are secure enough to meet all of these requirements.

To obtain compliance with regulations such as the Federal Information Security Management Act (FISMA), the Health Insurance Portability and Accountability Act (HIPAA), and the Sarbanes–Oxley Act in the United States, the Data Protection Directive in the European Union, and the credit card industry's Payment Card Industry's Data Security Standard (PCI DSS), cloud computing customers may have to adopt hybrid deployment modes that are typically more expensive and may offer restricted benefits. This process is how, for example, Google is able to "manage and meet additional government policy requirements beyond FISMA," and Rackspace (**www.rackspace.com**) is able to claim PCI compliance. FISMA requires each federal agency to develop, document, and implement a program to provide information security for the information and information systems that support the operations of the agency, including those provided by contractors. PCI DSS is a set of requirements designed to ensure that all companies that process, store, or transmit credit card information maintain a secure environment.

Concern 6: Criminal Use of Cloud Computing

Cloud computing makes available a well-managed, generally reliable, scalable global infrastructure that is, unfortunately, as well suited to illegal computing activities as it is to legitimate business activities. We look here at a number of possible illegal activities.

The huge amount of information stored in the cloud makes it an attractive target for data thieves. Also, the distributed nature of cloud computing makes it very difficult to catch criminals.

Cloud computing makes immense processing power available to anyone. Criminals using cloud computing have access to encryption technology and anonymous communication channels that make it difficult for authorities to detect their activities. When law enforcement pursues criminals, the wrongdoers can rapidly shut down computing resources in the cloud, thus greatly decreasing the chances that there will be any clues left for forensic analysis. When criminals no longer need a machine and shut it down, other clients of cloud vendors immediately reuse the storage and computational capacity allocated to that machine. Therefore, the criminal information is overwritten by data from legitimate customers. It is nearly impossible to recover any data after the machine has been *de-provisioned*.

Criminals are registering for an account (with assumed names and stolen credit cards, of course) with a cloud vendor and "legitimately" using services for illegal purposes. For example, criminals are using Gmail or the text-sharing website Pastebin (**www.pastebin.com**) to plan crimes and share stolen information. Another example is that criminals use cloud computing in brute-force password cracking (see Chapter 4). Although such uses are prohibited by most company's terms-of-service agreements, policing the cloud is expensive and not very rewarding for cloud providers.

Many cloud vendors offer geographical diversity—that is, virtual machines that are located in different physical locations around the world. Criminals can use this feature in transnational attacks. Such attacks place political and technical obstacles in the way of authorities seeking to trace a cyberattack back to its source.

Another weakness exploited by criminals arises from the Web-based applications, or SaaS offerings, provided by cloud vendors. With millions of users commingling on tens of thousands of servers, a criminal can easily mix in among legitimate users.

Even more complicated for authorities and victims, cyberattacks can originate within cloud programs that we use and trust. For example, researchers at the security firm F-Secure reported that they had detected several phishing sites hosted within Google Docs. What made the attacks possible is a feature within Google's spreadsheet system that lets users create Web-based forms, with titles such as "Webmail Account Upgrade" and "Report a Bug." These forms, located on a Google server, were authenticated with Google's encryption certificate. Significantly, they requested sensitive information such as the user's full name, username, Google password, and so on, according to the F-Secure researchers.

Before you go on . . .

1. Discuss the various risks of cloud computing.
2. In your opinion, which risk is the greatest? Support your answer.

TG 3.7 Web Services and Service-Oriented Architecture

Author Lecture Videos are available exclusively in *WileyPLUS.*
Apply the Concept activities are available in the Appendix and in *WileyPLUS.*

Thus far, we have explained how cloud computing can deliver a variety of functionality to users in the form of services (think IaaS, PaaS, and SaaS). We conclude by examining Web services and service-oriented architecture.

Web services are applications delivered over the Internet (the cloud) that MIS professionals can select and combine through almost any device, from personal computers to mobile phones. By using a set of shared standards, or protocols, these applications permit different systems to "talk" with one another—that is, to share data and services—without requiring human beings to translate the conversations. Web services have enormous potential because they can be employed in a variety of environments: over the Internet, on an intranet inside a corporate firewall, or on an extranet set up by business partners. They can also perform a wide variety of tasks, from automating business processes to integrating components of an enterprisewide system to streamlining online buying and selling.

Web services provide numerous benefits for organizations:

- The organization can use the existing Internet infrastructure without having to implement any new technologies.
- Organizational personnel can access remote or local data without having to understand the complexities of this process.
- The organization can create new applications quickly and easily.

The collection of Web services that are used to build a firm's IT applications constitutes a **service-oriented architecture**. Businesses accomplish their processes by executing a series of these services. One of the major benefits of Web services is that they can be reused across an organization in other applications. For example, a Web service that checks a consumer's credit could be used with a service that processes a mortgage application or a credit card application.

Web services are based on four key protocols: XML, SOAP, WSDL, and UDDI. **Extensible markup language (XML)** is a computer language that makes it easier to exchange data among a variety of applications and to validate and interpret these data. XML is a more powerful and flexible markup language than **hypertext markup language (HTML)**. HTML is a page-description language for specifying how text, graphics, video, and sound are placed on a Web page document. HTML was originally designed to create and link static documents composed primarily of text (**Figure TG 3.5**). Today, however, the Web is much more social and interactive, and many Web pages have multimedia elements, such as images, audio, and video. To integrate these rich media into Web pages, users had to rely on third-party plug-in applications such as Flash, Silverlight, and Java. Unfortunately for users, these add-ons require both additional programming and extensive computer processing.

The next evolution of HTML, called **HTML5**, solves this problem by enabling users to embed images, audio, and video directly into a document without the add-ons. HTML5 also makes it easier for Web pages to function across different display devices, including mobile devices and desktops. HTML5 also supports offline data storage for apps that run over the Web. Web pages will execute more quickly, and they will resemble smartphone apps. HTML5 is used in a number of Internet platforms, including Apple's Safari browser, Google Chrome, and the Firefox browser. Google's Gmail and Google Reader also use HTML5. Websites listed as "iPad ready" are using HTML5 extensively. Examples of such sites are CNN, the *New York Times,* and CBS.

Where HTML is limited to describing how data should be presented in the form of Web pages, XML can present, communicate, and store data. For example, in XML, a number is not simply a number. The XML tag also specifies whether the number represents a price, a date,

(a) html

```
<!DOCTYPE HTML PUBLIC "-//W3C//DTD XHTML 1.0 Transitional//EN" http://www.wiley.com/college/gisslen/0470179961/video/video111
<html xmlns="http://www.wiley.com/college/rainer/0470179061/video/video111.html"><head>
<meta http-equiv="content-Type" content="text/html; charset=ISO-8859-1">
<title>CSS Text Wrapper</title>
<link type="text/css" rel="stylesheet" href="css/stylesheet.css">
</head><body id="examples">

<div id="container">
        <div class="wrapper">
                <div class="ex">
                        <script type="text/javascript">shapewrapp
er("15","7.5,141,145|22.5,89,89|37.5,68,69|52.5,46,50|67.5,3
height: 15px; width: 39px;"></div><div style="float: left; clear: left; height: 15px; width: 27px;"></div><div style="float:
15px; width: 4px;"></div><div style="float: left; clear: left; height: 15px; width: 6px;"></div><div style="float:
right; cle
width: 43px;"></div><div style="float: left; clear: left; height: 15px; width: 57px;"></div><div style="float: right; clear:
                        <span style="font-size: 13px;" class=c">
```

(b) XML

```
<feature numbered="no" xml:id="c08-fea-0001">
    <titleGroup>
        <title type="featureName">OPENING CASE</title>
        <title type="main">Tiger Tans and Gifts</title>
    </titleGroup>
    <section xml:id="c08-sec-0002">
        <p>
            <blockFixed onlyChannels="print" type="graphic">
                <mediaResource alt="p0310" copyright="John Wiley &amp; Sons, Inc." eRights="yes"
                    href="urn:x-wiley:9781118443590:media:rainer9781118443590c08:p0310" pRights="yes"/>
            </blockFixed>
            Lisa Keiling owns & tanning salon in Wedowee, Alabama, that does very well from January to May....
        </p>
    </section>
</feature>
```

FIGURE TG 3.5 (a) Screenshot of an HTML wrapper. This wrapper gives instructions on how to open a video associated with this book. (b) Example of XML tagging.

or a zip code. Consider this example of XML, which identifies the contact information for Jane Smith:

```
<contact-info>

<name>Jane Smith</name>

<company>AT&T</company>

<phone>(212) 555-4567</phone>

</contact-info>
```

Simple object access protocol (SOAP) is a set of rules that define how messages can be exchanged among different network systems and applications through the use of XML. These rules essentially establish a common protocol that allows different Web services to interoperate. For example, Visual Basic clients can use SOAP to access a Java server. SOAP runs on all hardware and software systems.

The *Web services description language (WSDL)* is used to create the XML document that describes the tasks performed by the various Web services. Tools such as VisualStudio.Net automate the process of accessing the WSDL, reading it, and coding the application to reference the specific Web service.

Universal description, discovery, and integration (UDDI) allows MIS professionals to search for needed Web services by creating public or private searchable directories of these services. In other words, UDDI is the registry of descriptions of Web services.

Examples of Web services abound. As one example, the Food and Nutrition Service (FNS) within the U.S. Department of Agriculture (USDA) uses Amazon Web Services successfully. The FNS administers the department's nutrition assistance programs. Its mission is to provide children and needy families with improved access to food and a healthier diet through its food assistance programs and comprehensive nutrition education efforts.

The Supplemental Nutrition Assistance Program, or SNAP, is the cornerstone of the USDA's nutrition assistance mission. More than 47 million people—most of them children—receive SNAP benefits each month. To help recipients, in 2010, the FNS created a Web application called the SNAP Retail Locator. Faced with limited budget and time to implement the solution, the FNS selected Amazon Web Services to host the application. As its name suggests, the SNAP Retail Locator, which receives 30,000 visitors each month, helps SNAP recipients find the closest SNAP-authorized store and also provides driving directions to the store. The application has been available 100 percent of the time since it was launched. By employing Amazon, the FNS also saved 90 percent of the cost it would have incurred had it hosted the application on-premises.

Before you go on . . .

1. What are Web services?
2. What is a service-oriented architecture?

What's in **IT** for me?

For All Business Majors

As with hardware (see Technology Guide 1), the design of enterprise IT architectures has profound impacts for businesspeople. Personal and organizational success can depend on an understanding of cloud computing and a commitment to knowing the opportunities and challenges they will bring.

At the organizational level, cloud computing has the potential to make the organization function more efficiently and effectively, while saving the organization money. Web services and SOA make the organization more flexible when deploying new IT applications.

At the individual level, you might use cloud computing yourself if you start your own business. Remember that cloud computing provides start-up companies with world-class IT capabilities at a very low cost.

Summary

TG3.1 Describe the problems that modern information technology departments face.

Traditional IT departments (on-premise computing) face many problems:

- They spend huge amounts on IT infrastructure and expert staffs to build and maintain complex IT systems. These expenses include software licenses, hardware, and staff training and salaries.
- They must manage an infrastructure that is not often used to its full capacity.
- They spend the majority of their budgets on maintaining existing IT infrastructure, with the remainder being spent on developing new systems.
- They have difficulty capturing, storing, managing, and analyzing all these data.
- They can actually inhibit an organization's ability to respond quickly and appropriately to rapidly changing dynamic environments.
- They are expensive.

TG3.2 Describe the key characteristics and advantages of cloud computing.

Cloud computing is a type of computing that delivers convenient, on-demand, pay-as-you-go access for multiple customers to a shared pool of configurable computing resources (e.g., servers, networks, storage, applications, and services) that can be rapidly and easily accessed over the Internet. The essential *characteristics* of cloud computing include the following:

- Cloud computing provides on-demand self-service.
- Cloud computing includes the characteristics of grid computing.
- Cloud computing includes the characteristics of utility computing.
- Cloud computing uses broad network access.
- Cloud computing pools computing resources.
- Cloud computing typically occurs on virtualized servers.

TG3.3 Describe each of the four types of clouds.

Public clouds are shared, easily accessible, multi-customer IT infrastructures that are available nonexclusively to any entity in the public (individuals, groups, and organizations). *Private clouds* (also known as *internal clouds* or *corporate clouds*) are IT infrastructures that are accessible only by a single entity, or by an exclusive group of related entities that share the same purpose and requirements, such as all the business units within a single organization. *Hybrid clouds* are composed of public and private clouds that remain unique entities but are bound together, offering the benefits of multiple deployment models. *Vertical clouds* serve specific industries.

TG3.4 Explain the operational model of each of the three types of cloud services.

With the *infrastructure-as-a-service* model, cloud computing providers offer remotely accessible servers, networks, and storage capacity. In the *platform-as-a-service* model, customers rent servers, operating systems, storage, a database, software development technologies such as Java and.NET, and network capacity over the Internet. With the *software-as-a-service* delivery model, cloud computing vendors provide software that is specific to their customers' requirements.

TG3.5 Identify the key benefits of cloud computing.

The benefits of cloud computing include making individuals more productive; facilitating collaboration; mining insights from data; developing and hosting applications; cost flexibility; business scalability; improved usage of hardware; market adaptability; and product and service customization.

TG3.6 Discuss the concerns and risks associated with cloud computing.

Cloud computing does raise concerns and has risks, which include "legacy spaghetti," cost, reliability, privacy, security, and the regulatory and legal environment.

TG3.7 Explain the role of Web services in building a firm's IT applications, and provide examples.

Web services are applications delivered over the Internet that MIS professionals can select and combine through almost any device, from personal computers to mobile phones. A *service-oriented architecture* makes it possible for MIS professionals to construct business applications using Web services.

Technology Guide Glossary

cloud computing A technology in which tasks are performed by computers physically removed from the user and accessed over a network, in particular the Internet.

extensible markup language (XML) A computer language that makes it easier to exchange data among a variety of applications and to validate and interpret these data.

grid computing A technology that applies the unused processing resources of many geographically dispersed computers in a network to form a virtual supercomputer.

HTML5 A page-description language that makes it possible to embed images, audio, and video directly into a document without add-ons. Also makes it easier for Web pages to function across different display devices, including mobile devices as well as desktops. It supports the storage of data offline.

hybrid clouds Clouds composed of public and private clouds that remain unique entities but are bound together, offering the benefits of multiple deployment models.

hypertext markup language (HTML) A page-description language for specifying how text, graphics, video, and sound are placed on a Web page document.

infrastructure-as-a-service (IaaS) A model with which cloud computing providers offer remotely accessible servers, networks, and storage capacity.

on-premise computing A model of IT management in which companies own their IT infrastructure (their software, hardware, networks, and data management) and maintain it in their data centers.

platform-as-a-service (PaaS) A model in which customers rent servers, operating systems, storage, a database, software development technologies such as Java and .NET, and network capacity over the Internet.

private clouds (also known *as internal clouds or corporate clouds*) IT infrastructures that are accessible only by a single entity or by an exclusive group of related entities that share the same purpose and requirements, such as all the business units within a single organization.

public clouds Shared, easily accessible, multi-customer IT infrastructures that are available nonexclusively to any entity in the general public (individuals, groups, and organizations).

server farms Massive data centers, which may contain hundreds of thousands of networked computer servers.

server virtualization A technology that uses software-based partitions to create multiple virtual servers (called *virtual machines*) on a single physical server.

service-oriented architecture An IT architecture that makes it possible to construct business applications using Web services.

software-as-a-service (SaaS) A delivery model in which cloud computing vendors provide software that is specific to their customers' requirements.

utility computing A technology whereby a service provider makes computing resources and infrastructure management available to a customer as needed.

Web services Applications delivered over the Internet that IT developers can select and combine through almost any device, from personal computers to mobile phones.

Discussion Questions

1. What is the value of server farms and virtualization to any large organization?

2. If you were the chief information officer of a firm, how would you explain the workings, benefits, and limitations of cloud computing?

3. What is the value of cloud computing to a small organization?

4. What is the value of cloud computing to an entrepreneur who is starting a business?

Problem-Solving Activities

1. Investigate the status of cloud computing by researching the offerings of the following leading vendors: Dell (**www.dell.com**), Oracle (**www. oracle.com**), IBM (**www.ibm.com**), Amazon (**www.amazon.com**), Microsoft (**www.microsoft.com**), and Google (**www.google.com**). Note any inhibitors to cloud computing.

Artificial Intelligence

TECHNOLOGY GUIDE OUTLINE	LEARNING OBJECTIVES
TG 4.1 Introduction to Artificial Intelligence	**TG 4.1** Explain the potential value and the potential limitations of artificial intelligence.
TG 4.2 Artificial Intelligence Technologies	**TG 4.2** Provide use case examples of expert systems, machine learning systems, deep learning systems, and neural networks.
TG 4.3 Artificial Intelligence Applications	**TG 4.3** Provide use case examples of computer vision, natural language processing, robotics, image recognition, and intelligent agents.

TG 4.1 Introduction to Artificial Intelligence

Artificial intelligence (AI) is a subfield of computer science that studies the thought processes of humans and re-creates the effects of those processes through information systems. We define **artificial intelligence** as the theory and development of information systems able to perform tasks that normally require human intelligence—that is, we define AI in terms of the tasks that humans perform, rather than how humans think.

This definition raises this question: "What is *intelligent behavior*?" The following capabilities are considered to be signs of intelligence: learning or understanding from experience, making sense of ambiguous or contradictory messages, and responding quickly and successfully to new situations.

The ultimate goal of AI is to build machines that mimic human intelligence. A widely used test to determine whether a computer exhibits intelligent behavior was designed by Alan Turing, a British AI pioneer. The *Turing test* proposes a scenario in which a man and a computer both pretend to be women or men, and a human interviewer has to identify which is the real human. Based on this standard, the intelligent systems exemplified in commercial AI products are far from exhibiting any significant intelligence.

We can better understand the potential value of AI by contrasting it with *natural (human) intelligence*. AI has several important commercial advantages over natural intelligence, but it also displays some limitations, as outlined in **Table TG 4.1.**

It is important to distinguish between strong artificial intelligence and weak artificial intelligence. **Strong AI** is *hypothetical* artificial intelligence that matches or exceeds human intelligence—the intelligence of a machine that could successfully perform any intellectual task that a human being can. Strong AI, therefore, could be considered to have consciousness

Author Lecture Videos are available exclusively in *WileyPLUS*.
Apply the Concept activities are available in the Appendix and in *WileyPLUS*.

TABLE TG 4.1	Comparison of the Capabilities of Natural Intelligence versus Artificial Intelligence	
Capabilities	**Natural Intelligence**	**Artificial Intelligence**
Preservation of knowledge	Perishable from an organizational point of view	Permanent
Duplication and dissemination of knowledge in a computer	Difficult, expensive, takes time	Easy, fast, and inexpensive
Total cost of knowledge	Can be erratic and inconsistent, incomplete at times	Consistent and thorough
Documentation of process and knowledge	Difficult, expensive	Fairly easy, inexpensive
Creativity	Can be very high	Low, uninspired
Use of sensory experiences	Direct and rich in possibilities	Must be interpreted first; limited
Recognizing patterns and relationships	Fast, easy to explain	Machine learning still not as good as people in most cases, but in some cases better than people
Reasoning	Making use of wide context of experiences	Good only in narrow, focused, and stable domains

or sentience. **Weak AI** (also called **narrow AI**) performs a useful and specific function that once required human intelligence to perform, and does so at human levels or better (for example, character recognition, speech recognition, machine vision, robotics, data mining, medical informatics, automated investing, and many other functions).

Today, systems that are labeled "artificial intelligence" are weak AI. Weak AI is already powerful enough to make a dramatic difference in human life. Weak AI applications enhance human endeavors by complementing what people can do. For example, when you call your bank and talk to an automated voice, you are probably talking to a weak AI program. Researchers at universities and companies around the world are building weak AI applications that are rapidly becoming more capable.

Consider chess, which weak AI systems now play better than any human. In 1997, IBM's Deep Blue system beat the world chess champion (Garry Kasparov) for the first time. Since that time, chess-playing systems have become significantly more powerful. However, the way these systems play chess has not changed. They search through all possible future moves to find the best move to make next.

Today, however, the best players in the world are not machines, but what Garry Kasparov, a grandmaster, calls "centaurs." Centaurs are teams of humans and chess-playing programs. In freestyle chess matches, competitors can play unassisted as humans, unassisted as chess-playing programs, or as centaurs. In the Freestyle Battle of 2014, pure chess-playing AI software won 42 games, while centaurs won 53 games.

In an interview in May 2018, Kasparov compared chess-playing entities (i.e., humans and software) using Elo ratings, which are scores that reflect the skill of chess players:

- Kasparov stated that his own highest Elo rating was 2,851.
- Magnus Carlsen, the world human chess champion in 2018, had an Elo rating of 2882.
- IBM's Deep Blue's Elo rating was above 2,700.
- Alphabet's (parent company of Google) DeepMind's AlphaZero had an Elo score of 3,600.

Interestingly, the advent of AI did not diminish the performance of purely human chess players—quite the opposite. Cheap, highly functional chess programs have inspired more people than ever to play chess and the players have become better than ever. In fact, today there are more than twice as many grandmasters as there were when Deep Blue beat Kasparov.

Similar to centaurs, physicians who are supported by AI will have an enhanced ability to spot cancer in medical images; speech recognition algorithms running on smartphones will bring the Internet to many millions of illiterate people in developing countries; digital assistants will suggest promising hypotheses for academic research; and image classification algorithms will allow wearable computers to layer useful digital information onto people's views of the real, physical world.

Weak AI does present challenges. For example, consider the power that AI brings to national security agencies, in both autocracies and democracies. The capacity to monitor billions of conversations and to pick out every citizen from the crowd by his or her voice or face poses serious threats to liberty. Also, many individuals could potentially lose their jobs as a result of advances in AI.

Several technological advancements have led to advancements in artificial intelligence. We take a brief look at each of them here.

- *Advancements in chip technology:* AI systems employ graphics processing units (called GPU chips). These chips were developed to meet the visual and parallel processing demands of video games. In fact, GPU chips facilitate parallel processing in neural networks, which are the primary information architecture of AI software. (We discuss neural networks later in this Technology Guide.)

- *Big Data:* As we discussed in Chapter 5, Big Data consists of diverse, high-volume, high-velocity information assets that require new types of processing to enable enhanced decision making, insight discovery, and process optimization. Big Data is now being used to train *deep learning* software. (We discuss deep learning later in this Technology Guide.)

- *The Internet and cloud computing:* The Internet (discussed in Chapter 6) and cloud computing (discussed in Technology Guide 3) make Big Data available to AI systems, specifically neural networks, and provide the computational capacity needed for AI systems.

- *Improved algorithms:* An **algorithm** is a problem-solving method expressed as a finite sequence of steps. Researchers are rapidly improving the capabilities of AI algorithms. AI algorithms also run much faster on GPU chips.

These technological advancements underlie four stages of artificial intelligence. Each stage of AI uses the AI technologies and the AI applications that we discuss in the next two sections of this guide.

First-stage AI applications consist mainly of recommendation systems. These systems learn from vast amounts of data to personalize online content for each of us. For example, consider Amazon's product recommendations and the "Up Next" YouTube video recommendations.

Second-stage AI applications analyze the data that traditional companies have collected and labeled in the past. For example, banks have issued loans and recorded successful and unsuccessful repayments. Hospitals archive diagnoses, imaging data, and subsequent health outcomes. Courts have recorded conviction history, recidivism (the tendency of convicted criminals to reoffend) rates, and flight rates. When these AI applications are applied to banking, medicine, and our legal system, loan default rates decrease, health outcomes improve, and recidivism and flight risks diminish.

In addition to the data analyzed by second-stage AI applications, *third-stage AI applications* analyze additional data from smart devices and sensors (see the Internet of Things in Chapter 8). These sensor-enabled smart devices transform physical-only entities into physical/digital entities. For example, consider hospitals, cars, schools, and many others.

For example, you walk into a grocery store, the store software scans your face, and shows you a list of your most common purchases. You then pick up your virtual assistant shopping cart. The cart adjusts your usual grocery list with voice input, reminds you to buy a card for your wife's birthday, and then guides you through the store.

Fourth-stage AI applications integrate the three previous stages and enable machines to sense and respond to the world around them. For example, swarms of drones selectively spray and harvest entire farms with computer vision and high levels of dexterity, heat-resistant drones put out forest fires more efficiently, and autonomous vehicles navigate roads and traffic.

Before you go on . . .

1. What is artificial intelligence?
2. Differentiate between artificial and human intelligence.
3. Differentiate between strong AI and weak AI.
4. Describe the four stages of AI applications.

TG 4.2 | Artificial Intelligence Technologies

A variety of technologies have been developed in the field of artificial intelligence. In this section, we begin our discussion with expert systems, one of the earliest AI technologies. We continue with two technologies that have relatively recently revolutionized the field of artificial intelligence: machine learning and deep learning. We then discuss neural networks that are essential to machine learning and deep learning.

Expert Systems

Expert systems (ESs) are computer systems that attempt to mimic human experts by applying expertise in a specific domain. Expert systems can either *support* decision makers or completely *replace* them.

Essentially, an ES transfers expertise from a domain expert (or other source) to the system. This knowledge is then stored in the system, which users can call on for specific advice as needed. The system can make inferences and arrive at conclusions. Then, like a human expert, it offers advice or recommendations. It can also explain the logic behind the advice. Because ESs can integrate and manipulate enormous amounts of data, they sometimes perform better than any single human expert. On the other hand, expert systems do present problems, which include the following:

- Transferring domain expertise from human experts to the expert system can be difficult because humans cannot always explain *how* they know and what they know. They are often not aware of their complete reasoning process.

- Even if the domain experts can explain their entire reasoning process, automating that process may not be possible. The process might be either too complex or too vague, or it might require too many rules. Essentially, it is very difficult to program all the possible decision paths in an expert system.

- In some contexts, there is a potential liability from the use of expert systems. Humans make errors occasionally, but they are generally "let off the hook" if they took reasonable care and applied generally accepted methods. An organization that uses an expert system, however, may lack this legal protection if problems arise later. The usual example of this issue is medical treatment, but it can also arise if a business decision driven by an expert system harms someone financially.

For example, in the case of medical treatment, consider a physician who consults with a medical expert system when treating a patient. If the patient's care goes poorly, then the question arises, who is liable? The physician? The expert system? The vendor of the expert system?

A large number of expert systems have been developed, such as MYCIN and PROSPECTOR. MYCIN was designed to identify bacteria causing infections and suggest appropriate antibiotics. PROSPECTOR was designed to help geologists in mineral exploration.

New developments in the field of artificial intelligence now largely take place in the areas of machine learning and deep learning. We turn our attention to these two technologies and then discuss how neural networks enable each technology.

Machine Learning

Machine learning develops algorithms that can learn from and make predictions about data. These algorithms operate by building a model from example inputs in order to make data-driven predictions or decisions, rather than following explicit instructions in a computer program. Therefore, we can say that **machine learning (ML)** is the ability to accurately perform new, unseen tasks, built on known properties learned from training or historical data that are labeled.

Machine learning systems have the ability to improve their performance by exposure to data without the need to follow explicitly programmed instructions. Essentially, machine learning automatically discovers patterns in data. Once discovered, the pattern can be used to make predictions. For example, presented with data about credit card transactions, including date, time, merchant, merchant location, price, and whether the transaction was legitimate or fraudulent, a machine learning system learns patterns that are predictive of fraud. The more transaction data the system processes, the better are the predictions expected from them.

For example, an ML system can be trained on e-mail messages to learn to distinguish between spam and nonspam messages. After learning, the system can then be used to classify new e-mail messages into spam and nonspam folders. The following are other examples of machine learning:

- **FIN** In banking, automated fraud detection systems use machine learning to identify behavior patterns that could indicate fraudulent payment activity.

- In the life sciences, ML systems are used to predict cause-and-effect relationships from biological data and the activities of compounds, helping pharmaceutical companies identify promising drugs.

- **POM** In the oil and gas industry, producers use machine learning in many applications, from locating mineral deposits to diagnosing mechanical problems with drilling equipment.

- **MKT** Retailers use machine learning to discover attractive cross-sell offers and effective promotions.

- **MIS** In 2014, Google announced that it had just completed mapping the exact location of every business, every household, and every street number in all of France. The process took Google one hour. How? The company used its street-view database containing hundreds of millions of images. Humans manually examined a few hundred of the images and circled the street numbers in them. Then Google fed those labeled images into a machine-learning algorithm that figured out what was unique about the circled objects. The software then looked for that type of object in the remainder of the images and read the numbers that it found.

- **MIS** Real estate broker REX Real Estate Exchange (**www.rexhomes.com/**) uses machine learning instead of real estate agents to sell homes. REX software analyzes over 100,000 data points to find likely buyers for a home and then targets them with digital ads. REX also uses robots at open houses to answer questions. The company charges a 2 percent commission rather than the 5–6 percent commission that real estate agents charge.

- **MKT** Retailers use machine learning to analyze customer sentiments (e.g., likes and dislikes) across various social media platforms and match customer profiles to their social experiences regarding a particular product. ML systems can therefore recommend products in real time, even as the customer shops.

- **MKT** Retailers use machine learning in *visual search*. Brands upload images of products in their inventory. When customers upload a picture of a product they like, ML software evaluates the picture for aspects such as brand, color, size, and other variables. The software then makes suggestions in real time on additional brands or products.

- **MKT** Chinese news aggregation app Toutiao (**www.toutiao.com**) uses machine learning to figure out users' interests and tastes and tailors its offerings accordingly to gain more users and more clicks. As users visit the website, the ML software gains knowledge and refines its recommendations. Toutiao is very successful, with over 80 million daily active users in 2018.

Deep Learning

Deep learning is a subset of machine learning in which the system discovers new patterns without being exposed to labeled historical or training data. Example applications of deep learning include speech recognition, image recognition, natural language processing, drug discovery and toxicology, and customer relationship management. Let's look at specific examples of deep learning.

- In June 2012, a Google deep learning system that had been shown 10 million images from YouTube videos correctly identified cats, human faces, yellow flowers, and other objects 16 percent of the time. The system identified these discrete objects even though no humans had ever defined or labeled them. The accuracy of the neural network was 70 percent better than any previous method.

- **MKT** **POM** eBay is using deep learning to categorize products in images posted by sellers. By studying images that have already been tagged, the system can tell the difference, for example, between a pair of flip-flops and a pair of flats. This process is helping eBay's search engine, particularly for products that have not been tagged very accurately.

- **MKT** **POM** Facebook is using deep learning to help filter the posts and ads that its users see. Specifically, Facebook applies deep learning to improve its users' news feeds, the personalized list of recent updates that Facebook calls its "killer app." The company already uses conventional machine learning techniques to manage the 1,500 updates that average Facebook users could potentially see down to 30 to 60 that are judged to be the most likely to be important to them. Facebook needs to become more effective at picking the best updates because of the growing volume of data that its users generate.

- **MIS** Deep learning has improved voice search on smartphones. Because the multiple layers of neurons in a neural network (discussed next) allow for more precise training on the many variants of a sound, the system can recognize sounds more reliably, especially in noisy environments, such as offices with high levels of background conversations or subway platforms. Because the system is more likely to understand what the user actually said, it is more likely to return more accurate results.

- At CERN, the world's largest particle physics laboratory, deep learning algorithms are more accurate at identifying subatomic particles than the software written by physicists.

- A team of researchers won a contest sponsored by Merck to identify molecules that could lead to new drugs. The group used deep learning to find molecules that would most likely bind to their targets.

- **FIN** A major U.S. insurance company is using deep learning to identify fraudulent claims.

Neural Networks

A **neural network** is a set of virtual neurons or central processing units (CPUs) that work in parallel in an attempt to simulate the way the human brain works, although in a greatly simplified form. The neural network assigns numerical values, or weights, to connections between the neurons.

Because of improvements in algorithms and increasingly powerful computer chips and storage, deep learning researchers are able to model many more layers of virtual neurons in neural networks than previously. Current neural networks are able to simulate billions of neurons. Let's look at how neural networks process an image and a sound.

Each layer of the neural network manages a different level of abstraction. To process an image, for example, the first layer is fed with raw images. That layer notes aspects of the images such as the brightness and colors of individual pixels, and how those properties are distributed across the image. The next layer analyzes the first layer's observations into more abstract categories, such as identifying edges, shadows, and so on. The next layer analyzes those edges and shadows, looking for combinations that signify features such as eyes, lips, and ears. The final layer combines these observations into a representation of a face.

To process a sound, the first layer of processors learns the smallest unit of speech sound, called a phoneme. The next layer finds combinations of sound waves that occur more often than they would by chance alone. The next layer looks for combinations of speech sounds such as words, and the final layer can recognize complete segments of speech.

Programmers train neural networks to detect an object or a sound by feeding the network with digitized images containing those objects or sounds containing those phonemes. If the neural network does not accurately recognize a particular object or sound, then an algorithm adjusts the weights or the strength of the connection between processors. The goal of the training is to teach the network to consistently recognize the patterns in sets of images or patterns in speech that humans know as, for example, image of a dog or the phoneme "d."

For a neural network to learn facial recognition, it will be presented with a "training set" of millions of images. Some will contain faces and some will not. Each image will be labeled by a human, for example, through Amazon's Mechanical Turk. The images act as inputs to the neural network and the labels ("face" or "not face") are the outputs. The network's task is to develop a statistical rule (operationalized through the weights between processors) that correlates inputs with correct outputs.

To accomplish this task, the network will search for those features that are common to the images showing faces. Once these correlations are strong enough (i.e., the weights, or strength of the connections between processors, are high enough) the network will be able to reliably differentiate faces from not-faces in its training set. The next step is to feed the neural network with a fresh set of unlabeled images to see if the facial recognition algorithms that the network has developed actually work with the new data.

Consider this example. In 2015, Matthew Lai created an artificial intelligence system called Giraffe that taught itself to play chess by evaluating positions much more like humans and in an entirely different way from conventional chess-playing programs. Giraffe's level of play is in the top 2 percent of all tournament chess players.

Lai's system uses a neural network that examines each position on the chessboard through three different analyses. The first analysis examines the global state of the game, such as the number and type of pieces on each side, which side is to move next, and other rules of the game. The second analysis examines piece-centric features such as the location of each piece on each side. The third analysis assesses the potential squares that each piece can attack and defend. That is, Giraffe derives its strength not from being able to see far ahead, but from being able to accurately evaluate tricky positions and understand complicated positional concepts that are intuitive to humans.

To train his system, Lai randomly chose 5 million positions from a database of computer chess games. He then created greater variety by adding a random legal move to each position before using it to train his neural network. In total, he generated 175 million positions in this manner.

Lai then had Giraffe play against itself with the goal of improving its prediction of its own future position. In this way, Giraffe learned which positions were strong and which were weak.

Before you go on . . .

1. Define expert systems and describe some problems that expert systems have.
2. Differentiate between machine learning and deep learning.
3. Describe how neural networks function.

TG 4.3   Artificial Intelligence Applications

The field of artificial intelligence has many applications. Note that these applications use machine learning, deep learning, and neural networks. In this section, we discuss computer vision, natural language processing, robotics, speech recognition, and intelligent agents.

Author Lecture Videos are available exclusively in *WileyPLUS*.
Apply the Concept activities are available in the Appendix and in *WileyPLUS*.

Computer Vision

Computer vision refers to the ability of information systems to identify objects, scenes, and activities in images. Computer vision applications are designed to operate in unconstrained environments. Computer vision has diverse applications:

- Medical imaging to improve prediction, diagnosis, and treatment of diseases:

    To the human eye, an X-ray is an unclear puzzle. But to an AI system, an X-ray—or a CT scan or MRI scan—is a data field that can be assessed down to the pixel level. Images are estimated to make up as much as 90 percent of all medical data today. Image recognition software gathers high-resolution image data from multiple sources—X-rays, MRI scans, ultrasounds, CT scans—and then groups together biological structures that share hard-to-detect similarities. For example, the software can examine several images of the same breast to measure tissue density. The software then color-codes tissues of similar densities so that humans can observe the pattern as well. The software finds and indexes pixels that share certain properties, even pixels that are far apart in one image or in a different image altogether. This process enables medical personnel to identify hidden features of diffuse structures.

    In 2015, IBM purchased Merge Healthcare for $1 billion. Merge specializes in handling all kinds of medical images, and its service is used by more than 7,500 hospitals and clinics in the United States, as well as clinical research organizations and pharmaceutical companies. The acquisition is part of an effort to draw on many data sources, including anonymized, text-based medical records, to help physicians make treatment decisions. Merge's data set contains some 30 billion images, which will be used to train the deep learning aspects of IBM Watson.

    IBM Watson is also being used to detect melanoma, a type of skin cancer. Detecting melanoma is difficult because of the variation in the way that it appears in individual patients. By feeding a deep learning system with many images of melanoma, it is possible to teach the system to recognize very subtle but important features associated with the disease.

    POM Enlitic (www.enlitic.com) is a start-up that uses deep learning and image analysis to help physicians make diagnoses and spot abnormalities in medical images. For example, Enlitic software could analyze medical images such as X-rays, MRIs, and CT scans for trends in the data or anomalies in individual images.

- **MIS** Facial recognition used by Facebook to automatically identify people in photographs and in security and surveillance to spot and identify suspects.

    Specifically, Facebook's Moments app uses facial recognition technology to group the photos on your phone, based on when they were taken and to identify which friends are in the photos.

    In 2014, Facebook unveiled an algorithm called DeepFace that can recognize specific human faces in images about 97 percent of the time, even when those faces are poorly lit or partially hidden. This performance is on par for what humans are able to do.

- **MKT** Shopping: Consumers now use smartphones to photograph products and be presented with purchase options.

- Self-driving cars: Computer vision systems can now help drive a car down a street and not hit anything or hurt anyone—that is, the systems are a high-stake exercise in computer vision that involves many different kinds of data in a constantly changing environment.

- **MKT** Pinterest is using a computer vision system combined with deep learning to enhance product recommendations by automatically recognizing specific objects contained within the image of a pin.

- Google Photos app uses computer vision combined with deep learning to automatically recognize, classify, and organize a user's photos.

- **MIS** Google and Microsoft Research are using computer vision combined with deep learning to improve object detection, classification, and labeling. For example, one computer vision system automatically summarizes a complex scene in a photo and generates captions that accurately describe the scene.

- **POM** Microsoft's Traffic Prediction Project uses Bing traffic maps, road cameras, sensors, and other data sources to predict traffic jams.

Natural Language Processing

Natural language processing refers to the ability of information systems to work with text the way that humans do. For example,, these systems can extract the meaning from text and can generate text that is readable, stylistically natural, and grammatically correct.

Because context is critically important, the practical applications of natural language processing typically address relatively narrow areas such as analyzing customer feedback about a particular product or service, automating discovery in civil litigation or government investigations (e-discovery), and automating writing of formulaic stories on topics such as corporate earnings or sports. Two other examples are as follows:

- IBM's Watson uses natural language processing to read and understand the vast amount of medical literature, hypothesis generation techniques to automate diagnosis, and machine learning to improve its accuracy.
- Built into Google's translation app, deep learning technology has the ability to translate printed text such as menus in a live view through your phone's camera. The app can translate among 27 different languages without needing an Internet connection.

Robotics

Integrating computer vision with tiny, high-performance sensors and actuators, a new generation of robots can work alongside people and flexibly perform many different tasks in unpredictable environments. Examples include unmanned aerial vehicles, *cobots* (cooperative robots) that share jobs with humans on the factory floor, robotic vacuum cleaners, and so on. Specifically, recall our discussion of Baxter in Chapter 1.

Speech recognition

Speech recognition focuses on automatically and accurately transcribing human speech. This technology must manage diverse accents, dialects, and background noise. Furthermore, it must distinguish between homophones and work at the speed of natural speech. Applications include medical dictation, hands-free writing, voice control of information systems, and telephone customer service applications.

POM Duncan Regional Hospital in Oklahoma wanted to improve efficiency in its patient care. Approximately 15 physicians at the hospital are improving their clinical documentation on laptops with Dragon speech recognition software from Nuance Communications.

The hospital also uses a secure, HIPAA-compliant messaging platform from Imprivata (**www.imprivata.com**). Instead of sending a text message, physicians speak their message rather than having to stop interacting with a patient. Nurses also use speech recognition software to enter clinical documentation, a critical need as the health care industry requires an increasing amount of documentation to meet HIPAA requirements as well as mandates for meaningful use of electronic health records.

Intelligent Agents

According to Gartner, by the end of 2016, two-thirds of consumers in the developed world were expected to regularly use virtual personal assistants in their daily lives. Virtual assistants are the most basic form of AI—the ability of a system to mimic human intelligence through experience and learning. For example, popular voice-based digital assistants, such as Apple Siri, Microsoft Cortana, Google Now, Amazon Alexa, and Facebook M, can understand our words, analyze our questions, and point us in the general direction of the right answer.

An **intelligent agent** is a software program that assists you, or acts on your behalf, in performing repetitive computer-related tasks. You may be familiar with an early type of intelligent agent—the paper clip (Clippy) that popped up in early versions of Microsoft Word. For example, if your document appeared as though it was going to be a business letter—that is, if you typed in a date, name, and address—the animated paper clip would offer helpful suggestions on how to proceed. Users objected so strenuously to this primitive intelligent agent that Microsoft eliminated it from subsequent versions.

Today, there are many intelligent agents (also called *bots*) used for a wide variety of tasks. The following sections examine three types of agents: information agents, monitoring and surveillance agents, and user or personal agents.

Information Agents.   **Information agents** search for information and display it to users. The best-known information agents are buyer agents. A **buyer agent**, also called a **shopping bot**, helps customers find the products and services they need on a website. There are many examples of information agents. We present a few illustrative cases next:

- **FIN** Companies in the insurance and financial services sector are using IBM Watson, which functions as a customer-facing intelligent advisor. For example, insurance company USAA (www.usaa.com) uses Watson in an application that lets USAA customers who are leaving military service ask questions about, for example, college tuition reimbursement or changes to their health benefits. USAA chose the topic of military separation because approximately 150,000 people separate from military service each year. USAA executives say that the goal of the system is to augment employees' expertise, not to replace them. The system offers better insight and information than the original USAA digital portal offered. Watson helps shorten service calls, offers more context to incoming calls, and reduces the amount of paperwork around customer interactions.

- **FIN** Australian bank ANZ deployed IBM's Watson Engagement Advisor. When a customer asks a financial planner about a company or an investment, the planner relays questions to Watson using natural language, by either speaking or typing. The system then analyzes vast amounts of information—such as annual reports, SEC filings, relevant news stories, and other analysts' views—and produces its own insight on the potential investment.

- **MKT** The information agents for **Amazon.com** display lists of books and other products that customers might like, based on past purchases.

- The Federal Electronic Research and Review Extraction Tool (FERRET) was developed jointly by the Census Bureau and the Bureau of Labor Statistics. You can use FERRET to find information on employment, health care, education, race and ethnicity, health insurance, housing, income and poverty, aging, and marriage and the family.

Monitoring and Surveillance Agents.   **Monitoring and surveillance agents**, also called **predictive agents**, constantly observe and report on some item of interest. There are many examples of predictive agents. Consider the following:

- **MIS** Allstate uses monitoring and surveillance agents to manage its large computer networks 24/7/365. Every five seconds, the agent measures 1,200 data points. It can predict a system crash 45 minutes before it happens. The agent also watches to detect electronic attacks early so that they can be prevented.

- **POM** Monitoring and surveillance agents can watch your competitors and notify you of price changes and special offers.

- Predictive agents can monitor Internet sites, discussion groups, and mailing lists for stock manipulations, insider trading, and rumors that might affect stock prices.

- These agents can search websites for updated information on topics of your choice, such as price changes on desired products (e.g., airline tickets).

User Agents.   **User agents**, also called **personal agents**, take action on your behalf. Let's look at what these agents can do (or will be able to do shortly):

- Check your e-mail, sort it according to your priority rules, and alert you when high-value e-mails appear in your inbox.

- Automatically fill out forms on the Web for you. They will also store your information for future use.

Before you go on . . .

1. Describe the advantages of computer vision, natural language processing, and speech recognition.
2. Describe how you might use intelligent agents, information agents, monitoring and surveillance agents, and user agents.

What's in **IT** for me?

ACCT For the Accounting Major

AI systems are used extensively in auditing to uncover irregularities. They are also used to uncover and prevent fraud. Today's CPAs use AI systems for many of their duties, ranging from risk analysis to cost control. Accounting personnel also use intelligent agents for mundane tasks such as managing accounts and monitoring employees' Internet use.

FIN For the Finance Major

People have been using computers for decades to solve financial problems. Innovative AI systems have been developed for activities such as making stock market decisions, refinancing bonds, assessing debt risks, analyzing financial conditions, predicting business failures, forecasting financial trends, and investing in global markets. AI systems can often facilitate the use of spreadsheets and other computerized systems used in finance. Finally, AI systems can help reduce fraud in credit cards, stocks, and other financial services.

MKT For the Marketing Major

Marketing personnel use AI systems in many applications, from allocating advertising budgets to evaluating alternative routings of salespeople. New marketing approaches such as targeted marketing and marketing transaction databases are heavily dependent on IT in general and on AI systems in particular. AI systems are especially useful for mining customer databases and predicting customer behavior. Successful AI applications appear in almost every area of marketing and sales, from analyzing the success of one-to-one advertising to supporting customer help desks. With customer service becoming increasingly important, the use of intelligent agents is critical for providing fast response.

POM For the Production/Operations Management Major

AI systems support complex operations and production decisions, from inventory to production planning. AI systems in the production/operations management field manage tasks ranging from diagnosing machine failures and prescribing repairs to complex production scheduling and inventory control. Some companies, such as DuPont and Kodak, have deployed hundreds of AI systems in the planning, organizing, and control of their operational systems.

HRM For the Human Resources Management Major

Human resources personnel employ AI systems for many applications. For example, recruiters use these systems to find applicants' resumes on the Web and sort them to match needed skills. HR managers also use AI systems to evaluate candidates (tests, interviews). HR personnel use AI systems to train and support employees in managing their fringe benefits and to predict employee job performance and future labor needs.

MIS For the MIS Major

The MIS function develops (or acquires) and maintains the organization's various AI systems, as well as the data and models that these systems use. MIS staffers also interact often with subject area experts to capture the expertise used in AI systems.

Summary

TG4.1 Explain the potential value and the potential limitations of artificial intelligence.

Table TG 4.1 differentiates between artificial and human intelligence on a number of characteristics.

TG4.2 Provide use case examples of expert systems, machine learning systems, deep learning systems, and neural networks.

Expert systems are computer systems that attempt to mimic human experts by applying expertise in a specific domain.

Machine learning is the ability to accurately perform new, unseen tasks, built on known properties learned from training or historical data that are labeled. Machine learning systems can distinguish between spam and nonspam messages; identify fraudulent banking transactions; help pharmaceutical companies identify promising drugs; and diagnose mechanical problems with drilling equipment.

Deep learning is a subset of machine learning in which the system discovers new patterns without being exposed to labeled historical or training data. Example applications of deep learning include speech recognition, image recognition, and natural language processing.

A *neural network* is a system of programs and data structures that simulate the underlying concepts of the human brain. Neural networks are used to detect weapons concealed in personal belongings, in research on various diseases, for financial forecasting, to detect fraud in credit card transactions, to fight crime, and many other applications.

TG4.3 Provide use case examples of computer vision, natural language processing, robotics, and intelligent agents.

Computer vision refers to the ability of computers to identify objects, scenes, and activities in images. Computer vision has diverse applications, examples of which include medical imaging, facial recognition, and self-driving cars.

Natural language processing refers to the ability of information systems to work with text the way that humans do. Applications of natural language processing include analyzing customer feedback about a particular product or service, automating discovery in civil litigation or government investigations (e-discovery), and automating writing of formulaic stories on topics such as corporate earnings or sports.

Robots integrate computer vision with sensors and actuators. Cooperative robots (called cobots) can work alongside people and flexibly perform many different tasks in unpredictable environments. Examples include unmanned aerial vehicles, "cobots" (cooperative robots) that share jobs with humans on the factory floor, robotic vacuum cleaners, and so on. Specifically, recall our discussion of Baxter in Chapter 1.

Speech recognition focuses on automatically and accurately transcribing human speech. Applications include medical dictation, hands-free writing, voice control of information systems, and telephone customer service applications.

Intelligent agents are software programs that assist you, or act on your behalf, in performing repetitive, computer-related tasks. Intelligent agents are used to display lists of books or other products that customers might like, based on past purchases; to find information; to manage and monitor large computer networks 24/7/365; to detect electronic attacks early so that they can be stopped; to watch competitors and send notices of price changes and special offers; to monitor Internet sites, discussion groups, and mailing lists for stock manipulations, insider trading, and rumors that might impact stock prices; to check e-mail, sort it according to established priority rules, and alert recipients when high-value e-mails appear in their inbox; and to automatically fill out forms on the Web.

Technology Guide Glossary

algorithm A problem-solving method expressed as a finite sequence of steps.

artificial intelligence (AI) A subfield of computer science that is concerned with studying the thought processes of humans and re-creating the effects of those processes with machines such as computers.

buyer agent (or **shopping bot**) An intelligent agent on a website that helps customers find products and services that they need.

computer vision The ability of information systems to identify objects, scenes, and activities in images.

deep learning The ability of information systems to discover new patterns without being exposed to labeled historical or training data.

expert systems (ESs) Information systems that attempt to mimic human experts by applying expertise in a specific domain.

information agent A type of intelligent agent that searches for information and displays it to users.

intelligent agent A software program that assists you, or acts on your behalf, in performing repetitive, computer-related tasks.

machine learning systems The ability of information systems to accurately perform new, unseen tasks, built on known properties learned from training or historical data that are labeled.

monitoring and surveillance agents (or predictive agents) Intelligent agents that constantly observe and report on some item of interest.

narrow AI See weak AI.

natural language processing The ability of information systems to work with text the way that humans do.

neural network A set of virtual neurons, placed in layers, which work in parallel in an attempt to simulate the way the human brain works, although in a greatly simplified form.

personal agents See user agents.

predictive agents See monitoring and surveillance agents.

shopping bot See buyer agent.

speech recognition The ability of information systems to automatically and accurately transcribe human speech.

strong AI Hypothetical artificial intelligence that matches or exceeds human intelligence and could perform any intellectual task that humans can.

user agents (or **personal agents**) Intelligent agents that take action on your behalf.

weak AI (also called *narrow AI*) Performs a useful and specific function that once required human intelligence to perform, and does so at human levels or better.

Discussion Questions

1. Explain how your university could employ an expert system in its admission process. Could it use a neural network?

What might happen if a student were denied admission to a university and his parents discovered that an expert system was involved in the admissions process?

2. One difference between a conventional business intelligence system and an expert system is that the former can explain *how* questions, whereas the latter can explain both *how* and *why* questions. Discuss the implications of this statement.

Problem-Solving Activities

1. You have decided to purchase a new "smart" television. To purchase it as inexpensively as possible and still get the features you want, you use a shopping bot. Visit several of the shopping bot websites that perform price comparisons for you. Begin with MySimon (**www.mysimon.com**), BizRate.com (**www.bizrate.com**), and Google Product Search.

Compare these shopping bots in regard to ease of use, number of product offerings, speed in obtaining information, thoroughness of information offered about products and sellers, and price selection. Which site or sites would you use, and why? Which television would you select and buy? How helpful were these sites in making your decision?

2. Access the MyMajors website (**www.mymajors.com**). This site contains a rule-based expert system to help students find majors. The expert system has more than 300 rules and 15,000 possible conclusions. The site ranks majors according to the likelihood that a student will succeed in them, and it provides six possible majors from among 60 alternative majors that a student might consider.

Take the quiz, and see if you are in the "right major" as defined by the expert system. You must register to take the quiz.

3. Access **www.exsys.com/demomain.html**. Try the various demos and report your results to your class.

Apply the Concept Activities

Apply the Concept 1.1

LEARNING OBJECTIVE 1.1

Identify the reasons why being an informed user of information systems is important in today's world.

STEP 1: Background (Here is what you are learning.)

Section 1.1 discussed how businesses are utilizing modern technologies to become more productive by connecting to their customers, suppliers, partners, and other parties. Those connections, however, do not exist simply to support the businesses. Do you realize how connected you are? Computers and information systems have become an essential feature of our everyday lives. Most of you have a cell phone within reach and have looked at it within the past 5 minutes. No longer is a phone just a phone; rather, it is your connection to family, friends, shopping, driving directions, entertainment (games, movies, music, etc.), and much more.

When you embark on your career, you likely will have to interface with information systems to post transactions and search for or record information. Accomplishing these tasks will require you to work effectively with computers, regardless of the industry in which you find yourself employed.

STEP 2: Activity (Here is what you do.)

Visit the websites of three local businesses: a bank, a dentist, and a retail shop. Examine their information to see if you can determine what types of information systems they use to support their operations. It is likely that you will find some similarities and differences among the three. Also, see if they have any open positions. If they do, what technical skills do these positions require? Summarize your findings in a paragraph or two.

STEP 3: Assignment (Here is what you turn in.)

Based on your research, identify five reasons why it is important for you to be an informed user of information technology. Reference your summarized findings to support your reasoning. Submit this list to your instructor, but also keep it in mind. You have just looked into the real world (your local world, in fact) and identified a reason for taking this course!

Apply the Concept 1.2

LEARNING OBJECTIVE 1.2

Classify the activities supported by various types of computer-based information systems in an organization.

STEP 1: Background

Section 1.2 discussed the various functional areas in which you most likely will be employed and the different IS that support them. It should be no surprise that these are the majors from which you can choose in most colleges of business. The four major functional areas are marketing/sales, finance/accounting, manufacturing, and human resources. Often, these areas will use the same database and networks within a company, but they will use them to support their specific needs. This activity will help you develop a solid understanding of the role of IS within the different functional areas.

STEP 2: Activity

Review the section material that describes the major functions of the four major functional areas. Then, review the basic functions of the following types of information systems: transaction processing, management information, and decision support.

After you have acquired a solid understanding of the functional areas and information systems that support them, you are ready to move forward with the activity!

STEP 3: Assignment

Create a table like the one shown below, and classify the activities supported by various types of computer-based information systems. To assist you, we have prefilled one item in each type of system. After you complete your chart, submit it to your professor.

	Transaction Processing	Management Information System	Decision Support System
Marketing/Sales	Enter Sales Data		
Accounting/Finance			
Human Resources			Comply with EEOC
Manufacturing		Inventory Reporting	

Apply the Concept 1.3

LEARNING OBJECTIVE 1.3

Discuss ways in which information technology can affect managers and nonmanagerial workers.

STEP 1: Background

Section 1.3 demonstrated that the essential reason businesses use information systems is to add value to their daily activities. In fact, IS have radically transformed the nature of both managerial and nonmanagerial work. Managers employ IT to instantly track information that previously was available only in monthly reports. Support staff can view calendars and schedules for all employees and can schedule meetings more easily. Sales representatives can view current product information while visiting with clients. This list does not even scratch the surface of the countless ways technology has added value to modern businesses.

STEP 2: Activity

Consider the restaurant industry. You have probably visited some "old-school" restaurants where your order is written down on a piece of paper and never entered into a computer system for preparation. You have most likely also been to a very modern restaurant where you enter your own order with a tablet, smartphone, or other piece of technology. Visit http://www.wiley.com/go/rainer/IS8e/applytheconcept and watch the two videos about using the restaurant table as the menu and ordering system.

STEP 3: Assignment

Imagine that you are a manager in each type of restaurant. How does working without technology impact how you do your job? How does adding the technology change your performance? Based on your thoughts from Step 2, imagine that you are explaining to your friend the ways that restaurants could benefit from IT. Prepare a paragraph or two that will discuss the ways that the traditional job of a restaurant manager and other employees has been changed by IT.

Apply the Concept 1.4

LEARNING OBJECTIVE 1.4

Identify positive and negative societal effects of the increased use of information technology.

STEP 1: Background

As you have just read, the increased use of IS has had a significant impact on society. Section 1.4 focused on three areas—quality-of-life improvements, robotics, and health care—to spark your interest in the ways our lives are being touched. Unfortunately, the technologies that provide quality-of-life improvements can also create economic and political problems. For example, robots that help streamline production also eliminate jobs. Similarly, health care improvements raise concerns regarding shared data and privacy violations.

STEP 2: Activity

Conduct a Web search for "technology and work–life balance." Look for programs, articles, research, suggestions, and other materials that help you understand the positive and negative effects of the increased use of information technologies.

STEP 3: Assignment

Create a table that identifies the positive and negative effects for the following areas: quality of life, robotics, health care, and work–life balance. Set your table up as in the example below, and submit it to your instructor.

	Positive	Negative
Quality of Life		
Robotics		
Health care		
Work–Life Balance		

Apply the Concept 2.1

LEARNING OBJECTIVE 2.1

Discuss ways in which information systems enable cross-functional business processes and business processes for a single functional area.

STEP 1: Background (This is what you are learning.)

This chapter defines a business process as an ongoing collection of related activities that create a product or a service of value to the organization, its business partners, and/or its customers. Normally, we do not see everything that goes into a process; rather, we observe only the results of the process. For example, when you shop at a grocery store, you see stocked shelves. However, the inventory-management processes that operate to keep the shelves stocked—as well as the information systems that support those processes—remain essentially invisible.

STEP 2: Activity (This is what you are doing.)

Visit http://www.wiley.com/go/rainer/IS8e/applytheconcept and click on the link provided for Section 2.1. This link will take you to a YouTube video that focuses on workflow and business process management in a health care environment. As you watch the video, look for the ways that information systems enable cross-functional business processes and make the flow of data much easier and quicker for everyone involved.

STEP 3: Deliverable (This is what you turn in.)

Based on the video from Step 2, write a brief description of how information systems enable both cross-functional business processes and business processes for a single functional area. Submit your description to your instructor.

Apply the Concept 2.2

LEARNING OBJECTIVE 2.2

Compare and contrast business process reengineering (BPR) and business process management (BPM) to determine the advantages and disadvantages of each.

STEP 1: Background

One of the most difficult decisions related to business processes is whether they need to be reengineered or simply managed. Reengineering business processes is a "clean-slate" approach in which you build completely new processes to accomplish current tasks. In contrast, managing these processes involves making current processes more efficient. Put simply, reengineering is radical, whereas management is incremental.

STEP 2: Activity

Consider the many processes involved in getting you (as a student) accepted, enrolled, registered, housed, fed, and, ultimately, educated. Do you recall the processes you went through to accomplish these tasks? Did any of these processes strike you as inefficient?

STEP 3: Deliverable

Imagine that you are a student representative on a committee whose task is to consider reengineering or modifying (managing) these business processes. Prepare a written statement for the committee that will compare and contrast BPR and BPM to determine the advantages and disadvantages of each strategy. Make a recommendation as to which one your university should follow, and present your recommendation to your instructor.

Apply the Concept 2.3

LEARNING OBJECTIVE 2.3

Identify effective IT responses to different kinds of business pressures.

STEP 1: Background (Here is what you are learning.)

Businesses face immense pressures today from every angle imaginable. The market is constantly shifting, technology becomes obsolete almost as quickly as it is implemented, society expects businesses to take more responsibility for the communities their work impacts, and legal compliance is required. Businesses increasingly employ cutting-edge technologies to navigate these difficult waters.

STEP 2: Activity (Here is what you do.)

Pick one business pressure from each of the three broad categories presented in the chapter: Market, Technology, and Societal/Political/Legal. Now search for a real-world business story related to each of the pressures you have chosen.

STEP 3: Deliverable (Here is what you turn in.)

After you have selected your three examples, identify an effective IT response to each one. Feel free to use the responses listed in the chapter. For each example, explain why you feel this is an appropriate response to the business pressure you have identified.

Perhaps there is a response outlined in the story you found. If so, determine whether the response was truly effective in dealing with the business pressure. Your submission should follow the outline below:

Broad Category: _____

Business Pressure: _____

IT Response: _____

Description: _____

Apply the Concept 2.4

LEARNING OBJECTIVE 2.4

Describe the strategies that organizations typically adopt to counter Porter's five competitive forces.

STEP 1: Background

This section has exposed you to Porter's five forces model, which explains how various forces can affect an organization. The threat of entry of new competitors, bargaining power of suppliers, bargaining power of customers, threat of substitute products or services, and rivalry among existing firms in the industry all have an impact on the organization's success. Based on this model, the chapter presents five strategies for competitive advantage: cost leadership, differentiation, innovation, operational effectiveness, and customer orientation.

Walmart is a worldwide company that focuses on a cost-leadership strategy. Review the ways Walmart uses the five forces (or controls them) to maintain their position as a global cost leader. Although it may be somewhat easy to perform this exercise with a global giant like Walmart, it is very difficult to apply these concepts to small businesses.

STEP 2: Activity

Visit your favorite restaurant and ask to speak to the manager. Asking only a few questions, evaluate whether the manager has a grasp of the five forces model. Do not ask anything specifically about Porter. Rather, inquire about rivals, substitutes, customers' bargaining power, suppliers' power, and so on. A good manager should be familiar with these concepts regardless of whether he or she uses the term *Porter's five forces*. Finally, ask the manager what strategy he or she uses. Then, try to classify that strategy as a cost leadership, differentiation, innovation, operational effectiveness, or customer orientation strategy.

STEP 3: Deliverable

Identify which of the five forces are at work based on the manager's feedback. Then, describe the strategies that *could* help deal with these particular forces, and explain *if* this is what the restaurant is currently attempting to do. If it is not, then explain what they should do differently. Your submission will have two parts: (1) a definition of the forces and (2) a description of the strategies at play in response to those forces.

Apply the Concept 3.1

LEARNING OBJECTIVE 3.1

Describe ethics, its three fundamental tenets, and the four categories of ethical issues related to information technology.

STEP 1: Background (Here is what you are learning.)

As you begin your career, you need to be aware of the current trends affecting the four areas of concern presented in Section 3.1. Privacy (what people know about you), property (who owns the data about you), accuracy (are the data about you accurate), and accessibility (who can access your data) are major topics in today's high-tech world. They are especially important in the migration to electronic health records, mobile wallets, social media, and government-run databases, to name a few.

STEP 2: Activity (Here is what you are doing.)

Visit http://www.wiley.com/go/rainer/IS8e/applytheconcept and read the article posted from November 2013. The article describes an unusual (or not-so-unusual) action on the part of Goldman Sachs. It seems they decided that their junior bankers should have weekends off!

Understand that it isn't illegal to require your employees to work weekends, nor is it illegal to give them time off. It also isn't illegal to work people 75 hours a week. Many of the talking points in this article focus expressly on ethics. An employer is trying to do the "right" thing, and they have used a new standard to define "right."

STEP 3: Deliverable (Here is what you turn in.)

Summarize the article for your professor. In your summary, make certain to define ethics and to describe how the three fundamental tenets of ethics (responsibility, liability, and accountability) played a role in Goldman Sachs' decision. Finally (not from the article), discuss how these same bankers deal with the four areas of ethical concern with regard to your financial information.

Apply the Concept 3.2

LEARNING OBJECTIVE 3.2

Discuss at least one potential threat to the privacy of the data stored in each of three places that store personal data.

STEP 1: Background

Section 3.2 has defined privacy as the right to be left alone and to be free of unreasonable personal intrusions. Information privacy is the right to determine when, and to what extent, information about you can be gathered and/or communicated to others. And, where our data are concerned, we are in control, right? If so, then why do people always seem to fear that "Big Brother" is spying on us and violating our privacy? The law generally assigns a higher priority to society's right to access information than to an individual's right to privacy.

The 2002 movie *Minority Report* presented a future in which a special police unit could predict when and where crimes were going to occur before they actually did. This unit could arrest "criminals" before they committed a crime. Along these same lines, a 2008 movie titled *Eagle Eye* focused on a highly intelligent computer system that chose to abide by the Constitution even if it meant having the president of the United States assassinated.

STEP 2: Activity

Movie night! If you have not seen the two films noted in Step 1, then schedule a movie night and watch them from the perspective of privacy and information security. Discuss the movies with your friends, and obtain their thoughts on these issues. If you don't have time to watch the movies, then visit http://www.wiley.com/go/rainer/IS8e/applytheconcept to read a synopsis of both films on IMDB.com.

STEP 3: Deliverable

After considering the plots in these movies, prepare a paper identifying three types of storage options you use for storing personal data. For each location, discuss at least one potential threat to your personal privacy that arises from storing your information there. Make them major threats . . . on the scale of the movies. Consider just how far your seemingly innocent decisions can take you! Present your paper to the class and submit it to your instructor.

Apply the Concept 4.1

LEARNING OBJECTIVE 4.1

Identify the five factors that contribute to the increasing vulnerability of information resources and specific examples of each factor.

STEP 1: Background (Here is what you are learning.)

Section 4.1 has taught you about the importance of information security, particularly when you are conducting business over the Web. It is important to note that a chain is only as strong as its weakest link. Therefore, although you may have been careful to maintain security across your network, if your business partners have not done so as well, then as your information passes over their networks it will be at risk.

STEP 2: Activity (Here is what you are doing.)

Visit http://www.wiley.com/go/rainer/IS8e/applytheconcept and click on the link to VeriSign's website. As you read this page, keep in mind that VeriSign is in the business of protecting websites and Web users, which is something we all appreciate. In fact, it is likely that you feel some level of comfort when you see the VeriSign symbol on an e-commerce site.

STEP 3: Deliverable (Here is what you turn in.)

After reading the article, compose a brief memo from VeriSign to a potential client. Identify the five factors that contribute to the increasing vulnerability of information resources and provide examples of how Verisign can help protect the client's digital assets against these threats. Submit your memo to your instructor.

Apply the Concept 4.2

LEARNING OBJECTIVE 4.2

Compare and contrast human mistakes and social engineering, along with specific examples of each one.

STEP 1: Background

Sensitive information is generally stored in a safe location, both physically and digitally. However, as you have just read, this information is often vulnerable to unintentional threats that result from careless mistakes. As one example, employees frequently use USB (flash) drives to take information home. Although these actions are perfectly legal, the USB drive makes it easy to lose the information or to copy it onto unauthorized machines. In fact, any device that stores information can become a threat to information security—backup drives, CDs, DVDs, and even printers! Printers?! Because people can "copy" information? Not quite. Continue the activity to find out more.

STEP 2: Activity

Go to http://www.wiley.com/go/rainer/IS8e/applytheconcept and click on the link provided for Apply the Concept 4.2. You will find an article about how the hard drive in a printer sometimes stores images of all the documents that have been copied. In the past, when these printers were discarded, their hard drives were not erased, leaving medical records, police reports, and other private information in a vulnerable state.

STEP 3: Deliverable

Compare and contrast human mistakes and social engineering using the example above. How might someone make a mistake with a printer? How might someone use social engineering to access or create copies of personal information? Put your thoughts into a report and submit it to your instructor.

Apply the Concept 4.3

LEARNING OBJECTIVE 4.3

Discuss the 10 types of deliberate attacks.

STEP 1: Background

Unfortunately there are many people who take advantage of others. Fraud, espionage, information extortion, identity theft, cyberterrorism, spamming, phishing, and many other deliberate acts have created a world where we must always confirm the identity of the people with whom we share information.

STEP 2: Activity

Go to http://www.wiley.com/go/rainer/IS8e/applytheconcept and click on the links provided for Apply the Concept 4.3. The link will take you to a video about foreign lotteries and a website the U.S. Postal Service provides to help people realize when they are being scammed. This type of scam has taken advantage of many people who are not aware that such scams exist. After watching the video, search the Web for other fraudulent activities that involve Craigslist, eBay, and any other sites you find.

STEP 3: Deliverable

Imagine you are the owner of a site such as Craigslist. Draft a memo to your users—both buyers and sellers—explaining your intention to run a "clean" site where all parties are safe. In your memo, discuss the 10 types of deliberate attacks that you want your users to be aware of as they conduct business on your site. Submit your memo to your instructor.

Apply the Concept 4.4

LEARNING OBJECTIVE 4.4

Describe the three risk mitigation strategies and provide examples of each one in the context of owning a home.

STEP 1: Background

Section 4.4 discussed at length the ways businesses deal with risk. Risk management is so important that companies frequently assign an entire department to oversee risk analysis and mitigation. When companies address risk, they have three basic methods from which to choose: risk acceptance, risk limitation, and risk transference. Significantly, we do the same thing when it comes to our personal assets.

Like businesses, homeowners face intentional and unintentional threats. To mitigate against these threats, almost all homeowners take certain actions. These actions reflect, among other things, where your home is located. For example, a home on the beach is much more susceptible to hurricanes than is a home in Nebraska. However, the home in Nebraska is (perhaps) more susceptible to tornadoes than is the home on the beach.

STEP 2: Activity

Imagine that you own your home. What risks do you need to manage? What property do you need to assess? What is the probability that any asset will be compromised? (*Note:* You will need to assess the risk to each asset.) What are the costs associated with each asset being compromised?

STEP 3: Deliverable

In a document, define the three risk management strategies and provide an example of each one in the context of owning a home. Submit your document to your instructor.

Apply the Concept 4.5

LEARNING OBJECTIVE 4.5

Identify the three major types of controls that organizations can use to protect their information resources and provide an example of each one.

STEP 1: Background

Security controls are designed to protect all components of an information system, including data, software, hardware, and networks. Because there are so many diverse threats, organizations utilize layers of controls. One security feature discussed in this chapter is public key encryption. This feature requires a public key and a private key. The public key is shared and is used to encrypt a message that only the individual's private key can decrypt.

STEP 2: Activity

Visit http://www.wiley.com/go/rainer/IS8e/applytheconcept and click on the link provided for Apply the Concept 4.5. The link will take you to an article about the 2004 movie *National Treasure*. Watching the actual film is preferable, but you may not have access to it. For this activity, reading about it will suffice. In this movie, Ben Gates (played by Nicholas Cage) steals one of our nation's most sacred documents—the Declaration of Independence. In the process, you see how the thief breaches all three of the major types of controls.

STEP 3: Deliverable

Identify the three major types of controls that the National Archives employs—and that Gates ultimately penetrates—and provide examples of them from the movie. Prepare a document with the three types of controls and examples from the movie and submit it to your instructor.

Apply the Concept 5.1

LEARNING OBJECTIVE 5.1

Discuss ways that common challenges in managing data can be addressed using data governance.

STEP 1: Background (Here is what you are learning.)

The amount of data we create today is absolutely mind-boggling. Dell EMC is a global company that focuses on helping organizations manage their data. Recently, the company sponsored a study to determine exactly how big the "digital universe" actually is and to envision its projected growth. There are some amazing findings in this study that point to a dramatic growth in data and an increase in virtual data centers. In the future, it will be possible to run your information systems in data centers that do not operate on your premises.

STEP 2: Activity (Here is what you do.)

Visit YouTube and search for a video titled *The Dawn of the Digital Era and Even Bigger Data*. Watch this video and consider how the trends it presents relate to the challenges discussed in this section. Now, imagine that your parents own their own business. It is successful, but it is also struggling under pressure to upgrade IT services for its employees and customers. How could you help them to look ahead to the future rather than keeping the status quo?

STEP 3: Deliverable (Here is what you turn in.)

Write an e-mail to your parents to explain how data and data management are likely to evolve over the next 10 years. Describe the common challenges they face and discuss how data governance can help address these issues. Also, based on the video, highlight the qualities they should look for in new employees. Finally, identify the types of training they should provide for their current employees.

Submit your e-mail to your instructor.

Apply the Concept 5.2

LEARNING OBJECTIVE 5.2

Discuss the advantages and disadvantages of relational databases.

STEP 1: Background

This section has introduced you to the advantages and disadvantages of using a relational database. This is one of those concepts that cannot really be appreciated until you work through the process of designing a database. Even though very few people go on to become database administrators, it is still valuable to have some understanding of how a database is built and administered. In this activity, you will be presented with a scenario, and you will then apply the concepts you have just read about. In the process, you will develop a solid foundation to discuss the advantages and disadvantages of relational databases.

STEP 2: Activity

You are employed as the coordinator of multiple ongoing projects within a company. Your responsibilities include keeping track of the company's commercial projects, its employees, and the employees' participation in each project. Usually, a project will have multiple team members, but some projects have not been assigned to any team members. For each project, the company must keep track of the project's title, description, location, estimated budget, and due date.

Each employee can be assigned to one or more projects. Some employees can also be on leave and therefore will not be working on any assignments. Project leaders usually need to know the following information about their team members: name, address, phone number, Social Security number, highest degree attained, and his/her expertise (for example, IS, accounting, marketing, finance).

Your manager has instructed you to present an overview of the advantages and disadvantages of a database that would support the company's efforts to manage the data described in this scenario. At a minimum, you should define the tables and the relationships among the key variables to provide structure to the information that would be included in the database.

STEP 3: Deliverable

Using the relational database design you created in Step 2, prepare a discussion of the advantages and disadvantages of this database. How will it benefit the company? What additional challenges might it create?

Submit your design and your discussion to your instructor.

Apply the Concept 5.3

LEARNING OBJECTIVE 5.3

Define Big Data and its basic characteristics.

STEP 1: Background

This section describes Big Data as an ongoing phenomenon that is providing businesses with access to vast amounts of information. The key "ingredients" that make the Big Data phenomenon a reality are volume, velocity, and variety.

STEP 2: Activity

TIBCO (www.tibco.com) is a company that provides a real-time event-processing software platform that brings customers and vendors together in a very interactive and engaging way. It uses vast amounts of data (volume), in real time (velocity), from multiple sources (variety) to bring this solution to its customers. Visit YouTube, and search for two videos—*Deliver Personalized Retail Experiences Using Big Data* and *Harnessing Big Data and Social Media to Engage Customers*. As you view these videos, watch carefully for the three "ingredients" mentioned above.

STEP 3: Deliverable

Choose one of the videos mentioned in Step 2 and write a review. In your review, define Big Data and discuss its basic characteristics relative to the video. Also in your review, note the functional areas of an organization referred to in each video.

Submit your review to your instructor.

Apply the Concept 5.4

LEARNING OBJECTIVE 5.4

Explain the elements necessary to successfully implement and maintain data warehouses.

STEP 1: Background

A set of general ingredients is required for organizations to effectively utilize the power of data marts and data warehouses. Figure 5.4 presents this information. Health care as an industry has not been centralized for many business, legal, and ethical reasons. However, the overall health implications of a centralized data warehouse are unimaginable.

STEP 2: Activity

Visit http://www.wiley.com/go/rainer/IS8e/applytheconcept and read the article in *Health-Tech* magazine from July 11, 2018, titled "Fitbit Pushes into the Clinical Space to Make Medicine More Personal." As you read the article, think about how Fitbit and Google are using data warehouses. (The term *warehouse* is not used, but the concept is applicable.)

STEP 3: Deliverable

To demonstrate that you recognize the environmental factors necessary to implement and maintain a data warehouse, imagine that the date is exactly five years in the future. Write a newspaper article titled "Data from Gadgets Like Fitbit Changed How Medical Data Was Used." In your article, imagine that all of the ingredients necessary in the environment have come together. Discuss what the environment was like five years ago (today) and how things have evolved to create the right mix of environmental factors.

Be aware that there is no right/wrong answer to this exercise. The objective is for you to recognize the necessary environment for a successful data warehouse implementation. The health care-related example simply provides a platform to accomplish this task.

Apply the Concept 5.5

LEARNING OBJECTIVE 5.5

Describe the benefits and challenges of implementing knowledge management systems in organizations.

STEP 1: Background

As you have learned in this text, data are captured, stored, analyzed, and shared to create knowledge within organizations. This knowledge is exposed in meetings when colleagues are interpreting the information they received from the latest report, in employee presentations, in e-mail among coworkers, and in numerous other scenarios. The problem many organizations face is that there are massive amounts of knowledge that are created and shared, but this information is not stored in a centralized, searchable format.

STEP 2: Activity

Visit http://www.wiley.com/go/rainer/IS8e/applytheconcept and click on the links provided for Apply the Concept 5.5. They will take you to two YouTube videos: *Discover What You Know* by user Ken Porter and *Lee Bryant—Knowledge Management* by user UsNowFilm. Both videos illustrate the importance of capturing knowledge within an organization so it can be shared with the right person at the right time to support effective decision making.

STEP 3: Deliverable

Write a short paragraph or two to discuss the benefits and challenges faced by companies when they attempt to implement a knowledge management system. How many of these elements are technical and how many are social? Also, discuss the ways that companies can use technologies to help capture and share knowledge.

Submit this essay to your instructor.

Apply the Concept 5.6

LEARNING OBJECTIVE 5.6

Understand the processes of querying a relational database, entity-relationship modeling, and normalization and joins.

STEP 1: Background

It is very important that you understand the connections among entities, attributes, and relationships. This section has defined each of these terms for you. Typically, entities are described by their attributes, and they are related to other entities. For example, if "student name" is the entity, then age, gender, country of origin, marital status, and other demographic data are the attributes (characteristics) of that particular student. That student is also related to other entities such as financial information, major, and course information.

STEP 2: Activity

An entity–relationship model is one of the most challenging aspects of designing a database because you have to (1) understand the rules that govern how processes work and (2) be able to define and describe these rules in a picture. This section has provided you with the necessary tools to draw a basic ER model.

Imagine the following scenario. You are designing a database for your local police department to keep track of traffic violations. The department has provided you with the following rules:

- Each officer can write multiple tickets.
- Each ticket will list only one officer.
- Each ticket will list only one driver.
- Drivers can receive multiple tickets.

STEP 3: Deliverable

Using the tools described in this section, demonstrate that you understand the process of ER modeling by drawing and submitting an ER model for the scenario provided in Step 2.

Apply the Concept 6.1

LEARNING OBJECTIVE 6.1

Compare and contrast the major types of networks.

STEP 1: Background (Here is what you are learning.)

Section 6.1 has introduced you to the different types of networks that connect businesses around the world. These networking capabilities enable modern organizations to operate over many geographic locations. Frequently, a company's headquarters are located in one city with various branches in other countries. In addition, employees often work from home rather than commute to a physical office. The computer network is the technology that allows all of this to happen. For a network to function, a few components are required. In this activity, you will place these components in the appropriate places to create a computer network.

STEP 2: Activity (Here is what you do.)

Consider the following company, called JLB TechWizards, and the following potential network components:

1. Headquarters: JLB TechWizards manufactures, sells, and services computer equipment. The company's headquarters, located in Chicago, house several key functions, including marketing, accounting, HR, and manufacturing. Each office has a number of PCs that connect to the main server. All offices share data and printers.

2. Salesforce: The company has technicians who service equipment sold within the United States. Each technician has a laptop that must connect to the database at headquarters about three hours each day to check inventory, enter repairs, and place orders. Technicians are constantly on the road and they need to be able to check inventory whether they are in a hotel or at a customer site. In addition, each evening the technicians must log on to check for updates and to post their daily activities.

3. Employees from home: JLB TechWizards has a number of employees who work from home part-time on flextime. These employees must have a fast, secure connection because some of them are dealing with financial data stored in the main computer and its databases at headquarters. They all live within 20 miles of their workplace.

STEP 3: Deliverable (Here is what you turn in.)

Use the description of JLB TechWizards presented above to compare and contrast the types of networks discussed in this section. Explain how these networks will or will not meet the needs of each situation. A table may be useful to present this information, but it is not required. Create a Word document with your description and explanations and submit it to your instructor.

Apply the Concept 6.2

LEARNING OBJECTIVE 6.2

Describe the wireline communications media and transmission technologies.

STEP 1: Background

Section 6.2 covers network channels, protocols, and other network fundamentals. These computer networks enable businesses to receive and share information with customers, suppliers, and employees. Made up of several possible cable types and protocols, they are quite literally the backbone of modern businesses.

STEP 2: Activity

Imagine that you work in the billing department of a midsized hospital. Recently, your supervisor stated that hospital growth had created a need for office space to be repurposed, and your work would now be done from home. You would be reimbursed for any expenses involved in preparing your home office, and your home Internet would also be reimbursed quarterly.

The only requirement is that you finalize the same number of bills each day from home as you did in the office. You can schedule your own time as long as your work gets done.

Visit http://www.wiley.com/go/rainer/IS8e/applytheconcept to watch a few videos about telecommuting.

STEP 3: Deliverable

Describe the wireline communication media and the transmission technologies (protocols) that you will need to be able to telecommute. Your description should (at a minimum) include the home Internet connection, use of the Web, and connections within the office. It should also describe the protocols that operate to support these connections. Submit your description to your instructor.

Apply the Concept 6.3

LEARNING OBJECTIVE 6.3

Describe the most common methods for accessing the Internet.

STEP 1: Background

Section 6.3 has explained the difference between the Internet and the World Wide Web. Although many people use these terms interchangeably, they are very different. Most computers today are continuously connected to the Internet, though they are not always accessing the Web. Offices and other places of employment typically set up an Internet connection via a local area network (LAN). However, at home you have several options to consider.

STEP 2: Activity

Visit http://www.wiley.com/go/rainer/IS8e/applytheconcept and watch the YouTube videos listed there. These videos go into a little more detail about the types of connections mentioned in Table 6.2. You will learn about advantages, disadvantages, and things to consider for the different methods of connecting to the Internet.

STEP 3: Deliverable

Imagine that your parents are "technologically challenged" (some of you may not have to imagine). They have just bought a house at the beach and they are getting ready to set up an Internet connection. At home, there is only one provider, so DSL versus cable versus cellular versus satellite is not an issue. However, there are several options at the beach and your parents do not know where to begin.

Compose an e-mail to your parents that describes the most common methods for accessing the Internet to help them develop criteria for making their choice.

Apply the Concept 6.4

LEARNING OBJECTIVE 6.4

Explain the impact that discovery network applications have had on business and everyday life.

STEP 1: Background

Section 6.4 has introduced you to the discovery aspect of networks, specifically, the Web. Search engines (of all kinds) open up doors of knowledge for anyone with a question. Translation tools allow you to even discover your answer from other languages. These, however, are very broad tools. Portals help to narrow them by focusing your search within a narrow realm of information. They also push very specific information to you rather than waiting on you to request everything.

STEP 2: Activity

Before there were online search tools, there was the library card catalog. It was a method of organizing information in a library so that you could easily retrieve the information you needed. Today, research is handled very differently. Visit http://www.wiley.com/go/rainer/IS8e/applytheconcept to watch a video about the use of the "old-school" library card catalog.

STEP 3: Deliverable

Search the Web for the book referenced in the YouTube video linked above. Use multiple search engines (such as google.com, yahoo.com, or bing.com), some meta search engines (such as dogpile.com, blingo.com, or excite.com), and your school's library system. Make note of the amount of and type of information you are able to find in just a few minutes about the book referenced in the YouTube video above. Write a paragraph that compares your experience to the card catalog system.

Now think even bigger. If discovery applications have made this much impact on something as simple as finding a book (or information on the book), how much bigger is the impact on business and everyday life? Prepare a second paragraph that discusses the latter question.

Submit both paragraphs to your instructor.

Apply the Concept 6.5

LEARNING OBJECTIVE 6.5

Explain the impact that communication network applications have had on business and everyday life.

STEP 1: Background

Section 6.5 has introduced you to the communication aspect of networks that have radically changed the way humans interact with each other. Most of these methods of communication are even available on our mobile devices now via a cellular connection. Such drastic changes have brought about many struggles and possibilities for businesses.

STEP 2: Activity

The methods that we use to communicate today vary greatly from just 50 years ago. Visit http://www.wiley.com/go/rainer/IS8e/applytheconcept to watch a YouTube video about how communication has changed. While it only goes up to 1965, you will still recognize the situations and the uses of improved communications.

STEP 3: Deliverable

Consider the various uses of communications in the video (work, personal, military, emergency, etc.). How do our modern technologies such as Internet, video, mobile, and text impact what is possible on these types of communication? Create a list of the ways that the technologies discussed in this section have changed the way we communicate on a personal level, at work, in emergencies, and in military situations and give a brief explanation of each. Discuss at least three changes for each area of communication. Submit your answers to your professor.

Apply the Concept 6.6

LEARNING OBJECTIVE 6.6

Explain the impact that collaboration network applications have had on business and everyday life.

STEP 1: Background

As you have seen, collaboration tools impact people inside and outside the organization. Some collaboration tools allow geographically separated employees to work together, while some allow those across the hall to work more effectively. Other tools just allow larger groups to brainstorm and be creative. The big idea here is that there is synergy created when people are able to work together via digital tools that overcome time and space.

STEP: Activity

Brightidea is a company that provides a suite of products that touches on many of the topics in the chapter. Visit http://www.wiley.com/go/rainer/IS8e/applytheconcept and watch the YouTube video that introduces the company. Then click the second link to visit the Brightidea website. There are several case studies, videos, and product explanations that will help you understand what this product offers.

STEP 3: Deliverable

As you peruse Brightidea's website, look for evidence that the software supports the topics discussed in this section: workflow, virtual collaboration, crowdsourcing, and teleconferencing. Prepare a set of presentation slides (use any tool at your disposal or at your instructor's request) that discusses the impact that collaboration network applications (such as Brightidea's products) have had on businesses. Present your slides to your class and professor.

Apply the Concept 6.7

LEARNING OBJECTIVE 6.7

Explain the impact that educational network applications have had on business and everyday life.

STEP 1: Background

Imagine that you are an expert in math. Someone hands you a piece of chalk and a small chalkboard and gives you a task of creating an educational experience to share your knowledge with other people. You would probably create a traditional classroom. Now imagine that you are not handed chalk, but are given the Internet, video capabilities, file sharing, collaboration, tools, and more! Imagine the possibilities!

STEP 2: Activity

Visit http://www.wiley.com/go/rainer/IS8e/applytheconcept and view the first video, and then visit the website about Brightspace. Be sure to look at the video about how technology has changed education. Brightspace (you may have heard it called by its former name, Desire2Learn) is a learning management system that several schools use as a platform to offer educational activities using the digital tools available today. This platform can be used to offer e-learning experiences, distance learning opportunities, or fully virtual classrooms.

There are many discussions about how these educational network applications impact an individual's everyday life. Single parents are able to go to school using educational network applications. Working professionals are able to pursue graduate degrees online. But what about the impact on businesses?

STEP 3: Deliverable

Many organizations use these tools to facilitate mandatory training or for onboarding new employees. Visit http://www.wiley.com/go/rainer/IS8e/applytheconcept and view the second link about Brightspace's enterprise offerings. Research their site to create and discuss a list of five ways that educational network applications impact businesses.

Apply the Concept 7.1

LEARNING OBJECTIVE 7.1

Describe the six common types of electronic commerce.

STEP 1: Background (Here is what you are learning.)

Today, there are many companies that specialize in making e-commerce a reality for small businesses. Amazon, Yahoo!, PayPal, and other entities offer services that provide everything a small business needs to sell products and accept payment over the Internet. In fact, many consumers prefer that their transactions go through these larger global companies because they trust these companies' security.

STEP 2: Activity (Here is what you are doing.)

Visit http://www.wiley.com/go/rainer/IS8e/applytheconcept and click on the link provided for Apply the Concept 7.1. This link will take you to PayPal's website. Click on the business link at the top of the page. You will find that PayPal offers easy solutions for both businesses and customers.

STEP 3: Deliverable (Here is what you turn in.)

Create and submit a table that lists and describes the six common types of e-commerce. Which ones are supported by PayPal and which are not? For the second group, can you explain why they are not supported? Should PayPal move into these areas of e-commerce as well?

Apply the Concept 7.2

LEARNING OBJECTIVE 7.2

Describe the various online services of business-to-consumer (B2C) commerce, along with specific examples of each.

STEP 1: Background

At this point in your "buying" career, you have probably purchased something online, visited an auction site (and possibly won a bid), and engaged in some form of online banking. Your generation is very comfortable with the retail side of e-commerce. While you were engaging in B2C e-commerce, you probably created an account with a few vendors and received some e-mail advertisements. No doubt you have also received some pop-up ads promoting products during your Internet searches. Another aspect of modern business that has changed is that companies now want you to do their advertising for them. The text refers to this development as viral marketing.

STEP 2: Activity

Imagine that you and some friends decide to start a new online thrift store. To become a member, an individual has to donate to the thrift. For every 10 items a person donates, he or she is awarded a two-month membership. However, you have no IT platform for e-commerce. After some research, you determine that Shopify is your best provider. Shopify is an e-commerce platform that enables individuals and businesses to create online stores.

Visit http://www.wiley.com/go/rainer/IS8e/applytheconcept and click on the link provided for Apply the Concept 7.2. This link will take you to Shopify's website. Near the top of the page, you will see a link to "Examples" of other providers. Look through the examples to identify ideas you would like to incorporate into your store.

STEP 3: Deliverable

After reviewing the Shopify site, prepare a presentation or a document that describes the various online services of B2C commerce provided by Shopify. Provide specific examples of services that attracted your attention and discuss how you would apply these services to your store.

Apply the Concept 7.3

LEARNING OBJECTIVE 7.3

Describe the three business models for business-to-business electronic commerce.

STEP 1: Background

Section 7.3 describes forward auctions, reverse auctions, and exchanges. Forward auctions are used when a seller is trying to reach several buyers, and reverse auctions are used when a buyer is soliciting from several sellers. In an exchange, both buyers and sellers come to a central website to quickly and easily establish a B2B relationship. Some of these websites or exchanges are for materials involved in manufacturing a product; others involve materials that help run the business.

STEP 2: Activity

Visit http://www.wiley.com/go/rainer/IS8e/applytheconcept and click on the link provided for Apply the Concept 7.3. This link will take you to one of the horizontal exchanges (an exchange for many buyers and sellers across industries) listed in the section. As you examine the available products, you should get a better understanding of the breadth of a horizontal exchange.

STEP 3: Deliverable

Describe the three business models for B2B e-commerce by comparing and contrasting them to Globalsource. Submit your description to your professor.

Apply the Concept 7.4

LEARNING OBJECTIVE 7.4

Discuss the ethical and legal issues related to electronic commerce, along with examples.

STEP 1: Background

Amazon.com is the world's largest online retailer. In fact, it is one of a kind in many ways. It competes with Apple, Google, Microsoft, and Walmart, some of the biggest names in the tech and retail universe (online and in-store).

However, for many years there was a huge controversy surrounding Amazon. Specifically, the retailer did not collect sales tax in all states. A recent Supreme Court Decision in 2017 has changed that.

STEP 2: Activity

Read the article in the *Los Angeles Times* titled "Small retailers who sold through Amazon are facing a tax time bomb" on May 1, 2019. What do you think about the Supreme Court decision and California's subsequent actions?

STEP 3: Deliverable

Take a little time to consider this controversy. Then, create a list of arguments for and against California's new requirements. Make certain your argument identifies both the ethical and legal aspects of this issue.

Apply the Concept 8.1

LEARNING OBJECTIVE 8.1

Identify advantages and disadvantages of each of the four main types of wireless transmission media.

STEP 1: Background (Here is what you are learning.)

As stated in this section, mobile communication has changed our world more rapidly and dramatically than any other technology. Although several wireless transmission media are available, rarely will one technology meet all of a business's needs by itself. Vislink is a global technology firm that collects and delivers high-quality video broadcasts. These broadcasts are utilized in sports, news, law enforcement, and other areas. Although Vislink specializes in video, they rely on multiple mobile transmission media to obtain live feeds from multiple locations. Rajant is one of the providers that Vislink has utilized for their wireless media.

STEP 2: Activity (Here is what you are doing.)

Visit http://www.wiley.com/go/rainer/IS8e/applytheconcept and click on the link provided for Apply the Concept 8.1. There are three links. One will take you to Vislink's website, another to Rajant's website, and the last to a YouTube video in which Vislink demonstrates how they can provide a live video feed to law enforcement agencies using Rajant's wireless mesh network.

STEP 3: Deliverable (Here is what you turn in.)

As you watch the video, listen for the wireless transmission media they mention and pay attention to how many of them are discussed in this section of the book. Write and submit a summary of your findings that highlights the advantages and disadvantages of the transmission media types and explains why they were or were not used in the product that Vislink/Rajant demonstrated.

Apply the Concept 8.2

LEARNING OBJECTIVE 8.2

Explain how businesses can use technology employed by short-range, medium-range, and long-range networks, respectively.

STEP 1: Background

Many cellular phones today, including both Apple and Android devices, contain multiple radios. These include Cellular, Bluetooth, Wi-Fi, infrared, GPS, and NFC chips. With all of these radios embedded in a small mobile device, the possibilities of connectivity are nearly endless because one device can utilize short-range, mid-range, and wide-range connectivity.

STEP 2: Activity

Visit http://www.wiley.com/go/rainer/IS8e/applytheconcept and view the video demonstration by Serial IO. There is also a link to their website, where you will find several examples of wireless products intended for business use. Although most of these products are short-range devices, you must assume they will be connected to some mid-range and/or wide-range wireless network. In fact, these devices support Windows, Mac, Android, iOS, BlackBerry, and other platforms.

STEP 3: Deliverable

Based on the video and the Serial IO website, create and submit a table to explain how businesses can use the technologies employed by short-range, medium-range, and long-range networks to achieve their business purposes.

Apply the Concept 8.3

LEARNING OBJECTIVE 8.3

Provide a specific example of how each of the five major m-commerce applications can benefit a business.

STEP 1: Background

Section 8.3 introduced you to five of the most popular mobile commerce applications. These applications are location-based applications, financial services, intrabusiness applications, accessing information, and telemetry. Although you may not have had experience with each of these, it is likely that you have experienced some.

STEP 2: Activity

Read (or reread) the section and consider the following questions related to your personal experiences with mobile commerce: Do you use a mobile wallet? Has using a mobile wallet replaced your traditional wallet? What location-based services do you allow on your mobile device? Do you freely share your location, or are you more private? What type of intrabusiness applications do you utilize as an employee or customer of an organization? What type of information do you access on a regular basis? Do you utilize any telemetry information (such as a wireless connection to your vehicle computer to record information on your mobile phone)?

STEP 3: Deliverable

Based on your answers to the questions in Step 2, build a table that provides a brief discussion of how each of the five major m-commerce applications benefit businesses and provide your personal experiences with each.

Apply the Concept 8.4

LEARNING OBJECTIVE 8.4

Describe the Internet of Things, along with examples of how organizations can utilize the Internet of Things.

STEP 1: Background

Section 8.4 has introduced the concept of the Internet of Things (IoT) and provided several examples. There is no doubt that the IoT will continue to grow and shape our lives. Many industries will change from reactive (correcting problems after they happen) to proactive (acting to prevent problems before they happen based on IoT data).

STEP 2: Activity

Visit http://www.wiley.com/go/rainer/IS8e/applytheconcept and watch the YouTube video. It describes examples of personal applications of IoT and professional uses of IoT. After watching the video, let your mind wander into the future to a time when everything is connected via the

IoT—not just the devices mentioned in the video (like your car) but also your coffee pot, bed, clothes, closet door, front door, toothbrush, and so much more are all connected to the IoT.

STEP 3: Deliverable

Write a paragraph or two to first describe the IoT, and then provide current examples of how it has impacted your life and is currently making a difference for businesses and industries. Finally, provide a few ideas of how the IoT will shape the future.

Apply the Concept 9.1

LEARNING OBJECTIVE 9.1

Describe five Web 2.0 tools and the two major types of Web 2.0 sites.

STEP 1: Background (Here is what you are learning.)

This section differentiates Web 1.0, which consists of places to visit, from Web 2.0, where users interact and share information. Whether or not you have thought of these media in these terms, you are familiar with these differences. No doubt you are much more accustomed to Web 2.0, and businesses have begun to integrate information sharing into their public sites.

STEP 2: Activity (Here is what you are doing.)

Visit http://www.wiley.com/go/rainer/IS8e/applytheconcept and click on the link for Apply the Concept 9.1. This video provides a valuable overview of Web 2.0 technologies. Take notes of the various features that Web 2.0 makes available, and then click on the second link. This link will take you to a CNN Money Web page that provides a rank-order list of the Fortune 500 companies. Visit the websites of the top 10 firms and identify the Web 2.0 technologies they employ on their site.

STEP 3: Deliverable (Here is what you turn in.)

Create a table that displays the following information about 5 of the top 10 companies on the CNN Money rankings:

- The company's name
- The company's rank
- The industry (e.g., retail, consulting services, communications)
- A description of the Web 2.0 technologies/applications that each company uses
- A description of the Web 2.0 tools the company does not use

Submit your table to your professor.

Apply the Concept 9.2

LEARNING OBJECTIVE 9.2

Describe the benefits and risks of social commerce to companies.

STEP 1: Background

Collaborative consumption has been fueled by social networks because it allows owners to share their goods with those who would rather rent something than permanently own it. Sharing also makes it cheaper to own because the cost of ownership is spread across many users. The sharing economy has changed drastically in recent years as companies like Uber and Airbnb continue to gain in popularity, and social media has driven this rise.

STEP 2: Activity

Visit https://davidbuckingham.net/ and read his 2017 critique, "Media and the Sharing Economy." Now think about how you can apply these lessons to bike sharing. Look up a company called CitiBikes.

STEP 3: Deliverable

Many of these companies, including CitiBike, got their start in big cities. Why do you think they started in such heavily populated areas? What advantages would a collaborative consumption business model have in a heavily populated area? What disadvantages would they face? In what ways might a college campus be a prime location to introduce users to collaborative consumption services? Create a table that compares the advantages and disadvantages of collaborative consumption for the biking industry. Submit your table to your instructor.

Apply the Concept 9.3

LEARNING OBJECTIVE 9.3

Identify the methods used for shopping socially.

STEP 1: Background

Section 9.3 defines shopping socially as taking the key aspects of social networks (e.g., groups, reviews, discussions) and applying them to shopping. This phenomenon is not new. People have shopped socially for years, through general conversation.

Today, most consumers conduct a lot of research before they make a purchase by reading reviews posted by other customers. Recently, however, the validity of these reviews has been questioned. As you learn about social shopping, you should also become aware of the potential fraud that takes place online.

STEP 2: Activity

Go to http://www.wiley.com/go/rainer/IS8e/applytheconcept and click on the link for Apply the Concept 9.3. This link will take you to an article from the *New York Times* and one from the *Denver Post*. Both articles deal with the issue of falsified recommendations and ratings. Talk to some of your classmates about this topic and record their feedback. How did they respond to the fact that product ratings may not be legitimate? Ask them the following questions:

- What star rating do you rely on when you are considering a product?
- Do you read reviews or simply notice the number of stars?
- If you read reviews, do you read only the good ones, only the bad ones, or a mixture of both?
- Do you rely on reviews more than a third-party organization such as Consumer Reports?

STEP 3: Deliverable

Considering the material you have read and your conversations with your classmates, identify various methods of shopping socially and discuss the role that trust plays in each method. Prepare a paper or presentation for your professor documenting what you have learned.

Apply the Concept 9.4

LEARNING OBJECTIVE 9.4

Discuss innovative ways to use social networking sites for advertising and market research.

STEP 1: Background

Section 9.4 presented the major uses of social computing in advertising and market research. Social advertising is simply a way of presenting information to potential customers via a social platform. Social market research makes use of these same social platforms to examine the ongoing communication between the company and its customer community for information that the company can use to improve products or services.

STEP 2: Activity

Visit http://www.wiley.com/go/rainer/IS8e/applytheconcept and find the two links. First, read the article about "20 Companies You Should Be Following on Social Media." Some of these companies are not specifically related to advertising or market research, but you will still enjoy learning about them. Next, read the article on Digimind.com about the innovative ways people are using social media as a rich pool of information.

STEP 3: Deliverable

After reviewing the examples in the articles linked in Step 2, prepare a discussion of the top three innovative ways that these companies are using social networking for advertising and the top three innovative ways that companies are using the information available on social networks as a mechanism for learning about their customers. Submit your discussion to your instructor.

Apply the Concept 9.5

LEARNING OBJECTIVE 9.5

Describe how social computing improves customer service.

STEP 1: Background

Social customer relationship management involves using social networks to maintain customer loyalty. One company that employs this strategy quite skillfully is ZAGG (Zealous About Great Gadgets; www.zagg.com). ZAGG makes and sells accessories for mobile devices such as smartphones and tablets. To help sell its products, the company has developed one of the best social customer relationship management plans around.

When ZAGG develops a new product, it not only posts notes about the product on its social networking page, but it also involves customers in the process. For example, when ZAGG was releasing its ZAGGFolio for the iPad, the company allowed fans to vote on the colors of the new product.

ZAGG is also proficient at monitoring the social network for product-related issues. It is not uncommon for a customer to complain and then receive feedback from a ZAGG employee. Not only does the company retain that individual customer, but it also develops a sense of trust with all of its customers, who are confident they would receive the same treatment.

STEP 2: Activity

Go to http://www.wiley.com/go/rainer/IS8e/applytheconcept and click on the link to ZAGG's website. At the bottom of the page you will find a link to all of the company's social networks. Visit their Facebook page and review their timeline. Search for customer complaints and for how the company deals with them. Did you find a customer representative present on the social networking site? Does the site offer any competitions? Polls? Give-aways? Can you reverse-engineer the company's social customer relationship management methodology?

STEP 3: Deliverable

Imagine that you are a marketing manager, and you have been selected to present a report to the president to describe how social computing improves customer service. Create the outline that you would use to make your points and present it to the class and to your instructor.

Apply the Concept 9.6

LEARNING OBJECTIVE 9.6

Discuss different ways in which human resource managers make use of social computing.

STEP 1: Background

Social human resource management is redefining the ways we search and apply for jobs and make hiring decisions. Going digital was a natural step, but it was also an awkward one. When position announcements went from the bulletin board and local newspaper to Monster.com, the number of positions and applicants exploded. We are so connected today that it is impossible to go back. After you graduate, you will no doubt use social networks to find and apply for jobs.

STEP 2: Activity

Visit LinkedIn, a professional social network. Create a profile that includes the college you currently attend. Connect to your classmates as they also complete this activity. You never know when you will need to call on one of these individuals.

Next, search the Web for "Job Search Websites," and see which ones will allow you to connect with your LinkedIn profile. As you connect with these professional sites, consider the differences between a professional and a personal social network.

STEP 3: Deliverable

In a paper, discuss the various ways in which human resources managers can make use of social computing and how you can best present yourself online. Present your paper to your instructor.

Apply the Concept 10.1

LEARNING OBJECTIVE 10.1

Explain the purpose of transaction processing systems.

STEP 1: Background (Here is what you are learning.)

Section 10.1 has explained that transaction processing systems (TPS) capture data and then automatically transmit those data to the various functional area systems. Most TPS are designed based on an organization's existing processes. To better understand how a TPS operates, you should consider the flow of data through the student application process.

STEP 2: Activity (Here is what you do.)

Visit http://www.wiley.com/go/rainer/IS8e/applytheconcept and click on the link provided for Apply the Concept 10.1. This link will take you to a Web page that describes the process of creating data flow diagrams (DFDs). The page uses the example of a college student application to demonstrate the flow of data through a university. Review this description and identify the transactions that take place throughout the process.

STEP 3: Deliverable (Here is what you turn in.)

Consider your student application process. Are there any pieces of your application that you feel were handled differently than the example described? Prepare a short description of the application process described in the video and discuss the purpose of the TPS for this process.

Apply The Concept 10.2

LEARNING OBJECTIVE 10.2

Explain the types of support that information systems can provide for each functional area of the organization.

STEP 1: Background

Section 10.2 introduced you to the concept of functional area information systems (FAIS). As you can see, every area of business has processes in place that define how data are stored, analyzed, applied, and distributed across the area. For example, inventory management is easy to manage with a computer system because it involves simply keeping track of your materials and products. However, when you integrate inventory management with production and operations management (POM), you have a very effective functional system that supports the internal production line.

STEP 2: Activity

Visit http://www.wiley.com/go/rainer/IS8e/applytheconcept and click on the link provided for Apply the Concept 10.2. You will be directed to four websites that present real-world examples of the information systems discussed in this section. Read over them, and look for any specific material that you can tie back into the concepts covered in the chapter.

STEP 3: Deliverable

Prepare a report that explains the types of support the IS reviewed in Step 2 can provide for each functional area within an organization. Submit your report to your instructor.

Apply The Concept 10.3

LEARNING OBJECTIVE 10.3

Identify advantages and drawbacks to businesses implementing an enterprise resource planning system.

STEP 1: Background

Section 10.3 explained that enterprise resource planning (ERP) works toward removing information silos within an organization by implementing a single system to support all of the functional areas. One example of an ERP system is SAP Business One. SAP is an industry-leading ERP company. In this activity, you will consider the advantages and drawbacks of using an ERP such as SAP.

STEP 2: Activity

Visit http://www.wiley.com/go/rainer/IS8e/applytheconcept and click on the link provided for Apply the Concept 10.3. This link will take you to a YouTube video titled *SAP-Business-One.wmv* by user angeltechdotit. As you watch the video, consider how many departments the representative would have to contact to find the information that SAP Business One can present in just a few moments. If this organization operated out of silos, the representative would have to take extensive notes, visit multiple departments, and call the customer back at a later time with the answers.

STEP 3: Deliverable

After considering how complicated it would be for OEC to handle the customer's requests without an ERP, identify the advantages and drawbacks to OEC of using the SAP Business One ERP. Submit your thoughts to your professor.

Apply The Concept 10.4

LEARNING OBJECTIVE 10.4

Describe the three main business processes supported by ERP systems.

STEP 1: Background

We have discussed reports that you can receive from TPS, FAIS, and ERP systems earlier in this chapter. In particular, these reports truly are the power of an ERP. Getting the right information to the right person at the right time to make the right decision is the underlying purpose for installing and utilizing an ERP. Recall from earlier in the text that managers need IT decision-support tools because decisions are becoming more complex, there is less time to make decisions, there are more options, and the costs of making incorrect decisions are increasing.

STEP 2: Activity

Visit http://www.wiley.com/go/rainer/IS8e/applytheconcept and click on the link provided for Apply the Concept 11.4. This link will take you to a YouTube video titled *Phoebus ERP—Customized Dashboard*. This video will introduce you to the dashboard tool provided by Phoebus, which individual users can customize to provide the specific information they need. This type of dashboard pulls together the many reports you have learned about in this chapter. As you watch the video, look for examples of the three major types of processes (procurement, fulfillment, and production) that are supported by ERP systems as discussed in this section.

STEP 3: Deliverable

Discuss the three major types of processes and the ways that an ERP can support them. Use what you learned in the dashboard video to discuss the types of information that could be presented in a dashboard to support these processes.

Apply the Concept 11.1

LEARNING OBJECTIVE 11.1

Identify the primary functions of both customer relationship management (CRM) and collaborative CRM strategies.

STEP 1: Background (Here is what you are learning.)

Section 11.1 introduced the concept of a CRM system, and it suggested that it is better to focus on relationships than on transactions. The idea is that relationships create transactions, so if you grow the relationship, you keep the customers (and the transactions)!

STEP 2: Activity (Here is what you are doing.)

Visit http://www.wiley.com/go/rainer/IS8e/applytheconcept and click on the link provided for Apply the Concept 11.1. This link will take you to a YouTube video that illustrates how Recreational Equipment Incorporated (REI) uses CRM to service their customers.

STEP 3: Deliverable (Here is what you submit.)

In a report, identify the primary functions of both customer relationship management (CRM) and collaborative CRM strategies. What are REI's approaches to CRM? Can you make any suggestions to help them improve? Submit your report to your professor.

Apply the Concept 11.2

LEARNING OBJECTIVE 11.2

Describe how businesses might utilize applications of each of the two major components of operational CRM systems.

STEP 1: Background

Section 11.2 introduced you to the concept of customer-facing and customer-touching CRM applications, the two major components of operational CRM systems. Many organizations use a combination of both types of systems to establish, develop, and maintain relationships with consumers. This activity will help you to see these systems in action when you do business on a website or in a brick-and-mortar business.

STEP 2: Activity

Visit a physical store where you like to shop (or recall a recent visit and discuss it with some friends), and visit the store's website. Make certain to select a company that has both an Internet site and a physical store so you can compare the two channels.

As you walked through the store, did you notice any cues that could tie a customer to a CRM? Did the business have a customer loyalty program? Are there any significant advantages to joining the program? Is the in-store membership tied to anything online? If so, how? Or, does the store seem to have separate in-store and online memberships?

STEP 3: Deliverable

After considering the points mentioned in Step 2, describe how businesses might utilize both the customer-facing and customer-touching applications of a CRM to integrate the online and traditional shopping experiences. Prepare a report and submit it to your instructor.

Apply the Concept 11.3

LEARNING OBJECTIVE 11.3

Explain the advantages and disadvantages of mobile CRM systems, on-demand CRM systems, open-source CRM systems, social CRM systems, and real-time CRM systems.

STEP 1: Background

Section 11.3 has outlined different CRM systems—not operational or analytical—but, instead, the different ways you can actually implement a CRM system. For example, you can run mobile CRM, open-source CRM, on-demand CRM (cloud), and more. You will have most—if not all—of these options with any system you plan to implement!

STEP 2: Activity

Visit and click on the links provided for Apply the Concept 11.3. One link will take you to a YouTube video that describes an on-demand CRM system (Salesforce). Another will take you to a video that highlights an open-source CRM (Sugar CRM). The final link will illustrate a hybrid approach, Sales Cloud (mobile-cloud CRM). Watch these videos, paying special attention to the advantages and disadvantages of each approach. The advantages will be easy to spot (these are promotional videos). The disadvantages of each one will become obvious as you compare the advantages of the others because you may notice particular functions that system one cannot perform but the others can.

STEP 3: Deliverable

Build a table that highlights the advantages and disadvantages of each approach. Do the differences reside in the capabilities of the software or in the user experience? Submit your table to your instructor.

Apply the Concept 11.4

LEARNING OBJECTIVE 11.4

Describe the three components and the three flows of a supply chain.

STEP 1: Background (Here is what you are learning.)

Section 11.4 focused on supply chain flows, materials, and "positions" (upstream, internal, and downstream). It is important to understand how products move in the supply chain because data move along with them every step of the way. In fact, the data that travel with materials and products are more important to the efficiency of the operation than the products themselves!

STEP 2: Activity (Here is what you are doing.)

Visit http://www.wiley.com/go/rainer/IS8e/applytheconcept and click on the link provided for Apply the Concept 11.4. This link will take you to a YouTube video titled *Module 1: What Is Supply Chain Management? (ASU-WPC-SCM)* by user W. P. Carey School. As you watch the video, consider the data that would be transferred with each product movement within the bottled water supply chain. Certain types of data, such as inventory updates, shipment information, quality checks, and supplier information, would deal just with the bottled water itself. In addition, there will be HR information, employee data, and machine data from the internal organization as well as from all of the suppliers!

STEP 3: Deliverable (Here is what you turn in.)

Using the example you learned about in Step 2, describe the three components and the three flows of a water bottle supply chain in a report. Submit your report to your instructor.

Apply the Concept 11.5

LEARNING OBJECTIVE 11.5

Identify popular strategies to solving different challenges of supply chains.

STEP 1: Background

Section 11.5 explained that managing a supply chain is not a simple task because consumer demand is so uncertain. Although organizations can forecast demand with some accuracy, actual demand almost inevitably will differ from the organizations' predictions. To manage demand fluctuations, organizations are moving toward JIT (just-in-time) inventory models. These data must be shared in a timely fashion if organizations are to remain flexible and capable of adapting to consumer demand.

STEP 2: Activity

Visit and click on the links provided for Apply the Concept 11.5. The first link will take you to an article that examines how the bullwhip effect wreaks havoc on the supply chain, and the second will take you to an activity in which you will manage a supply chain for beer. This latter task might not sound difficult until you consider that there are serious timing issues due to the perishable nature of the product. The simulation begins with your supply chain in equilibrium, but it then suddenly shifts. Your job is to put things back in order!

As you work through the simulation, pay attention to how much information needs to be shared across the supply chain to make the entire operation function smoothly.

STEP 3: Deliverable

Based on your experience, discuss how the popular strategies for dealing with supply chain challenges (building inventory, JIT inventory, vendor-managed inventory) would or would not work for this product. Write a report and submit it to your instructor.

Apply the Concept 11.6

LEARNING OBJECTIVE 11.6

Explain the utility of each of the three major technologies that support supply chain management.

STEP 1: Background

Electronic data interchange (EDI) is defined in this section as a communication standard that enables business partners to exchange routine documents, such as purchasing orders, electronically. You should understand the need for electronic sharing of information if you completed the activity in Apply the Concept 11.6. That activity required you to manage a supply chain on your own. Imagine the challenge of performing this function without being able to share data electronically!

STEP 2: Activity

Visit http://www.wiley.com/go/rainer/IS8e/applytheconcept and click on the links provided for Apply the Concept 11.6. The link will take you to a YouTube video titled *What is EDI* by user Hitek Equipment. You will also link to an article that defines EDI and discusses some of its standards.

As you watch the video, pay attention to the important components that are necessary to share information between two organizations. Then, consider the fact that suppliers rarely operate in only a single supply chain. In fact, suppliers typically have multiple customers, which means they are sharing information with many organizations via EDI.

STEP 3: Deliverable

Based on the content of this section and the video you watched in Step 2, explain the utility of each of the three major technologies (EDI, extranets, and corporate portals) that support supply chain management. In other words, how might these technologies interact to enable the participating parties to exchange data? Put your explanation in a report and submit it to your instructor.

Apply the Concept 12.1

LEARNING OBJECTIVE 12.1

Use a decision support framework to demonstrate how technology supports managerial decision making at each phase of the decision-making process.

STEP 1: Background (Here is what you are learning.)

If you look back through this section, you will see that Henry Mintzberg's 1973 book, *The Nature of Managerial Work*, was referenced when the three basic roles of a manager were presented. This text focuses on the decisional role because that is the one that is most supported by information systems. However, Mintzberg's work goes well beyond the decisional role.

STEP 2: Activity (Here is what you do.)

Visit http://www.wiley.com/go/rainer/IS8e/applytheconcept and click on the link provided for Apply the Concept 12.1. The link will take you to a YouTube video titled *Data-Driven Decision Making* by user Minnetonka Schools. This video mentions a strategic plan, operational control, and decisional control. As you view the video, make certain to watch for these key points, and pay special attention to how they are supported by data.

STEP 3: Deliverable (Here is what you turn in.)

Write a short paper (a couple of paragraphs is plenty) for your professor that will identify the phases in the decision-making process for Minnetonka Schools. Be sure to demonstrate how technology supports their decision making in each phase.

Apply the Concept 12.2

LEARNING OBJECTIVE 12.2

Describe each phase of the business analytics process.

STEP 1: Background

In this section you learned that BA is a concept that encompasses everything from the collection, analysis, and dissemination of data to the technology tools that enable this process to take place. In particular, organizations use BA to support the following:

- Specific departmental needs
- Organizational change

STEP 2: Activity

There are several companies that provide data management and BA tools to help make decisions. Two of these companies are Avitas and Intricity. Visit http://www.wiley.com/go/rainer/IS8e/applytheconcept to watch a short YouTube video about BA by each of these companies. While you watch, look for examples of how their tools support departments, enterprises, and/or organizational change.

STEP 3: Deliverable

Write a short description of how Avitas and Intricity help users work through the BA process (see Figure 12.3). Try to show how the process is supported, but also be aware that there might be gaps. Make note of any areas for improvement as well, if you find any.

Apply the Concept 12.3

LEARNING OBJECTIVE 12.3

Describe each of the various analytics tools and examples of their uses.

STEP 1: Background

This section explained that data are more abundant today than ever before. One thing we are learning is that there is much we can know that we do not know. In fact, there are many questions we are not even aware we should be asking! For such questions, we use multidimensional analysis and data-mining tools to extract valuable insights from the data. When we know the questions, we frequently employ decision support systems to run sensitivity, what-if, or goal-seeking analysis.

STEP 2: Activity

Consider your university. Various departments focus on teaching, student academic support, financial aid, admissions, recruitment, administration, and much more. Each of these departments has its special purpose, but overall the enterprise exists to support student learning.

Visit your university's website, and look for these various functions. What can you learn about their purpose? Based on this knowledge, what can you imply about the types of BA applications they might use?

STEP 3: Deliverable

Within the context of higher education, describe the various tools and provide an example of how each could be used to support your campus. Submit your response to your instructor.

Apply the Concept 12.4

LEARNING OBJECTIVE 12.4

Provide a definition and a use case example for predictive analytics.

STEP 1: Background

According to the text, predictive analytics attempts to detect patterns that can be used to predict, or forecast, future events. While trends change, when you look at them over time, they can show periods of growth and decline. This information is invaluable to managers who are required to make decisions about resource allocation to prepare for the future.

STEP 2: Activity

Imagine that you work for a fast-food restaurant. You have been there for a long time, but the new boss is just figuring things out. Last week, your boss stopped you and asked for some help planning labor for various times of the day and days of the week. Obviously, once the crowd arrives it is too late to bring in more labor. But the restaurant cannot afford to keep a full staff all of the time. What kind of analytics could help?

STEP 3: Deliverable

Put together a short report for your boss that defines predictive analytics and explains how you intend to use them in the restaurant. Use the example above to give context to the solution. Discuss ways that data from past weeks, months, and years can help inform patterns that can be used to determine labor needs for the future.

Apply the Concept 12.5

LEARNING OBJECTIVE 12.5

Provide a definition and a use case example for descriptive analytics, predictive analytics, and prescriptive analytics.

STEP 1: Background

Section 12.5 discusses descriptive, predictive, and prescriptive analytics. Descriptive analytics describe what has happened, predictive analytics predict what might happen, and prescriptive analytics prescribe probabilities to future outcomes based on future activities.

STEP 2: Activity

Visit http://www.wiley.com/go/rainer/IS8e/applytheconcept and click on the link provided for Apply the Concept 12.5. This link will take you to a video that describes prescriptive analytics to help a rock climber determine the best path to the top based on certain decisions. While this is a simple example, it illustrates the need to think past the next choice and to see how this choice will impact the overall probability of reaching the desired outcome.

STEP 3: Deliverable

Based on the video and any of your own Web research, describe and give examples of how a rock climber might use descriptive analytics, predictive analytics, and prescriptive analytics to determine the best path to the goal.

Apply the Concept 12.6

LEARNING OBJECTIVE 12.6:

Identify and discuss two examples of presentation tools.

Step 1: Background

Visual aids have been around for a long time. In fact, most of our communication is through visual aids. Letters represent sounds and from them, we can put together words and meaning. Additionally, today a growing number of messages are sent primarily using emojis! Liking pictures and images on Instagram or similar platform is a regular activity for many people. Sharing data is no different. Graphs and charts have been used for years to help viewers quickly grasp the meaning of data.

Step 2: Activity

Imagine that you manage a children's clothing store. Each month you make decisions on products, quantities, prices, timing of sales, and much more. What kind of information do you think you would you like to see? Sales by department? Sales over time? Product Line Comparisons? What else?

Step 3: Deliverable

Sketch an example of a dashboard that would provide at least six visual aids to understand the data you might want to see as a clothing store manager.

Apply the Concept 13.1

LEARNING OBJECTIVE 13.1

Discuss the different cost–benefit analyses that companies must take into account when formulating an IT strategic plan.

STEP 1: Background (Here is what you are learning.)

You may not realize it, but you perform cost–benefit analyses all the time. Imagine that you want to go to the beach for the weekend, but you decide not to because you would have to drive eight hours each way and therefore would not get to spend much time there. In this case, the costs outweigh the benefits. However, if you could extend your stay another day, then the benefits might outweigh the costs. The difficulty in this example is that the benefits are difficult to measure. A cost–benefit analysis is designed to quantify all of the key elements, and sometimes there are subjective benefits for which there are no clear-cut numerical values.

STEP 2: Activity (Here is what you are doing.)

Visit http://www.wiley.com/go/rainer/IS8e/applytheconcept and click on the links provided for Apply the Concept 13.1. You will watch three short videos that offer a financial explanation for net present value (NPV), return on investment (ROI), and break-even analysis. The business case approach is not a financial approach, and it does not require further explanation.

STEP 3: Deliverable (Here is what you turn in.)

Imagine you are creating a website to sell promotional items. You have no experience developing a site, so you will have to pay someone to do this for you. You research this service and discover that the site you have in mind will cost $3,500. (For this example, assume there are no monthly hosting fees.) This design will last five years, after which you will need to update it. You anticipate that you can make $500 in year 1, $750 in year 2, $750 in year 3, $1,000 in year 4, and $1,500 in year 5 from the site. Calculate the NPV, ROI, and break-even analysis for this case, and discuss which metric is most helpful. Also, explain how a business case analysis would be helpful beyond what the numbers provide. Prepare a document with your figures and present it to your instructor.

Apply the Concept 13.2

LEARNING OBJECTIVE 13.2

Discuss the four business decisions that companies must make when they acquire new applications.

STEP 1: Background

Section 13.2 discusses the many options available to acquire information systems. One of the more popular methods is software-as-a-service (SaaS). SaaS is popular because it eliminates the need for the company purchasing the software to maintain the hardware on which the software will run. They simply need an Internet connection to access the software from the host company.

STEP 2: Activity

Visit http://www.wiley.com/go/rainer/IS8e/applytheconcept and click on the links provided for Apply the Concept 13.2. There are two videos linked there that illustrate SaaS. As you watch these videos, consider the types of hardware that are required on both sides of the relationship. Also, give some thought to the legal nature of the relationship, given that the data will likely reside with the service provider.

STEP 3: Deliverable

Imagine that a company has decided to use an SaaS model to acquire a new piece of software. Prepare a paper discussing the four business decisions they have made in light of this type of acquisition. Submit your paper to your instructor.

Apply the Concept 13.3

LEARNING OBJECTIVE 13.3

Enumerate the primary tasks and the importance of each of the six processes involved in the systems development life cycle.

STEP 1: Background

The systems development life cycle uses a very systematic approach in which each stage builds on work completed at an earlier stage. It is an excellent model to follow, assuming that the right decisions are made at each stage of the SDLC and are appropriately communicated to the next stage of the SDLC.

STEP 2: Activity

Visit http://www.wiley.com/go/rainer/IS8e/applytheconcept and watch the video titled *Software Development Life Cycle*, which is linked to Apply the Concept 13.3. The video conveys a realistic (though perhaps a bit pessimistic) view of how poor communication can severely damage the software-development process.

STEP 3: Deliverable

After watching the video, build an outline that specifies the primary tasks and the importance of each of the six processes involved in the SDLC. Make certain to discuss the importance of communication from one step to the next.

Apply the Concept 13.4

LEARNING OBJECTIVE 13.4

Describe alternative development methods and the tools that augment development methods.

STEP 1: Background

The systems development life cycle is a very thorough method of development. However, it is also very time consuming and expensive. Section 13.4 discusses several alternative methods. Joint application design, rapid application development, and agile development are used in conjunction with several tools for systems development.

STEP 2: Activity

Visit http://www.wiley.com/go/rainer/IS8e/applytheconcept and click on the link provided for Apply the Concept 13.4. This link will take you to a Vimeo about prototyping. Imagine that you are a developer of iPhone apps. At lunch the other day, someone mentioned a very cool idea for a new camera app that would enable users to take pictures simply by opening the app and saying "click" rather than having to push a button.

Describe the idea to a couple of friends to develop a list of user needs and preferences. From this list, make a sketch of the app. Then let the same people review your design and make suggestions. Use the second set of suggestions to create your "final" drawings of the app.

STEP 3: Deliverable

Write a short report documenting the alternative development methods you have used and how the tools discussed in this section might help you to actually develop your app. Be sure to mention how you might use different tools at different stages of development.

Apply the Concept Technology Guide 1.1

LEARNING OBJECTIVE TG 1.1

Identify the major hardware components of a computer system.

STEP 1: Background (Here is what you are learning.)

At a basic level, a computer is a computer, just like an automobile is an automobile. The purpose of the automobile drives its size, design, build, price, and much more. Similarly, the purpose of a computer dictates its build requirements, storage capability, and price.

STEP 2: Activity (Here is what you do.)

Imagine a colleague has been asked to create high-quality training videos for internal purposes. The project will take 6 months to complete and she has been given a $1,500 budget for purchasing any needed equipment. After searching, she finds out that a 4K webcam will cost $150 and a high-quality USB microphone will cost $125. This leaves $1,225 for a new computer. Think of which features will be most important for your colleague's uses and how they will function in conjunction with the webcam and microphone.

STEP 3: Deliverable (Here is what you turn in.)

Review the definitions of central processing and primary and secondary storage that are detailed in this tech guide. Then visit Dell's website and customize a computer that would meet your friend's needs and stay within the budget. Write a memo to your professor describing your selection with a justification for the choices.

Apply the Concept Technology Guide 1.2

LEARNING OBJECTIVE TG1.2

Discuss strategic issues that link hardware design to business strategy.

STEP 1: Background

In the modern business environment, computer hardware components are inextricably linked to business strategy. Put simply, computers are tools that allow businesses to automate some transactions and make others more efficient. As technology evolves, businesses need to evolve the ways they use that technology to execute their business strategies. The generally accepted rule is that technology should *not* drive business strategy, but business strategy *must* consider how the organization can implement new types of hardware to achieve its goals.

STEP 2: Activity

Consider Lowe's (www.lowes.com). A large home improvement warehouse store might seem very distant from the use of information technology. However, in 2011 Lowe's made significant improvements to its customer experience by implementing a type of hardware. What hardware is that? The answer is—smartphones.

Visit http://www.wiley.com/go/rainer/IS8e/applytheconcept and click on the link provided for Apply the Concept TG1.2. This link will take you to a *U.S. News and World Report* article that discusses how Lowe's implemented smartphone technology for their employees and their customers.

STEP 3: Deliverable (Here is what you will turn in.)

Discuss strategic issues that link hardware design to business strategy, using the Lowe's case to illustrate these links. Put your discussion in a Word document and submit it to your professor.

Apply the Concept Technology Guide 1.3

LEARNING OBJECTIVE:

Describe the various types of computers in the computer hierarchy.

STEP 1: Background

All computers require processing power and storage capability. But, as you move along the computer hierarchy, that processing and storage can sometimes be distributed to another location. We refer to this as fat and thin clients.

STEP 2: Activity

You are an inventory manager for a local tire shop. You have well over 2,000 SKUs that you are responsible for. Inventory management has been managed on paper by keeping up with invoices for items in stock and receipts of items sold. Monthly reconciliation has been sufficient, but now upper management is seeking daily clarity on inventory and there is a need for an up-to-date system.

STEP 3: Deliverable

Search the Web for inventory management software and review the type of computers that are used in the specific inventory management system. It is likely that it will have some type of server, desktop PC, and mobile devices. Prepare a list of those and describe each one relative to the computer hierarchy.

Apply the Concept Technology Guide 1.4

LEARNING OBJECTIVE TG1.4

Differentiate the various types of input and output technologies and their uses.

STEP 1: Background

Computers in and of themselves are not very useful to us. They are usually boxes that make some noise and create some heat. However, it is our ability to interact with their power that makes them invaluable to us. Input and output technologies allow us to engage with the processing power of the computer and all the "knowledge" of the Internet to be able to make decisions.

STEP 2: Activity

Traditional input and output technologies have relied heavily on keyboards, mice, and flat displays. However, this is changing rapidly. New technologies are allowing for more virtual interaction that is changing what is possible with computers.

STEP 3: Deliverable

Search the Web for virtual and augmented reality. As you read about them, consider the different forms of input and output technologies. Prepare a table that describes these innovative tools for interacting with a computer!

Apply the Concept Technology Guide 2.1

LEARNING OBJECTIVE 2.1

Discuss the major software issues that confront modern organizations.

STEP 1: Background (Here is what you are learning.)

Today's organizations deal with many decisions when it comes to technology. Will it meet our needs? Will it be flexible enough to meet our needs in the future? Will there be support for problems? Will it be user-friendly? Can we afford it? Will the licensing change in the future? Is there some technology that will make this useless in the next three to five years? These are just a few of the questions that will be considered when looking at software.

STEP 2: Activity (Here is what you do.)

Imagine that you are meeting with your boss about a new software package for the Human Resources Department of your organization. A focus group has created a list of user requirements for the new system to be functional and supportive, and your boss is meeting with them next week.

STEP 3: Deliverable (Here is what you turn in.)

Help prepare a list of questions that the boss should discuss concerning the software from an administrative perspective. Remember, the group has focused on what they "want and need," not necessarily what is best for the organization (or what is feasible).

Apply the Concept Technology Guide 2.2

LEARNING OBJECTIVE TG2.2

Describe the general functions of the operating system.

STEP 1: Background

There are a lot of computing terms that are commonly used in the wrong way. For example, most of the time when people say they have a "PC," they are referring to a computer that runs some version of the Microsoft Windows OS. This was even used in the Mac versus PC commercials that Apple ran a few years ago. In reality, though, a PC is just a personal computer and could run any operating system.

STEP 2: Activity

Operating systems are a necessary part of the computer. Without them, the computer will not function. Imagine that you are helping your friend pick out a computer. He just wants to pick out the color, shape, and size of the computer, but you are trying to help him understand the differences in computers.

STEP 3: Deliverable

One major difference is the type of operating system. Write a paragraph that describes what an operating system does and why it is important to be careful about your selection!

Apply the Concept Technology Guide 2.3

LEARNING OBJECTIVE TG2.3

Differentiate between the two major types of software.

STEP 1: Background

There are two types of software (systems and application), two general ways of obtaining software licenses (proprietary versus open-source), and two general types of uses (traditional versus mobile). You should be sufficiently familiar with software to be able to categorize programs that you use.

STEP 2: Activity

Visit http://www.wiley.com/go/rainer/IS8e/applytheconcept and click on the link for Apply the Concept TG2.3. This link will take you to CNET's Download.com. At this website, you should immediately notice one of the categories mentioned above. At the time of this writing, the site automatically recognized the type of computer operating system on the user's computer. For example, this author is writing on a Mac, and the system recognized the Mac OS and defaulted to the Mac software page. Review the available software and differentiate between the operating systems and the applications. Within applications, differentiate by method of obtaining a license—some you have to pay for, and some are available by open-source or freeware licensing.

STEP 3: Deliverable

Build a table that differentiates between the two major types of software. To complete this task, list 10 applications you reviewed on the website mentioned in Step 2. Use the template provided below. Turn your completed table in to your instructor.

Application	Operating System	Licensing

Apply the Concept Technology Guide 3.1

LEARNING OBJECTIVE TG3.1

Describe the problems that modern information technology departments face.

STEP 1: Background (Here is what you are learning.)

This section discussed the evolution of computer infrastructure over time. Early computing models were called "terminal to host"; today we have "cloud," or "distributed computing," models available. A knowledge of how infrastructure models have changed can help you understand the challenges confronting modern IT departments.

STEP 2: Activity (Here is what you do.)

Review the evolution of IT infrastructure as presented in this section. It is likely that all businesses today have some form of a local area network (LAN) in the client/server model of computing. Beginning with that stage, consider the problems that modern IT departments face as their systems evolve.

Imagine that your boss has asked your advice on moving from traditional LAN computing, in which each department operates a separate network, toward enterprise or cloud computing. What type of challenges could you help your boss anticipate?

STEP 3: Deliverable (Here is what you turn in.)

Write a letter to your boss (your instructor) that describes the problems that modern IT departments must address as they evolve toward enterprise and cloud computing.

Apply the Concept Technology Guide 3.2

LEARNING OBJECTIVE TG3.2

Describe the key characteristics and advantages of cloud computing.

STEP 1: Background

One of the more popular virtual servers is a virtual Web server offered by Web hosting companies. Historically, someone would simply purchase and share space on a server that would host his or her files. However, many people today need dedicated servers that guarantee performance for their consumers.

STEP 2: Activity

Visit http://www.wiley.com/go/rainer/IS8e/applytheconcept and click on the link provided for Apply the Concept TG3.2. This link will take you to a case study on an offshore drilling company, Seadrill, that migrated from in-house data centers to a virtual private cloud data center. As you review the site, focus carefully on the advantages and concerns mentioned in the case study.

STEP 3: Deliverable

In a Word document, describe the key characteristics and advantages of cloud computing for Seadrill. Submit your document to your instructor.

Apply the Concept Technology Guide 3.3

LEARNING OBJECTIVE TG3.3

Identify a use case scenario for each of the four types of clouds.

STEP 1: Background

This section describes four types of clouds: public, private, hybrid, and vertical. The common feature among all four types is that resources are hosted remotely and made available to a wide range of devices over high-speed Internet connections. All four types display the basic features of the cloud that were presented in earlier sections. However, the applications of these features differ for each type.

STEP 2: Activity

Refer to the Boeing example presented in this section. Boeing employs a hybrid cloud. As you have seen, there are many possible strategies for utilizing the cloud. Imagine a use case scenario for Boeing for each type of cloud.

STEP 3: Deliverable

Build a table that identifies a use case scenario for each of the four types of clouds for Boeing.

Apply the Concept Technology Guide 3.4

LEARNING OBJECTIVE TG3.4

Explain the operational model of each of the three types of cloud services.

STEP 1: Background

Infrastructure-as-a-service, platform-as-a-service, and software-as-a-service are relatively new processing models made available by the rise in dependable, high-speed Internet access and powerful "host-computer" processing capabilities. The three cloud models are differentiated by how users employ them and which services providers offer with each one.

STEP 2: Activity

Review the material in this section. For each operational model, consider who owns the infrastructure, the operating systems, and the applications.

STEP 3: Deliverable

In a Word document, explain the operational model for each of the three types of cloud services by highlighting the differences in who is responsible for the infrastructure, the operating systems, and the applications for each model. Submit your document to your instructor.

Apply the Concept Technology Guide 3.5

LEARNING OBJECTIVE TG3.5

Identify the key benefits of cloud computing.

STEP 1: Background

This section has outlined the benefits that are driving many organizations to transition to cloud computing. Productivity, cost reductions, collaboration, more robust data mining, flexibility, and scope expansion are just the beginning. Cloud computing is a powerful tool that is changing the ways we do business.

STEP 2: Activity

Visit the Amazon Web Services (AWS) site (www.aws.amazon.com) and learn about the variety of cloud computing services Amazon provides. This site contains video of several customer testimonials. As you watch them, look for common benefits the various customers receive from cloud computing.

STEP 3: Deliverable

Based on the video and the material in this section, identify the key benefits of cloud computing that amazon.com offers its business customers. Detail these benefits in a memo to your boss (instructor).

Apply the Concept Technology Guide 3.6

LEARNING OBJECTIVE TG3.6

Discuss the concerns and risks associated with cloud computing.

STEP 1: Background

This section discussed why the risks associated with cloud computing outweigh the benefits for some organizations. The statistics provided early on that cloud computing will remain a small portion of IT spending reflect concerns regarding these risks.

STEP 2: Activity

Visit http://www.wiley.com/go/rainer/IS8e/applytheconcept and click on the link provided for TG3.6. This link will take you to an article that addresses some of the risks of cloud computing that senior managers need to consider. As you read the article, try to organize the managers' thoughts according to the concerns presented in this section: legacy systems, costs, reliability, security, privacy, and regulatory and legal environment. Imagine you have just overheard a conversation about how wonderful cloud computing is that mentioned all of the positives and none of the negatives. How would you respond?

STEP 3: Deliverable

Based on the material contained in this section and the information conveyed in the article, write a response to the above scenario that discusses the concerns and risks associated with cloud computing.

Apply the Concept Technology Guide 3.7

LEARNING OBJECTIVE TG3.7

Explain the role of Web services in building a firm's IT applications and provide examples.

STEP 1: Background

Web services allow companies to increase functionality with minimal effort by using standard protocols to access and share data. The advantage of using Web services is that they standardize the Web platform. Using the same Web protocols that allow you to access any website makes sharing data much easier.

STEP 2: Activity

Imagine you work for a bank and you want to display some financial data on your intranet to keep your employees up to date on major market trends. One option is to gather data, perform an analysis, build and share charts and graphs, and then keep everything current. This probably sounds like a lot of work. But, suppose someone else had done all of the work for you?

Visit http://www.wiley.com/go/rainer/IS8e/applytheconcept and click on the link provided for Apply the Concept TG3.7. This link will take you to a website that discusses the available "widgets" (another name for an embeddable Web service) that businesses can select to display on their sites. Review the available information and consider how it would help you add content to your bank's intranet with minimal effort.

STEP 3: Deliverable

Write a summary that explains the role of Web services in building a firm's IT applications. Include a few examples based on the options you viewed in Step 2.

Apply the Concept Technology Guide 4.1

LEARNING OBJECTIVE TG4.1:

Explain the potential value and the potential limitations of artificial intelligence.

STEP 1: Background (Here is what you are learning.)

This section introduced you to several applications of artificial intelligence. One of these applications was the Google self-driving car. This innovation presents a scenario in which technology could potentially greatly enhance the safety of motorists, pedestrians, and passengers. However, there are also significant risks posed by turning over the keys to the computer.

STEP 2: Activity (Here is what you do.)

Visit YouTube and watch a video titled *Self-Driving Car Test: Steve Mahan* that introduces the Google self-driving car. Although this innovation is very exciting, it can also be very scary! While you are watching the video, imagine the advantages and disadvantages of this type of intelligent system. Would it function best as a "pilot" or a very helpful "copilot"?

STEP 3: Deliverable (Here is what you turn in.)

Build a table that displays both the potential value (advantages) and the potential limitations (disadvantages) of artificial intelligence for different scenarios illustrated in the example below.

	Advantages	Disadvantages
Tired driver		
Distracted driver (texting)		
Sick/stressed driver		
Ambulance driver		
School bus driver		
Soccer mom, minivan driver		

Apply the Concept Technology Guide 4.2

LEARNING OBJECTIVE TG4.2

Provide use case examples of expert systems, machine learning systems, deep learning systems, and neural networks.

STEP 1: Background

Throughout much of human history, expertise was transferred from a master to an apprentice through years of training. Only after the apprentice had mastered all of the "tricks of the trade" was he or she considered ready to perform on his or her own. We still employ a similar system for doctors, who must participate in a residency program under the guidance of the resident doctor before they can begin their own practice. This approach is not appropriate, however, for many non–life-threatening situations. In some cases, being able to make an expert decision is simply a matter of having access to the experts' knowledge and experiences. If this knowledge can be captured in a computer-based information system, then it can be distributed for other people to use in similar scenarios. Although this sounds great, there are many challenges to developing this type of system.

STEP 2: Activity

Visit http://www.wiley.com/go/rainer/IS8e/applytheconcept and watch the YouTube video linked for Apply the Concept TG4.2. This video will show you a short demonstration of an expert cooking system. The video mentions that you are responsible for building and testing an expert system, but that is not part of this activity. As you watch the video, pay particular attention to the miscommunication between the cook and the computer. You will find this interaction to be quite comical.

STEP 3: Deliverable

Based on the video and material in this section, provide examples of the benefits, applications, and limitations of using artificial intelligence in the world of cooking. Create a Word document to submit to your instructor. Based on the video and material in this section, provide examples of the benefits, applications, and limitations of using artificial intelligence in the world of cooking. Create a Word document to submit to your instructor.

Index